An Introduction

to the History

of the Western Tradition

An Introduction

to the History

of the Western Tradition

by
EDGAR N. JOHNSON
Brandeis University
formerly of the
University of Nebraska

volume I

GINN AND COMPANY

BOSTON   NEW YORK   CHICAGO
ATLANTA   DALLAS   PALO ALTO   TORONTO   LONDON

To

Emily, John, and Tim

Preface

This book introduces the American undergraduate to some of the many strands that form a Western Tradition he may be called upon to defend with his life. It suggests that this tradition has been shaped in part by a conflict between two points of view: the humanistic, represented by the ancient Greeks, and the ascetic, represented in general by Christianity. It suggests also that these two have tried, at times, to combine into an outlook often called Christian humanism. The writer is not so Hegelian as this approach would seem to make out, and he is well aware of the dangers involved in reducing so much history to so simple a theme. He merely hopes that the theme will promote understanding and that the text itself will reveal that the actual history was more complicated.

The author is heavily indebted to many persons and many things for aid in bringing this work to an end. There is the great and colorful fabric of the human past, ready and willing always to be re-mended and re-woven. There is the long line of distinguished men and women who, on previous occasions and in their several ways, have been engaged in preserving and explaining this past. I have tried to acknowledge some of my obligation to them in footnotes. I only wish I could have read larger amounts as well as what more of them had to say. I have had to remember, however, if I were ever to conclude, Salvemini's counsel about the mathematical ratio of what one knows to what one does not know: it is always as one to infinity.

My former university, the University of Nebraska, permitted two annual leaves that afforded time for study and writing. It made available additional hours and the assistance of students in preparing the text. These young people are Orville Zabel, Cecily Raysor, the late Fred Pelton, James Brundage, William Christiansen, Richard Rowen, and Robert Frank. The staff of the Love Library at the University of Nebraska has always been generous with its services. To Columbia University I am obligated for the privileges, on two occasions, of a Visiting Scholar.

Colleagues and friends have been kindly willing to read parts of what I have written. Before his death C. H. Oldfather saw some of the material on the ancient period. Samuel Eddy has read all the chapters on the ancient world. Glenn Gray has seen most of the material on England. Paula and Eugene N. Anderson, before going off to the University of California at Los Angeles, read some of the material then ready. Orin Stepanek read the early manuscript of Volume I, Jerome Ritter and Miguel Basoco the chapter on science in the seventeenth century, and the latter also the material on Greek science and mathematics. Besides preparing the students' manual to accompany the text Orville Zabel read the earlier chapters in manuscript. To all of these I am obligated for many corrections and suggestions that in no way absolve me from my responsibility. Dorothy Forward has always been bountiful with her help, whenever asked. The book would have been difficult to do without the support and encouragement of Dr. Richard Thornton of Ginn and Company. My family has rewarded me, to say no more, with loyal interest, warm encouragement, and infinite patience during the slow completion of the writing.

EDGAR N. JOHNSON

Cambridge
September 1958

Contents

An Introduction

to the History

of the Western Tradition

volume I

chapter one

A POINT OF VIEW

CHE MEANING OF HISTORY.　The title of this book—*An Introduction to the History of the Western Tradition*—has been carefully chosen, for the book lays no claim to possess what no man's thought or word possesses: the dignity, beauty, or value of absolute truth.　It tries, however, always to use what are called facts.　It tries also to give some meaning to these facts, for its author does not think very highly of meaningless history. The manner in which he interprets these facts depends ultimately upon the meaning he gives to life upon this earth.　This attitude depends, in turn, upon his experience, into which has gone, among other things, the acquisition of knowledge.　The adequacy of his, or any historian's, interpretation of the facts depends upon the variety of his experience and the wealth of his knowledge; it depends also upon the ripeness of his wisdom.　To be fair to his reader, every historian should preface his work with a statement of his point of view.　What follows is an attempt to do this by stating (1) what the author's conception of history is, and (2) how he has applied it to his knowledge of the past.

A DEFINITION OF HISTORY

A Dutch historian has defined history as "the intellectual form in which a generation renders account to itself of its past."[1]　This suggests that the interpretation of the past that any historian makes will reflect the outlook of his generation.　The outlook of his generation will depend upon its great needs, and the point of view of the historian will therefore reflect

[1]See J. Huizinga, "History," in *Essays Presented to Ernst Cassirer*.

the great needs of his generation. This further suggests that the interpretation of history will vary from generation to generation, as the great needs vary from generation to generation. Opinions will also vary among members of any given generation as to what its great needs are. That historical interpretation will be most adequate that attempts to rise above these individual opinions and estimate the needs of a generation as a whole. In the estimate of these needs of a whole generation the historian will want to summon all his resources in order to put his own in the line of past and future generations, to measure the needs of his time against the story of mankind, and mankind itself against eternity.

HISTORY AND THE GREAT NEEDS OF OUR GENERATION

It would be difficult for a historian who is a member of the present generation not to say that its chief need is to find workable answers to two momentous questions: (1) how to control the rapidly accumulating knowledge and technique of modern science, and, closely related to this, (2) how to avoid another total war in which this knowledge and technique would be applied by society to its own destruction. The fate of the civilization of the West, and of the world, seems at present to hang upon these issues. The answer to the first question would appear to lie among a tangle of complexities and implications: What is the importance and purpose of man's knowledge? What is its relation to life? What is its final meaning or value for mankind? In a more basic formulation it becomes the question: What is the relation of man to the universe in which he finds himself? With all his knowledge, what are his ultimate goals? Is knowledge to be controlled and directed toward the service of an earthly happiness—toward goals that are tangible, experiential, human? Or is it to be aimed at the intangible, the abstract, the superhuman? And what is the correct balance between freedom of inquiry and control? Inevitably, in their implementation, these problems become further complicated by the subsidiary purposes and problems of the organizations, institutions, and societies that deal with them. The question of the relation of man to the universe becomes, through its immediate application, a question of the relation of man to man. Living with his fellows in society, how can man be secure and still progress? How, in a world of independent sovereignties, may a nation maintain its power and still allow its citizens to be free? Among nations or within nations, what is the correct relationship between freedom and security? In the modern world a nation's program and ideology may depend upon the degree of technological advancement that it has so far attained, or it may depend equally upon its cultural tradition, or its geographical situation, or all of these. In any case, if the first question of the control of scientific knowledge and technique is successfully to be met, the answer to the second question, avoidance of total war, must first be found. Differences in interest, in ideology, in policy between the West and the rest of the world must first be understood, adjusted, then eventually resolved. To carry out this task soberly, effectively, we in the West must be able to represent our point of view. We must know what both we and our opponents believe. Fundamentally, the mode of action of the contending parties will be shaped by their idea of what it is that influences the opinions of mankind; upon, in other words, their belief about the nature of man.

If this analysis is correct, then a historian reflecting the needs of the contemporary generation and wishing to minister to them will interpret the past in the light of those needs. He will wish to search for what the past tells concerning (1) the relative advantages and disadvantages of war and peace, (2) the origins and growth of the conflict between East and West, and (3) the origins and development of the western and eastern points of view, including ideas on the nature of man. This does not mean that he can ever escape from the obligation to look at history in the light of a single category: man, and man himself under the aspect of eternity.

THE MEANING OF TRADITION AND WESTERN

This book professes to be an introduction to the history of the western tradition. By *tradition* is meant what the past teaches as the best way of thinking about or doing certain things. As a historian, the author works within the tradition established by past historians. They have had certain opinions about what history is or ought to be, and they have tried to put their theories into practice. The value of their opinions and the success of their applications have been debated down through the centuries for as long as there have been any historians. The results of this debate are what constitute for the historian his tradition. He must come to terms with it. Does he believe that what past historians have said about history is accurate, and will he try to write his history according to their rules? If there is no consensus, then there is really no tradition. It has long been a part of the historical tradition that a historian should go out of his way to use only those facts that are accurate. If he is writing a biography of Julius Caesar, he must do his best to verify all the facts that he wishes to use. Carelessness in this respect is inexcusable; it disqualifies a man as a reputable historian. It has long been a part of the historical tradition, also, that a historian, to give an adequate interpretation of his facts, must look at them from as many angles as possible. If he is writing a history of the decline and fall of the Roman Empire, he must be careful, after collecting all his facts, not to attribute the decline and fall to one thing alone (let us say, depopulation) unless all the facts unquestionably point to this one explanation. Any historian who gives a narrow or limited interpretation of his facts, however accurate, cannot be taken seriously. He is likely to be a crank or a fanatic. This is a tradition established among western historians. By *western* is meant, in this connection, the Ancient Near East, Greece, Rome, and those nations that grew up when the Germans and other barbarians took over the Latin Christian half of the Roman Empire.

From these original western European nations other western European and non-European nations have sprung. The western tradition of writing history is, therefore, what has been considered the best historical thought and practice among historians from the above geographical areas. It might well be shared by historians who come from other areas. It would not be shared, at least publicly, by practicing historians of Communist-ruled countries, for these are obliged to give only one, that is, the official Communist interpretation of their facts, however accurate.

THE LIMITATION AND EMPHASIS OF THE BOOK

In the sense that there is a western tradition about the best way to write history, there is also a western tradition about the best way to build houses, or the best way to paint pictures and write poetry. There are some things in violation of these traditions that no ordinary architect, painter, or poet would risk doing. There has likewise begun to crystallize a western tradition about the best way to govern a state, to organize a society, and to do the things necessary to achieve not only the political and social but indeed all the other bests. Ideally this book should contain an account of the development of all these traditions, major and minor. This is for many reasons impossible. The book claims to be only an *introduction* to the history of the western tradition, and as such it must limit itself to an elementary consideration of the development of only the major western traditions. Because its author feels that what an individual believes determines to a large extent what he does, it will concentrate on the development of a general western attitude, or point of view, and emphasize what religion, philosophy, and science have to say about this attitude. Because, also, the author believes that when man is exercising his creative imagination and talent as an artist he is at his best, the book will try not to under-emphasize the western artistic tradition: its painting, its architecture, its poetry, and especially its music.

A WESTERN FAITH

The western tradition has established certain conclusions with respect not only to history but to ideas about how best to govern a state and organize a society. These ideas center about the word democracy and associate with democracy the convictions that (1) men must be free to govern themselves, (2) governments must recognize the principle of equality before the law, and (3) there must be equality of opportunity to develop individual potentialities. The West has developed the additional concept that in a society organized according to these principles there will be progress; man will correct his mistakes and improve the conditions under which he lives. Behind these ideas is the belief that man is essentially good, and that under proper circumstances he will establish a world in which he and his fellow humans may be happy.

It is largely the experience of the twentieth century that has impressed western man with the necessity of establishing democratic states and societies. For the undemocratic states of this century, the fascist and Communist states, have turned the world into a battlefield and continue to threaten its civilized existence. The conviction has thus become general in the West that if man is to give meaning and hope to his existence this can only be done in a democratic world at peace.

WESTERN NEEDS

Peace, then, is essential to the successful functioning of democratic states and societies. Their members need also a certain vital faith in the noble qualities of the human being and in his will and capacity to give quality and beauty to earthly life. Only a world of meaning, satisfaction, and promise can inspire the wish to stave off the holocaust of another world war. For such a world makes it unthinkable to most human beings not to want to be alive for as long as possible in order to comprehend the meaning, enjoy the satisfaction, and share the responsibility of realizing the promise.

To assume, however, that human life has any importance or promise is to ignore what we have been taught to believe by some of our scientists. To assume that man is capable alone of creating his own kingdom of heaven on earth is to rebel against established religions.

COPERNICUS

Man's curiosity has always been engaged by the starry vault of heaven. Until a comparatively recent date his ideas of the relationship of the moving earth to the moving stars have not obliged him to question the relative importance of his terrestrial home. For the orderly procession of the stars and planets through the sky was determined by the earth, the central point of the universe. Man's abode was the universal pivot. But since 1543, the date of the publication of Copernicus's *On the Revolutions of the Celestial Bodies*, or rather since the acceptance of Copernicus's theory, men have been obliged to reject their proud notions of the supreme importance of their dwelling place. Copernicus came to the conclusion that the universe was not geocentric (with the earth as its center) but heliocentric (with the sun as its center). The spinning earth, like the other planets, at regular intervals revolved about the sun.

Men did not easily accept this displacement of the earth as the true account. Not, indeed, until many astronomers had pointed their new telescopes toward the heavens, and many mathematicians had plotted the new orbits of the planets, was the concept of a solar system held valid. The astronomers, however, did not content themselves with this insult to man's dignity. As they accumulated knowledge with their improved instruments, they robbed man of his possible pride in the uniqueness of his own solar system. His solar system was but one in an infinite number of similar systems, his family of solar systems but one in an infinite number of similar families of similar systems. In so far as they could and can yet tell, the universe extends, and is actually expanding, into infinite space.

THE ORIGIN OF LIFE

To restore his self-confidence man turned his attention to the nature and history of the earth. Having detached it from the sun as the result of what he thought might be the gravitational pull of an approaching planet, set it to whirling on its axis and revolving about its parent mass, he set his geologists to tracing its history under the climatic conditions of the solar system. At a wonderful moment in its history life appeared upon the earth. Just how, the geologist could not and cannot explain. He can suggest when, and can describe the general conditions under which the single living cell was born. He can even hope some day so to understand the mechanism of life that he will be able to explain precisely how it arose. As yet, however, what is of most interest to man must, for the scientist or those who follow his lead, remain a mystery.

DARWIN AND EVOLUTION

Now that at a specific moment in time, and as a result of what most scientists would insist was a purely physical process, life appeared upon a weathering earth, the biologist was asked to explain how that simple cell could eventuate in the human animal. It had long been a notion of civilized man that this development was from simple to complex and accompanied the adaptation of living forms to the environment of a changing earth. Not, however, until after the publication, in 1859, of Darwin's *Origin of Species* did educated men generally accept this emergence as the result of an evolution, according to which: "once life got started it began to change at once in adaptation to diversified conditions in the environment; that, in general, the changes . . . proceeded from more plastic, generalized types to less plastic, specialized types; that immense numbers of highly developed types . . . appeared, . . . thrived for a time, and then . . . died off; . . . that the forms living today are merely the present end-products of thousands of lines of specialization, each descended from the simplest form of life."[2] Man, according to this law of nature, was, to begin with, an animal, one of the species of anthropoid apes.

These conclusions of the scientists have obliged men who rely upon scientists alone to accept the position of highly specialized animals, the most recent in a vast series of such specializations, struggling to adapt themselves to the physical environment of an earth that in its present phase is in an interlude between two glacial epochs. This earth is but an inconspicuous dot in a universe decomposing through radioactivity.

[2]Reprinted from *The Nature of the World and of Man*, ed. H. H. Newman, p. 192, by permission of The University of Chicago Press. Copyright 1927 by The University of Chicago Press.

Western man has resisted being classified as an evolving animal on an evolving earth in an evolving universe largely because he has been taught otherwise by his religion. The Christian Scriptures were written within the framework of a geocentric, not a heliocentric, universe. According to the interpretation of the Scriptures by early theologians, this universe was the spectacularly rapid creation of God. In creating man God made not simply another specialized kind of animal but a creature in his own image, a divine being destined to enjoy the bliss of a terrestrial paradise for as long as he remained obedient to the will of his Creator. Even after he had forfeited this bliss through the sin of disobedience, and had been condemned by God to death, it was still possible for him, with divine aid, to recapture his earlier divine nature and, if not on earth, then in heaven, to enjoy the eternal bliss of communion with his God. This is a supernatural, rather than a natural, interpretation of man's place in the universe. It is God's will and power, rather than nature's will and power, that supply the meaning of his existence.

THE ASCETIC OUTLOOK

From the above it is evident that early Christianity was concerned not so much to give man an explanation of his origins in the universe as to instruct him in the reasons for, and the possibilities of, his existence. The environment of the Roman Empire, in which Christianity grew to be a religion of universal stature, was such that the new religion sought nothing more at first than to escape it. Christianity's growing popularity in this empire rested in large part upon the promise to redress the unavoidable misery and injustice of this world with the joy and perfection of the heavenly world that was to come. Like other eastern religions, it was an enemy of the world in which it was born. It was only the Kingdom of God that mattered. Its instruction to man, therefore, was to avoid the world as a plague and to follow the Savior, Jesus, the Christ. If its attitude toward the contemporary world was hostile, and toward the future of this world pessimistic, its opinion of man also was not flattering. Man, because of his sin, had fallen away from the perfection with which he had originally been endowed by his God. This original sin, it came to be taught, was physically inherited by all the children of Adam. It explained the miserable state of affairs to which men had brought their world. Indeed, early Christian theologians went on, because of this sin man lost the ability that he possessed in the Garden of Eden of directing his own future, of making his own choices, of exercising his free will. It was only with divine intervention and with constant divine aid that this free will could be restored, and then not for the purpose of reforming the world but of meeting the conditions set up by God for the attainment of eternal life. Thus the men who began the Christian civilization of which we are still a part were taught by their religion to loathe their ordinary selves and the world in which they dwelt and to devote their efforts to meriting a divine aid that would help them to become sinless and reward them with eternal contemplation of their God. Let us call this point of view ascetic, and say that it assigns to man as his chief function moral reformation, and as his chief good immortal life.[3]

THE GREEK HUMANISTIC OUTLOOK

This ascetic point of view became official in the Roman Empire at the end of the fourth century A.D. It supplanted what we may call the humanistic point of view of the Greeks, which, with modifications, had been taken over by the Romans and made the dominant philosophy of their universal state. The Greek humanists did not turn to a God for an explanation of the origins of the universe, this earth, or the human creature. Nor did they rely upon a God for their interpretation of the meaning of man's life on earth. Their religion was elaborated by poets and artists, not by theologians, and accordingly it never became authoritative or dogmatic. Indeed, the Greek humanist had an unbounded faith in the ability of man himself to work out an accurate account of the nature of the world and man. It was enough for him to put his mind to this end, to use his reason. Such an approach produced an interpretation of the world in terms of science and mathematics, and of man in terms of philosophy. As a rational animal, man's chief task was to discover the art of living in this world rather than to subject himself to the discipline of preparing for the next one. The art of living in this world had chiefly to do with adapting the individual to life in a political society. As a responsible citizen of a state, the individual was to seek to realize his full human stature. This stature, at its best, avoided extremes or excesses in any direction. It was composed of a harmonious balance between reason and emotion, thought and action. It cultivated beauty, in whatever form, as a necessary enrichment of human character. The Greek humanist, in placing upon man the responsibility of achieving the good life on earth, gave him little or no supernatural support. Gods made in the image of men, and only too often setting them a very bad example, he made over into the defenders of a moral order or else reduced to the creatures of a picturesque mythology. There was no reward for the achievement of a good life except the satisfaction of having lived well. Ultimately these men came to conceive of mankind as a universal brotherhood.[4]

THE REVIVAL OF HUMANISM

The official substitution of the ascetic for the humanistic outlook by the Roman emperors of the late fourth century is the most important fact to

[3]This meaning of "ascetic," as enlarged in Chap. viii, will be used throughout this work.
[4]This meaning of "humanistic," as enlarged in Chap. iv, will be used throughout this work.

date in the cultural history of the civilization to which we belong. That substitution, in fact, marks the disappearance of a civilization that we call classical or Hellenic (essentially Greek) for our own western European one. The facts, however, were not quite as simple as we have stated them. The Christian ascetic point of view, while it became official and dominant, absorbed some of the features of Greek humanism. It could not and did not destroy those features that it rejected. They began to reassert their hold upon men's minds and hearts again when the environment of western Europe had so improved that it was no longer necessary utterly to reject the world. This was the moment when the Church, that institution that had been entrusted with leading men to their otherworldly goal, was itself forfeiting men's confidence through its negation of its own ideal.

A SYNTHESIS BETWEEN ASCETICISM AND HUMANISM

Man in the West was then faced with the difficult task of reconciling Greek humanism and Christian asceticism in a synthesis that we may call Christian humanism. It is a task upon which he is still engaged. At the moment in our history when this synthesis became necessary if the West were to preserve a common point of view, the results of early modern science tended to discredit the dogmatic statements of Christian churches and to support the humanistic tradition. For, after all, the marvelous discoveries of the scientists and their application to the improvement of man's earthly lot were the work of men pursuing what was essentially the goal of the Greeks. Under this pressure, and that of the development of modern industrialism, men sought to enlarge the traditional interpretation of Christianity by giving it a social as well as an individual aim, by entrusting it with a reformation of the world through a reformation of men. What, then, mankind at the present moment seems to be trying to do is to balance Christianity's emphasis upon the moral nature of man with the tolerant, rational emphasis of scientific humanism upon the discoverable ways of earthly betterment. Until this balance can be achieved in a way satisfactory enough to become the dominant view of our civilization, we shall obviously continue to be the victims of a bewildering dichotomy.

THE WESTERN TRADITION AND TOTALITARIANISM

The western tradition was seriously threatened by the rise of dictatorships after World War I. While men had come to no agreement on a synthesis of the Christian ascetic and Greek humanistic points of view, they felt the common democratic aspects of these two views threatened by the ideologies and the aggressive character of these totalitarian states. Under the guidance of the English, French, and Americans, the western world had fashioned the machinery of a democratic state, whose power rested ultimately upon the choice of the people expressed through the ballot. In such a state the opinions of the people were to be formed through the freedom of the individual to think what he pleased, and to express these thoughts in private or in public meetings, in the press, in education, and in art. In addition to such freedom of expression, the democratic state upheld the ideal of freedom of opportunity, the notion that it should be the object of society to enable every person to develop those capacities that make it possible to live the life of a civilized human being. The democratic state, moreover, had begun to guarantee to those who were in various ways victimized by industrial society a minimum of social security. Its law was based on the theory that it was to offer protection to all, irrespective of social or economic station.

THE TOTALITARIAN DENIAL OF DEMOCRACY

After World War I it seemed for a while to some observers as if the new Communist regime set up in Russia by the 1917 revolution, with its advanced social and economic policies, represented a hopeful step forward in the struggle toward human betterment. But as the peoples of the West have watched the development of this regime and learned more of its character, it has become apparent that, as in the old Russia, in the new Russia human values have been sacrificed to the power of the state and the ideology of its ruling group. Authoritarian practices in Russia are not new and can perhaps be better understood in the light of Russian historical and cultural development. Between the wars, however, totalitarian beliefs and practices developed great strength in western Europe itself, notably in the fascist and Nazi regimes in Italy and Germany. These nations had grown up in the western tradition, and the authoritarianism of their governments, while learning some of its techniques from the Russian Communists, represented a peculiarly western challenge.

The fascist rejected with contempt the democratic state. For it he substituted the totalitarian state directed by a single political party. The people existed for this all-powerful state. The state did not exist for the people. The prohibition of all political opinion except that of the leadership of the single party was a deliberate negation of the democratic principle of freedom of thought. This prohibition went beyond the political into all fields upon which the single party held definite views. Since the party professed to have a philosophy, these fields included most of what men had occasion to think about. Freedom of opportunity did not exist in the fascist state inasmuch as it held theories of race that regarded one group of people (such as Jews or Slavs) as inferior to other groups (such as Germans or Italians). It denied them, accordingly, not merely the opportunity to develop their talents but even the right to live. In the fascist state there was no equality of law. Law was virtually the expression of the will of the leaders of the single party, and its judgments were directed against those who found fault with fascist tyranny. The fascist state was not only a negation of the democratic content of the western tradition; it was essentially a negation of western civilization itself, and indeed of all civilization. It was often led by unbalanced criminals who, in order to impose their authority, resorted to inconceivable cruelty and murder on a large scale, carried out with special zeal behind the barbed wire of the concentration camp.

THE DEMOCRATIC HOPE

The fascist powers were defeated by the democratic powers—with the considerable assistance of Russia—in World War II. Totalitarianism as a philosophy, a force, and a mode of organization and action, however, cannot really be exterminated in the world until the conditions that breed it have been altered. Today totalitarian attitudes and methods hold full power and sway among the eastern Communist states and constitute for the West an explicit political and military threat. But in the West itself totalitarian attitudes and methods, whether Communist or fascist, exist implicitly in the thinking and the actions of many individuals and groups. The democratic ideal, whether explicitly or implicitly, is still under heavy and dangerous attack. Yet this ideal, conceived within the Christian ascetic–Greek humanistic framework, remains to date the finest work of man. This must be the conviction of the West. Its larger realization is the greatest hope of man. It is the meaning, the satisfaction, and the promise that give vitality to the will to survive. It is the point of view that can restore to our bewildered mentality the common outlook that Christianity alone once gave, and, to all appearances, can no longer give. It is therefore our obligation to set to work to understand the content of this tradition in order properly to assume the responsibility of making it prevail. Whether it is to prevail or not cannot be predetermined. For all practical purposes, it still rests upon human choice and action.

THE WESTERN AND OTHER TRADITIONS

Once we have met this obligation we shall be in a proper position to try to understand the cultural traditions guiding the actions of the other peoples upon whose co-operation our survival depends. To attempt this understanding without first understanding ourselves would produce abortive results. Thus, in order to help to avoid the possible catastrophe that lies before us and to go on with the noble and difficult task of refashioning human society in accordance with our best knowledge and ability, we must first study our own cultural heritage, seeking thereby to acquire sufficient wisdom to assist us in measuring its value in relation to the heritages of other peoples. With this wisdom, we may hope to participate in the defense of what is best in it, and to modify what is not good, in the light of the best of our own and of other traditions. This fusion of the best in mankind's history can form the basis of a world tradition to guide the actions and inspire the hopes of the citizens of a world society to come.

chapter two

THE RELIGIOUS TRADITION OF THE ANCIENT NEAR EAST

*T*HE INFLUENCE OF DEAD CIVILIZATIONS. It is the opinion of some historians that, in spite of all appearances to the contrary, the only civilization that is healthy today is our own—the western European civilization. All others are sick unto death if not actually expiring. The history of man, from one point of view, is merely an account of the tragic deaths of civilizations that once enjoyed the greatest vitality. To learn the secret of a society's health, or, inversely, what can prevent its sickness and death, is the ultimate reason for the study of history.

Dead civilizations leave remains, the physical and spiritual residues of their ways of life. If these civilizations while alive have caused other civilizations to imitate them, they live on, in spite of their own deaths, because of their creative power to inspire. They may thus achieve immortality. It is not at all necessary that a civilization's ability to inspire be contemporaneous with its actual career. This is notably the case with the civilizations of the Ancient Near East. By Ancient Near East is meant the area bounded on the west by the Nile Valley, on the east by the Tigris-Euphrates Valley, the two valleys being connected by the Fertile Crescent, the strip north and west of the Arabian Desert along the eastern Mediterranean coast. The original civilizations of the two river valleys were a contemporaneous inspiration to their neighbors, and in this way succeeded in perpetuating themselves among their descendants. Their inspiration, however, was only partial. The civilizations as a whole perished, and with them perished an accurate knowledge of them, and even of the languages in which their history was recorded. The ancient world of the Near East had to be discovered in the nineteenth century.

JAMES H. BREASTED

It was discovered by scholars of the western European civilization which, indirectly, it had inspired. "You know," said an Egyptian official to one of these discoverers, Professor James H. Breasted of the University of Chicago, "Egypt has no civilization except what comes to us from Europe and America. We *must* rely on foreign scientists." This discovery of the Ancient Near East in the nineteenth century, involving as it did a vast improvement in the techniques of the archaeologist and of the philologist, who laboriously deciphered the ancient languages, is one of the noble and exciting chapters in the history of the scientific spirit applied to the study of man. The American discoverer mentioned above wrote to his father at the threshold of his career, "I have tried to find some phrase which would sum up what I want to do, or *can* do. It is this: I want to read to my fellow men the *oldest* chapter in the story of human progress. I would rather do this than gain countless wealth." To prepare for this reading to his fellow man, Breasted felt he had to "copy, translate and publish *every* known ancient Egyptian historical inscription—in the Cairo Museum, the museums of Europe and America, and on the ancient monuments and temple walls of the entire Nile valley itself." Early in December, 1894, he was, for example, at Luxor: "For three days, from dawn till dark, I never lost a moment copying inscriptions—and on one night at Karnak I copied by moonlight. The silver light streamed down through the broken roof of the vast colonnaded hall, splashing with bright patches the dusky outlines of the enormous columns. . . . Imagine a forest of 134 columns, the middle two rows sixty-nine feet high and twelve feet thick, with capitals eleven feet high; and carved upon them in deep relief the tall figures of gods and kings, with legends in hieroglyphic. . . . I shall remember that evening until my dying day." In November, 1922, he was permitted to see the newly opened tomb of the Pharaoh Tutankhamon (1362–1352 B.C.): "We saw an incredible vision, an impossible scene from a fairy tale, an enchanted property-room from the opera house of some great composer's dreams. Opposite us were three couches upon which a king had lain, all about were chests, caskets, alabaster vases, gold-embellished stools and chairs—the heaped-up riches of a Pharaoh who had died some three thousand two hundred and fifty years ago. . . . In the brilliant light, against the white limestone wall, the colors of all these things were vibrant yet soft—a medley of brown, yellow, blue, amber, gold, russet, and black. . . . Never was anything so dramatic in the whole range of archaeological discovery as this first view of what must surely be Tutankhamon's tomb."[1]

[1]Reprinted from *Pioneer to the Past* by Charles Breasted, pp. 389, 78, 65, 72, 335–336; used by permission of the publishers, Charles Scribner's Sons.

Breasted's study of the material life of ancient Egypt led him finally to study its spiritual life and to write a book entitled *The Dawn of Conscience*. "It will furnish," the author wrote, "the first *historical* demonstration that the evolutionary process which seems to have operated so largely in the rise and development of material forms, has culminated in ideals of human conduct and has thus produced an age of character which we have little more than begun."[2] His preface argued that: "Man began as an unmoral savage. . . . Out of prehistoric savagery, . . . [and] his own experience, [he] arose to visions of character, . . . to a world of inner values transcending matter. . . . Not projected from the outside into a world of unworthy men by some mystic process called inspiration or revelation, but springing out of man's own life two thousand years before the theologians' 'age of revelation' began, illuminating the darkness of social disillusionment and inner conflict, a glorious vindication of the worth of man, the dawn of the age of conscience and character broke upon the world. No conception of a spotlight of Divine Providence shining exclusively on Palestine shall despoil man of this crowning glory of his life on earth, the discovery of character. It is the greatest discovery in the whole sweep of the evolutionary process as far as it is known to us. . . . The human adventure has no value or significance except as we see it rising . . . toward . . . the Age of Character."[3]

THE ANCIENT NEAR EAST AND THE PRESENT

If the ancient Egyptians discovered character, they did not influence directly its development among the peoples of western Europe until it was learned that they had done this. It was then possible to use this discovery to estimate the moment at which man set up moral ideals for himself, and thus to gain temporal perspective in regard to the development of man himself. "As a young Orientalist I [Breasted] found that the Egyptians had possessed a standard of morals far superior to that of the Decalogue over a thousand years before the Decalogue was written."[4] But the oriental concept of character that helped most to shape the development of the West was that contained in the Old Testament. Accordingly, the discovery of the civilizations of the Ancient Near East made it possible for them to inspire the present stage in the development of the civilization of the West as they were not able to inspire its formation. When an American architect drew his plans for the capitol of the state of Nebraska, he could conceive them within the general framework of the ancient architecture of the Tigris-Euphrates Valley as a Roman architect,

[2]C. Breasted, *Pioneer*, p. 404.
[3]Reprinted from *The Dawn of Conscience* by James H. Breasted; used by permission of the publishers, Charles Scribner's Sons, quoted in C. Breasted, *Pioneer*, pp. 406–407.
[4]C. Breasted, *Pioneer*, p. 407.

CHRONOLOGY — Religious Tradition of Ancient Near East

B.C.	Mesopotamia	Egypt	Palestine	Persia
2000				
	Hammurabi (reigned ca. 1728–1686)			
1500				
		Ikhnaton (r. ca. 1375–1358) Tutankhamon (r. ca. 1362–1352)		
1000			Solomon (r. ca. 960–922) Elijah (fl. 9th c.) Amos (fl. 750) Isaiah (fl. 720) Holiness Code (after 586) Ezekiel (fl. 550) Priest Code (ca. 500)	Zoroaster (fl. 560) Cyrus (r. ca. 550–530)
	Nebuchadnezzar II (r. ca. 605–561)			

building his capitol, could not have done. To the Roman this architecture was unknown and dead. To the American it was rediscovered and alive. The latter could, therefore, correct history in his architecture and put beside the Moses of the Decalogue the Hammurabi of the Code and the father-in-law of Tutankhamon, Ikhnaton, who conceived of a kind of monotheism long before the Hebrew prophets.

THE INFLUENCE OF THE OLD TESTAMENT

At the same time that western scholars were discovering the civilizations of the Ancient Near East they were establishing also, partly in the light of this discovery, how the books composing the Old Testament came to be written and edited. This particular collection of Hebrew literature had become one of the chief means of civilizing the West. The fact that Jesus was a Jew and that Christianity began as an attempt to reform Judaism, the religion of the Jews, made the literature of Judaism of particular moment to Christians. Since, too, the career of Jesus as the Messianic Savior of mankind was believed by early Christian scholars to have been announced previously in various passages of the Old Testament, it became inevitably a part of Christian literature. This joining of the Old Testament to the New Testament to form the sacred Christian Scriptures meant, of course, that the finest literary heritage of the Ancient Near East became a most important part of the spiritual and intellectual nourishment of the civilization of the West. Because the Bible for so long a period in western history was almost the only book that was read, and because it has remained, in spite of the attacks upon its sacred character, the most enduringly popular book of the West, the history of the Old Testament becomes inevitably the most valuable history of the Ancient Near East for explaining the content of the western tradition. This popularity, of course, rests far more upon the authoritatively sacred character of these writings than upon their literary quality, great as that is. The God of the Hebrews became through Jesus the God of the Christians. The Old Testament, to the rabbis the sacred word of Yahweh, became to the Christians the sacred word of God. Accordingly, nothing more authoritative could be found to regulate not only the large affairs of state and society but all the individual affairs of man, his relations both to his fellow men and to his God. The early history of the western tradition, therefore, is bound up with men's interpretation of the sacred Hebrew Scriptures.

This is not the whole story of the importance of this collection. The Old Testament is, of course, a part of the Bible of Greek Orthodox Christians and occupies the same position in the history of eastern as of western Europe. It would, moreover, be impossible to understand adequately the religion of Mohammed without understanding the Old Testament, since Mohammed, too, regarded it as authoritative for a religious revelation previous to his own. Thus, in addition to Jewish history, the Old Testament is bound up intimately with the history of three other civilizations. Since Judaism did not die with the early expiration of the Jewish state but has been carried by Jews to the ends of the earth, and now back again to Palestine, it remains a living universal religion, and the Old Testament continues to serve its original purpose as an authoritative and sacred guide for Jewish life. Certainly it has been given to few peoples to play so large a part in the civilizations of the world.

THE SCHOLARLY STUDY OF THE OLD TESTAMENT

The study by western scholars of the nature and composition of the books collected together in the Old Testament was motivated by discontent with the mere assumption of their sacred character as the word of God. These scholars hoped to establish their validity as historical documents upon which could be built a critical history of the Jewish people in the setting of the Ancient Near East. The result has not been to deprive the Old Testament of its unique position among the literatures of the Ancient Near East or, indeed, of the world. Rather this patient work has succeeded in exalting the human spirit that was capable of producing such a body of writings. By establishing, in so far as it was possible, the authorship of the various books and the manner in which the authors wrote, by showing how at various times it seemed necessary for priests and scribes to edit, combine, or rearrange older materials, scholars were able to relate these books to a particular historical or human setting, and to interpret them as the expressions of the experience of a people. It was possible, by utilizing the contemporary work of the discoverers of the other civilizations of the Ancient Near East, to show how the Hebrews in Palestine were at the cultural as well as the military and commercial crossroads of the Fertile Crescent and how, in many respects, the Old Testament reflects the cultural borrowings of the Jews from more powerful neighbors on either side of them. This chapter chooses, therefore, in its treatment of these societies to emphasize the history of the Jews. It does this not only because of the relationship between Jewish history and the formation of the western tradition, but also because this history was itself inspired by neighboring civilizations of the Near East.

THE HEBREWS

About the time Pharaoh Tutankhamon ascended the imperial throne of Egypt (1362 B.C.), nomadic Hebrew tribes were beginning to filter into the western Fertile Crescent from the hot sands of the Arabian Desert. They entered an area already occupied by the Canaanites, another Semitic people. This area, following the Greek historian Herodotus, is called Palestine, or land of the Philistines, because it had been invaded by Philistines, a seafaring Mediterranean people who settled the western section. The Semitic Phoenicians, in any event, took to the sea from Syrian ports to the north (Sidon, Tyre, Byblus). These Phoenicians, who first spread the alphabet from which ours is derived, not only traded throughout the

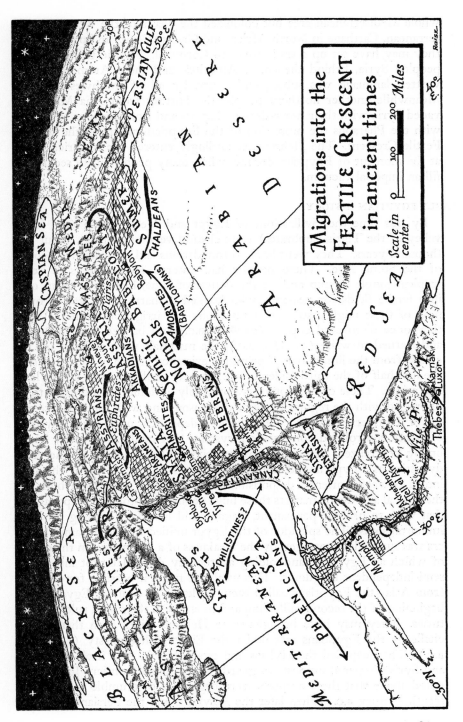

Migrations into the
FERTILE CRESCENT
in ancient times

Scale in
center

0   100   200   Miles

whole Mediterranean area but colonized the coasts of the western Mediterranean, Carthage in North Africa, and Gades (Cadiz) in Spain, whence they may have set up a trade route to Cornwall. Semitic tribes had also peopled Syria, behind the coast: Amorites, and those Arameans whose written language was subsequently used by all of southwestern Asia. Meanwhile another northern people, the Hittites from Asia Minor, invaded Syria with their horse-drawn chariots and iron weapons to contest with the Pharaohs the possession of the Egyptian empire in the western Fertile Crescent. The Hebrews accordingly entered the historical scene at the moment of Egyptian decline, when many peoples were seeking to fill an imperial vacuum.

EARLY EGYPTIAN HISTORY

By this time the civilizations of Egypt and Mesopotamia (the lower valley of the Tigris-Euphrates) were already very old, that is, about two thousand years. They went back to foundations laid by primitive peoples of the Stone Age. These peoples had entered river valleys of semi-tropical jungle swamp and, in the course of time, had made them over into fertile fields for peasants, who learned to harness the yearly overflow of these mighty streams in reservoirs and irrigation ditches. When they once discovered copper (*ca.* 4000 B.C.) and bronze (*ca.* 3000 B.C.) and learned to write (*ca.* 3200 B.C.), the materials were at hand for the escape from the limitations of primitive existence. Already by the end of the first half of the third millenium (2500 B.C.) civilizations of a high level had arisen. These civilizations were primarily agricultural and came to be impressed with the regular cycle of the seasons and with the vital rise and fall of the rivers. Their very lives became dependent upon unified systems of water control and conservation, systems that could most easily be set up by centralized, autocratic governments. The Pharaohs of the early dynasties of Egypt united the city-kingdoms of the valley of the Nile into a powerful oriental despotism, whose enslaved population built for their royal and divine masters those huge geometrical tombs, the pyramids, that were to provide permanent, elegant, and luxurious housing for their immortal souls. The splendor of the Egypt unified by the pyramid builders was succeeded, however, by the weakness of a feudal age, in the course of which an Egyptian landholding aristocracy divided Egypt into many semi-independent kingdoms. This weakness made it possible for invaders from Asia (the Egyptians called them Hyksos) to conquer Egypt at the beginning of the second millenium and to establish their own rule for centuries. They may have brought some Hebrew tribes with them. This challenge the Egyptians met under the Eighteenth Dynasty (1570-1320 B.C.). They expelled the Hyksos and established in Asia itself (Palestine and Syria) imperial outposts to guard the Egyptian frontier. It has been noted above that these outposts were beginning to crumble in the fourteenth century B.C. When later the Assyrians and the Persians sought to

On some of the huge columns in the temple of the sun-god Amon-Re at Karnak are carved records of the expansion of Egypt under Thutmose III (1490–1436 B.C.).

An oriental theocrat: the sublime Egyptian Pharaoh Khaf-Re (2560 B.C.).

Plate 2
Sculpture in the Egyptian Museum, Cairo

Plate 3

Sculpture in the State Museum, Berlin

The revolutionary Pharaoh Ikhnaton (*ca.* 1375–1358 B.C.).

Nefertiti, the sister-wife of Ikhnaton.

Plate 4

Sculpture in the State Museum, Berlin
Verlag Gebr. Mann, Berlin
Artext Prints, Inc., Westport, Connecticut

breach the gates leading from Asia through the Sinai Peninsula into Egypt, enfeebled Pharaohs had to surrender the Nile Valley to the conquerors.

EARLY MESOPOTAMIAN HISTORY

The foundations of Mesopotamian civilization were laid in those cities founded in the delta of the Two Rivers by the Sumerians, cities which were governed by priest-kings. They were sufficiently prosperous to tempt, from time to time, Semitic tribes from the Arabian Desert to conquer them. The first of these, the Akkadians, were able to gather the Sumerian cities into a kingdom including all Mesopotamia. The second, Amorites from Syria, forged the Sumerian-Akkadian state into what became known as the Babylonian empire, which under Hammurabi (1728–1686 B.C.) represented Mesopotamian society at its most grand if not at its best. After an interlude of foreign conquest by mountaineer horsemen, the Kassites, the Babylonian empire was destroyed by the third group of Semites, the Assyrians, from their early city at Assur and later from Nineveh. In campaigns of ruthless savagery, these Assyrians, the first essentially militaristic power, reduced the peoples of the Ancient Near East, including the Hebrews, to satellites of a new empire. When this military tyranny was brought to an end by the Medes and Chaldeans, an unknown Hebrew prophet poured out in song the joy and gratitude of his people. In so doing he was likewise voicing the exultant relief of millions of other oppressed Assyrian subjects.

THE INFLUENCE OF MESOPOTAMIA AND EGYPT UPON THE HEBREWS

Syria and Palestine were a crossroads for many peoples of various racial stocks from the surrounding areas: Indo-Europeans (Hittites), Semites (Phoenicians, Amorites, Aramaeans, and Hebrews) from the north and east, and Egyptians from the south. From the civilizations of Egypt and Mesopotamia especially they were inspired to borrow much. This can best be illustrated by parts of the Old Testament, which are now recognized to be closely akin to Egyptian and Mesopotamian religious literature.

THE HYMN TO ATON

Reference has already been made to Pharaoh Ikhnaton as a religious innovator who reigned at a moment when the Hebrews were beginning to enter Palestine.[5] It is not likely, as Egyptologists formerly suggested, that Ikhnaton, with his new god, wished to provide a religion which might help to hold a tottering empire together. In any case, the change from Amon to Aton (Ikhnaton means "Aton is satisfied") involved the abandonment of an old for a new sun god, who was to predominate over all other deities in the state and empire.[6] Aton was represented as the sun's disk,

[5]See p. 23.
[6]See J. A. Wilson, *The Burden of Egypt*, Chap. ix, for the exact nature of this revolution.

rather than in human or animal form, and in one of the hymns composed for his worship he is referred to as:

> O living Aton, Beginning of life!
> When thou risest in the eastern horizon of heaven,
> Thou fillest every land with thy beauty
> For thou art beautiful, great, glittering, high over the earth;
> Thy rays, they encompass the lands, even all thou hast made.
> Thou art Re, and thou hast carried them all away captive;
> Thou bindest them by thy love.
> Though thou art afar, thy rays are on earth;
> Though thou art on high, thy footprints are the day.[7]

As the hymn goes on it becomes reminiscent of the 104th Psalm. But that this religious revolution may have influenced the development of Hebrew monotheism is no longer taken seriously by orientalists.[8]

HEBREW, MESOPOTAMIAN, AND EGYPTIAN LITERATURE

The "wisdom literature" of Egypt and Babylonia seems to have been known to the authors of Ecclesiastes and Proverbs. The following advice is given in Ecclesiastes 9:7-9:

> Go thy way, eat thy bread with joy,
> And drink thy wine with a merry heart;
> For God now accepteth thy works.
> Let thy garments be always white;
> And let thy head lack no ointment.
> Live joyfully with the wife whom thou lovest
> All the days of the life of thy vanity,
> Which He hath given thee under the sun.[9]

This advice appears earlier in the Babylonian epic concerning the search of Gilgamesh for eternal life:

> Why, O Gilgamesh, dost thou wander about?
> The life that thou seekest, thou wilt not find.
> When the Gods created man,
> Death they ordained for man,
> Life they kept in their hands.
> Thou, O Gilgamesh, fill thy belly,
> Day and night be joyful!
> Daily be glad!
> Day and night make merry!

---

[7]Reprinted from *A History of the Ancient Egyptians* by James H. Breasted, p. 273; used by permission of the publishers, Charles Scribner's Sons. Cf. trans. J. A. Wilson, in *Ancient Near Eastern Texts*, ed. J. B. Pritchard, p. 370.

[8]A. T. Olmstead, *History of Palestine and Syria*, p. 172, argues for this view; but see Wilson, *The Burden of Egypt*; also T. J. Meek, "The Origin of Hebrew Monotheism," *Hebrew Origins*.

[9]Trans. J. A. Bewer, in *The Literature of the Old Testament in Its Historical Development*, pp. 334-335.

Let thy garments be white,
Anoint thy head, and purify thyself!
With the children at thy side,
Enjoy the wife of thy bosom![10]

and in the Egyptian "Song of the Harper":

So long as thou livest
Put myrrh on thy head
And clothe thyself in fine linen. . . .
Follow thy heart and thy inclination.[11]

The following counsel is given by the Hebrew author of Proverbs (King James):

Better is little with the fear of the Lord
Than great treasure and trouble therewith.
Better is a dinner of herbs where love is,
Than a stalled ox and hatred therewith. (15:16–17)

Divers weights, and divers measures,
Both of them are alike abomination to the Lord. (20:10)

Seest thou a man diligent in his business?
He shall stand before kings;
He shall not stand before mean men. (22:29)

Lying lips are abomination to the Lord:
But they that deal truly are his delight. (12:22)

This is so close to the text of *The Teachings of Amen-em-opet* that it must be assumed the latter was used by the authors of the Old Testament:

Better is poverty in the hand of God
Than wealth in the storehouse.
Better is bread with a happy heart
Than wealth with trouble.

Move not the scales, and falsify not the weights,
And diminish not the parts of the corn-measure.
A scribe who is skilful in his office
Findeth himself worthy to be a courtier.

Speak not to a man in falsehood
—The abomination of God—
Sever not thy heart from thy tongue,
That all thy ways may be successful.[12]

The account in Genesis of the creation of the universe and man is similar to a corresponding Babylonian epic of creation. The account in

[10]Bewer, *Development*, p. 335. Cf. trans. E. A. Speiser, in *Ancient Near Eastern Texts*, p. 90.
[11]Trans. W. L. Wardle, in *The History and Religion of Israel*, p. 220.
[12]Wardle, p. 221. Cf. Wilson, *Ancient Near Eastern Texts*, pp. 422–424.

Genesis of Noah and the Deluge has its Babylonian counterpart in Utnapishtim of the Gilgamesh epic referred to above.[13] The law of Hammurabi's Code is similar to and often identical with the early law of the Jews contained in the Book of the Covenant (Exodus 20:22–23:33). *Sheol*, the murky underground abode of Hebrew souls after death, is much like the Babylonian *Arallu*. A common humanity as well as a common civilization is reflected in these parallels.

THEOCRATIC SOCIETIES OF THE NEAR EAST

The character of the Hebrew state and society likewise resembled that of the Nile Valley and Mesopotamia. Indeed, the institutions grouped about the oriental monarchical despotisms became, through the Old Testament itself, and through the perpetuation of these institutions until they were assimilated by the Roman Empire, a part of the western tradition that finally had to be rejected. Briefly stated, the form which these oriental societies took was a theocracy. The theocratic notion of society assumes that its origin and functioning have a divine source, that government is by a god (the literal meaning of theocracy) in societies with a monotheistic religion, or by gods in polytheistic societies. These gods must be kept well disposed toward mankind if the society is to survive and flourish. If no moral regimen is attributed to the gods, divine beneficence may be won by appropriate religious ceremonies, including sacrifice. If the divine powers are moral powers, their support is not to be had simply by appeasement; it must be earned by obedience to what is taken to be the divine law. In a theocratic society there is little justification for human existence except to maintain the equanimity of often rather temperamental deities. In the societies of the Ancient Near East the ordinary human being was made constantly aware of the insignificance of his existence by the awful proximity of his gods in the persons of his kings, who were either regarded as gods themselves, as descendants of gods, or as the immediate vice-regents of gods. The Egyptian Pharaohs were divine, the sons of the Sun God. The kings of the Sumerian city-states were the chief priests of their tutelary deities. The monarchs of Babylonia were the vice-regents of Marduk; those of Assyria, of Ashur; those of Israel, by analogy, of Yahweh. One could not disobey or disregard the will of the gods with impunity. Consequently one could not disregard the commands of their human incarnations or agents, the priest-kings. These societies were organized for the benefit of their royal masters and those who assisted them in getting what they wanted.[14]

[13]One recension of this epic has Nwh for Utnapishtim.

[14]The word "theocratic" will be used throughout this work to describe an absolute state whose government has a divine sanction. A distinction is later made (Chaps. xii–xiii) between a secular and an ecclesiastical theocracy. The former is an absolute state of divine origin, government, or purpose, subordinating and absorbing the church and ruled by a layman. The latter is an absolute church, subordinating and absorbing the state and ruled by a priest.

THE PILLARS OF THEOCRACY

In a theocracy it follows that next to the divine presence of the ruler the most important group is the priesthood, those skilled in the art and technique of placating the gods. In societies where the great masses are illiterate, those who know how to write—the scribes, the bureaucrats, the keepers of the account books of king and priest, the collectors of the revenues from their vast estates—are also important mainstays of the divine government. And in a world where gods were martial and even imperialistic, leading their followers into battle, the general was an inevitable adjutant to the royal chief priest. Thus the governments of the societies of the Ancient Near East were divine despotisms whose ruling groups were composed of royal families, hereditary priesthoods, subservient bureaucracies, and the military. Beneath them was the mass of slaves, serfs, peasants, working classes, merchants, and skilled artisans whose privilege it was to worship and work, often at forced labor, for the maintenance of what in the last analysis was conceived to be an unalterable, divine economy.

THE HEBREW THEOCRACY OF SOLOMON

The specific character of oriental theocracies can be examined in the Jewish monarchy under Solomon (*ca.* 960–922 B.C.). At the moment of his accession to the throne the kingdom was only about fifty years old. Jewish nomads from the desert and from Egypt under the leadership of individual tribes for centuries had been wresting Palestine from the Canaanites. This conquest and settlement required a severe adjustment in manner of life, the adjustment from a migrant tender of flocks to a settled farmer or townsman. In the course of it, the perpetuation of jealousy among the tribal units weakened their resistance to the Canaanites and the invading Philistines. They attempted, therefore, to establish unity under a king. With their first kings, Saul and David (*ca.* 1000–960 B. C.), the conquest of the land had been completed, a national and religious capital set up at Jerusalem, and a beginning made of assimilating the rich urban life of the area.

The new boy-king Solomon was anointed by the chief priest Zadok with holy oil from the tent where the ark of Yahweh was kept. "So far as he was able, Solomon made his court a replica of that at Thebes or Babylon or Ashur [Assur]." Its officials were a prime minister, a director of the *corvée* (forced labor owed the king), a chief priest, royal scribes, a chief eunuch (master of the household, which included a harem), a king's companion, and a director of the administration of the twelve provinces to which both Hebrews and Canaanites were subjected. "Their men were levied as soldiers or for plowing and reaping the crown lands with their own animals, or for manufacturing weapons and chariots; their women were enrolled as perfumers, cooks and bakers. The best of their fields, vineyards, and olive orchards were confiscated and granted to the king's

The HEBREW KINGDOM of DAVID and SOLOMON 1000 –922 B.C.

supporters. A tithe was demanded of the seed, wine, and flocks, and the 'king's mowing' took the first cutting of the grass. Every day the court consumed thirty cors of fine flour and sixty measures of meal, ten fat oxen, twenty pasture-fed oxen, a hundred sheep, not to mention harts, gazelles, and fatted fowl. Barley and straw must be provided for the horses, of which he had four thousand stalls, and food for the twelve thousand horsemen."[15] Trade in this kingdom was a royal monopoly.

The profits of the monarchy were spent in part on public works. To make his palace more like those of monarchs who really counted in the world Solomon had to import cedars of Lebanon from the realm of the Phoenician King Hiram of Tyre. To pay for what he needed he had to export 20,000 cors of wheat and 20,000 baths of olive oil and cede to Hiram twenty Galilean towns. A labor force of 30,000 drafted men was required

[15]Reprinted from *History of Palestine and Syria* by A. T. Olmstead, p. 341; used by permission of the publishers, Charles Scribner's Sons.

to procure these trees from Lebanon. Other forced-labor contingents had to transport them from the sea to Jerusalem and to work the quarries for their foundations. The trees were used to adorn not only the king's own residence but other buildings of the royal quarter, the House of the Forest of Lebanon, the house for his Egyptian queen, the Porch of Pillars, and the Porch of Judgment.

THE HABITATION OF YAHWEH

That tribal war god Yahweh, the source of all Israel's prosperity, who hitherto had been confined to the habitation of a tent, was made to share the larger fortunes of the kingdom in a new temple. Its entrance was flanked by two columns with capitals, "cast in bronze, seven and a half feet high, and covered with trellis work and two rows of pomegranates . . . cult objects pure and simple, relics of the days when standing stones were themselves objects of worship," imitations of the two columns of gold and "emerald" which the artist "had seen in the temple of Baal Melkart in his home city." At the far end of the outer room of the temple was Yahweh's gold altar. "Double folding doors of olive wood, carved with cherubs, palm trees, and open flowers, gave access to the inner shrine, a cube of thirty feet which imitated the primitive cave. Touching its goldplated walls were the outstretched wings of two cherubs, winged bulls such as are found in Assyrian ruins, and covered with gold." When removed from its tent, its nomadic dwelling, to this "exalted house" Yahweh's ark had a "place of . . . dwelling forever."[16]

THE HISTORY OF THE HEBREW KINGDOM

The history of a united Jewish kingdom, trying to ape the great kingdoms of the surrounding world, is a short and comparatively barbaric one. The Jews of northern Palestine found the rule of Solomon intolerable and, at his death, seceded and founded a separate kingdom of their own, the Kingdom of Israel, with Samaria as its capital. The Jews of southern Palestine, with Jerusalem as their political and religious capital, remained the subjects of a Kingdom of Judah. This separation into a northern and a southern kingdom was the result in part of the incompatibility between nomads who had been completely assimilated into the settled rural and urban life bordering on the Phoenician and Syrian worlds, and nomads of the south who retained their shepherd way of life. In any event, it was impossible for these little kingdoms to preserve their independence from the expanding Semitic kingdoms of the Tigris-Euphrates Valley. The northern kingdom fell before the Assyrian army in 722 B.C., and the influential part of its population, in accordance with Assyrian policy, was deported. The southern kingdom, utilizing a precarious diplomacy in the struggle between Assyria and Egypt, managed to preserve its existence until 586

[16]Olmstead, pp. 347–349.

B.C., when Jerusalem was partly razed and depopulated by the Chaldean emperor Nebuchadnezzar II. The Chaldeans, likewise Semitic nomads from the desert, had first fastened themselves upon the delta of the Tigris-Euphrates, and in 612 B.C. had participated in the destruction of the Assyrian capital at Nineveh. From their own capital, a restored Babylon, they had swept the whole Fertile Crescent into a Chaldean empire. After Jerusalem's destruction, the Jews of the southern kingdom were deported, this time to Babylonia, leaving in all Palestine but an insignificant number of peasants. The exile in Babylonia was terminated in 538 B.C. after the destruction of the Chaldean empire by the Persians under Cyrus in 539 B.C. The Jewish exiles were then permitted to re-establish themselves in Palestine as an autonomous state under priestly leadership. Henceforth, except for a brief interval, the Hebrews never regained their independence until the formation of the state of Israel in A.D. 1948. They formed a part of Alexander's empire when the Persian empire fell to him, a part of the empire of his successors in Egypt (the Ptolemies) and in Syria (the Seleucids), and finally a part of the all-embracing Roman Empire.

THE HEBREWS AND YAHWEH

If the political, social, and economic history of the Hebrews is but the story of their unsuccessful attempts to fit ancient oriental institutions to their own needs, their interpretation of this history in the light of their religion is one of the supreme human accomplishments of all time. It was made possible by enlarging the concepts of a primitive nomadic religion as it moved into a more advanced environment. Originally, the Yahweh of the Hebrews was only a local storm god of the desert. His adoption by Hebrew tribes can be attributed to the influence of Moses. The particular nature of this event is difficult to determine, inasmuch as the priests who later edited early Hebrew historical writings gave them a meaning they found useful to themselves. At any event, it came to be taught and believed that Yahweh had made a pact or covenant with the Hebrews. In return for their undivided allegiance and obedience to his law (the Mosaic Code), he promised to lead them to their Palestinian home and remain their jealous protector. Yahweh's acceptance as the special god of the Jews became more widespread in the course of Judah's settlement in southern Palestine. To his character as a storm god he added the attributes of a war god, while retaining his role as the defender of his law. With the establishment of the united kingdom at Jerusalem his cult spread to the Jewish settlers in northern Palestine.

YAHWEH AND THE BAALS

In entering Palestine Yahweh came into competition with the local gods and goddesses of the Canaanites, the enemies of his chosen people. He was unable to defeat them. They were the baals and baaliths, the guarantors of the fertility of nature, the gods who determined whether, after the death of vegetation in the winter, there was to be a resurrection in the spring. Their favor was sought at altars in the "high places" and in temples in the cities where, among other rites, the productivity of the soil was encouraged by promoting the fertility of temple prostitutes. The incoming Jewish settlers did not feel secure enough with Yahweh at their head to disregard these local guarantors of a means of livelihood. Consequently there ensued an identification of Yahweh with baal worship that took many forms. The oppressive character of the new Jewish monarchy, moreover, and the injustices caused by the development of superior and inferior social classes seemed to some to be departures from the traditional principles of leadership and equality common to nomadic life. The loss of unity after Solomon and the threat of a loss of independence from abroad also thwarted the long-held trust in Yahweh and seemed to call for special explanation.

THE RISE OF THE PROPHETS

Under these circumstances the prophets arose in Israel. These men were of the type of religious leader who is able, through various means, to establish what he regards as direct communication with God, so that God then uses him as his mouthpiece to speak to men. The moments of direct communication are described ordinarily in terms of ecstasy or trance, and the prophet sees visions that it is necessary to interpret. The Hebrew prophets regarded themselves, as the result of such experiences, as the spokesmen of Yahweh, and spoke directly in his name. This is also to say, in effect, that these men, often from the ranks of the underprivileged, were giving a divine sanction to their own criticisms of the evils that they found among their people. Yet they were much more than mere poetic denouncers of contemporary evils. They sought to, and did, institute practical reforms, and they tried to guide the policy of the ruling groups of their society. Accordingly, with the Hebrew prophets we have a popular reform movement, if not a real social revolution. In associating reform with the demands of religion, in seeking to establish justice as the vindication of the laws of God, they helped to establish the tradition which made Christianity, the religion of the West, an activist religion, impelled by its God to go out into the world and right its wrongs.

ELIJAH

This bold spirit of reform appeared splendidly in the person of Elijah, to whom Yahweh spoke "in the sound of a soft stillness" after being announced by "a great and strong wind" which tore the mountains and broke the rocks. The fiery defender of Yahweh had to deal with a worthless king of Israel (Ahab) and his foreign queen (Jezebel of Tyre), who had brought the Baal Melkart of Tyre with her to Samaria, where he was worshiped in a temple which Ahab himself had erected. Elijah had to demonstrate the powerlessness of this false god and to destroy his priests

(450 of them) with his own hands (1 Kings 18:21–46). Moreover, it had to be made clear that Yahweh did not permit kings to slay subjects and confiscate their lands. This had happened in the case of Naboth, a citizen of Jezreel, whom Jezebel had managed to have stoned so that Ahab might confiscate his vineyard next to the royal palace. When Ahab went to take possession of the vineyard the prophet was on the spot to meet him. "And Ahab said to Elijah, Hast thou found me, O mine enemy?" Elijah confronted him with the dire prediction of Yahweh, "Hast thou killed, and also taken possession? . . . In the place where dogs licked the blood of Naboth shall dogs lick thy blood even thine. . . . The dogs shall eat Jezebel by the wall of Jezreel." (1 Kings 21:19–29)

THE PROPHETS AND ETHICAL MONOTHEISM

Under such an impulse the prophets of the eighth century, Amos, Hosea, Isaiah, and Micah, worked out the conception of an ethical monotheism unique in the annals of the Ancient Near East. They pilloried a corrupt religion which mistook the meticulous performance of ritual and sacrifice for right conduct and a pure heart, and condemned people who did not carry out the prescriptions of divine justice in their social dealings with their fellow men. The Yahweh which they thus raised to the conception of a righteous God, the defender of a moral order, in the opinion of Amos and Hosea had condemned such a people to their unalterable doom. In their concern with a divine sanction for the moral order these men came to see that it could not be limited to the Jews alone, and they began to extend Yahweh's dominion beyond the confines of Palestine. As the century drew to its end and the Assyrian advance promised the extinction of their national existence this onslaught was interpreted as Yahweh's use of Israel's enemies to punish her for her iniquity. Yet for all the monotheistic emphasis of these prophets they were not able to forget completely the notion of Yahweh's special covenant with Israel, nor could they believe that he would utterly abandon them. If the righteous God demanded vengeance for their transgressions, the loving God would reward those who repented or remained obedient to his law. The God who brought the Assyrian scourge upon Israel would save the loyal in Judah, and after this deliverance a savior-king would usher in the peaceful golden age.

YAHWEH AND SACRIFICE

It was intolerable, therefore, for Yahweh to have to witness the increase of altars and "goodly images" of the local nature gods. "He shall break down their altars, he shall spoil their images." The sacred "calf of Samaria shall be broken in pieces." It was folly to suppose that the piling up of offering upon offering was a proper substitute for the observance of the moral law. "For I desired mercy, and not sacrifice; and the knowledge of God more than burnt offerings. . . . I hate, I despise your feast days, and

I will not smell in your solemn assemblies. Though ye offer me burnt offerings and your meat offerings, I will not accept them: neither will I regard the peace offerings of your fat beasts. Take thou away from me the noise of thy songs; for I will not hear the melody of thy viols. But let judgment run down as waters, and righteousness as a mighty stream." (Amos 5:21-24)

What could Yahweh do with a society whose greedy rich fed upon the misery of the poor?   They sell "the righteous for silver, and the poor for a pair of shoes" and "pant after the dust of the earth on the head of the poor, and turn aside the way of the meek." The "fat rich women" of Samaria, "kine" Amos calls them, "oppress the poor, crush the needy and say to their masters, 'Bring and let us drink.' " Yahweh will take in hand the "haughty" women of Jerusalem who "walk with stretched forth necks and wanton eyes, walking and mincing as they go, and making a tinkling with their feet. . . . The Lord will take away the bravery of their tinkling ornaments." It will be the same for those that "tread upon the poor" and "take from him burdens of wheat" and "built houses of hewn stone, . . . lie upon beds of ivory, and stretch themselves upon their couches, . . . eat the lambs out of the flock, and the calves out of the midst of the stall, . . . chant to the sound of the viol, and invent to themselves instruments of musick, like David; . . . drink wine in bowls, and anoint themselves with the chief ointments."

Isaiah continued the burden of this complaint. Yahweh looked for justice but "behold oppression; for righteousness, but behold a cry. Woe unto them that join house to house, that lay field to field, till there be no place, that they may be placed alone in the midst of the earth! . . . Woe unto them that rise up early in the morning, that they may follow strong drink; that continue until night, till wine inflame them! And the harp, and the viol, the tabret, and pipe, and wine, are in their feasts." It is to be remembered that "the Lord of hosts shall be exalted in judgment, and God that is holy shall be sanctified in righteousness." (Isaiah 5:7-8, 11-12, 16)

YAHWEH AND THE ASSYRIANS; THE PRINCE OF PEACE

For these evils Yahweh had brought on the Assyrians. "O Assyrian, the rod of mine anger . . . I will send him against an hypocritical nation, and against the people of my wrath will I give him a charge, to take the spoil, and to take the prey, and to tread them down like the mire of the streets." Yet a blasphemous Assyria that did not recognize itself to be the instrument of Yahweh could not be permitted to destroy the city of Zion. "I will break the Assyrian in my land, and upon my mountains tread him under foot." After the fall of Samaria (722 B.C.), when the Assyrian armies were obliged to desist from further attack upon Jerusalem, it was as if Isaiah had been vindicated. God had taken his people again under his protection, "though your sins be as scarlet, they shall be as white as snow." Isaiah was able also to express his joy over the deliverance from the Assyrians and to renew his people's hope by predicting the future coming of the Messiah, whose name was to be "Wonderful, Counsellor, the mighty God, the everlasting Father, the Prince of Peace. Of the increase of his government and peace there shall be no end." Such a prince "shall not judge after the sight of his eyes, neither reprove after the hearing of his ears: but with righteousness shall he judge the poor, and reprove with equity for the meek of the earth . . . and righteousness shall be the girdle of his loins, and faithfulness the girdle of his reins. The wolf also shall dwell with the lamb, and the leopard shall lie down with the kid. . . . And the sucking child shall play on the hole of the asp. . . . They shall not hurt nor destroy in all my holy mountain: for the earth shall be full of the knowledge of the Lord, as the waters cover the sea."

When this had happened, the prophet foresaw the world subjecting itself to Yahweh's righteous judgment and the advent of a reign of universal peace. "It shall come to pass in the last days, that the mountain of the Lord's house shall be established in the top of the mountains, and shall be exalted above the hills; and all nations shall flow unto it. And many people shall go and say, Come ye, and let us go up to the mountain of the Lord, to the house of the God of Jacob; and he will teach us of his ways, and we will walk in his paths: for out of Zion shall go forth the law, and the word of the Lord from Jerusalem. And he shall judge among the nations, and shall rebuke many people: and they shall beat their swords into plowshares, and their spears into pruninghooks: nation shall not lift up sword against nation, neither shall they learn war any more."

YAHWEH AND EXILE

The prophets had felt called upon to explain, in terms of punishment by Yahweh for sin, the destruction of the two kingdoms of Israel and Judah and the deportation of their populations. Likewise the exigencies of exile obliged them, as with most exiles, to look forward to the restoration of a new Jerusalem by Yahweh and to inspire their people with this hope. In dwelling upon the misery of their fate in exile, some came to substitute for the relationship between Yahweh and his people the relationship between Yahweh and the individual Jew, and to interpret religion as essentially the assumption by the individual person of moral responsibility to his God. Others came to lay greater emphasis upon the proper execution of a new code of divine law, when once the temple was restored in Jerusalem, to be based upon that codification which had been introduced in Judah in 621 B.C. by King Josiah under the direct influence of the prophetic movement. Others, in considering the wonderful events which led to the overthrow of Babylon (Chaldea) by Cyrus the Persian and the freeing of the Jews from their exile, chose to interpret these large historical movements as further evidence of Yahweh's universal dominion and to emphasize that they were calculated to prepare a special mission for the Jewish people. Their suffering for their own sins was made to appear so intense that not only did it seem to Yahweh to atone for their transgressions against his law but it atoned as well for the sins of all the people in the world. Israel, indeed, was transformed into Yahweh's Suffering Servant, whom repentance and pain had made worthy to act as his missionary to the whole world. The result of this missionary endeavor was to be the establishment of the reign of Yahweh, the universal God, over all the peoples of the earth. Israel's fate in the hands of her God was to be the instrument for founding a world theocratic government. Among the prophets of exile who contributed most to this magnificent development was Ezekiel, and the Second, or Deutero-Isaiah.

YAHWEH AND THE RESTORATION OF THE TEMPLE

While the Psalmist was singing:

> By the rivers of Babylon,
> There we sat down, yea, we wept,
> When we remembered Zion.
> We hanged our harps
> Upon the willows in the midst thereof.
> For there they that carried us away captive . . .
> And they that wasted us required of us mirth,
> Saying, Sing us one of the songs of Zion.
> How shall we sing the Lord's song in a strange land?

a pastor among the exiles, Ezekiel, was reminding them, in the same manner as had Jeremiah, that religion was an individual and not a national matter; that each might be expected to be punished for his own sins and not for those of the nation. "Yahweh is righteous and will judge every one after his own ways." Yahweh would also demonstrate to the nations surrounding Palestine who had been gloating over its end that he was merely punishing his people for violating the law, and that, accordingly, he would now restore them to their former homes. There they would again have a king and enjoy forever the peace and joy that had been denied them. After this restoration Yahweh would then defeat the armies of those nations that still held to false gods and establish his universal dominion. Not only would the nation be restored but the temple also would be rebuilt as the "place of my throne, and the place of the soles of my feet, where I will dwell in the midst of the children of Israel for ever." The old ceremonies would be revived, and the restored temple, as it had not previously, would assert control over the life of the new kingdom. Yahweh in the midst of his priests would govern his people.

YAHWEH AS A UNIVERSAL GOD

The confident shouts of a Yahweh who knows that he is the only God echo through the pages of Deutero-Isaiah. "I am he: before me there was no God formed, neither shall there be after me. . . . I am the first, and I am the last; and beside me there is no God. . . . I am the Lord that maketh all things; that stretcheth forth the heavens alone; that spreadeth abroad the earth by myself. . . . I am the Lord, and there is none else. . . . There is no God else beside me; a just God and a Saviour; there is none beside me. . . . The God of the whole earth shall he be called." This was the Yahweh who had made Cyrus his anointed, "whose right hand I have holden, to subdue nations before him. . . . He is my shepherd, and shall perform all my pleasure: even saying to Jerusalem, Thou shalt be built; and to the temple, Thy foundation shall be laid." This is the Yahweh who can announce to his people in exile: "Comfort ye, comfort ye my people. . . . Speak ye comfortably to Jerusalem, and cry unto her, that her warfare is accomplished, that her iniquity is pardoned: for she hath received of the Lord's hand double for all her sins."

This is the Lord who will lead his people personally back to Jerusalem. "Prepare ye the way of the Lord, make straight in the desert a highway for our God. Every valley shall be exalted, and every mountain and hill shall be made low: and the crooked shall be made straight, and the rough places plain." Those at home must be prepared to receive their God. "O Zion, that bringest good tidings, get thee up into the high mountain; O Jerusalem, that bringest good tidings, lift up thy voice with strength; lift it up, be not afraid; say unto the cities of Judah, Behold your God! . . . he shall feed his flock like a shepherd: he shall gather the lambs with his arm, and carry them in his bosom, and shall gently lead those that are with young." If, however, Israel is the specially beloved of Yahweh he has prepared a special task for her, worthy of his love. The rule of Yahweh must extend over the earth. "Look unto me, and be ye saved, all the ends of the earth: for I am God, and there is none else. . . . unto me every knee shall bow, every tongue shall swear. . . . My righteousness shall be for ever, and my salvation from generation to generation." The world that knew not Yahweh would come to realize that he had made his people to suffer for its sake. "Surely he hath borne our griefs, and carried our sorrows: yet we did esteem him stricken, smitten of God, and afflicted. But he was wounded for our transgressions, he was bruised for our iniquities: the chastisement of our peace was upon him; and with his stripes we are healed." Yahweh would use this Suffering Servant to win over the heathen. "It is a light thing that thou shouldest be my Servant to raise up the tribes of Jacob, and to restore the preserved of Israel: I will also give thee for a light to the Gentiles, that thou mayest be my salavation unto the end of the earth." Here again, to repeat, is the god of the nation, made to control the enemies of the people and finally transformed into the creator of the world and universal God who will not only free his people from exile but use them to establish his universality. Nor would this mission fail. "He shall not fail nor be discouraged, till he have set judgment in the earth: and the isles shall wait for his law."

Yet he, that is, the Hebrew, did fail. He failed both to make the spiritual character of Yahwism prevail and to establish God's justice upon the whole face of the earth. When the Jews were reassembled in Palestine after being released by Cyrus, they conceived of the reconstruction of their state in the narrow terms of a theocracy administered by a priest-hood (hierocracy), headed by the chief priest of the restored temple. The religion that this priesthood sought to enforce was a religion of the law, the law that prescribed in minute detail the routine of service and sacrifice by which Yahweh might be appeased and by which the Jews might be kept clean. The prophets had denounced and rejected this ritualistic law as the basis for religion. They did not convince their people. The codification of Jewish law accepted by Josiah in 621 B.C. (Deuteronomy) did away with the local nature cults and their priests and concentrated the national religion in the temple at Jerusalem. In addition to prescribing a unique Yahweh worship it also sought to express the social teachings of the prophets in religious law. It set up as its ideal the total abolition of poverty ("save when there shall be no poor among you") and ameliorated the condition of orphan and widow, foreigner, slave, and laborer. But they could not dare to hope to abolish the cult: they could hope only to reform it.[17] The elaborate temple worship that made a burdensome priesthood necessary still remained.

THE HOLINESS CODE AND PRIEST CODE

The revision of the law, the Holiness Code, was made soon after the destruction of Jerusalem in 586 B.C. (Leviticus 17–26). It preserved the social reforms contained in the Josiah codification, and admonished, "Thou shalt not hate thy brother in thine heart: thou shalt not in any wise rebuke thy neighbor, and not suffer sin upon him. Thou shalt not avenge, nor bear any grudge against the children of thy people, but thou shalt love thy neighbor as thyself: I am the Lord." Yet in this codification the holiness of Yahweh's worshipers is conceived in terms of ritual purity: how sacrificial animals must be slaughtered and what foods can be eaten. This led directly after the re-establishment of the temple to a further codification, the Priest Code, or Priestly Law (*ca.* 500 B.C.). It prescribed the details of temple ritual, the observance of the Sabbath, circumcision, the Passover, and prohibited the eating of blood: in fact the whole gamut of prescriptions that the Jew must observe to atone for his sin and keep himself clean.[18] The Priest Code, which incorporated the Holiness Code, was adopted by the people as part of the law of the

[17]Bewer, *Development*, p. 135: "They tried to effect a spiritual reformation by the change of the cult, while it can be accomplished only by a change of heart."

[18]Bewer, p. 272, n. 1, indicates the amounts needed yearly to take care of public sacrifices: 1093 lambs, 113 bullocks, 37 rams, 32 goats, 5487.86 litters of fine flour, 2076.43 litters each of wine and oil.

theocratic state of Judah. Thus, under a succession of foreign masters, the Jewish people bowed down to the administration of a hereditary priesthood enforcing a law sanctifying many primitive practices. As this system hardened with the further elaboration of the law, a favorable environment was created for the renewal of the prophetic spirit which came with Jesus. Meanwhile, the dreams of Jewish visionaries concentrated on the appearance of the Messianic Savior who would remove the scourge of foreign domination.

THE JEWISH DISPERSION

The dreams of the prophets that the reconstructed Jewish nation would bring the world to Yahweh were likewise left unrealized. Before the Babylonian Exile the Jews had begun the migration (dispersion, or *Diaspora*) that carried them ultimately to the ends of the earth. They took their Scriptures, their law, and the synagogue with them, but they went out not to convert the world as missionaries but to seek the wider economic opportunities denied them at home. In this respect they were so successful that, once this commercial skill had been combined with their proud, jealous, and exclusive loyalty to their own God and his religious law, they brought down on their heads the envy and resentment, the hatred and persecution of those peoples in whose midst they settled. It remained for Christianity, under the stimulus of the prophetic zeal of Jesus, to return to the universalism of the Old Testament in Deutero-Isaiah. It seems strange today that many of the leaders of this people, after their melancholy search for safety from their tormentors, and after being virtually exterminated in Europe in the Nazi concentration camps, should have turned once again to the exclusive national hope of Zion, a special Palestine of their own. The best of their early prophets had pointed to another and more difficult way.

THE JEWISH POINT OF VIEW

For the history of the peoples of the western tradition this failure of the Jews of the Ancient Near East, through the instrumentality of their religion, to realize the good society at home and to spread it abroad has had the incalculable importance of inspiring them to succeed where the Jews failed. It need not be emphasized again[19] how the record of this failure, the Old Testament, came to be a part of the Sacred Scriptures of Christians. When a new western civilization began to emerge from the later Roman Empire, conditions were such that another opportunity was afforded to build a new society upon the basis of a new religion, Christianity. The manner in which the Jewish experience was used by the peoples of the West it will be important to trace. Meanwhile we should bear in mind the main principles for the ordering of human society which Jewish experience emphasized. It held that the fate of mankind

[19]See p. 19.

rests, in the last analysis, upon forces outside the control of man, namely, in what God wishes to do with the universe he has created. This is obviously a confession of man's inability to determine his own fate. Yet in its insistence upon a universal God, upon monotheism, this Jewish faith was a wonderful and, of course, revolutionary simplification of the extraordinary variety of local divinities in the ancient world. It made possible the abolition of all local religious loyalties. Such an abolition would make practicable the religious unification of the world, a necessary counterpart of its political and economic unification. What God wished to do was to save this world. Salvation, in Jewish eyes, concerned this earth and not another world that was to come. The Jews were not especially troubled about immortality. This world was conceived of as a moral order, and the moral principles governing it were of divine ordination. They were God's law. Salvation was to be had by conforming to this law, a compliance which would result in the establishment of a peaceful temporal society whose maintenance depended upon the continued observance of the law.

According to this view man was constantly threatened with the loss of his temporal felicity for failure to live up to the moral law. God suspended a perpetual doom over his head. To be sure, this main emphasis was not the whole one. God might become impatient and lose trust in man, but composure was regained, God forgave, and, in spite of all man's laxity, loved the wayward creature he had created. If the divine plans for a broad national salvation did not work out God also provided for individual salvation, the inward peace and joy that came from individual adherence to the moral law. Inasmuch as these ideas were put in the form of a covenant between God and his chosen ones, whereby salvation was meted out to all alike in return for a common observance of the pact, there are notions here of spiritual equality and a contractual form of government important to the subsequent development of democratic ideas. In the strenuous insistence that individual morality must have a social application, that there must be no difference between private and public morality, that this social application must help to remove social differences created by the development of human society, there is a source of our democratic heritage. Thus the Jewish failure became a Christian hope when, under different circumstances and with a different, Christian emphasis, the western world set out once again to make the Jewish theocracy, a particular adaptation of the theocracy of the Ancient Near East, a practical instrument of government to realize the good society.

OTHER NEAR–EASTERN RELIGIONS

Before the ethical monotheism of the Hebrews became, in its Christian form, the official doctrine of the Roman Empire it had to contend with and vanquish other religions that emerged from the Ancient Near East. These were the religions of Persian origin, which are called Zoroastrianism,

Mithraism, and Manichaeanism. In addition, there were various mystery cults, the most influential of which were those centering about pairs of ancient fertility deities, Isis and Osiris, Ishtar and Tammuz, the Great Mother and Attis, and Venus and Adonis. Ethical monotheism had to come to terms, too, with an attitude toward life that was rooted in Babylonian astrology.

ZOROASTRIANISM

Of the Persian religions, Manichaeanism need not concern us here. It was a later development within the Roman Empire, derived, however, from older, Persian sources. The prophet Zoroaster is believed to have been active at the end of the seventh and the beginning of the sixth century B.C., that is, at the moment when the Persians were about to gather the whole Near East into their empire. The reforms he introduced, like the original Yahweh reform, may be conceived of as an attempt to introduce a kind of monotheism into Persian belief to take the place of a complicated worship of nature deities. The god raised to this position was Ahura-Mazda, or as he was later called, Ormazd. He was a righteous god, a god of light. The distinctive note in Zoroastrianism, however, was its treatment of the problem of evil in the human heart. In Babylonian thought, in the Old Testament, and in Christianity evil is equated with the idea of sin, a defect of being, a kind of heritable instinct caused by a primal violation of the moral law. It is simple to attribute man's resistance to, and violation of, the moral law to divine, that is, supernatural forces, whose sole purpose it is to lead him astray. In this way, evil (as well as good) may be attributed to a god, and the struggle to achieve the good life may be interpreted as a battle between a god of good and a god of evil. Zoroaster's god of evil, equated also with darkness, was Ahriman, about whom, as auxiliary demons, were grouped all the local deities of earlier Persian religion. Zoroaster was not content, however, to leave the issue between good and evil to be decided by a mere heavenly struggle between Ahura-Mazda and Ahriman. The heavenly battle was one in which men had to join. Man himself had to decide which of the heavenly hosts he would serve. Nor was Zoroaster content to leave undetermined the issue of the struggle between the two gods, their respective demoniac aids, and their human supporters. It was, to be sure, a desperate struggle, but the outcome was predetermined. The end was to witness the triumph of good, of Ahura-Mazda, and final settlement was to be made at a last judgment, when the individual's choice would be rewarded or punished; rewarded with blessed immortality if he chose aright, with a kind of hell if he joined with Ahriman. Thus the dualistic character of Zoroastrianism, the constant struggle between good and evil led by Ahura-Mazda and Ahriman, was subordinated to ethical monotheism. Evil was real and divinely supported, but it could and would be beaten.

Features of Zoroastrianism spread with the Persian empire. The hierarchy of angels supporting Ahura-Mazda were transferred to Yahweh's angelic hosts, and in later Judaism Ahriman, in the form of Satan, or the Devil, began his mischievous career. This dualism and the concept of a last judgment came also to be fitted into Christianity although the latter leaves hell unpurged, whereas Zoroaster provided for its ultimate destruction. Zoroastrianism today remains a living religion for a few thousand Persians and the Parsis of India. To some of these it is essentially a humanistic creed. "The imperfect world is man's opportunity. The perfect world is in the making. God has planned it and entrusted man with the duty of completing it. The world is certainly not hell, but neither is it paradise; it is merely purgatory, we may say, with God-given guarantee of its ultimate conversion into paradise by human endeavor."[20]

MITHRAISM

One of Ahura-Mazda's aids in his constant struggle with Ahriman was Mithra, whose popularity in the Mediterranean world was to be far greater than that of his lord. Indeed, he was an older god, for he came into Iran and India with the Aryan ancestors of the Medes and Persians. In early Hindu religious literature, the Vedas, he is a god of light, the defender of truth, and the enemy of error. In the Avesta, the divine scriptures of the Persians, which contains the literature of the Zoroastrian reform, his light is the source of the fertility of the earth and accordingly of man's life and happiness. He is the "truth speaking, undeceived God to whom nobody must lie," and hence the protector of contracts. "On whichever side there is one who has lied to Mithra, on that side Mithra stands forth angry, and offended, and his wrath is slow to relent." Mithra is the great champion of Ahura-Mazda in his struggle against Ahriman. As the Persian army swept over the Near East he became their lord and the special guardian of their royal commanders. When he entered Babylonia he acquired a consort in Anahita, a fertility goddess, and became acquainted with the stars. When the Persian armies fell before Alexander, Mithra's popularity had already spread to Asia Minor whence, after many more transformations,[21] he was to become a great favorite of the Roman legions and a powerful rival of Jesus.

THE MYSTERY CULTS

If Yahweh had to struggle with the local fertility cults of Palestine (the baals and baaliths) and, at least for a while, to compromise with them, his Christian counterpart had to engage in a corresponding struggle with what were essentially similar cults. The Persian empire and those succeeding it permitted these cults to spread far beyond the confines of

[20]Manekji Dhalla, *Our Perfecting World*, quoted in A. G. Widgery, *Living Religions and Modern Thought*, pp. 158–159.
[21]See pp. 294 ff.

their original homes. The Phrygian Great Mother and Attis achieved a wide popularity in Asia Minor; so did the Babylonian Tammuz and Ishtar, the Syrian Venus and Adonis in the Fertile Crescent, and the Egyptian Isis and Osiris beyond Egypt. The legends crystallizing about these divinities are of a heterogeneous nature and have their origins in primitive religious attitudes, but in every case they emphasize the position of the gods as the source of all fertility, human or otherwise, and explain the seasonal alternation of the earth's productivity. Yet, even before the end of the Persian period these divinities were beginning to be worshiped as more than the guarantors of the fertility of the earth and the life it gives; they were becoming the guarantors of personal immortality. This boon they granted to initiates who took part in religious ceremonies that afforded the worshipers emotional experiences of an essentially new kind. They were thus, in part, an escape for mortals for whom the oriental despotisms afforded no real status in the world. When these oriental societies came under the domination of Alexander and his successors, and finally of the Romans, the mystery cults were able to extend their influence throughout both the Greek and Roman worlds.[22]

ORIENTAL ASTROLOGY

With them went astrology, which, as it spread from Babylonia, lent them additional power and continues to the present day to give satisfaction and comfort to the bewildered. It is not difficult to understand why prolonged observation of the heavens should have induced the Babylonian scholars to urge upon men the abandonment of their own initiative to the fate that is written in the stars. Long and careful observation demonstrated that the movement of the heavenly bodies was not capricious but orderly and predictable. Where the planets had once been they would again be. Any given relationship of sun, moon, stars, and planets would be recurrent. If, as it was not difficult to assume, what went on in the heavens had something to do with what went on on earth, then the human future was as fixed and predetermined as the movement of the heavens. If, moreover, the heavenly orderliness was of divine ordination, and if the heavenly bodies themselves were identified with gods and goddesses, as of course they were, then what was happening under a given set of stellar circumstances was in accordance with divine will. What would once happen under certain circumstances would always happen under the same circumstances. The future, then, was written in the stars for men to read. It was not in their own hands. He who could read it was man's only reliable guide. If such an interpretation did not promote man's initiative it did promote his fortitude to bear what was in store for him. Job had been concerned with the capriciousness of a Yahweh who, from all appearances, did not seem to govern his actions according to the moral

[22]See p. 112.

law. The astrologers' divine stars were not capricious; they apparently were responsible for the way things were; and the way they were, they would always be. This fatalistic view later carried over into Stoicism and made it possible to advocate living according to the laws of nature.[23]

Thus the men of the Ancient Near East interpreted their world almost entirely in religious terms. In Yahwism and Zoroastrianism they summoned themselves to support and attempt to achieve a human moral order of divine sanction. In astrology, however, they asked only that men bear what their astral gods imposed. The important issue of whether man is free to choose a moral life in a moral world or whether man's efforts are divinely determined had thus been joined.

[23]See p. 242.

chapter three

GREEK DEMOCRACY

$\mathcal{H}$EBRAISM AND HELLENISM.   The spirit of the Hebrew, who would have been classified as a barbarian by the Greeks (all foreigners were "barbarians" to them), and the spirit of the Greek, who would have been classified as among the unchosen of Yahweh (that is, a Gentile) by the Hebrews, have both been guides in the western search for a point of view. Matthew Arnold has contrasted these two spirits: "The uppermost idea with Hellenism [Greek is Hellene] is to see things as they really are; the uppermost idea with Hebraism is conduct and obedience. . . . The governing idea of Hellenism is *spontaneity of consciousness*; that of Hebraism, *strictness of conscience*. As Hellenism speaks of thinking clearly, seeing things in their essence and beauty, as a grand and precious feat for man to achieve, so Hebraism speaks of becoming conscious of sin, of awakening to a sense of sin, as a feat of this kind."[1]

HERODOTUS

Herodotus, the "father of Greek history," to whom Palestine was the land of the Philistines and not the Hebrews, had no way of knowing how influential the religious history of the, to him, comparatively unknown Hebrew people was to be. Nor could Herodotus foresee what the liberty of Greece was to mean to Europe. Yet he does exhibit the increasingly analytical quality of the Greek spirit in his *History*, in which he systematically relates cause and effect. The Greeks were defending their liberty

[1]*Works* (Macmillan), VI, 123 ff.

against the despotic power of the Persian empire. He wrote, he said, "in order that the actions of men may not be effaced by time, nor the great and wondrous deeds displayed both by Greeks and barbarians deprived of renown." "His glory," accordingly, was "in human virtue and achievement wherever [it was] to be found." His impelling desire "to see things as they really are," to understand the world in which he lived, made him one of the world's first great historians. In search of material for his chosen theme, he traveled as few if any other private individuals traveled in the Mediterranean world before the establishment of the Roman Empire. A native of Halicarnassus, a Greek city on the western coast of Asia Minor, Herodotus went northward to Byzantium on the Bosporus, to Olbia at the mouth of the Bug, westward across the Aegean into European Greece, to the Greek colonies in southern Italy, and southward to Tyre and Egypt. His lively interest in all phases of human life thus enabled him to write extensively of the civilizations of the eastern Mediterranean world, as well as of a "united Hellas [Greece] . . . transfigured and glorified by the repulse of the 'Barbarian.' "[2]

THE GREEK POLIS

If it had been successful, the Persian invasion of 490 B.C. would have reduced Greece to a Persian province. That it was not successful must be attributed, among other reasons, to the intense loyalty of many Greek city-states, led by Athens, to the way of life they had created for themselves. This way of life had been worked out within the confines of what the Greeks called the *polis*, or city-state, in the course of several centuries. The Ancient Near East, of course, had a highly developed urban culture, but these cities had been swallowed up in the growth of despotic kingdoms and empires that deprived them of their original independence. What replaced the local loyalty to the city was the enforced obedience to the divine ruler. This was now the fate that confronted the Greeks: the loss of their local independence to a vast empire, the attachment of their supreme loyalty, interests, and hopes to a remote barbarian ruler.

THE INDO–EUROPEAN PEOPLES

The Greeks were Indo-Europeans; that is, they belonged to a group of people who spread into Asia (India) and Europe, where they developed languages that, as we know them today, are still so similar that it is clear they must have a common origin. Where the Indo-Europeans originally dwelt cannot be said with certainty, but when their descendants moved into southwestern Asia and Europe they probably came from the areas north of the Black and Caspian seas. Such were the Aryans who moved into India, the Hittites, and the Medes and Persians. The Greeks, al-

[2]R. W. Macan, "Herodotus and Thucydides," *Cambridge Ancient History*, ed. J. B. Bury et al., V, 417.

though only an offshoot of the Indo-European peoples, exerted a decisive influence upon the course of European development.

GREEKS (HELLENES) AND MINOANS

They came into the Balkan peninsula in waves from the north, the first of these a wave of Achaeans, the second a wave of Dorians. These invaders encountered an indigenous folk belonging to a civilization created by a maritime people, the Minoans, whose center was on the island of Crete. This was a fresh and vigorous civilization, coextensive with not only the Greek mainland but also the islands of the Aegean, the western coast of Asia Minor, and the Syrian littoral. This civilization was engulfed by the invading Greeks as they swept from the mainland over the islands of the Aegean to the coast of Asia Minor. The Achaean settlers, driven out in their turn by the Dorians, were forced to abandon their mainland strongholds. In so doing they split into the two groups known as the Aeolian and Ionian Greeks, who occupied respectively the northern and southern halves of the coast of Asia Minor.

EARLY GREEK SETTLEMENTS
1400 – 700 B.C.

40°

Troy

A S I A

Area of Achaean
and Aeolian Greeks

M I N O R

Smyrna

Mycenae   Athens
Argos
Tirynths

Area of
Ionian Greeks

Miletus

AEGEAN SEA

Sparta

36°

Area of
Dorian Greeks

Cnossus

○ Centers of Minoan culture

C R E T E

Miles   0   50   100

22°   26°   palacios

THE FORMATION OF THE POLIS

As Greek warriors settled down in the midst of a conquered people they built walled fortresses on the hilltops of a mountainous land, and

	Political Persons and Events	Writers
1200 B.C.		
	Trojan War (ca. 1184)	
	Solon (ca. 639–559) Darius I (r. 521–486) Cleisthenes (fl. 508)	
500		
	Persian War (499–479) Xerxes I (r. 486–465) Pericles (495–429)	
		Herodotus (484–428) Euripides (ca. 480–406) Thucydides (460–400) Aristophanes (ca. 438–380)
	Peloponnesian War (431–404) Demosthenes (ca. 384–322) Philip II of Macedon (382–336) Alexander (356–323)	

here they also housed their gods. This enclosure was the *Acropolis*, the "high city." In time, the merchant, tradesman, and artisan gathered beneath in the market place, or *agora*. Around this fortified trading center, often located by the sea, the members of the various tribes, bound together by clan and family loyalties, settled as shepherds and husbandmen. Therewith began the slow process of transforming a loyalty cemented by kin into a loyalty stimulated by a common life in a small political community, a common life of citizens of the *polis*. So rich was the life of many of these independent city-states that no Greek could conceive of wanting any other form of political organization. Even after they had lost their independence to Macedonia, those who wrote about political theory still regarded the city-state as the ideal political form, to whose welfare all else was to be subordinated.

LIMITATIONS OF GREEK DEMOCRACY

It was in the Greek *polis* that the first systems of democratic government were worked out. These, however, were exclusive little democracies which jealously guarded the ranks of the citizens privileged to share in their government. Citizenship was not extended to foreigners or aliens, who carried on a large share of industry and trade. Nor did it extend to women or slaves. This denial of the privileges of citizenship to many of the inhabitants of the city-state who made its good life possible was, of course, a serious limitation upon Greek democracy. Indeed Greeks such as Aristotle were disturbed by it.

GREEK PATRIOTISM

Greek political growth was also fatally limited by the jealous regard for the independence of the local city. This narrow loyalty was so strong that after the initial victory over the Persians the Greek cities were unable to create institutions to maintain peace among themselves. The freedom enjoyed within many of the Greek city-states—for example, Athens—enabled their citizens to live rich and fruitful lives, but their fierce determination to defend their individual sovereignties at any cost ultimately destroyed this way of life. A peaceful unity, which the hundreds of Greek city-states could not preserve among themselves, was at last imposed upon them from without. That *polis* which Aristotle defined as "an association formed for the maintenance of complete and self-sufficient life," wherein man could exercise fully his "political" nature, was a cause of both the greatness and the degradation of Greece.

GREEK COLONIZATION

The character of Greek life in the early *polis* during the period of the Trojan War (which Greek sources place in the twelfth century B.C.) is described in the exciting heroic poetry of Homer's *Iliad* and *Odyssey*. This *polis* was usually situated on a hill in a walled citadel (for example,

Mycenae or Tiryns) and was ruled by a king and occasionally a council of elders. But in the sixth and fifth centuries B.C., Greek society underwent a notable economic transformation and a further expansion which went far toward destroying the old order. The transformation had to do, in part at least, with the pressure of a growing population upon the limited means of subsistence in both European and Asiatic Greece. The Greek solution of the problem was to take to the sea again and plant colonies wherever prospects of a satisfactory life existed and the expansion of other peoples did not forbid. They thus went westward along the northern shore of the Mediterranean as far as Spain, as the Phoenicians had gone westward along the southern shore. Near the mouth of the Rhone they planted Marseilles (Massilia). In Sicily, where the Phoenicians were colonizing the western part of the island, they founded Agrigentum (Acragas), Syracuse, and Messina; in southern Italy, Reggio, Sybaris, and Tarentum. The northwestern and northeastern coasts of the Balkan peninsula and the northern shores of the Aegean received new colonies. Byzantium was situated at the mouth of the Bosporus, and Chalcedon across from it in Asia Minor. Greek colonies were located on all the shores of the Black Sea. The colonies were in no sense politically controlled by their mother cities. They were new, independent city-states which, as they grew and prospered, rendered Greek political life almost impossibly complicated.

EFFECT OF COLONIZATION UPON MOTHER CITIES

This large Greek colonial world helped to transform the older world of the mother cities. The promise of a rich exchange of home products with those of the new colonial markets brought about economic and social changes at home that called for political changes. The shepherds and husbandmen were pushed to the wall by the development of large estates for the purpose of cultivating the vine and olive, whose products were exchanged for cereals from the colonial areas. At Athens an elegant pottery industry emerged to supply the containers in which these products were carried abroad by an efficient merchant marine. The development of an exchange economy resulted in the growth of a powerful middle class of merchants and industrialists who controlled the trade of the eastern Mediterranean, ousting the Phoenicians, and contesting political control of the city-state with the older aristocracy. The harassed small farmer, the artisan, and the sailor became new social groups to which political attention had to be given.

DEMOCRATIC DEVELOPMENT OF THE CONSTITUTION OF ATHENS

These changes are the setting for the development of the Athenian constitution, the most democratic of the constitutions of any of the hundreds of Greek city-states, if not "a democracy the most complete that the world has ever known."[3] It will be recalled that the democracy here

[3]E. M. Walker, "The Confederacy of Delos," *Cambridge Ancient History*, V, 74.

referred to was a very exclusive one. The citizens who participated in its government were limited to those of the *polis* of Athens-Attica. They did not, as we have said, include the women. They did not include the "foreigners," Greeks as well as others, who were known as *metics*, and to whom the Athenians, with a certain aversion to the corrupting influence of money, were willing to entrust a large share of their trade and industry. They did not include the slaves. The citizen body was, accordingly, a kind of élite, perhaps numbering in the fifth century 150,000 to 170,000, while the metics at the same period numbered 35,000 to 40,000, and the slaves 80,000 to 100,000.[4] It cannot be said, however, with the exception of the slaves employed in the state silver mines of Laurium, that either slaves or metics were a horribly exploited minority. The metics were in a position not much more restricted than that of unnaturalized immigrants in the contemporary United States, and an effect to liberalize their admission to citizenship was made, but was stopped by Pericles. Although slaves later took advantage of the Peloponnesian War to leave Athens, they were never used in gangs as agricultural laborers on large estates, as the Romans used them. Among Athenian citizens themselves there was substantial political and legal equality.

RATIONAL CHARACTER OF ATHENIAN POLITICAL REFORM

The rather slow and, in general, nonviolent elaboration of a democratic constitution by the Athenians was in striking contrast to the political history of the Ancient Near East, where nothing of the sort took place. This constitution was the outcome of the development of rather sharp differences in the class structure of Athens-Attica. In order to iron out these differences and to avoid civil war at critical moments, more and more political power was entrusted to the simple Athenian citizen. Unlike the situation in Israel, where political reform was urged by religious leaders (the prophets), reform in Athens was undertaken by political leaders themselves as a rational approach calculated to produce a healthier state. It contained no religious element. The Athenians who were primarily responsible for the democratic constitution of Athens were Solon, Cleisthenes, and Pericles.

THE REFORMS OF SOLON

The city-state of Athens initially was a monarchy, whose king eventually lost his position to the landowning aristocracy. Yet the security of the state required more than the military service of its citizens of noble birth. At an early date, citizens were divided into four classes on the basis of income rather than birth, and to these classes corresponding military obligations were assigned. These were (1) those whose estates yielded 500 bushels of grain or more annually, (2) those whose estates

[4]Walker, "Delos," p. 11.

yielded 300 bushels, (3) those whose farms yielded from 200 bushels, and (4) small farmers and laborers without a fixed income. The first two classes owed service as mounted infantry; a member of the first coming with two horses, one for himself and one for his squire; a member of the second with one. The third class served as heavily armored infantrymen, and the fourth as light infantry or rowers. By the beginning of the sixth century (*ca.* 594) the development of the large estate devoted to vineyards and olive culture had gone so far that many small landholders found themselves squeezed out of their land or hopelessly in debt, and others were deprived of freedom because of unpaid mortgages or other debts. The numbers were so great that the chief magistrate (*archon*) for 594 B.C., the aristocratic Solon, undertook by legislation to remedy the situation, and at the same time to give Athenian political institutions a broader social foundation. To curb the growth of large estates, the size of individual holdings was limited by law. Land lost through mortgages was restored to its original owners, and the mortgages quashed. It was forbidden to loan money on the security of land or persons, and those who had lost their personal freedom in this way regained it. Grain was not to be exported at the risk of diminishing the food supply of the state.

THE CONSTITUTION OF SOLON

After putting through these remedial measures Solon broadened the popular basis of the constitution. Income from wine and oil as well as from grain was used to determine the division of Athenians into economic classes. The civil officials of the state, the *archons*, were to be chosen from the first two classes alone, those who served in the mounted infantry. Up to this moment, also, the popular assembly of Athens, the *ecclesia*, which selected the magistrates, had been composed of only the first three classes. Solon enlarged its membership by including in it the small landowners and workers without property. Thus by the beginning of the sixth century B.C. all adult Athenian male citizens were members of the popular assembly. Solon took one step further in elaborating the democratic character of the constitution. He instituted a popular law court, the *heliaea*, as a supreme court to hear appeals from the judicial decisions of the *archons* and to try the cases of suspected magistrates who were leaving office. Citizens from all the four classes were made eligible to the *heliaea*. In his own poetry Solon summarized his reforms: "I removed the mortgage pillars which stood in many places. . . . To Athens, our country divinely founded, I restored many men who had been sold, one illegally, another under the law . . . . others held here in unseemly slavery, and trembling under their masters' caprices, I set free. This I did by my power, uniting force with justice. . . . I gave the commons as much power as sufficed, neither detracting from their honor nor adding thereto. Those who possessed might and were illustrious in wealth, for them I planned that

they should suffer naught unseemly. . . . Thus the commons would best follow their leaders, neither given too much rein nor yet oppressed."[5]
After Solon Athenian government could be controlled by all the citizens.

THE REFORMS OF CLEISTHENES

At the end of the sixth century, after a long experience with what the Greeks called *tyranny*, essentially an alliance between a strong man and the populace against the aristocracy, Cleisthenes made a further attempt to enlarge the democratic foundations of the state. In accordance with a definite plan he fitted the Solonic reforms into a larger framework. His purpose was to promote the transference of all the loyalties still attaching the Athenian to such nonpolitical institutions as the tribe, the clan, the family, and the class to the democratic state. The core of the reforms was the institution of a new tribal unit to take the place of the four old tribes, which were now abolished. In the formation of the new tribes, recognition was given to the social organization of the Athenians in the various geographical areas of Attica. The coastal area contained the fishermen and those who manned and loaded the ships of the merchant marine and navy. In the city of Athens itself lived the chief mercantile and industrial classes. Outside the city and coastal area the population was agricultural, including both the owners of large estates and of small farms. Cleisthenes organized these three areas into a number of what were called *demes*, or townships, with the local villages as centers. The inhabitants of the *deme* at the time of its creation were registered as its official members, and accordingly as Athenian citizens. Within the area of the *deme* was set up a wholly democratic system of local government which has been called the nursery of the democracy of the government of Athens-Attica. In each of the three geographical areas mentioned above the new *demes* were organized into a larger unit, called the *trittys*, a definite territorial district, of which there were ten of approximately equal population in each area. These *trittyes* were given, however, no political organization. Thus the *demes* of the three geographical areas of Athens-Attica were divided into thirty *trittyes*. From these were formed ten new tribes by taking one *trittys* by lot from each of the three geographical areas (coast, city, plain). Thus the new tribal unit might or might not form a geographical unit, but it was composed of approximately one-tenth of the population of the city-state, apportioned among landowning, commercial, and working-class elements of the population.

THE COUNCIL OF 500

The new tribal organization now became the basis of the central government. The older Council of 400 was now enlarged to 500, made repre-

[5]The selection from G. W. Botsford, *Hellenic History*, pp. 112, 114, copyright 1956 by The Macmillan Co., and used with The Macmillan Co.'s permission.

sentative of the tribes, and, in fact, became the chief executive in the government of the city-state, the "first endeavour to govern by means of a House of Representatives."[6] Each of the ten tribes furnished fifty members to the Council of 500. The fifty were chosen by lot from lists of candidates selected by the *demes*, whose population determined the number of candidates each proposed. The Council of 500 thus directly represented the tribe, and indirectly the *deme*. In order to make it possible for 500 men to act as an executive authority, the year was divided into ten equal periods or *prytanies*, and the fifty representatives of each tribe were in turn assigned to administer current business for their respective *prytanies*. For every day of the *prytany* one of the fifty was chosen as chairman, president, or mayor, and the fifty themselves were available day and night. Minor current affairs were thus managed by a group of fifty members of the Council, presided over by a chairman. The larger affairs of state, having to do with financial, military, and foreign policy, were acted upon in the deliberations of the Council as a whole.

BOARDS OF OFFICIALS

The policy decisions of the Council were carried out by boards of officials, who, when not elected by the tribes or the assembly, came to be chosen by lot and held office for one year only. They were also under the close supervision of the Council of 500. There was, for example, a board of nine *archons*, a board of financial officials, and a board of ten elected generals (*strategoi*), each of which commanded the regiment of his tribe and took turns as commander in chief of the whole Athenian army in turn. After the Persian Wars the Board of Generals took over the leading administrative positions, and in fact became a sort of cabinet. It was as a member of the Board of Generals, for example, that Pericles was able to exercise his dominant influence upon Athenian politics. The magistracies were ultimately open to all classes except the fourth, and the practice of choosing some of them by lot emphasized the democratic notion that any citizen who could get on a list from which lots were drawn could exercise satisfactorily the duties of his office.

THE ASSEMBLY

This representative executive council of the Athenian state and its administrative boards were always subject to the will of the Athenian Assembly, the fundamental institution of Athenian democracy. Theoretically, at this date, the Assembly was open to all Athenian citizens. Practically, however, it was open to all who could afford to attend, since governmental service of all kinds was as yet unpaid. The frequency of the meetings of the Assembly came to be regularized under Pericles to four a *prytany*, or forty a year, in addition to any special sessions that

[6]M. I. Rostovtzeff, *A History of the Ancient World*, I, 226.

might be called. The Council of 500 drew up the agenda for these meetings. It also drafted and presented the laws which they were to consider. Every Athenian citizen could, of course, speak at these meetings. In his hands rested the authority of making the law. Here the conduct of the magistrates was examined, and those suspected of improper conduct were suspended from office and turned over to the courts. In order to avoid the possible extremes of civil war, Cleisthenes empowered the Assembly once a year to ostracize, that is, send into exile for ten years, any member it considered dangerous to the state. To be ostracized an individual had to be condemned by a plurality of the votes of an assembly at which at least six thousand were present. There was, accordingly, no matter of public or private interest that could not be brought up by an Athenian citizen before the popular assembly. The Council of 500 and the Assembly together constituted a kind of bicameral legislature, the former representative of the tribes, the latter containing potentially all the citizens.

THE HELIAEA

Popular control of legislation and administration was further augmented by the *heliaea*, the popular jury court. By the time of Pericles it had absorbed the authority of the older judges, the *archons*, who now acted as presiding officers of the *heliaea* and prepared cases for its decision. By this time also the number of jurors had reached 6000, or 600 for each of the ten tribes, chosen annually by lot upon presentation by the *demes*, as in the case of the Council of 500. The jurors were ordinarily divided into panels of 501, and they determined guilt or innocence, and inflicted punishment, by a majority vote. After 462 B.C. they were paid for their services in order that the court might not be restricted to those who could afford to serve. Before this assembly of Athenian citizens the defendant had to plead his own case without benefit of counsel. Before them came the accused magistrates. Special groups of jurors came to be used by the Assembly to pass on legislation proposed by the Council of 500. The jury was used also to test the legality of measures proposed in the Assembly. By the fifth century any citizen could stop deliberations in the Assembly on any measure with the announcement, under oath, that he intended to test the legality (we should say constitutionality) of the measure before a popular court. Such a citizen had, himself, to prosecute the sponsor of the measure. If he failed to secure one-fifth of the votes of the jury he was heavily fined and prohibited thenceforth from bringing forward more announcements of prosecution. This procedure was used against political enemies in the Assembly and came to supplant ostracism.

PAYMENT FOR GOVERNMENTAL SERVICE

During the Periclean age payment was made for government service other than jury service. The Council of 500 and all except the military magistrates received a daily wage. A wage was likewise paid for service in the armed forces. It was not, however, until the fourth century that members of the Assembly were paid for attendance. Until this was done, the Assembly represented chiefly the city of Athens and not the *demes* of the countryside. Thus the urban demagogue came to exercise a preponderant influence on the democratic machinery.

PERICLES ON ATHENIAN DEMOCRACY

It was this democratic government that Pericles extolled in the famous speech reported by Thucydides, delivered in 430 B.C., by way of comfort to the Athenians who had lost their husbands, sons, and relatives in the first year of the Peloponnesian War. He wished to point out, he said, "by what sort of training we have come to our present position, and with what political institutions and as the result of what manner of life our empire became great.

"We live under a form of government which does not emulate the institutions of our neighbours; on the contrary, we are ourselves a model which some follow, rather than the imitators of other peoples. It is true that our government is called a democracy, because its administration is in the hands, not of the few, but of the many; yet while as regards the law all men are on an equality for the settlement of their private disputes, as regards the value set on them it is as each man is in any way distinguished that he is preferred to public honours, not because he belongs to a particular class, but because of personal merits; nor, again, on the ground of poverty is a man barred from a public career by obscurity of rank if he but has it in him to do the state a service. . . .

"When we come to the test we show ourselves fully as brave as those who are always toiling; and so our city is worthy of admiration in these respects, as well as in others. For we are lovers of beauty yet with no extravagence and lovers of wisdom yet without weakness. Wealth we employ rather as an opportunity for action than as a subject for boasting; and with us it is not a shame for a man to acknowledge poverty, but the greater shame is for him not to do his best to avoid it. And you will find united in the same persons an interest at once in private and in public affairs, and in others of us who give attention chiefly to business, you will find no lack of insight into political matters. For we alone regard the man who takes no part in public affairs, not as one who minds his own business, but as good for nothing; and we Athenians decide public questions for ourselves or at least endeavour to arrive at a sound understanding of them, in the belief that it is not debate that is a hindrance to action, but rather not to be instructed by debate before the time comes for action. For in truth we have this point also of superiority over other men, to be most daring in action and yet at the same time most given to reflection upon the ventures we mean to undertake; with other men, on the contrary, boldness means ignorance and reflection brings hesitation. . . .

"In a word, then, I say that our city as a whole is the school of Hellas, and that, as it seems to me, each individual amongst us could in his own person, with the utmost grace and versatility, prove himself self-sufficient in the most varied forms of activity. And that this is no mere boast inspired by the occasion, but actual truth, is attested by the very power of our city, a power which we have acquired in consequence of these qualities. For Athens alone among her contemporaries, when put to the test, is superior to the report of her, and she alone neither affords to the enemy who comes against her cause for irritation at the character of the foe by whom he is defeated, nor to her subject cause for complaint that his masters are unworthy. Many are the proofs which we have given of our power and assuredly it does not lack witnesses, and therefore we shall be the wonder not only of the men of to-day but of after times; we shall need no Homer to sing our praise nor any other poet whose verses may perhaps delight for the moment but whose presentation of the facts will be discredited by the truth. Nay, we have compelled every sea and every land to grant access to our daring, and have everywhere planted everlasting memorials both of evil to foes and of good to friends. Such, then, is the city for which these men nobly fought and died, deeming it their duty not to let her be taken from them; and it is fitting that every man who is left behind should suffer willingly for her sake." (I, 323–333)[7]

In spite of this proud bravery of Athens and her leaders, the Peloponnesian War was eventually to enfeeble Athenian and all Hellenic civilization. At this moment, however, Pericles had every reason to feel proud of what his own city-state had been able to accomplish. It had, in short, been able to do three things: (1) it had led the Greeks in withstanding the Persian peril; (2) it had continued an offensive against the Persians that drove them from the Aegean Sea, and in the course of this offensive it had founded an empire; and (3) it had made itself the center of civilization for the whole Greek world by nurturing an astounding and incomparable cultural life within its own city walls, and attracting from the cities of the larger colonial world the leading men in the arts and sciences. This last accomplishment must be the subject of the following chapter.

THE EXPANSION OF PERSIA

By the time that the constitution of Cleisthenes was put to the test of the Persian War, Persia had brought the whole Ancient Near East into its empire. Expanding from their homeland in Iran, after incorporating the Medes, the Persians had overthrown the Chaldean empire. Then, before embarking upon their conquest of the western Fertile Crescent and Egypt, they had reduced Asia Minor, dominated at the time by the kingdom of Lydia, which had already conquered the Aeolian and Ionian cities on the western coast. These earlier conquests had been the work of Cyrus.

[7]Citations from Thucydides in my text are to *Peloponnesian War*, trans. C. Forster Smith, Loeb Classical Library (hereafter cited as Loeb), Nos. 108, 109, 110, 169, 4 vols.

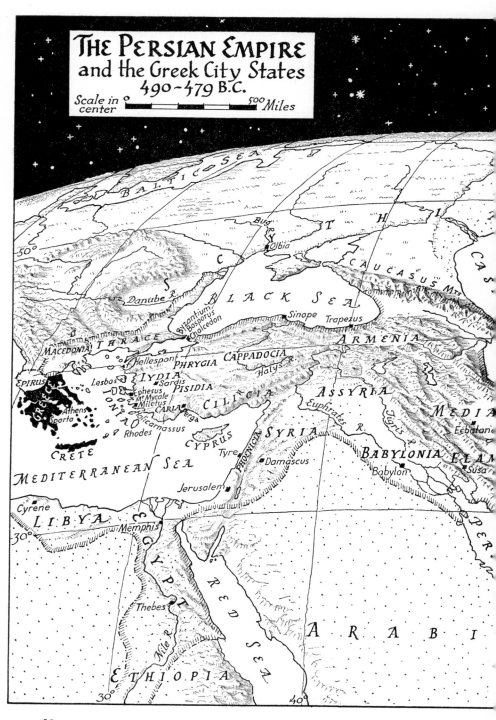

THE PERSIAN EMPIRE
and the Greek City States
490–479 B.C.

Scale in
center

0   500 Miles

BALTIC SEA

50°

Bug R.

Olbia

T H   I

C A U C A S U S Mrs.

Danube R.

BLACK SEA

CAS

Byzantium
Bosporus
Chalcedon

Sinope

Trapezus

MACEDONIA

THRACE

Hellespont

PHRYGIA

CAPPADOCIA

ARMENIA

EPIRUS

Lesbos

LYDIA
Sardis

Halys R.

ASSYRIA

MEDIA

Athens
Sparta

Ephesus
Mt. Mycale
Miletus

PISIDIA

CILICIA

Euphrates R.

Ecbatana

IONIA

CARIA

Perga

Tigris R.

Halicarnassus

CYPRUS

SYRIA

BABYLONIA

ELAM

Rhodes

Tyre

PHOENICIA

Damascus

Babylon

Susa

CRETE

MEDITERRANEAN SEA

Jerusalem

PER

Cyrene

LIBYA

Memphis

30°

E
G
Y
P
T

RED SEA

A R A B I

Thebes

Nile R.

ETHIOPIA

30°

40°

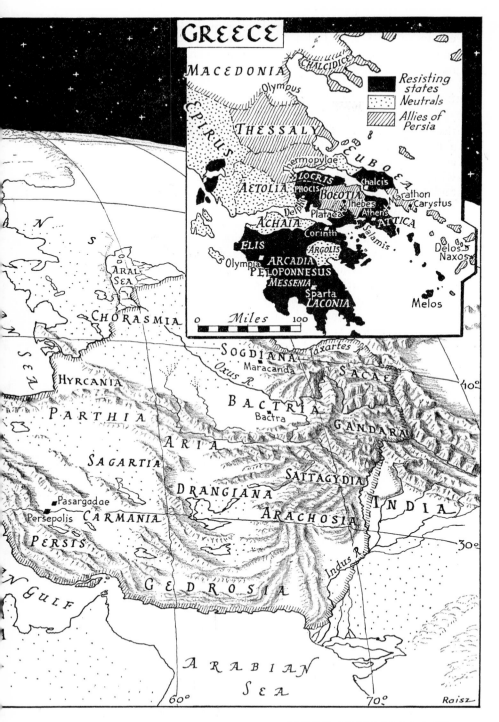

GREECE

Resisting states
Neutrals
Allies of Persia

MACEDONIA
CHALCIDICE
Olympus
EPIRUS
THESSALY
EUBOEA
Thermopylae
LOCRIS
AETOLIA
PHOCIS
Chalcis
Delphi
BOEOTIA
Marathon
Thebes
Carystus
Plataea
Athens
ACHAIA
Corinth
ATTICA
Salamis
ELIS
ARGOLIS
Delos
Naxos
Olympia
ARCADIA
PELOPONNESUS
MESSENIA
Sparta
LACONIA
Melos

0   Miles   100

N
S
ARAL SEA
CHORASMIA
HYRCANIA
SOGDIANA
Jaxartes R.
Maracanda
Oxus R.
SACAE
BACTRIA
Bactra
GANDARA
PARTHIA
ARIA
SAGARTIA
SATTAGYDIA
INDIA
DRANGIANA
Pasargadae
Persepolis
CARMANIA
ARACHOSIA
PERSIS
GEDROSIA
Indus R.
GULF
ARABIAN
SEA

40°
30°
60°
70°

Raisz

It was his son Cambyses who finally added Egypt (525 B.C.). The vast empire, after 512, had also been extended into Europe, as a result of a campaign against the Thracians in northern Greece and the Scythians north of the Black Sea.

THE GREEK (ATHENIAN) DEFEAT OF PERSIA

The Greek cities of Asia Minor, however, were not content to bear the comparatively mild Persian rule. They tried to free themselves by a combined revolt (499–494 B.C.), in the course of which they were assisted by Athens. To make his northwestern frontier secure the Persian King Darius planned the reduction of that Athens which had dared to interfere with his administration of the satrapy (province) of Ionia. In 490 B.C. he launched by sea an expedition against Athens which landed on the eastern Attic coast not far from the plain of Marathon. Here he was met by the Athenians alone, and so conclusively defeated that he knew that much more extensive and careful preparations had to be made before he could be secure from the Greeks. It was left to his son Xerxes to make a second attempt after ten years of preparation. Gathering together at Sardis, his advanced headquarters, what was described by Herodotus as a spectacular assortment, including barbarian contingents, from all parts of his empire, Xerxes marched to the Hellespont (Dardanelles), bridged it with ships, and proceeded along the north Aegean coast toward Greece. It was not a united Greece that met him. Those who were prepared to give in without a struggle had been supported in their attitude by the oracle of Apollo at Delphi. It was Athens again that finally bore the brunt of the campaign. It had been planned to stop Xerxes at the pass of Thermopylae, but these plans were thwarted by treachery. The Persian troops then marched toward Athens without hindrance. Meanwhile the Athenians had evacuated the whole population of the city to Salamis, whence could be seen the flames that Persian torches had lit in their beloved city. The Athenian general Themistocles had decided to risk all upon a naval engagement, knowing that without the supplies furnished by the Persian fleet the Persian army could not survive on Greek soil. The Persian fleet was drawn into the Bay of Salamis (480) and there hopelessly destroyed. In the next year, the Athenians joined the Spartans against the Persians in a decisive land battle at Plataea which, together with a second Athenian naval victory at Mycale, obliged the Persians to return to Asia. They were never to tread again upon the European continent.

ATHENS AND THE DELIAN LEAGUE

While the other Greek states, notably Sparta, were content to relax after this signal accomplishment of Greek arms, the Athenians went ahead to capitalize on the fear of the island city-states of the Aegean that the Persians might reappear. In the years following Salamis they organized an offensive campaign calculated to prevent the Persians from threatening the islands and the western coast of Asia Minor. The result was an alliance system constructed by Athens that at its greatest extent included over two hundred cities of the whole Aegean area. These alliances took the form of a confederation, or league, with Delos as its center. This Delian League, which Athens soon came to dominate, was conceived as a confederation of equals sending delegates to a common assembly and making contributions to a joint treasury at Delos. All were to furnish money or ships for a unified navy directed by Athens. The confederation in its early stages furnishes the best example of successful co-operative effort on the part of the Greek states when faced with a danger common to them all. Within a few years the purpose of eliminating Persian interference in Aegean affairs was accomplished. Not only the cities of the Aegean islands but also those of the Thracian coast, of the Hellespont, and of the western coast of Asia Minor joined in forcing the Persians to withdraw from this area. By 448 the Persians were content to make peace on terms that excluded them from the affairs of the cities of the League.[8] This did not mean that Persia henceforth ceased to be a factor in the internal and external politics of Greece. But it was Persian money and diplomacy rather than Persian armed forces that played the determining part. Persia was no military match for Greece. The forced levies of an oriental despotism had failed to reduce the militias of free cities.

DELIAN LEAGUE AND ATHENIAN EMPIRE

What began, however, as the Delian League ended as the Athenian empire. The city-state that was thoroughly democratic at home was unwilling to maintain the early democratic character of the League. The tolerated leadership of Athens had become, by the time of the opening of the Peloponnesian War, an Athenian tyranny, hated by the members of the League and feared by the Greek states of the mainland. Athens used the League, for example, to establish her economic hegemony in the whole Aegean and Black Sea area. When Pericles said that "our city is so great that all the products of all the earth flow in upon us, and ours is the happy lot to gather in the good fruits of our own soil with no more home-felt security of enjoyment than we do those of other lands" or that "we have compelled every sea and every land to grant access to our daring, and have everywhere planted everlasting memorials both of evil to foes and of good to friends," he was speaking of the benefits of this policy. The Athenians not only used the League to establish their own economic fortunes, they used its funds to expand and embellish their democracy at home. The treasury of the League was removed from Delos to Athens, and its surplus funds used to pay the numerous officials of an expanding bureaucracy and even to build public works in Athens. The imperializa-

---

[8]Botsford's date, *Hellenic History*, p. 238. For the question of the treaty and date, see *Cambridge Ancient History*, V, 469, n. 3.

tion went further. The common assembly of the League ceased to meet. The Athenians determined the character of the governments of the allied cities, permitting nothing but democracies to exist. Gradually disputes and violations of the law were settled not in local but in Athenian courts. All commercial disputes and the more important criminal cases were tried before the popular courts in Athens, which thus reaped the financial rewards. As the imperial policy grew more oppressive individual states attempted to revolt. Democratic Athens was to many of them no better than despotic Persia. When revolts occurred Athens put them down by force and punished the dissentients remorselessly. Athenian garrisons were imposed locally and Athenian colonists sent out to keep watch on suspected communities. When, for example, the island of Naxos revolted in 469, she was crushed by force, her walls were torn down and her fleet confiscated, tribute was imposed, and her freedom was destroyed. Other revolts were treated in similar fashion. After the outbreak of the Peloponnesian War, the Athenians had to use even more stringent means to keep their subjects in line.

ATHENS AND MELOS

This cynical and callous imperialism is best illustrated from the history of Thucydides. He describes the refusal of the inhabitants of the island of Melos, a Spartan colony, to come into the empire, and their resistance to the attempt of the Athenians to force them in. Before making a final reduction of the city an Athenian embassy was sent to Melos to convince its citizens of the futility of resistance. In the course of the discussion the Athenians reminded the Melian magistrates that in spite of the fact that "we hold sway justly because we overthrew the Persians" there was no point in discussing such matters, since "what is just is arrived at in human arguments only when the necessity on both sides is equal . . . the powerful exact what they can, while the weak yield what they must" (III, 159-179). When the Melians objected to becoming Athenian slaves they were told, "It would be to your advantage to submit before suffering the most horrible fate, and we should gain by not destroying you. . . . To say nothing of our enlarging our empire, you would afford us security by being subdued, especially if you, an insular power, and weaker than other islanders, should fail to show yourselves superior to a power which is master of the sea." It was useless for the Melians to hope for a successful military outcome. "Hope is indeed a solace in danger, and for those who have other resources in abundance, though she may injure, she does not ruin them; but for those who stake their all on a single throw—hope being by nature prodigal—it is only when disaster has befallen that her true nature is recognized." When the Melians remarked, "We trust that, in point of fortune, we shall through the divine favour be at no disadvantage because we are God-fearing men standing our ground against men who are unjust," the Athenians replied, "Well, as to the kindness of the divine favour, neither do we expect to fall short of you therein. . . . For of the Gods we hold the belief, and of men we know, that by a necessity of their nature wherever they have power they always rule." In fact, "self-interest goes hand in hand with security, while justice and honour are practised with danger. . . . You will not consider it degrading . . . when a choice is given you of war or safety, not to hold out stubbornly for the worse alternative." When, in spite of Athenian argument, the Melians chose the "worst," and were defeated, "the Athenians thereupon slew all the adult males whom they had taken and made slaves of the children and women. But the place they then peopled with new settlers from Athens, sending thither at a later time five hundred colonists." (I, 43)

No matter what may be said to justify the Athenian transformation of the Delian League into an empire, or of the great advantage it was for the Aegean cities to share the superior culture of their master, those contemporaries of Pericles who saw in Athenian imperial policy a negation of the best that Athens stood for were certainly right; this policy, in fact, was a supreme example of that overbearing insolence (*hubris*) for which Aeschylus had condemned Xerxes in *The Persians*. Eleven years after the annihilation of Melos, nemesis came for Athens in the loss of her empire and the occupation of the Acropolis by Spartan troops.

THE CAUSE OF THE PELOPONNESIAN WAR

It was no accident that the dissatisfied imperial subjects of Athens allied themselves with Sparta to bring about this event. In his analysis of the causes of the Peloponnesian War (431–404 B.C.), Thucydides, its great historian, asserts that he believed "the truest explanation, although it has been the least often advanced, . . . to have been the growth of the Athenians to greatness, which brought fear to the Lacedaemonians [Spartans] and forced them to war." The fear thus expressed was that the Athenian empire, based essentially upon sea power, would extend itself in Greece proper, and thus become a land power. Such an extension of Athenian power in Greece would challenge the position of Sparta in the Peloponnesus and in fact threaten the very existence of the Spartan state. Inasmuch as Sparta allowed to her allies more local independence than Athens tolerated in her empire, the related issue of the struggle was the degree of subjection to which the Greek cities, who would be forced to take issue in the struggle, would submit. Sparta was thus, in the eyes of her allies, the champion of the undiminished independence of the city-state; Athens, the ruthless and cynical imperialist power, to whom any independence other than her own was a matter of power politics, and of moral indifference.

FURTHER ISSUES IN THE PELOPONNESIAN WAR

At the same time, the choice of the Greek city-states between Athens and Sparta was made more difficult in that Athens was, after all, a political democracy, where the people did control their state. Sparta, on the contrary, was an authoritarian state governed by an oligarchy representing the army. She relied upon governments of a similar oligarchical character for her allies. The Athenian empire, if it restricted local independence, left the residue of power in popular hands. The Spartan League, though it respected local independence, left this authority in the hands of privileged groups. That there was really no greater promise of freedom under Sparta than under Athens Thucydides makes clear in a speech of an Athenian delegate to the Spartans at the outbreak of the war: "If others should seize our power, they would, we think, exhibit the best proof that we show some moderation. . . . The present yoke is always heavy to subjects. Certainly you, should you overthrow us and obtain supremacy, would soon lose the good will which you have gained through fear of us—if indeed you mean again to show such temper as you gave a glimpse of at that time when for a little while you had the hegemony against the Persian. For the institutions that prevail among you at home are incompatible with those of other peoples, and, besides, each one of you when he goes abroad uses neither these nor those which the rest of Greece is accustomed to." (I, 131–133)

SPARTAN POLITICAL INSTITUTIONS

The incompatible Spartan institutions to which Thucydides refers were not so much her political as her social and economic institutions. To be sure, the Spartans continued to be governed by two kings long after monarchy had disappeared elsewhere in Greece. These kings, along with twenty-eight members chosen from the leading families of the hereditary aristocracy, were members of the Council of Elders, who had to be at least sixty years of age. This Council, corresponding to the Athenian Council of 500, was the executive body of the Spartan *polis*. It was chosen by an assembly of all Spartan citizens, the *apella*, corresponding to the Athenian *ecclesia*. Unlike the latter, the Spartan assembly merely voted *yes* or *no*, without further discussion, on matters or laws presented to it by the Council.

THE PERIOECI

As in Athens the citizen body was rigidly limited. It did not include the *perioeci*, those "dwelling around," who occupied the towns and territory on the outskirts of the strictly Spartan domain, and who were subject to restrictions varying in accordance with their individual cities. Although they were not politically classified as aliens, as were the Athenian metics, they did occupy a position similar to that of the metics in economic life. The Spartans' attitude toward trade and industry is clear from their retention of cumbersome iron "money" long after it was abolished elsewhere in Greece. The *perioeci* and not the Spartan citizens were, therefore, the

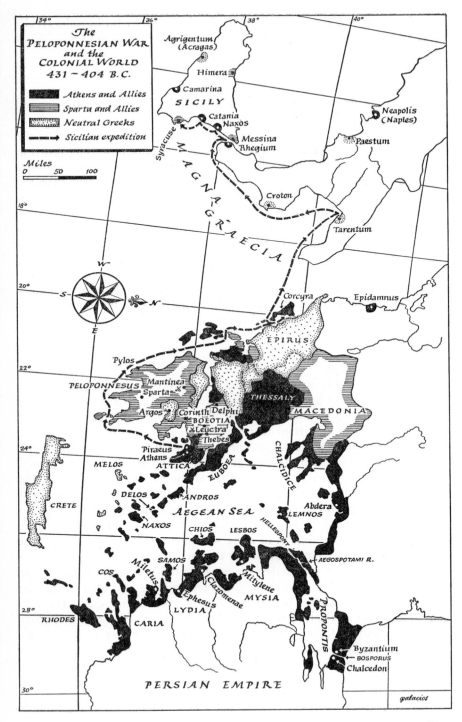

The
PELOPONNESIAN WAR
and the
COLONIAL WORLD
431 – 404 B.C.

- Athens and Allies
- Sparta and Allies
- Neutral Greeks
- - → Sicilian expedition

Miles
0   50   100

Agrigentum (Acragas)
Himera
Camarina
SICILY
Catania
Naxos
Messina
Rhegium
Neapolis (Naples)
Paestum
Syracuse

MAGNA GRAECIA

Croton

Tarentum

Corcyra
Epidamnus

EPIRUS

Pylos
PELOPONNESUS
Mantinea
Sparta
Argos
Corinth
Delphi
BOEOTIA
Leuctra
Thebes
Piraeus
Athens
ATTICA

THESSALY
MACEDONIA
CHALCIDICE

MELOS
DELOS
ANDROS
NAXOS
EUBOEA
Abdera
LEMNOS

CRETE

AEGEAN SEA

CHIOS
LESBOS
HELLESPONT
AEGOSPOTAMI R.

SAMOS
Miletus
COS
Clazomenae
Mitylene
MYSIA
Ephesus
LYDIA
RHODES
CARIA

PROPONTIS
Byzantium
BOSPORUS
Chalcedon

PERSIAN EMPIRE

galacios

manufacturers and the merchants. As for foreigners who introduced the ideas and customs of the outside world, the Spartans simply would not tolerate them.

THE HELOTS

Indeed, the city-state of Sparta was organized as a perpetual armed camp composed of citizen members of the armed forces ready to fight at any time. The chief fact which helps to explain this organization of the state for constant readiness in war is that the Spartans, in settling down in Laconia as conquerors, had enslaved (or kept enslaved) as agricultural workers a local population about twenty times more numerous than the Spartans themselves. This group of agricultural slaves were called *helots*. They are described by the Spartan poet Tyrtaeus as "labouring like asses under heavy loads, and forced by bitter compulsion to bring their masters half of all the produce of their fields. . . . And whenever one of their masters died, they and their wives must go to his funeral and lament for him."[9] The lands which the helots cultivated for the Spartan citizens were state property, allocated to provide for the maintenance of the military élite, the Spartan citizens, who thus had nothing to do but develop their athletic and military prowess and perform their duties as members of the assembly.

SPARTAN INSTITUTIONS

To keep the helots in terror the Spartans had organized a secret police (*crypteia*) of young Spartans, who worked at night to kill off any helots thought dangerous to the Spartan system. Military service to the state was regarded as so important that neither the education of youth nor the training of the adult was thought compatible with family life. The youth who survived physical inspection at birth, which condemned weaklings to exposure, was taken from his mother at the age of seven to begin his training as a member of the army. He was taught to endure annual competitive floggings, to be resourceful by learning how to steal without being caught, above all, to be courageous and to look upon death in battle as the glorious consummation of a life well spent. Tyrtaeus sings to these youth the disparagement of all virtue except "warlike valour. . . . For no one is a good man in war, unless he can bear to see bloody slaughter and can press hard on the enemy, standing face to face. . . . That is the best and fairest prize which a young man can win among men. . . . He who falls among the foremost fighters and loses his dear life in winning glory for his city and his fellow-citizens and his father—his breast and his bossed shield and his breastplate pierced with many wounds in front—he is lamented by young and old together, and the whole city mourns for him in sad grief; and his tomb and his children are honoured among men, and

[9]Werner Jaeger, *Paideia: The Ideals of Greek Culture*, trans. Gilbert Highet, I, 83.

his children's children likewise and his whole race after him; never is his name and fair fame destroyed, but though he lies beneath the earth he becomes immortal."[10]

At the age of twenty, when the young Spartan was ready for duty in the field, he might marry, but he did not live at home. His was a barracks life. With his fellow citizen-soldiers he ate and slept and exercised and drilled. As the bearers of the future citizens of the Spartan state, women were given similar training. Aristophanes, the Athenian comic poet, introduces one of them, Lampito, into his play *Lysistrata*, "brown with the sun and 'strong enough to choke an ox.' "[11] To maintain this system of iron discipline, the Spartan assembly elected "overseers" (*ephors*) who ultimately displaced the kings as the directors of the Spartan state.

The Peloponnesian War was thus a conflict between two imperial systems, the one led by a democratic, the other by an authoritarian and military state. After Sparta emerged successful from the conflict political speculation regarded somewhat wistfully the disciplined devotion of the Spartan to his city when compared, for example, with the selfish individualism of the Athenian. In the ideal cities imagined by the philosophers some Spartan institutions were set up for imitation. In many more than Spartan hearts the civic patriotism of Tyrtaeus found a warm response.

THE BEGINNING OF THE WAR

The incidents that precipitated the struggle between Athens and Sparta reveal clearly the imperial character of the contest. They show that what Pericles and Athenian democrats had in mind was an extension of the Athenian empire to the Greek cities in Italy and Sicily, of which Syracuse, a Dorian colony, was the most important. The Athenian pottery industry had made large inroads into the markets of these cities long before 500 B.C. The cities of Peloponnesian Greece were dependent on the western colonies for imports of food and raw materials. If Athens should secure control of these vital imports the Peloponnesians would thus come to depend upon Athens for their livelihood. Athens' opportunity to secure control of the trade routes from western Greece to southern Italy and Sicily came when Corcyra, at war with her mother city, Corinth, offered an alliance to Athens and pointed out, according to Thucydides, that "Corcyra is favourably situated for a coasting voyage either to Italy or Sicily, so that you could prevent a fleet from coming thence to join the Peloponnesians, or could convoy thither a fleet from here." The Athenian acceptance of this offer brought about the war.

PERICLEAN STRATEGY

The events of the war itself made only too clear this preoccupation of Athens with a western empire and the determination of southern Greece

[10] Jaeger, I, 88-89.
[11] Gilbert Murray, *Aristophanes: A Study*, p. 166.

to thwart it. Pericles, the real architect of Athens' future, survived the beginning of the war by only two years (429 B.C.). The Athenian democracy had hitherto depended for its leadership upon the old aristocratic families of Athens. At this point, however, leaders emerged from the middle classes and from the people (Cleon, for example) whose immediate fortunes were tied up with the commercial expansion of the city. These men lacked the ability to hold the Athenians to a balanced course. Their methods were scoffed at by the Athenian conservatives, who called them demagogues. Pericles' plan of defense had been to maintain Athenian sea power intact while permitting Sparta and her allies regularly to devastate the farms of Attica, whose occupants he evacuated to well-fortified Athens. Until the Athenian fleet could successfully blockade the whole Peloponnesus, the war could only result in a stalemate. Its very first year cost Athens about one-third of its population, when into the midst of this greatly overcrowded city a plague of African origin struck. As the war went on year by year without any decisive engagements, and as the Athenian farmers and landholders could see no end to the annual ravaging of Attican territory, a peace party, led by Nicias, arose, demanding a cessation of hostilities. The response on the part of the Spartan League, torn by destructive party conflicts, was such that a temporary respite was arranged in 421 (Peace of Nicias), but it did not end the conflict.

THE SICILIAN EXPEDITION

When the war began again it centered about Athens' attempt to decide the issue once and for all by the successful conquest of the western colonial world. The main architect of this plan was Alcibiades, a nephew of Pericles, personally ambitious, an ardent imperialist, and to the Athenian Assembly a flashy and tempting, if suspected and hated, spokesman. The issue of a Sicilian campaign against Syracuse was put to the Athenian Assembly by Nicias, who opposed it as follows: "On behalf of our country, which is now running the greatest risk it has ever run, hold up your hands in opposition and vote that the Siceliots, keeping the same boundaries with respect to us as at present . . . shall enjoy their own possessions and settle their own quarrels among themselves" (III, 207). Alcibiades' answer, in the same Assembly, was "We acquired our empire—both we and all others that have ever won empire—by coming zealously to the aid of those, whether barbarians or Hellenes, who have at any time appealed to us; whereas, if we should all keep quiet . . . we should add but little to our empire and should rather run a risk of losing that empire itself. For against a superior one does not merely defend oneself when he attacks, but even takes precaution that he shall not attack at all. And it is not possible for us to exercise a careful stewardship of the limits we would set to our empire; but, since we are placed in this position, it is necessary to plot against some and not let go our hold upon others, because there is a danger of coming ourselves under the empire of others, should we not ourselves hold empire over other peoples. . . . Calculating, then, that we shall rather strengthen our power here if we go over there, let us make the voyage." (III, 217–219)

The Assembly supported Alcibiades. The great expedition set sail for Sicily in 415. "It was the longest voyage from home as yet attempted and undertaken with the highest hopes for the future as compared with . . . present resources." (III, 239) The details of this undoing of Athenian greatness must not detain us. They are best sought in the account of Thucydides himself. The campaign proved a miserable and tragic failure. Thucydides closed his account of it with the statement: "This event proved to be the greatest of all that had happened in the course of this war, and, as it seems to me, of all Hellenic events of which we have record—for the victors most splendid, for the vanquished most disastrous. For the vanquished, beaten utterly at every point and having suffered no slight ill in any respect—having met, as the saying goes, with utter destruction—land-force and fleet and everything perished, and few out of many came back home. Such was the course of events in Sicily." (IV, 179, 181)

THE END OF THE PELOPONNESIAN WAR

Athens made a desperate effort to recover from this disaster, but to no avail. The Spartan League, which had closely co-operated with Syracuse in Greece, now sought and received Persian aid. The plan was to further undermine Athenian hegemony in a tottering empire by cutting Athens off from her Black Sea colonies, thereby robbing her of a chief source of her food supply. In 405, at the mouth of the Aegospotami River in northwestern Asia Minor, a Spartan fleet caught by surprise the "last possible" Athenian fleet, "manned with their last available crews," and utterly destroyed it. A surviving dispatch ship (the *Paralus*) was sent to the Athenian port of Piraeus to bring the news. "It was night when the *Paralus* reached Athens with her evil tidings, on receipt of which a bitter wail of woe broke forth. From Peiraeus [Piraeus], following the line of the Long Walls up to the heart of the city, it swept and swelled, as each man to his neighbor passed on the news. On that night no man slept. There was mourning and sorrow for those that were lost, but the lamentation for the dead was merged in even deeper sorrow for themselves, as they pictured the evils they were about to suffer, the like of which they had themselves inflicted on the Melians . . . and on many other Hellenes."[12] This defeat brought the final revolt of the whole empire, a Spartan fleet to the harbor of Piraeus, and a Spartan army to besiege Athens itself. Athens submitted in 404. Although there were many members of the Spartan League who would have liked to see Athens wiped out and her population exterminated, the actual terms read: "That the Long Walls and the fortifications of Peiraeus should be destroyed; that the Athenian fleet with the excep-

[12]The selection from G. W. Botsford, *Hellenic History*, p. 327, copyright 1956 by The Macmillan Co., and used with The Macmillan Co.'s permission.

tion of twelve ships should be surrendered . . . and lastly that the Athenians should acknowledge the headship of Lacedaemon in peace and war, leaving to her the choice of friends and foes, and following her lead by land and sea."

THUCYDIDES' ESTIMATE OF PERICLES

Thucydides says of his account of the Peloponnesian War that "it may well be that the absence of the fabulous from my narrative will seem less pleasing to the ear; but whoever shall wish to have a clear view both of the events which have happened and of those which will some day, in all human probability, happen again in the same or a similar way—for these to adjudge my history profitable will be enough for me. And, indeed, it has been composed, not as a prize-essay to be heard for the moment, but as a possession for all time." (I, 39, 41) His lofty treatment of the particular issues involved in the war makes his history a classic description of imperialistic struggles. Not that he himself felt that the war was predetermined by any large cosmic forces. As a participant he knew the importance for the final outcome of the decisions that were made from day to day, and he felt the limitations placed upon the hazardous enterprise of war by subjecting its conduct to capricious democratic control. It was for this reason that he came to feel that Pericles, had he lived, would have carried the war to a successful conclusion. For Pericles would not have risked the Sicilian expedition. "He had told the Athenians that if they would maintain a defensive policy . . . and not seek to extend their sway during the war . . . they would prove superior. But they not only acted contrary to his advice in all these things, but also in matters that apparently had no connection with the war they were led by private ambition and private greed to adopt policies which proved injurious both to themselves and their allies." (I, 375, 377) The quality of Pericles' leadership in peace made him, in Thucydides' estimation, an ideal leader in war, when more than ever it was necessary to calm the emotions of the multitude. "Pericles, who owed his influence to his recognized standing and ability, and had proved himself clearly incorruptible in the highest degree, restrained the multitude while respecting their liberties, and led them rather than was led by them, because he did not resort to flattery, seeking power by dishonest means, but was able on the strength of his high reputation to oppose them and even provoke their wrath. . . . And so Athens, though in name a democracy, gradually became in fact a government ruled by its foremost citizen." (I, 377)[13]

GREEK DEMANDS FOR PEACE

Greek civilization was ruined by this war, and therefore by a devotion to parochial independence that made it impossible for the two lead-

[13]See also the essay of Jaeger on Thucydides in *Paideia*, I, 379–408.

ing city-states and their satellites to make the compromises necessary to establish the institutions of a common peace. Certain men of Athens at the time were also aware, not only of the corruption of public character that the Athenian empire brought about, but also of the fact that Greece could not really survive the war. They could not see why it was impossible for the Athenian empire and the Spartan League to live at peace, and thus to insure the continuation of the high civilization that the Greeks had achieved. They began, therefore, to damn the treatment that the Athenians were meting out to their allies, to ridicule the imperialistic warmongers who were pandering to the lusts of the Athenian populace, to demand a cessation of the war, and, by trying to understand the Spartan point of view and praising Spartan virtues, to build up public sentiment to the point at which a permanent Athenian-Spartan alliance might guarantee peace to a ravished Greek community.

Two of these men were dramatic poets, namely, Aristophanes, who wrote comedy, and Euripides, who wrote tragedy. They were sufficiently courageous to present their unpopular views to the Athenian populace at the annual state dramatic festivals, and, it must be added, the Athenian state itself was sufficiently liberal to award prizes to the plays containing these views and to pay for their production on the Athenian stage. We may appreciate this endowment of freedom of speech if we try to imagine a situation in which a modern state awarded a prize to a native dramatist who branded the government leaders warmongers, held up the virtues of the enemy for admiration, and demanded peace and the establishment of an alliance with the enemy.

ARISTOPHANES

Aristophanes was born around the middle of the fifth century B.C. He came of an old conservative Attic family who taught him to treasure the decencies of Periclean Athens and to love and memorize its literature and that of all Greece. He lived through the Peloponnesian War, observed its destruction, watched how it put the democratic machinery of the city at the mercy of demagogues, and saw how it led to an imperialist policy of terror. He decided to protest in his plays against what he regarded as the evil trend of events. Five of them were especially devoted to these themes: *The Babylonians, The Acharnians, The Knights, The Peace,* and finally *Lysistrata.* His program was a simple one: that the two leading powers of Greece, Athens and Sparta, each with her own virtues and vices, should compose their differences and establish co-operatively a peaceful Greek world where Greek culture could really flourish.

"THE BABYLONIANS"

His first protest, *The Babylonians,* came in the spring of 426, six years after the beginning of the war. It was produced at a time when representatives of all the allies could be present to witness it. Although it is preserved only in fragments, there can be little doubt that its theme was the unmerciful character of Athenian imperial policy under the direction of Cleon, Pericles' successor, who to Thucydides was "the most violent of the citizens" and to Aristophanes was "a whale that keeps a public-house and has a voice like a pig on fire." In this play Aristophanes attacks "all the Athenian officials, whether elected or chosen by lot, and, above all, Cleon." The Greek cities in the empire were made to form a chorus of branded Babylonian slaves working at a mill under the supervision of the Athenian people. The play seems to make constant reference to the exploitation of the allies in the form of military service, to plundering, and to the corruption rife among Athenian officials. It was too much for Cleon, who apparently prosecuted Aristophanes for his impudent lack of public respect. At least, when Aristophanes put on his next play, *The Acharnians*, in 426, he referred to Cleon's prosecution:

> . . . I know what I myself endured
> At Cleon's hands for last year's Comedy.
> How to the Council-house he haled me off,
> And slanged, and lied, and slandered, and betongued me,
> Roaring Cycloborus-wise; till I well nigh
> Was done to death, bemiryslushified. (I, 39–41)[14]

"THE KNIGHTS"

In 424 B.C. Aristophanes continued his attack on Cleon in *The Knights*. Cleon is represented in the play as the toady of Demus, the Athenian populace. "Last new moon," we are told,

> He [Demus] bought a slave, a tanner, Paphlagon [Blusterer],
> The greatest rogue and liar in the world.
> This tanning-Paphlagon, he soon finds out
> Master's weak points; and cringing down before him
> Flatters, and fawns, and wheedles, and cajoles,
> With little apish leather-snippings. . . . (I, 129)

His rival, a sausage seller, charges that

> . . . the peace which, unsought, Archeptolemus brought, you were quick from the city to scout
> And as for the embassies coming to treat, you spanked them and chivied them out. (I, 201)

The tanner answers, however, that he did so "That over all Hellas our Demus may rule." After a contest between Cleon and the sausage seller for the favor of the Athenian Assembly, in which Aristophanes pours scathing and raucous ridicule upon the fickle, greedy, and ignorant mob,

[14]Citations from Aristophanes in my text are to his works trans. B. B. Rogers, Loeb, Nos. 178, 179, 180, 3 vols. See Gilbert Murray, *Aristophanes and the War Party*.

Cleon is deposed and succeeded by the sausage seller, who proclaims that for punishment

> . . . he shall ply my trade,
> Sole sausage-seller at the City gates.
> There let him dogs'-meat mix with asses' flesh,
> There let him, tipsy, with the harlots wrangle,
> And drink the filthy scouring of the bath. (I, 257–259)

With this Cleon is carried off, "that so the strangers [the allies?], whom he wronged, may see him."

"THE ACHARNIANS"

In *The Acharnians*, *The Peace*, and *Lysistrata*, Aristophanes took up the peace theme more directly. The first of these, *The Acharnians*, was produced in 426 B.C., and *Lysistrata* in 411 B.C. In *The Acharnians*, Dicaeopolis, an inhabitant of the deme of Acharnae and a victim of the regular devastation of Attic farms carried on by the armies of the Spartan League, comes to the Athenian Assembly at daybreak to plead for a treaty of peace.

> . . . I am always first of all to come, [he says]
> And here I take my seat; then, all alone,
> I pass the time complaining, yawning, stretching,
> I fidget, write, twitch hairs out, do my sums,
> Gaze fondly country-wards, longing for Peace,
> Loathing the town, sick for my village-home,
> Which never cried, *Come, buy my charcoal*, or
> *My vinegar, my oil, my* anything;
> But freely gave us all; no *buy*-word there.
> So here I'm waiting, thoroughly prepared
> To riot, wrangle, interrupt the speakers
> Whene'er they speak of anything but Peace. (I, 9)

But the assembly chooses to listen to its ambassadors to Persia rather than to talk of peace. Dicaeopolis, therefore, determines to "do a great and startling deed." He gives an agent eight drachmae and directs him to

> . . . take them; and with all
> The Lacedaemonians make a private peace
> For me, my wife and children: none besides.

The man who brings back Dicaeopolis' treaties of peace is pursued by

> . . . some veterans . . .
> Acharnians, men of Marathon, hard in grain
> As their own oak and maple, rough and tough,

who cry,

> O villain, dare you
> Bring treaties when our vineyards are cut down?

When Dicaeopolis himself is attacked by the Acharnians for treating,

> . . . when with Sparta
>   no engagement sacred stands,
> Not the altar, not the oath-pledge,
>   not the faith of clasped right hands!

he replies,

> Yet I know that these our foemen,
>   who our bitter wrath excite,
> Were not always wrong entirely,
>   nor ourselves entirely right.
>   . . . . .
>   I can prove by reasons strong
> That in many points the Spartans
>   at our hands have suffered wrong.
>   . . . . .
> I'll speak my mind for Lacedaemon's folk. (I, 33, 39)

In speaking before the assembly Dicaeopolis says that, of course, he detests the Spartans,

> For I, like you, have had my vines cut down.
> But after all—for none but friends are here—
> Why the Laconians do we blame for this?
> For men of ours, I do not say the State,
> Remember this, I do not say the State,
> But worthless fellows of a worthless stamp,
> Ill-coined, ill-minted, spurious little chaps,
> Kept on denouncing Megara's little coats [the staple manufacture of Megara].
> And if a cucumber or hare they saw,
> Or sucking-pig, or garlic, or lump-salt,
> All were Megarian, and were sold off-hand. (I, 51)

In his account of the petty incidents that started the war he blames the Athenians as much as the Spartans.

> Ye'll say *They should not* [declare war on such slight provocation]; but
>   what should they, then?
> Come now, had some Laconian, sailing out,
> Denounced and sold a small Seriphian dog,
> Would you have sat unmoved? Far, far from that!
> Ye would have launched three hundred ships of war,
> And all the City had at once been full
> Of shouting troops, of fuss with trierarchs . . .
> Of wineskins, oarloops, bargaining for casks,
> Of nets of onions, olives, garlic-heads,
> Of chaplets, pilchards, flute-girls, and black eyes.
> And all the arsenal had rung with noise
> Of oar-spars planed, pegs hammered, oarloops fitted,

Of boatswains' calls, and flutes, and trills, and whistles.
This had ye done; and shall not Telephus,[15]
Think we, do this? we've got no brains at all. (I, 53–55)

Having concluded his private peace, Dicaeopolis opens his private market
place, proclaiming that,

> . . . I to all the Peloponnesian folk,
> Megarians and Boeotians [the former enemies], give full leave
> To trade with me; but not to Lamachus.

The benefits of peace are not for Lamachus, since he is the Athenian
general who has proclaimed,

> . . . I with all the Peloponnesian folk
> Will always fight, and vex them everyway,
> By land, by sea, with all my might and main. (I, 61)

The first trader in the market is a poor Megarian, whose whole town
has been ruined by the war. He asks his two little daughters whether
they would rather be starved or sold, and they answer, in the Dorian
dialect, "Liefer be sellt! Liefer be sellt!"[16] He disguises them as little
pigs, instructs them in grunting, and after much canny bargaining and
after proving that they have at least the appetites of pigs, succeeds in
getting Dicaeopolis to buy them for "a tie o' garlic" and "half a peck o'
saut." A Boeotian comes bringing, "Mats, dittany, pennyroyal, lantern-
wicks . . . Plivers an' divers . . . geese . . . easels an' weasels, urchins, moles,
an' cats, An' otters too, an' eels frae Loch Copaïs. . . . Let me salute the
eels, if eels you bring," says Dicaeopolis. "O loved, and lost, and longed
for, thou art come. . . . Six years a truant, scarce returning now." Others
come to beg him for a bit of his peace, a husbandman who is ruined by the
loss of his two oxen and a bridesmaid who brings a message from the
bride begging for a little peace "to keep her bridegroom safely by her
side." While Lamachus is being ordered off to war by the generals ("O
generals, great in numbers, small in worth!") Dicaeopolis is invited to a
feast by the priest of Bacchus.

> . . . All things . . . are ready and prepared,
> The couches, tables, sofa-cushions, rugs,
> Wreaths, sweetmeats, myrrh, the harlotry are there,
> Whole-meal cakes, cheese-cakes, sesame-honey-cakes,
> And dancing-girls. . . .

[15]Telephus, son of Heracles, specifically a Dorian hero and therefore a symbol of
all the Peloponnesian people.
[16]The translator here uses Scottish dialect to approximate the effect of the Doric
speech in which these passages were originally written.

As the chorus sings,

> Off to your duties, my heroes bold.
> Different truly the paths ye tread;
> One to drink with wreaths on his head;
> One to watch, and shiver with cold,

the play ends with the general nursing his wounds and Dicaeopolis triumphing in a Bacchic revel. (I, 105, 111)

"THE PEACE"

Aristophanes' *The Peace* was produced in 423, two years before the abortive Peace of Nicias was signed. In it Trygaeus is moved to seek peace from the gods.

> My master's mad [says one of his servants]; a novel kind of madness,
> Not your old style, but quite a new invention.
> For all day long he gazes at the sky,
> His mouth wide open, thus; and rails at Zeus:
> O Zeus, says he, *what seekest thou to do?*
> *Lay down thy besom, sweep not Hellas bare!*
> . . . . Thou wilt drain
> The lifeblood from our cities ere thou knowest! (II, 9)

Trygaeus then mounts his dung beetle for heaven in order to see Zeus personally. "My flight for the sake of all Hellas I take," he proclaims. But when he gets there, he finds that the Gods have abandoned heaven:

> They were so vexed with Hellas: therefore here
> Where they were dwelling, they've established War,
> And given you up entirely to his will.
> But they themselves have settled up aloft,
> As high as they can go; that they no more
> May see your fightings or receive your prayers. . . .
> Because, though They were oftentimes for Peace,
> You always would have War. (II, 21)

War is possessed of a great mortar, which "He means to put the cities in and pound them." Peace has been buried in a deep pit from which Trygaeus proposes to rescue her, summoning to his aid "farmers, merchants, artisans . . . craftsmen, aliens, sojourners . . . O all ye peoples." But the Greeks do not pull well together on the rope that is to bring the goddess Peace from her pit. It is only when no one but farmers are on the rope that she is rescued and greeted by Trygaeus,

> Giver of grapes, O how shall I address you?
> O for a word ten thousand buckets big
> Wherewith to accost you . . . (II, 49)

The peaceful earth can now be surveyed from above. "See how the rec-onciled cities greet and blend/In peaceful intercourse, and laugh for joy." But the munitions makers and suppliers of military equipment are not pleased. The crest maker is "tearing his hair," the pike maker is be-having even worse, the sickle maker is "joking and poking the spear-burnisher." The breastplate maker can exclaim, "O what's the use of this habergeon now?/So splendidly got up: cost forty pounds." And so with the trumpet maker and the helmet maker. With Peace on earth, the play ends in a festive revel, and the chorus sings:

> What a pleasure, what a treasure,
> What a great delight to me,
> From the cheese and from the onions
> And the helmet to be free.
> For I can't enjoy a battle,
> But I love to pass my days
> With my wine and boon companions
> Round the merry, merry blaze,
> When the logs are dry and seasoned,
> And the fire is burning bright,
> And I roast the pease and chestnuts
> In the embers all alight,
> —Flirting too with Thratta
> When my wife is out of sight. (II, 105)

"THE DAUGHTERS OF TROY" OF EURIPIDES

Euripides, one of the great Athenian tragic poets of the fifth century, was born at Salamis on the day in 480 B.C. when the Athenian navy over-whelmed the Persian fleet. His play *The Daughters of Troy* was pre-sented in Athens in 415, that is, just after the annihilation of Melos had shocked the Greek world, and on the eve of the departure of the Athenian fleet for Sicily. Through the medium of this play Euripides was protest-ing against the brutal practices of Athenian imperialism. Athena, the patron goddess of Athens, and Poseidon, the lord of the sea, resolve to destroy the Greeks on their way home from Troy for their shameful desecration, in the course of the war, of the shrines of the gods. He is a "fool," says Poseidon, "that in sack of towns lays temples waste,/And tombs, the sanctuaries of the dead!/He, sowing desolation, reaps destruc-tion." Under this cloud of doom the play unfolds the final atrocities com-mitted by the Greeks upon the Trojans. The Trojan women are being carried away by the Achaeans as slaves and concubines, among them Hecuba, the wife of Priam, the aged king of Troy, who is made in the play to bear the sufferings of her people. She herself is to become a slave of Odysseus of Ithaca. Her daughter, Cassandra, "Phoebus' maiden," (a consecrated virgin priestess of Apollo,) has been chosen by Agamem-non. Her daughter Polyxena is "slain at Achilles' tomb . . . a gift to a life-less corpse." Andromache, the wife of her son Hector, is to be taken by Achilles' son, Neoptolemus. Astyanax, Andromache's son, "O darling child, O prized above all price . . . must . . . die by foes! . . . He must be hurled from battlements of Troy." Menelaus of Sparta orders Helen to be dragged from her tent by the hair. "And I was minded . . . to bear [her] to Greece, to yield her there to death,/Avenging all my friends in Ilium slain. . . . Thou, to the stoners hence!" (I, 357–459)[17] The culmination of these brutalities for Hecuba comes when she learns that, as the parting touch, Troy is to be burned. With the city all in flames, she is dragged away to the Achaean ships, while the citadel of Troy crashes into the ruins. This attack on the glorious tradition of the Trojan War was a veiled attack upon Athenian treatment of her defeated enemies. The Achaeans in the play are the Athenians, and the Trojans the Melians. The doom pronounced by the gods upon the Achaeans was the doom that was to accompany the expedition to Syracuse. After the production of this play Euripides abandoned Athens for the "barbarian" court of Macedon.

"LYSISTRATA"

Aristophanes' last play on the theme of peace, *Lysistrata*, was produced in the spring of 411 B.C., four years after *The Daughters of Troy*, and two after the disaster of the Sicilian expedition. In spite of the loss of her army, navy, and empire, Athens was continuing the war. Aristophanes thus felt compelled to appeal to a city that had gone mad, with the hilarious suggestion that what Greek men had not been able to do perhaps Greek women could do. He entrusts to Lysistrata (Dismisser of Armies) the task of organizing the Greek women in a revolution which will force the men to make peace. Her proposal to them, when they are finally assembled, is that "if we really mean/To make the men make Peace, there's but one way,/We must abstain . . . each—from the joys of Love." There are protests ("I'll never do it. Let the war go on. . . . Ask anything but this."); but when the Spartan representative, fresh from her gymnastics, insists that "we maun hae Peace, at a' risks," the women, planning also to occupy the Acropolis, swear an oath beginning, "I will abstain from Love and Love's delights." They seize the treasury because Lysistrata says that money is the cause of the war "and all other disputes that there are." After the danger of some defection from the feminine ranks has been overcome, the plan succeeds. Husbands come pleading to their wives to come home ("No, no, I won't, unless you stop the war,/And all make friends"). Finally a herald comes from Sparta "anent a Peace." At Sparta "they're sair bested, Spartans, allies, an' a'." A peace conference is arranged between the "fellow sufferers," which Lysistrata addresses:

> . . . I wish to chide you both,
> That ye, all of one blood, all brethren sprinkling
> The selfsame altars from the selfsame laver,

[17]Citations from Euripides in my text are to *Tragedies*, trans. Arthur S. Way, Loeb, Nos. 9, 10, 11, 12, 4 vols. The interpretation is that of Gilbert Norwood in *Greek Tragedy*.

At Pylae, Pytho, and Olympia, ay
And many others which 'twere long to name,
That ye, Hellenes—with barbarian foes
Armed, looking on—fight and destroy Hellenes! (III, 109)

She reminds them of times past when they have come to each others' aid,
and they agree to sign a peace. At the banquet celebrating the peace the
Athenians find the Laconians "cheery fellows," and a Spartan decides to
"tak' up the pipes an' blaw" and dance and sing for the Athenians. The
play ends with a Spartan chorus praying to Artemis,

> Come wi' thy stoutest tether,
> To knit our sauls [souls] thegither,
> An' gie us Peace in store,
> An' Luve for evermore;

and an Athenian chorus inviting the gods to "witness the peace and the
harmony,/This which divine Aphrodite has made." (III, 121) The departing envoys take their wives home with them.

SPARTAN AND THEBAN HEGEMONY

Athens had failed to organize her empire on a democratic basis, and had
failed to compose her differences with the Peloponnesian League. The
price she paid for these failures was the loss of the opportunity to carry
her own brilliant life of the middle fifth century to still nobler heights
and to spread it more intensively abroad. It was now (404 B.C.) the turn
of Sparta to try, by profiting from the Athenian experience, to construct
a large organization of the Greek city-states that would satisfy their
aspirations to live at peace and preserve their own local independence.
However, as the Athenians had foreseen, the Spartan attempt to reorganize Greece was likewise a failure. The practices of Spartan rulers were
far more burdensome than those of Athens. "The little finger of her
tyranny was thicker than the loins of Athens had ever been."[18] When,
after a revival of war with Persia, Spartan predominance had seemed only
to bring, in the peace of 387, a surrender of the Greek cities of Asia Minor
to the enemy, her leadership became all the more insupportable. It was
destroyed by Thebes at the Battle of Leuctra in 371. Thebes attempted to
do what Athens and Sparta had not succeeded in doing, namely, to organize a strong Boeotian state to form the basis of Theban hegemony in
Greece. Although Thebes succeeded in freeing the Spartan helots in 369,
she was no more imaginative in organizing the Greeks than others had
been. After being held at bay by an anti-Theban coalition at Mantinea in
362, the brief rule of Thebes over Greece collapsed. Greece then fell
back into an anarchy of warring city-states, a situation about which no
one seemed able to do anything.

[18]W. G. De Burgh, *The Legacy of the Ancient World*, p. 155.

The final chapter in the history of the Greek attempt to preserve the liberty of the city-state is no less heroic than tragic. Its heroism is exemplified in the career of the Athenian statesman and orator Demosthenes; its tragedy in the relentless advance of the northern barbarian power Macedon, under Philip and Alexander. It had been argued by many Greeks after the Peloponnesian War that the only effective way to destroy the fratricidal warfare among them was to organize a war against Persia. Such a war would unite them in a common enterprise and forever prevent Persia from inciting the Greeks against each other. How this war was to be led remained uncertain until a power arose on the northeastern boundaries of Greece which promised to compose Greek differences and lead them in a glorious crusade against their traditional enemies. When Macedon first appeared in this guise, the politically conscious Greeks were immediately divided into two parties, a pro-Macedonian and an anti-Macedonian party. The issue at stake between them was the old one of whether the independence of the city-state was worth preserving. For it was clear to all that the acceptance by Greece of Macedonian leadership in whatever holy cause put the fate of the liberty of the Greeks in other than their own hands. The pro-Macedonian party felt that the failure of the Greeks to achieve a peaceful solution of their internal conflicts was so final and disastrous that the very principle of local independence must be sacrificed. Only a unity imposed from without could achieve for the Greeks the large position in the world to which their culture and abilities entitled them. The anti-Macedonian party, on the contrary, felt that under no circumstances should the Greeks abandon the task upon which they had vainly spent so much effort. No matter what the consequences, they themselves had to settle the question of their own unity. No price was so great as that which would subject their own self-determination to the calculated interest of a foreign power that they considered barbaric.

DEMOSTHENES

The incarnation of this anti-Macedonian attitude was Demosthenes, a rare kind of practical political idealist who saw clearly that if Athens was to regain its old position in Greek affairs it must be in defense of this proposition. The Athens that was to guide Greece along this line must also be a new Athens, aware of the folly she had once committed in attempting to dominate Greece with traditional, imperialistic methods. She must now lead a confederacy of equals bound together by common interests and mutual confidence. Whether in the struggle of Greek against Greek, or of barbarian against Greek, she must support the cause of democratic freedom; and in her own midst, in Athens herself, she must maintain the lofty example of a devoted, democratic state. In the finest oratory the ancient world knew he expounded these principles to Athens and to all Greece, and in his own life, to the very end, tried his best to carry them out. The tradition of the Athenian empire had to go.

PHILIP OF MACEDON AND THE HELLENIC LEAGUE

Philip of Macedon came to the throne in 359, after having spent three years as an apprentice in Greek affairs at Thebes. At the head of a kingdom already unified by his predecessor Amyntas (390-369), he inaugurated a program of expansion that carried his kingdom to the Aegean Sea and along its northern coast to the Hellespont. Philip planned to incorporate Thessaly and to establish for Macedon a dominant position in Greek affairs. This expansion, utterly ruthless to resisters, involved war with Athens, since it took over Athenian colonies or threatened Athenian allies. In a series of fiery speeches against Philip (*Philippics*), Demosthenes tried to persuade his fellow citizens to pursue this war with plan and energy. Yet it was not until Philip, through intervention in a war against Phocis, utterly destroyed that city and took its place on a council regulating the affairs of the Delphic Confederacy, a religious organization based on the oracle at Delphi, that the Athenians and Greeks began to listen to Demosthenes. In 344, in an attempt to rouse them against Macedon, he visited the cities of the Peloponnesus and succeeded in organizing an impressive confederation to meet Philip when he should strike his final blow. It came at Chaeronea in 338, when, after suffering defeat, the Greek confederation dissolved, leaving Philip the master and arbiter of the Greek states. Thereupon Philip, having meted out proper punishment to his Greek enemies, called a congress at Corinth which drew up a plan for a Hellenic League under his leadership. This league took the form of a defensive and offensive alliance with Philip, who was to be the commander in chief of its forces, some 200,000 infantry and 15,000 cavalry.[19] The Greek states composing the League, represented in a governing council, were to be independent and self-governing under the constitutions they then enjoyed. They were to tolerate no revolutionary violations of property rights such as confiscations of property, partitions of large estates, remissions of debt, or emancipation of slaves. There was to be no payment of tribute and no stationing of garrisons. Greek states were not to infringe upon their mutual independence but were to live at peace. The Hellenic League was not only to accept Philip as its commander in chief; it was to promise never to destroy the power of his house. He alone was to have the right to summon the council of the League. This arrangement, guaranteeing the position of Macedon as the guardian of Greek order and tranquillity, was conceived as a permanent one. Its first mission was to carry on war against Persia. The Greeks, unable to provide themselves with a unity that was able to withstand Philip's military power, had succumbed for the time being to force. Demosthenes' warnings had not been enough. The city-state had essentially met its doom.

[19]Botsford, *Hellenic History*, p. 391.

While Alexander (336-323) was establishing his Macedonian empire, and thus reducing Athens and the whole world of the old Greek city-states to comparative political insignificance, Demosthenes remained at Athens devotedly performing the tasks of a loyal citizen. It had been proposed that as a reward for his services he be given a gold crown, a proposal that became the occasion for his best oration, "the most finished, the most splendid, and the most pathetic work of ancient eloquence—the immortal oration 'On the Crown.' " For refusing to let Athens become too involved in the affairs of a traitorous Macedonian official who had fled to Athens Demosthenes was fined and imprisoned. From the exile to which he had escaped he was later recalled, upon Alexander's death, to organize a revolt against a continuation of Macedonian domination. The revolt was a failure, and Athens was obliged to give over those of her citizens, including Demosthenes, who had helped to instigate the uprising. Demosthenes, instead, fled to a sanctuary of Poseidon on the island of Calauria, and, rather than be captured by the Macedonians who pursued him, took poison. His faith in the correctness of his point of view stayed with him to the last. In "On the Crown" he cries out, "I say that, if the event had been manifest to the whole world beforehand, not even then ought Athens to have forsaken this course, if Athens had any regard for her glory, or for her past, or for the ages to come."[20]

ALEXANDER

Meanwhile Philip's brilliant, unstable, and romantic young son, Alexander, had reminded disaffected Greeks of their real position by destroying Thebes. As the president of the league established at Corinth by his father he had completed the offensive against Persia that Athens had long before begun. In a remarkably short time the entire Ancient Near East, as well as the Greek states in the Balkan peninsula, was added to Macedonia. In three years (334-331) Alexander brought Asia Minor, Syria, Phoenicia, Palestine, and Egypt into his expanding state, and in 331, at Gaugamela in the Tigris Valley, finished off the Persian empire. The years following were spent in campaigns to reduce the northeastern satrapies in Bactria and in northwestern India (Punjab). When his troops would no longer tolerate the rigors of the Indian campaign he was obliged to return to Babylon, to prepare for the exploration of the Arabian coast and the possible conquest of the peninsula. In the midst of these preparations he fell prey to a fever at the age of thirty-two. After his death rival generals divided his empire into independent kingdoms. By the beginning of the third century three had become dominant: (1) Macedonia (which included Greece) under the Antigonid dynasty, (2) Egypt under the Ptolemaic dynasty, and (3) the Seleucid kingdom, which included Syria,

[20]R. C. Jebb, "Demosthenes," *Encyclopaedia Britannica.*

a large part of Asia Minor, and Mesopotamia. The rivalries of these three and their constant wars made possible the ultimate intervention of Rome.

ALEXANDER'S IMPERIAL POLICY

Although in itself short-lived, Alexander's Macedonian empire, and later the kingdoms that succeeded it, introduced remarkable changes into the life of the whole area of the Ancient Near East and Greece. Alexander himself, as a youth, had been a student of Aristotle, one of the greatest philosophers and scientists of Greece. His whole campaign had been planned as a means to extend, under Macedonian patronage, since the Macedonians had no civilization of their own, the influence of Greek civilization into the Orient. This was to be accomplished by the settlement of Greeks in all parts of the Ancient Near East, but especially in newly established colonies. This program was promoted with vigor both by Alexander himself and his successors. He gave his own name to many of these cities, notably to Alexandria in Egypt, and is credited with the founding of twenty such colonies. His successors increased this number into the hundreds. This was the third phase of Greek expansion, the first being the expansion from the European mainland to the islands of the Aegean and the western coast of Asia Minor, and the second, the establishment of colonies in Italy and Sicily and on the shores of the Black Sea. Yet Alexander was not simply interested in the Hellenization of the East. His own attitude toward the older civilizations that he added to his semi-barbarian state was accommodating, so accommodating that it produced resentment among his Macedonian followers. Like the Persians, he did not interfere with the local religions, for example, but took over the relationships previous rulers had maintained with local divinities. He obviously was interested in breaking down the old Greek prejudices against the foreigner by promoting marriages between Persians, Macedonians, and Greeks. He set the example when he married Roxana, a Persian, and encouraged mass marriages between his troops and native women. It is likewise clear that he had no notions of preserving as a monopoly for Macedonians and Greeks the administration and army of the new empire. Defeated Persians were also to become administrators of the cosmopolitan state born of a fusion of Greek with oriental civilizations. Although Aristotle himself was unwilling to consider the new empire as a suitable basis for the government of a state, other philosophers, notably the Stoics, were willing to drop the city-state, the *polis*, that had now been effectively reduced in importance, and to talk of the new state as a *cosmopolis*, a world city, of which all men, united in brotherhood by their common humanity, were citizens.[21] How far Alexander would have continued in this direction, had he lived, it is impossible to say. Under his successors, however, the fusion between Greek and Oriental progressed so far that historians

[21]W. W. Tarn, *Alexander the Great and the Unity of Mankind*, attributes to Alexander himself exciting ideas of this kind.

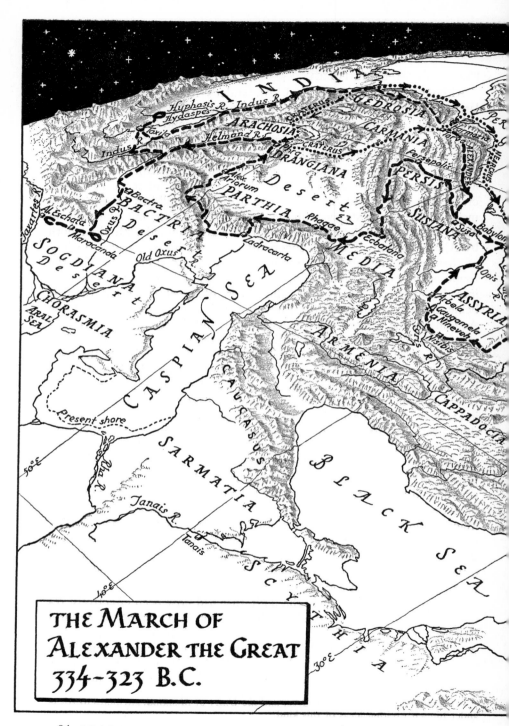

THE MARCH OF
ALEXANDER THE GREAT
334–323 B.C.

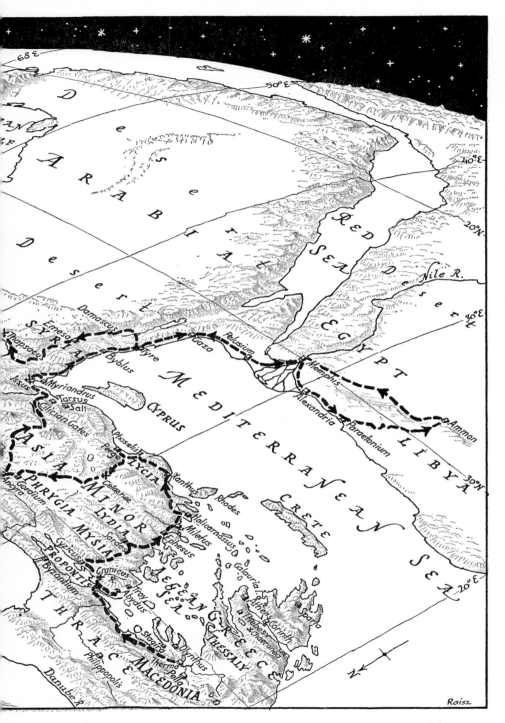

describe the age with the term *Hellenistic*, that is, similar to the Hellenic. This last phase of Greek culture before its absorption and dissemination by Rome will be discussed in subsequent chapters.

ALEXANDER AND THE THEOCRATIC TRADITION

While the new Greek colonies in the Near East took the form of the Greek city, neither they nor the older cities in the Hellenistic world may be said to have been an extension of the free and independent Greek city-state of the Greek homeland. It has been noted previously that the characteristic form of government of the Ancient Near East was a theocracy. In the course of establishing his empire Alexander, for both personal and political reasons, succumbed to this political tradition. When, in Egypt, he visited the oracle of the god Ammon as the new Pharaoh, he was greeted as the son of Ammon. After the death of the Persian King Darius he wore Persian dress and adopted Persian court ceremonial. He went so far as to demand of Persians, Macedonians, and Greeks alike prostration upon coming into his presence. This ritual signified nothing but formal etiquette to the Persians, but involved the notion of worship for a Greek or Macedonian. Already, indeed, he was thinking of becoming a god for his Greek, as well as his oriental, subjects. As president of the Corinthian League it would be embarrassing for him to have to violate its terms. As a god he was above them. In 324 he let the Greek cities know that he wanted them to recognize him as a god. The Spartans replied, "Since Alexander wishes to be a god, let him be one," and at Athens, where there was not much faith left in the traditional gods, Demosthenes urged, "Let us acknowledge him the son of Zeus for all I care, or the son of Poseidon, if he prefers it." Identified with the god Dionysus, he was put into the city's pantheon. The Greeks were unwilling to risk the consequences of a refusal. Alexander's successors followed suit. They too became "gods manifest" and "saviours." Thus the institution of the oriental theocracy was perpetuated by Alexander and his successors. In Egypt it took its most extreme form, since here the divine Pharaoh actually owned the state. Rome took it over when the eastern Mediterranean became hers. Theocracy became also the form of organization of the Christian Church. These two institutions passed the concept on to western and eastern Europe, where it has not yet been completely eradicated.

THE GREEK FEDERAL LEAGUES

When Rome, at the beginning of the second century, was ready to intervene in the affairs of Greece, the city-states under Macedonian tutelage had at last, through the instrument of the federally organized League, arrived at a partial solution of their chronic disunity. There came to be two, the Aetolian League of northern Greece and the Achaean League of the south. Each possessed an assembly of citizens of the member states and a council representing the cities on the basis of population. The assemblies elected the magistrates, the chief of whom was the general. Such a federal government had control over weights, measures, and foreign

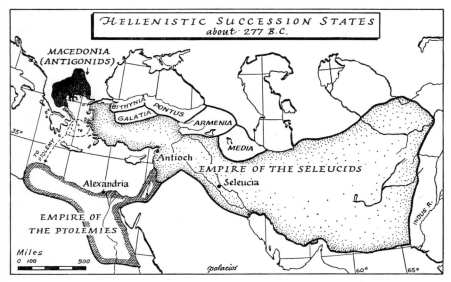

HELLENISTIC SUCCESSION STATES
about 277 B.C.

MACEDONIA
(ANTIGONIDS)

BITHYNIA
GALATIA
PONTUS
ARMENIA

MEDIA

Antioch

EMPIRE OF THE SELEUCIDS

Alexandria   Seleucia

EMPIRE OF
THE PTOLEMIES

Miles
0 100   500

palacios

policy, including the declaration of war and the making of alliances, and the federal army. Beneath this federal government each member city retained its own autonomy. Although Greece herself was still split into two leagues and was thus unable to develop strength equal to a contest with Rome, this "does not detract from the truth that the federal union was the most highly developed political creation of the world before the rise of modern representative democracies, such as those of Great Britain and the United States."[22]

THE IMPORTANCE OF GREEK POLITICAL EXPERIENCE

What, in conclusion, may be said to be the importance for us of the political experience of the Greek people? Their experience was that of citizens of a city-state rather than, as in the Ancient Near East, subjects of a theocracy. The experience was democratic rather than autocratic. It required that the individual citizen co-operate actively with his fellow citizens in determining the course that his own political community was to follow, and therefore the kind of life that he was to enjoy. The community of citizens thus learned to do things for themselves with the general public interest in view, rather than to have things done for them by a divine despot whose interest was primarily his own. Thus the democratic political ideal was established: the building of a good life for all members of the community by the sharing of a common political responsibility for the fate of the community. At the same time practical democratic ma-

[22]Botsford, *Hellenic History*, p. 470.

chinery was invented in the form, for example, of the Athenian constitution of the fifth century. The Greeks had also learned what the constant threat and prosecution of war did to democratic institutions.

It was not possible, however, for the city-state to live in isolation. Endeavoring to protect itself from Persia and then from Macedon it was faced with the problem of working out effective relationships between city-states. This it was unable to do. The difficulty lay first in creating a loyalty which went beyond the city-state to the larger Greek community, or, in other words, in sacrificing the independence of the individual city-state to the peace of all the city-states. The Greeks made many experiments with this aim in view: the Delian League, the Peloponnesian League, and finally the Aetolian and Achaean leagues. In the case of the first two the experiments resulted essentially in tyranny and almost constant war. The result was so to weaken city-state loyalty that it was unable to protect the Greek states from the dictation of Philip of Macedon. Under these circumstances the more successful federal experiments of the Aetolian and Achaean leagues came too late. The careers of Philip and Alexander re-established despotic theocracy as the dominant political tradition within which all others had to operate. Thus it may be said that the Greek democratic spirit, whether expressed in popular institutions of local government or in love of local independence, was unable to create institutions for a community of city-states that would provide for the extension and deepening of this spirit. This inability produced chronic war, which destroyed not only the civilization of the city-state but its democracy as well. The reversion to the oriental theocrat, however, did not completely demolish the democratic ideal nor the memory of its practice. It introduced a competition between autocracy and democracy to see which could produce the more satisfactory society for its members. That competition is as yet undecided.

The Greek experience becomes all the more instructive when viewed in the light of recent and contemporary events. The unit of political society today has come to be the nation not the city-state. Within the national states varying degrees of political democracy have been established. The western nations in general have developed an intense devotion to the democratic ideal and have incorporated it more or less successfully into their political practice. Some of the eastern nations, on the contrary, have reacted to the democratic challenge by building larger and more menacing autocracies. This is the old contrast between Athens and Sparta. These national states have not lived in isolation. It has been necessary for them to establish international relationships. When these have been of an imperial character (as in the Athenian empire) the democratic states of the West have not always been willing to share their political democracy with dependent peoples. As national states they have not known how to establish international relationships that could prevent the rise of the tyrant state (such as Macedon or Nazi Germany) and preserve the peace. At present, however, the western nations, through such various combinations as the United Nations, the North Atlantic Treaty Organization, and the like, are trying to rid themselves of this same old incapacity of the Greeks. If they do not overcome it they may be overwhelmed by the same fate: war that will destroy their democratic civilizations and the superimposition of a universal theocratic despotism whose god will be Power.

chapter four

GREEK HUMANISM

Introduction

The western tradition has had to contend with two points of view, the asceticism that it received from Christianity and the humanism that it received from the Greeks.[1] The religious foundations of Christian asceticism in Hebraism have been alluded to. The previous chapter has described the political environment in which the Greeks worked out their humanistic point of view. This chapter must enlarge upon the earlier, simple definition of Greek humanism.[2]

HUMANISM

A start may be made with the statement of the Greek teacher Protagoras[3] that "man is the measure of all things." The appropriate contrast to this statement would be "God is the measure of all things," representing the attitude of the Ancient Near East. By "man is the measure of all things" we may understand, "man is the meaning of all things." Nothing accordingly has a meaning except in human terms, and it is for man to supply these terms by applying his reason to an analysis of his life. All things

---

[1]This is not to deny the ascetic aspects of Greek thought. See p. 139; also I. G. Whitchurch, *The Philosophical Bases of Asceticism in the Platonic Writings*; also C. W. Moore, "Greek and Roman Ascetic Tendencies," *Harvard Essays on Classical Subjects*, ed. H. M. Smyth.

[2]See pp. 10 f.

[3]See pp. 122 f.

must go through the mind of man, as through a measure. Every manifestation of human life must be evaluated from the standpoint of the human being.

HUMANISM, RATIONAL AND ANTHROPOCENTRIC

Such an attitude is striking because of its confidence in the ability of man to evaluate the circumstances of his existence. It lays primary emphasis upon man as a rational being, capable of reducing his world and himself to order, that is, to an intellectual discipline. It is striking also because of its unwillingness to resort to a divine rather than a human, a religious rather than a secular explanation. One might express this by saying that the humanist's view is primarily anthropocentric, the ascetic's theocentric. In his *History of the Persian Wars*, Herodotus, though at times sceptical of the play of divine forces in human affairs, generally allowed for them. Thucydides, on the contrary, rigorously excluded them.

GREEK INVENTIVENESS

With sheer virtuosity the Greeks set about in almost all fields of human endeavor to create standards of human excellence that have remained unsurpassed, or, as it is ordinarily put, have become classic. Outside the field of religion they were the architects of the western mind, and in this field also they made their own characteristic contribution. For the most part their achievement was independent of the Ancient Near East, although future work in archaeology may upset this opinion. When the historian begins to describe the various accomplishments of the Greeks in the fields of the arts, politics, and science, he is usually obliged to preface his remarks with, "The Greeks were the first to do this,"[4] and, when he concludes, to indicate that the Greek accomplishment has remained an enduring model or standard.

FURTHER DEFINITION OF HUMANISM

As far as we know the Greeks were the first to work out a democratic system of government in the city-state. They were the first to discuss political theory; that is, they established political science. They founded political economy and history as well. For the West, epic poetry begins with Homer rather than with the author of the Gilgamesh epic. Many of the forms of western lyric poetry also are the creation of the Greeks. Western drama is their invention. They were the first to develop systematic literary criticism. They were the first to speculate about nature, and, as a result, to found mathematics and the physical and natural sciences in all their many branches, including medicine. They were the first phi-

[4]See T. L. Heath, "Mathematics and Astronomy," *The Legacy of Greece*, p. 98: "The Greeks laid down the principles, fixed the terminology, and invented the methods *ab initio*"; or E. Zimmern, "Political Thought," *Legacy*, p. 331: "The first valuable contribution the Greeks made to political study was that they invented it."

losophers, in a special as well as a general sense. They were the first to draw up rules for logical thinking. In their art they first gave devoted attention to the ideal human form. "The beginnings of nearly all the great things that progressive minds now care for were . . . laid in Greece. . . . The seeds of almost all that we count best in human progress were sown in Greece. . . . The conception of beauty as a joy in itself and as a guide in life was first and most vividly expressed in Greece, and the very laws by which things are beautiful or ugly were to a great extent discovered there and laid down. The conception of Freedom and Justice, freedom in body, in speech and in mind, justice between the strong and the weak, the rich and the poor, penetrates the whole of Greek political thought. . . . The conception of Truth as an end to pursue for its own sake, a thing to discover and puzzle out by experiment and imagination and especially by Reason, a conception essentially allied with that of Freedom and opposed both to anarchy and to blind obedience, has perhaps never in the world been more clearly grasped than by the early Greek writers on science and philosophy."[5] This amounts to saying that the Greeks were the first to discover man and to glorify him, that they were the first to explore and exalt the almost infinite capacity of man to make life purposeful and beautiful. They first stressed the importance of releasing this capacity, of removing the obstructions to the realization of all that is potentially best in human nature. This positive faith in the human being and this high value placed upon all that he does to give meaning and beauty to human existence may be characterized as humanism.

RELATIVISM AND ABSOLUTISM

It must not be assumed that because the Greeks were unwilling to make God the measure of all things, the best of them were any less interested than the Hebrew prophets in the moral foundations of public and private life. Indeed, the very statement of Protagoras that "man is the measure of all things" posed for them a very difficult problem. Man's measurement of things may vary from man to man. It may vary from man to man and from time to time. It may vary from man to man, from time to time, and from place to place. If man's measurements do vary the result may be a bewildering variety of conclusions as to what constitutes truth. There will be no one standard of morality, for example. Morality will be relative to the person, the time, and the place. What will be moral to Socrates in fifth-century Athens will not be moral to Alexander in fourth-century Macedon. Such an attitude is called relativism, and its contrary belief in a permanent and fixed body of truth is called absolutism. The Greeks were not content to adopt a relativist position. Rather, however, than adopt the position of the theocrat, or, let us say, of the Hebrew prophets, that truth is absolute and established by God, they preferred to build their system of absolute

[5]Gilbert Murray, "The Value of Greece to the Future of the World," *Legacy*, pp. 21–22.

	Art and Literature	Mathematics and Science	Philosophy
750 B.C.	Homer (before 700) Hesiod (fl. 750) Alcaeus of Mytilene (fl. 620) Sappho (fl. 600) Anacreon of Teos (ca. 570–485) Simonides of Ceos (ca. 556–467) Aeschylus (ca. 525–456) Pindar (ca. 522–438)		Thales (ca. 640–546) Anaximander (ca. 611–547) Anaximenes (fl. 6th c.) Pythagoras (fl. 530) Heraclitus (fl. 6th–5th c.)
500	Phidias (ca. 500–432) Sophocles (ca. 496–406) Euripides (ca. 485–406) Aristophanes (ca. 438–380) Scopas (fl. 4th c.) Praxiteles (ca. 370–330)	Hippocrates of Chios (fl. 470) Hippocrates of Cos (fl. 400) Eudoxus (408–355) Heracleides of Pontus (388–315) Menaechmus (375–325) Theophrastus (ca. 372–287) Euclid (330–275) Aristarchus of Samos (ca. 310–230)	Parmenides (fl. 5th c.) Empedocles (fl. 5th c.) Leucippus (fl. 5th c.) Anaxagoras (ca. 500–428) Protagoras (ca. 480–410) Socrates (ca. 469–399) Democritus (fl. 5th–4th c.) Plato (ca. 428–347) Aristotle (385–322)
300		Herophilus of Chalcedon (fl. 3d c.) Erasistratus (fl. 3d c.) Archimedes (287–212) Eratosthenes (ca. 276–195) Diophantus (fl. 250) Apollonius of Perga (247–205) Hipparchus of Nicaea (ca. 190–120)	
100 B.C.			
100 A.D.		Galen (fl. 131) Nicomachus of Gerasa (fl. 150) Ptolemy (fl. 168) Pappus (fl. 3d c.)	

truth upon the foundation of human reason. Merely because truth was not accepted as a divine revelation it was not necessarily thereby thought to be variable. Its absolute nature was recognized in the universality of human experience as interpreted and demonstrated by the exercise of man's reasoning faculty.

Political Thought

PLATO AND ARISTOTLE AS CONSERVATIVES

This attitude can be illustrated from Greek political theory as presented in Plato's *Republic* and Aristotle's *Politics*. Both these men, although radical enough for their time, were what today we should call conservatives, and both wrote in the fourth century during the melancholy political circumstances referred to in the previous chapter. Aristotle wrote later in the century by way of supplementing and correcting his teacher Plato. Plato (428?–347 B.C.) was a student of Socrates in the last years of the fifth century, that is, the last years of the Peloponnesian War, when, to his mind, Athenian democracy was degenerating in the hands of an ignorant mob led by irresponsible demagogues. This democratic government had put his beloved master Socrates to death, and he could not forgive it. Aristotle (b. 385 B.C.), writing at a time when Macedon, and not Athens, was the dominant power in the Greek world shared his teacher's scepticism of democracy. Together, their fundamental attitudes go back to those of Socrates, from whom, indeed, stem all subsequent attempts to meet the problem of relativism.

PLATO'S "REPUBLIC"

In the *Republic* Plato pictures Socrates disputing with men holding views on law and justice that he regards as immoral and subversive. Some of these men ridicule man's attempt to set up a system of law which improves upon the law of nature. These say, for example, that nature does not know slavery. It establishes rather a common kinship among men. But man's law, "the tyrant of mankind," has established such differences as those between Athenian citizens, metics, and slaves. Others say that "the right life according to nature is to live in domination over others." Human laws to restrain this domination cannot, therefore, be taken seriously. Nature justifies "the advantage of the stronger." Thrasymachus in the *Republic* argues that what is called justice is merely the justification of this interest or advantage of the stronger. Those who control the state merely enact laws in their own interest. It is further suggested in the *Republic* that if justice is not simply this will of the ruler or of the ruling group it is the result of a compromise. Men who in a state of nature suffered the injustice of the strong compacted with each other to circumvent this natural law of domination by the stronger by agreeing "neither to commit nor to suffer injustice." The resulting human law to enforce this compact is thus but a "compromise between the best, which is to do wrong with impunity, and the worst, which is to be wronged and be impotent to get one's revenge." In any case, Plato finds it necessary to arrive at a definition of justice which avoids a law of nature that is outrageous to a sense of human decency, and to avoid a law of men that is a mere expression of the will of the dominant elements in the state, or a temporary and wholly artificial compromise of their interests. Justice must be something more than this.

PLATO'S ORGANIC STATE

To Plato, then, there would not be three justices, divine, natural, and human, but one absolute and unalterable, universally applicable justice. His attempt to give it political meaning is understandable only from the point of view of his own concept of the state. In the *Republic* this state is conceived of in literal political terms, that is, in terms of the *polis*. This was also Aristotle's view. The tutor of a world emperor found abhorrent a state whose assembled citizens could not all hear the voice of a herald. Plato does not regard this small community as the scene of a tug of war between self-seeking individuals or self-seeking classes. It is an organism, a whole, with its own life. The purpose of this organism is not simply to provide its members with the means of livelihood or to protect its independence from without. It is to direct them in the path of the good life, whose chief expression is devotion to the good life of the whole community. The chief responsibility of the individual is to the collective good of the community. Justice is that sense of moral obligation to the common good that makes it possible for the citizen to be content to serve this good in the manner in which he is best fitted.

THE STATE AN ETHICAL AND EDUCATIONAL INSTITUTION

Since the state has essentially an ethical aim, that is, to promote the collective good, conceived of also as the collective goodness, Plato's political theory amounts to a branch of ethics, or else ethics is but a branch of his political theory. Since, too, the devotion of the individual citizen to the common good is something that has to be inculcated, and those who inculcate it have to be trained, the state is by necessity an educational institution. It indoctrinates its citizens with its own morality, which is a copy of the absolute system of morality. Plato conceives the just state to be merely an enlargement of the just citizen or the good man. He builds its social organization upon his analysis of the human soul. This soul, he thinks, is possessed of three elements: (1) the appetitive, consisting of man's basic desires, the primal urges to eat, drink, and love; (2) the spirited, consisting of the willingness to defend and protect, and equivalent to honor; and (3) the rational. The justice of the individual consists in a sense of harmony, which puts each of these elements in its

proper place, subjecting passion and spirit to reason, and thus producing the good man, who, in his moderation, is also the happy man.

THE THREE CLASSES IN THE STATE

The class of citizens in the state corresponding to the appetitive element of the soul is composed of the farmer, the artisan, the merchant, and
the industrialist. This is the economic class, providing through its specialized talents the basic needs of the community. All others are the guardians
of the state. The class of guardians or guards corresponding to the spirited
element of the soul is the military. That class of guardians corresponding
to the rational element is the administrative class, or the actual governors.
The guardians, whether military or administrative, are chosen on the
basis of intelligence, knowledge, and character, and owe their positions
neither to birth nor to wealth.

THE EDUCATION OF THE GUARDIANS OF THE STATE

The civic duties of these guardians were regarded by Plato as so sacred
that he considered their education of paramount importance. The military guardians needed to be educated only in the traditional Greek subjects
of gymnastics and music, and then not to produce the professional athlete
or the aesthete but the well-rounded citizen of moral character. Because
training in music involved instruction in literature, Plato was willing to
go to extreme limits in prescribing the kind of music and literature that
was to be taught. Since the purpose of the instruction was morally to
uplift, this criterion was made the basis of choice. The drama, for example,
Plato excluded. His course in literature was limited to heroic, that is, epic,
poetry. From Homer he removed all those passages which celebrate the
immorality of the gods. In order that the guardians might be free to devote all their time and attention to their civic duties Plato deprived them
of property and wives. They were to live like Spartans in state barracks
where the necessities of life were supplied. They were to mate with suitable female guardians, at the proper time, and the children of such matings,
like their mothers, were to be regarded as common to all the guardians.

PHILOSOPHERS AS RULERS

Those guardians who were entrusted with the governing of the state
had to go through a still more rigorous intellectual and moral discipline.
They were obliged to master the mathematical and scientific subjects
and spend at least five years in the study of dialectics, that is, logic. The
purpose of such training was to produce a philosopher, a man capable of
understanding such things as truth, beauty, wisdom, courage, temperance,
justice, and, above all, what was meant by the idea of the good. To Plato
the chief task of the ruler was to mold his state in the light of these virtues, and, without knowing what they were, no ruler could administer
them. The ideal ruler, therefore, was the philosopher, governing in the

interests of all the citizens, in accordance with the noblest principles conceivable. "Unless . . . either philosophers become kings in our states or those whom we now call our kings and rulers take to the pursuit of philosophy seriously and adequately, and there is a conjunction of these two things, political power and philosophic intelligence . . . there can be no cessation of troubles . . . for our states, nor . . . for the human race either." (Shorey, No. 276, p. 509)[6] A city governed and educated in such a philosophic spirit would be guided so perfectly by a sense of justice that it would have no need for courts and lawyers. Plato accordingly made no provision for them. It would have no need for physicians. Physicians only cure disease and in the ideal state there would be no disease. Indeed, it would have no use for law, since the will of the philosopher-king is law.

PLATO'S VIEWS ON DEMOCRACY

If not quite, as it has been called, a "philosophic autocracy,"[7] Plato's ideal state is, from his point of view, literally an aristocracy, meaning a government by the best. It rejects the popular control of the Athenian democracy. Of democracy Plato had no high opinion, regarding it only, in his classification of states, as preferable to tyranny. It develops through the decay of oligarchy "when the poor, winning the victory, put to death some of the other party, drive out others, and grant the rest of the citizens an equal share in both citizenship and offices—and for the most part these offices are assigned by lot" (to Plato, an utter negation of the principle of excellence). Socrates, in the *Republic*, ridicules and distorts democracy's individualistic freedom. There is "freedom from all compulsion to hold office in such a city, even if you are qualified, or again, to submit to rule, unless you please . . . how superbly it [democracy] tramples under foot all such ideals [as the necessary training of a good man], caring nothing from what practices and way of life a man turns to politics, but honouring him if only he says that he loves the people!" Democracy, Socrates continues in the same vein, is "a delightful form of government, anarchic and motley, assigning a kind of equality indiscriminately to equals and unequals alike!" Indeed, the excesses of freedom in a democracy produce an anarchy whose ultimate outcome is tyranny. "The father habitually tries to resemble the child and is afraid of his sons, and the son likens himself to the father and feels no awe or fear of his parents . . . the resident alien feels himself equal to the citizen and the citizen to him . . . the teacher in such case fears and fawns upon the pupils, and the pupils pay no heed to the teacher . . . the old, accommodating themselves to the young, are full of pleasantry and graciousness, imitating the young for fear they may be thought disagreeable and authoritative. . . . And the climax of popular liberty . . . is attained in such a city when the purchased slaves, male and

[6]Citations from Plato in my text are to the several translators and the Loeb series numbers.
[7]The phrase in Ernest Barker, *Greek Political Theory*, p. 173.

female, are no less free than the owners who paid for them. . . . Without experience of it no one would believe how much freer the very beasts subject to men are in such a city than elsewhere. The dogs literally verify the adage and 'like their mistresses become.' And likewise the horses and asses are wont to hold on their way with the utmost freedom and dignity, bumping into everyone who meets them and who does not step aside. . . . All things everywhere are just bursting with the spirit of liberty." (No. 276, pp. 285, 291, 307, 309)

ARISTOTLE ON DEMOCRACY

Aristotle, with his remark that "political fellowship must . . . be deemed to exist for the sake of noble actions," indicates his general affinity with Plato's idea of the state. He rejects the notion, however, that the guardians of the state should be deprived both of families and of property. He goes out of his way to justify slavery as a natural institution which enables the best men, by relieving them of the bother of supplying their means of livelihood, to devote their talents to the interests of the state. Democracy, Aristotle says, exists "when those who are free are in the majority and have sovereignty over the government." Oligarchy exists "when the rich and more well born are few and sovereign." He is careful to distinguish different forms of democracies, reserving his harshest criticism for the "fifth form," in which not the law but the multitude have the supreme power and supersede the law by their decrees. This is the state of affairs brought about by the demagogues. When it comes to determining what is the best form of government attainable in this world (the ideal form would be, as in Plato's view, a true aristocracy) Aristotle has recourse to a principle announced in his *Ethics*, "that the happy life is the life that is lived without impediment in accordance with virtue." Since "virtue is a middle course, it necessarily follows that the middle course of life is the best—such a middle course as it is possible for each class of men to attain." This middle course, Aristotle concludes, is the mean between very rich and very poor. For "the former turn more to insolence and grand wickedness, and the latter overmuch to malice and petty wickedness. . . . The latter class do not know how to govern but know how to submit to government of a servile kind, while the former class do not know how to submit to any government, and only know how to govern in the manner of a master. The result is a state consisting of slaves and masters. . . . But surely the ideal of the state is to consist as much as possible of persons that are equal and alike, and this similarity is most found in the middle classes; therefore the middle-class state will necessarily be best constituted in respect of those elements of which we say that the state is by nature composed." (Rackham, No. 73, pp. 327, 329, 331)[8] This is to Aristotle a suitable compromise between oligarchy and democracy.

[8]Citations from Aristotle in my text are to the several translators and the Loeb series numbers.

GREEK ANTHROPOMORPHIC POLYTHEISM

Since man was to be regarded as a political animal, the Greek thinkers gave their attention to the principles of the best or ideal state. But man was also, they clearly recognized, a religious animal. Greek thinkers, when compared with Hebrew, were almost nonreligious. The Greeks had in their midst no such figure as the Hebrew prophet. It is difficult to imagine that a prophet would have been understood or listened to had he appeared. The Greek approach to religion was through man, not God. With respect even to physical appearance the Greeks fashioned their gods in the image of men, while the Hebrews taught that men were fashioned in the image of God.[9] This seemed quite natural to one of the philosophers, Xenophanes of Colophon, who, after explaining that "mortals deem that the gods are begotten as they are [that is, mortals], and have clothes like theirs, and voice and form," goes on to remark: "Yes, and if oxen and horses or lions had hands, and could paint with their hands, and produce works of art as men do, horses would paint the forms of the gods like horses, and oxen like oxen, and make their bodies in the image of their several kinds. . . . The Ethiopians make their gods black and snub-nosed; the Thracians say theirs have blue eyes and red hair."[10] What took the place of the prophet in Greek religious life was the philosopher, and he became its critic. It was the philosopher who suggested a monotheism of an abstract, impersonal, and ideational kind, hardly comparable to the angry, vengeful, and despotic Yahweh of some of the Hebrew prophets. Monotheism of this character was the result of the effort of the philosopher to rationalize the popular and, to him, immoral polytheism of the ordinary Greek. This polytheism, because of its human character, may be called *anthropomorphic polytheism.*

THE GODS OF HOMER

Its character is best sought in the *Iliad* and *Odyssey* of Homer, who, together with the poet Hesiod (*ca.* 750 B.C.), according to Herodotus, "taught the Greeks of the descent of the gods, and gave to all their several names, and honours, and arts, and declared their outward forms."[11] This poetic establishment of the gods of Olympus remained characteristic of the development of Greek religion. Its interpreters were not theologians or priests but poets, whose poems were the closest approach to a bible the Greeks ever knew.

The gods of Homer were glorified human beings, radiant in their immortal, youthful beauty. If superior to man in size, strength, and wisdom, and superior in their control over the forces of nature, they were yet the

[9]See W. W. Hyde, *Greek Religion and Its Survivals*, pp. 17 ff.
[10]John Burnet, *Early Greek Philosophy*, p. 131.
[11]*History of the Persian Wars*, trans. A. D. Godley, Loeb, No. 117, p. 341.

victims of all his pains and passions. Nothing could have kept them at Olympus while the Trojan War was going on, nor could they refrain from participating in it. They thus helped to maintain, if they did not establish, the tradition that the gods support both sides in war. When they had made up their minds whom to support they did not remain loyal. Part of the difficulty was always in the royal ménage of the gods, where Zeus, married to his sister, "ox-eyed" Hera, had difficulty in maintaining the independence of a self-respecting husband and the dignity of the lord of the immortals. For fear of becoming too henpecked he had, on occasion, to discipline her. In the *Iliad* he recalls to her, in one instance, the unpleasant moment "when thou wast hung from on high, and from thy feet I suspended two anvils, and about thy wrists cast a band of gold that might not be broken! And in the air amid the clouds thou didst hang." (II, 107)[12] Those gods who tried to keep him from beating her were treated roughly.

ZEUS AND HERA

Zeus himself was inclined to support the Trojans, and Hera favored the Greeks. At a desperate moment in the war, when the Trojans were driving the Greeks back to their ships, drawn up on the beach, Hera thought it necessary to keep Zeus inactive for the moment and allow Poseidon to turn the tide of battle. "And Zeus she marked seated on the topmost peak of many-fountained Ida, and hateful was he to her heart. Then she took thought, the ox-eyed, queenly Hera, how she might beguile the mind of Zeus that beareth the aegis. And this plan seemed to her mind the best—to go to Ida, when she had beauteously adorned her person, if so be he might desire to lie by her side and embrace her body in love, and she might shed a warm and gentle sleep upon his eyelids and his cunning mind. So she went her way to her chamber, that her dear son Hephaestus had fashioned for her, and had fitted strong doors to the door-posts with a secret bolt, that no other god might open. Therein she entered, and closed the bright doors. With ambrosia first did she cleanse from her lovely body every stain, and anointed her richly with oil, ambrosial, soft, and of rich fragrance; were this but shaken in the palace of Zeus with threshold of bronze, even so would the savour thereof reach unto earth and heaven. Therewith she anointed her lovely body, and she combed her hair, and with her hands plaited the bright tresses, fair and ambrosial, that streamed from her immortal head. Then she clothed her about in a robe ambrosial, which Athene had wrought for her with cunning skill, and had set thereon broideries full many; and she pinned it upon her breast with brooches of gold, and she girt about her a girdle set with an hundred tassels, and in her pierced ears she put earrings with three clustering drops; and abundant grace shone therefrom.

[12]Citations from Homer in my text are to *Iliad*, trans. A. T. Murray, Loeb, Nos. 170, 171, 2 vols., and *Odyssey*, trans. Murray, Loeb, Nos. 104, 105, 2 vols.

And with a veil over all did the bright goddess veil herself, a fair veil, all glistering, and white was it as the sun; and beneath her shining feet she bound her fair sandals." (II, 79-81) When she had received from Aphrodite "the broidered zone, curiously-wrought, wherein are fashioned all manner of allurements; therein is love, therein desire, therein dalliance— beguilement that steals the wits even of the wise, . . . ox-eyed, queenly Hera smiled." She then enlisted the help of Sleep, "the brother of Death," and thus fortified proved irresistible to Zeus. "Never yet," he says, "did desire for goddess or mortal woman so shed itself about me and overmaster the heart within my breast." (II, 83-91)

"Therewith the son of Cronos clasped his wife in his arms, and beneath them the divine earth made fresh-sprung grass to grow, and dewy lotus, and crocus, and hyacinth, thick and soft, that upbare them from the ground. Therein lay the twain, and were clothed about with a cloud, fair and golden, wherefrom fell drops of glistering dew." While the Father thus slept, Sleep went to the ships of the Greeks and spoke to Poseidon. "With a ready heart now, Poseidon, do thou bear aid to the Danaans [Greeks], and vouchsafe them glory, though it be for a little space, while yet Zeus sleepeth; for over him have I shed soft slumber, and Hera hath beguiled him to couch with her in love." (II, 93)

THE OLYMPIANS AND THE TROJAN WAR

The frequent lack of harmony in the supreme Olympian household tainted as well the relationship among the remaining gods and goddesses. In part, for the same reason; the Trojan War split them into two armed camps. At another moment in the war, after Hera, Hephaestus, Poseidon, and Athena had come to the aid of Achilles, "upon the other gods fell strife heavy and grievous. . . . Together then they clashed with a mighty din, and the wide earth rang, and round about great heaven pealed as with a trumpet. And Zeus heard it where he sat upon Olympus, and the heart within him laughed aloud in joy, as he beheld the gods joining in strife. Then no more held they long aloof, for Ares, piercer of shields, began the fray, and first leapt upon Athene, brazen spear in hand. . . . He smote upon her tasselled aegis—the awful aegis against which not even the lightning of Zeus can prevail. . . . But she gave ground, and seized with her stout hand a stone that lay upon the plain, black and jagged and great. . . . Therewith she smote furious Ares on the neck, and loosed his limbs. Over seven roods he stretched in his fall, and befouled his hair with dust, and about him his armour clanged." When Aphrodite took the groaning god of war by the hand and led him away Athene, at the behest of "white-armed" Hera, "sped in pursuit, glad at heart, and rushing upon her she smote Aphrodite on the breast with her stout hand; and her knees were loosened where she stood, and her heart melted. So the twain lay upon the bounteous earth, and vaunting over them Athene spake winged words: 'In such plight let all now be that are aiders of the Trojans when they fight against the mail-clad Argives.' " To end it all Hera interfered to upbraid Artemis when she taunted Apollo for not fighting with Poseidon. "Therewith she caught both the other's hands by the wrist with her left hand, and with her right took the bow and its gear from her shoulders, and with these self-same weapons, smiling the while, she beat her about the ears, as she turned this way and that." Artemis then went back to Olympus and "sat down weeping upon her father's [Zeus's] knees, while about her the fragrant robe quivered." Artemis, "the fair-crowned huntress of the echoing chase," then told Father Zeus all about the contentious Hera. With a mutual bond of sympathy, "on this wise spake they one to the other." (II, 437–447)

CONTRACTUAL NATURE OF GREEK POLYTHEISM

These all-too-human Olympians were a pleasant method for Greeks to use in establishing their rapport with the fearful and uncertain ways of nature and of men. It was not difficult to keep them appeased. They were as hungry for the roasted flesh of the sacrificial feast and as thirsty for the red wine of the libation as the Greek participants themselves. So long as, and to the degree that, their altars were properly maintained and supplied they rendered their services to man. These Homeric divinities were hardly aware of sin. They demanded no higher standard of morality from men than they imposed upon themselves. The relationship between the Greek and his gods was thus in the nature of a contract, so much given for so much received, a contract whose equal terms the gods were jealous to maintain. As the Greeks possessed no religious books except poetry and no dogma except mythology they likewise permitted no priestly caste to develop as the special servitors of the gods. Religious ceremonies were conducted by civic officials, administering what was only a function of the state. There could thus be no church led by an organized clergy since there were no clergy as such.

EARTHLY CHARACTER OF GREEK RELIGION

The Olympian pantheon of Homer and Hesiod, common to all the Greeks, was often localized to meet the special needs of the particular city. Athena, although an Olympian, was also the patron goddess of Athens. In addition to the major gods there were many minor divinities caring for the untold lesser needs of troubled humans at the local temple and shrine. Greek religion was a local affair, as multifarious in its manifestations as the city-states were numerous. It served primarily man's earthly needs, refusing to torture him with a sense of sin that must be atoned for, and taking care to uplift his spirit with poetry and the arts. It might occasionally warn him of a fate common to gods and men alike, but it did not hold up the joys of heaven for the ordinary man's yearning nor threaten him with the pain of hell. Death was an event that the Greeks, with their enjoyment of all the good things of life, did not care to dwell upon. In the *Odyssey* Achilles took no comfort from his exalted position in Hades among the "unheeding dead, the phantoms of men outworn." He told Odysseus, when he reminded him of it, "Nay, seek not to speak soothingly to me of death, glorious Odysseus. I should choose, so I might live on earth, to serve as the hireling of another, of some portionless man whose livelihood was but small, rather than to be lord over all the dead that have perished." (I, 419, 421) The early Christians poured lofty scorn upon these indulgent deities and then in chastened and altered form made some of them saints.

THE LYRIC POETS AND THE GODS

If religion were to be used as a support of human morality the gods of Homer obviously had to be reinterpreted. This task was undertaken by succeeding poets, and after them by philosophers. The object of the poets was to make the gods the defenders, and even the sanction, of an immutable moral order, the violation of which involved divine punishment. Hesiod, for example, after putting the confused genealogies of the gods in order in his *Theogony*, in his *Works and Days* makes Zeus the avenger of injustice and personifies Justice as Zeus's daughter. Many of the lyric poets of the seventh and sixth centuries, who were creating for all time the forms, the meter and verse, of lyric poetry continued the same theme. By the time of Pindar (b. *ca.* 522 B.C.) the Olympians had become well-nigh omnipotent and omniscient. Truth, "the foundation of virtue," also had joined Justice as a daughter of Zeus. Indeed Pindar, like Plato after him, chose to forget the phases of Greek mythology that seemed unfitted for gods who were to uphold the moral order. They could not be made guilty of things it was improper for mortals to do. "I may not," he says, "call any one of the blessed gods a cannibal." The particular sin that he and others condemned in man was the combination of selfish insolence and pride (*hubris*), often to be found in the wealthy and powerful, which caused them to be unmindful of the rights of gods and men, a sin based upon an "illimitable lust for self-assertion and domination." The *hubris* of the individual or the nation provoked the righteous indignation (*nemesis*) of the gods and men, and therewith the sinner's doom. Over and against it was to be set *sophrosyne*, the virtue of self-restraint in the face of self-knowledge, of sane judgment in the face of temptation, and of proper subordination of the individual to the whole.[13] It was excess, then, which Pindar condemned and moderation which he praised. Man must be ever mindful of his mortality. "If a man shall have wealth and excel other men in beauty, and if in the games he hath exhibited his strength and gained distinction, let him still remember that his garment wraps mortal limbs and that earth shall be the raiment of all in the end."[14]

[13]See W. G. De Burgh, *Legacy of the Ancient World*, pp. 94–95.
[14]C. H. Moore, *The Religious Thought of the Greeks*, p. 87.

These poets who set the standards of lyric poetry for the Romans and the succeeding western world did not only sing songs justifying the ways of Zeus to man. They wrote also to celebrate human joys and earthly satisfactions. Alcaeus of Mytilene (b. *ca.* 620 B.C.) could emphasize man's importance to the city-state:

> It is not streets where proud-roofed mansions stand,
> Nor masonry of ramparts deftly planned,
>   It is not dockyard, quay, or jetty,
>   That, in themselves, can make a city—
> But *men*, with hearts to use what comes to hand.[15]

He wrote drinking songs also:

> Zeus rains; a storm comes in its might
> From heav'n, and freezes rivers tight . . .
>
> Put down the storm! Pile up the fire,
> Mix the sweet wine to your desire,
>   And round your forehead set
>   A dainty coronet.
>
> To woe the heart must not give in.
> In grief's no help. One medicine,
>   My friend, alone is fit—
> Wine—, and get drunk on it.
>
>   . . . . .
>
> Drink! Why wait for lamps? The day
> Has not another inch to fall.
> Fetch the biggest beakers—they
> Hang on pegs alone the wall.
>
> Bacchus, son of Semelê
> And of Zeus, discovered wine
> Giving it to man to be
> Care's oblivious anodyne.
>
> Pour in water two to one,
> Fill them full to overflowing;
> When the first is drained and done,
> Set another cup a-going![16]

Alcaeus' compatriot, the distinguished poetess Sappho (b. *ca.* 610 B.C.) sang of her *Beloved*:

> Him I hold as happy as God in Heaven,
> Who can sit and gaze on your face before him,
> Who can sit and hear from your lips that sweetest
>   Music they utter—

[15]The selection from F. L. Lucas, *Greek Poetry for Everyman*, trans. J. M. Edmonds, p. 242, copyright 1956 by The Macmillan Co., and used with The Macmillan Co.'s permission.

[16]*Oxford Book of Greek Verse in Translation*, eds. and trans. T. F. Higham and C. M. Bowra, pp. 201-202.

Hear your lovely laughter, that sets a-tremble
All my heart with flutterings wild as terror.
For, when I behold you an instant, straightway
    All my words fail me;

Helpless halts my tongue; a devouring fever
Runs in flame through every vein within me;
Darkness veils my vision; my ears are deafened,
    Beating like hammers;

Cold the sweat runs down me; a sudden trembling
Sets my limbs a-quiver; my face grows paler
Than the grass in summer; I see before me
    Death stand, and madness. (Lucas, pp. 244–245)

She could also immortalize her little daughter Cleïs:

I have a child; so fair
As golden flowers is she,
My Cleïs, all my care.
I'd not give her away
For Lydia's wide sway
Nor lands men long to see. (Bowra, p. 211)

Other bits that remain from her poetry are:

My Lady Moon has set,
The Pleiads too are gone;
'Tis midnight, th' hours pass,
Yet still I sleep alone.[17]

. . . . .

Sweet mother, let the weaving be,
    My hand is faint to move.
Frail Aphrodite masters me;
I long for my young love. (Higham, p. 210)

Bridegroom dear, to what shall I compare thee?
    To a slim green rod best do I compare thee.
        (*Oxford*, trans. anon., p. 210)

Thou, Hesper, bringest homeward all
    That radiant dawn sped far and wide:
The sheep to fold, the goat to stall,
    The children to their mother's side.[18]

Theognis of Megara (*ca.* 540 B.C.) bemoans the passage of youth:

Now is the time to surrender our hearts to merry-making,
    While life's fair things can give us a joy that is not vain.

[17]C. T. Murphy, K. Guinagh, and W. J. Oates, *Greek and Roman Classics in Translation*, trans. C. T. Murphy, p. 148.

[18]*Love, Worship and Death: Some Renderings from the Greek Anthology*, ed. and trans. Sir Rennell Rodd, p. 5.

For the glory of youth goes by us, swift as a thought, o'ertaking
    Even the speed of steeds whose charging hoofs amain
Whirl some king in his car to the press of the spear-fought fray,
Over the young green furrows, exulting on their way.
       . . . . .

Make merry, heart within me. Others shall come to birth
So soon, and I be lying but blackened earth in earth. (Lucas, p. 253)

Anacreon of Teos (*ca.* 570—*ca.* 485 B.C.) writes of his lady:

Thracian filly, why so heartless? Why, so shyly sidelong glancing,
    Hold me ever at a distance, like a fool with wit untried?
I could clap a bridle on ye, very well, for all your prancing;
    Down the course I well could rein ye, make ye wheel the way I guide.
Yet a while, across the pastures, go your ways with light feet dancing—
    You have still to find the master that shall curb ye and shall ride. (Lucas,
      p. 256)

Simonides of Ceos (556–467 B.C.) thought that:

      Virtue dwells, so runs the tale,
      On precipices hard to scale.
      Swift holy Nymphs attend her place;
      No mortal eyes may see her face,
      But only he, who with distress
      Of soul and sweating heart can press
      On to the height in manliness. (Bowra, p. 236)

Pindar of Thebes, the creator of the ode, uses it to celebrate the feats of the winners at the Olympic games and the beauties of spring:

When the Seasons clothed with purple have flung their chamber wide,
And fragrant Spring leads back her flowers, as nectar sweet,
Then on the earth divine beneath men's feet
Are violets strewn; then rose-wreathed locks blow free,
And flute and song resound on every side,
And dancers praise the diademed Sémele. (Lucas, p. 266)

THE TRAGIC POETS AND THE GODS

At least the first two of the three great tragic poets of the fifth century, Aeschylus (525–456 B.C.) and Sophocles (496–406 B.C.), continued the work of the earlier lyric poets in exalting the moral stature of the gods. These were the men who were creating European drama and setting up such high standards for it that their plays have never been excelled. The achievement is to be explained not only by the genius of the poets but by the happy combination of the arts of the dance and of music with poetry, all under the patronage of the government of the free city-state, in this instance, Athens. For the history of Greek drama is almost entirely the history of the drama of Athens.

Both tragedy and comedy were religious in origin and had to do with the worship of the god of the vine, Dionysus.[19] This religious origin, no matter how modified in the course of the development of the drama, was never wholly obscured. The drama always possessed characteristics of ritual. At Athens it was presented during the seasons of religious festival: the city *Dionysia* (March–April), the *Lenaea*, or Festival of the Wine Press (January–February), and the rural *Dionysia* (December–January). The plays were given in an open-air theater on the southeastern slope of the Acropolis, within an area sacred to the god and close to his temple. In the center of the orchestra was an altar to Dionysus, and his priest occupied the best seat. The subject matter of tragedy, which, in Aristotle's view, must be an imitation of noble action arousing the emotions of pity and fear, came from the epic tradition. The form of the lyrics sung and danced by the chorus came from both the earlier lyric poets and earlier hymns, the choral odes, written to be sung and danced for divine worship. The author was accordingly not only a poet but a musical composer and choreographer; the actor not only a declaimer but a singer. Literally tragedy is a "goat song," the song sung and danced by the satyrs, the peculiar devotees of Dionysus.

THE DRAMATIC COMPETITIONS

The dramatic festivals in honor of Dionysus were staged under the supervision of the state and were competitive. The *archon*, who acted for the state, granted a chorus to the poet whose play was accepted for performance. The expenses of production were borne by a rich citizen, the *choregus*, as a public service. At the city *Dionysia* three tragic poets competed with four plays each, and five comic poets with one each. A board of five judges decided upon the winner, who, together with his *choregus*, was crowned with ivy. Year in and year out, accordingly, as a part of their civic religious duty, the Athenian citizens crowded to these festivals where they heard the best tragedy and comedy, written and acted by their fellow citizens, that mankind has produced. Of the 280 plays written by Aeschylus, Sophocles, and Euripedes only thirty-three have survived. Of Aristophanes' comedies only eleven are extant. Of some two thousand plays staged at Athens during the fifth century this is all we have.

AESCHYLUS

Aeschylus, much more than Sophocles, is concerned with the problem of religion, of the ways of gods with men. He believes that "around and above men is a divine government about which many things may be obscure, but of which we surely know that it is righteous and the guardian of righteousness. Man enters by sin into collision with the law. The drama of Aeschylus is based on his study of man's will and moral con-

[19]See p. 114.

sciousness, struggling to understand, to justify to itself, and to obey that law. Supreme justice working itself out in terms of human will—such is his theme."[20] The will of Zeus, in his plays, is thus made supreme; it absorbs and colors the immutable laws of Fate, and its righteousness the human may not ignore with impunity. This theme may be illustrated by reference to *Prometheus Bound* and to the *Orestes* trilogy.

"PROMETHEUS"

In *Prometheus Bound* Zeus has recently succeeded in wresting power from an older generation of gods and is having difficulty in establishing his sovereignty over the divine world. Utterly disgusted with the race of men he has decided to destroy them and create a new race. He is thwarted in this by the Titan Prometheus, who steals fire from the gods and gives it to men and through his other gifts makes it possible for them to develop a rich civilization. This thwarting of the divine purpose "is his offence; wherefore he is bound to make requital to the gods, that so he may be lessoned to brook the sovereignty of Zeus and forbear his championship of man." He is therefore chained to a wild Scythian crag, where he pours out his defiance to all who will hear him. The chorus, the daughters of Ocean, ask him, "Didst thou not behold the helpless infirmity, no better than a dream, wherein the purblind generation of men is shackled? Never shall the counsels of mortal men transgress the ordering of Zeus." Prometheus knows, however, that Zeus's rule is doomed by a future revolution among the gods such as Zeus himself instigated. When Zeus approaches him with the offer of release from his chains for the knowledge of how to avert this future upset, Prometheus refuses. Zeus's messenger, however, reminds him now that it is through his own choice that he is subjecting himself to further torture. "Nor ever say that it was Zeus who cast you into suffering unforeseen. Not so, but blame yourselves. For well forewarned, and not at unawares or secretly, shall ye be entangled in the inextricable net of calamity by reason of your folly."[21] It is in the lost sequel *Prometheus Unbound* that Aeschylus resolved this conflict. The young Zeus of *Prometheus Bound*, a tyrant ruling by sheer force, has learned to identify himself with eternal righteousness, and to oblige Prometheus to recognize the *hubris* of his defiance and to become reconciled. In so doing Zeus acquires the wisdom of Prometheus, the benefactor of mankind, who becomes a local Attic deity. Zeus as a wise and all-powerful lord assumes responsibility for the destiny of heaven and earth alike.

THE "ORESTEIA"

In the *Oresteia*, the trilogy composed of *Agamemnon*, *The Libation-Bearers*, and *The Furies*, Aeschylus describes the fate of a noble house

[20]Gilbert Norwood, *Greek Tragedy*, p. 125.
[21]*Tragedies*, trans. H. W. Smyth, Loeb, No. 145, p. 313.

stained by murderous blood guilt. Agamemnon, upon his return from Troy, is murdered by his wife, Clytaemnestra, out of revenge for Agamemnon's sacrifice of his own daughter in order to secure a favorable wind to carry the Greek fleet to Troy. The gods punish Clytaemnestra with death at the hands of Orestes, her son, who has been ordered to the deed by Apollo. To vindicate divine justice the Furies pursue Orestes to Athens where, upon the intervention of Athena, he is spared their vengeance when his case is turned over to a secular court, the court of the Areopagus. In this instance Orestes is driven on by the inherited guilt of his house, a kind of original sin. But he acts also in accordance with the will of Zeus who, exerting his will through Apollo, urges him to his foul deed. Accordingly, it is not the Olympians but the Furies who insist upon his punishment. Since this cannot be, inasmuch as Zeus himself has undertaken to justify the curse of blood guilt by commanding Orestes to murder, the Furies surrender their jurisdiction to Zeus in return for a local worship as fertility deities in Attica. The vote of the jury of the Areopagus is a tie, which Athena resolves by a vote to acquit. The final decision thus rests with the Olympians, whose justice is the power behind human justice.

"OEDIPUS THE KING" OF SOPHOCLES

Sophocles does not question the divine order. In his most powerful play, *Oedipus the King*, the chorus sings of the obligation

> To follow still those laws ordained on high
> Whose birthplace is the bright ethereal sky
> No mortal birth they own,
> Olympus their progenitor alone!

Or,

> All wise are Zeus and Apollo, and nothing is hid from their ken;
> They are gods;

accordingly,

> The proud sinner, or in word or deed,
> That will not Justice heed,
> Nor reverence the shrine
> Of images divine,
> Perdition seize his vain imaginings,
>   If, urged by greed profane,
>   He grasps at ill-got gain,
> And lays an impious hand on holiest things.
>   Who when such deeds are done
>   Can hope heaven's bolts to shun?[22]

[22]*Tragedies*, trans. F. Storr, Loeb, No. 20, p. 81.

Man's duty, then, is to submit to what may seem to be an inscrutable divine justice, "for nothing to which the gods lead man is base." Sophocles is not interested in questioning the justice of the gods but in observing how man reacts to it. There may be many wonders, he says, but "naught more wondrous than man."

Oedipus, the king of Thebes, is the victim of a divine prophecy condemning him to murder his father and marry his mother. When he becomes aware of the possibility that he may in all innocence be the cause of the ruin of his kingdom, he leaves no stone unturned to obtain the evidence that will prove whether he has actually murdered his father and married his mother. When the evidence is clear he does not cry out against the justice of the gods who have made him "a wretch, in birth, in wedlock cursed, a parricide, incestuous, triply cursed." It is but "All-seeing Time [that] hath caught Guilt, and to justice brought the son and sire commingled in one bed." When in his frenzied misery he comes upon Jocasta, his mother and wife, "hanging there, a running noose entwined about her neck," he blinds himself with "the golden brooches that upheld her queenly robes," and thinks only to inflict upon himself the exile he had decreed for the person whom the oracle had indicated as, because of blood guilt, bringing disaster to Thebes. With a swift pace that leaves one stunned and shaken at the end, Sophocles rushes the mad Oedipus, "abhorred of gods, accursed of men," to his doom. The blinded father's farewell to his two young daughters is shattering in its emotional impact. He would take them with him into exile, but urged to "crave not mastery in all, for the mastery that raised thee was thy bane and wrought thy fall," Oedipus then submits himself to the inevitable punishment of divine justice. The play ends with the chorus's reminder:

Therefore wait to see life's ending ere thou count one mortal blest;
Wait till free from pain and sorrow he has gained his final rest. (I, 139)

THE MYSTERY CULTS

It would be difficult to determine how much the religious message of the tragic poets impressed the minds and hearts of the audiences before whom their plays were performed. Many Greeks, however, found the civic religion of the *polis* inadequate for their religious needs. No matter how beautiful the public ritual and how plentiful the sacrifices, the Olympian cult did not give the ordinary individual an explanation of his place in the universe; it did not offer him a means to free himself of what he felt to be his own imperfections or sins; it made available no escape from the ordinary routine of daily life that ended in death; it held out no hope that man could resemble the gods and share their divinity. These needs came to be supplied by a group of cults known as the mystery cults, of which three were influential: (1) the Eleusinian mysteries, (2) the cult of Dionysus, and (3) the cult of Orpheus. The last came to be organized into definite brotherhoods, of which that founded by Pythagoras is best known.

It will be recalled that similar mystery cults grew up in the Ancient Near East and spread with the Persian empire.[23] Together with these, the Greek cults likewise spread with the empire of Alexander. When the Romans gave imperial unity to the Mediterranean basin these mystery cults became a kind of universal religion for their empire. As such, they exercised a powerful influence upon the transformation of Christianity from a local Hebrew cult into a universal religion. These Greek mystery cults, therefore, have much more than a local interest. To describe their general character is to describe the nature of the oriental cults, and some of the features of early Christianity.

THE THEORY OF THE MYSTERY CULTS

They were called mystery cults by the Greeks because to those who were not initiated, and this must have been most of the Greeks, what went on in the course of their religious services was actually a mystery; their rites were secret. Thus these cults made an individual and not a group or corporate appeal. Unlike the official anthropomorphic polytheism of the *polis*, whose services were public and in which all could participate, these cults were private and open only to those who had become members. Their concept of the human being was unlike that of the ordinary Greek, for they did not look upon him merely as a mortal of great and various capacity whose task it was to develop his many-sidedness in and for the local community. They regarded man if not as originally divine, as in the case of the Orphics, at least as potentially divine or one who was capable of assimilating the divine. This divine part or quality of the human being was associated with what was called a soul or spirit. The human soul, however, had become corrupted or impure through its contamination with the body and all its physical ills and passions. The Orphics spoke of the soul's being imprisoned in the tomb of the body. The goal of the human being was to regain his original divine stature or to realize his divine potentialities. To regain one's original divine stature meant, to the Orphic, to release the soul from its death in the bodily tomb. This was not easy, for the Orphics taught that the soul could be released forever from bondage only after a succession of purges in several bodies, human or animal. They believed, that is, in the transmigration of souls. The soul, after the death of the body in which it was first imprisoned, entered into another body, and then into another, until, after a period of a thousand years, or according to some Orphics, ten thousand years, it was finally cleansed of all contamination of the flesh and, regaining its original spiritual state,

[23]See pp. 39 ff.

became immortal. The life of the body, according to this interpretation, was the death of the soul; the death of the body, the life of the soul. Accepting this interpretation, Plato could quote Socrates as saying that the life of the philosopher was a preparation for death. The purification of the soul, according to the Orphics, could be assisted by following various ascetic practices, such as wearing certain kinds of clothing and eating certain kinds of food.

In the Eleusinian mysteries and in the cult of Dionysus, divine stature for the human being was achieved by making it possible for the individual to become temporarily divine, either by an emotional identification with the fate of the divine hero or by a sacrament consisting of the actual eating of the god or of something symbolic of the god. Emotional identification with the god is mysticism. The sacramental eating of the god is religious cannibalism; a person becomes physically divine through nourishment by the divine body and blood. In the case of human nourishment upon what is symbolic of the god the sacramental cannibalism is indirect.

THE ELEUSINIAN MYSTERIES

Mystical fusion with, and physical nourishment upon, the divine is achieved through the ritual. Because of the secret nature of these cults it is difficult to know exactly what ritual was performed. The ritual of the Eleusinian mysteries grew up around the legend of the earth mother, the goddess Demeter, who lost her daughter, Persephone, to Pluto, the god of the underworld. After a long, sorrowful search she regained her, only to have to share her with Pluto thereafter for a definite part of each year. The meaning given to this legend was made to fit the original powers of Demeter as a fertility goddess responsible for the alternation of the seasons, the annual death and resurrection of vegetation. The months of the year which Persephone spent with Pluto symbolized the death of vegetation in winter; the months spent with her mother symbolized the rebirth of vegetation in the spring, its gradual maturity, and its final harvest in the autumn. After preliminary services in the spring, during which the candidate was purified by ocean baths (baptism), and made sacrifices, the major part of the mysteries was performed at Eleusis, near Athens, in the fall. This included partaking of a sacramental cereal drink and witnessing a ritualistic passion play concerning the life of Demeter. It was in the course of these ceremonies, performed by priests and accompanied by sensuous devices calculated to heighten their emotional effect, that the initiate partook of, and became identified with, his goddess Demeter. This temporary fusion with a godhead responsible for the recurrent change in the seasons assured the now divinized mortal that death did not terminate his life or send him to a murky underworld but that, like his nature goddess and nature herself, he was immortal. This pagan belief has never since entirely lacked support.

The ritual of the cult of Dionysus can be best understood from Euripides' tragedy the *Bacchanals* (the bacchanals, or bacchantes, are the *maenads*, the women followers of Bacchus, or Dionysus). It was one of his last plays, written after he had left Athens in disgust for the Macedonian court in the course of a "simple Homeric life in Macedonian forests and mountains, and perhaps even [after] the sight of real Bacchantes dancing there."[24] Dionysus, like Demeter a vegetation deity and, more specifically, the god of the vine, came into Greece from Thrace. Euripides' play opens with Dionysus' appearance in his first Greek city, Thebes, that "I first thrilled, there with fawn-skin girt her limbs,/And gave her hand the ivied thyrsus-spear." He announces his intention to force his worship upon the city, orders his Asiatic votaries to "Uplift the cymbals to the Phrygian towns/Native . . . And smite them, compassing yon royal halls/Of Pentheus [the king]." (III, 9–11)[25] He then leaves to dance with his bacchantes in the valleys of Mount Cithaeron.

Immediately the chorus establishes the wild religious note of the play:

> O happy to whom is the blessedness given
> To be taught in the Mysteries sent from heaven,
> Who is pure in his life, through whose soul the unsleeping
>   Revel goes sweeping! . . .
>
> Thebes, nursing-town of Semele, crown
>   With the ivy thy brows, and be
> All bloom, embowered in the starry-flowered
>   Lush green of the briony,
> While the oak and pine thy tresses entwine
>   In thy bacchanal-ecstasy.
> And thy fawn-skin flecked, with a fringe be it decked
>   Of wool white-glistering
> In silvery tassels;—O Bacchus' vassals,
>   High-tossed let the wild wands swing!
> One dancing-band shall be all the land
>   When, led by the Clamour-king,
> His revel-rout fills the hills. . . .
>
> O trance of rapture, when, reeling aside
>   From the Bacchanal rout o'er the mountains flying,
> One sinks to the earth, and the fawn's flecked hide
>   Covers him lying
> With its sacred vesture, wherein he hath chased
> The goat to the death for its blood—for the taste
>   Of the feast raw-reeking, when over the hills
> Of Phrygia, of Lydia, the wild feet haste,
>   And the Clamour-king leads, and his "Evoë!" thrills
>   Our hearts replying! . . .

[24]Gilbert Murray, *Euripides and His Age*, p. 197.
[25]Citations from *Euripides* in my text are to *Tragedies*, trans. Arthur S. Way, Loeb, Nos. 9, 10, 11, 12, 4 vols.

> "On, Bacchanal-rout . . .
> Blend the acclaim of your chant with the timbrels thunder-knelling,
>   Glad-pealing the glad God's praises out
> With Phrygian cries and the voice of singing,
>   When upsoareth the sound of the melody-fountain,
> Of the hallowed ringing of flutes far-flinging
>   The notes that chime with the feet that climb
>   The pilgrim-path to the mountain!"
> And with rapture the Bacchanal onward racing,
>   With gambollings fleet
> As of foals round the mares in the meads that are grazing,
>   Speedeth her feet. (III, 11-17)

The king, Pentheus, is frantic at this invasion of his kingdom by a foreign god, "A juggling sorcerer from Lydia-land,/With essenced hair in golden tresses tossed,/Wine-flushed, Love's witching graces in his eyes," and amazed to find that his blind diviner and his own father, "in dappled fawnskins clad" and "tossing the reed-wand," are about to join the worshipers in the mountains. But the old blind convert's faith is not to be shaken. "Two chiefest Powers," he says to the king, "among men there are: divine Demeter—/Earth is she, name her by which name thou wilt;—/She upon dry food nurtureth mortal men:/Then followeth Semele's Son [Dionysus]; to match her gift/The cluster's flowing draught he found, and gave/To mortals, which gives rest from grief to men/Woe-worn, soon as the vine's stream filleth them./And sleep, the oblivion of our daily ills,/He gives—there is none other balm for toils. . . . Yet shalt thou see him even on Delphi's crags/With pine-brands leaping o'er the cloven crest,/Tossing on high and waving Bacchus' bough,—/Yea, great through Hellas." As the two old men go off to the rites supporting each other the chorus exclaims:

> Our God, the begotten of Zeus, hath pleasure
>   In the glee of the feast where his chalices shine;
> And Peace doth he love, who is giver of treasure,
>   Who of Youth is the nursing-mother divine.
> On the high, on the low, doth his bounty bestow
> The joyance that maketh an end of woe,
>   The joyance of wine.
> But he hateth the man that in scorn refuseth
>   A life that on pinions of happiness flies
> Through its days and its nights, nor the good part chooseth.
>   Wisely shalt thou from the over-wise
>   Hold thee apart: but the faith of the heart
>   Of the people, that lives in the works of the mart,
>   For me shall suffice. (III, 35-37)

After the king has failed in an attempt to arrest and imprison the god and his votaries, a cowherd reports the strange goings on of Dionysian initiates in the neighboring mountains. These women possessed with divine madness "First down their shoulders let . . . stream their hair:/Then looped they up their fawnskins . . . and girt the dappled fells/Round them with snakes that licked their cheeks the while./Some, cradling fawns or wolf-cubs in their arms,/Gave to the wild things of their own white milk. . . . Then did they wreath their heads/With ivy, oak, and flower-starred briony." When the women discovered that the cowherds were spying upon them they, led by the king's mother, Agave, attacked their herds.

> Then hadst thou seen thy mother with her hands
> Rend a deep-uddered heifer bellowing loud:
> And others tore the calves in crimson shreds.
> Ribs hadst thou seen and cloven hoofs far hurled
> This way and that, and flakes of flesh that hung
> And dripped all blood-bedabbled 'neath the pines.
>
> Bulls chafing, lowering fiercely along the horn
> Erewhile, were tripped and hurled unto the earth,
> Dragged down by countless-clutching maiden hands.
> More swiftly was the flesh that lapped their bones
> Stripped, than thou couldst have closed thy kingly eyes. (III, 63)

At the conclusion of this attack they returned

> To those same founts the God sent up for them,
> And washed the gore, while from their cheeks the snakes
> Were licking with their tongues the blood-gouts clean. (III, 65)

The king cannot, thereupon, resist the temptation of the god to go himself to spy upon the secret revels. Aware of his approach, the chorus of bacchanals summon the god:

> O Dionysus, reveal thee!—appear as a bull to behold,
> Or be thou seen as a dragon, a monster of heads manifold,
> Or as a lion with splendours of flame round the limbs of him rolled.
>
> Come to us, Bacchus, and smiling in mockery compass him round
> Now with the toils of destruction, and so shall the hunter be bound,
> Trapped mid the throng the Maenads, the quarry his questing hath found.
> (III, 89)

Agave orders the bacchantes to seize the king "that he may not proclaim abroad/Our God's mysterious rites!" They set upon him as if he were the sacred bull whose blood and flesh they were to eat. Agave, "with foaming lips and eyes that rolled/Wildly, and reckless madness-clouded soul," began the attack.

> One awful blended cry
> Rose—the king's screams while life was yet in him,
> And triumph-yells from them. One bare an arm,
> One a foot sandal-shod. His ribs were stripped
> In mangled shreds: with blood-bedabbled hands
> Each to and fro was tossing Pentheus' flesh. (III, 97)

Still possessed, Agave bears Pentheus' head to Thebes, "Impaled upon her thyrsus-point . . . Like [a] mountain-lion's." The play ends as Agave, recovering her senses, discovers with horror that she has murdered her own son. With her exile and the ruin of her house, the triumph of Dionysus is made complete, even if, as Euripides comments, "It fits not that in wrath Gods be as men."

NATURE OF DIONYSIAN RITUAL

From this account it is clear that the Dionysian ritual combined intoxication with wine (conceived as a communion with, or possession by, the god or his energy), a sacrament of sacrificing and eating the raw flesh and drinking the blood of an animal sacred to the god, and nocturnal dances in secluded mountain valleys performed in special sacred vestments to the music of the drum, the tambourine, and the flute. Plato did not like it. He remarked that the immortality of drunkenness seemed to be considered the Dionysian reward of virtue. Nor did the Christian Fathers approve. One complained that "the Bacchi hold orgies in honor of a mad Dionysus. They celebrate a divine madness by the eating of raw flesh. The final accomplishment of their rite is the distribution of the flesh of butchered victims. They are crowned with snakes, and shriek out the name of Eva, that Eve through whom sin came into the world, and the symbol of their Bacchic orgies is the consecrated serpent."[26] Another referred to the "feasts of raw flesh in which with feigned frenzy and loss of a sane mind you twine snakes about you, and to show yourselves full of the divinity and majesty of the god, you demolish with gory mouths the entrails of goats bleating for mercy." This was, of course, an elemental, barbaric attempt periodically to attain the divine nature and find release from the restraints of civilized human society. Yet it will be easily recognized that the methods used have been employed at all times, then as well as now, to secure the same ends.

EURIPIDES AND RELIGION

Euripides' interest in the mystery religions may have come from his profound dissatisfaction with the moral inadequacy of popular religion. As a critical thinker he had been forced to come to terms with other phases of Greek thought which were inimical to traditional religion, that of the scientists and of the Sophists. They had made of him a thoroughgoing sceptic, if not an out-and-out rationalist. It was possible for him to have one of his characters say: "We are slaves of gods, whatever gods may be." He devoted a play to the theme of denial of the justice of the gods in which another character exclaimed, "Doth any feign there is a god in heaven? There is none, none!"[27] The discrediting of the older religion

[26]Reprinted from *Pagan Regeneration* by H. R. Willoughby, p. 77, by permission of The University of Chicago Press. Copyright 1929 by The University of Chicago Press.
[27]Murray, *Euripides*, p. 191.

by the poets, the indifference of the scientists to traditional religion, and the apparent undermining of the moral foundations of society by the Sophists made necessary a reconstruction of Greek belief. This was undertaken by Socrates and Plato.

Early Science

SOCRATES AND SCIENCE

In the *Phaedo* Plato has Socrates describe the attraction which science held for him as a youth, and the disillusion which came over him when he discovered that it had only materialistic and not moral answers for his questions. "When I was young," Socrates says, "I was tremendously eager for the kind of wisdom which they call investigation of nature. I thought it was a glorious thing to know the causes of everything, why each thing comes into being and why it perishes and why it exists." He turned especially to the books of Anaxagoras, the sceptical friend of Pericles, because of his argument that "it is the mind that arranges and causes all things. . . . My glorious hope . . . was quickly snatched away from me. As I went on with my readings I saw that the man made no use of intelligence, and did not assign any real causes for the ordering of things, but mentioned as causes air and ether and water and many other absurdities . . . in truth they give no thought to the good, which must embrace and hold together all things." (Fowler, No. 36, pp. 331, 335, 339, 341)

EARLY SPECULATION ON SCIENCE

The Greeks were the first in the West to philosophize in a rational manner, and so well did they do it that they stimulated all subsequent study of philosophy in Europe. Their philosophy began with what we should call science (a distinction that the Greeks did not make). Their earliest thought, when not religious, had to do with nature (*physis*): the nature not only of the immediately surrounding physical world but also of the whole universe. Their early speculation concerning nature went beyond merely supplying a description of it, based upon observations made with the limited instruments at their disposal. It asked fundamental questions about nature's ultimate constitution and drew up hypotheses to answer these questions. The Greeks saw the world about them, the world of their senses, in a process of constant growth and decay or, as some of them put it, in a state of everlasting becoming and passing away. They sought to find through reason some element of order and unity, some essential permanence behind the evanescent phenomena. And so remarkable was their capacity for rational thought that they invented and applied to their scientific and philosophical arguments both mathematics and logic.

What, they asked, was the fundamental substance or substances out of which arose the changing world of nature, and what were the principles in accordance with which this substance was, or substances were, modified to form the world of our senses? They began, that is, by asking the most important questions of the contemporary scientist, namely, What is the real or true, the irreducible unit of all matter, and in accordance with what laws does it compose itself to form the objects of the natural world? When once formed, in accordance with what principles does it decompose? The earliest Greek thinkers were bound by the notion of an orderly universe, formed of a few elements functioning according to principles that could be expressed in logical (rational) or mathematical terms. This has been the basic notion of all science ever since. We have been engaged only in making the Greek notion more explicit.

OPINIONS OF THE EARLY NATURAL PHILOSOPHERS

The men first engaged in this work were not Athenians but colonial Greeks, the most important of whom were active at Miletus in Asia Minor (Thales, Anaximander, Anaximenes) in the sixth century, and in the Greek world of southern Italy (Pythagoras, Parmenides). Their successors likewise came from the colonial world (Heraclitus of Ephesus, Anaxagoras of Clazomenae, Leucippus of Miletus, and Democritus of Abdera). In a limited sense the whole approach of these various schools was materialistic or at least secular. They dealt with material substances as the essential reality, or if they spoke in religious terms, went beyond the limits of traditional religion. Thales, for example, thought simply that the universe was composed of water. Anaximander spoke of the cause and first element of things as "the Infinite . . . from which arises all the heavens and the worlds within them. . . . And besides this there was an eternal motion, in the course of which was brought about the origin of the worlds." Anaximenes said likewise that the underlying substance was one and infinite, but he identified it with air. Pythagoras was a brilliant mathematician and theoretical musician[28] as well as the leader of a religious brotherhood. He added to the principles regarded as governing the cosmos the notion of harmony, and thought that all realities could be identified with specific numbers. Heraclitus was responsible for the remark that "this order, which is the same in all things, no one of gods or men has made; but it was ever, is now, and ever shall be an everliving Fire." He also said that Homer "was wrong in saying: 'would that strife might perish from among gods and men!' He did not see that he was praying for the destruction of the universe; for, if his prayer were heard, all things would pass away. . . . War is the father of all and the king of all. . . . All things come into being and pass away through strife. . . . The quick and the dead, the waking and the sleeping, the young and the old

[28]See pp. 149 ff.

are the same; the former are changed and become the latter, and the latter in turn are changed into the former." The real, Heraclitus was inclined to say, is in a state of constant change or flux. "You cannot step twice into the same rivers; for fresh waters are ever flowing in upon you." (pp. 149-152)[29] His followers carried this thought to its logical extremes and declared that you could not step into the same river once.

By the end of the fifth century these various views had crystallized into more definite and contrasting attitudes. In part this was the result of the work of Parmenides. From the notion of earlier philosophers that the variety of nature was reducible to one material element, Parmenides went on to deny that our imperfect senses could give us more than an illusory conception of the variety of nature. He was inclined to think that what we call nature was an illusion. The essential reality of the universe was in any case spiritual and not material.[30] This abrupt denial of Heraclitus's reality of change was followed by attempts to make the reality behind nature many rather than one, yet still corporeal. Empedocles of Agrigentum sought in water, air, fire, and earth the indestructible elements of reality. "Out of these," as a result of a conflict between love and hate, "are all things formed and fitted together, and by these do men think and feel pleasure and pain." Anaxagoras sought to explain motion among an infinite number of material elements as the result of a quasi-mechanical mind—an idea that, as we have already noted, disappointed Socrates. Leucippus and his pupil Democritus hit upon an explanation of the universe in terms of the mechanical motion of purposeless atoms. "There are an infinite number of them, and they are invisible owing to the smallness of their bulk. They move in the void (for there is a void); and by their coming together they effect coming into being; by their separation, passing away. . . . He [Leucippus] says that the worlds arise when many bodies are collected together into the mighty void from the surrounding space and rush together. They come into collision, and those which are of similar shape and like form become entangled, and from their entanglement the heavenly bodies arise."

SCIENCE AND RELIGION

An atomic universe such as this seemed to imply a godless universe. Its fate, if not blind, is in the hands of men. These natural philosophers were either indifferent or antagonistic to the gods of popular religion. Xenophanes' opinion of the gods has already been alluded to.[31] "She that they call Iris [a messenger of the gods] is a cloud likewise, purple, scarlet, and green to behold. . . . Homer and Hesiod have ascribed to the gods all

[29]Citations from Anaximander, Heraclitus, Empedocles, Leucippus, Xenophanes, and Anaxagoras are to ed. O. J. Thatcher, *The Ideas That Have Influenced Civilization* (Roberts-Manchester, 1901), Vol. II.
[30]See p. 135.
[31]See p. 100.

things that are a shame and a disgrace among men, thefts and adulteries and deception of one another." Heraclitus could agree: "Homer should be turned out of the lists and whipped, and Archilochos [a lyric poet] likewise." When Anaxagoras insisted that "the sun and the moon and all the stars are fiery stones ignited by the rotation of the ether" and not divine, popular indignation obliged him to leave Athens. The trend here, too, was toward atheism. The long and bitter fight between science and religion that has so impeded the forward march of mankind was herewith joined.

Philosophy

THE SOPHISTS

The conflict was intensified by men who tried to teach the Greeks that their world, now that the gods had disappeared, was of their own making. These were the Sophists, a term used today in the disparaging sense of "a captious and fallacious reasoner." Socrates and Plato, their great antagonists, gave the word this meaning. It is clear now, however, that the views of the Sophists are not simply to be condemned, unless we wish wholly to adopt the point of view of Socrates and Plato. They arose in the Greek world in response to great needs, and in their attempts to meet these needs brought the Greeks, and all those who have inherited their tradition, face to face with the implications of a naked humanism. Likewise, as professional teachers they supplied the Greeks, and Europe since that day, with a curriculum for higher education. Finally, through their fundamental doctrines they provoked Socrates and Plato to define a new religious and philosophical position.[32]

The great Sophists came to Athens from other parts of the Greek world as professional teachers. They came at a time when Athens, after the victory over Persia, was building, externally, her Mediterranean empire and, internally, her democratic city-state. Athens was in need of the trained legal and political expert, the man who knew his way about the popular courts and the assembly, who could manipulate public opinion to support a sound domestic and foreign policy, who could understand the necessities of good local and imperial administration, the all-round statesman. This kind of a man the Sophists claimed they could train. Since they demanded fees for their services—for their concern for money Socrates and Plato, men of higher motivation, had nothing but scorn—it was inevitably the sons of the rich Athenians who came to them for training. These young men came from an environment hostile to the growing forces of Athenian democracy. The teachings and training of the Sophists they thought to use as a means to control the state in their own interests and to justify their right to control and even to subvert it. Some Sophists adapted

[32]See the interpretation in Jaeger, *Paidaea*, I, 283-329.

themselves cynically to this political and social setting and incurred the wrath of old, conservative, aristocratic families, who resented the intrusion of the new bourgeoisie. Other Sophists were merely ignorant pedagogues who thought by their new methods alone to pave the royal road to learning. Others, again, were enlightened and open-minded professors, well acquainted with the new science and its implications for religion, men who did not hesitate, in defiance of accepted notions, to discuss freely ideas that threatened the foundations of Athenian society. Plato's quarrel with these men is the subject of many of his dialogues, notably the *Protagoras*, the *Gorgias*, and the *Theaetetus*. We have already met the Sophist Thrasymachus in the *Republic*.[33] It is Protagoras whom Plato seeks especially to demolish.

THE CURRICULUM OF THE SOPHISTS

Because they set out to train the future leaders of the state, the Sophists laid great store by oratory, an art in which they sought to give a complete training. They concentrated their attention on formal training in language, not only grammar—and they were the first grammarians—but also the embellishment of written and oral discourse, or rhetoric—and they were the first rhetoricians. They had to train young men in the use of the logic of persuasion (dialectics), and were accused of being indifferent to what men were to be persuaded of. Young men acting as lawyers before the popular courts needed to be eloquent and convincing on both sides of any question. There were Sophists who specialized in this. Young men acting as speakers in the assembly had to know how to confuse as well as plead. For this purpose verbiage was necessary. There were specialists, such as Prodicus, in the "philosophy of synonyms." But in addition to grammar, rhetoric, and dialectics, which, as the *trivium*, subsequently became the core of European higher education, the Sophists did not neglect the new mathematics and science. Arithmetic and geometry, astronomy and music, later grouped together as the *quadrivium*, were included in their curriculum. It was a broad training that the best Sophists insisted upon, no matter how perverted may have been the application of it by individual Sophists or their pupils.

PROTAGORAS A RELATIVIST

Although the Sophists were not professional philosophers or scientists they adapted certain trends of the earlier schools to their own purposes. Protagoras, for example, according to Plato, was an out-and-out religious sceptic. He is quoted as saying, "Excellent boys and old men, there you sit together declaiming to the people, and you bring in the gods, the question of whose existence or non-existence I exclude from oral and written discussion." This was to question the traditional notion of an un-

[33]See p. 95.

alterable and divinely sanctioned truth, and indeed Protagoras took his stand on his statement that man, not God, "is the measure of all things."[34] In Plato's elaboration of this statement, Protagoras is not made the defender of the humanistic point of view. He is made rather the defender of a particular theory of knowledge that, in the tradition of Heraclitus, insists that we know only through our senses, and that—since the senses err— truth is to be conceived of as subjective, temporary, and evanescent. There is no universal and eternal truth. This attitude we have already defined as the position of the relativists and the opposing position as that of the absolutists.[35]

PLATO'S "THEAETETUS"

Relativism is attacked by Socrates in the *Theaetetus* in the following way: "I don't see why he [Protagoras] does not say in the beginning of his *Truth* that a pig or a dog-faced baboon or some still stranger creature of those that have sensations is the measure of all things. Then he might have begun to speak to us very imposingly and condescendingly, showing that while we were honouring him like a god for his wisdom, he was af- ter all no better in intellect than any other man, or, for that matter, than a tadpole. . . . For if that opinion is true to each person which he acquires through sensation, and no one man can discern another's condition better than he himself, and one man has no better right to investigate whether an- other's opinion is true or false than he himself, but, as we have said several times, each man is to form his own opinions by himself, and these opinions are always right and true, why in the world, my friend, was Protagoras wise, so that he could rightly be thought worthy to be the teacher of other men and to be well paid, and why were we ignorant creatures and obliged to go to school to him, if each person is the measure of his own wisdom? . . . For would not the investigation of one another's fancies and opinions, and the attempt to refute them, when each man's must be right, be tedious and blatant folly, if the *Truth* of Protagoras is true and he was not jesting when he uttered his oracles from the shrine of his book?" (Fowler, No. 123, pp. 77-79)

PLATO'S "GORGIAS"

The Sophist theory of the subjective nature of truth puts a grave re- sponsibility upon the individual human being that Socrates in this dialogue was not willing to assume. In the *Gorgias* the Sophists are made to defend a theory concerning the nature of political society that we have already encountered in the position of Thrasymachus in the *Republic*. It is that the growth of democratic society has really upset the course of nature, which in truth justifies might as right. As elaborated by Callicles the

[34]The student might as well memorize this phrase as the password of (sophistic) humanism.
[35]See pp. 93 f.

argument runs: "the makers of the laws are the weaker sort of men, and the more numerous. So it is with a view to themselves and their own interest that they make their laws and distribute their praises and censures; and to terrorize the stronger sort of folk who are able to get an advantage, and to prevent them from getting one over *them*, they tell them that such aggrandizement is foul and unjust, and that wrongdoing is just this endeavour to get the advantage of one's neighbours: for I expect they are well content to see themselves on an equality, when they are so inferior. So this is why by convention it is termed unjust and foul to aim at an advantage over the majority, and why they call it wrongdoing: but nature, in my opinion, herself proclaims the fact that it is right for the better to have advantage of the worse, and the abler of the feebler. It is obvious in many cases that this is so . . . that right has been decided to consist in the sway and advantage of the stronger over the weaker. . . . Why, surely these men [such as Xerxes] follow nature—the nature of right—in acting thus; yes, on my soul, and follow the law of nature—though not that, I dare say, which is made by us; we mould the best and strongest amongst us, taking them from their infancy like young lions, and utterly enthral them by our spells and witchcraft, telling them the while that they must have but their equal share, and that this is what is fair and just. But, I fancy, when some man arises with a nature of sufficient force, he shakes off all that we have taught him, bursts his bonds, and breaks free; he tramples underfoot our codes and juggleries, our charms and laws, which are all against nature; our slave rises in revolt and shows himself our master, and there dawns the full light of natural justice. . . . No, in good truth, Socrates—which you claim to be seeking—the fact is this: luxury and licentiousness and liberty, if they have the support of force, are virtue and happiness, and the rest of these embellishments—the unnatural covenants of mankind—are all mere stuff and nonsense." (Lamb, No. 166, pp. 385, 387, 413) The statement of Callicles, a pupil of the Sophists, has been called the "most eloquent statement of the immoralist's case in European literature."[36]

"THE CLOUDS" OF ARISTOPHANES

The controversies injected into the intellectual life of Athens by the infiltration of new scientific ideas and the invasion of the Sophists are well illustrated by the comedy of Aristophanes, produced in 423 B.C., which he called *The Clouds*. The play uses Socrates as the representative of the new sophistic learning and, however careless of presenting Socrates' real outlook, does contain authentic details of his person. It may not have been a dangerous attack upon him in 423, but in 399, when standing before a popular jury attempting to defend himself against a charge of impiety, he complains that it is well nigh impossible to dissipate the legend created by this play. The present text is a rewritten version composed af-

[36]Paul Shorey, *What Plato Said*, p. 154.

ter the initial failure of the play in 423, a revision that attempts to make clearer than did the original Aristophanes' lack of sympathy with the educational novelties that were becoming so popular.

In the play Strepsiades, a farmer, seeks relief from the debts in which his horse-racing son, Pheidippides, has involved him by urging his son to enter "the thinking-house of sapient souls" where "they'll teach (only they'll want some money),/How one may speak and conquer, right or wrong." Presumably with this aid he will make it unnecessary for his father to pay his debts. Pheidippides, however, will have nothing to do with "Those rank pedants,/Those palefaced, barefoot vagabonds . . . That Socrates, poor wretch," and the father is compelled to enter the school himself. He discovers Socrates engaged in such problems as "How many feet of its own a flea could jump" and whether "the gnats/Hummed through their mouth, or backwards, through the tail." He finds the school well supplied with globes and charts for the study of astronomy and geometry. Socrates himself, at the moment of his approach, is suspended in the air in a basket and tells him, "I walk on air, and contemplate the Sun." Strepsiades informs him of his purpose to learn the false method of reasoning and promises, "Name your own price, by all the Gods I'll pay it." He is informed "the Gods with us/Don't pass for current coin," and is put through an initiation, intended to take off a mystery-cult initiation, during which the clouds, the special patron goddesses of the school, are summoned. Socrates explains, "These, these then alone, for true Deities own, the rest are all Godships of straw." This shocks Strepsiades, and he asks, "Let Zeus be left out: He's a God beyond doubt: come, that you can scarcely deny." Socrates counters with "Zeus, indeed! there's no Zeus: don't you be so obtuse," and gives an elaborate proof of his own new creed.

> Now then you agree in rejecting with me
> the Gods you believed in when young,
> And *my* creed you'll embrace *"I believe in wide space,*
> *in the Clouds, in the eloquent Tongue."* (I, 307)[37]

But Socrates abandons Strepsiades as unteachable, and he is instructed to send his son in his stead.

When Pheidippides arrives Aristophanes introduces a contest between Right Logic and Wrong Logic, to see which is to instruct him. Wrong Logic maintains, "There never *was* Justice or Truth" and says that Right Logic, who praises "the Discipline rare which flourished in Athens of yore/When Honour and Truth were in fashion with youth and Sobriety bloomed on our shore," is "quite out of date." Right Logic warns Pheidippides against following the new education, insisting that

> . . . if you pursue what men nowadays do,
> You will have, to begin, a cold pallid skin,

[37] Trans. B. B. Rogers, Loeb, Nos. 178, 179, 180, 3 vols.

Arms small and chest weak, tongue practised to speak,
Special laws very long, and the symptoms all strong
Which show that your life is licentious and wrong.
And your mind he'll prepare so that foul to be fair
And fair to be foul you shall always declare. (I, 359)

Wrong Logic pleads with him,

. . . take this chastity, young man:
                                    sift it inside and out:
Count all the pleasures, all the joys,
                            it bids you live without:
No kind of dames, no kind of games,
                        no laughing, feasting, drinking,—
Why, life itself is little worth
                        without these joys, I'm thinking.
Well, I must notice now the wants
                            by Nature's self implanted;
You love, seduce, you can't help that,
                        you're caught, convicted. Granted.
You're done for; you can't say one word:
                            while if you follow me
Indulge your genius, laugh and quaff,
                            hold nothing base to be.
Why if you're in adultery caught,
                        your pleas will still be ample:
You've done no wrong, you'll say, and then
                        bring Zeus as your example.
He fell before the wondrous powers
                        by Love and Beauty wielded:
And how can you, the Mortal, stand,
                    where He, the Immortal, yielded? (I, 365)

Aristophanes gives Wrong Logic the victory, and he undertakes the instruction of Pheidippides. Unlike his father, the son learns his lessons well,
so well that besides teaching his father how to get rid of his creditors he
beats him. His father had wanted him to sing something from Aeschylus,
but Pheidippides, taught to think of Aeschylus as "That rough, un-
polished, turgid bard, that mouther of bombast," sang instead from
Euripides, "most sapient bard." He not only beats his father but defends
his right to do so, and says, "By the same Logic I can prove 'tis right to
beat my mother." This is too much for Strepsiades, and, leaving his son
to his opinion that "There is *no* Zeus. Young Vortex reigns, and he has
turned out Zeus," he sets off to burn down the thinking house with its
occupants. As the flames shoot up, Socrates calls, "Hallo! what are you
at, up on our roof?" and Strepsiades replies, "I walk on air, and contemplate the Sun." (I, 401)

SOCRATES

The man whom Aristophanes had burned as a Sophist for teaching immoral doctrine was judicially murdered by the Athenian state in 399 B.C.

It had come to the point in Athenian political life when the democracy could not tolerate a magnificently self-contained individual who held up to the state its shortcomings in the light of what he conceived to be virtue. The man whom the Athenians sentenced to death was one of the finest and noblest specimens the human race has produced. This greatness is to be measured not only by the complete integrity of his own personality but also by the almost incomparable influence he exerted on his own fellow citizens and on all subsequent mankind. Almost all that is known of him is to be found in the *Dialogues* of Plato and in Xenophon's *Memoirs of Socrates* (*Memorabilia*). He never bothered to write anything himself. In the *Dialogues* it is very difficult to separate Socrates from Plato. Yet the real Socrates appears in the *Dialogues* on his trial and death (*Apology*, *Crito*, *Phaedo*) if anywhere. Plato was present at the trial and certainly did not misrepresent these last tragic days of a beloved teacher.

It was a portly old man of seventy years, in the *Apology*, "with bald head, snub nose, thick lips and protruding eyes," who rose in the jury court to defend himself against what he called the charges of his ancient enemies that "Socrates is a criminal and a busybody, investigating the things beneath the earth and in the heavens and making the weaker argument stronger and teaching others these same things." His recent enemies charged that "Socrates is a wrongdoer because he corrupts the youth and does not believe in the gods the state believes in, but in other new spiritual beings." He was a familiar figure to his fellow citizens. For decades he had been haunting their public places and private dwellings, barefoot and poorly dressed, talking and talking about what it meant to be good. His pupils used the image of Silenus (the leader of the satyrs) to describe his face; they joked about his snub nose, and one speaks of his " 'strutting like a proud marsh-goose, with ever a sidelong glance,' turning a calm sidelong look on friend and foe alike." (No. 36, pp. 75, 91) Even though he had no great faith that majority rule was the rule of the best he had been an intensely loyal citizen and had won renown in all the city's wars. At Potidaea, said one of his comrades, he "made his way more easily over the ice unshod than the rest of us did in our shoes. The soldiers looked askance at him, thinking that he despised them." His students had often seen him transfixed in deep thought, and some had wept to hear his words. Alcibiades in the *Symposium* confesses that "I find my heart leaping and my tears gushing forth at the sound of his speech, and I see great numbers of other people having the same experience. When I listened to Pericles and other skilled orators I thought them eloquent, but I never felt anything like this." (No. 166, p. 221)

SOCRATES IN HIS OWN DEFENSE

Before the assembly of his fellow citizens Socrates does not fawn for his life. He is accused, he says, because he is hated. He is hated by men because he has revealed to them their ignorance, and he has been compelled to reveal their ignorance because of the oracle of Apollo at Delphi, who said he was the wisest man. He had to find out in what sense this was true by questioning other men. It was true, he discovered, in the sense that he knew that he was not wise and those whom he questioned did not know that they were not. "Therefore I am still even now going about and searching and investigating at the god's behest anyone, whether citizen or foreigner, who I think is wise; and when he does not seem so to me, I give aid to the god and show that he is not wise." If he is to be destroyed, Socrates says, he will be destroyed by the envy and detraction of the world, which "has condemned many other good men, and there is no danger that it will stop with me." (No. 36, pp. 87, 89)

He is not afraid to die because that would be to presume to know that there is life after death and that it is unpleasant. This he does not pretend to know. "For to fear death, gentlemen, is nothing else than to think one is wise when one is not; for it is thinking one knows what one does not know. For no one knows whether death be not even the greatest of all blessings to man, but they fear it as if they knew that it is the greatest of evils." Even if acquitted he would not alter his ways. "For I go about doing nothing else than urging you, young and old, not to care for your persons or your property more than for the perfection of your souls, or even so much; and I tell you that virtue does not come from money, but from virtue comes money and all other good things to man, both to the individual and to the state. If by saying these things I corrupt the youth, these things must be injurious . . . either acquit me, or not, knowing that I shall not change my conduct even if I am to die many times over." (No. 36, pp. 107, 109)

Before the vote of the jury he said: "And so, men of Athens, I am now making my defence not for my own sake, as one might imagine, but far more for yours, that you may not by condemning me err in your treatment of the gift the god gave you. For if you put me to death, you will not easily find another, who . . . attaches himself to the city as a gadfly to a horse, which, though large and well bred, is sluggish on account of his size and needs to be aroused by stinging. I think the god fastened me upon the city in some such capacity. . . . Such another is not likely to come to you, gentlemen; but if you take my advice, you will spare me." The verdict was thirty votes short of an acquittal. In accordance with Athenian law he could propose a suitable penalty. He proposed "what is fitting for a poor man who is your benefactor, and who needs leisure to exhort you, . . . that such a man be given his meals in the prytaneum," that is, public support for the rest of his life (the *prytaneum* was the building where the governing *prytany*[38] was housed and fed). For "to talk every day about virtue and the other things about which you hear me talking and examining myself and others is the greatest good to man . . . the unexamined life is not worth living." Reflecting that if death is "uncon-

[38]See p. 54.

sciousness, like a sleep in which the sleeper does not even dream, death would be a wonderful gain . . . for in that case, all time seems to be no longer than one night." If it is "a change of habitation from here to some other place," then with the illustrious dead he will be able, he said, "to pass my time in examining and investigating the people there, as I do those here, to find out who among them is wise and who thinks he is when he is not. . . . At any rate, the folk there do not kill people for it." Finally he bids farewell to his judges, "the time has come to go away. I go to die, and you to live; but which of us goes to the better lot, is known to none but God." (No. 36, pp. 111-145)

THE DEATH OF SOCRATES

The closing scene of the *Phaedo* describing Socrates' death has been called "perhaps the greatest passage in all prose literature."[39] He had spent the hours before his death talking over with his close friends the most serious problems of philosophy. When the moment came to prepare the hemlock, his jailer, calling him "the noblest and gentlest and best man who has ever come here," broke into tears and went out. When the jailer returned with the poison Socrates said, " 'Well, my good man, you know about these things; what must I do?' 'Nothing,' he replied, 'except drink the poison and walk about till your legs feel heavy; then lie down, and the poison will take effect of itself.' At the same time he held out the cup to Socrates. He took it, and very gently . . . without trembling or changing colour or expression, but looking up at the man with wide open eyes, as was his custom . . . raised the cup to his lips and very cheerfully and quietly drained it." At this point his friends could stand it no longer. Everyone broke down and wept "except Socrates himself. But he said, 'What conduct is this, you strange men! I sent the women away chiefly for this very reason, that they might not behave in this absurd way; for I have heard that it is best to die in silence. Keep quiet and be brave.' . . . He walked about and, when he said his legs were heavy, lay down on his back, for such was the advice of the attendant. The man who had administered the poison laid his hands on him and after a while examined his feet and legs, then pinched his foot hard and asked if he felt it. He said 'No'; then after that, his thighs; and passing upwards in this way he showed us that he was growing cold and rigid. And again he touched him and said that when it reached his heart, he would be gone. The chill had now reached the region about the groin, and uncovering his face, which had been covered, he said—and these were his last words—'Crito, we owe a cock to Aesculapius [the god of healing]. Pay it and do not neglect it.' 'That,' said Crito, 'shall be done; but see if you have anything else to say.' To this question he made no reply, but after a little while he moved; the attendant uncovered him; his eyes were fixed. And Crito when he saw it,

[39]De Burgh, *Legacy*, p. 139, n. 1.

closed his mouth and eyes. Such was the end . . . of our friend, who was, as we may say, of all those of his time whom we have known, the best and wisest and most righteous man." (No. 36, pp. 379, 401, 403)

THE POINT OF VIEW OF SOCRATES

Because Socrates lived and thought, the whole outlook of the western world has been changed. Greek philosophical thought first centered on an interpretation of nature and came to materialistic and mechanistic conclusions. The natural philosophers were followed by the Sophists, offering, without much concern for ethical propriety, to teach men how to become practical successes in this life. Socrates was indifferent to the scientists and hostile to the Sophists. He had a new outlook. Plato quotes him as saying that "the noblest of all investigations is the study of what man should be, and what he should pursue." In other words, Socrates was primarily interested in moral or ethical problems. He was not, as was Aeschylus, trying to justify God's ways to man; rather, he was trying to persuade man to justify to himself his own ways in the light of the highest conceivable virtue, namely, the good.

Socrates did not put it as vaguely as this. To express what he meant he gave an old Greek word an entirely new meaning. This word was soul (*psyche*). For him the soul was the mind, and especially that part of it which had to do with morality. Socrates' charge to his fellow citizens was that they should take care of their souls. By this he meant that they should so cultivate their minds and their sense of morality that, by clearing away the brush of inferior values, they might see what was good and might direct their whole lives in accordance with it. Man's life had a purpose other than to be a cog in nature's machine or to attain some kind of material success. That purpose was to achieve the good. If one did not know what this good was, life was aimless and not worth living. The soul was not, in his view, something separate from the body. Body and soul were a common ingredient of human nature. But if the body could be trained in the gymnasium, the soul could be disciplined by man's thought. The soul should dominate the body; the mind, the passions; principle, mere expediency. Proper care of the soul meant self-control, the attainment of moral autonomy, individual emancipation from physical, external circumstance. Individual moral freedom was so much a quality of the soul and not of the person that the slave might be truly free while the free man might be actually a slave.

Socrates did not believe that the virtue of goodness, unless equated with knowledge, could be taught, as the Sophists claimed.[40] All that he could do, he thought, was to assist men by cross-examination to come to recognize it for themselves. This method would oblige them to acknowledge the utter folly of the inferior virtues they clung to and the conduct

[40]See Plato's dialogue the *Protagoras*.

resulting therefrom. Thus he had no system of morals of his own to impart. Certain of his opinions, however, he held with such tenacity that they constituted a kind of personal creed. He insisted (1) that virtue or goodness is knowledge, and that this virtue is indivisible; in other words, that to be and do good one must know what is good. Without such knowledge an art of living is impossible. Nor can virtue be really broken down into virtues of courage, prudence, temperance, and the like. Goodness consists of them all and they of it. He insisted also, so high was his conception of human potentiality, (2) that no one does wrong willingly; if one chooses to do what is wrong it is because he does not understand what, in the largest view, is actually the best for him. He insisted constantly that to do injustice is much worse than to suffer it. The true end of life, therefore, is virtue or goodness, to be achieved here and now on this earth. Only this, within every man's reach, can bring happiness.

In this way Socrates enlarged the concept of Greek humanism. To the notion that man, or at least the free-born man, is to have the opportunity within his community to develop the various capacities that ennoble him, and to do this in accordance with his own best lights rather than in accordance with the unalterable instruction of some divine power, Socrates added the notion that the art of living is worthless unless it is practiced in accordance with an ideal of the good which the individual has discovered for himself. This is to suggest that there is not much hope in society until the individuals who compose it have given an ethical meaning and order to their lives. It is difficult to be sure to what extent Socrates conceived of ethics in religious terms. He himself conformed to the religious practices of his own *polis*. He talked about an inner, divine check which always warned him not to do things, even if it gave him no positive guidance. He insisted that in carrying on his mission of helping men to discover the good for themselves he was carrying on a divine mission. Yet Socrates did not think that what he had to teach was in any sense the instruction of a god. He was not the bearer of any special divine revelation to man. He was not concerned with an afterlife in which man would be rewarded or punished in proportion to his earthly obedience to divine precept. He was interested in the earthly life of his *polis*. As a tough-minded thinker he delighted in the exercise of his reason and was impatient with the indifference of his fellow citizens to the use of their reason. He believed that man could come to his own conclusions if he applied his thought to what he knew, and if his knowledge were abundant. The most important knowledge concerned the ends of life, and these were moral. When a man achieved this moral knowledge and acted in accordance with it he was fulfilling supremely his human qualities. He was doing more than this. He was acting divinely, acting as a god should act, and certainly not as the gods of popular mythology were accustomed to act. Socrates thus summoned man to act in superhuman fashion. He pleaded with him to assume the heroic moral stature of which he was capable. Such virtue was not to deny other qualities that enabled man to act as a member of a family or community. It merely enhanced these others and ordered them in terms of what were man's best qualities. These were what made him good. At this point Greek humanism reached its climax. To this point western man has since sought periodically to return.

It was for Plato to make this outlook somewhat more specific and to clothe it in the imperishable language of a poet. From then until our own day his thought has constituted an elevated idealism from which western man, when frustrated by the limitations of his physical environment and surfeited by the accomplishments of his own folly, has drawn sustenance and inspiration. When used by Christian theologians to interpret the religion of Jesus this Platonism became a refuge for the tired and a goal for the courageous.

PLATO IN DEFENSE OF PHILOSOPHY

It is easy to become lost in, and irritated by, the attempts of minds less gifted than Plato's to make a philosophic system of his thought. He was one of the greatest of the philosophers of the West. Many of the loftiest passages in his *Dialogues* have to do with a defense of the philosophic way of life and with an idealization of the philosopher. When, for example, in the *Gorgias* the hard-bitten Callicles expresses disgust for the kind of person who spends too much time with philosophy, Socrates rises to a heroic defense. Philosophy, says Callicles, may be all right for a youth to dabble in with moderation, but "if he continues to spend his time on it too long, it is ruin to any man. However well endowed one may be, if one philosophizes far on into life, one must needs find oneself ignorant of everything that ought to be familiar to the man who would be a thorough gentleman and make a good figure in the world. For such people are shown to be ignorant of the laws of their city, and of the terms which have to be used in negotiating agreements with their fellows in private or in public affairs, and of human pleasures and desires; and, in short, to be utterly inexperienced in men's characters." Callicles goes on to say that when he sees a man continue the study of philosophy beyond youth, "that is the gentleman, Socrates, whom I think in need of a whipping. For as I said just now, this person, however well endowed he may be, is bound to become unmanly through shunning the centres and marts of the city, in which, as the poet said, 'men get them note and glory'; he must cower down and spend the rest of his days whispering in a corner with three or four lads, and never utter anything free or high or spirited." (No. 166, pp. 389, 391, 393)

Plato's answer may be taken from the *Theaetetus*. To be sure, he says, the philosopher is not to be found in the market place, the assembly, or the courts. "His mind, considering all these things petty and of no account, disdains them and is borne in all directions . . . measuring the surface of the earth . . . studying the stars, and investigating the universal nature of every thing that is, each in its entirety, never lowering itself to anything close at hand." The philosopher is enquiring "what a human being is and what is proper for such a nature to do or bear different from any other. . . . When he hears a panegyric of a despot or a king he fancies he is listening to the praises of some herdsman . . . who gets much milk from his beasts. . . . And when he hears that someone is amazingly rich, because he owns ten thousand acres of land or more, to him, accustomed as he is to think of the whole earth, this seems very little." His concern is "the investigation of abstract right and wrong, to inquire what each of them is and wherein they differ from each other and from all other things," his "the investigation of royalty and of human happiness and wretchedness in general, to see what the nature of each is and in what way man is naturally fitted to gain the one and escape the other." It is the task of the philosopher "to persuade people that the reason generally advanced for the pursuit of virtue and the avoidance of vice—namely, in order that a man may not seem bad and may seem good—is not the reason why the one should be practised and the other not. . . . Let us give the true reason. God is in no wise and in no manner unrighteous, but utterly and perfectly righteous, and there is nothing so like him as that one of us who in turn becomes most nearly perfect in righteousness . . . the knowledge of this is wisdom or true virtue, and ignorance of it is folly or manifest wickedness; and all the other kinds of seeming cleverness and wisdom are paltry when they appear in public affairs and vulgar in the arts." (No. 123, pp. 121–129) Or we might take the defense in the *Phaedo*, where, under the influence of the Orphic doctrine,[41] Socrates describes the philosopher as a type of ascetic, fleeing the pleasures of eating and drinking, the pleasures of love, "the possession of fine clothes and shoes and the other personal adornments," despising them, "except so far as it is necessary to have them," and attending rather the soul. In dissevering "the soul from communion with the body," employing "pure, absolute reason in his attempt to search out the pure, absolute essence of things," he is at his best, for the soul "thinks best when none of these things troubles it, neither hearing nor sight, nor pain nor any pleasure, but it is, so far as possible, alone by itself, and takes leave of the body, and avoiding, so far as it can, all association or contact with the body, reaches out toward the reality." This desire to separate soul from body, which is what is meant by death, makes the "true philosophers practise dying, and death is less terrible to them than to any other men." The philosopher indeed is "the spectator of all time and all existence." (No. 36, pp. 225, 235)

THE SPIRIT OF PLATO

The reader of the *Dialogues* is aware, in spite of the dogmatic conservatism of a sour old age that appears in the *Laws*, of a constant effort to

[41]See p. 139.

arrive at a balanced point of view and of the willingness to test all positions by further argument. This is the larger significance of Plato. Essentially, his is the demand for the free play of the intellect in its search for truth. To read a Hebrew prophet and a dialogue of Plato is to sense this. The prophet emerges from a theocratic environment. "Thus saith the Lord" to his slaves. The spirit of the dialogue is "Let us sit down together, talk these things over, and avoiding no difficulty in the tough exercise of our minds, see if we can arrive at conclusions with which we may all agree." The spirit of the former is intolerant conformity; of the latter, a tolerance which recognizes the need of contributions of many points of view before a balanced and harmonious one can be achieved. For the prophet, God disposes; for Plato, man. He is thus at his best an apostle of the tolerant exercise of intellectual freedom.

PLATO AN ABSOLUTIST

Plato crystallized the trend of thought initiated by Socrates into a definite point of view. This point of view we have characterized earlier in this chapter as absolutist[42] to distinguish it from relativist. It is a point of view called realist[43] by medieval philosophers, and by recent and contemporary philosophers, idealist, or, more concretely, absolute idealist. It is concerned with what the technical philosophers call epistemology; in other words, with the theory of knowledge. It asks the most fundamental of all questions, namely, what can be known, or, to use other words, what is reality, what is truth? The general answer given to this question by the theologian is that that is true which has been revealed by God. The general answers given to this question by philosophers have been the following: (1) that is true which is known through the senses; (2) that is true which is discovered by the rational processes of the mind; or (3) that is true which results from a rational exercise of the mind upon the data of the senses.

SUMMARY STATEMENT OF EARLIER VIEWS

Long before Plato these issues had been raised by Greek thinkers. No classical Greek ever believed that the gods revealed, in our ordinary meaning of this term, any kind of truth. What these gods revealed made the best thinkers among the Greeks a bit ashamed. Some effort was necessary to transform the gods into upholders of a vague moral order. Some of the natural philosophers had been inclined, like Heraclitus, to see reality only in terms of the perpetual change or flux apparent to our senses, or, like Democritus, to conceive of it in the mechanistic terms of an atomic system. The Heraclitan view had been strengthened by those Sophists who, like Protagoras, talked about truth's being measured by the individual man, so that however arrived at, whether through the bare mechanism of

[42]See p. 93.
[43]See pp. 643 f.

the senses, or through reason, or through a combination of both, it had no permanent or enduring value. Some of the earlier philosophers, Parmenides for instance, had conceived of an eternally real unity behind the illusory, transient world of the senses. And Socrates, in opposition to the scientific materialists and the Sophists, thought that truth was essentially a body of moral principles, intelligible to man through the use of his reason.

Now Plato, following his master Socrates, rejected the Sophists' notion of relative truth, refused to identify the Heraclitan flux with reality, and returned rather to the tradition of Parmenides. According to Plato there is no real knowledge about individual things in the transient world to be gained through the senses. The world revealed in this way is actually unreal, an illusion, a dream. At best it supplies a type of knowledge of an inferior order, which is to be described as opinion and not truth. To have opinions about the world revealed through the senses is to know nothing truthful about it, even though the opinions themselves may be useful. What you can know, what is the immutable and eternal truth, has to do with the common characteristics of the individual things in a changing world. These are the qualities which classify them. These are the universal characteristics of particulars.

PLATO'S IDEAS, OR FORMS

One can, for example, know what man is, but not through an approach to the individual men of his acquaintance. About these he can only have opinions based upon experiences with them. When he begins to compare men with other men he discovers that they have common qualities. They all seem to have the capacity to reason; they are rational, they possess rationality. Rationality, one says, is a quality of mankind. Or upon further analysis it is discovered that individual men have certain human qualities; they are just, temperate, virtuous, or brave. They are possessed of certain qualities of humanity. These qualities are what Plato called ideas, or forms.

Plato's notion is that only these general ideas, concepts, or universals are knowable: man, rationality, justice, temperance, virtue, courage, and humanity. We come to know or understand them through that part of our soul which he identifies with our reasoning faculty. The ideas, then, constitute reality; they are the substance of truth. Plato, moreover, regarded these ideas as possessing a peculiar spiritual reality of their own utterly different from the physical substance of those individual things we know through the senses. He went so far as to insist that the world about us is real only in so far as it partakes of, reflects, shares in, imitates, or has actually assimilated this higher and different world of reality. A man is human in so far as he reflects the true idea of humanity, just in so far as he partakes of justice, rational in so far as he shares in the real quality of rationality. It is accordingly only the intelligible world of the understanding that is true, real, permanent, and eternal. It alone gives meaning and value to the sensations imparted by the external world. It is therefore only the unsensed world of the general concept that can be really known. This constitutes the absolute and unchanging truth of which our world is but a pale reflection and toward which it ever aspires. If we care to use the more speculative language of the metaphysician we may say that about us is an unreal, evanescent world of becoming. The world of being consists of real, absolute, and true ideas.

THE PLATONIC THEORY OF IDEAS

Because Plato uses the word "idea" or "form" to define these general concepts, the above is a statement of what is called his "theory of ideas." In the Platonic sense, one who believes in the reality of the ideas alone is an idealist or, in the medieval sense, a realist. In the sense that this ideal reality is unvarying they are both absolutist. The theory can be best illustrated from Plato's *Parmenides*, in which he offers many objections to it, and from the *Phaedo*. In the former Socrates asks Zeno, a follower of Parmenides, "But tell me, do you not believe there is an idea of likeness in the abstract, and another idea of unlikeness, the opposite of the first, and that you and I and all things which we call many partake of these two? And that those which partake of likeness become like, and those which partake of unlikeness become unlike, and those which partake of both become both like and unlike, all in the manner and degree of their participation?" Socrates assents when Parmenides asks, "Do you think there is such a thing as abstract likeness apart from the likeness which we possess . . . ? And also . . . abstract ideas of the just, the beautiful, the good, and all such conceptions?" (Fowler, No. 167, pp. 207-211) In the *Phaedo*, Simmias agrees with Socrates that there is "such a thing as absolute justice" and "absolute beauty and goodness" which cannot be seen or reached with the eyes or "any of the bodily senses." Socrates goes on, "I am speaking of all such things, as size, health, strength, and in short the essence or underlying quality of everything. Is their true nature contemplated by means of the body? Is it not rather the case that he who prepares himself most carefully to understand the true essence of each thing that he examines would come nearest to the knowledge of it?" Further Socrates insists: "Would not that man do this most perfectly who approaches each thing, so far as possible, with the reason alone, not introducing sight into his reasoning nor dragging in any of the other senses along with his thinking, but who employs pure, absolute reason in his attempt to search out the pure, absolute essence of things, and who removes himself, so far as possible, from eyes and ears, and, in a word, from his whole body, because he feels that its companionship disturbs the soul and hinders it from attaining truth and wisdom? Is not this the man, Simmias, if anyone, to attain to the knowledge of reality?" (No. 167, pp. 227-229)

The most important of the ideas that one must know are the moral ideas, since these give reality to human conduct. They can be known through the exercise of the rational faculty of the soul. They may also be glimpsed at rare moments through the operation of the passionate or erotic faculty of the soul driven by love. An awareness of the reality of the ideas may be cultivated by training the rational faculty in dialectics, advancing from a low and narrow generality to a higher and broader generality to the highest and best generality, which is goodness, or it may be God. For this ascent the disciplines of logic and mathematics are essential. At moments even Plato, like the Pythagoreans, is inclined to see truth clothed in a mathematical, that is, geometrical, form. Yet the final awareness of reality is often in the nature of an intuitive flash, a spark of divine madness, that is to be associated with the mystic's approach to the truth. One may speak, therefore, of Plato's intellectual mysticism.

This mysticism is best illustrated by the *Symposium*, in which Socrates and other Athenian notables, under the stimulation of wine (Socrates drinks them all under the table), take to discoursing about love. Socrates has reached the point of explaining how it has been made clear to him that "what men love is simply and solely the good . . . they love it to be not merely theirs but theirs always" and that "from what has been admitted, we needs must yearn for immortality no less than for good, since love loves good to be one's own for ever. And hence it necessarily follows that love is of immortality." Socrates then proceeds to give instruction on how one may come to know love of this exalted kind. The youth should begin by encountering "beautiful bodies" and come to "be in love with one particular body, and engender beautiful converse therein; but next he must remark how the beauty attached to this or that body is cognate to that which is attached to any other," and he will "regard as one and the same the beauty belonging to all." Thus he becomes not a lover of beauty in one body but "a lover of all beautiful bodies. . . . But his next advance will be to set a higher value on the beauty of souls than on that of the body." Then he will be "constrained to contemplate the beautiful as appearing in our observances and our laws. . . . From observances he should be led on to the branches of knowledge, that there also he may behold a province of beauty, and by looking thus on beauty in the mass may escape from the mean, meticulous slavery of a single instance . . . and turning rather towards the main ocean of the beautiful may by contemplation of this bring forth in all their splendour many fair fruits of discourse and meditation in a plenteous crop of philosophy; until with the strength and increase there acquired he descries a certain single knowledge connected with a beauty which has yet to be told. . . . When a man has been thus far tutored in the lore of love, passing from view to view of beautiful things, in the right and regular ascent, suddenly he will have revealed to him, as he draws to the close of his dealings in love, a wondrous vision, beautiful in its nature . . . [the beautiful] existing ever in singularity of form independent by itself, while all the multitude of beautiful things partake of it in such wise that, though all of them are coming to be and perishing, it grows neither greater nor less, and is affected by nothing." Socrates puts it in other words. One proceeds "from personal beauty . . . to beautiful observances, from observance to beautiful learning, and from learning at last to that particular study which is concerned with the beautiful itself and that alone; so that in the end [one] comes to know the very essence of beauty. . . . In that state of life above all others . . . a man finds it truly worth while to live, as he contemplates essential beauty. . . . What would happen if one of you had the fortune to look upon essential beauty entire, pure and unalloyed; not infected with the flesh and colour of humanity, and ever so much more of mortal trash? What if he could behold the divine beauty itself, in its unique form? . . . There only will it befall him, as he sees the beautiful through that which makes it visible, to breed not illusions but true examples of virtue, since his contact is not with illusion but with truth. So when he has begotten a true virtue and has reared it up he is destined to win the friendship of Heaven; he, above all men, is immortal." (Lamb, No. 166, pp. 189-209)

THE PHILOSOPHER AS KING

Not all men, in Plato's view, can reach these heights of understanding. They are reserved chiefly for philosophers. To the degree that one can reach them one is in a position to order his life in accordance with true ends. The search for an understanding of the ideas leads to the only worthy art of living. The person, therefore, who achieves a complete knowledge of the truth of the ideas is the person who should direct those who remain in a state of incomplete knowledge. Thus, ideally the philosopher should be king.

THE "TIMAEUS"

This approach to the knowledge of truth in Plato's old age terminates in religion. Not in the sense that truth is a revelation of God, but that these things that man aspires to understand and to live by are apart from man's ordinary world—permanent, immutable, eternal, and thus divine. Man is himself, as in the case of the mysteries, capable of sharing in divinity. It is not easy to determine exactly what Plato means by God. At one moment he seems to equate him with the idea of the good, as goodness or righteousness itself. At another, God is conceived of as the highest of many kinds of soul, the soul being defined as the source of life and motion, God thus becoming the formal source of life, the first cause of motion. In the *Timaeus*, Plato's elaborate and difficult treatise on cosmology, there is sketched the pattern of a god, responsible for creating the universe and for giving it a soul, the soul of the universe, and thus a divine purpose. God created the universe, using the forms or ideas as archtypes. God thus framed the universe in accordance with truth. But the ideas were impressed upon a primeval chaos, and thus the universe was but a reflection of, a sharer in, an aspirant of, the ideal world of God's truth. In this scheme human souls are made of the material left over from the creation of the soul of the universe, and thus are divine. Plato at no time abandoned the employment of the term *gods*, but we can be sure that he did not conceive of them in a popular sense.

PLATO AS A RELIGIOUS TEACHER AND THEOLOGIAN

Platonism, moreover, is religious in that it utilizes the Orphic doctrine of the dualism of soul and body. In the *Phaedo* Socrates insists that "so long as we have the body, and the soul is contaminated by such an evil, we shall never attain completely what we desire, that is, the truth. . . . If we are ever to know anything absolutely, we must be free from the body and must behold the actual realities with the eye of the soul alone. . . . And while we live, we shall, I think, be nearest to knowledge when we avoid, so far as possible, intercourse and communion with the body, except what is absolutely necessary, and are not filled with its nature, but keep ourselves pure from it until God himself sets us free." Then, "being pure, we shall, I think, be with the pure and shall know of ourselves all that is pure,—and that is, perhaps, the truth." Since death is "the release and separation of the soul from the body . . . the true philosophers practise dying, and death is less terrible to them than to any other men. . . . Shall he who is really in love with wisdom and has a firm belief that he can find it nowhere else than in the other world grieve when he dies and not be glad to go there?" (No. 36, pp. 229-235) In all this there is an ascetic, otherworldly note. The humanistic optimism for this world gives way to pessimism. Man is only happy when he is immortal. In the *Laws* Plato becomes authoritarian and excludes from society the heretic who is an atheist, or, if a believer in gods, thinks they are not interested in men or that they can be bribed to do what men wish.

Plato may thus be called a theologian, a rationalist theologian who, rejecting the sophist "man is the measure of all things," substitutes God for man. It would not be accurate to say that Plato became a convert of the Hebraic point of view. His monotheism is not Yahwism. If God be self-existent goodness, the embodiment of all truth, or if he be the highest soul, he is at least no tyrant imposing his truth upon mankind. Rather, he is the intelligible creature of human reason, discoverable through man's noblest faculties, and once discovered or understood, the object of imitation upon earth. Man is to be the "friend of God" and not his servant. It is quite obvious how easily Christianity could become Platonic.

POLITICAL EFFORTS

Plato's dominant interest, like that of every good Greek, was political, namely, to create a moral *polis*. This is evident from his most extensive dialogues, the *Republic* and the *Laws*. When offered the opportunity to transform the tyrants of Syracuse into philosophers he attempted it but did not succeed. He then thought to establish a training school for philosophers, the first university of its kind. In a grove sacred to the hero Academus he set up his Academy, the inscription over whose door is said to have reminded entering students that without a knowledge of geometry they might not hope to succeed. Here Plato continued to write and teach until he died, an old man of eighty. His Academy lived on after him, a center of philosophic study in the Mediterranean world, until closed by the Christian Byzantine emperor Justinian in A.D. 529.

ARISTOTLE

The most brilliant student of this Academy was Aristotle. He came to Athens at the age of eighteen from Stagira on the Chalcidice peninsula. At Athens he had the incomparable advantage of studying for twenty years with the most distinguished philosopher of all Greece. Just as the personal association of Socrates and Plato brought forth the exciting Platonic dialogues, so the close and prolonged association of Plato and Aristotle produced, if not the exciting, then the tough, rugged, at times baffling and dull, but withal amazing and inspiring formal treatises of Aristotle. After Plato's death (347 B.C.) Aristotle withdrew for a short while to Asia Minor, whence he was called by Philip of Macedon to act as tutor for his son Alexander. How fruitful this association was can be judged only from the career of Alexander himself. For Aristotle it had the subsequent advantage of providing him, through Alexander's munificence, with the means for pursuing research upon a large scale. When Alexander became a regent of Macedon, Aristotle returned to Athens and founded the Lyceum, a companion school to Plato's Academy. There he walked and talked with his students and delivered formal lectures on the subjects with which he was wrestling in his own mind. After Alexander's death he was caught in a wave of anti-Macedonian feeling that swept over Athens and was suspected of unorthodox religious opinions. Rather, he said with Socrates in mind, than permit Athens a second time to sin against philosophy, he withdrew to Chalcis on the island of Euboea, where he died in 322 B.C., when Alexander's empire was breaking to pieces.

ARISTOTLE ON POLITICS

No more can be indicated here than how Aristotle exemplifies the spirit of Greek humanism and what his immense importance has been for the intellectual history of the western world. He has already been encountered as the author of the *Politics*, subordinating ethics to politics and the individual to his community, and emphasizing, as Plato had emphasized in the *Republic*, the importance of the state as the setting for the achievement of noble living.[44] The best form of society for such a state, he

44See p. 96.

thought, was a mean between two extremes, one in which the middle class predominated. It has also been noted[45] that he was strangely indifferent to the political revolution shaking the Greek and eastern Mediterranean worlds of his day. While a world empire was being shaped by his former pupil he clung to the notion that the best political organization for the Greek peoples was their ancient *polis*. This primary concern with politics as a means of promoting the good life and his desire to make the standards of private morality prevail in the public domain emphasized old tenets of Greek humanism.

ARISTOTLE AND LEARNING

Aristotle introduces his *Metaphysics*, the most difficult of all his books and "probably the most difficult book in existence,"[46] with the remark that "all men naturally desire knowledge." This hits upon one of man's most redeeming features: the impetuous and irrepressible passion to explore the nature of his own being and that of the surrounding world. Certainly of all men Aristotle illustrates most vividly the driving impulse to know everything, not merely in the sense of being acquainted with the facts (although as a good scientist he was interested in the facts), but more in the sense of reducing the vast body of facts to interrelated principles that the human mind can comprehend. The scope of his learning, and he was one of the most learned of all men, can be indicated by mentioning the more important of his surviving treatises.

THE WORKS OF ARISTOTLE

For the writing of his *Politics*, Aristotle is known to have collected information on no less than 158 specific constitutions of the Greek states. His *Constitution of Athens* is a commentary on one of these. The *Politics*, to which the *Ethics* was an introduction, was undertaken "in order that the philosophy of human life may be made as complete as possible." Similar treatises related closely to civic life were the *Rhetoric*, knowledge of which was essential to one wishing to influence public opinion in a democratic state, and the *Poetics*, a consideration of the nature, structure, and purpose of drama, quite useful to the intelligent Athenian citizen. The moral, cultural, and political man was also seen as a part of the larger world of nature, which itself had to be regarded from the vantage point of the universe. Accordingly, in his *Physics*, Aristotle set about to consider the nature of the physical world, and in his monumental *History of Animals*, based on large-scale co-operative research, he created the science of biology. After the *Physics* he wished to consider the most fundamental questions of human existence, the problems involved in the first philosophy. This first philosophy he was inclined to identify with theology.

---

[45]See p. 95.
[46]Gilbert Norwood and J. W. Duff, *The Writers of Greece and Rome*, p. 112.

"If there is not some other substance besides those which are naturally composed, physics will be the primary science; but if there is a substance which is immutable, the science which studies this will be prior to physics, and will be primary philosophy, and universal in this sense, that it is primary. And it will be the province of this science to study Being *qua* Being; what it is, and what the attributes are which belong to it *qua* Being." (Tredennick, No. 271, pp. 297-299) Questions of this fundamental nature he considered in the *Metaphysics*.

THE WORKS ON LOGIC

Aristotle, moreover, felt it necessary to come to terms with the method of arriving at truth in all fields of learning. The mere satisfaction of idle curiosity, no matter how imperious, was not his concern. In the *Metaphysics* he says that "two innovations . . . may fairly be ascribed to Socrates: inductive reasoning and general definition. Both of these are associated with the starting-point of scientific knowledge." (No. 271, p. 197) Induction, as a method, Aristotle can define as "the process whereby, after experience of a certain number of particular instances, the mind grasps a universal truth which then and afterwards is seen to be self-evident."[47] In other words, induction is the use of reason to arrive at valid generalizations, first principles, definitions, and axioms after a consideration of the facts elicited by observation and experiment. Aristotle went beyond this to invent deductive logic, or the method of arriving at truthful statements by considering the interrelationship of the valid generalizations, first principles, definitions, and axioms established by inductive reasoning. The particular form of statement invented by him in this connection is the syllogism. This consists of a preliminary generalization held as self-evident (the major premise), such as "the world cannot survive another war"; this is followed by a supplementary statement considered obvious (the minor premise), such as "another war is sure to come." These are then followed by the conclusion, "the world will not survive." This form of reasoning is the basis of Euclid's geometry. Aristotle explored all its possibilities in a series of six logical works which are collectively known as the *Organon* (Instrument), applicable to all the sciences (*The Categories, Concerning Interpretation, Prior Analytics, Posterior Analytics, Topics, Concerning Spurious Refutations*). Thus for all subsequent time Aristotle provided men with this new tool for sharpening their wits. His tough and capacious mind was evidently differentiating the fields of philosophy and science and marking the boundaries of their specific provinces. Philosophy was separated into the fields of metaphysics, politics, ethics, and aesthetics; science, into the physical and biological fields. Logic was the instrument with which to pursue them both. Only in the field of mathematics did Aristotle fail to display his all-round originality. Yet the work

[47]F. M. Cornford, "The Athenian Philosophical Schools," *Cambridge Ancient History*, VI, 340-341.

he accomplished was enough to establish him even for subsequent ages as, in Dante's words, "the master of those who know." To many today the only cure for the contemporary scourge of vague, undifferentiated imaginings that often are called thought is to begin again with Aristotle.

ARISTOTLE'S "ETHICS"

It is worth illustrating from the *Ethics*, and from Aristotle's modification of Plato's point of view, his essential reasonableness and the stability he gave to Greek humanism after its rather lofty flight with Plato. We may take the priority of the *Ethics* to the *Politics* to mean that Aristotle thought that there was little hope in the mere form which a political society took if that form were not based on the moral character of the individual citizen actively expressed. Although he recognizes that there is conduct which is involuntary, yet he places squarely upon the shoulders of every individual the responsibility for making the right rather than the wrong decisions, and for acting in accordance with these decisions. This responsibility he bases upon his faith in the power of man's reason to make the proper choice between alternatives. "The function of man," Aristotle says in the *Ethics*, is "the active exercise of the soul's faculties in conformity with rational principle," and of a good man, "to perform these activities well and rightly," that is, "in conformity with excellence or virtue, or if there be several human excellences or virtues, in conformity with the best and most perfect among them. Moreover this activity must occupy a complete lifetime." (Rackham, No. 73, p. 33)

THE DOCTRINE OF THE GOLDEN MEAN

This action in accordance with virtue brings man his chief good, which is happiness, "a form of good life or doing well . . . the best, the noblest, and the pleasantest of things," but withal a virtue which Aristotle is frank to acknowledge cannot easily be practiced without "the addition of external prosperity." Since happiness is to be associated with virtuous action, Aristotle feels obliged to consider the nature of virtue, which he regards as being intellectual (wisdom, prudence), or moral (liberality, temperance), and not physical, and to be acquired only through practice. "Moral dispositions are formed as a result of the corresponding activities. . . . We have consequently to carry our enquiry into the region of conduct, and to ask how we are to act rightly; since our actions, as we have said, determine the quality of our dispositions." In the case of virtuous actions it is what Aristotle calls "excess and deficiency" which are fatal. "The man who runs away from everything in fear and never endures anything becomes a coward; the man who fears nothing whatsoever but encounters everything becomes rash. Similarly he that indulges in every pleasure and refrains from none turns out a profligate, and he that shuns all pleasure, as boorish persons do, becomes what may be called insensible. Thus Temperance and Courage are destroyed by excess and deficiency, and preserved by the observance of the mean. . . . Virtue, therefore, is a mean state in the sense that it is able to hit the mean." It is "a settled disposition of the mind determining the choice of actions and emotions, consisting essentially in the observance of the mean relative to us, this being determined by principle, that is, as the prudent man would determine it." This is the doctrine of the golden mean (*aurea mediocritas*, in the words of the Roman poet Horace). "Nothing too much" was another way the Greeks had of putting it.[48]

In bringing the *Ethics* to conclusion, Aristotle returns again to the notion of happiness. Earlier, in his discussion of friendship, he felt obliged to consider the question of the propriety of self-love. In so doing he emphasizes again man's rationality as his noblest quality. "The terms 'self-restrained' and 'unrestrained' denote being restrained or not by one's intellect, and thus imply that the intellect is the man himself. Also . . . it is our reasoned acts that are felt to be in the fullest sense *our own* acts, *voluntary* acts. It is therefore clear that a man is or is chiefly the dominant part of himself, and that a good man values this part of himself most. Hence the good man will be a lover of self in the fullest degree, though in another sense than the lover of self so-called by way of reproach, from whom he differs as much as living by principle differs from living by passion, and aiming at what is noble from aiming at what seems expedient." (No. 73, p. 553)

ARISTOTLE ON HAPPINESS

Happiness, then, man's chief good, is to be achieved through action, meaning the action of man's noblest faculty, his reason, in choosing the mean between the extremes of excess and deficiency as a guide for further action. Happiness is to be associated with reason. "That happiness consists in contemplation may be accepted as agreeing both with the results already reached and with the truth. For contemplation is . . . the highest form of activity (since the intellect is the highest thing in us, and the objects with which the intellect deals are the highest things that can be known). . . . Activity in accordance with wisdom is admittedly the most pleasant of the activities in accordance with virtue." Aristotle is inclined to see in this life of reason something more than merely human. "Such a life as this however will be higher than the human level: not in virtue of his humanity will a man achieve it, but in virtue of something within him that is divine; and by as much as this something is superior to his composite nature, by so much is its activity superior to the exercise of the other forms of virtue. If then the intellect is something divine in comparison with man,

[48]In Chap. vii of Bk. II of the *Ethics*, Aristotle gives what is virtually a table of the mean states between the excesses and deficiencies of the chief virtues. Magnificence, for example, is a mean between vulgarity and meanness; wittiness, between buffoonery and boorishness; modesty, between bashfulness and shamelessness. He then goes on to discuss these mean virtues in some detail.

so is the life of the intellect divine in comparison with human life. Nor ought we to obey those who enjoin that a man should have man's thoughts and a mortal the thoughts of mortality, but we ought so far as possible to achieve immortality, and do all that man may to live in accordance with the highest thing in him; for though this be small in bulk, in power and value it far surpasses all the rest." (No. 73, pp. 613, 617) According to Aristotle, then, the speculative wisdom with which contemplation is concerned, in other words, the activity of the philosopher, is the highest, best, most divine, and, indeed, most practical human activity.

ARISTOTLE ON GOD

This deification of man's reasoning faculty is carried to further lengths in the *Metaphysics*. There, as a means of explaining the origin of the movement which he saw in the heavens and on earth—and he included in the idea of movement the growth and decay of organic nature—he posited a first or prime mover, himself unmoved. There, as a means of describing the origin of his system of causes, which explained the development of individual things, he set up a first, or final, cause. This prime mover and first cause he called God, and to it (it is hardly accurate here to use the anthropomorphic *him*) he gave as its only function pure contemplation, and contemplation unrelated to anything else but contemplation, pure "thinking about thinking." He stated it as follows in the *Metaphysics*: "There is something—X—which moves while being itself unmoved. . . . For the primary kind of change is locomotion, and of locomotion circular locomotion; and this is the motion which X induces. Thus X is necessarily existent; and *qua* necessary it is good, and is in this sense a first principle. . . . Such, then, is the first principle upon which depend the sensible universe and the world of nature. And its life is like the best which we temporarily enjoy . . . its active contemplation is that which is most pleasant and best. If, then, the happiness which God always enjoys is as great as that which we enjoy sometimes, it is marvellous; and if it is greater, this is still more marvellous. Nevertheless it is so. Moreover, life belongs to God. For the actuality of thought is life, and God is that actuality; and the essential actuality of God is life most good and eternal. We hold, then, that God is a living being, eternal, most good; and therefore life and a continuous eternal existence belong to God; for that is what God is. . . . It causes motion as being an object of love, whereas all other things cause motion because they are themselves in motion." (No. 287, pp. 149, 151) If the ordinary Greek's concept of the gods reflected much of himself, the God of Aristotle is a deification of the rational, contemplative faculty of the Greek philosopher.

Aristotle's monotheism is intellectual rather than religious. Unconcerned with the creation or the end of the world, this God is neither a creator nor a final judge of man's conduct. He is not even man's provider. When Christianity came to use Aristotle to bolster up its theology, these omissions, pointed out by Mohammedan students of Aristotle,[49] proved embarrassing. Aristotle's God is indifferent to the world; he does not in fact know the world. He exists only as the intellectual necessity to explain how the world moves. He is quite unconcerned with morality. The isolated suggestion that he "causes motion as being an object of love" Aristotle does not analyze or develop. Aristotle places man's fate in human rather than divine hands; he makes it dependent upon the proper exercise of what is man's chief glory, his divine reason. The time was to come when Plato's idea of the good and Aristotle's unmoved mover were to be fused with Yahweh to form the Christian God. Such a fusion, however, doubtless would have astounded both Plato and Aristotle.

ARISTOTLE AND PLATO

Aristotle discarded some of Plato's essential teachings, without at the same time discarding what was meant to be their emphasis. Plato assumed a real world of ethereal universals knowable through the exercise of dialectical reasoning. The world of the senses was real only in so far as it caught hold in some vague way of this eternal other world. To Aristotle this seemed nonsense. The real world was not the superstructure of intelligible ideas or forms. It was the actual world of particulars in which we live.[50] It is not humanity that is real; it is the individual man. Aristotle, however, did not discard the notion of the universal, or idea, or form. He used it to explain how the real individual thing becomes what it is.

THE DOCTRINE OF CAUSES

An individual man is the product of something called matter and the idea, or form, of humanity. The form of humanity determines the growth of the matter of the child into a particular, real man. The form of the oak tree determines the growth of the matter of the acorn into a particular, real oak tree. Aristotle employs other language to elucidate this process of becoming real. He uses, for example, a doctrine of causes to explain it. These causes he lists as four: the material, the efficient, the formal, and the final causes. To explain an individual, real marble statue of a victor at the Olympic games would be to explain how a block of marble (the material cause) is chipped away by the sculptor (the efficient cause) in accordance with what he thinks the statue of the Olympian victor ought to be (the formal cause), thus revealing at the completion of his work the finished statue (the final cause). Or, to return to the example of the individual real man, in the language of the *Metaphysics*, "What is the material cause of a man? The menses. What is the moving [efficient] cause? The semen. What is the formal cause? The essence. What is the final cause? The end."

[49]See p. 651.
[50]Generally speaking, this is what the medieval scholastics called the nominalist (rather than the realist) position. See p. 644.

This doctrine of causes reduces the explanation of organic change producing the real to the combining of matter and form. Aristotle also uses the concepts of potentiality and actuality to explain this process. The marble is potentially a statue; it is actually one when it has achieved its proper form. The child is potentially a man; it is actually a man when it has achieved its proper form. Thus in Aristotle's general scheme of things there is the notion of purpose, known technically as teleology. It is the purpose of matter to realize its appropriate form. While there is the suggestion in Aristotle that God is the most perfect form (or being, or essence) and that the purpose of the world is to realize this perfection, there is no development of this notion. Aristotle never says that the forms are God's purpose for the world. God has no purpose for the world. He does not love. We are thus left with the notion that the ideas or forms are the creation of man's reasoning faculty and are divine only in the sense that this faculty is divine. Man thus creates his own purpose in accordance with his best lights. He is ever struggling to transform the potentiality of his nature into the actuality of his most highly conceived ideals. In this way Aristotle preserves the aspiring character of the Platonic system. In this general sense, if not in the particular Platonic sense, he may be called an idealist.

PLATO AND ARISTOTLE AND MATHEMATICS

It has been remarked of Aristotle that "he dissected fishes with Plato's thoughts in his head."[51] This is essentially the method of modern science, the verification of a hypothesis by means of experiment. Together Plato and Aristotle, aside from their importance in philosophy, are the founders of modern science, the essence of whose method is the complementary employment of induction and deduction upon a given body of factual data. In a particular sense Plato is the father of modern science because of his divination of the importance of mathematics as a means to understand the workings of nature. Plato in his late years, profoundly impressed by the work of the Pythagoreans, came to regard the naked truths of mathematics as the essential truth of nature. The fundamental working principle of modern science has been to express its findings in mathematical formulas. Without the development of modern mathematics the progress of recent science is inconceivable. Newton's mathematical formulation of the law of gravitation and Einstein's formulation of the law of the transformation of matter into energy are two brilliant vindications of Plato's intuition.

[51]The selection from A. N. Whitehead, *Adventures of Ideas*, p. 136, copyright 1933 by The Macmillan Co., and used with The Macmillan Co.'s permission.

THE MUSEUM

After Aristotle's death the intellectual center of the eastern Mediterranean world shifted from Athens to the newly founded Alexandria. Here it was to remain until the formulation of Christian doctrine by eastern theologians seemed to make unnecessary any further concern with secular science. Theology, the queen of the sciences, at that subsequent moment established her rule. As a counterpart to the Academy and the Lyceum at Athens, which, of course, continued to function as learned institutions, the first of the Ptolemies founded the Museum. Here the best scientists and scholars of the eastern world gathered to teach and engage in research in what was the first state-endowed university. To enhance the glory of the theocratic successors of the Pharaohs, scholarship was provided with the best equipment available. Its chief resource was a magnificent library, variously estimated at from 400,000 to 700,000 volumes, which remained intact until A.D. 390, when it was in great part destroyed by what were believed to be the orders of Archbishop Theophilus. The end of the Museum itself came in 642 when the armies of the Caliph Omar occupied Alexandria. On this occasion he is reported to have said that "if these writings of the Greeks agree with the book of God [the Koran], they are useless, and need not be preserved; if they disagree, they are pernicious, and ought to be destroyed." Although the Arabs closed the Museum, at a later date they gave evidence of the finest scholarship and became munificent patrons of learning.[52]

HELLENISTIC CULTURE

The shift from the civilization of the Greek city-state to the civilization of Ptolemaic Egypt and the other Hellenistic[53] centers of the East was accompanied by a transformation in the character of learning and scholarship. If the earlier Hellenism was an attempt to realize in all provinces of the human spirit "a great ideal of perfection," in the Hellenistic epoch its genius turned to the foundation of "the special sciences" and the stabilization of learning. Learning was thus "furnished with methodologies, and was handed over to university professors of the modern type. Doctors of Medicine, Mathematicians, Astronomers, Grammarians, Theologians, for more than six hundred years dominated the schools of Alexandria, issuing text-books, treatises, controversies, and dogmatic definitions. Literature was replaced by Grammar, and Speculation by the Learned Tradition."[54] The grammarian's funeral would be celebrated later.

[52]See pp. 496 f.
[53]See p. 87.
[54]The selection from A. N. Whitehead, *Adventures of Ideas*, p. 133, copyright 1933 by The Macmillan Co., and used with The Macmillan Co.'s permission.

The Hellenistic scholar brought to fruition work which had been begun by the Greeks in mathematics, astronomy, and medicine.[55] It was in the former field that the Greek capacity for, and insistence upon, clear, logical thinking found a characteristic and distinguished outlet. Greek science was essentially mathematical; when it had run its course arithmetical theory had been founded, geometry completed until the days of Descartes, and algebra, trigonometry, and the integral calculus adumbrated if not worked out in detail. It was the genius of the Greeks which lifted mathematics from a practical method of measurement to a highly abstract form of numerical and figurative deductive logic. The Pythagoreans were concerned with arithmetic not as a means of counting but as a theory of numbers (odd, even, prime, perfect, amicable), and with the possibility that number might be the actual real substance of the universe. The revelation that back of the pleasure of musical sound lay the reality of numerical proportion contributed to this notion. It was Pythagoras who discovered the proportion between the sounds of the octave and the lengths of the strings giving forth the sound. The Pythagoreans are also credited with puzzling over the peculiar features of such a number as the $\sqrt{2}$. This is not the kind of problem which disturbs many people, but it can be understood that for one who can give a precise characterization of the kind of numbers represented by our Arabic numerals, and who sees in these numbers a representation of actual reality, a precise definition of what the $\sqrt{2}$ is might be confusing. One who knew the proof of the Pythagorean theorem and who used it to determine the length of the diagonal of a ten-inch square might well wonder about a hypotenuse that was represented by the symbol $\sqrt{200}$. This kind of number is what is now called an irrational number. Its nature continued to puzzle subsequent Greek mathematicians and it is still a subject of controversy in the modern foundations of mathematics. Yet the original work of the Pythagoreans was not notably augmented by succeeding mathematicians. What was accomplished was conveniently summarized by, among others, a Syrian scholar, Nicomachus of Gerasa (*ca.* A.D. 150). Nicomachus's *Introduction to Arithmetic* is of especial interest inasmuch as its translation by Boethius[56] made it the starting point for the study of arithmetic in western Europe.

GREEK GEOMETRY

In geometry the Greeks left no field uncultivated. Clouds of dust arose from the geometrical figures drawn in sand upon the floors of the palace of Dionysius II of Syracuse when Plato was attempting to teach his court-

[55]Since the chief Hellenistic philosophies, Stoicism and Epicureanism, were further developed by the Romans, they will be considered in Chap. vi, "The Romans and Greek Humanism."
[56]See pp. 414 ff.

iers how to be wise and virtuous. By the time of Pythagoras the Greeks had reached the point of rediscovering what is now known as the Pythagorean theorem (known to Babylonian mathematicians), that the square of the hypotenuse of a right triangle is equal to the sum of the squares of the other two sides, "a corner-stone—perhaps *the* corner-stone —of the science of geometry."[57] They proved also that the sum of the three angles of a triangle is equal to two right angles. And they gave much attention to the properties of the regular solids, of which they knew four (cube, tetrahedron, octahedron, and icosahedron). So much work was done by the fifth century that it could be summarized in the first textbook of geometry by Hippocrates of Chios (*ca.* 470) and lead to such problems as the squaring of a circle, the trisection of any angle, and the duplication of a cube. Eudoxus (408–355 B.C.) extended the field of geometry by investigating methods for measuring curvilinear areas and solids. Menaechmus (375–325) initiated the study of conic sections (ellipses, parabolas, and hyperbolas). By the end of the third century there was room for another summary, the summary to end all summaries, Euclid's (*ca.* 330–275) *Elements of Geometry.* "No work presumably, except the Bible, has had such a reign; and future generations will come back to it again and again as they tire of the variegated substitutes for it and the confusion resulting from their bewildering multiplicity."[58] Euclid was the curator and librarian of the mathematical division of the library of the Museum. "To him belongs indisputably the merit of having developed and coordinated into a faultless logic all the geometrical work accomplished before him."[59] It is difficult to imagine the influence of this one book in disciplining the young minds of countless generations. If it is being supplemented today by non-Euclidean geometries to meet the needs of a new physics, the new geometries can do no better than to employ Euclid's rather spectacular application of Aristotle's deductive logic.

Euclid's *Principles* did not stop further geometrical speculation. Apollonius of Perga (second half of the third century B.C.), continuing the work of Menaechmus and his successors, wrote a work on conic sections of such inclusiveness that it was not superseded for centuries. The great Archimedes (287–212 B.C.) was a prolific writer of original mathematical treatises. Continuing the work of Eudoxus on the measurement of curvilinear areas and solids, he was responsible for πr^2 as the area of a circle, $4 \pi r^2$ and $\frac{4}{3} \pi r^3$ for the surface and volume of a sphere, and similar formulas for cones and pyramids. He improved upon Eudoxus' method of finding the area of a circle by inscribing in it ever-more-sided regular polygons to exhaust the area and approach the circumference; and by then circumscribing the circle as well with similar figures approaching its circumference, he is credited with the invention of the infinitesimal integral

[57]Sir James Jeans, *The Growth of Physical Science*, p. 30.
[58]T. L. Heath, "Mathematics and Astronomy," *Legacy*, p. 120.
[59]A. Reymond, *History of the Sciences in Graeco-Roman Antiquity*, p. 67.

calculus. In so doing he arrived at a figure for π between 3.1409 and 3.1429 that was only improved upon by Apollonius himself. Diophantus (*ca.* 250 B.C.) is credited with the introduction of symbols for numerals in arithmetic to initiate algebra. Hipparchus of Nicaea (*ca.* 190–120 B.C.) invented trigonometry. The *Sphaerica* of Menelaus (*ca.* A.D. 100) used spherical trigonometry. After a period of stagnation, an attempt was made by Pappus (end of the third century A.D.) to revive geometrical study by a comprehensive survey (the *Collection*) of the whole field from its very beginnings. Thereafter mathematics slumbered in the Christian world until reawakened by the Arabs[60] and by the introduction of these very works into the learned circles of the West.

GREEK ASTRONOMY

In astronomy likewise, with the help of the work at Seleucia and in the observatory of the Museum and with the application of their mathematics to the heavens, the Greeks were able to systematize the work of the Babylonians so that the geocentric theory of the universe was considered irrefutable until the time of Copernicus.[61] The same daring speculation, however, that produced such notable results in philosophy and mathematics led also to the conception of a heliocentric universe. This Greek conception was, in fact, the starting point for Copernicus's own later restatement of the theory. But, while typically concerned with the general nature of the universe, the Greeks also developed more precise notions of the particular relations of the earth to the sun, the planets, and the fixed stars, and of the very size and motion of the earth itself.

The Greek universe was a limited and finite one, spherical in shape, the motion of whose parts was circular. Its center was the earth. Different geometrical theories were held to explain the relationship of the circular movements of the stars, planets, sun, and earth to each other. What came to be the classic work in defense of this geocentric universe was written by the Alexandrian astronomer Ptolemy (*ca.* A.D. 168) and known in the Greek as the *Syntaxis*, in the Arabic as *al-Majisti*, and in the corrupted English form as the *Almagest*. It was the mathematical structure of this work that Copernicus, with the aid of the contrary Greek theories, undermined.

Pythagoras was the first to maintain that the centrally located earth was spherical in shape. His followers Hicetas and Philolaus were already conceiving that the earth, sun, moon, and the planets made a circular rotation about a "central fire." Anaxagoras was clear about the sun's illumination of the moon, and of the moon's eclipse when it comes within the shadow of the earth. Heracleides of Pontus (388–315 B.C.) held to the notion that the sun and major planets revolve around a fixed earth rotating on its axis once every twenty-four hours, but that Venus and Mercury revolve

[60]See pp. 496 f.
[61]See p. 7.

about the moving sun. Finally Aristarchus of Samos (*ca.* 310–230 B.C.), in the words of Archimedes, refuted the definition of "the term world, as it is defined by most astronomers," namely, "a sphere of the heavens, whose center coincides with the center of the earth, and whose semi-diameter is the distance from the center of the earth to the center of the sun." He has given it "a far more extensive signification; for according to his hypothesis, neither the fixed stars nor the sun are subject to any motion; but the earth annually revolves round the sun in the circumference of a circle, in the center of which the sun remains fixed."[62]

This original displacement of man's home from the center of the universe was, unfortunately, not taken seriously. It was Ptolemy rather than Aristarchus who determined man's notion of the universe until the sixteenth century A.D. There was no organized Christian Church to threaten Aristarchus as an early Galileo with torture for his boldness. There were, however, comparable frames of mind. At least we are informed that Cleanthes the Stoic thought that Aristarchus ought to be indicted on the charge of impiety for setting the hearth of the universe in motion.

The above constitute but a part of the remarkable scientific accomplishments of the Greeks. Aristarchus was interested in the size of the sun and moon when compared with the earth and in the distances between the heavenly bodies. He prepared better estimates on these matters than his predecessors. Eratosthenes (*ca.* 276–195 B.C.), the creator of geography, came within 225 miles of an accurate measurement of the circumference of the earth. Hipparchus of Nicaea (*ca.* 190–120 B.C.), learning from Eratosthenes, affirmed the importance by locating by means of latitude and longitude. "No one could tell whether Alexandria in Egypt were north or south of Babylon, without observing the latitudes. Again, the only means we possess of becoming acquainted with the longitudes of different places is afforded by the eclipses of the sun and moon." These men founded the branch of physics we know as optics. Archimedes established mechanics with his discovery of the laws of the lever (*On Plane Equilibriums*) and hydrostatics with his *On Floating Bodies*. Theophrastus (*ca.* 372–287 B.C.), the head of the Lyceum at Athens, applied Aristotle's system of classification of animals to plants and became the first "systematic botanist" (*Enquiry into Plants*). This brief mention of only outstanding names is perhaps enough to indicate the vital heritage of Greek and Alexandrian mathematics and science. Yet this science did not, in the end, penetrate beneath the upper stratum of the learned to shape the point of view of the large masses. The science of the older world of the Ancient Near East was for the few only. It had been concerned with magic and astrology. The power of these was not seriously limited by Greek science and mathematics. When the tyranny of the Hellenistic theocrats was supplanted by the tyranny of the Romans, the influence of magic and astrology was widened, and they became the foundation of popular re-

[62]G. W. Botsford and E. G. Sihler, *Hellenic Civilization*, p. 640.

ligion. Long before the victory of Christianity the popular and even the learned religion of the Roman Empire became increasingly astral. The summarizer of Greek astronomy, Ptolemy, felt obliged also to write a learned work on astrology (the *Tetrabiblos*).

GREEK MEDICINE

Nothing is more characteristic of the spirit of Greek humanism than application by Greek medicine of the method of science to the curing of disease. If in other fields of science examples of the application of the experimental method are limited, in Greek medicine there is abundant evidence of the regular employment of close observation of human disease in order to work out the nature of its causes and the methods of its cure. There is evidence likewise of the dissection of animals and dead human bodies in order to build up the store of anatomical facts upon which surgery and medical practice had to be based. Indeed, we are told that some Alexandrian physicians engaged in the inhuman practice, attributed recently to some Nazi physicians in German concentration camps, of experimenting upon living human bodies. At least the Roman writer Celsus (first century A.D.) reports that "Herophilus and Erasistratus . . . cut into criminals received from the kings out of prison, while living, and . . . observed, before breathing ceased, those things which nature formerly had kept under seal."[63]

The shift in point of view from one that regarded disease as the result of supernatural causes that could be cured by the intervention of a god to one that regarded it as the result of natural causes that could be cured by scientific treatment is, of course, striking. The Greek god of healing was Aesculapius, and it was a common Greek practice, taken over by the healing saints of the Christian Church, for those stricken with disease to spend the night in his temple, after proper offerings and sacrifice, in order that the god himself might intervene and effect a cure. An inscription recording such a cure runs as follows: "A man had an abdominal abscess. He saw a vision and thought that the god ordered the slaves who accompanied him to lift him up and hold him, so that his abdomen could be cut open. The man tried to get away, but his slaves caught him and bound him. So Aesculapius cut him open, rid him of the abscess, and then stitched him up again, releasing him from his bonds. Straightway he departed cured." The attitude behind the history of a probable case of diphtheria, as reported in the large collection of medical treatises known as the *Hippocratean Corpus*, is quite in contrast: "The woman with quinsy, who lodged with Aristion: her complaint began in the tongue; voice inarticulate; tongue red and parched. *First day*, shivered, then became heated. *Third day*, rigor, acute fever; reddish and hard swelling on both sides of neck and chest; extremities cold and livid; respiration elevated; drink returned by the nose; she could not swallow; alvine and urinary

[63]Botsford and Sihler, p. 632.

discharges suppressed. *Fourth day*, all symptoms exacerbated. *Fifth day*, she died." It is unfortunate that in this case the physician was not as successful as Aesculapius. He has not always been able to compete successfully with the god. But if men have learned to go to the physician as a first resort, and to the god only when all his art and science fail, it is because the physician deliberately set out to profit from his failures and to seek the natural causes of the diseases he was supposed to cure. The author of one of the treatises in the *Hippocratean Corpus* reports that "the Scythians attribute a certain physical disability to a god . . . but it appears to me that these affections are just as much divine as are all others and that no disease is either more divine or more human than another, but that all are equally divine, for each of them has its own nature, and none of them arise without a natural cause."[64]

Greek medicine illustrated Greek humanism in another way. It was not concerned with the use of scientific information merely to improve the lot of man, an attitude we may describe as scientific humanism. It approached its tasks in a large philosophic spirit related to the whole art of living and permeated with an ethical concern for the proprieties of medical practice. Scientific and philosophic medicine grew out of the early Greek concern with the nature of the world and man. It sought to make its knowledge an essential part of human culture. If early Greek medical writers gave doctors the advice which they have never taken seriously, namely, "it is particularly necessary in talking about this art to speak so that laymen can understand," they were uncertain at first whether, for successful medical practice, it was necessary to understand the general character of the world and man. The source of the above advice, for example, protests against the notion of some "physicians and sophists [that] no one can understand medicine without knowing what man is, how he originated, and what stuff he is made on." He was interested rather not in "what man is in himself, but 'what he is in relation to what he eats and drinks and how he lives and how all that affects him.' "[65]

In fact the Greeks were more interested in healthy living and in its relation to healthy thinking than they were in the mere curing of disease. It was the sound and beautiful body as the receptacle for the sound and beautiful spirit that they emphasized. The preservation of health and the prevention of disease made it possible for the human being to exercise all his capacities. Nature herself was the best doctor; the task of the physician was to make it possible for nature to function properly. They were quick to recognize the physician's incapacity to do more than assist nature. "Most doctors are like bad pilots. As long as the weather is all right their inexpertness is not noticeable, but in a bad storm everyone sees that they are useless. . . . The patient's nature is the doctor that cures his illness. . . . Nature finds her own ways and means, without conscious in-

[64]Charles Singer, "Medicine," *Legacy*, pp. 222, 220, 214.
[65]Jaeger, *Paideia*, III, 13, 18–19.

telligence."[66] The problem of curing disease was the problem of restoring nature to her proper equilibrium in order to permit her to carry on her curative functions. Lack of natural balance was conceived as the disproportion of wet, dry, hot, and cold qualities of the elements which made up the human body (air, earth, fire, water) and also as the improper mixture of bodily humors (blood, phlegm, yellow and black bile). The condition of health came from the proper harmony of the bodily factors. These it was the physician's job to maintain. Medical practice emphasized therefore proper hygiene and proper diet. This included the proper amount of exercise in the *palaestra* under the supervision of a gymnastic trainer to whom the physician was subordinate. Health was a matter of daily routine, part of the practice of an art of living.

An ideal routine can be illustrated from the advice of a well-known Greek physician, Diocles of Carystus, a younger contemporary of Aristotle, who practiced in Athens. It was necessary to get up before sunrise, but not to get up immediately upon waking but "wait till the heaviness of sleep leaves our limbs, and then rub our neck and head at the places where they pressed on the pillow." Upon rising the whole body should be rubbed "lightly and equally" with oil, and the joints flexed. "The hands should be washed and the face and eyes bathed in pure cold water." Teeth, nose, ears, hair, and scalp must then be attended to. For those who have work to do a morning walk before or after breakfast will have to be omitted. For those who have no work it is but a prelude for exercise. "Then young men should go to the gymnasium, and old people and invalids to the bath, or to some other sunny place, to be anointed with oil." Exercise must be proportioned to age. "For elderly men, it is enough to be gently massaged, to move about a little, and then to have a bath. . . . Luncheon . . . should be light and not filling, so that it can be digested before the gymnastics of the afternoon." It should be followed—wonderful counsel—by "a short siesta in a dark and cool, but not draughty, place; and then more business at home, a walk, and finally (after another short rest) the afternoon's exercise."[67] Dinner came before sunset in summer and later in winter.[68] This routine is obviously that of a gentleman of leisure who had nothing much more to do than to look after his health. It may be considered an ideal for the ordinary Greek. "And yet perhaps the life led by a citizen of a Greek city-state in the fourth century allowed him more time to spend on the culture of his spirit and the care of his body than any other life ever lived by man."[69]

HIPPOCRATES

The literature in which this early Greek medical practice is described (the *Hippocratean Corpus*) consists of some sixty or seventy treatises

[66]Jaeger, III, 18, 19.
[67]Jaeger, III, 42–43.
[68]Compare this with the daily routine of a good Stoic, p. 248.
[69]Jaeger, III, 44.

collected at Alexandria in the early third century B.C. The name comes from the attribution of much of it to the father of Greek medicine, Hippocrates of Cos, who was active around 400 B.C. "Hippocrates will ever remain the type of the perfect physician. Learned, observant, humane, with a profound reverence for the claims of his patients, but an overmastering desire that his experience shall benefit others, orderly and calm, disturbed only by anxiety to record his knowledge for the use of his brother physicians and for the relief of suffering, grave, thoughtful and reticent, pure of mind and master of his passions . . . the Father of Medicine . . . is a figure of character and virtue which has had an ethical value to medical men of all ages comparable only to the influence exerted on their followers by the founders of the great religions. If one needed a maxim to place upon the statue of Hippocrates, none could be found better than that from the book . . . *Precepts* [one of the Hippocratean collection]: 'where the love of man is, there also is love of the Art.' " This high ethical standard, not always followed by the modern physician who is preoccupied with the accumulation of wealth, is expressed in the words of the "Hippocratic oath, . . . the watchword of the profession of medicine: . . . I will look upon him who shall have taught me this art even as on mine own parents. . . . The regimen I adopt shall be for the benefit of the patients to the best of my power and judgment, not for their injury or for any wrongful purpose. I will not give a deadly drug to anyone, thought it be asked of me, nor will I lead the way in such counsel; and likewise I will not give a woman a pessary to procure abortion. But I will keep my life and my art in purity and holiness. Whatsoever house I enter, I will enter for the benefit of the sick, refraining from all voluntary wrongdoing and corruption, especially seduction of male or female, bond or free. Whatsoever things I see or hear concerning the life of men, in my attendance on the sick or even apart from my attendance, which ought not to be blabbed abroad, I will keep silence on them, counting such things to be as religious secrets. If I fulfil this oath and confound it not, be it mine to enjoy life and art alike, with good repute among all men for all time to come; but may the contrary befall me if I transgress and violate my oath."[70]

ALEXANDRIAN MEDICINE

The insufficiency of the training of earlier doctors in physiology, pathology, and anatomy was made good by the experimental school at Alexandria. The outstanding names here, mentioned above in connection with the vivisection of criminals, are Herophilus of Chalcedon and Erasistratus. The former is responsible for the discovery of "the function of the nerves and their classification into sensory and motor." For him the brain was the seat of the mind. He also discovered the function of the

[70]Singer, "Medicine," *Legacy*, pp. 212–214.

arteries in carrying blood pumped by the heart throughout the body, and therewith the importance of the pulse as an indication of health; that is, he knew the principle of the circulation of the blood. The Roman writer Pliny[71] refers to his discussion of the pulse: "The pulsation of the arteries is more perceptible on the surface of the limbs, and affords indications of nearly every disease, being either stationary, quickened or retarded, conformably to certain measures and metrical laws . . . described with remarkable skill by Herophilus, who has been regarded as a prophet in the wondrous art of medicine."[72] Erasistratus, a younger contemporary of Herophilus (third century B.C.), made many technical advances in the fields of Herophilus's chief interest.

GALEN

The creative period in Greek medicine was brought to a close by Galen (*ca.* A.D. 131), who, after studying in the East, became for a time the physician of Marcus Aurelius, and then returned to his birthplace at Pergamum to work and write. What Euclid was to geometry and Ptolemy to astronomy Galen was to Greek medicine. His works, constituting about one-half the total volume of the surviving Greek medical literature, comprise twenty-two volumes. Because of his intimate acquaintance with the whole history of the theory and practice of Greek medicine in its various fields, Galen, together with Hippocrates, dominated all subsequent medicine until at least the sixteenth century. He was a contentious and aggressive personality. He had no use for those physicians who saw no large purpose in the workings of nature. "Some of these people," he wrote, "have even expressly declared that the souls possess no reasoning faculty, but that we are led like cattle by the impression of our senses, and are unable to refuse or dissent from anything." Following Hippocrates, he rejected this notion. He wondered whether it was really possible to teach anything to the "moderns," and warned the young how necessary it is to dig in and work. "I am not, however, unaware that I shall achieve either nothing at all or else very little. For I find that a great many things which have been conclusively demonstrated by the Ancients are unintelligible to the bulk of the Moderns owing to their ignorance—nay, that, by reason of their laziness, they will not even make an attempt to comprehend them. . . . The fact is that he whose purpose is to know anything better than the multitude do must far surpass all others both as regards his nature and his early training. And when he reaches early adolescence he must become possessed with an ardent love for truth, like one inspired; neither day nor night may he cease to urge and strain himself in order to learn thoroughly all that has been said by the most illustrious of the Ancients. And when he has learnt this, then for a prolonged period he must test and prove it, observing what part of it is in agreement, and what in disagreement with

71See pp. 257 f.
72Botsford and Sihler, *Hellenic Civilization*, p. 634.

obvious fact. . . . To such an one my hope has been that my treatise would prove of the very greatest assistance. . . . Still, such people may be expected to be quite few in number, while, as for the others, this book will be as superfluous to them as a tale told to an ass."[73]

Greek Art

THE GREEKS AND ART

It would have been enough to merit our warm gratitude had the Greeks contented themselves with the accomplishments sketched above. But if man's history is distinguished by his love of knowledge and by the good uses to which that knowledge can be put, it is no less distinguished by his love of beauty and by the good uses to which that beauty can be put. Certainly it is one of the glories of the human being that he is so gifted artistically, and one of the great satisfactions of human existence that the products of his genius can be made to give joyous meaning and purpose to each day's life. The Greeks chose to emphasize man's aesthetic gifts and capacities no less than his reason. In their minds a successful life was conceived in terms of a lovely and proportionate art in which the parts were as beautiful as the whole, but were in part beautiful because they were harmoniously subordinate to the whole. An important ingredient in Greek education was music, a subject which included not only the enjoyment of beautiful sound but its enjoyment in relation to poetry and the dance. It is not easy to imagine what might happen to us as a people if from the earliest days of our youth we were led to absorb instead of the cheap substitutes with which our children are now plagued the beauties of sound and of form that are contained in our best musical, poetic, and choreographic tradition. Plato and Aristotle were convinced of the importance of art in the making of the good life. But they wanted good art not merely in the sense of technically proficient or formally beautiful art; they wanted it good also in an ethical sense—good in its ability to arouse goodness in the hearts of those who shared in it.[74] Aristotle thus wrote, "It may be impossible that there should be such people as Zeuxis used to paint, but it would be better if there were; for the type should improve on the actual." And Plato: "We must look for those craftsmen who by the happy gift of nature are capable of following the trail of true beauty and grace, that our young men, dwelling as it were in a salubrious region, may receive benefit from all things about them, whence the influence that emanates from works of beauty may waft itself to eye or ear like a breeze that brings from wholesome places health, and so from earliest childhood insensibly guide them to likeness, to friendship, to harmony with beautiful reason."

[73]George Howe and G. A. Harrer, *Greek Literature in Translation*, pp. 595–597.
[74]See G. L. Dickinson, *The Greek View of Life*, Chap. iv.

The Parthenon.

Plate 5

Davis Pratt, from Rapho-Guillumette

Oxen to be sacrificed. From the frieze of the Parthenon
(the Panathenaic procession, see pp. 162 f.).

Plate 6
Alinari

Plate 7
Alinari

Water boys. Parthenon frieze.

Cavalry. Parthenon frieze.

Cavalry. Parthenon frieze.

"Wealthy young men rode upon beautifully groomed thoroughbreds." Parthenon frieze.

Plate 10

© **British Museum**

Plate 11

Magistrates awaiting the procession. Parthenon frieze.

Poseidon, Dionysus, and Demeter awaiting the procession. Parthenon frieze.

Plate 12
Alinari

It is useless to say much about Greek art without actual objects or illustrations before us. It is the deeply felt experience of the beauty of a Greek temple, or statue, or vase that is alone convincing. It is possible, however, to illustrate once again, from the general character of that art, the qualities of Greek humanism. This illustration can be made precise by reference to one of the most beautiful of all temples, the Parthenon at Athens, which was adorned with some of the most beautiful of all sculpture.

GREEK ART AND HUMANISM

As it has been traced in this chapter, the Greek view attempted to subordinate human activities to the needs of the *polis*. Its anthropomorphic polytheism was essentially a civic religion that explained the gods in terms of what was best in man. When that religion was criticized by the poets, philosophers, and scientists it was criticized in the name of an immutable, divine moral order, of an exalted idealism, and of a disregard for the external facts of human existence. Greek humanism, moreover, laid no less emphasis upon the cultivation of the rational faculty of man than it did upon the perfection of his body. It sought proper balance between the claims of mind and body, a fitting harmony between the ideal and the real, an essential unity in the whole life of man devoted to the task of making the best that could be made of life here on earth.

THE GREEK TEMPLE

Here Greek art struck no discordant note. It strove to enhance the beauty of what was a public life spent in the open. The chief expressions of public art are, of course, architecture and sculpture. Greek architecture, except for that of the open-air theater, was chiefly the architecture of the temple, and on the Greek mainland, chiefly the architecture of the Doric temple. The temple itself was the home of the anthropomorphic god himself represented by sculpture. The temple was also the spot at which sacrifices were made to the god and goddess. It was centrally, if not dramatically, located in Athens in the Acropolis, at Paestum and Agrigentum on the shore of the "life-giving and wine-dark sea." The temples were modest, low-lying buildings with which man could retain an intimate relation. Their colored marble exteriors were bathed in the bright light of the warm Mediterranean sun, which had access, through widely spaced colonnades and porticoes, to all parts of the building; their interiors were only the comparatively small rooms that housed the statues of the gods. Here was no vast, interior, mystic gloom such as was characteristic of the Egyptian temple. Columns were not used as an impressive and forbidding façade but as a means of access, an invitation to enter a building of civic and this-worldly character. The columns were placed around all four sides of the centrally located temples, throwing them wide open to the gods, the elements, and to the daily life and ordinary citizens of the city-state. These temples were part of a religion more related to life than to death. Harmonious unity was sought in their design. No one part of the building must be permitted to dominate the other; no conflicting lines, no disproportionate sculpture, to distract attention from the total architectural effect. In fact, except for the cult statue, the best Greek temples possessed little or no sculpture that was not in the form of relief. In the case of the cult statue itself they did not hesitate to violate their sense of proportion. The Zeus at Olympia and the Athena of the Parthenon rose up from their pedestals almost to the ceilings of their cells (*cellae*). Today these temples are largely ruins. Those parts that remain have lost the brilliance of their original marble and color. The centuries have weathered them to a golden brown. When subsequently transformed into Christian churches their external appeal was changed to an internal appeal. The light was shut out by filling in the spaces between the outside row of columns. Windows were introduced and the old god or goddess either driven out by the Christian Trinity or obliged to occupy a more modest position as one of the saints.

GREEK SCULPTURE

Yahweh did not permit himself to be represented in artistic form for the benefit of lowly man. In this characteristic he was to be followed by Allah. It was not so with the immortals of Olympus. The anthropomorphic gods were sculptured, yet when that art was at its best they were given not just any human form but the most beautiful and the most idealized human form. As one observer stated: "The Greek custom is to represent the gods by the most beautiful things on earth—pure material, the human form, consummate art. The idea of those who make divine images in human shape is quite reasonable, since the spirit of man is nearest of all things to God and most godlike."[75] Greek sculptors were the first to use the form of the naked male. Since it was the practice of Greek gymnasts and athletes to perform in the nude, artists became easily acquainted with the beauties of the male form and re-created them in their superb athletic sculpture. The foremost artists of the fifth century, Phidias, for example, did not undertake to represent the beauties of the female form without the use of drapery. But this hesitance was dropped in the fourth century by such men as Praxiteles and Scopas. While never deviating far from the natural human form, the best Greek sculptors, with an inexplicable genius, suffused their Zeus's, Apollo's, and Aphrodite's with an idealistic beauty that has remained the highest standard of accomplishment for all subsequent sculptors not ignorant or indifferent to this past. Its quality may be judged from the Parthenon frieze.[76]

[75]Percy Gardner, "The Lamps of Greek Art," *Legacy*, p. 359.
[76]See pp. 162 f.

Art was not only used to enhance the beauty of civic religion and of sport. It was also an intimate part of domestic life. The student of Greek coins or seals notes the exquisitely patient care required in rendering them objects of beauty. In the manufacture of pottery the Greek painter excelled in making the useful beautiful. His subject matter was often religious, mythological, or heroic; he might, as in similar themes in sculpture, represent the external conflict between *hubris* and *sophrosyne*,[77] or lift from obscurity into permanence some more prosaic scene from daily life. In any case his treatment made the Greek vase, the oil jar, the wine jug, the lamp, the bowl and cup elegant objects of art. Athenian pottery was an essential item in her Mediterranean trade, and of course it was widely copied.

THE PARTHENON

The temple of Athena Parthenos, Athena the Virgin Goddess, the patron deity of Athens, stands as a monument to the genius of the greatest of all cities at its peak under Pericles. The temple was begun around 447 B.C. and finished, in white marble, about nine years later. If the great sculptor Phidias did not actually superintend its construction, he did carve some of the reliefs and the colossal statue of the goddess, made of ivory and gold, that stood in the sanctuary of the temple. The temple was paid for by contributions from, and actual raids upon, the treasury of the Athenian empire, involving a compromise between religion and imperialism. It was built, at least in part, by the work of slaves.[78] On a base measuring 250 by 150 feet, the temple, approached by three steps, was surrounded by a Doric colonnade, eight columns in width and seventeen in length, rising about thirty-four feet in height. These columns with a base diameter of 6.25 feet inclined inward, and their shafts swelled to a "maximum deviation from a straight line" of about 2.25 inches. Because of their position the corner columns were heavier than the rest, and more closely spaced. The steps and the floor upon which the outside columns rested were not actually horizontal but convex, at one point the middle rising to about nine inches higher than the corners. The walls of the *cella* sloped slightly inward. All these sensitive deviations from the straight line "mark the difference between the frigidity and hardness of mere architectural precision and the warmth and elasticity of a masterpiece of art. . . . The true

---

[77]See T. B. L. Webster, *Greek Art and Literature*, Chap. ii.

[78]Some idea of the share of slaves in the construction may be had from the expenditures in 408 for the building of the Erechtheum, a neighboring temple on the Acropolis. Of the 81 identifiable men engaged in the work for this year, 24 were Athenian citizens, 40 metics, and 17 slaves. It is highly interesting to note, however, that citizen, metic, and slave, "underling and architect," all received the same daily wage. See Botsford and Sihler, pp. 360–361.

explanation of the effect on the eye . . . is psychological."[79] The approach to the statue of Athena in the *cella* was made through an eastern portico of six columns. The *cella* itself (ninety-eight by sixty-three feet) contained an inner colonnade of three sides surrounding the statue of the goddess. Behind the *cella* was the treasury of the goddess, its roof supported by four Ionic columns. From this room one proceeded through a balancing portico to the western end of the temple. The pediment on the eastern end of the temple was decorated with a relief celebrating the birth of Athena, the western pediment with the "contest of Poseidon with Athena for the land." Beneath the cornice and architrave, around the whole temple, ran a series of ninety-two reliefs (*metopes*) separated by a design consisting of three vertical lines (*triglyphs*). These metopes rehearsed familiar mythological themes, some of which had to do directly with Athens (such as the conflict of Athenians and Amazons). Running some five hundred and twenty-four feet around the whole sanctuary, 3.25 feet in height, some forty feet above the floor and containing about six hundred figures, was the frieze reproducing the Panathenaic procession. This large collection of the greatest sculpture which man has produced was the combined and anonymous work of the sculptors of Athens.

THE PANATHENAEA

Athens of the fifth century comes to life in this frieze. The religious festival of the Panathenaea was held every four years at the foot of the temple.[80] After days of gymnastic exercises, chariot races, competitions in the recitation of poetry, singing, and flute playing, a beauty contest for men, a weapon dance, and a race with burning torches, a procession was formed on the final day in order to present to the goddess a new, richly embroidered yellow robe, woven by the women and girls of Athens. The procession was headed by girls bearing gold and silver bowls containing the things necessary for the sacrifice, "woollen fillets to wind around the animals, barley which was strewn in the altar-flames, and the knives for slaughter." Next in line were the sacrificial animals, the sheep and oxen, some of them contributed by Athenian colonies (Pl. 6). There followed groups of musicians, of the "aged yet still handsome men with fruit-laden branches," magistrates, foreign ambassadors, and the victors in the contests. Athenian military power was represented with infantry, cavalry (Pls. 8, 9), and charioteers. The procession was terminated by the golden robe of Athena herself. "It was hung upon a mast and yard, like a sail, visible to all from afar, and the cart which bore it was fitted out like a ship. With this the official procession was at an end, and the population of Athens joined it in a merry confused crowd. Whoever possessed

[79]The selection from C. H. Weller, *Athens and Its Monuments*, p. 282, copyright 1913 by The Macmillan Co., and used with The Macmillan Co.'s permission.
[80]This account is after Martin Schede, *The Acropolis of Athens*, and C. H. Weller, *Athens and Its Monuments*.

weapons displayed them proudly. The wealthy young men rode upon beautifully groomed thorough-breds, while all the others traipsed through sun and dust."[81] (Pl. 10) The procession marched toward the Acropolis, where it was received by the magistrates (Pl. 11) and, on the frieze, by the gods and goddesses who had been watching its approach (Pl. 12). Finally the girls who made Athena's robe carried it up to her temple and delivered it to her priest.

The fate of the Parthenon was the fate of classical civilization. In the fifth century A.D. it became a Christian church, dedicated finally to another virgin "goddess," Mary, the Mother of God, and remodeled accordingly. After the occupation of Athens by the Turks (1456) the Christian church became a Mohammedan mosque. In the course of the siege of Athens by the Venetians in 1687 the central portion of the Parthenon was destroyed. It remained a mosque after the Turks retook Athens until the Greek people won their independence (1821-1829). Before this event, the earl of Elgin, in 1801 and the years following, under authority of the Turks "to take away any pieces of stone with old inscriptions or figures thereon, appropriated and later shipped to England nearly all the remaining statues of the pediments, much of the frieze, and numerous metopes, and other fragments."[82] Their arrival in the British Museum helped to arouse an appreciation of the supremacy of Greek sculpture compared with that of the early nineteenth century. Since that day there have been many who in regarding this beautiful fixation in marble of a moment of joyous life in fifth-century Athens, now imprisoned within the walls of a museum, have been moved to tears.

[81]Schede, p. 80.
[82]The selection from C. H. Weller, *Athens and Its Monuments*, p. 306, copyright 1913 by The Macmillan Co., and used with The Macmillan Co.'s permission.

chapter five

THE PAX ROMANA

$\mathcal{S}$UMMARY. To this point we have been concerned with an area of the globe called the eastern Mediterranean. The political history of the Ancient Near East we characterized with the word *theocracy*; that of Athens with the word *democracy*. The tragedy of Greek politics we saw to consist (1) in the inability of the city-states to maintain peace among themselves by suppressing their local patriotism, and (2) in the inability of Athens to extend democratic institutions to a larger political unit than the *polis*. The result was the emergence again of the divine ruler and the theocratic empire (with Alexander and the succession-states into which his empire fell). The cultural achievement of the Ancient Near East that contributed most to our western tradition was the ethical monotheism of the Hebrew. Out of the amazing creativeness of the Greeks in almost every field of endeavor came the outlook we call humanism. The movement of the Greeks into the Near East carried humanism into older theocratic civilizations and brought about a cultural fusion that historians label Hellenistic. We have already looked at the mathematical and scientific achievements of this fusion.

SIMILARITY OF GREEK AND ROMAN HISTORY

With this chapter it is necessary to move westward and to consider the extraordinary political accomplishments of another Indo-European people, the Romans. At first glance they would seem to be but a repetition on a larger scale of Greek failure. Like the Greeks, the Romans were first faced with the task of creating a constitution for the city-state (*civitas*) of

Rome. Like the Greeks, they were obliged to modify the original monarchical and aristocratic character of its constitution to meet the demands of the majority of citizens; that is, to refashion the state along democratic lines. The Athenians prepared for their downfall by transforming the Delian League into an Athenian empire with which they did not share their democratic institutions. Rome, the city-state, began early in her history to acquire an empire. She too was faced with the tremendous task of creating for this empire suitable instruments of government. If we say that suitable instruments of government would have been those that kept intact the democratic form of the Republic and made possible the extension of these forms on an international scale, then Rome also failed. For the Roman Republic fell a victim to the generals who conquered part of its empire. The result was not an international, imperial Roman Republic but, by the time of Augustus, an international, imperial Roman monarchy, which in the course of centuries grew into a theocratic despotism. Under these circumstances the Roman Empire went to pieces, as had the Greek world previously. It was necessary to begin all over again.

THE ROMAN ACHIEVEMENT

The above statement, however, does not go deep enough. For if we accept the traditional date 753–752 B.C. to mark the founding of the city of Rome, and the traditional date A.D. 476 to mark the dissolution of the Empire, the transformation from an urban monarchy to an oriental despotism took over 1200 years. While we may look upon these centuries as the second great political tragedy in the history of the West, in so doing we should not fail to recognize what was in fact the real achievement of the Romans. The tragedy of the ultimate downfall of their empire made necessary the reconstruction we know as our western European civilization. The example of this empire, however, supplied this reconstruction with what has been its greatest political hope—the establishment of a peaceful world state.

For, no matter in what form, this is what the Romans succeeded in doing. Roman history is like the history of no other city on earth. A small community of farmers dwelling near the mouth of the Tiber River built an empire that at its height reached from the North Sea to the Sahara Desert, from Britain to Persia, from the Black Sea to the Atlantic, including all the civilized centers of the Ancient Near East and Greece. These farmers not only succeeded in conquering this area but, what is more important, they gave it a common law, the Roman law. They managed also to create a universal citizenship within this world state governed by a common law. Within the frontiers of their world they established a wellnigh universal peace which lasted for two centuries. If they had done no more—if, that is, they had not spread the Graeco-oriental civilization of the eastern Mediterranean throughout the western Mediterranean and made possible by the mere fact of the existence of their empire the transformation of a Jewish cult into a universal Christian religion—they would have done enough to call forth the respect and admiration of later generations. Yet they did more. Under the tutelage of the Greeks they developed a distinguished literary, artistic, and philosophical culture of their own, and in other fields gave evidence of their own originality. Our interest in Roman history must accordingly concentrate on (1) the establishment of the Roman world state; (2) the government and society of this world state; (3) the Roman appropriation of Greek humanism; and finally (4) the decline, fall, and heritage of Rome. Items one and two will be the subject of this chapter; three and four, of subsequent chapters.

The Establishment of the Roman World State

THE CHANGE IN IMPERIAL POLICY

The history of the establishment of the Roman world state not only provides us with information concerning the advantages of international organization but instructs us as well in the dangers of imperial expansion when that expansion is undertaken by a ruling class unwilling to assume full responsibility for those whom it is forcing to submit to its rule. It can be well argued that the Romans did not set out deliberately to conquer the Mediterranean world. Yet they did not hesitate to push farther afield when it seemed necessary to protect what they regarded as their interests and their honor. In the early stages of the expansion, the conquest of Italy, they pursued a liberal policy of federation with defeated states, a policy that resulted in a healthy imperial structure. But when once they became so powerful that they could not be challenged with impunity they treated the conquered less as allies than as exploitable subjects. A practical and efficient people with an ever-growing experience in politics, they easily grew intolerant of the inability of others, especially the Greeks, to manage their own affairs. Therefore, instead of co-operating patiently with others in the solution of common political problems they often preferred to use strong-arm and harsh methods to impose their will. They succumbed ultimately, after their dominant position had been maintained for centuries, to the temptation of the oriental despots, who solved all problems by fiat from above. Thus the Romans, corrupted by the power and wealth of empire, were able only partially to utilize their political talents. The early promise of a Mediterranean world organized into a mutually profitable federation about Rome failed to develop. Instead the later Roman Empire appears to be but an extension of the earlier Egyptian, Assyrian, Persian, and Alexandrian empires to the whole Mediterranean basin.

EMPIRE AND LOCAL INDEPENDENCE

The establishment of ancient empires usually snuffed out local independence and undermined the human loyalty attached thereto. If the

CHRONOLOGY — The Pax Romana

300

B.C.

Samnite Wars (343–290)
Pyrrhus (ca. 318–272)

200

First Punic War (265–241)
Scipio (237–183)
Second Punic War (218–201)
Hannibal (247–183)
Philip V of Macedon (228–179)
Antiochus III (223–187)

100

Tiberius Gracchus (163–133)
Marius (155–86)
Gaius Gracchus (153–121)
Third Punic War (149–146)
Sulla (138–78)
Mithridates (131–63)
Spartacus (d. 71)
Crassus (115–53)
Pompey (106–48)
Cicero (106–43)
Julius Caesar (100–44)
Marcus Brutus (85–42)
Cassius (d. 42)
Mark Antony (83–30)
Cleopatra (69–30)
Augustus (63 B.C.–A.D. 14)
Claudius I (10 B.C.–A.D. 54)

B.C.

A.D.

Caligula (12–41)
Nero (37–68)
Vespasian (9–79)
Domitian (51–96)
Nerva (30–98)
Trajan (52–117)
Pliny the Younger (62–113)
Hadrian (76–138)

100

Marcus Aurelius (121–180)
Commodus (161–192)
Septimius Severus (146–211)

Aelius Aristides (fl. 2d c.)

conqueror treated his imperial subjects well he succeeded ultimately in re-shaping their old loyalties into a new loyalty for the imperial state. Much of the history of the western world has to do with the abandonment of an old for a new political loyalty based upon a larger territorial and political unit. Twentieth-century Americans are now, for example, expected to transform their loyalty from their nation and nationality into a series of allegiances: to the Atlantic community, the western world, the United Nations, and mankind. That western Europe could develop as a group of nationalities was in part a result of the work of Rome. For it was Rome that first destroyed within the boundaries of what came to be called "na-tions" those attachments to tribe and locality that prevented attachment to a larger territorial unit such as an empire. In accomplishing this, Rome facilitated the subsequent development of loyalty to such units as Italy, Spain, Gaul, and Britain, when empire failed to satisfy human hopes.

ROME AND HER NEIGHBORS

Originally the Romans were but one in a group of Latin peoples who migrated to Italy and settled on, and south of, the lower Tiber River. The Latin peoples themselves were but one of several other immigrant groups. As colonists from their mother cities, the Greeks had occupied harbor sites on the southwestern coast of the peninsula (Cumae, Capua, Naples) and on the southern coast (Thurii, Rhegium, Tarentum). These Greek cities were harassed by primitive inland mountain peoples, the Samnites, the Lucanians, and the Bruttians, all of whom were, like the Latins, Indo-European immigrants to the peninsula. The Latins, including those in Rome, were constantly threatened by Volscians to the south, and to the east and north by Marsians, Aequians, and Sabines. North of the Tiber and stretching to the Apennines were immigrants from Asia Minor, the Etruscans, bordering on Umbrians to the east. In the valley of the Po River Celtic Gauls had settled and, with fresh reinforcements from south-ern Germany, were a constant threat to the rest of Italy. Out of these varied peoples, in the centuries following the Roman conquest, was fash-ioned an Italian people.

LATIN LEAGUE AND ITALIAN FEDERATION

The Roman conquest of Italy took about two hundred and fifty years. It began soon after the establishment of the Republic, when Rome was able, in a treaty of alliance with the other Latin cities, to maintain a posi-tion equal in power to all of them combined, and therefore superior to any one. The rise of a dominant power on the Tiber promised pro-tection to other Italians who felt themselves threatened and guaranteed ultimate peace, at least among the peoples of the peninsula. After the Gauls had burned and looted Rome (*ca.* 390 B.C.), the Greek cities of Campania appealed to her for protection against the tribes of Samnites in the Apennines. The favorable response of the Roman Senate initiated the

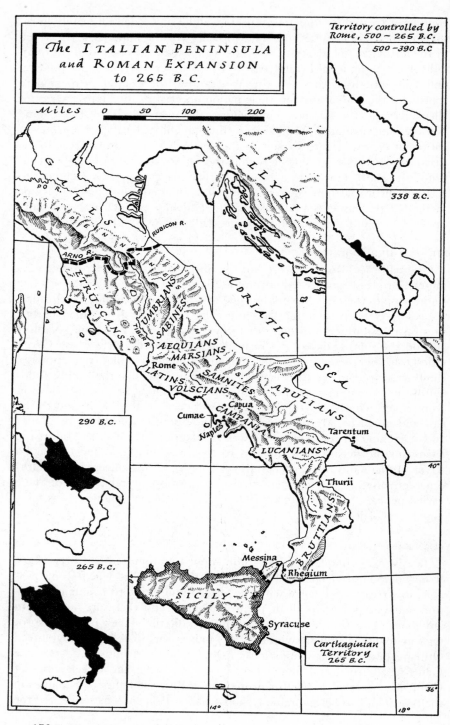

The ITALIAN PENINSULA and ROMAN EXPANSION to 265 B.C.

Miles
0   50   100   200

Territory controlled by Rome, 500 – 265 B.C.
500 – 390 B.C.

338 B.C.

GAULS

PO R.

A P E N N I N E S

ARNO R.

RUBICON R.

ETRUSCANS

TIBER R.

UMBRIANS

SABINES

AEQUIANS

MARSIANS

Rome

LATINS

VOLSCIANS

SAMNITES

APULIANS

ILLYRIA

ADRIATIC SEA

Capua

Cumae

CAMPANIA

Naples

Tarentum

LUCANIANS

Thurii

BRUTTIANS

290 B.C.

265 B.C.

Messina

Rhegium

SICILY

Syracuse

Carthaginian Territory 265 B.C.

40°

36°

14°   18°

Samnite Wars (343–290 B.C.). At the end of the first of these Rome controlled Campania, and Rome's Latin allies, fearful of the results of the increase of Roman power, demanded full Roman citizenship. This was denied. Instead the Romans dissolved the old Latin League, however favorable to themselves, and made individual treaties with the separate Latin cities, in which each was treated according to what Rome considered its deserts. Roman citizenship without the vote was granted in some treaties. In others no grant of citizenship was made, but rights of self-government were guaranteed. Further gradations in status were made in other treaties. Rome promised military protection and a share of the booty, especially the right to help to establish colonies on newly conquered ground, but she demanded from her allies military help and surrender of independence in foreign affairs. Rome's policy here can be seen to involve the prevention of the growth of any common Latin allegiance at the cost of allegiance to Rome. The relations of the Latins were to be with Rome and not among themselves. The Romans meant to be generous and fair. Roman citizenship and self-government were not to be denied when merited, and they could be earned by proper attitudes and services. The new treaties with the Latins (338 B.C.) were a device which Rome also used to extend her control over non-Latin peoples. After military defeat, that is, she offered to the Italian peoples similar treaties, thus building up an Italian federation. Before they were finally defeated the Samnites had brought Latins, Etruscans, Gauls, and others into an alliance against Rome in an effort to defend their common independence and to prevent Roman unification of the peninsula. But when the Samnites were finally defeated (290 B.C.) they were permitted to come into the Italian federation on terms similar to those previously granted the Latins. By 280 B.C. Rome had completed the conquest of the Etruscan cities, which were likewise permitted to enter the federation.

THE CONQUEST OF THE GREEK CITIES

The Romans were summoned to protect the Greek cities of southern Italy from attacks of Lucanians and Bruttians and even from wars among themselves. When the Romans intervened against Tarentum some Greek cities summoned a Hellenistic adventurer from Greece, Pyrrhus, the king of Epirus, to protect them from what they regarded as the Roman barbarians. Pyrrhus failed, and after his defeat by the Romans Tarentum (272 B.C.) and, subsequently, the other Greek cities of southern Italy were permitted to become allies of Rome, that is, members of the Italian federation. By this time Rome had advanced northward to the Apennines by subduing the Umbrians and Gauls. The Italian peninsula, with the exception of the Po Valley, was thus unified in a federation of Rome with her Latin and Italian allies. For the Roman army of 700,000 infantry and 70,000 cavalry the Latin and Italian allies now supplied 400,000 and 44,000 respectively. To hasten the unification of these peoples the Romans were quick to connect their principal cities with superb and well-nigh imperishable roads. Also they hastened to send out Roman or Latin colonies, primarily military or naval, which were placed in strategic spots to hold conquered lands and extend Roman influence. Thus by means of treaties, roads, colonies, Roman officials, and the Roman army, that process of Romanization was begun which, in the course of centuries, made of the originally diverse Italian peoples one Roman-Italian people.

THE PROBLEM OF EXPANSION BEYOND ITALY

In becoming an Italian power Rome had also become, whether she wished it or not, an Adriatic and a western Mediterranean power. Unless she were to isolate herself she had to be concerned with the larger politics of these areas. Having assumed a protectorate over the Greek cities of southern Italy she could not ignore their relations with the Greeks of Sicily, and, once involved in Sicilian affairs, she then faced Carthage, a former Phoenician colony in North Africa which, at the moment, was attempting to wrest Sicily from the Greeks. To challenge Carthage in Sicily was to challenge the Carthaginian position as a commercial power claiming a monopoly over the trade and shipping of the western seas. To challenge Carthage meant that Rome had to decide to become a commercial and naval power herself and suffer her stalwart peasant sons to be corrupted by greed for traders' profits. Her expansion to the eastern coast of Italy meant, moreover, that she had also to protect allies on this coast from Illyrian pirates roving over the Adriatic Sea and, accordingly, to intervene in the politics of western Greece. There was no way out of it. To go beyond Italy was to choose the path leading to world empire.

THE FIRST PUNIC WAR

Rome's first war with Carthage (the First Punic War, 265–241 B.C.) began with an attempt to prevent the Straits of Messina from falling into enemy hands but developed shortly into a war to drive Carthage from Sicily. When it was won Rome levied a heavy war indemnity ($3,500,000) upon the Carthagianians and took over Sicily not as a member of the Roman federation but as the first of Rome's overseas provinces. While membership in the federation was extended to certain Sicilian cities, for most of the island Rome chose to maintain the methods of government of the tyrants of Syracuse and the rulers of Carthage, methods which had been imported into Sicily by these governments directly from the theocratic courts of Hellenistic monarchs. To a Hellenistic ruler, the state owned most of the land of the kingdom, and its inhabitants were tenants of state lands and thus owed the state rent in the form of tribute. From the Sicilians Rome took this tribute, amounting to about a million dollars a year, in the form of a tithe on crops. The lands of cities that had resisted Rome now became Roman public land and were leased to their former owners by Roman officials. The Romans were not ready with a new system of government for this or any other province. They did not concern themselves at this moment with the building of an imperial civil service but merely adapted to the new provinces the city-state government of Rome.[1] They left the collection of income not to Roman officials but to those private citizens who bid highest for this privilege. This amounted, of course, to leaving it in the hands of the heaviest exploiters. Cicero protested against the misgovernment and extortion practiced by subsequent Roman governors in Sicily in his *Orations against Verres*. Sicily, unfortunately, was to be the model for other new provinces in the West.

THE SECOND PUNIC WAR

It was the model, for example, for the new province of Sardinia and Corsica, which Carthage was obliged to cede to Rome in 238 B.C. Spain became a Roman province at the conclusion of the Second Punic War (281–201 B.C.) after Rome had fought a life-and-death struggle on Italian soil with the Carthaginian general Hannibal. Carthage had sought to make good her loss of Sicily by expansion in Spain and the exploitation of rich silver mines there. Hannibal, son of a Carthaginian general, decided to use Spain as the jumping-off place for an attack on Italy, an attack that was first to strip Rome of her Italian allies and then destroy her, if, once isolated, she dared to resist. The Romans had warned Carthage that she was not to cross Spain's Ebro River under arms, and that in any event they would not tolerate an attack on Italy from Spain and southern Gaul, where the old Greek colony of Massilia was also an ally of Rome. But Rome was unable to prevent Hannibal's crossing of the Pyrenees and the passage through southern Gaul, his ascent of the Alps and descent into the valley of the Po, accompanied by infantry, cavalry, and elephants (winter of 218–217). From this moment until Hannibal's evacuation of Italy (203 B.C.) Rome and her allies had to suffer the devastation and humiliation of more or less constant military defeat. Indeed, at Cannae in Apulia (216 B.C.) Rome lost some eighty thousand men and eighty senators. Hannibal, however, unable to induce the Italian allies to join forces with him, was finally forced onto the defensive. The Romans then came to realize that the war would be decided in Sicily, Spain, and Africa, not in Italy. To punish Syracuse for deserting to Carthage Rome in 212 B.C. gave over the city to rapine. "Robbed of its wealth, its temples ravaged, its priceless art treasures sacrificed to the insatiate god of war, stripped of its artistic glories to adorn the homes of the new-rich Romans, the proud city became henceforth tributary to Rome, a part of the province of Sicily. But the supreme loss to civilization was the death of Archimedes, brutally struck down by a Roman soldier while drawing a mathematical figure on the sand."[2] Scipio conquered Spain from Hasdrubal (210–206 B.C.) and prevented him from joining his brother Hannibal in Italy.

[1] For details see pp. 205 f.
[2] Albert A. Trever, *History of Ancient Civilization*, II, 94–95.

It was to Scipio that Rome now entrusted the waging of offensive war in North Africa itself. By 203 B.C. he had been so successful as to force upon Carthage a preliminary treaty calling for the withdrawal of Hannibal and his army from Italy. After the return of Hannibal to Africa, however, the Carthaginians decided to risk one more battle against the Romans, a battle which Hannibal lost to Scipio at Zama (202 B.C.). The treaty concluding the war obliged the Carthaginians to give up all their territory except Carthage itself and the land about it. They were required to pay an annual indemnity of $12,000,000 for fifty years and to abandon their navy. They were, moreover, not to wage war in Africa or beyond without Rome's consent. Under a native chieftain, Numidia was set up as an ally of Rome to keep watch over a Carthage whose career in the western Mediterranean had once and for all been terminated. Rome then annexed Spain as another Roman province and subjected it to the same kind of oriental, imperial government that had been established in Sicily. Thus the foundations of another western European nation were laid. In a manner similar to the experience of the peoples of Italy, the primitive Iberian tribes entered the circle of western peoples about to be civilized under Roman leadership. They suffered long and bitterly before abandoning finally their hope of native independence. Though Carthage was not yet a Roman province,[3] a Romanized western North Africa and a Romanized western Europe were now a certainty. The fate of those primitive peoples in the West not yet brought within the Roman orbit had also been determined. Rome had become the great western power. Upon her shoulders rested the responsibility of introducing to primitive peoples the principles and practices of a more ordered and dignified life than was possible to a world of warring tribes.

After the Third Macedonian War (171–167 B.C.) Rome brought 1000 Greek hostages to Italy for a period of seventeen years. One of these, the historian Polybius, was so impressed with Rome's extraordinary advance to world power that he chose the theme for his history "by what means and under what system of polity the Romans in less than fifty-three years have succeeded in subjecting nearly the whole inhabited world to their sole government." (I, 3, 5)[4] The fifty-three years Polybius had in mind were those between the outbreak of the Second Punic War and the partition of Macedonia in 167 B.C. Certainly we can be no less amazed than Polybius. History knows of few such spectacular seizures of power.

ROME TURNS TO THE EAST

It would have required a resolute delimitation of Rome's future for the shapers of her foreign policy to have refused to enter the field of eastern Mediterranean, or Hellenistic, politics. For the first time in classical history

[3]See pp. 178 f.
[4]Citations from Polybius in my text are to *Histories*, trans. W. R. Paton, Loeb, Nos. 128, 137, 138, 159–161, 6 vols.

the field of international politics could no longer be confined to one part of the Mediterranean; it had to concern the whole of it. To protect the Italian allies from the ravages of Illyrian pirates, in the course of the Punic Wars the Romans had been forced to reduce Illyria to a protectorate. If now, after Zama, Rome had to defend her newly won position in the western Mediterranean she was obliged also to concern herself with eastern politics, since Hannibal was seeking to retrieve the fortunes of Carthage by alliance with Macedonia and Syria. Only suicide put an end to his consuming desire to undo the Roman victory over his country.

THE POLITICAL SITUATION IN THE EAST

The political situation in the eastern Mediterranean after the death of Alexander the Great (323 B.C.) has been described earlier.[5] His empire fell to his generals: Egypt came under the Ptolemies, the descendants of Ptolemy Lagus; Syria, Babylonia, and parts of Asia Minor went to the Seleucids, the descendants of Seleucus; and Macedonia, to the Antigonids, the descendants of Antigonus. The lesser powers in the Hellenistic world were Rhodes, Pergamum in Asia Minor, and the Aetolian and Achaean leagues.[6] Each one of the leading dynasties was imbued with the theocratic imperial policies of Alexander himself, and their efforts to impose their wills upon each other resulted finally in the establishment of a balance of power, into which the lesser powers were required to fit. At the conclusion of the Second Punic War the balance of power among them was threatened by the efforts of both Macedonia and the Seleucids to partition the overseas possessions of Egypt. The aggressions of Philip V and Antiochus II were a threat, moreover, not only to the imperial position of Egypt but also to the lesser states in the East, the Greek leagues, Pergamum, and Rhodes. During the closing years of the Second Punic War, Egypt, the Aetolian League, Rhodes, and Pergamum had all appealed to Rome, the new star on the western horizon, for aid against these two rulers. On the face of it this was an appeal of the weaker states of the East that Rome intervene to protect the devotion of the Greek to the independence of his local city. If it had been possible at this moment for Macedonia, the Seleucid empire, and Egypt to present a united front against Rome, then Roman intervention might have been warded off. The Roman conquerors, who for centuries had known how to direct a policy of *divide et impera* (divide and rule), saw this possibility. There can be no doubt that Rome's intervention in eastern affairs was in part the result of an unwillingness to see her future circumscribed by union of the great powers of the East.

[5]See pp. 82 f.
[6]See pp. 86 f.

Yet it is also clear that Rome's motives at this moment were not wholly determined by considerations of her own future freedom of action. The leading group in Roman public affairs at the time, men such as the Scipios, had become sensitive to the taunts of "barbarian" which the Greeks hurled at them. Deeply appreciative of the high level of culture in the cities of Greece and the Hellenistic East and aware of what this culture might do to widen the intellectual and spiritual horizon of the Roman peasant and soldier, some Romans showed themselves eager to participate in eastern politics in defense of Greek independence. In 200 B.C. Rome therefore took up the appeals of the weak powers of the East and turned first against Philip V of Macedon, declaring war when he refused to abandon his aggressions against Egypt, the Greek cities, Pergamum, and Rhodes. A Roman victory at Cynoscephalae (Dogs' Heads) in Thessaly in 197 B.C. led Philip to accept terms of peace which provided for the autonomy of all Greek states, the surrender of all but six ships of the Macedonian navy, a war indemnity of $1,200,000, and the entrance of Macedonia into the circle of Rome's allies. In the next year (196 B.C.) at the Isthmian games, the Roman general who had defeated Philip, Titus Flamininus, himself a philhellene, ordered his herald to announce to the assembled representatives of the Greek cities that "the Senate of Rome . . . having overcome King Philip and the Macedonians, leave the following peoples free, without garrisons and subject to no tribute and governed by their countries' laws—the Corinthians, Phocians, Locrians, Euboeans, Achaeans, Magnesians, Thessalians." These were the people whom Macedonia had subjected. The reaction of the crowd to this generous liberation is described by Polybius: "At once at the very commencement a tremendous shout arose, and some did not even hear the proclamation, while others wanted to hear it again. . . . But when the herald, coming forward to the middle of the stadium and again silencing the noise by his bugler, made the same identical proclamation, such a mighty burst of cheering arose that those who listen to the tale to-day cannot easily conceive what it was. When at length the noise had subsided, not a soul took any further interest in the athletes, but all, talking either to their neighbours or to themselves, were almost like men beside themselves. So much so indeed that after the games were over they very nearly put an end to Flamininus by their expressions of thanks. For some of them, longing to look him in the face and call him their saviour, others in their anxiety to grasp his hand, and the greater number throwing crowns and fillets on him, they all but tore the man in pieces." (V, 189, 191)

THE WAR WITH ANTIOCHUS

In the same year Roman envoys to Antiochus announced that "none of the Greeks were any longer being attacked by anyone or the subjects of anyone." Roman words, however, could not restrain Antiochus. In the next few years he conquered Greek cities on the coast of Asia Minor and, bent upon the conquest of Thrace, invaded Europe. This was followed by intervention in Greece to support the Aetolian League in a move to build up an anti-Roman coalition in the peninsula. Rome chose to accept the challenge to her position as a defender of Greek liberty by a declaration of war against Antiochus. He was beaten in Greece at Thermopylae, in Asia at Magnesia (190 B.C.), and was obliged by treaty to withdraw behind the Taurus mountains in Asia Minor, to surrender his war elephants and all but ten ships of his navy, and to pay a war indemnity of no less than $18,000,000. Rome thereupon restored their freedom to some of the Greek cities in Asia Minor and divided Antiochus's conquests between Rhodes and Pergamum. The two Hellenistic aggressors, Antigonid and Seleucid, had now been put in their places, and the lesser states in the East, Greek and non-Greek, had been freed and strengthened. Rome had annexed no territory in these wars, but she could do so whenever she chose.

THE CHANGE IN ROMAN IMPERIAL POLICY

The philhellenic idealism which moved the Roman Senate when it first began to concern itself with eastern affairs was soon succeeded by a conservative, coldly realistic and selfish imperialism typified by men such as Cato. They "cared little whether or not Athenian orators pronounced them uncivilized for living outside the pale of Greek politics. Philhellenism, particularism, and applause at Greek games did not seem to them things for which one should spill Roman blood and appropriate public moneys. . . . Men like Cato pointed out that the soldiers who had fought in Greece and the East came home with new-found vices and that the generals' staff brought back an un-Roman taste for everything from Greek cooking to marble statuary."[7] Men of this stamp were impatient with the political incapacity of the Greeks and with the refusal of others to be content with the limitations Rome had put upon them. Empire was no sentimental adventure. The Roman expenditure of effort, blood, and treasure should bring tangible material advantages to the state and its citizens. They thought it unnecessary to apologize for the imposition of Roman rule or to avoid the inevitable by postponing the actual subjection of non-Roman peoples to provincial government.

MACEDONIA A PROVINCE

The results of this reversal of attitude on the part of the Roman Senate are to be seen in the addition to the Roman provinces made after the war with Antiochus. Rome was quick to intervene when Philip's son Perseus, with the aid of dissatisfied Greek cities, sought to restore the position his father had lost. This time, after the defeat of Pydna (168 B.C.), Perseus

[7]The selection from Tenney Frank, *Roman Imperialism*, p. 191, copyright 1914 by The Macmillan Co., and used with The Macmillan Co.'s permission.

was dethroned and the Macedonian kingdom destroyed. The Roman general who defeated Perseus, Aemilius Paulus, celebrated a triumph in Rome in which "two hundred and fifty wagons bore the spoils of war, art, arms, silver, furniture, and four hundred golden crowns from the Greek cities. . . . So enormous was the booty taken from Perseus and Greece that the war tax on the property of Roman citizens . . . was not again levied until 43 B.C."[8] For a time Rome tried the experiment of dividing Macedonia into four autonomous republics under her supervision. But when again (149 B.C.) Macedonia withdrew from Roman protection to support Andriscus, who claimed to be a son of Perseus, Rome reduced Macedonia to a province (148 B.C.).

THE SUBJECTION OF THE GREEK CITIES AND CARTHAGE

The Greek cities and Carthage experienced even more ruthless Roman treatment. After the liberation of the Greek cities from the aggression of Philip V Rome had sought to strengthen her position in Greece by supporting local governments of a conservative, pro-Roman character. This sort of puppet regime was not what many Greeks meant when they talked of freedom. In the war against Perseus Rome found a number of Greek cities supporting Macedonia, since she encouraged democratic, anti-Roman factions in the cities. After the war "the anti-Roman leaders throughout Greece were punished with death or exile." It was at this moment that Rome, as mentioned above, took as hostages 1000 of the leading citizens of the Achaean League.[9] Epirus paid for its support of Macedonia by having seventy of its towns sacked and 150,000 of its people sold into slavery. After the war against Andriscus, the popular, anti-Roman party in the Achaean League undertook to revolt from Rome. The revolt was immediately crushed (146 B.C.), and as a warning to future freedom-minded cities "Thebes and Chalcis were partly ravaged, and Corinth, the rich commercial center of Greece, was barbarously plundered and completely destroyed. Those inhabitants who had not escaped from the doomed city were sold into slavery. . . . Its splendid art treasures were sold or carried off to Rome. Polybius, an eyewitness of the sack, tells how he saw the rough soldiers . . . scornfully cast costly pictures to the ground and play checkers upon them." The Achaean League was broken up, its members, except Athens and Sparta, subjected to Rome and obliged to accept conservative, oligarchic governments in accordance with charters Rome drew up. Greece was not yet reduced to a province, but "henceforth, deprived of initiative under pro-Roman officials and a victim of the greed of Roman speculators and generals like Sulla,[10] Greece sank ever further to social, economic, and cultural decay. Carthage's end came in the same year (146 B.C.). To Polybius, Rome's purpose was to get rid of "a

[8]Trever, II, 110.
[9]See p. 174.
[10]See pp. 208 ff.

perpetual menace" and to destroy "a city which had disputed the supremacy with her and *might still do so if opportunity offered*." The destruction of Carthage had been endlessly advocated by no less a man than Cato, who, after 153 B.C., concluded all his speeches in the Senate with the demand: "Carthage must be destroyed (*delenda est Carthago*)." The Carthaginians resisted destruction with great energy and courage. When the city finally fell, its remaining and starving citizens were sold into slavery, its walls were leveled to the ground, "the site . . . plowed, salt . . . sown in the furrows, and a solemn curse . . . pronounced against it."[11] That part of the city's holdings not turned over to Rome's African allies was made into another Roman province.

THE FIRST PROVINCE IN ASIA

In 133 B.C. Attalus III, the king of Pergamum, made Rome the heir of his large kingdom in Asia Minor. Pergamum had long been the steady friend of Rome in the East and had been constantly rewarded by extensions of territory. Whether or not the legacy was a recognition on the part of Attalus of a certain inevitability in the turn of political events, Rome, after grants of territory to her friends in Asia, set up the remainder of the inheritance as her first province in Asia (129 B.C.). "For a century Asia was the happy hunting ground for every selfish Roman exploiter from governors and capitalists to lowest officials, and finally the once rich kingdom was made hopelessly bankrupt by the brutal exactions of the Roman general Sulla."[12] During the century following the completion of the

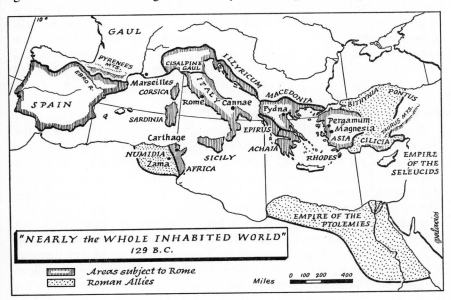

"NEARLY the WHOLE INHABITED WORLD"
129 B.C.

Areas subject to Rome
Roman Allies

Miles   0 100 200   400

[11]Trever, II, 118–119.
[12]Trever, II, 120.

unification of Italy, Rome thus established her mastery of the whole Mediterranean by annexing as provinces Sicily (227 B.C.), Sardinia and Corsica (227 B.C.), Spain (197 B.C.), Macedonia (148 B.C.), Carthage (146 B.C.), and Pergamum (129 B.C.). Subjected but not yet reduced to provincial status were Greece, Cisalpine Gaul, and Illyricum. These annexations, however, still stopped far short of the whole: in the first century B.C. Roman power penetrated further into Asia, Africa, and Europe.

THE NATURE OF ROMAN EXPANSION IN THE FIRST CENTURY B.C.

Roman imperial policy in the first century B.C., the last century of the Republic, was determined in large part by the exigencies of Roman party politics. In a manner we shall describe subsequently[13] there had emerged in Rome what we may call a radical, or popular, party and a conservative, or aristocratic, party, each struggling to control the vast power of the Roman Republic and its huge resources. It became a settled practice for the leaders of the respective parties to secure positions in the empire for themselves in order to build up influence, fortune, and military power, which could then be used to settle the issues of party politics at home. Indeed, the problems created by the empire were so formidable and complicated and their solution required such great talent and effort that the man who dealt with them successfully, and who had thereby made his fortune and built up a private army, could, if he chose, disregard the limitations of republican government. In this manner lust for political power led to further imperial expansion and exploitation, and these in turn trained and fashioned men who were ultimately to abandon the pretense of governing the empire as a republic and instead to turn to outright despotic methods with which they had become only too familiar in the provinces. The leading figures among such men in the first century B.C. were Marius, Sulla, Pompey, Caesar, Antony, and finally Octavian (Augustus), the actual founder of the empire.

MARIUS AND THE NEW PROLETARIAN ARMY

Marius was a popular leader who won great renown at the turn of the first century B.C. as a successful general against a horde of Germanic and Celtic tribes, the Cimbri and Teutons, who were attempting to terminate a long trek from the southern shores of the North Sea through Gaul by invading and settling in Italy. His reputation was further enhanced by his success in helping to subdue Jugurtha, a slippery Numidian prince who boasted of his success in bribing Roman senators, generals, and officials sent to keep him in his proper place. Marius finally brought him to Rome to grace his triumph and to die in prison. To achieve these military victories Marius took what turned out to be a step fateful for Roman republican institutions. Not content with the additional levies of soldiers supplied him by the Senate from the ranks of propertied Roman citizens, he started on

[13]See pp. 193 ff.

his own authority to enlist troops from groups of citizens hitherto un-qualified for the army. He took them from the unpropertied citizens of Rome, formerly used as legionnaries only in times of crisis, and enlisted them "for a definite period of service, and in all probability for twenty years." This innovation marked the transition from an amateur public army composed of the wealthier citizens to a private professional army composed of the poorer citizens. "The policy inaugurated by Marius in the teeth of senatorial opposition of enlisting troops on his own initiative set a dangerous precedent which was followed by subsequent generals till the end of the Republic. The result was that generals raised armies for their own purposes, paid their soldiers from the booty which they gained, and when their work was finished compelled the state to find land for their veterans. Thus, so far from there being a state army in the last cen-tury of the Republic, there was rather a succession of armies owing loyalty to their respective generals."[14]

SULLA AND MITHRIDATES

The imperial ambitions of Mithridates, king of Pontus in Asia Minor, gave Rome her next opportunity to expand in the East, and it was Lucius Cornelius Sulla, the leader of the conservative party in Rome, who seized this opportunity for himself. Posing as the great liberator of the peoples of Asia Minor and European Greece, Mithridates had expanded westward from his native Pontus, incorporating the Roman province of Asia (Pergamum) and the Greek cities of western Asia Minor, and invading European Greece. He had aroused great enthusiasm for his western march into the Roman province and the territory of dependent Greek cities by promising to undo the work of the Roman taxgatherers, bankers, and merchants who had rushed into the area after the Roman conquest. In fact he gave orders that on a certain day "all Romans and Italians, adults and children, free men and slaves" were to be put to death. Their bodies were to be left unburied and their property divided between the murder-ers and the king himself. Slaves who murdered their masters were to be freed, and debtors who killed their creditors were to be free of half their indebtedness. We are assured that under this stimulus 80,000 Romans and Italians suffered the wrath of the inhabitants. If the conquests of Mithri-dates were not enough to arouse Rome, this slaughter of Roman citizens and allies was. Sulla marched into Greece (87 B.C.), in spite of the fact that he had been deposed by the popular party in Rome, defeated an army of Mithridates at Chaeronea and another at Orchomenus, and by 85 B.C. was able to land in Asia Minor. Mithridates was obliged to accept a Roman peace which cost him his conquests beyond his own kingdom of Pontus, the loss of part of his fleet, and 3000 talents.

Sulla then settled down for the winter to deal with those provincials who

[14]H. M. D. Parker, *The Roman Legions*, p. 26.

had opened their gates to Mithridates and had murdered Roman citizens and allies. He quartered his troops on the inhabitants. Each householder was obliged to furnish a Roman soldier with meals for himself and as many of his friends as the soldier desired to invite. He was obliged in addition to pay sixteen drachmae a day for a private soldier and more for an officer, and to furnish the former two suits of clothes. Upon the provincials Sulla levied an indemnity of no less than 20,000 talents ($24,000,000) to cover not only the cost of the war but possibly also arrears in taxes. Roman and Italian moneylenders appeared to take the place of their murdered colleagues and made this money available at interest rates that went as high as 48 per cent. It is reported that in 71 B.C., thirteen years after the indemnity had been imposed, "although twice the original amount of 20,000 talents had been paid to the moneylenders, the total indebtedness of the province, as the result, evidently, of the compounding of the arrears of interest, had risen to the almost incredible sum of 120,000 talents."[15] Lucullus, the Roman governor of the province after Sulla's departure, managed by a levy of 25 per cent on crops and a special tax on slaves and buildings, among other remedial measures, to reduce the total indebtedness to 40,000 talents. It was then paid off in four years. Sulla left Asia Minor for Rome in 84 B.C., ready to take similar vengeance upon the popular party. At his triumph he boasted that he had taken 1500 pounds of gold and 115,000 pounds of silver while in the East. He left behind him Greek states which "had suffered most severely for their disloyalty. Their lands in Attica and Boeotia were ravaged, Athens and Peiraeus were depopulated and laid waste, the sacred shrines had been looted of their costly treasures, and the coasts had been harried by the fleet of Mithradates. Of all the devastations of this long-suffering land, this of Sulla was the worst. From its blight, Hellas never entirely recovered."[16]

POMPEY AND THE PIRATES

The problems of the East left unsolved by Sulla were taken in hand by Pompey, Sulla's successor as the leader of Roman politics. Pompey showed himself an ardent imperialist, a popular leader, and a representative especially of those financial interests in Rome that were cashing in on the needs of the provinces. These men, eager to increase their opportunities by annexing new provinces, looked upon Pompey as their man. His emergence as a dominant leader in Roman public life had come in 67 B.C., when he was entrusted with an extraordinary command to deal with the domination of the Mediterranean by the Cilician pirates. The rise of the Cilician pirate state—for it was almost that—had come about as a result of Rome's destruction of the leading eastern powers while she herself, preoccupied with expansion, had not been able to devote sufficient atten-

[15]For these and many more amazing details see David Magie, *Roman Rule in Asia Minor*, Vol. I, Chaps. ix and x, especially pp. 216–217, 252.
[16]Trever, II, 184.

tion to this threat. As early as 167 B.C. Rome had made the Greek island of Delos a free port in order to create a commercial rival for Rhodes. Delos had subsequently become the great slave market of the Mediterranean world. To this market the depredations of the pirates upon the coasts of the Mediterranean furnished the 10,000 slaves that, it is reported, could be sold there daily. The pirate fleet numbered more than a thousand ships built, manned, and directed by enterprising and intelligent chieftains whose boldness knew no limits. They did not hesitate, in fact, to attack the coasts of Italy and to destroy a Roman fleet in the harbor at Ostia. They were thus in a position to cut off all Rome's communications with her overseas possessions. With the power granted him by his extraordinary command Pompey was able to crush them speedily. In less than three months from the beginning of his campaign and seven weeks from his departure for the East he had forced them back to the coast of Cilicia, had destroyed their fleet, and then had pursued them inland. Those who survived and surrendered were transformed from slaves into prosperous colonists of such new towns as Soli and Pompeiopolis, and Cilicia itself was made into a Roman province.[17]

POMPEY AND MITHRIDATES

Such efficiency was rewarded with a similar command in 66 B.C. against Mithridates, not yet reconciled to the position to which he had been forced by Sulla. In 75 B.C. the kingdom of Bithynia had been bequeathed to Rome by its King Nicomedes III and had been converted into a Roman province. When Mithridates disputed this claim, Rome declared war. In the period just previous to Pompey's assumption of the command this war had not gone well for Rome. Now Pompey defeated Mithridates at Nicopolis, and his kingdom of Pontus was made into a Roman province, governed together with Bithynia. Mithridates fled to the Crimea, on the northern shore of the Black Sea, and contemplated the conquest of Rome, with the help of the Celts, by an invasion down the Danube and into Italy. Thwarted in these hopes, the old monarch, rather than surrender to a traitorous son and grace a Roman province, took poison. When it failed to take effect he turned to one of his Gallic officers and persuaded him to do what poison could not.

POMPEY AND THE SELEUCIDS

Before returning home in triumph Pompey put an end to the reign of the Seleucids in Syria by deposing the last monarch of the line, Antiochus XIII, and annexing his dominions as the Roman province of Syria (63 B.C.). After marching into Jerusalem, massacring its citizens, leveling its walls, and besieging the Temple, Pompey abolished Jewish independence under the Maccabees and added Judea to the Syrian province. He started for home in 62 B.C., and eight months after his arrival he was granted the most

[17]See Magie, *Roman Rule*, I, 300 ff.

splendid triumph Rome had ever staged. "For two whole days the populace was dazzled by the display of the conqueror's exploits, including both his successes against the pirates and his victories over the kings of the East. Placards boasted that in addition to destroying the forces and ships of the corsairs, the General had conquered fourteen nations, extending from the Crimea to the Red Sea. . . . Six kings besides Mithradates had been overcome in war, eight hundred and forty-six pirate-ships had been destroyed or captured and fifteen hundred and thirty-eight towns and strongholds taken. The amount of gold and silver, in money and plate, that accrued to the public treasury was set at one hundred and twenty million denarii, and the annual revenues from the newly-acquired provinces were estimated at eight-five millions—nearly twice the total amount that Rome had hitherto received from her dependencies. Waggons and litters bore ornaments and trophies, jewelled vessels and crowns, golden chariots and banqueting-couches, among them a couch said to have belonged to the Persian monarch Darius . . . also golden statues of the gods, silver statues of Pharnaces I of Pontus and Mithradates, besides a colossal statue of the latter, made of solid gold. On the second day of the triumph—Pompey's own birthday —were displayed the notable captives, three hundred and twenty-four in number: pirate-chieftains, royal women taken from the Scythians . . . Aristobulus, the vanquished claimant to the Jewish High Priesthood, together with three of his children, five sons and two daughters of Mithradates, and Tigranes, the prince of Armenia, with his wife and daughter and one of his harem. Paintings of Mithradates and Tigranes the elder were exhibited, showing them in battle or in flight, and the death of the Pontic monarch was also depicted. Finally, attended by the officers who had shared in his wars, came the Conqueror himself, riding in a four-horse chariot, bedecked with jewels and arrayed in a cloak which, it was said, once belonged to Alexander the Great."[18]

THE FIRST TRIUMVIRATE

In 60 B.C., the year following his triumph, Pompey, disgruntled over the refusal of the Senate to reward his veterans with land or to confirm his arrangements in the East, allied with two ardent imperialists in the city, Crassus and Julius Caesar, to form the First Triumvirate. Like Pompey, Crassus, the wealthiest man in Rome, represented the interests of the bankers, taxgatherers, and loan sharks, who at the moment were pressing

---

[18]Magie, I, 366–367. Frank, *Roman Imperialism*, pp. 321–322, remarks: "The new annual tribute that Pompey acquired for the state from all these provinces and princes amounted to 35,000,000 drachmas, whereas the whole annual revenue of the state before his arrival in the East had been only 50,000,000 drachmas all told. We may fairly estimate that the acquisitions of Pompey about quintupled the amount of revenue that the province of Asia had hitherto yielded." Trever, *Ancient Civilization*, II, 199, says: "He increased the Roman revenue in annual tribute from 200,000,000 to 340,000,000 sesterces ($10,000,000 to $17,000,000). Besides, he paid a bonus of 384,000,000 sesterces to his soldiers and turned into the Roman treasury 480,000,000 more."

for more favorable terms on the state contracts for collection of the eastern revenue. He had seen in Julius Caesar the future big man of the Roman state and, according to Plutarch, had lent him no less than 830 talents (almost a million dollars) to satisfy his creditors before he went off on his first imperial mission to Spain. Caesar had borrowed this money to buy his way into the favor of the Roman populace and, as a result of an unscrupulous and demagogic career, was now in a position to pave the way for military achievements that would permit him to challenge Pompey's leading position in the state. He understood only too well that the way to political power was through imperial expansion, and there can be little doubt that his joining with Pompey and Crassus was planned to make this possible. Indeed in 59 B.C. he arranged to have assigned to him the provinces of Illyricum, Cisalpine and Transalpine Gaul, with four legions, for a period of five years. When the First Triumvirate was renewed in 56 B.C. this command was renewed for another five years, to date from 54 B.C. Crassus was allotted Syria for five years, and Pompey, Spain and Africa.

CAESAR'S CONQUEST OF GAUL

Transalpine Gaul, established as a province in 121 B.C., included the strip of coastal territory running from Italy to the Pyrenees, the two leading ports of which were Narbonne and Marseilles. Beyond it to the north, bounded on the west by the Atlantic and on the north and east by the Rhine and the Alps, lay the fair lands inhabited by Celtic tribes who had moved into the area under pressure from the Germans. In the centuries following their occupation the Gauls had established a civilization far above the level of primitive barbarism. Those along the Atlantic coast had extensive trade relations with their kinsmen in the British Isles, Britons, Irish, and Scots, who had originally crossed the English Channel from Gaul. Beyond the Rhine were the formidable Germans, and in the western Alps the Helvetians. Transalpine Gaul, at the moment of Caesar's arrival in the province, was threatened by both the Helvetians and the Germans. The grandiose project presented itself to Caesar of conquering the Gauls while protecting them from Helvetians and Germans, and possibly even extending the Roman state to Britain and Germany. It is hard to believe that Caesar did not from the start envisage the implications of this project not only for himself but for the Roman Empire. During his first year in Gaul he defeated the Helvetians and the Germans under their King Ariovistus, thus establishing the Rhine River as the Roman boundary. In the following two years, by defeating the Aquitanians of southern Gaul, the maritime Veneti of the Normandy and Brittany coasts, and the Belgians of northern Gaul, he practically subdued all Gaul. In 55–54 B.C. he was in a position to make a show of Roman arms across the Rhine from Coblenz and in Britain. Of the Rhine crossing after the speedy building of the first bridge across this river, Plutarch says that Caesar "coveted the fame of being the first man to cross the Rhine with an army," and of his crossing into Britain he remarks that it "was celebrated for its daring. For he was the first to launch a fleet upon the western ocean and to sail through the Atlantic sea carrying an army to wage war. The island was of incredible magnitude, and furnished much matter of dispute to multitudes of writers, some of whom averred that its name and story had been fabricated, since it never had existed and did not then exist; and in his attempt to occupy it he carried the Roman supremacy beyond the confines of the inhabited world." (VII, 499)[19] It is interesting to speculate upon just what thoughts were running through Caesar's mind as he marched over his bridge into Germany or first saw the British mainland. These events pointed to the future. Meanwhile he had to consolidate the conquest of Gaul.

In the last year of Caesar's extraordinary command he had to crush the revolts of the Gauls, whom the speed of Roman conquest had left too stunned to realize that their turbulent independence had come to an end. At its height the revolt included almost all the conquered Gauls, led by Vercingetorix of the tribe of the Arverni. Such events as the Roman massacre of 40,000 inhabitants of Avaricum, including old men, women, and children, inspired the hatred of the rebels. Vercingetorix and his army were bottled up in Alesia, where they were starved into surrender. By 51 B.C. Gaul had been pacified, and, while not yet reduced to the status of a Roman province, it was forced to pay an annual tribute of something less than $2,000,000 a year. Vercingetorix was sent in chains to Rome to await Caesar's triumph.

The death of Crassus on his Parthian campaign (55–53 B.C.) left Pompey the master of Rome, a position he used to prepare for the final struggle with Caesar.[20] Caesar crossed the Rubicon River, the boundary between his province of Cisalpine Gaul and Italy, on 10 January, 49 B.C., to answer Pompey's challenge.[21] He left behind a conquest of unusual importance for the history of western Europe. Henceforth the Celtic tribes of Gaul, as well as the Iberian peoples of Spain, were subjected as provincials to the discipline of Roman civilization. When once the Roman Empire in the West had gone to pieces, a thoroughly Romanized Gaul was to be the heart of the revived civilization of western Europe. In the course of centuries this Romanized Gaul was to become France, and without her Roman experience France would never have been able to make her incalculable contributions to the growth of a western tradition. Moreover, Caesar had left behind him Britain and Germany as possible future provinces of the Roman state.

[19]Citations from Plutarch in my text are to *Parallel Lives*, trans. B. Perrin, Loeb, Nos. 46, 47, 65, 80, 87, 98–103, 11 vols.

[20]See p. 212.

[21]It will be more convenient to deal with the political consequences of this act and of Caesar's later career in another place and to consider here the implications of this further expansion.

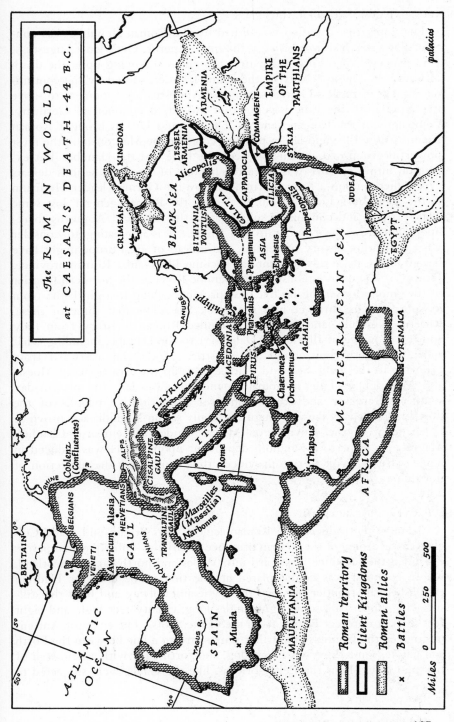

The ROMAN WORLD
at CAESAR'S DEATH · 44 B.C.

BRITAIN

ATLANTIC OCEAN

VENETI
BELGIANS
Coblenz (Confluentes)
Rhine R.
Avaricum Alesia
HELVETIANS
ALPS
AQUITANIANS
GAUL
TRANSALPINE GAUL
CISALPINE GAUL
Marseilles (Massilia)
Narbonne
SPAIN
Munda
TAGUS R.
MAURETANIA

DANUBE R.
ILLYRICUM
ITALY
Rome
EPIRUS
MACEDONIA
Philippi
Pharsalus
Chaeronea
Orchomenus
ACHAIA
Thapsus
AFRICA

CRIMEAN KINGDOM
BLACK SEA
BITHYNIA-PONTUS
Nicopolis
LESSER ARMENIA
ARMENIA
GALATIA
CAPPADOCIA
COMMAGENE
Pergamum
ASIA
Ephesus
CILICIA
SYRIA
Pompeiopolis
MEDITERRANEAN SEA
CYRENAICA
EGYPT
JUDEA
EMPIRE OF THE PARTHIANS

palacios

Roman territory
Client Kingdoms
Roman allies
× Battles

Miles
0   250   500

The imperialist tradition established by the Roman Republic was continued at a much slower pace by the first emperor, Octavian (Augustus), who managed to restore order after the chaos following upon the death of Caesar.[22] The insecurity of the Rhine frontier, caused by the continuous attacks of restless Germans, tempted Augustus for a moment to move this frontier to the Elbe River, if not indeed to conquer all Germany. Campaigns of the Roman generals Tiberius and Drusus brought Roman legions to the Elbe and led to plans to conquer the Marcomanni, the most powerful group of Germans between the Elbe and the Danube. But expansion into Germany was thwarted by one of the most serious defeats ever inflicted upon a Roman army, that by the German leader Hermann in the Teutoburg Forest in A.D. 9. Varus, the Roman general, lost some 20,000 troops and committed suicide after the disgrace. Augustus thereupon withdrew the frontier to the Rhine. It is interesting to consider what the future history of central, and indeed of all, Europe might have been if Germany at this moment had become, like Gaul, a Roman province. However, Augustus established the Danube River as the northern frontier of the empire by setting up five new provinces along its right bank, from its source to its entrance into the Black Sea. The first three of these, Rhaetia, Noricum, and Pannonia, extended Roman territory from Italy and the province of Illyricum (Dalmatia) to the Danube, including what today is eastern Switzerland and Austria. Moesia ran eastward from Dalmatia to the Black Sea, and Thrace took up the area between Moesia and Macedonia. Thus a Roman foundation was laid for present-day southern Germany and Austria and for the primitive peoples of the northern Balkans. Likewise Augustus finally set up Numidia as a province independent of the province of Africa. Under the emperor Claudius, Mauretania, hitherto a kingdom dependent upon Rome, was reduced in A.D. 45 after a revolt to two provinces, thus completing the subjection of northwest Africa.

THE PROVINCE OF BRITAIN

Claudius reintroduced the Roman legions into Britain and made Colchester the capital of the Roman province of Britain. Subsequent emperors expanded the province westward into Wales and northward to Scotland, whose conquest was contemplated at one time. The emperor Hadrian established the frontier between the Tyne and Solway and built the still-surviving stone wall, some eighty miles long, twenty feet high, and eight feet thick, to protect Britain from the Celtic Scots. The emperor Antoninus moved the frontier still farther northward to a line between the Forth and Clyde, some thirty-six miles long, and fortified it with a new wall of turf and clay. Thus the Celtic Britons, like the Gauls, were subjected to

[22]See pp. 213 ff.

the process of Romanization, especially in southeastern and central England if not in the north, and although the Romanization of Britain was not to be of such fundamental importance to the future England as the corresponding Romanization of Gaul, Spain, and Italy, still another group of Celts had been brought into the domain of the civilization of the Mediterranean.

THE TITHED LANDS AND DACIA

Two extensions beyond the Rhine-Danube frontier were made during the first century. The first, the triangle of southwestern Germany between the upper Danube and Rhine, begun by the emperor Vespasian and continued by Domitian, amounted to an extension of the provinces of upper Germany and Rhaetia. When completed, these Tithed Lands, as they were called from the rents paid by the colonists, were protected from the Germans by a ditch and palisade 228 miles long, from Rheinbrohl on the Rhine to Pfahlbronn, and by a stone wall for 108 miles, from Pfahlbronn to Eining on the Danube. The second extension came from the conquest of the area of modern Roumania north of the lower Danube, inhabited by primitive Dacians. The conquest was completed by the emperor Trajan in A.D. 107 and the area made into a Roman province and settled, after a fairly thorough extermination of the Dacians, "by forcible colonization from 'all over the Empire,' especially from the Danube lands, Asia Minor, and Syria."[23] When, in A.D. 167, the Danube frontier from Rhaetia to Moesia was overrun by the German tribes of the Marcomanni and Quadi, the emperor Marcus Aurelius immediately rushed to the defense of these provinces and succeeded in two campaigns in holding the Danube frontier. Had it not been for his death at Vienna in A.D. 180, it is altogether likely that the earlier plans of Augustus to reduce the Marcomanni to provincial status would have been completed, with an extension of the Roman frontier beyond the Danube to the Carpathians.

THE END OF THE PTOLEMIES

In the East, likewise, the Roman state expanded noticeably under the empire. After his defeat of Antony and Cleopatra at Actium, Augustus entered and annexed Egypt, bringing to an end the dynasty of the Ptolemies. Egypt, however, was not made an ordinary Roman province. The Ptolemies owned Egypt as their own private property and, in return for their maintenance of the system of irrigation upon which the population depended, received rents for their lands from what were essentially serfs of the Egyptian king. Augustus, as the successor of the Ptolemies, took over this position as virtual Egyptian king, the private owner of Egypt, and to this position the subsequent emperors succeeded. The rents of the imperial Egyptian serfs went into the personal treasury of the

[23] Trever, II, 520.

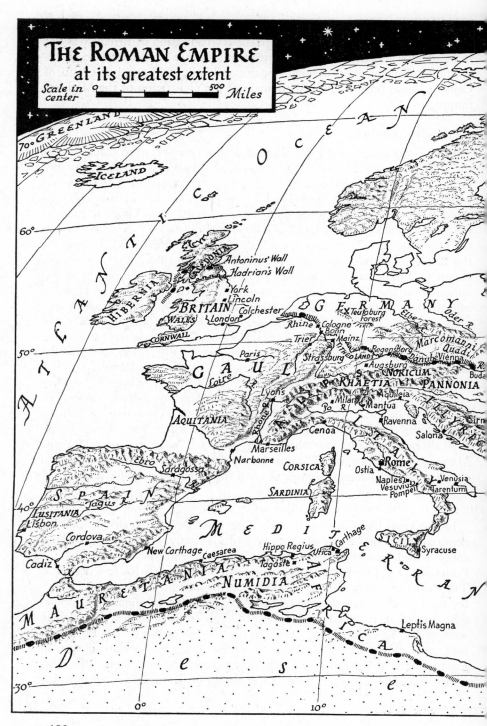

THE ROMAN EMPIRE
at its greatest extent

Scale in center 0 —————— 500 Miles

GREENLAND

70°

ICELAND

ATLANTIC OCEAN

60°

HIBERNIA

CALEDONIA

Antoninus' Wall
Hadrian's Wall

York
Lincoln
BRITAIN
WALES
London
Colchester
CORNWALL

GERMANY

Teutoburg forest

Rhine
Cologne
Bonn
Trier
Mainz

Marcomanni
Quadi

50°

Paris

GAUL
Loire

Strassburg
Augsburg
NORICUM
Regensburg
Danube Vienna
PANNONIA
Buda

Lyons
RHAETIA
Milan
Mantua
Aquileia

AQUITANIA

Rhone R.
Po R.

Ravenna
Salona

Genoa

Marseilles
Narbonne

CORSICA

ITALY

Rome
Ostia
Naples
Vesuvius
Pompeii
Venusia
Tarentum

SPAIN

Ebro
Saragossa

SARDINIA

MEDITERRANEAN

SICILY
Syracuse

40°

LUSITANIA
Lisbon
Tagus R.

Cordova

Cadiz

New Carthage
Caesarea
Hippo Regius
Tagaste
Utica
Carthage

MAURETANIA
NUMIDIA
AFRICA

Leptis Magna

DESERT

30°

0°
10°

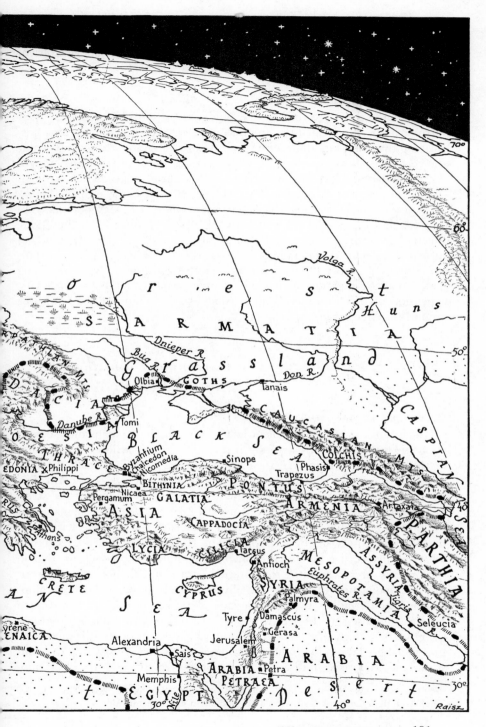

emperors, and with Egypt as a model this method of exploitation was adopted for other imperial estates. "Egypt, then, furnishes the chief, though not the only, link between the feudal system of the ancient Orient and that of medieval Europe."[24]

FROM EXPANSION TO DEFENSE

Trajan, the conqueror of Dacia, extended the eastern boundaries to their farthest limit. He pushed the empire into the Arabian peninsula by transforming the client kingdom of the Nabataean Arabs into what soon became the very prosperous province of Arabia Petraea. Six years later he entered Armenia, deposed its king, and made it a Roman province. As a result of successful campaigns against Parthia the lands of the upper Tigris-Euphrates Valley became the Roman provinces of Mesopotamia and Assyria, and the rest of the valley to the Persian Gulf a client kingdom. But his successor, Hadrian, abandoned this old path of Alexander and returned Armenia, Mesopotamia, and Assyria to the Parthian king. This emperor, who also built walls to protect Britain and southwestern Germany, may be regarded as having brought to an end the extraordinary expansion of the little city Rome to include the whole of the land area around the Mediterranean Sea.

The Government and the Society of the Roman World State

SUMMARY OF ROMAN POLITICAL DEVELOPMENT

Our interest in the government and society of the Romans must center upon the transformations wrought in each by the expansion traced earlier in this chapter. These transformations can be simply described. Like Athens, Rome, after the dethronement of her early kings, was controlled by a patrician oligarchy, or aristocracy. This oligarchy, under the stress of the expansion of the city, was forced to give way to the demands of the simple, nonnoble Roman citizens, or plebeians, and to share with them the political power of the Republic. The Roman Republic thus assumed what we may call a democratic form. It is quite clear, however, that in spite of the preservation of the external forms of a democratic constitution the acquisition of empire actually thwarted the democratic development of the Republic. It did this in two ways: (1) by making the Roman Senate, composed of the wealthy, conservative, officeholding aristocracy, the governing body of the state; and (2) by giving to successful generals or provincial governors the military and financial means to override the constitutional limitations of power whenever they saw fit to do so. The demo-

[24]The selection from Tenney Frank, *Roman Imperialism*, p. 351, copyright 1914 by The Macmillan Co., and used with The Macmillan Co.'s permission.

cratic promise of the early Republic was thus never realized, and the Republic itself was succeeded by a monarchy that quickly destroyed the remnants of the republican constitution. This monarchy, in the first and second centuries A.D., established the Pax Romana of the Mediterranean world. Its absolute and divine emperor brought security briefly to a limited few and took away liberty or the promise of liberty from all. Of such a transformation it could be asked—What price peace?

SUMMARY OF SOCIAL DEVELOPMENT

The social transformation brought about by expansion was similarly tragic. It destroyed the early democratic character of Roman society, founded upon the small landowning farmer. Imperial war ruined this farmer. It made of him a tenant on a large estate or an unemployed member of an urban proletariat living on the public dole. It turned over his farm and the public lands acquired by conquest to the capitalistic large-estate owner, who used the slave gang, the captives of war, for labor. Expansion, moreover, created a middle class composed of merchants and industrialists whose profits often came from war and who thrived on the opportunities created by empire. Among these were also contractors for the right to collect provincial taxes, to build public works, and to exploit state properties; and in addition there were bankers to lend funds to imperial subjects made needy by the demands of the conqueror. Expansion created as well a new class of professional soldiers more loyal to their commanding generals and to their pocketbooks than to the state. It set up, finally, after the imperial monarchy had been established, a new aristocracy of trained bureaucrats to serve the needs of a universal despotism. Ultimately, as we shall see, this complex society created by expansion hardened into something approaching a caste system.

PATRICIANS AND PLEBEIANS

This is the very general picture that a view of many centuries presents. Such a view, however, obscures the temporary developments and achievements that fit into the main picture. Let us examine it more closely and bring to light some of this detail. The creation along democratic lines of the republican constitution of Rome took some three centuries following the revolutionary overthrow of the early monarchy (ca. 509 B.C.). The destruction of the monarchy, whose last kings were Etruscan, was the work of the patrician clans (gentes), and it produced an undying hatred for tyrannical kingship. The origin of the patrician clans is to be traced back to the original conquerors of Rome, and that of the plebeians to the conquered and to those foreigners (compare the Athenian thetes) who had moved into the city after its foundation. Originally there had been as many as seventy-three of these noble, privileged clans, but by the end of the third century B.C. they had declined to twenty, and with this decline in actual numbers is to be associated the loss of their exclusive political power. By the same time the number of Roman citizens had grown to about one million. Of these the far greater number were plebeians who had been called upon to share the obligations, military and financial, incurred by the early expansion. The history of the making of a democratic, republican constitution is the history of begrudging concession on the part of the patrician nobles to the demands of the plebeians (*plebs*), increasingly conscious of their indispensability. These concessions, however, never went to the length of establishing a real city-state democracy such as that of the Athenians.

THE REPUBLICAN MAGISTRATES

The first task of the patrician revolutionaries of 509 B.C. was to set up with proper safeguards a substitute for the abandoned king. This was the consul, the chief magistrate in possession of executive power (*imperium*). For the life tenure of the king, however, was substituted the annual tenure of the magistrate, and in order to avoid the abuse of power on the part of the consul for even one year he was given a colleague who, as a magistrate of equal power, could veto his acts. The increase in the size of the city, together with its expansion, called for additional magistrates. The first to be added were two quaestors to take charge of the public treasury and two aediles to exercise police power in the city and to be responsible for the administration of public works, streets, games, markets, and the grain supply. To these were added the censors, whose original duty was to compile the census, or list of citizens, with property ratings suitable for assignment to military service and for the payment of taxes. These censors acquired great additional authority, becoming virtually ministers of finance, responsible for the collection of taxes and the expenditure of public funds. Thus they were charged with the management of revenues from the provinces, including the exploitation of these by the private corporations of Roman citizens (the publicans). They ultimately received the authority to draw up the list of members of the Senate, whom they selected not only by wealth but by reputation and character. Their power to draft the census and membership lists of the Senate made them to a large extent the arbiters of public morals. Finally, there were the praetors, the judicial magistrates. Of these there came to be two categories, the urban praetor (*praetor urbanus*), who judged cases between Roman citizens, and the peregrine praetor (*praetor peregrinus*), who judged cases between Romans and non-Romans.[25] In time the specific conditions for holding the magistracies became fixed, and the order in which they might be held (*cursus honorum*), determined. Beginning with the quaestor, the order ran through the offices of aedile, censor, and praetor, to the consulship. Ultimately these magistrates came automatically to be members of the Senate, filling in the ranks of the declining patrician clans. It can easily be imagined that a magistrate, himself a patrician and

[25]See p. 254.

holding office for only one year, sharing his authority with one or more colleagues, and finally entering into the membership of the august Senate, was not likely to be tempted to challenge the position of the Senate.

THE SENATE, "COMITIA CURIATA," AND "COMITIA CENTURIATA"

The patricians preserved from the monarchical period those political institutions in which they were dominant: the council of clan leaders (the Senate) and the curiate assembly (*comitia curiata*), composed of all citizen members of the clans (*curiae*). At some time near 500 B.C. the centuriate assembly (*comitia centuriata*) was created, set up as a new assembly representing the body of citizens as an army. This assembly was based on a division of the Roman citizenry into classes on the basis of ownership of property made by the censor for purposes of military conscription and taxation. To each class was assigned so many centuries, or companies, for the purpose of voting in the assembly, each century possessing one vote. To the wealthiest class serving in the cavalry were given eighteen centuries, or votes, and to the wealthiest class serving in the infantry, eighty centuries. Of a total of 193 centuries assigned to all classes the men of wealth possessed a majority (98), and the landless proletariat, in contrast, one century. Since the centuries representing the wealthiest class voted first, and since voting was stopped when a majority was reached, it was ordinarily not necessary to listen to the votes of the poorer classes. During the early Republic this centuriate assembly of the nation in arms took over most of the powers of the older curiate assembly of clan members. It elected the consuls and the chief republican magistrates. Under the presidency, usually, of a consul, it passed laws subject to the confirmation of the Senate. As long as the very wealthy controlled it its existence caused no great concern to the patricians. Indeed it was but part of the monopoly of political power which they held. The plebeian majority, counting for nothing in this assembly, was likewise excluded from the Senate and the magistracies. In the absence of a codification of the law the plebeians felt themselves the victims of patrician judges. They considered themselves exploited also by the laws on debt, and discriminated against in the assignment of public lands. Moreover, they were prevented from intermarrying with patrician families. The people who belonged to the class containing the vast majority of the citizens, formed the great mass of the army, and made the largest contribution to the public treasury were held down to the status of political, economic, and social pariahs by a small aristocracy of birth.

THE PLEBEIAN PROGRAM OF REFORM

It is thus possible to speak of a plebeian program for the correction of their virtual exclusion from public life. Its main demands were (1) a plebeian assembly with appropriate electoral, judicial, and legislative powers; (2) a reform of the composition of the centuriate assembly that would give proper recognition to the plebeian class; (3) extension to plebeians of the right to stand for election to the chief magistracies and to be included among the members of the Senate; (4) the codification into law of the customs of the people; (5) the redrafting of the inhuman laws on debt and the enactment of new laws on landowning that would keep the small farmer from being pushed to the wall; and finally (6) the removal of the social discrimination contained in the marriage laws.

The long struggle of the fifth, fourth, and third centuries B.C. to achieve these reforms constitutes one of the fine chapters in the history of human liberty, and it has been a constant inspiration to subsequent groups bent upon similar reform. At least once the plebeian leaders were obliged to use the weapon of a kind of general strike to force the patricians to make concessions. They threatened to have the *plebs* pack up and leave the city to the patricians. By and large, however, both parties avoided extreme measures, and in the end a temporary balance of political forces was achieved that recognized, in theory, that the source of political power was the people or, as we say, that sovereignty was popular in origin. This was the work of those early, sturdy Romans, uncorrupted by empire, who had been responsible for the rather liberal policy used in unifying the Italian peninsula. By the time of the First Punic War the reformed republican constitution had already been elaborated.

THE "COMITIA TRIBUTA" AND THE TRIBUNE

Some features of the new constitution need to be treated in detail. The incorporation into the political machinery of the state of a special assembly representing the *plebs* was the most important of these reforms. This assembly, the *comitia tributa*, or tribal assembly, was based on a former organization of Roman citizens into tribes. These tribes were simply composed of the citizens, patrician as well as plebeian, who resided in the wards or territorial divisions of the city-state of Rome. There came to be four urban and thirty-one rural wards, and thus thirty-five tribes. Additional citizens were customarily enrolled in these thirty-five tribes. The patricians constituted a small minority while the majority was composed of Roman farmers of the rural areas. When legally organized into an assembly the vote was taken according to tribes, the majority thus coming from the countryside. The new assembly elected its own presiding officer, the tribune (*tribunus plebis*), and the original power granted him was meant to protect the *plebs* against a hostile or arbitrary government. There ultimately were ten such officials. The tribune was authorized to veto the acts of other magistrates and to summon the tribes together to make or pass decisions (plebiscites) of their own, originally binding upon the *plebs* only. Plebeian leaders, however, sought to have the plebiscites of the tribal assembly considered as law for the whole citizen body, patrician and plebeian alike. This was first secured by requiring Senate approval to make plebiscites into law. Not until the Hortensian Law (287

B.C.) were plebiscites of the tribal assembly recognized as the law of the Roman state without such confirmation, an independence never achieved by the centuriate assembly. Thus laws could be passed by two assemblies during the Republic, the centuriate and the tribal. Ultimately special spheres of legislation were divided between them: the centuriate assembly lost its general lawmaking authority to the *comitia tributa* and limited itself to questions of war, peace, and alliance. A corresponding separation of authority also came to be made between the two assemblies in respect to judicial and electoral questions. The centuriate assembly acted as a court of appeal in cases calling for capital punishment, the tribal in cases involving only large fines. The former came to elect the chief magistrates, the consuls, censors, and praetors; and the latter, the lesser magistrates.

THE REFORM OF THE "COMITIA CENTURIATA" AND THE SENATE

The reform of the centuriate assembly in the middle of the third century made it a less plutocratic assembly. Each class in this assembly was now given seventy centuries, or votes, that is, two for each tribe. This raised the number of centuries and votes in this assembly from 193 to 373. A majority in this reformed assembly was now 187 instead of the former 98. To get a majority it was necessary to include more votes than the centuries of the wealthiest class. The procedure still limited the majority to the wealthy, but some liberalization had taken place. Those whose vote it was now necessary to take in the centuriate in order to get a majority were the same rural middle-class farmers who controlled the tribal assembly as members of the thirty-one rural tribes. Thus the social basis of political power had widened to include the middle as well as the wealthiest (aristocratic) class.

The campaign to permit plebeians to stand for the magistracies was a prelude to their inclusion in the Senate itself. Beginning with the quaestorship in 421 B.C., the magistracies were gradually opened to the plebeians, the consulship being finally made available to them in 367 B.C. The office of tribune was likewise enhanced by making it possible for the tribune to convoke the Senate, to act as its presiding officer, and to demand its vote. After 400 B.C. the Senate itself was not necessarily limited to those of patrician rank, and about 312 B.C., when the determination of membership in the Senate was given to the censor, it was provided that the censor must take new senators (they were appointed for life) from those who had previously been magistrates. Thus it was possible for a plebeian who had become a magistrate to enter the body formerly limited to patricians alone.

LIMITATIONS OF THE REPUBLICAN CONSTITUTION

When the legal custom of Rome was codified in the form of the Twelve Tables (451 B.C.),[26] the plebeians had removed any possible discrimination

[26]See pp. 252 f.

that might come from patrician judges. A few years later the Canuleian Law removed the social stigma which forbade marriage between a patrician and a plebeian. Despite numerous attempts, however, no satisfactory solution of the agrarian problem was reached during this early period. For this failure the Roman state was to pay heavily.

Although one may speak of the equalization of the patrician and plebeian orders in the ways mentioned above, of the elaboration of a constitution with democratic features, and of a Roman doctrine of popular sovereignty, certain limitations must be kept in mind. The first was the lack of popular initiative. "The people could convene for no business whatever unless summoned by a magistrate. They could consider no other subject than that proposed to them by the president; they could take no part in the deliberation excepting in so far as the president granted permission to individuals; they could merely vote yes or no on the question presented to them. Notwithstanding the theory of popular sovereignty these conditions prevented the rise of a real democracy; they placed the assemblies under the control of the magistrates, who as a rule, including even the tribunes, were willing ministers of the Senate."[27] The second was that the leaders of the plebeians, when admitted to the magistracies and through them to the Senate, became essentially the members of a new nobility composed of those families who had held public office. These men, when enriched by the spoils of empire, saw to it that the democratic trend in Roman society did not reach the point of establishing more democracy in the actual operation of the government nor extend to the economic and social spheres.

POLYBIUS ON THE ROMAN CONSTITUTION

These limitations were of no concern to the Greek Polybius, the first historian of Rome. If Pericles extolled the virtues of Athenian democracy, Polybius was no less eulogistic of the constitution of the Republic at the middle of the second century. He saw in it a wonderful balance between those three forms of government that Greek political theorists loved to discuss: monarchy, aristocracy, and democracy. "For," he said, "if one fixed one's eyes on the power of the consuls, the constitution seemed completely monarchical and royal; if on that of the senate it seemed again to be aristocratic; and when one looked at the power of the masses, it seemed clearly to be a democracy. . . . It was impossible even for a native to pronounce with certainty whether the whole system was aristocratic, democratic, or monarchical." Because of this balance of political powers, Polybius said, "it is impossible to find a better political system than this." When such a state is faced with critical issues in times either of war or peace the constitution creates unity of action on the part of the citizen body. "For when one part having grown out of proportion to the others

[27]The selection from G. W. Botsford, *The Roman Assemblies*, pp. 345–346, copyright 1909 by The Macmillan Co., and used with The Macmillan Co.'s permission.

aims at supremacy and tends to become too predominant, it is evident
that, as . . . none of the three [that is, the monarchical, aristocratic, and
democratic] is absolute, but the purpose of the one can be counterworked
and thwarted by the others, none of them will excessively outgrow the
others or treat them with contempt. . . . Any aggressive impulse is sure
to be checked and from the outset each estate stands in dread of being interfered with by the others." (III, 297, 309, 311, 318)

THE INADAPTABILITY OF THE REPUBLICAN CONSTITUTION

The stability of a constitution, the political organization of society,
depends in part upon the stability of the society itself and in part upon
the flexibility of the constitution, that is, its ability to adapt itself to the
needs of a changing society. The Roman society upon which the republican constitution was based was composed of a small minority of
wealthy senatorial nobles and a majority of middle-class peasant proprietors. This social structure was considerably modified in the course of the
second and first centuries B.C. as a result of imperial expansion. If the
machinery of a republican constitution could be used successfully to control these radical social changes and to direct them in the spirit which had
determined its own formation, in the democratic spirit of extending political privilege and power beyond a small aristocratic clique, then the Republic might live and grow. If it could not do this, then obviously the
Republic was doomed. The answer of history is that it could not, and to
this inability we must now turn.

SOCIAL CHANGES DURING THE REPUBLIC

The social changes that could not be controlled or directed by the republican constitution and that in turn transformed it first into an oligarchy, then into a dictatorship, and finally into a monarchy were (1) the
enlargement of the older patrician aristocracy into a patrician-plebeian
aristocracy of officeholders and ex-officeholders; (2) the formation of a
new equestrian class (the *equites* or knights) of businessmen (*negotia-
tores*), public contractors, bankers, and private collectors of imperial
revenue and leasers of public property (publicans); (3) the decline of the
free peasantry, with a corresponding increase in slaves and urban proletariat; and (4) the rise of the professional soldiery supporting the ambitious conquerors of new provinces. Together these changes destroyed the
possibility of strengthening the democratic character of the republican
constitution and of building a responsible administration for the expanding state. Together they meant that whatever were to be the achievements
of Roman civilization and culture their benefits would largely be monopolized by an élite. The exclusion of the large majority of the people
from these benefits rendered them indifferent or hostile to the state, thus
contributing directly to what historians refer to as the decline and fall of
the Roman Empire.

No sooner was the earlier supremacy of the patricians limited by the extension of political privileges to the plebeians than a new and enlarged aristocracy took shape. This development may be interpreted as an attempt on the part of the older aristocracy to save itself from extinction by incorporating new elements into its privileged circle, a phenomenon that is not limited to Roman society. In any case, the patrician group was enlarged by those plebeians who came to hold the republican magistracies and thus entered the Senate, the continuing stronghold of the new oligarchy. The new patrician-plebeian aristocracy numbered by the end of the Republic some six hundred intermarried families. By the end of the third century (219 B.C.) they were prevented from directly entering the newly opened world of imperial trade and commerce by a law that prohibited senators and their sons from owning ships large enough to engage in extensive overseas trade. The same law probably prevented them from taking contracts from the government. In origin the law was an attempt on the part of the Roman peasant to keep the nobility from sharing the commercial opportunities opened up by the conquest, and thus to remove those who governed from the temptation of shaping policy to accord with profits, present and future. As a matter of fact it did not prevent the senatorial aristocracy from participating in these profits, for they secretly joined the companies organized to exploit them; while for those inclined to obey the law it encouraged investment of capital in Italian land, contributing thus to the ruin of the small, independent Roman farmer. Such legislation helped to establish the notion that a genuine aristocracy does not stain its hands with filthy lucre but concentrates on the business of government. For the enlarged aristocracy of the second and first centuries this concentration was directed toward guarding the prerogatives of the Senate, directing the magistrates, and manipulating the operations of the assemblies.

THE NEW CLASS OF EQUESTRIANS

The political monopoly of the Senate was challenged in the late Republic by the new and small class of businessmen, or knights. Their rise is to be explained in part by the fact that the government of the Republic found it impossible to set up public institutions to administer public needs and properties and to create an imperial civil service. There thus arose, as Polybius states, "a vast number of contracts" which the censors gave out "for the construction and repair of public buildings" and for work on "navigable rivers, harbours, gardens, mines, lands, in fact everything that forms part of the Roman dominion. . . . Everyone is interested in these contracts and the work they involve. For certain people are the actual purchasers from the censors of the contracts, others are the partners of these first, others stand surety for them, others pledge their own fortunes to the state for this purpose." We have already met these entrepreneurs in

Sicily and Asia undertaking to collect new imperial taxes and rents imposed upon the provincials, and lending money with which to pay their tribute to hard-pressed, newly conquered areas.[28] Their vital interest in expansion can be easily understood, and thus their eagerness to influence if not to control politics. Like many men of their kind, they preferred to actually control by the use of their wealth those who did govern rather than to govern personally. What they finally succeeded in wresting from the senatorial oligarchy was exclusive membership in juries of the ordinary and special criminal courts, which enabled them to avoid punishment for illegal use of their money to influence policy and to practice outrageous exploitation of the provincials. The political struggle between senators and knights was a disturbing factor in late republican politics, and popular leaders tried to use the latter to destroy the political monopoly of the former. Yet the political battle between an aristocracy of birth and office-holding and the new possessors of mobile wealth did not prevent their co-operation when needed to share the profits of government at home and abroad.

THE OWNER OF THE LARGE ESTATE

These men came to own gorgeous country villas about Rome and invested their surpluses in large estates in Italy and elsewhere. That the small, landowning Roman peasant found himself obliged to sell out to these men is one of the most important facts helping to explain the breakdown of the Roman Republic. Yeomen farmers of the rural middle class had made up the early republican armies, paid the expenses of early expansion, broken down the patrician ascendancy, and composed the majority in the most influential of the assemblies, the *tributa*, and an important segment in the *centuriata*. Later Roman writers looked back with nostalgia on the days when these farmers, together with the Senate, ruled Rome. One of these authors, Columella, a writer on agriculture of the first century A.D., thinks back on Quinctius Cincinnatus, "summoned from the plough to the dictatorship to be the deliverer of a beleaguered consul and his army, and then, again laying down the power which he relinquished after victory more hastily than he had assumed it for command, to return to the same bullocks and his small ancestral inheritance of four *iugera*." He thinks also of the "other renowned captains of Roman stock [who] were invariably distinguished in this twofold pursuit of either defending or tilling their ancestral or acquired estates" and reflects that "yesterday's morals and strenuous manner of living are out of tune with our present extravagance and devotion to pleasure. For, even as Marcus Varro complained in the days of our grandfathers,[29] all of us who are heads of families have quit the sickle and the plough and have crept within the city-walls; and we ply our hands in the circuses and theatres rather than

[28]See pp. 172 f.
[29]Varro published a work on agriculture in 26 B.C.

in the grain fields and vineyards; and we gaze in astonished admiration at the posturings of effeminate males, because they counterfeit by their womanish motions a sex which nature has denied to men, and deceive the eyes of the spectators. And presently, then, that we may come to our gluttonous feasts in proper fettle, we steam out our daily indigestion in sweat-baths, and by drying out the moisture of our bodies we arouse a thirst; we spend our nights in licentiousness and drunkenness, our days in gaming or in sleeping, and account ourselves blessed by fortune in that 'we behold neither the rising of the sun nor its setting.' The consequence is that ill health attends so slothful a manner of living; for the bodies of our young men are so flabby and enervated that death seems likely to make no change in them." Since it is impossible to return the absentee owner of the large estate to the country, Columella instructs him in the running of his estate with overseers directing slave gangs. He must "inspect the inmates of the workhouse, to find out whether they are carefully chained, whether the places of confinement are quite safe and properly guarded, [and] whether the overseer has put anyone in fetters or removed his shackles without the master's knowledge." He must reward "women . . . who are unusually prolific . . . for the bearing of a certain number of offspring." To cultivate vineyards fettered slaves should be used. Of these, "squads should be formed, not to exceed ten men each . . . because that limited number [is] most conveniently guarded while at work." Such an "arrangement not only stimulates rivalry, but also it discloses the slothful; for, when a task is enlivened by competition, punishment inflicted on the laggards appears just and free from censure."[30]

THE DECLINE OF THE SMALL FARMER

The plight of the small Roman farmer was in part the result of continuous war, war which took him away from his fields when it did not, as in the case of the Hannibalic wars, actually ruin them and kill him in large numbers. The other uncertainties of agriculture led the small farmer easily into debt, and Roman laws on debtors were unusually harsh. Competition with grain imported from new provinces such as Sicily put small Roman farmers at a disadvantage. Slave labor became abundant as a result of imperial war and was employed on larger estates specializing in a capitalistic production of cattle, the vine, and the olive.[31] Small farms were sold by discouraged owners unable to reduce production costs sufficiently to compete, or they were lost through debt. The allotment of public lands acquired through conquest worked in favor of wealthy

[30] *On Agriculture*, trans. H. B. Ash, Loeb, No. 361, pp. 13–15, 93–101.

[31] Ralph Turner, *The Great Cultural Traditions*, II, 868, gives some figures: After the First Samnite War 36,000 were sold into slavery; after the destruction of Carthage 50,000. "In 101 B.C. Marius sent 100,000 Cimbri south to the slave pens of Italy; during the Gallic Wars, it is said, Caesar sent 400,000 captives across the Alps." Trever, *Ancient Civilization*, II, 277, gives 4,000,000 as the estimate for the Roman slave population at the end of the Republic.

Roman senators or knights. Appian, a Greek historian of Rome, writing in the second century A.D., explains that "of the land acquired by war," the Romans, having "assigned the cultivated part forthwith to the colonists . . . made proclamation that in the meantime those who were willing to work [the uncultivated lands] might do so for a toll of the yearly crops. . . . From those who kept flocks was required a toll of the animals, both oxen and small cattle. They did these things in order to multiply the Italian race, which they considered the most laborious of peoples, so that they might have plenty of allies at home.

"But the very opposite thing happened; for the rich, getting possession of the greater part of the undistributed lands, and being emboldened by the lapse of time to believe that they would never be dispossessed, absorbing any adjacent strips and their poor neighbours' allotments, partly by purchase under persuasion and partly by force, came to cultivate vast tracts instead of single estates, using slaves as labourers and herdsmen, lest free labourers should be drawn from agriculture into the army. At the same time the ownership of slaves brought them great gain from the multitude of their progeny, who increased because they were exempt from military service. Thus certain powerful men became extremely rich and the race of slaves multiplied throughout the country, while the Italian people dwindled in numbers and strength, being oppressed by penury, taxes, and military service."[32]

THE URBAN PROLETARIAT

Ruined or dispossessed farmers might become tenants on large estates, but more often they moved to Rome to swell the numbers of an urban proletariat that the city could not employ and that became dependent upon public bounties. This development shook the foundations of sound, stable democratic politics in accordance with the republican constitution. The Roman citizen, like the Greek citizen, had to be present to exercise his voting privileges in an assembly. Before the weakening of the Roman farmer class, the work of the assemblies depended upon the citizens present in Rome. Rome unfortunately never hit upon the practice of representation to avoid this situation. When important legislation was up, Roman farmers did come into the city to participate. But with the growth of the large estate and the ruin of the peasantry, the latter were present in the city mostly in the role of indigent proletarians. The rural tribes were left in the hands of the wealthy, whose influence in the assemblies now became paramount. The assemblies were attended by growing numbers of urban citizens whose interests centered on what the state had to offer by way of food, employment, and the profits of empire, and who were not averse to selling their votes. Buying and selling votes became a public business in republican Rome. A hungry, idle, illiterate, and undisciplined urban citizenry is no satisfactory body upon which to build a democratic

[32]*Roman History*, trans. H. White, Loeb, No. 4, pp. 15, 17.

state or empire. The peculiar nature of the social development of the Republic put its political machinery inevitably in the hands of the senatorial oligarchy, who had no democratic sympathies themselves and were to prove to be incompetent managers of the state.[33]

THE PROFESSIONAL SOLDIER

Nothing can be more serious for a society with democratic aspirations than to place its military in a position to exercise undue political power. For an army has never been in itself a democratic institution, and the generals, when given political power, are often tempted to direct states as they direct armies, which means giving orders to subordinates. The Roman state, once it began to expand beyond Italy, was never able to keep its military subordinate to civilian interests. This difficulty arose from the fact that the chief republican executive magistrate of Rome, the consul, was at the same time a general. As long as the consul could be kept in control by such practices as annual tenure of office and the necessity of sharing his supreme power (*imperium*) with a colleague, as long as the army was a citizen army composed mostly of small peasant owners, the danger was not great that consular military power would supersede consular civilian power. But if the army should be composed of those who were not interested in the opportunities of civilian life, and if the consuls should be granted more than one-year tenure, obviously there would be danger. Something like this happened in the first century B.C.

MARIUS, FOUNDER OF THE NEW ARMY

Such a development began with Marius.[34] The ruin of the Roman peasant made it no longer possible to rely exclusively upon this class in recruiting the Roman army. Indeed the Roman historian Sallust says of Marius in connection with the Jugurthan War: "He . . . enrolled soldiers. not according to the classes in the manner of our forefathers, but allowing anyone to volunteer, for the most part the proletariat. Some say that he did this through lack of good men, others because of a desire to curry favour, since that class had given him honour and rank. As a matter of fact, to one who aspires to power the poorest man is the most helpful, since he has no regard for his property, having none, and considers anything honourable for which he receives pay. The result was that Marius set sail for Africa with a considerably greater contingent than had been authorized."[35] To take care of Jugurtha, and moreover to meet the serious threat of the Cimbri and Teutons, Marius was elected to the consul-

---

[33] Trever, II, 279: "Perhaps in no other great society has the antithesis between 'millionaires and beggars' been so glaring without the mediation of a prosperous middle class, as in the parasitic society of the last days of the Roman Republic."
[34] See pp. 180 f.
[35] *War with Jugurtha*, trans. J. C. Rolfe, Loeb, No. 116, p. 323.

ship no less than five times, in violation of republican practice. Here was an ominous combination. Marius as a man of the people gathers about him an enthusiastic army, acquires prolonged consular power, and in the name of democracy attacks a Senate incapable of solving the pressing military problems in any other fashion than by permitting the constitution to be violated.

THE ABSOLUTE PROVINCIAL GOVERNOR

The imperial problem of Numidia made possible this development. Indeed, it may be said that it was Rome's failure to extend the democratic controls of a city-state constitution to the administration of an empire, or to provide some substitute for these, that made possible the rise of the absolute military governor. It was difficult enough under ordinary circumstances to administer the city-state with a Senate, three assemblies, and some twenty republican magistrates. We can see now that, when she came to possess provinces, Rome should have set up an entirely new system of administration for them, one that separated the military and civilian administrations and made both responsible to the city-state government itself. To have done this would have demanded a ready political genius of a high order. For not being able to produce this genius Rome and the Mediterranean world paid heavily. Instead of being ready with plans, or developing them quickly, the Romans preferred to temporize. When it came to organizing their first province, Sicily, they did extend the principle of federation, used in Italy, to those cities that had remained loyal to Rome.[36] Beyond this they took over the oriental practices of Syracuse and Carthage with respect to the ownership of provincial land and the collection of provincial revenue. To the subsequent provinces Rome merely sent out men who had completed their turn of office in Rome; that is, the consul, after his annual tenure in Rome, was sent with similar power to a province as proconsul, and to assist him were sent praetors and quaestors as propraetors and proquaestors. With few exceptions these men therefore came from the patrician-plebeian aristocracy. They could look forward to imperial careers after their municipal ones, and of course looked forward to governing the largest and wealthiest provinces. They were sent out to distant areas with an army, with absolute power (proconsular imperium), and without being subject to any supervision or control. Only upon their return to civilian life in Rome could they be called to account, if indeed they ever were.

The situation in many provinces called for a government more permanent than the annual tenure of the promagistrates. Accordingly, as at Rome, their appointments were often extended beyond a year. Ambitious men who, as governors of large provinces, possessed the absolute powers of a monarch and commanded armies that were devoted to them personally, men who, if not already rich, had made their fortunes by exploiting

[36]See pp. 169 ff.

their uncontrolled imperial positions found it difficult, after returning to Rome, to submit to the petty restrictions of republican politics. Their minds had come to scan the vast horizon of world politics and to conceive of plans for the reorganization of the Republic which substituted monarchical for republican principles. Rome in the first century B.C. thus became a battleground where such men fought among themselves for the supreme power of the empire. Of such calibre were Sulla, Pompey, Caesar, Antony, and Octavian. The civil wars between rival, imperially minded provincial governors finally established one of them as the kingly master of the state. Therewith the Roman democratic experiment was over. Meanwhile the Roman provinces had been sucked dry, Roman society irretrievably transformed, and the whole state permanently crippled by the ravages of constant civil war. Cicero could declare in the course of his prosecution of Verres of Sicily, one of the most rascally of the provincial governors: "Because of Roman greed and Roman injustice, all our provinces are mourning, all our free communities are complaining, and even foreign kingdoms are protesting. As far as the bounds of Ocean there is no spot now so distant or so obscure that the wanton and oppressive deeds of Romans have not penetrated thither. Not against the onset of the armies of the world in war, but against its groans and tears and lamentation, can Rome hold out no longer. When such are the facts, and such the prevailing moral standards, if any prosecuted person, upon his crimes being clearly demonstrated, shall plead that others have done the like, he will not find himself without precedents: but Rome will find herself without hope of escaping doom, if the precedents set by one scoundrel are to secure the acquittal and impunity of another."[37] After his success in bribing influential Romans, Jugurtha, the princely murderer of Numidia, could well believe, Sallust tells us, that "at Rome anything could be bought," and when, having subsequently escaped punishment for his crimes, he was ordered by the Senate to leave Italy "he often looked back at Rome in silence and finally said, 'A city for sale and doomed to speedy destruction if it finds a purchaser.'"[38]

THE REFORM PROGRAM OF THE GRACCHI BROTHERS

Before the destruction of the republican government by monarchically minded provincial governors an attempt was made at the end of the second century to reform Roman society and remodel republican institutions in order that Rome might function as a healthy city-state democracy. The attempt was made by two brothers, Tiberius and Gaius Gracchus, liberal representatives of the Roman nobility whom a noble mother, Cornelia, had schooled in the best traditions of Greece and Rome. The essential part of their program was to revive the class of small Roman peasant proprietors and Italian farmers whom the large-estate system was destroying, and

[37]*The Verrine Orations*, trans. L. H. G. Greenwood, Loeb, No. 293, p. 225.
[38]*War with Jugurtha*, pp. 179, 213.

thus restore stability to the assemblies, whose meetings the Roman proletariat was coming to dominate. This was to be done by new agrarian legislation to put public lands that had been taken over by the large-estate holders into the hands of the landless citizens, who were to be helped with state subsidies to establish themselves on the land. It was to be done also by establishing new colonies of landless citizens both inside and outside Italy, for example, at destroyed Carthage. For those urban citizens who did not take up the now available public lands or become colonists, some security was to be furnished by providing them with regular allotments of imported grain at considerably less than market prices. The Gracchi were also willing to strengthen the democratic machinery of the state at the cost of the senatorial oligarchy. They were willing that the tribunes of the people have more than an annual tenure of office. To keep the Senate from interfering in the work of the *tributa* by having tribunes of the senatorial party veto proposed liberal legislation, they were willing to have a recalcitrant tribune recalled by a vote of the assembly (Tiberius actually did this) and replaced by a newly elected tribune willing to co-operate in reform. Indeed, the Gracchi were willing to rely upon the assembly alone, as in Athens, to carry on the business of government. Moreover, they were desirous of widening the social basis for the attack on senatorial privilege, not only by strengthening the ordinary citizen in the above ways, but by giving the knights important taxing-collecting contracts in the provinces and substituting them for senators on juries trying men for extortion of the provincials. Finally, they were convinced that the actual citizen basis of the Roman Republic was too narrow, that full citizenship should be given to the Latin and Italian allies as these allies were beginning to demand, and thus that Italy, and not merely Rome, should become the homeland of the empire.

THE DEATH OF TIBERIUS

The attempt to turn this program quickly into law stirred the senatorial clique to violence and caused the death of both reformers. In his biography of Tiberius Gracchus Plutarch says that his determination to do something about the agrarian problem came when he actually saw in Tuscany "the dearth of inhabitants in the country, and that those who tilled its soil or tended its flocks there were imported barbarian slaves." After becoming a tribune in 133 B.C. Tiberius supported his bill for turning over usurped public land to landless citizens by such remarks as "The wild beasts that roam over Italy have every one of them a cave or lair to lurk in; but the men who fight and die for Italy enjoy the common air and light, indeed, but nothing else; houseless and homeless they wander about with their wives and children. . . . Not a man [of the soldiers] has an hereditary altar, not one of all these many Romans an ancestral tomb, but they fight and die to support others in wealth and luxury, and though they are styled masters of the world, they have not a single clod of earth that is their own." By having an opposing tribune recalled by the *comitia tributa* he secured the passage of his bill. To prevent his own election to the tribunate a second time, the Senate itself finally resorted to violence when it could not get a consul to do so. Accompanied by attendants who "carried clubs and staves," this venerable body rushed to a tumultuous meeting of the *tributa*, picked up the "fragments and legs of the benches" which the crowd had broken in making way for them, and "went up against Tiberius, at the same time smiting those who were drawn up to protect him. . . . Of these there was a rout and a slaughter." As Tiberius fled, "he stumbled and fell to the ground among some bodies that lay in front of him. As he strove to rise to his feet, he received his first blow . . . on the head with the leg of a bench. . . . And of the rest more than three hundred were slain by blows from sticks and stones. . . . Nor was this all; they banished some of his friends without a trial and others they arrested and put to death." (No. 102, pp. 163-167, 191-193)

THE DEATH OF GAIUS

Gaius became a tribune in 123 B.C. He was resolved to implement his brother's agrarian legislation and to carry out the other parts of their reform program. In the end he and his followers were obliged to arm themselves against an attack of the senatorial party, which, when it came, cost the lives of more hundreds and Gaius's suicide. Subsequently no less than 3000 of the popular party were put to death without trial. The era of violence had been ushered in, and the conservative and popular groups in Rome were now organized into definite factions. The victorious senatorials allowed the agrarian laws of Tiberius, re-enacted by Gaius, to lapse for want of financial support, thus leaving the problem of the large estate in Italy to remain unsolved until this very day.[39] Subsequent developments of party politics kept the remaining items of the program from having the effect originally intended by the Gracchi. The Italian and Latin allies secured citizenship only as the result of a war of secession that aimed to set up a federal Italian state independent of Rome (90–88 B.C.). But in yielding to the rebels Rome nevertheless denied herself the full advantages of a generous extension of citizenship by enrolling the new citizens in but eight of the thirty-five tribes, thus guaranteeing the predominance of the older citizen body in the Roman assemblies.

SULLA

The Gracchan reforms opened up a period of almost unimaginable violence, marked by raging conservative and popular factions, intervening proconsuls and civil wars, and leading to the dictatorship of Julius Caesar

---

[39]The present government of Italy is undertaking hesitantly to attack this problem again. For literary descriptions of the large estate in southern Italy, see C. Levi, *Christ Stopped at Eboli*; also I. Silone's chapter in *The God That Failed*, ed. R. H. S. Crossman.

and the monarchy of Augustus. The evil character of the period has already been attributed to a disastrous social development and the inadequacy of a republican city-state constitution in dealing with the extraordinary problems of a rapidly expanding state. The career of Sulla illustrates these points. We have already met him as the man chosen to deal with Mithridates.[40] He has been characterized as one of the many "young bloods of his day" in whom "the luxurious and chaotic Roman society suddenly enriched by foreign conquest had bred . . . a cynical contempt for all moral principle and a brutal disregard for all human values."[41] Before he could start for the East he was deprived of his command by vote of the assembly in favor of Marius, and his legions ordered to come to Rome to receive their new general. Instead, Sulla, always popular with his troops, marched on Rome (the first time this had happened), took it with ease, forced the assembly to declare the popular leaders "outlaws and enemies of the Roman people," and in 87 B.C. set forth for the East.

While he was carrying on his high-handed operations in Greece and Asia Minor, the popular leaders, including Marius with an army of slaves, took Rome by force, instituted a violent and bloody popular regime, and declared Sulla an outlaw and enemy of the state. He, the cashiered general, returned to Italy in 83 B.C. with an army of 40,000 men more loyal to him than ever, destroyed the armies of the Marian party, outlawed and proscribed his enemies to the number of 4700, including ninety senators and 2600 knights, confiscated and sold their property, and proceeded as dictator to reform the republican constitution in a manner to restore power to the senatorial oligarchy. Before reconstituting the state he turned over to his veterans lands confiscated from the revolting allies and freed 10,000 slaves of those he had proscribed to act as his personal gang in Rome. To a purged Senate he added 300 equestrian members and restored its power over legislation by laws requiring its approval before bills could be presented to the assemblies and after they had been voted by the assemblies. He also attacked the power of the tribune by depriving him of his right to initiate legislation, by making his re-election impossible until after an interval of ten years, and by keeping him from holding any other office. He struck as well at the practice of re-election to the magistracies by providing a similar period of ten years before re-election. In order to avoid the ambitious struggle for imperial office and the granting of extraordinary commands to magistrates and in order, too, to limit the danger from the proconsul who threatened to overturn the state with his army, he increased the number of praetors to eight and provided that they and the consuls after the year of office in Rome should go to the provinces as proconsuls and propraetors. The provincial governor was forbidden to cross the frontier of his own province with an army or to start wars on his own responsibility. When these reforms were accomplished Sulla

[40]See pp. 181 f.
[41]Trever, II, 182.

resigned his dictatorship and retired to private life. The reforms were an interesting attempt to ameliorate an anomalous situation by a man who knew only too well from personal experience what was possible under it. Yet they left the fundamental evils untouched. The city-state constitution had not been modified sufficiently to take care of the new Latin and Italian citizens or to circumscribe the power of the promagistrate. It had merely been given over to a Senate enlarged by men in possession of mobile wealth. The situation of the urban proletariat was actually worsened by depriving them of the grain dole. And there was no safeguard that future proconsuls, following Sulla's example, would not reorganize the state at their pleasure as he had done, and in as partisan a manner. The massacre of their opponents by conservatives and populars alike left behind bitter resentments it would take long to heal, and the future was still open to the ambitious politician promising to restore the popular party to power.

POMPEY

The Senate, with its power restored by Sulla, was unable to solve the social and imperial problems of the succeeding period without resort to unconstitutional methods that again brought the victorious general and his army to the fore. When Sertorius, a member of the popular party, successfully undertook to lead a rebellion of badly exploited Spanish provincials it was Pompey to whom the senators entrusted an extraordinary command to defeat the rebels (77-71 B.C.). When, after a series of dangerous revolts of slaves in Sicily and Delos, 70,000 of them joined the revolt of the gladiators under Spartacus in 73 B.C., special powers to put down the revolt had to be given to Crassus, a man who had made a fortune dealing in the confiscated property of the victims of Sulla's proscriptions. It is not pleasant to contemplate the character of a social system, or the mentality of the conqueror, responsible for the crucifixion of 6000 slaves after the suppression of this revolt. The prosecution of Verres' scandalous misgovernment of Sicily came in 70 B.C. When it became necessary to deal with the pirates in 67 B.C., extraordinary authority again had to be given to Pompey.[42] The Gabinian Law, embodying the terms of this grant, provided that he was "to have power for three years over the entire Mediterranean and equal authority with the provincial governors over its coast for fifty miles inland; all princes and communities were to furnish aid at his request; he was to have supreme control over the entire naval resources of Rome, the right to draw on the public treasury and full power to enlist both soldiers and crews; he might also name fifteen subordinates to act under his direction." When Sulla's efforts against Mithridates proved insufficient, Pompey was ultimately granted another extraordinary command by the Manilian Law (66 B.C.). "He was vested with unlimited powers over all Asia Minor and the surrounding seas, and the governors

[42]See pp. 182 f.

of the Asianic provinces were ordered to resign in his favour both their posts and their armies. He was also authorized to appoint legates in addition to those who had served against the pirates."[43] Both these measures were pushed through by the popular assembly in spite of the opposition of the Senate. While Pompey was in the East it was with some difficulty that Cicero, a "new man," was able to rout the gang of bankrupt noblemen, descendants of those proscribed by Sulla, bonus-hungry veterans, and desperadoes under Catiline who were willing to do almost anything to inspire terror and take over the government of the state. Returned from the East, Pompey joined with Crassus and Julius Caesar to form the First Triumvirate in 60 B.C., a trio of bosses, impatient of constitutions, who set out to divide the Roman world between them.[44]

JULIUS CAESAR

It was reported that Caesar supported the Manilian Law because it was what the people wanted, and he hoped to be the recipient of similar powers in the future. He urged only moderate measures against five of the members of Catiline's conspiracy, without being greatly involved in its plots. A cousin of Marius whom Sulla had spared with the remark "that they had no sense if they did not see many Mariuses in this boy," Caesar is described by Plutarch as "of a spare habit" with "a soft and white skin," suffering "from distemper in the head," and epileptic. We have met him before as the conqueror of Gaul.[45] Whatever may be said of his general capacity, and these estimates have been varied and extravagant,[46] there can be no doubt that he was the man who deliberately brought the Roman Republic to an end. Instead of trying to reshape it in line with its earlier democratic tradition he preferred to substitute for it an absolute monarchy, which, in hands less enlightened than his, could and did develop into a despotism ruinous to Roman civilization. For this preference he paid with his life.

CAESAR'S EARLIER CAREER

Caesar undertook a career of cold calculation aimed at taking advantage of the weaknesses in Roman society and politics to acquire personal power. He saw early in his career that it was necessary to pander to the urban proletariat at Rome to gain popularity and office, and in this art he became a master, borrowing huge sums to meet these expenses. Plutarch reports that "by lavish provision besides for theatrical performances, processions, and public banquets, he washed away all memory of the ambitious efforts of his predecessors in the office. By these means he put the people

[43]Magie, *Roman Rule*, I, 298.
[44]See pp. 184 f.
[45]See pp. 185 f.
[46]Trever, II, 241: "He was the greatest genius Rome produced, and in the combined fields of war and politics, few have been his equal in world history."

in such a humour that every man of them was seeking out new offices and new honours with which to requite him." Such a leader is usually called a demagogue. He saw clearly that imperial office meant the opportunity to make a fortune, acquire a powerful military following, and achieve a military reputation. His service in Spain and Gaul did this for him. While in Gaul he stood above no dishonorable political conduct in order to build up his Roman machine. "The candidates for office there [enjoyed] his assistance, and [won] their elections by corrupting the people with money from him, and [did] everything which was likely to enhance his power." (No. 99, pp. 453, 459)

CAESAR AND POMPEY

After Crassus' death in the Parthian campaign (53 B.C.) Rome became the victim of the resulting struggle between the remaining triumvirs, Pompey and Caesar, for supreme power in the state. When it became clear to Caesar that Pompey and the Senate would not permit him to return to a leading position in civilian life, and that no compromise was possible between them, he did not hesitate to precipitate three years of civil war by crossing the Rubicon River, the boundary between his province of Cisalpine Gaul and Italy, with his troops on 10 January, 49 B.C. In the spring of 48 B.C. he caught up with Pompey in Thessaly and defeated him at Pharsalus. Following him to Egypt, where Pompey was assassinated, Caesar was captivated and detained for too long a time by the stunning and resourceful Cleopatra. Returning to Rome in 46 B.C., after disposing in the famous *veni, vidi, vici* campaign of the attempts of Pharnaces, the son of Mithridates, to recapture his father's position, he left quickly for Africa and Spain to wipe out the remaining Pompeian forces. The African opposition was destroyed at Thapsus (46 B.C.) and the Spanish at Munda (45 B.C.), and Caesar had finally reached the goal of his desire, the mastery of the Roman world. Plutarch tells the story of one of Caesar's captains who had been sent to Rome during the campaign in Gaul in order to report on Caesar's fortunes in the city. "As he stood in front of the Senate-house and learned that the Senate would not give Caesar an extension of his term of command," he "slapped the handle of his sword and said: 'But this will give it.'" (No. 99, p. 517) And it did for as long a time as Caesar lived.

CAESAR'S MONARCHICAL POWER

Before his assassination (15 March, 44 B.C.) a servile and cowed Senate and people had given him all the necessary attributes of monarchy except the title of king. He was made dictator for life and sole consul. He was given the power of the tribune and the censor. He acquired the power to appoint one-half the magistrates in Rome and the provinces, to make war and peace without taking the Senate into consideration, and to exercise complete command over the army and navy and unlimited control over the public purse. "In 44 the senate voted a wholesale ratification of all his future acts and required all magistrates henceforth to take oath to uphold them!"[47] Although he was not actually deified until after his death, before it a temple had been dedicated to him, and he had been given the title Jupiter Julius. If he, the supposed descendant of a king and a goddess, could have assumed the title of king without outraging too much the antiroyal feelings of public opinion it is likely that he would have taken it, as Plutarch indicates, even though it added nothing to his power. That in some respects he exercised his dictatorship with moderation, vigor, and imagination there can be no doubt. There was no slaughter of his political enemies. He was interested in rehabilitating the urban proletariat by reforming the grain dole, undertaking public works, carrying out an extensive colonization program, and breaking up the political gangs in Rome. Without trying to strike at the system of large estates in Italy he did attempt to diminish the slave population on them by insisting upon the replacement of one-third of their slaves with free labor. He also interested himself in the reform of the provincial administration, substituting an annual tax for the tithe system of certain provinces and legislating against the abuses of the tax collectors. He is credited as well with a policy aiming to replace the independent governor who used his provinces as a source of private income with a responsible official concerned with the welfare of his subjects. His generous enfranchisement of provincials and his introduction of them into the Senate make it seem possible that he was not interested in prolonging the predominance of Rome and Italy over the whole empire but looked forward to an equalization of provinces under the autocratic ruler. His reformed calendar, with modifications, has persisted to date. But in the minds of those to whom one-man power—making slaves of the citizen body—was odious, the positive features of Caesar's dictatorship did not excuse his abandonment of the republican tradition. As he prepared to go east on a campaign against Parthia to avenge the defeat and death of Crassus, there were those who feared that this move was but a preliminary step to the establishment of a hereditary monarchy upon a Hellenistic model. After all, Cleopatra had given him a son—Caesarion.

THE IDES OF MARCH

In any event, a group of devoted republicans and less idealistically minded conspirators decided that it was necessary to do away with Caesar. They attacked him on the eve of his departure for Parthia, on the ides of March, as he was sitting in the Senate chamber listening to petitions. "Those who had prepared themselves for the murder bared each of them his dagger, and Caesar, hemmed in on all sides, whichever way he turned confronting blows of weapons aimed at his face and eyes, driven hither and thither like a wild beast, was entangled in the hands of all; for all had

[47]Trever, II, 232.

to take part in the sacrifice and taste of the slaughter. Therefore Brutus also gave him one blow in the groin. . . . When he saw that Brutus had drawn his dagger, he pulled his toga down over his head and sank . . . against the pedestal on which the statue of Pompey stood. And the pedestal was drenched with his blood." (No. 99, p. 599)

The murder of Caesar postponed the solution of the constitutional crisis that had arisen with the formation of the empire and the emergence of the military proconsul. That crisis, as we have seen, revolved about the problem of whether the government of a city-state with democratic forms could be satisfactorily adapted to the administration of an empire, or, conversely, whether the maintenance of empire required the abandonment of republican institutions. Caesar's solution had been essentially to abandon the Republic for an absolute monarchy, to be patterned possibly on the Hellenistic model. His solution had been premature and caused his death. Before a second notable attempt could be made by Augustus another savage struggle for mastery of the state took place which disposed the population of the empire to look with relief upon any form of government that would bring peace.

THE SECOND TRIUMVIRATE

In his will Caesar had designated as his heir his grandnephew and adopted son, the young Octavian. The man who filled the immediate power vacuum after Caesar's death was the consul, Mark Antony. In 43 B.C. these two essentially hard and ruthless rivals for supreme power joined with Lepidus, Caesar's Master of Horse and head of the state religion, to seize and divide, irrespective of law, the power and resources of the state. Thus was formed what is known as the Second Triumvirate. With the unrefined brutality of a Sulla they began to rule by offering large rewards for the murder of political opponents whom they had proscribed. They took special vengeance on the senators and knights, having some three hundred of the former and two thousand of the latter butchered. Nor did they, upon the special urging of Antony, spare Cicero, who, whatever his faults (he too had cashed in as a provincial governor), was among the few relatively decent Romans left in public life. As Plutarch puts it: "So far did anger and fury lead them to renounce their human sentiments, or rather, they showed that no wild beast is more savage than man when his passion is supplemented by power." The assassins caught Cicero being carried in a litter to the seashore. When he saw them he "ordered the servants to set the litter down where they were. Then he himself, clasping his chin with his left hand, as was his wont, looked steadfastly at his slayers, his head all squalid and unkempt, and his face wasted with anxiety. . . . He stretched his neck forth from the litter and was slain, being then in his sixty-fourth year." His head and hands were cut off and sent to Rome to Antony, who with peculiar delicacy had them "placed over the ships' beaks on the rostra." (No. 99, pp. 201, 207)

ANTONY AND CLEOPATRA

The proscriptions over, Octavian and Antony set out for Greece to defeat the armies of Caesar's murderers led by Brutus and Cassius. These defenders of the republican tradition had meanwhile mulcted the eastern provinces of their coin to prepare for the showdown. The crucial battle occurred at Philippi in Macedonia (42 B.C.), ending in a victory for the triumvirs and the suicide of both Brutus and Cassius. After the battle Octavian returned to Italy, and Antony went to the East to establish control and prepare for an eventual campaign against Parthia. At Ephesus he was hailed as the incarnation of the god Dionysus, and at Tarsus, whither he had summoned Cleopatra to answer for her support of Cassius, he was instead taken over by the "royal wench."

THE VICTORY OF OCTAVIAN OVER ANTONY

This capitulation to Cleopatra upon their first encounter was the beginning of a conquest of ten years' duration that worked the transformation of a crude Roman general into a Hellenistic theocrat who would gladly have reduced the whole empire to his sole rule. And Cleopatra was quite willing to become the queen of the Roman Empire. As it was, she did become Antony's wife and the mother of his three children, two boys and a girl. What was in the air was revealed clearly when, after his marriage, he assumed the title of King of Kings; and again when, in 34 B.C., after an unsuccessful campaign against Parthia and a successful one against Armenia, he celebrated a royal triumph in Alexandria. Here in the guise of the god Dionysus, with Cleopatra as the goddess Isis, he proceeded to make her Queen of Kings, and Caesar's son a King of Kings. To his own children by Cleopatra he granted away large portions of the eastern provinces. This outrage to Roman public opinion resulted in a final split between East and West, between Antony and Octavian, followed by a naval engagement in the Gulf of Actium (Battle of Actium, 31 B.C.). Here Octavian's navy won a complete victory, and Antony fled the battle with his Ptolemaic queen. When Octavian entered Egypt the following year Antony's troops deserted to him, and the incarnation of Dionysus committed suicide. Isis herself, when she discovered that the new Roman Caesar was interested in her only as a wonderful trophy for his triumph, likewise committed suicide. Octavian now entered into the inheritance of the Ptolemies[48] and, after thirteen years of civil war which had reduced the empire to anarchy, into the inheritance of the whole Mediterranean world. In grateful relief many heralded him as a savior. From the East, where rulers were automatically gods, petitions soon came to him requesting that he permit himself to be worshiped. In Rome the Senate called him Augustus, one to be revered, if not a god then something more than human, the son of that Julius who had already been deified. At

[48]See pp. 189 f.

the moment when the constitutional problem was to receive its final settlement, and the Republic to yield permanently to Caesar, the spirit of the East hovered subtly over the change.

Octavian Augustus, the grandnephew and adopted son of Julius Caesar, was no republican. But he "had every interest in saving appearances and draping a constitutional cloak over the crude nakedness of things."[49] The "constitutional cloak" was the republican form; "the crude nakedness of things," the absolute monarchy of Caesar. Augustus knew only too well how Caesar's dictatorship had terminated, and yet he was convinced that Caesar's solution was the correct, if extreme, one. He knew how he himself had been able to profit from Antony's more overt acceptance of oriental monarchy, and such unpopularity he did not wish to court. His political revolution must take a more moderate form and yet be no less a revolution. The more moderate form was the Principate, so called from the Latin *princeps civium*, the chief, or first of the citizens, a title conferred upon Augustus by the Senate. That is to say, Augustus, after the "extralegal" period of the civil war was over, was to take "control of everything" and be "above all in authority," not as dictator or king, but as one chosen by the proper constitutional authority and subject to law. Augustus therefore went through the motions of what he called transferring "the government from my hands to those of the Senate and Roman People" and accepting "no function contrary to the usages of our fathers."

THE POWERS OF THE "PRINCEPS"

When these functions are put together it is clear that they total up to the powers of Caesar's dictatorship, the model, indeed, of Augustus' reorganization. To be more specific: Augustus was *Imperator*, the recognized commander in chief of the military forces. As such, after 31 B.C., there was no one man or group of men who were in a position to challenge anything he wished to do. For nine successive years after 31 B.C. he was also consul, and in fact sole consul, possessing that supreme executive authority that the Romans called *imperium*, the substance of the power of the *imperator*. In possession of the power he did not bother much with the office after 23 B.C. He was content to make others consul. The Romans came to make a distinction between the *imperium* of a consul and that of a proconsul, the former being limited to Rome and Italy, the latter constituting the supreme power of the governor of the extra-Italian provinces. After 23 B.C. Augustus assumed the proconsular *imperium*, thus giving himself supreme authority over the whole Mediterranean world. The Romans had set up the tribunate to protect the people

[49]Léon Pol Homo, *Roman Political Institutions from City to State*, trans. M. R. Dobie, p. 205.

from the arbitrary and unjust authority of the regular magistrates. As the representative of the people the person of the tribune had been made inviolable, and it was he who had presided over the popular assemblies. The power and position of the tribune were granted to Augustus for life after 23 B.C. Finally, he was made the chief priest (*pontifex maximus*) of the state religion. This gave him supreme spiritual as well as temporal power. In fact, as the object of an imperial cult with its temples and priesthoods throughout the empire, he was virtually a divine person, a god. With these various powers in the possession of one man it made very little actual difference whether, for the sake of appearance, the Senate and assemblies, the magistracies and the elections were retained. The actual ruler of the state was the *princeps*, Augustus, whose power no one was in a position to limit except the *princeps* himself.

THE REFORMS OF AUGUSTUS

Augustus did in fact choose to limit his own power. He assumed control over only those provinces that were on the frontier and in which troops were stationed; the interior and more pacified provinces he left to the Senate. He did not, however, hesitate to interfere in the management of the senatorial provinces, and for his own provinces he sent out his own governors (*legati*) as paid officials for as long as they rendered efficient service, thus abandoning the old republican system of promagistrates. Indeed, the establishment of the principate was accompanied by a wholesale attempt to renovate Roman society, religion, and morals as well as government. This was done in the spirit of the conservative old Roman, eager to rescue his people from contamination with foreign peoples, to free them from the corruption and degradation of great wealth, and to make vital again those virtues of the peasant-soldier that had been responsible for Rome's greatness. To this end Augustus was unwilling to extend Roman citizenship beyond Italy, sought to prevent intermarriage among Rome's social classes, and tried to restore to the religious calendar festivals, now dead, that had originally been associated with the life of the early peasant community. Although none too good an example himself he was anxious to restore the institution of Roman marriage and to encourage the raising of large families. He tried to legislate bachelors and spinsters out of existence, and offered rewards to the founders of large families. Adultery became a crime and the extravagant display of luxury was forbidden. To support this moral rejuvenation, as well as his political program, he organized a rather brilliant literary propaganda.[50] In these things, however, he was doomed to disappointment, as were so many rulers after him. The decadence of Roman society continued to grow, its religion failed increasingly to inspire, and the future was thus opened to the spread of new religions from the East.

[50]See pp. 233 ff.

Augustus' victory at Actium in 31 B.C. marked the beginning of what the title of this chapter calls *Pax Romana*, the Roman Peace which lasted until the close of the second century A.D. "Government by one man," the Roman historian Tacitus remarks, "became the condition of peace." It has been usual among historians to characterize this era as the Roman counterpart of Greece's fifth century B.C., an era when classical civilization reached a second and all-embracing climax, and when, if ever, mankind was at its best. Edward Gibbon, the distinguished English historian of the *Decline and Fall of the Roman Empire*, called the second of these two centuries the Century of all Centuries, "during which the condition of the human race was most happy and prosperous." Contemporaries also felt that something unique and imperishable had been achieved by the Romans. Aelius Aristides, a second-century Greek teacher of rhetoric in Smyrna, Asia Minor, one who in our own day would be an excellent public-relations officer for the United Nations, speaks, in his *Roman Speech*, of "a democracy of the whole earth" having been established "under a single and admirable ruler. . . . No other way of life is left," he says. "A single harmonious, all-embracing state has been created." The nations "have exchanged mutual quarrels and disorders for a collective supremacy, and suddenly come again to life. Wars seem beyond credence. . . . The whole world keeps holiday, and laying aside its ancient dress of steel has turned in freedom to adornment and all delights. The cities have abandoned their old quarrels, and are occupied by a single rivalry, each ambitious to be most pleasant and beautiful. Everywhere are playgrounds, fountains, arcades, temples, workshops, schools. . . . The world sick from creation has recovered its health. . . . Festivals never cease, but move from people to people and are always being celebrated somewhere. You [Rome] have best shown the truth of the universal legend that earth is the common mother and fatherland of all. To-day Greek or foreigner may travel freely where he will . . . as though he was passing from homeland to homeland. . . . To be safe, it is enough to be a Roman, or rather a subject of yours. . . . You have meted out the whole world, bridled rivers with many a bridge, cut mountains into carriage roads, filled the deserts with outposts, and civilized all things with settled discipline and life." To Aristides, the emperor is the "Great Governor and Universal President" who can "sit in comfort at home and guide the world by letters, which reach their destination almost as soon as they are written," letters to provincial governors in whom "more fear and respect" have been instilled than in a slave before his master. Thinking of the turbulent Greek city-state democracies, he adds, "There when the people has once given its vote, you cannot go elsewhere or to a further tribunal, but must accept the decision. But here [in Rome] there is another great court of appeal, which no point of justice ever escapes. Here is a great and proper equality between the small and the great, between the obscure and the illustrious, between the poor and the rich and well-born." And then the crucial question, of immeasurably greater impact now than it was then: "Is not this better than any democracy?"[51]

THE FAILURE OF THE REPUBLIC

For Aristides the question was answered in the affirmative by a contrast between the old Greek system of wars between independent city-states or Hellenistic theocracies and the stable autocracy of a universal Mediterranean empire governed in accordance with a common law. For us the contrast is not quite so simple. We have to think about the promise and failure of the Roman Republic and of what the international organization of the Mediterranean world would have been like if that promise had been fulfilled and the failure avoided. A successful republican policy would have meant that the earlier equalization of political power between patrician and plebeian in Rome would have been made effective rather than nullified by the maintenance of the ultimate authority of a conservative, oligarchical Senate. It would have meant also that gradually, and without the necessity for civil war (90–88 B.C.), the privileges of Roman citizenship would have been extended to the conquered inhabitants of the Italian peninsula. Among these privileges would have been actual participation in the government of the state through some kind of a representative system. It would have meant, also, as the Roman state expanded beyond Italy, that the attitude taken toward the inhabitants of the provinces would have been more than naked exploitation. The administration set up for the empire would have been controlled by specially created organs of a reasonably democratic government at home, and controlled in the interest not only of the Roman state but also of the provincials. Such an organization would have obviated the anomalous situation in which the upper classes of a single city, Rome, so manipulated the machinery of city-state government that they were able to govern in nobody's interest but their own. Thus the promise, we may believe, would have tended toward the formation of a democratic republican empire. It was not realized, and the history of the Pax Romana has to be related with this failure in mind. For the opportunity lost could not be regained.

THE CHARACTER OF THE PAX ROMANA

The Pax Romana was the peace of a military autocracy verging toward an outright oriental despotism. Tacitus, the Roman historian, was unkind enough to repeat the words of a provincial Briton, that where the Romans "make a desert they call it peace."[52] There is considerable truth in this remark. For the peace of the Roman world was the peace of a conquered world, and certainly enough has been said of that conquest to indicate that it was the work of rather ruthless, cruel, and rapacious conquerors. As

[51]R. W. Livingstone, *The Mission of Greece*, pp. 256 ff.
[52]Ubi solitudinem faciunt, pacem appellant. *Agricola*, Loeb, No. 35, p. 30.

long as there were worlds that could within reason be conquered, there was no peace. If we were to consider the history of the Roman frontier during the Pax Romana more thoroughly than we have,[53] we should see that actually there was no peace. It was the Germans themselves who blocked the grandiose project of a conquest of central Europe beyond the Rhine and the Danube. It was the same with Parthia and the project for going beyond the Tigris and the Euphrates. No love of peace kept the Roman emperors from continuing with expansion but rather the frank recognition that there were limits to the ability of the Roman state to expand. If we were to pursue in detail the internal development of the empire during the Pax Romana we should see also that it was hardly what we should call peaceful. The predominance of the military, the interference of the military in the making of emperors, the prevalence of conspiracy, plot, and revolt, and the latent and sometimes overt war between the military and the aristocracy suggest rather an armed peace—the armed peace of the autocratic government of the conqueror.

THE PROBLEM OF SUCCESSION

The problem of succession to the reigning *princeps* was never satisfactorily solved during the empire and remained a constant source of weakness and disturbance. Republican magistracies were elective, and in theory at least the *princeps* was the choice of the Senate. But in practice the emperors sought to establish hereditary dynasties and therefore to be succeeded by their own sons if they had them or by adopted sons from inside or outside the imperial family.[54] The heir designated by the ruling *princeps* was usually associated with him in the government and presented to the Senate for confirmation. Yet orderly dynastic succession was constantly threatened by the military in the form of (1) the Praetorian Guard, the personal bodyguard of the emperor set up in Rome by Augustus, and (2) the frontier legions, erected into a professional standing army by Augustus. By the end of the reign of Nero, as Tacitus remarks, "the secret of empire was now disclosed, that an emperor could be made elsewhere than at Rome." In the year A.D. 68-69 civil war broke out between no less than four candidates for the imperial throne, backed by the Spanish, Rhenish, and eastern legions, and one of these, Titus Flavius Vespasian, legate of Judaea and the candidate of the eastern legions, founded the Flavian line. Nerva was the choice of the Senate, but his position was guaranteed only by adopting a powerful general on the Rhine frontier, Marcus Ulpius Trajan, the legate of Upper Germany, and associating him in

[53]See pp. 188 ff.
[54]The three dynasties of the first two centuries were (1) the Julio-Claudian (31 B.C.–A.D. 68), including Augustus (31 B.C.–A.D. 14), Tiberius (A.D. 14–37), Caligula (37–41), Claudius (41–54), Nero (54–68); (2) the Flavian (69–96), including Vespasian (69–79), Titus (79–81), Domitian (81–96); and (3) the "Good Emperors" and Antonines (96–193), including Nerva (96–98), Trajan (98–114), Hadrian (114–138), Antoninus Pius (138–161), Marcus Aurelius (161–180), and Commodus (180–192).

the government. When the Antonine dynasty was brought to an end by the murder of Commodus, that profligate and degenerate gladiator son of the Stoic emperor Marcus Aurelius, the Praetorian Guard murdered his successor and sold the imperial office to the highest bidder. Then, as in A.D. 68, the legions took over with their candidates and fought a civil war until one of the candidates, Septimius Severus, the general from Upper Pannonia, was successful (A.D. 194). Subsequently there was not much question of the army's right to determine the succession.

THE DEVELOPMENT OF CENTRALIZED TYRANNY

The political history of the principate during the Pax Romana is largely the story of the gradual removal of the "constitutional cloak" referred to above, revealing the "nakedness of things," and the reclothing of autocracy with a new centralized imperial administration. In other words, the republican machinery retained by Augustus was permitted in the course of centuries to waste away when it was not actually attacked and destroyed. It was superseded by a government dependent upon the will of the emperor. The manner of succession to the principate permitted the most outrageous as well as the most enlightened characters to direct this transformation, utterly monstrous tyrants setting themselves up as gods alongside Stoic philosophers. The insane tyrant Caligula, offering his toes to be kissed by worshipful subjects, was followed after a few years by the incredible Nero. This pupil of Seneca, the most distinguished Stoic philosopher of his day, could not ruin the administration of the empire or prevent, in the earlier years of his reign, Seneca and Burrus, the captain of the Praetorians, from governing well. Once he escaped the tutelage of his mother, Agrippina, he revolted public opinion by outrageous profligacy, injustice, and cruelty, and by his pretensions as a would-be athlete and lyre player. After provoking a conspiracy against his life, the suppression of which cost the lives of the leading literary and philosophical figures of his day (Lucan, Petronius, Seneca), and after inaugurating the first persecution of the Christians he ended his life, while his legions were in revolt, in a miserable suicide, exclaiming, it is reported, "What an artist perishes in me!" Only less despicable was the last of the Flavians, the "lord" and "god" Domitian. The rule of the liberal Antonines, on the contrary, "was as near to constitutional monarchy as the ancient world ever came" and marked "essentially the triumph of the Stoic conception of the ruler as the servant of all, ruling under law and by right reason."[55]

THE CENTRAL ADMINISTRATION

If, however, one overlooks the vicissitudes of the personal rule of the individual emperors it is clear that the autocracy was continuously strengthened and provided with organs of administration. The Senate became little more than a craven sanction of the imperial will and was

[55]For characterizations of the individual emperors, see Trever, II, 503–506.

gradually supplanted by the private Imperial Council of the emperor (*concilium principis*), which under Hadrian received its final organization. From the end of the second century this council was the chief central organ of imperial administration. Under the principate the assemblies quickly ceased to legislate altogether, this function being taken over by the emperor. The old republican magistracies were deprived of their essential powers, now taken over by new imperial officials. Chief among the imperial officials came to be the Prefect of the Praetorium, the commander in chief of the troops in Rome and Italy, a member of the Imperial Council and its presiding officer in the absence of the emperor. Law cases appealed to the emperor came first to him, and in the end he became a kind of prime minister, in charge of such important departments as interior, justice, war, and the navy. Other leading figures in the imperial administration came to be the Minister, later Procurator, of Finance, the Procurator of the Private Property of the Empire, and the Prefect of Vehicles, a kind of postmaster-general. A huge imperial secretariat was soon departmentalized to transmit communications adequately to and from the central government. The Office of Correspondence (*Ab epistolis*) handled all the administrative correspondence to and from the emperor; the Office of Petitions (*A libellis*) replied to requests coming to the emperor; the Office of Inquiries (*A cognitionibus*) prepared the cases to come before the imperial court, and the Office of Preliminary Examinations (*A studiis*) prepared reports necessary to the emperor in dealing with administrative and judicial problems. The leading positions in these central departments of administration came to be held by freedmen and knights, not senators. The city of Rome, together with Italy, came likewise to be governed by a new set of officials "on the model of similar officials in Alexandria."[56] These were the Prefect of the City, responsible for public safety; the Prefect of the Corn Supply, responsible for the provisioning, distribution, and sale of food to the city; and the Prefect of the Watch, responsible for protecting the city at night with police, and at all times from fire. In addition there were special commissions for Rome and Italy, such as the Water Commission, responsible for the water supply of the city, the Commission of Public Buildings, the Commission of the Bed and Bank of the Tiber, and the Curators of Italian Roads.

IMPERIAL GOVERNMENT IN THE PROVINCES

The provinces likewise received a new deal under the empire. The original differences between Italy and the remaining provinces, Egypt and the remaining provinces, and senatorial and imperial provinces slowly disappeared, reducing all to an identical administration. The provinces themselves, after the second century, were multiplied and reduced in size to provide for more efficiency. Augustus' system of legate-governors ap-

[56]Homo, *Roman Political Institutions*, p. 313.

pointed by the emperor was maintained and extended to the senatorial provinces. The legate, a military as well as civil official, was supplied with special financial officers, and thus the publicans, the private contractors for the collection of direct taxes who flourished with such ill effect under the Republic, were removed. Augustus himself began the practice of taking regular property surveys of the whole empire in order that taxes might be equitably assessed. Yet many provincial governors still had to be prosecuted for extortion. Under the Pax Romana the emperor also promoted a widespread extension of urban life into those areas which did not yet know the city-state. These cities, with a municipal government patterned on that of Rome, enjoyed local autonomy for the most part, their relations with the central government being regulated by individual treaties characteristic of Rome's early treaties with her Latin and Italian allies. Most of them, however, were tributary, that is, their local governments were obliged to make annual payments of tribute to the central government. The conditions of relative peace, the absence of internal barriers to the flow of commerce and trade, and the excellent system of roads penetrating into all parts of the empire contributed to a vigorous revival of prosperity, which facilitated the movement to the West of the more specialized arts, crafts, and industries of the older East. Nothing like this was to be known again until comparatively recent times. Simultaneously Roman citizenship was gradually extended beyond Italy to the remaining provinces until in A.D. 212 citizenship became universal for all free men. At the same time Roman law was developing into a magnificent system for the binding together of a world state.[57] From the letters of the emperor Trajan to Pliny, his governor in Pontus and Bythinia, the new imperial administration can be seen working at its best. The system, it will be noted, was paternalistic to the extreme. There was scarcely any detail of local life about which Pliny did not feel it worth while to seek advice from the emperor, and Trajan's replies are those of the born administrator, careful of all these details. The great weakness of the revived city life under the empire is also apparent here. In their zeal for beautiful public buildings and more efficient public works, these cities did not concern themselves much with balancing the budget. This meant that the central government had to intervene with troubleshooters (*correctores*), since bankrupt cities, in turn, were of no assistance in upholding the imperial finances. The letters also reveal the great contribution the Romans had to make to the provinces in the field of civil engineering.

THE ROMANIZATION OF THE WEST

Under these circumstances the gigantic process of Romanization—standardization, we might also call it—of the West took place. In western North Africa the municipal system penetrated the sands of the Sahara,

[57]See pp. 251 ff.

where ruins still stand to impress the visitor with the vitality and expansive strength of Roman civilization. Into Spain also the city-state penetrated. Under Augustus there were in all at least a hundred of these cities, one-half with full citizen rights. From them came many of the leading figures in Roman public and literary life of the early empire, the emperors Trajan and Hadrian, and such writers as Seneca, Lucan, Martial, Quintilian, and Columella. The emperor Antoninus Pius came from Gaul; and here too, especially in southern Gaul, the original Transalpine Gaul, and in Aquitaine the Roman municipality flourished. Elsewhere in Gaul the degree of Romanization was not so great. Yet the Rhine legions, recruited and supplied from Gaul, furnished with their camp sites centers for considerable Rhine towns (Cologne, Bonn, Mainz, Strassburg), and until very recently the ruins of one of them, Trier, mingled with the ruins of the modern city of World War II. London was the largest Roman town in Britain, followed by Lincoln, Gloucester, York, and Colchester; but, as in Africa, Spain, and Gaul, Latin speech had not as yet penetrated deeply into the countryside. Along the Danube Regensburg, Augsburg, Vienna, and Budapest developed as frontier towns to take care of the needs of the Danube legions. Before these provinces were overrun by German barbarians centuries more of existence under the Roman Empire intensified and expanded further the degree and extent of Romanization.

THE PAX ROMANA AND SOCIAL CHANGE

In spite of what we may call the brilliance of certain aspects of Roman life under the Pax Romana it must be remembered that the system depended upon a growing autocracy. Nor did the Pax Romana produce any amelioration in the structure of Roman society. The substantial achievements were reserved primarily for the rich to enjoy, and the price they were beginning to pay for this enjoyment was increasing subjection to the growing administrative apparatus of the state. The institution of slavery remained unchallenged. To be sure, under the influence of Stoic jurists some improvements were made in the status of the slave, and the relative cessation of warfare reduced the number of slaves for sale. The freeing of slaves resulted often, during the early empire at least, in remarkable careers, public as well as private, for the freedmen. Slavery continued, however, to be taken for granted as a necessary foundation of economic and domestic life. Nor can we say that there was any change in the position of the urban proletariat. Rather, one can say it spread from Rome to other cities. Devices originated under the Republic to keep this social element placated, the cheap grain, the races, and the wild-animal and gladiatorial fights, were maintained. The latter became unexampled spectacles of brutality, making use of condemned criminals, prisoners of war, and slaves. This phenomenon was an unhealthy product of the unhealthy life to which the underprivileged of Rome were subjected.

Little, moreover, was done in agriculture to relieve the pressure on the small farmer of the growth of the large estate, or *villa* (*latifundia*). The decline in the numbers of slaves transformed its organization to some extent. The slave was supplemented by the tenant (*colonus*) holding land from an absentee landlord under conditions that gradually reduced him to a position approaching serfdom. The system of large estates, moreover, was expanded as a means of exploitation of state property. Egypt, which was a kind of huge state enterprise under its own prefect, exercised a powerful example. Nero confiscated the estates of six men who are reported to have owned one-half of Africa. There were large state domains in almost all the provinces, and they were leased out to private agents (*conductores*), with the results that usually follow from such a system. In the state mines the criminal and the slave formed the labor supply. Social conditions in the Italian cities became so serious that the emperors of the second century had to intervene. With rare concern for the welfare of the children of poor families, Nerva set up a state fund administered by the municipalities to make loans to small farmers. The interest from these loans was to be used to help to care for poor children of the locality. Supplemented by private benevolence these funds became a major enterprise, in Italy first, and then in the provinces. In the second century public funds were also used to help to pay the salaries of elementary teachers for the children of the middle classes in the towns. However, the masses of the empire, the slaves, the urban proletariat, and the peasants on large estates, were excluded from the benefits of the prosperity and the higher level of civilization resulting from the Pax Romana. These were reserved for the middle classes in the towns, the knights, and the senatorial nobles of Rome itself. The failure of Augustus and others to curb the vulgar display of luxury and the corruption of family life became only too evident in the following centuries. "Never in history was there a time when money was more the measure of the man than in the Rome of Claudius and Nero."[58]

Thus we must say that the Roman peace, however brilliant and epoch-making in its universal aspects, was a peace achieved at the cost of liberty, since it was the work of a sham-republican autocracy and a growing bureaucracy. It was likewise achieved at the cost of social improvement by maintaining a stratification that kept the great majority of the inhabitants of this empire from fully sharing its benefits. We must also say that under it, and because of these very costs, the empire did not attain the stability and resilience, the promise of progress and benefit, and accordingly the loyalty of citizens and subjects that might have enabled it to withstand the strains of the third century and to prevent what is called the "decline and fall." But, as we know, there is always a heavy price to pay for peace, and after the failure of the promise of the Republic, the Romans found it impossible to achieve peace at any other price.

[58]Trever, II, 441.

chapter six

THE ROMANS AND GREEK HUMANISM

This chapter must consider the culture of the Roman world state. It means by culture not the all-inclusive category of the sociologist or anthropologist. For this use of culture the historian has a perfectly satisfactory word: civilization. Rather, by culture is meant the discipline and delight which man gives his mind and heart by the products of his creative imagination and his consequent ennobling of daily life with purpose, dignity, and beauty. It is his chief glory.

ROMAN CULTURE

In considering the culture of the Roman world state one is seriously confronted for the first time in the history of the West with the question of tradition. As the Romans expanded they came into contact with the major traditions of the Near East and the Greeks. In Italy, Sicily, and the Greek peninsula they met the tradition of Hellenism. In Sicily (Syracuse), and North Africa (Carthage), they met the spirit of the Orient. In Asia Minor, Egypt, and the intervening lands they met the combination of these two that we have described as Hellenistic. The Romans had a great capacity to learn from others. They absorbed these Hellenic, Hellenistic, and oriental traditions and adapted them to their own needs. The Romans, however, were not without special talents and experiences of their own. These talents were strongest in the fields of war, politics, administration, law, and engineering, those elements that went into the making and retaining of a world state. The results of Rome's use of these many traditions to express and to supplement her own talents we may call Roman culture.

By means of Romanization it was her privilege and obligation to make this culture available to less fortunate, more primitive (chiefly western and northern) parts of her empire.

EARLIER ROMAN CULTURE

In the formation of the Roman world state, therefore, the cultural problem was whether Greek democracy and humanism were to prevail or oriental theocracy and religion. Under circumstances of the "decline and fall" of the Roman Empire oriental theocracy and religion prevailed, and the particular form they assumed was the Christian Church. Before the Church matured, however, the Romans had made an earlier adaptation of Greek and oriental traditions. This chapter treats of this earlier Roman culture. The following chapter will consider the victory of the Orient under the circumstances of "decline and fall," and this will inevitably be followed by an analysis of victorious Christianity and its Church.

CATO AND GREEK CULTURE

The Romans entered the arena of eastern Mediterranean politics to defend Greek freedom against greedy Hellenistic tyrants.[1] Such idealism was quickly succeeded by a cold, realistic, imperial policy guided by strictly Roman considerations. The Roman attitude toward Greek culture changed in a similar way. There were Romans who recognized its superior qualities and the necessity of building upon them. The more practical Romans holding this view did not wish to do over again, simply to make it Roman, something that had already been done by the Greeks. Other Romans did not wish to corrupt the sturdy Roman character by contamination with the refined, and so some thought, effeminate Greek and eastern cultures. We have seen old Cato the Censor, who boasted that he never caressed his wife except when it thundered badly, representing the hard-boiled view of Roman imperialism. Such a man could not and did not feel kindly toward the cultivation of Greek literature and philosophy. Plutarch reports of him that when two Greek philosophers arrived in Rome as ambassadors and succeeded in arousing the enthusiasm of the young Romans for philosophy and Greek literature, Cato, "when this zeal for discussion came pouring into the city, was distressed, fearing lest the young men, by giving this direction to their ambition, should come to love a reputation based on mere words more than one achieved by martial deeds." He arranged accordingly to have these philosophers sent home as soon as possible in order that "the youth of Rome give ear to their laws and magistrates, as heretofore."[2]

QUINTILIAN AND GREEK

Cato and his kind—cultural isolationists—did not succeed in cutting Rome off from the Greek tradition. The latter was too creative, vital, and funda-

[1]See pp. 171 f.
[2]*Parallel Lives*, trans. B. Perrin, Loeb, No. 47, p. 371.

mental to all that distinguished man from beast. An empire half of which used Greek as its learned and international language could not dispense with this tongue. Thus it was that the education of the Roman who looked forward to a public career, or who merely wanted training in the liberal arts, necessarily included Greek as well as Latin and a thorough grounding in Greek literature and philosophy. To complete higher education one often went to Athens or Rhodes. When Quintilian, a Spanish professor of rhetoric at Rome in the first century A.D., came to write his famous and influential book on the *Education of the Orator* (*Institutio Oratoria*). he took it for granted that this education would include not only the Greek language but a liberal training in the whole Greek tradition. "I prefer that a boy should begin with the Greek language," he says, "because he will acquire Latin, which is in general use, even though we tried to prevent him, and because, at the same time, he ought first to be instructed in Greek learning, from which ours is derived." In the first century A.D., with the decline of the Senate and the public assemblies, oratory was not so necessary as formerly to make a career in politics. Yet Quintilian felt that the orator, "a good man skilled in speaking," needed for his eloquence a broad liberal as well as technical education. It was not enough "to have read the poets only; every class of writers must be studied." The grammar necessary to the orator was not complete "without a knowledge of music, since the grammarian has to speak of metre and rhythm; nor, if he is ignorant of astronomy, can he understand the poets, who, to say nothing of other matters, so often allude to the rising and setting of the stars in marking the seasons"; nor must he be unacquainted with philosophy because of the philosophers who have "committed the precepts of philosophy to verse." The Romans thus recognized that in order to acquire the humanity (*humanitas*) that should distinguish the cultivated gentleman it was necessary to be bilingual. Greek was necessary to explore that large world of the human spirit which the Greeks had opened up. Thus Horace, one of Rome's finest poets, says,

> At Rome I had my schooling, and was taught
> Achilles' wrath, and all the woes it brought;
> At classic Athens, where I went ere long,
> I learnt to draw the line 'twixt right and wrong,
> And search for truth, if so she might be seen,
> In academic groves of blissful green. (p. 373)[3]

He also refers to captive Greece's taking her rude conqueror captive.

ROMAN DRAMA AND GREEK DRAMA

Latin literature accordingly became a chapter in the history of the influence of Greek literature, the first of many such chapters reaching to date. But it was, of course, much more than this. For if the Roman writer

[3]George Howe and G. A. Harrer, *Roman Literature in Translation*. Further citations from these authors will appear in my text.

CHRONOLOGY — The Romans and Greek Humanism

	Philosophy, Science, History, and Law	Literature
450 B.C.		
	Twelve Tables (451–450)	
	Zeno (ca. 350–260) Epicurus (341–270)	
		Menander (ca. 342–291)
		Plautus (ca. 254–184)
	Cato the Censor (234–149)	
		Terence (ca. 190–159)
	Cicero (106–43)	
100		
	Lucretius (ca. 99–55)	Catullus (ca. 84–54) Vergil (70–19) Horace (65–8) Tibullus (ca. 55–19)
	Livy (59 B.C.–A.D. 17)	Propertius (ca. 50–16) Ovid (43 B.C.–A.D. 18)
B.C. **A.D.**		
	Pliny the Elder (ca. 23–79)	Seneca (4 B.C.–A.D. 65) Petronius (d. ca. 66) Quintilian (ca. 35–95)
	Epictetus (fl. 60) Vitruvius (fl. 1st c.) Frontinus (fl. late 1st c.) Tacitus (ca. 55–120)	Martial (40–104) Juvenal (ca. 55–130) Suetonius (ca. 70–130) Apuleius (2d c.)
100		
	Marcus Aurelius (121–180)	
500		
	Justinian Code (529)	

used the forms, techniques, and even the subject matter of Greek literature, he still had to make of his Latin tongue an elegant instrument for the
expression of his own creative genius. Because the Greeks had created the
form of the drama, both comedy and tragedy, the meters in which its
poetry was written, and the plots of its subject matter did not mean that
the Romans, by pre-empting these, could produce great drama. In fact,
the Romans never did produce great drama. They were never very much
interested in tragedy, and although the tragedies of Seneca (*ca.* 4 B.C.–A.D.
65) have had considerable influence upon the development of European
drama, they are a far cry from the work of the great Athenian writers of
tragedy. Similarly, the comedies of Aristophanes found no comparable
expression on the part of the Romans. The Roman writers of comedy,
Plautus (*ca.* 254–184 B.C.) and Terence (*ca.* 190–159 B.C.), preferred to
use as their models the plays of the Hellenistic author Menander (*ca.* 342–
291 B.C.), who had dropped the chorus and the vigorous public criticism
of the Aristophanic comedy. The Roman adaptations of Greek settings,
Greek plots, and Greek characters, with results as interesting and funny
as they sometimes still are, never succeeded in making the Romans enthusiastic playgoers like the Greeks. They came to prefer the spectacles of
the arena and the entertainments of the circus to the theater.

LATIN LYRIC POETRY

Latin lyric poetry reached its perfection during the last century of the
Republic and the reign of Augustus in the work of such distinguished poets
as Catullus, Propertius, Tibullus, Ovid, Horace, and Vergil. Like Plautus
and Terence, the first four of these men were influenced chiefly by
Hellenistic (Alexandrian) poets rather than by the earlier Greek lyricists.
Only to Horace and Vergil did the earlier Greek lyric and epic poets,
such men as Anacreon and Homer, become sources of inspiration. These
Roman writers, like lyric poets at all times and places, were occupied
with the theme of love: Catullus for his Lesbia, Propertius for his Cynthia,
Tibullus for his Delia, and Ovid for his Corinna. As members of an elegant, luxurious, decadent aristocracy they exploited all the possibilities of
polished Latin verse to describe the vicissitudes of by no means conventional passion. Catullus urged Lesbia, the wife of a friend, to

> Give me kisses thousand-fold,
>   Add to them a hundred more;
> Other thousands still be told,
>   Other hundreds o'er and o'er. (p. 266)

and Tibullus, Delia,

> Then let us worship Venus while we may,
> With brow unblushing, burst the bolted door
> And join with rapture in the midnight fray,
> Your leader I—Love's soldier proved of yore. (p. 353)

In a different mood Propertius asked,

> Whence, O my Cynthia! shall I date thy scorn?
> When was it first that Cynthia bade me mourn?
> I, who late bore a happy lover's name,
> Now see my passion doom'd to fatal shame! (p. 443)

OVID

Ovid, whose Corinna may have been only imaginary, tempered his fashionable love poetry with wit and established himself in his *Art of Love* as the undisputed authority on the subject:

> In Cupid's school whoe'er would take degree,
> Must learn his rudiments by reading me.
> . . . . .
> Experience makes my work; a truth so try'd
> You may believe. (pp. 455–456)

THE "ART OF LOVE"

These men did not limit themselves to the theme of love. The *Attis*[4] of Catullus is a powerful expression of the emotions stirred up by the mystery cult of the Magna Mater. Ovid in his *Metamorphoses* summarized for all posterity the chief tales of Greek mythology. His *Art of Love*, a handbook on seduction, was, however, more than the emperor Augustus could take. Augustus, it will be remembered, was seriously interested in reforming the morals of Roman society. At about the moment when the *Art of Love* was published his only daughter, Julia, was involved in a scandalous adultery leading to her banishment. Augustus suffered acutely from her very bad reputation. Seneca reports of her that "she had been accessible to scores of paramours, that in nocturnal revels she had roamed about the city, that the very forum and the rostrum, from which her father had proposed a law against adultery, had been chosen by the daughter for her debaucheries." It is possible that for his part in promoting frivolous moral views and in the scandal associated with Augustus' own daughter Ovid himself was banished to Tomi on the Black Sea. He continued to write poetry (*Tristia* and *Letters from the Pontus*) and in the former admits that "my *Art of Love* is not a serious work. But it contains nothing contrary to the laws. Besides, it is not addressed to Roman ladies; it is a light work for light women." It is useless in any case to trust to censorship for "there is no good thing but can also do harm. And where should one stop? If poetry corrupts, plays also offer the seeds of vice. Have all the theatres put down, which have given so many cause for sinning! Put down the Circus; there the young girl sits next to a complete stranger! Why is that portico left open? Some women walk there to meet their lovers! And an honest woman should avoid the temples. In the Temple

---

[4]See pp. 287 ff.

of Jupiter she will at once think how many women the god made mothers. At the Temple of Mars the statue of Venus stands before the door, together with her mate, the Avenger. . . . Everything can corrupt perverse minds."[5]

HORACE

It was not necessary for Augustus to banish Horace (65–8 B.C.) or Vergil (70–19 B.C.). These supreme masters of Latin verse, the beneficiaries of imperial patronage, were in a sense political poets. At any rate they were so impressed with the achievement of Augustus, and so sympathetic with his aims in establishing the principate, that they did not hesitate to use their talent in his behalf. Neither of these men, and this could be said for all the writers mentioned so far, was, strictly speaking, a Roman. Horace, a freedman's son, came from Venusia in southern Italy, and Vergil, of peasant stock, was born in a village near Mantua in northern Italy. Both preferred the life of a country gentleman to that of a man about town. Horace's poetry takes many forms (*Epodes*, *Satires*, *Odes*, and *Epistles*), and he is frank to acknowledge his dependence upon such Greek poets as Sappho, Alcaeus, and Anacreon. When he is not praising Augustus he likes to emphasize the simple rural joys to be pursued on his Sabine farm (Augustus was much interested in the Roman farmer) and to recommend the Epicurean approach of seizing upon the moment for the pleasure it may bring. Augustus, Horace calls in one ode:

> Father and guardian of the human race—
>   Offspring of Saturn—thine by destiny,
> Great Caesar's charge. Thou art supreme; his place
>   Second to none but thee. (p. 359)

And in another:

> Augustus Caesar, thou on earth shall be
>   Enthroned a present Deity;
> Britons and Parthian hordes to Rome
>   Their proud necks yielding. (p. 364)

In another he says:

> While we have Caesar at our head,
>   Serene custodian of the State,
> No civil fury shall we dread,
>   Nor feuds that cities desolate;
> The rage that fires barbarian hordes
> Shall never sharpen Roman swords. (p. 360)

[5]Reprinted from *The Roman Spirit in Religion, Thought, and Art* (trans. M. R. Dobie), p. 289, by Albert Grenier, by permission of Alfred A. Knopf, Inc. Copyright 1926 by Alfred A. Knopf, Inc.

In one he praises the simple life:

> Why build—to win but envy thus—
>   A pillared mansion huge and strange?
>   Or why my Sabine vale exchange
> For riches more laborious?
>
> . . . . .
>
> The golden mean who loves, lives safely free
> From filth of foreworn house, and quiet lives,
>   Releas'd from court, where envy needs must be.
>
> . . . . .
>
>   Happiest to whom high Heaven
> Enough—no more—with sparing hand has given. (pp. 363–366)

In another he advises Leuconoe:

> Strive not . . . to know what end
> The gods above to me or thee will send:
> Nor with astrologers consult at all,
> That thou mayst better know what can befall;
> Whether thou liv'st more winters, or thy last
> Be this, which Tyrrhen waves 'gainst rocks do cast.
> Be wise! Drink free, and in so short a space
> Do not protracted hopes of life embrace:
> Whilst we are talking, envious time doth slide;
> This day's thine own; the next may be denied. (p. 389)

VERGIL

Vergil had no difficulty in taking up the imperial emphasis upon agriculture and ancient Italian religious rites. He himself was a son of the soil and relished as a part of his inheritance the beauties of the countryside and the simple virtues it encouraged. In his *Eclogues*, or *Bucolics*, imitating the Hellenistic poet Theocritus, he sings pastoral, or shepherd, songs. The fourth of these won for him Christian praise as a prophet, for it speaks, as of the Christ to come, of "the new-born babe—who first shall end that age of iron" and "bid a golden dawn upon the broad world." His *Georgics* is ostensibly a poetic manual on how to run the farm, but it does much more in holding up for praise the life of that peasant who

> With crooked ploughs the fertile fallows tills;
> And the round year with daily labour fills.
> And hence the country-markets are supply'd:
> Enough remains for household charge beside:
> His wife and tender children to sustain,
> And gratefully to feed his dumb deserving train.
>
> . . . . .
>
> And this rude life our homely fathers chose.
> Old Rome from such a race deriv'd her birth,
>
> . . . . .
>
> Which now on seven high hills triumphant reigns,
> And in that compass all the world contains. (p. 351)

But it is as the master of majestic epic verse that Vergil, placing himself beside Homer, has earned the gratitude of mankind, and especially of Dante, who called him

> My master and my author verily,
> Thou only art the one from whom I took
> The seemly style for which men honor me.

THE "AENEID"

In his *Aeneid*, Vergil not only tells the story of a mythological hero but uses the dignity of the hexameter to compose a truly patriotic epic, one to enhance the glory of the Roman golden age introduced by Augustus. Rome was destined to be founded by a Trojan hero, that special favorite of the gods, *pius Aeneas*, who realized how his career and, accordingly, that of the Romans, having been determined by the immortals, could be endangered in the beginning by the oriental princess Dido of Carthage. Aeneas, the symbol of all that was best in Roman character and destined to found a universal state, in the sixth book of the *Aeneid* descends to the underworld to meet his old father, Anchises, and to seek guidance for the future. Here he sees Rome's worthies and is told:

> Now fix your sight, and stand intent, to see
> Your Roman race, and Julian progeny.
> There mighty Caesar waits his vital hour,
> Impatient for the world, and grasps his promised pow'r.
> But next behold the youth of form divine—
> Caesar himself, exalted in his line—
> Augustus, promised oft, and long foretold,
> Sent to the realm that Saturn ruled of old;
> Born to restore a better age of gold.
> Afric and India shall his pow'r obey;
> He shall extend his propagated sway
> Beyond the solar year, without the starry way,
> Where Atlas turns the rolling heav'ns round,
> And his broad shoulders with their lights are crown'd.

Anchises then says of Rome:

> But Rome! 'tis thine alone, with awful sway,
> To rule mankind, and make the world obey.
> Disposing peace and war thy own majestic way;
> To tame the proud, the fetter'd slave to free:
> These are imperial arts, and worthy thee. (pp. 316–318)

THE SATIRISTS

If the Greek writers inspired these Roman poets, such can hardly be said of the Roman satirists. Here was a poetic form that Quintilian claimed to be wholly Roman (*Satura quidem tota nostra est*). While Greek literature is not without satire it is not clear that it had anything to do with the work of the earlier satirists, Lucilius and Horace, or with the brilliant writing of the Spaniard Martial (A.D. 40-104) or of Juvenal (*ca.* A.D. 55-130). It is to these men that one must go for an intimate and detailed picture of the often sordid daily life of the capital of the world in the first century of the Pax Romana. It was a world to which Martial reacted in the form of light-hearted and often witty epigram (he was the first epigrammatist of the West), and Juvenal in poems seething with what he called savage indignation. This was the century of growing despotism, of the informer, of Nero and Domitian, an age when "literature had either to be silent or to be servile"; when, without daring to criticize the prince, one could dare to attack the idle and immoral rich and the notorious weaknesses of all human beings. Martial was servile enough in the presence of his tyrants, "unconfined controllers of the earth" and "propitious parents of mankind!" Between an invitation from Jove and Caesar he would prefer, "though that the stars were near, Rome more remote," to accept the one from his "Jupiter on earth." Juvenal, however, could refer to the time

> When the last Flavius, drunk with fury, tore
> The prostrate world, which bled at every pore,
> And Rome beheld, in body as in mind,
> A bald-pate Nero rise, to curse mankind. (pp. 500-501)

Martial, who prided himself on his "stiff Spanish hair" and his "hairy legs and cheeks," had not much use for the Roman fop:

> You are everywhere thought just too lovely to live.
> You must be: I hear and believe it.
> But, Cotilus, pray be so good as to say
> What's a lovely man, as you conceive it?

> "Well, a lovely man must have his hair combed and curled,
>   Of perfumes he mustn't be chary,
> Must hum the last strain from the Nile and from Spain,
>   Must dance well and mustn't be hairy.

> "He must linger all day by some lady friend's chair,
>   With murmured remarks must regale her,
> Must get billets doux and respond to them, too;
>   Must be firm and precise with his tailor.

> "He must always be posted on every intrigue
>   And must whirl in the gay social vortex;
> Each family tree through all years A. U. C. [*Ab Urbe Condita*]
>   He must know from medulla to cortex."

> That will do! This will make a man lovely, you say?
>   I'm not in position to doubt it—
> But when I want to pass for a thorough-bred ass
>   I can see how I'd best set about it. (p. 571)

Juvenal had little respect for foreigners, especially those Greeks who were crowding into Rome.

> A flattering, cringing, treacherous, artful race,
> Of torrent tongue, and never-blushing face;
> Which shifts to every form, and shines in all:
> Grammarian, painter, augur, rhetorician,
> Rope-dancer, conjurer, fiddler, physician,
> All trades his own your hungry Greekling counts. (p. 578)

And those women who were taking to Greek:

> Some faults, though small, no husband yet can bear:
> 'Tis now the nauseous cant, that none is fair,
> Unless her thoughts in Attic terms she dress;
> . . . . .
> All now is Greek: in Greek their souls they pour,
> In Greek their fears, hopes, joys;—what would you more?
> In Greek they clasp their lovers. We allow
> These fooleries to girls: but thou, O thou,
> Who tremblest at the verge of eighty-eight,
> To Greek it still!—'tis now a day too late.
> Foh! how it savors of the dregs of lust,
> When an old hag, whose blandishments disgust,
> Affects the infant lisp, the girlish squeak,
> And mumbles out, "My life!" "My soul!" in Greek. (pp. 579–580)

LATIN PROSE

The Greek language conditioned the development of Latin prose as well as verse. In the marvelously balanced cadences of Cicero, trained in the rhetorical tradition of Isocrates and Demosthenes, prose reached its apogee. Cicero had completed his training for public life by studying with the famous rhetorician Molon at Rhodes and had learned how to temper the extravagances of the Asiatic manner popular before his day. He used his prose not only to prosecute corrupt provincial governors and sinister conspirators but also to extoll the advantages of that humanism bestowed by an education in Greek culture. A typical Greek in his participation in public life, he used his leisure to make known to the Romans in popular form the philosophy and the political thought of the Greeks. Only the prose of the historian Tacitus (*ca.* A.D. 55-120) can compare in brilliance with Cicero's, possessing, in addition, a tough, terse, epigrammatic originality of its own and expressing, like Juvenal's, a bitter hostility toward the growing loss of liberty in Roman public life. The Roman gift for satire was carried over into prose by Petronius's extraordinary novel the *Satyricon*, a hilarious parody of the vulgar display of the nouveau riche in the first century A.D. The novel, itself an invention of the Hellenistic Greeks, was further developed by the African writer of the second century A.D. Apuleius, whose romantic tale the *Golden Ass* contains a vivid and intimate account of the cult of the Egyptian goddess Isis. Together with the imperial biographer Suetonius (*ca.* A.D. 70–130), Martial, Juvenal, Tacitus, and Petronius offer incomparable fare for an understanding of the surging life of the first capital of the world.

ROMAN RELIGION: ANIMISM

Greek literature not only helped to stimulate and transform Latin literature but contributed as well to the transformation of the old Roman religion into something that resembled Greek anthropomorphic polytheism.[6] The early religion of the Roman peasant was concerned with spirits (*numina*) rather than with gods and goddesses. It is thus called an animism rather than a theism. These spirits, dwelling in natural objects or localities, had charge over specialized human activities, and it was necessary to establish peace with them (*pax numinum*). Varro complained that the Romans and Italians recognized some thirty thousand of these spirits. Their departments were indeed highly specialized. It took the co-operation of many to bring up a child: Cunina to watch over the cradle, Rumina to teach him to nurse, Educa and Potina to make him eat and drink, Statulinus to hold him upright, and Fabulinus to make him talk. For a peasant it was a matter of life and death to preserve good relations with the spirits of the fields, woods, and streams and with those who controlled the weather and the fertility of crops. It was not difficult to secure these good relations with the spirits if one knew how, at the proper time, in the proper place, and in the proper manner, to conciliate them with the correct ritualistic deference and offerings. Like the Greeks, the Romans conceived of their relationship with the spirits as in the nature of a contract, so much given for so much received. A Roman peasant would thus pray to the spirit, "I offer thee this cake and pray my prayer aright, *in order that* thou mayest be kind and propitious to me and my children, to my house and household."

THE RELIGION OF THE CITY-STATE

The propitiation of the spirits controlling agriculture and the life of the family constituted the religion of the early Roman. The *lares*, the spirits of the fields, were brought into the house to become domestic spirits; the *penates* were a group of spirits controlling the store cupboard, and thus the food supply. Janus, the spirit of the doorway, connected the house with the outside world; and Vesta was the spirit of the hearth flame. With all these spirits the head of the family, the *paterfamilias*, conducted the proper rites. He joined as well with his peasant neighbors in celebrating festivals in honor of the spirits of the boundary stones (*Terminalia*), of prosperity (*Ambarvalia*), and of the grain to be sown (*Saturnalia*). When the peasant communities coalesced into Rome the city-state, this

[6]See p. 100.

religion came to be regarded as a proper field in which the state might function. Accordingly, in the course of time, a special priesthood, headed by a chief priest (*pontifex maximus*), was set up to administer and protect the divine law (*ius divinum*). Yet the objects of worship of this state cult remained the older spirits of household and field, and its festivals the old celebrations of an agricultural community. Janus was now the doorway of the state, open in time of war, closed in time of peace; Vesta now the hearth of the state, whose eternal flame was tended by vestal virgins. The *lares* and *penates* also became part of the state cult. Here was danger. A priesthood, regarded as officials of the state, took over from the private Roman citizen and the individual locality the obligation of maintaining the peace of the spirits. It is no wonder that the Roman ceased to consider his religion as a personal matter and even, in the case of local agricultural spirits, services for whom were retained by a metropolitan state, forgot their names or, in case they had been made gods or goddesses, forgot their sex.

ROMAN RELIGION AND GREEK RELIGION

Varro, the prolific writer on Roman antiquities of the first century B.C., remarks that for 170 years the Romans worshiped gods and goddesses without giving them human form, and he adds that "those who first made images of the gods for the nations, both removed fear from their states and added error." With this remark Varro seems to say: a god is not a human, but while you may fear the invisible spirit of a dark and gloomy grove you cannot fear a beautiful nymph. Romans first learned from the Etruscans, and then directly from the Greeks, to give their spirits human form. They took over gods and goddesses of the Italians and the Greeks and gave them Latin names. Thus Jupiter, Juno, Minerva, and Venus were added to the Roman pantheon and identified with the Greek Zeus, Hera, Athena, and Aphrodite. From the Etruscans the Romans learned how to build temples and carve statues for their gods. From the Greeks they took, further, Apollo, Demeter, Dionysus, Persephone, Aesculapius, Hermes (Mercury), and Poseidon (Neptune). With the Greek gods came features of the Greek ritual, and with Greek literature the Romans learned how to humanize their spirits with personal descriptions, characterizations, and the biographies of mythology. Roman religion thus adopted the anthropomorphic polytheism of the Greeks. It ceased being Roman and became Graeco-Roman.

THE RELIGIOUS REFORM OF AUGUSTUS

When Roman religion became a political or state matter and not a personal, private one, it lost much of its appeal. Chief priests and priestly colleges, manipulating religion in the interests of politics, gave occasion for cynical scepticism. From the literature of the Greeks the Romans absorbed the criticism of popular Greek religion contained there, and with the philosophy of the Greeks they acquired, for the learned and sophisticated at least, a substitute for a discredited popular Graeco-Roman polytheism. The decline of the old Roman religion and what has been called its cold, unenthusiastic, "grave and severely official" character made room, however much resisted at first, for the popularity among all classes of the Greek and oriental mystery religions,[7] thus introducing to the practical Roman an entirely new religious experience. In any case, religious indifference and cynicism had gone so far by the end of the Republic that Augustus felt it necessary to identify his rule with a religious reform. Varro thought that the Roman gods might perish from the neglect of Roman citizens themselves. Augustus' reform, associated with moral reform, was of a dual nature. He sought to revive the old religion of the countryside that the state had taken over and deadened. He thus restored the neglected temples and festivals of half-forgotten gods as part of a movement to revive the virtues of the early Roman peasant-soldier. The success of this part of his reform was only temporary.

EMPEROR WORSHIP

At the same time, as if he recognized the impossibility of reviving the old Roman religion, he permitted the establishment in the West of the worship of the emperor as a divine being. To be sure, the precise nature of the emperor worship that Augustus tolerated was not exactly the worship of the emperor personally as a living god (only poets were permitted this). It was the emperor together with the goddess Roma, the spirit of Rome, to whom temples went up over the empire. Most of the early emperors were apotheosized at their deaths. "I feel I am becoming a god," Vespasian said humorously when he recognized the symptoms of a fatal malady. But by the end of the third century the very person of the living emperor was considered divine. In essence Augustus had permitted the theocracy of the Orient to be established. Emperor worship became, however, just another political religion. It provided the symbolism with which to gather about the Roman Empire the loyalty of the various peoples of the Mediterranean. It did not provide a substitute for decadent Graeco-Roman polytheism at a time when the empire was sorely tried. The religious history of the empire shows instead the growths of oriental mystery cults and Christianity, their conflict, and the victory of the latter.

ROMAN PHILOSOPHY

To the extent, likewise, that the well-bred and educated Roman became interested in philosophy it was Greek philosophy that claimed his interest, since there could hardly be said to be any other. What interested him especially in Greek philosophy was what it said about morality and conduct, subjects about which the Romans, in their dealings with other

[7]See pp. 111 ff., 41 f.

peoples, needed to know much. In other words, Roman interest in philosophy was not a purely intellectual or technical interest concerned, for example, with a definition of truth or reality but essentially a religious interest, concerned with the question of how man's relation with the divine promoted decent behavior. The Romans, therefore, did not cultivate the earlier Platonic or Aristotelian schools, although many were well acquainted with both. They took rather to the two main subsequent schools developed in Athens in the late fourth and early third centuries, the Epicurean and the Stoic. The former was founded by Epicurus (341–270 B.C.), a Greek from the island of Samos; the latter by Zeno (350–260 B.C.), an ascetic half-Semite from the island of Cyprus. That a Semitic prophet could go to Athens in the fourth century and found a popular school of philosophy is a good example of what was happening in the Hellenistic world. In this world, now that the political unit of the city-state had lost its importance, the Greek had to adjust himself to the absolutism of the Hellenistic monarchies. It often happens that when this kind of adjustment is imposed upon the individual he turns to the last refuge of his freedom, his mind, and builds up individualistic philosophies aiming to teach him how to be happy in spite of tyranny and insecurity. In religious terms these philosophers were concerned with the salvation of the individual, while some of them considered as well the practical relationship of the individual to the new political unit, the theocratic empire.

LUCRETIUS

The early reaction of Roman conservatives to Greek philosophy turned its teachers out of Rome. Such rejection, however, did not prevent Greek philosophy from spreading to the West. By the middle of the first century B.C. it was being popularized by no less a person than Cicero. Already in this century one of the two leading Hellenistic schools of Athens, the Epicurean, had received classic expression in poetry by the Roman Lucretius, who felt that he could make his passionate devotion to Epicureanism more influential if he worked it out in hexameter verse. The result was a poetic as well as a philosophical masterpiece, *The Nature of Things (De Rerum Natura)*, a unique work of its kind.

FEARS INSPIRED BY RELIGION

In the course of this work Lucretius remarks that "much more keenly in evil days do men turn their minds to religion," and he was well aware of the evil character of his own century. But he did not write his philosophical poem to provide a religious answer to the question of human happiness. As a staunch and orthodox Epicurean he thought that happiness was essentially a matter of pleasure (hedonism) and that pleasure, the source of happiness, was mental. It was mental calm or intellectual contentment that constituted the pleasure responsible for happiness. He saw as the chief obstacles to mental calm the fears inspired by conventional religion. There were two of these especially: (1) the fear that the gods interfered in and regulated the life of man; and (2) the fear that there was a life after death, when man was punished for his evil life on earth. Lucretius states the first fear as follows: "For when we look upwards to the celestial regions of the great firmament, to the ether studded with glittering stars, when we think of the ways of the sun and moon, into our hearts already crushed with other woes a new anxious care awakening begins to lift up its head, whether by any chance we have to do with some immeasurable power of the gods, able to make the bright stars revolve with their different movements? . . . Whose mind does not shrink up with fear of the gods, whose limbs do not crawl with terror, when the scorched earth quakes with the shivering shock of a thunderbolt and rumblings run through the mighty sky? . . . When the whole earth trembles beneath our feet, when cities are shaken and fall or threaten to fall, what wonder if the sons of men feel contempt for themselves, and acknowledge the great potency and wondrous might of gods in the world to govern all things?" With respect to the second he says: "If men saw that a limit has been set to tribulation they would have some degree of strength to defy religious fears and the threatenings of the priests; but as it is there is no way of resistance and no power, because everlasting punishment is to be feared after death."[8] (pp. 9, 11, 427, 429)

LUCRETIUS AND THE ATOMIC THEORY

Mankind, Lucretius continues, "had no reason for the most part to roll the sad waves of trouble with their breasts. . . . This terror of [the] mind . . . must be dispelled . . . by the aspect and law of nature"; in other words, by science, for Lucretius had recourse to the atomic theory of Democritus[9] to explain away these two religious fears. The universe and all its works are to be explained in materialistic terms, in terms of the movements of atoms in the void. There has been no divine creation out of the void, for "we must confess that nothing comes from nothing, since all things must have seed from which each severally being created may be brought forth into the soft air. . . . All nature therefore, as it is in itself, is made up of two things; for there are bodies, and there is void, in which these bodies are and through which they move this way and that." These bodies are composed of atoms, so small that our senses are unable to perceive them. We can, however, best get at the larger truth of this illimitable, mechanistic, atomic universe through our sensations, for "what can we find more certain than the senses themselves to mark for us truth and falsehood?" (pp. 13, 17, 31, 53)

[8]Trans. W. H. D. Rouse, Loeb, No. 181. Further citations from Lucretius will be made in my text.
[9]See pp. 119 f.

It is absurd, he goes on, to imagine that the operations of the universe are to be explained in terms of gods and goddesses rather than of atoms moving in the void. "If Jupiter and other gods," asks Lucretius, "shake the shining regions of heaven with appalling din, if they cast fire whither it may be the pleasure of each one, why do they not see to it that those who have not refrained from some abominable crime, shall be struck? . . . Why rather does one with no base guilt on his conscience roll in flames all innocent, suddenly involved in a tornado from heaven and taken off by fire?" Further, asks Lucretius, "Why does he [Jupiter] shatter holy shrines of the gods and even illustrious habitations with the fatal thunderbolt, why smash fine-wrought images of the gods and rob his own statues of their grandeur with a violent stroke?" Lucretius does not go so far as to say there are no gods. They are, like everything and everyone else, mere atomic compounds themselves. But it is the "very nature of divinity . . . [to] enjoy immortal life in the deepest peace, far removed and separated from our troubles; for without any pain, without danger, itself mighty by its own resources, needing us not at all, it is neither propitiated with services nor touched by wrath." These materialistic gods and goddesses, dwelling in the vast interstellar spaces, who "in tranquil peace pass untroubled days and a life serene," have thus, it seems, achieved the Epicurean happiness and spend their time discussing, perhaps chanting, if not the *Nature of Things* then Democritus or Epicurus himself. Accordingly, "it is no piety to show oneself often with covered head, turning towards a stone and approaching every altar, none to fall prostrate upon the ground and to spread open the palms before shrines of the gods, none to sprinkle altars with the blood of beasts in showers and to link vow to vow; but rather to be able to survey all things with mind at peace." The gods, then, do not interfere in human affairs, and do not themselves wish to be disturbed with human appeals. It is because of "their ignorance of causes that men refer events to the dominion of the gods, and yield them the place of kings." (pp. 131, 163, 425, 449)

LUCRETIUS AND IMMORTALITY

There is a similar explanation for the fear that after death the soul will be punished for the sins committed during life. To Lucretius there is no such thing as an immortal soul. Indeed, there is no distinction between soul and body. The soul is a very specialized combination of material atoms. Death, like some atomic explosion, breaks up the soul into its atomic components. "Therefore when the body has died, we must admit that the soul has perished, wrenched away throughout the body. . . . Accordingly we may be sure that there is nothing to be feared after death, and that he who is not, cannot be miserable. . . . No one awakens and rises whom the cold stoppage of life has once overtaken."

When once through freedom from fear, fear of an intervention of the gods in human affairs, and fear of a tortured life after death, one achieves the philosophic calm that is the chief and intellectual pleasure of Epicureanism, there is no exhortation to go ahead to achieve a more positive happiness. The system does not encourage, for example, any active participation in government or society. Its advocacy of a withdrawal from the more active life to achieve intellectual pleasure is somewhat ascetic. The younger and more profligate set of Roman aristocratic society took Epicureanism to mean nothing more than physical hedonism, a rejection of divine guidance and immortality in order to seek the immediate, frank, and sensual pleasures of the flesh. This interpretation was a complete distortion. For the Epicureans rejected sensual gratification as the basis of true pleasure (and therefore happiness) because such pleasures were obviously transitory and futile. The lasting pleasures were exclusively and necessarily mental or spiritual. The Epicurean philosophy, because of its intellectual and antireligious character, never secured a large Roman following. Yet it defended passionately man's rational ability to figure things out for himself. "Nothing," according to Lucretius, "hinders us [with the help of reason, of course] from living a life worthy of the gods."

THE ROMAN STOICS

If Lucretius sought to teach the Romans how to escape the fears inspired by religion, the Roman Stoics, on the contrary, developed the religious implications of Zeno's philosophy. They did it to such an extent that Stoicism promoted an outlook closely resembling Christianity, which, in fact, borrowed much from it.[10] As the result of the activity of early Stoic teachers in Rome Stoicism was well known by the first century B.C., when Cicero, in his work *Concerning Duties* (*De Officiis*), expounded its doctrines. Roman Stoicism was systematized during the principate of the first two centuries. Its first important representative was Seneca (*ca.* 3 B.C.–A.D. 65), a Spanish-born son of Latin colonists. He had been entrusted with the emperor Nero's education, and during the early years of his pupil's reign he took part in an enlightened administration of the state. On the charge, however, of having been party to a conspiracy against Nero he was forced to commit suicide. His philosophical reflections are contained in his *Moral Essays*. His successor as a leading Stoic teacher was Epictetus (b. *ca.* A.D. 60), the lame Phrygian slave of one of Nero's courtiers. Together with other philosophers he was expelled from Rome by Domitian in A.D. 90 and settled in Greece, where a devoted student published his teachings in the form of the *Discourses* and the *Handbook*. The last and most noble representative of Roman Stoicism was the emperor Marcus Aurelius (A.D. 121–180), who, while in camp on the

[10]See p. 355.

German frontier, jotted down his ideas in Greek in his *Meditations*.[11] Stoicism may thus be said to have been the philosophy of the empire under the Pax Romana. While it reveals characteristics of a philosophy of despotism it expresses also some of the loftiest aspirations of the empire— its universalism and humanitarianism. It paid with the martyrdom of some of its followers for opposition to the despotism of Nero, and Epictetus was among the philosophic exiles of Domitian because he was held to share the Stoic hostility to Domitian's tyranny.

THE STOIC ATTITUDE

Stoicism, like Epicureanism, was originally an effort to provide the individual with guidance through a difficult and insecure world. The Epicurean teaching urged man to avoid the discomforts of pain and fear and seek the intellectual pleasure that such avoidance brought. The Stoic preached independence of heart and mind by recognizing the inevitability of fate in those spheres of human activity where man's conduct seemed to be determined; or, as the Stoic was inclined to put it, he taught man to be indifferent to the externals of life and death, prosperity and poverty, health and disease. It was the obligation of the Stoic as a man of reason and as the possessor of free will in the field of personality and character, where man's conduct seemed open to choice, to build, and grow, and do his best in the job allotted him to do. He saw no excuse for sacrificing one's personal integrity or failing to do one's duty, no matter what the outcome.

STOIC PHYSICAL THEORY

The Stoic outlook rested upon definite ideas of the physical composition of the universe. Where the Epicurean sought to explain everything in terms of the atom, the Stoic made use of a combination of the elements of air and fire. The substance of the universe he called a materialistic and yet living "fiery breath," directing the whole course of events. This ultimate and governing reality, the "fiery breath," Stoic teaching identified with reason, or, let us say, universal reason, since it permeated everything. The universe thus became an entirely rational thing, functioning according to law. The Stoic was inclined to identify this universal reason with nature, and, accordingly, saw the orderliness of the universe as the workings of natural law. The inexorability of natural law was identified with fate, but not a blind fate, since the law that governed the universe operated in accordance with the divine reason and was therefore the law of Providence, or of God, and necessarily in the best interests of all concerned, man included. This bridges the gap between early Greek philosophy (elemental fire) and Christianity.

[11]See pp. 249 ff.

According to Stoic teaching, man, as a part of the universe, possesses a spark of the "fiery breath" within him. This spark is a part of the divine reason, or nature, that permeates and directs the universe. It may be called man's soul, and it makes of man more than a mere mortal. Through it he partakes of the divine reason or nature; indeed, as a rational creature he is himself a divine being. Given then this divine nature of man, and of the very universe itself, it is man's chief function, according to Stoic doctrine, to live in harmony with nature, his own nature, and the nature of the universe. This is to say, in view of the Stoic identification of nature with reason and God, the chief task of man is to live in accordance with reason and its universal law, or God and his universal law. Man is to submit to the laws of nature, or of reason, or of God. He is not to be a rebel, for in these matters it is futile to be a rebel. When the workings of the world discomfort, annoy, inflict pain upon, or humiliate man, he must not let himself become a victim of his emotions: of anger, sympathy, pity, grief, or scorn; he must recognize that his emotions cannot affect the total situation. He is to remain indifferent or apathetic to situations such as these in the firm belief that the actions of Providence cannot be mistaken, even if he does not understand them. Whatever is must be right, and must accordingly be accepted without loss of human dignity. Essentially this is a conservative outlook. It is what was meant previously by referring to Stoicism as the philosophy of a growing despotism. Despotism could be interpreted as the incomprehensible functioning of divine reason, the inescapable workings of a natural destiny.

THE STOIC POINT OF VIEW

For an elaboration of this point of view one may turn most profitably to the Stoic writers themselves: "Do we ask what cause is? It is surely creative Reason,—in other words God." "What then is the true nature of God? It is intelligence, knowledge, right reason." "You are a being of primary importance, you are a fragment of God; you have within you a part of Him. . . . God is near you, he is with you, he is within you . . . a holy spirit indwells within us, one who marks our good and bad deeds, and is our guardian." "The peculiar property of man. Do you ask what this is? It is soul, and reason brought to perfection in the soul. For man is a reasoning animal. Therefore, man's highest good is attained, if he has fulfilled the good for which nature designed him at birth. And what is it which this reason demands of him? The easiest thing in the world, to live in accordance with his own nature." "Being by nature noble, and high-minded, and free, the rational animal, man, sees that he has some of the things which are about him free from hindrance and under his control, but that others are subject to hindrance and under the control of others. Free from hindrance are those things which be in the sphere of moral purpose, and subject to hindrance are those which be outside the sphere of moral purpose. . . . Always I wish rather the thing which takes place. For I regard God's will as better than my will . . . my will is one with his will. . . . We cannot change this order of things; but what we can do is to acquire stout hearts, worthy of good men, thereby courageously enduring chance and placing ourselves in harmony with Nature. . . . Whatever happens, assume that it was bound to happen, and do not be willing to rail at nature. That which you cannot reform, it is best to endure, and to attend uncomplainingly upon the God under whose guidance everything progresses. It is a bad soldier who grumbles when following his commander. . . . Let Fate find us ready and alert. Here is your great soul— the man who has given himself over to Fate; on the other hand that man is a weakling and a degenerate who struggles and maligns the order of the universe and would rather reform the gods than reform himself."

STOICISM AND HUMAN BROTHERHOOD

Stoic writers used language that reflects the rise of empires and world states as much as resignation to the will of God. The doctrine that all men possessed a spark of that divinity that was God meant that all men were divine, and divinely equal. It meant also that they were brothers and common citizens of the world of gods and men—the great cosmopolis. From these statements Roman lawyers drew extraordinary conclusions.[12] As "sons of God," Stoics referred to themselves as citizens of the universe. Marcus Aurelius, for example, said, "To me as Antoninus my city is Rome, but as a man it is the universe."

STOICISM AS AN ASCETIC DISCIPLINE

In the hands of the Roman writers Seneca, Epictetus, and Marcus Aurelius Stoicism became less a system of philosophy and more a religion or, at least, a guide for daily living. The god that earlier Stoicism inclined to identify with reason and nature now came to be described in more personal terms and was made to absorb, under various aspects, the many gods of Roman popular religion. It was a god to whom one sang hymns and addressed prayers. The virtues that Stoicism upheld were found to be the old Republican virtues of Cato and of the early peasant-soldier. These virtues were now to be developed by daily practice, as if Stoicism had become an ascetic discipline to be performed by Stoic monks. It was recognized that the perfect embodiment of Stoic virtues could be attained only by a kind of saint—the Stoic Wise Man—and much was made of the rude, monkish Stoic missionary to the Romans, the un-Stoic heathen. At the same time members of the Roman aristocracy kept Stoic confessors in their houses to direct the morals of the inmates. In his correspondence Seneca thus set himself up as a kind of moral adviser.

[12] See pp. 254 ff.

The rules of Stoic living were carried over into everyday life. "In the early morning he [the Stoic] shakes off sleep, rousing himself to do the day's work of a man. Having clothed himself, he turns his mind towards his Maker, and sings his praises; he resolves during the coming day to cooperate in his purposes, and to bear cheerfully any burden that may be placed upon him. He will then give a short time to gymnastic exercises for the good of his health; after which, if his strength allows it, he will take, winter or summer, a plunge into the cold bath; next comes the slightest of meals. . . . Food that requires no cooking has an advantage, as ripe fruit, some vegetables, milk, cheese, and honey. Flesh food is for many reasons objectionable. It is heavy and impedes thought; the exhalations from it are turbid and overshadow the soul. Men should imitate the gods, who feed on the light exhalations of earth and water." The Stoic must be careful as to dress. "It is against nature to be averse to neatness in appearance. . . . A sensible man will conform to fashion, nor will he wish to make the name of philosopher still more unpopular than it is. . . . To men the beard should be an object of just pride, for it is more becoming than the cock's comb, or the lion's mane . . . the beard may be trimmed; for, as Zeno has observed, nature provides rather against the 'too little' than against the 'too much,' and reason must come to her help." After breakfast comes a short nap or reverie and then "the day's studies, being careful to alternate reading and writing, so that his mind may be neither exhausted by the latter nor relaxed by the former. Later on he will consider his practical duties towards his relatives, his friends, and society in general. . . . He will visit his friends, saying a word here and there in season, but not . . . to all and sundry. He will encourage those who are making progress in virtue, and sharply warn those who are in danger of a fall. He advises a young mother to nurse her child at her own breast; and when he meets with objections, points out the wisdom and propriety of obeying the prescriptions of nature. Returning home, he will again enjoy some slight bodily exercise, joining perhaps in a game of ball; his thoughts however will not always turn on success in the game, but he will consider how many principles in physics and ethics may be illustrated by it. Now that evening comes on, he sits down to a meal (not over-elaborate) in the company of one or two favourite pupils. . . . Retiring to his chamber, he will examine his conscience, review the events of the past day, and be at peace with himself before he sleeps."[13]

SENECA

Seneca, in one of his dialogues, advises that in order to acquire peace of mind one must avoid sloth, for "an unhappy sloth favours the growth of envy, and men who cannot succeed themselves wish everyone else to be

[13]E. Vernon Arnold, *Roman Stoicism*, pp. 359, 346, 365, 360.

ruined. . . . Let us learn to increase our continence, to repress luxury, to set bounds to our pride, to assuage our anger, to look upon poverty without prejudice, to practise thrift . . . to keep all undisciplined hopes and aspirations as it were under lock and key. . . . All life is slavery: let each man therefore reconcile himself to his lot, complain of it as little as possible, and lay hold of whatever good lies within his reach. No condition can be so wretched that an impartial mind can find no compensation in it. . . . He who knows that this fate [to die] was laid upon him as soon as he was conceived will live according to it, and by this strength of mind will gain this further advantage, that nothing can befall him unexpectedly; for by looking forward to everything which can happen as though it would happen to him, he takes the sting out of all evils. . . . Know then that every station of life is transitory; and that what has ever happened to anybody may happen to you also. . . . It is better to accept public morals and human vices calmly without bursting into either laughter or tears; for to be hurt by the sufferings of others is to be forever miserable, while to enjoy the sufferings of others is an inhuman pleasure, just as it is a useless piece of humanity to weep and pull a long face because someone is burying his son. . . . A man cannot live well if he knowns not how to die well."

MARCUS AURELIUS

From Stoic opposition to tyranny to a Stoic on the imperial throne is a considerable change in position. Marcus Aurelius, the last emperor of the Pax Romana, the most noble, humane, and civilized of all Romans, owed his character in part to his Stoic training. A hater of aggressive war who regarded conquerors as no better than spiders, just plain robbers, he had to spend most of his reign on the German frontier. An heir to the tradition of tyranny, he thought, as he considered the names of the Stoic martyrs to tyranny, Thrasea and Helvidius, and the names of Cato the Younger and Brutus, "of a polity in which there is the same law for all, a polity administered with regard to equal rights and equal freedom of speech, and the idea of a kingly government which respects most of all the freedom of the governed."[14] He was convinced of a great harmonious unity of the universe: "All things intertwine one with another, in a holy bond; scarce one thing is disconnected from another. In due coordination they combine for one and the same order. For the world-order is one made out of all things, and god is one prevading all."

This god is Providence. He asks, "Is it the portion assigned to you in the universe, at which you chafe?" and answers, "Recall to mind the alternative—either a foreseeing providence, or blind atoms. . . . The world is either a welter of alternate combination and dispersion [the Epicurean view], or a unity of order and providence. If the former, why crave to

---

[14]*The Meditations of the Emperor Marcus Aurelius*, trans. George Long (A. L. Burt Co.), p. 135.

linger on in such a random medley and confusion? why take thought for anything except the eventual dust to dust? why vex myself? do what I will, dispersion will overtake me. But on the other alternative I reverence, I stand steadfast, I find heart in the power that disposes all." Again with the Epicurean doctrine in mind he says, "If indeed they [the gods] take no thought for anything at all—an impious creed—then let us have done with sacrifice and prayer and oaths, and all other observances by which we own the presence and the nearness of the gods." To him they exist, because "from my continual experience of their power, I have the conviction that they exist, and yield respect."[15]

MARCUS AURELIUS ON STOIC CHARACTER

For him strength of character is paramount: "Be like the headland, on which the billows dash themselves continually; . . . it stands fast, till about its base the boiling breakers are lulled to rest." Do not say, "How unfortunate for me that this should have happened," but rather, "How fortunate, that in spite of this, I own no pang, uncrushed by the present, unterrified at the future!"[16] Firmness of character must, however, be accompanied by goodness, kindness, love of mankind, and the willingness to forgive. "Do not act as if thou wert going to live ten thousand years. Death hangs over thee. While thou livest, while it is in thy power, be good. . . . Keep thyself . . . simple, good, pure, serious, free from affectation, a friend of justice, a worshiper of the gods, kind, affectionate, strenuous in all proper acts. . . . Adapt thyself to the things with which thy lot has been cast; and the men among whom thou hast received thy portion, love them. . . . This, too, is a property of the rational soul, love of one's neighbor. . . . When a man has done thee any wrong, immediately consider with what opinion about good or evil he has done wrong. For when thou hast seen this, thou wilt pity him, and wilt neither wonder nor be angry. . . . It is satisfaction to a man to do the proper works of a man. Now it is a proper work of a man to be benevolent to his own kind. . . . He who acts unjustly acts impiously. For since the universal nature has made rational animals for the sake of one another to help one another according to their deserts, but in noway to injure one another, he who transgresses her will, is clearly guilty of impiety toward the highest divinity. . . . Shall any man hate me? Let him look to it. But I will be mild and benevolent toward every man, and ready to show even him his mistake, not reproachfully, nor yet as making a display of my endurance, but nobly and honestly. . . . Am I doing anything? I do it with reference to the good of mankind. . . . Have I done something for the general interest? Well then I have had my reward."[17]

[15]Arnold, pp. 123–124.
[16]Ibid., p. 124.
[17]*Meditations of Marcus Aurelius*, pp. 165 ff.

THE STOICS AND IMMORTALITY

On the question of the immortality of the soul the Stoics took varying points of view. Most of the Greek Stoics talked of an ultimate conflagration in the course of which those bits of the fiery breath which constitute the human soul would be joined with the fiery breath which permeates the universe in a very impersonal but substantial and everlasting union. This, of course, was nothing like a personal survival after death. Seneca took a different view. He has the soul say, "When the day comes to separate the heavenly from [the] earthly . . . I shall leave the body here where I found it and shall of my own volition betake myself to the gods. I am not apart from them now, but am merely detained in a heavy and earthly prison. . . . These delays of mortal existence," Seneca says, "are a prelude to the longer and better life. . . . That day, which you fear as being the end of all things, is the birthday of your eternity." We must work "to meet the gods' approval, to prepare ourselves to join them at some future time, and to plan for immortality." Epictetus and Marcus Aurelius are not quite so sure or so joyful. Epictetus says, "Shall I then no longer exist? You will not exist, but you will be something else." Marcus says, "You exist but as a part inherent in a greater whole. You will vanish into that which gave you being; or rather, you will be re-transmuted into the seminal and universal reason. Death put Alexander of Macedon and his stable boy on a par. Either they were received into the seminal principles of the universe, or were alike dispersed into atoms." In any case a good Stoic may not fear death, for it is something beyond his control. "Contemn not death, but give it welcome; is not death too a part of nature's will? As youth and age, as growth and prime, as the coming of teeth and beard and grey hairs, as begetting and pregnancy and the bearing of children, as all other operations of nature, even such is dissolution. Therefore the rational man should not treat death with impatience or repugnance or disdain, but wait for it as one of nature's operations. O for the soul ready, when the hour of dissolution comes, for extinction or dispersion or survival! But such readiness must proceed from inward conviction. Serenely you await the end, be it extinction or transmutation. While the hour yet tarries, what help is there? what, but to reverence and bless the gods, to do good to men, 'to endure and to refrain'? and of all that lies outside the bounds of flesh and breath, to remember that it is not yours, nor in your power."[18]

THE ROMAN LEGAL GENIUS

Although the Roman was not what could be called a technical philosopher in the general sense, he could be called a philosopher of law in a particular sense. Law was a field in which he exercised a genius peculiarly his own without much help from the Greek, a genius closely related to

[18]Arnold, pp. 125–126.

his ability as builder and governor of a world state. It will be noted that aside from the Bible no other book has so influenced the development of Europe as the book containing the summary of Roman law made by the emperor Justinian and known as the Justinian Code.[19] For this Code made usable the experience of over a thousand years of a people especially gifted in the law. This experience had to do not only with the elaboration of a law for the founders of the city-state of Rome but also for the empire of these Romans. Early Roman law had to be adapted to the peoples of the provinces as they were added to the state, and vice versa, the law of the peoples of the provinces had to be adapted to the use of the Romans. Through mutual adaptation a common, universal law was set up for the world state when all its free inhabitants became Roman citizens (A.D. 212). With the help of Greek scholars, the Romans went beyond this to set up the notion of an ideal system of law for all mankind, the provisions of which must not be violated by any particular or local system of law. They thus conceived of the legal unification of the globe.

THE WRITTEN LAW

The actual development of a body of Roman law capable of governing an empire was necessarily a reflection of the political history of that empire. It can be traced by using the words of Justinian's codifiers as a guide. "Our law," they say, "is partly written, partly unwritten. . . . The unwritten law is that which usage has approved: for ancient customs, when approved by consent of those who follow them, are like statute." The ancient customs of the Romans were not written down in the Twelve Tables until 451–450 B.C.,[20] and then only after long insistence on the part of plebeians who felt that as long as they were unwritten they could be used by the patrician magistrates to protect the interests of their class. Not until the middle of the third century B.C. was the interpretation of the provisions of the Twelve Tables removed from the hands of the religious authorities and opened to lay lawyers. Justinian's summarizers say that "the written law consists of statutes, plebiscites, senatusconsults, enactments of the Emperors, edicts of the magistrates, and answers of those learned in the law." The statutes were thus laws passed by the *curiata* and *centuriata* assemblies, the plebiscites those passed by the *tributa* assembly. "A senatusconsult is a command and ordinance of the senate, for when the Roman people had been so increased that it was difficult to assemble it together for the purpose of enacting statutes, it seemed right that the senate should be consulted instead of the people."[21] The "edicts of the magistrates" were those of the two praetors, the urban praetor and the peregrine praetor.[22] The urban praetor was the judicial

[19]See pp. 465 f.
[20]See pp. 197 f.
[21]*The Institutes of Justinian*, trans. J. B. Moyle, pp. 5–6.
[22]See p. 194.

magistrate for Roman citizens; the peregrine praetor for cases involving, or wholly concerning, non-Romans or aliens. It became the practice of both these praetors upon the assumption of their offices to issue an edict containing a statement of the principles and procedures they would use in administering the customary and statute law. In most instances these principles and procedures amounted to a modification of the strict letter of the law in the name of what the Romans called equity (*aequitas*).

THE JURIS-CONSULTS

With the establishment of the principate, the "answers of those learned in the law" and the "enactments of the Emperors" became an important source of the statute law. "Those learned in the law" are the class of what we should call lawyers (the Romans called them juris-consults), a group which began to emerge when the interpretation of the law was taken out of the exclusive hands of the priestly colleges. Augustus picked out the more distinguished of these men and licensed them to give opinions upon cases submitted to them upon his (the emperor's) authority. Such opinions, reduced to writing, sealed, and sent to the judges calling for them, were held to be definitive. These licensed juris-consults became an extremely important group in the early empire, entering into the emperor's privy council, given a definite organization of their own by Hadrian, and occupying major posts in the civil service. Together with the edicts of the praetors their opinions offered another opportunity for escaping from the technicalities and the letter of the law. Their opinions thus constituted a growing body of precedent and enlightened commentary upon the actual texts of the laws themselves.

THE EMPEROR'S WILL AS LAW

The history of Roman law during the empire is an account of the emperor's becoming the sole source of law. The decline of the assemblies and the Senate diminished the importance of these bodies in this respect. The emperor Hadrian put a stop to the further development of the praetors' edicts by ordering in A.D. 131 a codification of all past and a cessation of all future ones. The juris-consults became more and more dependent upon designation by the emperor, and by the end of the third century were dropped altogether. Long before this the "enactments of the Emperors" had become law. In technical language these enactments were called constitutions, and were further classified as (1) edicts, corresponding to the earlier praetors' edicts; (2) rescripts, written opinions of the emperor on petitions sent to him by private persons or magistrates; (3) decrees, decisions on judicial appeals to the emperor; and (4) mandates, the instructions given to the governors of provinces. After the third century the absolute emperor had become the sole source of law, or, as Justinian's lawyers put it, "what the Emperor determines [wishes] has the force of a statute [*quod principi placuit, legis habet vigorem*]"; and this, be it noted, because the people have "conferred on him all their authority and power by the *lex regia*, which was passed concerning his office and authority [*cum lege regia quae de imperio ejus lata est, populus ei et in eum omne suum imperium et potestatem concessit*]."[23] The emperor might be absolute, but the source of his absolutism was popular.

"IUS GENTIUM"

Before the sources of Roman law had been restricted to the legislation of the emperor-god, Roman law had been enriched by the interpretations of the juris-consults and by Roman political theory as developed in the reflections of such men as Cicero and Seneca. Roman law was held finally to include much more than the civil law that pertains to those "rules which a state enacts for its own members" and are "peculiar to itself." Roman law incorporated also the law of nations (*ius gentium*). Justinian's lawyers defined this law as "those rules prescribed by natural reason for all men" and "observed by all peoples alike. . . . The law of nations is common to the whole human race; for nations have settled certain things for themselves as occasion and the necessities of human life required." It "is the source of almost all contracts; for instance, sale, hire, partnership, deposit, loan for consumption, and very many others."[24] In other words, the law of nations was the product of the jurisdiction of the peregrine praetor. As the Roman state expanded, as it became a commercial power, it had to settle disputes between Roman citizens and non-Romans and between non-Romans apart. It found that certain legal practices of the Romans were not known to other peoples, and the reverse. It found, moreover, that these divergent practices could be harmonized and that the principles and procedures used to harmonize divergent practices could be incorporated into the civil law, whose constant expansion in this manner enabled it to become the unifying law of an expanding state.

NATURAL LAW

Roman law incorporated the principles and procedures of the law of nations, and it contained as well principles and practices of more fundamental law common to the whole human race. These principles formed a body of natural law (*ius naturale*). Natural law was originally a Stoic conception, and the Roman juris-consults absorbed the notion with Stoicism itself. At first they were inclined to identify the natural law with the law of nations. But in the course of time they differentiated the two. "The law of nature," says the Code of Justinian, echoing the juris-consult Ulpian, "is that which she has taught all animals; a law not peculiar to the human

[23]*Institutes*, p. 5.
[24]*Institutes*, p. 4.

race, but shared by all living creatures. . . . Captivity and slavery," recognized by the law of nations, are "contrary to the law of nature; for by the law of nature all men from the beginning were born free."[25] Later the Code says, "the laws of nature, which are observed by all nations alike, are established, as it were, by divine providence, and remain ever fixed and immutable." Examples of it, says another juris-consult, are our "obligations to the gods and the duty of submission to parents or country" or "the right to repel violence and wrong, for it is according to this law, that an act done for the protection of one's person is held to be rightful, and since nature has established a kind of kinship between us, as a consequence it is impious for one man to lie in wait for another." The liberation of slaves had its origin in the *ius gentium*, "for by the law of nature all would have been born free and manumission would therefore be unheard of since slavery itself would be unknown." "Liberty," says another, "belongs to natural law; lordship was introduced from the law of nations." Cicero, echoing Stoic notions concerning a natural law, speaks of that "true law [which] is right reason consonant with nature, diffused among all men, constant, eternal; which summons to duty by its command and hinders from fraud by its prohibition, which neither commands nor forbids good men in vain nor moves bad ones by either. To make enactments infringing this law, religion forbids, neither may it be repealed even in part, nor have we power through Senate or people to free ourselves from it. It needs no interpreters or expounder but itself, nor will there be one law in Rome and another in Athens, one in the present and another in time to come, but one law and that eternal and immutable shall embrace all peoples and for all time, and there shall be as it were one common master and ruler, the god of all, the author and judge and proposer of this law. . . . This whole world must be thought of as one great state common to gods and men. . . . There is one common equal rule of life among men."[26]

THE STATE OF NATURE

Some of this language has a modern note. It is, indeed, at this moment, in the notions of Cicero, Seneca, the Stoics, and the juris-consults, that a change comes over the political theory of the classical world. Aristotle had talked about the natural inequality of mankind and went out of his way to justify slavery. We now hear of a primitive golden age into which men were born free and equal, an original state of nature governing by the laws of nature an innocent and brotherly mankind. Here there was no coercive state, no private property, no inequality, and no slavery. These are contrary to the law of nature. But the golden age could not be maintained, for man's nature was corrupted "by vice and wrong-doing." It

[25]*Institutes*, pp. 4, 6.
[26]The selection from C. H. McIlwain, *The Growth of Political Thought in the West*, pp. 126, 11, 116, copyright 1956 by The Macmillan Co., and used with The Macmillan Co.'s permission.

was necessary to set up a state, Cicero suggests, as the result of a "sort of compact . . . made between the people and the powerful men," and with this state came lordship, slavery, and private property. Ideally the state will be neither a monarchy, an aristocracy, nor a democracy. It will possess the mixed constitution of the Roman state. However, it can never tolerate the tyrant, "than whom no animal more foul and loathsome to gods and men or more detested can be imagined; who, though he have the figure of a man, outdoes the most monstrous of beasts in the excess of his vices."[27]

THE ROMAN HERITAGE

The state must be "a partnership in law," for the state is "an assemblage of men associated in consent to law."[28] The state, then, must be founded upon the consent of the whole people. These notions of liberty, equality, and fraternity guaranteed by natural law, of a higher immutable law based on universal reason to which all local law must conform, of a world unified by a law of nations composed of the harmonized experience of mankind, and of nations bound together by consent to the rule of law, are all precious beginnings of a western political tradition.

ROMAN SCIENCE

It remains to consider the relationship of the Roman to the Greek humanistic tradition in science and the arts. In science the Romans produced no great figure. But it is well to consider whether any people faced with the immediate problems the Romans had to contend with could have done more with the tremendous Greek heritage in science[29] than the Romans did; that is, absorb it, make what use of it they could, and pass it on to the West. Cicero praised the gods because the Romans were not like the Greeks in their love for pure mathematics. The Romans were content with the practical application of mathematics, and this outlook characterizes their attitude toward science as a whole. Theirs was the attitude of the engineer rather than the pure scientist, and as engineers they were distinguished. The Romans made advances in no science, but they did write practical treatises of various kinds and displayed more than usual curiosity in natural history. Vitruvius, one of Augustus' architects, wrote a handbook on architecture that, for all its accumulation of miscellaneous information from Greek sources, is essentially a practical treatise on erecting public buildings (theaters, baths, harbors) and on town planning. Frontinus, a superintendent of the water supply of Rome in A.D. 97, wrote an extensive treatise on *Aqueducts* and the administration of the public water supply of the city.

[27]McIlwain, pp. 117, 109.
[28]Ibid., p. 116.
[29]See pp. 149 ff.

Pliny the Elder (*ca.* A.D. 23–79) gives one indication of the Roman attitude toward scientific matters in his *Natural History*, first published in A.D. 77 and sent with fulsome praise to the emperor Titus. He claims his thirty-seven books to be an original project, for "there is not one person to be found among us who has made the same venture, nor yet one among the Greeks who has tackled single-handed all departments of the subject." He claims also that "by perusing about 2000 volumes, very few of which, owing to the abstruseness of their contents, are ever handled by students, we have collected in thirty-six volumes 20,000 noteworthy facts obtained from one hundred authors." He reminds his readers that his scholarly work had to be confined to the evening hours, for as a public official, "the days we spend on you, the public." From his nephew, Pliny the Younger, whom we have met as a scrupulous imperial administrator,[30] we get a more detailed picture of this hard-working collector of information. "He had a keen intelligence, incredible devotion to study, and a remarkable capacity for dispensing with sleep. . . . Before dawn he used to wait on the Emperor Vespasian, who also worked during the night; and then he went off to the duty assigned to him. After returning home he gave all the time that was left to study. Very often after lunch . . . in the summer, if he had no engagements, he used to lie in the sun and have a book read to him, from which he made notes and extracts; he read nothing without making extracts from it—indeed he used to say that no book is so bad but that some part of it has value. After this rest in the sun he usually took a cold bath, and then a snack of food and a very short siesta, and then he put in what was virtually a second day's work, going on with his studies till dinnertime. Over his dinner a book was read aloud to him and notes were made, and that at a rapid pace. I remember that one of his friends, when the reader had rendered a passage badly, called him back and had it repeated; but my uncle said to him, 'Surely you got the sense?' and on his nodding assent continued, 'Then what did you call him back for? This interruption of yours has cost us ten more lines!' Such was his economy of time. He used to leave the dinner table before sunset in summer and less than an hour after it in winter—this rule had with him the force of law. These were his habits when in the thick of his engagements and amid the turmoil of town. In vacation, only the time of the bath was exempted from study; and when I say the bath I mean the more central portions of that ritual, for while he was being shampooed and rubbed down he used to have something read to him or to dictate. On a journey he seemed to throw aside all other interests and used the opportunity for study only: he had a secretary at his elbow with book and tablets, his hands in winter protected by mittens so that even the inclemency of the weather might not steal any time from his studies; and with this object he used to go about in a chair even

[30]See p. 223.

in Rome. Once I remember his pulling me up for going somewhere on foot, saying 'You need not have wasted those hours!'—he thought all time not spent in study wasted. This resolute application enabled him to get through all those volumes, and he bequeathed to me 160 sets of notes on selected books, written on both sides of the paper in an extremely small hand, a method that multiplies this number of volumes! He used to tell how during his Lieutenant-governorship in Spain he had an opportunity of selling these notes for £3,500; and at that date they were considerably fewer in number."[31]

PLINY'S "NATURAL HISTORY"

It ill becomes any scholar who has spent most of his life in a similar way to condemn Pliny's collection of information on astronomy, meteorology, geography, mineralogy, zoology, and botany. There are few people so utterly devoid of curiosity as not to be tempted by some entries in his elaborate table of contents. Not by "Thunderbolts, why attributed to Jove"; "Music from the stars"; "Showers of milk, blood, flesh, iron, wool, bricks"; or "The first clock"? Not by "Human generation: periods of pregnancy from 7 months to 13 shown by famous examples"; "Cases of eminence in the sciences and arts, astronomy, philology, medicine, geometry, architecture, painting, sculpture in bronze, in marble, in ivory; engraving"; or "Date of earliest barbers"? Not by "Elephants, their sense; when first harnessed; their docility; remarkable achievements of; instinctive sense of dangers in wild animals; elephants, when first seen in Italy; fights between elephants; modes of capture; modes of domestication; their propagation, and general physiology"? Pliny, a lawyer and public administrator, was no scientist, and did not pretend to be one; he was only an encyclopedist. He was wonderfully curious and had a penchant for the marvelous. He thought he was avoiding the fascination of magic in what he included in his natural history, but actually he could not. He was not rigid in distinguishing between the true and false and often was gullible and credulous. He mixed fable and folklore together with the science learned from the Greeks. He wanted, however, to preserve what was known, even if he could not enlarge the store of this knowledge, and the attitude he reveals toward facts and fable, science and fiction, truth and falsehood is a sharp reminder of how unscientific in any sense the first century A.D. was. It was Pliny who supplied to the encyclopedists of the Middle Ages those compilations of pseudo-science that later generations have taken such delight in condemning.

ROMAN ENGINEERING

In the field of civil engineering the Romans showed more distinction than in mathematics and pure science. Their discovery of concrete as a

[31] Trans. H. Rackham, Loeb, No. 330, pp. 9–13, x–xii.

building material and their extensive use of the arch and vault made it possible for them to build on a scale of truly imperial magnitude. They built a system of roads for the empire, bringing together the Mediterranean world as it had never been brought together before, and as it was never to be united again until the nineteenth century. There were some 180,000 miles of these main and secondary roads over which an imperial post traveled normally at five or six miles an hour. These roads, increasing in mileage as the empire expanded, were set down with the notion of permanence, or at least with the thought that they would not need to be maintained. Lasting ordinarily from seventy to one hundred years, in some instances they have survived to the present. Associated with the Roman road is the Roman bridge; for example, one crossing the Tagus River near Alcantara on six arches for a distance of 600 feet, and one (Pont du Gard) over the Gard River in southern Gaul, 900 feet long and 150 feet high, carrying an aqueduct as well as a road and carrying them very beautifully. The aqueduct, as well as the road and bridge, is an example of the Roman skill in engineering. In Frontinus's day it took 700 people of the Board of Water Supply to administer the system that supplied Rome with the 270 million gallons of water used daily in the city. This supply was brought in over fourteen aqueducts. In medieval Rome these aqueducts were no longer maintained, and the city had to rely on the Tiber. The amount brought in by the imperial aqueducts was about three times the amount used in contemporary Rome. This water supplied, in part, the 591 fountains in the city and the thirty-nine public baths (such as the bath [*thermae*] of Diocletian). Together with the amphitheater the public bath is to be found wherever Romans extended their empire, including the military camps on the frontier. For the Roman who could afford it the private bath became a necessary part of his dwelling. An English writer, commenting upon the abandonment of the Roman camp at Tomen-y-mur in northern Wales, remarks: "It is extremely probable that after the abandonment of the site, the grass-covered baths of Tomen-y-mur were the only baths that the county of Merioneth ever possessed until the nineteenth century was well advanced; and even then, the innovations were substitutes that any Roman would have regarded with the utmost disdain, even if he had considered that a modern bathroom could be dignified with the name of a bath at all."[32]

ROMAN AND GREEK ART

The recognition by the Romans of the superiority of Greek art led originally to the wholesale looting of Greek cities. Most of the statues in Rome at the time of Augustus are said to have come from Corinth. "The city and the State warehouses were packed with the artistic loot of two centuries of victories."[33] Greek artists had likewise been predominant in

[32]H. J. Randall, *The Creative Centuries*, p. 108.
[33]Grenier, *Roman Spirit*, p. 233.

republican Rome and continued to form the majority of artists under the empire. In this direct way the Romans absorbed the spirit as well as the forms and technique of Greek art. The Roman temple, originally Etruscan in inspiration, was transformed, like Roman religion, into something Greek.

ART AND EMPIRE

From the Hellenistic East the Romans learned the relationship of art to despotism. They learned the importance of luxury and sheer size in making an impression of theocratic power upon the illiterate masses. They learned, in other words, the significance of art as a symbol of wealth and power and as a means of imperial propaganda. Italy possessed its own artistic traditions, stretching back to the Etruscans. The Romans had their own artistic capacities and their own notions about the uses of art. "To them art was neither the expression of ideas nor the attainment of beauty, but a method of making actions known and of committing them to posterity."[34] By the time of Augustus these various influences and capacities had combined, under the need for a dynastic and imperial art, to produce work of the finest character, imperial altars of peace, for example, and portrait statues of emperors. When once produced in Rome this work could be imitated in the provinces and made to exalt the divine person of the emperor and the beneficent results of his rule. Of these monuments, two that are very typical and very beautiful may be considered: the *Ara Pacis* (Altar of Peace) of Augustus (Pl. 13) and the statue of Augustus from Prima Porta (Pl. 24), "one of the most imposing creations of European portrait art." The former was built between 13 and 9 B.C. to commemorate the return of Augustus to Rome after a long absence in the East, in Gaul, and in Spain, establishing the Pax Romana. It was to be the point at which a long procession of grateful Roman citizens who had gone out to meet the emperor from the Porta del Popolo was to terminate with a thanksgiving ceremony and sacrifice. The statue of Augustus, found in the ruins of an imperial villa in the village of Prima Porta, is usually dated around 20 B.C., but there are those who find this dating too early for the masterful technique some features of the statue display.

THE ALTAR OF PEACE

The Altar of Peace itself was surrounded by a wall some ten to thirteen feet high and thirty-eight feet square. Upon the upper exterior of this wall was a frieze representing the emperor and his family marching in solemn procession with the citizens of Rome to the altar (Pls. 14–18). Elsewhere there are friezes with symbolical and mythological themes. The procession frieze, to be compared obviously with the procession of Athenian citizens at the Panathenaea on the Parthenon,[35] contains a wonderful series of

[34]Eugenie Strong, "The Art of the Augustan Age," *Cambridge Ancient History*, eds. S. A. Cook et al., X, 545, 555.
[35]See pp. 162 f.

portraits of Roman officials, members of the imperial family, and ordinary Roman citizens—men, women, and children. The children are especially charming, babies being dragged along on sturdy legs (Pl. 18), youngsters obviously uncomfortable in their heavy togas, and a sister smiling down upon a younger brother. When this frieze is placed beside the Panathenaean frieze it is clear that the Roman sculptor had no interest in endowing his persons with the idealistic beauty of the Greek figures. He wanted to represent his human beings as they really were, to faithfully copy his living models. It is a superb example of an artistic realm in which the Romans were unsurpassed: realistic portrait sculpture. The beautiful figure of the Earth Mother (or is it Italy?) (Pl. 19) in another frieze is symbolic of the temporary prosperity brought to agriculture by the Augustan peace and may have specific references to Vergil's *Georgics*. The frieze representing Aeneas pouring a libation to the *penates* (Pl. 20) calls to mind Augustus' religious policy (he restored a temple to the *penates*) and the patriotic praise of the new regime contained in Vergil's *Aeneid*.

THE STATUE OF AUGUSTUS FROM PRIMA PORTA

The statue of Augustus from Prima Porta shows the *princeps* as a military chief clad in cuirass. The figures on the cuirass (Pl. 25) are symbolic of the emperor victorious upon earth. In the center is the god Mars receiving a Roman standard from a Parthian (referring to an actual event of 20 B.C.). The central figure is flanked right and left by two figures representing provinces "mourning"—possibly Gaul and Spain. Below this central group is another Earth Mother, made fruitful and prosperous by the Roman Peace. Above the central group is "an allegory of empire." Heaven, above, spreads out his mantle to protect the Roman sphere, as the Dawn heralds the new order represented by the Sun in his four-horsed chariot. "The features of the Emperor are delicate and refined: the clear ossature of the face shows beneath the firmly modelled flesh; the luminous eyes look steadily out into space; the mouth has the beauty of line familiar in portraits of the Julio-Claudians; the comparatively small chin is without weakness, the line of cranium and neck of incomparable harmony."[36] (Pl. 26) The workmanship is that of an ideal head, but idealism is strictly subordinated to resemblance.

SUMMARY

The humanism of Greek culture acted as a powerful stimulus upon the more prosaic Romans. When first they came in contact with it they recognized its superiority and understood that in so far as this was possible they would have to make this culture their own. In thus absorbing Greek humanism into the Latin tongue, where it became what the Romans called *humanitas*, the Romans made possible its spread with the Latin

[36]Strong, pp. 557–558.

language. Those who encountered it there were constantly impelled to go back to its original in the Greek. This is only another way of saying that the Romans were mediators of the Greek way to the West. It does not mean that the Romans became a nation of humanists. Some of them, let us say Cicero, Horace, Vergil, and Marcus Aurelius, are remarkable examples of the transforming nature of Greek culture. As a people, however, the Romans remained Romans, a rather sober, hard-headed, practical, and utilitarian band, none too original or creative. But their lack of originality can be exaggerated. We have had occasion in this chapter to see that in spite of the tremendous influence of Greece upon Rome Greek culture was not simply copied and imitated. It was transformed into something that the Romans could use. In certain fields the Romans stood out as original creators, as in the case of the satirical form in literature. They were almost wholly responsible for the magnificent system of Roman law. They were the inaugurators of an impressive and world-wide civil engineering and the creators of a remarkable portrait sculpture. Such creativity is enough to ask of any people. In the fields of literature and philosophy they managed to make the Greek tradition their own. In the creation and administration of a world state they provided an actual setting for the realization of Greek dreams of human brotherhood, though, practically, they failed to realize these dreams.

The Altar of Peace (*Ara Pacis*) of Augustus (see pp. 260 f.).

Priests and members of the imperial family in procession. Bas-relief from the frieze of the Altar of Peace.

Plate 14

D. Anderson

Children and adult members of the imperial family in procession. Frieze, Altar of Peace.

Plate 15

D. Anderson

Priests and senators in procession. Frieze, Altar of Peace.

Plate 16

D. Anderson

Senators and citizens in procession. Frieze, Altar of Peace.

Plate 17

D. Anderson

"Carry me!" Frieze, Altar of Peace.

Plate 18

D. Anderson

Figures representing Mother Earth (center) together with Air and Water. Frieze, Altar of Peace.

Plate 19

D. Anderson

Aeneas pouring a libation to the Penates. Frieze, Altar of Peace.

Plate 20

D. Anderson

Naturalistic decorative detail of the Altar of Peace.

Plate 21

D. Anderson

Plate 22
D. Anderson

The festoon on an interior wall of the Altar of Peace.

Decorative detail on fragments of the Altar of Peace.

Plate 23
D. Anderson

The statue of Augustus from Prima Porta (see p. 261).

Plate 24

Sculpture in the Vatican Museum

The cuirass of Augustus from Prima Porta.

The head of Augustus from Prima Porta.

Plate 26
Alinari

THE DECLINE AND FALL OF THE
ROMAN EMPIRE

*I*n 1430, more than a thousand years after a tribe of German barbarians had first attacked Rome, two scholars sat viewing its ruins from the Capitoline Hill. As they thought of the former imperial splendor they said to each other: "This spectacle of the world, how it is fallen! how changed! how defaced! The path of victory is obliterated by vines, and the benches of the senators are concealed by a dunghill. Cast your eyes on the Palatine hill, and seek, among the shapeless and enormous fragments, the marble theatre, the obelisks, the colossal statues, the porticoes of Nero's palace: survey the other hills of the city, the vacant space is interrupted only by ruins and gardens. The forum of the Roman people, where they assembled to enact their laws and elect their magistrates, is now inclosed for the cultivation of pot-herbs or thrown open for the reception of swine and buffaloes. The public and private edifices, that were founded for eternity, lie prostrate, naked, and broken, like the limbs of a mighty giant; and the ruin is the more visible, from the stupendous relics that have survived the injuries of time and fortune."[1]

GIBBON'S "DECLINE AND FALL OF THE ROMAN EMPIRE"

More than three hundred years later the distinguished English historian who reports this incident was himself approaching Rome for the first time in his life. He approached it, he says in his *Autobiography*, with

[1]Edward Gibbon, *The History of the Decline and Fall of the Roman Empire*, ed. J. B. Bury, 8 vols., VII, 302.

"strong emotions which agitated my mind." The morning after his arrival, following a sleepless night, "I trod," he writes, "with a lofty step, the ruins of the Forum; each memorable spot where Romulus stood, or Tully [Cicero] spoke, or Caesar fell, was at once present to my eye." Later in that October of 1764 he sat "musing amidst the ruins of the Capitol, while the bare-footed fryars were singing vespers in the temple of Jupiter." In the quiet of that evening, while the chants of Christian monks rose from a former pagan temple and settled in the ruins of pagan glory, he was inspired to write a history of how such a thing could come about; how, that is, the former capital of a world state could crumble to ruins and be succeeded by the capital of another world state dedicated to the universal victory of Christ. Edward Gibbon spent the better part of the remainder of his life writing the great work he called the *History of the Decline and Fall of the Roman Empire*. Twenty-three years after his original resolution he finished his work, about midnight, in a summer house in the garden of his dwelling at Lausanne, Switzerland, on the shores of Lake Geneva. He then passed, he writes, through a "covered walk of acacias, which commands a prospect of the country, the lake, and the mountains. The air was temperate, the sky was serene, the silver orb of the moon was reflected from the waters, and all nature was silent. I will not dissemble the first emotions of joy on the recovery of my freedom, and, perhaps, the establishment of my fame. But my pride was soon humbled, and a sober melancholy was spread over my mind, by the idea that I had taken an everlasting leave of an old and agreeable companion, and that whatsoever might be the future date of my History, the life of the historian must be short and precarious." In the last chapter of his last volume Gibbon wrote: "In the preceding volumes of this History, I have described the triumph of barbarism and religion." To him the decline and fall was brought about by the German barbarian invasions and the victory of Christianity.

IMPORTANCE OF THE PROBLEM OF DECLINE AND FALL

Gibbon had indeed picked a worthy and magnificent theme upon which to spend a life of scholarship. In this he has been followed by many historians, for there is no more important problem in all historical scholarship. To explain how it is that civilizations rise to some kind of original climax only subsequently to lose their vigor and creative power is the chief justification for the historian's work. The contemporary English historian, Arnold Toynbee, following in the footsteps of Gibbon, has devoted ten large volumes to this question (*A Study of History*).[2] The problem is especially important for present and future generations. It is just possible that what we, at the middle of the twentieth century, are witnessing is the beginning of the end of our own western European civili-

[2]There is a good summary in two volumes by D. C. Somervell.

zation. If so, to the extent that the historian can explain the decline and fall of classical civilization, he is in a position to instruct us in ways to avoid a modern repetition of that event. For, although it would not be wise to assume that an analysis of its causes would necessarily, in every respect, apply to our own civilization, the character of human society has not fundamentally altered since classical days. What is basically true with respect to the decline and fall of classical civilization applies to the decline and fall of all civilizations, including our own. If, in spite of the differences in historical circumstances, the political, economic, social, intellectual, religious, or military developments in Roman history that brought an end to her power and world position are allowed to take place in a similar manner in our present society, these same political, economic, social, intellectual, religious, or military developments will bring about our own decline and fall.

THE MEANING OF "FALL"

In pursuing this problem it is necessary first to define what is meant by the decline and fall of the Roman Empire. It is not difficult to give precise meaning to the word *fall*. It means, simply, "end." The fall of the Roman Empire, is, therefore, its end. The later Roman emperors came to realize that the empire was too large to govern from one center—Rome. Diocletian (284–305) tried the experiment of governing it in four parts, or prefectures. Constantine (324–337) recognized the need for a new capital, which he founded upon the site of the old Greek colony at Byzantium. This he called the city of Constantine—Constantinople (Istanbul). At his death in 395 the emperor Theodosius divided the empire between his two sons, with the western, or Latin, half being governed from Ravenna in Italy, and the eastern, or Greek-oriental, half being governed from Constantinople. This western half came to an end in 476. What took its place was a group of German kingdoms, formed as a result of some hundred years of barbarian migrations, and without any of the lights of civilization of the now dead and unlamented Athens of Pericles. The eastern half persisted in greatly altered form until 1453, when it was destroyed by the Ottoman Turks. Historically speaking, what is meant by the fall of the Roman Empire is the end of its western half, in other words, the displacement of Roman emperors by German kings after 476. To explain the fall of the Roman Empire, accordingly, is to explain how it was impossible to prevent its western half from coming into the possession of German chieftains. This would seem to be a military problem in the same sense that the tragic "fall of France" in the spring of 1940 was a military problem. But it requires only a bit of reflection to realize that what is involved is much more than a military problem. What is involved is the larger question: Why is a state or nation unwilling or unable to defend itself against the enemy, barbarian or otherwise?

CHRONOLOGY — The Decline and Fall of the Roman Empire

	Reigns and Political Persons	Philosophy and Religion
50 B.C.		
		Philo (ca. 20 B.C.–A.D. 50)
100 A.D.		
		Marcus Aurelius (121–180)
		Tertullian (ca. 150–230)
	Septimius Severus (193–211)	
200		
		Cyprian (ca. 200–258)
		Plotinus (204–270)
	Caracalla (211–217)	
	Elagabalus (218–222)	
	Alexander Severus (222–235)	Mani (ca. 216–274)
		Porphyry (233–304)
	Decius (249–251)	
	Aurelian (270–275)	
	Diocletian (284–305)	
	Maximian (286–305)	
300		
	Galerius (305–311)	
		Edict of Milan (313)
	Constantine (324–337)	
		Iamblichus (d. ca. 330)
		Ulfilas (311–383)
	Ammianus Marcellinus (b. ca. 330–d. 400)	Saint Chrysostom (347–407)
		Saint Jerome (347–419)
		Saint Augustine (354–430)
	Theodosius (379–395)	
	Alaric (b. 370–d. 410)	
	Stilicho (b. ca. 359–d. 408)	
400		
	Attila (ca. 433–453)	
	Zeno (474–491)	
	Romulus Augustulus (475–476)	
	Odovacar (476–493)	
	Clovis (481–511)	
500		
	Justinian I (527–565)	

It is not so easy to come to terms with the phrase "decline of the Roman Empire." To be sure, it would make sense to say that all those factors that could be shown to have contributed to the unwillingness of the empire to defend itself would be evidences of decline. On the other hand, it could be argued that some of the evidences of decline had outwardly very little to do with the problem of defense. After the second century A.D. there were no poets of the stature of Vergil, Horace, and Ovid, and only one historian (Ammianus) of the stature of Livy or Tacitus. The historians of literature speak of a "silver age" following a golden one. There seems to have been a definite decline in the ability to write distinguished Latin verse or prose in the older humanistic vein. The same was true in the field of sculpture. The brilliant ability of the artists of the Altar of Peace or of the portrait sculptors of the first and second centuries vanished in the subsequent period. There was thus a decline in the ability to carve. But it may not really have been a decline in the *ability* to write or carve, for there is every reason to believe that human capacity in these fields remains more or less constant. It may have been a decline in the opportunity to learn how to write or sculpture well or a lack of stimulation to use one's talents to the utmost. Such a decline in the opportunity to learn may have resulted from a growing belief that it was unimportant whether or not there was any excellent writing or art or interest in politics or concern with humane achievement. And such a belief might have had something to do with a conviction that one's country or nation was not worth defending. In any case, to the extent that decline was not directly related to the problem of defense it may nevertheless have been related to a change in point of view that was itself fundamentally responsible for the failure in defense.

THE THEME OF ORIENTALIZATION

The history of the later Roman Empire, in fact, does show a fundamental shift in point of view. It is a shift which could be described as the orientalization of that empire. We have had occasion to show how the Romans absorbed and adapted to their needs the spirit of Greek humanism. We had occasion to suggest also that, in so far as we may speak of the Hellenization of the empire, it was confined to a small élite. We have also referred to the fact that the Romans, rather than provide their own solutions to pressing problems, in the course of their expansion occasionally had recourse to oriental solutions. We pointed to this fact in connection with the treatment of provincials,[3] and we have said repeatedly that the failure of the Republic and the establishment of the Empire were the outcome of the adoption of an oriental solution for the problem of central government: the divine monarch. This adoption of oriental

[3] See pp. 205 f.

solutions certainly betrays a lack of inventiveness or of creative ability, combined with a repudiation of the Hellenically oriented background.

THE SHIFT FROM HUMANISM TO ASCETICISM

One can, however, speak of orientalization in more senses than the adoption of eastern theocratic forms of government. For the orientalization of the Roman Empire involved a complete shift in point of view, indeed, one of the most dramatic and most decisive shifts in all history, a change from an outlook we have called humanistic to one that we shall call ascetic or religious. Earlier chapters in this book have pointed to the growth of mystery religions in the Orient and Greece.[4] We have also described how Stoicism, as an imperial philosophy, became more religious. It is a fact that during the late Republic and early Empire the mystery religions of Greece and the Orient became more popular in Rome, Italy, and the West, and together with them oriental astrology and magic. In the third century A.D. something like a synthesis of the oriental mystery religions became the dominant religion of the empire. What was left of the rational tradition in Greek philosophy was largely abandoned for a religious mysticism, chiefly the system of thought of the Egyptian Plotinus known as Neoplatonism. This receptivity of the Roman world to mystery religions and mystical philosophy was the prelude to its acceptance of another oriental religion, namely, Christianity. The heyday of the oriental religions and of Neoplatonism in the third century was followed by the victory of Christianity in the fourth. Constantine tolerated and favored Christianity, and Theodosius made it the exclusive religion of the Roman state. This shift from a dominant humanistic to a dominant religious or ascetic outlook marked, on the part of the individual, a loss of self-confidence and a growing indifference to the external world. The turn to theocracy was a confession that the Romans could not hope to achieve a satisfactory political organization by working together along republican lines. The turn to religion was a confession that the external world had little to offer the individual. He was no longer interested in how the good life could be lived on this earth but rather in the salvation of his soul. These things happened in chronological sequence. The Republic fell, and theocracy appeared. As the theocracy became established the oriental religions and philosophies took root, reaching a peak of influence in the third century. They were followed by the victory of Christianity in the fourth century. The German victory came in the fifth. May we adopt the easy solution and say *post hoc ergo propter hoc* ("after this, therefore on account of it")? In other words, may we say that what answers best our question of decline and fall is what we have called the failure of the Republic? Let us reserve our final answer until the end of this chapter. Meanwhile there is one more preliminary consideration to be discussed.

[4] See pp. 41 f., 111 ff.

In speaking of the decline and fall of the ancient world we put ourselves in a melancholy mood. We say it is unfortunate for the human race that Greek and Roman culture could not have maintained their brilliance and gone on to even more spectacular achievements. We declare that the political history of the Roman people, like the political history of the Greek people, ended in failure and tragedy. The failure was the inability of the empire to realize the promise that the Republic had already failed to realize. The tragedy was that the blessings of two centuries of peace could not have been made more permanent and used to extend the values of a high civilization to those who were not yet able to enjoy them. We regret that the cultural experiences of the citizens of the empire were thus limited, not only by the failure to perpetuate and increase their quality, but by the failure to make this culture available to everybody in the state possessing the capacity to absorb it and to be enriched by it. The regret we have in speaking of the decline and fall is occasioned also by thought of ourselves. The violence of the classical world occasioned the physical loss of much that was excellent. We ourselves should have been greatly enriched and better instructed if there had been no decline and fall.

THE CHRISTIAN AND THE DECLINE AND FALL

We may be sure, however, that then and now there would be those who did not, and do not, regard this phase of ancient history as either failure or tragedy. This would be true of the Christian, to whom this was a vile, pagan world. Its decline and fall were, therefore, only glorious history making way for the Christian Church and the Christian state. Tertullian, an important Christian writer of the third century, had all the contempt of the extreme ascetic for this world: "I owe no obligation to forum, campus, or senate. I stay awake for no public function, I make no effort to monopolize the platform, I pay no heed to any administrative duty, I shun the voter's booth, the juryman's bench. . . . I serve neither as magistrate nor soldier, I have withdrawn from the life of secular society. . . . My only concern is for myself, careful of nothing except that I should have no care. . . . What greater pleasure than contempt for pleasure, than scorn for the activities of the world!"[5] The sooner the Roman world passed for such a man, the better.[6] Thus what we may look upon as an unfortunate chapter in human history may be regarded by others in an entirely different light. Since, they may argue further, the debacle of this ancient world made way for the reconstruction we know as western European civilization, we may rejoice the more over this event. If, that is, there had been no decline and fall we may assume there would not have been a new western European civilization. There would have

[5]C. N. Cochrane, *Christianity and Classical Culture*, p. 213.
[6]Indeed, Jerome, one of the Latin Fathers, could say: "The Roman world is falling; yet we hold up our heads instead of bowing them."—H. C. Baker, *The Dignity of Man*, p. 134.

been only a further development of classical civilization, a large part of which would have taken the form of a continued Romanization of the primitive peoples of Europe. This also, in a sense, is what actually happened. The great difference between what might have been and what actually was is the difference produced by the emergence of the Christian Church. But let us inquire more closely into all these things.

THE DEVELOPMENT OF THEOCRACY

The century and a half between the reigns of Marcus Aurelius (d. 180) and of Constantine (d. 337) transformed the principate of the Pax Romana into an oriental theocracy, into an absolute state whose monarch was considered divine or the agent of divinity. This development, already begun before the third century, can be explained by the persistence of old, unsolved political problems and by the appearance of new menacing frontier ones. The chief old problem remaining unsolved was the subordination of the military to the civilian element in the state; the new frontier problems had to do with the German Goths and Sassanid Persia. So serious was the situation by the end of the third century that the emperors Diocletian and Constantine felt obliged to undertake a thoroughgoing reform of the empire that in its effects enslaved the Roman citizen to an omnipotent state in the person of an unlimited sovereign. The large economic background of this political development was a crisis marked by inflation and a decline in production that, as a consequence, forced the government to impose rigid controls over the economy. The new military dictators, for that is essentially what these third-century emperors were, invoked oriental gods to sanction their autocracy. The state was desperate, and its solution was to subordinate all things and all people to its stark survival. It was no accident that Constantine moved the capital to Constantinople at a time when Christianity was first legally tolerated and the farmers of the empire were made serfs.

THE EMPERORS OF THE THIRD CENTURY

The first emperor of the Severan dynasty, Septimius Severus (193–211), was a general of the troops stationed in Upper Pannonia (modern Hungary) who won out over two rival generals commanding troops in Britain and Syria.[7] The regime thus introduced was frankly military. Since the Romans had never managed to provide a regular, constitutional method for imperial succession, nothing was left for the usurper to do but to attempt to found a dynasty. He was succeeded by his son, the "cruel, vindictive, vicious, cowardly, despotic" Caracalla, who told his peasant and mercenary soldiers, "I am one of you. . . . All the treasuries are yours. . . . It is for you, and not myself, that I rule."[8] It was he who in 212 extended the tax lists by granting Roman citizenship to all the free inhabitants of the em-

[7]See pp. 188 f.
[8]Albert A. Trever, *History of Ancient Civilization*, II, 635–636.

pire. After a short interval the Syrian troops raised the adolescent grand-nephew of the Syrian wife of Septimius Severus to the throne—a lad called Elagabalus since he was a hereditary priest of the sun god of that name worshiped at Emesa. The representation of this god, a black conical stone, was brought to Rome and enshrined near the residence of the emperor, who tried to make this local baal predominant and universal in the whole empire. "The incongruity of a circumcised Augustus, who abstained from the flesh of swine to perform with a ritual purity the obscenities of a Syrian cult and who paraded in public tricked out in the effeminate finery prescribed by its ceremonial, offended a public opinion which was not exacting in morals but expected a traditional decorum from its rulers."[9] In the end he was killed by the Praetorian Guard, dragged through the streets of Rome, and thrown into the Tiber. He was suc-ceeded by his cousin, Alexander Severus (222–235), another adolescent, who was ruled by his mother, Julia Mamaea, and who, to be absolutely safe with divine power, included Abraham and Christ among the gods he worshiped in his private chapel. The murder of both Alexander and his mother by the troops brought to the throne a Thracian peasant giant, Maximinus, who had risen from the ranks and who doubled the pay of the army soon after his accession. His rule introduced a period of unparal-leled anarchy (235–285) interrupted only by the emperor Aurelian (270–275). Only one of the many emperors (at least eighteen) who ruled during the chaos of civil war and German invasion died a natural death; the rest were creatures and victims of an army which had lost "all sense of loyalty either to the Empire or to the generals."[10]

THE GERMANS IN THE THIRD CENTURY

The first successful barbarian threat to the empire came in the third century. The Goths completed their long trek from southern Scandinavia to the northern shore of the Black Sea, and from here conducted raids into Asia Minor, the islands of the Aegean, and above all across the lower Danube into the Balkan peninsula. Eventually the large province of Dacia[11] was abandoned to them, and the city walls of Rome itself were repaired and put in order to withstand siege. The Alamanni and others were constantly harassing the mid-Danubian provinces and making incur-sions into Italy. Ultimately the Tithed Lands were surrendered to them.[12] Across the lower Rhine came frequent incursions of the Franks. Under these circumstances the empire threatened to disintegrate. The West gathered for a while around a usurper who set up an empire of Gaul, with Spain and Britain as dependent provinces. In the East, as a result of con-

[9]S. N. Miller, "The Army and the Imperial House," *Cambridge Ancient History*, XII, 55.
[10]Trever, II, 641.
[11]See p. 189.
[12]See p. 189.

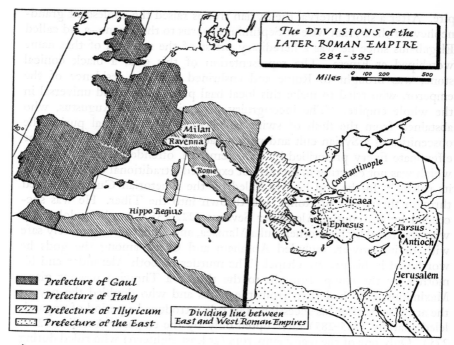

The DIVISIONS of the
LATER ROMAN EMPIRE
284-395

Miles 0 100 200 500

Prefecture of Gaul
Prefecture of Italy
Prefecture of Illyricum
Prefecture of the East

Dividing line between
East and West Roman Empires

tinuous struggle with Sassanid Persia, an independent state grew up at
Palmyra. As if military anarchy, barbarian invasion, and territorial disintegration were not enough, a long plague of some fifteen years' duration
decimated the empire at the middle of the century. Aurelian (270–275)
restored the state to some semblance of its former stability, but it was
necessary for the Illyrian soldier Diocletian and his successor, Constantine,
to undertake, in the spirit of Augustus, their all-embracing world reform.
It was Aurelian, calling himself a born lord and god, who sought to rein-
troduce Elagabalus's cult of sun worship and assumed for himself the diadem
of the Invincible Sun. It was Diocletian and Maximian who, aware of his
military prowess, "solemnly consecrated Mithra as chief tutelary deity
of the empire, and represented themselves as his counterparts on earth."[13]

THE REFORMS OF DIOCLETIAN AND CONSTANTINE

The reforms introduced by Diocletian and Constantine under the pressure of events and the influence of Persia were in large part a confirmation
of desperate measures already taken by emperors of the third century to
keep the state erect. They mark the effective transformation of the empire
into a theocratic despotism of the most relentless sort, with an economy
that has been described as an ancient state socialism[14] with a castelike

[13]Cochrane, p. 3.
[14]F. Oertel, "The Economic Life of the Empire," *Cambridge Ancient History*,
XII, 270 ff.

society. Diocletian attempted to introduce a new system of succession to the throne. Feeling that the state was too large and now too complex to be successfully governed by one man, he determined to set up two *Augusti*, one for the West and one for the East. Recognizing as well the danger of the ambitious usurper, he provided that each Augustus was to be provided with a Caesar who was to succeed him after twenty years' rule. Diocletian abdicated properly enough in 305, but a civil war immediately broke out between more *Augusti* and Caesars than Diocletian had provided for. The new scheme had to be discarded immediately and the old dynastic principle was reintroduced. At this moment also there was introduced a fundamental territorial and administrative reorganization based on strict centralization and calculated to render the empire easier to govern. The whole empire was divided into four large prefectures (Gaul, Italy, Illyricum, East), each governed by a prefect. The prefecture was further subdivided into dioceses governed by vicars, and the dioceses split up into about one hundred and twenty provinces. Within the provinces were the urban (*civitas*) and rural (*villa*) units of administration.

THE DIVINE EMPEROR

As was quite proper for an emperor considered to be divine, or at least charged with divinity, the court and administration surrounding the lord and god (*dominus et deus*) had to suggest the life and habitation of the immortals. Anything connected with the emperor was called sacred. He lived in a sacred palace, he issued sacred constitutions, and he had a sacred mint (*sacra moneta*). "Hidden in the depths of his palace, like an idol in its shrine," he could be approached, when once the curtains of the audience chamber had been pulled, as no ordinary mortal. It was necessary to prostrate oneself before him and to kiss the hem of the silken imperial robe, if not his hand or foot. Like an eastern prince, he wore a diadem set with precious stones, and carried a scepter with eagle and globe. He sat on a special chair, or throne, "originally the seat of the gods."[15] He was surrounded by a huge household in which the eunuch occupied a place of honor and the ceremony of the court was directed in accordance with a stiff and elaborate etiquette. The central administration now contained such offices as the Provost of the Sacred Bedchamber and the Count of the Sacred Largesses.

CONSTANTINOPLE

That Rome was no longer regarded as the center and capital of this state is symbolic of what was happening to the empire as a whole. As Italy had absorbed Rome the Mediterranean area had now absorbed Italy. Not only did it seem impossible to defend the far-flung frontiers of such a huge state from Rome but, like a moth to the flame, the empire was

[15]Léon Pol Homo, *Roman Political Institutions from City to State*, p. 278.

attracted to those mystic elements in Greek and oriental civilizations which had influenced it most. Thus it was that in 330 Constantine founded the new capital of the empire at the strategic spot on the frontier between Europe and Asia that he called Constantinople. The establishment of this city, perhaps in itself a recognition of the cultural dichotomy between the western and eastern, the Latin and Graeco-oriental, halves of the empire may be said also to mark the beginning of that cleavage in Europe into East and West that still plagues the world. For just as the new barbarian (German) nations of the West began to group themselves about Rome, the new barbarian (Slavic) nations of eastern Europe began to group themselves about Constantinople. And just as about Christian Rome there began to develop a new western European civilization based upon the classical tradition, so about Christian Constantinople there began to develop what in many respects was a new Byzantine civilization (from Byzantium, the original Greek colony on the site of Constantinople). From 330 until 1453 there ruled in the East an almost unbroken succession of emperors who were fanatically insistent upon their position as legitimate successors of the Romans.

THE ECONOMIC REFORMS

The economic and social reforms instituted by Diocletian and Constantine stemmed in large part from earlier attempts to keep the state solvent in the midst of an economic crisis caused to some extent by the enormous increase of military expenses. The crisis has been explained as the outcome of the very nature of Roman imperialism itself. This imperialism provided for the exploitation of the provinces by the seizure of their economic surpluses, the constant draining away of further resources by taxes, tributes, and financial services, and the failure "to make investments or develop enterprises that expanded production, or, in other words, they [the Romans] extracted wealth from an economy whose productive capacity they did not increase. . . . When confronted with the inevitable consequence of the failure to create new wealth, namely, the decline of production, they could do no more than attempt to hold their share of the decreasing production by resorting to violence and, along with this resort, by a tightening of controls over all kinds of labor—in fine, a progressive regimentation of economic life."[16] Not only did the state interfere in private business but it directed large enterprises of its own. "The State (or the emperor) [was] the largest landed proprietor, it was also the biggest owner of mines and quarries, and in course of time came to be the greatest industrialist, having gained control of a specific category of industries . . . (mints, builders' yards, brick-kilns, textile-mills, iron-foundries, . . . armourers' workshops). . . . A system of forced labour

[16]By permission from *The Great Cultural Traditions*, by R. E. Turner, II, 935–936, 940. Copyright, 1941. McGraw-Hill Book Company, Inc.

was imposed on the workers in the manufactories, in much the same way as on workers for the Ptolemaic State-monopolies." The state interfered constantly in wholesale and retail trade. "Transport was also largely nationalized."[17] In 301 Diocletian attempted to call a halt to inflation by imposing a rigid system of price control upon the whole economy, labor as well as commodities.

THE HEREDITARY CLASSES: THE SERF

The social outcome of the attempt of the state to control the economy in its own interest was to create a hereditary, castelike society. In the interests of a more equitable system of taxation Diocletian undertook an economic survey of the empire, the like of which had not been made since Augustus. But its result was, for purposes of assessment, to attach the peasant (*colonus*) so closely to the land that he was not permitted to leave it. Such a status is ordinarily called servile. This late Roman serfdom was legalized by Constantine in 332. It completed a process that had been going on in Italian and western agriculture since the establishment of the empire. Rome never succeeded, we have insisted, in solving the problem of the growth of the large estate (*villa*) and the consequent ruin of the small peasant proprietor. In the late days of the Republic these large estates were cultivated by slave gangs. But the Pax Romana lessened the supply of slaves for agriculture, and the large-estate owners, often absentee, undertook to exploit their estates by leasing them out to tenants in comparatively small plots. In return for this grant of land the tenant was usually held to labor services on other land reserved for the direct exploitation of the owner of the *villa*. The huge complexes of state property were also managed in this fashion. The large estates continued to grow in number throughout the course of the empire, often the result of special favoritism shown by the military emperors to the military. When the urban conditions became unsatisfactory many of the large *villa* owners moved onto their estates and so lived in the midst of their peasants. They thus came to constitute the hereditary senatorial aristocracy of the later empire. It is quite clear that from the third century on, as the state had increasingly to attempt to control the economy, wealthy and individualistic landlords began to move to their *villas* as a protest against the encroachments of the state. They undertook, in fact, to make of their large domains little private states as independent as possible of the public state. And when the public state could not protect them from invasion and civil war they sought to protect themselves by means of private military forces. These forces were also quite convenient for keeping the tax collector off the estate, when he could not be otherwise persuaded. They undertook also to settle disputes among their tenantry in local courts on the *villa*. They were, accordingly, not at all averse to having their labor supply guaran-

[17]Oertel, XII, 272-273.

teed by the creation of a hereditary class of serfs. It was then possible for them to pursue and chain a runaway serf. These circumstances helped to transform the *villa* into a self-sufficient economic unit, making the tools and goods it needed and raising its own food. Such a localization of the centers of production served, as well, to hasten economic decline and to foster a return to an economy in the West that was almost wholly rural, a reversion to the centuries of an earlier Iron Age. It is evident that here, with the noble senator and his hereditary serf, with the new economic, military, and judicial unit of the large estate, or *villa*, we have conditions that are ordinarily described as medieval. The despotic state enslaved the peasant, who, for the sake of security and the right to cultivate land, abandoned his liberty to a rural aristocracy.

THE "CURIALES" AND "COLLEGIA"

The ruralization of the empire was furthered by the attack of the state upon the liberty and prosperity of the towns. The chief glory of the Roman state had been that it multiplied the number of city-states, chiefly in the West, and promoted the prosperity of the urban community. The autonomous, if not self-governing, town had flourished, and the local middle classes had distinguished themselves in the provision of public monuments and services to their local communities. The empire has, indeed, often been described as a confederation of such city-states. The economic crisis of the third century hit the prosperity of the towns as well as of agriculture and increased their tax burdens. It became so difficult for the urban governments to collect the tax assessments while the amount of taxes going to the central government became so small that the latter held the local officials, the *curiales* (so called because of membership in the local *curia*, or senate), personally responsible for the collection of the local assessments; that is, if the amount assessed was not collected the *curiales* had to make up the difference from their own pockets. This kind of public service is obviously far too much to ask of ordinary citizens. They refused to assume it by refusing to take office and become members of the curial class. The state thereupon undertook to force this obligation upon them and, in order to guarantee that there would always be *curiales* to do the collecting, proceeded to make them a hereditary class by having their sons become members of the class at eighteen, with corresponding obligations. It can be understood why, under these circumstances, the state had to intervene to keep these *curiales* from fleeing their cities or entering the clergy, a class exempt from paying taxes. The notion of fixed class membership was also attached to another group, the workers in the towns, who were organized into something like the later guilds (*collegia*). Obviously in a city like Rome, or in correspondingly important centers, the guilds responsible for maintaining the food supply could not be permitted to shirk their responsibility. It was similar with *collegia* responsible for transport, or for munitions, or for guaranteeing the water supply. From these guilds necessary and minimum quantities of goods and labor had to be required, and, in order to ensure an adequate supply of skilled labor in these trades, some *collegia* were made hereditary, with sons obliged to follow in their fathers' footsteps. This kind of forced labor for the state on the part of *curiales* and *collegia* was multiplied everywhere when the debased coinage became worthless and the state took its taxes in goods and services. The roads and postal services had to be maintained by local labor and supplies. The transport of taxes in kind to state warehouses had to be furnished locally. The support of government officials had to be undertaken by those in whose communities they were working. It was the first of the Severi, Septimius, who made the *curiales* responsible for the local collection of taxes. It was the last of the Severi, Alexander, who subjected the *collegia* of Rome to government control. It was Diocletian and Constantine who completed and legalized the subjection of the urban middle classes and regularized the practice of forced labor for the state. "It is this above all else that constitutes the tragedy of the Roman Empire in the third century, the reduction of individual citizens of all classes to the compulsory service of the state . . . the rapid submergence of the citizens of all classes to slavish subjects of a relentless military despotism."[18]

THE ARMY

Since the growing theocracy of the empire was military as well as religious it is well to note the character of the army that was the foundation of this state. It was an army recruited necessarily from the less civilized portions of the empire and one whose officers and men became, in part, hereditary members of a military class. It was, moreover, an army increasingly supplemented by mercenary units, infantry as well as cavalry, recruited among noncitizen barbarians. Under the Severi the recruits came from the peasantry "of the less-developed provinces," and the officers from the provinces rather than from Italy. Lands were also offered to frontier soldiers on a hereditary basis, that is, in return for the obligation to render military service. In fact, there was something like an attempt to form a proletarian army that would support the despotism in its attack upon the Senate, the provincial aristocracy, and the monied classes generally. Maximinus, for example, the Thracian peasant emperor, "removed all officers of senatorial rank from the army and instituted a policy of systematic extermination of the propertied classes and wholesale plunder of private and even public property of the cities." As the military crisis developed the number of legions was increased; with the rise in prices the wages of the legionaries were increased. During the military anarchy (235-270) these class-conscious legions got out of hand and set out to

[18]Trever, II, 655.

plunder the state. The result was, by way of reform, to take even larger numbers of troops as mercenaries from the less Romanized barbarian population: Illyrians, Moors, Thracians, Arabs, Britons, Germans, and Sarmatians. Many of these rose to high position in the army and civil service when the senatorials were pushed out of leading positions, since a commission in the army brought equestrian rank and, consequently, privileges in the civil service. The army became "an alien, hereditary caste, supported by the people of the Empire to fight its foreign battles. Yet its leaders now formed the ruling aristocracy of the Empire and furnished its administrative personnel, even the emperors themselves."[19] As part of their administrative reforms, Diocletian and Constantine, while not changing the character of the army itself, did separate civil from military authority throughout the administration.

CONTEMPORARY WRITERS ON THE DECLINE AND FALL

These symptoms of a collapsing state are well reflected in the literary sources of the period. The Christian Fathers had no hesitancy in commenting on a passing pagan world. Cyprian, a third-century bishop of North Africa, speaks of the world "proclaiming by the evidence of universal decay her imminent collapse." Nature herself had gone back on the pagans. "No longer is there sufficient rain in winter to nourish the crops, or heat in summer to bring them to maturity. Spring no longer makes provision for the sowing, nor autumn for her fruits. Less and less are blocks of marble wrested from the exhausted hills; less and less the worn-out mines yield their stores of gold and silver; daily the impoverished veins become shorter until they fail. The field lacks labourers, the sea mariners, the camp soldiers. Innocence departs from the forum, justice from the court, concord from friendship, skill from art, discipline from conduct."[20] Saint Chrysostom speaks out against the incipient feudal lords of the late empire: "Who could be more oppressive than landlords? If you look at the way in which they treat their miserable tenants, you will find them more savage than barbarians. They lay intolerable and continual imposts upon men who are weakened with hunger and toil throughout their lives and they put upon them the burden of oppressive services. They use their bodies like asses and mules, or rather like stones, hardly letting them breathe, and they strain them equally in good years and bad, never giving the slightest relief. . . . The tortures and beatings, the exactions and ruthless demands of services which such men suffer from agents [of absentee landlords] are worse than hunger. Who could recount the ways in which these agents use them for profit and then cheat them? Their labour turns the agent's olive-press; but they receive not a scrap of the produce which they are compelled illegally to bottle for

[19]Trever, II, 642, 654.
[20]Cochrane, *Christianity*, pp. 154–155.

278 CHAPTER SEVEN

the agent, receiving only a tiny sum for this work. Moreover the agent extorts more oppressive interest than even pagan law allows, not twelve but fifty per cent from a man with a wife and children, who is filling the agent's barn and olive-store by his own labour."[21]

AMMIANUS MARCELLINUS

Ammianus Marcellinus, the last distinguished historian of the Roman Empire, a Syrian provincial writing in Latin and describing conditions of the last half of the fourth century, could declare: "He [the emperor] opened the door to plunder, which doors are daily more and more opened by the depravity of judges and advocates, who are all of the same mind and who sell the interests of the poor to the military commanders or the persons of influence within the palace, by which conduct they themselves have gained riches and high rank. . . . The emperor . . . considered nothing but how he might amass money from all quarters, without any distinction between just and unjust actions. . . . Every class and profession was exposed to annoyance, being called upon to furnish arms, clothes, military engines, and even gold and silver and abundant stores of provisions and various kinds of animals. . . . Detestable collectors [came] among them, extorting money and exaggerating accusations in order to build up wealth and influence for themselves, and to procure their own safety and prosperity by draining the natives. . . . The misery of these times was further increased by the insatiable covetousness of his [the emperor's] tax collectors who brought him more odium than money. . . . The natives, from weariness of the severe rule under which they were, were eager for any change whatever. . . . Lastly, the burdens of all tributes and taxes were augmented in a manifold degree, and drove some of the highest nobles from fear of the worst to emigrate from their homes. Some also after being drained to the utmost by the cruelty of the revenue officers, as they really had nothing more to give, were thrown into prison, of which they became permanent inmates. And some, becoming weary of life and light, sought a release from the miseries by hanging themselves . . . the treasury is empty, the cities are exhausted, the finances are stripped bare." The city of Rome is "declining into old age."[22]

THE GERMAN INVASIONS

The reform of the empire by Diocletian and Constantine, if we may dignify the fixation of tyranny as a reform, including as it did financial and military measures enabled the state to survive in the West until the onslaught of the Germans at the end of the fourth century. Then from 376 to 476, except for central Gaul, the empire in the West was reduced to

[21]C. E. Stevens, "Agriculture and Rural Life in the Late Roman Empire," *Cambridge Economic History of Europe*, eds. J. H. Clapham and Eileen Power, I, 116.
[22]*The Roman History of Ammianus Marcellinus*, trans. C. D. Yonge, Bohn's Classical Library, p. 560.

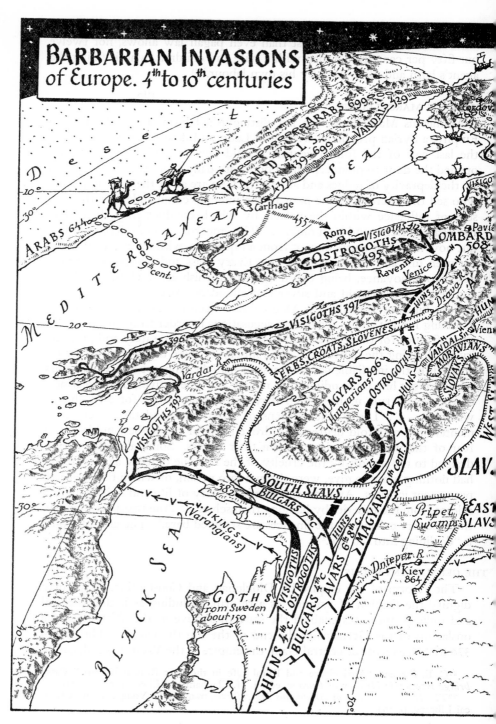

BARBARIAN INVASIONS
of Europe. 4th to 10th centuries

Viking raids 9th-10th century

ATLANTIC OCEAN

SIGOTHS
Toledo 414-711 SUEVI

to Iceland 874
to Greenland 986
and Vinland

Poitiers
119 VANDALS
Toulouse
412

Loire
106
Seine
Paris
Châlons
451
Mainz

5th-6th centuries
London

BURGUNDIANS

HUNS

H H H

Regensburg
401

FRANKS

SAXONS
FRISIANS

Angles

9th and 10th cent.

Jutes

NORTH SEA

10°

10°

VANDALS LOMBARDS

CHS

Elbe
R.

WENDS

GERMANS

Vistula R.

BALTIC SEA

NORTHMEN
(Vikings, Danes)

10°

PRUSSIANS LETTS

LIVS R.

Dvina

RUS VIKINGS
Portages

ESTHS

FINNS LAPPS

20°

V Volkhov R.
Novgorod
862

60°

30°

Raisz

THE DECLINE AND FALL OF THE ROMAN EMPIRE 281

a memory and an influence or a longed-for dream. For the Germans the occupation of the western empire was the end of a long trek toward the civilized coast lands of the Mediterranean. It was a trek that began from southern Scandinavia and northern Europe between the Weser and Oder, whither the Germans, an Indo-European people, had moved at a time and in a fashion quite unknown to us. In the course of their movement southward toward the Rhine and the Danube they met the Celts in southern Germany, with whom they in part intermarried and whom they in part drove out.[23] By the time of Julius Caesar they had reached the Rhine and Danube rivers and were stopped by him at the Rhine. Subsequently the Romans expanded beyond the Rhine and Danube into the Tithed Lands and Dacia, but were obliged to vacate these lands to the Goths and the confederation of the Alamanni when the Germans began to exert pressure upon this frontier in the third century.[24] Before the tribes of Goths continued the German trek within the boundaries of the empire the emperors had already sought to buttress a weakening state by using primitive German strength. Famine, plague, and the decline in population had left a good deal of public and private land uncultivated. To remedy this situation the emperors brought in a great many Germans as colonists. Some of these, when settled upon vacant public land, were given leases obliging them to render military service when called upon. Other Germans were taken as individuals or as groups into the army as mercenary soldiers. With military service came citizenship, and with citizenship public office, whether military or civilian. At moments of severe crisis the empire often had to depend upon German officials and a Germanized army to defend the state against German invaders, certainly an anomalous situation. Moreover, the Romans had taken whole tribes into their protection as allies (*foederati*) against the potential German enemy. Thus we may speak of a peaceful German infiltration of the empire which, for about a century after the abandonment of Dacia and the Tithed Lands, had acquired considerable momentum.

THE HUNS

This peaceful infiltration was interrupted by the mass migration of whole tribes and confederations of tribes into the empire in search of a place of permanent settlement. When events in southeastern Europe forced the Germans to move across the Roman frontier they knew that if they acted concertedly they could not be refused entrance and a place of settlement. These events had to do with the entrance of the nomadic Mongolian Huns into the southern Russian steppes, the first of many such migrations that were to continue for about a thousand years. Since the time of their arrival in southeastern Europe the Goths had split into two

[23]See p. 188.
[24]See p. 189.

groups: the eastern, or Ostrogoths, dwelling north of the Black Sea, and the western, or Visigoths, occupying the former province of Dacia. Both groups had been converted to Christianity by the missionary Ulfilas (fourth century), who at the same time inaugurated Germanic literature with his translation of most of the Scriptures into Gothic. Ulfilas, however, was what by this time was called an Arian rather than an orthodox Christian,[25] and he had converted the Goths to this heretical form of the faith. From the Goths the Arian form of Christianity spread to the other eastern German peoples, that is, to the Vandals, the Burgundians, and the Lombards, of whom the two former, like the Visigoths and Ostrogoths, were already Christian when they entered the empire. After conquering many of the Ostrogoths and forcing the remainder to join the Visigoths in begging the Roman state for permission to cross the Danube, the Huns established in present-day Hungary the first Asiatic state in Europe. Inasmuch as this state included many smaller German tribes north of the Danube, the Huns became the same kind of threat to the Germans on the middle and upper Danube and on the Rhine as they had been to the Goths. If the frontier legions and fortifications did not hold, the empire would be inundated not only by Germans but also by Huns. This is precisely what happened, and in order to clarify as well as simplify the events of this chaotic century it is necessary to know the chief tribes or confederations located on the Rhine-Danube frontier.

LOCATION OF GERMANIC TRIBES ON THE RHINE-DANUBE FRONTIER

The center of the Hunnic empire was in the valley of the Theiss River. Below on the lower Danube the Visigoths were located. Above them on the middle Danube was a German confederation called, in the fifth century, the Bavarians, formed chiefly from the remainders of the Marcomanni and Quadi whom Marcus Aurelius had fought. In the bend of the upper Danube and Rhine, the former Tithed Lands, was the confederation of the Alamanni, containing large numbers of Suevi (Swabians). The Burgundians and Vandals occupied the valley of the Main. Below them on the right bank of the Rhine was the confederation of the Ripuarian Franks. On the lower Rhine, partly within the empire as allies (*foederati*) and partly on the right bank, was the confederation of the Salian Franks. Beyond these frontier peoples, in the interior of Germany, the important groups were (1) the Frisians, situated on the North Sea; (2) the Saxon confederation, between the Weser and Elbe; (3) the Angles and Jutes in Schleswig-Holstein and Denmark; (4) below the Saxons, in the area of the Harz mountains, the Thuringian confederation; (5) to the east of the Elbe, in an area subsequently to be occupied by Slavs, remnants of the Suevi and Vandals; and (6) in the valley of the Oder, the Lombards. If the eastern Germans were Arian Christians when they came into the empire,

[25]See pp. 331 f.

the western Germans who entered, the Bavarians, Alamanni, Franks, Angles, Saxons, Jutes, and Frisians, still clung to their old deities. In any case, whether heretic or pagan, they were a challenge to the western Church.

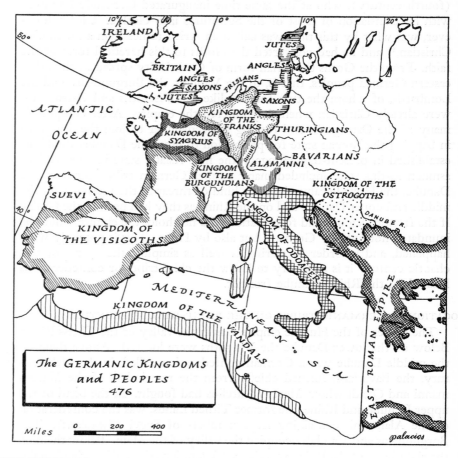

The GERMANIC KINGDOMS and PEOPLES 476

THE VISIGOTHS

It was beyond the capacity of the Roman emperors of this century to settle the German tribes and confederations peacefully within the empire as citizens or prospective citizens, even as it was beyond their strength to keep them out. In 376 the Visigoths were permitted to cross the Danube as refugees from the Huns and to settle in Thrace as allies of the Roman state. But Roman officials were not content to let them settle down as satisfied colonists. Instead they were driven to rebellion, then and repeatedly thereafter, and entered again upon a long trek that the Romans were unable to halt. Under their king, Alaric, they moved through the lower Balkans and into Italy, plundered Rome for two or three days in 410, and, after failing in an attempt to move to North Africa, left Italy for southern Gaul, where in 418, some forty-two years after their crossing of the Danube, they were settled between the Garonne and the Loire as an allied kingdom with sovereignty only over Goths. In 426 they were made an independent kingdom and soon expanded to include all southern Gaul to the Pyrenees and all except northwestern Spain.

THE COLLAPSE OF THE RHINE-DANUBE FRONTIER

Meanwhile, to protect Italy and the West, Stilicho, its Vandal defender, had withdrawn so many troops from the Rhine frontier that it could no longer be held. It was necessary subsequently to do the same with the Danubian troops and to withdraw the legions from Britain. The result was that Angles, Saxons, Jutes, and Frisians crossed the sea to Britain, pushed the Christianized Celts back into Wales and Cornwall or drove them to the continent (Brittany). All of these except the Frisians established kingdoms of their own in Britain. The weakening of the Rhenish defense enabled the Ripuarian Franks and the Alamanni to move to the left bank of the river, making from this time on (early fifth century) a German left bank of the Rhine. It also enabled the Burgundians to cross the river and settle first around Mainz and Worms, and then in the valley of the Rhone. The Vandals meanwhile had moved across Gaul to Spain (409), and under pressure from the Visigothic allies of Rome crossed into North Africa (424), out of which they made an independent Vandal kingdom that by 455 was sacking Rome. The Alamanni not only crossed the Rhine into what was to become Alsace but crossed the upper Danube into future western Switzerland. The Bavarians moved south of the Danube.

THE END OF THE WESTERN EMPIRE

In 451 the Huns, under Attila, followed the Germans into Gaul but withdrew when they were faced with a coalition of Roman, Frankish, Burgundian, and Visigothic troops. At Attila's death (454) the Hunnic empire went to pieces and the Germans subject to it were freed. In the years following, Italy was taken over by the German mercenary troops stationed in the peninsula, the Suevian general Ricimer being the first to set up a puppet emperor, followed by the Burgundian Gundobald. When finally the eastern emperor Zeno set up a western emperor of his own (474), the latter was driven out of Italy by his own master of troops, Orestes, a former officer in Attila's army. Orestes thereupon raised his young son Romulus Augustulus to be the last Roman emperor of the West. When denied a grant of one-third of the public lands in Italy, the German mercenary troops crowned one of their leaders, Odovacar, a Scirian chieftain, as king, murdered Orestes, and deposed Romulus (476). Within a few years what was left of the Roman Empire in central Gaul under the loyal governor Aëtius was taken over by Clovis, the king of the Salian Franks.

The ease with which these tribes and confederations moved through the empire of course illustrates its weakness. It does more. It illustrates the indifference with which the citizens of the empire abandoned their state to the Germans. Only in a few places, however, were the numbers of these tribes large enough to bring about a fundamental ethnic change in the West. Except for Celtic Wales and Cornwall, Britain became a German land. The same may be said for the region south of the lower Rhine colonized by the Salian Franks, and for the whole remaining left bank of the Rhine settled by the Ripuarians and Alamanni. The right bank of the Danube also became German. Germany proper thus bulged beyond its Rhine-Danube frontier. Elsewhere the Germans in the new kingdoms were not numerous enough to bring about a complete ethnic change and thus give to these kingdoms a strong native foundation. Instead the Germans were a small, alien minority governing Roman citizens. They were, moreover, a small, alien, heretical (Arian), or pagan minority ruling an orthodox population who were members of a powerful church. The kingdoms were thus short-lived. The Vandals were conquered by Justinian,[26] the Visigoths in Spain by the Moslems.[27] The Visigoths in southern Gaul, the Burgundians in the Rhone valley, and all the Germans in Europe, within or without the boundaries of the Roman Empire, were swallowed up in the expanding Frankish state.[28]

THE MYSTERY CULTS

It has been suggested that the shift toward theocracy in Roman imperial life, particularly marked after the third century, was accompanied by a growing interest in a kind of personal religion not characteristic of the anthropomorphic polytheism of the Greeks and Romans. The new personal religion was centered in the mystery cults and Christianity. The former have already been alluded to, and the general characteristics of the Greek mysteries described.[29] It is now necessary to describe the characteristics and trace the spread to Italy and the West of the more popular of the oriental cults: the cult of the Great Mother (Magna Mater), of Isis, of Mithra, and, besides, the religion of the Persian prophet Mani. The mystery cults preserved features of religions that went back to primitive fertility cults, to practices that not only caused plants to grow and ripen out of fertile soil but animals and humans to be born out of fertile wombs. The gods and goddesses associated with them were therefore considered to be the immediate causes of the great alternations of the seasons and the fundamental rhythmic cycles of human and animal life. As they adapted themselves to more civilized societies they became less magical and more

[26]See p. 284.
[27]See p. 284.
[28]See p. 284.
[29]See pp. 41 f. for the oriental, and pp. 111 ff. for the Greek mystery cults.

symbolical, preserving, however, suggestions of their original character. Finally they were made to serve man's need of a guarantee that he is more than a mere animal sentenced by some decree of unavoidable fate to death, that he is capable of becoming a divine being like the gods and goddesses whom he worships, and like them of dying of course, but only temporarily. For these divinities had conquered death, had arisen from the tomb, and man, too, by being assimilated to their divine nature would conquer death and live an immortal life. Whatever the simplicity of the legend or the crudity of the ritual, these were cults aiming to satisfy in a definite way powerful human needs of an elemental kind.

CATULLUS'S "ATYS"

The Roman poet Catullus (84–54? B.C.)[30] tried to capture the spirit of the Magna Mater cult in a poem addressed to the Great Mother's male consort, Attis. In it she is given her Greek name, Cybele, but the setting is Phrygia, in central Asia Minor, supposedly the original place of her worship. That part of the legend is here told in which Attis (Atys in the poem), a young shepherd born of a virgin mother and a lover of Cybele, castrates himself in a fit of frenzy as an act of devotion toward the goddess:

Atys o'er the distant waters, driving in his rapid bark,
Soon with foot of wild impatience touch'd the Phrygian forest dark,
Where amid the awful shades possess'd by mighty Cybele,
In his zealous frenzy blind,
And wand'ring in his hapless mind,
With flinty knife he gave to earth the weights that stamp virility.
Then as the widow'd being saw its wretched limbs bereft of man,
And the unaccustom'd blood that on the ground polluting ran,
With snowy hand it snatch'd in haste the timbrel's airy round on high,
That opens with the trumpet's blast thy rites, Maternal Mystery;
And upon its whirling fingers, while the hollow parchment rung,
Thus in outcry tremulous to its wild companions sung:—
    "Now come along, come along with me,
    Worshippers of Cybele,
    To the lofty groves of the deity!
    Ye vagabond herds that bear the name
    Of the Dindymenian dame!
Who seeking strange lands, like the banish'd of home,
With Atys, with Atys distractedly roam;
Who your limbs have unmann'd in a desperate hour,
With a frantic disdain of the Cyprian power;
Who have carried my sect through the dreadful salt sea,
Rouse, rouse your wild spirits careeringly!
    No delay, no delay,
    But together away,
And follow me up to the Dame all-compelling,
To her high Phrygian groves, and her dark Phrygian dwelling,

[30]See p. 231.

Where the cymbals they clash, and the drums they resound,
And the Phrygian's curved pipe pours its mourning around;
Where the ivy-crown'd priestesses toss with their brows,
And send the shrill howl through their deity's house;
Where they shriek, and they scour, and they madden about,—
'Tis there we go bounding in mystical rout."
    No sooner had spoken
    This voice half-broken,
When suddenly from quivering tongues arose the universal cry.
The timbrels with a boom resound, the cymbals with a clash reply,
And up the verdant Ida with a quicken'd step the chorus flew,
While Atys with the timbrels' smite the terrible procession drew;
Raging, panting, wild, and witless, through the sullen shades it broke,
Like the fierce, unconquer'd heifer bursting from her galling yoke;
And on pursue the sacred crew, till at the door of Cybele,
Faint and fasting, down they sink, in pale immovability:
The heavy sleep—the heavy sleep—grows o'er their failing eyes,
And lock'd in dead repose the rabid frenzy lies.
But when the Sun look'd out with eyes of light,
Found the firm earth, wild seas, and skies of morning white,
    Scaring the lingering shades
    With echo-footed steeds,
Sleep took his flight from Atys, hurrying
To his Pasithea's arms on tremulous wing;
And the poor dreamer woke, oppress'd with sadness,
To memory woke, and to collected madness.—
Struck with its loss, with what it was, and where,
Back trod the wretched being in despair
To the sea-shore, and stretching forth its eye
O'er the wide waste of waters and of sky,
Thus to its country cried with tears of misery:—
"My country, oh my country, parent state,
Whom like a very slave and runagate,
Wretch that I am, I left for wilds like these,
This wilderness of snows and matted trees,
To house with shivering beasts and learn their wants,
A fierce intruder on their sullen haunts,—
Where shall I fancy thee? Where cheat mine eye
With tricking out thy quarter in the sky?
Fain, while my wits a little space are free,
Would my poor eye-balls strain their points on thee!
Am I then torn from home and far away!
Doom'd through these woods to trample day by day,
Far from my kindred friends and native soil,
The mall, the race, and wrestlers bright with oil?
Ah wretch, bewail, bewail; and think for this
On all thy past variety of bliss.
I was the charm of life, the social spring,
First in the race, and brightest in the ring:
Warm with the stir of welcome was my home;
And when I rose betimes, my friends would come
Smiling and pressing in officious scores,
Thick as the flowers that hang at lovers' doors:—
And shall I then a minist'ring madman be

To angry gods? A howling devotee?—
A slave to bear what never senses can,—
Half of myself, sexless,—a sterile man?
And must I feel, with never-varied woes,
The o'erhanging winter of these mountain snows,
Skulking through ghastly woods for evermore,
Like the lean stag, or the brute vagrant boar?
Ah me! ah me! Already I repent;
E'en now, e'en now I feel my shame and punishment!"
As thus with rosy lips the wretch grew loud,
Startling the ears of heaven's imperial crowd,
The Mighty Mistress o'er her lion yoke
Bow'd in her wrath,—and loosening as she spoke
The left-hand savage, scatterer of herds,
Roused his fell nature with impetuous words.
"Fly, ruffian, fly, indignant and amain,
And scare this being, who resists my reign,
Back to the horror-breathing woods again.
Lash thee, and fly and shake with sinewy might
Thine ireful hair, and as at dead of night
Fill the wild echoes with rebellowing fright."
Threatening she spoke, and loosed the vengeance dire,
Who gathering all his rage and glaring fire,
Starts with a roar, and scours beneath her eyes,
Scattering the splinter'd bushes as he flies:
Down by the sea he spies the wretch at last,
And springs precipitous:—the wretch as fast,
Flies raving back into his living grave,
And there for ever dwells, a savage and a slave.
O Goddess! Mistress! Cybele! dread name!
O mighty power! O Dindymenian dame!
Far from my home thy visitations be:
Drive others mad, not me:
Drive others into impulse wild, and fierce insanity.[31]

THE CULT OF THE GREAT MOTHER

In the developed legend Attis dies, whether because of his self-mutilation
or otherwise, and the Magna Mater enters upon a prolonged and intensive
period of mourning for her dead beloved. Finally she is responsible for
bringing him to life again, and now as a deified human he enjoys immortality. The spring festival of the Magna Mater at Rome aimed to repeat
this legend in ritual form in such a way as to make it possible for the
participant to become another Attis who could be regenerated by the
goddess into a divine person enjoying immortality. On the second day
of the festival in March a pine tree representing the dead Attis was
brought into the temple of Cybele. "The trunk was swathed like a corpse
with woollen bands and decked with wreaths of violets, for violets were
said to have sprung from the blood of Attis . . . and the effigy of a young

[31]"Atys," trans. Leigh Hunt, in G. Howe and G. A. Harrer, *Roman Literature in
Translation*, pp. 272-274.

man, doubtless Attis himself, was tied to the middle of the stem." After a day of fasting and mourning the climax of the festival, the Day of Blood, a kind of barbaric Good Friday, was celebrated. "The Archigallus or high-priest drew blood from his arms and presented it as an offering. Nor was he alone in making this bloody sacrifice. Stirred by the wild barbaric music of clashing cymbals, rumbling drums, droning horns, and screaming flutes, the inferior clergy whirled about in the dance with waggling heads and streaming hair, until, rapt into a frenzy of excitement and insensible to pain, they gashed their bodies with potsherds or slashed them with knives in order to bespatter the altar and the sacred tree with their flowing blood." During this frenzy those who intended to become priests, or *galli*, of the goddess emasculated themselves, like Attis. To conclude the extraordinary ceremonies the pine tree, symbolic of Attis dead, was buried, and those who had made the supreme sacrifice, considered now as new Attises, were brought to spend the night in the marriage chamber of the goddess. The Day of Blood was followed by a Day of Joy (*Hilaria*), a kind of pagan Easter rejoicing over the resurrection of Attis by the Magna Mater. "When night [of the Day of Blood] had fallen, the sorrow of the worshippers was turned to joy. For suddenly a light shone in the darkness: the tomb was opened: the god had risen from the dead; and as the priest touched the lips of the weeping mourners with balm, he softly whispered in their ears the glad tidings of salvation. The resurrection of the god was hailed by his disciples as a promise that they too would issue triumphant from the corruption of the grave."[32] The closing day of the festival was marked by the washing of the goddess in the Almo, a rite considered necessary after her mystical marriage with her new priests.

"TAUROBOLIUM"

The Magna Mater cult also used the ceremony of baptism in the blood of a sacred bull (*taurobolium*) or ram (*criobolium*) to mark the rebirth or regeneration of the neophyte. In this the would-be member of the cult descended into a pit over which had been built an altar, upon which the sacred bull or ram was sacrificed. In the words of a Christian poet, he "receives the falling drops on his head, clothes and body. He leans backward to have his cheeks, his ears, his lips, and his nostrils wetted. He pours the liquid over his eyes and does not even spare his palate, for he moistens his tongue with blood and drinks it eagerly."[33] By this baptismal bath the neophyte was cleansed of his sin and was born again into eternity (*renatus in aeternum*). Other ceremonies of a private character point to a communion meal. These primitive and barbaric rites, similar in some

[32]The selection from James G. Frazer, *The Golden Bough*, pp. 348–350, copyright 1940 by The Macmillan Company of Canada, Ltd., and used with their permission.
[33]Reprinted from *Pagan Regeneration* by H. R. Willoughby, p. 5, by permission of The University of Chicago Press. Copyright 1929 by The University of Chicago Press.

respects to those of Dionysus, aimed by means of ceremonies of identification and communion with the divine hero to transform the human being into a god who was master of even the fate that spells death. By means of wild rites that stirred his most primitive emotions the individual was lifted from the hopeless world about him to share the society of the many-breasted Mother of all nature and to partake of the actual being of her deified husband.

THE CULT OF ISIS-OSIRIS

For our purposes the nature of the Isis-Osiris cult can best be understood from the account in Apuleius's *The Golden Ass.* In this work the Egyptian goddess has become identified with all the great goddesses of antiquity. The legend around which the ritual of the cult developed is much like that of the Magna Mater-Attis legend. Isis is the sister and wife of Osiris (Serapis) and Horus is their son. Osiris loses his life at the hands of his brother Set, who puts him in a chest and throws him into the Nile. Isis goes in search of her husband, suffering and mourning greatly in the course of her travels, and finally comes across the chest. But Set once again gets the body and scatters it in fourteen parts about Egypt. Isis gathers together these parts, buries them, and then restores her dead husband to life, he becoming the god and judge of the dead. The devotees of Isis, in the course of witnessing the passion play rehearsing her life, are mystically identified with the god, and thus will share in the goddess' gracious gift of immortality. In becoming one with Osiris they partake of his divinity. As the public ceremonies of the cult are revealed by Apuleius it is impossible not to see in them much that was to become a part of the Christian Church.

APULEIUS'S "THE GOLDEN ASS"

Lucius, the hero of Apuleius's tale, has in the course of his travels been magically transformed into an ass and is led to believe that he can regain his human form through the miraculous power of the goddess. After purifying himself by plunging his head seven times into the sea, he prays to her as the great and superior synthesis of all the goddesses of antiquity: "O blessed queen of heaven, whether Thou be the Dame Ceres which art the original and motherly nurse of all fruitful things in the earth . . . or whether Thou be the celestial Venus, who, in the beginning of the world, didst couple together male and female with an engendered love, and didst so make an eternal propagation of human kind . . . Thou, which dost luminate all the cities of the earth by Thy feminine light; Thou, which nourishest all the seeds of the world by Thy damp heat . . . by whatsoever name or fashion or shape it is lawful to call upon Thee. . . . Remove from me the hateful shape of mine ass, and render me to my kindred and to mine own self Lucius." Apuleius describes the goddess as she appears to

Lucius. "She had a great abundance of hair, flowing and curling, dispersed and scattered about her divine neck; on the crown of her head she bare many garlands interlaced with flowers, and in the middle of her forehead was a plain circlet in fashion of a mirror, or rather resembling the moon by the light that it gave forth; and this was borne up on either side by serpents that seemed to rise from the furrows of the earth, and above it were blades of corn set out. Her vestment was of finest linen yielding divers colours, somewhere white and shining, somewhere yellow like the crocus flower, somewhere rosy red, somewhere flaming; . . . her cloak was utterly dark. . . . Here and there upon the edge thereof and throughout its surface the stars glimpsed, and in the middle of them was placed the moon in mid-month, which shone like a flame of fire. . . . Her odoriferous feet were covered with shoes interlaced and wrought with victorious palm. Thus the divine shape, breathing out the pleasant spice of fertile Arabia" speaks to him, describing herself as "the natural mother of all things, mistress and governess of all the elements, the initial progeny of worlds, chief of the powers divine, queen of all that are in hell, the principal of them that dwell in heaven, manifested alone and under one form of all the gods and goddesses. At my will the planets of the sky, the wholesome winds of the seas, and the lamentable silences of hell be disposed; my name, my divinity is adored throughout all the world, in divers manners, in variable customs, and by many names [Mother of the gods, Minerva, Venus, Proserpine, Ceres, Juno, Bellona, Hecate, Rhamnusia]." She promises Lucius that on the morrow, in the course of a grand procession in her honor, he will be restored to his human form by her great priest. But in return for this miracle Lucius is to know "that the residue of thy life until the hour of death shall be bound and subject to me. . . . And if I perceive that thou art obedient to my commandment and addict to my religon, meriting by thy constant chastity my divine grace, know thou that I alone may prolong thy days above the time that the fates have appointed and ordained."[34]

AN ISAIC PROCESSION

Apuleius describes in detail the grand Isaic procession of the following day. There was one "attired in a robe of silk, and socks of gold, with fine ornament, having long hair added and fixed upon his head, and walked delicately in form of a woman," and another "with a mantle, a staff, a pair of pantofles, and with a beard as long as any goat's, signifying a philosopher." There was "a meek and tame bear," and "an ape with a bonnet. . . . An ass had wings glued to his back and went after an old man, whereby you would judge the one to be Pegasus and the other Bellerophon, and at both would you laugh well." Women attendants of the goddess followed. "Then came a great number, as well of men as of women, with lamps,

[34]Trans. W. Adlington, rev. S. Gaselec, Loeb, No. 44, pp. 541-551.

candles, torches, and other lights, doing honour thereby to her that was born of the celestial stars. After that sounded the musical harmony of instruments, pipes and flutes in most pleasant measure. . . . Then came the great company of men and women of all stations and of every age which were initiate and had taken divine orders, whose garments, being of the whitest linen, glistened all the streets over. The women had their hair anointed, and their heads covered with light linen; but the men had their crowns shaven and shining bright, as being the terrene stars of the goddess, and held in their hands timbrels of brass, silver, aye and gold, which rendered forth a shrill and pleasant sound. The principal priests, . . . apparelled with white surplices drawn tight about their breasts and hanging down to the ground, bare the relics of all the most puissant gods. . . . Another was there that bare in his bosom (thrice happy he!) the venerable figure of the godhead." Finally came the great priest who gave to Lucius the garland of roses to eat that released him from his lamentable state and restored him suddenly and miraculously to his human shape. "Then the people began to marvel, and the religious honoured the goddess for so evident a miracle."[35]

PRE-INITIATION CEREMONIES

What follows in Apuleius is the account of Lucius' preparation for, and initiation into, the priesthood of Isis. He "hired . . . a house within the cloister of the temple . . . so that I might ordinarily frequent the company of the priests." He attended the public services in the temple after "the opening of the gates in the morning. . . . I went in, and when the white curtains were drawn aside, I began to pray before the face of the goddess, while the priest prepared and set the divine things on every altar with solemn supplications, and fetched out of the sanctuary the holy water for the libation. When all things were duly performed, the religious began to sing the matins of the morning, testifying thereby the hour of prime." He had to "refrain from profane and unlawful meats, as those priests which were already received, to the end I might come more apt and clean to the knowledge of the secrets of the religion." When the day of Lucius' initiation was set he was given over to the charge of a great priest who took him "when he found that the time was at hand, to the next baths, accompanied with all the religious sort, and demanding pardon of the gods, washed me and purified my body according to the custom. . . . After this . . . he brought me back again to the temple and presented me before the feet of the goddess, giving me a charge of certain secret things unlawful to be uttered, and commanding me generally before all the rest to fast by the space of ten continual days, without eating of any beast or drinking of any wine."[36]

[35]*Golden Ass*, pp. 553–561.
[36]Ibid., pp. 571–579.

On the evening of the day of initiation "there arrived on every coast a great multitude of priests. . . . Then was all the laity and profane people commanded to depart, and when they had put on my back a new linen robe, the priest took my hand and brought me to the most secret and sacred place of the temple." Lucius says it is unlawful for him to tell "what was said and done there." He can only indicate vaguely that "I approached near unto hell, even to the gates of Prosperine, and after that I was ravished throughout all the elements, I returned to my proper place: about midnight I saw the sun brightly shine, I saw likewise the gods celestial and the gods infernal, before whom I presented myself and worshipped them. . . . When morning came and . . . the solemnities were finished, I came forth sanctified with twelve stoles and in a religious habit. . . . There I was commanded to stand upon a pulpit of wood which stood in the middle of the temple, before the figure . . . of the goddess; my vestment was of fine linen, covered and embroidered with flowers; I had a precious cope upon my shoulders, hanging down behind me to the ground, whereon were beasts wrought of divers colours, as Indian dragons, and Hyperborean griffins. . . . In my right hand I carried a lighted torch, and a garland of flowers was upon my head, with white palm-leaves sprouting out on every side like rays; thus I was adorned like unto the sun, and made in fashion of an image, when the curtains were drawn aside and all the people compassed about to behold me. Then they began to solemnise the feast, the nativity of my holy order, with sumptuous banquets and pleasant meats." Having now been made a priest, Lucius departed for home, after "I had fallen prostrate before the face of the goddess and wiped her feet with my face" and addressed her "O holy and blessed dame, the perpetual comfort of human kind, . . . Thou are she that puttest away all storms and dangers from men's life by stretching forth Thy right hand, whereby likewise Thou dost unweave even the inextricable and tangled web of fate, and . . . keepest back the harmful course of the stars. . . . Thou dost make all the earth to turn, Thou givest light to the sun. . . . By Thy mean . . . the seasons return, . . . the elements serve . . . the seeds prosper, and the fruits do grow." On the way home Lucius was initiated into the priesthood of Osiris at Rome after ten more days of fasting and after "I . . . did shave my head." He was then called "to receive a third order of religion," which enabled him, he frankly confesses, to gain "much money in pleading of causes."[37]

THE CULT OF MITHRA

Along with the cult of the Magna Mater and Isis, the worship of the Persian Mithra spread westward[38] and became probably even more popular

[37]*Golden Ass*, pp. 579–595.
[38]See p. 41.

than the other two. It was a religion open only to men and was found wherever the legions were stationed. It summoned the male fraternity to stand by Mithra in his fight on behalf of Ahura Mazda against the forces of evil and darkness. Unlike the other cults it is impossible to describe its nature from literature. Such a description can only come from the architectural and sculptural remains of its sanctuaries. Mithra was born, according to the legend, on the banks of a stream under the shade of a sacred tree, observed by shepherds watching their flocks. As a young man he defeated Ahura Mazda in combat and then become his good friend and ally in the battle against evil. Mithra also killed the bull, the first living creature made by Ahura Mazda, and from its blood and thus directly through Mithra came all the beneficial plants and animals of the earth. Indeed, Mithra's whole life was spent in protecting the first humans against the activities of the evil god Ahriman. When his earthly life was over Mithra had a last supper with the sun and other companions, and was taken by the sun (Ahura Mazda) to dwell with the immortals in the stars, protecting from this abode all those who remain faithful to him.[39] Whether the wives of his followers were included is not known.

MITHRAIC CEREMONIES

The Mithraists were organized in small congregations and met in underground chapels or caves to witness the ritual rehearsing the life story of the god. Final initiation into the cult came only after going through at least seven stages. The stages were marked by ceremonial baths or baptisms to wash away sin. Mithraism also used the *taurobolium*. At one point in the ceremonies there was something like a confirmation, with Mithra burning a sign on the forehead of his followers. There were ceremonies of consecrating bread and of mixing water with wine and of offering them to the initiates. In one relief representing this communion ceremony the bread is marked with a cross. This communion service was taken to be a commemoration of the last supper between Mithra and Ahura Mazda before his ascension to heaven. There were special feast days to be celebrated, and among these the twenty-fifth of December, the birthday of the Invincible Sun.

MITHRAISM AND CHRISTIANITY

The Mithraist was held to obey his god's commandments, including those calling for perfect purity, perfect loyalty, and fraternity to comrades. Mithra would preside at a last judgment at which the eternal destiny of the initiate would be determined from the quality of his earthly life. He showed the way to the other world and presided over it. There were even some groups of Mithraists who believed in the second coming of Mithra to earth, a physical resurrection of the dead, the destruction of the

[39]See F. V. M. Cumont, *The Mysteries of Mithra*.

wicked, and the rejuvenation of the universe. It cannot be wondered at if some Christian writers were exercised over the similarity between Mithraism and Christianity, and accused the former of a diabolical imitation of the latter. Tertullian wrote, with respect to the Mithraic baptisms: "The Devil, whose business is to pervert the truth, mimics the exact circumstances of the divine sacraments in the mysteries of idols. He himself baptizes some, that is to say, his believers and followers; he promises forgiveness of sins in the sacred fount, and thus initiates them into the religion of Mithra." And another wrote of the Mithraic communion service: "The wicked demons have imitated this [the Christian Eucharist] in the mysteries of Mithra, commanding the same thing to be done. For that bread and a cup of water are placed before the initiate with certain incantations in these mysteries, you either know or can learn."[40]

THE WESTWARD SPREAD OF THE CULTS

The Greek and oriental mystery cults moved westward with the Greeks and orientals themselves. They came westward with the eastern merchants and with eastern slaves who, like the Sicilians bringing Santa Lucia to New York City, could not do without the protection of their old gods in their new homes. They came westward also with the legionary recruits from the eastern provinces and with those who had been stationed long on eastern frontiers. The Magna Mater was first introduced to Romans in 204 B.C., when she was brought to do what the local Italian and Roman gods seemed unable to do, that is, win the war with Carthage. But the Romans were horrified at the undignified excesses of the members of this cult—"tambourine-bangers, not worth a nutshell"—and forbade Roman citizens to become the goddess's priests. They were alarmed also at the ease with which the cult of Dionysus spread from the Greek colonies in southern Italy to the rest of Italy, alarmed at men who "as though frenzied, uttered soothsaying with a fanatical tossing of their bodies," and at "matrons attired as Bacchants with hair loosed" who "rushed to the Tiber with blazing torches." When the Romans ordered the cult stopped "there was a panic in Rome and all over Italy. . . . Numbers were arrested. Some of the initiates, both men and women, killed themselves. Those who pleaded guilty were executed, and the rest were kept in prison. Those slain were more than those imprisoned. The women were handed over to their relations or to those under whose authority they were, for private punishment."[41] When, likewise, the Isis cult spread to Rome the Senate, on numerous occasions in the first century B.C., ordered its altars and statues destroyed.

---

[40]Reprinted from *Pagan Regeneration* by H. R. Willoughby, pp. 160, 162, by permission of The University of Chicago Press. Copyright 1929 by The University of Chicago Press.
[41]Grenier, *The Roman Spirit*, p. 162.

The cults, however, were accepted and regularized under the empire and spread extensively throughout the western provinces. With them came an emphasis upon solar worship and an almost universal trust in Babylonian astrology with its depressing teaching of a fate contained in the movement of the heavens, a fate which these oriental deities were to circumvent. Astrology had been made poetical as early as Augustus, in Manilius's *Astronomica*, and it had been made learned and authoritative by Ptolemy's summary of the subject.[42] It was probably in the third century that ancient paganism, under the dominance of the Orient, reached a kind of synthetic stability[43] around the worship of the Roman monarch, the Unconquerable Sun (*Sol Invictus*), and the Magna Mater.

It is not difficult to understand the popularity of these worships. They became prominent and influential at a time of political absolutism and economic and social decay, when for the ordinary mortal there was little to give meaning to life. As Graeco-Roman polytheism never succeeded in doing, these cults seized upon the individual and, in return for practices which we may call ascetic and as a result of special mystical ceremonies, made him a divine creature by making him one with his lord. Thus the immortalized human no longer needed to make his peace with the circumscribed life of a world going to pieces. He enjoyed the special protection of the god or goddess to whom he had specially dedicated himself through initiation ceremonies and from whom he might expect a blessed immortality when he departed this vale of tears. He achieved this security, moreover, in highly stimulating and exciting ways. The gods and goddesses themselves came from the fabulous and exotic East. Their religious services were directed by a special authoritative priesthood who could read holy books written in fanciful characters and who dressed in extravagant and luxurious vestments. These services, moreover, were deeply emotional. They used music, wine, and special sacramental mysteries to help the participant to lose touch with the world about him and make him feel a part of the world above.

MANI AND MANICHAEANISM

One more non-Christian oriental religion spread westward into the Roman Empire, that of the Persian prophet Mani (Manichaeanism). Mani began to preach at Ctesiphon in 242 and was executed some thirty-four years later by the Sassanid Persian king Bahram I. By the middle of the fourth century his faith had spread into the Latin West, the greatest Father of the Latin church, Saint Augustine, becoming a Manichee for nine years. A powerful rival of Christianity, final remnants of its belief were

[42]See p. 153.
[43]Cumont, in *Oriental Religions in Roman Paganism*, pp. 197 ff., has tried to describe this synthesis.

later to be found among the Albigensian heretics in medieval Europe.[44] Mani went back to the older Zoroastrian dualism for his conception of the two eternal substances of Light and Dark that, although originally separate, are hopelessly interconnected in this present world and are to be forever separate in the future. For it is the mixture of light and dark that is evil, a reflection of the terrible mixture of good and bad that constitutes human beings. Indeed, this earth of ours has been made by a Primal Man, a fallen creature, out of the excrement of the evil demons of darkness. Into the strange mythology used to explain how the evil mixture of light and darkness came about Mani introduced an Adam, a creation also of the evil demons of darkness and a mixture of light and darkness. Jesus, a heavenly being, appears to this Adam, and by making him eat of the Tree of Life reveals to him the impossible and evil mixture that he is. "By continence and renunciation he must set free little by little the Divine Substance [light] within him, thereby joining in the great work of distillation with which God is occupied in the universe."[45] Had Adam not been corrupted by Eve, God's purpose would have been completed and Adam's descendants, mixtures of light and darkness, never been born. Mani, however, the last of the prophets (Buddha, Zoroaster, and Jesus), teaches how to bring about the ultimate distillation between light and dark. When the light goes, the earth will burn for 1468 years.

THE MANICHAEAN ELECT

Mani's followers were divided into two groups, the Elect, or clergy, and the Hearers, or laity. "All Manichees were vegetarians, but the Elect abstained from wine, from marriage, and from property." The actions of the Elect were so restricted (they could not even break their own bread "lest they pain the Light which was mixed with it") that they were accompanied by disciple-servants. The Hearers provided food for the Elect, who, partaking of it through the filter of their own purity, were able to retain the light particles until their deaths caused them to join the realm of light. Thus the Elect were necessary to the distillation process. The Manichaeans took a very dim view of the present world and of man himself, but they did not despair of the eventual separation of the good from the evil, of the light from the dark; and this realm of light, into which the light particles imprisoned in the individual would ultimately disappear, was to them a realm "altogether swayed by Intelligence, Reason, Mind, good Imagination, and good Intention."[46]

NEOPLATONISM

As Manichaeanism was essentially the last pre-Christian religion to help to give meaning to the phrase "orientalization of the Roman Empire," so

[44]See pp. 609 f.
[45]F. C. Burkitt, "The Christian Church in the East," *Cambridge Ancient History*, XII, 507–508. [46]Ibid., pp. 510–514.

Neoplatonism was the last pagan philosophy to do so. As the mystery religions helped the inhabitants of the empire to escape a melancholy world and attend to the salvation of their own souls, so Neoplatonism also contributed to this end. It is curious that whenever the world seems to be in need of the greatest reformation so many humans are inclined to reject or deny it. The founder of the new Platonism was the Egyptian philosopher Plotinus (204–270), whose school lasted as long as any pagan school of philosophy, that is, until closed by the emperor Justinian in 529. Plotinus studied in Alexandria and actually wished to absorb firsthand the philosophies of Persia and India. When this proved impossible he established a school in Rome. Because, according to his disciple and biographer, Porphyry, "the emperor Gallienus and his wife Salonia greatly honored, even worshiped, Plotinus," he sought to receive their support for the rebuilding of what was thought to have once been a City of Philosophers in Campania. The city was to be called Platonopolis, and the population was intended to live under Plato's laws. But the plan did not work out. It was Porphyry, too, who, after Plotinus's death, edited the manuscripts of his lectures and published them as the *Enneads*.

Neoplatonism, then, was the adaptation of the philosophy of Plato (and Aristotle) to the needs of the inhabitants of a declining world state. It illustrates the way philosophers had come to interpret the original teachings of Plato. Plato's philosophy, in spite of its general humanistic quality, possessed certain ascetic and mystic features.[47] The ascetic had to do with the dualism between body and soul that Plato took over from the Orphics, and the mystic with the exalted contemplation of ultimate reality, that is, of those transcendent ideas that give reality to things. It was the ascetic and mystical phases of Plato's thought that came to be emphasized by Hellenistic writers and those Platonists who, after the second century A.D., brought about the revival of Platonism that culminated in Neoplatonism. It is quite clear that Plotinus's chief emphases are ascetic and mystical.

HELLENISTIC DEFINITIONS OF GOD

There was, however, another feature common to post-Platonic and Aristotelian philosophy that is to be found culminating in Plotinus. This is the effort to arrive at a satisfactory definition of God and to relate God to the human scene. It will be recalled that we cannot be too sure of Plato's exact notion of divinity and that Aristotle's definition was the "unmoved mover."[48] Plato's concept of divinity was related to his concept of the absolute ideas. It was the highest of these ideas, the idea of the good, or the quintessence of these ideas: an absolute composed of beauty, goodness, nobility, love, and the rest. Aristotle's God was related to his

[47]See pp. 137 f.
[48]See p. 145.

theory of causes[49] as the first cause. Subsequent philosophers and theologians in defining God tried to combine the notion of God as a supreme absolute and as a first cause, to fuse the Platonic and Aristotelian ideas. In other words, Hellenistic philosophers were endeavoring to establish a kind of Greek monotheism of a severely impersonal, abstract, and intellectual kind, quite unlike the monotheism of the Hebrews. Moreover, they were trying to explain the universe in terms of such a God. How could what was defined as a combination of first cause and abstract quality actually influence the world of human affairs? To some this could be explained on the analogy of God and the Sun. Just as the Sun, without outside help and without suffering any loss, gives off rays of heat, light, and power, so God is the source of radiation of divine power responsible for the life, beauty, and orderliness of the universe. Some Hellenistic philosophers liked to compare the workings of this God with the workings of an oriental theocrat who, from the depth of his divine palace, sent out his stream of royal power through his agents. God thus sent out his divine ray of power to be administered by agents or mediators between himself and man. Others, and this was more common, who interpreted God essentially as mind referred to the Divine Mind's expressing itself in a "stream of Utterance,"[50] written or oral, and this utterance was called in Greek the divine *logos*, or as it is translated in the Fourth Gospel, the "Word."[51] The intellectual God therefore makes and maintains the universe through his spoken word or the written word that he has inspired. God is related to the world only through his logos, his word. If, accordingly, the purpose of life is to escape life (ascetic) and to seek to become identified with the divine source from which it comes (mystic), the approach must be made through God's mediator, the logos.

PHILO

It is obvious that these Greek efforts to define God and relate him to man were quite unlike those of the Jewish prophets, and yet they were so influential that when the Greek world penetrated the East attempts were made to transform Judaism into a Greek mystery religion. These attempts were of tremendous influence, not only upon Neoplatonism, but upon Christian thought itself. A conspicuous attempt of this kind to harmonize Jewish religion and Greek thought is found in the writings of Philo, an Alexandrian Jewish contemporary of Jesus. Yahweh becomes for him a

---

[49]See pp. 146 f.

[50]The phrase in E. R. Goodenough, *Religious Tradition and Myth*, p. 48.

[51]There seem to be Egyptian and Babylonian sources also for this idea of the logos. Thus, "all the divine order really came into being through what the heart [of Ptah] thought and the tongue commanded."—Pritchard, *Ancient Near Eastern Texts*, pp. 5, 66. In the Babylonian creation epic, Marduk is given power to "wreck or create" by opening his mouth, and the gods rejoice in the "fruit of his word."—J. A. Wilson, *Intellectual Adventure of Ancient Man*, pp. 56 ff. Yahweh also creates in this way in Genesis I.

Greek absolute, and Moses, Abraham, and Isaac incarnations of the logos, or word, of Yahweh through whom man was saved and returned to his divine source. Moses did not die but was received into heaven to become the intercessor for all men, and as they become "initiates of Moses, they are freed from the body, [and] brought to the life of the spirit or *logos*, as once he had lead them out of Egypt." And this life of the spirit prepares them for the supreme religious experience, the vision of, and union with, God, about which mystic writers are never very clear even though they express this vagueness in vivid language. Philo, for instance, asks, "What lovelier or more fitting garland could be woven for the victorious soul, than the power, with clear vision to gaze on him who is? Truly splendid is the prize held out to the wrestling soul—to be equipped with eyesight so as to perceive without dimness him who is alone worthy of contemplation." At the crucial moment he may "appear to you visibly, causing incorporeal rays to shine upon you, granting visions of his nature, undreamed of and ineffable, which are the overflowing sources of all other blessings." This is not only an intellectual but a highly emotional experience. "By divine possession," Philo says, "I fell into a rapture and became ignorant of everything, the place, those present, myself and what was spoken or written." Under these circumstances the soul "is kindled into a flame of thanksgiving to God and becomes drunken with that drunkenness which does not intoxicate. . . . In the case of the God-possessed not only is the soul wont to be stirred and driven into frenzy, but to be flushed and inflamed, since the joy which wells up within and makes the spirit glow transmits the experience to the outward parts."[52]

THE NEOPLATONIC TRINITY

In the mind of Plotinus the new Platonism became a very rigid, difficult, and ascetic system of religious mysticism and, it may be said at once, the source of the philosophical mysticism in Christianity. For Plotinus God could not be expressed in positive terms at all. As a kind of ultimate, ineffable, absolute unity, the source of all being, he is simply the One. "We can say," he says, "what it *is not*, but not what it *is*." Still it is "greater than all we call being, greater and better than reason and intelligence and sense, though it is that which gives them whatsoever reality they have."[53] From this indefinable and unknowable One the universe and world of man have emanated, but not directly; rather through mediators. The first emanation, or irradiation, is Divine Mind, or Thought, which is a kind of universal intelligence and contains within it all the Platonic ideas in accordance with which the world was fashioned. These ideas can of course be known or understood. But the Divine Mind is not the active and immediate creator

[52]Reprinted from *Pagan Regeneration* by H. R. Willoughby, pp. 245–248, by permission of The University of Chicago Press. Copyright 1929 by The University of Chicago Press.
[53]Edward Caird, *Evolution of Theology in the Greek Philosophers*, p. 219.

of this world. For from the Divine Mind there proceeds another emanation: World, or Universal Soul, which impregnates the formless matter of the world with the divine ideas that make the world about us what it is. In this way man receives from the World Soul his individual soul, and thus reality enters the universe. For formless matter is itself nothing at all without this impregnation with the ideas contained in the Divine Mind. In fact, it is worse than nothing. It is what Plotinus calls evil, and is thus something to be avoided or shunned. The body as something material is evil and to be put aside. Indeed, the individual soul inherits from the World Soul the desire to return to the divine source from which it came. Thus all emanations from the One seek to be reabsorbed in the One, as in the Manichaean system all particles of light seek to be reabsorbed in the realm of light.

NEOPLATONIC MYSTICISM

The general method to be used in preparing the individual soul for its ascent or return to the One is a combination of asceticism and contemplation. The unpurified soul cannot hope to return. But by ascetic exercises the soul may be taught to get along without body and matter; and by contemplation it may avoid the sensual in the search for the eternal. Under circumstances such as these it is possible for the individual to achieve at rare moments during his lifetime an ecstatic vision of the One, which actually absorbs him into it and for an incredible moment makes him wholly godlike. Plotinus, we are told, achieved this state on four occasions.

Plotinus uses extraordinary language to express the emanative process and the return to the One. "Over against the body stands the Principle [the One], self-caused, which neither is born nor passes away and whose dissolution would mean the end of all things never to be restored. . . . There is the Divine Mind living the purely intellective life. . . . But immediately following upon It there is that [the World Soul] which desires to produce order on the model of what it has seen in the Intellectual Realm; pregnant by those Beings [the ideas] and in pain to the birth, it is eager to create. In this new zest it strains towards the realm of sense. It is partly in body, partly outside of it. It has plunged from among the primals and entered this sphere of the third rank. Thus Divine Mind while remaining in Itself operates through Soul to flood the universe with beauty and penetrant order—immortal Mind, eternal in its unfailing energy, acting through immortal Soul." Yet "the soul by nature loves God and longs to be at one with Him in the noble love of a daughter for a noble father; but coming to human birth and lured by the courtships of this sphere, she takes up with another love, a mortal, leaves her father and falls. But one day coming to hate her shame, she puts off evil, once more seeks her father and finds peace. . . . The soul takes on another life as it approaches God; thus restored, it feels that the Dispenser of true Life is There and that we must put aside all else and rest in This alone, This become, This alone, all the earthly environmnt done away, in haste to be free, impatient of any bond holding us to the baser, so that with our entire being we may cling about This, no part in us remaining but through it we may touch God.

"Thus we have all the vision that may be of Him and of ourselves; but it is of a self wrought to splendor, brimmed with the Intellectual light, *become* that very light, pure, buoyant, unburdened, raised to Godhood, rather identical with God, all aflame then, but flickering out if it should take up again the discarded burden. . . . This is the life of gods and of godlike and blessed men,—liberation from the alien that besets us here, a life taking no pleasure in the things of earth—a flight of the alone to the Alone."[54]

LATER DISCIPLES OF PLOTINUS

The severe and exalted character of Plotinus's mysticism was not maintained by his disciples and followers. Neoplatonism, as the last refuge of the pagan world, took up the battle with Christianity, which to its best minds was "a fabulous and formless darkness mastering the loveliness of the world."[55] Porphyry, for example, wrote a very famous book, *Against the Christians*, which earned for him from the intemperate Christian Father Jerome such epithets as "a scoundrel, an impudent fellow, a vilifier, a sycophant, a lunatic and a mad dog."[56] But in coming to the defense of pagan culture Neoplatonism had to come to the defense of an orientalized Graeco-Roman paganism and, accordingly, of the superstitious, magical practices of popular religion. With these it compromised as Stoicism had compromised. Iamblichus (d. 330), the Neoplatonist authority at the moment of Christianity's toleration, admitted the existence of as many as 360 divine entities, twenty-one so-called lords of the world, and forty-two gods of nature.[57] Those who came after him transformed Neoplatonism into a complicated system of theurgy, a system of magical compulsion of the gods. At the same time, however, the dependence of Plotinus upon Plato and Aristotle kept the school busy with reading and commenting upon their works at a time when Jerome rejoiced, "What a handful now reads Aristotle! How many know the books or the name of Plato? Hardly do old men at leisure study them in seclusion." Indeed, it has been remarked, with nice appreciation, that "the closing of the [Neoplatonic] Academy at Athens in A.D. 529 is not so remarkable as its continued existence till that date."[58]

[54]G. H. Turnbull, *The Essence of Plotinus*, pp. 142, 145, 219–220, 222.
[55]E. R. Dodds, *Select Passages Illustrative of Neoplatonism*, p. 8.
[56]J. Bidez, "Literature and Philosophy in the Eastern Half of the Empire," *Cambridge Ancient History*, XII, 634.
[57]Bidez, XII, 636.
[58]A. D. Nock, *Sallustius*, p. xxv.

CHRISTIANITY AND THE ROMAN STATE

In his *Confessions*[59] Saint Augustine points out how his study of Neo-platonism made it possible for him to understand some of the Christian teachings that had hitherto been a puzzle to him, and how this new understanding made easier his conversion to Christianity. What was true for Saint Augustine was undoubtedly true for many Romans educated in Greek philosophy. For those who were initiates of, or were acquainted with, the Greek and oriental mystery cults Christianity might seem somewhat familiar. Yet the final stage in the orientalization of the Roman Empire, its turning to Christianity, was only in part the result of a preparation made by other Graeco-oriental religions and Graeco-oriental philosophy. It came also after some four centuries of intermittent struggle with the Roman state. This struggle is of great importance to the history of the western tradition, not simply because Christianity was victorious, but because of the very issue involved: whether the state, a political despotism, could successfully dictate to all its citizens in questions of conscience. The fundamental issue was concerned with freedom of the mind and heart from political tyranny.

ATTITUDE OF THE STATE TOWARD RELIGION

In religious matters the Roman state was fairly tolerant. It did not concern itself with the religious beliefs of its citizens in so far as those beliefs did not have political implications or very serious social or moral implications—for instance, the practice of human sacrifice in Druidism. Indeed, any polytheistic system very easily adds gods and goddesses to its pantheon. Accordingly, the Roman pantheon had expanded as the empire itself had expanded. Upon the religious calendar of the *pontifex maximus* were put the festivals first of Roman, then of Greek, and finally of oriental gods. There is a sense, however, in which Roman public religion was altogether political, that is, concerned with the state. The purpose of this public religion was not to save individual souls but to maintain the peace of the gods (*pax deorum*). Unwillingness to participate in the services conducted by the official priesthoods to maintain the peace of the gods meant, obviously, that one was not interested in seeing that this peace was maintained. Such an attitude was unpatriotic.

EMPEROR WORSHIP AND POLITICS

The development of emperor worship added to the political nature of public religion. Originally Augustus was worshiped together with the goddess Roma (Rome), clearly a recognition of the divine hegemony over the world of the city of Rome as well as of its ruler. As, from the third century on, every living emperor came to be regarded as a god, emperor worship was a divine sanction for a particular form of govern-

[59]See pp. 344 f.

ment, namely tyranny. A refusal, therefore, to participate in the public services acknowledging the emperor to be divine was tantamount to a refusal to recognize the divine hegemony of Rome and the divine character of its government. Such an attitude, from the Roman point of view, was clearly subversive.

The early Christians put themselves into the category of unpatriotic and subversive citizens by refusing to participate in public religious services. This they did to uphold their belief in ethical monotheism. Having once won his battle with the gods and goddesses of Palestine, the Christian Yahweh did not intend to compromise with Graeco-Roman polytheism. And while Graeco-Roman polytheism could understand a supreme god, one over all the others, it could not understand an exclusive one-and-only god that took over all the little specialized functions of the rest. When the Roman emperors from about the middle of the third century decided to exterminate Christianity it was because they felt that Christians were an unreliable political element in society at a moment when, if ever, the Roman Empire needed reliable citizens.

EARLY PERSECUTION OF THE CHRISTIANS

Before this (*ca.* A.D. 250) there was not much persecution of Christians. What there was was local rather than widespread, and sporadic rather than persistent. It resulted, moreover, from local popular hostility rather than from a deliberate policy of the central government. The early Christians were to the ordinary Roman strange, unsocial, fanatical creatures. They held to impossible beliefs about the speedy termination of this world, followed by the inauguration of another by their Lord. This certain event made all preoccupation with the Roman world unnecessary and futile. While they held to the immediate coming of the Lord they refused, if a recognition of pagan worship was necessary, to support those institutions that held the Roman state upright. They could not serve in the army and often denounced the military. They could not hold public office. They could not participate in pagan festivals and games. In addition, the Roman state was very fearful of private meetings of its citizens. It did not like to have even the fire brigades meet to discuss their affairs. The secret nightly meetings of subversive initiates into the mystery of Christ, often in underground cemeteries, gave rise to rumors inflaming the hostility of pagan mobs. Were not these Christians guilty of cannibalism and incest as well as subversion? Officials bowing before popular passions of this kind were responsible for persecutions in Rome, Vienne, and Lyons in the first and second centuries. The policy of the central government is stated in Trajan's answer to Pliny the Younger:[60] the Christians had to be dealt with if they were publicly accused, but officials were not to seek them out, and they were to take care that accusations were based on more than

[60]See p. 223.

private grievances. This meant that, for about two centuries and a half, the Christians, by and large, were unmolested in their new sanctuaries.

MODIFICATION OF CHRISTIAN HOSTILITY TO THE STATE

As it became necessary to postpone the second coming of the Lord into the remote future the hostility between Christians and Roman society became less bitter. The Roman Empire was still, as Augustine was to say, an earthly kingdom founded by the devil and would disappear some day before the victorious heavenly kingdom founded by God, but, until that time came, Christians did have to live in this world, and if they wished to share in the advantages it had to offer they had better share its burdens. More and more Christians did serve in the army and hold public office. They made it clear that they did not oppose the state as such, that, on the contrary, their religon taught them to respect authority. And if they could not worship pagan gods and a pagan emperor they could at least pray to their God on behalf of a pagan emperor.

TOLERATION OF CHRISTIANITY

Such an attitude on the part of Christians made it clear to the political leaders that Christians were not necessarily subversive or antisocial. The attempts of the reforming emperors after Decius (Valerian, Aurelian, Galerius, and Diocletian) to exterminate Christianity thus seemed unnecessarily cruel. The Christians, moreover, were not all to be intimidated. The steadfast refusal of their heroes to renounce their faith for their lives made an impression upon the pagan world. Tertullian pointed out that "the blood of the martyrs is the seed of the Church." Magistrates and officials went out of their way to make it easy for Christians to seem to have performed the necessary rites for compliance with the state cult. Local populations became obviously sympathetic with persecuted Christians whom they knew well as neighbors. In any case, persecution, followed up as it always was by respite and hesitation to go to the full length of extermination, always permitted the Church, increasingly well-organized and fervent, to recover its strength. The Christians were gaining in numbers, not losing, and obviously could not be destroyed except at costs which the state was unwilling to expend. The number of victims was greatest in the decade before 311, when Galerius, repenting his cruelty on his deathbed, granted toleration to Christians. He was followed in this by Constantine, the first Christian emperor, who, it will be remembered, founded a new Christian capital at Constantinople. Constantine, although baptized into the Arian form of Christianity only at the point of death (337), had long before this regarded himself as a Christian. He had come to believe that in his struggle for the imperial throne he was supported by the Christian God, and he came to realize the importance of building a decadent state anew upon the enthusiasm and strength of the Christians, no matter how small a minority they might be at that time. The document containing the grant of toleration is known as the Edict of Milan (313). It states that "it accords with the good order of the realm and the peacefulness of our times that each should have freedom to worship God after his own choice; and we do not intend to detract from the honor due to any religion or its followers."[61] Actually the legislation of Constantine's sole rule indicates that he did far more than merely tolerate Christianity. He granted it a position among the religions of the empire from which it sprang inevitably to favor.

THE VICTORY OF CHRISTIANITY

It is unfortunate that paganism could not have tolerated Christianity before Constantine. It is likewise unfortunate that Christianity could not have tolerated paganism after Constantine. We might then have had a completely peaceful solution of the religious problem of the empire. No Christian, however, could regard it as a victory to be put on a par with a pagan worshiper. It was, on the contrary, an insult to the Christian God to be made an equal of the pagan demons. There could be no victory until Christianity was made not merely a tolerated religion but the only religion tolerated in the Roman Empire, that is, the exclusive Roman religion. Only the emperors could do this. In addition, from the point of view of certain Christians there could be no adequate solution of the religious problem until orthodox Christianity was made the exclusive state religion and heretical Christianity was outlawed. Both of these things Christianity achieved by the end of the fourth century, during the reign of the emperor Theodosius (379–395). During the years 361 to 363 the scholarly emperor Julian tried to restore paganism upon the philosophical basis of Neoplatonism, with certain improvements in organization and social service borrowed from Christianity. This he felt should be done peacefully. "Men should be taught and won over by reason, not by blows, insults and corporal punishments. . . . Those who are in the wrong in matters of supreme importance are objects of pity rather than of hate." But paganism could not be restored at this date in this or in any other way. The legislation of Theodosius made sacrifice to pagan gods illegal, indeed, an act of treason. It distinguished also between "Catholic Christians" and "the others . . . foolish madmen," who were to be branded "with the ignominious name of heretics, and shall not presume to give to their conventicles the name of churches."[62]

THE NATURE OF THE CHRISTIAN VICTORY

Thus a despotic Roman government with a divine emperor (secular theocracy) was obliged to admit that it could not eradicate a religion that

[61]Henry Bettenson, *Documents of the Christian Church*, p. 23.
[62]Ibid., pp. 29, 30–31.

refused to recognize its divine foundation. Christianity was tolerated, and this was a victory for intellectual and spiritual, in short religious, freedom. But this victory was comparatively short-lived. For the tolerated Christian Church was itself neither politically nor religiously tolerant. It could not tolerate as rulers other than Christian emperors (it made no difference how despotic) any more than it could tolerate other than Christians as citizens. In fact, the Christian Church, as we shall see more fully later,[63] was developing the characteristics of an ecclesiastical theocracy—a church-state headed by a chief priest. This ecclesiastical theocracy, the possessor and enforcer of the divinely revealed truth, was less tolerant than the Roman secular theocracy. It was called upon, as others were, to support the state, and how could it in conscience sanction anything that was not in conformity with what it believed to be the truth—the revealed Christian truth? The complete victory of Christianity by the end of the fourth century had nothing to do with either political or religious freedom. The Roman state continued to be a despotism, supported by a single, intolerant religion. From the Christian point of view there had been a great victory, inasmuch as Christian truth had been substituted for pagan error. But the history of Christianity in the last years of the fourth and the early years of the fifth century included the forceful and often violently fanatical uprooting of a pagan religion that refused to die simply because it had been legally condemned, the work, often, of mobs led by hysterical monks and clergy.

AGAIN THE PROBLEM OF DECLINE AND FALL

Let us now come back to our original problem. Can we point with any confidence to the causes of the decline and fall of the Roman Empire, that have been sketched above? We could, of course, supply an answer with greater confidence if our social sciences had proved without doubt what it is that keeps a society alive, vigorous, and at its peak. Without this positive assurance we must do our best with the facts available, the suggestions that have been made, and our experience with our own civilization. We have already taken *fall* to mean the loss of the Latin West to a group of German kings and *decline* to mean (1) whatever contributed to this fall and (2) the growing absence of creative ability in literature and the fine arts. If, with this definition in mind, we should rephrase our problem we should have to ask, Why was Rome unable to maintain the Rhine and Danube frontiers against the barbarian? And if we could answer this problem satisfactorily we should still have to ask—for keeping out the barbarian would not have stemmed what we have called decline but at most would have prolonged it—Why did the Roman people cease to be creative?[64]

[63]See p. 337.
[64]That is, in a pagan sense. For the history of Christianity is the history of creativity.

The inability of the Romans to maintain their frontiers had to do in part with the inability of the Roman state to support a military force large enough to hold such very long frontiers everywhere, and the inability of the Roman state to support a huge military force had to do with the unwillingness of Roman citizens to undertake the large sacrifices necessary to maintain such a military establishment. Indications of that unwillingness are to be seen in the fact that the Roman state was unable to rely upon its best citizens to fight in its army. They came finally from the less civilized regions of the empire. In fact, the Roman state could not even rely exclusively upon its own citizens to man its army. As we have seen, it had to employ the barbarian mercenary in ever-increasing numbers. Indeed, to obtain recruits for the legions it was necessary to offer special inducements to citizens and mercenaries alike and these inducements were grants of land on the frontier. When, in the third century, military leaders whose power rested upon the support of the army rose to the purple, the public treasury and public lands were turned over by emperors to the soldiers. In the civil wars between rival generals for the imperial office, a chronic situation in the third century, the empire itself became an object of plunder for rival armies. Thus it can certainly be said that the inability of the otherwise practical Romans to work out a regular system for succession to the imperial authority helped to produce those chronic disorders at the end of every reign that made it possible for the army to interfere and supply its own candidate, the general. In this way the Empire became a military state. The very expansion of the state during the Republic had upset the relationship between civilian and military control, and the insecurity of the frontiers after, and even during, the Pax Romana helped to maintain this imbalance. War, without doubt, contributed to the decline and fall.

In attributing the fall to the unwillingness of the Roman citizen to assume the obligations necessary to maintain a sufficiently large military establishment we approach also the essential reason for what we have described as the growing absence of creative activity: the fact that to the great bulk of citizens this state was not worth defending or doing one's best for. Here we are dealing with the "dull resentment [of the citizens] towards the Empire with its expensive and cumbrous machinery which did so little for them. . . . When soldiers of the Empire were branded, like runaway slaves, it was obvious that men were no longer willing to fight for it: and in many provinces barbarian invaders found an eager welcome from the subject classes, for under a barbarian king, though their status was not improved, they had no longer to bear the expenses of Roman government. Thus the Empire was forced to depend upon highly subsidised barbarians for its defence, and when with the loss of Africa the West could no longer pay its defenders, they turned and broke it."[65]

[65]Stevens, "Agriculture and Rural Life," *Cambridge Economic History*, I, 117.

In the *Politics* Aristotle remarks that "a tyrant is fond of making wars, as a means of keeping his subjects in employment and in continual need of a commander." This statement follows his analysis of other measures taken by tyrants "to prevent mutual confidence among the citizens, to incapacitate them for action, and to degrade their spirit." These are "the practice of cutting off prominent characters and putting out of the way the high spirits in the state; the prohibition of common meals, political clubs, high culture and everything else of the same kind; precautionary measures against all that tends to produce two results, *viz.*, spirit and confidence; the opposition offered to literary *réunions* or any other meetings of a literary kind, and the endeavor by every possible means to produce the greatest mutual ignorance among all the citizens, as it is acquaintance that tends to produce mutual confidence. . . . Another expedient is the endeavor to prevent any word or action of any subject from escaping detection by a system of spies. . . . For the citizens are then less free of speech for fear of the spies and, if they do speak freely, are more easily discovered."[66] Aristotle's acute observations suggest that it was the breakdown of republican institutions in the course of expansion and the resulting development of one-man power culminating in the principate to which is to be traced the fundamental cause of the indifference of the citizen to the state. In other words, the inability of the Roman to realize the democratic implications of the Republic not only for the city-state of Rome but for the whole empire led straight to tyranny, to theocracy, or, as we may also put it, to a Roman totalitarian state. Having failed to deal properly with serious political, economic, and social problems as they arose, the Romans were finally led to abandon all responsibility to the sacred despot. Despotic methods destroyed the hopes, ambition, and initiative of all classes of citizens and made all, except the upper crust of the military, court officials, bureaucracy, and landed senatorials, the slaves—in many cases the virtually hereditary slaves—of an omnipotent state. The individual citizen was accordingly denied the opportunity to develop his capacities. If the despot destroyed the liberty of the individual citizen and the freedom of action of all classes, he also liquidated and impoverished those who looked back to the good old republican days: the senatorial class in Rome and the curial class in the provinces. Upon these classes, moreover, and especially upon the urban middle classes of the provincial towns, had rested, during the centuries of the Pax Romana, the responsibility for maintaining a high level of civilized existence. This liquidation of the older social classes was the result of civil struggles for power and for the profits of power. It was, in a sense, the result of a social war that had been produced by the inequalities in wealth, prestige, and power brought about by the growth of empire and the resulting exploitation of its physical and human resources.

[66]C. H. McIlwain, *Constitutionalism, Ancient and Modern*, pp. 39–40.

The liquidation of the old and the establishment of new privileged classes brought cultural decline, the cessation of creative activity, reversion to primitive conditions and to a primitive mentality. What had previously been a process of civilization, Romanization, and assimilation from top to bottom, from aristocrat to plutocrat, from privileged to unprivileged, from Roman to provincial, from civilized to barbarian, was now reversed before it had been completed. It was now ignorance, superstition, bad taste, violence, brute force, servility, and irresponsibility that triumphed. Since hope, promise, liberty, and even security were increasingly denied; since, in other words, what we have called the humanistic ideal, never passionately cultivated by the Romans, was rudely abandoned; since this world became a hard, ruthless battle for survival, men turned, as they have always turned under similar circumstances, to the comforts of religions and philosophies that emphasized compensation and self-realization in another world. And this, we have to say, was an abdication of human responsibility, however understandable, brought about by those who really had no respect for the larger interests of mankind. It was, moreover, a turn to a new kind of despotism or theocracy, spiritual and ecclesiastical this time: the theocracy of a church that absorbed, in the course of its spread, the whole culture of the Roman Empire in its declining days. Thus we may suggest that among the larger reasons for the decline and fall of the Roman state were (1) the prevalence of war, which preserved the imbalance between civil and military interests first brought about by the creation of the empire; (2) the tyrannical imperial government, which reduced the citizens to slaves of the state; (3) the inability of the ruling classes to extend the advantages of civilized society to all members of the state; and (4) the general acceptance of otherworldly religions and philosophies that helped to create the notion that the world was hopelessly evil and, consequently, that it was best to concern oneself with the salvation of one's own soul. This is to suggest that the failure of classical civilization to fulfill its democratic and humanistic promise deprived it of the support of the vast mass of its citizens, or it is to say that the failure of the ancient world is basically concerned with the triumph of the Ancient Near East (in Roman form) over Greece.

If we used the somewhat more technical language of Professor Toynbee[67] to explain this decline and fall—and he would say every other decline and fall—it would be something like this: The Romans failed to respond to the challenge of properly governing a world state and extending the blessings of a high civilization to all its members. Its *creative minority*, that is, its wealthy, aristocratic governing class, ceased to create; failed, we

[67]See p. 264. Cf. Toynbee, IV, 61, where the interpretation is different in detail.

should say, to solve adequately the complicated problems ensuing from the establishment of a world state, abandoning thereby its roles of leadership and modes of conduct that might have inspired lesser men to higher things. It transformed itself into a merely *dominant minority*, a tyrannical minority ready to use force and ever more force to maintain its irresponsible and exploitative position. When this condition had persisted for some time it automatically produced a revolt of the proletariat. Toynbee speaks of the revolt of the *internal proletariat*, which abandoned a state that had never taken it seriously. The internal proletariat transferred its faith to religion. He speaks also of the *external proletariat*—the barbarian world on the frontier—which took advantage of the revolution of the internal proletariat to march in and take over a state thus incapable of defending itself.

THE ROMANS AND AMERICANS

Now what, considering the character of the world in which we live today, may we say is the meaning of this Roman experience for us Americans? We are often compared with the Romans and not in a very complimentary way. We are the cultureless boors of the world threatening its future with the imposition of a drab Pax Americana. Like the Romans we have no soul, being devoted only to dollars and technology. Like the Romans we have no taste, cultivating only what is big, brassy, and expensive. Like them we passionately pursue comfort and cleanliness with gadgets and plumbing; and, with our wealth and our engineering, we aim to impose a materialistic civilization whose symbols are the automobile and the television set.

Those who talk or write this way do not know Americans very well. Yet this is not to say that the history of the Romans is not an instructive one for a people who find themselves, as we do, in a position of world leadership, a position such as the Romans were in after the Punic Wars. Our position of world leadership is challenged by the Soviet Union and her Communist satellites as the Roman position, of course, was never challenged. We are, therefore, more properly, the leader of the western European nations and of those nations whose civilizations have been determined by western influences. This position of leadership has come to us as a result of two world wars, which, largely fought in Europe, have to a great extent destroyed the wealth and power of the leading nations of western Europe, leaving us with our vast economic resources comparatively intact. We are trying to perform a leading role among western nations in the defense of a tradition common to them all—what is called the western tradition, having to do with democratic government, democratic societies, and essentially democratic cultures. We stand in relationship to this tradition in much the same position as the Romans did to the democratic and humanistic tradition of the Greeks. We are the products of it, and however much we may have contributed to it we have in the past been constantly dependent upon the stimulus of the culture of the western European nations. We are thus in the position of the Romans on the eve of their entrance into eastern Mediterranean politics. They went in to help to defend the Greek world against the ambitions of an aggressive oriental world that existed beyond it. We find ourselves going in to help to defend a western European world against the ambitions of an aggressive eastern world that exists beyond it.

In the course of her expansion Rome permitted this earlier idealism to be supplanted by a hard, cruel, selfish, and exploitative imperialism. Indeed, she may be said to have learned nothing from Athenian, Spartan, or Carthaginian imperialism. She went her own way. The result was, first of all, to crush the democratic promise of the early republican government and society by turning over this government and society to the leadership of military-minded dictators catering to the profiteers of imperialism. Thus, as Athens failed to extend her city-state democracy to her empire, so Rome, having ceased to develop as a city-state democracy, or even to resemble one, was in no position to extend democracy to her world-wide empire. Her ruling classes failed to share the sympathies and aspirations not only of all Romans but of all peoples whom the Romans conquered. There was, to be sure, the interlude of the Pax Romana, but by and large the Roman Empire developed as a despotism. She could not prevent herself from being overwhelmed by oriental rather than Greek notions of government, economics, society, religion, and philosophy. In so doing she lost the support of her citizens, who ceased to care finally whether a state and civilization so indifferent to their needs and hopes really stood or not.

At the moment when America is entering upon her career of world leadership the democratic development of her own domestic political, economical, social, and cultural institutions has by no means been completed. How incomplete they are her critics and enemies love to point out. If the pursuit of a world career should mean for Americans that this democratic development will be cut short and that, as in the case of Rome, the results of participation in world politics will be even to reverse this development and, to pursue the analogy, bring about a permanent imbalance between civilian and military needs (establishing the military in the chief offices of government and transforming the nation into a permanent army), then it can be supposed that Americans will quickly return to their isolationism and cultivate a decided apathy for governments pursuing such policies. That Americans will follow in the footsteps of Roman imperialism is less likely, for we, as well as others, have learned much from the history of this and other imperialisms. Moreover, international organizations such as the United Nations, the North Atlantic Pact, and the Pan-American Union have been set up to safeguard against such an eventuality. Yet there is always danger that Americans, like the Romans, will grow impatient at the slowness of international machinery and at the lack of efficiency displayed by our friends in making contributions to the common effort or in raising their own standards of living. There is always the crude American nationalist who thinks that because he pays his dollars he should run the show. There is danger that Americans, as the task of leadership becomes ever greater and more complicated, will be tempted to by-pass international organizations and go their own way in the world, without taking into consideration the needs and aspirations not only of their friends and allies in the western world but of all those whom they wish to wean away from international communism and bring to the democratic way. The Roman experience would suggest that if Americans succumb to this temptation to dominate rather than to share, they will undermine the loyalty of their friends, forfeit the friendship of those undecided, and immeasurably strengthen their enemies. As in the case of Rome, this is the way to decline and fall.

CULTURE AND DEMOCRACY

There is a final point to be mentioned in this connection. A distinguished American historian of the ancient world, in discussing the problem of the decline, remarks, "The main phenomenon which underlies the process of decline is the gradual absorption of the educated classes by the masses and the consequent simplification of all the functions of political, social, economic, and intellectual life, which we call the barbarization of the ancient world." He then goes on to ask the question, "Is it possible to extend a higher civilization to the lower classes without debasing its standard and diluting its quality to the vanishing point? Is not every civilization bound to decay as soon as it begins to penetrate the masses?"[68] For Americans and all adherents of the western tradition this is a crucial question, for it suggests, of course, that democracy and a high civilization are incompatible, and it would use Roman history as evidence. To many it would seem today that in our western world, and particularly in America, there is in effect an inability to pass on to the mass of citizens the cultural heritage of the past intact, not to mention improved. They argue that with the development of democratic education its quality seems to be diluted. They show that the new methods of mass education and communication, the press, the movies, radio, and television, cater, for the sake of their profits, especially to the worst and cheapest rather than to the best and noblest that is in the human being. They would suggest that the failure of Roman society to pass on to the underprivileged, as well as to the privileged, the inspiration and enrichment of the best that its best men had done is being repeated in our own society, and that if this process is not checked we may look forward to the same cheapening and barbarization of our inheritance as befell the classical inheritance in the later centuries

[68]M. I. Rostovtzeff, *The Social and Economic History of the Roman Empire*, pp. 486–487.

of the empire. Our American historian suggests also that this barbarizing process follows inevitably from the attempt to extend the blessings of a high civilization beyond a small privileged élite. It is our suggestion, on the contrary, that the Roman evidence shows that the failure of Rome to do just this, to pass on the blessings of civilization beyond a mere élite, is partly responsible for the decline and fall. If, likewise, we do not somehow check the tendency toward, or oppose the danger of, barbarization in our midst, if we do not learn to make democracy and a high civilization compatible, we may expect this failure to contribute to our own decline and fall before we have reached our peak or realized our potentialities.

THE CLASSICAL TRADITION

It remains to be pointed out that, although in reference to Roman power and culture we use these words *decline* and *fall*, we may not properly speak of *disappearance*. We have already said that there was a real fall only in the West. In the East, in the area around Constantinople, the decadent empire continued in Christian Byzantine form. In both East and West the traditions of the pagan empire persisted. They included in their turn certain aspects of the traditions of the Ancient Near East and of the Greeks. Together these are commonly referred to as the "classical tradition."[69] It is to be contrasted with the Christian tradition (considered in the following chapter), which is itself a compound of oriental, Greek, and Roman elements. It is these two, the classical and the Christian, that formed the early tradition of the West. The Christian tradition became dominant in the West in the fourth century. But at regular intervals in the history of the West its leaders have turned to the classical tradition for inspiration, enjoyment, and guidance: to its literature, art, thought, and institutions. These intervals are usually referred to as renascences, that is, rebirths or revivals of a concern with the meaning of the classical period in all its wonderful variety. We shall have to be concerned with them in this book, and although the influence of the classical tradition has become relatively less great upon recent western, and particularly American, generations, it is still vital and under proper auspices can become more vital. We have associated it with such large words as democracy and humanism, with universalism in politics and citizenship, with prolonged and widespread peace, and with the rule of law, popular in origin and universal. It will not be easy to destroy the ideas, emotions, and institutions back of these words. For as long as they exist and are vital their sources in the classical world will be a matter of precious concern to western man.

[69]See G. Highet, *The Classical Tradition.*

chapter eight

CHRISTIAN ASCETICISM

*P*ROGRAM OF THE CHAPTER. The previous chapter told of Christianity's fight with the Roman state for toleration and then for monopoly. The fact that such a powerful state was unable to exterminate Christianity is a good example of the limitations of political power when faced with a belief fervently held by a large number. The subsequent extermination of paganism is also a good example of the unlimited power of despotism when supported by the fanatical intolerance of a majority. What would have happened to Christianity without the support of the state is an interesting speculation. Surely we may not say that its victory was wholly political in character. It must accordingly be the purpose of this chapter to make clear the extent to which it was more than political. One of the points we shall have to make is that in spite of its peculiar and original features Christianity was a very eclectic and adaptive faith. At the time of its victory in the Roman Empire it had become something we may call Jewish, Greek, and Roman. It had undergone a complete transformation that has always bothered the purists in its ranks, whether Protestant or Catholic. For these prefer to see Christianity directing the historical process rather than being contaminated or changed by it. In spite, however, of what we may say is Jewish or Greek or Roman in Christianity it did succeed by the end of the classical period in elaborating in its orthodox theology a very definite point of view. This Christian point of view supplanted in the main the humanism of the Greeks and Romans. This chapter, then, must consider (1) an explanation for the Christian victory that also will illustrate (2) its adaptive genius, (3) the Christian point of view, and (4) the relationship of this point of view to classical humanism.

An Explanation for Christianity's Victory
in the Roman Empire

BASIC RELIGIOUS NEEDS

We may assume, in discussing the reasons for Christianity's victory in the Roman Empire, that its superiority was ultimately religious and that in its competition with the older Graeco-Roman paganism and the newer mystery cults it catered better than these to the fundamental religious needs of the empire's inhabitants. These fundamental religious needs are similar at all times and places. They give meaning to the phrase that man is a religious animal. If they are not taken care of in one way then they are in another. They include the following: the need for help to combat what appears to be an indifferent and even hostile world of nature and to understand what is mysterious in it and the world of man; the need for companionship and comfort to overcome the essential loneliness and tragedy of existence and to be able to believe that man is something more than a beast, and life something more than a mere struggle for physical survival. The latter need requires sanction that life has a larger, nobler meaning than seems apparent and that man's pursuit of this meaning, his nobler actions in support of it, will be rewarded and the contrary punished. This is man's need for support outside himself to realize his better nature. Finally, there is the great need to be assured that all effort does not terminate in the tomb. Graeco-Roman polytheism attempted to fill these needs in a mechanical way by propitiating the gods with ritual and sacrifice. The mystery cults sought to use ritual not so much to pacify the gods as to realize the divine potentiality of the worshiper. In doing this they had to rely on ancient legend.

THE JEWISH INHERITANCE OF CHRISTIANITY[1]

Unlike its competitors, Christianity was the religion of a book and possessed an authenticated antiquity. A part of this book (the Bible) was the Jewish Scriptures, for although Christianity cut itself loose from formal Judaism it retained the Old Testament. It insisted that this Old Testament contained the divine prophecy of which Christianity was the fulfillment. In retaining the Old Testament it appropriated for itself essential Jewish teachings, and above all ethical monotheism. In this manner the Yahweh of the Old Testament became the Christian God.

---

[1]This inheritance is greatly enlarged by the material in the Dead Sea Scrolls, discovered in 1947 in a cave at 'Ain Fesh Kha near the north end of the Dead Sea. The Scrolls emphasize the debt owed the dissident sects in Judaism such as the monastic community of Qumran. The language and ideas of the New Testament are so close to those of the Qumran community that one scholar can speak of Jesus as "an astonishing reincarnation of the teacher of righteousness," a leader of this sect.—Miller Burrows, *The Dead Sea Scrolls* (Viking). See also H. H. Rowley, *The Zadokite Fragments and the Dead Sea Scrolls*; and Edmund Wilson, *The Scrolls from the Dead Sea*.

Hence the Christian state and society, like the Jewish, were to be interpreted as the result of a covenant with God binding the rulers to the maintenance of his righteousness. To both Judaism and Christianity theocracy was the proper political organization. It is not easy to imagine the great change in religious thinking involved in the substitution of Jewish ethical monotheism for the variegated polytheism of the classical world. To be sure, the impact was softened when paganism came to conceive of a supreme god with many divine mediators and Christianity modified its monotheism with the doctrine of the Trinity and the veneration of saints. Yet for all its modifications Christianity retained its Jewish monotheism and refused to compromise with it.

SACRED SCRIPTURES

Christianity came to have also a New Testament, concerning whose books there was general agreement by the middle of the second century. This testament contained the record of Jesus' life and the work of his followers and an account of the fulfillment of Old Testament prophecy. Together these two testaments were not simply, in the belief of Christians, a historical account of Christianity and its Jewish background. They were the sacred Word of God. The new religion accordingly had a precise and definite literature giving it what it believed to be a holy authority.

JESUS

Christianity also received from Judaism its founder, the Rabbi Jesus, who set out to free his people's religion from dependence upon the letter of the law. He was no dim figure of myth but a warm, historical personality, preaching a way of life that, if taken seriously, in the ways of previous prophets, would have upset the world. However few and unreliable the details of his career as given by the New Testament, he had, for his faith, undoubtedly encountered the hostility of both church and state and paid with his life. The humiliating and cruel death by crucifixion, a death accorded the common criminal, was felt all the more poignantly by his followers, since it came to be believed that Jesus was the Son of God and that he had assumed human form, suffering all the indignities that human flesh is heir to, in order to atone to his Father, God, for the miserable sins of the human race. Thus Jesus, both human and divine, had sacrificed his life on the cross in order that mankind might inherit eternal life. This tragic act of love on his part called forth in turn from his followers feelings of gratitude and sorrow. Perhaps no one who has not wept over the death of Jesus can expect to understand Christianity. These feelings of love, tenderness, gratitude, devotion, and unutterable grief over his death are well approached through the American Negro spiritual "Were You There When They Crucified My Lord?" Neither Attis, Osiris, nor Mithra could be confounded with Jesus. The

CHRONOLOGY — Christian Asceticism

Emperors, Popes, and Councils	Important Persons in the Early Church
	Jesus (ca. 4 B.C.–A.D. 29)
	Philo (ca. 20 B.C.–A.D. 50)

B.C.

A.D.

Emperors, Popes, and Councils	Important Persons in the Early Church
	Saint Paul (d. ca. 67)
	Tertullian (ca. 150–230)
	Origen (ca. 185–254)
	Plotinus (ca. 205–270)
	Saint Anthony (ca. 251–350)
	Arius (ca. 256–336)
	Saint Pachomius (d. ca. 340)
	Athanasius (295–373)
Constantine (r. 324–337)	Saint Martin of Tours (ca. 316–397)
Council of Nicaea (325)	Saint Basil (ca. 330–373)
	Saint Ambrose (ca. 339–397)
	Saint Jerome (ca. 347–419)
	Saint Augustine (354–430)
	Pelagius (ca. 355–425)
Theodosius (r. 379–395)	John Cassian (ca. 360–435)

400

Emperors, Popes, and Councils	Important Persons in the Early Church
Council of Ephesus (431)	
Council of Chalcedon (451)	
	Nestorius (d. ca. 451)
	Eutyches (ca. 378–452)
Gelasius I (r. 492–496)	Saint Simeon Stylites (ca. 390–459)
Anastasius (r. 491–518)	
Gregory the Great (r. 590–604)	

tragedy of his life, symbolic of the tragedy of all life, was enhanced by the belief that Jesus was also the Messiah of God, that as such he had been commissioned to inaugurate a new Kingdom of God. Thus his death postponed into an unknown future the establishment of that divine society that was to terminate melancholy and evil human existence.

JESUS AS THE MESSIAH

In this fashion Christianity took from Judaism the incomparable advantages of the Old Testament and Jesus and the organization of a sect. Its own originality would seem to consist in the special emphasis that Jesus gave to the teachings of the Jewish prophets, of whom he may be regarded as one. For if in the absence of much information about him we trust some of his modern interpreters, there is little reason to believe that, as a good Jew, he conceived of the spread of his religious ideas beyond the Jewish community. He associated himself with many ardent Jews who believed that a time was soon coming when God would bring to an end the interminable suffering and humiliation of their people by a spectacular intervention in human affairs. God would send a special agent of his own, a Messiah (Christ), to establish his Kingdom. Whether or not Jesus felt himself to be this Messiah is a question of serious dispute among scholars of the New Testament. In any case his disciples, recognizing in him God's Messiah, were utterly bewildered and depressed when the authorities, both Jewish and Roman, co-operated in removing this threat to the established order by having Jesus crucified. What then seemed to them impossible later became possible when it was held that Jesus was not dead but had risen from the tomb to heaven, whence he would come at a later time as the Messiah. It was now the task of the disciples to prepare for the speedy reappearance of Jesus. He had urged the Jews to repent, for the Kingdom of God was at hand. It was still at hand, postponed only slightly. It would be inaugurated only after a final judgment to determine its true citizens. That Jesus was the Jewish Messiah the Jews as a people could not accept. Christianity, therefore, was in its earliest form restricted to a very small sect among them. As a reform movement of a Messianic character within Judaism it failed.[2]

THE CHRISTIAN MESSAGE

To Jesus and his disciples the Kingdom of God was soon at hand. Just exactly what they meant by the phrase is not perfectly clear, although

[2]Other similar movements had failed before it. The Qumran community of the Dead Sea Scrolls incorporated such a movement. Its "teacher of righteousness" led a sect looking for the coming of the Messiah of Aaron and Israel. The leader was persecuted, seems to have suffered martyrdom, and, in the opinion of some scholars, was expected to rise again. The sect goes back to the second century B.C. at a time when the Jews, under the leadership of the Maccabees, were resisting the introduction of Greek culture. It came to be housed in a monastery north of the Dead Sea and lasted until the destruction of Jerusalem by the Roman emperor Titus in A.D. 70.

there is every reason to believe that Jesus' earlier notions were of a wholly spiritual kingdom, where charity and the rule of love reigned in every man's heart. Jesus himself was a simple, poetically gifted, and comparatively unlettered Jew, preaching to unlettered herdsmen, farmers, fishermen, and craftsmen in Galilee about a loving and merciful God, the Father, whose worship, or loving, consisted in the love of man by man as neighbors or even brothers. Jesus preached to them in the Sermon on the Mount:

> Blessed are you who are poor, for the Kingdom of God is yours!
> Blessed are you who are hungry now, for you will be satisfied!
> Blessed are you who weep now, for you will laugh!
> Blessed are you when people hate you and exclude you and denounce you and spurn the name you bear as evil, on account of the Son of Man. Be glad when that happens, and leap for joy, for you will be richly rewarded in heaven, for that is the way their forefathers treated the prophets.
>
> But alas for you who are rich, for you have had your comfort!
> Alas for you who have plenty to eat now, for you will be hungry!
> Alas for you who laugh now, for you will mourn and weep!
> Alas for you when everyone speaks well of you, for that is the way their forefathers treated the false prophets!
>
> But I tell you who hear me, love your enemies, treat those who hate you well, bless those who curse you, pray for those who abuse you. To the man that strikes you on the cheek, offer the other also, and from the man who takes away your coat, do not keep back your shirt either. Give to everyone that asks of you, and if anyone takes away what is yours, do not demand it back. And treat men just as you wish them to treat you. If you love only those who love you, what merit is there in that? For even godless people love those who love them. And if you help only those who help you, what merit is there in that? Even godless people act in that way. And if you lend only to people from whom you expect to get something, what merit is there in that? Even godless people lend to godless people, meaning to get it back again in full. But love your enemies, and help them and lend to them, never despairing, and you will be richly rewarded, and you will be sons of the Most High, for he is kind even to the ungrateful and the wicked. You must be merciful, just as your Father is. Do not judge others, and they will not judge you. Do not condemn them, and they will not condemn you. Excuse others and they will excuse you. Give, and they will give to you; good measure, pressed down, shaken together, and running over, they will pour into your lap. For the measure you use with others they will in turn use with you. (pp. 147–149)[3]

Saint Paul echoed the same teaching:

> If I can speak the languages of men and even of angels, but have no love, I am only a noisy gong or a clashing cymbal. If I am inspired to preach and know all secret truths and possess all knowledge, and if I have such perfect

[3]Reprinted from *The Parallel New Testament* translated by Edgar J. Goodspeed by permission of The University of Chicago Press. Copyright 1943 by The University of Chicago Press. Further citations from this translation will appear in my text.

faith that I can move mountains, but have no love, I am nothing. Even if I give away everything I own, and give myself up, but do it in pride, not love, it does me no good. Love is patient and kind. Love is not envious or boastful. It does not put on airs. It is not rude. It does not insist on its rights. It does not become angry. It is not resentful. It is not happy over injustice, it is only happy with truth. It will bear anything, believe anything, hope for anything, endure anything. Love will never die out. If there is inspired preaching, it will pass away. If there is ecstatic speaking, it will cease. If there is knowledge, it will pass away. For our knowledge is imperfect and our preaching is imperfect. But when perfection comes, what is imperfect will pass away. When I was a child, I talked like a child, I thought like a child, I reasoned like a child. When I became a man, I put aside my childish ways. For now we are looking at a dim reflection in a mirror, but then we shall see face to face. Now my knowledge is imperfect, but then I shall know as fully as God knows me. So faith, hope, and love endure. These are the great three, and the greatest of them is love. (pp. 401–402)

The ethical system thus prescribed by Jesus is so difficult that it has been practiced only by a very few; if this is Christianity the western world has never been, and is never likely to be, really Christian. Indeed, this teaching is so severe that it has been conceived by some to be only a system of "interim ethics," a system, that is, to be used in preparation for the almost immediate coming of the Messiah. The implications of the ethics here laid down as the practice of religion are clearly social. Religion bears fruit in social good—in the noblest altruistic behavior. The West's acceptance of this code as a part of its religion, without ever having been able to live up to it, has given its religious history a moral tension that has carried over into other activities of life and has made its general history uniquely dynamic. Jesus did not use these teachings as the basis for a social or economic message of revolutionary import. They were rather his way of preparing his people for divine judgment. But he had no way of controlling their subsequent use. The spirit that animates the competition between western nations in securing economic markets abroad, that urges modern corporations and individuals to help themselves above all is hardly the spirit of Jesus.

SAINT PAUL

Many would argue that it was Saint Paul and not Jesus who was the real founder of historical Christianity. They would argue thus because it was he, a Jew educated in Greek and a Roman citizen, who took the steps necessary to save Christianity from perishing as a Jewish sect, inasmuch as he adapted it to the larger, gentile world and carried it to that world. This was, of course, the Graeco-Roman world of the first century of the Pax Romana, devoted to the gods and goddesses of the Greek and oriental mystery cults and to the older divinities of the Graeco-Roman pantheon. The figure of a martyred Jewish prophet, or a crucified and risen Jewish Messiah, could hardly be expected to cause this extra-

Palestinian world to desert its old divinities. Since there had been no thought among Christians of divorcing the new faith from the observance of Jewish law, and accordingly from such practices as circumcision and the dietary regulations, no great future for Christianity could be seen outside Jewish circles. But if Christianity could cut itself loose from Judaism, if it could consider itself an independent religion, if the figure of the crucified and risen Messiah could be interpreted in the light of the Lord and Savior of a new mystery religion, then, with a vigorous missionary propaganda it could be hoped that Christianity would make its way in the world. This is what Paul succeeded in doing. Originally an ardent persecutor of Christians, he became, after his conversion, the leader of those who would separate Christianity from Judaism. As he said in his Letter to the Galatians: "There is no room for 'Jew' and 'Greek'; there is no room for 'slave' and 'freeman'; there is no room for 'male' and 'female'; for in union with Christ Jesus you are all one." This union was the mysticism seen in the oriental religions, for Paul a kind of permanent "indwelling of Christ" in the human soul. It was achieved by loyal devotion or faith in the Lord. Paul interpreted Jesus' death as a sacrifice to God for the sins of mankind, an atonement for human wickedness. Those who, in union with their Lord, died with him in the flesh and rose again in the spirit were guaranteed the blessings of immortality. Since Jesus was the Divine Lord he was differentiated from God and called Son of God. All those, indeed, who were united by faith with their Savior were sons of God. By such a faith they were justified, that is, forgiven their sins and saved from eternal punishment. Paul began to interpret the purification bath of the Jews and the common meals of Jesus' disciples as special sacramental ceremonies. To him must be credited the initiative of planning and carrying out a widespread missionary campaign to the leading Greek and Roman cities. In the course of it he suffered a martyr's death in the Rome of Nero. By his correspondence with the young churches he had founded or visited he gave a sense of unity to the movement as well as an interpretation of Christianity as not only another mystery cult but also a severe ascetic code tolerating no pampering of the flesh.[4] "The things our physical nature does are clear enough—immorality, impurity, licentiousness, idolatry, sorcery, enmity, quarreling, jealousy, anger, selfishness, dissension, party-spirit, envy, drunkeness, carousing, and the like. I warn you as I did before that people who do such things will have no share in the Kingdom of God. But what the Spirit produces is love, joy, peace, patience, kindness, goodness, faithfulness, gentleness, self-control. There is no law against such things. Those who belong to Jesus the Christ have crucified the physical nature with its propensities and cravings." (pp. 358, 440)

[4]For the striking parallels between the Christianity of Paul and the religion of the Qumran community of the Dead Sea Scrolls, see Millar Burrows, *The Dead Sea Scrolls.*

The Adaptive Genius of Christianity

By removing the specific Jewish limitations upon Christianity and interpreting it as a mystery cult, Paul made possible the spread among the gentiles that he himself promoted. It was accepted first by those groups that, like its earliest followers in Palestine, constituted the simple, illiterate, underprivileged population of the great Mediterranean seaports: the slaves, the dock hands, and the laborers. In the course of this acceptance it adapted itself in practice as well as in theory to the popular cults competing for the allegiance of the urban populations and became actually a new mystery cult in their midst. Origen, a Christian Alexandrian theologian of the third century, could speak of "initiation into the mysteries of Jesus." Thus Christianity became a specific body of religious lore based on holy books and confided only to those who were willing to undergo initiation. It became, as well, an intricate ritual centering upon the dramatic and tragic life story or passion play of Jesus the man-god, Lord and Savior of the cult. The important ceremonies of this ritual were the sacraments. Religious lore and ritual were entrusted for safekeeping and performance to a group of priests set apart from the ordinary Christian by special training, special garb, special manner of life, and, it was hoped, special saintliness. Baptism and the Eucharist were the chief sacraments. Baptism washed away previous sin and symbolized a rebirth into a new Christian life. As a ceremony, it has always retained some of the blood symbolism of the primitive mystery-cult baptisms ("Wash me in the blood and I shall be whiter than snow"; "There is a fountain filled with blood"). The Eucharist also retained features of primitive barbaric rites that had to do with eating the body and drinking the blood of the god. For the central part of the ritual came to be what is called the Mass, a re-enactment of the tragic and atoning sacrifice of Christ upon the cross. It came to be the interpretation of the theologians, and it is still the teaching of the Catholic Church, that by virtue of his holy power the priest performs a miracle at the altar. This miracle consists of transforming (transubstantiating) the elements of the Eucharist, the bread and wine of the Last Supper, into the actual body and blood of the Lord and Savior. Thus in the ceremony of the Mass the priest repeats the original sacrifice of Jesus upon the cross to atone to God for men's sins. Because Christ has re-entered the bread and wine and they have become his actual body and blood, the priest is resacrificing in "unbloody" fashion the real Christ to God. The ceremony of the Eucharist, concluding the Mass, consists in the priest's offering to the faithful in the form of the bread and wine the actual body of the Lord to eat and his blood to drink (the wine is no longer offered to the laity in the Catholic ceremony). In this way the faithful actually feed upon the Lord, take him as nourishment into their bodies, and he becomes part of them. In other words, they become in part physically divine. A

Christian Father speaks of the flesh that "feeds on the body and blood of Christ in order that the soul also may fatten on God." Because they have absorbed their Lord they are bound to be as imperishable and immortal as he. So interpreted, the Eucharist is a process of glorification for the participant, a physical union of the neophyte with his God. Performed, as it came to be, in an impressive architectural setting by gorgeously garbed clergy in accordance with an elaborate ritual using such sensuous stimulants as music and incense, it provided, and still provides, an intense emotional excitement of a mystical kind, in which the ordinary mortal, for a brief moment, tremblingly becomes one with his Savior. The ways in which Christianity may have been influenced by the mysteries in detail as well as in theory have already been hinted at by a consideration of these cults themselves.[5] Of the general transformation there can be little doubt.

CHRISTIANITY AS POLYTHEISM

Christianity became then a new mystery cult of salvation. It became, also, a new kind of polytheism. For no matter how the theologians came to define the Trinity as a Unity, to many simple people Christians seemed to worship a Father, a Son, and a Holy Ghost. To them, the monotheism of the Hebrews had been but precariously preserved. Polytheism in Christianity, however, is better illustrated by the cult of the Virgin and the saints than by the Trinity. To be sure, the Catholic Church, which retains this cult, does not teach that the Virgin and the saints are to be worshiped as the Triune God is to be worshiped. They are merely to be venerated for their sanctity, miraculous power, and ability to intercede with God on behalf of man. Christianity showed an extraordinary insight when it adapted Graeco-Roman polytheism to its own purposes by permitting a special Christian cult of the Virgin and saints to supplant pagan polytheism. Since it became an established admonition of the Church to her missionaries never to destroy pagan practices, and thus unnecessarily offend her future converts when these practices could be Christianized, it may be assumed that she acquired this wisdom in the course of her first contacts with the Graeco-Roman world.[6] In any case, the many special services that pagan gods and goddesses performed for their devotees Christianity permitted its martyrs and ascetic heroes to perform as saints. And if the saints were not to be worshiped as gods and goddesses, it was hard to make this teaching clear to the great body of the faithful. In those lands that once were a part of the Roman Empire it is still a difficult matter to explain. The Church has always had to combat, and still has to combat, the very understandable preference of individuals for the saints, who can perform greatly needed special services, over such a difficult abstraction as the Trinity. The clergy still have to remind the faithful that if they do not first address their prayers to the Trinity they may not expect to

[5]See pp. 286 f.
[6]See Gregory the Great's instructions to the Anglo-Saxon mission, p. 402.

receive any favors from the saints. The very heart of popular Christianity in ancient and medieval times, and in Catholic populations since the Reformation, has been the cult of the Virgin and the saints. Thus the Virgin, the sinless (Immaculate Conception) Mother of God, who, as the Church now teaches (the Assumption) was upon her death received directly into heaven, became the most powerful intercessor with her Son when once he had faded away into the philosophical logos.[7] Out of all those powerful human needs that had made the great goddesses of antiquity so popular (Aphrodite, Venus, Hera, Diana, Ceres, Magna Mater, Demeter, Isis) now rose the cult of the Ever Virgin Mother of God. If Isis became a synthesis of all the pagan goddesses, Mary became her Christian successor. Once inaugurated the cult of the Virgin had, and continues to have, an extraordinary development. Popular religion made her, the lovely young mother with the divine baby at her breast or on her lap, the supreme object of devotion. Indeed, she had so much to do for her devotees that she had to divide her work among various local manifestations of herself. The Virgin Mother, Sovereign of the Universe, had to work through Our Lady of Paris, and of Chartres, and of Lourdes, and of Alt-Ötting.

THE SAINTS

What the Virgin had to leave undone was taken care of by the saints, theoretically by intercession but as everyone really believed, directly. Thus in Spain it was Saint John the Baptist who would take care of your headache, and in southern Italy Saint Joseph who could help interpret your dreams. And these saintly helpers of mankind, available at the nearest chapel, developed into a mighty legion which is still growing. An American list of patron saints[8] recommends the invocation of Saint James against arthritis and rheumatism, of Saint Eulalia against drought, Saint Eustachius against family troubles, Saint Christopher against the hazards of travel, Saint Erasmus against intestinal disorders, Saint Apollonia against backache, and Saint Giles against sterility. An English scholar refers to "Our Lady of the Stiletto" in the church of Saint Agostino all Zecca in Naples. "In front of one of the altars stands a very remarkable realistic figure, life-size, in glazed and coloured terra-cotta. I seem to remember that they told me it represented Sta. Agata. She raises her outspread hands and is about to stagger backwards, while a dagger sticks to the hilt under her collar-bone and pierces to the heart. This realism comes home to the population of Naples, where stabbing affrays are far more frequent than in any other European city of similar population. This little church, therefore, has become consecrated in the popular mind to what we may call Our Lady of the Stiletto. The man who has a vendetta on hand vows it to this altar in case of success, just as the mother has vowed a head of wax (or silver, if she is rich enough) for her child's life, or the lover a

[7]See p. 300.
[8]*Is It a Saint's Name?* comp. Rev. William P. Dunne.

heart for success in his love. Thus the altar is hung with dozens of triumphant stiletti; moreover, the boards erected to receive them show also a considerable number of empty nails, which tell an even more gruesome tale. For, here and there, some other man has vowed his own particular vendetta, and has reinforced the religious force of that vow by borrowing one of the consecrated stiletti to do the job with. He has never come back to replace it; and each empty nail stands for two murders at least. The objects speak plainly enough for themselves; but I took care to get full corroboration. The sacristan, questioned on the subject, admitted reluctantly that each of these daggers stood for a *mala morte*. Thence I drifted across the street to get my hair cut, and the barber told the same tale in plainer language."[9]

PAGANISM IN CHRISTIANITY

Nor did the older gods and goddesses of Graeco-Roman antiquity fade completely away before their Christian competitors. In some instances pagan gods and goddesses actually became Christian saints; in others Christian saints took over the specific attributes of pagan gods. Pagan shrines and temples were occupied by Christian shrines and churches dedicated to corresponding saints. Pagan holidays and festivals were supplanted by Christian holidays and festivals, sometimes with a deliberate substitution of the Christian for the pagan festival. Artemis became Saint Artemidus, and Demeter became Saint Demetrius, or, at Eleusis, an uncanonized Saint Demetra. On Naxos, the legendary home of Dionysus, can be traced a Saint Dionysius, associated with the vine. Saint Nicholas, "the sailor," took over the duties of Poseidon. Saint Catherine helped the Virgin with the functions of Aphrodite, and a Saint Venere in Albania performed the duties of Venus. Aphrodite Pelagia, the marine Aphrodite, became merely Saint Pelagia. In Sienna a temple of Quirinus was taken over by the church of Saint Quirinus. The Virgin succeeded Athena at the Parthenon in Athens, and, generally speaking, all the great goddesses in their temples (Diana of the Ephesians, often the Magna Mater, and the sanctuaries of Ceres in Sicily). The pagan *Saturnalia* became a part of the Christmas festivities, as the twenty-fifth of December, the birthday of the Invincible Sun, became the birthday of Jesus. The Roman worship of the dead (*Parentalia*) was taken over by All Saints (1 November) and All Souls (2 November). In the world of art this transfer from pagan to Christian usage was quite common. Pagan temples became Christian churches, pagan images were used for the Virgin and saints (for example, Isis and Child Horus for Virgin and Child), pagan tombs became Christian altars, and pagan representations of Apollo, Orpheus, and Aesculapius were used for Jesus.

[9]G. G. Coulton, *Fourscore Years*, pp. 232–233.

The Gospel according to John begins, "In the beginning the Word existed. The Word was with God, and the Word was divine. It was he that was with God in the beginning. Everything came into existence through him, and apart from him nothing came to be.[10] It was by him that life came into existence, and that life was the light of mankind. The light is still shining in the darkness, for the darkness has never put it out." This Gospel continues at a later point, "So the Word became flesh and blood and lived for a while among us, abounding in blessing and truth, and we saw the honor God had given him, such honor as an only son receives from his father." (Goodspeed, pp. 209-210) The Greek for "Word" in the above passages is *logos*. The passages themselves are not distinguished for their clarity. They refer to a divine personification of the Word (logos), originally a part of God ("the Word was with God"). This divine personification (Word, logos) was the sole creator. The life created by the Word was also light, and still exists. This Word, originally spirit, became living flesh and blood for a while, and in this form was honored by God as a Son. If we say that the Word in these passages is Jesus, the passages may become somewhat clearer. Jesus, then, is said to be the divine Word (logos), originally a part of God, and the sole creator. Jesus was originally spirit but became living flesh and blood for a while, and as such was honored by God as his Son. We may simplify the above by using another traditional sentence, "Jesus was the incarnation of the divine logos," but we should hardly clarify it. To refer to Jesus as the divine logos incarnate is to speak of him in a new capacity. He has been spoken of as the Messiah or Christ and as the new Lord and Savior of a Christian mystery cult. But the incarnation of a divine logos? Indeed, the phrase cannot very well be explained at all without a somewhat technical knowledge of the terms of Greek philosophy from its earliest days.

The transformation of Jesus into the "incarnation of the divine logos" was an attempt to make Christianity philosophically respectable as well as to emphasize the divinity of Jesus. It was inevitable that as Christianity became more popular in the larger urban centers it should be attacked by pagan intellectuals. It was just as inevitable that these should be answered by Christian intellectuals (the Apologists). It could be expected that pagan attacks upon Christianity would arise out of a background of the leading

[10]There is a doctrine of the Word (or logos, see p. 300) in the literature of the Qumran community of the Dead Sea Scrolls, where this sentence is paralleled: "Everything that is he establishes by his purpose and without him it is not done."—Burrows, p. 338. Indeed, the language and ideas of the Fourth Gospel are so close to those of the Qumran community that it is not necessary to look for some of them (e.g., the logos) in Greek (Platonic) philosophy. There is back of both the Gospel and the literature of the community "a wider background in the general stream of Iranian influence in Judaism and in other religions of western Asia," but "the scrolls thus show— and this has not always been recognized—that we do not have to look outside of Palestinian Judaism for the soil in which Johannine [the Gospel of Saint John] theology grew."—Burrows, pp. 339-340.

schools of philosophy, the Platonic and Stoic, and that the answers of the Christian apologists would have to come to terms with this philosophical language. Indeed, pagan critics of Christianity liked to mock it for being quite innocent of philosophy. Christian theologians consequently borrowed what they needed from Greek philosophy and introduced their borrowings into Christian tradition. The result was that just as in its popular religious forms Christianity came to have a cult similar to those long popular in the Roman Empire so it came to have a philosophy (theology) similar to the popular philosophies of the Roman state. It adapted itself, in other words, to the needs of the intellectuals as well as of the masses. Men like Clement and that Christian Attis, the castrated Origen, heads of a theological school in Alexandria in the early third century, could argue that while the simple and illiterate accepted Christianity only by faith the educated Christian needed the whole wealth of pagan culture before he could understand fully the Christian Scriptures. Christianity was a divine science or philosophy that had to be understood as well as believed.

JESUS AS THE LOGOS

If one should study the Christian science, or theology, that Clement and Origen were writing about he would soon become aware that they, like Philo with Jewish religion,[11] were trying to incorporate into Christianity as much philosophy as possible. He would likewise become aware that the kind of philosophy they were trying to incorporate was similar to the system of Plotinus. Clement and Origen, that is, were trying to utilize the definitions of God arrived at by Greek philosophers, and, in order to give Jesus philosophic importance, were trying to utilize the attempts of Greek philosophers to relate an infinite God to this finite world. We have already observed that the Greeks came to define God in terms of pure negative abstraction, culminating in Plotinus's "the One." We have also noted that in trying to relate this ineffable and incomprehensible One to the material universe the Greek philosophers made use of the device of mediators between God and man. Plotinus used two of these—the Divine Mind and the World Soul. The mediator between God and the world was often conceived of as God's reason, and the latter as his creative word, or utterance, written or spoken. And the Greek word used for reason, or word, in this sense was *logos*. The problem of the Christian theologian was thus to relate the personal Jewish and Christian Yahweh, God the Father, to the philosophical Greek One, and Jesus, the Christian Messiah and Lord and Savior, to the logos. The solution was, simply stated, to identify them. Jehovah was the One. Jesus was the incarnation of the divine logos. Jesus was also the Son of God. In somewhat more detail it was explained that Jesus, the Son of God, had an earthly and a pre-earthly existence. In his pre-earthly existence he, the spiritual Son of God, was

[11]See pp. 300 f.

the divine logos, the divine reason, the divine creator. In his earthly existence he was the divine spiritual logos incarnate in the human Jesus, in other words, the God-man.

THEOLOGICAL CONTROVERSY

Such a mixture of Jewish and Greek, of personal religion and philosophy, could obviously not have taken place without controversy. If Jesus were to be considered the incarnation of the divine logos, or Word, it looked as if Christianity were abandoning its monotheistic tradition and adopting the worship of at least two gods, Jehovah and Jesus. Possibly three, if the Holy Spirit, or Holy Ghost, were to be considered a deity. And just how was the incarnation of the divine logos to be understood? How could a divine spirit become flesh and blood? These were very important questions to Christians. If once Christianity were to abandon its monotheistic tradition and turn to the worship of two or three gods there was little to stop it from making a complete compromise with classical religions and becoming altogether polytheistic. The question of just how the incarnation was to be understood was also vital to the existence of Christianity as a popular and effective mystery cult. In this cult the initiate was rendered divine by partaking of the body and blood of the Savior in the sacrament of the Eucharist. If this incarnate logos were to be considered more human than divine the glorification of the human being through the Eucharist might be considered to be incomplete; if more divine than human, the possibility of glorification would be more remote. If Christianity were to become philosophical it would have to become rational, or at least submit to tampering under the tyranny of logic. Once begun, there was no stopping until a more or less complete Christian theology had been worked out. It was at this moment (third century A.D.) that theology began to supplant philosophy as the chief form of western man's intellectual activity. It continued in that position until the hopes of making Christianity completely rational proved illusory.[12]

ARIANISM

The first major controversy to split the Church was that over Arianism. The argument arose as a dispute between two local Alexandrian clerics, Arius and Athanasius, the latter subsequently the bishop of Alexandria, over the precise way in which God was considered to be related to his Son Jesus, the incarnate logos. Before it was settled the controversy threatened to disrupt the Church completely at the very moment of its official toleration by the state. To the emperor Constantine, who had turned to Christianity as a source of unity, so much fuss over what seemed to him a question of phraseology was undignified. In 325 he intervened, to call and preside over the first general, or ecumenical, council of the Church at Nicaea, where the issue was first decided.

[12]See p. 675.

The point of view of Arius may be gathered from a letter he wrote, perhaps in 321, to his friend Eusebius, the bishop of Nicomedia. He was being driven out of Alexandria, he said, because he did not concur when his bishop publicly preaches, "God always, the Son always; at the same time the Father, at the same time the Son; the Son coexists with God, unbegotten; he is ever-begotten, he is not born-by-begetting; neither by thought nor by any moment of time does God precede the Son; God always, Son always, the Son exists from God himself." Arius then tells Eusebius that he believes "that the Son is not unbegotten, nor part of the unbegotten in any way, nor is he derived from any substance; but that by his own will and counsel he existed before times and ages fully God, only-begotten, unchangeable. And before he was begotten or created or appointed or established, he did not exist; for he was not unbegotten. We are persecuted because we say that the Son has a beginning, but God is without beginning."[13]

It is notable here that the personality of Jesus is not a question for discussion. What he did or what he said seems to matter little. It is what he was that counts, and what he was has to do with how he was created. That Jesus is the Son of God is not questioned, that in his prenatal and pre-earthly existence he was the divine logos is not questioned. What is questioned is how this divine-logos Son of God came into being. Arius objects to saying that the Son-logos has existed as long as God the Father, that he is accordingly unbegotten, or that he is of the same stuff or substance as the Father. Rather, Arius insists, the Father came before the Son, created the Son, and in fact begat him; the Son, accordingly, was not of the same stuff or substance as the Father. This is not to say that the Son of God has not from the time of his creation been "fully God." It is only to say that he has been begotten (created) in time, or, as Arius puts it, that the Son had a beginning. What concerns Arius is to maintain the lofty pre-eminence of the one God and the peculiar significance of Jesus. The Son of God became incarnate in Jesus without question. If he were the same as God the Father (coexistent, unbegotten, of the same substance), then God lowered his dignity in becoming a human. And if Jesus were the incarnation of such a completely divine Word, then he had lost his significance as a human of heroic moral stature. To Arius, what he called God did not become human flesh and blood, or, in other words, incarnate. What did become incarnate was a separately created substance, no matter how unique and divine. In the mystery-cult theory of redemption he apparently was not much interested. To him, Jesus revealed God and enlightened his followers with a knowledge of God and thus pointed out to them the way of salvation. Jesus was thus a special prophet of perfect human proportions who had been sent to help man.

---

[13]Bettenson, *Documents of the Christian Church*, p. 55.

This last was what particularly annoyed Athanasius and the more conservative churchmen. Christianity by this time had become a mystery cult of salvation. Salvation was to be had through the sacraments uniting the devotee with the immortal Lord of the cult. If Arius's description of the Son of God were permitted to stand, then Jesus was not a completely divine person in the same sense that God the One was. Union, therefore, with this kind of Jesus was union with a not completely divine person, and such a union did not make salvation and immortality absolutely secure. The Son of God that became incarnate in Jesus had to be coexistent with God, without beginning, unbegotten, and of the same stuff and substance, if salvation through union were to be absolutely certain. Setting up, moreover, a Jesus who was divine in some way but less than divine in the sense that God was divine seemed to these men to be setting up a second divinity, and therefore to be compromising with Christian monotheism. Such a matter became all the more delicate in that Christian tradition also preserved what was called the Holy Spirit, or Ghost. If this Holy Spirit were to be interpreted in the same way as Arius's interpretation of the Son of God, then there was danger that Christianity would possess three gods instead of one.

HE COUNCIL OF NICAEA

The Council of Nicaea rejected the position of Arius and his followers and adopted a compromise formula proclaiming that "We believe in one God the Father, All-sovereign, maker of all things visible and invisible; and in one Lord Jesus Christ, the Son of God, begotten of the Father, only-begotten that is, of the substance of the Father, God of God, Light of Light, true God of true God, begotten not made, of one substance with the Father, through whom all things were made . . . who for us men and for our salvation came down and was made flesh, and became man, suffered, and rose on the third day, ascended into the heavens, is coming to judge the living and dead; and in the Holy Spirit." And to make sure that it was understood that Arius was condemned, the Council went on: "And those that say 'There was once when he was not' and 'Before he was begotten he was not' and that 'He came into being from what-is-not,' or those who allege that the Son of God is 'of another substance or essence,' or 'created' or 'changeable' or 'alterable' these the Catholic and Apostolic Church anathematizes."[14] That the beginnings of the formulation of dogma should be accompanied by the pronouncement of anathema is a melancholy accomplishment of the first Christian general council. In any event the decision of Nicaea did not settle the matter, and in the succeeding years the controversy raged on. Arian emperors repeatedly exiled Athanasius from his see. The Arians themselves split into divergent

[14]Bettenson, p. 36.

groups. A group of theologians from Cappadocia in Asia Minor resolved the controversy by taking advantage of the technical distinction in Greek philosophy between "substance" and "person." The Christian monotheistic tradition could be preserved, and the differences between Arian and Athanasian avoided, if it were acknowledged that Father, Son, and Holy Spirit constituted a unity in trinity, that is, the Trinity of Father, Son, and Holy Spirit was "one substance in three persons, . . . a common nature or substance or essence possessed by three individual beings or persons."[15] The Christian God thus turned out to be much more complicated than the mere identification of Yahweh with the One, or even of Jesus with the divine logos.

NESTORIUS ON THE NATURE OF CHRIST

While it was a little difficult after the Arian controversy to dispute that a divine logos had become incarnate in the human Jesus, it was still a vital question as to how that incarnation had taken place. Here again the question was not merely one of curiosity, how in fact does God take on human flesh; the efficacy of sacramental rites was involved. If the union of God and man were to be conceived in such a way that God completely absorbed man, there did not seem to be much point in such an incarnation; the body and blood of such an incarnate God appeared little less than a derogation of divinity, and its consumption in the Eucharist therefore of questionable saving value. If, on the contrary, the human element remaining in this incarnation was overemphasized at the expense of the divine, the possibility of complete glorification was brought into question. The immediate problem of the statesmen, the practical churchmen, and the moderate theologians was to arrive at a compromise formula for extremely opposite views. These two views were of the Greek theologians Nestorius and Eutyches. Nestorius was concerned with maintaining the figure of the human Christ as a being possessed of free will and undergoing an independent moral development of his own, and therefore of value to mankind as a heroic, ethical example. Nestorius also disliked the paganism involved in the growing cult of the Virgin Mary and the willingness of her devotees to call her the Mother, or Bearer, of God. According to Nestorius, the Incarnate God, Jesus, was not of course to be denied a divine nature, but what was to be emphasized was his preservation, after the incarnation, of a separate and distinct human nature. He did not believe, either, that the human Virgin Mary could be said to be the Mother of God. A human does not give birth to a God. She may have provided flesh and blood in her womb for something already divine, but she could not properly be spoken of as the mother of this divine element. Jesus' human mother accordingly emphasized his humanity.

[15] A. C. McGiffert, *History of Christian Thought*, I, 266 ff.

The extreme, opposing opinion of Eutyches was the Monophysite view. It contended that after the incarnation of God Jesus possessed but one, inseparable, divine-human (theanthropic) nature. According to this view the human Jesus had been completely absorbed by the divine logos. Involved in these disputes was still, as at Nicaea, the desire of the emperor to maintain religious peace and unity. Theology was definitely a political matter. For a moment after the Council of Ephesus, in 431, the emperor Theodosius was so angry at the mutual anathemas and depositions of the Nestorians and their Alexandrine opponents that he had the leaders of both parties arrested. Likewise involved in the controversies were questions of prestige for the leading patriarchs of the East (Alexandria, Antioch, and Constantinople) and indeed for Rome.

`HE COUNCIL OF CHALCEDON

After decades of conflict it was finally realized that the dispute had better be presented before a general council. At Chalcedon, accordingly, in 451, the dispute over the nature of Christ after the Incarnation was mediated with the following words: "Following, therefore, the holy Fathers, we confess and all teach with one accord one and the same Son, our Lord Jesus Christ, at once perfect [complete] in Godhead and perfect [complete] in manhood, truly God and truly man, and, further, of a reasonable soul and body; of one essence with the Father as regards his Godhead, and at the same time of one essence with us as regards his manhood, in all respects like us, apart from sin; as regards his Godhead begotten of the Father before the ages, but yet as regards his manhood—on account of us and our salvation—begotten in the last days of Mary the Virgin, bearer of God; one and the same Christ, Son, Lord, Only-begotten, proclaimed in two natures, without confusion, without change, without division, without separation; the difference of the natures being in no way destroyed on account of the union, but rather the peculiar property of each nature being preserved and concurring in one person . . . not as though parted or divided into two persons, but one and the same Son and Only-begotten God the Logos, Lord, Jesus Christ." It would be interesting to know if the Jesus of the gospels could really have identified himself from this highly metaphysical definition of his nature. The Fathers at Chalcedon went ahead to provide that "no one shall be permitted to bring forward a different faith, nor to write, nor to put together, nor to excogitate, nor to teach it to others."[16] This prohibition proved to be beyond their powers. In fact, they were unable to satisfy the Nestorians and the Monophysites with this mediating definition. These two groups subsequently organized churches of their own, and these churches still exist in various regions of the Near East. As a result of trying to express its faith

[16]J. F. Bethune-Baker, *An Introduction to the Early History of Christian Doctrine*, p. 287.

precisely and of trying to impose a dogmatic expression upon all, the Christian Church thus began to disintegrate into various sects at this early point in its history. A fifth-century western summary of the decisions taken at Nicaea and Chalcedon, known as the Athanasian Creed, defines the Catholic faith as follows: "We worship one God in trinity, and trinity in unity; neither confounding the persons nor dividing the substance, for there is one person of the Father, another of the Son, and another of the Holy Spirit. But the divinity of the Father, of the Son, and of the Holy Spirit is all one, equal in glory, coeternal in majesty; . . . We believe and confess that our Lord Jesus Christ, the Son of God, is God and man; God of the substance of the Father; begotten before the worlds; and man, of the substance of his mother, born in the world; perfect God and perfect man, of a reasonable soul and human flesh subsisting; equal to the Father in regard to his divinity, and less than the Father in regard to his humanity who, although he be God and man, is still not two but one Christ; one, however, not by conversion of divinity into flesh, but by assumption of humanity into God; wholly one, not by confusion of substance but by unity of persons; for as the reasonable soul and flesh is one man, so God and man is one Christ."[17]

THE WESTERN EMPHASIS

When objection was made to Tertullian, an early Father of the western Church at Carthage, that it would have been impossible for God to be crucified or for his Son to die, because, from the very nature of divinity, such events would have been absurd, he answered that it was this very impossibility or absurdity that made these events certain. Tertullian may have been expressing on this occasion the impatience of a Roman with the Greek habit of putting everything to the test of reason. Western churchmen were perfectly willing to have Greeks make their theological decisions for them, but they did not believe it necessary to go on interminably, until the very last theological subtlety had been ironed out. Indeed, with notable exceptions, the Roman West preserved to the end its distaste for abstract philosophy. It preferred to see in Christianity less a mystical philosophy than a code of law, in God less a philosophical absolute than a maker of this law, and in Jesus less the incarnation of the logos than a revealer of this new law and a judge of sinful, lawbreaking mankind. It showed less interest in providing Christianity with a logically airtight system of belief than in giving it the organization and the law it needed to survive and grow.

THE CHRISTIAN CHURCH

Thus Christianity, like all powerfully felt social movements, emerged as an institution, a church, conceived in catholic (universal) terms, as

[17]Reprinted from *Jesus through the Centuries* by Shirley Case, pp. 230–231, by permission of The University of Chicago Press. Copyright 1932 by The University of Chicago Press.

founded upon the revealed truth of the one and only God, administering salvation to all mankind, and maintaining a commonly held belief. In charge of this church were clergy, set apart from the laity or membership at large by special garb, symbols (for example, tonsure), and a special sanctity acquired by special religous rites (ordination) enabling the clergy to perform the sacraments, the rites necessary to the salvation of mankind. With the clergy a new feature in Graeco-Roman society was thus set up: a highly organized and privileged spiritual élite, which became in time also an intellectual élite. Upon these men, as the agents of God, rested the salvation of mankind. The clergy then became the dominant element in that church, and its members were indeed inclined to identify themselves with it. Christianity was taken over by a church that almost supplanted it. The western Roman Empire was succeeded not only by barbarian kingdoms but by this church.

THE CHURCH A THEOCRACY

The pattern for the development of the organized clergy of the Church was undoubtedly the secular administration of the empire after the reorganization of Diocletian and Constantine. We have described this administration as that of a centralized, absolute monarchy, the divine attributes of whose ruler make it possible to speak of it also as a centralized theocracy. In saying that the Church followed the pattern of the state we are obliged accordingly to say that the Church itself developed as a centralized theocracy. We may differentiate the theocracy of a church from the theocracy of a state by calling the former an ecclesiastical theocracy (in the hands of the clergy) and the latter a secular theocracy (in the hands of lay officials).[18] The development of the Church as an ecclesiastical theocracy was a slow process. It did not reach its peak until the thirteenth and fourteenth centuries A.D.,[19] but by the end of the classical period the main lines of its program were already sketched.

CENTRALIZATION OF THE CHURCH

The lowest unit in the administration came to be the parish, administered by the parish priest, corresponding in the rural areas to the *villa* and in the urban areas to the wards of the city. The parish was a part of the diocese, a term borrowed from the civil administration, and the administrator of the diocese was the bishop. Actually, the dioceses of the Church were the equivalent of the city-states, or *civitates*, of the state. The diocese was a unit of the ecclesiastical province, headed by the metropolitan or archbishop, which was the equivalent of the civil province, headed by the provincial governor. A larger administrative unit than the province appeared for a while in the East with the exarchate, headed by

[18]This distinction will be used later in this book. For a more precise definition, see p. 26, n. 14.
[19]See Chap. xiii.

the exarch, the equivalent of the civil diocese, headed by the vicar. Among the metropolitans there developed for the oldest and most distinguished churches the title of patriarch (Alexandria, Jerusalem, Antioch, Constantinople, Rome), an official who may be compared with the praetorian prefect of the prefecture. To head the whole organization, or hierarchy, as the equivalent of the Roman secular theocrat or emperor was the bishop of Rome, the pope. Since his jurisdiction was never recognized by the eastern churches, the patriarch of Constantinople rose in the East to succeed him.

AUTHORITARIAN CHARACTER OF THE CHURCH

That the Church developed as an authoritarian monarchy, however, cannot be explained merely as a process of adaptation to Roman models. Any organization that claims to possess and administer a divinely revealed system of absolute truth is almost certain to become authoritarian. The possessors of divinely revealed truth are likely to feel that it must be obeyed. Yet, as we have seen, there was difficulty in agreeing upon the proper interpretation of the truth handed down in the Scriptures. Christianity very soon threatened to break up into small sects. The early Church could survive as a group of democratically organized congregations, and early doctrinal difficulties could be settled by the use of the democratic council. When councils contradicted themselves, however, centralized authority was felt necessary to keep the divergent in line. Thus arose the notion of orthodoxy and of an orthodox church whose obligation it was to suppress, by force if necessary, the heterodox, or heretic. For, as Saint Augustine said, "Heresy is a crime more atrocious than forgery or murder. If a heretic dies in sin, and if you might have saved him by using force, will not your tolerance be actual hatred? It is better to save with harshness than to destroy with gentleness."

THE BISHOP OF ROME

That the bishop of Rome became the pope or monarch of the western Church contradicted the principle of unity upon which the early Church was built, namely, the equality of all bishops. This equality was based upon the idea, established when the Church first sought a principle of authority, that the bishops were to be considered the successors of the apostles of Christ who first established churches. If, in the conflict among several opinions, an authoritative answer were to be sought it should be sought from the bishop or bishops, since the tradition of their sees went straight back to the apostles who founded them, and thus to Christ and God the Father. Apostolic succession was the guarantee of apostolic tradition and sanctioned equality in authority. Now, it could be expected that the Roman church, the church of the capital of the empire, would gain some prominence in the West. It was felt to enjoy a particular authority because it had been founded by, or associated with, two apostles,

Peter and Paul, and its bishop was thus the successor of two apostles. As early as the third century Roman bishops began to point out that as successors of Peter they enjoyed a special authority, for Christ had made Peter the founder of his church and given him unlimited power. The verses of Scripture used to support this claim were especially those of Matthew XVI: 18-19: "Thou art Peter, and upon this rock I will build my church, and the gates of hell shall not prevail against it. And I will give unto thee the keys of the kingdom of heaven; and whatsoever thou shalt bind on earth shall be bound in heaven, and whatsoever thou shalt loose on earth shall be loosed in heaven." The bishops of Rome, as successors of Peter, are thus the divinely appointed heads of the Church. Possessing the power of the keys, they are to do what they please on earth with the knowledge that their decisions and actions will be confirmed by heavenly authority. This claim to headship, the Petrine Theory, as it has been called, was never taken seriously by the churches of the Greek East; but it was hearkened to sufficiently by the churches of the West to give to the bishop of Rome a position of primacy, if not of actual headship, by the end of the classical period.

PIRITUAL AND TEMPORAL POWER OF THE ROMAN BISHOP

The development of the power of the popes in accordance with the claims of the Petrine Theory may be considered from two angles, spiritual and temporal. The development of an unlimited spiritual power of the popes has to do with their right to determine, upon appeal or otherwise, all local disputes over discipline, concerning either clergy or laity. Such power would give to the Roman bishop the decision over all questions of church personnel. Obviously it would also give him an ultimate decision on all questions of belief or dogma. For example, if a dispute arose over the proper administration of a rite that could not be settled locally, it could be carried to Rome. If a local bishop proved to be immoral the Roman bishop could discipline, transfer, or remove him. If a dispute arose over the dogma of the Trinity that could not be solved locally, the Roman bishop would settle the question. It can easily be seen that the inability to make local decisions such as these created a demand for centralized authority. It can also be understood that ambitious and power-loving popes (holy office does not stamp out these traits) were eager to extend their authority. In the course of time the popes issued decretals of their own to regulate these matters, and these decrees became part of the Church's canon law, administered by a system of ecclesiastical courts culminating in the papal courts.

TEMPORAL POWER OF THE PAPACY

If spiritual power concerns supervision of, and control over, men and clergy as Christians and officers of the Church, temporal power has to do with supervision of, and control over, men simply as men, that is, with the acquisition of property and political rights, or, in other words, with the growth cf the Church as a state. After its toleration by the empire the Church, endowed by the faithful, quickly became a very wealthy institution. In the first instance its political power was associated with the city and environs of Rome. After Rome ceased to be the political capital of the West (330), and there were no longer any western emperors (476), the popes came to be *de facto* rulers of a state comprising Rome and central Italy called the Patrimony of Saint Peter, or the Papal States. Vatican City is today a small remnant of it. This acquisition of wealth and political power may be looked upon as unfortunate. It gave to the Church's potential critics the opportunity to say that all papal decisions and actions were made to enhance economic and political rather than spiritual power.

A church directed by wealthy and often aristocratic political princes could not be expected to lead Christianity in the spirit of Jesus, the poor reformer who came from the lower classes. Political and economic power made necessary an increasingly great concern with secular rather than spiritual matters. And, indeed, the possession of wealth and political power brought up questions not only of the relationship of the two to religion but of the particular relationship of the Christian Church to the Christian state, and of the head of that Church-state, the pope, to the other heads of Christian states. These matters have continued to agitate the West.

CHURCH AND STATE IN THE EAST

The relationship of Church and state developed differently in the eastern and western halves of the empire. Before this split the state cult was administered by a layman, who, although called *pontifex maximus* (the chief priest), was a political official. Before the toleration of Christianity the Roman state controlled religion. It intended to control Christianity after its recognition. Constantine, for example, insisted upon a settlement of the Arian controversy and personally presided over the Council of Nicaea (325). He also moved the capital of the Roman Empire to Constantinople, around which an eastern Roman, or Byzantine, Empire maintained itself until 1453. The form in which this eastern Roman Empire persisted was the form it had acquired in the early centuries A.D., namely, a secular theocracy. In such a state there is no room for a theocratic church. The patriarch of Constantinople came to be recognized as the head of the Orthodox Greek Church, but the patriarch occupied a position corresponding to the Roman *pontifex maximus*. He was appointed by the emperor. His office was political as well as religious, his church a department of state. The eastern emperor, the divine lord, was the ultimate authority in religious matters. Like the western pope, he possessed the supreme spiritual as well as temporal power. He determined the belief of his church.[20] In the East, then, the Church was absorbed into the state and became a sanction for the theocratic tyranny of the emperor of Constantinople.

CHURCH AND STATE IN THE WEST

The western development was different. It differed because the Church did not have to contend with the secular power of the Roman state after 476, and before 476 this weak state was anxiously looking about for allies. Together with the Germanic kingdoms the Church gradually supplanted the Roman state in the West. Here the Church came to insist upon its freedom to administer its own affairs as it pleased. It was a state within a state, possessing its own law and capable of, and by right entitled to, the regulation of its own affairs, including of course freedom from interference in matters of belief. This amounted to the affirmation of a powerful and vital principle: that the state may not coerce in matters of conscience, except, we have to add, when it is invited or commanded to do so by the church. If the state may not interfere in the affairs of the church except when the church orders it to, then the church is using the state as its agent in the enforcement of orthodoxy. The state, for this purpose, becomes a department of the church. Secular has become subordinate to ecclesiastical authority.

AUGUSTINE AND AMBROSE ON CHURCH AND STATE

Such, for example, was the point of view of Saint Augustine when he considered the relationship between church and state. What actually can be the ultimate purpose of the state if it is not to assist the church in the salvation of the soul of mankind, and if it is thus to serve must it not be subject to the direction of the church? When the emperor Theodosius made Christianity the official state religion, Ambrose, another western Church Father and bishop of Milan, considered the matter in another way. To a man like Ambrose a Christian state quite obviously demanded a Christian emperor, that is, a man who in his public capacity as emperor conducted himself as a private Christian, obedient to the moral teachings of his religion. If he conducted himself otherwise he was no less subject to the punitive discipline of the Church than any other Christian. Theodosius got into repeated difficulties with Ambrose over this view. For having massacred certain citizens of Thessalonica, for instance, contrary to Christian teachings, Ambrose excluded him from his church. This general point of view also states a powerful and vital principle of western development. It is the demand, first, that there should be no difference between private and public morality. It also makes the Church the arbiter of politics, for who but the Church is capable of determining whether or not a given policy or act is Christian? Thus in an effort to make rulers

[20]See p. 468.

and states Christian the Church took up the position that the state is essentially subordinate to the church. It must aid the church in saving mankind and, in its own sphere, adopt Christian policies and actions. The demand of the popes for unlimited spiritual and, consequently, unlimited temporal authority, for an unqualified position as vicars of Christ and successors of Saint Peter, or as ecclesiastical theocrats, introduced much tension and conflict into western history. The bishops of the West, as equal successors of the apostles, long resisted the attempts of the bishop of Rome to establish his spiritual authority. Likewise the western state, in whatever form, jealous of its own jurisdiction, resisted, and continues to resist, the efforts of the Church to tell it what to do and how to do it.

THE GELASIAN THEORY

At the end of the fifth century, just after the fall of the western empire, Pope Gelasius (492–496) made what has become a classical and authoritative statement of the relationship that should exist between church and state. It is commonly known as the *Theory of the two powers or swords.* In a letter to the eastern emperor Anastasius he says, "There are two [powers], August Emperor, by which this world is chiefly governed." The two powers are the holy authority of the pontiffs and the royal power (*auctoritas sacrata pontificum et regalis potestas*). Of the two "the charge of the priests [*sacerdotes*] is heavier, in that they have to render an account in the Divine judgment for even the kings of men. For you know, most gracious son, that, though you preside over humankind by virtue of your office, you bow your neck piously to those who are in charge of things divine and from them you ask the things of your salvation; and hence you realize that in receiving the heavenly mysteries and making proper arrangement for them, you must in the order of religion submit yourself rather than control, and that in these matters you are dependent on their judgment and do not desire them to be subject to your will. For if, as far as the sphere of civil order is concerned, the bishops themselves, recognizing that the imperial office has been conferred upon you by Divine disposition, obey your laws . . . with what zeal, I ask you, should you not obey those who are deputed to dispense the sacred mysteries?" In a subsequent work he wrote that "Christ, mindful of human weakness and of what would be good for men's salvation, so divided the duties of the two powers that the Christian emperors would need the pontiffs for their eternal salvation and the pontiffs would use the imperial orderings for the course of temporal things. . . . When all this is taken into consideration, it is evident that a pontiff cannot be bound or loosed by the secular power."[21] It seems clear from these words of Gelasius that however much he wished to separate civil from religious power he could not avoid looking upon the religious as the more important, responsible to

[21]A. K. Ziegler, "Pope Gelasius I and His Teaching on the Relation of Church and State," *Catholic Historical Review,* XXVII (January, 1942), 432–435.

God for the conduct of the civil power, and quite independent, in the final analysis, of civilian control.

THE TRANSFORMATION OF CHRISTIANITY

The adaptability of Christianity to the religious needs of the empire explains in part its victory. These adaptations were its development as (1) a mystery cult of salvation, (2) a quasi-polytheistic religion, (3) a Greek philosophy (theology), and (4) a monarchical (theocratic) church. Altogether these adaptations amounted to a vast transformation of Christianity from a reform movement within Judaism led by the prophet Jesus to an almost universal religion in the hands of a hierarchical church. That transformation, after centuries more of development in the Middle Ages, became more pronounced and has been described by a French Protestant scholar: "When we think of Christianity in the Middle Ages these are the features that stand out: it is universalist in temper and given to warfare; exclusive, violently intolerant, to the Jews especially menacing; bristling with peremptory dogmas which set reason at defiance; worked by complex elaborate rites, mighty in their potency and mysterious, cluttered up with innumerable special devotions addressed to a good many Virgins fairly distinguishable from one another, and also to a good many specialized Saints; directed by a clergy in control of the faith and conscience of the laity who already form a strict hierarchy and tend more and more to take their orders from one sole center; kept up to the mark by a formidable army of monks and kept in check by a quibbling troop of acute theologians. If we first look upon the countless magnificent churches in which it has its abode, and the splendid ceremonies carried out therein surrounded by the symbols which inspire them, and then compare it with the religion of the Galilean prophet, humble and gentle, who claimed only to announce to his brethren the Glad Tidings of the coming of the Kingdom and to make them worthy of receiving it, compare it, I repeat with the religion of this same Jesus, whose simple piety lifted his soul toward the God of his fathers by its childlike confidence, it is difficult to discover what these two have in common. It seems as if it is the philosophical and religious form of paganism with all its contrarieties and incoherences that has taken a fresh life under the name of Christ and triumphed over the religion 'in spirit and in truth' which the Jewish-born Master had taught and lived."[22] This transformation or contrast is vital, as the above quotation reveals, to an understanding of Protestantism. For when medieval Christians became dissatisfied with their Church and their religion, and at the same time became aware of this transformation, a program of reform became clear to them: return to the original Christianity of the Scriptures, before, that is, this transformation had taken place.

[22]The selection from C. A. H. Guignebert, *Christianity, Past and Present*, pp. 184–185, copyright 1927 by The Macmillan Co., and used with The Macmillan Co.'s permission.

However much the reasons for Christianity's triumph may be analyzed it must be obvious that this new belief never would have captured the Mediterranean basin had its fundamental point of view not been more satisfactory to the inhabitants of these lands than the religions to which they had hitherto subscribed. After the long period of adaptation and controversy was over this Christian point of view came to be summarized in the works of the Greek and Latin Fathers of the Church. The four Latin Fathers were the three contemporaries Saints Ambrose, Jerome, and Augustine (354-430) and Pope Gregory the Great (590-604). Inasmuch as Saint Augustine was the most influential of these men, indeed a theologian with whom all subsequent theologians, and others as well, have had to come to terms, he may be chosen as a suitable guide to the Christian point of view of late antiquity.

SAINT AUGUSTINE

The outlines of Augustine's life summarize the experiences of the intellectuals of the classical world of his day. They are to be found for the early part of his life in his autobiographical *Confessions*, a frank account of his highly emotional and lusty, if not over-sexed, youth as well as of his intense striving for religious and philosophical peace, all written to edify those who were having similar difficulties. Augustine came from Tagaste in North Africa. His father, a member of the local *curia*,[23] was a pagan, and his mother, Monica, a Christian. He was trained to be a teacher of rhetoric, and he read voraciously in the Latin classics. Among the great Latin writers his favorite was Cicero, from whom he derived his first serious interest in philosophy. Before he was twenty this interest led to his becoming not a Christian but a Manichaean,[24] which he remained for nine years. Philosophy caused him to abandon Manichaeanism and even what his mother had taught him of Christianity. He became an out-and-out sceptic. "The notion began to grow in me," he says in the *Confessions*, "that the philosophers whom they call Academics were wiser than the rest, because they held that everything should be treated as matter of doubt and affirmed that no truth can be understood by men." He was rescued from this scepticism by Plotinus, whose notions of God, of the nature of evil, and of mysticism were thoroughly absorbed by Augustine and made a part of his Christianity. Neoplatonism led him straight to Christianity, into which, under the influence of Ambrose, he was baptized together with his illegitimate son, Adeodatus, at Milan on Easter, 387. Augustine's unwillingness to put aside his concubine postponed his coming to Christianity. "I was bound by this need of the flesh and dragged with

[23]See p. 276.
[24]See pp. 297 f.

me the chain of its poisonous delight, fearing to be set free." "I . . . begged you for chastity, saying: 'Grant me chastity and continence, but not yet.' For I was afraid that you would hear my prayer too soon, and too soon would heal me from the disease of lust which I wanted satisfied rather than extinguished."[25] After his baptism he returned to North Africa and in 391 became a priest in the church of Hippo Regius. Within a few years he became its bishop and spent the remainder of his life fighting pagans and heretics. He died in 430, at a moment when the Vandals were about to attack his episcopal city.

THE FALL OF MAN

Augustine's religious outlook is dominated by his exalted notion of God, his harsh opinion of man, and his views of the Church. God to him was the Neoplatonic One, endowed with the almighty will and power of Jehovah. The universe was his creation, and his glory was its justification. The original divine economy—God in the midst of his admiring and obedient angels—had been disrupted when Lucifer, one of these angels, had tempted a small group to rebel against God. For this act he and his angelic minions had been cast out of heaven, leaving, accordingly, a gap in the angelic hosts. For this purpose, among others, man was created on earth. As originally created in the Garden of Eden he was made sinless in the image of God and endowed with all those virtues and powers, including free will, that would have enabled him to live an eternal life of bliss in the earthly paradise. But this primal man of God's creation turned out to possess no less audacity or foolhardiness than Lucifer himself. When tempted by the serpent to disobey God's command not to eat of the fruit of the tree of the knowledge of good and evil, he succumbed, fell, sinned, and had to be cast out of the earthly paradise.

ORIGINAL SIN

This sin of Adam, the result of his own choice, was the original sin. As described by Augustine, it was a mighty one: "Even in that one sin . . . a number of distinct sins may be observed, if it be analyzed as it were into its separate elements. For there is in it pride, because man chose to be under his own dominion rather than under the dominion of God; and blasphemy because he did not believe God; and murder for he brought death on himself; and spiritual fornication, for the purity of the human soul was corrupted by the seducing blandishments of the serpent; and theft, for man turned to his own use food he had been forbidden to touch; and avarice, for he had a craving for more than should have been sufficient for him."[26] This original sin was catastrophic. It so corrupted his generative powers that Adam handed it down to all his descendants, even

[25] Trans. F. J. Sheed, pp. 96, 123, 170.
[26] Edward M. Pickman, *The Mind of Latin Christendom*, p. 79.

to you and me. All mankind has been and always will be born with original sin. As punishment for his sin God removed Adam from Eden and set him to work and to suffer. Abandoned to his vicious self, he became a mass of perdition, a servant of the Devil, and a foul slave of sin. For, Augustine explained, Adam had been helped by God in the Garden of Eden to live the perfect life. In more technical language he had been the recipient of God's grace. The result of Adam's sin was that God withdrew his aid or grace, and man, victimized now by the taint of original sin, was no longer able to live the good life. In fact, Augustine explained, because of original sin man had lost his original free will. After his fall from grace man could no longer will the good. He could only will evil. Thus he was perpetually guilty and perpetually punishable. Indeed, he was subject to death, damnation, and eternal punishment. Vile and unredeemed man in this state is the subject of Augustine's most vituperative rhetoric. Augustine warns man, lest he be subject to pride, always to remember exactly how he was conceived and how and precisely where he was born.

PREDESTINATION

Had it not been for the intervention of God man would have been eternally condemned to this unlovely state. God chose, however, to redeem mankind from eternal punishment by sending his Son, Jesus, to earth and permitting him to be crucified as a common criminal. Jesus in this way atoned for man's sins by offering his life as a ransom or sacrifice to God, or the Devil, or justice (theologians explained the atonement in different ways). In Augustine's view, Jesus permitted himself to be killed in order to show sinful mankind how much he loved it. For when men realized that Jesus had died for their sins they would become contrite, and in a contrite state they could be pardoned and again helped by God. In other words, God, because of Jesus' atonement, decided to extend his grace once again to sinful mankind. Strictly speaking, this grace needed to be extended only to a few, only to as many as were needed to restore the divine economy to its original perfection, that is, to the number of the fallen angels cast down from heaven. It came to be Augustine's opinion that those "elected" to receive God's grace would be chosen not because of any virtuous results of their contrition but only because of God's good pleasure. In other words, God had predestined some to election and condemned or preordained others to damnation or reprobation to suit his own almighty will. Nothing man might do could condition God's action. This was just inasmuch as man, because of his original sin and his sinful tendency, deserved to be damned eternally. Those who were thus condemned received only what was coming to them. Those who were elected to salvation had every reason to be grateful. In any case, no one could know whether he had been elected to salvation or not. Many were called, and few chosen.

God re-extended his grace to those whom he had determined to save. This grace instilled in man the necessary faith in Christ's sacrifice to merit salvation and to permit the will to turn from evil to good. God does not extend his grace directly but indirectly through his church, outside of which there can be no salvation. The specific medium of grace is the sacraments administered by the clergy. In Augustine's view it was the proper administration of the sacraments and not the moral character of the clerical ministrant that determined their efficacy. As he put it, "between an apostle and a drunken man there is a great difference, but between the baptism of Christ which an apostle gives and that which a drunken man gives there is no difference." It was the sacrament of Baptism that washed away original sin and all sin committed to the date of Baptism. It thus initiated the regenerative process. Postbaptismal sin came to be forgiven through the sacrament of Penance, at this moment in the development of the ritual a public affair. The sacrament of the Eucharist provided for a more or less continuous feeding on Christ. As a practical churchman Augustine knew that he must make room for the idea that the sinful individual through his own initiative may develop a longing for virtue and accumulate sufficient good works to merit salvation at God's hands. But he was never able to make the system of salvation wholly dependent upon God's grace, freely and irresistibly given to whom he chose, jibe with the system of salvation allowing for human merit. His conception of Almighty God left little room for him who had shown himself irrefutably as a puny and despicable man.

"THE CITY OF GOD"

In the last years of his life Augustine wrote his second most influential book, *The City of God* (*Civitas Dei*). He wrote it to defend Christianity from the pagan charge that the gods were using the German barbarians, as witness the Visigothic sack of Rome in A.D. 410, to punish the Romans for turning to the Christian God. Augustine, however, took advantage of this opportunity to write an apology for Christianity and to present his view of the meaning of past and future history. In it Augustine reduces all history, present, past, and future, to a contrast and struggle between what he calls the City of God and the Earthly City (*Civitas Terrena*). The struggle begins with the God who is without beginning, and ends with the establishment of the two cities on the eternal basis of heaven and hell. What has determined the course of this history from the beginning and will determine it to the end is no imaginary set of secular causes but the very will of God. This is providential, or as the philosophers like to say, teleological history, that is, history with a purpose. God then is the "designer." The course of human history is paved by fiat. "The whole connection and train of causes which makes everything become what it does become is [thus] the will of God, not Fate. . . . To know the will of God is to know the most infallible and powerful of all causes."[27]

THE FOUNDATIONS OF THE TWO CITIES

The heavenly foundation of the City of God is to be seen in those good angels who maintained "their allegiance to God, and never were or ever shall be apostate." They are the "partners of the eternal light which is the unchangeable wisdom of God." The heavenly foundation of the Earthly City is to be seen in those bad angels who joined with Lucifer in the revolt against God, who bartered "the lofty dignity of eternity for the inflation of pride." Behold then, Augustine says, the two groups of good and bad angels, "the one led by God, the other by the Devil, . . . the one enjoying God, the other swelling with pride, the one blazing with the holy love of God, the other reeking with the unclean lust of self-advancement, the one tranquil in the brightness of piety, the other tempest-tost with be-clouding desires, the one tenderly succouring and justly avenging, the other boiling with lust of subduing and hurting." Lucifer, or the Devil, the founder and king of the Earthly City, was originally a creation of God, and his fall had been prearranged by God, for in this way God had created the potential evil of the world to be used for good. God embellished "the course of the ages as it were with an exquisite poem set off with antitheses. . . . For as the beauty of a picture is increased by well-arranged shadows, so to the eye that has skill to discern it the universe is beautified even by sinners, though considered by themselves, their deformity is a sad blemish."

THE EARTHLY FOUNDATION

An earthly counterpart of the heavenly foundations of the City of God and of the Earthly City was made possible by God's creation of Adam, the primal man. For God "made man in His own image, . . . created [with] a soul endowed with reason and intelligence." Man was, indeed, "to be a mean between the angelic and bestial . . . created in such a sort that if he remained in subjection to his Creator he should pass into the company of the Angels and obtain without the intervention of death a blessed and endless immortality, but if he offended the Lord his God by a proud and disobedient use of his free will, he should become subject to death and live as the beasts do, the slave of appetite and doomed to eternal punishment after death. God commanded obedience which, in a sort, is the mother and guardian of all the virtues in the reasonable creature."

THE CITIZENS OF THE TWO CITIES

Adam was disobedient and fell from divine grace, and "the death . . . of the soul takes place when God forsakes it, as the death of the body

[27]*The City of God*, trans. and ed. Rev. Marcus Dods.

when the soul forsakes it. . . . No sooner do we begin to live in this dying body than we begin to move ceaselessly towards death. Our whole life is nothing but a race towards death, in which no one is allowed to stand still for a little space or to go somewhat more slowly, but all are driven forwards with an impartial movement and with equal rapidity." The death of the soul comes because we inherit Adam's original sin, for "man being of his own will corrupted, and justly condemned, begot corrupted and condemned children. . . . And thus from the bad use of free will, there originated the whole train of evil, which, with its concatenation of miseries, convoys the human race from its depraved origin, as from a corrupt root, on to the destruction of the second death, which has no end, those only being excepted who are freed by the grace of God." Those then who proudly follow the fallen Adam are citizens of the Earthly City, and those who humbly seek to follow Jesus, citizens of the City of God. "There are two kinds of societies: the one consists of those who wish to live after the flesh, the other of those who wish to live after the spirit." The Earthly City was formed "by the love of self, even to the contempt of God, the heavenly by the love of God, even to the contempt of self . . . the one seeks glory from men but the greatest glory of the other is God, the witness of conscience. The one, the society of godly men is to live eternally with God; the other the society of the ungodly to suffer eternal punishment with the devil."

THE HISTORY OF THE TWO CITIES

The actual earthly founder of the Earthly City was Cain, a fratricide and "archtype of crime," who was moved by that "diabolical envious hatred with which the evil regard the good." Abel belonged to the City of God and was "the first to show by a kind of foreshadowing of the sojourning City of God what iniquitous persecutions the city should suffer at the hands of wicked and as it were earth-born men." His son Seth was its actual human founder. Augustine then carries the citizens of the Earthly City and the citizens of the City of God through a long history of five ages down to the birth of Christ. This history is treated in parallel fashion, the history of the City of God being largely the history of the Hebrews, and the history of the Earthly City being non-Jewish history, whose most conspicuous examples were Assyria and Rome. "We ought," Augustine says, "where it is needful to mention the Assyrian kings, that it may appear how Babylon like a first Rome ran its course along with the City of God, which is a stranger in this world. . . . The City of Rome was founded like another Babylon, and as it were the daughter of the former Babylon, by which God was pleased to conquer the whole world, and subdue it far and wide by bringing it into one fellowship of government and laws. . . . At the time when Rome was founded then the people of Israel had been in the land of promise 718 years." Yet Augustine deigns to say that "it cannot be denied that there have been certain men even of the other nations [than the Jewish] who belonged not by earthly but heavenly fellowship to the true Israelites, the citizens of the country that is above."

THE LAST DAYS

Having brought down his history to the birth of Christ and the beginning of the Sixth Age, Augustine loses interest in the Earthly City about him and becomes primarily concerned with the end of the struggle, admitting that "in vain do we attempt to compute definitely the years that remain in this world." He suggests that the City of God is to be equated with the history of the Church, and the Earthly City with the history of pagan Rome, but the definite equation is never made. Still he was primarily concerned with the history of the Church and relegated to an inferior position the history of secular society. It is really only the desertion of the "temples of the demons" and "the human race running to the name of the liberating mediator" that matters. The end that the City of God seeks is the eternal life of its members, and this "peace of the celestial city is the perfectly ordered and harmonious enjoyment of God and of one another in God." While making its pilgrimage on earth the City of God is to seek peace. It is to "call citizens out of all nations" and gather together "a society of pilgrims of all languages, not scrupling about diversities in the manners, laws, and institutions whereby earthly peace is secured and maintained, but recognizing that however various these are, they all tend to one and the same end of earthly peace which it will make use of until the mortal condition which necessitates it shall pass away." Before the final separation between citizens of the City of God and of the Earthly City is made at the Last Judgment God will let loose the Devil, or Anti-Christ, to make a last attempt at victory. He will "go out . . . and burst forth from lurking hatred into open persecution. He shall rage with the whole force of himself and his angels for three years and six months and those with whom he makes war shall have power to withstand all his violence and stratagems." In fact, God releases the Devil only to test the City of God. "This persecution is the last which shall be endured by the Holy City throughout the world, the whole City of Christ being assailed by the whole City of the Devil as each exists upon earth."

HELL

The end of the Earthly City is hell, and "what God has said about the punishment of the damned shall come to pass. . . . Hell . . . will be material fire, and will torment the bodies of the damned whether men or devils. . . . The eternal fire will be proportioned to the deserts of the wicked, so that to some it will be more and to others less painful whether this result be accomplished by a variation in the temperature itself, graduated according to every one's merit, or whether it be that the heat remains the same but that all do not feel it with equal intensity of torment."

The end of the City of God is heaven, and "those dismissed into the life without death by the Last Judgment shall no longer be animal but spiritual, having indeed the substance of flesh but without any fleshly corruption. . . . Who can conceive," asks Augustine, "not to say describe what degrees of honour and glory shall be awarded to the various degrees of merit? . . . How great shall be that felicity which shall be tainted with no evil, which shall lack no good, and which shall afford leisure for the praises of God, who shall be all in all. . . . This shall be the great Sabbath which has no evening. . . . When we are restored by him and perfected with greater grace we shall have eternal leisure to see that he is God, for we shall be full of him and he shall be all in all."[28]

SUMMARY OF "THE CITY OF GOD"

History, then, from the early Christian point of view was but an account of the unfolding of the will of an omnipotent God. This is the original and enduring cause of all history, without an understanding of which all history is meaningless. The chief sources of this history are the Old and New Testaments properly interpreted. Beyond these history concerns primarily those Christians everywhere who are organized into the Church. Of supreme importance is what furthers the interests of the Church and carries forth into new lands the banner of Christianity. History in this sense is concerned with a vast struggle between light and darkness, flesh and spirit, good and evil, God and the Devil, the City of God and the Earthly City. It begins with the very creation of the angels themselves, continues with the fall of the bad angels, and on earth with the creation of man. Human history is a continuation of the heavenly struggle, relieved by the possibility that through Christ God may save vicious, lustful, and fallen man from the consequences of his fall. This struggle has little meaning as a moral struggle, since it is one that God allows to begin and continue and whose end he determines. The City of God, as Augustine came finally to conceive of it, was the little band of predestined Christians—only enough to make up for the number of fallen angels. Only these elect will enjoy the eternal felicity of God, and the limitation is because he has willed it so. The vast majority of the human race, the great mass doomed to perdition, will receive what they deserve, the eternal fire of hell. This conception of history is a human-hating and God-loving one. Upon the mysterious and inscrutable will of an omnipotent God it breaks the back of most of the human race. To the extent that that will is clear, it has nothing more in store for man than filling in the ranks of the angels who praise God. But Augustine does summon the historian to take up the large themes, even as the scope of his divine historical drama reached from the beginning to the end of time. He does suggest that to

[28]Trans. Dods.

be a good historian one must be a kind of philosopher or, preferably, a theologian. In any case, the historian must be able to give some meaning to the panorama of human existence. Further, he has obliged all subsequent historians to consider whether his particular interpretation of history is correct. If it is, the historian may throw away most of his books and documents and concentrate on understanding the will of God. If he should come to understand it, Augustine further suggests, he can do nothing better than follow it.

PELAGIUS

There was one feature in particular of Augustine's view that subsequent churchmen could not stomach. They came to oppose what he had to say about God's predestination of a limited number of human beings to salvation, and condemnation of the rest to damnation, all for no other reason than that he pleased to do so. Augustine had been led to this position as a result of controversy with Pelagius, a British monk. Pelagius, for example, had no use for the doctrine of original sin, believing that sin is in no sense hereditary but individual and voluntary. And men are free, as Adam was, to choose between good and evil—their wills are unconstrained by any almighty will of God. Each is thus able to create his own character and settle his own fate. To give man so much moral independence appeared unreasonable to Augustine. But for Augustine to wipe away the foundations of moral life by making the human being the slave of an inscrutable will of God, and so condemning most of mankind to hell, appeared insupportable to his successors. Moreover, if, as Augustine taught, God has settled the whole matter of salvation by predestination, there actually is little room for a church dispensing the grace of God through sacraments, for there is no need of these sacraments. All has been prearranged.

THE SETTLEMENT OF THE PREDESTINATION CONTROVERSY

The controversy over predestination and free will went on for a full century after the death of Augustine before it was settled in a form that the western Church was quite willing to accept officially. It was carried on by theologians of southern Gaul, both bishops and monks, who were interested not only in preserving some moral initiative for the individual but also some role for the Church in the salvation of the individual. They accepted the doctrine of original sin and thus made salvation impossible without the intervening grace of God. This grace, however, coming first through the sacrament of Baptism and making man for the moment sinless, restored to him his free will, and henceforth by his choice of good or evil he determined his own fate. If he could endure the prospects of hellfire, he was free to sin. If he chose the good, he acquired personal immortality, with God's help. This view not only restored moral independence to man but also gave the grace-dispensing Church a part in human salvation, for without the Church there could be no sacraments. These men preferred to keep the idea of predestination, but in a non-Augustinian form. God's original decree of election to salvation was based not on his own good pleasure in saving a limited number. It was based rather on his foreknowledge. That is, God's nature was such that he could look ahead and forward down all the centuries that were to be. He could thus see for all time those who used their free will to choose the good and those who abused it to choose evil. From this foreknowledge God drew up his decree of election. Thus the number of the elect was not willfully fixed, and a man's own merit or demerit with God determined his salvation or damnation. Dogmatic statements of these principles were drawn up at a local Council of Orange in 529 and were accepted by Pope Gregory the Great as officially Augustinian.

THE SAINTLY IDEAL

We may characterize this conception of human history and the meaning of human life by the words *ascetic, otherworldly,* and *theocentric:* ascetic inasmuch as it involves subjecting the individual to the discipline of a church, and training him for the constant battle between the flesh and the spirit; otherworldly inasmuch as it conceives of physical human life on this earth only as a means of acquiring spiritual life forever in heaven; and theocentric in that not only is everything to be explained by the will of God, and all conduct to be motivated by the love of God, but the final and eternal joy of heaven is none other than mystic absorption in God. "Its ideal," it has been said, "is the saint whose distinguishing attribute is the love of God. The saint has no interest in the world. Completely holy, he does not sin. He submits patiently to bodily suffering, poverty, and persecution. He envies neither the rich nor the powerful. He forgives those who injure him and loves those who declare their enmity to him. He is kind to all men, particularly to the weak, the poor, and the afflicted. He avoids contention, anger, and violence. He is meek, gentle, patient, and magnanimous. He is chaste. In the face of pain and evil he is courageous and long-suffering. He is obedient to authority and respectful to the law. In brotherly love he manifests his love of God. Repudiation of the world is a mark of moral worth, but not the goal of spiritual striving. This goal is attained only when the saint, infused with the saving grace, is sanctified, *i.e.,* when he becomes incapable of all else but the love of God. The way to this goal is beset with temptation, but with eyes fixed on eternal things the saint struggles on, certain that because he loves God, God's love makes his attainment of perfection possible. . . . For the few sainthood is possible in this world; for all the faithful it is the reward of heaven. In this world sainthood is a miracle of God's mercy; in the next world it is a full realization of God's purpose for men."[29]

[29]By permission from *The Great Cultural Traditions,* by R. E. Turner, II, 1161-1162. Copyright, 1941. McGraw-Hill Book Company, Inc.

Such an interpretation of the meaning of history and human life makes everything but the salvation of the soul seem unimportant. It makes attention to learning or to political, economic, and social matters unrelated to salvation seem a waste of time. Augustine was very clear on this point. "Wretched is he who knows all this [science] and knows not Thee; blessed is he who knows Thee, even though he knows nought of all this; he who knows Thee and these things also is not more blessed through them but through Thee alone. . . . More praiseworthy is the mind which knows its own weakness, than the mind which thinks not of this, but searches out the courses of the stars, even though it shall or does already know them, and knows not the way to salvation and abiding strength. . . . Be not much concerned if thou knowest not the courses of the stars or the numbers of bodies in the heavens or the earth: behold the beauty of the world, and praise the wisdom of the Creator; behold what He made, praise Him who made it, love Him who made it; for thee also, who lovest Him, He made in His own image."[30] Again Augustine says, "It is customary to inquire what the form and figure of the heavens was supposed to be according to our Scriptures. For many dispute much about subjects which with greater prudence our writers have omitted because they are of no profit to those who are learning the blessed life and what is worse, consume much precious time which ought to be spent on matters pertaining to salvation. For how does it concern me whether the heavens enclose the earth on every side like a sphere, or cover it only on one side like a disc?"[31] Saint Ambrose in a work on the creation remarks, "To discuss the nature and position of the earth does not help us in our hope of the life to come. It is enough to know what Scripture states, 'that he hung up the earth from nothing' [Job XXVI:7]. Why then argue whether He hung it up in air or upon the water and raise a controversy as to how the thin air could sustain the earth. . . . Not because the earth is in the middle, as if suspended on even balance, but because the majesty of God constrains it by the law of his will does it endure stable upon the unstable and void."[32] Thus all learning not concerned with explaining the revelation of God in the Scriptures is unimportant learning. It is therefore theology that is the queen of the sciences, and it must start with the authority of Scripture, for as Augustine stated, "the authority of Scripture is higher than all effort of human intelligence." Faith, the unquestioning acceptance of what authority states to be true, is more praiseworthy than the desire to reason. Tertullian believed because it was absurd to believe, and Augustine thought faith to be the foundation of knowledge and not knowledge the foundation of faith. "I do not know," he said, "in order that I may believe."

[30]Sydney H. Mellone, *Western Christian Thought in the Middle Ages*, p. 51.
[31]McGiffert, *Christian Thought*, II, 120 ff.
[32]Henry O. Taylor, *The Mediaeval Mind*, I, 73.

The early Christian outlook was not especially concerned with social institutions, except as obstacles to Christian progress, and certainly not with reforming them. The importance of reforming society was small compared with the importance of reforming individuals, and the former without the latter was of little value or permanence. The Latin Fathers, however, did learn a great deal about the nature of society from the writings of the Stoics and the Roman juris-consults.[33] They incorporated much of this theory in a Christianized form into their own speculation. The Stoics thought of an earlier golden age, when men, free and equal, lived in accordance with a natural law. For the Stoic golden age, the Christian Fathers substituted the earthly paradise before the fall of man, and for natural law they substituted the law of God. Otherwise they managed to maintain the Stoic view. Christianity thus came to teach that over and above all positive law there was a higher law, God's law, to which all other law should conform. In the earthly paradise, when this natural, divine law was in actual operation, there was no need for coercive government, and none existed. In this Christian golden age, before the fall, men were free and equal, and there was no slavery. Indeed, there was no private property. The fall of man had made necessary government, slavery, and private property, not only because man became vicious, but because he had to be punished for his sin. These institutions were therefore regarded by the theologians as the results of, and the remedy for, sin. They were not part of the original divine establishment; nor would they be part of the final one. They were regarded as less than sacred and as subject to limitations. Augustine maintained that God did not make men as rational beings to be lords over each other but to be lords over irrational creatures. Gregory the Great declared, "for by nature we are all equal." All insisted that property was to be used to relieve distress and suffering. Ambrose argued that nature produced only a common, not a private right to property; only use and habit produced a private right. Augustine maintained that it was not the law of God but the law of the state that distributed property to men. They were all inclined to agree that the right of property was limited by the use to which it was put.[34] The importance to the history of the western tradition of this group of ideas, as originally elaborated by the Stoics and Roman juris-consults and now confirmed by the Christian Fathers, has already been emphasized.[35] When this point of view spread among those who suffered from the very existence of these things (slavery, private property) it was used as a program of action to return to the days when they did not exist. As it came to be said, "When Adam delved and Eve span, who was then the gentleman?"

[33]See p. 253.
[34]See Carlyle and Carlyle, "Political Theory of the New Testament and the Fathers," *Medieval Political Theory in the West*, Vol. I.
[35]See pp. 244 f.

As long as political, social, and economic institutions were regarded as a remedy for sin they could not be subjected to much serious Christian criticism. After all, it was not one's material condition that mattered but the condition of his immortal soul. Why concern oneself with the evils of a society that would ultimately be swept away? Since before God all souls were equal, what matter if actually the conditions of men were glaringly unequal? Slavery as an institution did not seriously disturb the Fathers of the Church, for it need not affect the condition of the soul. Christianity, however, had first taken root among poor and simple souls, and however much this fact might be obscured when Christianity became respectable, the social and economic implications of its gospel of love could not be permanently or altogether lost sight of. There was not much to be said for the mere accumulation of wealth. "Why, then," Ambrose asked, "do you vainly occupy yourself with spinning, as it were, webs of useless wealth which are as worthless and unprofitable as the webs of spiders?"[36] The whole occupation of the merchant, banker, and trader was tainted with the cardinal sin of avarice. Usury was an unpardonable exploitation of the poor. A Greek Father called it "the last extremity of inhumanity. You are making profit out of misfortune; you are levying a tax upon tears. You are strangling the naked. You are dealing blows on the starving. There are such people as twelve-per-cent and ten-per-cent men; I shudder to mention their names. They are exactors by the month like the demons who produce epilepsy, attacking the poor as the changes of the moon come round." If wealth could be justified for what it was able to do for the poor it was not easily allied with virtue. Indeed, poverty was the Christian ideal. "Remember the Apostles who lived in hunger and in thirst and nakedness, the prophets, the patriarchs, the just men, and you will find all these not among the rich or luxurious, but amongst the poor, the afflicted and the distressed. . . . If any one were to offer thee sovereignty and political power and wealth and luxury and then having set against them poverty, were to give thee thy choice to take which thou wouldst, thou wouldst straightway seize upon poverty, if indeed thou knewest the beauty thereof."[37]

[36]By permission from *The Great Cultural Traditions*, by R. E. Turner, II, 1211, 1214, 1215. Copyright, 1941. McGraw-Hill Book Company, Inc.

[37]Herbert Butterfield, *Christianity in European History*, pp. 14–15, speaks of the importance of Christian teaching in bringing about "a softening of manners." "In the ancient Roman empire it stressed the sanctity of human life, the importance of the family, the evils of sexual license and divorce, and the wickedness of either suicide or the gladiatorial combats or the murder of infants. In all this Christianity was standing for a higher estimation of personality, based on the view of man as a spiritual creature. Furthermore, the organization of charity was carried by the Christian Church to the point at which we can regard it as an original contribution to the life of the time. And in the fundamental place which it gave to love, in its emphasis on gentleness, humility, joy, and peace, the Church was parting from the ethical ideas of the pagan world, and promoting a different kind of personality, a different posture for human beings under the sun."

ASCETICISM

The word ascetic has been used to describe the Christian point of view, inasmuch as it subjected the individual to the discipline of the Church and trained him for the battle between flesh and spirit. In Greek, asceticism (from *ascesis*, "I practice") was literally the discipline or training given the soldier or athlete. Christian asceticism in its simplest meaning is accordingly the discipline or training needed to live the life of a Christian. For the ordinary Christian it was enough to submit to the obligations of membership in the Church. There came, however, to be a group who felt that such an easy way of acquiring salvation was undignified and unheroic, and who accordingly turned their backs on the world, denying its comforts as well as rejecting its obligations in order to acquire salvation the more difficult way.[38] This way, conceived in the light of the old Platonic contrast between body and spirit as emphasized by Saint Paul, was a struggle with demons tempting one to physical indulgence. The regimes set up to win this struggle, whether that of the hermit (anchorite) or monk in a monastery (cenobite), were calculated to subdue first of all that old devil sex and to minimize anything connected with the body. The individual was thus free to live the Christian life of the spirit, and salvation was more definitely assured.

ASCETICISM AND CIVILIZATION

Looked upon in its noblest aspects, this way of life involves the willingness to abandon immediate physical pleasures for an ultimate spiritual good. In this larger view asceticism is what civilization is all about: the willingness to undergo momentary self-discipline for the sake of a more permanent common good. As such it is of course not uniquely Christian; it will be found in most religions and in every civilization. Soldiers on the battlefield are asked to be temporarily ascetic for the sake of what a military victory may bring. American civilians have been asked to make moderate sacrifices in order to bring about conditions in Europe and the world at large that, it is hoped, will prevent another disastrous war and check the growth of tyranny, Communist or otherwise. The establishment of some kind of international order and the maintenance of peace is, from this point of view, an ascetic problem, for it involves the abandonment of the petty joys of national sovereignty for the salvation—the future

---

[38] The sources of Christian asceticism in the narrow sense of the life of the hermit or monk are not only Greek but Jewish and Egyptian. The Qumran community of the Dead Sea Scrolls was monastic, and its rule (The Manual of Discipline) may be read in Burrows, pp. 371-390. This community was either identical with, or closely related to, the ascetic Essenes, or Holy Ones. Philo, in a work on *The Contemplative Life*, trans. F. H. Colson, Loeb, No. 363, pp. 113-115, speaks of a group of Egyptian ascetics outside of Alexandria called *therapeutae*, who "profess an art of healing better than that current in the cities which cures only the bodies, while theirs treats also souls oppressed with grievous and well-nigh incurable diseases, inflicted by pleasures and desires and griefs and fears, by acts of covetousness, folly and injustice and the countless host of the other passions and vices."

peace, prosperity, and happiness—of all mankind. The asceticism of the hermit or monk involves the renunciation of the flesh for the sake of personal salvation. For this and other reasons the monk became the ideal of what the Christian ought to be, and so remained for many centuries.

SAINT ANTHONY

The Christian hermitage or monastery transforms the ascetic ideal into an institution. The former arose first in the deserts of Egypt, and its earliest hero was Saint Anthony (*ca.* 251–350). His *Life*, the first example of a new literary form, the biography of a saint, was written by his friend, the strenuous opponent of Arianism, Bishop Athanasius of Alexandria. Anthony came from noble and moderately wealthy parents and was moved to take up the ascetic life when he was about eighteen or twenty by the gospel passage reading, "If thou wilt be perfect, go and sell all that thou hast, and give to the poor, and come and follow me, and thou shalt have treasure in Heaven." His early asceticism was made more difficult than ordinary by attacks of the Devil, who "would assume, by night, the form and imitate the deportment of a woman." But the black "spirit of fornication" was no match for Anthony, and the Devil "fled in terror at his word, not daring longer to be near the man."[39]

Moving from his native village to some neighboring tombs, "he entered one of the tombs, which was closed by his friend, and he was left alone." Here he was again assaulted by the Devil and his demons, who assumed the forms of "lions, bears, leopards, bulls, serpents, asps, scorpions and wolves," but Anthony's soul was "fearless and vigilant." Subsequently he went to the desert where "he lived a solitary ascetic life for nearly twenty years, never going out and rarely seen by any one." His example was quickly imitated, and "in a short time, by his persuasions, many monasteries were established, over all of which he presided as a father." Longing to become a martyr, he went to Alexandria during the persecution of Maximian and refused to obey the judge and depart, thus "showing the boldness of us Christians." But he was not martyred and returned to the desert. He then "increased the severity of his ascetic practices; for he fasted continually and had his inner garment of hair cloth and his outer of leather, which he kept till his death. He never washed his body with water to cleanse it from filth nor his feet, and even abstained from putting them in water except from necessity." To escape the multitudes who came to him for counsel and cures he withdrew still further into the desert, taking up his abode about a certain mountain and growing his own food. Here "the fruit of the ascetic life" was good, and visions were "often the solace of labors."

Anthony "never communed with" schismatics, "nor did he have familiar intercourse with the Manichaeans or any other heretics. . . . So likewise

[39]*Life of Saint Anthony*, trans. Ralph Emerson, quoted in C. W. Jones, *Medieval Literature in Translation*, pp. 15 ff.

did he abhor the heresy of the Arians and warned all neither to go nigh them nor hold their corrupt doctrine. Accordingly when some of the Ario-maniacs came to him, on examining and finding them impious, he drove them from the mountain saying, 'Their words were worse than the poison of serpents.'" He even went to Alexandria to denounce the Arians. He was consulted by philosophers even though "unacquainted with letters." For he believed that "to one . . . who has a sound mind, letters are not necessary." Constantine and his sons wrote to him for advice, but letters from emperors did not impress him. He wrote back to them "to know that Christ is the only true and eternal king. He also entreated them to be humane and mindful of justice and of the poor." When, according to Athanasius, he was approaching one hundred years of age he took ill and died in a desert mountain cell.

SAINT PACHOMIUS AND SAINT BASIL

Athanasius mentions that Anthony's asceticism became so renowned, and he accumulated so many disciples, that monasteries had to be set up. Thus alongside the individualistic and often exhibitionistic ascetic virtuoso there grew up communities of monks for whom common rules (*regulae*) were written. Monks are accordingly known as the *regular* clergy, that is, living according to a rule. Men such as priests or bishops who serve the Church in the world (*saeculum*) rather than away from it are known as the *secular* clergy. The beginnings of regular monastic life in Egypt are to be associated with Saint Pachomius, who about 340 founded and drew up a rule for a monastery at Tabenna, an island in the Nile. Both types of asceticism, that of the hermit and that of the monk, spread from Egypt throughout the East. The anchorite is to be met in such extravagant types as grazing hermits, those living on grass or herbs, and pillar saints such as Saint Simeon Stylites, who spent some thirty years atop a sixty-foot pillar. But while the eccentric hermit became notorious his was not the normal type of ascetic life. In the East it was Saint Basil, the bishop of Neo-Caesarea in Cappadocia (*ca.* 330–373), who supplanted Saint Pachomius as the legislator for the monastery. In fact, the Basilian Rule became and remains the standard rule for eastern Mediterranean lands, that of Byzantine and Slavic monasticism. It is still today the foundation for the regulations guiding the group of monasteries constituting the Holy Mountain of Athos.

EARLY ASCETICISM IN THE WEST

Eastern asceticism spread westward in both its forms. During one of his exiles Athanasius lectured to Roman audiences on Egyptian practices, and his life of Saint Anthony was translated into Latin. Saint Jerome made available a Latin version of the Rule of Saint Pachomius, and the Rule of Saint Basil was soon known. In the West Egyptian practices were first established in Gaul. Saint Martin of Tours set up a house at Ligugé, and, after becoming bishop of Tours, moved it to Marmoutier on the Loire. In the early fifth century Honoratus, later the bishop of Arles (426–429), founded the monastery of Lérins on an island off Cannes. During the same period John Cassian founded houses for men (Saint Victor's) and women at Marseilles, and, building upon his experiences with eastern monasteries, wrote two works, the *Institutes* and the *Collations*, aiming in part to adapt the more strenuous eastern practices to the West. To these houses came British and Irish students who carried Egyptian asceticism back home with them. And in these houses, especially Lérins, the rigors of Augustine's predestination were softened. At the same time that monasticism was being introduced into southern Gaul it was also being introduced to Germans on the middle Danube by Saint Severinus. Indeed, it is quite clear that the monastery was beginning to supply other needs than those of the seeker after the more difficult way of salvation. To Saint Martin and Saint Severinus it offered the careers of missionaries. To many in that most violent century it must have offered, as it has continued to offer today, a security unattainable elsewhere and a retreat for those for whom the world had no place. Always a place of penance for the sinful and occasionally the criminal, for those who were lonely or grief-stricken, it became, as it was to remain, a means of escape from the prison-house of reality.

SAINT JEROME

The monastic movement was supported with enthusiasm by the Latin Fathers, of whom the last, Pope Gregory the Great, was himself the first monk to become a pope. Augustine, while sensitive to the abuses of long-haired fake ascetics who wished only to substitute an assumed piety for work, himself extended the monastic ideal to his cathedral clergy. The most extreme defender of ascetic practices among the Fathers was Saint Jerome. He combined his own ascetic practices with scholarship, a combination that has long endured, and endeavored to guide well-born Roman ladies in a successful practice of the ascetic life. He was willing to combat all who dared to impugn the sanctity of virginity, whether in men, women, or the Virgin Mother of Christ herself. From his picturesque letters we get a statement of his own difficulties with the ascetic life and of his instructions to the Roman matrons who wished to follow the new discipline. One trouble, Jerome says, was that he could not forget the gay Rome he abandoned for the Palestinian desert: "Oh, how often, when I was living in the desert, in that lonely waste, scorched by the burning sun, which affords to hermits a savage dwelling-place, how often did I fancy myself surrounded by the pleasures of Rome! I used to sit alone; for I was filled with bitterness. My unkempt limbs were covered in shapeless sackcloth; my skin through long neglect had become as rough and black as an Ethiopian's. Tears and groans were every day my portion;

and if sleep ever overcame my resistance and fell upon my eyes, I bruised my restless bones against the naked earth. Of food and drink I will not speak. Hermits have nothing but cold water even when they are sick, and for them it is sinful luxury to partake of cooked dishes. But though in my fear of hell I had condemned myself to this prison-house, where my only companions were scorpions and wild beasts, I often found myself surrounded by bands of dancing girls. My face was pale with fasting; but though my limbs were cold as ice my mind was burning with desire, and the fires of lust kept bubbling up before me when my flesh was as good as dead.

"And so, when all other help failed me, I used to fling myself at Jesus' feet; I watered them with my tears, I wiped them with my hair; and if my flesh still rebelled I subdued it by weeks of fasting. I do not blush to confess my misery; nay, rather, I lament that I am not now what once I was. I remember that often I joined night to day with my wailings and ceased not from beating my breast till tranquillity returned to me at the Lord's behest. I used to dread my poor cell as though it knew my secret thoughts. Filled with stiff anger against myself, I would make my way alone into the desert; and when I came upon some hollow valley or rough mountain or precipitous cliff, there I would set up my oratory, and make that spot a place of torture for my unhappy flesh. There sometimes also— the Lord Himself is my witness—after many a tear and straining of my eyes to heaven, I felt myself in the presence of the angelic hosts and in joy and gladness would sing: 'Because of the savour of thy good ointments we will run after thee.' "[40]

SAINT JEROME A CICERONIAN

Another trouble Jerome confesses was his inability to abandon classical literature, an inability which led him to take his library with him to the desert with almost fatal results. "But even when I was on my way to Jerusalem to fight the good fight there, I could not bring myself to forgo the library which with great care and labour I had got together at Rome. And so, miserable man that I was, I would fast, only to read Cicero afterwards. I would spend long nights in vigil, I would shed bitter tears called from my inmost heart by the remembrance of my past sins; and then I would take up Plautus again. Whenever I returned to my right senses and began to read the prophets, their language seemed harsh and barbarous. With my blind eyes I could not see the light: but I attributed the fault not to my eyes but to the sun. While the old serpent was thus mocking me, about the middle of Lent a fever attacked my weakened body and spread through my inmost veins. It may sound incredible, but the ravages it wrought on my unhappy frame were so persistent that at last my bones scarcely held together.

[40]*Select Letters*, trans. F. A. Wight, Loeb, No. 262, p. 53.

"Meantime preparations were made for my funeral: my whole body grew gradually cold, and life's vital warmth only lingered faintly in my poor throbbing breast. Suddenly I was caught up in the spirit and dragged before the Judge's judgment seat: and here the light was so dazzling, and the brightness shining from those who stood around so radiant, that I flung myself upon the ground and did not dare to look up. I was asked to state my condition and replied that I was a Christian. But He who presided said: 'Thou liest; thou art a Ciceronian, not a Christian. For where thy treasure is there will thy heart be also.'"

SAINT JEROME AND EUSTOCHIUM

Eustochium was one of the young ladies whom Jerome undertook to instruct in the proper way to persist in a sacred life of unmarried virginity. She must always, Jerome advises, keep in mind the disadvantages of marriage, "such as pregnancy, a crying baby, the tortures of jealousy, the cares of household management, and the cutting short by death of all its fancied blessings." As for himself, Jerome says, "I praise wedlock, I praise marriage; but it is because they produce me virgins." Eustochium must abandon her former enjoyment of luxuries. She must "avoid wine as you would avoid poison. . . . Wine is the first weapon that devils use in attacking the young." She must also avoid good food. "Not that God . . . takes any delight in the rumbling of our intestines or the emptiness of our stomach, or the inflammation of our lungs; but because this is the only way of preserving chastity." She must avoid the company of such women "as only wish to seem and not to be virgins." She must not see too much of married women or "frequent the houses of the great," for if there is one place where asceticism is not respected it is in the houses of women "puffed up by their husbands' honours, who surround themselves with troops of eunuchs and wear robes inwrought with fine threads of gold." She must avoid widows "who ride in their roomy litters with a row of eunuchs walking in front: see their red lips and their plump sleek skins; you would not think they had lost a husband, you would fancy they were looking for one. . . . Let your companions be those who are pale of face and thin with fasting."

But if certain classes of women are dangerous men are inevitably more so, and among these the clergy. For some "only seek the office of presbyter and deacon that they may be able to visit women freely. These fellows think of nothing but dress; they must be nicely scented, and their shoes must fit without a crease. Their hair is curled and still shows traces of the tongs; their fingers glisten with rings; and if there is wet on the road they walk across on tiptoe so as not to splash their feet. When you see these gentry, think of them rather as potential bridegrooms than as clergymen. Indeed, some of them devote their whole life and all their energies to finding out about the names, the households, and the characters of married ladies."

If it is necessary to go out, "Let your dress be neither elegant nor slovenly, and let it not be noticeable by any strangeness that might attract the notice of passers-by and make people point their fingers at you." It is better, however, to stay at home. "Let the seclusion of your own chamber ever guard you." Stay home and read. "Read often and learn all you can. Let sleep steal upon you with a book in your hand and let the sacred page catch your drooping head." But read sacred, not secular, literature. For "what has Horace to do with the Psalter, Virgil with the Gospels and Cicero with Paul? . . . We should rise from our bed two or three times in the night, and go over those passages of Scripture which we know by heart." Such a regime will not seem hard to one "who regards all the pomp of this world as dross, and holds everything under the sun as vain, if only he may win Christ." Finally he says to her, "As often as this world's vain display delights you; as often as you see in life some empty glory, transport yourself in thought to Paradise and begin to be now what you will be hereafter."[41]

ASCETICISM AND HUMANISM

The Christian victory in the pagan world meant the supersession of the point of view we have called classical humanism by what we have called Christian asceticism. In concluding this chapter it is necessary to reinforce this contrast and to ask whether in its adaptation to the Graeco-Roman world Christianity did not also adapt itself to humanism and thus produce something that could be called Christian humanism, if not humanistic Christianity.

Humanism preferred to look at the world of nature and of man primarily through human eyes. Man was the measure of all things. It was anthropocentric. Christianity, on the contrary, looked upon the universe primarily from a supernatural point of view. It concerned itself with a God, the creator and director of the universe, to whom man was subject. It was theocentric. Humanism preferred to emphasize the importance of man's life here on the earth and to seek means of perfecting an art of living upon it. It was essentially worldly. Christian asceticism, on the contrary, looked upon man's life on this earth as an unfortunate necessity brought about by his fall. It could hardly be made an art, but could rather become a discipline by which man could be trained for the life to come. Life on earth was to be avoided or endured, being compensated for by the heavenly life. Christianity was otherworldly. Humanism felt that an art of living could be realized upon earth because man was essentially a good and noble creature possessed of the abilities or potentialities necessary to the realization of the good life. What was necessary was to provide those conditions under which the human being could unfold his capacities in order both to develop his own personality and contribute to the common good. Christianity's description of man after the fall made

[41]*Select Letters*, p. 159.

him evil and depraved and incapable of any good. There was no hope in this vile creature unless he were restored by the grace of God to his condition before the fall. And, once restored, his sinful tendency always caused him to suffer little falls. Thus life on earth could not be made an art because man was always sinning. He did, however, have divine potentialities, and under the guidance of the Church he could use his life on earth as a way to the perpetual enjoyment of God in an afterlife.

Humanism felt that a part of man's goodness and nobility, indeed the chief glory that made it possible for him to create an art of living, was his rationality, his power to reason, and thus his ability to choose properly between alternatives. The universe was an intelligible thing, life was comprehensible, and what made them so was the application of man's mind to a study of the way in which they functioned. Since man could come to understand the laws of nature he could develop ways of adapting himself to them. He was intellectually a free person. He possessed free will. Christianity taught that man before the fall was a rational and intelligent creature. But original sin had contaminated this aspect of his nature. Sin and the sinful tendency made him a creature of dark and monstrous irrationality, the victim of passionate lust. By the acceptance of God's grace man's rationality could be sufficiently restored to enable him to choose between good and evil. Whatever choice he made, however, was within the larger pattern of God's providence. Man could not be trusted to make choices that would fashion the world simply according to his heart's desire. If humanism made man the master of his own fate, capable of directing his own life in a responsible manner, Christianity made him dependent upon God, who directs him in the way he is to go.

Humanism, moreover, trusted man because it believed he was a political and social animal seeking rationally to realize a good life in the society of free men whose potentialities were like his and to be realized with his. This good life was one of moderation and measure that aimed at the whole expression of the many-sided individual, a life which chose to accept philosophy rather than religion as its moral guide. Its purposes included not only the widest and profoundest possible exercise of the intellect in the fields of philosophy, science, and mathematics but the cultivation of the best in art, literature, and music. It was good-natured and tolerant. It made man the slave of no form of dogmatic belief, and if it gloried and exulted in his capacity for achievement it could smile with indulgence at his weakness.

That man was a political or social animal was of little concern to the Christian outlook. Moderation and measure had no meaning when it came to the defense of Christ. If humanism looked upon the state as the chief institution at man's service, Christianity substituted the Church, the possessor and interpreter of the divine truth contained primarily in the Bible and in what the Church called tradition. By the end of the classical period the Church was a monarchical institution administering a common way of salvation to all mankind and ready to impose, by force if necessary, a uniform body of belief. It asked man not to question but to accept. It made a virtue of faith, and it made this faith originally the gift of God. Whatever in life did not relate to the promotion of salvation was of slight consequence. Learning was of importance only in so far as it helped to clear away the obscurities of Scripture and tradition. Without revelation it was completely valueless. Art was now to put beauty at the service of Christian ritual and Christian faith. Life for the Christian was a matter of such desperate earnestness; it was so necessary to participate correctly in the unique historical transformation that was going on that there was little time for smiling and not much indulgence for the sinner dawdling by the way. A longer experience with the human race taught Christianity how to smile and how to be indulgent.

CHRISTIAN HUMANISM

It could be argued that these two viewpoints, Greek humanism and Christian asceticism, are incompatible, and that, accordingly, if the original meaning of these phrases is kept, Christian humanism is a contradiction. It is certainly true that the history of the western tradition is concerned largely with the attempt to harmonize them and that the very difficulty of the attempt has given vitality to this history. It is therefore necessary to point out that by the end of the classical period Christianity had adopted some tenets that we have called humanistic, even if in its own way. It had discovered that it could not get along without reason if it wished to keep from dissolving into mutually hostile sects. The Scriptures were not clear, and it was possible to derive differing interpretations from them and from tradition. Allegory was not sufficient to wipe away these ambiguities and divergencies. Reason was necessary. Even Greek philosophy, as we have had occasion to point out, was necessary in both its Platonic and Stoic forms. Christian theologians, therefore, maintained and have continued to maintain that the Christian scholar needed at least some training in classical philosophy. Thereupon was raised the issue of eliminating the boundaries of faith and making Christianity as rational as possible. This question of the proper relationship between faith and reason has been a constant preoccupation of Christian thinkers.

ASCETIC REASON AND FREE WILL

We have indicated that Christian theologians were not content to let Augustine take away man's moral initiative and give it wholly to God. They insisted that when once man's evil nature was purged by divine grace man was capable henceforth of choosing his own path. In this way Christianity came to adopt a fundamental tenet of humanism: that man possesses freedom of the will. We must add, however, if the phrases are permissible, that it is an ascetic reason and an ascetic free will that is meant here. For in the Christian view man's reason is subordinated to his credulity. Reason is tolerable only when revelation is not altogether clear. Its purpose is to explain the content of faith not to question that faith. Man's free will is a gift of God through grace, and he cannot be trusted to use it well. Restoring it to him did not mean that he should have intellectual freedom. It was dangerous for him to use it in a way not approved by ecclesiastical authority. In this limited way, then, it may be said that it was quite clear to the leaders of the Church, as we have indicated, that if there was to be a Christian literature and art as well as a Christian philosophy it would be impossible to do without training in classical languages and a knowledge of classical literature and art. In order to give the world his translation of the Scriptures into Latin (the Vulgate), Saint Jerome had to know Hebrew and Greek.

THE EQUALITY OF SOULS

However circumscribed in its humanistic approach, early Christianity nevertheless contributed certain powerful ideas to the individualistic tradition of the West. Humanism may be said to have emphasized the dignity of the whole man, body and soul, heart and mind, and to have advocated a balanced relationship between them. Christianity, while denying the dignity of the body, preserved the dignity of the soul. This divine soul raised man above the level of the beasts. A unique possession, it made possible his glorification and immortality. In making man a potential god Christianity immeasureably enhanced his dignity and sacred quality. The common possession of this immortal soul made all human beings equal, equal not necessarily in endowment or station but equal before God, and alike liable to eternal glory or eternal punishment. Through its retention of the Stoic notion of natural law and of a primeval state where men were free and equal Christianity reinforced the idea of equality and kept alive the idea that what man once was he could again become. The principle of the equality of souls before God could have subsequent implications that would involve more than the soul.

The Christian insistence in the West upon a separation of Church from state in matters of religion made possible the subsequent insistence that politics could not morally coerce conscience. Its theocratic politics, while absolutist and authoritarian, subscribed to the notion that the state must adhere to the principles of morality no less than the individual. There was no distinction of a public as opposed to a private morality. These views have made it possible for some Christians to resist modern dictatorship.

CHRISTIAN LOVE

Christianity arose out of the needs of the simple people of Palestine. It was a protest against the control of Judaism by an exclusive priesthood. Jesus and his followers were simple folk looking for some religious escape from the miseries of their environment. It was among the humble that

Christianity first spread around the Mediterranean. Among pagan thinkers it was only the Stoics who had talked about humanity, human brotherhood, and a common citizenship in the universe. Yet, however noble these sentiments, they were not tinged with compassion for the sorry lot of all humans, a compassion expressing itself in a love of man for man that took the form of loving action and thus had a social application. In preaching the love of man for man Christianity took up the tradition of social righteousness taught by the Hebrew prophets, a righteousness to be realized in public as well as personal life. This compassion for the tragic lot of man, especially the poor and humble, is the core of the ethic of Jesus. It is a religiously motivated love. The love of neighbor must be the result of the love of God. It is the mutual love of children flowing from the love of a common, just, and merciful Father. To be sure, this gospel tenet of brotherly love was somewhat obscured by the transformations through which Christianity went as it spread through classical society. But it was never lost, even if it came to be something rather preached about than acted upon, and something that an occasional saint, if not an ordinary Christian, might take seriously. Yet it was the Church that set aside a definite portion of its revenues for the sake of the poor and looked to the care of the outcast, the criminal, the widow, and orphan; the Church, too, that provided care for the sick in hospitals. Its thinkers were known to speak out against the exploitation of the poor and to criticize certain forms of economic activity that led to the vain accumulation of wealth. If the compassionate love of man for man, not so much as a religious obligation, but simply as a human obligation based upon a common human dignity and capacity, had been a tenet of Greek humanism, and if it could have been acted upon in any notable way in the classical world, we may surmise that there might not have been a victorious Christianity. The Christian humanism of love and compassion, far more vital than any other kind of humanism, in addition to the other democratic implications of Christian asceticism may have had more to do with its acceptance by an exploited society than any other feature. Christianity, however much absorbed by the status quo, bred a perpetual discontent. There had once been an earthly paradise. Jesus was the Christ who would come to establish the perfect society. If the Kingdom of God were a heavenly kingdom to be established at some time in a remote future there would be Christians impractical enough to insist that while waiting for it to come something might be done to make more of a utopia of man's earthly habitat. Christian impatience over the delay of the new kingdom was to blossom forth one day in a doctrine of progress. Likewise, if at the end of the classical period the tradition of Christian asceticism had become somewhat diluted, the mere fact of its asceticism was, and has always been, a constant reminder that the ends of life are not merely material, that happiness requires more than mere bodily comfort, and that there can be no peace for which a sacrifice is not made.

chapter nine

THE WESTERN TRADITION IN THE
EARLY MIDDLE AGES

$\mathcal{T}$HE MIDDLE AGES. The period of about a thousand years after the fall of the western empire (476) is customarily referred to as the Middle Age (*medium aevum*), or Middle Ages, or medieval period. This terminology is an inheritance from those scholars who, under the influence of the earliest enthusiastic revival of classical learning, were devoted to the study of the Graeco-Roman period, which seemed to them the first important epoch in the history of mankind. Their own age, the modern, seemed the second. The age intervening between the classical and the modern was, they thought, because of its barbaric ignorance and the extremes of its Christian asceticism to be passed over as an insignificant interlude, a mere transitional, or middle, age. Indeed, the term Dark Ages has come to be popular for the medieval period. The darkness has been associated with ignorance, cruelty, superstition, and barbarism.

EARLY WESTERN DEVELOPMENT

Ignorance, cruelty, superstition, and barbarism were plentiful enough in the Middle Ages, as in all ages, but it is neither accurate nor helpful to look upon the period simply from this point of view. Later Roman historians record a growing ignorance, cruelty, superstition, and barbarism. In the midst of a society with these characteristics Christianity grew and conquered. After 476 the leading western institutions were the German monarchies and the Christian Church. The historian's general interest must center not upon the extent and depth of the darkness but upon the success of these two institutions in stemming and then reversing the downward trend. The reversal produced the early development of western European civilization.

THE PROSPECT OF A CHRISTIAN CIVILIZATION

The primitive, barbarized, pauperized, illiterate, and class-ridden society of early western Europe lived under the guidance of the western tradition, formed essentially by Greek humanism and Christian asceticism. At the moment when the barbarian kings began their independent careers the Christian part of this tradition had totally supplanted or absorbed the humanistic. The new civilization of western Europe emerged under Christian auspices, and whether they were creative enough to give it character and substance was doubtful. Would Christianity be able to afford the West an ample outlet for the expression of its various capacities? Would the ascetic point of view be adequate to retain an exclusive hold upon the mind and heart of western mankind? Could it supply the inspiration for a new western literature? Would it offer the architect, the sculptor, or the painter a chance to unfold and develop his genius? Would it support the scholar? And would it undertake to change, in accordance with its gospel of love, the harsh political, economic, and social conditions of the age?

THE CHRISTIAN PROGRAM

The Church went out to convert the barbarians from paganism and heresy, and did so. It thus enormously extended its organization, power, wealth, and prestige. If what we have said about asceticism is true, the Church could offer to the barbarian kingdoms no secular program of political, economic, or social reconstruction. In such things it was only very indirectly interested. It was interested, we may say, only to the extent that they were necessary to its own survival, expansion, and prosperity. What it did offer was a program of moral reconstruction or spiritual regeneration calculated to save the decadent, barbarian West from its sin. In so far as learning and the arts were necessary for this program it would use them. There would be a Christian literature, learning, and art. In the main, however, ascetic otherworldliness regarded the external world as something to endure rather than to reform.

POLITICAL INSECURITY IN THE WEST

The basic needs of early western society appeared to be secular rather than religious. The West had desperate need for the political security and peace that the Germanic kingdoms did not supply. Their kings, considering their kingdoms as little private patrimonies, were brutal and unrestrained in their aggressions. After 476 two new groups of German barbarians settled in Italy. The Arian Ostrogoths moved from Pannonia

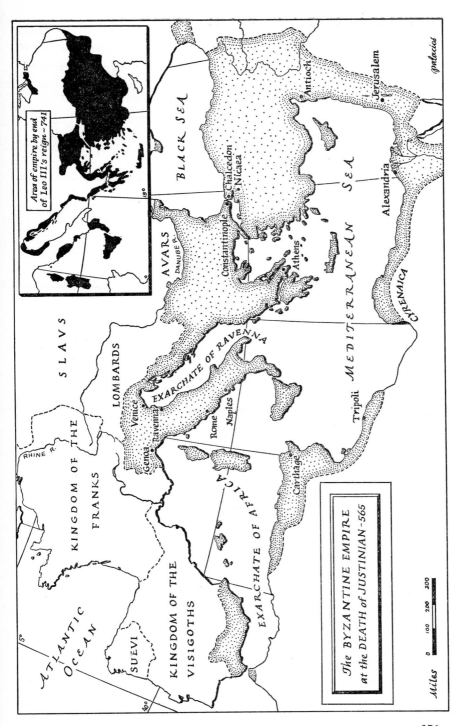

Area of empire by end of Leo III's reign – 741

BLACK SEA

AVARS

DANUBE R.

SLAVS

LOMBARDS

Venice
Ravenna
Genoa

EXARCHATE OF RAVENNA

Constantinople
Chalcedon
Nicaea

Athens

Rome

Naples

EXARCHATE OF AFRICA

Carthage

Tripoli

MEDITERRANEAN SEA

CYRENAICA

Antioch

Jerusalem

Alexandria

Palestina

RHINE R.

KINGDOM OF THE FRANKS

ATLANTIC OCEAN

SUEVI

KINGDOM OF THE VISIGOTHS

The BYZANTINE EMPIRE at the DEATH of JUSTINIAN – 565

Miles

0   100   200   300

CHRONOLOGY — The Early Middle Ages

	Reigns and Events	The Church	Literature
300			
		Saint Patrick (ca. 385–461)	Prudentius (ca. 348–410) Orosius (ca. 385–420)
400			
	Theodoric the Ostrogoth (474–526) Clovis (481–511)	Saint Benedict (480–544)	Boethius (ca. 475–525) Cassiodorus (ca. 480–575)
500			
	Justinian (527–565)	Saint Columba (521–597) Saint Columban (ca. 540–615) Pope Gregory the Great (r. 590–604) Saint Augustine (English missionary, d. 604)	Fortunatus (ca. 530–610) Gregory of Tours (538–594) Isidore of Seville (ca. 560–636)
600			
		Saint Benedict Biscop (ca. 628–690) Synod of Whitby (663) Saint Boniface (ca. 680–755)	Bishop Aldhelm (ca. 640–709) Caedmon (fl. 670) Venerable Bede (ca. 672–735)
700			
	Charles Martel (715–741) Battle of Tours (732) Pepin the Short (751–768) Charlemagne (781–814)	Pope Stephen II (r. 752–757) Pope Leo III (r. 795–816)	Cynewulf (fl. 750) Alcuin (ca. 735–804) Theodulphus (d. 821) Einhard (ca. 770–840)
800			
	Louis the Pious (814–841) Treaty of Verdun (843) Alfred the Great (871–899) Treaty of Mersen (870)	Pope Nicholas I (r. 858–867)	John Scotus Erigena (ca. 810–880) Notker of St. Gall (ca. 840–912)

under the leadership of their King Theodoric, destroyed Odovacar's kingdom,[1] and founded one of their own. This in turn was destroyed when Justinian (527-565), the eastern Byzantine emperor, made the Italian peninsula a part of his empire. Justinian's successors were unable to prevent the Arian Lombards, after 568, from fixing the capital of their kingdom at Pavia and partitioning the rest of the peninsula with the East. Both the rivalry of German kings and further barabarian invasions prolonged the insecurity of the West. The Slavic peoples, pushed on by the Mongolian Avars, moved westward to fill the vacuum left by the Germans.[2] The Arabs moved westward along the southern shore of the Mediterranean Sea,[3] cutting off North Africa and also, for a considerable time, Spain, as an area within which the new western civilization could take root. In the ninth and tenth centuries western Europe was attacked on all sides by barbarians—on the north by the Scandinavian Vikings (Danes, Norwegians, and Swedes), on the east by the Mongolian Hungarians (Magyars), and on the south by Moslems. Not until the eleventh century was western Europe relatively free from external barbarian aggressions, and when these ceased it was convulsed by a new kind of internal violence, namely, that of feudalism.

THE CHURCH AND SECULAR TASKS

Against barbarian attack the Church could offer little protection except prayers. It had rather to seek protection. Nor could it do anything to relieve the economic stagnation of the western world, a condition that likewise was to last until the eleventh century. It enhanced the castelike structure of early medieval society by adding to it its own clergy, a part of whom were aristocratic and all of whom were privileged. The formidable secular tasks of defense, of escape from economic stagnation and social immobility—the enormous job of keeping western society alive—required the talents of men who commanded more than an otherworldly point of view. If the Church was to become socially vital the virtuous conduct for which Christianity offered eternal rewards had to concern itself with improving the earthly lot of man.

It is fair to say that the barbarian leaders of the West, while formally adopting the Christian outlook, never took it so seriously as forthwith to abandon all attempts to work out the political, economic, and social problems facing them. While they were not unconcerned about their own and their subjects' souls, salvation was primarily a matter for the Church. Keeping the Church thus occupied freed them for more immediate, secular tasks. They also recognized, and were quick to support, the Church for its ability to act as a civilizing institution outside the purely spiritual

[1]See p. 284.
[2]See pp. 280-281.
[3]Justinian had also destroyed the Vandal kingdom in North Africa. This area was therefore taken by the Arabs from the Byzantine Empire.

sphere. For the Church, when possible, helped the barbarian leaders to perform the necessary secular tasks. No matter how much it set itself above the state, for example, in trying to induce these barbarian kings to observe the simplest rules of Christian morality, it supported the state as a sacred institution. At a time when there were no literate laymen to conduct the simple administration of the state the Church supplied literate churchmen. The upper clergy, the aristocratic bishops and archbishops, were the rulers of their episcopal towns and the administrators of huge estates. Asceticism in its monastic form[4] became somewhat practical. To the extent, then, that Christianity did not limit itself to otherworldly ends at a time when state and society desperately needed its help, it acquired the deeper allegiance of this society.

Evil political, economic, and social conditions in the Roman Empire had helped Christianity to victory. Their continuance in early medieval society served to prolong an exclusively Christian outlook. As the western world began slowly to climb out of the depths of the later Roman and early medieval worlds it began as slowly to abandon an exclusively ascetic point of view. To the extent that the Church, in spite of its concern with heaven, worked to ameliorate conditions on earth, and to the extent that it was able to adapt itself to an increasingly less ascetic and more humanistic outlook, it survived and prospered as a vital social institution. It always recognized that there was a certain danger in this approach. For if there was to be a heaven on earth, what then was to become of heaven in the heavens. After adapting itself to the needs of the classical world and producing what we have defined as Christian humanism, Christianity had to adapt itself further to the needs of the medieval world and enlarge the content of this humanism.

GERMANIC POLITICAL INSTITUTIONS

The dominant political tradition of early medieval Europe was theocratic. Theocracy had taken the form of a national monarchy (Jewish kingdom), an empire (Egyptian, Roman), and a church (Judaism, Christianity). The political tradition of the West, however, was not exclusively theocratic. It concerned also the democratic city-state (Athens, republican Rome). In so far as tradition was concerned, western Europe had to choose between theocracy and democracy. Its choice came to be determined to some extent by the character of the institution that the Germans brought with them into the empire. Tribal societies, like the German, possess a certain primitive democracy. Since their chieftains must consider the opinions of councils of elders and tribal assemblies, they are in no position to control the activities of the tribe as despots. When in the course of their invasion the German tribes became monarchies, their new kings were elected by the tribe and were limited by the decisions of tribal

[4]See p. 392.

elders and assemblies. The notion persisted that no king was quite wise enough to rule alone. The law of primitive societies, such as the German, is unwritten custom and, properly speaking, is never made, but grows. For the purpose of administering justice it was always necessary to consult those who knew the custom. The administration of justice was thus a co-operative affair. In this kind of society everyone, even the king, was limited by the custom or law of the group. The king was not, as Roman law said of the emperor, freed from the laws (*legibus solutus*). German customary law was personal. A person who grew up in the midst of a certain body of customs (for example, Saxon or Bavarian) retained the right to be tried according to these customs no matter where he might be. This personal right enhanced the dignity of membership in a tribe. German society was composed largely of freemen of no great distinction in wealth; of peasant warriors whose agriculture rested upon ancient practice, when land was commonly and not privately owned. The German peasant had common rights in the fields, forests, and streams, and the village itself was a co-operative organization.

THE FUTURE OF THE WESTERN TRADITION

The early Germans thus introduced new features into the political, social, and economic tradition of the West. Its major tradition would now have to develop out of something more than a conflict between humanism and asceticism or between democracy and theocracy. It would develop from a conflict between despotism and primitive notions of responsible government; between written and territorial notions of law (Roman) and unwritten, customary, personal notions of law; between a stratified, castelike society, where most men were dependent serfs, and a society in which, as warriors and peasants and also as Christians, men retained some dignity and freedom. In the formation of the new West primitive notions of government, law, and society did not disappear in the face of the Graeco-Roman-Christian heritage. These notions persisted most strongly in those sections of the empire where the German peoples actually succeeded in supplanting, or largely supplanting, the Roman populations. These areas were not many, and Anglo-Saxon England was the most important of them. The clash between the old and the new was to produce in the long run some of the characteristic features of western civilization: (1) the limited monarchy, (2) the English common law (on the Continent, the Roman law was ultimately victorious), (3) the co-operative village community, and (4) the mobile (rather than the hereditary) class structure. The western tradition was not, however, to be forged exclusively by those Romanized and Germanic peoples who were contained within the boundaries of a former Roman Empire. For in the spirit of the Roman conqueror the western Church went out beyond the boundaries of that empire to gather in the primitive Germanic,

Scandinavian, and Slavic peoples of central and northern Europe, besides the un-Romanized Celts of the British Isles. It was in this larger area that the final tradition was to be wrought. In tracing its early history (A.D. 500–1000) we must consider the development of (1) a western secular (German) theocracy, (2) an ecclesiastical theocracy, (3) a western asceticism, and (4) a western Christian culture.

Development of a Western Secular (German) Theocracy

THE SALIAN FRANKS BECOME CHRISTIAN

The first attempt to build an imperial theocracy in the West was made by the Salian Franks,[5] who in 476 were located in northern Gaul. The political history of their state and empire, persisting until 987 in France (the land of the Franks), became the history of all those Germanic peoples, except those in Britain, who settled within or remained outside the Roman Empire. The theocratic nature of their state was not fully apparent until the reign of their greatest king and emperor, Charles the Great, Charlemagne (781–814). But certain features of the Frankish empire can be discerned as the Franks began to expand under Clovis, their first important king (481–511). A tough wielder of the battle-ax, Clovis, with his people, was pagan at the beginning of his reign and, if we may believe his biographer, the good bishop-historian Gregory of Tours in his *History of the Franks*, he might have remained so had not God miraculously intervened in the course of his war with the Alamanni. Gregory has Clovis say to God, "On Thee am I fain to believe, if but I may be plucked out of the hands of mine adversaries," and reports that "as he said this, lo, the Alamanni turned their backs and began to flee." Clovis was subsequently baptized by the archbishop of Rheims in his cathedral church, and "like a new Constantine . . . moved forward to the [baptismal] water, to blot out the former leprosy." (pp. 68, 69)[6]

CLOVIS CONQUERS THE VISIGOTHS

It was fortunate that the church of northern Gaul was not an Arian but an orthodox church, for this fact meant that the Frankish monarchs would be able to establish cordial relations with the orthodox head of the western Church at Rome. Indeed, as over against the Arian Visigoths and Burgundians of southern Gaul, Clovis could pose as the champion of western orthodoxy and sanctify his conquests in the name of religion. Gregory reports him as saying, "It irketh me sore that these Arians hold a part of Gaul. Let us go forth, then, and with God's aid bring the land

[5]See p. 379.
[6]Trans. O. M. Dalton, Vol. II. Further citations from this volume will be made in my text.

under our own sway." (p. 75) The land here referred to is the land of the Visigoths whom Clovis defeated and forced back into Spain. He not only conquered the Visigoths in Gaul but also made the Burgundian kingdom dependent.

CLOVIS'S FURTHER CONQUESTS

Clovis's conquest of the Alamanni extended the Frankish state beyond the Rhine, for their confederation had occupied both banks. The defeat of the related group of Ripuarian Franks[7] did likewise, for they too had held both banks of the Rhine below the Alamanni. It is apparent that Clovis's policy of conquest meant to include not only the remaining German states in Gaul but, if necessary, those beyond the Rhine. By trickery and brutality he succeeded in destroying the other little kingdoms into which the Salian Franks were divided. After having King Sigibert and his son murdered, he annexed the former's kingdom. This acquisition Gregory describes as the Lord's reward for "an upright heart" and for doing "that which was pleasing in His sight." He had Chararic and his son beheaded. After defeating King Ragnachar of Cambrai in battle, "he raised his axe and buried it in his head. . . . He caused many other kings to be slain, and the near relatives whom he suspected of usurping his kingdom; in this way he extended his dominion over all Gaul." (pp. 79–81)

GREGORY OF TOURS AND SIXTH-CENTURY GAUL

Gregory of Tours' account of the Frankish state and society in the sixth century makes clear how difficult it was for uncivilized German princes to establish an orderly society among the ruins of Roman Gaul. Much of the political history of the latter part of the century had to do with the attempts of Brunhilde, a fierce Visigothic princess and wife of the Frankish King Sigibert of Austrasia (northern Gaul), to keep the throne in the hands of her son and his descendants, and to take vengeance on Chilperic, the king of Neustria, and his Queen Fredegund. Chilperic's first wife had been Brunhilde's sister, Galswintha. After her murder, possibly with Fredegund's connivance, he had married Fredegund, his mistress. The latter was a vicious character, almost a professional murderess and instigator of murders, sparing neither high churchmen nor her daughter. Gregory reports that she tried to murder her daughter Rigunth by catching her head with the lid of a chest when she was reaching into it. "She bore upon it with all her strength, until the edge of the chest beneath pressed the girl's throat so hard that her eyes seemed to start from her head." (p. 406) The difficulties of ferocious royalty were augmented by an utterly decadent clergy unable to resist the temptations made possible by the wealth of clerical office. Bishop Gregory does not fail to mention

[7]See p. 283.

these. Salonius of Embrun and Sagittarius of Gap, he says, were armed "not with the heavenly cross, but with the helm and mail shirt of the world, and are said to have slain many of the foe with their own hands. . . . They passed most of their nights in feasting and drinking, so that while the clergy were celebrating matins in the cathedral church, they were calling for fresh cups and keeping up their libations. . . . Not until the return of dawn did they rise up from the banquet; then they put on soft garments, and all bedrowsed and sunk in wine, slept on until the third hour of the day; nor did there fail them women with whom to be defiled. When they arose, they took a bath, and lay down to feast anew; leaving the table at evening, they were soon greedy for their supper again. . . . Thus they did day after day." (pp. 151, 197) In spite of this decadence the successors of Clovis managed to further expand the Frankish kingdom. In Gaul, the Burgundian kingdom and Provence were incorporated; beyond the Rhine, the kingdom of the Thuringians was destroyed, and the Bavarians were made dependent. Thus the process of expansion to include all Germans went relentlessly on.

EINHARD ON THE LAST MEROVINGIANS

The dynasty of Clovis is called the Merovingian. It lasted until *ca.* 751, when it was supplanted by the Carolingian. The circumstances of the change are described by Einhard, the biographer of Charles the Great. He says that Childeric, the last of the Merovingians, "was deposed, shaved, and thrust into the cloister by command of the Roman pontiff Stephen. But although, to all outward appearance, it [the Merovingian dynasty] ended with him, it had long since been devoid of vital strength, and conspicuous only from bearing the empty epithet Royal; the real power and authority in the kingdom lay in the hands of the chief officer of the court, the so-called Mayor of the Palace, and he was at the head of affairs." The king "had nothing that he could call his own beyond his vain title of King, and the precarious support allowed by the Mayor of the Palace in his discretion, except a single country-seat, that brought him but a very small income. There was a dwelling house upon this, and a small number of servants attached to it, sufficient to perform the necessary offices. When he had to go abroad, he used to ride in a cart, drawn by a yoke of oxen, driven, peasant-fashion, by a ploughman; he rode in this way to the palace and to the general assembly of the people, that met once a year for the welfare of the kingdom, and he returned home in like manner. The Mayor of the Palace took charge of the government, and of everything that had to be planned or executed at home or abroad."[8] The mayor of the palace who turned to Pope Stephen for sanction to dethrone Childeric was Pepin the Short, the son of Charles Martel. Pepin was thus the first of the Carolingians. He came to the throne at a time when the Frankish kingdom

[8] *Life of Charlemagne*, trans. S. E. Turner, pp. 15-17.

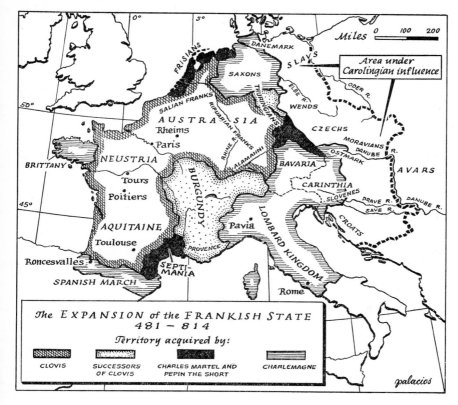

The EXPANSION of the FRANKISH STATE
481 – 814
Territory acquired by:

| CLOVIS | SUCCESSORS OF CLOVIS | CHARLES MARTEL AND PEPIN THE SHORT | CHARLEMAGNE |

palacios

was threatened with dissolution, a dissolution brought about by the suicidal practice of dividing the realm at the death of the king among his male heirs and by the efforts of a powerful aristocracy to control the government. The mayors of the palace were at first the representatives of this aristocracy.

THE SPANISH MARCH

The Carolingian mayors of the palace not only represented the interests of the aristocracy over and against the crown but Charles Martel had already brought the dynasty great military renown by stopping the northward advance of the Moslems from Spain, in 732, at Tours. Pepin had inaugurated the offensive that by 759 drove them out of Gaul, and the great Charles himself continued it beyond the Pyrenees. Here he founded the Spanish March and became for posterity a heroic crusader against the infidel. An incident of this campaign against Spain developed into a legend used by the writer of the first French epic, the *Chanson de Roland*. Roland was the governor of the March of Brittany, and on the return from Spain was killed by Christian Basques or Gascons in a pass of the Pyrenees called Roncevalles.

The march, or mark, was a frontier area similar to the American territory, set up for special defense. That there should have been a March of Brittany on the western boundary of Frankland and a Spanish March on the southern boundary is characteristic of the manner in which Charlemagne pursued the ancient Frankish policy of expansion to include all the Germans in Europe. How much of a German he was in appearance Einhard reveals in spite of his desire to make him resemble a Roman emperor. He was "large and strong, and of lofty stature . . . the upper part of his head was round, his eyes very large and animated, nose a little long, hair fair, and face laughing and merry . . . his neck was thick and somewhat short and his belly rather prominent."[9] By the end of his reign the continental Germans were a part of the Frankish kingdom. The Lombard kingdom in Italy,[10] which the Franks as allies of the papacy had long attacked, was destroyed by Charles and added to his state. The king of the Franks assumed now also the title of king of the Lombards, and actually his frontier extended to the holdings of the Byzantine Empire in southern Italy.

FURTHER CONQUESTS OF CHARLEMAGNE

Beyond the Rhine the Bavarians and Saxons were outside the Frankish realm, and the latter was still pagan. Charles refused to tolerate the disloyalty of Duke Tassilo of Bavaria any longer and finally annexed the whole area together with its Slavic dependency of Carinthia. The Germans now bordered on Slavs in the southeast and were faced by the Mongolian Avars in modern Hungary. The conquest of the Saxons, the last Germans to remain pagan, was a prolonged and wanton affair. Not only did the Saxons resolutely defend their tribal independence but they had no wish to become Christian. In exasperation Charles finally used outright slaughter and deportation to break their resistance, bringing in Franks to take the place of displaced Saxons. The Saxons were given a choice between Christianity and death, a complete reversal of the practice hitherto used by the Church in converting peoples, that of proceeding peacefully with their princes or kings. After the conquest and annexation of Saxony the Frankish state faced the pagan Danes on its northern frontier and the pagan Slavs, or Wends, on its eastern frontier, Slavs that for some time had been moving westward to fill in the area abandoned by migrating Germans. Here on the northern and eastern, as well as on the southern and western, frontiers Charles set up a string of border marches to protect the German from the non-German peoples; on the north the *Danemark* (Denmark), and over against the Slavs reaching from the Baltic to the Adriatic five additional marches. Of these the *Ostmark* (East March) was erected after the destruction of the Avar power in Hungary.

[9]Turner, p. 56.
[10]See p. 379.

These marches are to be understood not merely as protecting a German state from non-German peoples but as the advance posts of a further expansion of Germans and Christians against non-Germanic and pagan peoples. The Spanish March, for example, was the beginning of those Christian states that ultimately were to drive the Moslems from Spain; the Wendish March the beginning of Mecklenburg and Brandenburg.

THE IMPERIAL CORONATION OF 25 DECEMBER, 800

Charlemagne's Germanic state did not last very long. It was merely the first of many subsequent attempts to establish a German hegemony in Europe. It has more than a passing interest, however, since it came to be concerned with, and was actually established as, a reformation of the Roman Empire in the West. It thus gave new vitality to the idea of a universal empire in a theocratic Christian form. For men with a knowledge of the classical past, that is, for churchmen, the expansion of the Frankish state was obviously analogous to the expanding Roman Empire. They did not see why it should not actually be called so. Accordingly, a rather extraordinary event took place in Rome on 25 December, 800. In a contemporary account it is described as follows: "At noon on the most holy festival of our Lord's birth, when the King arose from kneeling in prayer . . . Pope Leo placed a crown upon his head and all the Roman people cried aloud, 'To Charles, Augustus, crowned of God, great and pacific Emperor of the Romans, life and victory.'" After the applause "he was adored by the Pope after the manner of the princes of old, and . . . called Emperor and Augustus."[11] It will be remembered that there had been no emperor in the West since 476. The only Roman emperor was the emperor of Constantinople, the Byzantine emperor. Reference is made in the quotation to the ritual of the coronation of the Roman (Byzantine) emperor by the patriarch of Constantinople. The Roman popes, for reasons of their own,[12] now turned from East to West, from the more distant emperor of Constantinople to the powerful king of the Franks. Exercising the functions of the patriarch of Constantinople, they were bold enough to establish by their coronation a new German emperor in the West. In so doing, they not only emphasized that the government of the West was properly universal and Christian but they also claimed that, in the form of a reincarnation of the Roman Empire, it had come into being under papal auspices. The Church had introduced into the West the practice of having clergy consecrate the newly elected German kings with holy oil, thus giving to them a sacrosanct character as agents of God. Charles's imperial coronation at the hands of a pope was a further extension of this practice; the imperial as well as the royal was a holy office. Such a concept of government we have called secular theocracy, secular because exercised by

[11]R. G. D. Laffan, *Select Documents of European History*, I, 6.
[12]See p. 387.

a lay person. Charles is reported by Einhard not to have liked the papal coronation, but what he did not like about it Einhard does not reveal.

THE SIGNIFICANCE OF THE CORONATION

In his governance of the Frankish state before and after the imperial coronation Charles conducted himself as a theocrat, without considering in any way that he was responsible to pope or bishop for his position. He had every desire to be a Christian king and to administer his realm in accordance with what he regarded as Christian principles. In so doing he would act as an agent of God. He was fully aware of the importance of the Church in the administration of the state, not only because it supplied literate administrators from its midst, but because it also trained laymen. To these ends Charles was careful to insist upon an efficient and alert church. Yet he had no intention of granting this church freedom from state control. He appointed the leading churchmen to their offices. He issued instructions to the clergy, whether pope or bishop, priest or monk. His legislation made no clear distinction between secular and ecclesiastical, or religious, matters and, in fact, was more concerned with the latter than the former. For him the Church was really a department of state. Thus, except for the imperial coronation at the hands of a pope, Charles returned to the practice of the later Roman Empire, when absolute emperors were considered divine and the Church part of the government. The incident of 25 December, 800, illustrates well the powerful influence of the Roman example. It created an institution, the Christian Germanic Empire, or, as it was to be called subsequently, the Holy Roman Empire, that persisted in varying forms until abolished by Napoleon in 1806. The Carolingian empire accordingly becomes a chapter in the long hard struggle for European unity.

THE DIVISIONS OF THE CAROLINGIAN EMPIRE

The empire did not long outlive its founder. That it did not may be explained by (1) the lack of devotion to the principle of unity on the part of Charles and his sons and successors, and (2) the inadequacy of the German principle as a basis for European unity. Charlemagne himself was much more interested in the power that unity provided than in the theory of its nature. Churchmen had long been trying to teach the barbarian kings that they held responsible positions. In the case of Charlemagne they had been notably successful. But they had not succeeded so well that Charles was ready to cling to the ideal of unity at any cost. Indeed, he was quite ready to partition the empire among his sons in order to avoid civil war. In 806 he drew up precise plans for such a partition. It so happened, however, that but one son finally succeeded him, namely, Louis the Pious (814-841). Imperial unity was thus accidentally preserved. Louis the Pious in his turn was not so fortunate. He, too, was confronted with the problem of how to preserve unity among greedy heirs who made

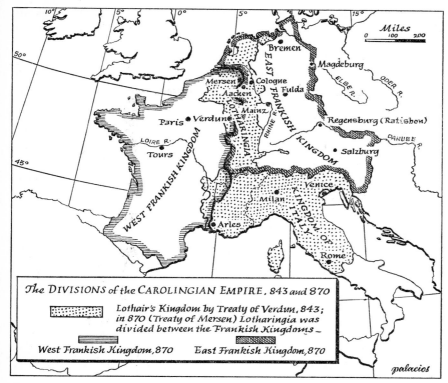

The DIVISIONS of the CAROLINGIAN EMPIRE, 843 and 870

Lothair's Kingdom by Treaty of Verdun, 843; in 870 (Treaty of Mersen) Lotharingia was divided between the Frankish Kingdoms

West Frankish Kingdom, 870   East Frankish Kingdom, 870

palacios

his life miserable with protests over his many partitions. At his death they fought among themselves over the inheritance and, in 843 in the Treaty of Verdun, divided it, creating a west Frankish kingdom, an east Frankish kingdom, and for Lothair, the eldest brother, a kingdom including Italy and a composite middle strip reaching from the North Sea to the Mediterranean. In 870, as a result of further partitions and wars over the middle strip, this area was divided (Treaty of Mersen) between the west and east Frankish kingdoms. By 870 the Carolingian empire had split into seemingly French, German, and Italian kingdoms. At the time that these partitions were made and civil wars fought over them, Europe was subjected to a new series of barbarian attacks, before which the little Carolingian kings were helpless. The imperial structure was fundamentally destroyed by the strong men who were able to protect their localities from barbarian attack. These were the new feudal lords. The political reorganization of Europe had now to start upward from the locality. Universal imperial organization had become more of a dream than ever.

THE VIKINGS

New barbarian peoples trying to break into central and western Europe at this moment, necessitating a larger than German basis for any future unity, were the Scandinavians (Danes, Norse, Swedes), the Magyars, or Hungarians, and the Moslems. The attacks of the Scandinavian Vikings revealed how fatal it was for the Carolingians not to have provided themselves with a navy. Except for the Mediterranean, the Vikings had almost complete control of European waters in the ninth, tenth, and early eleventh centuries, attacked whatever coasts they pleased, and went up the rivers deep into the interior, carrying their ships at times from the headwaters of one stream to another. Their terrifying, plundering raids soon settled down into positive attempts to trade, colonize, and discover, and all these they accomplished with amazing vitality. By *ca.* 862 they had founded a Swedish state in Russia at Novgorod and, subsequently, as they moved toward the Black and Caspian seas, the Grand Duchy of Kiev, which mark the beginning of Russian political history. Via Constantinople they connected early Russia with Byzantium and ensured its adoption of Byzantine civilization. The Danes acquired from Alfred the Great (871-899) northwestern England, or the *Danelaw*, which they then colonized. From the west-Frankish King Charles the Simple, the Norse secured in 911 about the mouth of the Seine the area that they colonized as the Duchy of Normandy. At the same time they founded flourishing city-kingdoms on the eastern coast of Ireland, colonized the Orkney, Faroe, Hebrides, and Shetland islands and the Isle of Man, settled Iceland, and discovered Greenland and North America. After enormous suffering the limited horizons of the inhabitants of western Europe were, in the end, much extended through the Viking incursions, while Denmark, Norway, and Sweden, emptied of their turbulent surplus population, settled down to become new members of a western family of Christian peoples.

MAGYARS AND MOSLEMS

The Hungarians, or Magyars, were the third important Mongolian people (the Huns and Avars had preceded them) to influence the course of western history. Their incursions up the Danube valley into the heart of Europe began in the late ninth century and continued until 955, when they were driven back into the valley of the Theiss. The German kings reorganized the East Mark (*Ostmark*) to protect Germany from further incursions, and by 1000 the Hungarians had accepted western Christianity, organized a kingdom, and joined the nascent group of western European states. The Moslems, who throughout the ninth century harassed the western coasts of Italy and the southern coasts of France, thus making the whole western Mediterranean unsafe for Christian shipping, came first of all from Tunisian Africa and later from Crete, Spain, and the Balearic Islands. They managed to take Sicily from the Byzantine Empire and to occupy Sardinia and Corsica. Barbarian invasions, partitions, and civil wars thus destroyed the Carolingian empire and made necessary the creation of a stop-gap government. The feudal system filled the vacuum.

For the moment universal secular theocracy became once again an ideal and impractical dream. The builders of future states would have to take the local feudal lords into account.

Development of a Western Ecclesiastical (Papal) Theocracy

POPE GREGORY THE GREAT

The development of the Frankish empire had important results for the growth of the papacy. The latter's program of spiritual supremacy over the Church and temporal supremacy over the state was rudely thwarted by the new Germanic kings of early western Europe who treated the churches within their boundaries as state churches. Before there could be an effective papal monarchy over a western Church, this church would have to be freed or separated from the state, a step no secular monarch was willing to undertake. Until the two could be separated the papacy would have to be content with building up its position of power and prestige in the West. To this end Pope Gregory the Great (590–604), the last of the Latin Fathers, made notable contributions.

GREGORY AND ASCETICISM

Gregory is a good example of the inability of western asceticism to wholly abandon the world. He came from a distinguished family and held important political positions in the city of Rome. He wished most of all to live the quiet life of a monk, and used his inheritance to endow some six monasteries, one of which, Saint Andrew's in Rome, he entered himself. He could not refuse, however, to serve the Roman Church at a time when it was hard pressed by aggressive Lombards and went for seven years as a legate to Constantinople, hoping to enlist the support of the Eastern emperor. Upon his return to Italy he became the abbot of Saint Andrew's, and in 590, in spite of his desire to remain in his monastery, he was elected to the papacy. Henceforth he had to limit his asceticism to praise of it in his writings, for he had little time to practice it.

GREGORY AND CLASSICAL LEARNING

His position as one of the four Latin Fathers of the Church came in large part from his writings: one, the *Pastoral Rule*, being a handbook for the guidance of bishops, and another, the *Moralia*, ostensibly a commentary on Job but in reality a work on theology. In these and others Gregory reveals himself to be a credulous propagator of a popular, superstitious, and magical Christianity, calculated to impress a primitive, barbarized, and ignorant western world. In his own commentaries on Scripture he says that he does not wish to be too much concerned with the rules of grammar, and he did not wish to have the clergy spending their time learning and teaching others grammar, since this meant becoming somewhat acquainted with classical literature. "It has been reported to me," he writes Bishop Desiderius of Vienne, "that your Fraternity is expounding the art of grammar to certain people. This news so vexed and so entirely disgusted me that I turned my previous words concerning you into lament and sorrow. One and the same mouth cannot hold the praise of Jupiter and Christ. Please do consider how serious, how unutterably wicked it is for a bishop to declaim aloud lines of poetry not even meet for a devout layman. . . . If hereafter it be shown that the report is clearly false and that you are not giving your energies to trifles such as pagan literature I shall give thanks to God."[13] When a bishop of Marseilles became so furious with the pagan adoration of the saints that he had their statues toppled over and broken into pieces, Gregory complained, "In truth I praise your zeal that nothing made by hands should be adored, but you should not have broken those images. A likeness made by art is put up in churches in order that the illiterate may read by their gazing on the walls what they cannot read in works. So your Fraternity ought both to preserve these statues and to keep the people from adoring them; so that they may neither sin nor lose the chance of gaining knowledge of history." On the question of the saints Gregory was enthusiastic. He recommended their use as "patrons in your trial before the severe judge; take these as your defenders in the day of the awful terror. . . . They wish to be asked. I may say they beg us to beg of them. Seek then, these to support your prayer; fly to these to protect you in your guilt; for the Judge Himself wills to be entreated that he may not punish sinners." To Gregory the acquisition of learning was but a form of pride. Man should rather "come to the consciousness of his ignorance, that he may fear. Let him fear, that he may humble himself. Let him humble himself, that he may place no confidence in himself. Let him place no confidence in himself, that he may learn to seek the help of his Creator; and, when he has come to know that in self-confidence nothing is to be found but death, he may, by appropriating the help of his Creator, return to life."[14]

GREGORY AS A THEOLOGIAN

Gregory has often been called the "Doctor of Angels and the Devil" (*doctor angelorum et diaboli*) because of his unusual interest in this phase of popular Christianity. He took great pains to distinguish between the nine orders of angels that unite the human with the divine: the Seraphim, Cherubim, Thrones, Dominations, Principalities, Powers, Virtues, Archangels, and Angels. The Devil, of course, was the leader of those fallen angels who had originally rebelled against God and were now demons

[13]The selection from Eleanor S. Duckett, *Gateway to the Middle Ages*, pp. 582–583, copyright 1938 by The Macmillan Co., and used with The Macmillan Co.'s permission.
[14]F. H. Dudden, *Gregory the Great*, II, 369–370, 289.

tempting man to sin. Though used by God in his discipline of the human race, the Devil will meet justice when Jesus appears for the Last Judgment. The Devil "will be smitten with eternal death, not in battle with the angels, not in contest with the saints, but through the coming of the Judge, by the breath of His Mouth alone,"[15] and will be cast into hell. With the Devil's pranks on earth Gregory is much concerned in his *Dialogues*, an assortment of interesting stories about monks and saints. As a theologian he is not much more than a popularizer of Augustine, whom he did not always understand. He lays special emphasis upon the notion of a purgatory for those who have yet to atone completely for their sin. And he makes the ceremony of the Mass a part of penance for sin, inasmuch as he interprets it as a repetition of the sacrifice of the Crucifixion, made by the priest on behalf of the sins of those present or of those for whom the Mass is said. One Protestant theologian has criticized Gregory's work as follows: "The darkest spot in medieval piety, the fact that it commanded constant contrition, while at the same time it incited the penitent to make calculations which deadened the moral verve and changed regret for sin into dread of punishment, this source of evil, which makes religious morality worse than non-religious, was from this time perpetuated in the Catholic Church of the West."[16]

GREGORY AND THE TEMPORAL POWER OF THE POPES

If the Christianity of Gregory was a further adaptation to the society of the barbaric West, his government of the Church enhanced the position of primacy that the papacy held among the western churches. His administration accomplished this in both the temporal and spiritual spheres. The founding of Constantinople and the termination of the line of western emperors strengthened the temporal position of the popes in the city of Rome. The popes of the fifth century had been able through negotiation to spare Rome some of the looting of the barbarian armies. Justinian's reconquest of Italy, however, put the popes in a dependent position, one made more serious by the aggressive Lombard kingdom. The notions of Byzantine emperors concerning the proper relationship between church and state were, as we have noted,[17] quite different from those of the popes. Nevertheless, the preoccupation of the emperors with eastern problems made it possible for the popes to extend their temporal position beyond the city to its environs, or so-called Duchy of Rome. The constant threat of the Lombard kings to absorb Byzantine as well as papal territory enabled capable popes, through negotiation, to uphold their independence from Constantinople. Gregory was one of these; he was determined not to adopt a subservient position toward the eastern emperor. "I am ready," he said, "to die rather than allow the Church of the Apostle St. Peter to

[15]Dudden, p. 367.
[16]Adolf von Harnack, *History of Dogma*, V, 271.
[17]See pp. 340 f.

degenerate in my days. . . . When I have once made up my mind to submit no longer, I face every danger with joy." When the patriarch of Constantinople assumed the title of Ecumenical (universal) Patriarch, Gregory was angry, for obviously "to all who know the Gospels it is plain that to St. Peter, Prince of the Apostles, our Lord committed the care of the whole Church." Yet it was not given to Gregory to solve the Byzantine-Lombard problem, even though his constant negotiations did much to strengthen the popes in Italy.

GREGORY AND SPIRITUAL POWER

We have noted that the western Church was in the hands of barbarian kings. The Arian church in Spain had become orthodox just before Gregory's accession to the papacy, and the Lombards were to turn to orthodox Christianity in the seventh century. Churches like Ravenna, under Byzantine control, and Milan, because of the tradition of Ambrose, were sensitive to any attempts of Rome to tell them what to do. Gregory, therefore, had to be tactful in asserting his spiritual authority. "I know of no bishop who is not subject to the Apostolic See when any fault has been committed," he said, but when "no fault exacts their submission, all are equal by the law of humility." He did his utmost to keep the administration of the Church efficient and its personnel respected. With the bishop of Carthage he intervened on behalf of an abbot whose monks, when disciplined "according to their Rule," leave "the monastery forthwith and wander without let wherever they will." When he heard of irregularities in Ravenna he could thank Almighty God that "the Lombards were posted between me and Ravenna. Else perhaps I should have been minded to show the world how severe I can be." He ordered an agent in Campania to call the bishops of the region together and lecture them for neglect of their work, and especially "my brother and fellow bishop Paschasius [who] is so lazy and neglectful everywhere that he is not recognized as a bishop at all." Over the large landholdings of the papacy at this date (possible reaching to some 1800 square miles and bringing in an income of $1,500,000) Gregory maintained a watchful administration. The agents of the pope in the Patrimony of Saint Peter were kept under rigorous control. In writing to them he did not need to be so careful to avoid offending local sensibilities. Peter the subdeacon, an overseer of papal lands in Sicily, he admonished, "Now please, after this warning, get busy and show us what you can do in the matter. . . . Now attend to what I say, for I am everlastingly talking to you about this business." When Peter sent him "a good-for-nothing hack to ride on," Gregory was amazed. "I cannot ride the hack, it is too wretched. . . . If you want to satisfy me, kindly send me something worthy of my position."[18]

[18]The selection from Eleanor S. Duckett, *Gateway to the Middle Ages*, pp. 572, 574, copyright 1938 by The Macmillan Co., and used with The Macmillan Co.'s permission.

The rise of the Carolingian mayors of the palace permitted the popes to escape from their tight Italian position. The popes, *de facto* rulers of the city of Rome and the surrounding duchy and owners of the large Patrimony of Saint Peter, were resentful of the control exercised over them by the Byzantine emperors. As long, however, as the Lombards were bent upon expanding the popes were dependent upon the emperors for military protection. Obviously, if this protection could come from the Franks rather than from the East, they could ignore Byzantine presumption. Their opportunity came in 751, when Pepin the Short turned to Pope Stephen II for permission to dethrone the last "do-nothing" Merovingian king and put him in a monastery. Permission was forthcoming; the request for it was a recognition of papal prestige in the West. When the Lombards succeeded in taking Byzantine Ravenna and started to move on Rome, Pope Stephen went personally to the Frankish court in 754, reanointed Pepin as king of the Franks, and in turn received promises of protection from the Lombards and, it seems, promises of all the territory that the Lombards had taken from the Byzantine Empire in Italy (the exarchate of Ravenna). In the ensuing years the Franks were in Italy fighting the Lombards, and in 756 they turned over the lands taken from them to the pope, as a temporal ruler. The grant, known as the Donation of Pepin, marks the beginning of the rule of the popes in Italy as *de jure* Italian princes, since it provided them with the legal foundation of their temporal or public power as contrasted with their private ownership of vast estates. From now on the popes ruled over the Papal States.

THE DONATION OF CONSTANTINE

How much more the popes really wanted than is contained in the Donation of Pepin is revealed by a forged document coming, most probably, out of the papal chancellery in the third quarter of the eighth century, either just before or after the Donation of Pepin. It is the notorious Donation of Constantine. It purports to be a grant of the Roman emperor Constantine to Pope Sylvester I in return for a miraculous cure of leprosy. Because Constantine has decided "it is not right that an earthly emperor should have authority there, where the rule of priests and the head of the Christian religion have been established by the Emperor of heaven," he is going to establish his government in a new city in the "province of Byzantium." For Pope Sylvester I he leaves behind "as a permanent possession . . . both our palace . . . and likewise all provinces, palaces, and districts of the city of Rome and Italy, and of the regions of the West." Moreover, Constantine orders that since "our imperial power is earthly . . . the sacred see of blessed Peter shall be gloriously exalted above our empire and earthly throne. . . . The pontiff who for the time being presides over that most holy Roman church shall be the highest and chief of all priests in the whole world. . . . We attribute to him the power and glorious dignity and strength and honor of the empire, and we ordain and decree that he shall have rule as well over the four principal sees, Antioch, Alexandria, Constantinople, and Jerusalem, as also over all the churches of God in all the world."[19] It would be impossible to find a better statement of the theocratic claims of the papacy. The Donation of Constantine became part of canon law, was often quoted in subsequent centuries to substantiate papal claims, and, although questioned, was not actually proved to be a forgery until the fifteenth century.[20]

Charlemagne confirmed the Donation of Pepin in 774, but how seriously he took the larger theocratic pretensions of the Roman bishops we have already noted. The coronation of 25 December, 800, was nevertheless related to the building up of theocratic precedent. It was, after all, a pope who crowned the first German to become a Roman emperor. Therewith the papacy finally severed its connection with the eastern empire at Constantinople and allied with the western Franks. The day was to come when it insisted that this western Roman Empire had been its creation. Because the pope had transferred the imperial crown from a Byzantine to a German head there could be no future western empire without papal authorization and coronation. The empire was dependent upon the Vicar of Christ and Successor of Saint Peter.

PSEUDO-ISIDORIAN DECRETALS

The dissolution of the Carolingian empire in the ninth century was accompanied by efforts of the Church and papacy to preserve the unity of the West and to supplant the feeble secular theocracy of the Carolingian state by an ecclesiastical one. The ambitions of the Frankish church are to be found in another forgery, the Pseudo-Isidorian Decretals, published in the neighborhood of Tours about the middle of the century. In these the pope is recognized as the head of the Church with supreme legislative and judicial power, and no doubt is left of the superiority of church to state, nor of the obligation of the latter to keep its hands off the former. These principles were established by forging decretals of popes and decisions of councils whose dates supposedly were before Constantine. The Donation of Constantine was also inserted into these decretals, which, like the Donation, were regarded as authentic and were used by the popes until the fifteenth century as part of the canon law. For a few years in the ninth century Pope Nicholas I (858–867) tried to govern in accordance with the principles of the decretals. In the end, however, the western Church became no less subject to the new feudal lords than it had previously been to the Germanic kingdoms. Effective ecclesiastical theocracy had done little more in these centuries than provide itself with useful precedent and forged documents.

[19]Laffan, *Select Documents*, I, 4–5.
[20]See pp. 764 f.

SAINT BENEDICT

The early monasticism[21] introduced into the western Roman Empire was Egyptian in origin, inspired by the anchorite more than the cenobite, and quite unregulated. The anomalies it produced aroused considerable criticism, and the question arose whether western Europe was actually suited to the extravagant asceticism of the East. Efforts were then made to moderate its principles and practices. Among them, those of Saint Benedict (480–544) were most successful, resulting in a monastic rule that established the normal type of Christian monastic life from that day to this. It is not certain whether Saint Gregory the Great's personally endowed monasteries were Benedictine, but the pope was very much interested in Benedict and wrote in his *Dialogues* an account of his life which, as a typical saint's biography, illustrates more the quality of Gregory's mind than Benedict's.

POPE GREGORY'S LIFE OF SAINT BENEDICT

Early in life, and shortly after the fall of the western empire, Benedict abandoned Rome, whither he had come from Nursia to study "humanity." He left for a retreat in the neighborhood of Subiaco, where for three years he lived as a hermit in a cave. Here he was tormented by the Devil, who so tempted him with visions of a former woman he had seen that "the representation of her did so mightily inflame with concupiscence the soul of God's servant . . . that, almost overcome with pleasure, he was of mind to have forsaken the wilderness. But suddenly assisted with God's grace, he came to himself and, seeing many thick briers and nettle-bushes to grow hard by, off he cast his apparel, and threw himself into the midst of these and there wallowed so long that, when he rose up, all his flesh was pitifully torn; and so by the wounds of his body he cured the wounds of his soul, in that he turned pleasure into pain, and by the outward burning of extreme smart quenched that fire which, being nourished before with the fuel of carnal cogitations, did inwardly burn in his soul." Benedict's austerities attracted many followers, and to escape them he decided to found a monastery in a more remote place. This proved to be a mountain in the immediate neighborhood of Cassino. Here, at this late date—and the situation was perhaps not unusual in the European countryside—"there was an ancient chapel in which the foolish and simple country people, according to the custom of the old gentiles, worshipped the god Apollo. Round upon it likewise upon all sides there were woods for the service of the devils, in which, even to that very time, the mad multitude of infidels did offer most wicked sacrifice. The man of God, coming thither, beat in pieces the idol, overthrew the altar, set fire on the woods, and in the

[21]See p. 358.

temple of Apollo he built the oratory of St. Martin, and where the altar of the same Apollo was he made an oratory of St. John." On this spot Benedict built his monastery—now being restored after its destruction in World War II as a German lookout—and for the monks established therein he wrote (*ca.* 529) his famous *Regula*, or *Rule*. Gregory calls it "both excellent for discretion and also eloquent for the style."[22]

THE BENEDICTINE RULE

In preparing the rule, Benedict hoped that it would "ordain nothing severe and nothing burdensome." In it he makes no place for the anchorite or hermit. He is writing for "the best kind" of monk, the cenobite. The monks are to form economically self-sufficient community, within which there is to be no private property and all of whose work is to be done by the monks themselves. The monk is to have "absolutely not anything: neither a book, nor tablets, nor a pen—nothing at all. For indeed it is not allowed to the monks to have their own bodies or wills in their own power." Within the community there are to be no social or economic distinctions. All monks are equal before the abbot and God, whose vice-regent the abbot is. The abbot's word, however, is final, even though he is obliged to take the monks into counsel on important matters. They are obliged to vow obedience to him. When the vow proves insufficient, discipline rests upon the lash. "The more honest and intelligent minds" the abbot is to "rebuke with words, with a first or second admonition; but the wicked and the hard-hearted and the proud, or the disobedient, let him restrain at the very beginning of their sin by castigation of the body, as it were, with whips." Again Benedict says, "concerning [him] who, being often rebuked, [does] not amend, . . . even after he has been excommunicated, . . . a more severe rebuke shall fall upon him, that is, the punishment of the lash. . . . As often as boys or youths or those who are less able to understand how great is the punishment of excommunication . . . offend they shall either be afflicted with excessive fasts, or coerced with severe blows, that they may be healed. . . . Children [who] make mistakes in the oratory . . . in saying a psalm, response or antiphon or lesson . . . shall be whipped."[23]

MONASTIC ROUTINE

The monk's task was to earn salvation by perfecting a way of life similar to that of the angels in heaven, chanting the praises of the Creator. His chief obligation was, and is, the work of God (*opus Dei*), that is, chanting daily the monastic services, consisting chiefly of psalms, beginning with vigils before dawn and ending with vespers before sunset. Since "idleness is the enemy of the soul," when not saying the monastic services the

[22]*Dialogues*, trans. P. W. Gardner, rev. E. G. Gardner, quoted in Jones, *Medieval Literature*, pp. 61, 65, 77.
[23]E. F. Henderson, *Select Historical Documents of the Middle Ages*, pp. 274 ff.

monk is to read, meditate, and do manual labor inside the monastery or outside in the fields, for "to work is to pray."

The monk is to "pronounce himself viler and more worthless than all [and] also believe it in the innermost workings of his heart." He is to "restrain his tongue from speaking; and, keeping silence," is not to "speak until he is spoken to." He is not to be "ready and easily inclined to laugh." He is to speak "slowly and without laughter, humbly with gravity, using few and reasonable words. . . . Everywhere, sitting or walking or standing, let him always be with his head inclined, his looks fixed upon the ground; remembering every hour that he is guilty of his sins."

When the bell rings for vigils (2:30 A.M.) the monks should get up "without delay . . . and when they rise for the service of God, they shall exhort each other mutually with moderation, on account of the excuses that those who are sleepy are inclined to make. . . . The use of baths shall be offered to the sick as often as necessary; to the healthy and especially to youths it shall not be so readily conceded." Food rations may be increased by the abbot if the work has been especially hard, "surfeiting above all things being guarded against, so that indigestion may never seize a monk. . . . The eating of the flesh of quadrupeds shall be abstained from altogether by everyone, excepting alone the weak and the sick. . . . We believe that a hemina [one-half pint] of wine a day is enough for each one. . . . The prior shall judge if either the needs of the place, or labor, or the heat of summer requires more; considering in all things lest satiety or drunkenness creep in. Indeed we read that wine is not suitable for monks at all. But because, in our day, it is not possible to persuade the monks of this, let us agree at least to drink sparingly."[24]

CASSIODORUS

Benedict himself did not consider that the monastery should be made a learned institution. That it became so is the result of the tradition established by his contemporary Cassiodorus. Unlike Benedict, Cassiodorus had not deserted the world for the monastery. Rather he had spent his young manhood helping Theodoric the Ostrogoth rule Italy. The aftermath of that rule was so disastrous for learning (Cassiodorus was disappointed in hopes to found a Christian seminary in Rome) that in his later years he founded a double monastery for hermits and monks on his ancestral estate in Squillace in southern Italy, and set his monks to work fighting the Devil "with pen and ink." He gathered together a considerable library of Christian and pagan works, and, after carefully training his monks as scribes or copyists, set them to making copies for libraries elsewhere. Thus, as the Benedictine monastery spread in western Europe, it spread not only as a band of ascetics but as a band of teachers and scholars—except for the secular clergy the only teachers and scholars in the midst of an illiterate population.

[24]Henderson, pp. 275 f.

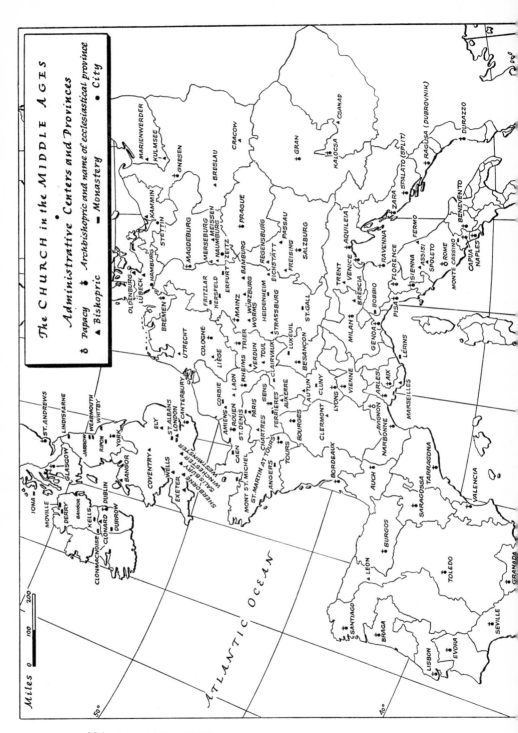

The CHURCH in the MIDDLE AGES

Administrative Centers and Provinces

ö Papacy   † Archbishopric and name of ecclesiastical province   • City
▲ Biskopric   ■ Monastery

Miles 0   100   200

ATLANTIC OCEAN

50°

40°

The Benedictine monastery came to be supported by the kings and aristocracy of western Europe not only because it set the example of a sacrificial Christian life but because it provided schools and made possible the preservation of the Christian and pagan learning of the past and the creation of learned works necessary for the proper functioning of contemporary society. Indeed, the monastery did much more than this. Benedict's rule makes it clear that in an age devoid of such institutions the monastery functioned as inn and hospital. The nobles came to use it as a supplement to, if not a substitute for, their own piety, inasmuch as the monks had time to pray for the souls of those who founded and endowed their houses. In so doing the monks built up huge landed estates for themselves and may thus be regarded as in some respects a heavily endowed "leisure class." The monastic estate was in itself an extremely important economic institution. It retained what remained of a scientific agriculture from the classical past and was a constant stimulus to less efficient neighbors. For this reason alone lords were eager to have a Benedictine monastery on their lands. For the papacy also the Benedictine monastery was a useful institution. It could, in the first place, carry on the work of the missionary and bring into the Christian fold the still-pagan peoples of Europe. In organizing the Christian Church in new areas it could also promote the recognition of the claims of Rome to spiritual headship. Western asceticism in its Benedictine form accordingly returned in many ways to the world it sought to abandon and in so doing made of itself a vital economic, social, and cultural, as well as religious, institution. Or, as has been said, "He [Benedict] redeemed the cloister from degenerating into a nursery of ineffectual dreamers and ascetics, and made it a school of useful workers whose ideal was, not merely to feel and suffer, but to do some good in their day and generation."[25]

IRISH MONASTICISM

Sometime between 595 and 600 Gregory the Great received a letter from an Irish monk in Burgundy begging him, "Please spare us the scandal of seeing you, our Father, at variance with Saint Jerome. For anyone in the Western Church who disagrees with *him* must be banned as a heretic, no matter who it be." The same monk, Columban by name, had refused to come to a council of Gallic bishops to discuss the question of the proper date for Easter, "lest I should show myself too contentious."[26] At this same time another Irish monk, Saint Columba, was closing his life on the island of Iona, off the western coast of Scotland, as the head of a mission working among the Picts and Scots. As the Benedictine rule spread

[25]Dudden, *Gregory the Great*, II, 169.
[26]The selection from Eleanor S. Duckett, *Gateway to the Middle Ages*, pp. 461, 464, copyright 1938 by The Macmillan Co., and used with The Macmillan Co.'s permission.

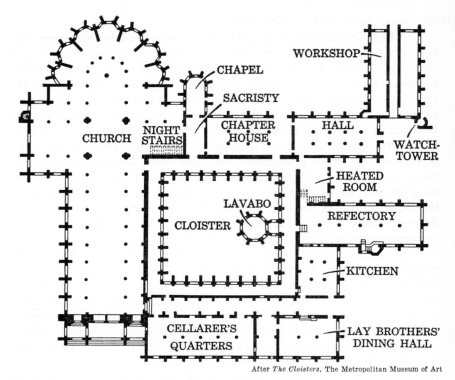

WORKSHOP

CHAPEL

SACRISTY

CHAPTER HOUSE

CHURCH   NIGHT STAIRS

HALL

WATCH-TOWER

HEATED ROOM

LAVABO

CLOISTER

REFECTORY

KITCHEN

CELLARER'S QUARTERS

LAY BROTHERS' DINING HALL

After *The Cloisters*, The Metropolitan Museum of Art

The ground plan of the Cistercian monastery of Royaumont. Royaumont, illustrating the principal characteristics of medieval monasteries, was founded by Saint Louis of France in the thirteenth century. The cloister adjoins the main church to the south.

from Italy throughout the West it had to contend with another form of asceticism contained in the Irish monasteries organized especially under the rule of Saint Columban. This expansive Irish Christianity stemmed from an Irish church that had grown up in the fifth century.

CELTIC CHRISTIANITY

Celtic Ireland, like Scotland, had not been a part of the Roman Empire. It knew Christianity from those British Celts who were pushed westward into Wales by the invasions of Angles, Saxons, and Jutes. A part of these Britons had crossed to the Continent to occupy Brittany, and together this Irish, Scottish, Welsh, and Breton Celtic world formed a Christianity apart from that beginning to center in Rome. Like the pagan and heretical groups, it too was a challenge to the centralizing plans of the papacy. The differences between it and Roman Christianity were not great, but they were serious enough to be decisive when backed by local patriotic differences, as, for example, those between the conquered Celt and the victorious German in Britain. They concerned only the date for celebrating Easter, the manner of wearing the tonsure, and the ritual for consecrating a bishop. Celtic Christianity was somewhat more rigorous than Roman inasmuch as it was inspired by the Egyptian asceticism prevalent in such monasteries as Lérins and Saint Victor's at Marseilles. The differences may be measured in the conflict between Pelagius, a British monk, and Saint Augustine.[27] They are better seen in the differences between the two churches in the practice of penance. The Roman Church had worked out a system of public penance whereby the sinner publicly proclaimed his misdemeanors before the assembled congregation and was, after proper punishment, publicly reconciled to the Church. In Ireland a system of private penance had been developed. In this the sinner confessed privately to the priest and was assigned penance in accordance with very rigorous written tariffs called penitentials. When Irish monks went abroad they took their penitentials and their private system of penance with them. After a long conflict with the older system of the Roman Church the Irish system won out and became accepted as the effective sacrament of Penance.

SAINT PATRICK

The work of Welsh monks in bringing Christianity to the Irish was supplemented by a British monk, Saint Patrick, the patron saint of Ireland, in the first half of the fifth century. When a youth, Patrick was carried off from Britain by Irish marauders, and, escaping from Ireland to Gaul, became for several years a monk at Lérins. Upon his return home he decided upon a mission to the land of his captivity and for this return he prepared himself by further long residence in Gaul as a student of the Welsh Saint Illtyd at Auxerre. He thus introduced into the Ireland, whose conversion he may be regarded as having completed and whose church he organized, the ascetic practices and the learning, both Latin and to a limited extent Greek, of the monasteries of southern Gaul. Indeed, the early Irish church, such as it is known to us, was essentially a monastic church, without dioceses, fitting into the tribal organization of a pagan society. Its abbots were so powerful that the word abbot in Irish came to mean any great power. Gregory the Great was the "abbot of Rome," Christ "the great abbot," God "our abbot," and the devil "the abbot of Hell."[28] The important houses over which these abbots presided, centers of learning for the western world, were Clonard, Moville, Clonmacnoise, Derry, Durrow, Bangor, and Kells.

SAINT COLUMBA AND SAINT COLUMBAN

To keep the Irish monk confined to a monastery, or indeed to Ireland, was hard. Irish asceticism had much more sympathy for the hermit recluse

[27]See p. 352.
[28]See Louis Gougaud, *Christianity in Celtic Lands*.

than the Benedictine came to have, and it was determined to carry its way of life to still-pagan lands or even to those insufficiently Christianized. Saint Columba, the founder of Derry and Durrow, left Ireland in 563 for Iona to work among the pagan Picts and his fellow Scots (*Scotus* is "Irishman") in Scotland. This mission, almost complete by the end of the sixth century, worked also among the pagan Northumbrians from the monastery of Lindisfarne, an island off the east coast of England. A student of Bangor, Saint Columban, with his group of twelve moved to the Gaul of Brunhilde to see what could be done to Christianize a countryside neglected by a decadent church. He complained to Gregory of bishops who were immoral and had bought Holy Orders. It was difficult for him to acquiesce in the morals of the Burgundian court, whose young twenty-year-old King Theodoric already had four illegitimate sons. When Brunhilde asked Columban to bless such progeny he referred to them as "children of a brothel" and warned their royal father to reform if he did not wish to be excommunicated. For this lack of discretion he was ejected from the monastery of Luxeuil he had founded in Burgundy and was asked to go home. Instead, after certain misadventures and references to "that dog Theodoric," he moved to the upper Rhine region and sought to Christianize the German Alamanni. Leaving behind him one of his followers, Saint Gall, upon the site of whose cell the famous monastery of Saint Gall was built, Columban left for Lombard Italy to found another scholarly house at Bobbio. He was the first of a line of Irish exiles to the Continent, where, in houses of their own foundation, or as guests in the houses of others, their Irish zeal, learning, wit, and genius enriched the nascent civilization of the West. When the scribe of a learned work is an Irish monk he usually lets himself be known by such personal remarks in the margins as "Let some of the better wine be given to the writer"; or "A blessing on the soul of Fergus. Amen. I am very cold"; or "Dubtach copied these verses in a brief space of time; pardon, reader, the errors you may notice"; or the plain colophon, "nightfall and time for supper."[29] In any case, as an Irish scribe himself confessed, it was fun. One wrote, "Pleasant is the glittering of the sun to-day upon these margins because it flickers so";[30] and another:

> The trees like a hedge surround me,
>   And a blackbird sings to me,
> And on my book and around me
>   The birds spill melody.
>
> From the topmost twig in the bushes falls
>   The gray-frock cuckoo's glee.
> O it's good to write in the dear Lord's sight
>   Under the greenwood tree.[31]

[29]Gougaud, pp. 362–363.
[30]Kenneth Jackson, *Studies in Early Celtic Nature Poetry*, Part II, introduction, p. 80.
[31]P. S. Allen and H. M. Jones, *The Romanesque Lyric*, p. 186.

The Cloisters. This building may be taken to represent a medieval monastery. Actually it is a branch of the Metropolitan Museum of Art that houses an outstanding part of its medieval collection in a characteristic setting. The Cloisters is situated near the Hudson River in Fort Tryon Park, New York City. Plates 28 to 34 are taken from the collection. The quotations are from a guide to *The Cloisters* (1951), prepared by its former director, James J. Rorimer, now the general director of the Metropolitan Museum.

Plate 27

The cloister. The architectural fragments which form the basis of this elegant cloister come from the Benedictine monastery of Saint-Guilhem-le-Désert in southern France, near Arles. It was built before 1206 in a style transitional from Romanesque to Gothic.

Plate 28

Plate 29

A detail of the Saint-Guilhem cloister. The great variety in the treatment of the shafts, capitals, and *abaci* (uppermost parts of the capitals) is to be noted. On the central capital delighted devils are jamming sinners condemned by the Last Judgment into the mouth of hell: ". . . a masterpiece of mediaeval sculpture."

Plate 30

The chapter house. The monks assembled daily in the chapter house after breakfast to conduct monastic business under the direction of the abbot. Here brothers were beaten for infractions of the rule. This simple, powerful Romanesque entrance (twelfth century) is from the chapter house of the former monastery of Notre-Dame-de-Pontaut in southwestern France.

The interior view of the Pontaut chapter house. The stone bench for the monks runs around the whole rectangular room. The variety in treatment of capital and *abacus* may again be noted.

Plate 31

Plate 32

A Romanesque doorway. Next to the Saint-Guilhem cloister at The Cloisters is the Romanesque hall to which this twelfth-century French doorway leads. The strength of the doorway is relieved by the delicate carving.

A Romanesque chapel. This chapel incorporates stonework and capitals from the church of Notre-Dame-du Bourg at Langon near Bordeaux. On the capital of the column to the left are "bending half-length" figures, resembling Greek caryatids, who seem to carry the load of the vault.

Plate 33

Plate 34

A capital from the Romanesque chapel. These startlingly realistic capitals may be portraits of Henry II of England and Eleanor of Aquitaine (see p. 720), who once visited in the neighborhood of Langon.

A page from the Book of Kells, an Irish manuscript of the early Middle Ages, containing the first words of the Gospel of Saint John: IN P/RINCI/PIO ERAT VER/BUM ET VERBUM. The CI of the second line may be also a harp player. The large figure at the top is Saint John; the smaller one to the right seems content with the thought of a drink from a cone-shaped cup. The elaborate and complicated interlacing patterns should be studied.

Plate 35

Trinity College, Dublin

A page from the Lindisfarne Gospels, written *ca.* 700, and generally thought to be earlier than the Book of Kells although decorated under the influence of Irish illumination. It contains the beginning of the Gospel of Saint Matthew: XPI / AUTEM GENE/RATIO SIC ERAT CUM / ESSET DESPONSATA / MATER EIUS MARIA JOSEPH.

Plate 36

© British Museum

Another page from the Lindisfarne Gospels containing the beginning of the Gospel of Saint Luke: QUO/NIAM / QUIDEM / MULTI CONA/TI SUNT ORDINA / RE NARRATIONEM.

Plate 37

A cruciform page from the Lindisfarne Gospels. The interlacing pattern of the cross is composed of twenty-four separate animals; that of the two upper panels of ten animals and ten birds each; that of the two lower panels of eleven animals and nineteen birds each, making a total for the page of sixty-six animals and fifty-eight birds.

Plate 38

© British Museum

No doubt pagan bards and Druid priests appeared at the primitive courts of Irish chieftains. Patrick brought Latin with him to Ireland as the learned language of the new religion, and soon Irish monks sang Christian songs in Latin and revealed an acquaintance with the pagan literature of Rome that would have scandalized Gregory the Great. Some had a mere smattering of Greek. But Christianity did not stop the flow of Gaelic song. Gaelic now became a written language, and Christian monks not only expressed their religious emotions in their native tongue but they also caught the moods of the natural world and the romantic, supernatural world of sprite and faery. Moreover, they reduced to writing in long cycles of prose and verse the tales of pagan heroes such as Cuchulainn, and Finn and his son Ossian. In so doing they, together with the Anglo-Saxons, started the vernacular literatures of the West centuries before their appearance on the Continent.

To the Gaelic poets, after winter, "the season of ice," when "Cold has seized the bird's wings" and "the wild goose has raised its accustomed cry, . . . May Day, a fair season," was a welcome time, a time when

> The loud hardy cuckoo calls,
> welcome noble summer.
>
> Man thrives, the maiden flourishes
> in her fine strong prime;
> fair is every wood from crest to ground,
> fair each great goodly plain.
>
> A mad ardour upon you to race horses,
> the serried host is ranged around,
> a bright shaft has been loosed into the land
> so that the iris is gold beneath it.
>
> A timid persistent frail creature
> sings at the top of his voice,
> the lark chants clear tidings;
> excellent May Day of quiet colors!

In summer itself:

> Green bursts out on every plant,
> wooded is the copse of the green oak-grove; . . .
>
> tangled hollies wound the hound.
>
> The hardy blackbird sings a strain,
> to whom the thorny wood is a hermitage;
> the sad turbulent sea is sleeping,
> the speckled salmon leaps.
>
> The sun smiles over every land, . . .
>
> hounds bark, stags assemble,
> ravens flourish, summer has come.[32]

[32]Jackson, pp. 24–25.

If the hermit could wish "for a hut to dwell in, a little hut, hidden where none has trod," and the simple satisfactions provided by "leeks and salmon and trout and bees, and a hen or two beside," life in the crowded monastery was more difficult. For here in the large choir it was not easy to keep one's thoughts on the words and music:

> During the psalms they wander on a path that is not right;
> They fash, they fret, they misbehave before the eyes of the great God.
>
> Through eager crowds, through companies of wanton women,
> Through woods, through cities—swifter they are than the wind.
>
> Now through paths of loveliness, anon of riotous shame!
> . . . . .
> Neither sword-edge nor crack of whip will keep them down strongly;
> As slippery as an eel's tail they glide out of my grasp.
> . . . . .
> Rule this heart of mine, O dread God of the elements,
> That Thou mayst be my love, that I may do Thy will.
>
> That I may reach Christ with His chosen companions, that we may be to-
> gether!
> They are neither fickle nor inconstant—not as I am.[33]

It is too easy while in choir to think of what one would like to do at a "Heavenly Banquet":

> To have the men of Heaven
>   in my own house,
> with vats of good cheer
>   laid out for them.
>
> I would like to have the three Marys,
>   their fame is so great.
> I would like people
>   from every corner of Heaven.
>
> I would like them to be cheerful
>   in their drinking.
> I would like to have Jesus, too,
>   here amongst them.
>
> I would like a great lake of beer
>   for the King of Kings.
> I would like to be watching Heaven's family
>   drinking it through all eternity.[34]

[33] Trans. Kuno Meyer, in Kathleen Hoagland, *1000 Years of Irish Poetry*, pp. 44–45.
[34] Trans. Sean O'Faolain, from *The Silver Branch*, comp. Sean O'Faolain, in Hoagland, pp. 48-49.

Or, as so many had done, get out of Ireland and row to distant lands:

Heia, fellows, Echo, resounding sends back our heia!
So that our emulous prow may cut the waves like a dolphin,
Row till the timbers groan and the ship leaps under your muscles—
Backward our whitened path flows in a lengthening furrow.[35]

There one might meet "Sons of queens and kings."

On their heads are
Beautiful golden-yellow manes.

With smooth comely bodies,
With bright blue-starred eyes,
With pure crystal teeth,
With their red lips.

Good they are at man-slaying,
Melodious in the ale-house.
Masterly at making songs,
Skilled at playing chess.[36]

Still, it is also nice to be at home in one's own monastery when you have a pussycat like Pangur to share your cell with you:

Pangur is proof the arts of cats
    And men are in alliance;
His mind is set on catching rats,
    And mine on snaring science.

I make my book, the world forgot,
    A kind of endless class-time;
My hobby Pangur envies not—
    He likes more childish pastime.

When we're at home time quickly flies—
    Around us no one bustles;
Untiringly we exercise
    Our intellectual muscles.

Caught in his diplomatic net,
    A mouse jumps down his gullet;
And sometimes I can half-way get
    A problem when I mull it.

He watches with his shining eye
    The wall that guards his earnings;
As for my eyesight—well, I try
    To match my stare with learning's.

[35] Allen and Jones, p. 166.
[36] Trans. Kuno Meyer, in Hoagland, p. 74.

His joy is in his lightning leap;
  Me—I'm a mental wizard;
My claws are sunk in problems deep,
  His, in a mousie's gizzard.

As comrades we admit we shine,
  For each observes his station;
He practices his special line,
  And I, my avocation.

Our rivalry you'll find is nice,
  If in the scale you weigh us;
Each day Pangur goes hunting mice,
  I bring forth light from chaos.[37]

THE ANGLO-SAXON MISSION

Pope Gregory the Great, we have seen, was in touch with Columban. We may assume that he knew of the Irish mission to Iona and Scotland. The good pope undoubtedly rejoiced over the expansion of Christianity, but he could not have been pleased that it was being spread by a church that was rather indifferent to the leadership of Rome. Accordingly, he seized the opportunity to convert the heathen Germans in Britain, and to do this utilized monastic asceticism, which in its Irish form had given such drive to Irish Christianity. A papally supported monastic mission would be certain to set up in newly conquered lands a church that would recognize the headship of Rome. Gregory used Augustine, the abbot of his monastery of Saint Andrew's, to head the mission to Britain. If not actually a Benedictine himself, Augustine must have been well acquainted with the rule of Saint Benedict, for we have already seen how devoted Gregory was to the tradition of the saint. A successful mission would thus spread the influence of the Benedictine rule. Gregory was careful to see that the mission would be successful. In instructions he sent to it after its arrival in England he warned "that the temples of the idols ought not to be destroyed." The idols themselves were to be destroyed and the pagan temples converted into Christian churches, so that the pagan Germans "may the more familiarly resort to the places to which they have been accustomed." Nor were the missionaries to forbid sacrifices. Rather, the pagans were to "kill cattle to the praise of God in their eating, and return thanks to the Giver of all things for their sustenance; to the end that, whilst some gratifications are outwardly permitted them, they may the more easily consent to the inward consolations of the grace of God. . . . For there is no doubt that it is impossible to efface everything at once from their obdurate minds."[38]

[37]Allen and Jones, p. 184.
[38]Dudden, *Gregory the Great*, II, 126.

402 CHAPTER NINE

Bede (*ca.* 672-735), the first historian of the English people, indicates that this advice was taken seriously by some of the Anglo-Saxon kings. King Redwald of East Anglia, for example, "in one temple erected an altar for the sacrifice of Christ and another little altar for burnt sacrifices to his idols and devils." Bede also tells the story that Gregory's attention was called to Britain when he saw handsome English youths in the slave market of Rome. "Alas, quoth he, it is a piteous case, that the author of darkness should possess such bright-beautied people, and men of so fair a face should inwardly bear so foul a soul." When told they were called Angles he remarked, "Truly not without cause they be called Angles, for they have an Angel's face. And it is meet such men were partakers and inheritors with the Angels in heaven."[39] Actually, Augustine did not go to the Angles but to the Jutish king of Kent (597). His conversion was soon brought about, and the English church was founded with an archbishopric and monastery at Canterbury. Gregory was delighted: "Lo! the Lord has joined in one faith the East and the West. Lo! the tongue of Britain, which before had known nothing but to make barbarous noise, now at length has begun to chant the Hebrew Alleluia."[40] Augustine's mission began the slow conversion, one by one, of the German kingdoms in Britain. It was not altogether the work of Rome through Canterbury. There were independent missions from Gaul. Above all, however, there was the Irish mission from Lindisfarne and elsewhere. It was almost inevitable therefore, that Irish and Roman Christianity should clash, and they did, especially at the Synod of Whitby in 663, called together by the king of Northumbria to settle the questions at issue between Irish and Romans. The king decided in favor of Rome, and his decision was adopted by the other English kings. The British and Irish clergy, however, did not easily submit; Iona not until 716, and the British not until 768. For the early culture of England this mixture and competition between Irish and Roman was a blessing.

ABBOT BENEDICT BISCOP

Soon after Whitby, in 669, Theodore of Tarsus, a Byzantine Greek, came to England as archbishop of Canterbury. He brought with him to preside over the monastic school at Canterbury Abbot Hadrian from Byzantine North Africa. The English church received a more thorough diocesan organization under its two archbishops of Canterbury and York and was brought together in general synods. By this time the kingdoms were well populated with new monasteries, many of which were Benedictine. What the new connection with western Europe, Italy, and Rome

[39]*History of the Church of England*, trans. T. Stapleton, p. 106. Cf. Helen Cam, *England before Elizabeth*, p. 30.
[40]The selection from Eleanor S. Duckett, *Gateway to the Middle Ages*, p. 586, copyright 1938 by The Macmillan Co., and used with The Macmillan Co.'s permission.

meant to the young English church and to the English people is made quite clear by Bede, who was a member of one of these Benedictine houses, Wearmouth-Jarrow in Northumbria. The monastery was founded in 674 by Benedict Biscop, a former thane of King Oswy of Northumbria. On his return from a first journey to Rome, before becoming abbot, he "came to the island of Lérins, where he joined the company of monks." While again at Rome he was appointed to conduct the new Archbishop Theodore to England, "a man learned in secular no less than in ecclesiastical philosophy, and that in both languages, Greek that is and Latin." On his third trip to Rome he "brought back many books of all subjects of divine learning, which had been either bought at a price or been given him freely of his friends." A year after the foundation of Wearmouth-Jarrow "Benedict crossed the ocean to France, where he required, procured, and brought away masons to build him a church of stone, after the Roman fashion which he always loved. . . . He sent messengers to France, which should bring over makers of glass (a sort of craftsman till that time unknown in Britain) to glaze the windows of the Church, its side-chapels and clerestory." These craftsmen "caused the English people thereby to understand and learn this manner of craft. . . . Moreover, this devout buyer, because he could not find them at home, took care to fetch from oversea all manner of things, to wit sacred vessels and vestments that were suitable to the ministry of the altar and the Church." From his fourth journey to Rome "he returned laden with a more abundant gain of spiritual merchandise than before. First, because he brought home a vast number of books of every kind: Secondly because he procured a plentiful grace of the relics of the blessed apostles and martyrs of Christ to be profitable to many English churches: Thirdly, because he introduced into his monastery the order of chanting, singing, and ministering in church according to the manner of the Roman usage." Indeed, Benedict brought a certain "John, archchanter of the church of the blessed apostle Peter and abbot of the monastery of the blessed Martin," to teach chanting in England. "Fifthly, he brought home sacred pictures to adorn the church . . . namely, the similitude of the blessed mother of God and ever Virgin Mary, and also of the twelve apostles . . . similitudes of the Gospel story . . . similitudes of the visions in the Revelation of the blessed John . . . in order that all men which entered the church, even if they might not read, should either look (whatsoever way they turned) upon the gracious countenance of Christ and His saints, though it were but in a picture; or might call to mind a more lively sense of the blessing of the Lord's incarnation, or having, as it were, before their eyes, the peril of the last judgment might remember more closely to examine themselves." A fifth visit to Rome brought "a great store indeed of sacred books [and more] sacred pictures." It brought also "two palls of silk of exceedingly goodly workmanship" with which the abbot purchased from the king "three hides of land." In short, it was a "glorious library of a very great store of books"[41] that he acquired, and the seeds and fruits of an older culture's art and craftsmanship unavailable in a still-primitive land.

BEDE

The conversion of England by Irish and Roman missionaries led to an astonishing development of English culture in the seventh and eighth centuries, a culture whose wealth made politically disunited England the greatest civilizing force in the eighth and early ninth centuries. Of this culture Bede of Wearmouth-Jarrow is a fine and quite lovable product. At the end of his *Ecclesiastical History of the English People* he gives a brief biography of himself and a list of his scholarly works. "I was delivered up by the hands of my kinsfolk to be brought up of the most reverend abbot Benedict [Benedict Biscop], and afterward of Ceolfrid; and from that time spending all the days of my life in the mansion of the same monastery, I applied all my diligence to the study of the Scriptures; and observing the regular discipline and keeping the daily service of singing in the church, I have taken delight always either to learn, or to teach, or to write." Among his many works he lists first the commentaries on Scripture that gave him his reputation as a biblical scholar. Of his biographies of saints he mentions "the Book of the life and passion of Saint Anastasius, which was ill translated from the Greek, and worse amended by some ignorant person," and which he "corrected to the sense as well as I was able." He lists his "history of the abbots of this monastery wherein I with joy do serve" and the "Ecclesiastical History of our island and nation, in five books." He lists, moreover, a "Martyrology of the birthdays of the holy martyrs, in which I have with all diligence endeavored to set down all whom I could find, and not only on what day, but also by what manner of contest, and under whom as judge they overcame the world; . . . a Book of Hymns in divers sorts of metre or rhythm, a Book of Epigrams in heroic or elegiac verse," and, especially for the use of his students in the monastery, books on science and chronology, on biblical figures of speech, on how to write poetry, and, alas, even then, "on Orthography, divided in the order of the alphabet."[42]

BEDE AS A SCHOLAR

We are in Bede's debt primarily for his *History*, in all respects an excellent piece of work distinguished for its Latin style (Bede does not apologize for his Latin as did Gregory of Tours) and for its scrupulous effort to get at the whole truth and to acknowledge properly those who have helped him to find it. For information on the mission of Saint Augustine the priest Nothelm searched for him, with permission of the pope, "the closets of the said holy church of Rome, where he found cer-

[41]*Historical Works*, trans. J. E. King, Loeb, No. 248, pp. 397–417. Cf. Jones, *Medieval Literature*, pp. 132 ff.
[42]*Historical Works*, pp. 383, 387, 389.

tain epistles of Saint Gregory and other bishops there." On the spread of Christianity among the kingdoms he had to rely on both written and oral information. "The history of the province of the Northumbers . . . we have gotten not by any one author, but by relation of many faithful witnesses . . . beside such things as by my own experience I knew." He referred to his sources in the margins of his text, and begged scribes not to omit these in their copies. The same diligence that he displayed in the *History* he displayed in other works, making available to an audience sadly in need of it the results of his wide reading in pagan as well as Christian writers. One of his biographies is a rendering of an earlier life in verse "in plainer words of prose for the benefit of many simple people." On another occasion he says he is trying to write clearly, concisely, and briefly because the English are mentally lazy and have failed to study Christianity. In his commentary on Luke he refers to the urgings of his bishop to write such a work, for although Saint Ambrose had covered the material, parts of Ambrose "only scholars can understand. . . . So will you please write your book on Saint Luke . . . in clear and plain words for those of plain education." And so Bede says, "I did begin this labour—a very difficult one, since, to say nothing of innumerable duties in the monastery, I have to make my own shorthand notes while reading my sources, to copy out the passages I take from these, and to write my books themselves with my own hand. And there are so many sources, so important and so impressive! I must diligently examine what blessed Ambrose, what Augustine, what Gregory, the apostle of our race, . . . what Jerome, what other fathers have said in their works about the words of Saint Luke. Then, since there is so much that is theirs for me to include and since I do not want to be thought a thief in putting down as mine what is really theirs, I have decided to place the first letter of the name of each authority in the margin, against each passage taken from his writings. . . . I don't really work 'night and day'; but it is quite true that I do toil hard to reach a right judgment on all that I read."[43]

BEDE'S DEATH

The writing of the *History* impaired Bede's health, but it did not stop his work. "His pouring over dim and difficult manuscripts had ruined his eyes, his bending over their sheets had stiffened his limbs, the eternal mists and fogs of England sending their damp cold into cell and dormitory and church, had brought rheumatism and bronchitis as familiar visitors."[44] Still during his last days he was concerned with making Scripture available to those who knew no Latin, and set to work translating the Gospel of Saint John "into the English tongue." He was working upon this when

[43] The selection from Eleanor S. Duckett, *Anglo-Saxon Saints and Scholars*, pp. 250, 275–277, copyright 1947 by The Macmillan Co., and used with The Macmillan Co.'s permission.
[44] Ibid., p. 321.

he was obliged to urge his students also to "learn quickly, for I do not know how long I shall last, nor if shortly my Maker shall take me." On the last day of his life one of his students reminded him, " 'Dearest master, one chapter of the book you are dictating is left yet to be done. Yet it seems hard of me to ask it of you.' But he answered, 'Nay it is easy, take pen and paper, and write simply.' And this he did." When on the evening of this day, after he had distributed among the brethren "the pepper and incense" he had accumulated, "the boy [Wallberche by name] said to him again: 'There is still dear master, one sentence not yet finished.' 'Write quickly,' he answered. Shortly after the boy said again, 'Now that sentence is finished.' 'Well hast thou spoken,' was his reply, 'it is finished. Hold my head on thy hands (for it pleases me to sit opposite my little shrine, where I have been wont to pray), so that I too seated may call upon my Father.' So on the floor of his cell, he sang the Glory be to the Father, and to the Son, and to the Holy Ghost, and as he spoke the word Holy Ghost, he gave up the ghost and so went to his heavenly kingdom."[45]

BEDE'S POPULARITY

The scholarly works of Bede have been much sought after even since his day. Outside his own country they spread first to Germany, where Anglo-Saxon missionaries were laboring to convert the heathen Germans beyond the Rhine. The leader of this enthusiastic band, Saint Boniface, wrote back to the abbot of Wearmouth-Jarrow, "We, labouring to plant the seeds of the Gospel among the wild and ignorant Germans beg you to send us something of the writings of Bede the monk, who of late was shining among you like a lantern with knowledge of the Scriptures. And if you could send us a bell also, it would be a great comfort to us in our exile." When later he repeated his request he added, "And we are sending by the bearer two small vats of wine, that you may have a day of joy with your monks." Boniface's English successor as the archbishop of Mainz, Lullus, wrote home, "I am sick and like to leave this vale of tears. I beg, as a consolation both of my exile and my illness for the book of Bede of blessed memory on the building of the Temple, or on the Song of Songs, or his epigrams in heroic or elegiac verse, all if possible, but, if not, the three books on the building of the Temple. Perhaps what I ask is difficult but I think nothing will be difficult to your charity."[46] The abbot who received this request wrote back, "I would have sent you more had I been able. But this winter the frost in our island has been so severe with terrible winds that the fingers of our boys have been unable to transcribe any more books."[47]

[45] Introd. Bede Jarrett, *History of the Church of England*, pp. xxviii–xxix.
[46] R. W. Chambers, "Bede," *Proceedings of the British Academy*, XXII, 147–148.
[47] Jarrett, p. xxv, n. 1.

Along with their scholarship the Irish developed an incredibly intricate and beautiful art of manuscript illumination.[48] Whether or not they introduced this into England and are thus to be credited with inspiring and supplying the example for the painting in the lovely Book of Lindisfarne (Pls. 36–38), or whether indeed the English taught the Irish, is a matter of academic dispute, which, unless one be unnecessarily patriotic, does not prevent enjoyment of, and wonder over, both. In the case of Bede we have referred to the fact that Christianity was responsible for the beginnings of a vernacular literature in England as well as in Ireland. Bede, one of his pupils tells us, "was learned in our songs" and on his deathbed "Sang one verse in our English tongue about the terrible separation of soul and body." Bede had fellow poets in Caedmon and Cynewulf, and their poetry, often quite pagan in spirit, was not always altered by the Christian scribes who wrote it down. A poem inscribed in runes on one of the sculptured stone crosses erected at this time in Ireland and England refers to "the young Hero that was God Almighty" who "stripped Himself, strong and steadfast, Bold in the sight of many, He mounted the high cross when He would redeem mankind. I [it is the cross speaking] trembled when he clasped me, yet I durst not bow to the ground."[49] It was at this moment (early eighth century) that some English poet wrote down in Old English an epic tale concerning Beowulf, the nephew of the Swedish King Hygelac, and his heroic struggle with the dragon Grendel, with Grendel's mother, and finally with a native monster. He thus revealed the continental background of the English, for the most part, in a pagan spirit. In both Ireland and England at this moment occurred that exciting development in the history of any nation, the reduction to writing of creative speech.

ANGLO-SAXON MISSION TO THE CONTINENT

Irish monastic Christianity transmitted its missionary zeal to the new Anglo-Saxon church. Missionaries, many of them trained in Irish monasteries, set to work to convert the still-pagan Germans on the Continent, the Frisians, and the Germans beyond the Rhine. This Anglo-Saxon church, strongly respectful of episcopal organization under papal leadership, was likewise devoted to the Benedictine monastery. Its mission to the Continent was accordingly entrusted to Benedictine monks or to clergy ready to work with them. It organized a German church under Rome, founded German Benedictine monasteries, and, following hard upon the Irish, introduced into the Continent, and especially Germany, a band of English men and women Benedictines who spread with the gospel the new Christian culture of their homeland.

[48]Its best example is the Book of Kells. See Pl. 35; also illustrations in O'Sullivan, *Book of Kells.*

[49]R. H. Hodgkin, *A History of the Anglo-Saxons*, I, 364.

The leading figure in this Anglo-Saxon mission was the West Saxon Winfred (Saint Boniface), who came to the Continent first in 716. He had been preceded by others of his countrymen. Wilfrid, the archbishop of York, who had defended the Roman cause at Whitby in 663, worked among the Frisians in the winter of 677–678 on his way to Rome. Others had failed before Willibrord, a Benedictine monk of Ripon and a former student in Ireland, managed, with the help of the Frankish mayor of the palace and the pope, to organize an archbishopric at Utrecht. Thus at this date (695–696) the expansion of Christianity on the Continent came under the protection of the Carolingian house. Boniface (672?–754) was a member of Willibrord's mission during its last years (719–722). Thereupon he turned to pagan areas in Germany, where his success was so great that Rome made him a bishop and Charles Martel supported him. After the secular church in the general area of Hesse and Thuringia had been organized into bishoprics (Buraburg, Eichstätt, Würzburg, and Erfurt), and after Benedictine houses had been set up at Fulda, Hersfeld, and Fritzlar to train the German missionaries, Boniface was rewarded with the title of archbishop. As a papal legate he completed the organization of the Bavarian church into four bishoprics (Passau, Salzburg, Regensburg, Freising), and as the site of an archbishopric for this new German church chose the Rhine city of Mainz. In the conversion of the Germans and the organization of their church he was assisted by many English men and women, both in Germany and in England.[50] The first bishops of Würzburg and Erfurt were English. English abbesses and nuns took over new German churches, in one instance the double monastery (with men and women as members) at Tauberbischofsheim in Baden; in another instance a similar monastery at Heidenheim in Württemburg. Boniface's successor at Mainz (Lullus) was an Englishman. Willehad, a missionary to the Saxons under Charlemagne who set up an episcopal see at Bremen, was "the last of the great evangelists who made the eighth century the heroic age of the Anglo-Saxon church."[51] Boniface, however, was not permitted to confine his efforts to Germany. The support of Charles Martel and then of his sons Karloman and Pepin led to his undertaking the reform of the Frankish church and the task of bringing it more definitely under the control of Rome. He was influential in those negotiations that led to the papal sanction of the switch from the Merovingian to the Carolingian house in 751–752, and it was he who first consecrated Pepin king of the Franks in 752. These activities did not exhaust his energy. His English correspondents kept him informed of conditions in the Anglo-Saxon kingdoms and churches, and he was concerned with reforming these. In the end, he returned to his first ambition: the conversion of the Frisians, by whom, together with more than fifty of his companions, he was massacred at Dockum on 4 June, 754.

[50]See F. M. Stenton, *Anglo-Saxon England*, pp. 168 ff.   [51]Ibid., p. 176.

Boniface's letters are a rich introduction to the problems of missionary work and reform in eighth-century Europe. He was anxious to get from his friend Daniel, the bishop of Winchester, careful instructions on the arguments to use in converting heathens to Christianity. He is told that a very effective one is to show how powerless the pagan gods are to punish "those who reject them. . . . How is it that they spare us Christians who are turning almost the whole earth away from their worship and overthrowing their idols?" From the popes Boniface received continuous instruction on how to meet the special problems of introducing Christianity to a recently converted land. "Within what degrees of relationship may marriage take place?" "What is a man to do if his wife is unable, on account of disease, to fulfill her wifely duty?" "If a father or mother shall have placed a young son or daughter in a cloister under the discipline of a rule, whether it is lawful for the child after reaching the years of discretion to leave the cloister and enter into marriage?" The answer: "This we absolutely forbid, since it is an impious thing that the restraints of desire should be relaxed for children offered to God by their parents." Boniface is informed that "jackdaws, crows, and storks . . . are absolutely forbidden as food for Christians. Beavers, horses, and wild horses are still more strictly prohibited." He is advised that bacon is not to be eaten "until it has been smoked or cooked over a fire. If, however, one prefers to eat it raw this should not be done until after Easter." Boniface is to take "the church tax of one *solidus* from each manse . . . without any hesitation, because from this you can give alms to the needy and maintain the upkeep of the sacred churches, as the canons prescribe." "As to whether it is permitted to flee from the persecution of the heathen or not?" "So long as it can be done, and you can find a suitable place, carry on your preaching; but if you cannot endure their assaults you have the Lord's authority to go into another city."[52]

THE CLERGY IN GAUL

The letters reveal also the conditions in the Frankish church that Karloman was anxious to get Boniface to reform. "Ecclesiastical discipline . . . for a long time, not less than sixty or seventy years, has been despoiled and trampled upon. . . . The Franks, according to their elders, have not held a council for more than eighty years. . . . For the most part the episcopal sees in cities are in the hands of greedy laymen or are exploited by adulterous and vicious clergymen and publicans for secular uses." Among these men are "so-called deacons who have spent their lives since boyhood in debauchery, adultery, and every kind of filthiness, who entered the diaconate with this reputation, and who now, while they have four or five concubines in their beds, still read the Gospel, nay rather,

---

[52]*The Letters of Saint Boniface*, trans. Ephraim Emerton, p. 163.

entering upon the priesthood, they continue the same vices, add sin to sin . . . and still worse, with such reputations advancing from step to step to nomination as bishop." There are also certain bishops among them "who, although they deny that they are fornicators or adulterers, are drunkards and shiftless men, given to hunting and to fighting in the army like soldiers, and by their own hands shedding blood whether of heathens or Christians." The decrees of the reforming synods (742-743), as announced by Karloman, provided that "a synod shall be held every year, so that in our presence the canonical decrees and the laws of the Church may be re-established and the Christian religion purified. . . . We have deprived false priests and adulterous or lustful deacons of their church incomes, have degraded them, and forced them to do penance." Clergy are not "to carry arms or fight, to enter the army or march against an enemy." They are not "to hunt or wander about the woods with dogs or to keep hawks and falcons." Bishops are to see to it that "the people of God perform no pagan rites, but reject and cast out all the foulness of the heathen, such as sacrifices to the dead, casting of lots, divinations, amulets and auguries, incantations, or offering of animals, which foolish folk perform in the churches, according to pagan custom, in the name of holy martyrs or confessors. . . . Any of the servants of God or the maids of Christ falling into carnal sin shall do penance in prison on bread and water. If it be an ordained priest he shall be imprisoned for two years, first flogged to bleeding and afterward further disciplined at the bishop's discretion. But if a clerk or monk fall into this sin, after a third flogging he shall be imprisoned for a year and there do penance. Likewise a veiled nun shall be bound to do the same penance, and all her hair shall be shaved."[53]

THE IMMORAL ENGLISH

A sensitive conscience like Boniface's could not tolerate the immorality of English kings or women. He joined some bishops in protesting to King Ethelred of Mercia that "you have never taken to yourself a lawful wife, . . . nor observed chastity for God's sake but, moved by desire, have defiled your good name before God and man by the crime of adulterous lust. . . . What is worse . . . these atrocious crimes are committed in convents with holy nuns and virgins consecrated to God." Ethelred should remember what happened to those other guilty English kings, his predecessor Ceolred, and Osred, king of Northumbria. Ceolred "while he sat feasting amidst his companions was suddenly stricken in his sins with madness by an evil spirit [and] without repentance or confession, raving mad, talking with devils and cursing the priests of God, he passed on, without doubt, from this life to the torments of hell. Osred also, driven by a spirit of license, pursued consecrated virgins in their convents, with

[53]*Letters of Saint Boniface*, pp. 91-93.

furious violence, until he lost his glorious kingdom, his young life, and his lustful soul by a miserable and shameful death." Boniface is worried about reports and charges "against us in France and Italy and even by the heathen themselves" that "the English people . . . are scorning lawful marriage and living in wanton adultery like people of Sodom." If this is so, then they, like the peoples of Spain, Provence, and Burgundy before them, will become "a degenerate and degraded people with unbridled desires." In fact Boniface advises Cuthbert, the archbishop of Canterbury, "it would be well and favorable for the honor and purity of your church, and provide a certain shield against vice, if your synod and your princes would forbid matrons and veiled women to make these frequent journeys back and forth to Rome. A great part of them perish and few keep their virtue. There are very few towns in Lombardy or Frankland or Gaul where there is not a courtesan or a harlot of English stock. It is a scandal and a disgrace to your whole church."[54]

Early Western Christian Culture

THE CHURCH AND CLASSICAL LITERATURE

This chapter has already indicated how two Christian institutions, the papacy and the monastery, made possible the development of a Christian culture in early western Europe and adapted that culture to the needs of a primitive Germanic society. The language of the Church, a Roman institution, was Latin. Just as the Romans spread their language with their empire, so the Church spread its language with its Christian empire. After the Roman Empire disappeared Latin therefore remained a learned international tongue. The Church did not permit rituals to grow up in the local vernacular dialects. The clergy had to learn to read and write Latin. They could, to be sure, learn their Latin from the best Christian authors, but, it was well recognized, this would not be the best Latin. To learn the best Latin the clergy had to be trained in pagan prose and poetry. Thus from the point of view of this need it was necessary to preserve Roman literature. Also, to teach the best Latin of pagan Rome textbooks would have to be used whose examples were drawn from the great pagan writers. Now obviously this concern with Roman literature was dangerous, for it was pagan literature and expressed in beautiful language ideas and emotions that no good Christian was supposed to have. To make the clergy good Latinists incurred the risk of making them good humanists. In troubled times it is difficult to cultivate the best. In times of desperate political insecurity it is impossible. Late Roman and early medieval times were of this kind. It became increasingly impossible to give instruction in the noblest Latin. The teachers and schools were not available. The audience that could understand it grew smaller. If the

[54]*Letters of Saint Boniface*, pp. 125–130, 140.

Church were to insist upon retaining Latin among populations whose spoken language was really no longer Latin, it would have to be content with retaining a simple, less grammatical Latin. And if it really wished to pass on the contents of Christian literature and Christian scholarship to an audience wider than the clergy, it would have to permit translation into the vernacular tongues. These were problems with which the Church was immediately confronted and that took centuries to resolve. Similar problems are still crucial for a society that desires to be democratic, as this society did not. For how can literature and learning be properly inspiring and useful if they are confined to an élite?

We have noted what men like Jerome[55] and Gregory the Great[56] thought of the study of classical literature. Their opinions on the subject became authoritative for the new German West. One of Gregory's contemporaries, the learned Spanish Bishop Isidore of Seville, equates a pagan with a heretical author and advises remaining ignorant of both. England's early scholar Bishop Aldhelm of Sherborne, writes to a friend who, he has heard, is going to Ireland to study: "I pray you, study that you may refute the lies of pagan poetry. How foolish to stray through the tangled and winding bypaths of these legends, to turn from the pure waters of Holy Scripture that you may quench your thirst in muddy pools, swarming with a myriad of black toads, noisy with the gutteral bark of frogs. What think you, does it profit a true believer to inquire busily into the foul love of Proserpina, to peer with curious eyes into things of which it is not even meet to speak—to desire to learn of Hermione and her various betrothals, to write in epic style the ritual of Priapus and the Luperci. Beware, my son, of evil women and their loves in legend, beware of them, too, in life."[57] Alcuin, the leading scholar of Charlemagne's court, wrote to his students, "The sacred poets are sufficient for you, and there is no reason why you should be corrupted by the luxuriance of Virgil's language." Since the Scriptures of the West were in Jerome's translation, the Latin Vulgate, and since the learned and theological works to elucidate these works were in Latin, a knowledge of Latin was necessary, and hence to acquire it something of Latin literature. As a Carolingian poet put it, "Ennius the poet, when one asked him what he sought in Virgil, replied: 'I seek gold in dung.' And as you know, just as dung prepares the field to bring forth corn more abundantly, so the words of the pagan poets, foul though they be, since they are not true, are yet of much aid in the comprehension of the divine word."[58] It was necessary therefore to preserve and study Vergil, and as long as this was the case men, being what they are, would always receive more from the study than merely a way to comprehend Scriptures.

[55]See pp. 360 f.
[56]See pp. 385 f.
[57]The selection from Eleanor S. Duckett, *Anglo-Saxon Saints and Scholars*, pp. 39–40, copyright 1947 by The Macmillan Co., and used with The Macmillan Co.'s permission.
[58]F. J. E. Raby, *A History of Secular Latin Poetry in the Middle Ages*, I, 239.

Gregory the Great despised classical literature. He also despised writing grammatically. "I have scorned to observe all art of style. . . . I avoid not the disorder of barbarisms. I despise a conformity to construction and moods and cases of prepositions. For I deem it exceedingly inept to fetter the words of the Heavenly Oracle to the rules of Donatus." (Donatus was Jerome's teacher of grammar.) This was because Gregory wished to adapt himself to his audience. Gregory of Tours was not proud of his Latin. In the first paragraph of his history of the Franks he says, "I beg indulgence of those who may read what I write, if . . . haply in letter or syllable I transgress the laws of Grammar, an art in which I am but ill versed." In another place he speaks about writing "without education in rhetoric and grammar" and refers to himself as "you who cannot distinguish between nouns, who often mix up your genders, who misplace your prepositions and confuse the ablative with the accusative." (p. 5) And yet, as Gregory says, if, because one did not possess a Ciceronian style he were not to write at all, who, then, in days such as he was living through would do the writing that needed to be done—the writing of history, for example? "In these times," he writes in the preface to his history, "when the practice of letters declines, nay, rather perishes in the cities of Gaul, there has been found no scholar trained in the art of ordered composition to present in prose or verse a picture of the things that have befallen. . . . Wherefore the voice of lament was oftimes raised, and men said: 'Alas, for these our days! the study of letters is perished from us, nor is any found among our peoples able to set forth in a book the events of this present time.' . . . Now when I heard these and like complaints ever repeated I was moved with however rude an utterance to hand down the memory of the past to future generations. . . . I was the more encouraged because I often heard with surprise our people say that while the accomplished writer is understood by few, it is the man of plain speech who has the general ear." On another occasion he reports that his mother urged him to write, saying, "Don't you know that if anyone talks in the way you do, just ordinary language, more people will listen to him? Now make no more ado, but set to work." (p. 2)[59] Bede, too, we have seen, was concerned with making his learning available to those less learned than he. He would translate Scriptures into Anglo-Saxon as others of his age would translate works of Latin literature into Anglo-Saxon. If one could read neither Latin nor the vernacular, there were, as Gregory the Great and Bede pointed out, the sculpture and paintings in the churches.

BOETHIUS AND GREEK LEARNING

One of the symptoms of the decline of the Roman Empire was the failure of its upper and educated classes to continue to preserve Greek as a

[59]Gregory of Tours, *History of the Franks*, trans. O. M. Dalton, Vol. II.

second language. By the time of Gregory the Great, indeed by the time of Augustine, a knowledge of Greek was a rare accomplishment, even as it is today. Inability to read Greek meant that, except indirectly through Latin literature, the whole vast learning and literature of the Greeks were lost to the West. The first man to understand this loss clearly and to do something about it was Boethius, who, together with Cassiodorus, sought to serve the barbarian King Theodoric the Ostrogoth, and to save what he could out of the wreckage of the past. By this time it was well recognized in educated circles that a proper education in the liberal arts involved what came to be called training in the *trivium*, the three-way, and in the *quadrivium*, the four-way, road to knowledge. The former consisted of grammar, rhetoric, and logic, or dialectics; the latter of arithmetic, geometry, astronomy, and music. For grammar the works of Donatus, Jerome's teacher, were available, and for rhetoric the standard textbook came to be Priscian's. For logic and the whole *quadrivium* there was nothing very satisfactory except Greek works, and, since few people in the West knew Greek, it was obvious to Boethius that unless translations were to be made from Greek into Latin instruction in these fields would be hopelessly barren. For arithmetic, Boethius translated the Syrian-Greek Nicomachus's *Introduction to Arithmetic*.[60] Cassiodorus speaks of Boethius's translation of Ptolemy, the Greek astronomer,[61] and it is possible that he may have written a treatise of his own on astronomy.[62] Boethius is also responsible for a translation into Latin of Euclid's *Elements of Geometry*,[63] and he may in addition have written a further work on geometry containing information about the Hindu (Arabic) numerals.[64] His work on *Music*, a compilation of information from Greek authors, was for centuries an authoritative textbook.

BOETHIUS'S WORKS ON LOGIC

For the study of logic and philosophy Boethius had grand plans. He intended to translate, with a commentary of his own, all the works of Aristotle available to him from Greek into Latin. "Furthermore," he wrote, "I will translate and comment on all the dialogues of Plato. And after finishing this I would not disdain, indeed, to bring the philosophy of Aristotle and Plato into some kind of harmony. . . . These tasks, if sufficiency of years and leisure be given me, I would accomplish with great advantage and also much labour." The political suspicions of a barbarian king kept Boethius from completing his plans and thus cost the West dearly. What he did manage to complete were the translations of the "Old Logic," that is, the two works of Aristotle called the *Categories*

[60]See p. 149.
[61]See p. 151.
[62]Duckett, *Gateway*, p. 157.
[63]See p. 150.
[64]Duckett, *Gateway*, p. 156.

and *On Interpretation*. He wrote commentaries on these as well. He also translated an *Introduction to Aristotle's Categories* by the Neoplatonist Porphyry,[65] and wrote a commentary on this work. It is possible, too, that he succeeded in translating the advanced logical works of Aristotle. He did write independent logical works of his own.

"THE CONSOLATION OF PHILOSOPHY"

As a result of the intellectual labors of this one man alert to the needs of his day, the West was supplied for about six centuries, until the twelfth century, with sound material for the study of all subjects on its curriculum except grammar and rhetoric. A great part of it was used. Nor was this all. The tragic outcome of Boethius's life was to supply the western world, for about a thousand years, with its most popular philosophical treatise, *The Consolation of Philosophy*. King Theodoric suspected Boethius of conspiracy with the emperor of Constantinople to bring about a Byzantine conquest of the Ostrogothic kingdom. He was accordingly imprisoned in 523 and subsequently executed. His death interrupted his work on the *Consolation*. That a man under sentence of death should have the courage to undertake to write a learned work in which sections of prose are joined together by poetry and in which philosophy undertakes to convince him that, in spite of what would seem to be the futile injustice of existence there is a Providence into whose ultimate plans his imprisonment fits, this circumstance was enough to recommend his work to all subsequent ages. The executioner came to take him from his prison cell as he was writing: "Fly vices, embrace virtues, possess your minds with worthy hopes, offer up humble prayers to your highest Prince. There is, if you will not dissemble, a great necessity of doing well imposed upon you, since you live in the sight of your Judge, who beholdeth all things."[66] The execution was somewhat crude: "A cord was tied around his head and drawn so tightly that at length his eyes burst from their sockets, and he was then dispatched by a blow from a club."

ISIDORE OF SEVILLE

Because of the stimulation of Cassiodorus the Benedictine monastery came to have a scriptorium where the scribe could increase the library of his own and other institutions. Because of the devotion of Boethius it came often to have a school providing training in the *trivium* and *quadrivium*. This school was not only for those who were to become monks but also for children of the neighboring aristocracy. For centuries it was the only kind of school available. After the early seventh century, students had available in most monastic libraraies an encyclopedia written by Bishop Isidore of Seville. He, too, was concerned with the decline of

[65]See p. 303.
[66]Trans. "I. T.," rev. H. F. Stewart, p. 411.

learning in the West and anxious to do what he could to stop it by summarizing in his work the learning of the past available to him. For example, he made extensive use of Pliny the Elder's *Natural History*.[67] The intellectual fare that the bishop provided is skimpy indeed, but a couple of centuries were to elapse before it was improved upon.

ART AND THE CHRISTIAN RITUAL

In his *Confessions* Augustine remarks that "at this time it was instituted [in Milan] that, after the manner of the Eastern Church, hymns and psalms should be sung, lest the people should pine away in the tediousness of sorrow; which custom, retained from then till now is imitated by many, yea, by almost all of Thy congregations throughout the rest of the world."[68] This introduction of congregational singing into the western Church was an opportunity for the Christian poet that the ritual confirmed when it adopted some of his hymns as a permanent and necessary part of its services. The fact that the Latin ritual was chanted and that the hymns were sung offered a similar creative opportunity for the composer of music. The fact that the services of the church had to be properly housed and that the performance of the ritual had to be properly beautiful offered creative opportunity for the architect and all those painters, sculptors, and craftsmen who decorated the church and furnished proper garb and utensils for performing the service. Christianity thus put new demands upon the imagination and craftsmanship of the artist.

LATIN POETRY

The poet found in Christianity inspiration and subject matter that went beyond the needs of congregational singing or the ritual. He used, for example, the subject matter of Scripture and the great themes of Christian history and theology. Nor did Christianity necessarily prevent him from dealing with secular themes, whether in Latin or the vernacular. By supplying a literate clergy to newly converted lands, the Church made possible the recording of older pagan poetry and stimulated the writing of new religious and secular poetry. On the Continent, as well as in Ireland and England, these early medieval centuries accordingly produced a thin stream of poetical writing.

PRUDENTIUS AND FORTUNATUS

Archbishop Ambrose wrote hymns that were quickly taken into the liturgy, as did his contemporary the Spaniard Prudentius, who notably expanded the scope of the subject matter suitable for Christian poetry. Prudentius wrote an epic on a historical incident of the pagan-Christian struggle. He used both Vergil and Lucretius to treat matters of theology and combat heretics. He wrote another allegorical epic, the *Psychomachia*,

[67]See p. 258.
[68]*Works*, trans. J. G. Pilkington, Vol. XIV, Bk. IX, Chap. vii, quoted in Jones, *Medieval Literature*, p. 43.

to tell the story of the battle between virtues and vices for the human soul, and he put the histories of Spanish and other martyrs into verse. One of Gregory of Tours' good friends, the Italian poet Fortunatus, was a successful writer of hymns, and in other poems celebrated the kindliness and beauty of Radegunde, the abbess of the nunnery of the Holy Cross at Poitiers, under whose protection he had come after a career as court poet. He had not been impressed with Frankish sensitivity to poetry. "I might just as well bawl as sing in this country, where people see no difference between the notes of a goose and a swan." However, he was much impressed with Radegunde, a Thuringian princess who had fled from a violent Frankish husband. As she was about to enter upon a retreat he wrote to her:

> Heavy with God, my friend, your mind you turn
> To feed the soul and let the body burn.
> You that are life to all your sisterhood
> Recur to that retreat which you found good,
> Keeping today your eternal vow—and we
> In spirit shall go after willingly.
> For from our eyes you take away the light
> So quickly, that for lack of you my sight
> Is darkened as with clouds more heavy than night.
> Excluding us, your cell you enter in;
> Yet, though you shut us out, we are within.
> It is most right that fleeing the brief days
> You hide away—but to each one who stays
> This month is longer than the lagging year.
> But you put time beneath your feet as though
> You'd not be seen by temporal lover so,
> (For such, when I behold you, do I seem)
> Yet that one vow together we shall dream;
> My soul shall follow after yours and slip
> Where in the flesh there is no fellowship![69]

The nunnery of the Holy Cross possessed a relic of the True Cross among its treasures. Under the influence of the cult that connected the fatal tree of the earthly paradise with the cross of the Crucifixion, Fortunatus wrote hymns, two of which (the *Crux Fidelis* and *Vexilla regis prodeunt*) were made a part of the Good Friday services of the Church and may still be heard on that day in Catholic churches. The *Crux Fidelis*, after addressing the

> Faithful cross, amidst all others,
> Noble tree alone art thou!
> There's no forest that hath yielded
> Flower as thine, or leaf or bough.
> Sweet thy wood, thy nails still sweeter,
> Sweetest weight thou bearest now,

[69]Allen and Jones, *Romanesque Lyric*, pp. 142-143.

refers to the fact that

> God, our Maker, led to pity
> By the guile which led astray
> Adam when he ate the apple,
> Bringing death no more can stay
> Marked this tree to crush the other,
> All the ills it bore allay.

The *Vexilla regis* addresses the Cross as

> O comely tree! thou radiant bride!
> By kingly purpose sanctified,
> Thou chosen from a high-born race
> God's hallowed members to embrace.
>
> O happy tree! to thee doth cling
> The sinful world's redeeming King,
> Thou, balance, where his body lies,
> To match from hell its stolen prize.
>
> O Cross, our only hope, all hail!
> This passion-tide, thy balm exhale:
> In loving hearts augment thy grace,
> The sinner's stains entire efface.[70]

CHARLEMAGNE AND LEARNING

Einhard, in his *Life of Charlemagne*, remarks that the emperor "most zealously cultivated the liberal arts, held those who taught them in great esteem and conferred great honours upon them. He took lessons in grammar of the deacon Peter of Pisa. . . . Another deacon, Albin of Britain, surnamed Alcuin, a man of Saxon extraction, who was the greatest scholar of the day, was his teacher in other branches of learning. . . . [The king] also tried to write, and used to keep tablets and blanks in bed under his pillow, that at leisure hours he might accustom his hand to form the letters; however, as he did not begin his efforts in due season, but later in life, they met with ill success" (pp. 61–62). Because of the support of the first German emperor of the Romans, the efforts of the early pioneers of a western Christian culture to lay new foundations in the midst of crumbling ruins were so successful that they could not be undone in the terrible ninth and tenth centuries. Boniface's work in reforming the Frankish clergy gave the emperor a reliable church to use for these purposes. To stimulate it further he used the liveliest scholars of the West, the English as represented by Alcuin, who came from Bede's Northumbria, and the Irish, represented by those "two Scots [who] came from Ireland to the coast of Gaul along with certain traders of Britain. These Scotchmen were unrivalled for their skill in sacred and secular learning; and day by

[70]*The New Roman Missal*, in Latin and English (New York: Benziger Brothers, Inc., 1937), pp. 487 ff., 490–492.

day, when the crowd gathered round them for traffic, they exhibited no wares for sale, but cried out and said, 'Ho! everyone that desires wisdom, let him draw near and take it at our hands; for it is wisdom that we have for sale.'" When Charles asked their price, they said, "We ask no price, O king; but we ask only for a fit place for teaching and quick minds to teach; and besides food to eat and raiment to put on, for without these we cannot accomplish our pilgrimage."[71]

CAROLINGIAN INTELLECTUAL ACTIVITY

As never before in the West, a German ruler now regarded the patronage of learning as a part of his government. In addition to English and Irish he also brought learned Italians and at least one Visigoth (Theodulph) from Spain to become members of a palace school that was to train capable administrators and churchmen from whatever social source and send them back to work in the world. The students destined for the church thus became local bishops and abbots and carried their zeal for the new learning throughout the whole new empire. Alcuin, for example, after directing the palace school, became the abbot of the famous house of Saint Martin at Tours, and his students are to be found in such far-removed places as Fulda. Theodulph, the Spanish poet, became the bishop of Tours and attempted to make schooling available in the parishes of his diocese. The new local centers of learning built up new libraries of their own, composed of manuscripts written in a reformed handwriting of great beauty, and these contained the basic works of the pagan Latin as well as of the Christian past. The archtypes, that is, the earliest surviving manuscripts, of most of the classical Latin writers came from these Carolingian scriptoria. Einhard could now use Suetonius's *Lives of the Caesars* to help to write his biography of Charlemagne. Lupus, the abbot of Ferrières, could now, with great enthusiasm, enlarge and correct his library of the works of Cicero; and Rabanus Maurus, the abbot of Fulda, Alcuin's pupil, could write a better encyclopedia than Isidore of Seville's. Another student of Fulda, the monk Gottschalk, after studying Saint Augustine's works on predestination, came to the conclusion that, contrary to what the Church had decided to be the true doctrine,[72] Augustine's theory of a double predestination to salvation or damnation was correct. Two monks of the monastery of Corbie, Ratbertus and Ratrammus, argued over the traditional interpretation of the sacrament of the Eucharist: whether, that is, as Ratbertus insisted, the priest actually transformed the bread and wine into the body and blood of Christ, or whether, as Ratrammus insisted, the bread and the wine were but symbols of Christ's body and blood. The new interest in scholarship produced also a scholar and philsopher of no ordinary caliber. He was John the Scot (Scotus Erigena), whose knowledge

[71]Notker of St. Gall, *The Early Lives of Charlemagne*, trans. A. J. Grant, quoted in Jones, *Medieval Literautre*, pp. 172–173.
[72]See pp. 352 f.

of Greek, continuing an old Irish tradition, was sufficient to enable him to translate into Latin the mystical works of a Greek writer of the late fifth century known as the Pseudo-Dionysius, works incorporating much of Plotinus. John, moreover, wrote a philosophical work of his own (*Concerning the Division of Nature*) that enraged his contemporaries with its originality and its boldness in defending reason over and against authority. When a papal librarian read his translation he exclaimed: "It is a wonderful thing how that barbarian, living at the ends of the earth, who might be supposed to be as far removed from the knowledge of this other language as he is from the familiar use of it, has been able to comprehend such ideas and translate them into another tongue."[73] Writers on political subjects repeated older treatises on the relation of church and state and emphasized again that the king or emperor was limited by the law and could not be tolerated if he became a tyrant.

SEDULIUS SCOTUS

The scholars of this learned revival also wrote large quantities of Christian and secular verse. The Irishman Sedulius first came to Liège with a few of his fellow countrymen to settle down as teachers in Bishop Hartgar's school, one of the many new episcopal schools. The weather was thoroughly nasty.

> We pious priests and scholars erudite,
> The swooping blast spares not our dignities.
> Its cruel beak tears all that it can seize.

From this plight "these wayworn Irish sages" were saved by Bishop Hartgar.

> The bishop, rare soul, calm and benevolent,
> Found means to tame the boisterous element.
> The three philosophers, bounteously he used them,
> And when they tired of talking, soon excused them;
> Nor clothes nor honors has he since refused them.
> Like a good shepherd, ever generous,
> Sheep of his pasture he has made of us. (p. 9)

There were also other things that the bishop could take care of. Sedulius complains:

> We're out of mead and beer and Bacchus' gifts we miss.
> Alas, what manifold shrinkings the fleshpots are subject to!
> And the earth so prodigal of fruits, and the air of dew.
>
> I'm a writer (I own it), an Orpheus, a second Musicus, I.
> I'm the ox that treads out corn—may someone profit thereby!
> Yes, I'm your knight of learning, armed with a poet's pen.
> Muse, ask our good father bishop: When do we drink again? (p. 11)

[73]Gougaud, *Christianity in Celtic Lands*, p. 309.

In a similar situation wine and mead fail:

> Small beer, that fell beast by the wise abhorred,
> Besets us now. Good Christ! relieve us, Lord!
> Unfit to taste or swallow is our brew,
> . . . . it beclouds the learned mind,
> Banishes joy and leaves remorse behind.
> O false-gold fraud! small beer of smallest worth!
> Ye gods, remove this blemish from the earth!
> The abortion, quick, in Lethe's wave submerge,
> Or bid the Styx arise and work a purge.
> This griping drench—the foul fiend guard it well—
> May take first prize among the pains of hell.
> Vain words! O father, what more can I say?
> Our twin affliction you alone can slay:
> Your man Sedulius, scoured by this disaster,
> Asks from your generous hand a healing plaster.

> The bishop read these lines, the plea succeeded,
> He laughed, the saint, and gave us all we needed. (p. 15)[74]

At the monastery of Angers they praised a monk of whom

> They say   each day   he cries out for wine to drink;
> Daylight   nor night   sees him pause or makes him shrink;
> That sot   does not   cease until he staggers by,
> Like a tree   that's wheeling
>   reeling underneath a blowing sky.[75]

THEODULPHUS

Theodulphus, one of the better poets at Charles's court, says of Alcuin that "his instruction is better and his reed has a better tune if he moistens the caverns of his learned chest." In a poem Theodulphus gives Charles's judges the benefit of his own experience as a judge. Those who brought cases before him always tried to bribe. "One promises a crystal and jewels from the East, if only he may win possession of another's lands. Another brings rich store of golden coins inscribed with Arabic letters or 'Roman' coins of paler silver; he desires estates and villas. Another comes, and in a low voice murmurs that he is the possessor of a wonderful and precious vase of antique workmanship. . . . I have seen judges slow in performing their duties; but not slow, I must admit, when it was a question of receiving bribes." If the litigants cannot get the judge himself to take the bribe, they show the presents to his wife, and she then comes to her husband. She "embraces the knees, the hands, the neck, and the cheeks of her lord; she speaks soft words, knowing well how to arm her own prayers with such poison as that wherewith an archer tips his arrows.

---

[74]*The Goliard Poets*, trans. George F. Whicher.
[75]Allen and Jones, *Romanesque Lyric*, p. 239,

If you are proof against all this, she will come back again with feigned sighs, complaining with tears that her prayers weigh nothing with you. Then a servant, or a nurse, or a handmaid joins in: 'Why do you refuse what my lady asks?' The lady herself sobs quietly. 'Other women get what they want. I alone never get anything.' The maid servants pull her towards her husband. 'Give him a kiss,' they say and to the husband, 'Why do you upset her?' This, says Theodulf, in effect, is the hardest trial the judge has to face. If he can resist feminine guile he can do anything."[76]

NOTKER OF SAINT GALL

Some seventy years after Charlemagne's death, Notker, a monk of the distinguished Irish foundation Saint Gall, wrote an account of the emperor's deeds. It is clear from it that the German West felt that, by this time, because it had done so much in cultural and, indeed, all other matters it had reached the level of the ancients and far surpassed the contemporary and decadent East. In referring to Alcuin's teaching the author remarks that it "bore such fruit among his pupils that the modern Gauls or Franks came to equal the ancient Romans or Athenians. . . . By reason of the glory of Charles, Gauls, Aquitanians, . . . Spaniards, Germans, and Bavarians thought that no small honour was paid to them if they were thought worthy to be called the servants of the Franks." Charles asked Rome for twelve clerks "deeply learned in divine song" in order that the music of the church of his empire might be co-ordinated and unified. But these clerks "like all Greeks and Romans [were] torn with envy of the glory of the Franks" and arranged among themselves to guarantee that the music of the realm should never be unified. To build the arches of the great bridge at Mainz "All Europe . . . laboured . . . in orderly co-operation." Charles's cathedral at Aachen was "half human and half divine"; the emperor himself, "after God, the greatest of judges." When envoys of the Persian king came to court at Aachen "they were so terrified at the sight of the most magnificent Charles that one might think they had never seen king or emperor before." They brought Charles "an elephant, monkeys, balsam, nard, unguents of various kinds, spices, scents and many kind of drugs, in such profusion that it seemed as if the east had been left bare that the west might be filled." Among the gifts which Charlemagne sent back to the Persian emperor were some superior hunting dogs. When they were set upon a Persian lion "the German dogs caught the Persian lion, and the envoys slew him with swords of northern metal which had already been tempered in the blood of the Saxons." In fact, the Persian emperor could not resist presenting Palestine to Charles and ruling over it as his representative. When, according to this same author, the Lombard king caught sight of the great Charles descending into Italy, clad in iron

[76]Raby, *Secular Latin Poetry*, pp. 191, 193 ff. For additional poetry see Helen Waddell, *Medieval Latin Lyrics*; Allen and Jones, *Romanesque Lyric*; and C. W. Jones, *Medieval Literature*.

and followed by an army similarly armored so that "the rays of the sun were thrown back by the gleam of iron, . . . he fell to the ground half dead."[77]

Charles's example made an impression upon that English king, Alfred the Great (871–899), who rallied the forces of his country to resist the Danes, confined them to a part of England (the Danelaw), and prepared for the reconquest of the whole land. Alfred was worried about what the Viking incursions had done to the glorious tradition of English learning. He knew "what wise men there formerly were among the English race, [and] how foreigners came to this land for wisdom and instruction." There were now "few on this side of Humber who could understand their mass-books in English, or translate a letter from Latin into English; and I ween that there were not many beyond the Humber." Alfred's remedy was in part to imitate Charlemagne, establish a school at court, gather foreigners to direct it, and include in it himself, his children, his nobles, and his clergy, and "even many of humble birth." We are told that "almost all the ealdormen, reeves, and thegns who had been illiterate from childhood took to their books, preferring to study laboriously the unaccustomed learning rather than to give up their posts."[78]

ALFRED AND TRANSLATIONS INTO ANGLO-SAXON

Alfred had also learned from the English past that he could promote the wisdom and learning of his subjects if he could get learned works translated from Latin into English. Even before the ravages of the Vikings, when English libraries were full, the clergy had "very little knowledge of the books, for they could not understand anything of them because they were not written in their language." The men of Bede's day he thought had not wished to translate into Anglo-Saxon because "they did not think that men would ever be so careless, and that learning would so decay; they deliberately abstained from it, since they wished that the wisdom in this land might increase with our knowledge of languages." But, Alfred reflected, all the great nations of the past, Greeks, Romans, and other Christian nations, had translated the important books of others into their own tongues. "Therefore it seems better to me . . . for us also to translate some books which are most needful for all men to know into the language which we can all understand, and so we can very easily bring it about, if we have tranquillity enough, that is, that all the youth now in England of free men, who are rich enough to be able to devote themselves to it, be set to learn as long as they are not fit for any other occupation, until they are able to read English writing well: and let those

[77]Notker, *Lives of Charlemagne*, quoted in Jones, *Medieval Literature*, pp. 173–191.
[78]Hodgkin, *The Anglo-Saxons*, II, 608, 609, 619.

be afterwards taught more in the Latin language who are to continue in learning, and be promoted to a higher rank."[79]

What Alfred thought fit to translate with the help of others included part of the writings of Augustine and two works of Pope Gregory the Great, the *Dialogues* and the *Pastoral Care (Rule)*.[80] Nor did he feel that the young men of England should be without Boethius's *Consolation of Philosophy*. Greatest stress of all he laid upon history, notably upon a summary of classical history written by Orosius, one of Augustine's students, to prove that Christianity had not, as pagans asserted, brought disaster upon the Mediterranean, since it had known plenty of misery under pagan gods (*Seven Books of History against the Pagans*). Also, no well-informed Englishman could be without the knowledge contained in Bede's *Ecclesiastical History of the English People*. And, in order to tie up the glorious annals of the English struggle against the Danes with Bede's work, he began the *Anglo-Saxon Chronicle*.

[79]Hodgkin, pp. 609, 618.
[80]See pp. 385 ff.

chapter ten

MEDIEVAL SOCIAL DEVELOPMENT AND THE WESTERN TRADITION

*I*t was suggested in the previous chapter that the Church could not create, and was not especially interested in creating, the conditions that western Europe needed to recover from the debacle of the later Roman Empire. These conditions were (1) political security, (2) economic prosperity, and (3) some mitigation of the rigid, castelike social structure. This chapter must consider how these things were recovered, and how, since it was largely the work of forces outside the Church, their recovery affected the Christian ascetic tradition of the West.

FEUDALISM

As the empire of Charlemagne went to pieces[1] Europe achieved a measure of political stability through the developing feudal system. Feudalism, first of all, was a form of decentralized government in which political power was exercised by the local possessor of wealth. In the period of which we are speaking, this person was the owner or holder of large landed estates. His blood was considered to have a special heritable quality that made him superior to ordinary mortals, a noble in fact, a member of the aristocracy. To this class belonged not only laymen but the upper clergy, consisting of bishops, archbishops, and the big abbots. The huge estates of this aristocracy were divided into units called manors,

[1]See pp. 382 f.

and these units were cultivated by ignoble peasants, most of whom were serfs. After Charlemagne western Europe ceased to be governed by a powerful Frankish king or emperor. It was ostensibly governed by the rulers of those kingdoms into which the Carolingian empire split. Actually, it was governed by the nobles who supported these kings and who, in return for this support, were granted additional lands and privileges.

A rural society governed by aristocratic landowners, who in turn are supported by peasant-serfs, was no new thing in the ninth and tenth centuries. It was, in fact, an inheritance from the later Roman Empire, with its senatorial nobility living on *villas* cultivated by *coloni*. As the central government of the Roman Empire weakened the senatorials were left almost independent on their *villas*. Some of them even had private armies. The German migrations did not change the situation. The ordinary free German became, in time, a servile cultivator on a large estate. The more important Germans became owners of large estates, often displacing the former Roman owners, or receiving grants of land from their kings. The largest owners of property were the German kings. They had taken over the public lands and sovereign powers of the Roman emperors, and they were thus able to impose themselves upon the rest—upon the aristocracy and peasants.

THE BENEFICE

Since this early German economy was based on the production and consumption of agricultural products and not on trade and commerce, there was a scarcity of actual cash money, and the only way the kings could get the business of government done was to pay for services in land and royal privileges. The payment of royal land for governmental services performed took the form of what were called *benefices*. That is, the benefice was a grant of land to be held for as long as the holder properly performed his administrative duties, as, for example, a royal judge or a royal tax collector. One of the services that the German kings came especially to need was that of the heavily armed cavalryman, an expensive form of service only to be performed by the wealthy. The kings, accordingly, granted out royal lands as benefices in return for this kind of military service. Political power rested in the last analysis upon the number of such benefice holders the kings could manage to acquire. A system in which the functions of government are performed by the holders of large plots of royal land can work as long as there is plenty of royal land to grant and as long as the kings can maintain the loyalty of their benefice holders. Every holder, of course, preferred to have his benefice without obligation or for as little as possible, and in no case would he ever wish to surrender it for regranting to a more efficient or loyal person. In the ninth and tenth centuries Carolingian royal, or crown, lands were exhausted, and benefice holders became unmanageable.

The crown lands were partitioned, together with the empire, under circumstances of constant civil war and new barbarian attacks. They went to benefice holders whom the weak kings could not control. With them went grants of local governmental powers that the kings were unable to exercise. At the same time, the regular officials of the empire and the holders of royal benefices took advantage of the general chaos to make themselves locally independent. They functioned as independent counts or dukes, rather than as officials of the crown, but they kept the royal benefices. Also, men who were neither officials nor the holders of benefices usurped powers of government in instances when there was no one else to perform them. As a result, in addition to the necessary dissipation of royal lands and powers there was much private usurpation of public authority. In some way or another this society had to be defended and governed. If the kings could not protect and govern, could not, that is, make it possible for this society to survive the new barbarian flood, then royal officials, benefice holders, and the landed aristocracy had to. A new class of rulers thus arose in the West. In the space of a generation or two a government that had appeared to be imperial became feudal.

THE COUNT OF CHAMPAGNE

Feudalism was a system of dependent landholding and personal relationship, as well as decentralized government. The new noble governors of western society did not rule their estates in isolation. To strengthen their position as the dominant lords they entered into mutual economic and personal relationships. Thus, for example, what was after 843 and 870 (treaties of Verdun and Mersen) the West Frankish kingdom headed by a Carolingian king dissolved into what was essentially a collection of independent counties and duchies (county of Flanders, duchy of Normandy, county of Champagne, duchy of Burgundy). What had happened to the Carolingian West Frankish kingdom had also happened to these smaller feudal principalities. Their rulers had only land with which to pay for administrative and military services, and they had not always been able to keep the recipients of this land under control. Let us take, for example, the count of Champagne. The county which he now ruled as a virtually independent feudal prince he or his ancestors formerly administered as a county of the Carolingian empire. For administering this county they were paid with royal lands in the county of Champagne, held from the emperor as a benefice. The chaos of the ninth century permitted them to retain this benefice as their own and to rule the county as independent princes, without serious concern for the West Frankish Carolingian king. The counts recognized that there still was something to be called the West Frankish "kingdom" with a sovereign king, but they were powerful enough to refuse obedience to the king and called themselves *lords* or *suzerains*, if not sovereigns. In order to build up their political

CHRONOLOGY — Medieval Social Development

Reigns and Events

700 ───────────────────────────────────────

Battle of Tours (732)

Charlemagne (781–814)

800 ───────────────────────────────────────

Treaty of Verdun (843)

900 ───────────────────────────────────────

1000 ───────────────────────────────────────

William the Conqueror (1066–1087)
Guibert de Nogent (b. 1053–d. 1124)

1100 ───────────────────────────────────────

Louis VI (1108–1137)

Henry II of England (1154–1189)
Philip Augustus (1180–1223)
Richard the Lion-Hearted (1189–1199)
King John (1199–1216)

1200 ───────────────────────────────────────

Battle of Bouvines (1214)
Magna Carta (1215)

1300 ───────────────────────────────────────

Hundred Years' War (1337–1453)

positions, to get their counties administered and protected, they too had to grant out their lands as benefices. By this time (ninth century), however, it was more usual to call the benefice a *fief* (*feudum*) in recognition of the fact that under ordinary circumstances it could be inherited. The fief, in other words, was a hereditary benefice. By this time also it was usual to call the holder of the fief a *vassal*. The count of Champagne had thus granted out his lands in the county as fiefs to vassals who, in return, rendered him various services.

HOMAGE AND FEALTY

The ceremonial grant of fief to the vassal was called *investiture*. In it the lord handed over some symbol of the fief, usually a piece of turf or straw, to the vassal. Before receiving his fief, however, the vassal was obliged to recognize the personal superiority of his lord and his obligation to serve the lord loyally, that is, he rendered him *homage* (*homagium*) and swore an oath of *fealty* (*fidelitas*). The vassal performed homage on bended knee by placing his cupped hands in his lord's hands (the attitude of prayer) and acknowledging his status as his lord's man. Thus the economic relationship between lord and vassal (the fief) was cemented by the personal relationship of homage and fealty.

MULTIPLE LORDSHIP

In the area of Champagne the count did not own all the land and therefore could not grant it all out as fiefs. Such feudal princes as the duke of Burgundy, the archbishop of Rheims, the bishop of Autun, and the abbot of Saint Denis owned land in the region. In order, therefore, to round out his holdings and to govern them as a unit the count of Champagne became the vassal of these lords for their lands in the county. After performing homage and fealty to them he was invested with these lands as fiefs. The count of Champagne was thus the lord of his own vassals and the vassal of many other lords. The fiefs he held from others he could regrant as if he owned them (subinfeudation). In about 1172, the count of Champagne received from his vassals the services of over two thousand knights. What the count of Champagne had done, moreover, his own vassals and the other great lords of the West Frankish kingdom had also done. Theoretically, at least, no land and no man in the kingdom were to be without a feudal overlord.

THE FEUDAL CONTRACT

The political, economic, and social relationship existing between the feudal lord and vassal was conceived as a private contract of mutual obligations. As long as these mutual obligations were loyally performed the contract stood. Should one party violate its terms, the other was freed from his obligation. Society was thus held together by personal arrangements. The terms of an ordinary feudal contract were as follows: The lord granted the vassal his source of livelihood, the fief. This was ordinarily a piece of land. It could, however, be any source of income, for example, the tolls from a bridge. In addition, the lord offered his vassal the protection of his court of justice and, in case of need, military aid. In return, the lord received military service or castle guard from his vassal. The number of knights the vassal was obliged to supply and the terms of their service depended, of course, upon the value of his fief. When traveling through a fief the lord might stop at his vassal's castle, where he could expect food, lodging, and entertainment for himself and his retinue. When the lord was holding court he had the right to expect his vassals to attend either to form a court of justice, or an advisory council. Since the relationship between lord and vassal was a noble one it could not be contaminated by the ignoble practice of paying taxes. The noble vassal rendered services instead. He helped his lord through financial emergencies by giving him what were called *aids* (*auxilia*). It was commonly recognized that there were three occasions upon which a lord might collect an aid from his vassals: to help to defray the expenses attendant upon (1) the knighting of his eldest son, (2) the marriage (usually only once) of his eldest daughter, and (3) to help to pay ransom if he were taken on the battlefield or elsewhere. The lords collected the payment known as *relief* from the heir of a fief, who, to validate his newly acquired inheritance, at the same time was obliged to renew homage and fealty. When the lord was succeeded by his heir the latter collected a relief and demanded a renewal of homage and fealty from all vassals. The lord also enjoyed certain rights called the feudal *incidents*. In case the vassal was succeeded by a minor heir the lord was the legal guardian and administered the fief during the minority of his ward. He had likewise to give his consent to the marriage of a lady-vassal and the remarriage of a widow-vassal. In case the vassal died without heirs the fief *escheated* (reverted) to the lord, who could then regrant it as he pleased. Should the vassal fail to carry out any of his contractual obligations he was considered to have forfeited his fief as a felon. Should the vassal consider the lord to have violated the terms of his obligation he could defy him and withdraw from the vassal relationship. For a lord successfully to deprive himself of a felonious vassal and regain his land or for a vassal to deprive himself of an unsatisfactory lord without losing his fief required superior military power. It can be well understood that no vassal voluntarily abandoned a lucrative fief.

FEUDAL MONARCHY

The feudal contract was thus a means for lords to exploit their lands, for vassals to increase their resources, and for society to protect and govern itself. The lord powerful enough to enforce the performance of his vassals' obligations was a strong lord. This power depended, for the most part, on the amount of land at his disposal and consequently on the number of his vassals. The Carolingian kings of the West Frankish kingdom dissipated their royal lands in the course of the ninth and tenth centuries. At the end, they retained little more than a small domain in the neighborhood of Laon. They were recognized as the overlords or suzerains of all the counts, dukes, and lords of the new feudal principalities into which the kingdom had dissolved; but as long as the kings were unable to enforce the terms of the feudal contract these vassals were a source of royal weakness. The kings were only nominal rulers and weak lords when men like the counts of Champagne ignored their feudal obligations with impunity.

SPREAD OF FEUDALISM

From its center in the West Frankish kingdom, or France, feudalism spread to the neighboring regions of central and western Europe. It spread into the Spanish peninsula, as the Christian states of the earlier Spanish March pushed southward against the Moslems; into Italy; and into the East Frankish kingdom, or Germany. From Germany it spread into eastern and northern Europe. In all these areas it was synonymous with weak monarchy and decentralized government. If, in these states, territories were ever to be unified, governments centralized, and monarchs made strong, feudalism would have to be destroyed. In only two areas of the West did feudalism become associated with centralized government and strong monarchy, namely, in the Norman kingdom of southern Italy and Sicily, and the Norman kingdom of England. Into both of these feudalism was introduced by conquerors from the duchy of Normandy, whose dukes had never permitted feudal vassals to become independent. These conquerors were able to impose upon their newly won lands conditions patterned on those at home.

FEUDAL CONTRACT AND THE DEMOCRATIC TRADITION

For the democratic aspects of the political tradition of the West the contractual nature of feudalism was of considerable importance. It buttressed similar features in the political traditions inherited from Christian antiquity and in those introduced by the Germans. In taking over the Old Testament as a part of its Sacred Scriptures, Christianity adopted the Jewish notion that society was the result of a compact or covenant between God and his people. If God were to fulfill his part of the agreement, then the people must be held to theirs or suffer accordingly. That God himself might be held to account the Jews would have regarded as a blasphemous idea.[2] The Stoics likewise conceived of an original state of nature from which mankind emerged with a government as a result of a contract between ruler and ruled.[3] The Roman juris-consults could say

[2]See p. 30.
[3]See pp. 254 ff.

that the emperor was absolute, because the people had conferred upon him their power.[4] The early German king was but an elected chieftain, assisted in his government by elders and people. The law that he enforced was not something that he made; it was the custom of the people, and therefore something to be discovered and learned if not already known. Further, it was binding upon the king as well as upon the people. The king was subject to, not above, the law. Feudalism conceived of the governmental function as a private contract between a noble lord and a noble vassal. It extended this notion to royal government. As feudal overlord, the king was held to the performance of certain obligations, in return for which he received certain definite services and payments from the noble barons of his kingdom. The aristocracy enjoyed certain feudal rights that the king could not violate: from his vassals the king must not demand more than his due. There was a body of custom by which he was bound. If he ignored his obligations, violated the rights of his nobles, and spurned feudal customs, he was a tyrant; he could be quite properly resisted and dethroned and another set up in his place. In the name of contract feudalism sanctioned rebellion against a tyrannous king. Together with coronation oaths, ceremonies of priestly consecration, and Germanic notions of law and kingship, it emphasized the conditional, we might say the constitutional, nature of kingship. It rejected implicitly the whole theocratic tradition.

MAGNA CARTA

The influence of feudalism in this regard can be seen in one of the most important of all feudal documents, the Great Charter, or Magna Carta, of 1215. Magna Carta was partly the result of the kind of feudalism introduced into England by William the Conqueror in 1066. William was well aware of what feudalism had done to destroy the power of the kings of France. As duke of Normandy, where independent feudal lords did not exist, he knew how to prevent a similar destruction of his own power. He disposed of the conquered resources of Anglo-Saxon England in such a way as to provide that no vassal could approach his wealth or power as feudal overlord of the Anglo-Norman baronage. In this position he made it impossible for a vassal to violate his feudal contract with impunity. William's Norman, and especially his Angevin, successors were able to implement this royal strength by creating powerful and efficient instruments of central government. After 1066 the kings of England were also dukes of Normandy. The accession of Henry II in 1154 brought under the English crown additional French feudal principalities: Maine, Anjou, Touraine, and Aquitaine. Such large holdings in France entailed almost constant war with the French kings and required the continuous residence of the English kings on the Continent. Richard I, the Lion-Hearted (1189–

[4]See pp. 253 f.

1199), who was also a crusader, spent but a few months of his reign in England. Yet the machinery of royal government[5] ran so smoothly that it could do without the presence of the king. Indeed, the royal government so overshadowed the feudal foundations of the monarchy that many of the barons feared the development of tyranny.

KING JOHN AND HIS BARONS

Under Richard's brother John (1199–1216) a great many barons felt that they were being governed by a tyrant. John's reign was decisive for the English empire on the Continent. The Carolingian kings of the West Frankish kingdom had been succeeded (987) by the kings of the Capetian line. Of these Capetian kings of France the dukes of Normandy were vassals, and even after 1066, when they became kings of England, as dukes of Normandy they remained vassals of the French kings. Not until John's reign did the French King Philip Augustus (1180–1223) feel strong enough to challenge the position of England in France. He did so by using the feudal contract. As a vassal John had to appear at the court of the French king if summoned. When the French count of La Marche appealed to his overlord, the French king, for justice against King John, another vassal of the French king, John was so summoned before the French court in 1202. He refused to come and accordingly was declared forfeit of his French fiefs for violation of the terms of the feudal contract. Philip's feudal court not only declared him forfeit as a contumacious vassal but the French king was powerful enough at this moment to deprive John of these holdings (all except Aquitaine) by force. Ten years later (1214), in a battle at Bouvines in northern France, he defeated an attempt by John and his continental allies to regain this lost French empire. The costs of the war to retain these English holdings in France had been enormous, and in the end futile. They did not make John a popular king. English barons felt that to raise these sums he had violated those terms of the feudal contract that brought money to the king. Without reference to feudal limitations he had arbitrarily and at will extorted money from them. This was notorious with reference to *scutage*, the money payment English vassals were permitted to make in lieu of military service. In other respects as well the barons felt their feudal rights to have been violated. To stop such violation and hold the king to his contractual agreement something would have to be done. Feudalism recognized the right of vassals to cast aside the overlord who did not keep to his agreement. When, after Bouvines, John returned to England and proceeded to govern as usual the barons formed a confederation, swore allegiance to it, and, when opposed by the king, took the field after presenting him with a defiance (*diffidatio*), a withdrawal of allegiance and actually a declaration of war. John was confronted with the alternative of negotiation or a hard

[5]See pp. 556 ff.

civil war, for a large proportion of, if by no means all, the barons were on the side of the rebels.[6] John decided to negotiate, hoping perhaps that his new overlord, Pope Innocent III,[7] would declare the results null and void. The terms were incorporated into Magna Carta and granted to the barons on 15 June, 1215, at Runnymede on the Thames.

FEUDAL PROVISIONS OF MAGNA CARTA

It is not difficult to illustrate that Magna Carta is a feudal document regulating the contract between the king and his vassals. Chapter Two, for example, determines the payment of relief and provides that an heir shall pay only what has been the customary relief for the inheritance of the fief ("the heir shall have his inheritance for the ancient relief"). The Charter carefully states what these customary reliefs are for the various sizes of fiefs. Chapters Three and Four regulate the practice of wardship. Three states that if the heir "is under age" and "in wardship, . . . he shall, when he comes of age, have his inheritance without relief. . . . The guardian of the land of such an heir [Chap. 4] who is under age shall not take from the land of the heir more than reasonable issues and reasonable customs and reasonable services, and this without destruction and waste of men or things." Chapter Eight provides that "no widow shall be forced to marry so long as she wishes to live without a husband, yet so that she shall give security against marrying without our consent if she hold of us, or without the consent of her lord is she holds of another." Chapters Twelve to Fourteen have to do with the very delicate matters of scutage and aids. Twelve provides that "scutage or aid shall be levied in our kingdom only by the common counsel of our kingdom, except for ransoming our body, for knighting our eldest son, and for once marrying our eldest daughter, and for these purposes only a reasonable aid shall be taken." Fourteen prescribes the manner in which the common counsel is to be secured for the levying of scutage and the extraordinary aids. Together these two paragraphs recognize the principle that the king may not assess the feudal dues without the consent of those who are to pay them. This provision was to be of subsequent importance in establishing the principle of "no taxation without representation." Further paragraphs have to do with protecting all freemen from the levy of excessive fines by the courts and in their liberty over and against the government. Chapter Thirty-eight provides that "no bailiff shall henceforth put anyone to his law by merely bringing suit against him without trustworthy witnesses presented for this purpose"; and Thirty-nine, "no freeman shall be captured or imprisoned or disseised [dispossessed] or outlawed or exiled or in any way destroyed nor will we go against him or send against him, except by the

[6]Cf. Sidney Painter, *The Reign of King John*: Of his 27 most powerful barons, only 13 were rebels.
[7]See p. 576.

lawful judgment of his peers or by the law of the land." Chapter Forty reads, "to no one will we sell, to no one will we deny or delay right or justice."[8] These provisions of Magna Carta foreshadow the later elaboration of such vital principles as "no person shall be held to answer for a capital or otherwise infamous crime unless on presentment or indictment of a grand jury"; "no warrants shall be issued but upon probable cause supported by oath or affirmation"; "no person shall be deprived of life, liberty or property without due process of law."[9]

CHAPTER SIXTY-ONE OF MAGNA CARTA

The last chapter of the Charter (61) undertook to guarantee its enforcement. It provides that "the barons shall elect twenty-five barons of the kingdom, whomsoever they please, who to the best of their ability should observe, hold, and cause to be observed, the peace and liberties that we have granted to them and have confirmed by this our present charter. . . . If we [the king] or our justiciar, or our bailiffs or any of our ministers are in any respect delinquent toward any one, or transgress any article of the peace or the security," and if this is made known to four of the above twenty-five barons, "those four barons shall come to us, or to our justiciar if we are out of the kingdom, to explain to us the wrong, asking that without delay we cause this wrong to be redressed." If the king or his officials do not redress the grievance within forty days, the case shall be referred to the twenty-five barons, and they "together with the community of the entire country, shall distress and injure us in all ways possible, namely by capturing our castles, lands, and possessions and in all ways that they can, until they secure redress according to their own decision, saving our person, and the person of our queen and the persons of our children. And when redress has been made they shall be obedient to us as they were before." The king even promises to force the neutrals to join the barons: "All those of the land who of themselves and by their own free will are unwilling to take the oath for the twenty-five barons, with them to distress and injure us, we will by our mandate cause to swear such an oath as aforesaid."[10] The above provision is a vivid statement of the feudal principle that rebellion is legal against a lord who does not adhere to his part of the feudal contract. When taken with those parts of the Charter that go beyond the terms of a feudal contract and the feudal classes it attempts to guarantee that the king must obey the fundamental law of the land. He is limited, as the ancient Germanic principle had it, by the customary law, which he violates at the risk of civil war. This, then, was the "first attempt ever made in history to put into constitutional form the principle that the government must obey the fundamental laws of the state."

[8]*Sources of English Constitutional History*, eds. and trans. Carl Stephenson and F. G. Marcham, pp. 116–117, 121.
[9]See George B. Adams, *Constitutional History of England*; also M. M. Knappen, *Constitutional and Legal History of England*, pp. 199 ff.
[10]Stephenson and Marcham, pp. 125–126.

Clause Sixty-one did not prevent a civil war in England, inasmuch as the barons refused to swallow the pope's declaration that the Charter was null and void and the barons themselves excommunicate. John died in the midst of this war. These events do not mean, however, that the Charter was not of fundamental importance to the history of the western tradition. It reaffirmed in England the Germanic and feudal principle that the king is not above the law and that, if he acts as if he were, he may be resisted as a tyrant. Because this was the affirmation of a group of hard-boiled and rapacious nobles defending their own selfish interests and local independence, and because it did not extend to the "unfree" peasants, we must not be led to deprecate it. Given the organization of English and medieval society at the moment, the rights of the élite had to be asserted and defended before they could become the rights of all. Subsequent English kings were obliged more or less regularly to subscribe to the terms of Magna Carta. It was reissued several times with modifications. Its method of redress, civil war and rebellion, did not become popular. Its main principle, however, the supremacy of law over both king and subjects, did. In the course of time the methods of discussion (parliament), rather than of force (rebellion), came to be the accepted means of securing the adherence of kings to the law and of redressing grievances. When, later in England, the parliament was attacked by absolute, theocratic kings (seventeenth century), its defenders took great solace from the action of the barons that produced Magna Carta and hailed it as a cornerstone of English liberties. As a justification for further rebellion against tyrannical and irresponsible monarchs, parliamentary political theorists enlarged the feudal notion of society as being held together by contract into the contract theory of the seventeenth and eighteenth centuries. This contract theory became the very justification for the English Glorious Revolution of 1688, the American and the French revolutions. The rights of the English aristocracy of 1215 became the rights of man in 1789. In this indirect way feudalism was a further source of the democratic tradition of the West.

MANORIALISM AND FEUDALISM

A Spanish author of the thirteenth century, writing on that virtue chivalry, that only the nobility was supposed to possess, said, "It is seemly that . . . men should plough and dig and work hard in order that the earth may yield the fruits from which the knight and his horse will live; and that the knight, who rides and does a lord's work, should get his wealth from the things on which his men are to spend much toil and fatigue."[11] This statement of Raymond Lully's reveals two things: that an essential

[11]Marc Bloch, "The Rise of Dependent Cultivation and Seigniorial Institutions," *Cambridge Economic History*, I, 277.

function performed by manorialism, the medieval system of cultivating the soil, was to support the aristocracy, and that there was a wide social gap between the aristocracy and the peasantry. In a sense manorialism may be regarded as a part of feudalism. The manor could be described, that is, as the lowest political unit in the feudal system. For the fiefs of the nobles were divided into manors, and it was in the manorial court, his private court, that the lord exercised his rights as a private governor and enforced his rights as a private landowner and holder. From the economic view, also, the manor was a part, the underside, of feudalism. The work of the peasant-serf upon the manor maintained the aristocracy of both the Church and lay society. One thing the noble did not do was to soil his hands by actual labor in fields or shop. From the social point of view, accordingly, these two systems were wide apart. Feudalism had to do with a noble, manorialism with an ignoble, caste. If the lord managed his own lands, these two classes came into contact on the manor. Ordinarily, however, the lord managed his estates through his bailiffs and was himself absentee, attending to the larger affairs of state and church. Since each class was a hereditary class whose virtues and vices were transmitted by birth there was no possibility, usually, for members of one class to enter the other. This was not altogether true, for under certain circumstances a peasant could enter the clergy as a priest or monk and, if he were enormously able, rise in the hierarchy to occupy positions normally held only by members of noble families. There are likewise examples of exceptionally capable serfs who were used in an administrative capacity by the nobility and rewarded with lands, and whose descendants were able in time to establish a minor grade of the nobility. For this to happen was, however, the rare exception and not the rule.

THE THREE ESTATES

Like Plato's social theory in the *Republic*,[12] that of the medieval churchman was organic. Society was a living organism of divine foundation in which each group had its specially assigned task necessary for the life of the whole community. The first of these groups, or classes, the clergy (first estate), had to pray to God on behalf of the sins of mankind. In this capacity of indirect savers of men's souls they were socially foremost. The second group, the nobility (second estate), had as the military to protect mankind with their arms. The group lowest in the social scale (third estate) had to do the world's necessary dirty work so that the other two could perform their tasks without too much concern for daily livelihood. It was composed for the most part of peasants. The analogy of the human body was often used to explain the organic nature of society. The directing head represented the first estate, the clergy; the protecting shoulders and arms, the second estate, the nobility; and the supporting limbs upon

[12]See pp. 95 ff.

which the rest necessarily depended if the whole were to function, the third estate, the peasantry. This is why peasants have stout legs.

THE PEASANT

Medieval literature reserved such precious virtues as gentility, courage, generosity, and chivalry for the aristocracy alone. The peasant was a clumsy, unrefined, subhuman beast of burden. Ordinarily the literature does not deign to mention him, since he does not belong to the aristocratic society with which it is preoccupied. When it does, it treats him as some hideous animal. For example, in the twelfth-century tale of Aucassin and Nicolette, the gentle, noble hero is searching the forest for his lost Nicolette. As he rides over the paths on his horse his tender flesh is torn and bruised by thorns and briars. "The blood sprang from his arms, and flanks, and legs in forty places or thirty." In the forest he met a peasant who had lost his ox Roger, "the best of my team." The author describes the peasant: "Tall was he, and great of growth, laidly and marvelous to look upon; his head huge, and black as charcoal, and more than the breadth of a hand between his two eyes and great cheeks, and a big nose and broad, big nostrils and ugly, and thick lips redder than a collop, and great teeth yellow and ugly, and he was shod with hosen and shoon of bull's hide bound with cords of bark over the knee, and all about him a great cloak twy-fold, and he leaned on a grievous cudgel."[13] In another source, an Italian clergyman recommends that "peasants must not eat fowls, but onions and cheese, nor rolls or white bread, but coarse bread, for base and coarse foods are to be given to base persons and delicate foods to noble folk."[14] "They have one squint eye and the other is blind. They have one good foot and the other is twisted." "The devil did not want the villeins [peasants] in hell because they smelled too badly." "They have such hard heads and stupid brains that nothing can penetrate them." The peasant deserves to be fed on "straw, thistles and thorns," or "beechmast and acorns like the swine that he is."[15]

SOCIETY THEORETICALLY UNALTERABLE

By its clerical theorists this castelike society was considered to be of divine foundation and therefore unalterable. The ideal member of society was patiently content with the position in life into which God had put him, knew his place and did not try to rise from it, and realized, as one cleric put it, that "Christ came to change men's hearts, not their conditions of life." Because of the spiritual equality of every soul in the sight of God the material conditions of life were unimportant. For this reason the Church had not attacked the slavery of the ancient world. In the course of time the Church itself possessed slaves and serfs in large num-

[13]Trans. Andrew Lang, quoted in Jones, *Medieval Literature*, p. 584.
[14]G. G. Coulton, *Medieval Village*, p. 316.
[15]Achille Luchaire, *Social France at the Time of Philip Augustus*, p. 389.

bers. It was then even more difficult to see that there was any contradiction between Christian love and slavery, for Christianity had nothing necessarily to do with personal freedom. If a slave became a Christian it was not necessary to emancipate him. "Rather she [the Church] hoped that, by faithful service, much better than that of his comrades who remained in sin, he would show to his master the loveliness of true religion."[16] Slavery persisted into the early medieval centuries, only to be gradually supplanted by serfdom, but the Church's fundamental attitude did not change. Indeed, the theologians, like the later American owners of Negro slaves, were very glad to make use of Aristotle's defense of Greek slavery to defend the slavery of their own day. Saint Thomas Aquinas, the leading orthodox theologian of the thirteenth century, agreed with Aristotle "that the peasant has no right to full citizenship in the ideal State; that the division between a fighting caste and a working caste is natural and profitable; that agriculture is a necessary but illiberal occupation; and that 'in the best state, the tillers of the soil, if they can be just as we wish, should be slaves [servos] robust of body, that they may well labour the earth, but deficient in understanding, lest they be inventors of wiles against their masters . . . poor spirited, and not of the same tribe; for thus they will be more useful for field work, and they will not grow insolent and plot against their lords.' "[17] It can be understood that the second estate joined with the aristocratic clergy in preferring a stable, static society in which every man knew his place and kept it.

MEDIEVAL SOCIAL CHANGES

As early as the fifth century, however, complaints were heard about the "dodges of those who will not stay in that state of life to which they are born." Those complaints and those "dodges" have continued to date. In the course of the long medieval centuries of our western history the castelike social organization of antiquity broke up. The class structure came to have more mobility and within it the ordinary individual, in accordance with his ambitions and abilities, might more occasionally rise. This development is a glorious chapter in the history of the West, and it has to do with four mighty changes in the social organization of early medieval Europe: (1) the gradual, if but temporary, disappearance of chattel slavery; (2) the widespread emancipation of the medieval serf; the emergence and articulation of what for medieval society were (3) a new middle, or bourgeois, class; and (4) a new class made up of skilled, organized workmen and an unskilled, unorganized urban proletariat. These social changes, the result largely of economic opportunities upon which the individual seized to improve his condition, introduced into western history the watchword of personal freedom.

[16]See Bloch, *Cambridge Economic History*, I, 237 ff.
[17]Coulton, p. 154, n. 3.

Slavery declined in the Roman Empire when imperial wars became fewer, and thus the number of war prisoners sold as slaves. When, with the barbarian invasions, more or less continuous war prevailed the supply of slaves increased, but not on a sufficient scale to permit a return to the old method of cultivating the lands of the *villa* with slave gangs. Indeed, as the number of slaves on the large estates declined the senatorial owners leased out larger amounts of their land to tenants who, after Constantine, were tied to the *villas* as soil-bound serfs. The wars of the early Middle Ages did not increase the supply of slaves to such an extent as to stop this process. Indeed, the period witnessed the frequent leasing of land to the slave as tenant, a lease accompanied often with emancipation. Christianity did not sanction the enslavement of Christians as a result of war, at any rate not of orthodox Christians; but its notions of humanity had not gone so far as to exclude the heretic or the eastern Orthodox Christian under the Byzantine church. Nor, of course, were infidels (Mohammedans) or pagans (trans-Elbean Slavs, Balts, or Finns) excluded. Expeditions directed by slave traders went into these areas to make captives. The results in numbers of slaves were not large, and they were sold in the Moslem and Byzantine, not western, markets. It thus happened that slavery gradually disappeared in the West. What was left of it was transformed into its medieval counterpart, serfdom. Accompanying the disappearance of slavery was the gradual reduction of freemen to the position of serfs. In a period of extreme poverty and insecurity landless men will take up land under the most humiliating conditions, and free farmers, for protection, will surrender lands to powerful neighbors and become serfs on their estates. Free peasants did not disappear in the West, but by about 1000 A.D. the great majority were serfs.[18]

THE INCIDENTS OF SERFDOM

Serfdom was a hereditary social stigma binding the peasant to a particular plot of ground and subjecting him to the unlimited demands of the lord for labor services and dues. Thus the peasant-serf, according to feudal law, enjoyed no freedom of movement. He was tied to the soil of the manor and could not work for whom he chose. If he tried to get away from his manor to seek better conditions he could be pursued by his lord within a definite period of time (usually four days), and without further ado brought back to the manor in chains. His was a kind of forced labor, never very remunerative for any lord. The serf was also limited in his choice of a marriage partner. To marry within or without the village community serving the manor the consent of the lord was necessary, and this consent was not given without payment of a fee (on English manors called *merchet*). The marriage of a female serf was an

[18]See Bloch, I, 234 ff.

especially delicate matter, inasmuch as, like the cow, she was the source of future labor power. The serf passed on his status to his children and thus could not guarantee to them any more freedom or any better fortune than he had had. If a serf-father wished his promising son to do something other than farm, to enter the clergy, for example, he had to secure the consent of the lord, inasmuch as the question, strictly speaking, had to do with the property rights of the lord in the serf. For the son to enter the clergy meant not only schooling away from the manor but also emancipation from serfdom, since the Church did not permit serfs to take orders. Negotiations had to be conducted with the lord on these matters and the proper fees paid.

PEASANT TAXES

The income of the serf was subject to the whim of the lord. Strictly speaking, what little property he managed to collect was at the lord's disposal. An English abbot reminded some revolting peasants that they actually possessed nothing more than their bellies. In addition to fees mentioned above there were other galling dues, including the *heriot*, or death duty. The lord took from the property of the deceased serf the best piece of property (an ox, a bed), and the Church took the next best. There were dues in kind made at the chief religious festivals of the year. The serf could be taxed by the lord, and taxed without restraint (taxable at will, *tailleable à merci*). This taxation took many forms, varying from region to region and from country to country. From the crops of the peasant the Church, too, took its often unwelcome tithe.

LABOR SERVICES

Not only was the serf unfree with respect to his person and his income but he was unfree with respect to his time, which was likewise at the disposal of the lord. Just as the fief was divided into those lands granted out to vassals as fiefs, and those retained by the lord as demesne farms to be exploited directly by him, so the cultivable lands of these farms were divided into two parts, that granted out to the peasants, and that retained by the lord (the demesne land) for his own use. The peasants on the manor supplied the labor for the cultivation of the lord's demesne land, and ordinarily this took about three days a week and was called "week work." This was not all the labor service demanded. At those special seasons of the farm year when the land had to be prepared or the seed sown or the crops harvested there was extra work to do on the lord's, as well as the peasant's, land. At these seasons the lord could call upon the peasants for more than their usual week work, that is, for the extra work that in England was called "boon work." A peasant had to cultivate his usual thirty-acre farm carefully if it was to suffice. Week work and boon work on somebody else's land, when the same could be applied to his own, were not especially to his liking. Nor did the fact that on certain manors the peasant could be beaten for not working hard enough stimulate his zeal. Tenures on the manor were given on conditions of service that included the use of the rod on boon days. On an English manor one "Walter Algerson . . . will come personally to all the boon-days holding his rod over the workers." On a German one the lord had the right of "moderate chastisement," interpreted as a "few boxes on the ear or a tolerable whipping."[19]

THE VILLAGE COMMUNITY

The peasant was a member of a village community of long standing, reaching back in many instances to primitive days, when lands were owned and cultivated in common. Upon these village communities lords had imposed themselves by force without being able to deprive the members of common rights to use the forest, streams, and wasteland. Because of the peculiar organization of the manorial lands this village community was co-operative. An ordinary serf-peasant held about thirty acres of land. These acres were divided among three fields, in order that the various types of land on the manor should be fairly distributed. Within each field the peasants' land consisted of unfenced strips whose size was determined originally by the medieval system of ploughing. Thus all the peasants holding strips in one field and planting an identical crop were subject to the same agricultural routine. No one, moreover, possessed the necessary equipment to cultivate his own strip independently. This equipment, including the draft animals, had accordingly to be pooled. There was not much chance under this system for one peasant to farm better than another. All were reduced to the same regime and bound by the same custom. This custom, often quite capricious, regulated the relations of the peasants to the lord or his agent. It was something the lord could not easily destroy or modify. Enforceable in the manorial court, it protected the serf from an arbitrary or vicious lord. The parish priest, often enough the son or a relative of a local peasant, was an integral part of this village. He, like the peasants, held strips in the three fields and in some instances can actually be shown to have worked on the lord's demesne land as a laborer. He was the appointee of the lord, and around him and his church much of the regular social life of the community centered. It can be readily understood that under conditions such as these, guaranteeing to the serf and his family but a scant livelihood, there should have developed strong desires to get out of the class in which one had been divinely stationed.

REASONS FOR PEASANT EMANCIPATION

The peasant's ability to alter his station depended upon his ambition and alertness in taking advantage of certain economic changes in western so-

[19]Coulton, pp. 51, 52.

ciety. Also, a very few of the aristocracy gradually came to realize that a system of forced labor was not the most satisfactory way to exploit one's property. Except in rare cases neither religious, humanitarian, nor benevolent feelings on the part of the owners of serfs, nor a change in the attitude of the Church suggesting that Christianity was incompatible with serfdom, had anything to do with peasant emancipation. The large estates of the upper secular and regular clergy were cultivated by serfs who were as much a part of the capital of ecclesiastical as of secular lands. Canon law, the law of the Church, forbade the alienation of this property by emancipation except in the case of strict necessity. The economic changes, in many instances, made it possible for the serf to accumulate enough money actually to buy his freedom from the lord. In some instances this was done by groups or whole villages of serfs who took advantage of his need of ready cash. It would not be fair, however, to say that all emancipations were inspired with the cynicism of the English bishop Grandisson, who, in a charter of 1355, justified a serf's emancipation thus: "Whereas thou being now come to thy fifty years hast no longer any wife or offspring lawfully begotten of thy body, and art so insufficient in worldly goods that thou must needs live from thine own labors, and knowest no art but that of a boatman, having learned none other from thy youth upward, therefore we cannot hold it unprofitable to us or to our Church of Exeter to restore thee to thy natural liberty."[20]

THE LARGE ECONOMIC CHANGES

The large economic changes referred to above caused a shift from an agriculture based on local consumption to one based on exchange, or, in other words, from a natural to a money economy. This, in turn, was part of the larger shift from an exclusively rural to a partly urban society. These changes began after Europe had recovered from the new barbarian invasions of the ninth and tenth centuries and had settled down to some measure of relative peace and security under the feudal system. The resulting increase in population made necessary an expansion of the arable land. Arable land could not be expanded except by recovering it from the sea and swamp, as in the Netherlands, or by cutting down the medieval forest. A third possibility was to leave those areas in western Europe where all the arable land had been taken up and move to new areas where the land was not all being cultivated, or where it was in the hands of infidels or pagans. The colonizing activities of the Norse were such a movement. Other areas in which arable land was to be had were Spain, held by Mohammedans, and Germany east of the Elbe River and south of the Baltic Sea, held by pagan Slavs, Balts, and Finnish peoples. Such work as pushing back the sea, draining the marsh and swamp, cutting down the forest, and extending the confines of Christian civilization were

[20]H. S. Bennett, *Life on the English Manor*, p. 283.

the activities of the pioneer. The pressure to expand the arable area created, then, both an internal and an external frontier, one within and one without the boundaries of Christian Europe. The pressure of an increasing population also caused an expansion overseas to the Near East and the Baltic areas that was, in turn, largely responsible for the reappearance of town life in central and western Europe and for the industry, trade, and commerce that nourished it. The re-enlivening of old towns and the creation of new towns, a very gradual urbanization of western society, began to transform fundamentally the nature of its economy. Manors had to provide not only for the local peasantry and aristocracy but also for the members of the middle and working classes in the new towns.

THE PEASANT AND ECONOMIC CHANGE

These were the changes that the peasants on the old, long-settled manors of western Europe had sense enough to take advantage of. Reclamation of land from the sea, swamp, marsh, and forest is no easy task. For landlords to hope to engage in and profit from such strenuous undertakings when there was no surplus labor, it was necessary to induce peasants to leave the old manors. To induce them to leave it was necessary to make of the new tasks an opportunity to get free from the social stigma and the burdens of serfdom. Thus the terms on which newly opened-up lands were offered to pioneer peasants were essentially those of a renter who was not held to labor services on the lord's demesne or to the unlimited payment of hated servile dues. What the personally free, pioneer peasant had to render for the use of the new arable land was not regulated by custom but put down in specific terms in a contract. It can be easily understood that to persuade peasants to pick up their meager goods and move long distances with their families to engage in reclamation work, or to take up new claims in pagan lands, one had to offer good terms such as abolishing serfdom and servile conditions. Those North German lords, lay and ecclesiastical, who summoned not only Germans but Flemings and Dutch to drain marshes and swamps in the valleys of the Weser, Elbe, and beyond offered those terms. The new towns were so desperately in need of labor that they encouraged the migration of peasants into their midst, holding out freedom if the peasant could disappear into the city for a year and a day without being discovered by his lord. The conservative lord, clinging tenaciously to the advantages serfdom brought him, found himself constantly threatened by the loss of his peasants, who slipped off in the darkness of night to a neighboring or far-distant estate where pioneer work was being done, or went no further than the neighboring town. To keep serfs on his manor the lord had to offer them conditions as fair as they could get elsewhere. Under these circumstances huge tracts of arable land were added to the older manors, and the forest was cut down for clearings. In fact, the work of internal colonization "came to an end about the year 1300, and in central and western Europe the cultivated area was not appreciably increased during the next five hundred years."[21] A good deal of this expansion was done in the form of what in England was called *assarting*. The assart was the bit of new arable land that the lord permitted the peasant to cut from the manorial wasteland or forest. Hard-working peasants could thus carve out holdings for their children or improve the size of their own, and inasmuch as these assarts were outside the regular field system of the manor the peasant might work them independently, as indeed he had to create them. Additional land made it possible to acquire that additional surplus with which to buy one's freedom.

PEASANT REVOLTS

Those lords who resisted this whole process learned that peasants were perfectly willing to take their fates in their own hands and revolt, if necessary, to secure an improvement in their condition. The revolts grew more numerous and extensive as the Middle Ages came to an end. While they were by no means always, or even frequently, successful, since the peasantry had no way of overcoming the superior military power of the aristocracy, they did contribute to the ultimate freedom of the serf and did lead to a new radical social theory that contrasted violently with the conservative organic view. These revolts were often joined by discontented workingmen in the towns and by the lower clergy, who were also interested in bringing about a revolution in the Church.

A chronicler reporting a revolt of Norman peasants against their duke about A.D. 1000 tells of the fate of delegates of the peasants who came to enumerate their grievances: "He [the agent of the duke] caught those delegates with certain other peasants; he cut off their hands and feet and sent them back thus useless to their own men, that they might restrain them from like doings, and that their fate might warn the rest. The peasants, after this experience, hastily abandoned their assemblies and returned to their ploughs." Serfs on the lands of a French abbey broke into rebellion, and "so great waxed their numbers and the popular tumult that they utterly refused to give fines for marrying their wives" and also the heriot. Revolting peasants on the lands of an English abbey (1229) were excommunicated; yet "they ceased not from their original fury and malice but, confessing themselves excommunicate, they said they would rather go down to hell than be beaten in this matter of tallage [taxation]." Peasants victimized by the ravaging of the early Hundred Years' War in France broke out into wild and hopeless revolt (1358). English peasants who resented the attempts of the king and aristocracy to keep them from taking advantage of the results of the Black Death to improve their condition broke out into revolt in 1381. At the close of the fifteenth and the

[21]Hans Nabholz, "Medieval Agrarian Society in Transition," *Cambridge Economic History*, I, 500.

beginning of the sixteenth century the peasants of the Rhineland were almost constantly in revolt. In 1502, for example, "the country-folk about Speyer gathered together against the lords and the parsons that they might cast off their tyranny and have all else free and common."[22] Stimulated by Luther's preaching the German peasants arose in furious and widespread revolt in 1524.

THE NEW SOCIAL THEORY

We have already noted the social circumstances under which Christianity arose and the teachings of the Christian Fathers about the original equality of all men.[23] It was in accordance with the latter that Jonas, the bishop of Orleans in the early ninth century, remarked that "rich and mighty folk" ought to "learn that both their bondfolk and the poor are by nature their own equals." The new social doctrine in the air in the later Middle Ages, when the peasant-serf was starting out on the road to freedom, can be illustrated by the following: Justice Herle, an English lawyer, wrote in 1309: "In the beginning every man in the world was free, and the law is so favourable to liberty that he who is once found free and of free estate in a court of record, shall be holden free forever unless it be that some later act of his own makes him villein."[24] A revolting English peasant in 1381 said, "We are men formed in Christ's likeness, and we are kept like beasts." Parliament in 1406 legislated that it is the right "of every man or woman, of what state or condition he be, to set their son or daughter to take learning at any school that pleaseth them within the realm." A Franciscan monk in papal employ in the early fourteenth century complained that the peasants "do not recognize God as the giver of the fruits of their fields and beasts and trees, but impute it to nature and their own labour." John Geiler, a reforming German priest, complained similarly (1510) "that no man is content with the class and rank which is given him by God but every man strives to climb higher. The peasant would fain be a citizen, the citizen a squire, the squire a baron, the baron a count." A contemporary of Geiler's wrote: "It is an unheard-of injustice, to which all Christendom must open its eyes, that there are men who can say to their fellow-man, 'Thou art my chattel.' Hath Christ suffered so sore for our freedom, and to loose us from all our bonds? There is no man in Christendom so lifted above another. He hath freed all states, whether nobles or commonalty, rich or poor, great or small; he who hath been baptized and believeth is a member of Jesus Christ."[25]

[22]Coulton, pp. 126, 129, 352.
[23]See p. 366.
[24]Bennett, pp. 309, 289.
[25]F. L. Ganshof, Hermann Aubin, N. Neilson, "Medieval Agrarian Society in Its Prime," *Cambridge Economic History*, Vol. I, and Nabholz, ". . . in Transition."

By 1500 the emancipation of serfdom in central and western Europe had gone so far that in most areas the end was in sight, and in only a few was this end to be postponed until the eighteenth and nineteenth centuries. In 1350 more than half of the inhabitants of England were serfs. By 1600 there was no serfdom left in England. In Normandy serfdom had disappeared as early as 1050. In the rest of France emancipation was the work of the twelfth, thirteenth, and early fourteenth centuries. By the end of the Middle Ages only some regions in central France, Burgundy and Franche-Comté, still had a servile peasantry that had to wait until the French Revolution to be freed. The free peasant was characteristic of such mountainous regions as Switzerland and Dauphiné in the thirteenth century. Indeed, the Swiss nation may be said to be the result of a peasant revolt against the German Hapsburgs. In Germany the advances made from the eleventh to the thirteenth century were cut short, and by the beginning of the sixteenth century Germany was smoldering with peasant discontent. Even in the colonial territory beyond the Elbe the early freedom of the pioneer farmer had in some areas been seriously restricted or altogether lost.

Because the peasant became a free renter, and in a few instances a small landowner, it must not be assumed that immediately the European countryside became a paradise. The free peasant was still subjected to the limitations of the village customs in cultivating the soil. Because he had commuted week work and boon work to money payments and escaped from servile dues such as merchet and heriot did not mean that he had gotten rid of all customary payments on the manor. He might still have to use the lord's bakery, winepress, or mill. He might still have to suffer the lord's hunting rights to damage his crops. We should not, however, minimize what had been accomplished. The fact that slavery and serfdom (for the most part) had disappeared in central and western Europe by 1500 is one of western man's most notable achievements. Its remnants and reappearances in Europe and, it is to be hoped, elsewhere on the globe were doomed.

TOWNS AND SOCIAL FREEDOM

The town not only furnished an asylum to the peasant who would be free but was itself a great liberating force. Its social impact was to fundamentally change the character of the third estate. In the early Middle Ages the third estate was composed of peasants. From the eleventh century on two new social groups came gradually to be added to it: (1) the burghers, or bourgeoisie, or middle class, composed of the medieval merchants, manufacturers, and bankers; and (2) a working class consisting of skilled artisans organized in guilds and of unskilled and unorganized workers, the latter a kind of medieval proletariat. Before the end of the medieval period, the middle class itself was further articulated into an upper and lower middle class and a professional, urban group of doctors, lawyers, teachers, and clergymen. As these two new elements in the third estate became established the history of western Europe and thus of the western tradition increasingly centered about their activities and ambitions. It is a history that still continues in the form of the workingman's attempts to win for himself a secure place in western society. When joined with the history of the emancipation of the tiller of the soil it is the liberation of the third estate, of the middle and working classes, that makes the history of the western tradition so much the history of an ever-wider social freedom, and thus of democracy.

COMMERCE WITH THE EAST

The reappearance of town life in western Europe after its decline and disappearance in the later centuries of the Roman Empire came with the establishment of more settled conditions by the medieval aristocracy, who finally put an end to the barbarian invasions of the ninth and tenth centuries. The ensuing increase in population with its pressure for an expansion of the area of arable land has just been considered. This was accompanied by the re-establishment of commerce between the Christian West and the Byzantine and Mohammedan East, and between the Christian West and a Christian-pagan Baltic area. The economic basis for this commerce was a growing western industry productive enough to export to both these regions. The impoverishment of the western Roman Empire had dried up the earlier sources of trade with the eastern Mediterranean, and what trade and industry remained became primarily a local matter confined to the *villa* or large estate. The expansion of the Arabs into Syria, Palestine, and Egypt and thence along the north shores of Africa into Spain and Gaul was cut off by Charles Martel at Tours (732). Together with the ninth-century expansion of the Moslems into Sicily, Sardinia, and Corsica, it made of the Mediterranean a Mohammedan lake from which Christian trade was excluded. The main exception to this Moslem control was the route from Constantinople to Venice at the head of the Adriatic, the control of which by the Venetian merchants gave such an early importance to their city. Until the rest of the Mediterranean came into Christian hands, and until the West itself was able to produce an exportable surplus to pay for eastern goods, western Europe remained a primitive, agricultural society. Charlemagne carried the offensive of western Christendom against Islam into the Spanish March, and by the end of the eleventh century the Christian states of Leon, Castile, and Aragon had advanced much beyond this point. At the same time, Genoa and Pisa drove the Moslems from Sardinia and Corsica and assisted the Normans in driving them from Sicily. Indeed, these two cities carried the Christian offensive to Tunis with the capture of Mahdia. By the end of the eleventh century the western Mediterranean was once again after a long interval securely in western hands.

The Crusades to the Near East[26] put the Genoese and Pisan merchants in the towns of Syria and Palestine. The Crusade to Constantinople in 1204 made Venice the mistress of that city and opened up the Black Sea area, and thus via caravan the Far East, to western business. The early Swedish-Russian Duchy of Kiev had previously established trading connections with Constantinople and had formed a route—the so-called Varangian route—connecting northern and western Europe with Byzantium via Russia and the Baltic. However, it was German merchants of the cities founded in the colonial territory beyond the Elbe (Lübeck) who really exploited the trading possibilities with northern and northeastern Europe. Organized into a league, the Hanseatic League, they were aided by the German crusading orders, the Livonian Brothers of the Sword and the Teutonic Knights, that were waging battle against pagan Prussians, Balts, and Finnish peoples.[27] Eastern luxuries and spices poured into southern Europe through the Italian towns, and the furs, forest products, and ultimately grain that came from the Baltic area, through the Flemish towns (Bruges). The southern products moving northward and the northern products moving southward met in the region of Champagne, where they were exchanged at the famous Champagne fairs. Together with them, products of the new western industry were exchanged, especially textiles manufactured in the Italian (Florence) and Flemish (Ghent) towns, and the wines of France and the Rhine. Not only goods from far-off lands and merchants and manufacturers of western Europe forgathered at the markets and fairs that began to multiply in the West. There came with them the money changer and the money lender, the new western bankers, in short, again primarily from the Italian towns (Genoa, Florence). From the eleventh century on, an isolated, agricultural western Europe began to establish commercial contacts with the rest of the world, as it has continued to do to this day.

THE FORMATION OF TOWNS

The effect of the economic revival was to transform into towns those administrative seats of bishops and monasteries that were suitably located to carry on the new trade and commerce. Since the new merchants and artisans needed protection, they often settled at the foot of, or outside the walls of, a suitably located castle (*urbs, burg, bourg*). They settled, that is, beneath the castle (*sub urbe*) or outside the bourg (*foris burgum* = *faubourg*), and constituted a new city (Neuburg, Neustadt), to be carefully differentiated from the old feudal burg or center (Altburg, Altstadt). The new inhabitants of such an enlarged burg were the burghers (*burgenses*). The burg might be located at suitable crossroads (Strassburg), or a town might grow up at a well-placed ford of a stream (Frankfurt,

[26]See Chap. xi.
[27]See pp. 510 ff.

Oxford) or bridge (Bruges, Cambridge). The growth of many towns can be easily traced: first the appearance of the suburbs near the old burg or episcopal center. Then the new community expands to enclose the older feudal center, necessitating a new walling-in of the whole. Occasionally a new suburb appeared outside the second wall, and the earlier process repeated itself. Not only were old feudal centers transformed into towns but enterprising lords, bishops, or abbots, eager to profit from the increased value of possible urban property, or from the fees of markets and fairs, often established new towns (*villes neuves*). When suitably located (Freiburg, Lübeck), these took their places with the older centers. They are to be found most frequently in new, colonial territory (Stettin, Danzig, Riga). Thus an actual process of urbanization that has continued to date began in rural western Europe. It would be unwise to think that it had gone very far by the end of the Middle Ages. Most of the towns were small and quasi-agricultural. At the same time, it would be absurd to underestimate the transforming power of the new capitalism.

URBAN REVOLUTIONS

The older, feudal-agricultural burg did not easily amalgamate with the new, urban-commercial suburb or faubourg. The former could not easily imagine the latter independent of the manorial regime, and therefore not liable to the services and dues of the peasant to the lord of the burg or town. The latter having grown up in a nonfeudal, essentially nonagricultural atmosphere, could not tolerate being subjected to the older regime, which in fact destroyed its whole manner of life. The inhabitants of the new towns, therefore, wished to be considered free, not servile, and to govern themselves; wished, that is, to hold their own courts, collect their own taxes, regulate their own economic affairs, and provide for their own protection. They wished to be independent or autonomous. There ensued, accordingly, a struggle between the old and new societies over this question. To carry it on, the townsmen found it necessary to organize themselves: into guilds at times, or into what were called *communes*, confederations of townsmen sworn to fight for and maintain the independence or autonomy of the urban community. Beginning, then, in the eleventh century, continuing at a peak in the twelfth, and quieting down in the thirteenth, occurred a series of revolts of the new townsmen, organized in their communes. In some instances, the employment of force was not necessary to secure charters of liberty from the lords. Some members of the aristocracy were farsighted enough to see the importance and inevitability of this movement and to support it. Others were quite willing to sell charters at a good price. As King Henry II said about the Londoners: "If they are willing to give those 3,000 marks they shall have their charter, but if not they shall not have their charter." As often as not the new burghers had to fight for their freedom from the feudal system in ugly, urban revolutions. In the eleventh century, revolting communes struggled against their episcopal overlords in the northern Italian and Rhine towns (especially Cologne), and in the twelfth century the struggle was continued elsewhere in the West, against secular and royal as well as ecclesiastical lords. The outcome was not always victory for the townsmen. Their charters granted varying degrees of independence or autonomy. When once received, independence or autonomy was not necessarily secure. It had to be maintained against a hostile feudality. Often enough, towns were unable to maintain their free or autonomous communities. To preserve hard-won freedom they frequently organized federations or leagues of communes, with all the apparatus of a nascent federal government (for example, the Lombard League).[28]

GUIBERT DE NOGENT AND LAON

How bitter these struggles could be may be illustrated from one that took place in the northern French town of Laon, as it is recorded for us by a capable French monk, Guibert de Nogent. Here the first revolt, in 1111, was against Bishop Renulf, a hard fighter and a voracious hunter who was followed about by his hangman, a Negro slave who did not hesitate to use churches for assassinations. The commune of Laon, formed during the absence of the bishop, was recognized in 1111 and destroyed the next year with the help of the French king, Louis VI. When Louis left the city, the townsmen rose in fury against the bishop and the church. A second intervention of the crown terminated this revived commune in 1114. Fourteen years later (1128) it was restored again with limited jurisdiction.

Guibert explains that "Commune is a new and a bad name of an arrangement for all the poorest classes to pay their usual due of servitude to their lords once only in the year, and to make good any breach of the laws they have committed by the payment fixed by law, and to be entirely free from all other exactions usually imposed on serfs. The people," he says, "seizing on this opportunity for freeing themselves gathered huge sums of money to fill the gaping mouths of so many greedy men. And they, pleased with the shower poured upon them, took oaths binding themselves in the matter. A pledge of mutual aid had been thus exchanged by the clergy and nobles with the people, when the Bishop returned with much wealth from England and being moved to anger against those responsible for this innovation, for a long time kept away from the city."

When the bishop, with the aid of the king, succeeded in having the commune annulled, the citizens were "no longer moved by mere anger, but goaded into a murderous lust for the death of the Bishop and his accomplices and bound themselves by oath to effect their purpose. Now they say that four hundred took the oath."

[28]See pp. 543 f.

On the day following the oath-taking, Easter Sunday, the "Bishop summoned a great number of country men from the episcopal manors and manned the towers of the church and gave orders that his palace should be guarded, although he was almost as much hated by them, as they knew that piles of money, which he had promised the king, must be drained from their own purses." When Guibert protested to the bishop he got as an answer, "What do ye think they can do by their riots? If John, my moor, were to take by the nose the most powerful man amongst them, he would not dare so much as to grunt. For just now I have compelled them to renounce what they call their Commune for so long as I live." On the fifth day in Easter week, after midday, "men shouting 'Commune!' . . . now entered the Bishop's court with swords, battle-axes, bows and hatchets . . . clubs and spears, a very great company." With "the outrageous mob . . . howling before . . . his palace," the bishop "put on the clothes of one of his servants and flying to the vaults of the Church hid himself in a cask, shut up in which with the head fastened on by a faithful follower, he thought himself safely hidden." Now the bishop was discovered by a "bondman of the Church of the Blessed Vincent" whom he (the bishop) "was wont in mockery to call Isengrin . . . because of his wolfish look, for so some people call wolves." When he had broken in the top of the cask where the bishop was hiding, "the wretch . . . says to the Bishop, 'Is this my Lord Isengrin stored away?' Renulf, therefore, sinner though he was, yet the Lord's anointed, was dragged forth from the cask by the hair, beaten with many blows and brought out into the open air in the narrow lane of the clergy's cloister before the house of the Chaplain Godfrey. And as he piteously implored them, ready to take oath that he would henceforth cease to be their Bishop, that he would give them unlimited riches, that he would leave the country, and as they with hardened hearts jeered at him, one named Bernard . . . lifting his battle-ax brutally dashed out the brains of that sacred, though sinner's head, and he slipping between the hands of those who held him, was dead before he reached the ground stricken by another thwart blow under the eye-sockets and across the middle of the nose. There brought to his end, his legs were cut off and many another wound inflicted. But Thibaut seeing the ring on the finger of the erstwhile prelate and not being able to draw it off, cut off the dead man's finger and took it. And so stripped to his skin he was thrown into a corner in front of his chaplain's house. My God, who shall recount the mocking words that were thrown at him by passersby, as he lay there, and with what clods and stones and dirt his corpse was covered?" The bishop's palace and church were set on fire, and the fire spread to other parts of town. The wife of a noble in the city was seized by "some of the women of the town . . . beaten with their fists and stripped of the costly clothes she was wearing."

The bishop was buried the following day. "One cannot describe the threats and abuse that were showered upon those who cared for his burial or with how many curses the dead man was pelted. Being carried to the church, he had at his funeral none at all of the offices that are paid to any Christian, much less a bishop. The earth being only half scraped out to receive him, the body was so tightly packed in the tiny coffin that the breast and belly were crushed even to bursting."

When Raoul, the archbishop of Rheims, came subsequently to the church of Saint Vincent, where the last rites for the bishop had been said, he "celebrated a solemn mass there for the first time on behalf of the Bishop"; and later he "preached a sermon on that accursed Commune, by which contrary to justice and right, serfs had violently withdrawn themselves from the claims of their lords. 'Servants,' saith the Apostle, 'be subject to your masters with all fear,' and let not servants impute hardness and greed to their masters; let them still obey, 'Not only the good and gentle, but also the forward. In the original canons they are distinctly banned who teach serfs to disobey their masters for religion's sake or to fly anywhere, much less to resist. A further proof of this is the fact that no one is admitted among clerks or into holy orders or to be a monk, unless he is free of servitude; moreover, when so admitted, he may by no means be kept against the demands of his master.' Many times he [the archbishop] maintained this principle in the King's court and at other times in various assemblies."[29]

DEMOCRATIC STRUGGLE IN THE TOWNS

Where, in the thirteenth century, kings were powerful and monarchical governments strong the communal movement did not produce completely independent towns (England and France). Where, on the contrary, as in the German empire (Flanders, Germany, Italy), the central government was weak, the independent town appeared. In any case, whether wholly independent or only autonomous, an institution comparable to the classical city-state now began to exercise a profound influence upon the general course of western history. That influence had to do in part with the wisdom acquired by townsmen in solving a great many entirely new problems. The town brought together large numbers of people within a small walled area. How were these people to be governed? How indeed were they to be fed? How were the trade and industry within the town walls to be regulated? And how, above all, was the town to be protected? The feeding of the town required, so it thought, control of the neighboring countryside, and thus territorial expansion, leading to municipal wars. The regulation of trade and industry was carried on through the guilds. The organization of the leading merchants, the merchants' guild, became in many towns synonymous with the government of the town. The regulation of industry was first done through the craft guilds. Both merchant and craft guilds sought to preserve the town market as a local, guild

[29]*The Autobiography of Guibert, Abbot of Nogent-sous Coucy*, trans. C. C. Swinton Bland, pp. 153–173.

monopoly. By the fourteenth century, the trade guilds were controlled by the wealthy masters, who excluded or restrained the eventual entrance of journeymen and apprentices. The big merchants, those who traded with distant lands far beyond the locality, had no need for the local merchant guild and escaped its control. Town governments came to be the monopolies of the rich merchants or manufacturers, who governed largely in their own interests. The fourteenth and fifteenth centuries accordingly witnessed bloody struggles within the city walls between the rich burghers and the poor, often unorganized (that is, outside a craft guild) workers for the control of municipal governments. For the first time in the history of the West, what has been called the proletariat was attempting to secure its place in the government and society of the town. These struggles took place first in the heavily industrialized towns (Ghent, Florence), but it is surprising how widespread they came to be. In some towns they brought a liberalization of town government for a time, but by and large they were not successful. Town governments remained a monopoly of the wealthy guilds. Yet here, in the attempts of these early medieval workingmen to win a share in their municipal governments, may be seen the earliest western political struggles of a democratic nature. Those policies first worked out by municipal governments to make the town a protected market for the exploitation of local monopoly, such as protective tariffs, were later taken over by monarchs who wished to do the same thing for kingdoms.

RESULTS OF THE URBAN REVOLUTION

When once western man recreated the town for himself, he opened up marvelous opportunities for the expansion of his ingenuity and the expression of his genius. The new fields of trade, commerce, and industry took him out of the locality into spheres of activity that one day were to penetrate to the very ends of the earth. They made possible the creation of a surplus wealth that could be used in, among other things, the cultivation of refinement, to enhance the dignity and beauty of human life on earth. The sharpening of the intelligence through contact with the wider world, and the necessity of solving new problems at home made possible the development of a new, cosmopolitan spirit. Indeed, with the new towns, the tempo of life in the West became accelerated, and the speed of change increased. In the midst of this more rapid change, the town acted as a modifier of medieval manorial and feudal institutions and ultimately of the ascetic Christian point of view. It has been mentioned that the town helped to break up the older static class structure by welcoming the serf into its midst and thus opening up to him, as a free man, the various opportunities of this new urban world. It widened the concept of a third estate by recreating a middle class of international traders, industrialists, and bankers on the one hand, and local business and professional men on the other. It enlarged this third estate further by creating an urban working class, composed of the skilled artisans in the crafts and of the unskilled, unorganized proletariat, into which the serf had first to enter. Nor did the new towns, with their bourgeoisie, leave the old, feudal aristocracy unaffected. The town was responsible for a serious modification of the old, rural economy based largely upon barter. For the town forced the manor into the competitive world of business, where money was the medium of exchange. Manorialism provided the peasantry with not much more than a meager living, and the aristocracy with the means for a stable and substantial way of life. More than this it did not aim to do, and with its system of production could not do. The urban world introduced a predominantly money economy, and although through its guilds it aimed, while supplying local employment, to divide somewhat equally the profits of exploiting the local market, it never succeeded in doing so. The international trader, manufacturer, and banker escaped its control and turned the economy in a capitalistic direction dominated by the spirit of making money. To carry on this type of economy new institutions had to be formed: the open fair, the bank, the trading company, the early factory, the improved mine, new systems of coinage, improved means of transportation and communication on sea and land, and indeed a more literate populace. The town required the food surplus from the neighboring countryside and was willing to pay for it. The lord and peasant could make money. An increased standard of living was possible. The aristocracy, in turn, in order to have the new clothes, foods, spices, and luxuries provided by the towns had to pay good money for them. Not only to keep one's serfs, but to keep one's head above water, the manorial system had to be adjusted to fit this money economy governed by a flexible price system. The enterprising lord could adapt himself in several ways. He could commute labor services and dues-in-kind to money. In shifting the tenures held by peasants from an hereditary basis of labor services and dues to a fixed rental basis, he could set them up on a short-term rather than long-term lease, adjusting the rents, with each renewal, to the level of cost. He could, and often did, actually withdraw from demesne farming on the manor, and lease the demesne land out on short terms. He thus became a *rentier*. Or he could transform the nature of cultivation on the manor by adapting it to the more intensive cultivation needed to supply garden crops, or, where the nature of the land made it possible, transform the manor into a sheep ranch to supply raw wool to the new manufacturers of woolen textiles. This meant getting rid of peasant cultivation of the soil and transforming peasant holdings into pasture. Those noble families who could not adjust in some such way as these were gradually ruined and found it helpful to marry into the wealthiest bourgeois families or to sell their lands to them. In Italy, nobles became town dwellers and participated directly in the new world of business. The towers of their urban fortresses or palaces became strongholds for the continuance of earlier feudal strifes as commercial family feuds.

Towns were a political challenge to the aristocracy. In fact, they may be said to have undermined feudalism as a system of government. This they did, first of all, by limiting the jurisdiction of the feudal suzerain over themselves. They fought free, or partially free, of the feudal system. To the same end, they supported the efforts of monarchs to weaken and destroy the feudal system. The new bourgeoisie supported monarchy because the kings could establish law and order over a larger territorial unit than the fief, namely, the kingdom, and so increase the opportunities for business. Kings could likewise support the overseas interests of international bankers and businessmen. The petty circumscriptions of economic activity, such as tolls, by provincially minded aristocrats were annoying to the new fortune hunters. It was from kings, however dependent upon the feudal system, that the new charters of municipal liberty often came. What the new towns had to offer that the kings did not have was that extraordinary solvent of so many troubles, currency. It took money to get charters, and it took money in the form of taxes to retain the privileges that the charters enumerated. Nobles never paid taxes. They only rendered services. In fact, we may say that kings and nobles began to compete for bourgeois money. The most effective thing a king could do with bourgeois money was to help pay a mercenary army. Mercenary armies made it less necessary to depend upon the troops that feudal vassals were obliged to supply. Mercenary troops supplemented by bourgeois militia often made possible the winning of crucial battles over feudal opponents. When, with the aid of taxes, bourgeois and otherwise, the kings could support a standing army and thus do without the feudal levies, they could begin to call their power absolute. Money from taxes could be used to transform the nature of the royal administration. As long as the economy was rural and based on barter, monarchs could get work done for them only by granting fiefs of land or other sources of income. Such fiefs were considered hereditary by the feudal mind, and the king thus found his activity limited by having the important offices of the crown continuously in the hands of the same noble family. If, however, the money resources of the royal treasury were sufficient to pay salaries instead of granting out fiefs, kings, quite free from the dictation of feudal interests, could hire and fire a royal administration as they saw fit. The new, educated bourgeoisie could supply the crown with the personnel of this administration. The early administration of kings was composed of churchmen and nobles, literate, to be sure, but under the circumstances untrained except by experience. From the ranks of the bourgeoisie could be drawn literate and trained administrators, trained not only in the large world of economic affairs, but also, when these towns came to have universities, in the law, and especially in that Roman law that when properly interpreted said perfectly splendid things about the power of monarchs. If the kings, as heads of the feudal system, were obliged to summon the lay and ecclesiastical aristocracy to court for counsel, they soon appreciated the wisdom of summoning as well these bourgeois members of the third estate who, in fact, became synonymous with the third estate. In due time, the bourgeoisie learned not only how to help the king to destroy feudalism but also how to help the king limit his own absolute power. By the time kings and bourgeoisie got through with the aristocracy—and the course of this struggle, varying from kingdom to kingdom, extended far into the modern period—the military power of the nobility was gone (they became the officers of the new standing armies), and their local political power and monopoly over the central administration were destroyed. As a privileged class they became, especially in France, the elegant and decorative social setting in which the absolute monarch could bask.

CULTURAL RESULTS

When once inaugurated, the urban revolution made possible those cultural changes, innovations, and influences that were to be the work of Rome, Paris, London, New York, and the lesser urban luminaries. With its new attractions and opportunities the town made rural life seem dull. From the countryside it enticed the most creative and enterprising spirits, beginning a movement from country to city that still continues. The new and ever-increasing surplus wealth produced by the town could be used to develop a new urban architecture, both secular and ecclesiastical, and to endow the painter, sculptor, and craftsman. A new bourgeois audience appeared to which the literary artist might appeal. To solve the new problems of urban life, special training was needed. The system of craft guilds provided for the necessary industrial education and built up traditions for all the major and minor arts. The new universities, an urban product, trained men in the law and in medicine. To the ranks of the intellectual élite, once monopolized by the clergy, were now added not only these new professional groups but the teacher as well. Training in the liberal arts added laymen to the body of educated men. The new agglomeration of people crowded within town walls developed anew the qualities of responsible citizenship and civic pride, resulting in a good deal of town rivalry.

TOWNS AND CHRISTIAN ASCETICISM

There remains the question of the relationship of the political, economic, and social changes covered by this chapter to the Christian ascetic tradition of the West and to the whole further development of the western tradition. Without doubt, these changes constituted the first serious challenge to (1) the social theory of the Church; (2) its ethical theory; (3) its fundamental teaching concerning the meaning of life; and (4) its notions concerning human dignity. We have said that Christian social theory was a modification of Plato's notions in the *Republic*. Society was an organic unity devised by God. Each man and woman was born into his proper station and should be content to remain in it in order that due authority might be properly exercised, and the work of the world be done with the least friction. It is quite clear from this chapter that neither the medieval serf, the medieval workingman, nor the medieval bourgeois took this conservative theory seriously. They not only regarded the contemporary organization of society as highly unsatisfactory, but also, ignoring what may have been its divine foundation, they undertook to change it— by force if necessary, and change it they did. Those groups left in its defense were the feudal aristocracy and the upper clergy. Elements in the lower or parish clergy showed themselves sympathetic with the efforts of the third estate to better itself. If only in a vague way there were many who felt the incompatibility between rigid social inequality and Christian teachings about spiritual equality and human brotherhood.

CHRISTIAN ATTEMPTS TO RESTRAIN THE TOWNS

Quite obviously, the Church felt that the fundamental trends introduced by the revival of trade, commerce, and industry were hostile to basic Christian teachings. For a man to wish to break loose from the pre-ordained, divine social scheme was to exhibit unholy ambition. For him to take satisfaction in the improvement of the conditions of his life was to display that greatest of all sins, that cause for man's primal fall, pride; and for him to work to accumulate a goodly share of this world's goods was avarice or covetousness. Indeed, the Church, having grown up in a class-ridden and poverty-stricken society that seemed to verify its pessimism, was uncomfortable in the face of social amelioration and the new capitalistic spirit. It sought to call a halt to the new social and economic tendencies by reminding Christians once again, as it had at an earlier time, of the virtues of poverty. It tried to teach those who were being carried headlong by the new tendencies that there was such a thing as a fair price, more than which it was a sin to collect. And this fair price was to allow a profit, not such as the traffic would bear, but only enough to keep a man and his family in the station of life to which they were accustomed. It also revived its earlier teachings about usury. It was nothing less than sinful to take interest, and without interest, that is, credit, the new society could not do. The new economic world would not be restrained in this way; indeed, it resented the attempt to restrain it. Numerous towns had secured their charters only as a result of organized rebellion against the ecclesiastical lords, and did not like the attempt of the Church to oppose the new course of events. To many, this kind of clerical opposition did not ring true from a church whose upper clergy were rich, landed magnates and temporal lords, and whose head was the ruler of a state; a church that, in spite of itself, could not keep its hands off the new money. In the end, the theologians and canon lawyers abandoned the Church's rigid doctrine about usury and came to regard it as quite legitimate when taken to cover economic risks, and not to exploit.

In bourgeois and urban circles, accordingly—and this was especially true of Italy—the ascetic point of view began to lose some of its appeal. Taking its place was a frankly secular outlook that did not think quite so badly of this world that it was transforming nor so deprecatingly of the human beings who were doing the transforming. This world, as a result of human effort, was becoming a better place in which to live. It was not so necessary to postpone until eternity one's hopes for the realization of some kind of happiness. That the peasant, the human beast of manorial capital equipment, should acquire freedom by his own efforts gave real meaning to the then limited concept of human dignity. Here were individuals whose capacities for improvement were actually opened up by themselves. The new urban classes were composed of men who, sprung up suddenly from no one knew quite where, without benefit of clergy or lay aristocracy successfully carved out a place for themselves in medieval society. Winning their own freedom gave them a feeling of their own inherent dignity and worth. Once more there were promise and hope in the world. This change in attitude, inconspicuous to begin with, has gained momentum with the succeeding centuries. It may be said to have constituted a return to the point of view that we have described as characteristic of antiquity, namely, the humanistic. Man was to seek his destiny in a rational adaptation to this world that utilized all his specifically human traits, but subordinated one to the other in accordance with deliberately chosen, good ends that could be realized here and now. Since this view already had been formulated by the writers of Greece and Rome it is not surprising that in the new scholarly circles classical literature and philosophy should have been taken up with enthusiasm.

CONTINUOUS INFLUENCE OF THE MEDIEVAL EXAMPLE

The medieval emphasis upon the humanistic phase of its inherited tradition was of great importance to the future development of the West. This medieval experience also had implications that were more than western. Medieval society began with a class structure inherited from the late Roman world. The barbarian invasions intensified it and gave it a pronounced military character. The feudalism that took root in the ninth and tenth centuries confirmed this earlier development and grafted upon Europe an aristocracy whose services had been and were still necessary to govern and protect it. With the rise of towns, what we may call capitalism, the middle class, the working class, skilled and unskilled, organized and unorganized, were thrown together in urban centers and these centers multiplied. The modification of the feudal system by this modern condition has been a continuous process to date. The outstanding initial social result was to free the serf and create the free middle and working classes. From the point of view of the castelike social structure of late antiquity this was social emancipation and social freedom, or, to use other words, an element of mobility was introduced into the class structure. The western tradition came to be associated in principle, and to a certain extent in practice, with what is called an "open" or a mobile society, suggestive of the Stoic golden age and the Christian earthly paradise. The examples of this early medieval social revolt were not forgotten. The fortunes of peasant and working class might not subsequently be as radiant as early freedom seemed to promise. New forms of slavery and serfdom might appear. What had been done once, however, could be done again. There was no need to resign oneself to the course of events. At least to a degree, man's fate could be influenced by his own choice. Protest, reform, revolution, improvement came to be a part of western history.

FEUDALISM AND THE WORLD

The political, social, and economic transformation of feudalism by what we have called the urban revolt has been a long, long process. It has been slowed up because rural feudalism was supplanted by a kind of industrial feudalism. Even in its agricultural form feudalism today is by no means gone. The existence of the large estate still owned by a nobility in the British Isles and almost everywhere in western Europe except France still challenges the ingenuity of the social reformer. If communism has taken hold in eastern Europe and Russia, this is in part because feudalism persisted in these areas for so long. Nor is feudalism simply a western European phenomenon. It emerges at all times and places where a strong government is lacking. As the local government of the wealthy, it is a global phenomenon, and the conditions it has created have today made the countries it dominates subject to the lure of a communism that promises, as one of its first reforms, to destroy the feudal aristocracy and divide up its large estates among the peasantry. The western world has for centuries been engaged in reforming the abuses of its own feudal system, both agricultural and industrial. It has still much to do in this regard. But its own experience now qualifies it to tackle feudalism elsewhere on the globe, and to help other societies to do what it has done for itself. Under these circumstances, there can be hardly anything more important to study today than the West's experience with feudalism.

chapter eleven

EAST AND WEST IN THE MIDDLE AGES

$\mathcal{P}$LAN OF THE CHAPTER.   The previous chapter has suggested that those feudal, manorial, and urban developments that broke up the rigid class structure of early medieval Europe were partly the outcome of economic expansion into the eastern Mediterranean and European areas. It must be the purpose of this chapter (1) to investigate further the influence of the medieval East upon the West, and (2) to consider the extent to which the contemporary East-and-West conflict has its roots in a comparable medieval conflict. By the medieval East is meant the area covered by (1) the Byzantine Empire and (2) eastern Europe. The Byzantine Empire was the temporal prolongation of the Graeco-oriental half of a decadent Roman Empire rejuvenated by Christianity. It was the Roman Empire after 476, with Constantinople, the new Rome, as its capital. Its fate was to be taken over by two groups of nomadic peoples: the Arabs and the Turks. In 1453, when Constantinople was captured by the Ottoman Turks, it ceased to exist, relinquishing the tradition of its leadership to the new, or "third," Rome of eastern Europe, Muscovite Russia. Eastern Europe includes the area not settled by the Germans, but for the most part inhabited by those peoples formed from the migration of the Slavs.

Byzantium and the West

BYZANTIUM IN THE WEST

The influence of the Byzantine East upon the medieval West was determined in part by the fact that for a considerable time some of this West belonged to the Byzantine Empire. The extension of the Byzantine state westward, it will be remembered,[1] came under the emperor Justinian, who had dreams of restoring the Roman Empire to the days of its former greatness under the Pax Romana. He formed a Byzantine exarchate of Africa out of Vandal North Africa and an exarchate of Ravenna out of Ostrogothic Italy and Sicily. North Africa was subsequently lost to the expanding Arabs,[2] while northern and a part of central Italy went to the expanding Lombards.[3] What was left of its western holdings, southern Italy and Sicily, remained Byzantine until the eleventh century, when the Normans, expanding from their duchy in France, took over this territory. Thus southern Italy and Sicily, the scene of earlier Greek colonization, for five centuries formed a part of the medieval Greek empire, and the rest of Italy did so for only lesser periods. In this way Greek Christianity, the Basilian monastery, and Greek artistic and literary culture spread westward.

BYZANTINE AND ROMANESQUE STYLE

Much of the splendor of early Byzantine art can be seen in the churches of Rome and Ravenna, and Saint Mark's at Venice is essentially a Byzantine church. By the time of Justinian, a distinctive Christian art had formed in the East, whose noblest monument is the church of Hagia Sophia (Holy Wisdom) in Constantinople. Its crowning glory is its dome, suspended almost in air over its central area. It is distinguished also for a rich and luxurious interior, made possible by colored marbles and brilliant mosaics of saints clad in stiff brocades and set in golden backgrounds. This oriental opulence entered into such an early Italian church as San Vitale at Ravenna. When Charlemagne wished to build an impressive palace church at Aachen he could think of nothing else but to imitate San Vitale and even pilfer some of its materials. The Byzantine became a part of the early western Romanesque style.

BYZANTINE AND RENAISSANCE PAINTING

The development of a Byzantine style was determined in part by the opposition to the representation of the human form in the round that came from the Iconoclastic struggle.[4] The result was that only the flat mosaic or painting could be used to represent the sacred images, or icons, of the saints. In any case, the icon and fresco painting of the Byzantine artist so influenced the early painting of Italy (for example, the Sienese school) that before Italian artists of the Renaissance could create a style of their own the authority of the Byzantine style had to be destroyed.

[1]See p. 371.
[2]See pp. 482 f.
[3]See p. 284.
[4]See pp. 469 f.

In the Byzantine monastery likewise were preserved the works of pagan Greek literature and philosophy. There seems, in fact, to have been less opposition in the East to the study of classical literature than in the West. When after a long interval the West was ready to resume the direct study of Greek literature and philosophy, the original impulse came from Greeks of southern Italy and Sicily who were educated in the Byzantine tradition. Among the early promoters of Greek studies in Renaissance Italy were Byzantine Greeks; and it was to the Byzantine East that the western scholar went to find original manuscripts in great abundance. To the efforts of Byzantine monks and scholars must, in part, be attributed the revival of the direct study of Greek humanism in the West. This is all the more important because, at the moment when the West began to restudy Greek, Byzantium itself had become a part of the empire of the Ottoman Turks. It is not to be assumed that the non-Greek, that is, the Slavic and Mongolian, inhabitants of eastern Europe were at this time in a position to take up the study of Greek civilization. Certainly the Ottoman Turks, who at that time could have understood little about it, were least of all interested in promoting the study of Greek culture. What is known in western Europe as the Renaissance did not, could not, take place in eastern Europe. This fact is of great importance in explaining the later divergence between West and East. Until a comparatively recent date the tradition of Greek humanism had no influence in eastern or southeastern Europe, not even, ironically enough, in the very land that first created it.

BYZANTIUM AND ROMAN LAW

Justinian made available to the West the fruits of Rome's legal genius through codification and summary in what is known as the Justinian Code. Private and public partial summaries of Roman law had been made before Justinian. The emperor Theodosius II, for example, brought together in 438 all the statute law from Constantine to his own reign. It was Justinian's idea that not only should the actual legislation of the emperors be collected for a longer period than that covered in Theodosius' code, but that also the writings of the juris-consults should be summarized. After his accession to the imperial throne he set up a commission headed by Tribonian to work on the imperial legislation from Hadrian to his own reign. The commission was to remove what was contradictory, repetitious, or obsolete, and to organize the remainder in a form which the teacher, student, and practitioner of law would find useful. The result was what is strictly speaking the Justinian Code (*Codex Justinianus*). Justinian then put his commission to work on the writings of the juris-consults. The result was the Digest, or Pandects (*Digesta, Pandecta*), providing the imperial law with the supplementary commentary of the best Roman legal minds. In order to make the new works even more useful to the law

	The West	Byzantium	Islam and the Slavs
400			
		(Emperors) Theodosius II (r. 408–450) Zeno (r. 474–491) Justinian I (r. 527–565) Heraclius (r. 610–641) Leo III (r. 717–741)	Mohammed (ca. 570–632)
700			
	Battle of Tours (732)		
		Cyril (827–869) Methodius (826–885)	Al-Kwarizmi (d. ca. 850)
	Otto I (r. 936; emperor, 962–973) Bishop Liutprand of Cremona (ca. 922–972)	Emperor Nicephorus Phocas (r. 963–969)	Saint Vladimir (ca. 956–1015) Avicenna (979–1037)
1000			
	Pope Leo IX (r. 1049–1054) Schism between Eastern and Western Churches (1054) Pope Urban II (r. 1088–1099) Council of Clermont (1095) First Crusade (1096–1099) Helmold (fl. 12th c.) Pope Adrian II (r. 1154–1159) Emperor Frederick Barbarossa (r. 1152–1190) Richard the Lion-Hearted (r. 1189–1199) Philip Augustus (r. 1180–1223) Third Crusade (1189–1192) Baldwin of Flanders (r. 1204–1205) Pope Innocent III (r. 1198–1216) Fourth Crusade (1202–1204) Geoffrey of Villehardouin (ca. 1150–1218) Philip of Swabia (r. 1198–1208) Albert of Bremen (d. 1230) Emperor Frederick II (r. 1212–1250) Saint Louis (r. 1226–1270)	Michael Cerularius (r. 1043–1059) Battle of Manzikert (1071) Emperor Alexius Comnenus (r. 1081–1118) Emperor Isaac II (r. 1185–1195; 1203–1204) Emperor Alexius III (r. 1195–1203)	Omar Khayyám (d. ca. 1123) Averroës (1126–1198) Saladin (1138–1193) Jenghiz Khan (ca. 1167–1227) Batu (d. 1255) Alexander Nevsky (ca. 1220–1263) Dmitri Donskoy (1350–1389) Battle of Kulikovo (1380) Prince Jagiello (1350–1434) Queen Jadwiga (1370–1399) Dynastic Union of Poland and Lithuania (1386) Battle of Kossovo (1389) Battle of Tannenberg (1410)
		Fall of Constantinople (1453)	Ivan III (1462–1505)

student Justinian then had both the Code and Digest summarized into a textbook on the Roman law (the *Institutes*). To bring his labors quite up to date he had his own legislation after 534 collected and published in Greek as the Novels (*Novellae Leges*). Together, the Code, Digest, Institutes, and Novels make up what is known as the Body of the Civil Law (*Corpus Iuris Civilis*).

The Corpus was preserved in southern Italy and became the text for the study of law in the medieval universities.[5] In this way Roman law not only influenced the development of the canon law of the Church but actually became the law of continental Europe. When the nations of western Europe, exclusive of England, expanded to cover the whole earth, they took this Roman law with them. Through them a law that had originally expanded from a city-state to a Mediterranean empire became the law of global empires. The universal capacity of the Roman law was further reinforced when, in the seventeenth century, men became concerned with establishing a law to govern relations between nations; in laying the foundations of international law they use and continue to use the concepts of a law of nations (*ius gentium*) and of a natural law (*ius naturale*) which Stoic juris-consults had worked out.

BYZANTIUM A BULWARK FOR THE WEST

It is often said that the Byzantine Empire acted as a bulwark to protect Europe from the invasions of nomadic peoples from Asia, the Arabs, Seljuk and, for a while, Ottoman Turks. The Arabs did fail in their attempts to occupy Byzantine Asia Minor and to take Constantinople, as they did not fail to take Visigothic Spain and advance into Gaul. It is interesting to speculate on what would have happened had the Arabs succeeded in penetrating southeastern as well as southwestern Europe, to ask whether some Slavic Charles Martel would have arisen to throw them back, or whether they would have gone on to join their fellow Arabs in the West. That the West was able subsequently to come to the aid of Byzantium against the Seljuk Turks may have had something to do with the fact—though this seems unlikely—that it was able to develop free of an Arab peril in southeastern Europe; Arabs who could not take Constantinople were not likely to get far in southeastern Europe. Nor is it altogether clear that the Seljuk Turks were any threat to southeastern Europe. In any case, the armies of western crusaders, responding to the call of Constantinople, did keep Seljuks busy in western Asia. The Ottoman Turks crossed over into Europe in about 1354.

HOSTILITY BETWEEN EAST AND WEST

In spite of these influences, the history of the relationship between western Europe and the Byzantine Empire was in fact one of growing

[5]See p. 666.

hostility, culminating in that aggressive attack upon Constantinople in 1204 that is known as the Fourth Crusade. The grounds for hostility are not far to seek and are of both a fundamental and petty character. The Byzantine state could never quite adjust itself to events in western Europe after 476. Its emperors yearned to establish themselves as the universal rulers of a revived empire. Justinian, in fact, had gone a long way toward doing so, but the activity of Germans in the West (Ostrogoths, Lombards) and the subsequent expansion of the Arabs exposed the futility of these yearnings. Even though their state contracted, the Byzantine emperors remained sensitive to all the titles and prerogatives of the name Roman emperor. When the Germans, with the aid of the pope, re-established a western empire in 800 and again, after its decline in the ninth and tenth centuries, in 962,[6] the revival was regarded at Constantinople as the effrontery of barbarians aided by a rebellious pope.

THE BYZANTINE EMPEROR

What developed at Constantinople after its foundation in 330 was a government of theocratic oriental despotism. The ceremonial etiquette of its court life and the elaborate structure of its bureaucracy had no counterpart in the simple, rude German monarchies of the West, whose representatives were always ill at ease and even resentful in the presence of the eastern court. These eastern monarchs, having been spared a German occupation of their territory, considered themselves not only the successors of the autocratic Caesars but also, as we have seen,[7] the heads of the Christian Church of this empire. Unlike the situation in the West, with its emperor and pope, they were both emperor and pope (caesaropapists), the patriarch of Constantinople being a mere religious official of the state.

THEOLOGICAL DIFFICULTIES BETWEEN EAST AND WEST

The contrasting political and ecclesiastical organization of the East helped to bring about a formal separation of eastern from western Christianity in the Greek Orthodox and Roman Catholic churches. The break (1054), which has never been healed, was long in preparation. Part of the difficulty lay in the dispute over the headship of the Church universal. We have seen that the Roman popes early in their history[8] made claim to this headship on the basis of the Petrine Theory. At no time was the claim recognized by the patriarch of Constantinople, nor could it be recognized by the Byzantine emperor, the secular head of the imperial Church. A further difficulty between the eastern and western churches arose from the willingness of the emperors as heads of the Church to pronounce upon theological questions when they felt it necessary. It will be remembered that two Christian groups, the Nestorians and the Monophy-

[6]See p. 528.
[7]See pp. 340 f.
[8]See pp. 338 f.

sites, had refused in the fourth and fifth centuries to accept the pronounce-
ments of the church councils. Since these divergent groups came to
represent the resistence of native elements in Syria, Palestine, and Egypt
to political domination from Constantinople, it was imperative, if possible,
to remove the sources of religious discontent. The emperors tried to do so
by issuing compromise dogmas of their own and expected the popes to
go along. As early as 492 the emperor Zeno, in an attempt to mediate between the view of Chalcedon that Christ had two natures and the view of
the Monophysites that he had only one, announced that Christ was "of
the same nature with the Father in the Godhead and also of the same nature with us in the manhood," and he condemned "all who have held, or
hold now or at any time, whether in Chalcedon or in any other synod
whatsoever, any different belief." In 638 the emperor Heraclius tried to
conciliate the Monophysites by proclaiming that if indeed Christ had two
natures, he had only one will. We can therefore well sympathize with
Constans II when, ten years later, he forbade "all the Orthodox subjects
. . . to contend and to quarrel with one another over one will or one
operation [energy] or two operations [energies] and two wills." In 680
at the Sixth Ecumenical Council in Constantinople Heraclius's imperial
dogma of only one will was condemned. Christ, according to this council,
had not only two natures but "two natural wills and operations [energies]
going together harmoniously for the salvation of the human race."[9] The
inability of the emperors to reconcile with their dogmas the Monophysites
in Syria, Palestine, and Egypt helped to pave the way for the Arab conquest of these areas. When the Sixth Ecumenical Council repudiated
Heraclius, the Monophysite churches tolerated in the new Arab state were
permanently alienated. Together with the Nestorians in the Near East
they remain to this day independent Christian churches. Imperial efforts
helped to alienate the Roman Latin as well as the oriental churches. The
popes did not hesitate to excommunicate Zeno and to pronounce the work
of Heraclius and Constans II heretical. It must be remembered that between Justinian's conquest and the Donation of Pepin Rome and its
environs were part of the Byzantine Empire, and that its bishop, the pope,
was regarded as a dependent of the emperor. For the popes to question
imperial infallibility was intolerably impudent.

ICONOCLASM

Relations between the Greek and Latin churches were further complicated by the Iconoclastic struggle in the Byzantine church. This struggle goes back to the compromise which Christianity made with paganism
when it introduced the cult of the Virgin and the saints and tolerated the
veneration of their images. Such images, whether paintings, mosaics, or
sculpture, were called icons. Those who resented this Christian compro-

[9]A. A. Vasiliev, *History of the Byzantine Empire*, I, 135, 272–273.

mise with idolatry and wished to do away with the practice of image worship were called image-breakers (iconoclasts), and the leading Iconoclasts were originally the emperors themselves, who not only disliked icons but thought there were too many of those who made them, namely, the monks. The attack on images was launched by the emperor Leo III with a decree against images in 725 or 726, and the struggle went on until 843, when images were restored. As a means of reconciling the reformers, however, it was provided that henceforth the icons must be flat and not in the round. The imperial decrees against icons had to be executed (in Italy) in Byzantine territory and called forth strong opposition from the popes, who were quite willing to excommunicate Iconoclasts. The tradition of Gregory the Great in this matter was not forgotten.[10] While the Iconoclasts received some little approval in the West, the popes were, generally speaking, supported in their opposition. Many centuries were to pass before a strong iconoclastic party developed in the western church.

THE BREAK BETWEEN THE EASTERN AND WESTERN CHURCHES

Less fundamental issues kept the two churches hostile. They quarreled over which was to convert the Slavs settling in the frontier regions between East and West.[11] They fought over minor differences in ecclesiastical usage. They became bitter, after their differences on iconoclasm, over a further theological issue, namely how the Holy Spirit came from the Father and the Son. The Greek church clung to the statement of the Council of Nicaea that the Holy Spirit proceeded from the Father *through* the Son, while the Latin church had come to describe the procession as from the Father *and* the Son (*ex patre filioque*) jointly. With the large question of Christian unity at stake it is difficult now to understand how minor theological questions of this kind could have seemed so all-important. The final break came at a time when Pope Leo IX was directing a reform program in the western church calculated, among other things, to translate the Petrine Theory into fact. The pope demanded as much obedience from the East as from the West, and Michael Cerularius, the patriarch of Constantinople, stubbornly refused to give it. The result was mutual excommunication in the summer of 1054. The patriarch and his followers were excommunicated as insolent heretics and consigned to the Devil. The papal legates were excommunicated and, together with their mission in Constantinople, described as having appeared "as a thunder or a famine, or better still . . . wild boors" who had come to "the God-guarded city . . . in order to overthrow truth."[12] It is difficult to read this history today without cynicism or, at least, a very heavy heart. It is impossible to read it without questioning very seriously those who tell us that Christianity or the Christian Church is not only the great bond of amity for the West

[10]See p. 386.
[11]See pp. 498 ff.
[12]Vasiliev, I, 411.

but for the whole globe in our own day. Christianity, a religion of brotherly love, began early to divide into hostile churches; first into separate Greek and oriental churches, and in 1054 into Greek and Latin churches, and later this disintegrating process was to continue further—even to accelerate. Existing division will have to be undone before Christianity can hope for another chance to unify the world.

The hostility between the Byzantine Empire and the West was essentially a conflict between levels of civilization, between the more highly developed East and a West that was more primitive. It expressed itself in corresponding superiority and inferiority complexes, the gloating pride of the East evoking the furious resentment of the West. This phase of the conflict can be illustrated from two historical accounts: (1) that of Bishop Liutprand of Cremona, who described an embassy he led to the Byzantine court in 968 on behalf of the German emperor Otto I; and (2) a contemporary and quasi-official account of the march through Byzantine territory of the crusading armies of the German emperor Frederick Barbarossa (1189–1190).

BISHOP LIUTPRAND OF CREMONA AND THE EAST

Otto I[13] had in 962 re-established the western German empire in a form more limited than that of Charlemagne's but in its theoretical pretensions no less universal. This revival was resented in Constantinople; in Byzantine southern Italy there was actual conflict. Bishop Liutprand's mission to the powerful military emperor Nicephorus Phocas (963–969) was to compose these differences, if possible, and to arrange for the marriage of a Byzantine princess to the heir to the German throne. From Liutprand's personal report to Otto I and his son Otto II it is clear that during his long stay in Constantinople (some four months) he was constantly annoyed and angry with everything he came across. He tells the Ottos that from the beginning "as a mark of disrespect to yourselves, being shamefully received, we were harshly and shamefully treated." He and his mission were housed in a "palace large enough, indeed, but uncovered, neither keeping out the cold nor warding off the heat" and provided with "insolent and tip-seeking servants." From this palace the Germans wore themselves out in walking to the imperial palace. "We did not ride." In general the food and drink were impossible. "To add to our calamity the Greek wine, on account of being mixed with pitch, resin, and plaster, was to us undrinkable." If they ate at the palace, they did so often "without a tablecloth," and what food! A "disgusting and foul meal which was washed down with oil after the manner of drunkards, and moistened also with a certain other exceedingly bad fish liquor." On one occasion Liutprand was obliged to eat with the servants of the palace, and the emperor sent him a "fat goat, of which he himself had partaken, deliciously [?]

[13]See pp. 528 ff.

stuffed with garlic, onions and leeks; steeped in fish sauce." In fact, the food always "smelt strongly of garlic and onions and was filthy with oil and fish-juice."[14]

The court that he had to attend was filled with shabby courtiers. When Nicephorus marched in procession to Hagia Sophia, the streets were lined with "a numerous multitude of tradesmen and lowborn persons . . . being disfigured by their little shields and wretched spears. . . . The greater part of this same crowd in his [Nicephorus's] honour, had marched with bare feet." The nobles who accompanied the emperor "through the plebeian and barefoot multitude were clad in tunics which were too large and which were torn through too great age. It would have been much more suitable had they marched in their everyday clothes. There was no one whose grandfather had owned one of these garments when it was new." The German nobles dressed much better: "One precious garment of thy nobles is worth a hundred of these, and more too." Neither the court ceremonial nor the bureaucracy impressed Liutprand. He did not like the "Attic eloquence" of chief chamberlains, marshals, chief state secretaries, and chief masters of the wardrobe. Even "although I was so weak that not only standing but even sitting seemed a heavy burden to me, he [the emperor] compelled me to stand before him with uncovered head, a thing which was entirely wrong in my state of health." There at court he ran into a general who was "a sort of man—a sort of, I say, because he has ceased to be a male and was not able to become a female." "Here you might find capon Greek bishops sipping their bathwater [wine] from a very small glass." In any case, it was a court composed of "soft, effeminate, long-sleeved, hooded, veiled, lying, neutral-gendered, idle creatures" who go around giving "kisses which were very sweet, very loving." Liutprand got some when he left.

The emperor was the most impossible of all, "a monstrosity of a man, a pygmy, fat-headed and like a mule as to the smallness of his eyes; disgusting with his short, broad, thick and half-hoary beard; disgraced by a neck an inch long; very bristly through the length and thickness of his hair; in colour an Ethiopian; one whom it would not be pleasant to meet in the middle of the night; with extensive belly, lean of loin, very long of hip, considering his short stature, small of shank, proportionate as to his heels and feet, clad in a garment costly but too old, and foul-smelling and faded through age . . . bold of tongue, a fox by nature, in perjury and lying a Ulysses." It seemed incredible that when such a man "like a creeping monster" entered the church of Hagia Sophia, "the singers cried out in adulation: 'behold the morning star approaches; Eos rises, he reflects in his glances the rays of the sun—he the pale death of the Saracens, Nicephorus the ruler . . . Long life to the ruler Nicephorus! Adore him, ye

[14]E. F. Henderson, *Select Historical Documents of the Middle Ages*, pp. 442 ff. The reader might like to imagine that a certain kind of American is visiting the Kremlin. See Toynbee, *Civilization on Trial*, pp. 176–177.

people, cherish him, bend the neck to him alone!' How much more truly might they have sung: 'Come thou burnt-out coal, thou fool, old woman in thy walk, wood-devil in thy look; thou peasant, thou frequenter of foul places, thou goat-foot, thou horn-head, thou double-limbed one; bristly, unruly, countrified, barbarian, harsh, hairy, a rebel.' "

It was a crowd like this that dared contest Otto's title, insult the western empire and popes, and in general abuse all Germans. Leo, the marshal of the court, "called ye not emperor, which is Basileus in his tongue, but to insult ye, Rex, which is king in ours." When envoys from Pope John referred to Nicephorus as "the emperor of the Greeks" and to Otto as "the august emperor of the Romans," the Greek courtiers said, "Was it not unpardonable to have called the universal emperor of the Romans, the august, great, only Nicephorus merely 'the emperor of the Greeks'; and a barbarian and a pauper, 'the august emperor of the Romans?'" Such envoys had to "languish in narrow confinement." They told Liutprand that such "a stupid silly pope does not know that the holy Constantine transferred hither the imperial sceptre, the senate, and all the Roman knighthood, and left in Rome nothing but vile minions, fishers, namely pedlars, bird catchers, bastards, plebeians, slaves."

To this Liutprand retorted that Romulus, "born in adultery," called together "insolvent debtors, fugitive slaves, homicides, and those who were worthy of death for their deeds [and] called them Romans. From such nobility these are descended whom you call world-rulers, that is, emperors, whom we, namely the Lombards, Saxons, Franks, Lotharingians, Bavarians, Swabians, Burgundians, so despise that when angry we can call our enemies nothing more scornful than Roman—comprehending in this one thing, that is in the name of the Romans, whatever there is of contemptibility, of timidity, of avarice, of luxury, of lying, in a word of viciousness." When the emperor twitted Liutprand about the Saxons from whom his emperor came, and about their recent conversion to Christianity, he replied that "all heresies have emanated from you, have flourished among you; by us, that is by the western nations they have been strangled, been put an end to." In fact, although Greeks and Franks "are both men, as the lion and the whelp are both animals, yet they differ in habits as much . . . as rational beings from those who have no reason. . . . The king of the Greeks wears long hair, a tunic, long sleeves, a hood; is lying, crafty, without pity, sly as a fox, proud, falsely humble, miserly and greedy; lives on garlic, onions, and leeks, and drinks bath-water. The king of the Franks, on the contrary, is beautifully shorn; wears a garment not at all like a woman's garment, and a hat; is truthful, without guile, merciful enough when it is right, severe when it is necessary, always truly humble, never miserly; does not live on garlic, onions and leeks. . . ."

With passing references to Saxony, the imperial birthplace "where the inhabitants wear the skins of wild beasts," Liutprand was asked whether in the West they had such parks as in Constantinople, "with wild asses and other animals." He replied, "Parks yes, but no wild asses." He was then shown the wild asses in the parks in the Byzantine capital and asks himself, "But why, I ask, wild asses? Our tame ones at Cremona are the same. Their colour, shape and ears are the same; they are equally melodious when they begin to bray." The only authentic wild ass in the East was the emperor Nicephorus. And Liutprand, after having been accused of being "a spy upon us while simulating peace," and after having been further insulted by being told that the envoy from the wild Bulgarians, although "shorn, unwashed, and girt with a brazen chain, is nevertheless a patrician" and that therefore "it would not be right to give a bishop, especially a Frankish one, the preference over him," concluded that Constantinople was a "half-starved, perjured, lying, wily, greedy, rapacious, avaricious [and] vainglorious city." "If I ever come back here again may Nicephorus present me with a crown and a golden sceptre!"[15]

THIRD CRUSADE AND BYZANTIUM

In the course of the Crusades the hostility grew so fierce that it led to an attack upon Constantinople in 1204. A Byzantine emperor, Alexius Comnenus, had seen fit in 1095 to summon the aid of the West against the Seljuk Turks. For quite understandable reasons, it was feared that the crusaders might take advantage of Byzantine weakness, destroy Constantinople, and set up a western Christian empire in its place. These fears, when combined with the experience of crusading armies plundering their way through Byzantine territory in the Balkans, soon cooled the Byzantine ardor for western help and led to a clumsy obstructive policy which only infuriated the crusaders and led them to think seriously of removing the Byzantine obstacle to their march eastward and capturing a rich prize as well. These feelings, revealed by Germans in the course of the Third Crusade, were expressed by Ansbert, the name given to a chronicler of the German contingent under the emperor Frederick Barbarossa. Frederick had decided to take the land route to the East. When the Byzantine emperor heard of the plans for the Third Crusade he suspected that "not only the [German] emperor but also the king of France would lead a hostile invasion into his realm." Before he left Germany in April, 1189, Frederick had to swear to Byzantine envoys that he intended no such harm, and that if his army were provided with the opportunities to buy food, the Byzantine Empire had nothing to fear from the German crusaders. The Byzantine emperor Isaac would not trust the Germans to keep their word. He allied with the Mohammedan sultan Saladin, and undertook to impede the progress of the German army eastward. He infuriated the Germans by arresting and holding in prison as hostages for the good conduct of German troops a distinguished embassy of German nobles sent ahead to negotiate with Isaac the details of the German

[15]Henderson, p. 468.

progress. In a letter sent back to Germany on 16 November, 1189, Frederick referred to Isaac's intention "to destroy us and all Christians," and to letters "written with great pomp" which "sang equally of threats. flattery and craft." After the arrest of the envoys "the whole army of the Cross became enraged, and took, shortly, to the uninterrupted ravaging and occupation of cities, castles and villages." Further delays brought on by the Greeks had led Frederick to have "no further faith in Greek vows and pretensions." He ordered plans to be made for Genoa, Venice, Ancona, and Pisa to supply "a squadron of galleys and smaller vessels, in order that, meeting us at Constantinople around the middle of March, they may besiege the city by sea and we by land." "Do not neglect," Frederick says in his letter, "to write the Lord Pope to send monks to the various provinces to exhort the people of God against the enemies of the Cross, and especially against the Greeks. For in the presence of our envoys . . . the Patriach of Constantinople publicly proclaimed in the church of St. Sophia that any Greek who killed one hundred pilgrims [crusaders], even if he were charged with murdering ten Greeks, would secure a pardon."[16]

The chronicler's narrative gives a further background to this letter. Roads through Bulgaria were blocked by "little double-dealing puny Greeks, Bulgars, Serbs, and half-civilized Vlachs." "Day after day ocurred the rout and murder of foragers and robbery by bandits who made sallies from the Greek side and incessantly stole horses and pillaged the carts which were proceeding without military escort." In one instance, Ansbert says, "We saw twenty-four of them [the Greeks] who had been tied to the tails of horses and brought back to camp, hung on one gibbet, like wolves, head downwards." Isaac's arrest of the envoys was "to the dishonor of the army of the Holy Cross and of all Christianity, since he desired to offer this favor to his friend and confederate Saladin . . . the enemy of the Cross and of all Christians." The envoys, when returned, reported "how they were shamefully taken prisoner, robbed, starved, mocked and insulted in various ways." The patriarch of Constantinople, that "pseudo-apostle," not only publicly encouraged Byzantine criminals to murder crusaders but called the latter "dogs" as well. The Germans became convinced that the Greeks were attempting to kill them with poisoned wine and that this was done upon imperial orders. Fortunately, the strong constitutions of the Germans preserved them from this treachery. "That same wine," which when forced down the throat of a recalcitrant Greek, caused him to turn pale, foam at the mouth, and wildly roll his eyes, "hardly so much as intoxicated some of our men." So it was that "the wine of the Greeks, steeped in poison and prepared for the destruction of our men, was deadly for the Greeks, but a healthy drink for our men." Nor were the Germans able to take with equanimity the taunting posters which Greek artists had painted in churches and public buildings. "When

[16]Quotations from the chronicle of Ansbert are from a translation by C. E. Wilcox in the library of the University of Nebraska.

they visited in force the region called Graditz they found in the pictures of churches and other buildings, Greeks astride the necks of pilgrims, and as if they were enemies, restraining them with bridles. Our men, enraged at this, set the churches and other buildings on fire, killed very many people with their swords, devastated that whole land, and took huge amounts of booty."

In the course of negotiations between Greeks and Germans there arose again that old, old question of title. "For that contemptible Greek with his usual pride, lyingly proclaimed himself to be the 'Emperor of the Romans' and our Most Serene August Lord himself to be not Emperor of the Romans but only 'King of Alamannia.'" When Frederick heard these titles he jumped up to explain to the Greek envoys the nature of the Roman Empire. "It is greatly to be wondered at," he said, "why my brother, your Lord and Emperor . . . should usurp this futile and undeserved title, and should glory foolishly in an honor which is, by all odds, not his, for clearly he understands that I am 'Frederick the ever August Emperor of the Romans' both in name and in fact." Frederick threatened that unless the Greek emperor "salutes me with due respect by the name of Roman Emperor . . . let him know that I, in reliance upon Divine Love, will unhesitatingly cut my way through with the sword." After calling Frederick "the Most Excellent Emperor of Alamannia," Isaac finally got around to calling him "the Most Noble Emperor of Ancient Rome."

BACKGROUND OF THE FOURTH CRUSADE

Special circumstances caused the hostility between West and East to break out into open warfare. The circumstances were that (1) in 1198 one of the western church's most ambitious popes, Innocent III, came to the throne; (2) the emperor of Constantinople, Isaac II, had been blinded and deposed by his brother Alexius III (10 April, 1195); and (3) the daughter of Isaac II, Irene, had married (25 May, 1197) Philip of Swabia, the Hohenstaufen emperor of Germany. The criminal Alexius wrote to the ambitious pope in 1198, "We are the only two world powers: the single Roman Church and the single Empire of the successors of Justinian; therefore we must unite and endeavor to prevent a new increase in the power of the western Emperor, our rival."[17] Innocent III and Philip of Swabia, "the Western Emperor," were engaged in an intense struggle for position in Italy and for the leadership of western Europe. Moreover, Venice, the Queen of the Adriatic, was at the moment fighting with Constantinople to rectify certain grievances and with her Italian urban rivals, chiefly Genoa, for commercial supremacy in Constantinople. She was governed at the moment by the blind old doge Dandolo, whom the Greeks were reported to have blinded while he was a hostage in Constantinople, "by means of a concave mirror which strongly reflected the rays of the sun."

[17]Vasiliev, II, 110.

These special circumstances were responsible for the notorius Fourth Crusade against Constantinople, one of the most extraordinary events in all history and a melancholy commentary upon some aspects of western civilization at the beginning of the thirteenth century.

VILLEHARDOUIN AND THE FOURTH CRUSADE

Among the English, German, Sicilian, but chiefly French knights who responded to Innocent's appeal for a new crusade to the Orient was Baldwin, the count of Flanders. With the intention of taking the sea route to Egypt, these representatives of western Christianity and western chivalry had forgathered at Venice in order to negotiate with the representatives of the new commercial spirit of the West about transport to the East. According to Geoffrey of Villehardouin, a Champagne knight on the crusade, the Venetians agreed to furnish transport for 85,000 marks. Indeed, they joined the crusade. Doge Dandolo promised: "For the love of God we will add to the fleet fifty armed galleys on condition that, so long as we act in company, of all conquests in land or money, whether at sea or on dry ground, we shall have the half and you the other half."[18]

By the time the crusade was ready to start from Venice the crusaders still owed Venice 34,000 of the promised 85,000 marks. But the Venetians had a plan. The city of Zara on the Dalmatian coast had recently revolted from Venice and come under the rule of the king of Hungary. Both the city and the king were planning to participate in the crusade. Dandolo's plan was to ask the crusading army to help conquer Zara. "Let us . . . ask them to help us reconquer it, and we will remit the payment of the debt of thirty-four thousand marks of silver, until such time as it shall please God to allow us to gain the moneys by conquest, we and they together." To this the crusading army finally agreed, and the crusade started off with an attack on, and destruction of, a Christian city (November, 1202). "Never before," wrote Geoffrey of Villehardouin, "had . . . as fine a fleet been seen. And then the pilgrims caused all the priests and clerks there present to get up into the castles of the ships and sing the *Veni Creator Spiritus*, and all, both the great and the small folk, wept for great joy and happiness. . . . It seemed as if the whole sea swarmed with ants, and the ships burned on the water, and the water itself were aflame with the great joy that they had."[19]

THE DIVERSION TO CONSTANTINOPLE

The son of the deposed and blinded emperor of Byzantium, whose name was also Alexius, had come to the West to plead with his brother-in-law, Philip of Swabia, to help to restore his father to the throne. Philip, at the moment engaged not only in a struggle with Innocent but also with a

[18]From *Memoirs of the Crusades* ("The Fourth Crusade," p. 6) by Villehardouin and DeJoinville, Everyman's Library. Published by E. P. Dutton and Company, Inc.
[19]Ibid., p. 16.

rival candidate for the German throne, could not come himself, but sent the young Alexius to Zara with a plea to the crusaders to take up his cause. Very likely at this moment the crusade became a part of the papal-imperial struggle in the West, and Philip was faced with the pleasant prospect of a brother-in-law upon the Byzantine throne. Again the crusaders hesitated, and again they agreed because of what young Alexius promised them in return for reseating his father on the throne. He promised to pay their debt to the Venetians, to unite the Greek with the Latin church, to contribute men, money, and supplies for an attack upon Egypt, and to provide a permanent guard for the Holy Land. In May, 1203, the crusading fleet set sail from Zara and at the end of June hove in sight of Constantinople. Villehardouin described the excitement on board: "Now you may know that those who had never before seen Constantinople looked upon it very earnestly, for they never thought there could be in all the world so rich a city; and they marked the high walls and strong towers that enclosed it round about, and the rich palaces, and mighty churches—of which there were so many that no one would have believed it who had not seen it with his eyes—and the height and length of that city which above all others was sovereign. And be it known to you that no man there was of such hardness but his flesh trembled; and it was no wonder, for never was so great an enterprise undertaken by any people since the creation of the world."[20] In July the city, for the first time in its history, fell to the crusaders, and both young Alexius and his father were placed on the throne.

THE CONQUEST OF THE BYZANTINE EMPIRE

The Greeks in Constantinople did not like the barbarian westerners in their midst. They came to resent the co-emperor, Alexius, who had brought them there, who was paying them money for their share in putting him on the throne, and who had promised them untold assistance to go on with their crusade to Egypt. Indeed, Alexius found it hard to pay the crusaders more than 100,000 marks. Of this the Venetians took their share of one half (50,000 marks) and added thereto the 34,000 owed them by the crusaders. In early 1204 a typical Byzantine palace revolution put both Alexius and his father in prison. Here Isaac II died, and the new emperor, Alexius IV, with that civilized refinement that on previous occasions had caused the murder or mutilation of an unwanted ruler, had the young Alexius strangled. The opportunity had now arisen for the Venetians and the French finally to come to terms with this hated obstacle to western political and economic ambition. They agreed to conquer the city for themselves and in March, 1204, signed an agreement as to how the empire and its spoils were to be divided. A committee of Venetians and French were to elect a new Latin emperor, and what he was not to pos-

[20]"Fourth Crusade," p. 31.

478 CHAPTER ELEVEN

sess in Constantinople and the empire was to be divided equally between the Venetians and the rest of the crusaders. Provisions for the election of a new patriarch and the details of a new feudal government were arranged, and the crusaders went to work to take Constantinople for the second time. On 13 April, 1204, it fell, and the emperor fled.

What happened in the city in the following three days reveals once again the ugly passions aroused by the religious and cultural differences of peoples when they take to war to resolve their conflicts. An eyewitness Byzantine historian (Nicetas) reports that in Hagia Sophia, "the sacred altar, formed of all kinds of precious materials, was broken into bits and distributed among the soldiers, as was all the other sacred wealth of so great and infinite splendor. . . . Mules and saddle horses [to carry away the booty] were led to the very sanctuary of the temple. Some of these, which were unable to keep their footing on the splendid and slippery pavement, were stabbed as they fell, so that the sacred pavement was polluted with blood and filth. Nay more, a certain harlot . . . sat on the patriarch's seat, singing an obscene song and dancing frequently. . . . In the alleys, in the streets, in the temples, complaints, weeping, lamentations, grief, the groaning of men, the shrieks of women, wounds, rape, captivity, the separation of those most closely united."[21] This picture is confirmed by Pope Innocent, who was appalled by what he had been instrumental in calling forth: "These defenders of Christ, who should have turned their swords only against infidels, have bathed in Christian blood. They have respected neither religion nor age nor sex. Matrons and virgins, even those vowed to God, were delivered to the ignominious brutality of the soldiers."[22]

Villehardouin reports, "The booty gained was so great that none could tell you of it. Gold and silver and vessels and precious stones and samite and cloth of silk and robes, vair and grey, and ermine and every choicest thing found upon the earth . . . never since the world was created, had so much booty been won in any city . . . greatly did they rejoice and give thanks because of the victory God had vouchsafed to them—for those who before had been poor were now in wealth and luxury. Thus they celebrated Palm Sunday and the Easter Day following in the joy and honour that God had bestowed upon them." (p. 65)

THE AFTERMATH OF THE CRUSADE

The disposition of the remains of the Byzantine state was in accordance with the arrangements made in March. Baldwin, the count of Flanders, was elected the new emperor of the Latin empire of Constantinople, and the Venetian Thomas Morosini was made the patriarch of Constantinople. The capital and the empire were divided between the emperor, the

[21]*Translations and Reprints of the University of Pennsylvania*, III, 16.
[22]*Cambridge Medieval History*, eds. J. R. Tanner, C. S. Previté-Orton, and Z. N. Brooke, IV, 420.

Venetians, and the crusaders. Venice got three-eighths of Constantinople, including Hagia Sophia, and took over territory securing control of the sea route from Constantinople home. She occupied Gallipoli, seaports in Thrace including Adrianople, and the Aegean islands of Naxos, Andros, Euboea, and Crete. She also took ports in the Peloponnesus, the Ionian Islands, and Durazzo. The lands taken by the crusaders were organized as feudal principalities whose holders were vassals of the emperor. Boniface of Montferrat set up the area around Thessalonica in Thrace as a kingdom of Thessalonica. Athens and Thebes became a feudal duchy under a Burgundian knight. The Peloponnesus became the Principality of Achaia, divided into twelve feudal baronies and governed ultimately by the Villehardouin family. Here in the East was a "new France."[23] Until 1261 there was no Greek empire at Constantinople, and when it was once again restored it had been so weakened by western attack that it was unable to prevent the expansion of the Ottoman Turks into Asia Minor and Europe. The perverted Fourth Crusade was an unpleasant early manifestation of what we have to call western imperialism.[24]

Islam and the West

MOHAMMED

The Crusades against Islam before the Fourth must be considered in a similar manner, that is, as a chapter in the imperialistic expansion of western feudal Europe.

This expansion had been provoked by the expansion of the Arabs. In the case of the Byzantine Empire the West was antagonized by what it regarded as a schismatic Christian religion, but in the case of the Arabs it was appalled and infuriated by a new religion that did not claim even to be Christian, and that seemed to combine religion and conquest in a way that Christianity had not yet learned. Mohammed, the creator of Islam (*ca.* 570–632), had, to be sure, been influenced by the Christian communities in the Arabian peninsula. But he had been impressed much more by the Jewish communities in the Hejaz. Indeed, Islam and Christianity must be regarded as outgrowths of a parent Judaism.[25] It is not that Mohammed was a close student of either Judaism or Christianity. According to Arab tradition he was illiterate. Whether he was actually illiterate or not, and this seems unlikely, he cannot be shown to have been acquainted with the actual texts of Jewish or Christian Scriptures. What he knew he had learned from observation or from the oral instruction of Jewish and Christian teachers. There can be no doubt that the religious reform that

[23]See Vasiliev, *Byzantine Empire*, II, 128-129.
[24]Treated in Vol. II.
[25]See pp. 19 f.

Mohammed intended for the Arabs was based upon the religion of Jews and Christians. Islam was to be, like the others, the religion of a book. As God had revealed himself to the Jews through the Old Testament, and to the Christians through the New Testament, so he was revealing himself to the Arabs through the Koran. Just as God revealed himself through prophets in the Old Testament and through Jesus Christ in the New, so, in the Koran, he was revealing himself through a new prophet, Mohammed. Just as Christians looked upon the revelation of the prophets in the Old Testament as a kind of early revelation that Christianity itself completed, and therefore included the Old Testament in their Scriptures, so, too, in the mind of Mohammed Judaism and Christianity were to be regarded as early manifestations of Islam. If Mohammed was not able to include the Jewish and Christian Scriptures among the Arab Scriptures, still he regarded such men as Adam, Noah, Abraham, Moses, and Jesus as prophets with whom God had made special agreements. To this line of specially chosen men he had been added by God (Allah) as the last and only really authoritative prophet. The final revelation of God, the one supplementing and supplanting all previous ones, was given to Mohammed in his abnormal trances, and its very words written down in the Koran. To this nothing could be added, and it was never intended that it should be translated into any other language than the sacred Arabic. The Prophet did not conceive of Islam merely as a new religion for Arabs; it was meant for Christians and Jews as a new universal religion for all mankind. Mohammed was bitter when his claims were rejected by Christians and Jews—as they had been at first by his fellow Arabs. Under such circumstances God revealed that Islam was to be a militant religion capable of fighting holy wars (the *jihad*). "Fight for Allah's cause against those who fight you; kill them wherever you find them and drive them from the place from which they have driven you; it is worse to tolerate their offense than to kill them . . . make war on them until there is no more offense and all men worship Allah alone."

THE MOSLEM

In revealing the nature of true religion to his prophet Mohammed, Allah was careful to adapt it to the needs of simple nomadic Arabs. There was no need to complicate the conception of God by ideas of a Trinity. If the primitive polytheism and animism of the Arabs were to be destroyed, it would be better to cling to the notion that God is one, and not three or three-in-one, avoiding in this way the difficulties of theological controversy and the development of an elaborate system of belief. For a nomadic people it was just as well to be without elaborate churches where services had to be performed in accordance with prescribed ritual by a special priesthood. In Islam there is no priesthood; the conductors of services are laymen. There are no sacraments, and one's religious obligations can be performed without the physical necessity of a church. The good

Moslem need only believe that "there is no God but Allah and Mohammed is the prophet of Allah"; and that God's revelation is contained in the infallible words of the Koran. He must pray five times a day. He must fast during the day for a month of the year. He must give to the poor, and, if possible, make a pilgrimage to the holy city of Mecca at least once in his lifetime. These things done, his loyalty will be rewarded after death in a very lovely paradise; his disloyalty, on the contrary, punished in a very unpleasant hell.

Mohammed and his successors, the caliphs, not only were the heads of a new religious community; they also were the heads of a new Mohammedan state. There was no separation between this church, if it may be so called, and the state. The legislation for the Mohammedan state was with Mohammed as much a matter of divine revelation as its religious belief. The Koran was thus a body of law introducing many reforms into Arabic society as well as retaining such institutions as polygamy and slavery. Since the law was based upon the revelation of God through his prophet, the Arab state took on the character of a new desert theocracy produced by the civilizations of western Asia. Since the caliph was the successor of Mohammed as prophetic head of a religious-political community, the Arab empire continued for some time to be a theocracy of this kind.

THE EXPANSION OF THE CALIPHATE

The expansion of the caliphate in the century after Mohammed's death (632–732) was an extraordinary phenomenon. It moved into the Tigris-Euphrates Valley to destroy the Neo-Persian empire and, for the most part, its Zoroastrian religion. At the same time it turned westward, where it was confronted by a Byzantine Empire not only weakened by its own long struggle with Persia but hated in Syria, Palestine, and Egypt by Christian minorities (Monophysites and Nestorians), persecuted Jews, and, in general, heavily exploited subjects. Except for isolated centers of Byzantine resistance, the Arab expansion into Syria, Palestine, and Egypt resembled a liberation. As a later Syrian historian put it, "the God of vengeance delivered us out of the hand of the Romans by means of the Arabs. . . . It profited us not a little to be saved from the cruelty of the Romans and their bitter hatred towards us."[26] By 650 the caliphate included Syria, Palestine, and Egypt and started to move westward across North Africa. By 698 it included Cyrenaica, Tripoli, and the Byzantine exarchate of Africa that Justinian had founded. For the first time in history the Berbers had been subdued by a foreign power. The expansion into Visigothic Spain (710) was the work primarily of Berbers led by a few Arabs. The conquest was again facilitated by rotten social conditions —a privileged secular and clerical aristocracy driving slaves and serfs into

[26]Bernard Lewis, *The Arabs in History*, p. 58.

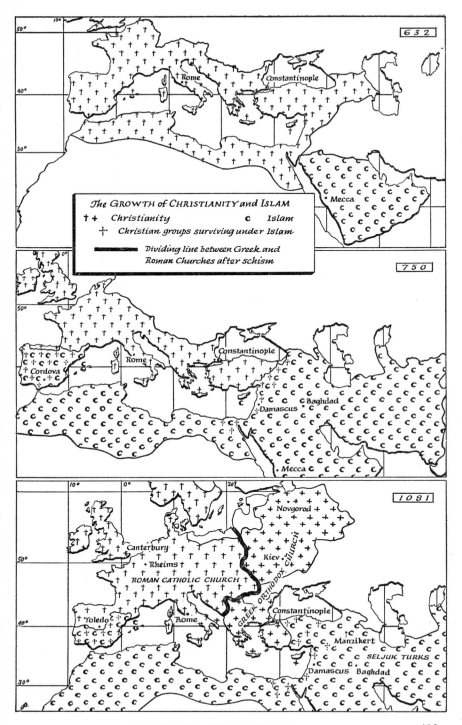

The GROWTH of CHRISTIANITY and ISLAM
† + Christianity   c   Islam
⸶ Christian groups surviving under Islam

━━━ Dividing line between Greek and
Roman Churches after schism

632

Rome   Constantinople

Mecca

750

Rome   Constantinople

Cordova

Baghdad

Damascus

Mecca c

1081

Novgorod

Canterbury

Kiev

Rheims

ROMAN CATHOLIC CHURCH

GREEK ORTHODOX CHURCH

Toledo

Rome   Constantinople

Manzikert

SELJUK TURKS

Damascus   Baghdad

rebellion, and an intolerant Christianity persecuting Jews. When the Moslems appeared many of the oppressed greeted them as liberators and joined their conquest. By 725 Visigothic Spain had been supplanted by a Moslem state and the Pyrenees crossed. Seven years later the Moslems were stopped in their northward march by Charles Martel at Tours.[27] In the ninth century further expansion, chiefly from Tunisia, brought Sicily, Sardinia, Corsica, and the Balearic Islands into their hands.

MOSLEM TOLERANCE

The expansion of Islam may not be interpreted simply as a holy war to spread the new faith. The caliphate was, as a matter of fact, tolerant of other religions. In Syria, Palestine, and Egypt not only the Greek Orthodox but the heretical Christian minorities were permitted to exist with their own organizations. In North Africa and Spain the situation was the same. The Christians in Spain (the Mozarabs) developed a special (Mozarabic) liturgy for their church, and in many respects the new Arabic administration was looked upon as enlightened when compared with its predecessor in Spain or the Frankish rule to the north. The Moslems destroyed the old secular and clerical aristocracy and distributed its lands among a new group of peasants. The literary culture introduced by the Arabs was so attractive that Christians complained that their fellow religionists preferred the study of Arabic and Arabic literature to Latin and Latin literature. A Christian of Cordova complained in the middle of the ninth century that "Many of my co-religionists read the poetry and tales of the Arabs, study the writings of Mohammedan theologians and philosophers, not in order to refute them, but to learn how to express themselves in Arabic with greater correctness and elegance. Where can one find today a layman who reads the Latin commentaries on the Holy Scriptures? Who among them studies the Gospels, the Prophets, the Apostles? All the young Christians noted for their gifts know only the language and literature of the Arabs, read and study with zeal Arabic books, building up great libraraies of them at enormous cost and loudly proclaiming everywhere that this literature is worthy of admiration. Among thousands of us there is hardly one who can write a passable Latin letter to a friend, but innumerable are those who can express themselves in Arabic and compose poetry in that language with greater art than the Arabs themselves."[28]

THE LOSS TO CHRISTIANITY

It must not be supposed that because Christianity was tolerated by the Moslems it remained as powerful after as before the Moslem conquests. The Moslems might not impose religious disabilities upon non-Moslems,

[27]See p. 379.
[28]Lewis, p. 123.

but they did impose political, economic, and social disabilities that made Christians an inferior minority and induced many of them to become converts to Islam in order to enjoy the privileges of the Mohammedan ruling class. Thus Islam proved to be a tremendous setback to Christianity, causing the loss of more of the faithful than any other rival heresy or religion and constituting the most serious threat to Christianity until the advent of communism.[29] In the course of time in Syria, Palestine, and Egypt Christianity became the religion of a minority and not a majority. In North Africa Christianity disappeared more quickly than elsewhere. Flight, as well as conversion, accounts for the disappearance, large numbers going to Spain, Italy, Greece, Gaul, and Germany. Gregory VII, the eleventh-century pope, will be found trying to revive the North African church, but by 1500 it had disappeared. In Spain the converts from Christianity (the *Muwallahs*) "may have formed the largest group of the population." If it survived, the Christian Church lost a great deal of its vitality because of having to live within a Moslem community. In Spain, for example, church councils were summoned by Moslem rulers, and Jews and Moslems were admitted to them. Church offices were purchased from Moslem rulers, and we have indicated that Christians preferred Arabic to Latin and Latin Christian literature. In consequence, not merely fear of conquest by the Arabs or Berbers inspired terror in western Europe. The weakness, in addition, of surviving Christian churches in Moslem lands and the great losses in numbers of the faithful to Islam contributed to this fear. Was it not possible that Christianity could be extinguished by this foe if it were permitted to continue to expand?

THE BEGINNING OF THE CRUSADES

The fear which seized western Europe in the face of agressive Islam may be understood in the light of the fear which seizes the western world today in the face of aggressive communism. At that time there resulted the organization of a military counter-offensive which we call the Crusades. The western inaugurator of the Crusades was Charles Martel. By 759 the Franks had succeeded in driving the Moslems out of Gaul. The offensive was continued when Charlemagne planted the Spanish March across the Pyrenees; and the march in turn split up into the little Christian states of Leon, Castile, Navarre, Aragon, and Barcelona. By 1086 Castile-Leon had taken Toledo, and by 1118 Aragon-Barcelona had taken Saragossa. The political and religious threat of Islam had already been augmented by an economic threat, the result of the expansion of the ninth century. As early as the beginning of the eleventh century, western Europe had recovered sufficiently from the decline and break-up of the Carolingian empire to experience a revival of trade and industry. This revival brought pressure to remove the Moslem control of the western Mediterranean. An

[29]See K. Latourette, *A History of the Expansion of Christianity*, II, Chap vi.

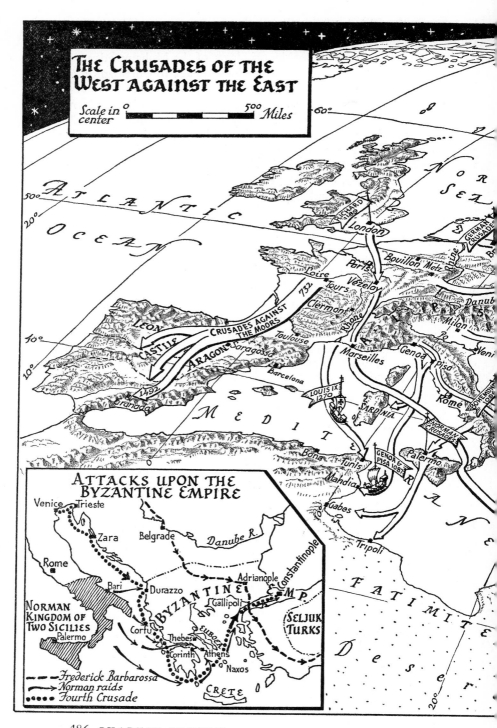

THE CRUSADES OF THE WEST AGAINST THE EAST

Scale in center

0   500
Miles

ATLANTIC OCEAN

ATTACKS UPON THE
BYZANTINE EMPIRE

NORMAN
KINGDOM OF
TWO SICILIES

- - - Frederick Barbarossa
→ Norman raids
•••• Fourth Crusade

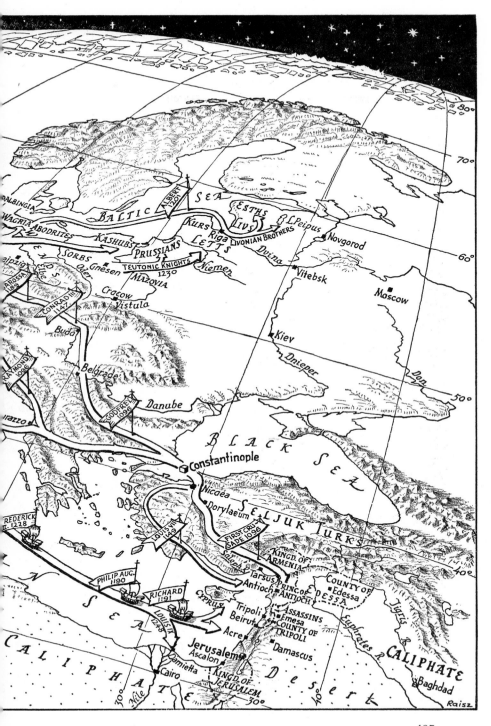

offensive against Islam on the sea joined the land offensive in Spain. The Normans, with the help of Genoa and Pisa, took Sicily from the Arabs by the end of the eleventh century. Earlier these two Italian cities had taken Sardinia and carried the offensive to North Africa.[30] The time was ripe for western Europe to carry the war against Islam into the eastern Mediterranean. What made the matter all the more urgent was the strengthening of Islam by the invasion of the Seljuk Turks into this area.

THE SELJUK TURKS

The Seljuk Turks had moved from central Asia into Iran, where they became Moslems, and then had taken the caliphate at Baghdad[31] under the protection of their sultans. A serious defeat of Byzantine troops at Manzikert (1071) opened Asia Minor to them, and Syria and Palestine as well. Their empire, which they called the Sultanate of Rum, broke up after 1092. Its central territories in Asia Minor became virtually independent, and so did the Turkish governors of Syria. Jerusalem was lost to the Fatimite caliphs of Egypt in 1098. At the same time that it was losing Asia Minor to the Seljuk Turks, the Byzantine Empire was being attacked from the European side by another group of Mongolian nomads, the Patzinaks, who in fact allied with the Seljuks for an attack upon Constantinople. Under these circumstances the Byzantine emperor Alexius Comnenus (1081–1118) appealed to the West for help. "Hasten with all your people, strain all your forces, lest such treasures [as Constantinople] fall into the hands of the Turks and Patzinaks. . . . Endeavor, so long as you have time, that the Christian Empire and, which is still more important, the Holy Sepulchre be not lost to you and that you may have in heaven no doom, but reward."[32] Ambassadors were sent to the Pope Urban II to urge the transference of the western crusade eastward.

MOTIVATION FOR THE CRUSADES

There can be no doubt that the West was interested for religious motives in widening the military offensive against Islam. It was ready to defend Christianity against further losses. It was capable of being outraged by the thought that those places made sacred by the birth, life, and death of the Lord should now be occupied by infidels who preyed upon Christian pilgrims journeying to these sites. For centuries the Christian nobles of the West felt the religious obligation of going on crusade. It would be naïve, however, to consider the movement as simply religious or, at its worst, as an example of crude and cruel religious fanaticism. If western knights were to do penance for their sins by going on crusade, they preferred to have that penance profitable in the form of booty, lands, and

[30]See p. 491.
[31]The capital of the caliphate was at Damascus under the Ommiads (660–750) and at Baghdad under the Abbasids (750–1258).
[32]Vasiliev, *Byzantine Empire*, II, 26.

privileges. They did not propose to go simply on behalf of the Byzantine emperors. What they thought of Byzantium we have already considered. Nor were the popes interested in the Crusades simply for religious reasons. They always looked upon them as a way to reunify the Church (after 1054) under their own leadership and as a means of enlarging their political power, either by setting up new Christian states in the East dependent upon themselves, of commandeering the kings, princes, and aristocracy of western Europe in their behalf, or actually of utilizing the idea of crusade to attack their political and religious enemies in the West.[33]

THE COUNCIL OF CLERMONT

When Pope Urban II presented the appeal of Byzantium for aid to the French at the Council of Clermont in 1095 he was careful to appeal to a variety of motives. Men were to remember how their ancestors the Franks, and especially Charlemagne, had begun the crusade in the West. They were to remember the horrible and cruel atrocities committed upon Christian pilgrims by infidel Turks. The pope was careful to remind his knightly audience that "this land which you inhabit, shut in on all sides by the sea and surrounded by mountain peaks, is too narrow for your large population; nor does it abound in wealth. . . . Enter upon the road to the Holy Sepulchre. That land which, as the Scripture says, 'floweth with milk and honey' was given by God into the possession of the children of Israel. Jerusalem is the navel of the world; the land is fruitful above others, like another paradise of delights." Pope Urban also thought it would be good for western Europe to be relieved of its surplus, bellicose, and even criminal nobility. "You," he said, "girt about with the badge of knighthood, are arrogant with great pride; you rage against your brothers and cut each other in pieces. . . . You, the oppressors of children, plunderers of widows; you guilty of homicide, of sacrilege, robbers of another's rights; you who await the pay of thieves for the shedding of Christian blood—as vultures smell fetid corpses, so do you sense battles from afar. . . . If, forsooth, you wish to be mindful of your souls, either lay down the girdle of such knighthood or advance boldly, as knights of Christ, and rush quickly as you can to the defence of the Eastern Church."[34] And if for many of the aristocracy who participated in this and subsequent crusades religion was a sanction for less worthy motives of greed and fame, for the merchants of the Italian towns, who furnished the transport and naval power as well as the supplies to maintain western outposts in Syria and Palestine, the crusade was a golden economic opportunity to open up the West to the East and the East to the West. The recipe was to be repeated time and again in western history.

[33]See pp. 526 ff.
[34]August C. Krey, *The First Crusade*, pp. 30 ff.

The knights responding to the pope's summons for a crusade were chiefly French, and their leaders were such men as Godfrey of Bouillon, duke of Lower Lorraine; his brother Baldwin; Raymond, the count of Toulouse; and Bohemund, the son of the Norman duke of southern Italy Robert Guiscard, who not long previously had failed in an attempted march upon Constantinople from Durazzo on the western coast of Greece. These men and their contingents, perhaps some 12,000 to 15,000 armed men, reached Syria after having journeyed to Constantinople by land, defeated the Seljuk Turks at Nicaea and Dorylaeum, and suffered great hardships in Asia Minor. On the way they lost Duke Godfrey's brother, Baldwin, who became the ruler of Armenian Edessa, where he set up the first crusading state in the East, the County of Edessa. Sweeping into their hands from the independent Seljuk governors some one hundred sixty-five Syrian towns and fortresses, they were finally able to take Antioch and protect it from a dangerous siege by the Turkish governor of Mosul. Here the Norman leader Bohemund established the Principality of Antioch and, like Baldwin, abandoned the crusade to Jerusalem. The remaining crusaders, under the leadership of Raymond of Toulouse, reached Jerusalem in 1099 and took it on 15 July. What happened in this city so holy to Christians is a further example of the barbarity of western Christianity and of unleashed religious passion. "When the hour approached on which our Lord Jesus Christ deigned to suffer on the Cross for us . . . one of our knights, Lethold, clambered up the wall of the city. . . . Our men followed, killing and slaying even in the Temple of Solomon, where the slaughter was so great that our men waded in blood up to the ankles. . . . When the pagans had been overcome, our men seized great numbers, both men and women, either killing them or keeping them captive, as they wished. . . . Afterward the army scattered throughout the city and took possession of the gold and silver, the horses and mules, and the houses filled with goods of all kinds. Later all of our people went to the Sepulchre of our Lord, rejoicing and weeping for joy, and they rendered up the offering that they owed.

"The amount of blood that they shed on that day is incredible. . . . Some of our men (and this was more merciful) cut off the heads of their enemies; others shot them with arrows, so that they fell from the towers; others tortured them longer by casting them into the flames. Piles of heads, hands, and feet were to be seen in the streets of the city. It was necessary to pick one's way over the bodies of men and horses. . . . At the Temple of Solomon, a place where religious services are ordinarily chanted . . . men rode in blood up to their knees and bridle reins. Indeed, it was a just and splendid judgment of God that this place should be filled with the blood of the unbelievers, since it had suffered so long from their blasphemies. The city was filled with corpses and blood. . . . No one even saw or heard of such slaughter of pagan people, for funeral pyres were formed from them like pyramids, and no one knows their number except God alone."[35] Subsequently a western chronicler reported further: "Those who were poor there, his God made rich here. Those who had a few pence there, have numberless gold pieces here; he who had not a village there possesses, with God as giver, a whole town here. Why then return to the West, when the East suits us as well?"[36]

THE LATIN KINGDOM OF JERUSALEM

The navies of Genoa, Pisa, and Venice helped the crusaders to capture, further, such coastal towns as Tripoli, Tyre, Arsuf, Caesarea, Acre, Sidon, Beirut, Haifa, Ascalon, Tortosa, Jubayl, and Laodicea, and for their aid they were richly rewarded with churches, trading quarters, and privileges. To all these and the earlier conquests the crusaders gave a political organization comparable to western feudalism. They set up a Latin Kingdom of Jerusalem, subdivided into the major fiefs of the County of Edessa, the Principality of Antioch, and the County of Tripoli. Godfrey of Bouillon, the duke of Lower Lorraine, was chosen to be, as the king was first called, the "Defender of the Church of the Holy Sepulchre," and, as feudal overlord, the recipient of the homage, fealty, dues, and services of the other western knights holding of him. No more in the East than in the West, however, did feudalism produce a strong state.

THE MOSLEM OFFENSIVE

The establishment of the Latin Kingdom of Jerusalem, the only major success of crusading imperialism in Syria and Palestine, had been made possible in large part by the disintegration of the Seljuk empire. If the Moslem world were to regain the unity it had lost the little western feudal kingdom on the eastern shores of the Mediterranean would be doomed. Under the leadership of Saladin the Moslem world did regain its unity. The unification began when Zangi, the lieutenant of the Turkish governor of Mosul, began to consolidate the Syrian cities in independent Turkish hands, and finally in 1144 almost destroyed Edessa and the first of the crusading states in the East, the County of Edessa. This event precipitated the so-called Second Crusade from the West, led by Kings Conrad III of Germany and Louis VII of France. The efforts of these armies accomplished nothing in Syria and Palestine. The Moslem offensive went on. In 1154 Damascus was taken by Zangi's son Nureddin, and the unification of the Moslem cities in Syria was completed. Thereupon Nureddin undertook to intervene in the politics of Egypt, where the Fatimite dynasty had long been established. In 1164 he sent a Turkish army under Shirkuh to Egypt, where Shirkuh was able to make himself vizier. At his death his nephew Saladin succeeded his as vizier of Egypt. When the

[35]Krey, pp. 256 ff.
[36]Lewis, *The Arabs in History*, pp. 150-151.

last Fatimite caliph died in 1171, Saladin became its master. Three years later he became its sultan. Within another decade Saladin had joined the Moslem cities of Syria and Mesopotamia to Egypt, and the Latin Kingdom of Jerusalem knew that its time had come. In 1187, after destroying an army of crusaders near Nazareth, Saladin took Jerusalem, leaving finally to the Kingdom of Jerusalem proper only the city of Tyre.

THE THIRD CRUSADE

The fall of Jerusalem called forth the imposing Third Crusade from the West. It was led by the German emperor Frederick Barbarossa, the French king Philip Augustus, and the English king Richard the Lion-Hearted. Had they been able to fight together as a unit, these armies, especially if aided by the Byzantine Empire, could have re-established the Latin Kingdom of Jerusalem. As it was, Frederick took his strong and well-organized army overland to Constantinople, where it was diverted and harassed by the Byzantine emperor.[37] After horrible suffering, it had almost completed the journey across Asia Minor when it lost its leader in a quite anticlimactic bath in the Saleph that resulted in Frederick's death by drowning. Only a small remnant of the German army joined the troops of the squabbling French and English kings, who were aiding the king of Jerusalem in a siege of Acre. Acre was recovered for the kingdom on 12 July, 1191, and Joppa and Ascalon as well. Thereupon Philip returned home, leaving Richard with the task of recovering Jerusalem, a task he could not perform. Instead, in 1192, he concluded a truce, giving the king of Jerusalem the strip of coast from Joppa to Acre and granting Christian pilgrims free access to Jerusalem. When Saladin died, in 1193, Antioch and Tripoli, as well as the Joppa-Acre strip, were still in Christian hands.

THE CRUSADES OF THE THIRTEENTH CENTURY

The foundation of the Latin empire of Constantinople in the course of the so-called Fourth Crusade made the re-establishment of the Latin Kingdom of Jerusalem more difficult, for it divided the West's efforts and resources between the capitals of the two kingdoms and revealed some of the crasser motives behind the whole venture. The Sixth Crusade (the Fifth was the short-lived capture of Damietta in 1219) was conducted by the excommunicated German emperor Frederick II[38] in the form not of a military expedition but of diplomatic negotiations with the Egyptian sultan Al-Kamil, which outraged the more conservative souls of the West. As a result of the treaty with Egypt Jerusalem, Bethlehem, and Nazareth were to come into Christian hands, and the strip of land connecting Jerusalem with the coastal strip, composing what remained of the kingdom, was ceded to Frederick. These arrangements lasted for fifteen years

[37]See pp. 486–487.
[38]See p. 545.

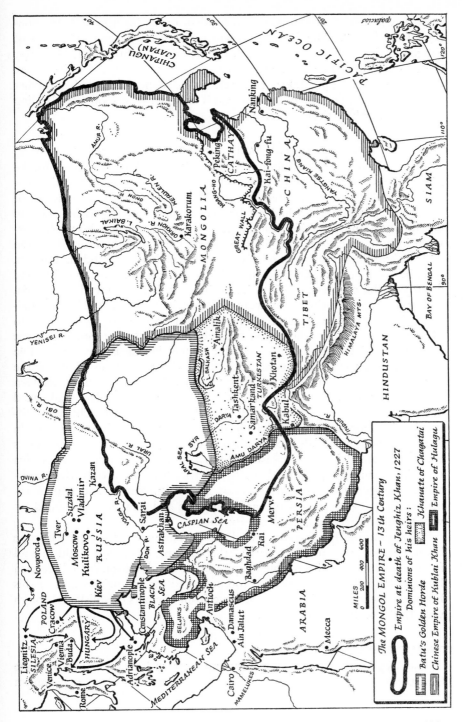

The MONGOL EMPIRE ~ 13th Century

● Empire at death of Jenghiz Khan, 1227

Dominions of his heirs :

▨ Batu's Golden Horde   ⬚ Ikhanate of Chagatai

▤ Chinese Empire of Kublai Khan   ▥ Empire of Hulagu

MILES
0   200   400   600

PACIFIC OCEAN

CHIPANGU (JAPAN)

CATHAY

Nanking

Peking

Kai-fong-fu

HOANG-HO

GREAT WALL

Karakorum

MONGOLIA

L. BAIKAL

AMUR R.

KERULEN R.

ONON R.

ORHON R.

YENISEI R.

CHINA

YANGTSE KIANG

TIBET

SIAM

BAY OF BENGAL

HIMALAYA MTS.

HINDUSTAN

INDUS R.

Kabul

Khotan

TURKESTAN

Samarkand

Tashkent

Amalik

L. BALKASH

SYR DARIA

AMU DARYA

OXUS

ARAL SEA

URAL R.

OB R.

IRTISH R.

Merv

Rai

PERSIA

Baghdad

Damascus

Antioch

Ain Jalut

MAMELUKES

Cairo

Mecca

ARABIA

MEDITERRANEAN SEA

SELJUKS

Constantinople

Adrianople

BLACK SEA

CASPIAN SEA

Astrakhan

Sarai

VOLGA R.

DON R.

Kazan

Vladimir

Suzdal

Moscow

Tver

Kulikovo

Kiev

RUSSIA

Novgorod

DVINA R.

Rome

Venice

Vienna

Buda

HUNGARY

POLAND

Cracow

SILESIA

Liegnitz

(1244), when Jerusalem reverted to Moslem hands for a period that continued until 1917. The fall of Jerusalem stirred Saint Louis, the king of France, to lead a further crusade to Egypt (the Seventh) in 1248. After the capture of Damietta, the crusaders, in a march toward Cairo, were defeated and the king taken prisoner. In 1270 he attempted a further attack upon Islam a little closer home in Tunis, but died soon after landing upon the North African shore.

THE MOSLEM CONQUEST OF THE LATIN KINGDOM OF JERUSALEM

The remnants of the Kingdom of Jerusalem fell into the hands of the Mameluke sultans of Egypt, who had risen to an important position because of their success in defending the Near East from new invasions of Mongols. Jenghiz Khan had established a huge and aggressive state in central Asia, and after his death (1227) the Mongolians advanced westward in two wings, one into the Russian steppes[39] and the other into Iran against the Seljuk Turks, the protectors of the caliphs at Baghdad. Hulagu, a nephew of Jenghiz, defeated the Seljuks at Baghdad, took the city, and destroyed the caliphate (1258). The Mongols then advanced into Syria, taking Christian Antioch but were defeated in Palestine (1260) by Baibars, the Mameluke general of Egypt, and forced to withdraw into Mesopotamia. Baibars thereupon became sultan of Egypt and began the reconquest of Palestine and Syria, including the Christian states. The conquest was completed by his successors with the taking of Acre, the last Christian stronghold in the East (1291). The first fruits of western expansion into the Near East, the Latin Kingdom of Jerusalem, had lasted in some form for two centuries (1099-1291). This ultimate Christian failure in the East was counterbalanced, however, by ultimate success in Spain. Although the advance of the eleventh and early twelfth centuries was interrupted by a fresh invasion of fanatical Berbers from North Africa (the Almohades), by the end of the thirteenth century only the southeastern Kingdom of Granada was left in Moslem hands, and here it remained until 1492. In this reconquest Castile and Aragon were aided by western crusaders from across the Pyrenees.

The Byzantine Empire influenced the development of western Europe because it possessed briefly a part of that Europe. As much could be said for the influence of the Arabic Empire upon the development of western Europe, for in Sicily and Spain it too possessed for centuries a part of this Europe. In each case the influence came from contacts established through war, trade, and ordinary travel.

ECONOMIC RESULTS OF THE CRUSADES

The Moslem threat to Christianity and western Europe helped to make Christianity aggressively militant, a trait stimulated also by the paganism

[39]See p. 493.

of Europe. It even transformed the western monk into a fighting knight through the military orders.[40] Nor did the centuries of intermittent warfare between Moslem and Christian hinder the efforts of the western, especially Italian, towns to open up the East to western trade. Here mutual economic advantage broke down religious hostility. Indeed, Mohammed had been careful to exalt the merchant, he himself having been one. "In the day of Judgment," he said, "the honest truthful Moslem merchant will take rank with the martyrs of the faith."[41] Saladin told the caliph in Baghdad that "the Venetians, the Genoese and the Pisans bring into Egypt choice products of the west, especially arms and war material. This constitutes an advantage for Islam and an injury for Christianity." While it is true that western Europe had begun to experience an economic revival long before the actual beginning of the Crusades to the East, nevertheless the urbanization and social mobility that the Crusades helped to bring about speeded up this revival. When once established, trade was not necessarily lost with the loss of the Latin Kingdom of Jerusalem. The Fourth Crusade introduced the Italian towns into the Black Sea region whence they had further contacts with the Far East. Not only by promoting urban development in the West was Moslem trade of consequence. Eastern goods, of a higher quality and technical perfection, stimulated western imitation. Such important things as paper, silk, the astrolabe, and the compass came from this trade, and the English vocabulary was itself enriched by such Arabic words as *check*, *magazine*, *risk*, *tariff*, *traffic*, *average*, and *admiral*.

MOSLEM OPINIONS OF WESTERNERS

The Mohammedan East influenced the Christian West in a still more fundamental way. In conquering the neighboring lands of Persia, Syria, Palestine, and Egypt, the Arabs were taking over lands whose culture was the original source of our western tradition and in most respects far richer and more complicated than the, at that time, rather primitive western culture. The fact that the Arabs introduced into this area a new religion and the Arabic language did not alter this situation. They were culturally superior to the West, and they knew it. A tenth-century Moslem geographer thought that the northern climate had contributed to the inferiority of the westerner. "The warm humour is lacking among them; their bodies are large, their natures gross, their manners harsh, their understanding dull and their tongues heavy . . . their religious beliefs lack solidity . . . those of them who are farthest to the north are the most subject to stupidity, grossness and brutishness." This opinion was confirmed by a Toledan scholar of the eleventh century, who, in describing "northern barbarians," wrote, "their bellies are big, their colour pale, their hair long and lank. They

[40]See p. 599.
[41]Lewis, pp. 91, 153.

lack keenness of understanding and clarity of intelligence, and are over-come by ignorance and foolishness, blindness and stupidity." And one of the most distinguished of Moslem historical scholars, Ibn Khaldun, doubted, as late as the fourteenth century, whether the West was con-cerned with anything that could be called learning. "We have heard of late," he wrote, "that in the lands of the Franks, that is, the country of Rome and its dependencies on the northern shore of the Mediterranean, the philosophic sciences flourish . . . and their students are plentiful. But God knows what goes on in those parts."[42]

TRANSLATIONS FROM HINDU AND GREEK INTO ARABIC

By the fourteenth century, western learning had begun to surpass the Moslem, but that it was doing so was only because of the help given earlier by Moslem scholars. Even before the migration of the Arabs, Christian scholars, Monophysites and Nestorians under the patronage of Persian monarchs, had begun to translate Hindu mathematics from Sanskrit into Persian and Greek geometry, astronomy, logic, and medicine from Greek into Syriac, and in cases from Syriac into Persian. Under the patronage of the caliphs at Baghdad in the late eighth and early ninth cen-turies, Nestorian Christians in well-established schools of translation rendered this material into Arabic, the new international language of the eastern world. To be more specific: in 772 a Hindu astronomer came to Baghdad bringing with him treatises on mathematics and astronomy. The works on astronomy, the earliest of Hindu scholarship, translated into Arabic by Ibrahim Al-Fazari (d. *ca.* 777), inaugurated the Arabic study of astronomy. More important is the fact that this translation introduced the Hindu numerals into Arabic. From it they were incorporated into the works of the noted mathematician Al-Kwarizmi (d. *ca.* 850), and from Al-Kwarizmi western scholars took them as "Arabic" numerals. From the first word of the title of Al-Kwarizmi's most important work on mathe-matics, Al-Jabr w-al-Muga-balah (Restoration and Equation), comes our word *algebra*.[43] Al-Kwarizmi in turn influenced the Persian mathematician Omar Khayyám, whom westerners know better as a poet from Edward Fitzgerald's translation of his *Rubáiyát*. In this way Moslem scholars learned from Hindu scholars their arithmetic, algebra, and trigonometry. Much of Greek learning was translated into Arabic, that is, the medical works of Hippocrates and Galen, Euclid's *Geometry*, Ptolemy's *Almagest*, and almost all Aristotle's works on logic and philosophy.

THE TRANSLATION OF ARABIC WORKS INTO LATIN

Upon this foundation, not so much Arab as Moslem, scholars built an impressive edifice of new learning. They did original work in algebra

[42]Lewis, p. 165.
[43]See E. J. Jurgi, *The Arab Heritage*, ed. N. A. Faris, p. 230.

and were "the founders of plane and spherical trigonometry" as well as of analytical geometry. They did distinguished work in other branches of science, in physics, for example, alchemy, astronomy, and, above all, medicine. The *Canon of Medicine* of Avicenna (979-1037), which brought together the work of Greek and Arabic medicine, was long a textbook in the West. Arabic scholars were close students of Aristotle, and many Christian scholars came to regard as indispensable the commentaries of the Spanish Moslem Averroës (d. 1198). As he moved into Mohammedan lands, first of all those of the West itself, Sicily and Spain, and then those of the Near East, the westerner found these riches of Arabic civilization. When he discovered in the libraries of Spain and Sicily both Greek and Arabic treasures that he never knew existed or was only dimly aware of, he realized that he was only a beginner and must make these treasures his own in order to compare with the mature Moslem scholar. Since the westerner knew no Arabic, he had to arrange for the translation of these works into a language he knew, namely, Latin. The translations in the twelfth century of Greek and Moslem works into Latin provided a tremendous stimulus to western learning. With the works themselves came the intellectual zeal that went into their making, and this zeal was instrumental in producing the western university and western science. Having lost its Greek, the West, in the form of Latin translations from the Arabic, regained a knowledge of part of the Greek heritage some three centuries before it could once more appropriate this heritage directly through a knowledge of Greek. Together with his art, literature, and music, the learning and craftsmanship of the infidel was, before the Italian Renaissance, the greatest stimulus to the maturity of western Europe.

The Slavs and the West

SLAVIC SETTLEMENT OF THE BALKANS

By the beginning of the sixth century the Slavs had reached the middle and lower Danube, the boundaries of the Byzantine Empire; and after Justinian's reign and in the following (seventh) century they poured into the Balkan peninsula under the impulsion, in part, of two Mongolian peoples, the Bulgars and the Avars. The Bulgars, a minority of nomadic Mongolian conquerors lording it over a Slavic majority, settled below the lower Danube, and in the course of time were completely absorbed by their Slavic subjects, abandoning their Bulgar language for a Slav tongue and developing as a Slavic people. Slavic tribes penetrated into the region of ancient Macedonia and Thrace and deep into Greece and the Peloponnesus, where they were soon absorbed by a Greek majority. Under the impulsion of the Avars, who succeeded the Bulgars in the steppes, additional Slavs moved into the northwestern part of the Balkan peninsula. For a time the Avars dominated a huge empire, including not only the steppes and the Balkan peninsula but Slavic peoples stretching from the Adriatic to the Baltic seas. Below the Danube and east of the Bavarians, in the area of present-day Austria and reaching beyond the headwaters of the Drave and Save rivers into Istria, the Slovenes settled. Beyond them, reaching from the Dalmatian coast to the middle valleys of the Drave and Save, the Croats settled, and in an area stretching from the Illyrian coast to the Danube, the Serbs. When Charlemagne crushed the Avar power, the Slavs north and south of the Danube were liberated. The Magyars[44] succeeded the Avars upon the steppes. When the Magyars occupied the lower Danube, invaded central Europe, and then settled down in Hungary, they drove a wedge between the Slavs north and south of the Danube. The Balkan Slavs thus came to be called the southern Slavs and those north of the Danube the western and the eastern Slavs.

EXPANSION OF WESTERN AND EASTERN SLAVS

The western Slavs are the Czechs (Bohemians), Moravians, Slovaks, Poles, Wends, and Lithuanians. The eastern Slavs are the various groups of Russians. On the southern shore of the Baltic Sea, between the Wends west of the Vistula and the Russians east of Lake Peipus, were a group of non-Slavic peoples called Balts, namely, the Prussians and the Letts, and a group of Finnish peoples: the Livs, Kurs, and Esthonians. Originally the Lithuanians were Balts but were absorbed by the Slavs, whom they conquered, and with whom they intermarried. Except for the Poles and Lithuanians the western Slavs spread to lands from which the Germans had migrated. The Poles, cut off from the Baltic by the Prussians, expanded from territory on the middle Vistula belonging to the original Slavic homeland. The Czechs, Moravians, and Slovaks moved into the abandoned former home of the Marcomanni and Quadi. The Wends, a general term referring to those many Slavic tribes moving westward across the Vistula as far as the Elbe and Saale rivers, which separated them from the Saxons, were occupying lands once traversed by Goths and inhabited before their migration by such German tribes as the Burgundians, Vandals, and Lombards. By the sixth century the eastern, or Russian, Slavs had moved northward from the original Slavic homeland down the valleys of the Niemen and the Dvina toward the Baltic, from which they were cut off by the Lithuanians, Letts, Livs, and Esths; northeastward toward the Gulf of Finland, until they ran into the Finnish people; eastward in the direction of Moscow; and southeastward in the direction of the Black Sea and the Don River.

SLAVS BETWEEN WEST AND EAST

The expansion of the Slavs brought them into contact with the two contrasting European civilizations: the one—the Latin West—represented by

[44]See p. 384.

the Roman church and the German, or Holy Roman, Empire; the other—the Greek East—represented by the Greek Orthodox church and the Byzantine Empire. Further, the Slav world was strongly influenced by Turko-Mongolian invasions which followed the Magyars, notably, those of the Tartars of Jenghiz Khan and of the Ottoman Turks. As the Mediterranean world had become divided into Christian and Moslem, and the Christian world itself had divided into West and East, so the Slavic world came to be divided culturally into a West and an East, depending upon whether it was converted to Christianity by the Roman church or by the Orthodox church. Only a few Slavs in the Balkans were ever converted to Islam. Since the respective churches were the important civilizers, the acceptance of a particular type of Christianity determined other features of Slavic civilization. Roman Catholic Slavs used the Latin alphabet to write their languages; Greek Orthodox, the Cyrillic, invented by disciples of Cyril (Constantine). The competition between western and eastern churches for conversion of the Slavs was certainly one factor driving the two branches of Christianity into schism.

ONSTANTINE AND METHODIUS IN MORAVIA

The competition can be well illustrated by the story of the conversion of the Moravians. In this case an aggressive ninth-century Carolingian empire, anxious to subject the Czechs and the Moravians, and supported by an ambitious Bavarian church, was resisted by a Moravian prince supported by missionaries sent out from Constantinople. The prince in this case was one Rostislav. To counteract the efforts of German missionaries from Salzburg, Regensburg, and Passau, he asked Constantinople for missionaries who could use the Slavic tongue (862), inasmuch as, unlike Rome, the Byzantine church was quite willing to permit the translation of the liturgy into the vernacular. He was sent two brothers, Constantine (Cyril) and Methodius, who had learned their Slavic in Macedonia. Of these Constantine at least conceived of the mission to Moravia in large terms. Just as Ulfilas had been responsible for translating the Scriptures into Gothic,[45] and Bede had turned the Fourth Gospel into Anglo-Saxon, Constantine meant to use the mission to make the Moravians literate. He invented an alphabet to use in translating into Slavic and himself translated passages from the gospels into the Slavic dialect he knew (a Bulgarian dialect). This was the start of a Slavic literature. When he arrived in Moravia (863), Constantine translated also the whole Latin liturgy into Slavic. In order to preclude the entrance of Moravia into the Byzantine church, Pope Adrian II summoned the brothers to Rome and authorized their use of the Slavic liturgy. After the death of Constantine in 869, he also made Methodius archbishop of Pannonia and papal legate to all the Slavs.

---

[45]See p. 283.

The appointment was more than the German clergy working in Moravia could take. Upon his return to his new see, Methodius was arrested and brought before a court of German bishops who chose to ignore his new position. One of them, the bishop of Passau, struck Methodius with his whip. The papacy intervened to restrain these Christian bishops and again, after some vacillation on the point, permitted the Slavic liturgy. After Methodius's death (885) his disciple and successor, Gorozd, and all the other Greek priests were driven out of Moravia, and some found themselves in the Venetian slave market. The work of Constantine and Methodius was undone; Czechs, Moravians, and Slovaks entered the western Latin Roman church under German auspices.

Nonetheless the efforts of Constantine and Methodius had not been completely in vain. Prince Boris of Bulgaria had decided in 862 to become a Christian and to lead his people to Christianity. A bitter fight between Rome and Constantinople ensued over which church the Bulgarians should enter. When Methodius's disciples were driven out of Moravia they were sent to Bulgaria to strengthen the hand of the Byzantine church there. Under Boris's son Simeon (d. 927) these missionaries, headed by one Clement, now made a bishop, founded a Slavic Christian literature in Bulgarian, using Byzantine sources. When the Russians finally turned to Christianity (989) this Bulgarian literature was introduced into Russia to become the foundation of Russian literature. The Serbs, as well as the Bulgarians, became Greek Orthodox Christians. The Slovenes and the Croats were converted by German and Italian Roman Catholic missionaries. Besides the Czechs, Moravians, and Slovaks, the Poles and Lithuanians also became Roman Christians, and the Russians, Greek. Thus the Slavic world was divided between the eastern and western churches: the Russians, Bulgarians, and Serbs adhering to Constantinople; the Croats, Slovenes, Czechs, Moravians, Slovaks, Poles, and Lithuanians adhering to Rome.

INFLUENCE OF BYZANTIUM UPON THE SLAVS

With the exception of the Croats and Slovenes, all the southern and eastern Slavs, through their adoption of Greek orthodoxy, were subjected to the cultural influence of Byzantium. This cultural influence was primarily that of the Greek church, whose essential mysticism and contemplative asceticism in the form of the Basilian monastery thus spread to the Slavs. The early vernacular literature of these peoples was likewise scriptural, theological, and liturgical; their art the architecture and icon painting of the Byzantine church. From the Byzantine church came, in addition, the veneration of the ruler as the agent of God and a willingness to be subject to his will in religious matters, to recognize the ruler as pope as well as caesar (caesaropapism). Shortly after these peoples were converted to eastern Christianity, the western and eastern churches separated

(1054), and the ensuing hostility was transmitted to the Slavs, who, partly as a result, were cut off from the West. However much we may admire certain aspects of the civilization of Byzantium it is quite certain that neither the Byzantine state nor church was able to do for the Slavs what the Roman church was able to do for the Romanized West. This inability of Byzantium helps to explain the present day divergence between East and West. The only secular equivalent to the Byzantine Empire in the West was the German, or Holy Roman, Empire. There was no Charlemagne in the East to bring together all the Slavs in eastern Europe as he brought together all the Germans. The Byzantine emperors before 1204 were always too harassed from both European and Asiatic sides to sustain an activity comparable to that of the emperors of the revived German empire (after 962). The Byzantine church was unable to bring to the Slavs, as the Roman church brought to the Germans, the tradition of classical learning, whether Greek or Latin. The Greek monastery was unable to develop the vitality of the Benedictine and subsequent western orders.[46] The Slavs were not enriched by outside contacts with western Europe and Asia as the West was enriched by Byzantium and Islam. The Mohammedan peoples who dominated the East, Turks and Tartars, were primitive peoples who did not develop a civilization comparable to that of the Arabs. The southern and eastern Slavs under the influence of Byzantium did not, therefore, have the rich cultural experience of western Europe in the twelfth and thirteenth centuries.[47] The southern and eastern Slavs were to have nothing corresponding to the Renaissance and Reformation of the West. At the moment when in the West theocracy, whether in political or ecclesiastical form, was being discredited[48] and a rigid class structure being somewhat broken up, theocracy in the form of tsardom was increasing its strength in the East, and the peasants were being bound to the soil as serfs. The civilization that Byzantium had to pass on to the Slavs has been described as follows:

"In intellectual and literary matters the Eastern Empire was conservative. It studied the past without rivaling it with the products of contemporary creative imagination. It was compilatory rather than original. Byzantine scholars were the most learned men of their day, but their learning was accumulative, not productive. Byzantine historians composed voluminous chronicles without evolving a philosophy of history, while Byzantine theologians dissipated their energy on amenities of dogma, argued with a bitterness which we should nowadays associate only with partisan politics. The Byzantine church was more political than the Roman, more closely affiliated with the state, and hence less fundamentally spiritual in outlook. The literary tradition transmitted by the Byzantine church was stiff and formalistic."[49]

[46]See pp. 594 ff.
[47]See Chaps. xiv, xv.
[48]See Chaps. xii, xiii.
[49]Samuel H. Cross, *Slavic Civilization through the Ages*, p. 101.

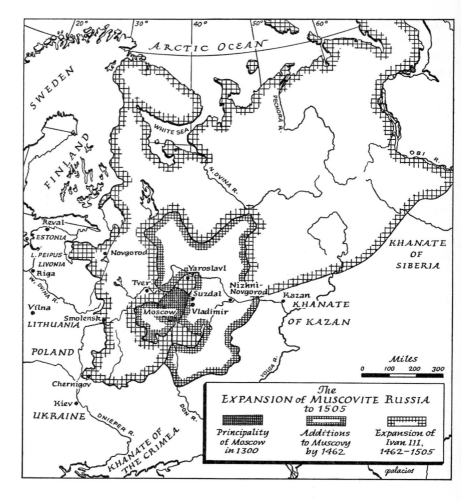

The map shows coordinates 20°, 30°, 40°, 50°, 60°

ARCTIC OCEAN

SWEDEN

FINLAND

WHITE SEA

N. DVINA R.

PECHORA R.

OBI R.

Reval

ESTONIA

L. PEIPUS

LIVONIA

Riga

W. DVINA R.

Vilna

Smolensk

LITHUANIA

POLAND

Novgorod

Yaroslavl

Tver

Suzdal

Nizhni-
Novgorod

Moscow

Vladimir

Kazan

KHANATE
OF
SIBERIA

KHANATE
OF KAZAN

VOLGA R.

Chernigov

Kiev

UKRAINE

DNIEPER R.

DON R.

KHANATE OF
THE CRIMEA

Miles

0 100 200 300

The
EXPANSION of MUSCOVITE RUSSIA
to 1505

Principality
of Moscow
in 1300

Additions
to Muscovy
by 1462

Expansion of
Ivan III,
1462–1505

palacios

RUSSIA AND THE MONGOLS

The fate of Russia under Byzantine influence is of supreme importance to us because of Russia's contemporary leadership of the eastern world. We have already pointed out that anything that might be called a Russian state emerged only in the ninth century under the leadership of immigrant Swedish Vikings (the original Rus) who founded the Duchy of Kiev. It was another century before the Russian Slavs under Vladimir, having absorbed the Swedes, accepted Christianity from Constantinople (989). That Kiev had finally to yield to Moscow as the future capital of the Russian state was largely the result of the invasion of Jenghiz Khan's Mongols or Tartars into the Russian steppes.[50] They came under Jenghiz' nephew Batu and destroyed Kiev in 1240. In the following year a

[50]See p. 493.

502 CHAPTER ELEVEN

northern wing moved as far west as Silesia, and a southern one through Hungary to the headwaters of the Adriatic and as far west as Vienna. These prongs proved impermanent. Meanwhile Batu's Golden Horde, after subjecting every important Russian town except Novgorod to the treatment given Kiev, established its capital at Sarai on the Volga River, and for over two centuries maintained its dominion over the Russian Slavs. It could not rule them directly, but it obliged the Russian princes to become its vassals, pay for the privilege of governing their states, and bring personally to Sarai the special head tax collected from their subjects. The princes of Moscow eventually freed the Russians from this Tartar overlordship, subjecting them in the process to their own domination. The Mongols were first beaten by a Muscovite prince, Dmitri Donskoy, in 1380 at Kulikovo. By 1412 these princes ceased bringing the Russian tribute to Sarai. In 1480 Ivan III (1462–1505) finally destroyed the power of the Golden Horde. This same Ivan married Zoë Palaeologus, the niece of the last emperor of Byzantium.

MONGOLIAN INFLUENCE UPON THE RUSSIANS

The two centuries of Mongolian dominance over Russia left an unfortunate inheritance with the Russian state and people. The Mongols, although they became Mohammedan, had no such treasures to offer the Slavs as the Arabs offered the Spaniards or the Germans of the West. Instead, they fortified the tradition of Byzantine theocracy with the example of their own cruel and uncivilized tyranny. The princes of Moscow became the successors of the Mongolian khans. During these centuries the Russian church was raised to an independent power, possessed of enormous wealth and of such great influence that no princely family could hope to dominate without its support. In the fifteenth century the metropolitan moved the seat of this church to Moscow and threw in its lot with the growing autocratic tsardom of the Muscovite princes. If Russian tsars came to insist not only upon their position as theocrats but upon the ownership of all Russian soil, the idea was in origin probably Mongolian. Their tax and military systems they borrowed from the Mongols. The use of torture, of the whip, the seclusion of women, and the inhumanity of superior to inferior have been attributed directly to Mongol influence.[51] What supplanted the influence of Byzantium upon the Russians was the influence of the Tartar. Although Russia, just emerging from Tartar domination, regarded herself, after the Byzantine Empire had been destroyed by the Turks (1453), as a "third Rome," she was in fact a primitive oriental autocracy embellished with the court ceremonial of a long-decadent Byzantine state. By this date the Russian church had come to look upon itself as the only supporter of the true Greek orthodoxy, for in 1438 the Byzantine church had proved itself traitorous by negotiating a

[51] See Cross, "Foundations of Russian Culture," *Slavic Civilization.*

union with the western Roman church at Ferrara-Florence.[52] "Moscow became not only . . . 'the third Rome,' but 'the second Jerusalem,' and 'the second Noah's Ark,' the sole guardian and repository of true orthodoxy; and Russia became 'Holy Russia,' signifying the ideal of complete and unconditional loyalty to the faith accepted, a conception of orthodoxy somewhat akin to the orthodoxy of communism."[53]

THE GERMAN ADVANCE EASTWARD

If the southern and eastern Slavs were the children of the Byzantine church and state, the western Slavs were the children of the Roman church and the German state. We have mentioned that the Croats, Slovenes, Czechs, Moravians, Slovaks, Poles, and Lithuanians became western Roman Christians. As such they were subjected to the influence of the more advanced civilization of the West. This civilization came not only through the Latin church but also through the Germans who moved into Slavic territory as conquerors and colonists.[54] The result of this German march eastward was ultimately a national reaction among the Slavs, who in the fifteenth century put a temporary end to the German eastward expansion. The animosity aroused during these centuries between German and Slav has continued to date, being intensified by subsequent events, and the fact that those western Slavs who became western Christians (Lithuanians, Poles, Czecho-Slovaks) are now satellites of Soviet Russian has something to do with this old antagonism. The nature of the German advance can best be illustrated by the history of the German expansion along the southern shores of the Baltic against the Slavic Wends, the Baltic Prussians and Letts, and the Finnish Livs, Kurs, and Esths. Elsewhere the advance of the Germans in Slavic territory was among Christian citizens of an already organized Slavic state. As a result of German colonization of the Ostmark[55] (Austria), the Slovenes were ultimately restricted to the extreme southern area south of the Drave River in Carinthia. In medieval Bohemia and Poland German colonization could be controlled by strong local princes and the central state itself. But along the southern shores of the Baltic there was no strong state to resist successfully the German church and the German people.

EXTINCTION OF THE WENDS

By the sixth century the Wends had moved as far west as the Elbe-Saale rivers dividing them from the Saxons. Charlemagne, after the conquest and forceful Christianization of the Saxons, prepared the way for the advance against the pagan Slavs by setting up marches on this frontier in much the same way as, by setting up the Spanish March, he inaugurated

[52]See p. 633.
[53]B. H. Summer, *Survey of Russian History*, p. 186.
[54]See pp. 507 f.
[55]See pp. 380 f.

the crusade against the Moors. The advance against the pagan Wends beyond the Elbe-Saale must be looked upon as a kind of crusade. Led at first by Saxons who themselves had been converted at the point of the sword, this crusade abandoned earlier methods of peaceful conversion and relied upon force. When even these methods did not suffice German princes finally realized that the Wends must be either exterminated, enslaved, or assimilated by the wholesale introduction of German colonists. The result has been that of the Wends originally inhabiting the area between the Elbe-Saale and the Vistula only two small groups survive, the Kashubs, northwest of Danzig on the Baltic coast, and the Sorbs, northeast of Leipzig on the Spree River. In the course of this bitter struggle nasty feelings were aroused, based not only upon constant warfare, but also upon differences between Christian and pagan, between those enjoying a more and a less advanced civilization, and even upon nationality differences between German and Slav. These attitudes, reinforced constantly by subsequent centuries, still persist. The ordinary German has no very high opinion of the Slav, and this feeling is in most instances heartily reciprocated.

REVOLTS OF THE WENDS

Until the middle of the twelfth century German efforts to conquer and Christianize the Wends were largely in vain and precipitated embittered revolts. The Wends resisted stubbornly the loss of their political independence, their pagan religion, their primitive customs, and their personal freedom. The efforts of the German king Otto I (936–973) to advance beyond the Elbe to the Oder were answered by the revolt of 983, which wiped out all the progress hitherto made on this frontier. The chronicler of this and of the subsequent revolts, Helmold, a parish priest in Slav territory at Bosau in the twelfth century, says of the Slavs in the early eleventh century that "they were pursued by the margrave [Dietrich] and Duke Bernhard [of Saxony] with such cruelty that they finally threw off the yoke of servitude, and had to take up arms in defense of their freedom." The revolt is described by Helmold: The Slavs "wasted first the whole of Nordalbingia with fire and sword. Then, roving about the rest of Slavia, they burned all the churches and destroyed them even to the ground. They murdered the priests and the other ministers of the churches with diverse tortures and left not a vestige of Christianity beyond the Elbe. At Hamburg, then and later, many clerics and citizens were led off into captivity and many more were put to death through hatred of Christianity." At Oldenburg "sixty priests (the rest had been slaughtered like cattle) were kept as objects of derision. The oldest of these . . . and others were martyred in this manner. After the skin of their heads had been cut in the form of a cross, the brain of each man was laid bare with an iron. With hands tied behind their backs, the confessors of God were then dragged through one Slavic town after another until they died . . . there were so many martyrs in Slavia that they can hardly be enumerated in a book. All the Slavs who dwelt between the Elbe and Oder and who had practiced the Christian religion . . . during the whole time of the reigns of the Ottos, in this manner cut themselves off from the body of Christ and of the Church with which they had before been united."[56]

A third revolt came in 1066. It was again precipitated according to Helmold by the "insatiable greed of the Saxons who . . . are ever more intent upon increasing the tribute than upon winning souls for the Lord. Through the perseverance of the priests Christianity would long ago have grown in the esteem of Slavia if the avarice of the Saxons had not stood in the way." In the course of this revolt an aged bishop John, "who had out of his love for roving come from Ireland to Saxony . . . was taken with other Christians in Magnopolis [Mecklenburg] and held for a triumph. And because he confessed Christ he was beaten with rods and then was led in mockery through one city of the Slavs after another. Since he could not be turned from the profession of Christ his hands and feet were lopped off and his body was thrown into the road. His head, however, the barbarians cut off, fixed on a spear and offered to their God Redigast in token of their victory. . . . And so all the Slavs who were sworn to a general conspiracy lapsed again into paganism after they had killed those who persisted in the faith. . . . And the see of Oldenburg was vacant for eighty-four years."[57]

SLAVIC CRUSADE OF 1147

Before resorting to large-scale colonization, in the realization that the Wend territory could never rest permanently under German or Christian control so long as it remained basically Slavic, one more effort was made to Christianize the Wends forcefully, the so-called Crusade of 1147—the Slavic counterpart of the Second Crusade to the East. For those Saxons who felt they could not go eastward because of the Slav danger at home, a crusade against the Wends was to be made the equal in spiritual rewards of the more difficult crusade to the East. Saint Bernard[58] gave it a watch-word: "Either the Wends or their religion are to be wiped out." Although Czechs and Poles and Swabians joined the Saxon army, and a Danish fleet stood by, nothing could be accomplished against the outraged and furious Slavs. "The Slavs," Helmold remarks, "immediately afterward became worse." (p. 181)

CHRISTIAN COLONIZATION OF WEND LANDS

Helmold reports on the colonization introduced by the Saxon nobles and the Saxon church into the lands of the Wends. It came not only from Saxony itself but beyond it, from those regions of Holland and Flanders

[56]*The Chronicle of the Slavs*, trans. F. J. Tschan, pp. 83–85.
[57]Ibid., pp. 95–99.
[58]See p. 596.

where men knew how to build dikes and drain marshes. He reports that Count Adolf of Holstein "sent messengers into all parts, namely, to Flanders and Holland, to Utrecht, Westphalia, and Frisia, proclaiming that all whosoever were in straits for lack of fields should come with their families [to Wagria] and receive a very good land,—a spacious land, rich in crops, abounding in fish and flesh and exceeding good pasturage." By the time Helmold finished his *Chronicle of the Slavs* (1172) the work of colonization was well on its way. He writes that "all the country of the Slavs, beginning at the Eider . . . and extending between the Baltic Sea and the Elbe River in a most lengthy sweep to Schwerin . . . was now through the help of God all made, as it were, into one colony of Saxons. And cities and villages grew up there and churches were built and the number of the ministers of Christ multiplied." "All the land of the Abodrites and the neighboring regions which belong to the realm of the Abodrites, had been wholly reduced to a solitude through unremitting warfare. . . . If there were any last remnants of Slavs remaining, they were on account of the want of grain and the desolation of the fields so reduced by hunger that they had to flee together to the Pomeranians and to the Danes, who, showing them no mercy, sold them to the Poles, Sorbs and Bohemians." "The Slavs who lived in the villages round about [Wagria] withdrew and Saxons came and dwelt there; and the Slavs little by little failed in the land." "Now . . . because God gave plentiful aid and victory to our Duke and to the other princes, the Slavs have been everywhere crushed and driven out. A people strong and without number have come from the bounds of the ocean, and taken possession of the territories of the Slavs. They have built cities and churches and have grown in riches beyond all estimation." (pp. 168, 281, 262, 225, 235–236)

RESULTS OF GERMAN COLONIZATION

By the end of the twelfth century the Wend territory between the Elbe and the Vistula had been taken over by German principalities, Holstein, Mecklenburg, Brandenburg, and Pomerania. The stream of German colonists was spilling over into Silesia, Bohemia, and Poland and was ready to make an assault upon Prussia and the Baltic lands. Beyond the Oder, at least, it was no longer necessary to push this movement by the sword. Slavic princes in Pomerania and Silesia sometimes welcomed into their lands the efficient and hard-working German colonists. Although the Slavs were no longer to be slaughtered, they were expected to become Christian, politically docile, and, if they did not wish to be expelled from their holdings, efficient, hard-working peasants. A Germanized, assimilated Slav soon appeared in the official documents. But German dominance meant, if not total extermination, then at least the partial extermination of a people and, with assimilation, the almost complete extermination of the Slavic culture, such as it was. Western Christianity in its highly organized secular and regular forms triumphed, bringing its stone churches, its elaborate services, its music, its art, and its tradition of learning. The Germans also brought the territorial state and the feudal institutions of the West, German law, the German town, a superior military, industrial, and mining technology, superior arts and crafts, and, to mention no more, a superior, even specialized, agriculture, using an iron rather than a wooden plow. To establish a more broadly balanced perspective, it is no longer sufficient merely to listen to the hopeful voices of the German colonists singing "to the East land we shall ride," and to exult in the eastward march of western Christian civilization. One is obliged to try to see the faces and understand the hearts of the Slav peasants as they watched the new colonists crowd in and threaten with extinction, if no longer themselves as persons, then certainly their way of life. One must listen to the sentiments of Slavic leaders who hated and reviled what was going on, and whose voices reverberated down the centuries. Helmold heard the reply of a Prince Pribislav to Bishop Gerold of Oldenburg, when of the Slavs assembled in the marketplace of Lübeck the bishop demanded that "they give up their idols and worship the one God who is in heaven." The Slavic prince said, "How shall we, ensnared by so many evils, enter upon this way? . . . Your princes rage against us with such severity that, because of the taxes and most burdensome services, death is better for us than life . . . every day we are outdone and oppressed even to the point of our exhaustion. . . . Were there but a place to which we could flee!" "You all know," said another Slavic leader to a group of his fellow countrymen, "what great calamities and what oppression have come upon our people through the violent might which the duke [of Saxony] has exerted against us. He has taken from us the inheritance of our fathers and settled foreigners in all its bounds—Flemings and Hollanders, Saxons and Westphalians, and diverse folk . . . no one save me is left who thinks of the good of our nation or wishes to raise up its ruins. Again pluck up your courage. . . . O men who are the remnants of the Slavic race, resume your daring spirit." (pp. 220, 256)

THE CONQUEST OF LIVONIA

In order to continue their advance against the pagan Balts (Prussians and Letts) and the pagan (Finnish) Livs, Kurs, and Esths, the Germans again had to use force in the form of another crusade. Albert of Bremen, the extraordinary bishop who conquered Livonia, a young, vigorous, and tough-minded Saxon noble, had learned from his two predecessors in Livonia how not to Christianize the pagans. The first of these had made clear to the Livonians that by accepting Christianity they would learn how to build the stone fortifications of the West and thus protect themselves from their Lithuanian enemies. But he had no troops and became a virtual prisoner of the Livs. His successor, Berthold, brought with him on his second journey to Livonia a Saxon army prepared to deal, he told the Livs, with "dogs" who had returned "to their vomit." The Livs asked him to send his army back to Saxony and to instruct them with "words and not with blows." He would not, and in the ensuing war the bishop was killed; "two of the Livonians surrounded him, a third, Ymaut by name, pierced him from the back with a lance, and others tore him to pieces." When the Saxon army withdrew after what it regarded as a general pacification those Livs who had received baptism concluded that this Christianity which had been so easily imposed with water could be as easily washed off and rushed to submerge themselves in the Dvina. Albert accordingly came with a well-organized plan of subjection. The conquest was to be entrusted to crusaders annually recruited from the West and to a standing army composed of the bishop's retainers and a new military order, the Brothers of the Militia of Christ, better known as the Livonian Brothers of the Sword. The powerful commercial interests behind the conquest and the occupation were to be secured by the creation of a permanent urban colony at the mouth of the Dvina, namely, Riga. Recruited from the North German cities, this colony would furnish a militia to supplement the permanent military establishment and would act as the capital city of the enterprise. Albert, an independent bishop in Livonia, was to transform a group of primitive communities of Finnish and Baltic peoples into a western church-state, a theocracy in miniature.

CONQUEST OF ESTHONIA

This machine quickly set to work to conquer and Christianize the Livs and the Letts. Then, with the enforced help of these, it turned eastward against the Esths, or Esthonians. The vicious character of these campaigns is well illustrated by the eyewitness chronicler Henry of Livonia. He describes the villages in Esthonia before these invasions as very beautiful, prosperous, and well populated. After them Esthonia was reduced to a wasteland. This is how the Germans converted the Esths to Christianity: "Moving into Saccala [an Esthonian province], the Christian army found the men, women, and little children in their homes in all the villages and localities. From morning until night the men killed those whom they found, the women as well as the children. They killed three hundred of the more prominent and leading men of the province and innumerable others until their hands and arms, because of excessive slaughter of the people, tired and failed them. All the villages were colored with the abundant blood of the pagans. On the following day they returned and collected much spoil in all the villages, oxen, cattle, and a great many little girls. They led them all back with them into their lands. . . . They killed here and there until, completely worn out, they and their horses with them, they could kill no more, and so with great joy they returned to Livonia, blessing God for the vengeance granted us against the pagans."[59]

[59]The quotations from Henry of Livonia are from a translation by J. A. Brundage in the library of the University of Nebraska.

The German and Christian domination in these Esthonian lands was set up over a waste of slaughtered natives and burned-out villages.

The conquest of Livonia and Esthonia brought the Germans into first-hand contact with the Russians, who had imposed tribute upon some Livs and introduced Greek Christianity in some areas. As the German power grew, and the resistance of the Livs and Esths became more desperate, the Russian princes of the region allied themselves with the revolting natives and showed more interest in introducing Greek Christianity. The struggle between German and native in this area developed into a conflict between German and Russian and between Latin and Greek Christianity for the possession of this part of the Baltic littoral. The Germans had no more respect for the Russian Slavs than for the other natives. They smiled when the Russians did not know how to use the new military machines of the West. "The Russians," says Henry, "made a little machine, in the fashion of the Germans, but not understanding the art of hurling stones they injured a great many of their men by hurling them into their backs." And if the Russians did not know how to use the new machines after they had built them they were in addition offensively indifferent to the rules of sanitation. When the Germans were about to occupy the recently abandoned Russian fort at Kokenhusen they found that "because of the lack of cleanliness on the part of the former inhabitants, it was filled with worms and snakes and had to be thoroughly cleaned before they would enter it."

In 1237 the Livonian Brothers of the Sword amalgamated with the Teutonic Knights, and the combined orders, attempting to absorb Novgorod, were defeated on Lake Peipus by Alexander Nevski, the Russian prince of Suzdal (1242). At a somewhat later date the papacy was perfectly willing to widen the campaign on the Baltic to a campaign against the Tartars controlling Russia, providing the Russian princes would come into the western church. Indeed, in 1260 the papacy went so far as to give the grand master of the Teutonic Order command of a campaign against the Tartars, promising the Order all lands that should be taken from resisting Russians and Tartars. The Russian princes were not to be had on these terms.

THE TEUTONIC KNIGHTS

Meanwhile the campaign on the Baltic took on more the nature of a crusade when the Teutonic Order entered the lists against the pagan Prussians. The Order had been founded in the Holy Land in 1198 and had come to Europe upon the invitation of King Andreas of Hungary to protect the eastern borders of his kingdom from the raids of heathen Mongolian Cumans. When it turned out to be more interested in building its own fortunes than in protecting Hungary, it was evicted from the kingdom (1225). Soon thereafter Duke Conrad of Masovia invited the Order to protect his principality against the pagan Baltic Prussians. The invitation was accepted only after prolonged negotiations guaranteeing to the German knights all the land they should take from the Prussians.

THE NATURE OF THE CONQUEST OF PRUSSIA

The conquest of Prussia began in the years following Bishop Albert of Bremen's death (1230) in Livonia. It lasted in the main for the rest of the thirteenth century, for only by this date may Prussia be said to have been actually subdued. It was accompanied by the completion of Albert's plans for the conquest of Livonia, and in both areas the general character of the conquest was identical. In both areas primitive tribes, without as yet any common political organization, were obliged hopelessly to protect their lives, their farms, their tribal independence, and their religion against the superior and experienced military might of the organized West, and against the fanaticism, compounded of crusading zeal and contempt for the non-Christian and the uncivilized, that animated it.

The Teutonic Knights, like the Livonian Brothers, could not manage the conquest alone. The two areas were, in fact, competitors for the aid of the aristocracy and burghers of northern Germany. During the years of conquest aid took the form of crusades, promoted by Rome and recruited by the agents of the orders themselves. The North German aristocracy, lay and ecclesiastical, that participated in these crusades had for centuries been successful colonizers of Slavic trans-Elbia. There were still huge landed estates to be had in Prussia, and these men were out to get them. Without their support the Knights could not hope to hold the area. The German burghers who participated in these crusades, the counterparts of those Venetians, Genoese, and Pisans on crusade to the Holy Land, were well acquainted with the economic potentialities of opening up the Baltic and its hinterland as a market for the vigorous young western industry, and importing therefrom raw products and the surplus of an improved agriculture. Prussia, then, as Livonia, was confronted not only by the highly organized Christianity of the West but by the new political, economic, and social forces breaking loose from the restrictions of a feudal society. No more than the other primitive peoples inhabiting the southern Baltic shores could the Prussians withstand this combination. They too were the sacrificial victims of the German expansion.

PRUSSIAN REVOLTS AND PEASANT COLONIZATION

In the course of its conquest the Order was confronted with furious Prussian revolts in 1240 and 1260, the second of which was put down with great ferocity. Some of the Prussian tribes were actually exterminated, some driven into Lithuania, and about one half of the land turned into a wilderness. Those Prussians who had not revolted (primarily the nobility) were given land and status equivalent to the German immigrants; those who had revolted lost their freedom and became serfs on the estates of the Order, of the German colonists, and of noble Prussians. The character of the suppression of this revolt made possible the subsequent disappearance of the Prussian people as such and opened up the way for further colonization. In the course of the actual conquest many German nobles and burghers were richly endowed with Prussian lands, and German towns were set up alongside the castles of the Order. Now that the conquest was completed, peasants streamed into Prussia for some sixty years, mostly from the region of Saxony, and in sufficient numbers to form some 1400 village communities. In addition to colonization from Germany proper there was a good deal of internal movement from older to newer Prussian settlements. German peasants, however, did not colonize Livonia and Esthonia; in these regions the Germans formed a thin uppercrust of alien aristocracy and burghers. Prussia was actually Germanized while Livonia was not. The German peasant moving eastward to Prussia with his superior agriculture escaped the limitations of the manorial system at home. He moved into an area where he was unquestionably a free man, cultivating a large amount of land on a rental basis only and free to dispose of his holding as and when he saw fit. He colonized more thickly where the Prussians had been wiped out or diminished by warfare. As a pioneer, he was given land to clear and forest to cut down, hard work that he was willing and able to do.

DYNASTIC UNION OF LITHUANIA AND POLAND

The Teutonic Order compensated for its inability to go beyond Esthonia by conquering eastern Pomerania, including Danzig (1308–1310) and the Neumark (1402). By the end of the thirteenth century the completed conquest of Prussia and Livonia brought the Knights into direct contact with the last remaining pagans in this area, the Lithuanian tribes of Samogitia and the Lithuanians themselves. If the two branches of the Order were to be able to co-operate with each other effectively inside Prussia and Livonia, or against Lithuania, it was necessary that the Samogitian gap between Prussia and Livonia be closed. The Order was never able to close the gap for any very long period and never tried very seriously, preferring to preserve this pagan neighbor as some justification for its existence as a crusading order. The potential threat, however, combined with the limitation put upon Poland and Lithuania by the growth of a strong German power on the Baltic, led to a dynastic union of Poland-Lithuania, formed by the marriage of Jagiello, the Lithuanian prince, to the Polish queen Jadwiga (1386). Conditions of the marriage were that Jagiello should become a Christian and undertake to recover for the Polish crown eastern Pomerania and the territory around Kulm.

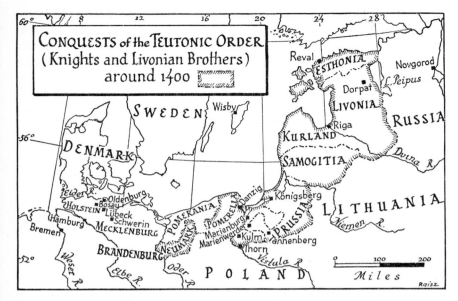

CONQUESTS of the TEUTONIC ORDER
(Knights and Livonian Brothers)
around 1400

THE STRUGGLE BETWEEN POLAND-LITHUANIA AND THE ORDER

The dynastic union of Poland-Lithuania marked the end of expansion for the Order. Already the signs of discontent with its government in Prussia were many. Both the Order and Poland-Lithuania prepared for war. When it came, the Order was badly defeated at Tannenberg (Grünwald) on 15 July, 1410. But the enemy, unable to take the Order's chief fortress, the Marienberg, was obliged to withdraw. Thus the First Treaty of Thorn (1411) was not disastrous for the Knights. They lost Samogitia and other small areas to Poland-Lithuania for the lives of the reigning princes of the latter, and paid a large war indemnity to Poland. After 1411 the German inhabitants of Prussia had to decide whether to sacrifice themselves to permit the Order to regain enough power to defeat Poland-Lithuania. To carry out this program the Order, on its part, would have had to build up in Prussia, among both Prussians and Germans, a far larger reserve of loyalty than it had in fact succeeded in winning. To an important section among all classes in Prussia the Order was an institution of the German aristocracy, organized to provide for a small number of hardly the most reputable or most talented of its younger sons living as a political, economic, and social élite in Prussia, an alien occupation of a few squabbling aristocrats for whom it was worth sacrificing nothing; or rather, since Prussia no longer needed the Order, to get rid of it was worth sacrificing much. This sentiment, which the Order was not able to placate, finally took the form (1440) of a Prussian League, organized to secure the autonomy of Prussia under the sovereignty of the Polish king. When the conditions of this autonomy had been negotiated, Poland declared war on the Order in February, 1454. The war lasted until 1466 (the Thirteen

Years' War), largely an unedifying struggle between the mercenary forces of each side. The combination of Poland-Lithuania and the Prussian League, however, was too much for the Order. The treaty concluding the struggle (Second Peace of Thorn, 19 October, 1466) gave eastern Pomerania (West Prussia) to Poland, and the rest of Prussia (East Prussia) was to be retained by the Order as a fief held by the grand master as a vassal of the king of Poland. The Second Treaty of Thorn formed what was, in later days, to be called a Polish Corridor to the Baltic (after the Treaty of Versailles, 1919); that is, it separated a less heavily Germanized West Prussia from a Germanized East Prussia. It was anathema to those later German nationalists who wished to join West as well as East Prussia to the Hohenzollern kingdom.

END OF THE TEUTONIC ORDER

In East Prussia, after 1466, the Order was unable to take measures to stem its own decline or to prevent the reduction of German and Prussian freemen to serfdom on the estates of the nobles, a class that, after 1466, was enlarged by mercenaries who had to be paid with Prussian land. The Order in Prussia was brought to an end in 1525. After the grand master, the Hohenzollern Margrave Albert of Brandenburg-Ansbach, had become Lutheran, together with many knights, East Prussia was made into a hereditary Duchy of Prussia, which the Hohenzollerns held as fiefs of the Polish crown. The Livonian branch of the Order prolonged its existence until 1561. At that moment the last master of the Livonian branch, Gotthard von Kettler, transformed Kurland (Courland) into a secular duchy held by him and his family as a fief from Poland-Lithuania. The remaining part of Livonia and Esthonia that was not annexed by Denmark, Sweden, and Russia was annexed by Poland-Lithuania. Here, too, the native peasants had become serfs on the large estates of alien masters. The German crusade against the pagans, Slav and Balt, thus resulted finally in the extermination, or assimilation, or enslavement of whole peoples (Wends, Prussians, Livs, Letts, Esthonians) and in the temporary elimination of the Germans from the struggle for the Baltic. This temporary elimination is to be explained in part by the inability of the German empire, long decomposed into little, quasi-independent territorial states, to support adequately the Baltic venture. It is to be explained as well by the fact that other nations, some on the Baltic (Denmark, Sweden) and others ambitious to be there (Poland-Lithuania, Russia), did not propose to relinquish the area to the Germans. The German Hanse, likewise, had begun to suffer from the competition of the merchants of other nations whose participation in Baltic-western trade had hitherto been excluded or limited. The Germans thus had to wait for the support of a stronger political organization (Brandenburg-Prussia, a unified Germany) before resuming the *Drang nach Osten.*

The OTTOMAN EMPIRE 1451 – 1481

KHANATE OF CRIMEA

SEA OF AZOV

BLACK SEA

WALLACHIA

DANUBE R.

BOSNIA
HERZEGO-
VINA
MONTE-
NEGRO

SERBIA
Nish
Kossovo

Ragusa

Scutari
Durazzo
ALBANIA

Nicopolis

Sofia
BULGARIA

Adrianople

Varna

BYZANTINE EMPIRE
Constantinople

EMPIRE OF TREBIZOND

Trebizond

OTTOMAN EMPIRE

Angora

Brusa

Athens

MOREA

KARAMAN

CIRCASSIAN MAMELUKES

CRETE

KINGDOM OF CYPRUS

Ottoman territory in 1451
Ottoman acquisitions 1451 – 1481
Venetian possessions

Miles
0   100   200

palacios

THE OTTOMAN TURKS INVADE THE BALKANS

Before Ivan III (1462–1505) finally destroyed the Golden Horde in
1480, the invasion of the Ottoman Turks struck fear into central and
western Europe and summoned it once again to a crusade. Around the
middle of the thirteenth century the Ottomans had established themselves
in northeastern Asia Minor and within a century had taken all of Asia
Minor from the Seljuk Turks and had crossed into southeastern Europe
(*ca.* 1354). Here they confronted an enfeebled Byzantine Empire, which
had been restored to Constantinople in 1261 by the Palaeologus family, and
which was in no position to block the advance of the Turks in any direction. A more serious obstacle to Turkish advance than the empire was
Serbia. The origins of an independent medieval Serbia go back to Stephen
Nemanja (1165–1196), whose dynasty at the moment of the Turkish crossing into Europe was represented by Stephen Dushan (1331–1355). Bulgaria, as well as Serbia, also had established independence from Byzantium
in the twelfth century under John and Peter Asen (the Asenid dynasty),
and at the moment of the Turkish crossing it had been made a vassal
state by the Serbian Dushan. It was Dushan's ambition to establish an independent Balkan state, destroy the Byzantine Empire, and take over its
capital at Constantinople. He was forestalled by Sultan Murad I (1359–

1389) at the Battle of Kossovo on 28 June, 1389. Thereupon not only Serbia, but medieval Bulgaria, the remainder of the crusading states, and indeed all Balkan territory to the Danube was added to the Ottoman holdings. This threat to central Europe was sufficiently serious to lead to two western attempts to halt the Turks. The first, made after Kossovo and the incorporation of Bulgaria into the Ottoman state, was strongly repulsed by the Turks at Nicopolis on the Danube (1396). The second came in 1444, after the Turkish conquest had been slowed up by the invasion of Tamerlane and his Mongolian horsemen into Asia Minor and their defeat of the Turks at Angora (1402). This crusading army, lead by the king of Hungary and Poland, Ladislav V, was successful at Nish but failed at Varna on the Black Sea. Re-established in the Balkan peninsula with the Danube as a frontier, the Turks under Mohammed II (1451-1481) finally took Constantinople, which they captured on 29 May, 1453. An oriental Mohammedan power thus actually succeeded Christian Byzantium, no matter how ardently Moscow, which had inherited the hostility of Byzantium to the West, claimed to be the real successor. The new Moslem Turkish state, again cutting off East from West, prolonged the crusades of West against East until the present century.

EAST AND WEST TODAY AND IN THE MIDDLE AGES

The contemporary conflict between East and West indubitably has its roots in the Middle Ages. These roots are to be seen first of all in the disintegration of the Pax Romana, resulting in a Graeco-oriental, or Byzantine, East and a Latin West. Divergence in religion emphasized this cultural diversity. The Byzantine Empire came to have its Greek Orthodox church, and the West its Roman Latin church, each regarding the other with the hate Christianity proscribes. Greek Christianity broke down further into Greek Orthodox and oriental (Monophysite and Nestorian) branches. The division into East and West was further deepened by the rise of an aggressive Islam that finally took over the Byzantine Empire and spread into both southwestern and southeastern Europe. The division between Byzantine and western Europe, and Mohammedan and Christian Europe, brought on western aggression, the aggression of the crusades, in reply to the earlier aggression of Islam. The conflict between East and West was thus expressed in war.

Muscovite Russia claimed to succeed to Byzantium after 1453. Together with all those Slavs who had been converted by the Byzantine church Russia inherited the tradition of hostility toward the western church and western civilization. This hostility was preserved and deepened by the Mohammedan Tartar domination over Russia and the conquest of the Balkan Slavs by the Ottoman Turks. But the opposition between East and West also expressed itself in the struggle between Germans and Slavs and Balts, having its roots in a Christian-pagan conflict and resulting in the Baltic crusades, the expropriation of Slavic and Baltic peoples, and the colonization of the area by Germans. Here, beyond Esthonia, the struggle took on the nature of a German-Russian rivalry based upon divergency in Christianity and upon differences in the level of civilization between West and East. In this Baltic region the conflict between East and West boiled over into constant war.

In spite of these fundamental and crippling divergencies, taking the form of continual warfare, it is to be observed that the Byzantine and Mohammedan East contributed greatly to the enrichment of western civilization just as western civilization began to spread among the western Slavs. These mutual gains were at a great cost in human life and human effort. Today West and East still face each other. That Russia leads a Communist eastern Europe against the West, that Russia has indeed established herself in Germany is partly to be explained by this old medieval German-Slav struggle. Nor has the Christian West as yet succeeded in overcoming the antagonisms and suspicions of Mohammedan countries. Differences in the level of civilization, as well as power politics and economic competition, are still creating hostility. It is still an open question whether, any more than in the Middle Ages, East and West can learn and mutually profit from each other without resort to the ever more extreme and awful expedient of war.

chapter twelve

THE REJECTION OF UNIVERSAL SECULAR THEOCRACY: HOLY ROMAN EMPIRE AND NATIONAL MONARCHIES

$\mathcal{E}$arly medieval society inherited from antiquity the idea that the world was best organized as a theocracy, either a secular theocracy such as the later Roman Empire, or an ecclesiastical theocracy such as the Christian Church headed by the papacy.[1] The histories of the attempt of the Carolingians to organize early western Europe as a secular theocracy, and of the popes to strengthen the claims of papal theocracy, have been traced.[2] In the end the new feudalism ruined the attempt of the Carolingians and put severe obstacles in the way of papal claims. The empire of Charlemagne dissolved into feudal kingdoms (France, Germany, and Italy), and these in turn dissolved into feudal principalities (Normandy, Champagne, Aquitaine, etc.). In the course of this feudal decomposition, the Church too came under the control of the feudal lords and kings.

PREVIEW OF THE CHAPTER

It might be expected that this would be the end of theocracy in western Europe; that political history thereafter would consist of the struggles between feudal princes for power and their attempts to provide western society with security and justice, together with the struggle of the Christian Church to free itself from the control of these feudal nobles and

[1]See p. 26, n. 14, where definitions are given for these terms.
[2]See pp. 378 ff.

kings. Such expectation would be false. The theocratic ideal was not so easily destroyed. It was taken up again by the German kings and by the popes. A fierce and prolonged struggle took place between them to decide whether secular or ecclesiastical theocracy was to prevail as western Europe's international organization. For a brief moment in the thirteenth century it was papal theocracy that won out.

In the end, however, medieval Europe was not to enjoy an international theocratic organization. The attempt of the German kings to establish for a second time their hegemony in Europe took the form of the Holy Roman Empire. It was destroyed by the popes in alliance with the feudal forces in Germany. Its destruction was so complete that the German kings lost not only their imperial but also their royal power. Feudal princes and towns filled the resulting political vacuum. The Holy Roman Empire survived more as a powerful idea and ideal than a reality. The brief victory of the popes in the thirteenth century aroused widespread discontent and opposition. It was brief because the pretensions of the popes were limited not only by the feudal princes and towns of the empire but by those feudal kings of France and England who had succeeded in subordinating the feudal system to the crown. These princes had often been supported by the popes themselves in pursuit of their own theocratic and anti-imperial policies. In France and England, if not in Germany and Italy, the national monarch and not the feudal lord was the political victor. Thus Europe was not to develop as a German or papal theocracy. After the interruption of the hard fight between empire and papacy, it was to resume its political development as a group of (1) feudal principalities, (2) towns or city-states, and (3) national monarchies. In each of these the main political issue came to be whether political power should be held absolutely by the prince or king or shared with a body representing the dominant social classes or estates (Estates-General, Parliament). In respect to this issue the kingdoms of France and England went divergent ways, the former in the direction of absolute, the latter in the direction of limited monarchy. If, therefore, theocracy was rejected, or, some might prefer, failed, on a universal or European scale, it was not rejected on a local, feudal, or monarchial scale. For the feudal lords and national kings often preferred to base their power theoretically upon divine rather than popular sanctions and to represent God rather than their subjects. The theocratic issue thus became local rather than universal.

Imperial and Papal Theory

CIVILIANS AND CANONISTS

The struggle between empire and papacy was accompanied, and in part determined, by a vigorous controversy among publicists and lawyers supporting the respective sides. The lawyers representing the imperial cause were the *civilians*, that is, men trained in the Roman law (*corpus iuris civilis*). They were opposed by the *canonists*, men trained in church, or canon, law (*corpus iuris canonici*).

DANTE'S "ON MONARCHY"

Although not a lawyer, Dante, the great Florentine poet, in a work *On Monarchy* defended the imperial cause.[3] He was a passionate Italian patriot who despaired over the disunity and turmoil that feudalism and warring city-states had introduced into his country. He saw in the Holy Roman Empire, to him also a continuation of the Roman Empire, a means of restoring unity and peace to Italy. He was especially hopeful about the expedition to Italy (1311–1313) of the German emperor Henry VII. As an adherent of the imperial party, Dante was what was called in Italy a Ghibelline. He hated the papal, or Guelf, party, supporting a church headed by a pope who, to him, was primarily interested in politics and not religion. To be sure, Dante's trust in empire at this moment was rather pathetic and unrealistic inasmuch as, by the time he was writing, the German empire was of little consequence in the field of actual politics. Yet the *On Monarchy*, a tightly reasoned defense of secular world government, is of great interest as illustrating the imperialist idealism of a poet whose reading of the classics had given him a vision of Roman glory.

Dante's deepest longing was for peace, the restoration of the Pax Romana. This longing was based on his high conception of human nature, whose noble potentialities could not be realized except in times of peace. He defined his "temporal monarchy" or "empire" as "a unique princedom extending over all persons in time." As a good humanist he thought the chief trait that glorified man was his rationality. "It is plain . . . ," he wrote, "that the specific potentiality of humanity as such is a potentiality or capacity of intellect." It is "in sedentary quietness [that] the individual man is perfected in knowledge and in wisdom," and accordingly it is "in the quiet or tranquillity of peace [that] the human race is most freely and favourably disposed towards the work proper to it. . . . Whence it is manifest that universal peace is the best of all those things which are ordained for our blessedness."

Dante believed that the best way to unify the human race was to subject it to a monarch or emperor. "The human race is . . . most one when it is all united in one, which cannot be save when it is subject in its totality to one prince." It is such a monarch who can best bring justice and freedom to the world, a freedom whose "first principle . . . [is] freedom of choice." "It is," moreover, "only when a monarch is reigning that the human race exists for its own sake, and not for the sake of something else," for it is the monarch who straightens out "perverted forms of government, . . . to wit, democracies, oligarchies, and tyrannies, which force the

[3]For Dante as a poet, see pp. 731 ff.

CHRONOLOGY — Holy Roman Empire and National Monarchies

	Empire (Reigns)	France (Reigns)	England (Reigns)	Papacy (Pontificates)
900	Henry I (the Fowler) (919–936) Otto I (the Great) (936–973)			
1000		Hugh Capet (987–996)		
	Henry IV (1056–1106)	Philip I (1060–1108)	William I (the Conqueror) (1066–1087)	Gregory VII (1073–1085)
1100	Frederick Barbarossa (1152–1190) Henry VI (1190–1197)	Louis VI (the Fat) (1108–1137) Louis VII (1137–1180) Philip Augustus (1180–1223)	Henry I (1100–1135) Henry II (1154–1189) Eleanor of Aquitaine (ca. 1122–1204) John (1199–1216)	Arnold of Brescia (b. ca. 1100–d. 1155) Concordat of Worms (1122)
1200	Frederick II (1212–1250) Dante Alighieri (b. 1265–d. 1321)	Louis IX (the Saint) (1226–1270) Charles of Anjou (1266–1285) Philip IV (the Fair) (1285–1314)	Henry III (1216–1272) Simon de Montfort (b. ca. 1208–d. 1265) Edward I (1272–1307) *Model Parliament* (1295)	Innocent IV (1243–1254) Urban IV (1261–1264) Clement IV (1265–1268) Boniface VIII (1294–1303)
1300	Henry VII (1308–1313) Charles IV (1347–1378) *Golden Bull* (1356)	*Hundred Years' War* (1337–1453)	Edward III (1327–1377)	
1400		Louis XI (1461–1483) Charles VIII (1483–1498)		

human race into slavery." He also establishes governments "conducted by kings, aristocrats . . . and zealots for the peoples' liberty." These latter governments "purpose freedom, to wit, that men should exist for their own sakes." In them the nation does not exist "for the sake of the king, but conversely . . . the king for the sake of the nation." Kings may be "masters of the rest as regards the way, yet as regards the end they are their servants; and the monarch most of all, for he must assuredly be regarded as the servant of all."[4]

It was obvious to Dante that the monarchy or empire that the world needed was the monarchy of the Roman Empire. Under this monarchy Christ chose to become man. "The world was never quiet on every side except under *divus Augustus*, the monarch, when there was a perfect monarchy." The Roman people responsible for this government was "the noblest," if for no other reason than that it produced "our divine poet Vergil." "Therefore it was meet for it to be set above all others." God, moreover, "did show forth miracles to perfect the Roman Empire." "The Roman people was ordained by nature to command. Therefore the Roman people, in subjecting the world to itself, attained to empire by right," inasmuch as "success amongst the athletes contending for the empire of the world must have followed the judgment of God." It was not difficult for Dante to think that in this government of the world the German empire succeeded the Roman Empire.

Dante worried "whether the authority of the Roman monarch . . . is immediately dependent upon God, or rather on some vicar or minister of God, by whom I understand the successor of Peter, who in very truth bears the keys of the kingdom of heaven?" In other words, is the emperor dependent upon God or upon the pope?[5] In this section of his book he had to contend with arguments based upon the Petrine Theory[6] and the Donation of Constantine.[7] He contends that the latter "has no force, because Constantine had no power to alienate the imperial dignity, nor had the church power to receive it." The Church had no power to receive it because it was told in Matthew: "Possess not gold nor silver, nor money in your girdles, nor purse for your journey." When, moreover, the Roman Empire came to power the Church did not exist, and it could therefore not be dependent upon it. In any case the Church as a spiritual institution has nothing to do with political power. "Virtue to authorize rule over our mortality is contrary" to its nature. Dante concludes that man has need "of a twofold directive power according to his twofold end, to wit, the supreme pontiff, to lead the human race in accordance with

[4]*The Latin Works of Dante*, trans. P. Wickstead, quoted in C. W. Jones, *Medieval Literature in Translation*, pp. 754 ff.

[5]Or, to use earlier phrases of this book, whether imperial government should be a secular theocracy (of direct divine sanction) or an ecclesiastical theocracy (of indirect sanction through a priest).

[6]See p. 339.

[7]See pp. 389 f.

things revealed, to eternal life; and the emperor, to direct the human race to temporal felicity in accordance with the teachings of philosophy."[8] What should make it possible for the Roman prince to ordain that "on this threshing floor of mortality life should be lived in freedom and in peace," is the fact that this world is dependent for its movements upon a greater universe governed by a providence that "weaves all things together, each in its due order." This is God and not the pope. "It is [thus] plain that the authority of the temporal monarch descends upon him [the emperor] . . . from the Fountain of universal authority. This does not mean that the emperor is entirely free of the pope for "mortal felicity is in a certain sense ordained with reference to immortal felicity. Let Caesar, therefore, observe that reverence to Peter which a first-born son should observe to a father, so that illuminated by the light of paternal grace he may with greater power irradiate the world, over which he is set by him alone who is ruler of all things spiritual and temporal."

THE ARGUMENTS OF THE CANONISTS

The defenders of the universal and absolute power of the popes used first of all the arguments of the Petrine Theory, which, grounded in Sacred Scripture, made of the pope the successor of Peter and the vicar of Christ. To them he was the vicar, if not, in a few bold instances the successor, of God. As such, there could be no limitation of his power in the world. The pope could do whatever God could do, and "whatever is done by the authority of the lord pope is done by the authority of God." The canonist transferred to the pope the absolute power of the Roman emperor;[9] whatever pleased the pope had the force of law. For just cause he could give men dispensation from the obligations of natural or divine law, and he needed no reason to dispense with human law. Indeed, he possessed what the canonists called "complete or full power" (*plenitudo potestatis*). This gave him unrivalled authority in both the spiritual and temporal spheres, and made everyone subject to his rule. "He had no equal on earth."[10]

The pope's power was universal in its extent, no matter what the religious beliefs of the inhabitants of the globe, whereas the power of the emperor was limited to Christians. Those non-Christian governments of the world that refused to recognize the superior world position of the popes could not be considered legitimate governments. The pope, as vicar of God, controlled the lives of non-Christian Jews, Mohammedans, and Gentiles, as well as Christians. As Pope Innocent IV put it: all men, "faithful and infidel alike are through their creation the sheep of Christ." "Nobody," one of the canonists held, "can claim to be outside the fold of the Church, and therefore everybody is subject to the jurisdictional power of

[8]This is Dante's version of the (Gelasian) Theory of the Two Swords. See pp. 342 f.
[9]See pp. 253 f.
[10]Walter Ullman, *Medieval Papalism*, pp. 50–51.

the Church." Such world power was not to be established by force. But the secular arm could, if necessary, be called upon to carry out the pope's will. Whenever a non-Christian violated natural law it was quite proper for the popes to intervene to punish and try such a person. Thus the pope could intervene to punish idolatry, which was a violation of natural law since "it was natural to worship one God only rather than the images of imaginary deities." Missionaries and representatives of the pope must be permitted freely to enter and work in non-Christian lands, and if this was refused them, according to Innocent IV, force could be used, whether by the pope or by his secular dependents. Yet Innocent did not go so far as to insist upon the right to compel non-Christians to become Christian, although this was a right often assumed by others. It was, however, quite proper to deny to Mohammedan envoys the rights and privileges demanded by Christian envoys in entering another's territory, for "we must not put ourselves on the same level as those people; because they are in error, and we walk in the path of truth." As the protector of Christians everywhere, the pope could interfere in the internal legislation of other countries, and Christians everywhere owed direct obedience to him alone. Innocent IV remarked that the pope as the vicar of Christ "has power not only over Christians but also over all infidels, since Christ himself had power over everybody." (pp. 119–120, 125, 130)

If the pope had such an exalted position in the universe as the head of a system of world government it can be well imagined that the papalists afforded only a modest position to the Holy Roman emperor. He was but one of the many Christian princes and kings over whom the pope stood. His position was that of "the most inferior servant of pope and church." The Donation of Constantine made impossible the exercise of any temporal, even imperial, power not conferred by the pope. Imperial power was popular in origin, whereas the source of papal power was divine. "The people can deprive the emperor of his power, but all the churches taken together could not do the same to the pope, since he does not receive his power from them, but they from him." Moreover, the empire had been transferred from the East to the West (Charlemagne) so that the Church could be better protected. There could be no empire outside the Church (*nullum imperium extra ecclesiam*). That the Germans should be selected as the recipients of imperial power from the popes pleased especially German canonists. If these emperors did not establish justice within their realms, if they were incapable or inefficient, and especially if they harbored enemies of the popes or of the Christian faith (heretics), they were to be driven from their thrones and supplanted by loyal Catholics (*catholici viri*). Any iniquitous prince could in fact be deposed by the pope. The pope had the obligation to supervise all secular legislation, no matter whose, to see that it was not sinful. "By reason of sin," says one canonist, "the Church can correct civil laws, and can draw civil matters into its own courts." In case of an imperial vacancy the pope could dispose of the government of the empire. The emperor had no temporal power until he was crowned by the pope. Indeed, the canonists argued, just as the soul is superior to the body, so is the pope superior to the emperor, and the emperor's power is justified only as it helps the pope to realize his own power. The Church, in fact, contains the empire (*ecclesia continet imperium*) and uses its power to facilitate man's spiritual welfare. In this capacity it must direct imperial policy if not actually govern and administer the empire. Canonists explained that it would be too "indecent and unworthy of the spiritual power . . . if it concerned itself with the vile works of government, since to the spiritual power belong the more dignified and powerful works" (pp. 140, 167, 171, 182, 187). The basis of world government must therefore be spiritual; to make the temporal of equal weight with the spiritual was heresy.

The Struggle between Empire and Papacy

MEDIEVAL POLITICAL ISSUES

The major issue of the political history of the Middle Ages, it has already been noted, was whether western Europe was to develop as a secular or an ecclesiastical theocracy—Holy Roman Empire or Holy Roman Church. Subsidiary issues were whether, in the absence of a successful international organization, the local political unit of Europe was to be the small feudal principality or the national monarchy, and, in either case, whether political power was to be absolute, or shared with representative bodies. Always the further question of the relation of church to state was involved. As the correct method of settling this latter issue, the papacy insisted upon the freedom of the church from the state, and in the name of spiritual supremacy, upon the subordination of the Church to itself.[11] It is now necessary to consider how these issues were tied up with the actual course of events in (1) the struggle between the German empire and the papacy, and (2) the feudo-monarchical developments in France and England.

THE FEUDALIZED CHURCH

The struggle between the Holy Roman Empire and the Holy Roman Church first became serious in the third quarter of the eleventh century, when Henry IV (1056-1106) was emperor and Gregory VII (1073-1085) was pope. It came at this time because of the character and ideas of each of these men, but it had long been brewing as a result of the feudalization of the western Church. This process of feudalization meant that the personnel and property of the Church were dependent upon either the new feudal aristocracy or the feudal monarchs. The patrons of the Church,

[11]See pp. 580 ff.

for example, were the feudal aristocracy. The lord of the manor chose the parish priest. The abbots of monasteries were appointed by the heads of families that had endowed them, and their lands granted out as fiefs at the will of these patrons. In some instances the baron did not bother with a regular abbot but appointed a layman instead or, as we should say, a local business manager. Under such circumstances, it can be imagined, the discipline of the monks became lax, the quality of abbots inferior, and the loss of monastic property to secular persons great. Likewise the leading offices in the secular church, the bishoprics and the archbishoprics, came into the hands of the powerful local lords who appointed them, obliged them to become their vassals, and dictated how they should grant out their property. From the point of view of the Church these developments were all illegal, that is, contrary to canon law. Canon law provided for the appointment of parish clergy by the proper bishop. Bishops and archbishops were to be elected by the clergy and the people. Monastic rules provided for the election of abbots by the monks themselves. Church property belonged, strictly speaking, to the patron saint of the church concerned. It could not properly be alienated. For bishops and abbots to become feudal lords and feudal vassals was to plunge them directly into the maelstrom of feudal politics, where it was often a hard fist rather than a gentle soul that determined issues. What made these new relationships more serious was their venality: church offices were for sale by their patrons, and well paid for by affluent candidates.

THE TRIBAL DUCHY IN GERMANY

As feudalism spread, these conditions became general in the West and notorious in Germany because of the peculiar circumstances of feudal development there. After the treaty of Mersen (870), the Carolingian dynasty continued to reign in Germany until 911. Then, and again in 919, instead of turning to the Carolingian rulers of France, important German nobles elected a king for themselves, choosing in 919 the duke of Saxony, Henry the Fowler, who founded the Saxon, or Ottonian, dynasty lasting until 1025. The fact that a duke of Saxony was chosen king reveals the special character of the German localism to which feudalism had to adapt itself. That is, Germany in the tenth century was divided into large duchies based upon long-established tribal differences (Saxony, Thuringia, Franconia, Swabia, Bavaria). The dukes of these subnationalities had risen to power as protectors of their fellow tribesmen against the invaders of the ninth and tenth centuries, the duke of Saxony against Danes and Wends, for instance, and the duke of Bavaria against the Magyars. It was thus a question whether an elected king of Germany, coming from the ranks of these dukes, could give any strength to the institution of German kingship, or whether under the circumstances the German king was not bound to remain a kind of honorary head of a federation of tribal duchies.

OTTO I AND THE CHURCH

The second of the new Saxon dynasty, Otto the Great (936–973), tried to strengthen the monarchy over and against the dukes by (1) relying heavily upon the Church and (2) reviving the Carolingian tradition of empire. He met with support from the German church because it preferred to escape the local control of tribal dukes by becoming, if necessary, the instrument of royal will and government. It thus happened that in Germany the leading clergy, the bishops, archbishops, and important abbots, in spite of the formalities of canon law, were actually appointed by the king. Not only this, but they received their lands and privileges as fiefs from the king after the performance of homage and fealty. In other words, the leading churchmen became feudal vassals of the king and paid him their share of the feudal contract. This was not, however, the end of the politicalization of the Church. According to the provisions of canon law, the bishop, at his consecration, received the symbols of his spiritual office, the ring (symbol of the marriage of the bishop to his flock) and the staff, or crozier (symbol of the bishop as shepherd of his flock), from the archbishop of his province. He was thus, to use proper feudal language, invested with his office by the proper ecclesiastical authority. What, however, became the practice in Germany and elsewhere was for the king to invest the new bishop, his appointee and vassal, with the ring and staff at court. This was the practice called *lay investiture*, the investing with spiritual office by a layman. Clearly, this kind of an alliance between crown and upper clergy brought considerable strength to the former and many additional privileges to the latter. It did not, however, please purists and reformers.

OTTO I AS EMPEROR

In 962 Otto I was crowned a Roman emperor by the pope. Before this, in 951, he had taken over the ancient kingdom of Lombardy in northern and central Italy. These events marked a deliberate revival by the Germans of a Carolingian empire that had gone to pieces in the ninth and tenth centuries. It was a revival supported by a papacy that was again very much in need of protection against its local enemies, having, in fact, summoned help from the north. Yet the circumstances of the reestablishment of the imperial tradition in western Europe must have been disappointing to a papacy with its own ambitions. Otto I and his successors looked upon the German emperor as the overlord of the Papal States and Rome, and indeed as the rightful possessor of Byzantine lands in southern Italy and Sicily. For his protection of the pope, Otto I insisted upon the condition that no pope must ever be elected to the Holy See without the previous consent of the German emperor. It looked very much as if the German empire were reducing the bishop of Rome to the position of a German bishop.

NORTH SEA

POMERANIA

FRIESLAND

ELBE R.

BRANDEN
BURG

Bremen

SAXONY

Brunswick

Magdeburg

Brandenburg

ODER R.

POLAND

LUSATIA

Dresden

Bruges

Cologne

Aachen

LOWER

LORRAINE

RHINE R.

THURINGIA

FRANCONIA

Mainz

Tribur

Worms

Speyer

Eger

Prague

BOHEMIA

MORAVIA

UPPER

LORRAINE

Metz

Bamberg

Regensburg

Châlons-
sur-
Marne

FRANCE

Chalon-
sur-
Saône

Besançon

KINGDOM OF BURGUNDY

Constance

Passau

BAVARIA

SWABIA

BRENNER
PASS

Salzburg

AUSTRIA

Vienna

DANUBE R.

HUNGARY

CARINTHIA

Cluny

Lyons

RHONE R.

MT. CENIS
PASS

Legnano

Milan

LOMBARDY

Brescia

Crema

Verona

Vicenza

Padua

Venice

CROATIA

Piacenza

PO R.

Tortona

Roncaglia

Genoa

Canossa

Bologna

Ravenna

DALMATIA

Avignon

Arles

Pisa

Florence

TUSCANY

Assisi

Fermo

CORSICA
(to Pisa – 11th C.)

Spoleto

ADRIATIC

PAPAL STATES

Rome

Tagliacozzo

= Monte Cassino

SEA

MEDITERRANEAN

SEA

40°

Benevento

Naples

SARDINIA
(to Pisa – 11th C.)

NORMAN KINGDOM of the TWO SICILIES

The HOLY ROMAN EMPIRE
10th – 11th Centuries

Miles   0   50   100

palacios

GERMAN EMPIRE AND NATIONAL MONARCHIES 529

The empire established by Otto I was a much smaller affair than Charlemagne's. It consisted originally of Germany and Italy, Byzantine territory in the south excepted. It was subsequently to include the kingdom of Burgundy in the Rhone valley and those areas added by a Germany expanding into new colonial territory: trans-Elbia, Prussia, Austria. It was strong enough at times to demand and secure a recognition of its overlordship over such neighboring states as Denmark, Poland, Bohemia, and Hungary. France and England never had to pay much attention to its international pretensions. In order to emphasize its theocratic character and its direct dependence upon God rather than the pope, it came during its struggle with the papacy to call itself "holy." As the Holy Roman Empire, it lasted in some shape or form until Napoleon put an end to it in 1806. It was, of course, the second attempt of the Germans to establish their hegemony in Europe. Aside from the fact that it was a further obstacle to the realization of the theocratic hopes of the papacy, and would thus incur papal opposition, it is difficult to see now how it could have hoped to be successful. The organization of central and western Europe was at the moment feudal. To superimpose upon this localized, feudal Europe an effective international organization would have required political gifts of a high order. As it was, the Germans found it difficult to set up an effective government even in Italy, and others in still-smaller areas.

THE CLUNIAC REFORM

Henry the Fowler added to the German kingdom that part of Lorraine that had gone to the western Carolingians in 870. It was from the monasteries of Lorraine that there first came men who wished to reform the conditions created when feudalism captured the Church. To these men were added reformers from the monastery of Cluny, which the duke of Aquitane founded in 910 as a reformed Benedictine house quite independent of any feudal or royal power. Cluny spread widely as a centralized monastic order throughout central and western Europe, with the mother house at Cluny directing its dependent priories. This monastic demand for independence from the feudal system, and subjection, if at all, to no power but Rome, has come to be known as the Cluniac reform. It would have been limited in its application had it not happened that Cluniac and reforming monks became members of the secular clergy and thus directed their attention to the reform of the secular, as well as the regular, church. The Cluniac movement was finally taken over by the clergy serving the popes, and they transformed it into a campaign to free the whole Church from the evil embraces of the state and make it liable to papal centralization.

What this reform program—often called the Gregorian reform because of its association with Gregory VII—came to demand were (1) the abolition of lay investiture and (2) the abolition of simony, its name for all violations of canon law and especially the flagrant purchase and sale of clerical office. It also entered upon the tremendous program of (3) establishing a celibate priesthood. This had become necessary because the parish clergy everywhere, contrary again to canon law, often lived quite openly with their wives or concubines, consequently creating the danger not only that family cares should engross the attention of the priesthood but, as Gregory VII himself complained, that the property and very offices of the Church might become hereditary. For the future of the Church, this beginning of a movement to establish a celibate clergy had an importance not easily imagined. The reform party in the Church split up into radical and moderate groups. Some few would have liked to see the Church free of the encumbrance of the Papal States in Italy and the enormous extent of landed property throughout Europe. Others wished to have restored to the Church all properties forcefully alienated from it. Most were willing to demand that the Church hold its endowment quite independently of any necessary feudal or royal obligations. It is quite obvious that such a program was a blow aimed at the power of the aristocratic ruling class of Europe, and that for such a state as Germany it asked the kings to abandon the great feudal support that the Church gave it. To ask for such a gift was to ask for more than the German kings, or indeed other feudal princes, were willing to concede. To persist in such a program, therefore, meant that the papacy was quite willing to enter upon a serious struggle with the feudal state. The Church could be freed in no other way, and unless it were freed there was no chance that it could be subordinated to the papacy in the mighty edifice of a centralized, monarchical, papal church. In other words, it is necessary to recognize that the reformers, however interested they were in correcting the abuses that had crept into the Church—and their sincerity is not to be questioned —were also interested in carrying to its completion (4) the spiritual supremacy of the pope over the Church. To carry out this program of reform and centralization, a man like Pope Gregory VII, convinced that only in this way could Europe be made properly Christian, was perfectly willing to rush headlong against the European princes and kings, and especially the German king. With the rash impatience of a fiery idealist who had a lust for rule and a passion to be obeyed, he attempted to establish the new order in church and state during his own pontificate. When he became pope in 1073, he had long been the moving spirit behind the reform program that the popes had launched in Europe. The first attack upon the empire had come in 1059, when a method for electing a new pope by the cardinal-clergy of Rome, and for gradually excluding the influence of the German emperor upon this election, was announced.

Shortly after Gregory's accession to the papal throne, he had his advisers on the canon law prepare a brief list of the powers that this law gave to the pope. It is clear from this list that there was little hesitancy in Rome to draw the proper conclusions from such claims as the Petrine Theory and such documents as the Donation of Constantine. These declarations establish the spiritual supremacy of the pope within the Church and his temporal supremacy over the state. They declare in part that "the Roman pontiff alone can with right be called universal. That he alone can depose or reinstate bishops. . . . That for him alone is it lawful, according to the needs of the time, to make new laws. . . . That he has power to ordain a clerk of any church he may wish. . . . That no chapter and no book shall be considered canonical without his authority. . . . That he himself may be judged by no one. . . . That the Roman church has never erred; nor will it err to all eternity, the Scripture bearing witness."[12] As for the relations of the papacy to the state, this list of papal rights (called the Dictate of the Pope) declares: "That . . . we ought not to remain in the same house with those excommunicated by him. . . . That he alone may use the imperial insignia. That of the pope alone all princes shall kiss the feet. . . . That his is the only name in the world. That it may be permitted to him to depose emperors. . . . That he who is not at peace with the Roman church shall not be considered catholic. That he may absolve subjects from their fealty to wicked men. . . ." In Gregory's letters these principles can be seen in action, together with the force of his imperious nature and his passion for reform.[13]

GREGORY VII IN HIS LETTERS

Gregory does not care to have papal legates, a relatively new institution at the time, careless in obeying orders. He writes to two of them in France: "We are very much surprised at your delay in returning here, especially since, after you had been ordered to return, and while we were long expecting you, you have not given us so much as a hint of reasons for your tardiness." To French feudal lords, about to go on a crusade to Spain, he writes, "We are sure that it is no secret to you that the kingdom of Spain was from ancient times subject to St. Peter in full sovereignty and . . . belongs of right to no mortal, but solely to the Apostolic See." He warns a recalcitrant archbishop of Rheims, "if . . . you shall refuse to reverence St. Peter in this matter . . . then beyond a doubt—we regret to say it—you will call down upon yourself our apostolic severity and wrath." He warns Duke Wratislaw of Bohemia that if his brother, the bishop of Prague, does not obey orders, "we shall confirm the sentence of deposition passed by our legates, and shall unsheath

[12]E. Henderson, *Select Historical Documents of the Middle Ages*, pp. 366–367.
[13]Ephraim Emerton, *The Correspondence of Pope Gregory VII*.

the sword of apostolic wrath against him even to his destruction, so that he, and through him many others, may learn by experience how great is the authority of this See." He promises the bishop of Chalon-sur-Saône that "either the king [Philip I] abandoning the evil merchandise of simoniacal heresy, shall allow suitable persons to be promoted to the government of the Church, or the French people, unless they desire to reject the Christian faith, shall be smitten by the sword of a general anathema and will refuse to obey him in future." Siegfrid, the archbishop of Mainz, is told, "You will understand that apostolic decisions cannot be reversed— I do not say by you but by any patriarch or primate. You are not to attribute to yourself any rights as against the Holy Roman Church nor make any attempt against her, seeing that without her abundant favour you cannot maintain yourself in the place you hold, as you well know." To the clergy of France he writes concerning King Philip I, "who is to be called a tyrant rather than a king," that they are to "declare to him as from our own lips that he shall no longer escape the sword of apostolic discipline." They are to separate themselves "from all service and communion with him and forbid throughout all France the celebration of public divine worship. But if even this discipline does not bring him to his senses we desire to leave no doubt in the mind of anyone that we shall, with God's help, make every possible effort to deprive him of his kingly rule in France. . . . And if we find you lacking in zeal in this great and necessary work, we shall no longer be in doubt that he remains incorrigible through his reliance upon your support, and shall smite you as allies and accomplices of his crimes with the spear of the same punishment and shall deprive you of your episcopal offices." The king of Hungary is informed that "the kingdom of Hungary was long since offered and devotedly surrendered to St. Peter by King Stephen as the full property of the Holy Roman Church under its complete jurisdiction and control." The archbishop of Bremen is ordered to come to Rome and "in consequence of the above mentioned offenses we suspend you from all episcopal functions until you shall appear before us." "Oh what insolence! Oh what audacity, that a bishop should despise the decrees of the Apostolic See," he tells the bishop of Constance. He orders the dukes of Swabia and Carinthia that, "no matter what bishops may say or not say," they are "not to recognize those whom you shall prove to have been promoted or ordained simoniacally or to be under charge of fornication. . . . You are to prevent such persons, to the best of your ability, even by force if that be necessary, from serving at the sacred mysteries." To the king of Denmark he can write, "Yet now we are so much the more strictly bound to care not only for kings and princes, but for all Christians as the universal government entrusted to us brings the interests of all men closer and more specifically to us." The bishop of Châlons-sur-Marne, "for his monstrous insolence of disobedience, ought to be deprived of his episcopal office." To the archbishop of Cologne: "It has ever been and ever shall be the province of the Holy Roman Church to provide new edicts and new remedies against newly increasing excesses, and these sent forth under the sanction of reason and authority, no human being may lawfully declare to be invalid." To Demetrius, the king of the Russians (grand prince of Kiev): "We finally gave our assent and in the name of St. Peter transferred the government of your kingdom to him [Dmitri's son, Yaropolk]." The people of Corsica are informed "that the island which you inhabit belongs by right of legal proprietorship to no mortal person and to no power but that of the Holy Roman Church." The archbishops of Milan and Ravenna, "who have risen against this holy catholic church with unexampled heresy and pride, we suspend absolutely from the episcopal and priestly office, and renew the anathema already laid upon them." A letter to King Alfonso of Leon refers to Saint Peter, "chief of the Apostles, to whom he [God] has made subject all principalities and powers of the earth, and has granted him the power of binding and loosing in Heaven and upon the earth." King Haakon of Denmark has to be told that one thing "must be sternly repressed by apostolic prohibition, namely that you ascribe to your priests the inclemency of the weather, foulness of the air, and certain ills of the body."

GREGORY'S LETTER TO THE BISHOP OF METZ

Gregory defended his excommunication and deposition of Henry IV in letters to the German people and clergy that describe in more detail his ideas about the relationship of empire to papacy. The most detailed of these is a letter he wrote to Hermann, the bishop of Metz, dated 15 March, 1081. Referring to the power of the keys mentioned in the Gospel of Matthew,[14] Gregory exclaims, "Are kings excepted here? Or are they not of the sheep which the Son of God committed to St. Peter? Who, I ask, thinks himself excluded from this universal grant of the power of binding and loosing to St. Peter?" Gregory maintains that the "holy fathers . . . have not only accepted her [the Roman church's] exposition of doctrine, and her instruction in [our] holy religion, but they have also recognized her judicial decisions. They have agreed as with one spirit and one voice that all major cases, all especially important affairs and the judgments of all churches ought to be referred to her as to their head and mother, that from her there shall be no appeal, that her judgments may not and cannot be reviewed or reversed by any one. . . . To whom, then, the power of opening and closing Heaven is given, shall he not be able to judge the earth? . . . God forbid! . . . Who does not know that kings and princes derive their origin from men ignorant of God who raised themselves above their fellows by pride, plunder, treachery, murder—in short, by every kind of crime—at the instigation of the Devil, the prince of this world, men blind with greed and intolerable in their audacity. . . . Does

[14]See p. 339.

anyone doubt that the priests of Christ are to be considered as fathers and masters of kings and princes and of all believers?" He quotes Pope Gelasius[15] as saying that of the two powers, priestly and temporal, "the priestly is by so much the greater as they will have to answer for kings themselves on the day of divine judgment. . . . Know [therefore] that you [the emperor] are subject to their judgment, not that they are to be subjected to your will." Gregory reminds the bishop of Metz that a pope once "deposed a king of the Franks, not so much on account of his evil deeds as because he was not equal to so great an office," and set in his place "Peppin, father of the emperor Charles the Great, releasing all the Franks from the oath of fealty which they had sworn to him." He recalls to him, too, the case of Ambrose and Theodosius[16] and quotes Ambrose as saying, "there is nothing in this world more excellent than a priest or more lofty than a bishop." Gregory sees the superiority of the priest in that he can perform the sacraments: "Who among them [the secular rulers] is able by his own word to create the body and blood of the Lord? or to whom among them is given the power to bind and loose in Heaven and upon earth? From this it is apparent how greatly superior in power is the priestly dignity. . . . Kings and princes of the earth, seduced by empty glory, prefer their own interests to the things of the spirit, whereas pious pontiffs, despising vainglory, set the things of God above the things of flesh."

THE OPENING OF THE INVESTITURE STRUGGLE

The struggle between Gregory VII and Henry IV was an intensely personal and dramatic affair. It broke out over the issue of lay investiture, when Gregory at the Lenten Synod of 1075 simply forbade the practice, and Henry, in the subsequent months, chose to ignore the prohibition and outraged the pope by appointments in northern Italy and even in papal territory (Fermo and Spoleto). At the end of the year, Gregory wrote to Henry a letter offering "greeting and the apostolic benediction— but with the understanding that he obeys the Apostolic See as becomes a Christian King." Gregory complained that "now, heaping wounds upon wounds you have handed over the sees of Fermo and Spoleto—if indeed a church may be given over by any human power—to persons entirely unknown to us. . . . This edict [against lay investiture]" he wrote Henry, "which some who place the honor of men above that of God call an intolerable burden, we, using the right word, call rather a truth and a light necessary for salvation, and we have given judgment that it is to be heartily accepted and obeyed, not only by you and your subjects but by all princes and peoples who confess and worship Christ." We are told that the legates who brought the letter threatened Henry with excommunication and deposition if he did not submit.

[15]See pp. 342 f.
[16]See pp. 341 f.

Consumed with wrath over such an intervention in German affairs, Henry immediately summoned a council of the German clergy for 24 January, 1076, at Worms. From this council the German clergy dispatched a letter to Pope Gregory. Referring to his "well-known arrogance," the bishops and archbishops complained that "as the lamentable state of the church universal proclaims and bemoans, thou dost with pertinacious continuance, fulfill the promises of thy evil beginnings through the still worse progress of thy actions and decrees. . . . Thou hast, with raging madness, scattered through all the churches of Italy, Germany, Gaul and Spain the flame of discord which, through thy ruinous factions, thou didst start in the Roman church." They complained bitterly that Gregory had turned revolutionary power over to the people against priests who did not obey the reform decrees, and charged that "now no one is bishop or priest over anyone unless he has bought this by most unworthy assent from thy magnificence." They assailed Gregory for usurping customary episcopal rights for himself and his legates. He was charged with "too familiar living together and cohabitation with a strange woman. . . . All the decrees of the apostolic see have been set in motion by women—in a word, through this new senate of women the whole circle of the church is administered." The German clergy concluded: "We renounce the obedience which we never promised to thee, nor shall we in future at all observe it. And since, as thou didst publicly proclaim, not one of us has been to thee thus far a bishop, so also shalt thou henceforth be pope for none of us."[17]

HENRY'S LETTER FROM WORMS

Henry IV also wrote an angry letter to Gregory from Worms. He referred to himself as "king not through usurpation but through the holy ordination of God" and addressed Gregory as "Hildebrand [his name before becoming pope] at present not pope but false monk." He stated that Gregory "hast understood our humility to be fear, and has not, accordingly, shunned to rise up against the royal power conferred upon us by God, daring to threaten to divest us of it. As if we had received our kingdom from thee! As if the kingdom and the empire were in thine and not in God's hand. . . . On me . . . thou hast lain thy hand; me who—as the tradition of the holy Father teaches . . . am subject to the judgment of God alone. . . . But thou who dost not fear God, dost dishonour in me his appointed one." Finally he broke out in conclusion: "Thou, therefore, damned by this curse and by the judgment of all our bishops and by our own, descend and relinquish the apostolic chair which thou hast usurped. Let another ascend the throne of St. Peter who shall not practice violence under the cloak of religion, but shall teach the sound doctrine of St. Peter.

[17]Henderson, *Select Historical Documents*, pp. 373–376.

I Henry, king by the grace of God, do say unto thee together with all our bishops: Descend, descend, to be damned throughout the ages." (pp. 372–373)

THE LENTEN SYNOD OF 1076

These letters were brought to Gregory at the Lenten Synod of 1076 in Rome. His answer quickly brought things to a head. The Synod threatened all the clergy of Germany and Italy who supported Henry with suspension from office, and Gregory replied to Henry with an excommunication and deposition whose Latin moves in somber cadence. It was addressed to Saint Peter: "By thy [Peter's] power, not by any works of mine, I believe that it is and has been thy will, that the Christian people especially committed to thee should render obedience to me, thy especially constituted representative. To me is given by thy grace the power of binding and loosing in Heaven and upon earth. Wherefore . . . through thy power and authority, I deprive King Henry . . . who has rebelled against thy church with unheard-of audacity, of the government over the whole kingdom of Germany and Italy, and I release all Christian men from the allegiance which they have sworn or may swear to him, and I forbid anyone to serve him as king. For it is fitting that he who seeks to diminish the glory of thy Church should lose the glory which he seems to have. . . . I bind him in the bonds of anathema in thy stead and I bind him thus as commissioned by thee, that the nations may know and be convinced that thou art Peter and that upon thy rock the son of the living God has built his church and the gates of hell shall not prevail against it." (pp. 376–377)

THE GERMAN REACTION

The excommunication and deposition of Henry IV offered a splendid chance to all the disaffected in Germany to strike with papal support against the king. These nobles resented the efforts of Henry to strengthen the monarchy by resuming rights long granted away and surrounding himself with a group of low-born Swabians as administrators and advisers. At this moment civil war was about to break out in Germany between feudal-papal and royal supporters, and, with interruptions, it was to last until the very end of Henry's reign (1106). The aristocratic enemies of the king first planned to take advantage of Henry's excommunication and deposition by getting rid of him and electing a new king. They decided in October, 1076, after a meeting at Tribur, that Henry was to withdraw from public life and retire to Speyer. If by 22 February, 1077, he had not released himself from the excommunication, he was not to be considered as king. In any case, Gregory was invited to come to Germany for a meeting at Augsburg to consider the fitness of Henry IV to be king, and if necessary to elect a new one. Soon after the receipt of this invitation Gregory, quite delighted at the prospect of playing a determining role in

German politics, set out for Germany, requesting meanwhile of the German nobles a safe conduct for his journey across the Alps.

CANOSSA

It was a serious moment for Henry. Not only was it necessary for him to get released from his excommunication. It was also necessary for him to forestall Pope Gregory's appearance in Germany at the head of a hostile assembly. The king decided to cross the Alps in the middle of the winter and, as a penitent sinner, demand forgiveness from the vicar of Christ as he made his way northward. Leaving Speyer, Henry crossed the Mont Cenis Pass and made straight for Canossa, a castle of Mathilda, the countess of Tuscany. Here, under the protection of one of his ardent Italian supporters, Gregory had taken refuge, not quite sure of what Henry was up to. Gregory had written to the Germans in 1076, after his excommunication of the king, that "if, under God's blessing, he shall return to his senses, no matter what he may be plotting against us, he shall find us always ready to receive him back into holy communion." He had also written them that if Henry did not seek release from his excommunication as a penitent sinner, "let another ruler of the kingdom be found by divine favor, such a one as shall bind himself by unquestionable obligations to carry out the measures we have indicated and any others that may be necessary for the safety of the Christian religion and of the whole empire. Further, in order that we may confirm your choice . . . inform us at the earliest possible moment as to the person, the character, and the occupation of the candidate." Now Henry at Canossa was beseeching Gregory for forgiveness. How he conducted himself Gregory described to the German princes in a letter written at the end of January, 1077. "Of his own accord and without any show of hostility or defiance he came with a few followers to the fortress of Canossa. . . . There, on three successive days, standing before the castle gate, laying aside all royal insignia, barefooted and in coarse attire, he ceased not with many tears to beseech the apostolic help and comfort until all who were present or who heard the story were so moved by pity and compassion that they pleaded his cause with prayers and tears. . . . At last overcome by his persistent show of penitence and the urgency of all present, we released him from the bonds of anathema and received him into the grace of Holy Mother Church." Gregory did not expect that this release from excommunication would keep him from Germany, nor did he regard the matter of his dispute with Henry as being in any way settled. But he was never able to get to Germany, and Henry was able to return with the stain of excommunication removed, and thus any doubt as to the legitimacy of his kingship. At the cost of what Gregory called "the king's penitential humiliation" Henry had won a tactical victory at Canossa. His papal and feudal enemies had been kept from joining hands.

Henry's German enemies did not intend to let what they must have regarded as Gregory's weakness interfere with their plans to get rid of the king. In March of 1077, with two papal legates present, the German princes elected Rudolf, the duke of Swabia, as their king. Civil war then broke out in all its fury between the two kings, between whom Gregory now took upon himself the right to choose. Demanding safe conducts from each, he declared himself "prepared, with the approval of those among you who fear God and love the Christian faith, to try the justice of the case impartially and give our support to the one whose government of the kingdom is decided to be the more according to right. . . . For if the See of St. Peter decides and gives judgment in heavenly and spiritual things, how much more in things earthly and secular?" In any case, no papal recognition could be made of any German king without his first becoming a vassal of the Holy See, turning over the suzerainty of the German empire to the pope. Although it seems quite impossible that Henry IV should ever have received the recognition of Gregory, the pope took three long years to make up his mind. On 2 March, 1080, he then excommunicated Henry IV a second time in a message addressed to both Saints Peter and Paul. In it he refers to Henry's coming to him "in confusion and humiliation . . . begging for release from his excommunication, . . . I restored him to communion only but did not reinstate him in the royal power from which I had deposed him." Henry has now "together with his supporters, not fearing the perils of disobedience—which is the crime of idolatry—incurred excommunication" by preventing a meeting of German princes that Gregory had summoned. "Wherefore . . . I place the aforesaid Henry, whom they call 'king' and all his supporters under excommunication and bind them with the chains of anathema. And again forbidding him in the name of Almighty God and of yourselves to govern in Germany and Italy, I take from him all royal power and state. I forbid all Christians to obey him as king, and I release all who have made or shall make oath to him as king from the obligation of their oath. . . . That Rudolf, whom the Germans have chosen for their king in loyalty to you, may rule and protect the kingdom of the Germans, I grant and allow in your name. . . . For as Henry is justly cast down from the royal dignity for his insolence, his disobedience and his deceit, so Rudolf, for his humility, his obedience, and his truthfulness is granted the power and the dignity of kingship. . . . And now, most holy fathers and princes, I pray you to take such action that the whole world may know and understand that . . . you are able . . . on earth to grant and to take away from everyone according to his deserts empires, kingdoms, principalities, dukedoms, marquisates, earldoms and the property of all men. . . . If you can give judgment in spiritual things what may we not believe as to your power over secular things? . . . Now let kings and princes . . . fear . . . the commands of your Church." (pp. 150–152)

This second excommunication was too much, even for the royal op-position in Germany. To be sure, after Rudolf of Swabia's death in battle in 1080 a few German nobles elected a successor, but he was never power-ful enough to cause Henry any trouble. Instead the king now proposed to give Gregory a little of his own medicine by providing him with a rival. A council of German and Italian clergy elected as pope, to supplant Gregory, Guibert, the archbishop of Ravenna, and in 1081 Henry marched with his pope into Italy. By 1084 he was able to install him in Gregory's place, being crowned himself, finally, as emperor. Gregory was obliged to withdraw from Rome and sought refuge in Monte Cassino, trying desper-ately still to govern the Church from this ancient home of Saint Benedict. He died in May, 1085, maintaining until the last that his fight had been only to help to make a supposedly Christian society really so. "I have loved justice," he said, "and hated iniquity, therefore I die in exile."

THE CONCORDAT OF WORMS, 1122

The struggle continued between Henry IV and the successors of Gregory VII. The papacy continued to follow Gregory's policy of supporting feudal rebellion in Germany, headed often by Henry's sons. By the end of his reign Henry had lost control of Italy and Germany to local German princes whose wealth and power he had been obliged to augment to secure their support. At the same time that they were carry-ing on their struggle against the German empire the popes were continuing the campaign for reform in France and England, where the hold of the kings upon the Church was only less powerful than under a monarch like Otto I. The papacy, taking up Gregory VII's plans to launch a crusade to the East, also promoted and organized the enthusiasm that led to the First Crusade.[18] Under the powerful stimulus of the crusading movement, when the Church was in need of all possible support from the feudal aristocracy, the reform program was less fanatically pushed, and its ex-treme aims, the establishment of temporal supremacy over the state and of spiritual supremacy over the whole Church, dropped for the time being. Instead, the leaders of the moderate wing of the reform party were per-mitted to negotiate settlements in England and France that concentrated upon getting rid of the practice of lay investiture, without insisting upon the complete absence of any royal control upon elections to high clerical office, or upon the complete separation of church and state in the sphere of feudal relationships. These settlements of the early twelfth century in England and France were the pattern upon which the German settlement, the Concordat of Worms, was negotiated in 1122. According to this agree-ment, a clear-cut distinction was to be made between the bishop as a tem-poral lord in possession of land and privileges granted to him by the crown

[18]See pp. 490 f.

540 CHAPTER TWELVE

(rights called regalian), and the bishop as a spiritual lord in possession of the power to save souls (the spiritual rights). Elections to clerical office in Germany were henceforth to be made in accordance with canon law, but they were to be made in the presence of the king or his representative, who was granted considerable influence in the case of disputed elections. The newly elected bishop was to receive his regalian rights from the king after he had sworn homage and fealty, and only after this had been done was he to be consecrated and granted his spiritual rights (ring and staff) by the proper archbishop. The German kings and aristocracy thus gave up, as in England and France, the practice of lay investiture, but the fact that feudal investiture with regalian rights preceded ecclesiastical investiture with spiritual rights weighed heavily in favor of the influence of the crown. For any bishop denied the regalian rights by the crown could scarcely maintain himself in possession of only his spiritual rights. The Concordat of Worms provided that in Burgundy and Italy investiture with spiritual powers was to be automatically followed by investiture with regalian rights. In these territories, then, the German king lost control over high clerical office.

RESULTS OF INVESTITURE STRUGGLE

The papacy thus was not able at this date to secure complete control over the clergy. Inasmuch as election in accordance with canon law (clergy and people) meant actually election by the cathedral chapter, which was normally composed of sons of the neighboring aristocracy, the upper clergy usually came from this social class. There can be no doubt that in the course of the investiture struggle in Germany the crown suffered heavily in power and prestige because of the necessity of paying a heavy price for the support of an ambitious feudal nobility. This price took the form of royal property and privileges. The late eleventh and early twelfth centuries, therefore, witnessed a more intensive feudalization of Germany than hitherto. To the extent that they had weakened the German crown the popes may be said to have been successful in their struggle to magnify the spiritual over the temporal power. But in permitting the aristocracy to be strengthened, they were not necessarily promoting the interests of their friends. From the larger view of creating a spiritual rather than a political church, the reforming popes were, of course, not successful. In promoting the campaigns to eradicate simony from the Church and establish a celibate clergy they were successfully promoting a more efficient church. The question was how the new efficiency was to be used: to promote spiritual or temporal interests? In any case, the real issue between secular and clerical theocracy, between empire and papacy, between church and state, had not yet been settled. It was now quite clear, however, in which direction the settlement was moving.

Henry IV belonged to the second medieval German dynasty, the Salian or Franconian (1025–1125). Ruling (like the Saxon dynasty) for about a century, it was then supplanted, through election of the princes, by the Hohenstaufens (1137–1254). Under the early Hohenstaufens (Frederick I, Henry VI) the Holy Roman Empire may be said to have reached its height for a brief moment, and under the later Hohenstaufens (Frederick II, Conrad IV, Manfred, Conradino) it may be said to have been finally defeated by the papacy. The way was thus opened for the settlement of the church-and-state problem in Germany, and for the development of Europe as a clerical theocracy.

THE HOHENSTAUFENS AND THE PAPACY

The struggle between the empire and the papacy during the Hohenstaufen period had much less the character of the Church struggling to reform itself and being resisted in this effort by the state than of an empire and a papacy fighting to see which would control the power and loyalty of the Christian Church. It also possessed to a great degree the nature of an intense political battle for the control of Italy. That is to say that neither the Saxon nor the Salian emperors were able to set up in Italy any satisfactory system of imperial government. They had to rely upon the local bishops and archbishops, or the local feudal aristocracy to rule for them, and this indirect rule had to be paid for in royal land and privileges. Even then there can hardly be said to have been any real German rule over Italy except when the German kings were present, and that was never for very long. The Germans were never able to penetrate into Byzantine southern Italy or Moslem Sicily. They were not able to prevent the advance of the Normans in southern Italy and Sicily in the eleventh century. After the papal electoral decrees of 1059, they found it difficult to control elections for a new pope, and they were unable to supplant papal government in the Papal States. After the Concordat of Worms they lost control of the Italian episcopate. Altogether, this was a situation that the Hohenstaufens sought to remedy. Much more thoroughly imbued with the principles of government of ancient Rome, as they were then being made known by the professors of law at the University of Bologna, the Hohenstaufens sought to introduce into northern and north-central Italy a direct control through an administration of their own. Because of events we shall presently narrate it was even possible for them to conceive of a unified Italy and Sicily under direct German control that would absorb Rome and the Papal States and supplant the Norman kingdom of southern Italy and Sicily. The papacy thus found itself threatened with the loss of its temporal power in Italy, that is, the loss of Rome and the Papal States. Since it could not conceive of itself as a purely spiritual institution, or rather, since it refused to contemplate such a complete subjection to the German state, a subjection that would mean a complete denial of its past and an abandonment of its plans for the future, it fought desperately with almost any weapon available to thwart these German plans. It was ready to ally with any other Italian power anxious to prevent their realization. In this way, the Norman princes and kings became vassals of the pope for their southern Italian and Sicilian state.

FREDERICK BARBAROSSA AND THE LOMBARD TOWNS

The other great power in Italy was the Lombard towns, the northern and north-central towns dominated by those of the Po Valley, of which Milan was the chief. By the time of the accession of Frederick I (Barbarossa) in 1152, the communal revolution had been completely victorious in northern Italy. The government of the towns had passed, often violently, from the control of bishops and archbishops to the control of local merchants, and the new self-governing towns, quite without reference to the German government, had assumed the powers necessary to govern their communities. To a man like Barbarossa this was an outrageous usurpation by ex-serfs of the sacred powers of imperial rule. Upon his second visit to Italy, in 1158, he called together four professors of the Roman law from the University of Bologna and representatives of twenty-eight Italian towns to meet at Roncaglia (the Diet of Roncaglia) to determine what were the regalian rights of the emperor in the new Italian towns. The conclusions to which this royal commission came were not tolerant of the new urban governments. If, it concluded, these towns were in possession of royal powers as a result of legal grants by the imperial government, well and good. If not, the royal rights were to be administered by officials to be appointed by Frederick himself with the consent of the people. The decisions of the commission were also to be entered into the Justinian Code by the professors of Bologna. It was thus clear to the Lombard towns that Hohenstaufen imperialism meant the extinction of their hard-won autonomy and independence.

The actual conduct of Frederick and his troops on Italian expeditions revealed only too clearly the hostility of the empire to the new urban developments. On his first Italian campaign (1154) he was opposed by Milan, and in return destroyed Milan's ally, Tortona. In Rome he obliged the pope, who was having trouble with a Roman commune, by hanging its leader, Arnold of Brescia.[19] On his second Italian journey (1158) he besieged Milan and forced her to promise to limit her controlling position in Lombardy. When it became clear that the towns would resist the decisions of the Diet of Roncaglia, Frederick attempted to terrorize them. He destroyed the town of Crema. He removed the fortifications of Piacenza and Brescia. After a year's siege he destroyed Milan and reduced its citizens to the status of peasants who had to render manorial services. It was thus obvious to the Italian towns that only their combined efforts could resist the Germans. Venice, with no desire to imitate Milan, in 1164

[19]See pp. 607 f.

organized the League of Verona (Venice, Verona, Vicenza, Padua). The success of this league against Frederick, upon his third Italian campaign, encouraged the Lombard towns to do likewise. In 1166 the two leagues, the Lombard and Veronese, fused, and the combined twenty-two towns set up a unique federal government to provide for the settlement of inter-urban disputes and a common army. When Frederick returned to Italy for his fifth campaign (1174–1178) he was defeated by the army of the League at Legnano (1176). After a truce of six years he signed with the League the Treaty of Constance (1183). The treaty did not deprive the German empire of all power in the Italian towns, but it did force Frederick to abandon the program of the Diet of Roncaglia. The autonomy of the Italian towns was recognized, and their desire to continue the Lombard League given imperial approval. The powerful German state could not suppress the organized resistance of the northern Italian towns. The blow at Legnano and the Treaty of Constance were thus first steps in the German loss of imperial power in Italy. Throughout the formation and the resistance of the League, the papacy had been its warm supporter. Consequently Legnano and Constance amounted to indirect papal victories in the long struggle to drive the Germans out of Italy.

GERMANY AND SOUTHERN ITALY AND SICILY

Although Frederick was obliged to yield to the Lombard towns he was able nevertheless to arrange for what seemed a brilliant future for the Hohenstaufen dynasty by marrying his son Henry to Constance, the heiress of William II, Norman king of southern Italy and Sicily (1186). The Norman conquest of southern Italy and Sicily from Byzantium and the Saracens had been completed by 1091, and in the twelfth century such capable monarchs as Roger II, William I (1154–1166), and William II (1166–1189) had been able to combine the diverse populations and traditions of this area into a prosperous, well-governed, for the most part unfeudal state, in much the same way as their kinsmen were doing in England.[20] Constance inherited the kingdom in 1189, and Henry VI (1190–1197) succeeded his father, Frederick, in the following year. Nevertheless, the Norman kingdom did not fall easily into German hands. It had to be conquered from Norman supporters who were aided by the papacy. Yet by 1194 Henry VI, with quite brutal methods, had succeeded in destroying the opposition in the south. The papacy was then confronted by Germans not only to the north but to the south as well, and it took no great foresight to see that the intervening gap might be closed and the temporal power of the papacy in Italy destroyed. At this moment, therefore, the papacy with even more energy tried to save itself from this fate.

[20]See pp. 556 ff.

In this last phase of the papal-imperial struggle the papacy was fortunate in having one of its most capable popes to guide it, Innocent III (1198–1216). It was fortunate as well in that Henry VI died in the midst of plans to establish a German hegemony in the eastern Mediterranean. After his death Germany was the scene of constant civil war between rival candidates for the throne: Henry's brother, Philip, duke of Swabia, and the Welf (Guelph), Otto of Brunswick. Upon her death in 1198 Constance left her young son by Henry VI, the future Frederick II, as a ward of the pope. With respect to the civil war in Germany Innocent III took on the role of mediator that Gregory VII had assumed after 1077, but in the end, when both Hohenstaufen and Welf candidates seemed bent upon pursuing the old imperial program in Italy and gathering in the kingdom of southern Italy and Sicily, he turned to his young ward Frederick, who, at a considerable price, contrived to have himself elected German king in 1211 and crowned in 1212. Henceforth, until his death in 1250, Frederick waged a bitter fight against Innocent III and his able successors. Half German and half Norman, Frederick was the most gifted member of his line, and much more imbued with the ancient example of the Roman Empire than any of his predecessors. It is quite evident that he saw no real possibility of establishing a strong government in Germany, where the feudal nobility had long been the actual rulers of their principalities. His whole emphasis was therefore upon Italy, which he hoped to unify with German aid. But he leaned most of all upon the resources of his Norman kingdom, which he brilliantly reorganized, and counted too easily upon subordinating the Lombard League. In fighting him the popes raised antikings in Germany and proclaimed crusades. There were the usual number of excommunications and depositions, and an irresponsible propaganda was unleashed by both papal and imperial sides. In the end, Frederick could not quite make it. He died without having established his control in either Italy or Germany. After his death the papacy pursued the Hohenstaufen house until there were no more heirs. Frederick's heir was his son Conrad IV, for whom Manfred, an illegitimate son of Frederick, ruled in Sicily. Conrad died in 1254, leaving his young son (Conradino) in the hands of the duke of Bavaria. To prevent the Germans from regaining the Norman kingdom, two French popes, Urban IV and Clement IV, worked out the plan of inviting Charles of Anjou, the brother of the French king, Louis IX, to take over the kingdom of the Normans. Charles came, entered the kingdom that Manfred was ruling in 1266, and defeated him in a battle at Benevento, where he was killed. The Ghibelline (imperial) party[21] then summoned young Conradino to Italy to take over the Hohenstaufen inheritance, and he and his imperial supporters were defeated at Tagliacozzo in 1268. Conradino, the last of the Hohenstaufens, was captured and subsequently beheaded at Naples.

[21]See pp. 520 ff.

This marked the end of the Hohenstaufen dynasty. In thus supporting the French campaign against the Hohenstaufens and the installation of a French kingdom in southern Italy, the popes were able to win in the struggle to prevent the Germans from establishing a strong imperial government in Italy. Henceforth no German king took seriously the re-establishment of German rule in Italy where a French kingdom ruled in the south, a papal state in the center, and a group of mutually hostile city-states in the north. The popes had prevented a German unification of Italy. In this way they thwarted such Italian patriots as Dante and his successors until the nineteenth century. For out of the disunity in which the imperial-papal struggle left it, Italy did not emerge until then.

RESULTS FOR GERMANY

To the struggle between empire and papacy may also be attributed the fact that Germany was unable to develop a strong monarchy during these early medieval centuries. The German kings who, after 962, pursued an imperial policy in Italy had to pay for the support of the German nobles with royal lands and privileges. When the crown became involved in a conflict with the popes, the German nobility found itself urged to revolt against kings whom the popes were opposing, and civil war became almost continuous in Germany between rival candidates for the throne. Under these circumstances the crown had to pay even more heavily with royal resources to maintain sufficient loyalty among the nobles. The resort to civil war and to antikings kept alive in Germany the principle of an elective kingship, inherited from the earliest days of Germanic monarchy, and the attempts of each succeeding dynasty to introduce a hereditary monarchy failed. German electors demanded heavy pay for their support. Thus by the beginning of the thirteenth century the old tribal duchies of Germany had broken up into hundreds of territorial duchies, margravates, burgravates, and counties, each striving for complete independence. Frederick II saw that there was nothing to do but to recognize this situation and, in fact, use it to secure the support of the nobles for his Italian program. In 1220 he granted to the German ecclesiastical princes, the bishops, archbishops, and leading abbots, and again in 1231 to the German secular princes, privileges that greatly strengthened their local independence. This independence in turn was still further augmented by the papacy's support of rebellion in Germany for the rest of Frederick II's reign.

The price the German kings had to pay for their unsuccessful imperial policy was the victory of feudalism at home. In obliging them to pay this price the popes had a large share. The German church, moreover, had secured from Frederick II in 1213 the Golden Bull of Eger, which freed it from the political control still left to the king by the Concordat of Worms, that is, it could now proceed with clerical elections without the presence of the king or his representative; royal influence upon disputed elections was abandoned; and to bishops and archbishops the same kind of freedom was granted in clerical as to the pope in papal elections. The king, moreover, was not to interfere with judicial appeals by German clergy to Rome. Thus the Golden Bull of Eger established for the German church that freedom from the state sought by the papacy from the earliest days of the investiture struggle. The way was now opened for the centralization of this church under the papacy.

These facts are of great importance for the future history of Italy and Germany, and indeed, for the future development of the papacy.[22] The fact that Italy and Germany did not achieve the kind of unification under a king that was the fortune of France and England postponed the political unification of these states until the nineteenth century and kept them from their proper share in the European partition of the globe. Accordingly, when what we call nationalism did come to Italy and Germany, it came in an especially virulent form, inasmuch as these peoples had felt themselves thwarted for so long. Reduced to political impotence by the medieval struggle between empire and papacy, they compensated themselves, after the early modern centuries had failed to improve their European status, by romantic delusions of grandeur that were to find ultimate twentieth-century expression in Mussolini and Hitler.

The Germanic attempt to revive the Roman Empire over feudal Europe was rejected by the papacy, which had its own plans for international organization. It was rejected by Italy because the character of German rule—the subordination of town life and the establishment of a uniform, centralized absolutism—did not allow for the free development of the Italian people, which had already begun. The German empire was unable to make any serious impression upon Germany's neighbors. Thus, with the effective collapse of the Holy Roman Empire, there was left as the alternate international organization for medieval Europe the Holy Roman Church. But the fact that this church had done so much to thwart the political ambitions of the German people meant that it had won the undying hatred of many Germans, a hatred that was increased by the subjection of the German church to Rome in the fourteenth and fifteenth centuries. This hatred was later to find expression in the Protestant Reformation. The extent to which the Church was able to organize an international theocracy will be considered in the next chapter. It will be argued that the West rejected international ecclesiastical, as well as international secular, theocracy. This rejection left as possibilities for the political future of Europe either (1) a multiplicity of little, sovereign, feudal states or (2) larger monarchies, whose kings had risen above the feudal lords. Germany and Italy took the first path. The rest of Europe, in the main, took the second. It was the rise of the feudal monarch that thus became the "normal" political development for Europe, and this feudal monarchy, providing various degrees of different kinds of political

[22]The results for the papacy will be considered in the following chapter.

unity for its kingdoms, was an early phase of something that, at the end of the Middle Ages, can be called national monarchy. Western Europe therefore rejected the Holy Roman Empire, the medieval form of secular theocracy, for the independent town, the feudal principality, and the feudal kingdom. To two of the latter, France and England, we must now turn.

The Political Development of France

MONARCHY AND PRIVATE WAR

The development of strong monarchy out of feudalism was a step forward in the political history of western Europe, inasmuch as loyalty to the monarch was an expansion of attachment to the locality. The attachment to village, town, and region is, of course, an inevitable sentiment, but when it goes no further it becomes a kind of stultifying, narrow provincialism that can make its possessors petty and bigoted. The feudal state could range in size from enough territory to support a single knight to a large duchy such as Normandy. A kingdom composed of a multitude of such states was a prey to constant war between suzerain-lords who, of all outrageous rights, maintained the worst, the right of private warfare. If the monarchy could offer these local lords a tribunal in which they could settle their grievances or the security of feeling themselves protected in their other essential rights, it could abolish private warfare. In this case the ensuing boon to the sufferers from war, always the great mass of mankind, would be incalculable.

MONARCHY AND ECONOMIC AND CULTURAL NEEDS

Looking upon his little state as the desirable end of all political development, the ordinary feudal lord attempted to penalize all economic development of an interregional or interfeudal kind. There would be tolls upon the roads, streams, and bridges, and fees at the local markets and fairs. If the monarchy could liberate trade and commerce from these local restrictive dues, if it could transform the local road into a royal highway, if it could consider the economic needs of the population of a kingdom rather than of a region, it would expand the activities of the worker, trader, and merchant and enlarge the benefits of trade and commerce. In the domain of culture, likewise, however important the contribution of the local dialect, the local artist, and the local school, the larger interests and resources of the monarchy permitted it to support cultural movements of more than local importance. In making persons the subjects of a kingdom rather than of a fief, these kings were associating mankind in larger than local enterprises and helping to establish their common needs, their common aspirations, and their common identity.

MONARCHY AND NATIONALISM

In the development of strong monarchy out of feudalism it was all-important whether the Germanic and feudal or the Roman and theocratic traditions of the past were more utilized, whether, that is, absolute or limited monarchy were to eventuate. In any case, it is well to remember at this point that the development of strong monarchy was a step in the production of what is called today the sovereign national state, animated often by the kind of superpatriotism called nationalism. It is quite well agreed today among leaders in all walks of life that this kind of state, agitated by this kind of sentiment, is no longer adequate to the necessary functioning of the globe, no more adequate to its proper functioning, in fact, than the feudal principality was adequate to the development of Europe after the ninth and tenth centuries. In other words, in the medieval struggle between feudalism and monarchy it was monarchy that represented the immediate step forward, in much the same way that regional federations today (NATO, Council of Europe, Pan-American Union) represent the intermediate step between the national state and the United Nations. And to push this analogy further is to say that just as feudalism contributed to the growth of monarchy the notion of contract, and therewith the protection of individual rights, so the national state today, whatever its form, suggests the idea that any future, successful world government must be federal in nature.

THE CAPETIANS

The Carolingian dynasty ruled in France until 987, some twenty-five years after Otto I of Germany was crowned a Roman emperor. In 987 the great feudal nobles of France elected as king one Hugh Capet, a member of a family that had acquired renown as the defender of the Seine Basin against the Normans. There was then founded the Capetian dynasty, which ruled France until 1328. During this time the Capetians succeeded in transforming the elective into an hereditary monarchy, and they were fortunate enough, until 1316, in having direct heirs to succeed them. In the course of these centuries they were able to transform France from a collection of quasi-independent feudal principalities into a strong, centralized monarchy with a well-organized system of government, and thus to aid in making France the most creative of the medieval states in the domain of literature, art, and learning.

THE CAPETIANS AS MONARCHS

In 987 Hugh Capet possessed a triple position. As the elected king of France he possessed all those rights of a sovereign that the ancient Germanic kings had once possessed and lost to the feudal nobles. That is, he was in theory the source of justice in the French kingdom, the man to whom all could come for a settlement of their disputes. He was, as well, the defender of the realm against its enemies and the protector of the defenseless—the widow, the orphan, and the Church. In this capacity he was crowned and consecrated by the Church after his election in ceremonies that made him an agent of God in the governance of his kingdom (the Lord's anointed) and indeed a special member of the clergy in the carrying out of his holy task as king. These traditional powers and these ceremonies gave to him a moral preponderance over the other nobles of the realm. Actually they gave him no power. They were, however, a potential source of power, and thus may be said to have suggested a program. The king, by divine right, was to be the chief judge, the commander in chief, and the chief promoter of the welfare of his subjects.

THE CAPETIANS AS SUZERAINS

Hugh Capet was more, however, than a nominal king possessed of theoretical powers that were to be realized in the future. He was recognized by feudal law to be the suzerain of all French feudal lords (thus responsible for the suzerain's side of the feudal contract) and the recipient of the obligations owed by his vassals. Hugh was also the suzerain of a particular domain, a narrow strip of land reaching from the Seine to the Loire, including Paris and Orléans, a domain known as the Île de France. This was in part cultivated directly for the crown and in part granted out as fiefs. In this domain the early Capetian kings were not the actual masters, for local nobles were able to terrorize the region with cruel and petty banditry. It can therefore be imagined that the early Capetians were in no position to make an impression upon the remaining great lords of France, whose domains were much larger and whose control of them was more complete than the Capetian. Thus the early Capetians were unable to perform their obligations as feudal suzerains and, consequently, were ignored by their vassals. In this situation the fact that the Capetians were kings made little difference. They were kings in possession of rights they could not exercise and suzerains in possession of rights and obligations they could not perform. It is therefore quite clear now, as it must have been quite clear then, that before they could rise in the feudal hierarchy they would have to become masters of their own domain in the Île de France. They would also have to increase the size of their domain to the point where it equalled or surpassed that of the strongest lords in France. This could be done only at the cost of other feudal lords. When it had been accomplished Capetians could perform their feudal obligations and expect to receive their feudal rights. They could function as powerful feudal suzerains. The power thus acquired could be used to enhance their position as monarchs, especially if, by being careful not to antagonize it, they could retain the great political, economic, and moral support of the Church. If, moreover, the prerogatives of the emperor as defined by Roman law could be applied to a king (the king is emperor in his own kingdom), then feudal powers might in the course of time be imperceptibly transformed into royal power. These steps constituted a program for the Capetian dynasty: (1) control the domain; (2) expand the domain; and (3) transform feudal suzerainty into royal sovereignty.

THE RISE OF THE ANGEVINS

It was Louis VI, the Fat (1108-1137), fourth in succession after Hugh, who managed to rid the domain of its lawless gangsters. It was his son and successor, Louis VII (1137-1180), who began to receive appeals to intervene in fiefs outside of the domain. It was Louis VII also who, by a famous marriage and divorce, built up the feudal holdings of the chief Capetian rivals in France, the house of Anjou (the Angevins). In 1066, it will be remembered, William the Conqueror, duke of Normandy, conquered England from the Anglo-Saxons. Henceforth, the Norman kings of England retained the Norman duchy as vassals of the French kings, vassals of power far superior to their suzerain's. The third Norman king of England, Henry I (1100-1135), married his daughter Matilda to Geoffrey, the heir to the county of Anjou, who became count in 1129. The counts of Anjou had already added Maine and Touraine to their domain. Upon the death of her father, Henry I, Matilda struggled against Stephen of Blois over the succession in England, and in her absence (1135) her husband, Geoffrey, the count of Anjou, Maine, and Touraine, conquered the duchy of Normandy. Geoffrey and Matilda's son Henry became duke of Normandy in 1150 and the next year succeeded his father as count of Anjou, Maine, and Touraine. This was but the beginning of his extraordinary accumulation of lands. In 1152 he married a very unusual and very capable French woman, Eleanor, the duchess of Aquitaine, who brought a large part of southern France, namely Aquitaine, into the Angevin holdings. When Eleanor was fifteen she had married Louis VII (1137), thus promising to add her inheritance to the Capetian domain. However, she was none too devoted to her monkish husband and, so it seemed to him after the birth of a second daughter, was unable to supply the crown with a male heir.[23] Accordingly, with supreme unconcern about Aquitaine, Louis VII secured a divorce on 21 March, 1152, and Eleanor, after being pursued by eligible bachelors from all sides, finally married Henry of Anjou on 18 May. In 1154 this same Henry became Henry II, the first and great Angevin king of England (1154-1189). Thus Louis VII and his successor, Philip Augustus (1180-1223), were confronted with a vassal who was not only the king of England but also lord of more than half of France: of Normandy, Maine, Anjou, Touraine, and, through his wife, of Aquitaine. It could not be expected that the Capetians would be taken seriously by such a king or that they could easily remove this Angevin obstacle to their advancement.

[23]See Amy Kelly, *Eleanor of Aquitaine and the Four Kings*; also C. H. Walker, *Eleanor of Aquitaine*.

Yet this is exactly what Philip Augustus succeeded in doing. Having secured the verdict of a French feudal court that for failure to answer a summons of his suzerain to appear before his court King John was a contumacious vassal and deprived of his French fiefs (1202),[24] Philip was able to take advantage of John's unpopularity on the Continent to conquer Normandy, Maine, Anjou, and Touraine (1204), leaving Eleanor's Aquitaine as the sole remnant of the English empire in France. The relation of these events to Magna Carta has been indicated previously.[25] To the Capetian future they meant that French kings now possessed the economic, and therewith the military, power (the Capetian domain had been doubled) to secure the adherence of French nobles to their feudal contract. Thus the feudal suzerainty of the Capetian king suddenly became a thing of substance rather than shadow, and every development of his feudal power enhanced his position as monarch. In the century after the acquisition of these holdings France under Saint Louis became a strong feudal kingdom, and under Philip the Fair (1285-1314) could summon the nation in assembly to support its policy and challenge the papacy of Boniface VIII.[26]

THE CAPETIANS AS STRONG SUZERAINS

As powerful feudal suzerains the Capetians could now take advantage of all the rights granted to them by the feudal contract. Vassals would appear at the court of their lord to act as a court of justice. Vassals would render military service or pay the equivalent in cash. Feudal aids and feudal relief would now be paid. Rights of wardship, marriage, escheat, and entertainment would now be carefully enforced, or their money equivalent collected. Favorable marriage alliances could now be made more easily, and more cash was now available for buying up fiefs and feudal privileges. In this way, by using perfectly legitimate feudal means and without antagonizing a feudal nobility pursuing the same policies, Philip and his successors could continue to expand the domain. Artois, Poitou, Perche, Mâcon, Languedoc, Toulouse, Navarre, and Champagne were among the more important additions to the domain made after the acquisition of the Angevin lands.

ROYAL FOR FEUDAL GOVERNMENT

The additions to the original Capetian domain of the remaining feudal principalities did not alone transform France into a strong monarchy. Feudal government had to be succeeded by monarchial government and to be introduced into the new jurisdictions. Feudal government was govern-

[24]See pp. 431 f.
[25]See pp. 434 ff.
[26]See p. 619.

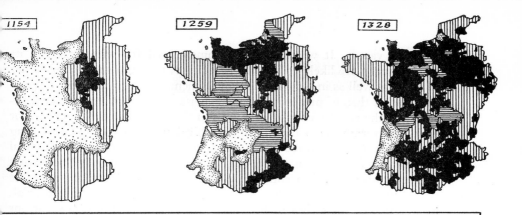

1154   1259   1328

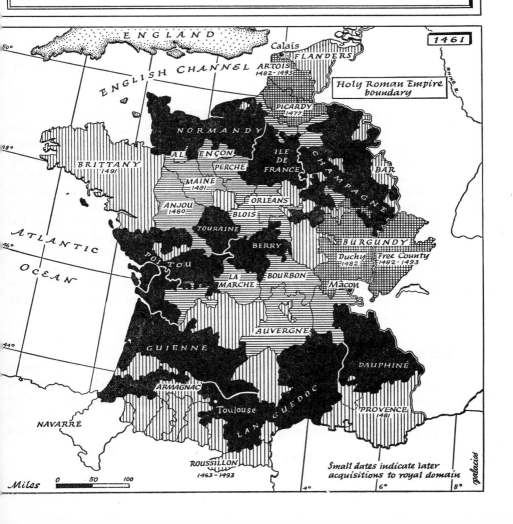

The
EXPANSION of the FRENCH ROYAL DOMAIN

Royal Domain   Appanages to the royal house   English territory   Burgundian territory   Other French fiefs

1461

ENGLAND
ENGLISH CHANNEL
Calais
FLANDERS
ARTOIS 1482-1493
Holy Roman Empire boundary
RHINE R.
PICARDY 1477
NORMANDY
ALENÇON
PERCHE
ILE DE FRANCE
CHAMPAGNE
BAR
BRITTANY 1491
MAINE 1481
ORLÉANS
BLOIS
ANJOU 1480
TOURAINE
BERRY
BURGUNDY
Duchy 1482
Free County 1482-1493
ATLANTIC OCEAN
POITOU
LA MARCHE
BOURBON
Mâcon
AUVERGNE
GUIENNE
DAUPHINÉ
ARMAGNAC
Toulouse
LANGUEDOC
PROVENCE 1481
NAVARRE
ROUSSILLON 1463-1493
Small dates indicate later acquisitions to royal domain

Miles 0   50   100

palacios

ment by vassals. It was thus a government paid for with fiefs, and its chief offices were likely to become hereditary, with son succeeding father in office as well as in fief. Feudal government was a government of amateurs rather than of professionals and experts. It was government dependent upon the regular counsel of vassals in the formulation of policy. For such a government to become monarchical would mean that the king possessed a military force independent of the limitations of the feudal contract. It would mean, moreover, that he possessed means of rendering justice to his subjects in addition to the institutions of feudal justice. It would mean, also, that in the choice of his central administrative officials he was free of the claims of heredity. Adequate monarchial government would mean that a royal administration dependent upon the king would penetrate the domain, as this domain expanded, and challenge the injustices of any feudal administration that remained. To build up a nonfeudal army and a nonfeudal administration the king would need a large cash income from which to pay salaries rather than invest with fiefs. Such an income, to be adequate, could come only from taxes. Feudal dues and income from crown lands were not enough.

CAPETIAN ACHIEVEMENT

By 1328 the Capetians had not yet liberated themselves from the limitations of a feudal army. They had begun to supplement this army with mercenaries, but they were not rich enough to keep a standing army. This would indicate that by 1328 they were not able as yet to collect direct taxes. They had, that is, to rely upon the income from their own domain, the Church, the feudal dues, and indirect taxes. For special financial aid from their subjects they had to negotiate with local assemblies. By this date, however, the framework of a new royal central administration and a new royal local administration had been established. It must, of course, be understood that this growth of new administrative institutions was not merely the result of a desire of the Capetians to get free of the limitations of the feudal system. It was also a response of the crown to new and more generalized needs of the more complex society that France was becoming. This was an adaptation of the crown to new needs by political invention, and a large part of the fascination of this theme consists in watching the human being spontaneously create more adequate political institutions under pressure of need.

THE ROYAL GOVERNMENT

The new central administration was created from the old feudal court of the king (*curia regis*), consisting of all the leading vassals of the crown, clerical and lay, who were held to service in court. By the time of Philip the Fair this court had split into two councils: the Great Council (*grand* or *plein conseil*), consisting of the more important vassals still summoned to court on irregular occasions, and the Small Council (*étroit conseil*), consisting of the permanent officials of the crown always at court. It was from this Small Council that professional staffs of specialized experts developed, and these, in turn, tended to separate into two groups: those having to do with the private administration of the royal household and those having to do with the public administration of the whole kingdom. By the beginning of the fourteenth century, for example, there was a special department for the royal household (*Hôtel du Roi*), a special household treasury (*Chambre aux deniers*), and a special household secretariat (*Chambre*). Much more important was the elaboration of a public treasury (*Chambre des Comptes*—Chamber of Accounts) and a public court specialized into separate groups, organized to receive and act upon appeals from any source in France and to investigate the local administration of justice. This court was the *parlement*. In addition, there was a public secretariat or chancellery (*chancellerie*). The local administration in the domain had depended first upon the provost (*prévôt*). Philip Augustus, however, felt that the *prévôts* needed to be carefully supervised by a new official, the bailiff (*bailli*), who administered a special district of his own (the *baillage*). Saint Louis (1226–1270) centralized this machinery further by setting up a new official to supervise the bailiff, the investigator (*enquêteur*). Bailiff and investigator were appointed by the crown, paid in cash, and thus dependent upon royal favor for their security. By the time of Saint Louis the king felt strong enough to issue ordinances for the realm without first considering the advice of his *curia regis*.

PHILIP IV AND THE STATES-GENERAL

Without a standing army and a system of direct taxation the French crown nevertheless remained essentially dependent upon feudal support. The popularity of a king like Saint Louis therefore rested upon his care not to offend the noble classes of the realm. He was a typically feudal king. But his grandson, Philip IV (the Fair), was a monarch of a different stamp. He surrounded himself with lawyers trained in the Roman law who exercised their talent in extending the prerogative of the crown. One of them, Peter du Bois, thought it would be quite a simplification of the complicated affairs of Europe if the French king were to be substituted for the emperor as the head of all Europe and take over, in addition, all the temporal power of the Church. Philip was hated for his ingenuity in forcing new revenue from his subjects. He did not hesitate to challenge the papacy successfully. He felt quite strong enough to summon representatives from the leading classes in France to meet together and organize support for his anti-papal and foreign policies. This first meeting of what was called the States-General (*États-Généraux*) took place in 1302 when, in what was essentially an enlarged meeting of the feudal *curia regis*, representatives of the lay and clerical vassals together with representatives of the communes, who since the reign of Philip Augustus had been a powerful royal support, were called together to consult with the king, or rather told what they must do to support the king. But this was the first time that representatives of the towns had been summoned together with representatives of the nobility and clergy. Out of similar beginnings in England was to come a political body (parliament) that forced the English monarchy to share power with it. In France, however, the States-General, while summoned occasionally by the French monarchy until 1614, never acquired the position of the English parliament until given this power by the French Revolution (1789). By the beginning of the fourteenth century the French monarchy had acquired sufficient strength to do without a partner in government. Historical circumstances of the fourteenth and fifteenth centuries were to confirm it in this position.

The Political Development of England

ANGLO-SAXON INHERITANCE OF WILLIAM THE CONQUEROR

It has already been necessary to deal with the political development of England in order to illustrate the importance of the feudal contract as a means of checking a tyrannical king. Magna Carta was used for this purpose.[27] It is now necessary to show why in England by the end of the Norman and Angevin dynasties (1399) a limited, rather than an absolute, monarchy was taking shape. In order to do this it is necessary to keep in mind the events that led to Magna Carta. After his conquest of England, William of Normandy introduced continental feudalism of the Norman type. The Anglo-Saxon baronage was supplanted by a new French-Norman baronage, and between these big tenants or major vassals of the crown and himself William set up feudal relationships far more favorable to the king than those prevailing in France and guaranteeing his position as a conquering overlord. The properties, for example, retained by the king himself after the conquest brought in an income of £17,650; those granted out to the 170 tenants in chief of the king brought in less than twice as much (£30,350).[28] William, in other words, was as strong after 1066 in comparison with his barons as the French kings became only in 1204 after Philip Augustus incorporated Normandy, Maine, Anjou, and Touraine. He was able to prohibit private warfare among his vassals and retain control over their castles. In addition the Conqueror was more powerful than his French counterparts, for he retained from the Anglo-Saxon government certain institutions that French feudalism never possessed. He retained the right to tax directly in case of an emergency. This was an inheritance from the days when Anglo-Saxons contributed the Danegeld to pay off the Vikings. He retained also the old German privi-

[27]See pp. 434 ff.
[28]W. J. Corbett, *Cambridge Medieval History*, V, Chap. xv.

lege of summoning the whole people to arms (the *fyrd*). He retained, moreover, the old Anglo-Saxon judicial and administrative divisions, the township, hundred, and shire (county). Through the sheriff (shire-reeve), the equivalent of Philip Augustus' bailiff (bailli), the Norman kings maintained an invaluable direct and nonfeudal channel of communication down to the village or manor.

NORMAN GOVERNMENT

Upon this strong foundation the Norman kings (William I, William Rufus, Henry I) began to erect institutions of central government partially independent of the feudal classes. They began also to take seriously the traditional obligations of the monarchy as the dispenser of justice to all freemen, that is, to look beyond its position as feudal overlord, and to consider whether the justice administered by the feudal courts of the barons was an adequate justice. Crown justices would say this was to consider what the "King's peace" actually covered and whether it was being too narrowly interpreted. The Normans also used an institution, the sworn inquest, which it is altogether likely they borrowed from the later Carolingians, incorporated into administrative practice in their duchy, and then imported into England. This was nothing more than the use of a local group of men, sworn to tell the truth, for purposes of gathering information needed by the crown. William the Conqueror used it in 1086 to gather information for a detailed economic survey of his newly conquered kingdom known as the Domesday Book, one of the most precious sources of information for historians interested in the changes in Anglo-Saxon England wrought by the Norman conquest. By the end of Henry I's reign (1135) organization of the central government had gone so far that the beginnings can be traced of such governmental departments as France was to possess only a century later during the reign of Saint Louis. The feudal court of the king (*curia regis*) had begun to break up into a Great Council and a Small Council, the former composed of tenants in chief of the crown, and the latter of the officials necessary to keep the business of government going. The needs of a state that included Normandy as well as England furthered the emergence of a secretarial staff, the chancery (chancellery), under a chancellor. A department of finance, the exchequer, with special subdivisions of its own, was also separating itself out of the unspecialized body of royal councillors. And, in addition, a special private administration for the king's household was organizing itself.

HENRY II AND THE PROBLEM OF JUSTICE

The strong government of the Normans was rudely shattered after 1135 during the civil war between Henry's daughter Matilda and his nephew, Count Stephen of Blois (1135-1154).[29] How easily power could

[29]See p. 551.

slip into the hands of the feudal nobility can be measured by the estimate of the chronicler that over one thousand unlicensed castles spread over England during this short period. When Henry II came to the throne in 1154, therefore, his subjects hoped that he would be able to restore strong monarchy again. This the great, restless, and, as some thought, demonic Angevin was able to do, building a strong central government the like of which was unknown on the continent. As the lord of Normandy, Maine, Anjou, Touraine, and Aquitaine, he possessed economic resources far beyond those of his Norman predecessors, and he had lofty imperial ambitions that, if realized, would have made him a competitor of his contemporary, Frederick Barbarossa. But Henry's greatness consisted in neither his administration nor his ambition. Rather, it consisted in the brilliant inventiveness with which he attacked the general problem of the administration of justice. Hitherto the king's court had concerned itself with the administration of a very limited king's peace among a very few noble Englishmen. With the private, feudal jurisdiction of the chief vassals of the crown the king had not as yet interfered. He had not concerned himself much with local difficulties between the powerful nobles and the simple, landholding freemen, nor with the legal relationships between the freemen themselves. The whole criminal jurisdiction was abandoned to the lower courts of hundred and shire. The king's court, therefore, had hitherto concerned itself mainly with justice for the upper classes. Such a situation left the small and weak at the mercy of the great and powerful, and contributed to the prevalent violence of the age. How violent it was even we, who have grown up in an age of international and domestic totalitarian violence, are in little position to appreciate. Even after the crown had begun to concern itself with these matters, we are told, when royal judges came to the comparatively small town of Lincoln in 1202 they had to deal with "114 cases of homicide, 89 of robbery (generally with violence), 65 of wounding, 49 of rape, besides a number of less serious crimes."[30]

ENGLISH SYSTEMS OF LAW

The legal system of England was, in fact, still chaotic, and the methods of determining guilt or innocence primitive, brutal, ineffective, and suspected. The English serf—and after 1066 the Normans preferred to consider all peasants serfs—was governed by the custom of the manor. In the hundred and shire courts local Anglo-Saxon law prevailed, varying from region to region in accordance with the customs of the tribe originally settling in the area. Norman feudal law governed the relationships among the baronage. Canon law regulated the affairs of the clergy. At the moment of Henry II's accession to the throne Roman law was being intensely studied in England. The methods of determining guilt or inno-

[30]A. L. Poole, *From Domesday Book to Magna Carta*, p. 392.

cence were still the pre-Christian, Germanic *compurgation, ordeal,* and *trial by combat,* which the Church had come to sanctify. If compurgation was used, one could establish one's innocence by employing oath-helpers to swear on oath that what one said was correct. In criminal cases it was customary to use the ordeal of cold water. "The trussed victim was lowered into a pool of water solemnly hallowed by the church. If he sank he was innocent; if he floated on the surface he was guilty, for the consecrated element would not receive a sinful body. If he failed at this ordeal, he must lose one of his feet and in this maimed condition abjure the realm." One also had to be ready to defend an accusation of crime with arms. "Unless he was too old or unless he was maimed, he must be prepared to fight and fight to the death. It was often mortal, for one or other of the combatants was either slain in battle, or, if he survived his defeat, was hanged or at least severely punished. . . . If they break their weapons, a late account of the duel relates, they must fight with their hands, fists, nails, teeth, feet and legs."[31]

HENRY II'S ATTACK UPON THE CONTEMPORARY JUDICIAL SYSTEM

Henry II attacked this anomalous situation in many ways: (1) he enlarged the scope of the king's peace, and therefore increased the number of "pleas of the crown" that could be tried in royal courts; (2) he made it possible to transfer certain cases from the private jurisdiction of his feudal vassals to the court of the king; (3) he used the sworn inquest to bring criminal cases before the king's court that had never before been the concern of any king; (4) he used the sworn inquest as a substitute for the primitive, Germanic methods of compurgation, ordeal, and trial by battle; (5) he developed central judicial machinery to take care of the expansion of royal justice and the opening of the king's court to any freeman; (6) he developed judicial machinery for supervising the local administration of hundred and shire and bringing royal justice to the locality; and finally (7) he insisted upon the primacy of the king's justice over all other forms of justice.

HENRY II'S NEW WRITS

Let us consider, for example, the manner in which Henry II went about (2) above, the attack upon the feudal jurisdiction of his barons. This attack, as in the case of so many other reforms of Henry II, was accomplished by the use of a writ, a "brief letter . . . of instruction, sent out by chancery clerks, to make sure that proper justice was done by those responsible for it, with the proviso that disobedience would be construed as contempt of the king and would result in their being summoned to answer for it before the king's justices."[32] Thus a person who felt that he

[31]Poole, pp. 402, 369.
[32]G. O. Sayles, *Medieval Foundations of England,* p. 133.

could not get justice from his lord could buy a *writ of right* from the chancery ordering his lord (the feudal lord of both plaintiff and defendant) to do justice if he did not wish the king to do it. A form of the writ of right called *Praecipe* ordered the sheriff to do justice immediately, the king in this case being supposed to be the nearest common feudal overlord of the two disputing parties. Such writs tended to bring cases concerning land disputes into the king's court. The way in which royal power was used to protect the small and weak against the great and powerful and at the same time employ the sworn-inquest procedure that was exclusively the king's can be seen in Henry's *Assize of Novel Disseisin* (Ordinance concerning Recent Dispossession), "one of the most momentous events in English history." It permitted any freeholder who had been recently deprived of his land by strong-arm methods to put the question of possession before a sworn inquest of his neighbors. In this case the sheriff, upon receipt of the writ, immediately put the plaintiff in possession of his property. A similar ordinance concerning inheritance (*Mort d'ancestor*, 1176) made it possible for a tenant whose overlord was keeping him from taking over the inheritance of his dead ancestor to secure a royal writ ordering that the question of rightful possession be put before a sworn inquest or jury of neighbors.

JURY FOR ORDEAL

The extension of the jury method to criminal cases to take the place of compurgation, ordeal, and trial by battle doomed the latter as judicial methods. The attitude of Henry's judges toward the ordeal is illustrated by the provision (the *Assize of Clarendon*, 1166) that if a man who actually passed the test of an ordeal had an extremely bad reputation he had nevertheless to leave the country as an outlaw. The provision of the Church in 1215 (Fourth Lateran Council) that henceforth no clergy were to participate in ordeals doomed this primitive method of determining guilt or innocence. The ordeal was based on the notion that God would interfere miraculously to defend the right. If the clergy were not to guarantee the sacredness of the method, this justification disappeared. Henry II's justices did not insist that the jury must necessarily be used instead of the older methods, nor was there subsequent law to this effect, but by 1275 it became virtually obligatory.

THE GRAND JURY

Henry used the jury not only as a method of determining guilt or innocence but also as a means of bringing serious crimes to the attention of the royal justices (our grand jury). The method is clearly set forth in the Assize of Clarendon (1166), in which Henry set out to discover what serious crimes had been committed since the beginning of his reign. He ordered that twelve men from the hundred, and four from every township were to report on oath before the sheriff in the county court, and before royal justices when they appeared locally, on who the robbers, murderers, thieves, or the harborers of these were reputed to be. Ten years later forgers and arsonists were added to this list. The assize also includes instructions to the sheriffs, who were made responsible for executing it, on how to get hold of, arrest, and imprison these suspects until they could be brought to trial.

THE DEVELOPMENT OF A COMMON LAW

It was Henry II who regularized the practice of sending royal judges on circuit to the shires to receive the reports of grand juries and administer justice to the enlarged number of litigants resulting from the new royal writs (Henry's justices invented some fifty of these). It can be understood that the popularity of the new writs and methods made necessary an increase in the number of justices serving Henry at court. Indeed, during this reign a beginning was made toward distinguishing between those justices who tried cases involving the king (the Court of King's Bench) and those trying cases not involving the king (the Court of Common Pleas). It was in 1178 that a central court was set up to hear the complaints of "all free men." Much later the chancellor developed a third central court of his own, the Court of Chancery. The great initiative shown by Henry II marked the beginning of a solution to the multiple systems of law in England. For the work of royal justices, moving from shire to shire year after year, giving verdicts based upon the work of local juries in an ever-increasing variety of criminal and civil cases, began to create a common law to supplant the special laws hitherto prevalent in England. This Common Law was the king's law based upon the decisions of the royal justices in central and local courts, decisions themselves based upon the declarations of local custom by men sworn to tell the truth. These justices, moving throughout all the English counties, dealt similarly everywhere with similar cases that came before them. They thus established in time a law common to all Englishmen, irrespective of class or wealth, as subjects of the crown. This common law was built, therefore, upon the individual decision of judges in particular cases. It employed the new jury methods. It venerated the zeal for justice and the subservience to law displayed by its real founder, Henry II, a king whose creativeness in the field of law had much to do with making the institution of monarchy popular among the English. Few peoples have ever revered so much, even today, their kings and queens.

IMPORTANCE OF THE COMMON LAW

The development of the Common Law is a matter of supreme concern to Americans because it has become, in both principle and substance, our own law. Just as the European nations that took over Roman law as their common law spread it into their overseas possessions, so the English colonists carried the common law to the uttermost parts of the earth. In its eventual effect, this judge-made law, resting upon the foundation of locally determined custom, joined hands with the feudal contract in promoting the institution of limited monarchy, for it took over the old Germanic notion of custom as a law from which no one, not even the king, is exempt. The strength and popularity of the Angevin monarchy after Henry II made it possible for his eldest son, Richard, to govern without being much in England. John, however, as we have seen, ran into the opposition of his baronage on feudal grounds. It can be said, also, that the outrage of the barons over the violation of feudal contract was supported by the common-law principle that the king is not above the law. If, for example, the provisions of Magna Carta that have to do with the legal and judicial innovations of Henry II were to be studied, it would be found that the barons were primarily concerned with making the new system of royal justice more efficient. From a more general point of view, the development of a system of common law promoted that tenet of humanism we have called rationalism. Roman and canon law were authoritarian and depended for expansion upon deductions from a text. The authority in common law was the collective body of decisions made by judges in a co-operative legal process. Here was faith in man's ability to arrive at just decisions through reason, after the give-and-take of trial in the courtroom.

PROVISIONS OF OXFORD

More important to the growth of limited monarchy in England, and her incomparable gift to the western and indeed to the whole world, is parliament, the fundament of government by discussion and, when properly used, the solvent of tyranny. One source of its strength in England was its success in effectively limiting royal absolutism where previous attempts had failed. The attempt of Magna Carta to set up a committee of twenty-five barons to supervise the administration of the Charter failed in the long run. In the middle of the thirteenth century a second notable attempt was made by the baronage to control the unpopular Henry III (1216-1272). This attempt came out of the discussions of an early parliament, the Oxford Parliament (1258), and is known as the Provisions of Oxford. It provided for a Council of Fifteen, appointed by king and nobles, to act as an adviser on all phases of royal policy and to correct abuses in government. To supervise this committee a Committee of Twelve, chosen by the barons from their own ranks, was to meet with the Committee of Fifteen at the three times a year when parliaments were to be convoked. Further attempts were made to control the chief offices of central and local government. But this machinery did not work successfully, and, with the co-operation of the pope, Henry III quashed the Provisions in 1261. The result was feudal rebellion led by Simon de Montfort (1264), who, to parliaments summoned by him, for the first time called representatives of the shires (knights of the shire) and towns. This rebellion did not disappear until 1267. It was, however, becoming clear to the baronage by this date that a better means of keeping the king in line than securing reissues of Magna Carta was to provide for regular meetings of his baronage in some kind of a gathering, no matter its name.

PARLIAMENT AS A COURT

A further source of the strength of Parliament came to be that it performed the function of the highest court in the land, where, in the form of petitions, the king's subjects could request and get reforms of the abuses of royal government. Beyond this, for the monarch wishing to reign without continual crises, Parliament came to be the most efficient way of getting along with his subjects. It was thus an extension of the methods of consultation used in such institutions as the Great Council and the Small Council. In Magna Carta the king had promised not to take more than the regular feudal aids without consulting his barons. In the course of the thirteenth century this practice became a principle of government. The king must consult with those from whom he expected to take money. Parliament, especially when enlarged by representatives of the shires and the towns, proved to be the most satisfactory way of securing this consent to be taxed. The association and representation in one body of such powerful motives of the king's subjects as the desire to be consulted and the desire to have grievances corrected, with the king's constant need for cash, led to that wonderful assumption of no grant of taxes without proper consultation and proper redress of grievances.

PARLIAMENT AS A COUNCIL

In origin, Parliament, like the States-General, was an institution depending upon royal initiative whose composition it is difficult to differentiate from the court of the king or the Great Council. It had nothing to do, at first, with the recognition of a right on the part of the king's subjects to be consulted regularly by the king. The institution went back to that feudal practice of a lord's, and hence a feudal king's, summoning his vassals to a court, at which fellow vassals were tried and questions of policy discussed. In England this feudal court of the king came to be called the Great Council. Together with the Small Council of the growing body of officials of the expanding royal administration, it constituted the court of the king (*curia regis*). Long after bodies met that were called parliaments, the Parliament was still regarded chiefly as a council. The Great Council of the king continued its existence in Parliament in the form of the House of Lords.

PARLIAMENT AND THE SWORN INQUEST

The representation of the shires and towns in Parliament may be said to be an extension of the use of the sworn inquest. Henry II used the sworn inquest as a means to detect crime (the grand jury) and as a means to determine guilt or innocence (trial jury). Earlier as well as later they were used for other purposes, namely, to secure information or opinions. The early House of Commons in Parliament was but the summoning of sworn inquests representing the shires and the towns before the king and his court or his Great Council for any purpose the king saw fit, including, of course, securing their opinion on a new contribution of taxes. What was called a Parliament in the thirteenth and fourteenth centuries did not necessarily include representatives of the shires or towns. From 1258 to 1286 some fifty parliaments were called together, but, of these, representatives of the nonfeudal classes were present in only six. Of thirty-four parliaments called together between 1290 and 1311, representatives of the shires and towns attended only thirteen. Of nineteen parliaments between 1311 and 1327, seventeen had representatives of the people, and in all the forty-eight parliaments of Edward III's reign (1327–1377) the shires and towns had representatives. In this early formative period the king could call whom he pleased, either knights of the shire or representatives of the towns or both, to meet with him and the Great Council or *curia regis*. What is called the Model Parliament of King Edward I (1295) had in it representatives of all the groups that had ever been brought together in a medieval parliament. In it were the tenants in chief, that is, the lords spiritual (bishops, archbishops, abbots, and priors) and the lords temporal (earls and barons), constituting the Great Council of the king. To these were added the leading permanent officials of the government, who usually constituted the Small Council. Two knights elected in the shire court came from each shire, and two burgesses elected by town councils came from each of the leading towns. In addition, this parliament included representatives of the lower clergy: archdeacons, parish priests, and cathedral chapters. The parliament met in three groups: (1) lords spiritual and temporal, officials, and knights of the shire; (2) townsmen; and (3) lower clergy. Each group came to its own terms with the king over the taxes he needed for wars on the Continent and in Flanders. A typical parliament of the early fourteenth century contained 52 lords spiritual (21 bishops, 31 abbots), 77 lords temporal (11 earls, 66 barons), 10 officials, 74 knights of the shire, 160 townsmen, and 141 representatives of the lower clergy, a total of 514.[33]

PARLIAMENT BECOMES BICAMERAL

By the end of the Angevin period (1399) Parliament had undergone changes in organization and acquired powers of its own that made it a partner in government and thus limited the prerogatives of the English monarch. By the middle of the fourteenth century it had become bicameral and therewith unique among similar medieval bodies. This came about

[33]T. F. T. Plucknett, in *The English Government at Work, 1327–1336*, eds. James F. Willard and William A. Morris, p. 105.

when the officials of the crown ceased to attend, except as they were tenants in chief or lords spiritual. The knights of the shire ceased to sit with the barons, as they had in 1295, and joined the representatives of the burgesses. The representatives of the lower clergy also dropped out of Parliament, preferring their own assembly of Convocation where they joined with the upper clergy, who, as tenants in chief of the crown, however, continued to attend the Great Council in Parliament. Thus Parliament came to be made up of a House of Lords (the Great Council), consisting of the lords spiritual and temporal, and a House of Commons, consisting of representatives of the counties and the towns.

PARLIAMENT ACQUIRES FINANCIAL AND LEGISLATIVE POWERS

The powers acquired in the fourteenth century were financial and legislative. The English kings, embarking upon the Hundred Years' War,[34] had to promise to levy no taxes without the consent of Parliament, whether these taxes were direct or indirect. Parliament, moreover, aimed to extend its control over not only the sources of revenue but also collection and expenditure. Parliamentary committees sought to audit the accounts of the exchequer. In any case, Parliament came to make no grants of taxes until its grievances had been redressed, or at least until promises to that effect had been received. It even sought, upon occasion, to make grants for specific purposes and thus in an indirect way to control governmental policy. Parliament early acquired the power to make law and thus became a legislature. It has been pointed out that Parliament was a great attraction for those representatives of shire and town who brought petitions with them for a correction of abuses and expected to have these petitions answered by the king before Parliament closed. This could be done nowhere else. But the representatives discovered that many of their individual, private petitions were similar, and that it would be more effective if they could present a petition from the body as a whole. These were called General, or Commons, petitions. They were considered so important that they were turned over to the Lords to examine. Thus what was originally a judicial process became a legislative process. The Commons were submitting laws to be approved by the Lords and the king. These Commons petitions, when approved by the Lords, were often modified by the king's officials before being inscribed among the statutes of the realm. It was desirable, therefore, for Parliament to secure control over this royal tampering with its expressed will. Before the end of the fourteenth century it did so by securing from Edward III (1327–1377) the promise that the fundamental law of the land would not be altered without the consent of Parliament. Parliament had less success during this period in securing control over the advisers of the king and thus over royal policy. It sought to have officials appointed with the con-

[34]See pp. 568 f.

sent of Parliament but did not succeed. It did, however, invent impeachment in 1376. It must not be concluded, of course, that by the acquisition of these powers Parliament deprived the king of all initiative in government. The crown always had private (crown land) sources of income that Parliament could not touch. In securing legislative power for itself it did not deprive the king of legislative initiative in Parliament. Nor did it deprive the king of the power to legislate by ordinance through his Great Council. The process of establishing a truly parliamentary government, that is, one in which Parliament is supreme, was to be a long one. But by the end of the fourteenth century Parliament had been firmly established as a necessary associate in government. This supreme political creativeness of the English was to save them untold misery in the future. Together with the legal unity being created by the common law Parliament helped to make of the English, sooner than elsewhere, something that can be called a nation. The share of the monarchy in this development both in the creation of the common law and in the establishment of Parliament gave it that popularity that made of it a truly national monarchy.

FOURTEENTH AND FIFTEENTH CENTURIES

The interpretation that has been given above to the political history of the earlier Middle Ages applies as well to the history of the fourteenth and fifteenth centuries. We have said that the second attempt of the Germans to establish a secular theocracy (Holy Roman Empire) failed in large part because of the opposition of the papacy.[35] The failure of the Holy Roman Empire to establish itself even in Italy left that country separated into a southern kingdom, a central collection of Papal States, and a northern group of independent city-states.[36] In Germany itself the monarchy acquired no power and was able to create no central or local administration. It was, rather, the local feudal magnate who emerged triumphant and who set about making his little territory as mighty a unit as possible.

The political history of Germany in the later Middle Ages is thus concerned with the petty dynasties heading these states and dominating all subsequent German history. They were in part ecclesiastical, for the big bishops, archbishops, and abbots headed independent clerical states. Among the clerical states, the Rhenish dominated with the archbishops of Cologne, Trier, and Mainz, and the bishops of Metz, Toul, Verdun, and Strassburg. The leading secular dynasties were the Hapsburgs, powerful in southwestern Germany and in Austria; the Luxemburgers, Rhenish princes and kings of Bohemia; the Wittelsbach dukes of Bavaria; and the rising Hohenzollerns of Brandenburg. These princes were concerned pri-

[35]See pp. 526 ff.
[36]See p. 543.

marily with the fortunes of their own houses, and if they sought the royal and imperial titles it was because these might serve to increase the size or augment the power of their own local states. The German monarchy remained an elective one.

THE GOLDEN BULL (1356)

In the thirteenth century the right of election of the king and emperor-elect came to be exercised by seven electors: the archbishops of Cologne, Trier, and Mainz, and the princes of Saxony-Wittenberg, Bohemia, Brandenberg, and the Bavarian Palatinate. In 1356 Charles IV of Bohemia (1347-1378), German elector, king, and emperor, did for these electors what every petty prince of Germany was anxious to do for himself. In the Golden Bull it was provided that the right to elect was, in the lay electorates, to be inherited by primogeniture. The electorates themselves were not to be divided. The Bull went a long way toward guaranteeing independence to the electors in their territories. For example, it prevented the summoning of any resident before a court outside the electorate or any appeal to an outside court. It forbade urban leagues. In setting up a formal procedure for the election of the king at Frankfort, and for his coronation at Aachen, the Golden Bull provided until 1806 an outward splendor to hide the meaninglessness of the titles of German king and emperor.

THE HANSE AND THE SWISS

There is much to be said, however, for the attitude that the important history of Germany in these later medieval centuries is to be sought not in details of local dynastic policies but in expansion in Livonia and Prussia,[37] or else in the striking organization and vigorous expansion of the North German towns in the Hanseatic League. The Hanse, dominated by such towns as Hamburg, Bremen, and Lübeck, was the most powerful of all medieval town leagues. It aimed at, and succeeded in achieving, a monopoly of the export and import trade from and into northern Europe and the Scandinavian countries. Organized around seventy to eighty German towns, with which some two hundred other towns, villages, and districts in Germany were associated, it set up outlying settlements in London, Bruges, Bergen, Wisby, and Novgorod. It participated actively in German expansion along the southern shores of the Baltic. At its height, its army and navy successfully fought the king of Denmark. But as native merchant classes grew strong in England, the Low Countries, Scandinavia, and Russia, the League lost its privileged position abroad and in the fifteenth century entered a sharp decline.

The influence of the Hanse upon the trade and commerce of the Scandinavian North was but a part of the German influence upon the de-

[37]See pp. 508 ff.

velopment of these lands. Christianity entered them from Germany and England. Feudalism spread northward from Germany. There was a good deal of intermarriage between German and Scandinavian noble families, and northern kings were frequently taken from the North German aristocracy. By the end of the Middle Ages, however, the Scandinavian kingdoms had thwarted the control of the German and English churches, Denmark had freed herself from an always loose recognition of the overlordship of the German empire, and the rising middle classes were helping to prepare for the building of national cultures. At the same time on the western and southwestern frontiers of the empire territories were being lost to the dukes of Burgundy, and peasants and townsmen in the Alps, through courage and federation, were winning their independence from the Hapsburgs and the German empire and creating a new republic, the Swiss Confederation.

THE HUNDRED YEARS' WAR

In western Europe, likewise, the political history of the fourteenth and fifteenth centuries illustrates the earlier developments—that of France into a strong (territorially unified) monarchy; that of England into a strong (territorially, judicially, and economically unified) monarchy limited by Parliament. These developments went on under the strain of war, the so-called Hundred Years' War (1337-1453). France under her Valois kings (1328-1589) was attempting to deprive England under her Lancastrian dynasty (1399-1461) of her last holdings on the Continent, namely, Aquitaine (Guienne and Gascony). For money to wage a war in France on behalf of the remnants of an empire that could not be permanently maintained, the Lancastrians had to pay with privileges to Parliament that make it possible to speak of the Lancastrian monarchy of the early fifteenth century as a parliamentary monarchy. When, in 1461, the dynasty terminated in civil war between the houses of Lancaster and York (Wars of the Roses) and thus reduced England to the anarchy it had once experienced under Stephen of Blois and Matilda (1135-1154), the need for strong government enabled the new dynasty of the Tudors to establish a virtual absolutism. But the Parliament, reinforced with its Lancastrian privileges, could not be totally ignored, even if a century or more had to pass before it could reassert its former influence (seventeenth century).

For the French Valois kings the Hundred Years' War was a defensive struggle to drive out the English and bring the remainder of southern France into the royal domain. At moments of great stress during the war the monarchy had to call upon the States-General for aid, and it then appeared as if this body might acquire some of the powers of a parliament. However, when the war became involved in a deadly factional strife between the dukes of Burgundy and Orléans, and it was clear to all that only a strong monarchy could win the war and reconstruct a country so completely ravished by foreign armies, mercenaries, plague, and peasant

SCOTLAND

NORTH
SEA

YORK

ENGLAND

WALES

• Warwick
Gloucester •
• Oxford
London •

Bristol •
Exeter •   Canterbury
        Southampton •   • Dover

CHANNEL

ENGLISH

ATLANTIC

OCEAN

1360 inset:
Calais
PONTHIEU
GUIENNE
GASCONY

RHINE R.

BRABANT

Calais •
FLANDERS
Boulogne •
Agincourt •
ARTOIS   • Arras
Crécy •
    • Amiens

• Rouen
SEINE R.
Bayeux •   Paris •   Rheims •
NORMANDY   CHAMPAGNE
            • Domremy
    Chartres •
BRITTANY   • Arc
    MAINE   Orleans •
        • Dijon
LOIRE R.   • Tours   BERRY   BURGUNDY
ANJOU   Bourges •   (DUCHY)   (COUNTY)
    • Poitiers
POITOU   BOURBON
    LA MARCHE
                Lyons •
    LIMOUSIN
            RHONE R.
        AUVERGNE   DAUPHINE

Bordeaux •
GUIENNE
    ARMAGNAC
        • Avignon
        PROVENCE
    • Toulouse

MEUSE R.

SAONE R.

1429

Boundary of the
Holy Roman Empire

ENGLAND in FRANCE
during the HUNDRED YEARS' WAR

English territory and areas
under English influence

French territory

Burgundian territory

Miles
0   50   100

palacios

MEDITERRANEAN SEA

GERMAN EMPIRE AND NATIONAL MONARCHIES 569

and feudal revolt, the States-General in 1439 granted to the king the right to levy a direct tax (*taille*) upon all persons for the purposes of building up a new military establishment independent of feudal limitations. The French monarchy, with the right of direct taxation and the right to build up a standing army, now possessed the weapons of absolutism, which it quickly used. The close of the war (1453) finally brought Aquitaine into the royal domain. During the reign of Louis XI (1461–1483) the Duchy of Burgundy and the Free County of Burgundy, among others, were added to the royal domain, and, finally, under Charles VIII (1483–1498), the Duchy of Brittany. Thus by the end of the Middle Ages the French kings, having under the Capetians built a strong feudal monarchy, were able under the Valois further to undermine its feudal basis and provide for an absolute state. At the same time they had brought the major fiefs of the original Capetian monarchy into the royal domain.

SUMMARY

Theocratic German empire was rejected by France and England as well as Germany and Italy. As a substitute for international tyranny these peoples chose the local monarch. In France, what we have referred to as the democratic implications of early Germanic government and feudalism were not strong enough to overcome the centralizing absolutism inherited in part from the tradition of Roman government. As a price for her territorial unity France had to pay with a theocracy on a local, dynastic scale. In England, on the contrary, Germanic principles of law and feudal principles of contract united to check the early powerful monarchy of the Angevins with common law, Magna Carta, and Parliament. The West, however, needed more experience with government on a national scale before it would be able to choose between the traditions represented by the English or by the French at the close of the medieval period. Meanwhile, monarchial development had thoroughly discredited the petty localism of feudalism.

chapter thirteen

THE REJECTION OF UNIVERSAL ECCLESIASTICAL THEOCRACY: HOLY ROMAN CHURCH AND NATIONAL CHURCHES

*P*ROGRAM OF THE CHAPTER.   In the last chapter it was argued that, with the help of the papacy, the German attempt to impose a secular theocracy upon Europe in the form of the Holy Roman Empire was a failure. That failure left as the only effective international organization in Europe the Holy Roman Church. This Church, headed by the papacy, has been previously described as an ecclesiastical theocracy, and it has been said that its theocrat, the pope, aimed at securing not only (1) spiritual supremacy within the Church, but also (2) temporal supremacy over the states of Europe. It must be one purpose of this chapter to ask the extent to which these two aims were accomplished. While making this clear it will be noticed (3) that considerable opposition developed to these papal aims and to the whole Church. In one important instance the Christian point of view itself was challenged. The methods that the papal theocracy used to crush this opposition will be found to have aroused so much antagonism that (4) the Christian unity of western Europe was broken, and (5) definite limits were put upon the papal program by the cities, princes, and kings of Europe. Thus western Europe rejected universal ecclesiastical as well as secular theocracy. In the course of this rejection such a strong reaction developed against the medieval adaptation of Christianity that many sought to restore the religion of Jesus in its original form.

Situated on the borders of the western world, not exactly belonging to it yet strongly influenced by its culture, Russian thinkers of the nineteenth century often showed penetrating insight in their criticism of western institutions. The great Russian novelist Dostoyevsky, in an extraordinary chapter of his novel *The Brothers Karamazov*, suggested the contrast between the religion of Jesus and the religion of the medieval Church. In it one of the brothers, the sceptical, cynical Ivan, is reading a poem to Alyosha, the sensitive, believing Christian novice, called *The Grand Inquisitor*. It concerns the return of Jesus to the Spanish town of Seville in the sixteenth century. "He came down to the hot pavement of the southern town in which on the day before almost a hundred heretics had, *ad majorem gloriam Dei*, been burnt by the cardinal, the Grand Inquisitor, in a magnificent *auto-da-fé*, in the presence of the king, the court, the knights, the cardinals, the most charming ladies of the court, and the whole population of Seville." While Jesus is raising a child from the dead in front of the cathedral, the Grand Inquisitor passes by. "He is an old man, almost ninety, tall and erect, with a withered face and sunken eyes, in which there is still a gleam of light." The crowd permits Jesus to be arrested by the guard of the Grand Inquisitor and to be imprisoned in the "close gloomy vaulted prison in the ancient palace of the Holy Inquisitor." That night the Grand Inquisitor visits him.

He tells Jesus that on the morrow he will be burnt at the stake "as the worst of heretics." For he had no business to return to earth, "no right to add anything to what Thou hadst said of old," or to "come to hinder us. . . . All has been given by Thee to the Pope . . . and all, therefore, is still in the Pope's hands, and there is no need for Thee to come now at all. Thou must not meddle for the time, at least." The freedom that Jesus promised men, the Inquisitor says, "now is ended and over for good. . . . Today, people are more persuaded than ever that they have perfect freedom, yet they have brought their freedom to us and laid it humbly at our feet." Now that freedom is gone "for the first time it has become possible to think of the happiness of men." Jesus thus had not known how to make men happy. "But fortunately departing Thou didst hand on the work to us. . . . Thou hast given to us the right to bind and to unbind, and now of course, Thou canst not think of taking it away."[1]

Jesus is told that in emphasizing freedom he was seriously mistaken. He was talking about something the ordinary man could not understand, indeed feared and dreaded, "for nothing has ever been more unsupportable for a man and a human society than freedom." Instead of freedom Jesus should have given bread. "Dost Thou know that the ages will pass and humanity will proclaim by the lips of their sages that there is no crime, and therefore no sin; there is only hunger?" " 'Feed men, and then ask

<hr>

[1]Trans. Constance Garnett, Part II, Book V, pp. 292-309.

of them virtue!' That's what they'll write on the banner which they will raise against Thee, and with which they will destroy Thy temple. . . . They will understand themselves, at last, that freedom and bread enough for all are inconceivable together, for never, never will they be able to share between them! They will be convinced too that they can never be free, for they are weak, vicious, worthless and rebellious." If, the Inquisitor goes on, Jesus had chosen bread, "Thou wouldst have satisfied the universal and everlasting craving of humanity—to find some one to worship. So long as man remains free he strives for nothing so incessantly and so painfully as to find some one to worship. But man seeks to worship what is established beyond dispute, so that all men would agree at once to worship it. For these pitiful creatures are concerned not only to find what one or the other can worship, but to find something that all would believe in and worship; what is essential is that all may be together in it. This craving for *community* of worship is the chief misery of every man individually and of all humanity from the beginning of time. For the sake of common worship they've slain each other with the sword. They have set up gods and challenged one another, 'Put away your gods and come and worship ours, or we will kill you and your gods.' And so it will be to the end of the world, even when gods disappear from the earth; they will fall down before idols just the same!"

Jesus is also blamed because "instead of taking men's freedom from them, Thou didst make it greater than ever! Didst Thou forget that man prefers peace, and even death, to freedom of choice in the knowledge of good and evil? Nothing is more seductive for man than this freedom of conscience, but nothing is a greater cause of suffering. And behold, instead of giving a firm foundation for setting the conscience of man at rest forever, Thou didst choose all that is exceptional, vague, and enigmatic. . . . In place of the rigid ancient law, man must hereafter with free heart decide for himself what is good and what is evil, having only Thy image before him as his guide. But didst Thou not know he would at last reject even Thy image and Thy truth, if he is weighed down with the fearful burden of free choice?"

The Inquisitor explains to Jesus that "there are three powers, three powers alone, able to conquer and to hold captive forever the conscience of these impotent rebels for their happiness." These powers are miracle, mystery, and authority. "Thou hast rejected all three and hast set the example for doing so. . . . Thou didst not come down from the Cross when they shouted to Thee, mocking and reviling thee, 'Come down from the cross and we will believe that Thou art He.' Thou didst not come down, for again Thou wouldst not enslave man by a miracle, and didst crave faith given freely, not based on miracle."

The Inquisitor then confesses, "We are not working with Thee, but with him [the Devil]—that is our mystery. It's long—eight centuries—since we have been on his side and not on Thine. Just eight centuries ago

CHRONOLOGY — Holy Roman Church and National Churches

	Reigns	Pontificates	Religious Personalities and Movements
900			
			Founding of Cluny (910)
1000			
		Gregory VII (1073–1085)	Bishop Odo (ca. 1030–1097) Archbishop Adalbert (ca. 1000–1072) Peter Abélard (1079–1142) *Carthusians* (1084) Arnold of Brescia (ca. 1090–1155) Saint Bernard (1091–1153) *First Crusade* (1096–1099) *Cistercians* (1098) *Augustinians* (late 11th c.)
1100			
	Louis VII of France (1137–1180) Henry II of England (1154–1189) Philip Augustus of France (1180–1223) Otto IV of Brunswick (1198–1215) John of England (1199–1216)	Alexander III (1159–1181) Innocent III (1198–1216)	John of Salisbury (ca. 1110–1180) Thomas à Becket (1117–1170) *Premonstratensians* (1119) Joachim of Fiore (ca. 1145–1202) *Second Crusade* (1147–1149) Stephen Langton (ca. 1155–1228) Peter Waldo (d. 1217) Saint Dominic (1170–1221) Saint Francis of Assisi (1182–1226)
1200			
	Saint Louis of France (1226–1270) Edward I of England (1272–1307) Philip IV of France (1285–1314)	*Fourth Lateran Council* (1215) Gregory IX (1227–1241) Boniface VIII (1294–1303)	*Albigensian Crusade* (1208–1213) Saint Thomas Aquinas (1225–1274) Duns Scotus (ca. 1265–1308) Marsiglio of Padua (ca. 1280–1342)
1300			
	Louis IV of Bavaria (1314–1347)	*Unam Sanctam* (1302) Clement V (1305–1314) *Residence at Avignon* (1305–1378) John XXII (1316–1334) Innocent VI (1352–1362) Urban V (1362–1370) *Great Schism* (1378–1417)	John Wycliffe (ca. 1328–1384) John Huss (ca. 1369–1415)
1400			
	Emperor Sigismund (1411–1437)		*Council of Pisa* (1409) *Council of Constance* (1414–1418) Joan of Arc (ca. 1412–1431) *Council of Basel* (1431–1449)

we took from him what Thou didst reject with scorn, that last gift he offered Thee, showing Thee all the kingdoms of the earth. We took from him Rome and the sword of Caesar, and proclaimed ourselves sole rulers of the earth. . . . Oh, the work is only beginning, but it has begun. . . . We shall triumph and shall be Caesars, and then we shall plan the universal happiness of man. . . . Why didst Thou reject that last gift? Hadst Thou accepted, Thou wouldst have accomplished all that man seeks on earth— that is, some one to worship, some one to keep his conscience, and some means of uniting all in one unanimous and harmonious ant heap. For the craving for universal unity in the third and last anguish of man. Mankind as a whole has always striven to organize a universal state. There have been many great nations and great histories, but the more highly they were developed, the more unhappy they were, for they felt more acutely than other people the craving for worldwide union. Hadst Thou taken the world and Caesar's purple, Thou wouldst have founded the universal state and have given universal peace. . . . I repeat, tomorrow Thou shalt see that obedient flock who at a sign from me will hasten to heap up the hot cinders about the pile on which I shall burn Thee for coming to hinder us. For if any one has ever deserved our fires, it is Thou. Tomorrow I shall burn Thee. *Dixi.*"

This is as if Dostoyevsky were saying that in turning away from the religion of Jesus to become a church striving for temporal power and supremacy, claiming to possess the authoritative truth and the right to burn all those who did not agree, offering security for freedom, the security of mind, soul, and body, Christianity turned from its founder to the worship of the devil and, in fact, became a "synagogue of Satan." This, as we shall note in this chapter, was the opinion of some of those groups called heretics. When the Church did not heed these complaints, they developed into the opinion of groups called Protestants.

FREEDOM FROM THEOCRATIC REGIMES

This attitude is what is meant when we refer to the rejection on the part of the West of universal ecclesiastical theocracy. In rejecting both universal secular and ecclesiastical theocracy, the West took refuge in the local town, territory, or monarchy to protect its freedom. This became in time taking refuge in nationalism, in which the West has, and continues to have, such great trust, in part because of its earlier experience with authoritarian, theocratic regimes. In its recognition of the right of the state to control the church within its boundaries, the West abandoned the earlier program of the Church for freedom, if not separation, from the state. Its rejection of theocratic universalism meant that when, as today, it has had to return to internationalism or universalism that return precludes any further resort to any kind or degree of theocracy. Its experience with national churches has led it in some cases to question the wisdom of this arrangement and to free the church from the state.

TEMPORAL VICTORIES OF INNOCENT III

The victory of the papacy over the empire in the thirteenth century left the papacy as the ruling international institution. If in that century the years were to be picked in which a pope best stood out as the theocratic lord of Europe, they would be the brief pontificate of Innocent III (1198– 1216). Some of the events associated with the rule of this outstanding pope have already been discussed. The Fourth Crusade took place early in his reign.[2] He was responsible for the organization of the devilish crusade against the Albigensians.[3] He assumed authority for settling the civil war in Germany between Welf (Guelph) and Hohenstaufen candidates for the throne. These occurrences brought recognition of his overlordship over the Latin Empire of Constantinople and the Holy Roman Empire. In addition to cities, towns, counties, and duchies, Innocent at other moments in his reign managed to establish his overlordship over England, Poland, Norway, Sweden, Denmark, Bohemia, Bulgaria, Serbia, Armenia, and the crusading Kingdom of Jerusalem. Previous to his accession, the papacy from Gregory VII on had already secured similar recognition from the Norman kings of southern Italy and Sicily, the king of Aragon, the prince of Kiev, the king of Croatia, and the king of Portugal. We have noted that Gregory VII insisted that Hungary and Spain belonged to Saint Peter. These temporal ambitions of the papacy can be further illustrated by reference to England.

THE ENGLISH CROWN AND THE PAPACY

From the days of the Conquest English kings were determined to keep the popes from interfering in the affairs of the English state or church. This could be done by keeping papal legates and decrees out of England unless they entered with royal consent, and by keeping Englishmen, clergy or otherwise, from visiting Rome or carrying appeals to Rome without the consent of the king. This was the policy of William the Conqueror. Gregory VII did not like it. "No king," he exclaimed, "not even a pagan king, has presumed to act against the apostolic see in the way that William unblushingly has acted; no one has been so irreverent and insolent as to prevent bishops and archbishops from coming to the threshold of the apostles." This barrier of England against Rome was, with little exception, maintained by William Rufus and Henry I. The situation changed during the anarchy of Stephen's reign,[4] when what the Church called its freedom was achieved. "Stephen had failed entirely to maintain the barrier set up by his predecessors. Papal bulls and papal legates freely entered the

---

[2]See pp. 476 ff.
[3]See pp. 610 f.
[4]See p. 551.

country; ecclesiastical synods and episcopal and abbatial elections were out of the king's control. In spite of his prohibition, bishops obeyed the papal summons, and ecclesiastical suits were taken to Rome without his leave being sought."[5]

HENRY II AND THOMAS BECKET

Henry II was determined to establish the *status quo ante* Stephen, but found himself thwarted by his archbishop of Canterbury, the impetuous and stubborn defender of papal interests, Thomas Becket. They clashed when Henry published as the Constitutions of Clarendon (1164) what he regarded as the ancient customs of the realm with respects to the relationships between church and state. One of these customs was to guarantee that a member of the clergy who had committed a crime should not escape with the lenient punishment of an ecclesiastical court. He should, the Constitutions state, after being tried and convicted by a court of the Church be given no further protection so that a royal officer could seize him and punish him, as a layman in like case would be punished. The Constitutions declared further that officials of the Church were not to leave the country and no appeals were to be carried to Rome without the king's consent. Other clauses provided that no chief vassals or officials of the king were to be excommunicated without royal consent. Becket's opposition to the Constitutions was supported by the pope, who condemned ten of them. The archbishop's relentless defense of the rights of his see, the Church, and Rome exasperated the king, who had raised him from obscurity to the chancellorship and expected him to be a loyal and obedient archbishop. At a moment when Henry had to suffer from Becket's suspension of clergy who defended the royal cause, the king angrily expressed his resentment over the fact that members of his court did not rid him of the archbishop. Therefore four knights betook themselves to Canterbury and murdered Becket in his cathedral. The public reaction was so hostile that Henry had finally to relent. The clause of the Constitutions demanding that punishment of clergy guilty of crime be equal to that of laymen was withdrawn. Henry had to promise not to prevent future appeals to Rome. As a result, "Canon law becomes at last completely valid in this country [England]." Pope Alexander III could send more decretals to England (over 400) "than to all the rest of Europe put together."

KING JOHN AND THE DISPUTED CANTERBURY ELECTION

This trend of affairs reached its climax in the difficulties between Innocent III and King John, who was no more religiously inclined than the previous members of his family. He was quite ready to interrupt preachers whose sermons interfered with his dinner, and he had no wish to sacri-

[5]Z. N. Brooke, *The English Church and the Papacy*, pp. 137, 188-189.

fice the rights of the crown with respect to the English church. His difficulties with Innocent arose over a disputed election to the arch-bishopric of Canterbury upon the death of Hubert Walter (13 July, 1205). The see of Canterbury was too important to the king to permit its being held by any but a royal candidate. Soon after the archbishop's death John arranged in person for a postponment of an election for six months. The electoral chapter of Canterbury was composed of the monks of Christ's Church. Anxious to prevent the bishops of the province of Canterbury or the king himself from intervening with the pope on behalf of their candidates, the monks of Canterbury secretly elected their own subprior Reginald as archbishop and sent him off with a delegation of monks to Rome, where he demanded the confirmation of the pope. When John heard of this election he went immediately to Canterbury where he so in-timidated the monks that they denied having made any election, and in the presence of the king elected his candidate, John de Gray, the bishop of Norwich. In the end (December, 1206), Innocent declared both these elections invalid and suggested to the Canterbury monks in Rome the election of a third candidate, Stephen Langton, an English cardinal-priest. The monks therefore elected Langton, and John was called upon to con-firm him. The king refused. His well-established rights in the election of an archbishop had been disregarded by a pope, and however English Langton might be, he had not been in England since about 1180 and had, moreover, been a professor of theology at the University of Paris and was actually a canon of the cathedral of Notre Dame de Paris. Instead, John took over the property of the Canterbury archbishopric, which brought in an income of £1492 10s. a year, and exiled all the monks of Christ's Church who were not too old to move.

INTERDICT FOR ENGLAND AND EXCOMMUNICATION FOR JOHN

In August, 1207, John was threatened with an interdict[6] for his kingdom if he did not receive Stephen Langton as archbishop of Canterbury. Before it was actually issued the king made plans to confiscate the property of any clergy refusing to perform the services of the Church in England. The interdict was published on 23 March, 1208, and for six years the English did without the regular administrations of the Church. Only "the Cis-tercians,[7] claiming the privilege of exemption, 'rang their bells, shouted their chants, and celebrated the divine offices with open doors' in defiance of the interdict."[8] John moved in on the property of the Church, and the profits were so large that he was not tempted to come to terms with Rome at any great sacrifice. Popular support of the king was so great that he had to order that those who did harm to the clergy or spoke evilly of them were to be hanged from the nearest oak tree. The king amused

[6]A prohibition of sacred public rites for groups or regions.
[7]See pp. 595 f.
[8]A. L. Poole, *From Domesday Book to Magna Carta*, p. 446.

himself, at considerable profit, by ordering his "agents to seize the mistresses of the members of the clergy and to hold them until their lovers ransomed them."[9] When personal excommunication of the king was added to interdict (November, 1209), John took it out still more on the Church, and English barons found that their contributions for war in England, Ireland, and Wales were reduced.

ENGLAND A PAPAL FIEF

The king was not seriously stirred to make peace until his difficulties began to have dangerous international repercussions, reaching within England itself. After his loss of Normandy and other continental holdings,[10] John was bent on nothing less than the recovery of these lands. This meant war against Philip Augustus, the king of France, and John planned it in co-operation with his nephew, the Welf (Guelph) Otto IV of Brunswick, the rival candidate for the imperial throne in Germany,[11] and with rebellious vassals of the French king. It so happened that in 1210 the pope abandoned his support of Otto IV of Brunswick because of the latter's plans to conquer southern Italy and Sicily, and turned to his young Hohenstaufen ward, Frederick II. Philip Augustus immediately allied with the Hohenstaufen against what was an English-Welf alliance, and was encouraged by Innocent in plans to invade England. Philip was also in touch with the English barons who were smarting under John's arbitrary government, and with the rebellious Welsh. Under these circumstances, John decided to make his peace if necessary at the pope's price, being urged thereto by papal threats of deposition. He was thinking of more than mere peace. In order to make of the pope a friend and supporter, and to guarantee that his enemies would also be considered the pope's enemies,[12] he would play up to Innocent's desire to be considered the overlord of Europe by turning England over to him as a fief and receiving it back after homage and fealty. The arrangement was concluded between John and a papal legate in May, 1213. John agreed to accept Stephen Langton as archbishop of Canterbury, to recall and reinstate all exiled clergy, and to compensate the Church for its financial losses. England was acknowledged to be a fief of the papacy, and in token thereof was to pay an annual tribute of 1000 marks a year. Shortly thereafter it was announced by the papal legate that "the lord king is another man by God's grace." As such, and as a vassal, Innocent could protect him against enemies abroad and at home, and, as John knew, when the time came, against Magna Carta itself, which Innocent called "a shame for England." "We are presented with the paradoxical situation of the pope's aiding the lately

[9]Sidney Painter, *The Reign of King John*, pp. 175–176.
[10]See pp. 435 f.
[11]See p. 545.
[12]Painter, p. 193. Poole, p. 457, agrees that it is probable that the idea originated in England and not in Rome.

excommunicated John, who was allied with the pope's bitterest enemy, the excommunicated Otto [IV, of Brunswick], against the pope's protégé, Frederick of Hohenstaufen, and his previous ally, the king of France."[13] It has even been suggested that what helped Innocent to see the changed man in John was not only recognition of papal overlordship but the fact that the king knew how to spend money judiciously in Rome. "It is clear that a large amount of sterling money was spent in Rome during the protracted negotiations, and it seems doubtful that it all went for the living expenses of John's agents. Then in 1213 and 1214 new pensions were established on the English exchequer. We find on the list Gualo, a future legate to England, the nephew of the bishop of Ostia, Count Richard, the pope's brother, and Stephen his son, Simon, nephew of Nicholas of Tusculum [the cardinal-bishop sent to England as a papal legate to see that the terms of John's surrender were carried out], and a fair number of other Romans, both clerics and laymen. The 1,000 marks a year promised in tribute was no paltry sum. Moreover, the English records show that Nicholas of Tusculum, who turned so benign an eye on the repentant king, was a very expensive 'angel of peace and safety.' His way of life in England was far from niggardly. One hesitates to use the term bribery—it always cost money to get things done in the papal court. But it certainly looks as if money well spent had smoothed the way for the pope's change of heart. The ironically inclined can well speculate as to how much of the booty pillaged from the English church ended in Roman strong-boxes."[14] Some of those who knew or came to know of these financial details must have wondered just what kind of an office the vicar of Christ and the successor of Saint Peter held.

Thus, in addition to their state in central Italy, the popes were able to make of the Donation of Constantine something more than a merely verbal claim, and to translate the deductions of their bold canonists into something more than the appearance of a papal world state. This state was conceived by the popes in terms of the contemporary feudalism. Holding the world in fief from Christ through his vassal Saint Peter, they were the overlords of the secular rulers of the earth, entitled to homage and fealty and to the services of the feudal contract or its equivalent. It was, however, the European church rather than the European states that they ruled with the centralized, bureaucratic absolutism of the later Roman Empire.

Papal Theocracy and Spiritual Supremacy

THE FOURTH LATERAN COUNCIL

This centralized church organization was of slow growth. If the papacy as a temporal power reached its height under Innocent III in the thirteenth

[13]Poole, p. 458.
[14]Painter, pp. 201–202.

century, the spiritual supremacy of the papacy, while recognized earlier, was not completely organized until the fourteenth century, at a time when the papacy was resident not in Rome but in the French town of Avignon. By spiritual supremacy of the papacy is meant the right of the popes to determine the personnel, the discipline, and the belief of the Church. Before the rise of the papal monarchy such questions, in so far as they were settled for the Church at large and not by the local bishops, were settled by ecumenical councils. By the beginning of the thirteenth century, however, the western church council had become an instrument of the papacy. The popes summoned such councils, prepared their agenda, presided over them, and confirmed their decisions. The Fourth Lateran Council, meeting in the last year of Innocent's pontificate (1215), is a good example of such a papally conducted council, at a moment when the Church was undoubtedly the dominant power in the western world. To read its decrees is to sense the power that these churchmen, under papal leadership, felt. The authorities of the state were ordered not to interfere with the administration of the Church by freely elected or appointed clergy. They were not to collect taxes from the clergy. Moreover, the Council boldly asserted that in no state could secular legislation inimical to the Church be considered valid.

The Council is also a good example of what is meant by the papal determination of the discipline and belief of the Church in the exercise of its spiritual supremacy. It used the Council to make obligatory a well-established discipline and to establish a long-argued dogma. The discipline in question was private confession to the priest; the dogma, transubstantiation.

The regulations of the Council provided that every member of the Church was to go to his priest once a year, make an oral confession of his sins, subject himself to the penalty assigned to atone for his sin, and thereafter participate in the sacrament of the Eucharist. The dogma of transubstantiation made necessary the belief on the part of every Christian that in the course of the ceremony of the Mass the priest, in consecrating the elements of the bread and wine, transforms them into the actual body and blood of Christ. As the result of this extraordinary priestly miracle, the Christian, in partaking of the Eucharist, actually consumes in his own body—and is thus physically sanctified—the very body and blood of Christ. These two prescriptions could be spoken of as the victory of Roman authoritarianism and of the pagan mystery cult in the Christian Church. They endowed the priest with God's power of forgiveness and of performing miracles. Without some appreciation of both it is impossible to understand the power of medieval and contemporary Catholic Christianity. The Council obliged every Christian who wished to remain in the Church to assuage his conscience in accordance with the terms of the Church.[15]

[15]See the discussion of Penance, pp. 590 f.

The spiritual supremacy of the papacy over the Church meant the centralization of the latter under the popes, after the Church had been freed from interference by the state. The legitimation of this supremacy was contained in canon law, upholding what has already been referred to as the *plenitudo potestatis*, or complete and absolute power of the pope. For canon law to become effective it had to become known and followed. This could not be accomplished without free access for Rome to the local churches and free access for the local churches to Rome. To provide for this access required the popes to be not only alert to the possibilities of intervention in the affairs of local churches but also surrounded by a central administration capable of intervening either from above or by receiving appeals from below, and thus protecting local churches in an independent position *vis à vis* the state. In addition to law and an administration to enforce it, provision had also to be made for means to support or pay the administrators. All these things the popes developed with an admirable and enviable efficiency.

THE PAPAL LEGATE

They needed, for example, someone to represent them locally, within a kingdom or principality, in order to provide that directions from above should be known and enforced, and that local churches should be subject to central supervision. This need the popes met with the papal legate. The legate could be appointed from the local clergy (as, for example, the archbishop of Canterbury as papal legate for England) or be sent out from Rome. He might be a permanent papal representative or one sent to deal with a particular and difficult problem. Such a legate would hold councils of the local churches, visit them, and be responsible for maintaining within them all the interests of Rome. The popes, however, did not rely solely upon the papal legate to centralize the Church. They leaned heavily upon the monasteries, which, more often than not, were freed by papal privilege from the control of the local bishop in whose diocese they were located and made responsible directly to Rome. They also encouraged the constant journeying to Rome of the local clergy. It was necessary for a newly elected archbishop, for example, to make a visit to Rome for his *pallium*. It was necessary to go to Rome for a decision on problems that could not be settled locally (for instance, clerical elections). Rome made itself the central court of appeal for all cases of violation of canon law that could not be handled in the local courts.

THE PAPAL CURIA

The centralization of the affairs of the Church in papal hands required the building of an administration, or *curia* (court), the leading positions in which went to the cardinals. The papal *curia*, as in the case of the *curia* of the king, became specialized into separate departments known by the thirteenth century as the chancery, the secretarial department, the penitentiary, the disciplinary department, and the *camera*, or treasury. Each of these acted as a court for the settlement of pertinent local appeals made to Rome. In the case of very special decisions, the pope, with or without a council of cardinals known as a consistory, acted as an appellate court. It was in the chancery that papal bulls were drawn up. The penitentiary was ultimately responsible for cases of excommunication and interdict and for dispensations from the provisions of canon law. This central machinery grew more complicated in the course of the thirteenth and fourteenth centuries. Its administration of divine affairs did not keep it from becoming venal. In the fourteenth century the luxurious, gorgeous, and corrupt papal court became a scandal to a great number of western Christians.

PAPAL CONTROL OVER THE PERSONNEL OF THE CLERGY

What made a greater impression upon the West than the judicial, disciplinary, and secretarial departments of the *curia* was the relentless way in which the popes were able to break down the local control of the personnel of the clergy, and to extract money from the Church. The fight for freedom from the state had previously meant that the Church was to choose its officials in accordance with canon law. But this freedom did not prevent local authorities, royal or aristocratic, from exercising an influence upon the choices made. Nor did it prevent the papacy from entering the lists in its own behalf, with the result that local authorities and the papacy contended for appointment to the offices of the Church as they fell vacant. The case of Stephen Langton illustrates how the papacy, by taking advantage of the many disputed local elections, could get its candidates into the most important sees. In the fourteenth century the popes at Avignon began to claim the right to appoint to large classes of ecclesiastical offices. They never succeeded in breaking the patronage of the local lord over the parish church, but they did reserve for themselves, as it was put (meaning take away from someone else), the right to appoint to all other church offices. That is, they took from monasteries the right to elect their own abbots, from cathedral chapters the right to elect bishops and archbishops, and from these officials the right to fill their own chapters. Urban V (1362–1370), for example, reserved for the papacy the right to appoint all patriarchs, archbishops, and bishops whose churches had an annual income of more than two hundred, and all abbots whose annual income was more than one hundred florins. Indeed this same pope later extended his list to include "all churches of the same types and also monasteries of women of whatever value, whenever he chose to dispose of them."[16] The popes facilitated their claims by accepting local

[16]William E. Lunt, *Papal Revenues in the Middle Ages*, I, 85.

suggestions as to how the vacancies should be filled. Yet this did not prevent the growth of considerable local hostility to foreign, that is, papal, intervention in what were properly considered local rights. In the fourteenth century this practice of papal reservation of appointments to local church offices became a complicated and lucrative business. For the popes were very glad to receive fees for appointments to local church offices and to receive them before the offices became vacant. If you wanted to become the abbot of a very wealthy monastery whose abbot was desperately ill, and to which the pope had reserved appointment, you journeyed to Avignon and paid the necessary "expectative" to the *camera* for the appointment. When there were many of the same mind, it was difficult for papal officials to avoid the temptation of receiving more than one expectative for the same office. Since by the end of the fifteenth century all the offices in the *curia* were for sale, the papal business in church offices flourished.

PAPAL INCOME

Avignon popes reserved for themselves not only appointments to local offices but also the adjudication of cases hitherto settled by local courts, and, more serious, certain fees hitherto collected by the local clergy. Innocent VI (1352-1362), for example, reserved for the papacy the fee called *procurations*, collected by a bishop or archbishop as expenses for making a local visitation. He also ordered his local collectors to perform the visitations. At Avignon the system of collecting local taxes by papal agents was completed with the organization of the whole western church into papal collectorates. Whether it was money paid to local collectors and transported to Rome, or money paid directly into the *camera* at Rome, the number of taxes collected by the popes from the Church made kings seem relatively amateurish in financial matters. Not to mention the income from the city of Rome and the Papal States, they collected what was called a *census* both from the monasteries exempted from episcopal control and from the vassals of the Holy See. From some states they collected Peter's Pence. The popes taxed the clergy to help pay for the crusades; they collected subsidies, the pope's feudal *aids*. If a churchman were appointed or confirmed by the pope he paid the fee known as *services*, supposedly one-third of the annual income of his office. When he did not pay services, he paid *annates*, supposedly the whole of the income of the first year of incumbency. The popes or papal officials on business collected the expenses of their journeys from the local clergy. This is only a part of the story. The administration of the papacy in all its spiritual and temporal glory was a costly affair, increasingly resented not only by the layman but by the clergy who shared in its expense.

SOCIAL CLEAVAGE AMONG THE SECULAR CLERGY

The subsidiary church over which the popes ruled was a vast international organization covering the areas in Europe, western Asia, and northern Africa into which western Christianity had spread or maintained a hold. It was divided among secular and regular (monastic) clergy. The organization of the former was essentially that which had been borrowed from the administration of the later Roman Empire,[17] that is, a centralized hierarchy. As it adapted itself to the rural society of the Middle Ages, however, it underwent certain modifications. This society was divided socially between a rural landowning aristocracy and a peasantry that worked its estates. The secular clergy reflected this split. The upper clergy, the archbishops, bishops, and the members of what were called the cathedral chapters, came as a rule from the noble families of the locality. The parish clergy, however, were recruited from the peasantry. At a time of social crisis this remained a very important cleavage. When peasants were seeking a larger measure of freedom they were often supported by their local priests. A similar relationship often grew up between the working classes in the towns and their priests. But in political, economic, and social matters the influence of the Church as a whole was aristocratic and conservative.

POPE AND ARCHBISHOPS

The hierarchy had developed historically by differentiation among bishops who were originally considered of equal authority. The pope was originally, and so remained, a bishop of Rome. The metropolitans, or as they came to be called, the archbishops, were originally bishops of their local cities, and as such they remained. The centralization promoted by Rome did much to subordinate the archbishop to the pope and to prevent his developing an intermediary power separating the ordinary bishop from the pope. The pope wished to be considered as the immediate superior (ordinary) of all the bishops as well as archbishops. Yet it was not possible wholly to destroy the special positions of such archbishops as those of Milan, Cologne, Hamburg-Bremen, Lyons, and Canterbury and York. The squabbles between the archbishops of Canterbury and York over precedence when in the presence of a papal legate are amusing, but to them no indignity could be spared when it came to maintaining the honor of rank and see.

THE EPISCOPATE

It was upon the bishops, the episcopate, that the administration of the Church chiefly rested, and, before the state possessed professional administrators, to an important degree the administration of the state as well. These younger sons of the ruling class were constantly engaged in the high politics of church and state. They were also powerful figures in the feudal system. And, as the papacy developed its own body of supporters among the monarchies of western Europe, they had also the interests of

[17]See pp. 337 f.

the Church and papacy to defend. They thus had little or no time for the ordinary tasks of administering salvation to their flocks. In fact, they spent a great deal of time away from their episcopal duties, attending to business elsewhere. When they did come home to their sees they often preferred to withdraw to the seclusion of their castles and country estates rather than concern themselves with the administrative details of an episcopal city. A fifteenth-century critic of Archbishop Kempe of York claims that he spent only two or three weeks in his see every ten to twelve years.[18]

BISHOP ODO OF BAYEUX

A half brother of William the Conqueror, Bishop Odo of Bayeux came to the episcopal throne when a lad of about fourteen (1049). As a feudal vassal of his brother, the duke of Normandy (and after 1066 the king of England), he owed the services of twenty knights. Among his own vassals he counted seven English earls, and altogether the lands of the bishopric returned the services of one hundred and twenty knights to the bishop. From his vassals he collected feudal aids "as often as he was obliged to go to Rome on the business of the church, whenever it was necessary to repair the cathedral, or when it was necessary to rebuild the episcopal dwellings after fires."[19] English chroniclers had no use for him, accusing him of "ambition, avarice, and singular cruelty. . . . One of them complains bitterly of his treatment of the poor, his inaccessibility to those seeking redress, and of his castles which were mighty nests of oppression." The chronicler giving him "the fairest treatment" concludes that he was essentially "an irreligious prelate, one in whom despite eloquence, generosity, and high spirits, the worldly predominated completely over the spiritual."

ARCHBISHOP ADALBERT OF HAMBURG-BREMEN

German bishops acquired a special reputation for being able to fight and swear hard. A contemporary of Bishop Odo of Bayeux, Archbishop Adalbert of Hamburg-Bremen, "was the wealthy son of parents related to the important Wettin family and the counts of Weimar."[20] He was extremely proud of his noble ancestry. "Not every bishop could put a German king or a Greek princess in his lineage. There was even a time when, as he looked back on the line of archbishops that preceded him, he could say they were all obscure men. . . . His noble enemies in bitter scorn reported that he even went as far as to announce in the presence of the king at a public mass that he and the king were in fact the sole survivors of the aristocracy." "His whole nature was permeated with such a love for the fantastic, such a hankering after the grandiose, as to make him appear

[18]See A. H. Thompson, *The English Clergy*, p. 47.
[19]S. E. Gleason, *An Ecclesiastical Barony of the Middle Ages*, pp. 16 ff.
[20]E. N. Johnson, "Adalbert of Hamburg-Bremen," *Speculum*, IX (April 1934), 147–179.

a strange eccentric being apart from the general run of his kind. . . . He was . . . delighted to add to his own court circle those skilled in many arts: doctors, . . . an Italian painter, a French versifier, actors, alchemists, those who had knowledge of the occult, interpreters of dreams, augurs, and a motley crew of fawning sycophants." He had grandiose plans for his see. He wanted to become the patriarch of the North for dioceses in Scandinavia and the Viking discoveries of the North Atlantic. He had ordained in Bremen the first bishop of the Orkneys and the first bishop of Iceland. The latter "took back with him to Iceland a letter from his new archbishop promising a personal visit to the new members of his flock, a letter addressed also to the Greenlanders. It is not at all beyond the realm of possibility, had Adalbert ever made good his promise and actually gone to Greenland, that the same ambitious *Wanderlust* that made him desire to go there might have taken him on to Vinland. For the existence of Vinland was well known in Bremen."[21] He planned also to complete the Christianization of trans-Elbia to justify his patriarchate. The Slavic revolt of 1066 ruined these plans, and Adalbert "was driven from the royal court as a lonely exile."

Alone at Bremen, he "withdrew into sullen rebellion against his own parishioners. . . . What was there to love in a people that remained stubbornly bound to their half-pagan manners and beliefs, who drank to excess, whose belly was their god, who were indifferent to the laws of the church, a violent gang of perjurers, fornicators, adulterers, polygamous, incestuous eaters of horse flesh? . . . In the face of their stubborn unwillingness to be corrected he had finally concluded that they were neither to be trusted nor spared; their mouths must be held in with bit and bridle, their transgression was to be punished with the rod. When he had an opportunity he put them in chains, confiscated their property, and, with an unpleasant laugh, asserted that bodily punishment was spiritually useful, loss of property an expiation for sin. In uncontrollable anger he was liable to break out in roaring curses, and to beat his officials with his own fist until he drew blood." In fact the archbishop was becoming insane. He "spent his time alone and appeared less often to the sight of a hostile people. He slept far into the day and spent his nights playing dice, or occasionally sought to assuage his depressed spirits with a harp player's music. . . . He became more a prey to superstitions. . . . His physical health began to give way under the strain, and more medicine from more doctors brought more discomfort. . . . [He became] cruel, intolerable, unhuman." A severe attack of dysentery wasted his handsome body away to the bones. And with this befouling illness he "died alone at high noon without the last rites of the church."[22] Clearly, among others, the Slavs had been too much for Adalbert.

[21] Johnson, p. 155.
[22] Johnson, p. 179.

During the Middle Ages the subsidiary administration between the bishop and the parish priest was worked out. To assist him in the administration of the diocese and to maintain the regular services in his church the bishop had a cathedral chapter. In some instances this chapter, as in Christ's Church Canterbury, was composed of monks, and next to the cathedral, therefore, was the monastery. More normally the chapter was composed of *canons*. These could be regular canons[23] living a common life according to monastic rule, or secular canons, in which case they lived independently in their own houses in the cathedral city. The chapter occupied the stalls in the choir of the church, and each canon held a benefice, or prebend, the landed endowment for his particular office. Often enough the conditions of holding a canon's prebend did not require the residence of the canon in the episcopal city. In this case the canon maintained a substitute in the stall. To grant a rich canonry not requiring attendance was a way to subsidize a promising university student. In some instances the canon held a parish in the diocese and maintained a substitute in the cathedral. The chapter held its own communal property separate from that of the bishop, and income from this was divided among the canons. It resented any interference from the bishop in its own affairs. Its elected head was the *dean*. Other officials were the *precentor*, in charge of the cathedral services, the *chancellor*, and the *treasurer*.

THE PARISH PRIEST

As his substitute when not at home the bishop had a *vicar-general*, and to administer his ecclesiastical court in his absence a person called simply the *official*. The diocese was divided into archdeaconries, headed by the *archdeacon*, and these in turn into several deaneries, headed by the rural dean, or *archpriest*. The archdeacon on the Continent often became a serious rival of the bishop. He it was who visited, that is, inspected, the monasteries and parishes in his archdeaconry. The archpriest, or rural dean, an appointee of the bishop from among the parish clergy, was responsible for the maintenance of ecclesiastical discipline in his little province, acting as an intermediary between archdeacon and the ordinary parish priest. Not infrequently parishes were not in the hands of regular parish priests but of their substitutes. In cases such as these, the parishes and their incomes (tithes) had often been turned over to monasteries in need of increases in income (the technical term is *appropriated*). The monasteries then maintained, at a small cost, vicars or curates to administer the sacraments and conduct the religious life of the parish.[24] The parish priest, whether rector or vicar or curate, was a man of the people, often

---

[23]See pp. 598 f.
[24]In the early 16th century the English county of York had 622 parish churches, of which 392, or 63 per cent, were appropriated. See A. H. Thompson, *The English Clergy*, p. 115.

ignorant, poorly trained, and not qualified to guide the spiritual lives of his flock. But when, like Chaucer's priest, he was "a learned man ... who Christ's own gospel saught to preach ... but first he followed it himselve," it was chiefly he who gave meaning to the endless toil of the peasant on the manor, through his administration of the sacraments, his preaching, and his availability as counsellor and friend.[25]

The Sacramental System

MODIFICATIONS OF SAINT AUGUSTINE'S POINT OF VIEW

Obviously there could have been no imposing centralized and theocratic western church governed by a body of canon law if the ascetic Christian point of view handed down from antiquity had not continued to be devotedly accepted by the peoples of central and western Europe. The definition of that point of view had, to a large extent, been made by Saint Augustine,[26] and, for the most part, his work did not need to be undone in the course of the Middle Ages. We have seen, however, that certain notions and contradictions of Augustine proved immediately troublesome to succeeding theologians.[27] They could not accept the extreme rigor of his doctrine of predestination, for no matter what he might say about the freedom of the human will, his predestination denied it and deprived man of moral responsibility. Likewise, no matter what he might say about the importance of the Church in the salvation of the soul, his predestination made the Church really unnecessary for the elect, and of no help to the damned. Men thus began to say that God's predestination was not based upon his arbitrary choice but upon his foreknowledge of the free choice men made between good and evil. They began to insist that fallen man could not regain his ability to choose between good and evil without the help of the Church dispensing God's grace through the sacraments. This view of the Semi-Pelagians was further developed during the medieval period, especially by theologians of the fourteenth and fifteenth centuries. A man like Duns Scotus, for example, did not hold with Augustine that original sin transforms man into a depraved, evil creature. In spite of original sin man remains essentially good. This sin merely causes him to be prone to use immoderately sensual things. He also keeps his free will. Scotus also believed that a man in possession of free will could of himself turn to God, and thus be rewarded by God's grace.

[25]See H. S. Bennett, *Life on the English Manor*, Chap. i.
[26]See pp. 344 ff.
[27]See pp. 352 f.

Man was left good and in possession of free will by most of these theologians, not that he might win God's grace through faith and love, but that he might choose to do the things that would earn him God's grace through the Church, or in other words, that he might, through good works, merit the divine grace necessary to salvation. The Church, that is —and the theologians tended to give their support to this position—preferred to make men feel secure about their salvation through participation in automatically efficacious rites and ceremonies. There was no deviation from the doctrine that the Church was the only dispenser of God's grace and that the method of dispensation was through the sacraments. It was generally recognized that there were seven of these (Baptism, Confirmation, Eucharist, Penance, Extreme Unction, Marriage, Holy Orders), and they were ordinarily defined as the "visible signs of invisible grace." Theologians, however, were not content to regard the sacraments as mere signs of grace. They insisted that they caused grace to exist in those who partook of them. "The sacramental rite thus itself possesses an inherent efficacy, and its symbolic significance is more or less displaced by the magical element in it. . . . They sanctify intrinscially." Indeed, there was considerable argument as to whether the sacraments automatically infused divine grace into the individual without his participating with an appropriate attitude or mood. A few made the efficacy depend upon such things as faith and repentance. Others thought that only a good disposition was necessary, "a sincerely religious spirit that aspires for grace and feels real contrition, and thus merits sacramental grace."[28] They were opposed by those who thought that only the "absence of a bad disposition (unbelief, contempt of the sacrament, mortal sin)" was necessary. In any case one can detect here the desire to relieve men of too much concern for their salvation by guaranteeing that under certain definite circumstances, God will not fail to extend his grace to them.

THE SACRAMENT OF PENANCE

The tendency of medieval Christianity to degenerate from an ardently felt faith to a series of mechanical rites can be illustrated by the sacrament of Penance. This sacrament concerns the extension of God's grace to forgive sin. It will be remembered[29] that the Fourth Lateran Council obliged every member of the Church to confess at least once a year to his parish priest. This system of private, or auricular, confession was introduced to the West by Irish monks[30] and gradually supplanted the older system of public penance. It has been one of the great sources of power of the Church. Christianity is much concerned with sin, that great obstacle to salvation. It aims to make the conscience sensitive to evil-doing and be

[28]James Mackinnon, *Luther and the Reformation*, I, 72, 81, 82.
[29]See pp. 580 f.
[30]See pp. 396 ff.

aroused by a sense of guilt. At the same time it offers the means of temporarily relieving the conscience of its sense of evil and guilt by providing for
the periodical emotional purge that comes from confessing one's guilt to
the priest, or, in other words, of talking it over with an agent of a gracious,
loving God eager to forgive mankind. The priest was the medieval man's
psychiatrist, and today he fears being supplanted by this modern rival.
Ever since antiquity theologians had been concerned with classifying sins,
separating the venial, or little, easily forgiven sins from the deadly or
mortal ones. They had come by the thirteenth century to agree that there
were seven of the latter (pride, envy, anger, sloth, avarice, gluttony,
lechery), and it was these that it was necessary to confess to the priest in
the confessional. By virtue of his ordination, which confers upon him
the power of the keys,[31] the priest is empowered to absolve the penitent
sinner from the penalty for the commission of mortal sin, namely, hellfire.
Immediately following upon confession, therefore, comes absolution,
which frees the sinner from worry about eternal punishment in hell. It
does not, however, free him from temporal or earthly punishment, so
that, following upon absolution, the priest assigns so much penance for
the sinner to perform—enough, it is hoped, to satisfy God's justice. If
insufficient penance has been assigned then the soul of the sinner must
purge itself awhile in purgatory before being released to the heavenly
paradise. There was a good deal of argument among the theologians as
to whether it was necessary for one to be *contrite*, that is, really sorry, for
one's sin before he could be forgiven in the sacrament of Penance, or
whether merely being *attrite*, that is, only afraid of the punishment for
sin, might suffice. The latter view, that attrition sufficed, was widespread
at the end of the medieval period and "certainly tended to demoralize
religion and to make the sacrament far too much a popular device for
escaping hell and ensuring heaven by priestly intervention without the
essentially religious spirit."[32]

INDULGENCES

If some theologians were ready to make it easier for the sinner by letting
attrition suffice for contrition, the Church was also anxious to provide
some security in respect to purgatory. This was provided through the
practice of granting what were called *indulgences*. These were granted
to the faithful in return for many kinds of good works: supporting a
crusade, making a pilgrimage, or visiting a shrine in possession of holy
relics. These indulgences released the sinner from temporal punishment
for his sin. If the indulgences were plenary they would free him from all
worry about the fires of pugatory by freeing him from the temporal
punishment for sin. If only partial, they provided for release from the
fires of purgatory for specific periods of time. It was thus possible for the

[31]See p. 339.
[32]Mackinnon, p. 87.

sinner, without making too careful a distinction between contrition and attrition, to confess to his priest, acquire indulgences, and free himself from worry about hell and purgatory. When these indulgences came to be sold, punishment for sin became something of a mockery.

POPULAR RELIGION

To the peasant on the manor it made little difference what the theologians said, though the official interpretations of the Church reached him through the sermons of his parish priest. To him the Church was vital not only because it provided a means of salvation but because it enhanced the dignity of the important events of human life: birth with Baptism, adolescence with Confirmation, marriage with a special sacrament of its own, and death with Extreme Unction. It provided the dead with special Masses reducing the time necessary for souls to spend in purgatory, and at all times there was available in the parish or neighboring churches a great host of saints to whose chapels one might repair for aid in every difficult circumstance, no matter how minor. And if these heavenly hosts were not able to move God to act on behalf of repentant and petitioning man, there was always the gracious Mother of God, the Virgin Mary, whose appeals Jesus could not resist. She could rescue man from almost any difficulty. It was told of a youth who had done homage to the Devil that the latter wished to have him repudiate not only Christ but his Mother, for "those whom the Son in His Justice casts away, the Mother, in her superfluity of mercy brings back again to indulgence." This the youth would not do, and when he repented of his deed he did not call upon "that terrible Majesty whom he had denied, but only importuned His most loving Mother with lamentable cries." When he did so before an altar upon which rested a statue of the Virgin and Child, "that blessed and singular advocate of Christians spoke thus through the lips of her statue, 'Sweetest Son, pity this man.' But the Child made no answer to His Mother, turning His face from her. When therefore she besought Him again, pleading that the youth had been misled, He turned His back upon His Mother, saying, 'This man hath denied me. What should I do to him?' Thereupon the statue rose, laid her Child upon the altar, and threw herself on the ground at His feet saying, 'I beseech Thee, Son, forgive him this sin for my sake.' Then the Child raised His Mother up and answered her. 'Mother, I could never deny Thee aught: behold, I forgive it all for Thy sake.' "[33] Monks who were afraid that Jesus would not help them threatened to tell his Mother on him. It was known that the Virgin took the place of knights at tournaments when they were delayed by doing homage to her at her chapels. Monks were known to dream of the sweet, chaste kiss she impressed upon their lips. She rescued them when they got into trouble, as, for example, when the monk who was

[33]G. G. Coulton, *Life in the Middle Ages*, I, 63, 65.

the treasurer of his monastery, taking the treasure with him, ran away with a matron who took with her "a sum of money which she secretly [stole] from her husband." When captured and imprisoned, both monk and matron appealed to the Virgin. "At length the Blessed Virgin appeared to them in great wrath, and after rebuking them bitterly she spoke thus: 'I might obtain from my Son the remission of your sin: but what can I do for so great a scandal? For ye have made the name of the Religious [the monks] to stink in the nostrils of the whole people, so that men will have no faith in them from henceforth; which is an almost irreparable loss.' At length the pitiful Virgin, overcome by their prayers, summoned to her presence the demons who had instigated this sin, and enjoined upon them, even as they had brought religion into disrepute, even so to put an end to this evil fame."[34]

THE VIRGIN MOTHER

The Virgin knew how to receive the homage of simple folk at its proper worth. At the monastery of Clairvaux a minstrel and tumbler had become a monk only, at first, to suffer severe embarrassment because he could not serve the Virgin as learnedly as the others. He finally decided to serve her as best he could. Before her statue in the crypt of the church, "he began to turn somersaults, now high, now low, first forwards, then backwards, and then he fell on his knees before the image, and bowed his head. 'Ah, very gentle Queen,' said he, 'of your pity, and of your generosity, despise not my service.' Then he tumbled, and leaped, and turned gaily the somersault of Metz. . . . And anon he turned the French somersault, and then the somersault of Champagne, and after that, those of Spain and of Brittany, and then that of Lorraine. . . . And after that, he did the Roman somersault, and then . . . turned him with great grace and looked very humbly at the image of the Mother of God. 'Lady,' said he, 'I do homage to you with my heart, and my body, and my feet, and my hands, for naught beside this do I understand. . . . Yonder they are singing, but I am come here to divert you. Lady, you who can protect me, for God's sake do not despise me.' " When he collapsed exhausted and perspiring upon the floor of the crypt, "the Mother of God . . . came to his succour. . . . Her vesture was all wrought with gold and precious stones, and with her were the angels and the archangels from the heavens above, who came around the tumbler, and solaced and sustained him. . . . The sweet and noble Queen took a white cloth, and with it she very gently fanned her minstrel before the altar. And the noble and gracious Lady fanned his neck and body and face to cool him, and greatly did she concern herself to aid him, and gave herself up to the care of him."[35]

[34]Coulton, IV, 214–215.
[35]Alice Kemp-Welch, *Of the Tumbler of Our Lady and Other Miracles*, quoted in C. W. Jones, *Medieval Literature in Translation*, pp. 595 ff.

MODIFICATION OF THE ASCETIC IDEAL

The regular, or monastic, clergy supporting the Church incorporated the ascetic point of view more intensively into their way of life. Yet, as we have seen,[36] western asceticism was a much more practical adaptation of this ideal than eastern. The Benedictines were organized to perform their proper services as monks, but they became colonies of expert farmers. Their large farms housed libraries, scholars, artists, and potential propagators or missionaries of the faith. Because, too, the monks offered to pray for the souls of their founders, their communities were heavily endowed, in spite of the fact that the Benedictine rule prohibited the monk from having private property. What, therefore, the monk could not own as an individual it was proper for the community of monks to own. Heavy endowment in land involved the monks in feudal politics and economics, and endangered the simple way of life contemplated by Saint Benedict in his rule. It is always difficult for heavily endowed idealism to maintain the lofty character of its first vision and the vigor of its earliest zeal. It can scarcely do so without the steady devotion of a long line of followers, which, over the course of centuries, it is not easy to acquire. The history of western monasticism is thus the history of periodic decay and reform, aiming to remove with new methods the deficiencies of the older institutions. These experiments with the way of life and organization of a monastic community are a tribute to the inventiveness and earnestness of the western mind. In the end they turned out to be further responses to the needs of a church functioning in the world, or of secular society itself. The early selfish ideal of individual salvation through living in an isolated, cloistered community was modified to include the performance of Christian tasks in the outside world. As it became more social, the ascetic ideal exhausted the possible forms of its organization and expression. At the close of the Middle Ages there was little in organization that it had not tried. In so far as older monastic organizations adopted the new forms of organization and expression—in so far, that is, as they became social as well as individual in their ends—they were maintained as important aids to the civilizing process. In so far as they did not, they were abandoned and ridiculed. Poor, desolate, and with discipline undermined, they were attacked by the Protestant reformer, who abolished them when he could.

THE CLUNIAC REFORM

The monastic Church was a standing protest against the organized pomp and wealth of the secular Church. As the individual monastic orders themselves decayed and were criticized, the critics of Christianity mul-

[36]See pp. 391 ff.

tiplied. And when the monastic reformer took hold, he could not ordinarily spare the secular Church from his criticism. We have had occasion to refer to the Cluniac reform,[37] the first major attempt to reform the Benedictine monasteries of the West. These reformers attributed the decay of the Benedictines to the fact that their wealth invited laxness in observing the provisions of their rule and also interference in their internal affairs by neighboring bishops or lords. They also thought that the autonomy of each individual Benedictine house was an organizational luxury, leading easily to local deviation and inviting local interference in its affairs. When the mother house of Cluny was founded (910) by the duke of Aquitaine, it was freed from the authority of bishops and laymen, and subjected only to the pope. Cluny expanded throughout the West, not by creating new independent houses, but by setting up dependent priories whose priors were appointed by the mother house. There was only one abbot of Cluny. Moreover, it took over older, decayed Benedictine houses that then lost their autonomy to the abbot of Cluny. The latter was responsible for maintaining the discipline of the subsidiary priories, and this he did by carrying out local visitations and holding annual meetings of the priors. Feudal autonomy was supplanted by a type of monarchical centralization. The disciplinary reform consisted of a return to the provisions of the Benedictine rule. The essential Cluniac modification was to minimize manual labor for a larger number of hours of psalmody in choir or of scholarship in scriptorium and library.

THE CISTERCIAN ORDER

After about two centuries the continued decay of the older Benedictine houses and the wealth and display of the Cluniac order led to another and, it so happened, final attempt at reform of the Benedictine system. This took the form of the Cistercian order, founded at Citeaux in Burgundy (1098) by monks from the Benedictine monastery of Molêsme who refused any longer to violate their monastic oaths by suffering infractions of the rule. Citeaux might have failed for lack of recruits had not a certain Burgundian nobleman, Bernard by name, entered it in 1112 with many of his relatives and friends. Thereafter its renown became so widespread that it began to establish daughter houses, over one of which, Clairvaux, Bernard became abbot. The organization of the Cistercians was a compromise between the older Benedictine autonomy and Cluniac centralization. Each Cistercian monastery elected its own abbot and had to be consulted before innovations could be introduced by the abbot of Citeaux. But the immediate control over the discipline of the houses was exercised by the four oldest daughter houses of Citeaux, each of which possessed the right of visiting and correcting its own daughter houses. Once a year a general chapter under the abbot of Citeaux was held, consisting of the four

[37]See p. 530.

abbots of the oldest daughter houses and five abbots chosen by each of the four filiations. Under certain circumstances the general chapter could depose the abbot of Citeaux.

SAINT BERNARD

It was rather Bernard, the abbot of Clairvaux, and not the abbots of Citeaux, who represented to Europe the spirit of Cistercian reform during the first half of the twelfth century. Indeed, Saint Bernard was to the early twelfth century what Pope Innocent III was to the early thirteenth century. He was a man of austere spirit, torn inwardly between hate for those who deviated from the teachings of the Church and love for his sweet Savior Jesus and his loving Virgin Mother. Bernard was in fact a mystic, seeking absorption not by God the Father but by Jesus the Son, and he would have preferred, no doubt, to remain in his cloister with his monks, cultivating his mysticism and asceticism. But a man of his ability the world could not do without; and no matter how ascetically inclined, he was a reformer by temperament, and reformers wish to do something about the world in which they live. Bernard was thus often away from Clairvaux, settling papal schisms, inaugurating the Second Crusade and its counterpart, the crusade against the Slavs, pursuing bold theological innovators like Abélard,[38] and persecuting and preaching against heretics. He therefore illustrates very well the impossibility of keeping western monasticism isolated from the world of affairs.

SAINT BERNARD ON THE CLUNIACS

The spirit of his reform can be seen in his criticisms of the Cluniacs. "I marvel," he says, "how such intemperance has been able to get itself established among monks; in revellings, garments, couches, horse-exercise, and the construction of buildings. Behold! economy is now held to be avarice; sobriety, austerity; and silence is considered equivalent to sadness. On the other hand, laziness is called discretion, profusion liberality, loquacity affability, laughter joyfulness, softness of clothing and trappings of horses are called dignity, the superfluous carefulness of readers elegance. . . . Nothing is done about the Scriptures, nothing for the salvation of souls; but trifles, and jests, and light words are thrown upon the air. At dinner the jaws are as much occupied with dainties as the ears are with nonsense, and wholly intent upon eating, you know no moderation in it. Dishes follow dishes, and in place of the meats from which abstinence is required, the great fishes are doubled in number. When you reach the second course, after being satiated with the first, you appear to yourselves to have tasted nothing. All things are prepared with such care and artifice of cooks that when four or five dishes have been disposed of, the first in no way interferes with the last, nor does satiety diminish ap-

[38]See pp. 646 ff.

petite. . . . Who can describe in how many ways the very eggs are tossed and tormented, with what eager care they are turned under and over, made soft and made hard, eaten up, fried, roasted, stuffed, now served minced with other things, and now by themselves. The very external appearance of the things is cared for, so that the eye may be charmed as well as the palate; and when the stomach, by frequent eructation, shows itself full, the curiosity is still not satisfied. . . . As to water, what can I say when no one takes water, even mixed with wine. As soon as we become monks we all have infirm stomachs, and do not neglect the needed injunction of the Apostle about taking wine—only, I know not on what ground, omitting the 'little' which his precept contains. Would that even with this we were content. When the wine is pure . . . you may see at one dinner three or four half-filled cups carried about, of wines rather smelled than tasted, or if tasted not fully drunk, that with quick discernment the strongest of all may be selected. On festival days some monks are said to observe the custom of having wines mixed with honey, and powdered with the dust of colored spices. Shall we say that this is done for infirmity of the stomach? . . . So clothing is sought, not for usefulness, but with respect to its fineness,—not to keep out the cold, but to minister to pride. . . . Our customary dress, which, I say it with grief, used to be a sign of humility, is worn by the monks of our time as a sign of haughtiness. We can hardly find in the provinces what we will condescend to wear. The soldier and the monk divide between them the same cloth, for head and tunic; and nobody in the secular world, though he were the King himself . . . would disdain to be robed in our garments, if after the fashion proper to him they were fitted and prepared. . . . Soft raiment shows effeminacy of soul. We should not so trouble ourselves to ornament the body unless the culture of the spirit in virtue had first been neglected."[39] Bernard's attitude toward the wonderful extravagance of Benedictine and Cluniac architecture was similar to these views on food, drink, and clothes.[40]

THE DECLINE OF THE CISTERCIANS

The Cistercians intended to restore the original provisions of the Benedictine rule, and especially the one pertaining to manual labor. They set out for remote and isolated locations where land was uncultivated or waste and swamp. Especially in northeastern Germany, beyond the Elbe and Saale, in territory taken from the Slavs, they acted as pioneer houses expanding the area of cultivated land and introducing German settlers on their estates. As missionaries they were active in these areas and in Livonia and Prussia. In England they specialized in sheep ranching, and their raw wool became indispensable to the textile industry in Flanders. The Cistercians, however, did not remain the agricultural laborers they set out to be. They

[39]R. S. Storrs, *Bernard of Clairvaux*, Charles Scribner's Sons, pp. 230–232.
[40]See pp. 746 f.

expanded rapidly, were heavily endowed by governments and aristocracy anxious to utilize their pioneer activities, and were soon possessed of large estates that they were unable to work wholly by themselves. To provide for the manual labor they needed, the Cistercians permitted workers and artisans called lay brothers to enter the order in a subsidiary capacity, thus permitting the Cistercian monks proper to concentrate on the work of the choir. The Cistercians then, like the Cluniacs, became a spiritual élite resting upon the labor of an inferior grade of monkhood in their houses. In the end, they found themselves in the same position as the Cluniacs whom Saint Bernard had set out to reform. Indeed the Cistercian reform, however related to the economic needs of the twelfth century, was the last reform of an order calculated to administer to the ascetic needs of an agricultural society. Meanwhile the towns had arisen in western Europe, and therewith the question of the relationship between asceticism and urban institutions. Within a hundred years after its foundation the Cistercian order was confronted by new monastic competitors for the support of western Europe, the friars.

THE CARTHUSIANS

Before Saint Francis and Saint Dominic revolutionized the older rural monasticism of western Europe, it had taken on other than Benedictine, Cluniac, and Cistercian forms. This extra-Benedictine expansion revealed also the vitality of the ascetic ideal and the experimental temper of the West. The older, eremitical asceticism of the East had never been very popular in western Europe, although the hermit was never a stranger. An attempt, and a very successful attempt, was made by a German cleric, Bruno of Cologne (1030–1101), to make the hermit ideal more acceptable by organizing hermits in communities. His first house was set up in the western Alps not far from Grenoble, where it was known as *La Grande Chartreuse*; it spread throughout western Europe as the Carthusian order.

THE REGULAR CANONS

It was felt also to be somewhat anomalous that the clergy serving the cathedrals and the larger churches (secular canons) should be permitted, in the face of the monastic example, to live independent and unregimented lives in their communities. There were, in fact, early, isolated examples of cathedral canons living in accordance with a monastic rule (regular canons). In the twelfth century two groups of regular canons were organized: the *Augustinians*, and the *Premonstratensians*. The former lived in accordance with a rule compounded of writings of Saint Augustine; the latter were organized (1119) in northern France, at Prémontré near Laon, by another German reformer, Norbert of Xanten, who became the archbishop of Magdeburg. The regular canons, unlike ordinary monks, were in orders, and could therefore serve as priests at the altar. Norbert intended that his canons should help to improve the standards of the parish clergy by undertaking to serve as parish priests. Like the Cistercians, they worked as missionaries and pioneers among the Slavs and other Baltic peoples in the area east of the Elbe.

THE MILITARY ORDERS

The most extraordinary medieval adaptation of the ascetic ideal was to imperialistic warfare in the form of the crusading orders, the chief of which were the *Knights Templars*, the *Hospitalers*, and the *Teutonic Knights*. These orders were built of a fighting élite, the aristocratic knights proper, whom a lesser rank of serving brothers aided on the battlefield and in the hospitals maintained by the orders for pilgrims to the East. There were also chaplains serving in the field and in the hospitals. It requires a certain stretch of the imagination to understand how, in the name of asceticism, the ordinary contemplative and mystical monk, being withdrawn from the world, could be transformed into an armed knight. Yet no less a man than Saint Bernard contemplated the slaughter of infidels and pagans with equanimity, and drew up a rule for the Templars based upon that of the Cistercians. The killing of human beings upon the battlefield has always been so horrible an affair that it has required the highest idealism to justify it. The fighting monk sanctified the slaughter in the name of defense of the faith. The modern army, though not monastic, is organized as a fighting order. The preparation for, and the character of its life in, actual combat is essentially ascetic. Like the medieval monk-knight, it too must fight in defense of a faith. The loss of the Kingdom of Jerusalem to the Moslems deprived the crusading orders of their principal justification. The Templars became the chief bankers of Europe, and were subsequently dissolved upon pressure of King Philip IV of France. The Teutonic Knights attempted to justify their existence by fighting primitive pagans in Europe.[41] When there were no longer any of these, their order was corrupted by the secular state it founded in Livonia and Prussia, and its Prussian branch was secularized in the sixteenth century.

THE DOMINICANS

At the moment when the last important monastic reform began the medieval Church was at the height of its temporal power. Saint Francis and Pope Innocent III were contemporaries. At this moment also the Church was faced by a serious defection in its ranks from Albigensian heretics in southern France. The order of friars (brothers) founded by the Spaniard Saint Dominic (1170–1221) and known, after him, as the Dominicans had as its chief task the suppression of heresy. Saint Dominic was intimately acquainted with heresy, for prior to the founding of his order he had dealt with it for ten years in southern France. He had come

[41]See pp. 510 f.

to the conclusion that it was best controlled by educating the secular clergy, and by preaching in their own tongue to the masses from which the heretics came. The members of his new order had therefore to become distinguished preachers, and this they have remained. They had accordingly to be well educated in the new universities, and, together with the Franciscans, they became the leading teachers in them. For his friars Dominic adopted the rule of the Augustinian canons and the regulations on poverty of the Franciscans. As the order spread, it developed a striking new organization of its own based on the principle of representation. The local chapter elected its own prior and a representative to the provincial chapter. The provinces sent representatives to the meeting of the general chapter of the whole order. Eventually the Dominicans came to abandon their early regulations on poverty and were soon entrusted with the direction of the Inquisition.

SAINT FRANCIS OF ASSISI

"All religions," said Machiavelli, "must be again and again rejuvenated by a return to their original principle. Christianity would have become entirely extinct had not St. Francis and St. Dominic renewed its life and kindled it afresh in the heart of man by their imitation of Jesus Christ. They saved religion, but they destroyed the church."[42] In his life of Saint Francis, Bonaventura tells that Innocent III saw in a dream "the Lateran Basilica about to fall, when a little poor man, of mean stature and humble aspect, propped it with his own back, and thus saved it from falling." This man Innocent identified as Saint Francis. Giotto painted this dream of Innocent III upon the walls of the cathedral church of Assisi. Machiavelli, as quoted above, is exaggerating in brilliant fashion. These men did not save religion or ruin the Church. But at a moment when the Church was preoccupied with its temporal position in the world, and Christianity had, for its priests and its sacraments, lost sight of its founder, there arose out of the merchant class of an Italian town a man of poetic nature who reminded this Church that its religion had something to do with the precepts of Jesus, with the love of mankind, and with the practice of rigid poverty. He not only held to this creed, he set out with a group of followers to practice it among his fellow men. And so unaccustomed was the western Europe of his day to the imitation of Christ, to the tender expression and practice of love for one's fellow human being, whether rich or poor, well or diseased, and to the utter renunciation of the wealth of this world, that it flocked to this man in greater numbers than he ever contemplated, demonstrating the power over the human heart of a lofty idealism sincerely felt and nobly practiced. Saint Francis was implying that the religion of the Church of his day was not really Christianity. In upholding an enthusiastic kind of evangelical piety he did rejuvenate

[42]The selection from R. M. Jones, *Studies in Mystical Religions*, p. 150, copyright 1909 by The Macmillan Co., and used with The Macmillan Co.'s permission.

the popular lay Christianity of his day, but he did not convert the Church. The Church went its own way along the path it had laid out for itself. In so doing it was laying the groundwork for the attack made upon it by reformers of the later Middle Ages and Reformation. It is in this sense that the Christianity of the friars "saved religion" and "destroyed the church."

THE ASCETIC IDEAL OF SAINT FRANCIS

Saint Francis wished to found an order based upon the model of Christ and his disciples. This amounted to a complete break with the chief idea of the older monastic orders, the salvation of the soul by ascetic exercises. For this meant that the monks were to go out into the world and preach and serve others and thus earn their own salvation by bringing it to others. "Go, teach," he said to his early followers. "God in His goodness has called us not alone for our own salvation but for the salvation of the people." The older orders were agricultural, and their houses, set in the midst of their fields, were isolated from the centers of medieval life. Francis was the son of a cloth merchant in the Italian town of Assisi. He understood what the town was doing to medieval society, and knew the suffering it brought to some classes of the population. He conceived of his order as urban rather than agricultural, ministering to the needs, spiritual as well as material, of the new towns, where, often enough, the critic of the Church and the heretic resided. In this sense, Francis' order was meant to do social work, to practice a positive rather than a negative asceticism.

FRANCISCAN FREEDOM

Francis did not imagine that his order would become European in scope. He evidently wished for only a small band of disciples, but for these he wanted the utmost freedom to work as they pleased. He understood well what had been the major source of the decay of the earlier orders. They had denied wealth to the individual monk without denying it to the community of monks. Saint Francis not only denied his followers the right to possess individual property, he was insistent that the order itself should have no property—no houses, no dwellings, no lands. The individual monk and the whole order were to be poor, and thus free of any material consideration. In this matter of poverty Francis was adamant and held up to himself ideals of great difficulty. He was embarrassed to come upon those poorer than he. Upon one occasion he met a poor man and remarked to his companions, "The poverty of that man brings great shame upon us, and much rebukes ours. For very great shame it is to me when I find anyone poorer than I am: since I have chosen holy poverty for my Lady, and for my spiritual and bodily riches." Franciscan monks had therefore either to work or to beg for their livelihood. Their begging brought them and those who imitated them the name of *mendicants*.

Saint Francis was careful, however, never to beg for too much. He told his brothers, "I have never been a thief concerning alms, in getting them or using them beyond necessity. Always have I taken less than I needed, lest I should defraud other poor folk of their portion, for to do the contrary would have been theft." Franciscan monks were not only to be free of possessions, they were to be free of restrictions to work as they pleased. Saint Francis had, to begin with, no idea that his monks should be governed by a rule. When he was urged to supply some sort of regulations for his brothers he merely culled from Scriptures those passages that had inspired him to imitate Christ and his disciples. Only when great numbers had flocked to him (and to the papacy it seemed dangerous to permit such numbers to go unregulated) did the Franciscans require a rule, and then from the pope and not Saint Francis. Francis also conceived of his order as a group of simple laymen working among their fellow men. They were not to be in orders, that is, clergy, and they were not to be educated men. "He wished them rather to be good by charity than smatterers through the desire of knowledge . . . he foreknew that knowledge which puffeth up should be an occasion of ruin."[43]

THE PERSONALITY OF SAINT FRANCIS

Francis' personality suffused the whole early order and has never ceased to inspire. In him were combined those rare qualities marking the saint and the mystic: simplicity, humility, a gentle love for all creation, and a joyful surrender to the Lord and his service. We are told that "drunken with the love and compassion of Christ, blessed Francis on a time did things such as these. For the most sweet melody of spirit boiling up within him frequently broke out in French speech, and the veins of murmuring which he heard secretly with his ears, broke forth into French-like rejoicing. And sometimes he picked up a branch from the earth, and laying it on his left arm, he drew in his right hand another stick like a bow over it, as if on a viol or other instrument, and making fitting gestures, sang with it in French unto the Lord Jesus Christ. But all this playing ended in tears, and this joy dissolved in compassion for the Passion of Christ. In these times he would draw sighs continually; and with deep-drawn groans, forgetful of those things which he held in his hands, he was raised to Heaven" (p. 267). He not only moved with tender solicitude among his fellow men, but like all saints felt a close kinship with his brother and sister animals. The wolves endangering the Italian countryside did so only because they were hungry. Saint Francis knew how to deal with them. They were "friar [brother] wolves" and needed only to be provided regularly with food. He was glad to preach to his "little sisters the birds." "They flew down to hear him," and while he was "uttering these words, all those birds began to open their beaks, and stretch their

[43]From *The Little Flowers of St. Francis*, pp. 195, 243. Everyman's Library, published by E. P. Dutton and Company, Inc.

necks, and spread their wings, and reverently to bow their heads to the ground, showing by their gestures and songs that the holy father's words gave them the greatest joy: and St. Francis was glad and rejoiced with them, and marvelled much at so great a multitude of birds and at their mainfold loveliness, and at their attention and familiarity: for which things he devoutly praised the Creator in them" (p. 30). He wished the emperor to make a law that "no man should take or kill sister larks, nor do them any harm." The mayors of towns and the lords of castles and villages "should be bound every year on Christmas day to compel men to throw wheat and other grains outside the cities and castles, that our sister larks may have something to eat, and also the other birds, on a day of such solemnity. And that for the reverence of the Son of God, Who rested on that night with the most blessed Virgin Mary between an ox and an ass in the manger, whoever shall have an ox or ass shall be bound to provide for them on that night the best of good fodder. Likewise on that day, all poor men should be satisfied by the rich with good food." (p. 290)

He could address the fire in a hot iron about to be used to cauterize his eyes: "My Brother Fire, noble and useful among all other creatures, be kindly to me in this hour, because formerly I have loved thee for the love of Him Who created thee. But I pray our Creator who created us, that He will so temper thy heat that I may be able to sustain it" (p. 291). He used to say to the brother gardener that he ought always to create a pleasure spot in some part of the garden; setting and planting there all sweet-smelling herbs and all herbs that bring forth fair flowers, that in their time they might call them that looked upon those herbs and flowers to the praise of God. For every creature cries aloud, "God made me for thee, O man!" His love for all creation he expressed in a poem, the so-called "Canticle of the Sun":

> Most High, Omnipotent, Good Lord.
> Thine be the praise, the glory, the honour, and all benediction.
> To Thee alone, Most High, they are due,
>   and no man is worthy to mention Thee.
>
> Be Thou praised, my Lord, with all Thy creatures,
>   above all Brother Sun
>   who gives the day and lightens us therewith.
>
> And he is beautiful and radiant with great splendour,
>   of Thee, Most High, he bears similitude.
>
> Be Thou praised, my Lord, of Sister Moon and the stars,
>   in the heaven hast Thou formed them, clear and precious and comely.
>
> Be Thou praised, my Lord, of Brother Wind,
>   and of the air, and the cloud, and of fair and of all weather,
>   by the which Thou givest to Thy creatures sustenance.
>
> Be Thou praised, my Lord, of Sister Water,
>   which is much useful and humble and precious and pure.

Be Thou praised, my Lord, of Brother Fire,
    by which Thou has lightened the night,
    and he is beautiful and joyful and robust and strong.

Be Thou praised, my Lord, of our Sister Mother Earth,
    which sustains and hath us in rule,
    and produces divers fruits with coloured flowers and herbs.

Be Thou praised, my Lord, of those who pardon for Thy love
    and endure sickness and tribulations.

Blessed are they who will endure it in peace,
    for by Thee, Most High, they shall be crowned.

Be Thou praised, my Lord, of our Sister Bodily Death,
    from whom no man living may escape.
    woe to those who die in mortal sin:

Blessed are they who are found in Thy most holy will,
    for the second death shall not work them ill.

Praise ye and bless my Lord, and give Him thanks,
    and serve Him with great humility. (pp. 294-295)

The spirit of Saint Francis was contagious enough to stimulate the foundation of an order of Franciscan nuns (Poor Clares) and to provide for laymen who wished to be associated with the order without becoming friars. This third order (the nuns were the second), or Tertiaries, refused in time to participate in offensive warfare, and, for a while, to bear arms at all. "They were allowed, though vassals, to refuse military service to their suzerains."

PAPAL MODIFICATION AND DECLINE OF THE FRANCISCANS

The papacy had had too much experience with heresy in the twelfth and early thirteenth centuries to be kindly disposed to the organization that Saint Francis contemplated for his order. It obliged him to give up his personal leadership in 1220, and it helped him to provide a rule for the order in 1223. After his death (1228) it set aside his last will and testament, which held fast to his original ideals, and finally had an official biography prepared, ordering all other lives destroyed so that there might be less chance of knowing what kind of a man he really was. The order was then permitted to compromise with Francis' ideas about individual and corporate holding of property. It took over the organization of the Dominicans and accepted privileges from the papacy authorizing it to go out into the parishes and preach and hear confessions without the consent of local ecclesiastical authorities. This made it a bitter rival of the parish priesthood. It meant also that Franciscans took orders and became priests and went to the universities for their education. The order, therefore, quickly lost the impassioned character given it by its saintly founder, willingly submitted to papal direction, and became soon enough the object of criticism for its rapid decline. Bonaventura, a minister-general of the order and the man entrusted with Saint Francis' official biography, described it by 1260 as composed of " 'legacy hunters'; extravagant alike in public buildings and in private expenses; 'contemptible in divers parts of the world' on account of their familiarity with women, and feared by the wayfarer, as armed robbers were feared. . . . I would willingly be ground to powder, if so the brethren might come to the purity of St. Francis and his companions, and to that which he prescribed for his Order.' "[44]

THE SPIRITUAL FRANCISCANS

There were those who refused to make the compromise with the original ideas of Saint Francis. They are known as the Spiritual Franciscans, as compared with the Conventuals, who were anxious for and abided by the change. The relationship between the two groups became one of open persecution. In 1318 four Spirituals were burnt at the stake as heretics in Marseilles "for asserting that the Rule of St. Francis was identical with Christ's Gospel and that even the Pope could not dispense Franciscans from their solemn vow of poverty."[45]

JOACHIM OF FIORE

Suffering from persecution, the Spirituals easily took to prophecies of doom for the Church and of glory for themselves. A group of them became strongly attached to the ideas of an abbot of a reformed Cistercian order in Calabria, Joachim of Fiore (d. 1202). Joachim's interpretation of history divided the past into two equal ages: (1) the 1260 years from Adam to Christ, and (2) the 1260 years from Christ to A.D. 1260. The first age was the Age of the Father, in which the Old Testament and the law prevailed; the second the Age of the Son, dominated by the spirit of the New Testament, an age in which the priesthood was most influential. Joachim believed, however, that the second age would soon come to an end. The third age to follow would be an Age of the Holy Ghost, "without priests and sacraments, without altar or sacrifice, an era of direct contemplation or perfect liberty."[46] "It shall be like unto the age of the Apostles, when men did not require earthly possessions or inheritances but rather sold them. . . . It will be a time of peace and truth over the whole earth."[47] In 1254 Gerard de Borgo San Donnino, a friar who was studying at the University of Paris, published a book called the *Eternal Gospel*, composed in large part of extracts from Joachim's writings with an introduction and notes of his own. The publication came during the adminis-

[44]Jones, *Mystical Religions*, p. 169.
[45]G. G. Coulton, *Ten Medieval Studies*, p. 171.
[46]The selection from R. M. Jones, *Studies in Mystical Religions*, p. 172, copyright 1909 by The Macmillan Co., and used with The Macmillan Co.'s permission.
[47]Émile Gebhart, *Mystics and Heretics in Italy at the End of the Middle Ages*, trans. and introd. Edward M. Hulme, p. 89.

tration of John of Parma, a Spiritual, as minister-general of the Franciscan order (1247–1257). Gerard's introduction and notes were intensely hostile "to the papacy, . . . to the corrupt and wealthy clergy . . . and show a loss of faith in the existing Church, and a vivid expectation of the end of the age in 1260, which was to usher in the new age of the Eternal Gospel. . . . Monks who are saintly and go barefooted are to take the place of easy-living priests; the entire sacerdotal system of the imperfect Church is to be swept away, and the religion of the Spirit was to take its place."[48] The papacy felt itself threatened by a great subversive movement stemming from the left wing of the Franciscans. In 1255 a papal commission pronounced the *Eternal Gospel* heretical and ordered it burned. John of Parma was driven from his office as minister-general, and Spiritual Franciscans who adhered to the teachings of Joachim were pursued and persecuted everywhere. In 1323 Pope John XXII declared the Spirituals heretics for teaching that Christ and his apostles possessed no common property but lived rather in absolute poverty. Driven to extremes, some Spirituals came to regard the Church itself as heretical, Saint Francis as the incarnation of Jesus, and themselves as the only true church.

Heresy and the Inquisition

THE CAUSES FOR HERESY

The efforts of the monks to reform themselves, and indirectly to reform the secular Church, produced in the left-wing, or Spiritual, branch of the Franciscans something that the popes condemned as heresy. Francis' effort to return to gospel Christianity made papal theocrats restless and unhappy until they had harnessed his order to the main wagon of the Church. Both Saint Norbert, the founder of the Premonstratensians, and Saint Bernard, the leading Cistercian abbot of his day, were active in combatting heretics, Norbert in Antwerp and Bernard in southern France. Indeed, in the twelfth century heretical groups became so numerous and so powerful that the Christian Church was actually threatened with the loss of a large part of the faithful. To account for this widespread defection, it has to be assumed that large numbers were no longer able to find spiritual satisfaction in the teachings and ritual of the Church. They therefore felt obliged to originate new teachings and new ceremonies to calm their uneasy souls. Moreover, since the heresies are often to be found anchored in the industrial populations of the new towns, especially among the textile workers, the dissatisfaction with the Church may well have expressed social and economic discontent that could not find its own proper expression. Since so much of the criticism has to do with the deviation of the Church from early Christianity, with its possession of

---

[48]Jones, *Mystical Religions*, p. 175.

great wealth and great political power, it is not incorrect to see in the heresies the protests of poor and simple people of town and countryside against an aristocratic church and a rich and privileged clergy who themselves often violated the teachings of it. If the monastic reforms were an attempt to make the asceticism of the regular clergy more vital, the heresies were an attempt to vitalize the secular Church by forcing it to concentrate on its spiritual rather than its temporal mission. The Church was called upon to abandon its theocratic program and to emphasize the salvation of individual souls in a more exacting way than by the mechanical performance of wonder-working sacraments.

ARNOLD OF BRESCIA

The combination of heresy, town, temporal power, and wealth can be observed clearly in the case of Arnold of Brescia. Arnold was a student of another critical spirit of the early twelfth century, Peter Abélard. For his inability to compromise with what he regarded as true Christianity, he was hounded over western Europe by no less a person than Saint Bernard. For organizing Brescia against its bishop during the latter's absence in Rome, he was expelled from Italy (1139) and ordered to keep quiet. He returned to France and taught theology at Paris in a very critical vein, sparing not even Bernard "as a seeker after vainglory who was jealous of all who had any reputation for learning or for religion, if they were not of his own way of thinking." He was condemned in France in 1141 and upon Bernard's urging expelled in 1142. After wanderings in Switzerland and Bohemia, he returned to Rome, of all places, where he joined the citizens in an attempt to deprive the pope of his political power in the city, and return it, as it was in Roman days, to a republican government of its citizens. For these pains he was tried and condemned as a heretic in 1155 and turned over to the emperor Frederick Barbarossa to be hanged and burned.

ARNOLD'S OPINIONS

Arnold's support of urban revolts against bishop and pope followed from his conviction that the Church should not now, no more than in its early history, possess political power or excessive wealth. John of Salisbury, the English scholar, remarks of him that he reserved his flattery for the laity alone and "was wont to say that neither clergy who possessed anything nor bishop who enjoyed *regalia*[49] nor monk who held property could by any means be saved." In Paris he is reported not to have spared bishops "for their avarice and love of filthy lucre and especially for their blemished living, and because they strove to build the Church of God in blood."[50] At Rome he stormed into the *curia* and in the presence of the pope condemned the cardinals for "the gold and silver vessels which

[49]See p. 528.
[50]Watkin Williams, *Bernard of Clairvaux*, pp. 321, 323.

adorned their tables and for the delicacies served at their banquets." For Arnold the College of Cardinals was but "the house of buying and selling and the den of thieves, who played the part of the scribes and pharisees toward the Christian people. . . . The Pope was no pope, because he was not an apostolic man and a shepherd of souls, but a man of blood who maintained his authority by killing and burning; a tormentor of churches; an oppressor of the innocent, who did nothing in the world but feed on flesh and fill his coffers and empty those of others. Nor was he apostolic, because he did not imitate the doctrine nor the life of the Apostles, and therefore no reverence nor obedience was due him." Further: "nothing in the government of the city pertains to the supreme pontiff: ecclesiastical jurisdiction ought to be enough for him." In fact, "the sacred laws did not sanction clerical possessions; the monks and priests had no right over the land; nor should the abbots relegate to themselves temporal power which belonged to the princes on the earth."[51] If this program cost Arnold his life it was an inspiration to many followers, the Arnoldists, after his death.

PETER WALDO AND THE WALDENSIANS

The heresy associated with the name of Peter Waldo of Lyons, the Waldensian, is closer in spirit to Saint Francis than to Arnold of Brescia. Peter Waldo was a merchant with a troubled conscience, anxious for the security of salvation. Like Saint Francis, he adopted the radical solution of the gospel for his difficulties: "If thou wilt be perfect, sell all thou hast and give to the poor and come and follow me." He summoned his fellow townsmen to do likewise and founded the lay order of the Poor Men of Lyons, who took preaching the gospel as their mission. They possessed translations of the New Testament in the vernacular, which they introduced to their congregations, and they made the features of New Testament Christianity familiar to those who listened. They also accepted as their mission working among the poor and sick of the towns. Here was another attempt to imitate Jesus and his disciples through work among the simple and afflicted. In 1179, at the Third Lateran Council, Peter Waldo secured permission to preach for his Poor Men, who were of course laymen and not priests, provided that they should secure the permission of their local clergy and remain under the jurisdiction of a bishop. It was not easy to secure the approval of clergy with whom they were competing, and whom in fact they were constantly criticizing for straying from the path of gospel Christianity. When the archbishop of Lyons ordered Peter and his followers to stop preaching, they refused, insisting that "we must obey God rather than men." This refusal was met with expulsion from the city. The movement thus became more than local; as it spread it came into contact with other heretical groups; and it developed as a large religious organization trying to free itself from clerical authority as well as to revive primitive Christianity.

[51]Ellen Davison, *Forerunners of St. Francis*, pp. 145–146.

Five years after being approved these "humble," or "Poor of Lyons," were anathematized by the Council of Verona (1184). "We include in the same perpetual anathema all who shall have presumed to preach, either publicly or privately . . . not having the authority of the Apostolic See or of the Bishop of the diocese."[52] Faced with this condemnation, the Waldensians decided that there was nothing left for them to do but to form their own church, "the true Church." Their teachings and practices then became more and more unorthodox.

WALDENSIANS AS EARLY PROTESTANTS

As laymen, they contended that ordination was not necessary to preach, nor indeed to conduct a religious service and administer sacraments. They had no objection to preaching by women. The validity of preaching and sacraments rested upon the moral character of the official, rather than upon the ceremony of ordination.[53] Confession to a good layman, therefore, was just as efficacious as to an ordained priest. They came to condemn indulgences, refused to take an oath, and some groups opposed war and capital punishment and denied transubstantiation. They came also to condemn holy images, purgatory, and the invocation of saints. It is thus clear that we have in the Waldensians a group of very early Protestants, contending that any good man can be his own priest, and rejecting the mediatorial and magical priesthood. They turned out, in fact, to be the earliest Protestants. For in spite of all repressive measures, the Church was unable to get rid of the Waldensians. They persisted in Bohemia, where they contributed to the radical reform movements inspired by John Huss, and in Piedmont, where French Protestant reformers of the sixteenth century were in contact with them. And still today in Italy and elsewhere the Waldensian church survives.

THE ALBIGENSIANS

The most powerful of the heresies with which the Church had to contend was that of the Cathari, or Albigensians,[54] who were themselves the medieval descendants of early Christian heretical sects the Church had never been able really to suppress. In fact, the Albigensians can hardly be included in the Christian heresies at all, for they go back to the fundamental teachings of such Persian reformers as Zoroaster and Mani.[55] Their point of view rests upon an oriental dualism that contrasts good and evil, spirit and matter, light and darkness with a rigidity unknown to Christian-

[52]The selection from R. M. Jones, *Studies in Mystical Religions*, p. 140, copyright 1909 by The Macmillan Co., and used with The Macmillan Co.'s permission.
[53]Cf. Augustine's view, p. 347.
[54]So called from their concentration in the town and region of Albi in southern France.
[55]See pp. 297 f.

ity. These contrasts were, of course, taken over by Christianity from the religions of the Near East, but they were subordinated to Christian monotheism. In taking over Satan from the Persians, Christianity left him as the captain of the forces of evil but subjected him wholly to God, who permits him to do whatever he does. The Albigensians held to the wholly independent, Persian God of Evil, who carries on, in his own behalf, the fight against the God of Good. He may eventually be defeated, but he is not a subordinate of the God of Good. Inheriting the doctrines of early Christians who did not want to graft Christianity onto the Old Testament, the Albigensians identified the God of Evil with the Jehovah of the Old Testament, thus rejecting the Old Testament, and identified their God of Good with the God of the New Testament. Since it was evident to the Albigensians that the Christian Church about them was a wealthy church, and that its clergy were occupied with such temporal and material matters as administering estates and governing states, the God of this Christian Church must be the God of Evil, Matter, and Darkness, and the Church the "Synagogue of Satan." With this church they could have absolutely nothing to do. The God of the Albigensian church was the God of Good, Spirit, and Light.

THE ALBIGENSIAN CHURCH

It was therefore necessary for the Albigensians to have their own church. Their clergy were called the perfect (*perfecti*), because they were regarded as the most completely purged of evil matter, the largest concentrations of divine light. Like the Christian clergy, they did not marry, since marriage resulted in perpetuating evil in the bodies of offspring. They ate only those things that were regarded as being asexually produced. The great community of Albigensians, called the believers, were not held to celibacy and fasting until they had entered the ranks of the *perfecti* by taking the sacrament of Consolation (*consolamentum*). The souls of those who failed to take the sacrament before death entered the bodies of animals, and had to pass through long cycles before again being offered the chance to be consoled. To avoid relapsing into evil, the perfect were often advised to commit suicide. As a whole, the Albigensians were pacifists, refused to take an oath, and were opposed to capital punishment. These unconventional attitudes, combined with their uncompromising hostility to the Church, account in part for the cruelty with which they were persecuted.

DEVELOPMENT OF THE IDEA OF A CRUSADE

In 1200, when papal theocracy was a vital force in western Europe, the Church had been under attack for more than a century by monastic reformers and dissentients called heretics. What these groups demanded was reform, a reform that would bring the Church closer to the Christianity of its founder. This reform the Church did not give. Instead, when it turned out that the reformers and heretics could not be peacefully persuaded to give up their complaints, the papacy sought to gain control of the reform movements, as in the case of the Franciscans, or to use force to suppress the heretics. Before this date, the Church had been known to deal peacefully with some of its enemies. The early missionary sought peaceful conversion, and the courts of the bishops dealt peacefully with the problem of dissenting opinion. The crusades, however, developed a military spirit in the Church. Christians used armies to fight the Moslem and the pagan Slav. The early thirteenth century witnessed the extension of the crusading idea. It was used not only against infidels and pagans, but against schismatics (the Byzantine Empire in the Fourth Crusade), political enemies (the crusades against Frederick II), and now the Albigensian heretics, with whom peaceful conversion by condescending Cistercian monks and papal legates did not succeed. The mighty theocrat Innocent III finally decided to utilize the desire of the French crown and northern French nobles to expand in southern France, where the Albigensian heresy was concentrated, by summoning them in 1208 to a crusade. It was a long, brutal one, which extinguished, together with the heresy, the flourishing culture of southern France, one of Europe's most advanced areas. "We spared neither dignity, nor sex, nor age," wrote Arnold of Citeaux, one of the monkish leaders; "nearly twenty thousand human beings perished by the sword. After the massacre, the town [Beziers] was plundered and burnt and the revenge of God seemed to rage upon it in a wonderful manner."[56]

THE INQUISITION

The popes well knew, however, that temporary force was not enough to keep down the heretics. A permanent system of terror was also necessary, and this was provided by the Inquisition. The failure of episcopal courts to extirpate heresy was demonstrated by its growth in the twelfth century. The Fourth Lateran Council of Innocent III confirmed the idea of a crusade against heretics by providing that "Catholics who assume the cross and devote themselves to the extermination of heretics shall enjoy the same indulgence and privilege as those who go to the Holy Land." It also provided for the excommunication of a temporal lord who neglected "to fulfill the demand of the Church that he shall purge his land of this contamination of heresy. . . . If he fails to make amends within a year, it shall be reported to the Supreme Pontiff who shall pronounce his vassals absolved from fealty to him and offer his land to Catholics. The latter shall exterminate the heretics, possess the land without dispute, and preserve it in the true faith."[57] Pope Gregory IX, in 1233, inaugurated the

[56]Reprinted from *A History of the Jews*, p. 194, by A. L. Sachar, by permission of Alfred A. Knopf, Inc., copyright, 1947.
[57]H. Bettenson, *Documents of the Christian Church*, pp. 188–189.

Inquisition, or Holy Office, by sending out permanent judges into the dioceses to set up machinery for discovering, trying, and punishing heretics. These positions were given primarily to the new Dominican friars, with whom the Franciscans were also sometimes associated.

The procedure of the Inquisition is offensive to all fair-minded persons, its use of torture an outrage, and its turning over of the convicted heretic to the state to be burned, with the hypocritical prayer that death or mutilation might be prevented, a crime against civilization as we now understand the meaning of this term. Only two witnesses were necessary to make an accusation of heresy, and they themselves might be "heretics, perjurers, excommunicated persons, or murderers." The aim of the inquisitor at the trial was to secure a confession and, after fitting punishment, to restore the heretic to the bosom of the Church. Bernard Gui, a Dominican inquisitor at Toulouse, recommended in his *Manual of the Inquisitor* that "when a person who is suspected of, denounced or reported for or accused of the crime of heresy, has been charged and refuses to confess, he shall be held in prison until the truth comes to light. . . . When an accused is strongly suspect and in all likelihood and probability guilty, and when the inquisitor is thoroughly convinced thereof; in such a case, when the person is obdurate in his testimony and persists in his denials, as I have observed time and time again, he should not be released for any reason whatever, but should be held for a number of years, in order that his trials may open his mind."[58] The accused was permitted no lawyer. He was not faced with his accusers or given their names, in order that they might be protected. After 1152, following the practice of Roman law, the inquisitors were permitted to use torture to secure a confession. If this did not suffice, the heretic was considered guilty until he could explain away the accusation, "a practically impossible undertaking. For if two witnesses, considered of good repute by the Inquisitor, agreed in accusing the prisoner, his fate was at once settled; whether he confessed or not, he was declared a heretic."[59] The heretic, whether confessed or not, was then given the opportunity to abjure or not. If he abjured, he was given the proper punishment. If he failed to abjure, he was turned over to the secular arm (the state) to be burned. If the state did not act, the officials concerned were excommunicated as supporters of heresy. The property of the condemned heretic was confiscated by the state.

CHRISTIANITY AND THE JEWS

The Church and western society had not only to contend with infidels, pagans, schismatics, radical reformers, and heretics; it felt it had also to deal with the Jews in its midst, and the record of these dealings is also shameful and horrible. This must be said not only for the combination of

[58]*Introduction to Contemporary Civilization in the West*, 2d ed., Columbia University Press (1954), I, 286–287.
[59]Elphège Vacandard, *The Inquisition*, trans. B. F. Conway, p. 128.

ignorance and fanaticism that produced slaughter but also for the fear, terror, and degradation that accompanied it. The persecution of the Jewish people began with the crusades. The early contingents of the First Crusade moved through the German Rhine cities in an anti-Jewish fury. "Perhaps as many as twelve thousand Jews perished." After the main body of the crusaders had taken Jerusalem "they drove all the Jews of the city into a synagogue and burnt them alive within it." Hatred of the Jews broke out again in the course of the Second Crusade, though Saint Bernard, its preacher, was free from it and risked his life to restrain it. The abbot of Cluny, however, "virtually called for the destruction of the hated race. It was of little use, he proclaimed, to smite the Saracens in far-off lands when there were so many blasphemers of the Saviour living in comfort among Christians. 'You ought not to kill them,' he advised [the French king] Louis VII, 'but to afflict them in a manner befitting their baseness.' . . . The crusades are a turning point in Jewish history. They mark the end of settled Jewish communal life in Europe, the beginning of intense race-aversions. They usher in the Jewish caricature who stalked through Europe until the eighteenth century, the pariah, with bent back and hunted look and obsequious manner, bitter over his yesterdays and fearful of his tomorrows."[60]

In the thirteenth century the Church obliged the Jews to wear a badge of identification; an attack was made upon their sacred literature; and they were expelled from many countries. Pope Innocent III could write, "The Jews, like the fratricide Cain, are doomed to wander about the earth as fugitives and vagabonds, and their faces must be covered in shame. They are under no circumstances to be protected by Christian princes, but, on the contrary, to be condemned to serfdom." In the course of the Albigensian crusade Jews were massacred as well as heretics. The Fourth Lateran Council (1215) forbade Jews to hold public office or employ Christian domestics, and ordered them to wear "a distinctive garment or a special badge, to set them apart from other men." "Nothing could have more quickly and more completely broken the proud spirit of Israel. The distinguishing mark called for ridicule and insult, and the ignorant populace was not slow to respond. The Jew was stoned and pelted, spat upon and cursed, compelled to slink through byways and side streets, in darkness and in shame. He ceased to dress with care, to walk with head erect. He lost the power to speak with ease, and, as he bowed and scraped his way through his tormentors, his self-respect disappeared. He was at last just what the Church had hoped he would become, a fugitive and a vagabond."[61]

Saint Louis (king of France, 1226–1270), a fanatical hater of Jews, inaugurated what was to be a long attack on the sacred literature of the

[60] I am relying here chiefly on Sachar, *A History of the Jews*, pp. 186, 189, 191, 192.
[61] Reprinted from *A History of the Jews*, pp. 193, 194, 195, by A. L. Sachar, by permission of Alfred A. Knopf, Inc., copyright, 1947.

Jews (the Talmud). After immense suffering, the Jews were expelled from England in 1290. In 1306 Jewish property was confiscated in France, and they were expelled from the land, an expulsion that in 1394 was made final for centuries. Assigned responsibility in popular imagination for the Black Death, they suffered unimaginable persecution. Even in Christian Spain, where their fate in the earlier Middle Ages had been fortunately unlike that in central and western Europe, they were eventually pounced upon. When the Inquisition was introduced into Spain by Ferdinand and Isabella, it was turned also against the Jews. Finally, an edict of 31 March, 1492, ordered all Jews on pain of death to leave Spain within four months, and at least one hundred and fifty thousand left the country.

JUSTIFICATION OF PERSECUTION

For the history of the western tradition, this use of force, bloodshed, and torture by the Church to secure religious uniformity, and the support of its use by the state and western society, is a matter of extreme critical importance. Before criticizing it, however, it is well to try to understand it by listening to the opinions and apologies of those who promoted it or who tolerated its use. Saint Augustine thought that "heresy is a crime more atrocious than forgery or murder. If a heretic dies in sin, and if you might have saved him by using force, will not your tolerance be actual hatred? It is better to save with harshness than to destroy with gentleness." Pope Innocent III remarked that inasmuch as the "civil law punishes traitors . . . all the more should we excommunicate and confiscate the property of those who are traitors to the faith of Jesus Christ. For it is an infinitely greater sin to offend the divine majesty than to attack the majesty of the sovereign." Saint Thomas Aquinas, the leading theologian of the thirteenth century, remarked: "There is the sin, whereby they deserve not only to be separated from the Church by excommunication, but also to be severed from the world by death. For it is a much graver matter to corrupt the faith which quickens the soul than to forge money, which supports temporal life. Wherefore if forgers of money and other evil-doers are forthwith condemned to death by the secular authorities, much more reason is there for heretics, as soon as they are convicted of heresy, to be not only excommunicated but even put to death." Aquinas then points out that by way of charity, "heretics who return after falling no matter how often, are admitted by the Church to Penance, whereby the way of salvation is opened to them." This provides for their spiritual good, which is the health of the soul. But there is "the other good . . . which charity considers secondarily, viz. temporal good, such as the life of the body, worldly possessions, good repute, ecclesiastical or secular dignity, for we are not bound by charity to wish others this good, except in relation to the eternal salvation of them and of others. Hence if the presence of one of these goods in one individual might be an obstacle to eternal salvation in many, we are not bound out of charity to wish such a good to that person, rather should we desire him to be without it, both because eternal salvation takes precedence of temporal good, and because the good of the many is to be preferred to the good of the one. Now if heretics were always received on their return, in order to save their lives and other temporal goods, this might be prejudicial to the salvation of others, both because they would infect others if they relapsed again, and because if they escaped without punishment, others would feel more assured in lapsing into heresy." When heretics, therefore, "fall again after having been received [back into the Church] this seems to prove them to be inconstant in faith, wherefore when they return again, they are admitted to Penance, but are not delivered from the pain of death."[62] Finally we may quote a sixteenth-century cardinal who had to contend with the great heresy of Protestantism (Cardinal Bellarmine): that the death penalty for heresy is justified "is proved . . . by natural reason. Heretics can be legally excommunicated, as all grant, therefore they can be killed, because excommunication is a greater penalty than temporal death. . . . Forgers merit death, in the judgment of all, and heretics are forgers of the words of God. All of these reasons support the execution of heretics. For they do more damage than any pirate or robber, since they kill the spirit, wreck the very foundations of all good, and fill the commonwealth with tumults which of necessity follow diversity in religions. Finally, it benefits obstinate heretics that they be cut off from this life; for the longer they live, thinking their several errors, the more they pervert, and the greater damnation they lay up for themselves."[63]

To paraphrase the above, one may say that there is a divine truth, established or revealed by God, and interpreted by the Church. In accordance with this divine truth or law, human affairs are to be governed. The Church is the divinely established institution for the administration of the law of God. It cannot permit this law to be violated. Violation is treason to God, the lord and ruler of the universe, and this treason is much more serious than treason to a mere secular ruler, which is punishable by death, or than many lesser crimes such as forgery, also punishable by death. To challenge the divine institution established by God for the maintenance of his truth is a serious act of subversion, for it challenges all the institutions of Christian society: the state and the social and economic organization, as well as the Church. It challenges the very principle of Christian authority. Obviously, the Waldensians were anarchistic, and the Albigensians pacifists and antisocial, with their teachings about marriage and suicide. Finally, the most important thing in the world is the salvation of the individual soul. You must love your neighbor so much

[62]From *Summa Theologiae*, quoted in Mendenhall, Henning, Foord, *Ideas and Institutions in European History*, I, 31–32.
[63]E. W. Nelson, "Theory of Persecution," *Essays in Honor of George Lincoln Burr*, p. 18.

that you will permit him to be killed if he does not adhere to the truth that alone will save that soul. Certainly he cannot be permitted to run wild in the world, endangering other souls as well as destroying his own.

The above quotations contain also the notion that religious uniformity is necessary, not only to maintain divine truth, but to preserve the peace by avoiding religious war. Further apologies on behalf of the Inquisition could argue that it was only a product of an intolerant age, and that it is unhistorical to expect it to have been tolerant when nothing else was tolerant.[64] The Inquisition, in regularizing the trial of heretics in accordance with fixed rules, was superior to the earlier system of episcopal courts or to submitting suspects to the furies of the ignorant mob. Moreover, to have weakened the Church by tolerating the heretic would have been to weaken the institution that was doing the most to promote a higher civilization in Europe by supplying the common point of view and the unity that would otherwise have been absent. Thus in acting as it did, in utilizing force to secure religious obedience, the Church may be seen as acting according to its best lights, and the support given to this conduct by western society likewise as enlightened conduct.

A CRITICISM OF PERSECUTION

In spite of its logical consistency, we of the twentieth century may not accept an explanation that in the name of divine truth makes possible the combination of religion and cruelty. To be sure, much that has happened since the fifteenth century makes this sort of explanation untenable. It is now not so certain that there is a body of unalterable divine truth entrusted to a church to enforce. It is not so certain that there is a body of any kind of unalterable and absolute truth entrusted to any kind of institution or individual to enforce. A general body of truth has been and is being built up upon the basis of human insight and experience. It is by no means complete, and will never be complete for as long as there are human beings undergoing new experiences. To be tolerant of nothing but an established body of truth is thus to prevent its being enlarged. To be intolerant is, in any case, to be cruel, for it is in the nature of some human beings to prefer death to the abandonment of what they hold to be true, and thus to get rid of ideas considered divergent from the truth it is necessary to put aside or kill human beings. History proves that even by killing men it is not always possible to get rid of their ideas. Thus from what we have learned since the days of the Inquisition we must

[64]This is to say, an age not much influenced by the doctrine of Christian love. "If Christianity found it a strength and an asset to have entered Europe as an exclusive religion, the pride of that position has also its terrible perils unless Christian charity prevails above all. . . . If Christians impute the cruelties to the brutality and the backwardness of the times, this argument carries with it important implications; for it means that Christianization according to the medieval system had not been sufficient. Time and the advance of civilization are necessary to co-operate with religion before gentleness can prevail." H. Butterfield, *Christianity in European History*, p. 33.

conclude that even if the Church and western society were acting in accordance with their best lights, they were wrong. The heretic should have been argued with and not forced. If that argument proved insufficient, the heretical groups should have been permitted to organize sects of their own within the Christian society. Only such conduct as this would have best served the interests of the western community. As it was, the Church, by the use of force, was actually unable to suppress all the heretical groups, as, for example, the Waldensians and the Hussites.

It is not easy even to be sure that the Church was acting in accordance with its best lights. To forgive it because it was a product of an intolerant society is to fall victim to a pernicious doctrine that individuals and institutions need only to conform and adjust to something that is called public opinion or society. There are many who would say that their duty is not merely to adjust but to lead. And so with the medieval Church. It is not possible to imagine that the leading men in the Church did not know what tolerance was. In many earlier writings churchmen had contended that religion was a matter of choice and not force. The Christian Church had been made possible only because of the tolerance of the Roman Empire. There must have been churchmen who knew this. Perhaps they knew it only too well—tolerated Christianity became victorious. And tolerated heresy? If their knowledge of history did not tell them what tolerance was, they had only to look about them in Moslem Spain, if no further, to see how both Christians and Jews were tolerated. If they refused to do this, they could have learned what toleration meant from those who wished to be tolerated. It is difficult to believe that medieval churchmen were so different from ourselves that they did not know what love of neighbor meant. It is difficult to imagine that they did not know all about the cruelty involved in crusades, torture, and burning at the stake. In fact there were some persons in the West, notably the troubadours,[65] who were critical of the conduct of the Church in these respects. The Church, then, and the ruling groups in western medieval society knew perfectly well what they were doing. They were not the helpless and innocent agents of impersonal historical processes. They used force because they believed in it, to be sure, but they did not believe in it because it was Christian. They used it because they were able to, and they used it to uphold the Church as a temporal as well as a spiritual institution. The Church was threatened by a movement urging return to the Christianity of the gospels. To have met this movement halfway would have involved a huge and difficult program of reform. For the most part the Church was unwilling to, and did not, undertake this reform. It felt, therefore, that it had to silence its critics and opponents by force if necessary if it were to preserve itself as the dominant institution that it was. The Church could have excommunicated and reformed. It was not necessary for it to torture and kill.

[65]See P. A. Throop, *Criticism of the Crusade.*

Thus we have to associate medieval Christian theocracy in the form of the monarchical Church with the willingness to be cruel in order to maintain religious uniformity. This was too heavy a price to pay for religious uniformity. It calls into question all those lovely qualities that medieval civilization is supposed to have possessed because it was a religious unity. The extent to which it was a real religious unity is of course questionable. Reformers and heresy are not a very good sign of unity. And to the extent that it was an imposed and not an agreed-upon unity, it was an unhealthy one.

MODERN PERSECUTION

The willingness to be cruel in order to maintain uniformity is as characteristic of the modern as of the medieval world. Today it is associated more with political, economic, and social uniformities than religious ones, because the West has had too much experience with the attempt to impose religious uniformities to trust them any longer. The willingness to torture to secure confessions is by no means simply a relic of a cruel past. It is a common practice of the police of most nations. One must spare some of his indignation over the cruelties inflicted upon human beings in the name of religion during the Middle Ages in order to have some left for contemporary cruelties. Mankind seems intent today upon establishing a unified world society. If it wishes to profit from the medieval experience with secular and ecclesiastical theocracies, it will hesitate to establish more unity than is necessary to keep the peace and to adapt to technological necessity. For unity and uniformity without divergence and variety are dull and dangerous.

Decline of the Church in the Fourteenth and Fifteenth Centuries

STEPS IN THE DECLINE OF THE CHURCH

In the thirteenth century the Church was at the height of its power and influence; in the fourteenth and fifteenth centuries it was on the decline. This decline was marked by (1) the limitations put upon the temporal and spiritual power of the papacy by the new national monarchs of western Europe, and also by German principalities; (2) the removal of the papacy to Avignon and the outbreak of schism; (3) the elaboration of new theories concerning the nature and organization of the Church; (4) the outbreak of new heresies as the result of the preaching of John Wycliffe and John Huss; and (5) the holding of new councils. Together, these events spelled the rejection by a large section of Europe of the papal theocracy of the earlier period, a rejection to be completed by the Protestant reformers of the sixteenth century.

REJECTION OF ECCLESIASTICAL THEOCRACY

International secular theocracy in the form of the Holy Roman Empire was rejected by the Church, by Italy, and indeed by Germany itself, and, whenever necessary or possible, by the monarchies of eastern and western Europe. The strongest of these new monarchies were not minded, now that they had defeated feudalism in their midst and rejected the German secular theocracy, to accept the ecclesiastical theocracy of the Holy Roman Church. This is quite evident in the case of France and England and, indeed, of Germany, which, although not a strong monarchy, successfully combatted the attempts of the popes once again to assert their control over German politics.

BONIFACE VIII

It was Pope Boniface VIII (1294–1303) who opened up the battle with the new national monarchies by insisting that, without the consent of the papacy, they did not have the right to tax the clergy within their boundaries, even when the income from such taxation was to be used for national defense. His position was stated in the bull *Clericis Laicos* (1296), which forbade, on pain of excommunication, "our prelates and ecclesiastical persons, religious or secular, of whatsoever orders, condition or standing . . . to pay or promise or agree to pay to lay persons collections or taxes."[66] All rulers were likewise forbidden to "impose, exact or receive such" collections or taxes. When King Edward I of England outlawed the clergy upon receipt of this bull, and Philip IV of France forbade the export of all money, jewels, and negotiable papers to Italy, Boniface withdrew his claims and indicated that the king had the right to determine when there was an emergency that made necessary collection of taxes from the clergy.

THE BULL "UNAM SANCTAM"

Boniface had further difficulties with Philip IV when he intervened to protect a bishop of Pamiers whom the king regarded as traitorous and against whom he had proceeded in the royal courts. This contravened the clerical privilege providing that criminal clergy were to be tried in ecclesiastical courts. Philip was told that he was a fool and a possible heretic if he thought he did not have a superior and was not subordinate "to the head of the ecclesiastical hierarchy." Philip's answer was to say to the pope, "Let your great fatuousness know that in temporalities we are subject to none. . . . Such as believe otherwise we account fools or madmen."[67] In addition, Philip protested with all the force of the nation by calling together the first meeting of the States-General,[68] but the pope

---

[66]Bettenson, *Documents of the Christian Church*, p. 160.
[67]Thomas S. R. Boase, *Boniface VIII*, p. 305.
[68]See pp. 555 f.

ROMAN CHURCH AND NATIONAL CHURCHES 619

merely remarked that "our predecessors have deposed three kings of France . . . and we will if need be depose Philip." There followed in 1302, in the bull *Unam Sanctam* (papal bulls are named from their first words), the most extreme statement of temporal supremacy over the state ever made by a pope. "There is," Boniface declared, "one Holy Catholic and Apostolic Church, and . . . outside this Church there is neither salvation nor remission of sins . . . In this Church and in her power are two swords, the spiritual and the temporal . . . Both are in the power of the Church, the spiritual sword and the material. But the latter is to be used for the Church, the former by her; the former by the priest, the latter by kings and captains but at the will and by the permission of the priest. The one sword then, should be under the other, and temporal authority subject to spiritual. . . . If, therefore, the earthly power err, it shall be judged by the spiritual power . . . and if a lesser power err, it shall be judged by a greater. But if the supreme power err, it can only be judged by God. . . . Furthermore we declare, state, define and pronounce that it is altogether necessary to salvation for every human creature to be subject to the Roman pontiff."[69]

THE AVIGNON PAPACY

Philip now decided to rid himself of this impossible pope. He planned to summon a general council to depose Boniface. The pope, meanwhile, was to be brought from Anagni, his home town in Italy, to France, a prisoner of the French king, and a new papal election was to be held. The papal palace in Anagni was invaded by Philip's followers and the pope put under guard, but the townsmen who had betrayed the pope to the French took courage from French indecision to drive them out again. Boniface was then escorted safely to Rome and died on 12 October, 1303, a victim of these royal intrigues. Although Philip IV was unable to bring the old pope to France, he took care that the next pope to be elected, Clement V (1305–1314), was a Frenchman. Clement took up his residence at Avignon, a town belonging to the French count of Provence. His appointees to the College of Cardinals made that body French. The new pope withdrew such bulls as *Clericis Laicos* and *Unam Sanctam* and absolved the French king from his share in the insult to Boniface VIII at Anagni. The pontificate of Clement, moreover, began a long residence of French popes at Avignon (until 1378), a period in papal history known as the French, or Avignon, papacy or, in Petrarch's words, the Babylonian Captivity of the Church. To Europe, and especially to France's enemies, it was something of a shock to have the vicar of Christ and the successor of Saint Peter abandon what had long been the Christian capital of the world for a little town on the left bank of the Rhone, and, as a resident of an imposing new palace, become a partisan of the French monarchy.

[69]Bettenson, pp. 161–163.

At first glance it appears strange that the popes at Avignon, supported by the French kings, should renew the old struggle with the German empire over which was the superior institution, inasmuch as both the papacy and empire were comparatively impotent at the moment. When it is explained that the French monarchy was using the papacy to weaken the German empire further, and that Louis IV of Bavaria (1314–1347), the German emperor, was strongly influenced by Spiritual Franciscans who wished to have the emperor reform the papacy, the real issues become a little clearer. What they pretended to be arguing over was whether the king elected by the German princes and subsequently crowned at Aachen possessed from these ceremonies sufficient authority to rule as German king (king of the Romans) and Holy Roman emperor, or whether he needed in addition the confirmation of the pope and an imperial coronation in Rome. The emperor contended that a German election and coronation were sufficient to give him this authority; the pope that, without papal consent, an oath of loyalty to the pope, and a coronation at Rome, a German election and coronation supplied no authority at all. These issues crystallized into actual events. Louis was excommunicated and deposed by Pope John XXII, and in reply went to Italy, accompanied by leading Spiritual Franciscans and Marsiglio of Padua.[70] He received the imperial crown from Roman municipal officials, then, after proclaiming him a heretic and a traitor, deposed the pope, named a Spiritual Franciscan to take his place, and invested the new pope with the symbols of his office. Later, in 1338, at Rense in Germany he summoned the German electors to his support. In the Declaration of Rense they ordained that "when anyone has been elected King of the Romans by the princes electors of the Empire . . . he does not need the nomination, approbation, confirmation, assent or authority of the Apostolic See in order to assume the administration of the rights and property of the Empire or the royal title." In the same year the German diet confirmed the Declaration by decreeing that "the imperial dignity and power proceeded in the beginning immediately from God alone. . . . The Emperor is made very Emperor solely by the election of those entitled to elect him."[71] When Charles of Bohemia had the electoral procedure regularized in the Golden Bull of 1356,[72] no mention was made of any participation by the pope. This declaration of independence from papal theocratic claims may have been some comfort to Germans whose ancestors had been put in their place by the popes of the eleventh to thirteenth centuries. In these days, instead of kings like Henry IV coming to Canossa because of imperious popes, popes were recognizing that "imperial dignity and power" were divine in origin and so began going to Avignon because of imperious kings.

[70]See pp. 624 f.
[71]R. G. D. Laffan, *Select Documents of European History*, I, 148.
[72]See p. 567.

It was the Avignon popes who perfected and centralized papal absolutism.[73] In so doing, they brought pressure to bear upon the local clergy, especially financial pressure, as it had never been brought before. These clergy now began to complain. In addition to those chronic abuses in the Church, immorality, simony, and nepotism, that had never been eradicated, there were now added the abuses that came from "reservations," "provisions," and new papal financial devices. What was more serious than all these was the Great Schism, which developed in 1378 and lasted until 1417. This split was the result of a double election to the papacy, after Gregory XI had returned to Rome in 1377. The cardinals first elected an Italian pope, Urban VI (1378-1389), and when he proved impossible they elected another French one, Clement VII (1378-1394), who returned to Avignon. This would not have been so serious (there had been popes and antipopes before) had the double election been soon corrected. It proved impossible, however, to re-establish immediately a single papacy at either Rome or Avignon. Europe was thus confronted by two popes, who spent much of their time saying uncomplimentary things about, and excommunicating, each other. Each pope, Roman and French, had his own College of Cardinals and his own *curia*. Each tried to maintain control over the local church, to appoint to church offices, and to collect taxes due from the clergy. That robe of Christ that the Church had always said was seamless was now rudely torn. Europe split into two parties, one supporting Rome, the other Avignon, and this division was determined in part by the animosities stirred up by the Hundred Years' War: France, of course, supporting the Avignon pope, and England the Roman pope. As the schism was prolonged year after year the sincere churchman and Christian realized that to retain the integrity of Christianity and the Church something extraordinary would have to be done, for less sincere Christians were beginning to smile and ridicule, and nothing is more harmful to any institution than for large numbers to make sport of it. Many of these anxious churchmen and Christians were in the Colleges of Cardinals serving the two popes and in the faculties of the universities of Europe.

NEW HERESIES

The sorry position into which the papal theocracy had put itself as a result of its struggle with Philip IV, its removal to Avignon, its renewal of disputes with the empire, and finally the outbreak of schisms led new groups of heretics to make attacks upon the theory of theocratic papal government and the system of Christian salvation. They led finally to demands that the very constitution of the Church be overhauled in a democratic fashion.

[73]See pp. 580 ff.

THE INFLUENCE OF ARISTOTLE'S "POLITICS"

The reintroduction of Greek learning into the West was partly responsible for these attacks.[74] A portion of this learning consisted of the works of Aristotle, who as a student of politics[75] had written a book called *Politics*, which medieval students now began to read. This book contained no discussion of theocracy or of the relations between church and state because the Greeks had no theocracy, and indeed no church relations with the state.[76] Aristotle's approach to the study of politics was secular and not religious; it was governed by the Greek experience with the city-state. At this point, with the reading of the *Politics* of Aristotle, the influence of the democratic tradition of the Greek city-state began to have an influence upon the West.

THE INFLUENCE OF THE UNIVERSITIES

The intellectual revival of the twelfth and thirteenth centuries produced also a new institution, the university,[77] where new works could be read, discussed, and debated, and where in the light of new knowledge the problems of the day could be discussed as well. The new revolutionary theorists, heretics, and defenders of the general council of the Church were all products of the new universities, institutions that had worked out for themselves self-governing organizations. The examples of the new Parliament, Estates-General, Cortes, Diet, and the representative assemblies of the mendicant orders may well have suggested to students of papal politics and ecclesiastical organization the possibility of forming similar institutions for the Church.

THE INFLUENCE OF THE SCRIPTURES

It has been noticed in the case of some of the monastic reformers and heretics, and it is true also of these new attackers of the fourteenth and fifteenth centuries, that they were becoming interested in early Christian as well as classical literature, and especially in the Scriptures. They were beginning to say that it was necessary to get back of the theologians and allegorists to the literal meaning of the text of the sacred Word, and to make this Word available in vernacular translations. When a greater number of people began to take this advice and to read the Scriptures carefully, they could not find in them some of the characteristic features of the Christianity of their day that seemed to be creating such scandal. They could not find the theocratic church headed by the papacy, the imposing and complicated system of theology, or even some of the features of the sacramental system. What they did find were the democratic features of early Christianity. Therefore, as the best way out of the mess into which

[74]See p. 679.
[75]See pp. 95 ff.
[76]See pp. 100 ff.
[77]See pp. 665 ff.

the Church had got itself, they began to urge a return to the authentic Christianity contained in the Scriptures and an abolition of all the historical accretions of the intervening centuries. For many of them this meant that the Church would have to give up its political power and program, its wealth and luxury, and content itself with its spiritual mission, the salvation of souls. Aristotle and the Scriptures reinforced each other.

MARSIGLIO OF PADUA

The most influential of the early critics of papal theocracy was Marsiglio of Padua (b. *ca.* 1280), who finished his quite radical treatise *Defender of the Peace* (*Defensor Pacis*) in 1324. Marsiglio, together with radical Spiritual Franciscans such as the Englishman William of Ockham, was a member of the court of the emperor Louis IV of Bavaria, to whose struggle with the papacy we have already referred.[78] He had been a rector of the University of Paris in 1313 and had joined Louis in 1326, having been obliged to leave Paris when it was discovered that he was the author of *Defensor Pacis*. The following year he was condemned as a heretic. This work not only frankly confessed having been written under the influence of Aristotle's *Politics*, but it also incorporated a knowledge of the democratic struggle in Marsiglio's home town of Padua, if not also of the other towns of northern Italy. In this work Marsiglio set out deliberately to combat what he called the "perverted opinion . . . pernicious to the human race" that the pope is endowed with complete power (*plenitudo potestatis*).[79]

"DEFENSOR PACIS"

Marsiglio removed the state from any papal jurisdiction by denying that it necessarily has anything to do with preparing the citizen for his heavenly home. Such preparation, in any case, is subject to the control of the state. Rather than with heaven, the state should concern itself with the "civil happiness which seems the best object of desire possible to man in this world, and the ultimate aim of human acts." Civil happiness is created by such things as peace, prosperity, and security. The source of political power in the state is not the pope but the people, to whom Marsiglio refers by the term *legislator*. The legislator is composed of the whole body of citizens, the citizen being defined as "one who participates in the civil community, in the governmental, deliberative, or judicial function, according to his rank." Only children, slaves, foreigners, and women are excluded from citizenship. In this body of citizens resides the sovereignty of the state. The citizen body, through an elected assembly, makes the laws, elects, and controls the government. Marsiglio, then, prefers a form of government where the ruler is responsible to the people, who are

[78]See p. 621.
[79]Alan Gewirth, *Marsilius of Padua*, I, 6.

sovereign.[80] The people are made self-governing because self-government is regarded as being essential to freedom, and laws, however good or bad, are better observed by citizens who look upon the laws as their own handiwork.

Such a republic, resting upon the principle of popular sovereignty and with only secular aims to accomplish for its citizens, has no use for the direction of a church. It is, in fact, a church, for Marsiglio defines the church as the whole body of the faithful (*universitas fidelium*), which is the equivalent of the citizen body (*universitas civium*). Thus the church is not the clergy, who are only a department of state and have no coercive power. The clergy are in fact to be restricted to teaching the faith and dispensing the sacraments. In this view the priesthood possesses no magical powers. In the sacrament of Penance it does not forgive sins. God forgives sins, and whatever priestly character is given by the sacrament of Ordination is given by God, not the bishop. There are no special grades of the priesthood, with some having power to administer sacraments that others cannot. Every priest has authority to administer "all the sacraments." The whole hierarchy, from pope down to parish priest, has no divine foundation. It is but the work of human beings. The pope is not the successor of Saint Peter. If the pope is the successor of anyone, he is the successor of Saint Paul. The bishop of Antioch is the real successor of Saint Peter.

Marsiglio then goes ahead in his argument to insist upon the democratic organization of the church. Its clergy are to be elected by the faithful. If the body of the citizens controls the ruler, the body of the faithful controls the pope through the instrumentality of an elected general council. Marsiglio was really the first to insist upon this relationship. The general council is guided by the Holy Spirit; it defines the articles of faith; its decisions are infallible, and belief in them necessary for salvation. This council, consisting of laymen as well as clergy, elects the pope, gives him whatever authority he possesses, and can depose him for cause. Thus the pope is entirely dependent upon the council. Since the clergy have no coercive authority, there may be complete freedom of religion if the people are willing. The final authority in the church should be the Scriptures, whose interpretation should not be left to pope or clergy but to a group of reasonable and learned men.

This was a rather dramatic substitution of popular for papal sovereignty in both state and church, calculated to draw absolute popes and monarchs into alliance. It was an expression of the new humanism being introduced with the study of the classics, and of the new secularism introduced by the medieval communes. Marsiglio does not want government to make men saints. He does not follow Aristotle to the extent of wanting government to make men virtuous. He wants men to be responsible, as citizen-governors, for what they want to make of themselves or for what they want their government to do. "The Marsilian doctrine represented an im-

[80]Gewirth, p. 237.

portant force for human enlightenment, not only through its negative attack on the theologico-political authoritarianism of the middle ages, but also through the confidence in the people's own abilities which it substituted for that authoritarianism. . . . The unlimited authority he gave to the whole people thus meant not merely, or even primarily, the subjection of the priests to the civil authority, but rather that the people could pursue its interests as it conceived them and control its destiny through its own laws and government, free from the constant coercion and interference of the priest invoking the divine law." (pp. 315–316)

THE CONCILIAR THEORISTS

Marsiglio was the first conciliarist, the first to suggest that the governance of the Church be handed over to a council. After the outbreak and prolongation of the schism, the number of such writers increased to such an extent that a regular school of conciliar theorists arose and continued for as long as there were any hopes of the salvation of the Church through a council. Such men were the French cardinal Pierre d'Ailly, John Gerson, the chancellor of the University of Paris, and the German Nicholas of Cusa. They did not go beyond the arguments advanced by Marsiglio in the *Defensor*. The power of the popes they regarded as having been permitted to arise by the Church and as being therefore subject to the control of the Church through a general council. The papacy was, in effect, a limited and not an absolute monarchy. The spiritual power of the Church resided ultimately in a representative body, which, in times of crisis, must take over and perform the functions the popes were administering so outrageously. It was not necessary to have the consent of the pope for such a council to meet. The emperor could summon it, or it could meet on its own accord. Once met, it could depose old and elect new popes, if necessary, and undertake all the necessary reforms and measures necessary to restore health to the Church.

THE COUNCIL OF PISA

By 1408 the demand for a council had become so strong that the majority of the cardinals of the rival Roman and French popes decided to try the proposal by summoning a general council at Pisa, which met in March, 1409, calling itself a "universal synod representing the Church universal." It deposed both the reigning popes and elected a new one, the cardinal of Milan, Alexander V. Upon his death in 1410 the Council made an impossible choice in Cardinal Baldassare Cossa, who had a good reputation as a former pirate and soldier, if not as a churchman. In fact, the Council was unable to establish its authority. The deposed popes refused to recognize its jurisdiction, and Cossa was unable to enforce the decree of deposition. The Council of Pisa, therefore, increased the number of popes from two to three.

When the German emperor Sigismund called together the second council of the fifteenth century, the Council of Constance (1414–1418), it declared itself a "General Council," representing the Catholic Church "with authority immediately from Christ." "All men, of every rank and condition, including the Pope himself, is [sic] bound to obey it in matters of Faith, the abolition of the schism, and the reformation of the Church of God in its head and its members. . . . Any one, of any rank and condition, who shall contumaciously refuse to obey the orders, decrees, statutes, or instructions, made or to be made by this holy council, or by any other lawfully assembled general council . . . shall, unless he comes to a right frame of mind, be subjected to fitting penance and punished appropriately."[81] This was putting conciliar theory into almost papal practice.

NEW HERETICS AND PATRIOTISM

The Council of Constance had to consider matters of faith, as well as schism and reform, because a second wave of heresy had arisen to threaten the very system of salvation, as well as the form of organization, of the Church. This wave was associated with the Englishman John Wycliffe, the Czech John Huss, and the French peasant girl Joan of Arc. In the case of each of these, heresy was connected with a kind of patriotism. John Wycliffe, before coming to the point of casting the whole sacramental system of the Church aside, was an active participant in the attempt of fourteenth-century Englishmen to keep the Avignon papacy from extending its system of spiritual supremacy over the English church. John Huss, while sharing these views, was also concerned with shaking off the German control of the Czech church and university. Joan, trying to raise the French monarchy from its torpor and to drive the English out of France, had to face the interference of the Church in what she considered her direct relationship with the saints and God. Papal theocracy thus pushed national resistance to the point of heresy, a combination it could not finally suppress.

JOHN WYCLIFFE

Fourteenth-century Englishmen did not like to feel that they were being mulcted by a papacy resident at Avignon and suspected of being an ally of the French crown, England's enemy in the Hundred Years' War. When, in 1365, Pope Urban V called for a payment of the current and all past tribute promised by King John as a vassal of the Holy See, Parliament refused and denied that, without its consent, John could have made England a fief of the papacy. In 1351 and 1353, in the *Statutes of Provisors and Praemunire*, Parliament had sought to thwart the appointment by the popes of foreigners to English church offices, and the appeal on

[81]Bettenson, *Documents of the Christian Church*, pp. 192–193.

the part of such men to the papal court for a settlement of their grievances. These efforts were repeated in the course of the century. Wycliffe ardently supported them, but he did not advance to extreme views until exasperated by the outbreak of the schism. On the subject of the propriety of the Church's holding property he was as bold as Saint Francis with respect to his order. Wycliffe held that no one could hold property legally unless he was in the grace of God. Every righteous man theoretically held all property, and together all righteous men should share in the enjoyment of all property. What should be done in the case of unrighteous laymen holding property he did not suggest, but he knew that, if the Scriptures were to be believed, the clergy had no business to own or possess property. They should live on the free-will offerings of the faithful. He did not hesitate, therefore, to recommend that all church property be confiscated by the state and divided among "poor gentlemen that wulden justly govern the people and maintain the land against enemies."

What he would have preferred to see was a revival of the Christianity and the organization of the Church that he found in the Scriptures. Indeed, he wished to see these Scriptures spread among an audience larger that the academic one, and was responsible for their translation into English for the first time. Such a Christianity would do without the hierarchic Church headed by the pope, and content itself with an organization without distinctions in rank. Such a church would not need the sacraments; Wycliffe attacked all of them except Marriage. Such a church would abolish the distinction between kinds of Christians introduced by the monastic system. It would do without the cult of saints and indulgences. It would eschew the use of the arts in religion. For the external, mechanical religion in the hands of priests mediating between God and man it would substitute a religion of personal purity, stemming from the love of the individual for Jesus Christ his Lord, and from the direct communication between the individual and his God. Nor was Wycliffe content, as a professor at Oxford, merely to put down his ideas in writing. He trained a body of men there, who came to be called Lollards and who traveled throughout England, bringing his message home to simple people.

THE LOLLARD'S CREED

By 1394, ten years after the death of Wycliffe, Lollards could say "That the pretended miracle of the sacrament of bread drives all men, but a few, to idolatry, because they think that the Body of Christ which is never away from heaven could by power of the priests' word be enclosed essentially in a little bread which they show the people . . . that exorcisms and blessings performed over wine, bread, water and oil, salt, wax and incense . . . are the genuine performance of necromancy rather than of sacred theology . . . that king and bishop in one person, prelate and judge in temporal causes, curate and officer in secular office, puts any kingdom beyond good rule . . . that pilgrimages, prayers, and offerings made to blind crosses or roods, and to deaf images of wood or stone are pretty well akin to idolatry . . . that auricular confession which is said to be so necessary to the salvation of a man, with its pretended power of absolution, exalts the arrogance of priests and gives them opportunity of other secret colloquies which we will not speak of; for both lords and ladies attest that, for fear of their confessors, they dare not speak the truth . . . that the abundance of unnecessary arts practiced in our realm nourishes much sin in waste, profusion, and disguise . . . that manslaughter in war, or by pretended law of justice for a temporal cause, without spiritual revelation, is expressly contrary to the New Testament, which indeed is the law of grace and full of mercies." Christ "specially taught a man to love his enemies, and to show them pity and not to slay them . . . the law of mercy, which is the New Testament, prohibits all manner of manslaughter, for in the Gospel: 'It was said unto them of old time, Thou shalt not kill.' . . . Jesus hates and threatens men who fight and kill, when He says: 'He who smites with the sword shall perish by the sword.' "[82] There was no Inquisition in England to try Wycliffe, and his powerful political and university connections kept him out of the episcopal courts. But he was condemned by the Church in England and in Rome, and the Council of Constance ordered his remains removed from consecrated ground. Because his views and the activities of the Lollards were associated falsely with the outbreak of peasant revolt in 1381, this early English Protestantism had no further outward success until the time of the English reformation. Indeed the reaction went so far that, after 1401, the English state was burning heretics at the stake.

JOHN HUSS

It was in Bohemia rather than in England that Wycliffe's views brought immediate results. His theological works were carried home by Czech students at Oxford and translated into Czech. They were taken up immediately by Czech masters at the University of Prague, and they set on fire a smouldering anti-papal reform movement that had been fed by remnants of the older Waldensian and Albigensian heresies. The Czech reform movement was patriotically anti-German, inasmuch as the University was controlled by the German masters, who were anti-Wycliffe, and these, in turn, were supported by the large German element in the Czech church. The Czech masters, in turn, were supported by the Czech element in the church. Back of this was the antagonism aroused by the earlier infiltration of numerous German colonists into the Czech towns. John Huss became the leader of the Czech reform movement. As a master of the University he had come under the influence of Wycliffe, whose works were assimilated into his own. After King Wenzel deprived the German masters of their control of the University of Prague Huss was

[82]Bettenson, pp. 249 ff.

elected rector. As a popular preacher of reform he was in constant trouble with the Church and, because of protests against papal-indulgence sellers, in 1412 was excommunicated and retired from public life. In 1414 he was anxious to vindicate himself and the whole Czech reform movement from the suspicions of heresy by appearing before the impressive assembly of the Council of Constance, to which he had been granted a safe-conduct by the emperor Sigismund. The safe-conduct was violated by the Council. The Council, to be sure, was anxious to demonstrate its ability to lead the Church by solving the schism and introducing measures of reform. But it had no intention of bringing itself into disrepute by being kind to suspected heretics. It had already condemned Wycliffe, and it wanted a recantation from Huss. He was not the kind of man from whom a recantation could be had for the mere asking, even under threat of torture and death by burning. He refused to recant opinions he said were not his, or those that could be substantiated by Scripture. He was therefore condemned as a heretic and turned over to the local authorities to be burned in early July, 1415. Before being put to the flames he protested again his innocence and said that all he had ever tried to do was "to save men from their sins. I die joyfully to-day in the truth of that gospel which I have written and taught and preached."[83] The Council thus got rid of Huss and, in the next year, of his follower Jerome of Prague, but it did not get rid of the Hussites, who now rose to the defense of their martyrs and their faith. The Church, having learned nothing in the course of the centuries, thought to deal with the Hussites as it had dealt with the Albigensians. It proclaimed a crusade against them.

JOAN OF ARC

In 1431, the year when the Council of Basel opened, the English burned Joan of Arc as a heretic and a sorceress in the market place of Rouen. She had been sentenced, after a long trial, by a court of the Inquisition, presided over by Pierre Cauchon, the bishop of Beauvais. To the English, a young, illiterate peasant girl who could inspire the French army to force them to begin a retreat from northern France[84] must necessarily be a witch. To the authorities of the Church, Joan's insistence that, as an agent of God, who directed her through the saints, she was quite independent of the clergy smacked of heresy. She told her judges on 4 May, 1431, "I trust in God my creator for every thing. I love Him with my whole heart. I trust in my Judge. He is the King of Heaven and of earth." It was explained to her that there was such a thing as the Church Militant to which she must submit, and that she had to believe in Boniface VIII's *Unam Sanctam*. She answered, "I believe indeed in the Church on earth; but for my words and deeds, as I have already declared, I trust and refer in everything to God who caused me to do what I have done." When she

[83]E. J. Kitts, *Pope John XXIII and Master John Hus of Bohemia*, p. 400.
[84]See p. 568.

was asked if she wished to say that she had no judge on earth, and that the pope was not her judge, she answered, "I will not say anything more. I have a good master our Lord to whom I refer everything and to none other." When she was told that if she did not believe in the Church and in *Unam Sanctam* she would be a heretic and be burned at the stake, she said, "I will say no more to you; and if I saw the fire, I should say all that I do now to you, and nothing more."[85]

On 9 May she was threatened with torture. "Many of the points were read and explained to her, and she was told that if she did not confess them truthfully she would be put to the torture, the instruments of which were shown to her all ready in the tower. There were also present by our instructions men ready to put her to the torture in order to restore her to the way and knowledge of truth, and by this means to procure the salvation of her body and soul which by her lying inventions she exposed to such grave perils." Joan replied to this threat of force: "Truly if you were to tear me limb from limb and separate my soul from my body, I would not tell you anything more; and if I did say anything, I should afterwards declare that you had compelled me to say it by force." She told her judges that she had been recently comforted by Saint Gabriel, and that her voices, the voices of her other saints, had told her when she asked them if she should submit to the Church, that if she desired the Lord to aid her she must wait upon him in all her doings. "Seeing the hardness of her heart and her manner of answering, we, the said judges, fearing that the torments of torture would be of little profit to her, decided to postpone their application until we had received more complete advice on the question." On 24 May, when her judges had completed reading the greater part of the sentence committing her to the flames, Joan did confess. She was horrified, she said, at the thought of her nice body being burned to ashes. She had lied about her voices; she was a sorceress; she should not have claimed to be directly inspired by God. Thereupon her judges sentenced her anew. "Inasmuch as you have rashly sinned against God and the Holy Church, we finally and definitely condemn you for salutary penance to perpetual imprisonment, with the bread of sorrow and water of affliction, that you may weep for your faults and never, henceforth, commit anything to occasion weeping."

When Joan was returned to prison she soon realized the irony of this sentence and the dishonesty of her confession. When her judges came to the prison "to observe her state and disposition" and asked her whether she had heard the voices of Saint Catherine and Saint Margaret recently, she said that she had. "God had sent word through the Saints of the great pity of this treason by which she consented to abjure and recant in order to save her life . . . she had damned herself to save her life. . . . She said that if she declared God had not sent her she would damn herself, for

---

[85]*The Trial of Jeanne d'Arc*, trans. W. P. Barrett, passim.

in truth she was sent from God. She said that her voices had told her that she had done a great evil in declaring that what she had done was wrong." She said that what she had declared and recanted "was done only for fear of the fire. . . . She recanted nothing which was not against the truth. She would rather do penance once and for all, that is to die, than endure any longer the suffering of her prison. Whatever they had made her deny, she had never done anything against God or the faith. She did not understand what was in the formula of abjuration. She did not mean to revoke anything except at God's good pleasure."

BERNARD SHAW AND JOAN

In his magnificent play *Saint Joan*, Bernard Shaw has Pierre Cauchon put Joan's case as follows: "She acts as if she herself were the Church . . . Has she ever in all her utterances said one word of the Church? Never. It is always God and herself." The Devil, says the bishop, has turned her head. "He is spreading this heresy everywhere. The man Hus, burnt only thirteen years ago at Constance, infected all Bohemia with it. A man named WcLeef, himself an anointed priest, spread the pestilence in England. . . . We have such people here in France too: I know the breed. . . . It is not the Mother of God now to whom we must look for inter- cession, but to Joan the Maid. What will the world be like when the Church's accumulated wisdom and knowledge and experience, its con- verts of learned, venerable, pious men, are thrust into the kennel by every ignorant laborer or dairymaid whom the devil can puff up with the monstrous self-conceit of being directly inspired from heaven? It will be a world of blood, of fury, of devastation, of each man striving for his own hand, . . . in the end, a world wrecked back into barbarism. . . . What will it be when every girl thinks herself a Joan and every man a Mahomet? I shudder to the very marrow of my bones when I think of it. I have fought it all my life; and I will fight it to the end. Let all this woman's sins be forgiven her except only this sin; for it is the sin against the Holy Ghost; and if she does not recant in the dust before the world, and submit to the last inch of her soul to her Church, to the fire she shall go if she once falls into my hand."[86]

After Joan's withdrawal of her recantation there was nothing for the court of the Inquisition to do but to condemn her as a relapsed heretic and turn her over to the English to be burned. She died at the stake on 30 May, with the name of Jesus on her lips. But in the eyes of the Church that condemned her she did not remain a heretic and sorceress. For, in order that it might not be said that the French monarchy was assisted by a heretic and sorceress, the papacy in 1456—a little late to help Joan—de- clared, after the case had been reheard, that the original trial was irregular

[86]*Saint Joan*, by George Bernard Shaw, pp. 69–71. Used by permission of The So- ciety of Authors and The Public Trustee.

and her punishment therefore unwarranted. In the late nineteenth century the French church, suffering the pains of official anticlericalism and wishing to demonstrate its close association with French patriotism, made her a popular heroine. In 1919 the girl who in 1431 was declared a sorceress and a heretic was declared a saint—a saint, in reality, of the new cult of nationalism.

THE WORK OF THE COUNCIL OF CONSTANCE

The opening of the Council of Constance was a moment of great hope for those Christians in the West who sought through it to bring about a permanent change in the constitution of the Church and a thorough reform from top to bottom. Its condemnation of Wycliffe and its burning of Huss and Jerome of Prague did not augur well for a judicial settlement of the main issues involved. To be sure, Constance did restore unity to the papacy. It finally succeeded in deposing John XXIII, arranged for the abdication of Gregory XII, and, when he had been deprived of all support, deposed Benedict XIII. It then elected as the new pope (1417) the Italian cardinal Otto Colonna, who took the name of Martin V. With the schism now gone, the new pope considered as his main task the undermining of the work of the Council and the destruction of the conciliar theory. Before he was able to dissolve Constance (1418), it had provided for the continuation of a series of general councils, one to be held in five, another in seven, and then regularly every ten years. Constance had been able to do little about the reform of the Church, and the reunified papacy kept it from interfering with the *curia*.

THE COUNCIL OF BASEL

In 1420 the papacy summoned Europe to a crusade against the Hussites. The response came from predominantly German crusading armies, who had no success against the Czech peasants and artisans led by Ziska and the priest Prokop. The Hussites were therefore invited to send delegates to the Council of Basel (1431) to negotiate a settlement. Meanwhile, the pope had dissolved the council called for Pavia-Siena in 1423, and was ready to dissolve Basel, too, when it assembled. The new pope, Eugenius IV, was thwarted, however, in this desire. The Fathers at Basel angrily refused to be dissolved. Eugenius then sought to split the Council apart by summoning a new one to meet at Ferrara in 1438 to deal with the question of a union of the western and eastern churches, in response to the pressure of the advancing Turks in the Balkans. The superficial success of Eugenius in negotiating this union (it never was actually put into effect) so angered the Council at Basel that it deposed him and elected as the new pope, in 1439, the duke of Savoy, a widower with several children, who took the name of Felix V. This act renewed the schism that the Council of Constance had succeeded in healing. It cost the Council of Basel the confidence of Europe.

Under these circumstances, the rulers of Europe took matters into their own hands. Eugenius himself was only too willing to negotiate settlements at the cost of the Council and of the conciliar theory. With the support of the French king, the French church undertook to establish its own relations with Rome in the Pragmatic Sanction of Bourges, in 1439. The German diet took similar steps, in the next year, for the German church. In negotiations with the emperor Frederick III and German princes Eugenius IV was able to work out compromise settlements lessening the power of the papacy locally, in return for abandonment of Basel and its conciliar program. These partial settlements were regularized in the German Concordat of 1448. Thereupon, after providing for the resignation of Felix V, the Council of Basel dissolved itself (1449). No council was to meet for about a century; not until the Church had been confronted with the Protestant Revolt.

THE MEANING OF PAPAL VICTORY OVER THE COUNCILS

What had happened was that the popes had succeeded in destroying the democratic hopes of the early fifteenth century. They succeeded by compromising with the states of central and western Europe on the question of who was to control the Church within their boundaries. The popes could not hope any longer to establish temporal control over these states after the events of the fourteenth and early fifteenth centuries. This phase of papal theocracy was now a thing of the past. To preserve the papal monarchy with its spiritual power at the cost of councils, conciliar theory, and the principles of a limited papal monarchy, if only to save the principle of authority in the administration of the Church, the papacy was willing to surrender to the states a large part of its control over the local churches. The princes had been supporting the councils, among other reasons, to secure reforms that would obstruct the papal monarchy and guarantee their own control over their respective churches. If the papacy was willing to make these concessions independently of the council, the princes had no further interest in supporting the council. The papacy therefore conceded to the princes the right to appoint to local church offices, collect taxes from the clergy, and draw cases from local ecclesiastical courts to their own. In surrendering papal for royal or princely control, the popes contributed to breaking up the theocratic Church into a series of national and territorial churches under the nominal spiritual leadership of Rome. In this way the popes managed to preserve their absolute position as monarchs over what there was left to rule. They were free of the limitations of a council as a permanent part of the constitutional structure of the Church. They thus preferred ecclesiastical absolutism in monarchical form to the spiritual substance of religion emphasized by the reformers. In surrendering power to the kings and princes rather than to representative institutions of the Church they preferred to strengthen the absolutism of their fellow secular monarchs rather than the power of the people. This choice cost them a great loss of authority.

The victory thus gained for papal absolutism, though limited in its scope, was at the expense of possible radical reform by papacy or councils. The negotiations between the Council of Basel and the Hussites paved the way for the establishment, in Bohemia in the fifteenth century, of what we may regard as the first Protestant churches. Elsewhere, the lack of reform left the reformers, conciliarists as well as nonconciliarists, bitterly disappointed. When the next crisis arose with Martin Luther, the reformers would be less patient in waiting for the Church to reform. They would undertake it themselves, with the support of the state. In supporting victorious heretics, some princes and kings of the sixteenth century would complete their assumption of control over the Church. The papal victory over the councils was accordingly only a phantom victory, at the ultimate cost of the religious unity of western Europe. It is in this sense that we may speak of the rejection of ecclesiastical theocracy in the fourteenth and fifteenth centuries by the strong monarchies and territorial states of the West, by the new revolutionary theorists and heretics, and, strange as it may seem, by the popes themselves, who in refusing to compromise with the demands for reform, while very willing to compromise with the state on the matter of control, limited papal theocracy and made Protestantism inevitable. The ghosts of the heretics whom the Church chose to burn in the Middle Ages rose to support the new Protestant heretics, demanding anew the right to believe as one's mind and conscience dictate.

chapter fourteen

THE WESTERN TRADITION IN THE LATER MIDDLE AGES: THOUGHT AND EDUCATION

HUMANISM AND ASCETICISM IN THE MIDDLE AGES.   It was asked in an earlier chapter[1] whether Christianity, as a result of its adaptation to the classical world, was so influenced by the humanistic point of view that it developed a Christian humanism. The answer given was that, while the obvious contrasts between humanism and asceticism persisted, the latter did, in its own way, adopt some humanistic tenets. It recognized the need of reason to explain its point of view, and it granted man a limited moral freedom. Its doctrine of love transcended the humanistic outlook. It has been pointed out[2] in another connection that, in so far as they were necessary to maintain and enrich the faith, the Church supported classical literature and learning. It promoted also a Christian literature and art. A consideration of the general features of the political, social, and economic history of the Middle Ages has revealed that, in pursuit of the powers of a theocratic state, Christianity violated its cardinal doctrine of love. The development of the national monarchy, of a more mobile arrangement of classes, and of an urban capitalistic society set up competing institutions and emphasized competing values. The new institutions were secular rather than ecclesiastical; the new values worldly rather than ascetic. It is necessary to ask in this chapter whether the intellectual and educational developments of the later Middle Ages tended to support the harmony or discord between humanism and asceticism.

[1]See Chap. viii.
[2]See pp. 412 ff.

The intellectual tradition of the post-Carolingian period rested upon the works of the Christian Fathers and of such men as Boethius, Isidore of Seville, Bede, Alcuin, John the Scot, and Rabanus Maurus. The tradition of the Fathers minimized learning for faith, insisting that, when one possessed the divine revelation of God in the Scriptures, all other learning was superfluous. "Divine learning does not need logic." Among the Fathers it was Augustine who was most influential in determining the tradition. To him, learning was subservient to belief (I believe in order to know), and, in any case, man after the Fall was not a creature whom learning could much benefit. He had lost the rationality that distinguished him before the Fall and had become a slave of appetite.

AUGUSTINE AND NEOPLATONIC MYSTICISM

What had brought Augustine to Christianity was his study of Neoplatonism, of which his religious philosophy was a Christian restatement. The general features of Neoplatonism we have already considered.[3] It is a compound of both Plato and Aristotle. Plotinus's God, in whom one can discern Plato's Idea of the Good as well as Aristotle's Unmoved Mover, was the all-inclusive One, who could be defined only in negative terms. This One, acting through such mediaries as Divine Mind and World Soul, created the universe in accordance with ideas that were the equivalent of the Platonic ideas, or forms, those absolute and eternal verities that give reality to the world about us. This world, originally composed of formless matter, God impregnated with the ideas. It is thus dependent upon the ideas in the mind of God for its development and end. As a system of salvation, Neoplatonism is a form of mysticism. It explains that the human soul, a divine idea imprisoned in the evil matter of the body, tries to escape and return to the Divine Mind from which it came. The moment of reabsorption into the mind of God is an experience attained only rarely and not easily described.

PLATONIC IDEALISM

In such a philosophy as that of Plotinus the one important thing to understand is God. To the extent that he can be understood by reason at all, it is best to try to understand him through the divine ideas that compose his mind. This is, in fact, the best way to come to understand the external world. For these ideas are the ultimate reality and determine the extent to which the world is real. God in this view is the supreme reality, of which the divine ideas are a part. The latter are such attributes as goodness, harmony, and beauty, whose presence determines the extent to which things about us are good, orderly, or beautiful. To understand why a tree is beautiful, according to this view, it would be an altogether

[3]See pp. 298 ff.

wrong approach to consider its shape, its color, its movement in the breeze, its background of blue sky. These are sensible qualities that change with every moment. It is impossible to seize hold of them. To understand the beauty of a tree, or the beauty of anything else, one must understand the divine idea of beauty, itself an objective reality, which determines the beauty of the tree. To the extent that the tree partakes of the divine idea of beauty, it is beautiful. To the extent that the man embodies the divine idea of the good, he is good. The understanding of these ideas or principles, therefore, cannot be achieved by considering the character of the particulars that partake of them. It must come through rational, logical, intuitive, or mystical processes free from the limitations of the world perceived by sense.[4]

CHRISTIAN IDEALISM

To make Neoplatonism Christian, Augustine had to identify Yahweh with the One, something already done by previous theologians. Christianity already possessed a Trinity to take the place of the Neoplatonic trinity. Into the number of ideas, or forms, comprising the divine mind of the Christian God it was necessary to introduce those specifically Christian ideas that the development of the faith had brought forth. There was the Fall, the Incarnation, and the Redemption, or Atonement. There was also Sin, Grace, Faith, and Immortality. The Christian God, the only supreme reality, could be understood only through an understanding of these specific Christian ideas. The world about us, and especially the world of man, could not be understood without comprehending these objectively real Christian ideas. Constituting God's providence, they determined the fate of the universe. They could not be understood by an approach through the natural world. It would be false to assume that because a man was handsome and talked reasonably that he was beautiful and rational. Man could not be understood without Sin and the Fall. If these general Christian ideas could not be understood by rational processes, they were to be accepted on faith as the authoritative teaching of the Church.

CHRISTIAN MYSTICISM

In any case, reason was an inadequate approach to the divine ideas and God. Some of the ideas had to be felt as well as understood. Did one know God without loving him, praying to him, adoring him? There was a point when reason became emotion. The supreme religious experience was the mystical one. To achieve it even momentarily, the heart as well as the mind had to be made ready. The supreme reward of Christian faith and conduct was the eternal prolongation of the mystical experience, the fusion with, and absorption in, God, the deification of the human mortal in a heavenly world. In his *Confessions* Augustine tries to make clear what

[4]Cf. M. H. Carré, *Phases of Thought in England*, p. 63.

CHRONOLOGY — Thought and Education in the Later Middle Ages

800 ⎯⎯⎯

Albumazar (ca. 805–885)

900 ⎯⎯⎯

Berengar (998–1088)

1000 ⎯⎯

Anselm of Bec (ca. 1034–1109)
Founding of University of Bologna (late 11th c.)
Peter Abélard (1079–1142)
Héloïse (d. ca. 1164)
Saint Bernard of Clairvaux (1091–1153)
Roscellin of Compiègne (fl. 1092–1119)

1100 ⎯⎯

Adelard of Bath (fl. 12th c.)
Founding of University of Paris (12th c.)
Peter Lombard (ca. 1100–1160)
Gerard of Cremona (ca. 1114–1187)
Founding of University of Oxford (ca. 1167)
Alexander Neckam (1157–1217)
Robert Grosseteste (ca. 1170–1250)
Albertus Magnus (1193–1280)

1200 ⎯⎯

Roger Bacon (ca. 1214–1294)
Saint Thomas Aquinas (1225–1274)

he and his mother thought this mystic experience in heaven would be like: "Suppose all the tumult of the flesh in us were hushed for ever, and all sensible images of earth and sea and air were put to silence: suppose the heavens were still, and even the soul spoke no words to itself, but passed beyond all thought of itself: suppose all dreams and revelations of imagination were hushed with every word and sign and everything that belongs to this transitory world: suppose they were all silenced—though, if they speak to one who hears, what they say is: 'We made not ourselves, but He made us who abides forever'—yet suppose they only uttered this, and then were silent, when they had turned the ears of the hearer to Him who made them, leaving Him to speak alone, not through them but through Himself, so that we could hear His words, not through any tongue of flesh nor by the voice of an angel, nor in thunder, nor, in any likeness that hides what it reveals; suppose, then, that the God whom through such manifestations we have learnt to love, were to be revealed to us directly without any such mediation—just as, but now, we reached out of ourselves and touched by a flash of insight the eternal wisdom that abides above all; suppose, lastly that this vision of God were to be prolonged for ever, and all other inferior modes of vision were to be taken away, so that this alone should ravish and absorb the beholder, and entrance him in mystic joy, and our life were for ever like the moment of clear insight and inspiration to which we rose—is not this just what is meant by the words 'Enter thou into the joy of thy Lord'?"[5]

AUGUSTINIANISM

Augustine's Christian adaptation of Neoplatonism may be called Augustinianism. There is no mistaking its ascetic, antihumanistic character. Following Plato and Plotinus, it turns man away from the world of particulars about him and asks him to consider only the specifically Christian ideas that this world embodies. Through an understanding of these ideas, one is to approach the comprehension of God. This is an otherworldly approach. Having no confidence in the ability of human reason to comprehend the Christian mystery, he lays supreme emphasis on faith, or on an emotional approach to this comprehension. Augustine is thus a mystic. He minimizes what the humanist regards as one of man's chief glories, his reasoning power. Other ways in which Augustinian views are to be considered ascetic and antihumanistic have been considered previously.[6] For the entire Middle Ages Augustinianism remained the fundamental interpretation of Christianity. No matter how much it was contended, under the influence of Aristotle, that Christianity could be made rational, there was always a point beyond which rationality could not seem to go, and thus the way was always open to the mystic. He always took it. There

---

[5]E. Caird, *The Evolution of Theology in the Greek Philosophers*, II, 287–288.
[6]See p. 353.

was a regular succession of theologians, clerics, and poets who exalted the approach of the mystic to Christian truth. Since the mystic does very well without a church, and even without a sacramental system—for his experience needs no mediator between himself and God—as the Church became more irresponsible and the Christian system of salvation more mechanical, the mystics grew in number and influence.

THE CORRECTION OF AUGUSTINE

The Church, however, always had to make room for those whom Augustinianism did not satisfy. Augustine's denial of human moral responsibility it quickly corrected.[7] His willingness to abandon reason for faith was also corrected when it became possible to think peacefully again, and when the instruments of thought were restored to western man. This was the time (eleventh century) when the feudal system had re-established a measure of order after the collapse of the Carolingian empire, and when (twelfth century) Greek and Mohammedan learning was introduced to the West.

ARISTOTELIAN LOGIC AND THE FAITH

Until this time the intellectual fare of the medieval western world had been comparatively meagre.[8] In the eleventh century, however, there were signs of a growing maturity, when a few men began to insist that it was not enough to go on accepting the contents of Christian dogma on mere faith. Men had an obligation to make this dogma as comprehensible as possible through the use of their reason. The tools available at this moment for the employment of human reason were those of logic or dialectics, and these were confined to the exposition given by Aristotle in his elementary treatises, the *Categories* and *On Interpretation* (the so-called Old Logic). These and further treatises on logic had been made available by Boethius.[9]

UNIVERSALS AND PARTICULARS

In taking up the study of Aristotelian logic, western scholars were obliged to come to terms with a question that had first been put by Plato and Aristotle concerning the relationship between what goes on in our minds and what exists outside them, or, put in other words, the relationship between universals and particulars. We speak of *a house* or *the house* as a particular thing, our own or someone else's. We speak also of *the house* as a general term to refer to a universal mode of shelter. We speak of *a man* or *the man* to refer to a definite, specific person. We speak of *man* or *humanity* to refer to all mankind. These general, abstract, all-

[7]See p. 347.
[8]It has been summarized in Chap. ix.
[9]See pp. 415 f.

inclusive terms (universals) are what Plato called ideas, or forms, and, it will be remembered,[10] he insisted that they make up the world of absolute, eternal, and immutable truth. They constitute, to repeat, the ultimate and only reality. They exist before particular things, and they can be comprehended by the human mind exercising its reasoning power. The world of particulars that we perceive through our senses is real to the extent only that it embodies, partakes, or reflects one of the absolute universals. *A house* or *the house* is real to the extent that it contains within it the universal idea *house*. The universal idea *house* may be regarded as the perfect or ideal house. The individual or particular house is real to the extent that it is patterned after and contains actual features of the perfect house. In this sense, a man is real in so far as he is perfect. This was a point of view that Aristotle did not accept. He insisted that particulars were real without relationship to any pre-existent idea of perfection, and instead of conceiving of universals as existing before things (*ante res*) and as giving things reality, he preferred to put universals (ideas, forms) in things (*in rebus*) as determinants of what they were going to be.[11] Thus an individual child is real enough, but what determines the kind of man he is to become is the presence in him of the idea, or form, *man*, which transforms his potentiality into actual manhood. A particular building is real, but what determines its special character of house is the idea *house*, implicit in its materials and structure.

REALISTS AND NOMINALISTS

The relationship of these ideas to Neoplatonism and Augustinianism has just been considered. During the Middle Ages those who took the Platonic (Neoplatonic, Augustinian) view that universals were the only reality were called Realists. Those who took the Aristotelian view were the moderate Realists. Those who said that universals were mere words or names (*nomina*) and in no sense real were called Nominalists. They argued that the particulars were real, came first, and determined the meaning of the words called universals.

IMPORTANCE OF THE REALIST-NOMINALIST QUESTION

The student may feel that to argue whether justice or just things constitute the ultimate reality is to quibble over words; that to try to determine whether, if universals are real, they existed before particulars or merely in particulars is a waste of time; and that to try to describe precisely how, if universals only are real, reality can enter into particular things is impossible. Such an attitude, however, would be seriously wrong. For if Augustinianism is correct, the world about us is an illusion, and to concern oneself with it a waste of time. If, on the contrary, the Nominal-

[10]See pp. 135 ff.
[11]See p. 146.

ists are correct, then the world of ideas, and these would include Christian ideas, is but a collection of words.

REALISM AND ABSOLUTISM

Realism was the approach that justified religion and deductive reasoning; nominalism the approach justifying science and inductive reasoning. If the universals are the only reality, then such a thing as the Church can have meaning as an entity. A nominalist such as Marsiglio of Padua would argue that the abstraction *Church* is unreal; only the individuals composing the Church have reality. A thorough-going realist can speak with confidence of the Fall of Man as a result of Adam's Original Sin, because to him the entity *man* is real. Adam is a part of it, in so far as he reflects the general idea, and in infecting himself can infect the whole. If the universals are the ultimate reality and truth, propositions can be deduced from them with confidence. Realists are thus what we have called absolutists. The universals are the eternal, immutable truths, the standards of perfection in the mind of God.

NOMINALISM AND RELATIVISM

Nominalists, in insisting upon the reality only of particulars, emphasize individual detail and not general principle. The world of objective detail is the world of science. If universals are mere words or names of characteristics common to particulars, the Nominalist can hardly do better than to concentrate on the description of particulars. The descriptions, however, may lead to general conclusions (induction). The Nominalist position leads easily to relativism, since descriptions of real particulars must vary as these particulars vary, and the conclusions drawn from varying descriptions must in themselves vary. Modern realists (absolutists) and nominalists (relativists) are still arguing with each other.

NOMINALIST ATTEMPTS TO RATIONALIZE CHRISTIANITY

Demands were being made in the eleventh century that Christian dogma be made rational, and attempts to do so raised the realist-nominalist issue. Berengar, a monk of St. Martin's at Tours, who argued against transubstantiation, contended that "It is a part of courage to have recourse to dialectic in all things, for recourse to dialectic is recourse to reason, and he who does not avail himself of reason abandons his chief honor, since by virtue of reason he was made in the image of God." Roscellin of Compiègne attacked the doctrine of the Trinity from the nominalist point of view. To him the Trinity as a composite yet unitary God meant nothing. It consisted of individuals, Father, Son, and Holy Ghost. He was attacked for this view by Anselm of the Norman monastery of Bec, a realist, a partisan of the attempt to rationalize Christian dogma, and a future archbishop of Canterbury. Contending that Roscellin "wishes to confess three gods or he does not understand what he says," Anselm declared that "those dialecticians, or rather dialectical heretics, of our times, who think that universal substances are nothing but words . . . should be wholly excluded from the discussion of spiritual questions. . . . For how can he who does not yet understand that many men are in species one man comprehend how in that lofty and mysterious nature a plurality of persons, each of whom single is perfect God, are one God?"[12]

ANSELM'S ARGUMENT FOR THE EXISTENCE OF GOD

Anselm did not care to have nominalists rationalize the faith, for their results were liable to be heretical. A realist could be trusted to come out with orthodox rationalizations. In his own theological treatises Anselm set out to prove two rather fundamental doctrines: (1) the existence of God, and (2) the necessity of Christ's death to atone for the sins of mankind. Dissatisfied with attempts to prove the existence of God by the use of many arguments, he tried, he says, "to seek within myself whether I might not discover one argument which needed nothing else than itself alone for its proof; and which by itself might suffice to show that truly God exists." The argument Anselm used is a typically realist one and depends upon the belief that the abstraction that can be properly conceived of in the mind actually exists; its intelligibility demonstrates its existence. God is defined in the argument as "something . . . than which nothing greater can be conceived." It is argued that "that than which a greater cannot be conceived cannot exist in the understanding alone. For if it be in the understanding alone, it is possible to conceive it as existing in reality."[13] Anselm was answered by a nominalist monk who contended in substance that "the existence of an idea in the mind does not entail the existence of a corresponding reality outside of the mind."[14] Because you can think of God does not prove that he exists. Because you can think "of an island, surpassing all lands in fertility" is not reason to think "it must indubitably exist in reality." When confronted with this argument Anselm could only say, "if a man will find me anything existing either in fact or in thought only, so excellent that nothing more excellent is conceivable, and if he be able to apply to it my train of argument, then will I discover and present to him his 'lost island,' to be lost no more."

ANSELM'S RATIONALIZATION OF THE ATONEMENT

Anselm's rationalization of the doctrine of the Atonement in a book called *Why God Became Man* (*Cur Deus Homo?*) was an attempt to improve upon earlier suggestions as to why Jesus had to die to save mankind from sin. Earlier suggestions had included the primitive notion that

[12]J. W. Thompson and E. N. Johnson, *An Introduction to Medieval Europe*, pp. 692, 696.
[13]Ibid., pp. 696–697.
[14]Bettenson, *Documents of the Christian Church*, p. 196.

God had to ransom mankind from the clutches of the Devil by the sacrificial death of his Son. Anselm, however, pursued a different theme. Sin he defined as failing to render God his due. To be saved, man must not only restore to God his due, but must render satisfaction to God or suffer punishment for having insulted him in this way. "To remit sin unpunished, would be treating the sinful and the sinless alike, which would be incongruous to God's nature. And incongruity is injustice." The satisfaction made to God for sin "ought to be in proportion to the sin." He contends quite arbitrarily that this amount is "something greater than the whole creation. All that is created, that is, all that is not God, cannot compensate the sin." It is obvious that no sinner can make this kind of satisfaction. Therefore, "Satisfaction cannot be made unless there be some One able to pay to God for man's sin something greater than all that is beside God. . . . Now nothing is greater than all that is not God, except God Himself. None therefore can make this satisfaction except God. And none ought to make it except man. . . . If, then, it be necessary that the kingdom of heaven be completed by man's admission, and if man cannot be admitted unless the aforesaid satisfaction for sin be first made, and if God only can, and man only ought to make this satisfaction, then necessarily One must make it who is both God and man." This explains why Jesus voluntarily offered his life to God on behalf of mankind. "What greater mercy can be conceived than that God the Father should say to the sinner—condemned to eternal torment, and unable to redeem himself—'Receive my only Son, and offer Him for thy self,' while the Son Himself said—'Take me, and redeem thy self'?"[15]

PETER ABÉLARD

Anselm was succeeded as the foremost dialectician of western Europe by Peter Abélard (1079-1142), whose fundamental attitude was quite the contrary of Anselm's. If Anselm joined Augustine in saying, "I believe in order to know," Abélard reversed this to say, "I know in order to believe." He was convinced that if Christianity was to survive as an authoritarian faith, dialectics would have to be used to harmonize the divergent opinions of the Fathers. For it took no great scholarship to show how various were the opinions of the Fathers on numerous points of doctrine. In a book called *Yes and No (Sic et Non)* Abélard cited these contradictory opinions of the Fathers and left them unreconciled, in order to have a lively source book on theology for his students. In his preface to this book he remarks: "We decided to collect the diverse statements of the holy fathers . . . raising an issue from their apparent repugnancy, which might incite the reader to search out the truth of the matter. . . . For the first key to wisdom is called interrogation, diligent and unceasing. . . . By doubting we are led to inquiry; and from inquiry we perceive the truth."

[15]Bettenson, pp. 197-198.

Such a spirit Saint Bernard could not tolerate. He thought Abélard was "trying to make void the merit of Christian faith, when he deems himself able by human reason to comprehend God altogether." In complaining to the pope about Abélard, Bernard declared, "On the threshold of his theology he defines faith as private judgment, as though in these mysteries everyone is allowed to think and speak as he pleases; as though the mysteries of our faith were to hang uncertainly in the midst of shifting and varying opinion. Is not our hope baseless if our faith is subject to inquiry?"[16] Bernard, the conservative mystic and monastic reformer, saw to it that a man as dangerous as Abélard was kept from spreading his ideas among his students and the multitude.

ABÉLARD'S AUTOBIOGRAPHY

In an interesting autobiography, *The Story of My Misfortunes (Historia Calamitatum)*, Abélard himself has recounted the difficulties into which his bold critical spirit got him. He was a Breton noble's son and preferred, he says, to flee "utterly from the court of Mars that I might win learning in the bosom of Minerva." This meant he had to go to Paris, where the cathedral school was one of the chief intellectual centers of the West. Here he listened to William of Champeaux, a realist, whom he occasionally conquered in debate and ultimately "compelled . . . by most potent reasoning first to alter his former opinion on the subject of the universals, and finally to abandon it altogether." Turning from dialectics to theology, he betook himself to the school of Anselm of Laon, where he was quickly disillusioned. "If any one came to him impelled by doubt on any subject, he went away more doubtful still." Abélard then outraged his masters by giving lectures on theology himself, and made himself so unwelcome that he returned to Paris to lecture in the cathedral school. "By this time [I] had come to regard myself as the only philosopher remaining in the whole world."[17]

ABÉLARD AND HÉLOÏSE

In Paris Abélard found it impossible to retain an ascetic way of life. For "there dwelt in that same city . . . a certain young girl named Héloïse, the niece of a canon [of the cathedral of Notre Dame] who was called Fulbert. . . . Of no mean beauty, she stood out above all by reason of her abundant knowledge of letters . . . [a virtue] rare among women, and for that very reason it doubly graced the maiden, and made her the most worthy of renown in the entire kingdom. It was this young girl whom I, after carefully considering all those qualities which are wont to attract lovers, determined to unite with myself in the bonds of love, and indeed the thing seemed to me very easy to be done. So distinguished

[16]Amy Kelly, *Eleanor of Aquitaine*, p. 15.
[17]Trans. H. A. Bellows.

was my name, and I possessed such advantages of youth and comeliness, that no matter what woman I might favour with my love, I dreaded rejection by none." Abélard arranged to become a member of Canon Fulbert's household as Héloïse's tutor. The canon's "simplicity," he thought, "was nothing short of astounding."

"We were united first in the dwelling that sheltered our love, and then in the hearts that burned with it. Under the pretext of study we spent our hours in the happiness of love, and learning held out to us the secret opportunities that our passion craved. Our speech was more of love than of the books which lay open before us; our kisses far outnumbered our reasoned words. Our hands sought less the book than each other's bosoms; love drew our eyes together far more than the lesson drew them to the pages of our text. In order that there might be no suspicion, there were, indeed, sometimes blows, but love gave them, not anger; they were the marks, not of wrath, but of a tenderness surpassing the most fragrant balm in sweetness. What followed? No degree in love's progress was left untried by our passion, and if love itself could imagine any wonder as yet unknown, we discovered it. And our inexperience of such delights made us all the more ardent in our pursuit of them, so that our thirst for one another was still unquenched. . . . I devoted ever less time to philosophy and to the work of the school. . . . My lecturing became utterly careless and lukewarm; I did nothing because of inspiration, but everything as a matter of habit. . . . I still wrote poems; they dealt with love, not with the secrets of philosophy. Of these songs . . . some have become widely known and have been sung in many lands, chiefly, methinks, by those who delighted in the things of this world. As for the sorrows, the groans, the lamentations of my students when they perceived the preoccupation, nay, rather the chaos, of my mind, it is hard even to imagine them."

When Canon Fulbert discovered what was happening, the lovers were separated. "Once the first wildness of shame had passed, it left us more shameless than before, and as shame died within us the cause of it seemed to us ever more desirable. And so it chanced with us as, in the stories that the poets tell, it once happened with Mars and Venus when they were caught together. . . . It was not long after this that Héloïse found that she was pregnant, and of this she wrote to me in the utmost exultation."

After the birth of their son, Astrolabe, they were married despite the protestations of Héloïse. "How unfitting, she thought [Abélard is writing], how lamentable it would be for me, whom nature had made for the whole world, to devote myself to one woman solely, and to subject myself to such humiliation! She vehemently rejected this marriage, which she felt would be in every way ignominious and burdensome to me." Abélard, in arrangements with Fulbert, had consented to the marriage, "provided only the thing could be kept secret, so that I might suffer no loss of reputation thereby." But Fulbert did not keep the matter quiet as he had promised, and Héloïse "denounced her own kin and swore that they were speaking the most absolute lies. . . . Her uncle, aroused to fury thereby, visited her repeatedly with punishments." Abélard thereupon sent her to a nunnery at Argenteuil, where she had been educated.

"When her uncle and his kinsmen heard of this, they were convinced that now I had completely played them false and had rid myself forever of Héloïse by forcing her to become a nun. Violently incensed, they laid a plot against me, and one night, while I, all unsuspecting, was asleep in a secret room in my lodgings, they broke in with the help of one of my servants, whom they had bribed. There they had vengeance on me with a most cruel and most shameful punishment, such as astounded the whole world, for they cut off those parts of my body with which I had done that which was the cause of their sorrow. This done, straightway they fled, but two of them were captured, and suffered the loss of their eyes and their genital organs."

Thereupon Héloïse became a nun at Argenteuil and Abélard a monk at the royal monastery of St. Denis. His life as a monk was stormy, for he had little patience with the ignorant and unreformed monasteries he encountered, and spoke out against them. When he abandoned the monastery to teach, he was always surrounded by crowds of loyal, enthusiastic students. For a while he was the abbot of St. Gildas, in Brittany. Here he had to do with monks who were "vile and untamable" in a region "uncivilized and lawless"; a monastery where there was "no property in common," and where each monk "with such resources as he possessed, supported himself and his concubines, as well as his sons and daughters"; and where they "stole and carried off whatever they could lay their hands on." When they tried to poison him, Abélard fled to Paris to resume his teaching. He had already been in difficulty with the ecclesiastical authorities, not over his sins of the flesh, but over his sins of the intellect, for he had written a suspicious book on the Trinity that they had obliged him to cast into the flames.

ABÉLARD AND SAINT BERNARD

Now, upon his return to Paris, the "indomitable rhinoceros," as he was known to his students, was pursued to the end by Bernard for the false opinions of his book on the Trinity. In 1141 he was hailed before a council at Soissons, over which Bernard presided. "The inquiry began briskly . . . and all bent to hear what he who put no trust in dialectic would do with the beautiful rhetoric of Master Abélard. The abbé [Bernard] simply did nothing with beautiful rhetoric. He read off straightly the damnable passages in the works of Master Abélard, one after the other, without pausing anywhere to call for the great logician's defensive eloquence. Those who had come to hear, let them hear. When Master Peter said that there would be no disputation, that the trial would be over in no time, and that he was already condemned by this tribunal, he stood forth and the voice that had enthralled the schools filled the choir. 'I refuse to be thus judged like a guilty clerk,' he cried. 'I appeal to Rome.' "[18] He died in a priory near Cluny, on the way to Rome with his appeal.

ABÉLARD'S CONCEPTUALISM

The brilliant and vain idol of the Parisian schools was thus condemned by the narrow and ignorant mystics whose authoritarian theology he had tried to rationalize. "A doctrine is not believed," he argued, "because God has said it but because we are convinced by reason that it is so."[19] Abélard was not only a popular teacher and poet but a daring theologian as well. His *Ethics* emphasized the moral freedom, and therewith the moral responsibility, of the individual. In his view, the virtue of conduct depended upon its motivation, not its performance. His sharp dialectics cut through the positions of realists and nominalists and took up a position midway between them that philosophers often call *conceptualism*. Abélard did not admit with the realists that only the universal was to be considered real. Nor did he admit with the nominalists that universals were only words, names, or signs. He preferred to see reality in the particulars rather than in the universals. But he also believed that those general concepts at which we arrive by comparing particulars and observing their common features are not to be dismissed as mere verbiage. By considering particular mountains we arrive at a concept *mountain*. Such concepts are a necessary part of human discourse. They have definite meaning. They may not have the kind of transcendent reality that the realist insisted enabled the universal to impart reality to the particular, but they have sufficient reality to justify their not being dismissed as mere noise. This common-sense point of view was taken over by the scholastics of the thirteenth century.

TRANSLATIONS FROM GREEK AND ARABIC INTO LATIN

Abélard's enthusiasm for dialectics and his confidence in human reason came from the limited learning of the early Middle Ages. In the last half of the twelfth century this body of knowledge was greatly reinforced by the introduction into the West of Greek and Mohammedan learning. The background for this introduction has already been sketched.[20] It has been shown how the expansion of the caliphate prepared the way for the translation into Arabic of Hellenic, Hellenistic, and Hindu philosophy, mathematics, and science (including medicine), and how the Moslem scholar added to this intellectual heritage. No sooner did the western world discover this Arabic literature in the libraries of Spain, Sicily, and the Near East than scholars from every western nation joined eagerly in translating it from Arabic into the Latin the western scholar could use. Only later, in the thirteenth century, were translations made directly from Greek into Latin.

[18]Kelly, *Eleanor of Aquitaine*, pp. 18–19.
[19]H. Baker, *The Dignity of Man*, p. 193, n. 22.
[20]See pp. 496 f.

In this new body of learning the Hellenic world was represented by translations from Plato and, above all, Aristotle. Of Plato nothing was directly known in the early Middle Ages. A part of his *Timaeus* had been translated into Latin. Now came translations of the *Meno* and *Phaedo*. Of Aristotle, only the elementary Old Logic was known during the earlier period. Now came translations of the New Logic, that is, the advanced works (*Prior* and *Posterior Analytics*, *Topics*, and *Sophistical Refutations*). It was, however, not only Aristotle the logician who was translated but also Aristotle the philosopher, scientist, and literary critic. The *Metaphysics* and *Ethics*, the *Physics* and *On Animals*, the *Poetics* and *Rhetoric*, the *Meteorology* and *On Generation and Corruption* were now done over in Latin; in the thirteenth century the *Politics* was translated directly from the Greek. The logical and philosophical works were accompanied by extensive commentaries by such Moslem scholars as Avicenna and Averroës. In addition, there came from the Hellenic world the medical works of Hippocrates. It will be noted that no Greek literature was introduced at this time, either directly or indirectly.

Translations of Euclid's *Elements of Geometry* and Ptolemy's *Almagest* made available the works of Hellenistic scholars. To these were added the medical works of Galen. In addition to Aristotelian commentaries, there came from the Moslem world the summary of medicine written by Avicenna (*Canon of Medicine*), the mathematics of al-Khwarizmi, Albumazar's *Introduction to Astrology*, and many works on physics, perspective, optics, and alchemy. From the Byzantine world came the summary of Greek theology written by John of Damascus. By the beginning of the thirteenth century, therefore, western Europe had become a cultural crossroads.

The introduction of Greek and Moslem learning brought about the West's first major intellectual crisis, one whose character was to be often repeated. The learning introduced was by no means Christian. Aristotle, for example, upheld views contradicting orthodox Christianity. The Unmoved Mover of his *Metaphysics* was hardly to be equated with the Christian God. He held to a theory of the eternity of matter that made impossible the Christian account of God's creation of the world. His attitude toward the question of universals[21] was also contrary to the traditional realist point of view. He was not only a pagan humanist upholding doctrines antithetic to Christianity; he was introduced, in addition, by commentaries made by distinguished Moslem scholars like Avicenna and

[21]Cf. p. 643.

Averroës, who developed his notions in a non-Christian manner. Averroës, for example, had a difficult doctrine of the "active intellect" that denied personal immortality to the individual, assimilating the human mind to the divine mind in Neoplatonic fashion. The spirit of the new learning was rationalistic for the most part, and tempted smart students in the schools to upset Christian belief. Its content had much to do with science, to which the Christian tradition had been indifferent, if not hostile. What would be the effect of this new learning upon the authoritative Christian truth revealed by God in the Scriptures?

WESTERN REACTIONS TO THE NEW LEARNING

Men's reactions to a situation of this kind always vary. Those whose power and influence the new doctrines threaten most directly try to prevent their dissemination. Many times in the thirteenth century the Church tried to prevent works containing what it regarded as dangerous doctrines from being read in classes at the new University of Paris. There always are those, also, whom the novelty of new and revolutionary ideas so captivates that they abandon the old for the new. Such, in Paris, were a small group who clung to the views of Averroës, and are thus known as the Averroists. In 1277 the Church felt obliged to condemn a long list of their errors (219), including such propositions as: "There is no higher life than the philosophic life"; "There are no wisdoms in the world except that of the philosophers"; "Nothing should be believed, save only that which either is self evident, or can be deduced from self-evident propositions"; "Christian Revelation is an obstacle to learning"; "One knows nothing more for knowing theology"; and "Theology rests upon fables." John of Jandun, who worked with Marsiglio of Padua on the *Defensor Pacis*, remarked, "I do believe that that is true; but I cannot prove it. Good luck to those who can. . . . I say that God can do that, but how, I don't know. God knows." Clever logicians claimed to be able to prove the existence of the Trinity in one breath and its nonexistence in another. One of the English translators interested in science, Adelard of Bath, expressed the spirit of many in a letter to a nephew: "It is hard to discuss with you, for I have learned one thing from the Arabs under the guidance of reason; you follow another halter, caught by the appearance of authority; for what is authority but a halter?"[22]

There are also those with compartmental minds who can hold to the theory of two truths: for example, that what is true in theology is not necessarily true in philosophy, and vice versa. Each establishes and teaches its own kind of truth. On the whole, however, the western Christian scholar took a liberal rather than an obscurantist or radical point of view. He did not reject the rationalist approach. He did not reject the new

[22]Reprinted from *Reason and Revelation in the Middle Ages*, pp. 63–64, by E. H. Gilson; used by permission of the publishers, Charles Scribner's Sons.

learning. He simply insisted, as did Saint Thomas Aquinas, that there were two realms of learning. One was built up from material furnished by our senses and was called natural theology (or philosophy); the other was built up from the authoritative revelation of God and was called revealed theology. There could not be two equally valid systems of truth. Natural and revealed theology were complementary and not contradictory, with revelation retaining a position of primacy. The moderates thus welcomed the new learning and at the same time retained their Christian belief. They argued, as the Christian Fathers had argued with respect to Latin learning, that the new learning must be put to the use of Christianity. It must not, however, be permitted to destroy it. Natural theology should go as far as it can go to establish the rationality of Christian faith, utilizing all knowledge to aid it. But because it cannot establish the rationality of all the articles of faith, it is not to reject those that appear irrational. These are to be accepted on faith, or made the object of the mystic's intuitive assent. They cannot be made completely clear until the Hereafter.

SCHOLASTICISM

The method used by the moderate scholars to Christianize the new learning is called *scholasticism*, and they themselves, *scholastics*. Their works took the form of commentaries upon the chief theological textbook of the schools, the *Sentences* of Peter Lombard, itself largely a collection of excerpts from the Fathers illustrating the divergences in the Christian tradition. They also wrote encyclopedias incorporating the new material, thus continuing the work of Isidore. More especially, they composed monumental summaries of theology. We may take two of the works of the greatest of scholastic philosophers, Saint Thomas Aquinas, to illustrate the scholastic method and approach: the one he wrote against the Averroists (the *Summa contra Gentiles*) and his own *Summary of Theology* (*Summa Theologiae*). Of especial interest to us are Saint Thomas's rational approach to theology as illustrated by his treatment of the problem of the existence of God, and his statement of the ultimate otherworldly and mystical end of man.

THE "SUMMARY OF THEOLOGY" OF SAINT THOMAS AQUINAS

Part I of the *Summary of Theology* consists of twenty-six questions concerning *God: The Divine Unity*. The first of these concerns "The Nature and Domain of Sacred Doctrine" and is divided into ten articles. The first article asks the fundamental question, "Whether, besides the philosophical sciences, any further doctrine is required?" Aquinas proceeds with two statements (objections), giving a negative answer to the question. The first objection, or negative statement, is in the form of a syllogism, arguing that we have no need of more than philosophy, "For man should not seek to know what is above reason," and since "whatever is not above reason is sufficiently considered in the philosophical sciences, . . . any other knowledge besides the philosophical sciences is superfluous." The two objections are followed by an opposing, affirmative argument in the form of a syllogism beginning with a quotation from Scripture. "On the contrary, it is written (2 Tim. iii:16): All Scripture inspired of God is profitable to teach, to reprove, to correct, to instruct in justice. Now Scripture, inspired of God, is not a part of the philosophical sciences discovered by human reason. Therefore it is useful that besides the philosophical sciences there should be another science—*i.e.*, inspired of God." Aquinas concludes, "I answer that . . . in order that the salvation of men might be brought about more fitly and more surely, it was necessary that they be taught divine truths by divine revelation. It was therefore necessary that, besides the philosophical disciplines investigated by reason, there should be a sacred doctrine by way of revelation." This passage is followed by Aquinas's answer to the two preceding objections (negative propositions). To the first he says, "Reply Obj. I. Although those things which are beyond man's knowledge may not be sought for by man through his reason, nevertheless, what is revealed by God must be accepted through faith." (I, 5-6)[23] The method pursued by the author is the same for each question: first, the negative or affirmative propositions, then the opposite propositions, then Aquinas' answer, and finally further answers to the first propositions.

The eighth article of the first question asks, "Whether sacred doctrine is argumentative?" In proof of "Objection 1. It seems this doctrine is not argumentative," a quotation from Ambrose is used: "Put arguments aside where faith is sought." Objection 2 is stated, "Further, if it is argumentative, the argument is either from authority or from reason. If it is from authority, it seems unbefitting its dignity, for the proof from authority is the weakest form of proof according to Boethius. But if from reason, this is unbefitting its end, because, according to Gregory, faith has no merit in those things of which human reason brings its own experience. Therefore sacred doctrine is not argumentative." The opposing (affirmative) answer is a quotation from Scripture: "On the contrary, the Scripture says that a bishop should embrace that faithful word which is according to doctrine, that he may be able to exhort in sound doctrine and to convince the gainsayers (Tit. i: 9)." Aquinas's answer reads: "I answer that, as the other sciences do not argue in proof of their principles, but argue from their principles to demonstrate other truths in these sciences, so this doctrine does not argue in proof of its principles, which are articles of faith, but from them it goes on to prove something else. . . . Since faith rests upon infallible truth, and since the contrary of a truth can never be demonstrated, it is clear that the proofs brought against faith are not demonstrations, but arguments that can be answered." In his answer to

[23]Citations from Aquinas in my text are to *Basic Writings of Saint Thomas Aquinas*, ed. A. C. Pegis, 2 vols.

Objection 2 he states, "sacred doctrine also makes use of human reason, not, indeed, to prove faith (for thereby the merit of faith would come to an end), but to make clear other things that are set forth in this doctrine. Since therefore grace does not destroy nature, but perfects it, natural reason should minister to faith as the natural inclination of the will ministers to charity.... Hence it is that sacred doctrine that makes use also of the authority of philosophers in these questions in which they were able to know the truth by natural reason. ... Nevertheless, sacred doctrine makes use of these authorities as extrinsic and probable arguments, but properly uses the authority of the canonical Scriptures as a necessary demonstration, and the authority of the doctors of the Church as one that may properly be used, yet merely as probable. For our faith rests upon the revelation made to the apostles and prophets, who wrote the canonical books, and not on the revelations (if any such there are) made to other doctors." (I, 12–14)

AQUINAS ON THE EXISTENCE OF GOD

Aquinas's second general question has to do with "The Existence of God." Its first article asks, "Whether the existence of God is self-evident?" Aquinas answers that "because we do not know the essence of God, the proposition is not self-evident to us, but needs to be demonstrated by things that are more known to us ... namely, by His effects." The second article asks, "Whether it can be demonstrated that God exists? Aquinas says yes, because "every effect depends upon its cause." If, therefore, the effect exists, "the cause must pre-exist. Hence the existence of God, in so far as it is not self-evident to us, can be demonstrated from those of His effects which are known to us." The third article puts the crucial question "Whether God exists." Aquinas answers negatively in two objections. The first uses the argument that "if one of two contraries be infinite, the other would be altogether destroyed. ... The name God means that He is infinite goodness. If, therefore, God existed, there would be no evil discoverable; but there is evil in the world. Therefore God does not exist." The second objection argues that "all natural things can be reduced to one principle, which is nature; and all voluntary things can be reduced to one principle, which is human reason or will. Therefore there is no need to suppose God's existence." For the opposite proposition Aquinas quotes Exodus iii: 14. "It is said in the person of God: I am Who am." Ignoring Saint Anselm's proof of the existence of God, Aquinas answers that "the existence of God can be proved in five ways." (I, 19–22)

GOD AS THE FIRST MOVER

By his first argument Aquinas arrives at Aristotle's Unmoved Mover. It is the argument from motion. "It is certain," he says, "that in the world some things are in motion. ... whatever is moved must be moved by another. If that by which it is moved be itself moved, then this also must needs be moved by another, and that by another again. But this cannot go on to infinity, because then there would be no first mover, and, consequently, no other mover, seeing that subsequent movers move only inasmuch as they are moved by the first mover; as the staff moves only because it is moved by the hand. Therefore it is necessary to arrive at a first mover, moved by no other; and this everyone understands to be God."

GOD AS THE FIRST EFFICIENT CAUSE

Aquinas's second argument is a restatement of that from motion in terms of Aristotle's efficient cause.[24] "In the world of sensible things we find there is an order of efficient causes. There is no case known (neither is it, indeed, possible) in which a thing is found to be the efficient cause of itself; for so it would be prior to itself, which is impossible. . . . Now to take away the cause is to take away the effect. Therefore, if there be no first cause among efficient causes, there will be no ultimate, nor any intermediate, cause. But if in efficient causes it is possible to go on to infinity, there will be no efficient cause, neither will there be an ultimate effect, nor any intermediate efficient causes; all of which is plainly false. Therefore it is necessary to admit a first efficient cause, to which everyone gives the name of God." (I, 22)

GOD AS THE ORIGINAL NECESSITY

The third argument is a restatement of the previous two in terms of "possibility and necessity." "If," Aquinas argues, "at one time nothing was in existence, it would have been impossible for anything to have begun to exist; and thus even now nothing would be in existence—which is absurd. Therefore, not all beings are merely possible, but there must exist something the existence of which is necessary. . . . Now it is impossible to go on to infinity in necessary things which have their necessity caused by another, as has been already proved in regard to efficient causes. Therefore we cannot but admit the existence of some being having of itself its own necessity, and not receiving it from another, but rather causing in others their necessity. This all men speak of as God.

GOD AS THE MAXIMUM

"The fourth way is taken from the gradation to be found in things. Among beings there are some more and some less good, true, noble and the like. But *more* and *less* are predicated of different things according as they resemble in their different ways something which is the maximum . . . so that there is something which is truest, something best, something noblest, and, consequently something which is most being for those things that are greatest in truth are greatest in being, as it is written in Metap. II

[24]See pp. 146 f.

[the Metaphysics of Aristotle]. Now the maximum in my genus is the cause of all in that genus. . . . Therefore there must also be something which is to all beings the cause of their being, goodness, and every other perfection; and this we call God.

GOD AS THE SUPREME ARCHER

"The fifth way is taken from the governance of the world. We see that things which lack knowledge, such as natural bodies, act for an end. . . . They achieve their end not fortuitously, but designedly. Now whatever lacks knowledge cannot move towards an end, unless it be directed by some being endowed with knowledge and intelligence; as the arrow is directed by the archer. Therefore some intelligent being exists by whom all natural things are directed to their end, and this being we call God." (I, 23)

AQUINAS AND THE KNOWLEDGE OF GOD

In this proof for the existence of God not much is left of the personal God who loves his creatures as they love him. God is the Unmoved Mover, First Cause, First Principle of Necessity, the Maximum of Being, and the Supreme Archer. The relationship established between this God and mankind is a completely theocratic and ascetic one. Although God may thus be proved to exist by rational means, according to Aquinas, he cannot be known in this life by natural reason. In answering the question (Article 12 of Question 12) "How God is known by us?" Aquinas says, "Our natural knowledge begins from sense. Hence our natural knowledge can go as far as it can be led by sensible things. But our intellect cannot be led by sense so far as to see the essence of God. . . . Hence from the knowledge of sensible things the whole power of God cannot be known; nor therefore can His essence be seen. But because they are His effects and depend on their cause, we can be led from them so far as to know of God whether He exists, and to know of Him what must necessarily belong to Him, as the first cause of all things, exceeding all things caused by Him." (I, 109) God can be known—and to know God is the end of life— only in the afterlife, and then not through reason, but through mystic contemplation.

AQUINAS ON MAN'S ULTIMATE HAPPINESS

In his *Summary against the Gentiles* Aquinas concludes that "man's ultimate happiness consists in the contemplation of truth." By the contemplation of truth is not meant trying to understand "first principles," for they lead only to an understanding of things. "Moreover, [trying to understand "first principles"] is the beginning and not the end of human inquiry, and comes to us from nature, and not through the pursuit of truth. . . . Man's ultimate happiness consists in wisdom, based on the consideration of divine things." It "consists solely in the contemplation of God." This happiness cannot be achieved in this life. The happiness that Aristotle talks about in the *Ethics*[25] is only an imperfect kind of human happiness. However, man is "able to reach perfect happiness after this life, since man has an immortal soul," and this happiness consists in a "knowledge of God which the human mind possesses after this life." The contemplation of God in heaven is but another name for the "beatific vision." It brings all knowledge at once, in a flash. This vision, moreover, "takes place in a kind of participation of eternity. . . . Those who obtain ultimate happiness from the divine vision never fall away from it." In the "happy state which results from the divine vision, man's every desire is fulfilled and his every end achieved. . . . In this life there is nothing so like this ultimate and perfect happiness as the life of those who contemplate the truth, as far as that is possible in this life." But "the contemplation of truth which begins in this life . . . will be consummated in the life to come." (II, 60)

REASON AND REVELATION IN AQUINAS

Thus Aquinas, in his approach to learning, was not afraid of rationality and not afraid of the new Greek and Arabic learning. This was not because he had any large confidence in the powers of human reason or in the ability of expanding secular knowledge to make the world more intelligible. Reason and secular learning were all right in their place, and their place was subordinate and auxiliary to God's revelation in Scripture as interpreted by the Church. Human reason could not go very far on this earth, and what man could come to understand here was not very important. The understanding of all things came only in the life to come. It came not through reason but through the sight of God, the beatific vision that brought immediate comprehension and joined one eternally to the Godhead. This was the mystic's "ecstatic swoon into the absolute" made permanent. However rational Aquinas's approach might be, it ended in mysticism. However much it accepted Aristotle's aid, it subordinated him to Plotinus and Augustine and to the irrationality of faith in divine revelation. Still, in providing a place, however subordinate, for the exercise of human reason within the Christian system, and in encouraging the enlargement of the bounds of secular knowledge in the West, Aquinas was taking the large, liberal view of his time. He was combatting the persecuting obscurantists who wished to keep men in ignorance, and those with compartmental minds who held to two systems of truth, a religious and a secular. His separation of natural from revealed theology made room for the pursuit of a philosophy independent of theology. For difficulties in working out a theology based upon evidence from the senses would lead to a shift from knowledge of God to knowledge of nature.

[25]See pp. 143 f.

Saint Thomas was the son of an Italian nobleman, and had entered the Dominican order as a youth. This order, founded to combat heretics, decided to capture the field of learning as well as preaching. At the moment when universities were first being established it sent its superior sons to study at these centers in order to become the leading scholars and teachers of the day. The Franciscans, despite the attitude of Saint Francis toward learning, soon followed this example. The rivalry between Dominican and Franciscan was thus intensified in the academic arena. Saint Thomas's most influential teacher was a German noble, Albert the Great (Albertus Magnus), an active churchman as well as a scholar who taught at Cologne and the University of Paris. Born in 1193, Albert came to maturity at the time when the great bulk of Greek and Arabic learning had been translated. He saw clearly that this material had to be made available to the West in a Christian form. He undertook, therefore, to write extensive commentaries on the works of Aristotle not only to make clear what Aristotle meant but also to explain that his doctrine was not offensive to orthodox Christian thought. His commentaries, however, turned out to be paraphrases rather than elucidations of a text, and Saint Thomas, in his various commentaries, accomplished what his master really left undone.

Albert was not only one of those anxious to absorb the new learning. He was also interested in its scientific aspects; and his acquaintance with Greek and Arabic mathematics and science stimulated in him a critical attitude marking the beginning of western science, in so far as that science realizes that authority, in order to be good authority, has to be tested with facts derived from observation and experiment. It is clear that Albert understood this. He says, in one instance, "We pass over what the ancients have written on this topic because their statements do not agree with experience." In a book on animals, he says that he is going to relate "what he knows by reason and what he sees by experience of the nature of animals." In one on plants, he remarks that "We satisfy the curiosity of our students rather than philosophy, for philosophy cannot deal with particulars." Science to him was not "simply receiving what one is told, but the investigation of causes in natural phenomena."[26] Adelard of Bath was likewise concerned with this question of causes. "The mind imbued with wonder and a sense of unfamiliarity, shudderingly contemplates from a distance effects without regard to the causes, and so never shakes off its perplexity. Look more closely, to the circumstances in their totality, set forth causes and then you will not be surprised at effects" was Adelard's good advice.[27]

[26]Lynn Thorndike, *A History of Magic and Experimental Science*, II, Chap. 59, pp. 517–593.
[27]M. H. Carré, *Phases of Thought in England*, pp. 76–77.

These "causes in natural phenomena" the medieval scientist did not feel were a world apart from, indifferent, or hostile to God. They were, in fact, the manner in which God operated the universe, and the scientist understood them as but a means of understanding the workings of God and therefore God himself. This did not mean, however, that these men and others like them did not remain primarily interested in the causes, whether they were ultimately those of God or not. A science dominated by a new spirit was, in fact, being born. It no longer needed to be concerned, as Augustine and the earlier Fathers wished it to be, simply with the elucidation of the Scriptures or with the Christian point of view. It was now lifted to the larger field of investigating causes, knowing that the causes discovered were inevitably divine causes. In the same manner, Albert's pupil Saint Thomas spoke of a natural theology or philosophy that, utilizing the new learning, might also contribute to a knowledge of theology, the Queen of Sciences. Science and philosophy, together concentrating upon their own special fields of investigation, would facilitate the comprehension of the Deity.

SCIENCE AT OXFORD

It was not so much the Dominicans, however, as the Franciscans who interested themselves in the fields of mathematics and science, and this in spite of the fact that they adhered to the older Augustinianism rather than to the newer scholasticism. Of the various Franciscan centers at the universities, the one at Oxford went farthest in the promotion of a scientific outlook. Its first member was the leading teacher of the University, Robert Grosseteste, who together with another member of the school, Adam Marsh, sought, it was said, "to unfold the causes of all things by the power of mathematics." It was said of Grosseteste, also, that he could not help but smile at the anxiety of those who sought to make Aristotle a good Christian. He was quite well aware of the ignorance of contemporary theologians of the writings of early Christianity, he himself belonging to that group who sought the inspiration of direct contact with the Scriptures and the earliest Christian writers. He realized the unsatisfactory nature of the translations from the Arabic, advocated direct translation from Greek, and translated some Aristotle from Greek himself. His critical bent was passed on to his best-known student, Roger Bacon.

ROGER BACON

A difficult and muddled person, Bacon in his fundamental religious outlook was as conservative as any of his colleagues. But he had a glimpse of what the new science had to offer and let his imagination stray into the far-distant future. He followed Grosseteste in his criticism of contemporary theologians. These preferred to study Peter Lombard's *Sentences* rather than Scripture. "Any one who would lecture on Scripture has to beg for a room and hour to be set him." They had to rely on translations of theological and philosophical works, when they ought to be able to read the original tongues themselves. Bacon spared the mathematicians and medical doctors no more than the theologians. The exciting parts of his writings, however, are not his attacks on his colleagues but his talk about the importance of experience and experiment to knowledge. He talks about an "experimental science which neglects arguments since they do not make certain," a science that seeks "by observation and experiment the lofty conclusions of all sciences." "Argument draws a conclusion and forces us to concede it, but does not make it certain or remove doubt, so that the mind may rest in the perception of truth, unless the mind find truth by the way of experience." Bacon was an experimenter himself and may have possessed a telescope or microscope. He wrote of "machines for navigating . . . without rowers, so that great ships, suited to river or ocean, guided by one man, may be borne with greater speed than if they were full of men. Likewise cars may be made so that without a draught animal they may be moved with unthinkable speed. . . . And flying machines are possible, so that a man may sit in the middle turning some device by which artificial wings may beat in the air in the manner of a flying bird."[28] Roger Bacon saw the utility of science not only for theology but also, if less emphatically than his later colleague, Francis Bacon, for all human life, and in this emphasis upon the relationship of science to the enrichment of human life he came close to the view of the subsequent scientific humanist.

MAGIC, ASTROLOGY, AND ALCHEMY

Albert the Great and Roger Bacon might talk about the necessity of going beyond authority to test conclusions with the facts of experience and experiment; not much of the latter was actually done. What we understand by scientific research hardly existed. The real "scientific" mood of the period is to be sought in the numerous treatises on magic, astrology, and alchemy, subjects of whose utility and importance the best minds were convinced. It may well be true that the pursuit of magic, astrology, and alchemy ultimately contributed to the advancement of science, but if so, then by wrong methods that had to be corrected, and with mischievous results that had to be overthrown. If useful information was discovered, as for example in alchemy, it was more often by accident rather than the result of purposeful experiment. The importance of magic, astrology, and alchemy in civilized societies today is but a reminder of how recently we have emerged from an intellectual environment in which these things were taken quite seriously. There are few men even today who can do without an occasional miracle or bit of magic to temper the cruel im--

[28]H. O. Taylor, *The Mediaeval Mind*, II, 532, 538.

personality of an inexorable natural law. Western man resisted for a long time the restrictions he claimed were put upon his mind by the rationality of modern science.

Saint Thomas, for example, whom we have taken to represent the scholastic mind at its best, could not quite throw aside magic. He goes out of his way to show "that the works of magicians do not result only from the influence of heavenly bodies. . . . In the works of magicians, doings appear that are exclusively the work of a rational nature; for instance, answers are given about stolen goods, and the like, and this could not be done except through an intellect. Therefore it is not true that all such effects are caused by the mere force of a heavenly body." In trying to get at the source of the efficiency of magicians, Aquinas argues that since "by learning we acquire, not the power to do a thing but the knowledge of how to do it," and since "some, by learning are rendered able to perform these magic works; therefore they must have only knowledge, and not the power, to produce these effects." Aquinas concludes therefore "that these effects are accomplished by an intellect to whom the discourse of the person uttering these [magical] words is addressed." Aquinas is not willing to say that the intellect which gives efficacy to the practices of magic is good "according to virtue." But neither is it actually evil. Rather than dwell on how these "intellectual substances, which we are wont to call demons or devils," may be unnaturally evil, Saint Thomas prefers "even though they are employed in order to further adultery, theft, murder and like malefices," and even though they "befriend and assist men of evil life, rather than any upright man," to be content to describe them as "not well disposed according to virtue." (II, 204, 207)

TRANSLATION OF WORKS ON ASTROLOGY

Saint Thomas illustrates also the changed attitude toward astrology that was introduced by the new learning. The influence of the astrologer grew considerably in later Roman society, and it was combatted without compromise by the early Christian Fathers. That man should be subject to a a fate determined by the movement of the heavens was a principle denying the power and providence of God as well as the limited freedom of the will that Christian theologians were willing to grant to men. But this hostility was softened when the treatises on astrology from the Hellenistic and Arabic worlds were introduced into the West and seemed, in turn, to be substantiated by certain treatises of Aristotle. Ptolemy's *Almagest* was the authoritative treatise on astronomy translated in the twelfth century. Ptolemy also wrote a serious work on astrology, called the *Tetrabiblos*.[29] This was translated in 1138 by Plato of Tivoli, be-

[29]See p. 153.

cause "The Latins . . . have not a single author [in astronomy]; for books they have only follies, dreams, and old wives' fables." Adelard of Bath, whose scientific temper we have already mentioned, translated into Latin the *Isagoge Minor* of Albumazar, "one of the standard textbooks of Arabian astrology." Herman of Dalmatia translated Albumazar's *Introduction to Astronomy*, a textbook on astrology than which no other "did more to make astrology acceptable to the church of the succeeding century."[30] Gerard of Cremona, the most prolific of the translators, translated the *Almagest* and the two treatises of Aristotle that helped make astrology seem quite reasonable and scientific: the *Meteorology* and *On Generation and Corruption*.

ALBUMAZAR ON ASTROLOGY

Aristotle's *Meteorology* and *On Generation and Corruption* had been introduced into astrology by the Arabs. Albumazar, in his *Introduction to Astronomy*, explains how the transparent and spherical stars, composed of a special fifth essence (this notion is Aristotle's, a substance that is neither earth, air, fire, nor water), move in a perpetual circular motion. When mixed together, the four elements beneath the celestial sphere are subject to the circular motion of generation and corruption. This motion runs in cycles, the degeneration of one substance becoming the generation of another, which in its turn degenerates, and then generates what was previously. It is the circular motion of the stars that determines this circular motion of generation and corruption, and thus influences all change. Aristotle had drawn a distinction between the regular motion of the fixed stars and the irregular motion of the planets. It was the planets that were responsible for change, and the stars that were responsible for the element of permanence. Albumazar, in explaining how "All that is born and dies on earth depends upon the motion of the constellations and of the stars," says that "To the sphere of the constellations is assigned a general rule; whereas to the wandering stars belongs the care over the details of earthly life. . . . The more rapidly a planet moves, and the stranger the course which it follows, the more powerful will be its influence on things below. The motion of the moon is swifter than that of any other planet; it has, accordingly, more to do than any other in regulating mundane affairs." Albumazar did not deny that, in addition to necessary actions determined by the movement of the heavens, there were also unpredictable, contingent actions that were influenced by the stars. Man has a reasoning soul that thinks and chooses for itself and rules over the body. But he points out that Aristotle teaches that the stars have a reasoning soul and a circular motion, and thus have the "power to modify the harmony existing between man's body and his soul."[31]

[30]T. O. Wedel, *The Medieval Attitude toward Astrology*, pp. 49, 50–51.
[31]Wedel, pp. 57–59.

The conservative Christian attitude toward astrology is to be seen in the treatise of the Englishman Alexander Neckam on the *Nature of Things*. "Let it not be supposed that the planets decide things here below by any inevitable law of necessity. . . . For the divine will is the unalterable and primal cause of things, to which not only the planets show obedience, but also created nature as a whole. It must be understood that, although superior bodies have some influence over inferior ones, yet the will is free [*arbitrium animae*], and is not impelled by necessity either this way or that."[32] With these limitations, astrology was welcomed with Ptolemy, Albumazar, and Aristotle.

AGRICULTURAL IMPROVEMENTS

The true medieval scientists were the peasant and the artisan who, from their own observation and deduction, discovered ways to improve the work on the farm and in the workshop, and inaugurated there the modern mechanization of the western world brought about by invention and technology. The advantages of the three-field over the two-field system of agriculture were discovered during the Carolingian period. It is difficult to believe that before the late ninth or early tenth centuries plowing was based on a system of harnessing so crude that if more than a force of seventy pounds was exerted by one horse he was in danger of choking. It was at this time that the horse collar was invented. The invention of the tandem harness and the horseshoe contributed further to facilitate the drawing of "the northern wheeled plow equipped with colter [or knife] to cut the grassy surface, horizontal plow-share for cutting the furrow itself, and a moldboard for turning over and pulverizing the soil."[33] With the cruder plows of ancient times the field had to be plowed twice, and the result was a square field. The northern plow made possible the strip of the manorial fields, and when drawn by oxen necessitated co-operative methods in plowing, for one peasant could not afford enough oxen to draw this plow. Together, the invention of the three-field system and the horse collar may have had much to do with making possible an increase in population and ultimately the rise of the medieval towns. The introduction of the stirrup during the early Middle Ages, an invention of the steppes, transformed horsemanship and the battle tactics based upon it.

WATER POWER

During the early Middle Ages the undershot and overshot water wheel sped northward from the lands surrounding the Mediterranean to become the power for grinding corn, moving the carpenter's saw, and operating the smith's bellows. They were joined by the windmill, an importation from

[32]Wedel, pp. 62, 67, 68, 69, 76.
[33]R. J. Forbes, *Man the Maker*, p. 110.

the East in the twelfth century. Water power was used for the tilt hammers and pounders used in fulling the cloth of the new textile industry, a
process that had to do with beating or compressing the woven cloth in
water, and that, before the use of the hammer, was done by feet, hands, or
clubs. Spinning was mechanized by the western invention of the spinning
wheel in the thirteenth century.

CAST IRON

"The greatest technical achievement of the Middle Ages was the production of cast iron."[34] It was made possible by the higher temperatures
produced in smelting furnaces when water wheels moved ever larger
bellows to force larger amounts of air into the furnaces. These new
methods made possible a regular production of Rhenish cast iron by 1300.
When gunpowder was invented in the West (1320–1330), cast iron became important in the manufacture of the early cannon, thus increasing
the problem of keeping an army up to date, and vastly speeding the
mechanization of warfare.

OTHER MEDIEVAL TECHNICAL IMPROVEMENTS

The medieval alchemist improved his distillation processes and produced alcohol, nitric acid, and, after 1150, sulfuric and muriatic acids.
The glassmaker enabled the chemist to improve his technique by improving the quality of glass and glazes. His stained glass provided the medium
for the great windows of the medieval cathedrals. The chemist improved
upon the Gaulish invention of soap, and made possible an active soap trade.
The Middle Ages also produced oil paints and increased the number of
pigments. "In the twelfth century the art of making white-lead paints
from lead and vinegar was discovered." "The development of the seagoing
sailing vessel is a major technical achievement of the Middle Ages,"[35] involving the invention of the rudder, which emancipated the size of the
sailing ship from the relation of man to steering oar, and made possible
the navigation of the open ocean. The introduction of paper from the
Arab world meant the end of parchment and vellum, and by the middle of
the fifteenth century printing from movable type had been invented by
Gutenberg or Coster. Altogether these are rather fundamental technological changes introduced into western life.

THE UNIVERSITY AND ITS CURRICULUM

The introduction of the new Greek and Arabic learning, combined with
other changes, brought about the formation of a new and precious institution in western Europe: the university. Hitherto the tradition of learn-

[34]Forbes, p. 117.
[35]Forbes, p. 130. Cf. E. H. Byrne, *Genoese Shipping in the Twelfth and Thirteenth
Centuries.*

ing and the business of teaching had been the work of the monastery and the cathedral school, and the student body consisted largely of future members of the clergy. The new books available to the reading public at the beginning of the thirteenth century expanded enormously the traditional curriculum of the schools. The grammar and rhetoric of the *trivium* were still taught from the manuals of Donatus and Priscian, but logic or dialectics could now make use of the New as well as the Old Logic of Aristotle. The *quadrivium* of the early Middle Ages was dominated by Boethius. Now arithmetic had the Arabic numerals, geometry Euclid's *Elements*, and astronomy Ptolemy's *Almagest*.[36] In addition to these, there were the new introductions into other phases of science, philosophy, and mathematics. These were made possible by works of Aristotle and Hellenistic and Arabic writers that did not fit nicely into the scheme of *trivium* and *quadrivium*. Here there was intellectual nourishment for more than the cleric. In addition, there was material for training in new secular professions. Peter Lombard's *Sentences* provided a textbook around which a course in theology could be built. The works of Hippocrates, Galen, and Avicenna formed the core for the training of the physician.[37] The discovery of the Justinian Code[38] in Italy in the eleventh century made possible the training of the civil lawyer, and Gratian's *Harmony of Conflicting Canons*, or *Decretum*, now afforded training in the canon law.

THE UNIVERSITY AND SOCIETY

The society out of which the university sprang was a semibarbarous, castelike, comparatively illiterate, and agrarian society struggling to emancipate itself from the limitations of centuries of political insecurity, the large estate, the domination of a feudal aristocracy, and the confinement of a narrow, ascetic point of view.[39] In shaking itself loose from the vested interests that thrived upon disorder, isolation, and ignorance, it created the university. A body of scholars was necessary to cultivate the new learning that now placed the West in the midst of the international intellectual world, and to discipline young minds in assimilating and passing on this heritage. The privileged position soon accorded these men acknowledged the insufficient character of a previous education in charge of monks and cathedral schools, training men only for the clergy. In their very enthusiasm for their task these scholars confessed the melancholy ignorance of earlier centuries and the unworthiness of the intellectual limitation that had characterized them. The prompt recognition of the university was an admission of the social value of the new learning to a society rapidly growing more complex.

[36]See p. 122 for origins of *trivium* and *quadrivium*.
[37]See pp. 153 ff.
[38]See pp. 252 ff.
[39]The following is taken from E. N. Johnson, "The Background of the University Tradition," in *Freedom and the University*.

THE UNIVERSITY, HERESY, AND PAGANISM

When the first universities were being founded, the Church, emerging victorious from its conflict with the empire, found itself challenged by heresy. Heresy was a state of mind involving conclusions about what Christianity and a church ought to be when compared with what Christianity and the Church actually were at the moment. Persuasion was necessary to deal with this state of mind. New methods of argument and a larger body of knowledge were now available. The trained theologian, in the person of the mendicant monk, proved to be the desirable and highly mobile weapon against heresy. It was, moreover, only the mature theologian who could defend intelligently old questions newly criticized. It is not surprising, therefore, that the theological faculty of the University of Paris should become the pampered child of the papacy. It is understandable that in the Albigensian territory of southern France a new Dominican University of Toulouse should add its argument to the sword of the crusader and the fire of the inquisitor. The Church was waging war, not only against heresy, but against the remains of heathendom in the countryside and on the frontier. When a new university was founded at Prague, it contained a large number of newly converted Lithuanians, and the masters of the University of Cracow found employment as bishops in Lithuania. The Teutonic Knights sought likewise to realize the advantages of having the professors follow up conquest with the proposed foundation of a university at Kulm, in Prussia. Only the trained priest or bishop could detect the remnants of ancient heathendom in the popular religion of the country folk.

CANON LAW AND THE CHURCH

The struggle with the empire was likewise argumentative and needed trained scholars. It was accompanied by the slow elaboration of a centralized administration for the ecclesiastical government of Europe. Both argument and the principles of administration were contained in the new works on the canon law now available for instruction of papalists and canon lawyers from whom the expanding hierarchy could draw its personnel. Together, then, the university courses in theology and canon law supplied the professional needs of an international institution that at the height of its influence seemed unable to adjust itself adequately to the new age.

THE UNIVERSITIES AND THE STATE

In its turn, the empire also needed argument to defend itself against the Church. Together with the rising monarchies of the West and the new towns, it sought to supplant primitive legal systems with the principles and procedure of the ancient imperial law. The day, moreover, when the Church could supply all the literate clerks and educated men necessary for the administration of new political institutions was over. The source of this new personnel was the group of lawyers educated in the Justinian Code. For the empire in its earlier days it was the University of Bologna that supplied the scholars who, because they knew what imperial law was, could guide the emperor in Italy. For the empire in its later days it was the state-created University of Naples that supplied the Roman precedent for Hohenstaufen absolutism and the officials for the complicated administration of the Kingdom of Southern Italy and Sicily. Since Paris had been reserved by the Church for theology, the servants of the French monarchy came chiefly from the law schools of Montpellier and Orléans. The universities of Germany opened up new careers for those strata of the population unable previously, because of the expense, to send their children to Italy or France for their higher instruction. These universities, in their turn, served the political needs of the rising German dynasts. The German Hanse founded its intellectual center in the University of Rostock, and in many an Italian town the university was founded or supported with the definite needs of the municipal administration in mind. Mayors, magistrates, judges, counselors, and ambassadors were drawn from the university circle. The payment of salaries to the law faculty was often contingent upon its giving legal advice. In these same towns there could also now be employed physicians trained in the new medicine.

THE NEW PROFESSIONS

For new and hitherto unimportant social strata possessed of the energy, ambition, and foresight to relate the new learning to social requirements here was the opportunity to create the professions of the theologian, the canonist, the lawyer, and the physician, to widen the middle classes of merchants, producers, and bankers, and to give them intellectual stature. Here was a further outlet for the capacities of the sons of the lesser nobility and the townsmen that gave some mobility to the class structure. The world, moreover, was in need not only of professions but also of a point of view adequate to its new environment. Preparation of this point of view required the collective effort of men concerned with all phases of knowledge, arguing over the nature of reality and the meaning of life. It required, in other words, an education for youth governed by philosophy and religion.

THE UNIVERSITY AS A GUILD

It is not merely in its attempt to release western Europe from its limitations that the tradition of the medieval university is to be sought but also in the spirit with which this attempt was made. The spirit of the university was that of the medieval guild. This is what the university first was: a guild, a society, a corporation (*universitas*). The earliest University of Paris was a group of teachers who undertook to provide those who wanted it with the learning at their command. They were carpenters of the mind. They arose quite spontaneously and freely when the desire and need for learning proved great enough. They undertook the organization of their guild in a democratic manner, elected their own officials, and assumed full responsiblity for laying down the necessary rules and regulations for those to follow who sought membership in the craft of teachers. The rules and regulations resulted in a prescribed curriculum of studies, in examinations for competence and for public admission into the guild. The student was the apprentice, or the journeyman. In a sense peculiar to the teacher's craft, he was also, when he had finished with his work, himself the masterpiece of his master. It was he, the masterpiece, whose task it was to produce other masterpieces. The university was thus a self-perpetuating, self-governing association of masters or students, or both. When once its free status had been secured and recognized, it sought fiercely to maintain this freedom over and against all who threatened to interfere with its doing its job as it saw fit.

UNIVERSITY OF BOLOGNA

Thus it was when the university of students at Bologna—which began as a students' corporation—found that its liberty to pursue learning as it saw fit was interfered with by the professors, who were in league for certain purposes with the citizens of Bologna. These professors, moreover, were not quite sufficiently aware of the need for these students to complete their work and get home to the jobs that awaited them. They did not understand the spirit of that Bologna student who, when summoned home to marry the girl his parents had chosen for him, replied that he did not have time to come. It would always be possible for him to secure a wife, but this was his one chance to get an education. The doctors did not start or end their lectures promptly. They liked to fill them with miscellaneous comment about bibliography. They did not cover the ground systematically. And, to use an example from another university, they often lectured too slowly. In addition, they were careless in missing class, whether by declaring holidays, or going off to a neighboring town on a vacation. These obstructions to expeditious learning brought back a unique student tyranny over teachers. Through a guild of students the professors were subordinated to the student rector, before whom, at any moment, they might be summoned out of their classes. They were instructed not to "create holidays at their pleasure" and, if they proposed to leave town, to deposit a sum of money to secure their return. In order to provide that the law texts were covered systematically, the professor was obliged at the beginning of a course to deposit ten Bologna pounds with the local banker. A time schedule for the lectures was then drawn up—so many lectures for a certain portion of the text. Should the poor doctor of the law get behind in his schedule, the banker, by order of the university officials, was obliged to deduct so much for each day's retardation. At

Paris it was not so easy to prescribe that lecturers should not drawl, but rather "bring out the words as rapidly as if nobody were writing before him." There were some students who wanted to take full notes. It was, therefore, thought wise to legislate against those who, "by shouting, hissing, groaning, and throwing stones," objected to speedy lecturers. At Bologna the students kept close watch on the professors through "denouncers of the doctors" (*denunciatores doctorum*).[40]

THE UNIVERSITY OF PARIS

The university of masters at Paris (here the university was first composed of teachers and not students) was fortunately able to avoid this melancholy state of affairs. Together with other universities of northern Europe, whose masters and students were regarded as clerics and thus amenable only to the jurisdiction of the Church, they had to struggle to maintain their privileged autonomy against the local hierarchy of the secular church: the officials of the cathedral chapters, the bishop, and the archbishop, and against the cardinals and legates of that Rome to which they often had to appeal for protection. They also had to protect themselves against the burghers, who more often resented their liberties and license than they understood the essential freedom for which they fought. Finally, they had to resist the encroachments of royal officials and ultimately of the king himself, who was their second final source of appeal.

THE UNIVERSITY'S STRUGGLE FOR LIBERTY

This fight on many fronts to preserve the liberty of the university, although in the end a losing one, was stubbornly conducted. Its chief weapons were *migration* and *cessation*. Professors who needed nothing much more than student fees to carry on their work were quick to move to another town when they felt their privileges locally abused. About half of the universities of medieval Europe, and among these some of the greatest, owe their foundation to this unwillingness on the part of teachers and students to tolerate any local oppression. When the matter was not important enough for an exodus or migration, it was often sufficient to stop lecturing (cessation). And while the refusal of the professors to go on talking was not always regarded as intolerable, revolting universities were never without a welcome elsewhere. The town council of Bologna finally tried to curb this impulse to get out, with the death penalty.

OXFORD AND WYCLIFFE

Some of the incidents of this large struggle for institutional freedom are worth citing. In the fourteenth century Oxford was the academic home of a master, John Wycliffe, whose heretical opinions the strenuous ef-

[40]For these and other illustrations, see Hastings Rashdall, *Universities of Europe in the Middle Ages*, eds. F. M. Powicke and A. B. Emden.

forts of neither pope nor archbishop could totally suppress. After Wycliffe's opinions had been condemned by Rome and by the archbishop of Canterbury, one of his former disciples, Nicholas Hereford, in a sermon before the University on Ascension Day, 1382, boldly asserted his sympathy with Wycliffe, as he had done on many occasions, and in his prayer deliberately omitted any mention of the pope. Yet he was not hindered in his progress toward a degree. On Corpus Christi of the same year he was again appointed to preach before the University by the chancellor, Robert Rugge. Before the day arrived, an order from the archbishop was served upon the chancellor directing him to publish the condemnation of Wycliffe's theses. The chancellor flatly refused to comply with the injunction. In his sermon on that day Hereford went on with his defense of Wycliffe, and "as the chancellor retired in state from S. Frideswide's [the church], followed by the whole concourse of doctors and masters, he made a point of waiting for the preacher at the church door, and walked home with him; 'laughing and great joy came upon the Lollards at such a sermon.'" The chancellor professed that he dared not, for fear of his life, publish the condemnation of Wycliffe in Oxford. "Then is Oxford," replied the archbishop, "the university of heresies, if she will not allow orthodox truths to be published."[41] In 1411 the archbishop, in spite of a papal exemption, cited the University to appear before him. The chancellor and the proctors refused to allow the archbishop to enter Oxford. The church at which they were to appear was fortified against him. The scholars appeared in the streets armed with bows and arrows and showed themselves quite prepared to use them against the primate and his retinue should the attempt be persisted in. When the town was laid under an interdict, a proctor broke open the doors of a University church and said Mass as usual. When the archbishop, complaining with "what insolency he had been received by a company of boys," took the matter to the king, who required the chancellor and proctors to resign, the University decreed a cessation, and when required to elect a new chancellor and proctors it persisted in its loyalty to Hereford and re-elected the old ones.

THE UNIVERSITY OF PARIS AND THE MONKS

The University of Paris had its difficulties with both the regular monks and the friars. Its masters and students were subject to attack from the Benedictines of St. Germain des Prés, who contested their right to walk and exercise in the fields outside the monastery gate. In 1278, "at the morrow of the Translation of S. Nicholas, the patron saint of scholars, the fields were crowded with the clerks [students] when the abbey bell was heard summoning the tenants and servants of the abbot and convent. By order of their black-robed masters an armed guard took possession of the only

[41]Rashdall, *Universities of Europe*, III, 127.

three gates which opened on to the Pré, so as to cut off the retreat of the scholars, while to the sound of horns and trumpets, and with shouts of 'death to the clerks' the convent and its retainers, headed by their provost, sallied forth upon the unarmed and defenseless boys and masters, and fell upon them with bow and arrow, club, sword, or iron-tipped stave. Many were badly wounded, some mortally, but they were nevertheless dragged off to the 'horrible dungeons' of the abbey. Those who fled (a doctor of divinity and a doctor of medicine were among them) were pursued far and wide over the country."[42] It was necessary to go to the king and papal legate and to threaten a cessation if redress were not granted within fifteen days.

PARIS AND THE FRIARS

It was as difficult to get the impudent friars to obey the statutes of the University as it was to get the chancellor of the cathedral chapter of Paris to respect its privileges. To tame the latter, an election of their own chancellor and even a dissolution of the University were tried. The general of the Dominicans complained that his friars were hard put to it in the course of their subjection. "It was dangerous for a friar to be seen abroad. . . . No sooner was he caught sight of . . . than he was surrounded by the human swarms that poured forth from every house and hostel in the narrow street 'hurrying as if to a spectacle.' Instantly the air was full of 'the tumult of shoutings, the barking of dogs, the roaring of bears, the hissing of serpents,' and every sort of insulting exclamation. Filthy rushes and straw off the floors of those unsavoury dwellings were poured upon the cowled heads from above; mud, stones, sometimes blows, greeted them from below." Arrows were shot against their convent, "which had henceforth to be guarded night and day by royal troops."[43]

OXFORD UNIVERSITY AND TOWN

The struggle between Oxford University and Oxford town was bitter and prolonged. It filled the coroner's rolls with records of murderous violence, which, when committed by the students, entailed for the majority "nothing worse . . . than being compelled to go to school at Cambridge." From intervention to protect the University from what is described as " 'air so corrupted and infected' by the filth in the streets 'that an abominable loathing' . . . is 'diffused among the aforesaid masters and scholars,' " and to ensure what was called "the correction of victuals" the University ultimately had to take over the virtual governance of the town.[44]

[42]Rashdall, III, 428.
[43]Rashdall, I, 389–390.
[44]Rashdall, III, 80.

Papal protection against one's local enemies was welcome enough, but not papal interference with local autonomy. A papal bull in 1221 had ordered the University of Paris to break a seal that the masters had recently made. When, four years later, a cardinal papal legate solemnly broke the University seal and forbade the University to make another, a mob of masters and scholars armed with swords and sticks attacked the legate's house, broke down the doors, and were about to get at the cardinal himself when the soldiers of the king arrived. It was a special satisfaction for the mere rector of the masters of arts at Paris when a dean of theology, who was also an archbishop and a papal legate, was "by the superior numbers and athletic prowess of the young Masters of Arts, and their younger pupils . . . forcibly expelled from the Rector's chair of State in the choir of S. Germain-des-Prés." After a riot or two the rector even succeeded in acquiring the dignity of sharing with the bishop of Paris the honor of bringing up the rear of public processions.

UNIVERSITIES AND INTELLECTUAL FREEDOM

The spirit of the early university is displayed not only in the defense of its institutional freedom but also, in so far as it was possible, against a powerful Church in the defense of its intellectual freedom. This is not to say that the medieval university distinguished itself in this struggle. At the very outset of university history it is discouraging to find Abélard— the man who was responsible for bringing to Paris the crowds of students who forced some form of organization upon the teachers—suffering the burning of his books and being sentenced to silence by what his students called a mumbling council of stupid, drunken prelates. It is no less disheartening to witness professors from the University of Paris, together with other university representatives, joining with other members of the Council of Constance to order the bones of a former professor at Oxford, John Wycliffe, exhumed and scattered to the winds, and to condemn to the stake for heresy a former rector of the University of Prague, John Huss. Nor is it edifying to watch these same professors of Paris, soon afterward, employing their learning to help condemn an illiterate young girl by the name of Joan.

Yet the class of teachers and scholars to which these men belonged played no mean part in raising the level of intelligence in the West, and in trying at least to remedy some of the evils of their day by forthright and courageous criticism and action. It has been pointed out above that[45] against the protests of the obscurantists they welcomed the opportunity to try to prove their faith intelligible and to reassert the right and dignity of man to be rational. Brushing aside the fears of those who did not know what Greek or Moslem philosophy and science might do to the untutored

[45]See p. 666.

minds of youth, they made the distinctions necessary to enable the whole new learning to be studied. Although the natural philosophy of Aristotle was proscribed at Paris by Rome, it was not so proscribed at Toulouse, and, in any case, masters went on teaching it in the arts course at Paris. Although the doctrines of Averroës were put on the black list at Paris early in the thirteenth century, they were at least current enough at a later date in the century to have to be repudiated in great volume, again and again. These professors did not, could not, stop talking about the essential problems of philosophy and theology. If, as a result of early controversy as to the nature of truth, the official theology of the Church became realist, that did not prevent the rise of a strong nominalist movement in the fourteenth century. In some of the German universities, at least, the dispute between realist and nominalist raged so hot that it was necessary to offer in the arts courses both a realist and nominalist approach to each book on philosophy and, for the sake of more than academic peace, to house the respective teachers and scholars separately.

PROFESSORS AND CHURCH REFORM

When, in spite of all they could do, that church that it was their chief task to serve began to become an offense to a growing number of western Christians, they again tried to reinvigorate it. It was in great part the work of the University of Paris that prepared public opinion in Europe for the great experiment of taking the organization of the Church out of the hands of decadent theocrats and turning it over to a council. Professors like John Wycliffe and John Huss not only sought to provide in the learned fields of philosophy and theology the principles for a revision of Christian belief; they also, as popular preachers, writers, and organizers, sought to kindle in the hearts of simple men the warmth of a more personal faith. In this regard, theirs was the harvest of a later day.

HUMANISM AND ASCETICISM AGAIN

It is now necessary to turn to the question posed in the first paragraph of this chapter, namely, whether the intellectual and educational development of the later Middle Ages tended to support harmony or discord between humanism and asceticism. Certainly, in trying to stress the rationality of Christianity, men like Anselm, Abélard, Albert the Great, and Saint Thomas were strengthening the efforts of some earlier Fathers to avoid limiting Christianity to the blind acceptance of what the Church took the revelation of God in the Scriptures to mean. Man had the ability to reason, and he should exercise this ability upon the articles of the faith. Man was also avid for knowledge, and there was no reason why he should not absorb the new learning and apply it as best he could to the support of the Christian outlook. This was a humanistic emphasis. But it never went so far as to suggest that the ascetic outlook could be questioned or corrected in its fundamentals. Reason was not to be permitted, on the basis of the wider knowledge, to suggest an outlook independent of Christianity. This would be heresy. Thus we must say that the fundamental dichotomy between humanism and asceticism remained, even if in the minds of some there was a fine confidence in the rationality and curiosity of the human being.

REASON AND FAITH

Upon further thought, however, it is clear that the dichotomy was actually widened. When Bishop Tempier of Paris, in 1277, felt obliged to condemn the errors of the Averroists, he included in his long list some errors that were held by Aquinas and his followers. Aquinas was also condemned at Oxford for some of his views. The Franciscans and many others were scandalized at the boldness with which he used the Aristotelian logic and learning to rationalize the tenets of the Christian faith. What might not a man do with Christian dogma who tackled the question of the existence of God as Aquinas tackled it! Indeed, Saint Thomas's scholastic theology produced an immediate reaction in intellectual circles from realism to nominalism, and from the emphasis upon the rational quality of Christian dogma to its lack of rationality. Christianity could not be proved; it could only be accepted upon faith. This, then, was to say that the efforts of Saint Thomas and all rationalists were in vain. There was no harmony between reason and faith; Christianity was not rational. Such an attitude opened the way for an extensive development of mysticism at the end of the Middle Ages.[46] It opened the way also for the development of an independent philosophy on the part of those who clung to the notion that man's reason was not helpless in building up a point of view. Those men who from now on took up the fields of science for study, who concentrated upon those natural causes that were assumed without further proof to be divine, strengthened the split between reason and faith. The principles of science were not revealed by God in Scripture. Faith in an authoritarian interpretation did not discover them. At this moment there began in the West a study of science independent of theology. The time was not far distant when the independent philosophy and the independent science were to join hands. At the close of the thirteenth century, therefore, it became clear that Christian asceticism could not absorb all the tenets of classical humanism. Nevertheless, this asceticism was not yet seriously challenged or attacked, and philosophy and science continued to accept its chief teachings. But that any real harmony could be established between humanism and asceticism was shown to be unlikely. That did not mean that men would stop trying. If Christianity could not absorb enough humanism to become fundamentally humanistic, perhaps humanism could absorb enough Christianity to remain Christian.

[46]See pp. 766 ff.

Most of these attempts and the debates over them were to be carried on in the new universities. It could be maintained that in the very long run the universities tended to support the humanistic outlook. Yet this would be a gross simplification. Universities became notoriously conservative institutions. Many were ecclesiastical to begin with, and preserved the ascetic outlook. Many have remained so. The fundamental debate still goes on within their walls, and it has not been decided. The university was the original home of scholasticism, the new mathematics, and science. Its tradition was receptive to the new learning, and, in spite of all obstacles, continued to be so. In other respects the early university established a tradition that remains vital today. It was a strong support of the leading international institutions of its day. Despite its local diversity, the university was itself an international institution. Its great professors moved with ease from one university to another. Its student bodies were recruited from all countries. Membership in the guild of one great university made one a member of the international guild of teachers and scholars, with the right to teach anywhere (*ius ubique docendi*). The language of the university, Latin, was an international one. We may perhaps again expect a time when all students will consider it a privilege to be as proficient in an international tongue as was the medieval freshman, who had to be able "to read, sing, and construe well" his Latin and compose "in it twenty-four verses on one subject in a day."

THE TRADITION OF THE UNIVERSITY

In a world dominated by force the university was a new instrument of persuasion. It enabled subsequent generations to complete the recovery of the classical tradition. Its rationalism was a foundation for the triumphs of the enlarged rationalism of the eighteenth century. With its theology and philosophy, it spent a good deal of its time preparing its students to grapple with the fundamental problems of life. It insisted that its professional training should come only after the acquisition of a philosophical outlook. It constituted itself a collective debating society in order to determine what were the important decisions upon which all action and thought had to be based. While the university has never since ceased to be an instrument of persuasion in a world dominated by force, it has abandoned much of the above tradition.

Not only a system of higher education integrated by philosophy and theology, the medieval university was also a corporation of teachers and students, a guild, or craft, founded on the principle of freedom of association, governing itself in a democratic manner, an autonomous body of scholars. In the course of its history it has lost much of this freedom to the twin powers of church and state. The great divergency in the traditions of western Europe and eastern Europe is to be explained, in part, by the fact that the West had universities with a strong tradition of freedom when the East had no universities at all. Neither the ruling groups of our own society nor the professors and students dare forget what a university first was and still is, even if only a few authentic universities remain.

Finally, the medieval university was the product of a feudal society's widening the base of its class structure. It contributed to this widening in its training of men for the new professions. At no time did it stand aloof from the major problems agitating this society. Rather, in its most vigorous moments it was helping to direct, often in conscious opposition to the status quo, the important courses of events. The university's obligation to keep widening the base of our present-day democratic class structure is a part of its tradition. Its obligation to help direct society persists to an even more formidable degree, now that the intellectual foundations of our culture are being molded in great degree by the technological media of mass communication. The tradition of the medieval university, as a part of the larger western tradition, comes to us in phrases that the cynical and disillusioned have made trite, but which are not and can never be trite for as long as men choose to give any meaning or promise to human existence: the subordination of the local to the international community; the obligation to persuade rather than to force, and thus to control passion with reason; the association of freedom with responsibility; and finally, the necessity for faith without fanaticism: a faith built upon knowledge of the past and hope for the future, trusting in man's reason to the limit of its capacity.

chapter fifteen

THE WESTERN TRADITION IN THE LATER MIDDLE AGES: LITERATURE, ART, AND MUSIC

THE TERM "RENAISSANCE."   It has long been customary to describe the cultural history of western Europe in terms of a Renaissance, or, to use the English word, Renascence. Such phraseology implies that during the course of the declining Roman world and the barbarian invasions culture died, or went into a long hibernation. Since the culture that supposedly died or hibernated was classical, the rebirth has unavoidably been associated with the renewed cultivation of classical culture, of Greek and Roman literature, art, science, and philosophy. We have associated the cultivation of classical culture with the humanist point of view. In a strict sense, a humanist is a serious and professional student of classical culture. In a wider and more meaningful sense, a humanist is one who believes in, and acts in accordance with, the tenets of humanism. Thus a humanist in a strict sense may or may not be a humanist in this wider sense. In any case, the renewed cultivation of classical culture marks the reappearance of the scholar whom we call the humanist, and of the point of view called humanism.

THE MEDIEVAL RENAISSANCE

It is usual to date the renewed cultivation of classical culture in the fourteenth century and to place it in Italy. Thus historians speak of the Italian Renaissance. But to one who has read the previous chapter it is obvious that there was a renewed cultivation of some aspects of Greek philosophy and science in the twelfth and thirteenth centuries throughout western Europe. This is what historians often call a part of the medieval, or twelfth-century, Renaissance. From this point of view, the so-called Italian Renaissance is but a continuation of the medieval, or twelfth-century, Renaissance. To those who have read earlier parts of this book it is clear that no matter how much the study of classical culture, or for that matter the pursuit of all learning, declined, it never really died or went into hibernation. The word Renaissance must be used with this reservation in mind. To be quite accurate, we must speak, rather, of a much more intensive study of classical culture, of there being more humanists, and more sympathy for humanism.

CULTURAL LIMITATIONS OF ASCETICISM

The decline in the cultivation of classical culture has been explained not so much as a result of the decline and fall of the ancient world as of the victory of Christianity and its ascetic point of view. No matter how much early Christianity may have emphasized the doctrine of brotherly love, the victory of the Christian Church amounted to a severe limitation upon the freedom of the human being to think, to feel, and to act. For there existed now an ecclesiastical organization with power and influence enough to use force to secure public uniformity of thought, feeling, and action within the orthodox Christian pattern. In confining the human mind and heart, the Church did not say that it totally rejected philosophy, science, literature, and art. It merely said that these cultural expressions must be subordinated to the Christian Church. Philosophy and science were to be limited to explaining the theology that had been elaborated as the meaning of God's revelation in Scripture; literature was to be used to embellish the liturgy or teach Christian morals; art had to be employed to enhance the Christian liturgy and elucidate its message. This was on the theory that the Christian God had revealed the one and only truth, and had entrusted its keeping to his Church.

HUMANISM AND MEDIEVAL CHRISTIANITY

The contrast between the humanistic and ascetic outlook has already been analyzed.[1] It has been said also that, in admitting that Christian theology needed rational substantiation and that the individual bore some responsibility for his salvation,[2] Christianity adopted two humanistic tenets. There are other senses in which medieval Christianity can be called humanistic. When it responded to the powerfully felt religious needs of the simple, illiterate masses of medieval Europe, we may call the results humanistic. In this sense classical polytheism was humanistic, that

[1]See pp. 9 ff.
[2]See p. 675.

is to say, it provided various kinds of security for the simple human being. Medieval Christianity was thus humanistic to the extent that it remained pagan or made adaptations similar to paganism. The concern of the Church and of the medieval theologians to see that everyone got to heaven without too much difficulty may be called humanistic: no human being who was at all co-operative was to be denied life's greatest good. The development of mariolatry, or the cult of the Virgin Mary, the Christian Magna Mater, was essentially humanistic. There could be nothing more human than the worship of the lovely Virgin with the Baby Jesus on her lap or at her breast, or the appeal to the Virgin to intercede with her Son to secure forgiveness for a quite human weakness of the flesh. The elaborate development of the cult of the saints, with pilgrimages to their shrines and veneration of their relics—Christianity's polytheism—was essentially humanistic in its response to very specific physical, economic, and spiritual needs. Yet the sense in which the above were humanistic is not the sense in which the term humanism has been used in the preceding chapters. For these were concessions made to support an otherworldly rather than a this-worldly approach to the solution of human problems. In the name of popular religion, these developments catered to human credulity by tolerating a wide variety of crudely superstitious practices. This did not conform with the humanistic emphasis upon rationality. In making morality dependent upon the mechanical performance of rites and cere-monies similar to the classical contractual arrangement between the gods and men, the above practices were not supporting the humanistic em-phasis upon individual responsibility and free will.

SECULARISM, HUMANISM, AND ASCETICISM

Because the Christian Church aimed to discipline the whole man, in preparation for his life in the other world, it sought inevitably to channel those aspects of his life that we have called cultural. It would make his thoughts, feelings, and actions in the fields of philosophy, science, litera-ture, art, and music as Christian as his political, economic, or social con-duct. It would create a wholly Christian culture. To do this, it had to make the world of men really Christian, and to take for granted that any encouragement or patronage given to creative minds would result in Christian expression. To make the world of men really Christian, Chris-tianity had to combat instinctive human animality or what it preferred to call Fallen Man, the man of Original Sin. Human animality, however disciplined by civilization, retains a good deal of its original conduct, and has its own crude system of values. The house dog may be domesticated and trained, but his life centers about his food, drink, sleep, play, and the perpetuation of his kind: immediate, instinctive sensual delights. However devoted to his master, he remains a selfish and greedy creature. The human being living in society retains much of his earlier animal con-

CHRONOLOGY — Late Medieval Literature

Latin Literature	Vernacular Literature

1000 ───────────────────────────────────

Latin Literature	Vernacular Literature
Peter Abélard (1079–1142)	Song of Roland (late 11th c.)
Saint Bernard of Clairvaux (1091–1153)	Suger (ca. 1081–1151)

1100 ───────────────────────────────────

Latin Literature	Vernacular Literature
Bernardus Sylvestris (fl. 12th c.)	
John of Salisbury (ca. 1110–1180)	
Alan of Lille (ca. 1114–1203)	
Emperor Frederick Barbarossa (ca. 1123–1190)	
Rainald of Dassel (fl. 12th c.)	
Adam of St. Victor (fl. 12th c.)	
Walter of Châtillon (fl. 12th c.)	Eleanor of Aquitaine (ca. 1122–1204)
	Andreas the Chaplain (late 12th c.)
	Wolfram von Eschenbach (ca. 1170–1220)
	Walter von der Vogelweide (1170–1230)
	Prose Edda (1179–1241)
	Nibelungenlied (1190–1205)
	Chrétien de Troyes (fl. late 12th c.)

1200 ───────────────────────────────────

Latin Literature	Vernacular Literature
	Guillaume de Lorris (d. ca. 1235)
	Jean de Meun (fl. 1270)
	Dante Alighieri (1265–1321)

1300 ───────────────────────────────────

Latin Literature	Vernacular Literature
	Geoffrey Chaucer (ca. 1343–1400)

duct. Although he has elaborately refined them, his life, too, centers about immediate, instinctive sensual delights, found in food, drink, sleep, play, and sex. He has not been quite so successful as some animals in getting others to take care of him, and has therefore to work. In addition to refining these instinctive sensual pleasures, man, because of his own peculiar physical endowment, has been able to develop additional sensual pleasures. His special sensitivity makes him responsive to beauty, whether in the natural world, or in a special world of art that he has created. His mental endowment has given meaning as well as beauty to his creations. And something called heart, or spirit, or soul, has irradiated this meaningful beauty with a special human relevance that lifts it above the commonplace and the ephemeral. Those human activities and values that go back to the barbarian, savage, and beast, and have to do with immediate sensual pleasures as selfish ends in themselves, we may call secular. The word *secular* is often used also to characterize nonreligious, if not irreligious, amoral, if not immoral, conduct and values. When secular activities and values are utilized or transformed in a rational way to enhance human dignity and realize human potentiality for good, we may call such activity humanistic. When secular and humanistic activity and values are suppressed or utilized in an authoritarian way to enhance the dignity of a god, the mystical ecstasy of an afterworld, or the power of a church, we may call such activity ascetic. The asceticism is Christian when the God, the afterworld, and the church are Christian.

AN INDEPENDENT PHILOSOPHY AND SCIENCE

The new science and philosophy of the twelfth century were made subservient to Christian asceticism. It was recognized that a body of learning could be built up on the transient phenomena of the surrounding world that would serve to explain and glorify God and his works. Even though this learning could not hope fully to comprehend God or the Christian outlook, it was a legitimate Christian pursuit. Such a recognition, however, contained the danger that philosophy and science might forget, or at least free themselves from, their Christian moorings and become independent, secular, or humanistic. If they became independent, they would then have the large task of replacing the Christian outlook with a valid new outlook of their own. If the new philosophy and science could not substantiate Christian asceticism, then at least they could try to build up a new moral outlook that would be colored by Christian, as well as classical, ethics or that would repudiate both. This has been the history of thought ever since: the working out of a point of view, wholly or in part independent of Christian asceticism.

THE PROBLEM OF A CHRISTIAN CULTURE

The Church was confronted by two powerful secular forces in the Middle Ages: (1) the lust for political power, incorporated in the different types of state that arose out of feudalism; and (2) the lust for economic power (wealth), incorporated in the new bourgeoisie that arose with the revival of trade and commerce. The Church itself, in its pursuit of theocracy and wealth, was corrupted by these two secular forces. It could hardly be argued that it really succeeded in subjecting the nascent medieval state. The trend was in the reverse direction. Nor could it be argued that the Church really succeeded in making nascent capitalism subservient to its point of view. Christianity made the new learning temporarily subservient under the terms referred to above. It is now necessary to see whether, in the fields of literature, architecture, and music, the Church, incorporating the spirit of Christian asceticism, was able to suppress, transform, or absorb those passions and outlooks that we have identified with secularism or humanism. To the extent that it did suppress, transform, or absorb them, in these aspects medieval culture may be described as Christian. To the extent that it failed to do so, this culture will have to be described as in part secular or humanistic.

This is a matter of more than the words to be used in an academic description. For we are often told that a culture in order to be vital, beautiful, and influential must have a religious foundation. Those who argue in this way point to the Middle Ages as a period when Christianity gave a vitality, beauty, and power to western culture that it has never had since, because of the intrusion of secular and humanistic forces. The same people argue that western culture cannot become vital again without a religious revival of some kind. Without such a revival, they say, its efforts to give direction to world society will be futile.[3] In opposition to this view of the Middle Ages, it might be said that to the extent that secular and humanistic forces in literature, art, music, and thought refused to be suppressed, transformed, or absorbed into Christianity, that is, made subservient to the Church, they were preserving the freedom of the human spirit to investigate and express other than a religious outlook. They could use this freedom to explore and express the whole wonderful character, personality, capacity, and genius of the human being, and not only his ability to sin and be saved. It was this refusal to become uniform and subservient to a dominant religious outlook incorporated in a powerful, persecuting Church that kept western culture from becoming decadent. Other forces, no less moral, could now influence the increasingly complex civilization of the West. The new secularism, untamed by authoritarian religion, might be influenced by points of view less extreme and more tolerant. In this sense, the failure of the Church completely to control the political, economic, social, and cultural life of western Europe at the beginning of its history was a stage in the liberation of the West contributing to the dynamic character of its growth. The extraordinary

---

[3]Cf. Toynbee, in *Civilization on Trial*; also Christopher Dawson, *Christianity and Western Culture*.

vitality of western culture during the period of its Renaissance was due likewise to this preserved freedom, this possible variety, this passion to investigate the whole.

Medieval Literature: Latin

MEDIEVAL LATIN

Medieval literature may be conveniently divided into two categories: that written in Latin, and that in the vernacular dialects. This division, already introduced in an earlier chapter,[4] persisted beyond the medieval period proper. Until succeeded by French in the seventeenth century, Latin remained an international tongue for central and western Europe. As such, it was not only the language of the Christian Church, but of politics, law, business, scholarship, science, education, and literature. In clerical and academic circles it was spoken as well as written. This medieval Latin, of course, was not the latin of Cicero and Vergil. Classical Latin was too difficult for the practical uses of medieval society. Gregory the Great and Gregory of Tours[5] refused, early in the Middle Ages, to take on the responsibility of writing correct classical Latin, and what a pope and bishop refused to do could hardly be expected of schoolmasters and boys. If it were to be kept alive as a means of communication in everyday life, its vocabulary had to change by giving old words new meanings and introducing new words from the vernaculars. Ignorance and different pronunciations tended to change its spelling. Its grammar and syntax became less rigid and complex. As a new adaptation of an old language, it acquired a special suppleness and grace of its own which found characteristic expression in the Latin verse of the Middle Ages. While retaining its superiority as a language of the professions until the seventeenth century, it lost its predominance as a vehicle of literature in the thirteenth century. This is not to say that Latin literature died in the thirteenth century. It was artificially stimulated by the humanists of the Renaissance, who prided themselves on being able to write an elegant classical prose and verse. Such an accomplishment, sprung from the schools and not from the heart, only temporarily prolonged the life of Latin literature.

LATIN LITERATURE IN THE SCHOOLS

For ability to speak and write in Latin, training that brought some acquaintance with the masterpieces of Latin literature was necessary. This training was given by courses in grammar and rhetoric that used books by the Roman authors Donatus and Priscian, containing examples from the best Latin authors. The libraries in monastic and cathedral schools con-

[4]See Chap. ix.
[5]See pp. 385 f.

tained copies of the classics, and these were read by a few men. Before the twelfth century, such reading had produced enthusiastic admirers of Roman authors and an awareness of how far medieval had deviated from classical Latin. Earlier in its history the Church had had to come to terms with the issue of whether it would support an active cultivation of pagan literature. The question always remained, and less trustful men in the twelfth and thirteenth centuries felt that the examples from classical literature in the textbooks ought to be supplanted by examples from Christian literature. Yet the Church did not oppose the study of Latin literature, because it felt that such study was useful. If it produced a few humanists, they would have to be tolerated and restrained. An elegant Christian Latin literature could only be written by men acquainted with the best in ancient literature.

LATIN LITERATURE IN THE UNIVERSITIES

In the late eleventh and twelfth centuries the monastic schools began to be supplanted by schools attached to the cathedrals. In some of these, notably the schools at Orléans and Chartres, men taught who were unqualified admirers of Roman literature, and they imparted a similar love to their students. An ardent humanism flourished in these centers. Out of some of these schools universities developed, universities in which courses in logic and training in the professions were dominant. These crowded or crushed out the enthusiasm for classical literature that had been fostered by the cathedral schools, and many were the laments poured out on this score.

CHRISTIAN ALLEGORY

Christianity retained classical polytheism in its cult of the Virgin and saints. When it was a little fearful of cultivating a pagan literature celebrating attractive divinities, it was assisted by a practice that it also took from classical antiquity: allegory. The principles of Christian allegory were worked out in antiquity, notably by Saint Augustine. They were used by Christian poets, as well as by theologians. As those who have tried it know, it is often very difficult to accept a literal interpretation of the Scriptures as the revelation of God. The hot oriental poetry of the Song of Solomon is a case in point. If it is taken as it stands, the sensuous eroticism fits ill with the ascetic spirit of Christianity. If, however, the lover and bridegroom is Christ, and the maiden, his bride, is the Church, why then it's all right. If the Shulamite maiden is really a prefiguration of the Virgin Mother, then it does no harm to describe her physical loveliness. Ingenious students worked out, and continue to do so, many allegorical meanings for the literal words of Scripture. They were particularly interested in interpreting the Old Testament as a prophetic anticipation of the New.

In about 1409 the duke of Berry, brother of King Charles V of France, commissioned Pol Malouel (Pol de Limbourg) to illuminate a prayer book. By the time of the duke's death in 1416 the work was unfinished. It was completed at the end of the century by Jean Colombe, an artist of the duke of Savoy. The prayer book has miniatures representing the months of the year, of which this page is July. Before the duke's triangular chateau of Poitiers, situated at the confluence of two streams, peasants are at work cutting wheat and shearing sheep.

Plate 39

The April page of the duke of Berry's prayer book. On the grounds of the ducal Château de Dourdan a small, select, and very stylish group of guests witness the betrothal of two tall, sedate, and aristocratic sweethearts, dressed for the occasion in beautifully decorated and flowing capes and gowns, and wearing fancy hats.

Plate 40

Musée Condé; Georges Viollon

The June page of the duke of Berry's prayer book. The view is of Paris from a window of the duke's town house on the left bank of the Seine. Beyond the river is the enclosed royal palace with the Sainte Chapelle built by Saint Louis. On this side of the river graceful peasants seem to dance a hay-making ballet.

Plate 41

Musée Condé; Georges Viollon

The October page of the duke of Berry's prayer book. The royal palace of the Louvre rises above its walls. While Parisians enjoy a walk along the Seine, peasants on the other side prepare fields for fall planting. To protect the sown field from the birds a scarecrow in the form of an archer stands in the midst of waving strips of white cloth tied to strings.

Plate 42

Musée Condé; Giraudon

This taking of the literal word as a symbol or personification of its real meaning was particularly congenial to Augustinianism, or Christian Neoplatonism.[6] According to this view, the world about us is an illusion. At best it symbolizes or personifies the real world of the divine ideas that are in the mind of God. To make this attitude concrete, allegorical symbolism is necessary. If the world is a struggle between virtue and vice for the soul of man, this is better understood if the real abstractions Virtue and Vice are personified; if, indeed, all the virtues and vices are personified. If the ancient pantheon and mythology could be fitted into the Christian mythology, here, in addition to saint worship, was another way of preserving classical polytheism, one making it necessary for the Christian scholar, or at least the Christian poet, to study Latin literature. The Christian poet could personify war with the god Mars without doing harm to the faith. He could personify love with Venus in the same manner, and continue the symbolical employment of her child Cupid. If he wanted these to communicate with each other he could retain Mercury. To allude to these learnedly he would need to be acquainted with classical mythology. Thus, through allegory, Christian Platonism was strengthened and classical literature retained. Ennodius, a Christian bishop of the late fifth and early sixth centuries, could describe in a marriage song Venus in all her naked beauty playing among the flowers. Her son Cupid comes to waken her from sleep and says: "We have lost our old empire. Cold virginity possesses the world. Arise! Shake off your sleep." Venus answers: "We shall be all the stronger for our rest. Let the nations learn that a goddess grows in power when no one thinks of her." A bridegroom is thereupon captured for Love. "If the gods had not died into allegory, the bishop would not have dared to use them; conversely, if he had not had allegorical gods for his mouthpiece, he could scarcely have put the 'case' of Venus against asceticism so strongly."[7] The classical tradition was not so easily forsaken.

ALLEGORY AT CHARTRES

The allegorical tradition established by early Christian poets was continued into the later Middle Ages. In some instances it was used to make classical literature acceptable, as when, for example, Vergil's *Aeneid* was made over into an allegory of the life of man. In the cathedral school of Chartres it was used to soften the hostility of orthodox Christianity toward those who had gone so far in their admiration of the classics as to accept Ovid's teachings on the subject of love in the *Ars Amatoria*, a questionable Christian classic.[8]

[6]See p. 638.
[7]C. S. Lewis, *The Allegory of Love*, pp. 77 ff.
[8]See pp. 232 f.

Ovid's popularity had gone far. A twelfth-century author had written a piece called the *Council of Remiremont*. The council was composed of nuns who had gathered together to discuss questions of love.

> When the virgin senate all
> Had filled the benches of the hall,
> Doctor Ovid's Rule instead
> Of the evangelists' was read.
> The reader of that gospel gay
> Was Sister Eva, who (they say)
> Understands the practick part
> Of the Amatory Art—
> She it was convoked them all,
> Little sisters, sisters tall.
> Sweetly they began to raise
> Songs in Love's melodious praise.

These preliminaries over, a Lady Cardinal rose to announce that:

> Love, the god of every lover,
> Sent me hither to discover
> All your life and conversation
> And conduct a Visitation.

She learns that the sisters have divided their favors among clerics and knights, and declares that only clerics are suitable for nuns. For nuns to consort with knights was rank heresy.

> Let all those who in their blindness
> Upon laymen waste their kindness
> Be a scorn and execration
> To the clerks of every nation,
> And let clerks at every meeting
> Pass them by without a greeting! (pp. 18–20)[9]

BERNARDUS SYLVESTRIS

Chartres was a school of Christian Platonists, where scholars were willing to try to reconcile Genesis with the *Timaeus*,[10] identify the Holy Ghost with the Neoplatonic World Soul, and study and reverence nature. One of its leading allegorical poets was Bernardus Sylvestris, who wrote a work on the creation of the world and man (*De Mundi Universitate*). It opens with Nature pleading with Reason to fill Matter with the Platonic Forms. These forms are generated as species in matter. When the elements are separated, soul and (finally) the world are created. In the second book Reason makes man. In this task she is assisted by Nature and

[9]Lewis, *The Allegory of Love.*
[10]See pp. 138 f.

by Physis, "organic nature." To give man the impress of divinity as well as of "organic nature" (Physis), Urania, a "heaven-spirit," is summoned. When Nature visits Urania, the latter explains that man's soul must be made acquainted before his birth with the influences of the stars, to which the soul will some day return:

> With me through all the expanse of heaven must go
> Man's soul, and I will make her know
> The laws of Fate allowing no repeal
> And Fortune's alterable wheel . . .
> Her godlike essence when her body dies
> Will seek again those kindred skies. (p. 95)

Together Nature and Urania descend to earth, where "wherever [it] . . . is most delightful, be it with grassy ridge or flowery mountain top, wherever it is brightened with streams or robed in woodland greenery, there Silvans, Pans, and Nerei, blameless of conversation, wear out the period of their longer life." They find Physis "deep in contemplation of the secret potencies of life," and under the personal direction of Reason proceed to make man, who is to be "heavenly, earthly." Of this man the sexual organs are created last. They are a part of man neither to be overemphasized nor underemphasized:

> Pleasant and fitting both their use will be
> When time and mode and measure do agree,
> Else withering from the root all lives would fail
> And that old Chaos o'er the wreck prevail.
> Conquerors of Death! they fill each empty place
> In Nature and immortalize the race. (pp. 95–97)

ALAN OF LILLE

Another poet of the Chartres school, Alan of Lille, in a poem called the *Anticlaudianus* described in Platonic allegory the creation of the perfect man. In this poem Nature calls her sisters, Concord, Youth, Laughter, Reason, Honesty, Prudence, Good Faith, Virtue, and Nobility, to tell them of her plan to create a human being possessed of all goodness. From God, Prudence and Reason secure a soul for the perfect man. The soul is then clothed with a perfect body and endowed with the virtues. They seem, however, to be not religious but secular virtues. The faith the perfect man is given is not Christian faith but "good faith"; the piety, rather pity than religious piety; he is endowed with popularity (*favor*), fertility (*copia*), youth (*juventus*), and nobility (*nobilitas*). He is advised by Reason not to be too modest in seeking for fame.

> Not swayed with popular applause, nor yet
> Spitting it out, unless it bear the stamp
> Of flattery and would purchase wealth for words;
> It smacks too much of sour austerity
> To scorn all fame.

It is no less a virtue than Modesty that counsels him to

> Let not the hair, too wanton-fine, appear
> Like woman's bravery and belie the man,
> Nor too unkempt, lacking its due regard
> Lest that proclaim thee by its tangled shock
> In thy fresh years too philosophical.

It becomes clear that, for Alan, the perfect man is a perfect gentleman. "Goodness does not mean asceticism; knighthood does not mean adultery. Both are brought together under the law of Natura, who is a vicar of God and essentially good. It is not a question of Grace redeeming Nature: it is a question of sin departing from Nature." The position is summed up in the advice given by Honestus to the perfect man:

> Let him love Nature who would flee from vice,
> Eschew what guilt or naughty will brought forth
> And to his breast clasp all that Nature made. (pp. 103–105)

The allegorical treatment of nature, the retention of the machinery of classical polytheism and mythology, and a humanistic exuberance in the expression of a "new love of the visible world" can be illustrated from another of Alan's poems, *The Complaint of Nature* (*De Planctu Naturae*), in which Nature is grief-stricken over the unnatural vices of mankind. When Nature appears "borne in a glassy coach . . . drawn of Juno's own birds . . . you would 'a thought that all the elements, as though they then renewed their kinds, did make festival. The heaven, to lighten (as it were) the maid's journey with his candles, gave order to his stars that they should shine beyond their wont; wherefore methought the daylight marvelled at their hardihood who durst so insolently be seen in his presence. Phoebus also, putting on a jollier countenance than he was used, poured forth all the riches of his light and made a show of it to meet her. . . . The air, putting off his weeping clouds, with serene and friendly cheer smiled upon her when she came, and whereas he was before grieved with the raging of Aquilo, now popularly took his ease in the bosom of Favonius. The birds, moved by a certain kindly inspiration, rejoicing with the plausive playing of their pinions, showed unto the virgin a worshipping countenance. Juno forsooth that before had scorned the kissings of Jupiter, was now with so great joy made drunken, that by a darting prologue of her glances she set her husband on fire for pleasing passages of love. The sea also that before was enraged with stormy waves, at the maid's coming made an holiday of peace and swore an everlasting calm; for Aeolus, lest they should move their wars (more than civil) in the virgin's presence, bound in their prisons the tempestuous winds. The fishes, even, swimming up to the eyebrows of the waves, so far forth as the lumpish kind of their sensuality suffered them, foretold by their glad cheer the coming of their lady; and Thetis, being at play with Nereus, bethought her that time to conceive another Achilles. Moreover certain maidens, the greatness of whose beauty was able not only to steal away the reason from a man but to make those in heaven also to forget their deity, coming forth out of places where streams sprang, brought unto her gifts of pigmentary's nectar, making as they should offer tithes to their newcome queen. And truly, the earth, that before lay stripped, by winter's robbery, of her garnishments, made shift to borrow from the largesse of the spring a scarlet smock of flowers, lest . . . she might not decently be seen before the virgin." (pp. 106–108)

JOHN OF SALISBURY

The humanism of the cathedral school at Chartres permeated also that Englishman John of Salisbury (ca. 1110–1180), who ended his life as bishop of Chartres, having defended the study of letters as the only sound basis of all concern with logic and philosophy. He had little use for logicians who argued "whether the pig led to market was held by the man or the rope." Deeply steeped in Latin literature he wrote a "supple and delicately shaded prose . . . doubtless the best which was written in the Middle Ages."[11]

THE GOLIARDS

A better illustration of the secular and humanistic flavor of medieval Latin literature than the allegorical work of the school of Chartres is the poetry of the wandering scholars and clerks, usually called the Goliards. They are so called from their mythical patron, Bishop Golias, a possible derivative from David's opponent Goliath, or it may be, since Saint Bernard called Abélard a Golias, a way Abélard's students took of making sport of the saint. It is not easy to identify the individuals composing the group of carefree and none-too-reputable academic and clerical tramps who sought support from the prominent and wealthy as they moved from town to town and school to school. One, Hugo of Orléans, called Primas, or the Primate, is referred to by contemporaries as "a most amusing rogue and a great versifier and extemporizer" and "a man of mean appearance and twisted face," whose verses moved everyone "to hearty laughter." "A phantom, hollow looking, meanly dressed, and racked by a consumptive cough" was a second, the famous Archpoet, who had Emperor Frederick Barbarossa's archchancellor, the archbishop of Cologne, Rainald of Dassel, for a patron. He says of himself:

The poet of all poets the poorest paid—that's me!
Without a stitch to call my own, except what you can see,
A thing which often grieves me, while you laugh at poverty;
It's not my fault—don't think I'm poor because I want to be!

[11]Maurice Hélin, *A History of Medieval Latin Literature*, p. 109.

A scholar dig to earn his keep! I neither will nor can.
I come of military stock, my sire's a fighting man;
But toils of war alarmed me, so it seemed a better plan
To stay at home with Virgil when you, Paris, led the van.

To beg for bread is a disgrace, I will not ask relief,
And thieves, though much falls to their clutch, are seldom free from grief.
What is there left for me to do, who hold no lands in fief?
I won't become a beggar, and I'd hate to be a thief.

Often the pinch of poverty makes me acquisitive,
The plaints I send to learned men sound far too purposive;
But laymen cannot understand that poets have to live,
And even to me, it's plain to see, they've no reward to give. (pp. 74, 102)[12]

Walter of Châtillon was not a vagrant scholar but an active cleric able to criticise the Church from a wide and varied inside knowledge. Most of the poems, however, are anonymous. Many come from a manuscript of the monastery of Benedict-Beuern in Bavaria, where no one dared to catalogue it (an "under-the-counter book," as the Roman classics were often under-the-pillow books).

THE ORDER OF GOLIARDS

This poetry can be learned, classical in reference, and satirical. It celebrates those sensual pleasures that have to do with drinking, lechery, and the dance. It parodies the liturgy and hymns. It is remarkably sensitive to the beauties as well as the joys of the natural world. But it can be very serious as well, serious and angry in its criticism of clerical abuses, and honest in its expression of other than merely frivolous emotions. One of the Goliards presumes to give the rules for the "vagrant order." The entrance requirement was not difficult:

We receive the shaven skull
Gladly as the hairy,
When a priest elopes or monk
Bolts the monastery;
Boys from school and masters too,
Parsons, clerks—we're flattered!
But your scholar is our prize,
Clad in robes untattered.

. . . . .

War mongers and pacifists,
Mild men and demonic,
Roman and Bohemian,
Slavic and Teutonic:
Men of medium size we take,
Likewise dwarfs and giants,
Humble folk, and those who still
Bid the gods defiance.

. . . . .

[12]*The Goliard Poets*, trans. George F. Whicher.

Of the vagrant order's laws
These are fundamental:
Generous must we be in life,
In demeanor gentle;
Also we must love a roast,
Dripping unctuous juices,
More than pecks of barley-meal
Fit for a hermit's uses.

. . . . .

Last, our order interdicts
All superfluous clothing;
One who sports an overcoat
We must view with loathing.
Let him pledge his needless wrap
At the shrine of Decius,
Soon his vest will follow too—
Dice are avaricious. (pp. 273, 277)

"THE CONFESSION OF GOLIAS"

In the same mood the Archpoet, in his "Confession of Golias," admits that

Dull and dour sobriety
    Never takes my money,
Give me loose society
    Where the jokes are funny;
Love will bring variety,
    Toil that's sweet as honey.
Pillars of propriety,
    Have you hearts as sunny?

Down the primrose path I post
    Straight to Satan's grotto,
Shunning virtue, doing most
    Things that I ought not to;

Little hope of heaven I boast,
    Charmed by pleasure's otto:
Since the soul is bound to roast
    Save the skin's my motto.

. . . . .

Much too hard it is, I find,
    So to change my essence
As to keep a virgin mind
    In a virgin's presence.
Rigid laws can never bind
    Youth to acquiescence;
Light o'loves must seek their kind,
    Bodies take their pleasance.

. . . . .

Next, I'm called in terms precise
    Monstrous fond of gaming;

Losing all my clothes at dice
    Gains me this worth naming:
While outside I'm cool as ice,
    Inwardly I'm flaming,
Then with daintiest device
    Poems and songs I'm framing.

Third, the tavern—here I dread
    Lies detraction's kernel:
Long on tavern joys I've fed,
    Never shall I spurn all
Till these eyes shall see instead
    Choirs from realms supernal
Chanting for the newly dead
    Requiem eternal.

My intention is to die
    In the tavern drinking;
Wine must be at hand, for I
    Want it when I'm sinking.
Angels when they come shall cry,
    At my frailties winking:
'Spare this drunkard, God, he's high,
    Absolutely stinking.'

    . . . . .

Let the verse be as the wine.
    Grasp this true technique well,
And like me, until you dine,
    Neither write nor speak well.
Fasting, while I peak and pine,
    Nothing comes in sequel;
Feast me, and these songs of mine
    Ovid could not equal. (pp. 107–113)

The joys confessed to by the Archpoet are fully elaborated by other Goliards.

Rudely blows the winter blast,
Withered leaves are falling fast,
Cold hath hushed the birds at last.
    While the heavens were warm and glowing,
        Nature's offspring loved in May;
    But man's heart no debt is owing
        To such change of month or day
        As the dumb brute-beasts obey.
Oh, the joys of this possessing!
How unspeakable the blessing
    That my Flora yields to-day!

Labour long I did not rue,
Ere I won my wages due,
And the prize I played for drew.

Flora with her brows of laughter,
　　Gazing on me, breathing bliss,
Draws my yearning spirit after,
　　Sucks my soul forth in a kiss:
　　Where's the pastime matched with this?
Oh, the joys of this possessing!
How unspeakable the blessing
　　Of my Flora's loveliness!

Truly mine is no harsh doom,
While in this secluded room
Venus lights for me the gloom!
　　Flora faultless as a blossom
　　　Bares her smooth limbs for mine eyes;
　　Softly shines her virgin bosom,
　　　And the breasts that gently rise
　　　Like the hills of Paradise.
Oh, the joys of this possessing!
How unspeakable the blessing
　　When my Flora is the prize!

From her tender breasts decline,
In a gradual curving line,
Flanks like swansdown white and fine.
　　On her skin the touch discerneth
　　　Naught of rough; 'tis soft as snow:
　　'Neath the waist her belly turneth
　　　Unto fulness, where below
　　　In Love's garden lilies blow.
Oh, the joys of this possessing!
How unspeakable the blessing!
　　Sweetest sweets from Flora flow!

Ah! should Jove but find my fair,
He would fall in love, I swear,
And to his old tricks repair:
　　In a cloud of gold descending
　　　As on Danae's brazen tower,
　　Or the sturdy bull's back bending,
　　　Or would veil his godhood's power
　　　In a swan's form for one hour.
Oh, the joys of this possessing!
How unspeakable the blessing!
　　How divine my Flora's flower![13]

The Bavarian monk at Benedict-Beuern might read of such forbidden joys as

When we're at the tavern, we
Care not what this world may be,
But we set ourselves to dicing—
Sport of all sports most enticing.
Would you glance at our high jinks
Where one small coin pours out the drinks?

[13] J. A. Symonds, *Wine, Women, and Song*, pp. 130–132.

Would you have that scene unfurled?
Listen to me, I'll tell the world.

We play, we drink, 'tis thus, my friends,
We burn the candle at both ends.
Of those who most frequent the game
Some lose their shirts and mourn the same,
Some pile fresh garments on their backs,
Some hide their nakedness in sacks;
All thought of death each man postpones
When for the drinks we roll the bones.

First we throw a round to settle
Who shall pay, like men of mettle;
Next we drink to captives, then
Drink a third to living men;
Fourth, to Christians truly bred;
Fifth, to cheer the faithful dead;
Sixth, vain woman when she errs,
Seventh, Diana's foresters.

Eighth, to brothers born to roister;
Ninth, to monks that slip the cloister;
Tenth, to voyagers and sailors;
Eleventh, to discord-making railers;
Twelfth, to all who penance pay;
Thirteenth, to wanderers by the way;
And at the last to king and pope
We all inordinately tope.

Host and hostess, *he* drinks, *she* drinks,
Even the parson on a spree drinks,
The captain drinks, nor drinks alone,
The tapster drinks with greasy Joan.
They drink, they drink, a motley rout,
The stay-at-home, the gadabout,
The ignorant, the erudite,
The swift, the slow, the black, the white.

They drink, the poor man ill at ease,
The no-account gone overseas;
They drink, the boy, the reverend man,
Prelate and dean both clink the can.
They drink, the sister with the brother,
They drink, they drink, old maid and mother;
What hundreds, nay, what thousands, think!
Drink, drink, drink, drink, drink, drink, drink.

To quench their thirst what would avail
A hundred mugs of penny-ale,
When all are drinking without measure
And all in drinking find their pleasure?
Whoever treats these thirsty folk
By morning will be stony broke.
They sponge on us? We treat? Not much!
Good fellows, listen! *This is Dutch.*[14]

[14]Whicher, pp. 227-229.

For the Goliard no less than for most medieval folk, spring was a blessing.

> The earth lies open-breasted
>   In gentleness of spring,
> Who lay so close and frozen
> In winter's blustering.
> The northern winds are quiet,
>   The west wind winnowing,
> In all this sweet renewing
>   How shall a man not sing?
>
> Now go the young men singing,
>   And singing every bird,
> Harder is he than iron
>   Whom beauty hath not stirred.
> And colder than the rocks is he
>   Who is not set on fire,
> When cloudless are our spirits,
>   Serene and still the air.
>
> Behold, all things are springing
>   With life come from the dead,
> The cold that wrought for evil
>   Is routed now and fled.
> The lovely earth hath brought to birth
>   All flowers, all fragrancy.
> Cato himself would soften
>   At such sweet instancy.
>
> The woods are green with branches
>   And sweet with nightingales,
> With gold and blue and scarlet
>   All flowered are the dales.
> Sweet it is to wander
>   In a place of trees,
> Sweeter to pluck roses
>   And the fleur-de-lys,
> But dalliance with a lovely lass
>   Far surpasseth these.
>
> And yet when all men's spirits
>   Are dreaming on delight,
> My heart is heavy in me,
>   And troubled at her sight:
> If she for whom I travail
>   Should still be cold to me,
> The birds sing unavailing,
>   'Tis winter still for me. (pp. 207–209)[15]

For youth it is the dance and not the book that calls:

> Let's away with study,
>   Folly's sweet.

[15]Helen Waddell, *Medieval Latin Lyrics.*

Treasure all the pleasure
        Of our youth:
Time enough for age
        To think on Truth.
So short a day,
And life so quickly hasting
And in study wasting
        Youth that would be gay!

'Tis our spring that's slipping,
        Winter draweth near,
        Life itself we're losing,
        And this sorry cheer
Dries the blood and chills the heart,
        Shrivels all delight.
Age and all its crowd of ills
        Terrifies our sight.
So short a day,
And life so quickly hasting,
And in study wasting
        Youth that would be gay!

Let us as the gods do,
        'Tis the wiser part:
Leisure and love's pleasure
        Seek the young in heart
Follow the old fashion,
        Down into the street!
Down among the maidens,
        And the dancing feet!
So short a day,
And life so quickly hasting,
And in study wasting
        Youth that would be gay!

There for the seeing
        Is all loveliness,
White limbs moving
        Light in wantonness.
Gay go the dancers,
        I stand and see,
Gaze, till their glances
        Steal myself from me.
So short a day,
And life so quickly hasting,
And in study wasting
        Youth that would be gay! (pp. 203–205)

WALTER OF CHÂTILLON

In his last days, Walter of Châtillon, polluted with leprosy, could see no
good to come from the corrupt world:

The harp so often plucked by Walter's hand
        Now sounds an elegy,

Not that he mourns his self-exile or, banned
   From clerics' company,
   Bewails his leprosy:
  But that he sees the dreadful face
  Of doom for all of mortal race
Rushing upon this unsuspecting world apace.

   Behold the Church's magistrates,
   How fallen from their high estates!
    More lost and gone astray
    Today than yesterday.

We can but dread the coming on of night
   When deepening shadows crowd
In valleys low, but if the mountains' height,
   The hills, and all things proud
   Are covered by a shroud
  Impenetrable, we may claim
  (And none will hold our words to blame)
That night has seized upon the world and rules the same.

The figure points, as you must understand,
   To lay-folk lapsed from awe,
Kings sunk in shame, the "valleys" of our land,
   Princes with greedy paw
   Defiant of the law,
  Whose fame is dimmed by lusts abhorred:
  Yet still the vengeance of the Lord
Threatens to strike them down with heaven's twice-sharpened sword.

And as for mountains that should tower so high,
   What can we find more fit
Than priests of Christ, those wells that never dry,
   Called "hills" in Holy Writ
   And sanctified by it:
  Their feet on Zion's top are based,
  And they above the world are placed,
A glass of truth, if not by law's abuse defaced.

  Our "hills" delight, in these degenerate days,
   To pillage the unwary.
  New customs now profane the ancient ways;
   God's holy sanctuary
   Is made hereditary;
  Christ's portion feeds the parasite
  And exile from true learning's light,
While prelates' minions gain rewards in heaven's despite.

   The bishop's "nephews," mark and see,
   Receive his offices in fee,
    And with their lord's entailings
    Inherit, too, his failings.

   O good Lord Jesus, may the end be nigh!
    Send us the promised year

Of jubilee, and quickly. I shall die,
    Nor live to see the spear
    Of Antichrist draw near;
Though now on sacramental ground
His vanguard stands, with creed unsound,
To levy in God's name tribute from all around. (pp. 137–139)[16]

The Goliards were sophisticated enough to take their religion with a smile. "The impulse to mock at the solemnities of liturgical ceremony gave rise to a whole series of parodies under such titles as the *Drunkards' Mass*, the *Office of the Ribalds*, the *Gluttons' Mass*, and so on, in French as well as in Latin, where *libamus* (let us drink) took the place of *oramus* (we pray) and the benediction was 'Fraud be with you.'" (p. 5) The following is a parody of a hymn to the Virgin:

Wine the good and bland, thou blessing
Of the good, the bad's distressing,
Sweet of taste by all confessing,
    Hail, thou world's felicity!
Hail thy hue, life's gloom dispelling;
Hail thy taste, all tastes excelling;
By thy power, in this thy dwelling
    Deign to make us drunk with thee!

Oh, how blest for bounteous uses
Is the birth of pure vine-juices!
Safe's the table which produces
    Wine in goodly quality.
Oh, in colour how auspicious!
Oh, in odour how delicious!
In the mouth how sweet, propitious
    To the tongue enthralled by thee!

Bless the man who first thee planted,
Called thee by thy name enchanted!
He whose cups have ne'er been scanted
    Dreads no danger that may be.
Blest the belly where thou bidest!
Blest the tongue where thou residest!
Blest the mouth through which thou glidest,
    And the lips thrice blest by thee!

Therefore let wine's praise be sounded,
Healths to topers all propounded;
We shall never be confounded,
    Toping for eternity!
Pray we: here be thou still flowing,
Plenty on our board bestowing,
While with jocund voice we're showing
    How we serve thee—Jubilee![17]

[16]Whicher.
[17]Symonds, *Wine, Women, and Song*, pp. 156–158.

Walter (Reginald) of Châtillon's take-off on the Gospel according to Mark is as follows: "The Beginning of the Gospel according to Marks of Silver. In those days said the Pope to the Romans: 'When the Son of Man shall come to the seat of our majesty, say first of all, "Friend, wherefore art Thou come hither?" And if He shall persevere in knocking and giving you nought, cast him forth into outer darkness.' Now it came to pass that a certain poor clerk came to the court of the lord Pope, and cried out, saying: 'Have pity on me, have pity on me, at least you the door-keepers of the Pope, because the hand of poverty hath touched me. For I am poor and in misery; wherefore I beseech you to succour my calamity and my wretchedness.' But they, hearing this, were moved to indignation and said: 'Friend, thy poverty perish with thee; get thee behind me, Satan! for thou savourest not the things that be of money. Verily, verily, I say unto thee, thou shalt not enter into the joy of the Lord until thou shalt have paid unto the last farthing.' The poor man therefore departed, and sold his cloak and his coat and all that he had, and gave to the cardinals and ushers and door-keepers. But they said: 'What is this among so many?' And they cast him forth from the doors; and going forth he wept bitterly, as one that could not be comforted. Afterwards there came to the courts a rich clerk, grown fat and thick and gross, who for sedition's sake had committed murder. He gave first to the door-keeper, then to the usher, and thirdly to the cardinals; but they thought within themselves that they should have received more. Now the lord Pope, hearing that his cardinals and ministers had received many gifts from this clerk, grew sick unto death; but the rich man sent unto him an electuary of gold and silver, and forthwith he grew whole again. Then the lord Pope called together his cardinals and ministers and said unto them: 'Brethren, take heed lest any man deceive you with vain words. For I give you an example, that as I take gifts, so should you do also.' "[18]

A PARODY ON THE CREED

Here, finally, is a dying Goliard's reworking of the Creed (*Credo in Deum patrem omnipotentem, creatorem coeli et terrae, et in Jhesum Christum filium eius unicum*—I believe in God the father almighty, maker of heaven and earth, and in Jesus Christ, his only son):

> *Credo*—in dice I well believe,
> That got me often bite and sup,
> And many a time hath had me drunk,
> And many a time delivered me
> From every stitch and every penny.
> *In Deum*—never with my will
> Gave Him a thought nor ever will.
>
> . . . . .

[18]G. G. Coulton, *Life in the Middle Ages*, I, 112-113.

Patrem—at St. Denis in France,
Good Sir, I had a father once,
Omnipotentem in his having,
Money and horses and fine wearing.

. . . . .

Creatorem who made all
I've desired—He has his will
Of me now. . . .
Coeli—of heaven ever think?
Nay, but the wine that I could drink.
Et terrae—there was all my joy.
Do you think that I believe
More in *Jhesum* than the tavern?
Better love I him who's host
There, than *Christum filium eius.*
Watch the roast turn on the spit,
And the wine that's clear and green,
Orléans, Rochelle, Auxerre,
That's the joy that's *unicum.*[19]

THE RELIGIOUS LYRIC IN THE SEQUENCE

The dominant note of medieval Latin poetry, however, was not secular or humanistic but ascetic. This asceticism is fresh and spontaneous because it is written in a new form and because it is an emancipation from the strict form of the liturgy set by the Roman missal. The meters of classical verse were based upon the quantity of the vowels, and did not use rhyme. Medieval Latin verse came to use meters based upon the natural stress, or accent, given the syllables in the spoken word, and it employed rhyme. Before the twelfth and thirteenth centuries, many hymns had been written in both classical and medieval forms and incorporated into the liturgy. To the monks the liturgy was an intensely personal thing, since through it they expressed the whole purpose of their way of life. But many felt that the prescribed form of the liturgy could bear a little tampering, or suffer a little expansion or a little creativeness, without at all interfering with its solemn purpose. In the service of the Mass a chant called the Alleluia may be inserted between the reading of the Epistle and the Gospel. Choirs could not resist prolonging the final *a* of the Alleluia in an extemporized melody. Then, for the chanted *a* came to be substituted a prose text supplied with a definite melody. In time, poetry, accented and rhymed, was substituted for the prose and also supplied with a melody. These prose and poetical continuations of the Alleluia chant in the Mass are called *sequences*. Most of the religious poetry of the twelfth and thirteenth century was in this form, written, that is, to be used for the Latin services of the Church and making the ritual a constant source of creativity.

[19]Helen Waddell, *The Wandering Scholars*, pp. 192-193.

It was also from additions to the liturgy that the medieval, and hence the modern, drama was born. It was not possible for classical drama to inspire a Christian imitation in the earlier Middle Ages; in fact, it was not until the tradition of the western drama was well established that the revival of Roman and Greek drama came to influence it strongly. The liturgical origin of the drama was the *trope*, which, like the sequence, was an insertion of words and music into the liturgy. The earliest form of trope known is one attached to the Introit for the Mass on Easter Sunday in the form of a dialogue. The angels guarding the tomb ask, "Whom seek ye in the sepulchre, O followers of Christ?" The Marys answer: "Jesus of Nazareth, which was crucified, O celestial ones." The angels reply: "He is not here; he is risen, just as he foretold. Go, announce that he is risen from the sepulchre." From such simple beginnings as these, sung antiphonally by the choir, came the medieval mystery, miracle, and morality plays, as well as the vernacular farces. As long as the texts were kept simple, they could be performed in the church by the clergy and choir. But as they grew more elaborate, they were removed to the church porch and market place, the actors became laymen instead of clergy, and the subject matter was gradually secularized.

ABÉLARD AS A POET

Abélard claimed to have written love songs of European renown.[20] This may be one of them, reminiscent of Héloïse:

My clouded heart hath dulled my eyes—
They were stars before.
And on my lips my laughter lies
Joyfully no more.
Grieving I aver.
She hath vanished, she my nearest;
Strength of heart was in my dearest,
And I cling to her!

All the band of maids that follow
Love, she hath outshone.
She that took from bright Apollo
His name for her own; [*helios* = Héloïse?]
And her face reflects
More than sunshine, and I burn for
Her I wish for, her I yearn for
This year and the next.

Now I mourn my time's diurnal
Solitariness!
Once I plundered (O nocturnal
Hours were apt for this!)

[20]See pp. 646 ff.

Kisses from her mouth:
'Tis a well of balsam flowing,
And her heart's a garden growing
Cassia from the south.

God! I waste away and know
Hope of solace not;
Flower o' youth, you dare not grow!
But if I could blot
Time that cuts and parts—
Could we meet again, ah surely
Plighted faith would bind securely
Our divided hearts![21]

Abélard also wrote religious verse of power. Here, for example, is one on *Good Friday*:

Alone, dear Lord, to sacrifice you go
submitting to the death your coming breaks.
What can we say when wretchedly we know
that you are suffering for our sinful sakes?

We, we have sinned, to us the pain is due:
why must you then be punished for our deed?
O pierce our breasts to suffer here with you,
then our compassion may for mercy plead.

Now in the dark we weep, a three days' space,
a dusk of loss where tears forever start,
until the dawn uplifts her joyous face
and Christ is risen in each sorrowing heart.

Christ, make us bleed with pity for your end,
that in your glory we may find a place.
When three long days in hopeless grief we spend,
you yield the laughter of your paschal grace.[22]

SAINT BERNARD AS A POET

Saint Bernard's

Jesu dulcis memoria
Dans vera cordi gaudia,
Sed super mel et omnia
Eius dulcis praesentia

has become in English the hymn:

Jesus—the very thought is sweet!
In that dear name all heart-joys meet;
But sweeter than the honey far
The glimpses of His Presence are.

. . . . .

[21]Reprinted from *Medieval Latin Lyrics*, edited by P. S. Allen, by permission of The University of Chicago Press. Copyright 1931 by The University of Chicago Press. Quoted in C. W. Jones, *Medieval Literature in Translation*, pp. 261–262.
[22]Jack Lindsay, *Medieval Latin Poets*, p. 152.

I seek for Jesus in repose,
When round my heart its chambers close;
Abroad, and when I shut the door,
I long for Jesus evermore.

With Mary, in the morning gloom,
I seek for Jesus at the tomb;
For Him, with love's most earnest cry,
I seek with heart, and not with eye . . .

. . . O Jesu! King of wondrous might!
O Victor, glorious from the fight!
Sweetness that may not be express'd,
And altogether loveliest!

Remain with us, O Lord, today!
In every heart thy grace display;
That, now the shades of night are fled,
On Thee our spirits may be fed.

More glorious than the sun to see,
More fragrant than the balsam-tree,
My heart's desire, and boast, and mirth,
Jesu, salvation of the earth.[23]

ADAM OF ST. VICTOR

In the Augustinian monastery of St. Victor's at Paris, the center of a profound mysticism, the monk Adam was writing in the twelfth century some of the loveliest of all the Latin sequences. They were, however, orthodox sequences:

Of the Trinity to reason	Digne loqui de personis
Leads to license or to treason	Vim transcendit rationis,
Punishment deserving.	Excedit ingenia.
What is birth and what procession	Quid sit gigni, quid processus,
Is not mine to make profession,	Me nescire sum professus,
Save with faith unswerving.	Sed fide non dubia.
Thus professing, thus believing,	Qui sic credit, non festinet,
Never insolently leaving	Et a via non declinet
The highway of our faith,	Insolenter regia.
Duty weighing, law obeying,	Servet fidem, formet mores,
Never shall we wander straying	Nec attendat ad errores
Where heresy is death.[24]	Quos damnat Ecclesia.

To the Holy Spirit he addressed the following prayer:

Oh, helper of the heavy-laden,	Oh, juvamen oppressorum,
Oh, solace of the miserable,	Oh, solamen miserorum,
Of the poor, the refuge,	Pauperum refugium,
Give contempt of earthly pleasures!	Da contemptum terrenorum!
To the love of heavenly treasures	Ad amorem supernorum
Lift our hearts' desire!	Trahe desiderium!

[23]Trans. John Mason Neale, quoted in Jones, *Medieval Literature*, pp. 264–265.
[24]Henry Adams, *Mont St. Michel and Chartres*, pp. 326-328.

Consolation and foundation,
Dearest friend and habitation
   Of the lowly-hearted,
Dispel our evil, cleanse our foulness,
And our discords turn to concord,
   And bring us succour!

Consolator et fundator,
Habitator et amator,
   Cordium humilium,
Pelle mala, terge sordes,
Et discordes fac concordes,
   Et affer praesidium!

The significance of the incarnation he put as follows:

To death condemned by awful sentence,
God recalled us to repentance,
   Sending His only Son;
Whom He loved He came to cherish;
Whom His justice doomed to perish,
   By grace to life He won.

Ne periret homo reus
Redemptorem misit Deus,
   Pater unigenitum;
Visitavit quos amavit
Nosque vitae revocavit
   Gratia non meritum.

Infinity, Immensity,
Whom no human eye can see
   Or human thought contain,
Made of Infinity a space,
Made of Immensity a place,
   To win us Life again.

Infinitus et Immensus,
Quem non capit ullus sensus
   Nec locorum spatia,
Ex eterno temporalis,
Ex immenso fit localis,
   Ut restauret omnia.

To him the Virgin comes as solace for man, the "Heir of sin, by nature son of wrath, condemned to exile . . . "

In this valley full of tears,
Nothing softens, nothing cheers,
   All is suspected lure;
What safety can we hope for, here,
When even virtue faints for fear
   Her victory be not sure!

In hac valle lacrimarum
Nihil dulce, nihil carum,
   Suspecta sunt omnia;
Quid his nobis erit tutum,
Cum nec ipsa vel virtutum
   Tuta sit victoria!

Within, the flesh a traitor is,
Without, the world encompasses,
   A deadly wound to bring.
The foe is greedy for our spoils,
Now clasping us within his coils,
   Or hiding now his sting.

Caro nobis adversatur
Mundus carni suffragatur
   In nostram perniciem;
Hostis instat, nos infestans
Nunc se palam manifestans,
   Nunc occultans rabiem.

We sin, and penalty must pay,
And we are caught, like beasts of prey,
   Within the hunter's snares.
Nearest to God! oh Mary Mother!
Hope can reach us from none other,
   Sweet refuge from our cares;

Et peccamus et punimur,
Et diversis irretimur
   Laqueis venantium.
O Maria, mater Dei,
Tu, post Deum, summa spei,
   Tu dulce refugium;

We have no strength to struggle longer,
For our bonds are more and stronger
   Than our hearts can bear!
You who rest the heavy-laden,
You who lead lost souls to Heaven,
   Burst the hunter's snare! (p. 332)

Tot et tantis irretiti,
Non valemus his reniti
   Ne vi nec industria;
Consolatrix miserorum,
Suscitatrix mortuorum,
   Mortis rompe retia!

The sequence form reached its perfection at the hands of the Franciscans in the thirteenth century in two poems, the *Stabat Mater* and *Dies Irae*, that have become a permanent part of the liturgy. The first calls for universal sympathy on behalf of the Mother, torn with grief at the crucifixion of her Son:

Next the cross in tears unceasing,
Worn by sorrow aye increasing,
Stood the Mother 'neath her Son.

Stabat Mater dolorosa
Juxta crucem lacrimosa
Dum pendebat Filius:

Through her soul already riven,
Simeon's sword divinely driven,
Edged with anguish, lo! hath run.

Cujus animam gementem,
Contristantem et dolentem,
Pertransiit gladius.

Sad, afflicted as no other,
Was that chosen blessed Mother,
Having none but Christ begot.

O quam tristis et afflicta
Fuit illa benedicta
Mater Unigeniti!

Faithful Mother! upward gazing,
Heart and hands to Son upraising,
Mourns and grieves his cruel lot.

Quae moerebat, et dolebat,
Pia Mater dum videbat
Nati poenas inclyti.

Hard the man his tears refraining,
Watching Mary uncomplaining
Bear a sorrow like to none.

Quis est homo qui non fleret,
Matrem Christi si videret,
In tanto supplicio?

Hard the man that shares no sorrow
With a Mother fain to borrow
Every pang that writhes her Son.

Quis non posset contristari,
Christi Matrem contemplari
Dolentem cum Filio?

Tortured, scourged in expiation
Of the sins that marred his nation,
Mary watched his every pang.

Pro peccatis suae gentis
Vidit Jesum in tormentis
Et flagellis subditum.

She beheld her dear Begotten,
Stretched in death by all forgotten,
As on hoisted rood he hung.[25]

Vidit suum dulcem natum,
Moriendo desolatum,
Dum emisit spiritum.

THE "DIES IRAE"

The *Dies Irae* (Day of Wrath, that is, the day of the Last Judgment) catches all the terror and hope of the fervent Christian soul faced with this awful event:

Dreaded day, that day of ire,
When the world shall melt in fire,
Told by Sybil and David's lyre.

Dies irae, dies illa,
Solvet saeclum in favilla,
Teste David cum Cibylla.

Fright men's hearts shall rudely shift,
As the Judge through gleaming rift
Comes each soul to closely sift.

Quantus tremor est futurus,
Quando Judex est venturus,
Cuncta stricte discussurus!

[25]*The New Roman Missal*, pp. 969–970.

Then, the trumpet's shrill refrain,
Piercing tombs by hill and plain,
Souls to judgment shall arraign.

Death and nature stand aghast,
As the bodies rising fast,
Hie to hear the sentence passed.

Then, before Him shall be placed,
That whereon the verdict's based,
Book wherein each deed is traced.

When the Judge his seat shall gain,
All that's hidden shall be plain,
Nothing shall unjudged remain.

Wretched man, what can I plead?
Whom to ask to intercede,
When the just much mercy need?

Thou, O awe-inspiring Lord,
Saving e'en when unimplored,
Save me, mercy's fount adored.

Ah! Sweet Jesus, mindful be,
That Thou cam'st on earth for me:
Cast me not this day from Thee.

Seeking me thy strength was spent,
Ransoming thy limbs were rent:
Is this toil to no intent?

Thou, awarding pains condign,
Mercy's ear to me incline,
Ere the reckoning Thou assign.

I, felon-like, my lot bewail,
Suffused cheeks my shame unveil:
God! O let my prayer prevail.

Mary's soul Thou madest white,
Didst to heaven the thief invite,
Hope in me these now excite.

Prayers of mine in vain ascend:
Thou art good and wilt forefend,
In quenchless fire my life to end.

'Mid thy sheep my place accord,
Keep me from the tainted horde,
Set me in thy sight, O Lord.

When the cursed by shame opprest,
Enter flames at thy behest,
Call me then to join the blest.

Prostrate, suppliant, now no more
Unrepenting, as of yore,
Save me dying, I implore.

Tuba mirum spargens sonum
Per sepulchra regionum,
Coget omnes ante thronum.

Mors stupebit et natura,
Cum resurget creatura,
Judicanti responsura.

Liber scriptus proferetur,
In quo datum continetur,
Unde mundus judicetur.

Judex ergo cum sedebit
Quidquid latet, apparebit:
Nil inultum remanebit.

Quid sum miser tunc dicturus?
Quem patronum rogatorus?
Cum vix justus sit securus.

Rex tremendae majestatis,
Qui salvandos salvas gratis,
Salva me fons pietatis.

Recordare Jesu pie,
Quod sum causa tuae viae,
Ne me perdas illa die.

Quaerens me sedisti lassus;
Redemisti crucem passus:
Tantus labor not sit cassus.

Juste Judex ultionis,
Donum fac remissionis,
Ante diem rationis.

Ingemisco tamquam reus:
Culpa rubet vultus meus:
Supplicanti parce Deus.

Qui Mariam absolvisti,
Et latronem exaudisti,
Mihi quoque spem dedisti.

Preces meae non sunt dignae;
Sed tu bonus fac benigne,
Ne perenni cremer igne.

Inter oves locum praesta,
Et ab hoedis me sequestra,
Statuens in parte dextra.

Confutatis maledictis,
Flammis acribus addictis,
Voca me cum benedictis.

Oro supplex et acclinis,
Cor contritum quasi cinis:
Gere curam mei finis.

Mournful day! that day of sighs,	Lacrimosa dies illa,
When from dust shall man arise,	Qua resurget ex favilla
Strained with guilt his doom to know,	Judicandus homo reus.
Mercy, Lord, on him bestow.	Huic ergo parce Deus:
Jesus, kind! Thy souls release,	Pie Jesu Domine,
Lead them thence to realms of peace.	Dona eis requiem.

(*The New Roman Missal*, pp. 1503–1505)

Medieval Literature: Vernacular

THE ETHICS OF CHIVALRY

The vernacular literatures in the later Middle Ages were in large part concerned with exemplifying the virtues that ought to be possessed by the true gentleman. In other words, they praised the ethics of chivalry, and consequently they record that process of refinement that transformed the raw feudal bully, crunching his sword through the skulls of his enemies, into a loyal vassal, devout son of the Church, and champion of the ladies. Feudal institutions themselves helped to initiate the process. The virtue of loyalty in the vassal strengthened and gave sanction to the feudal contract, and thus enabled it to work. Feudalism produced its own disciplinary system, the training in and about the castle that made the knight. The knight was primarily a soldier, schooled originally in the hard fighting of the ninth and tenth centuries. His virtues were necessarily martial: strength, valor, skill, and endurance, all those summarized by the word "prowess."[26] The knight was also a vassal and fief holder, and as such he had regularly to perform the terms of the feudal contract and to exhibit the personal devotion to his lord symbolized by such ceremonies as homage and fealty. Loyalty, fidelity, and integrity were the noble virtues of a good vassal. They were stimulated when the lord maintained a bounteous court and was generous to his followers.

The cultivation of such virtues the feudal class made its own business. To be chivalrous was to possess them. As the new feudal families of the post-Carolingian period hardened into a noble cast of which knighthood was the badge of honor, so these virtues were made peculiar to the members of the ruling aristocracy. Only the noble could be a gentleman, and only the nobility could really fight, serve, and govern.

THE CHURCH AND MARTIAL VIRTUES

The Church had need of such a nobility to protect its persons and property. Its own upper ranks were manned by the younger sons of these aristocratic families, and its lands were involved in the whole nexus of feudal relationships. It was in its interests, too, to see that the feudal virtues

[26]See Sidney Painter, *French Chivalry*, Chap. ii.

were upheld. Yet it sought also to correct the abuses called forth by martial fury and to raise the knight's vision above the mere accumulation of earthly glory and fortune. It sought with the Peace of God to exempt certain classes from the outcome of unrestrained private warfare. The decent knight would not molest the clergy and property of the Church; he would protect such noncombatants as women, children, and merchants on the highway. When such measures failed, it sought with the Truce of God to exempt such crucial times from feudal warfare as when the peasant was plowing, sowing, and harvesting his fields. Finally, when the Moslems invaded western Europe and spread over the Middle East for a second time, the Church decided to utilize the martial abilities of the aristocracy for a crusade. The true knight refrained from attacking the Church and its property; he also fought for it as a crusader. He fought not only against infidels but also against pagans, schismatics, heretics, and political enemies of the papacy. The ideal knight, the Church finally taught, was a fighting monk, a member of a crusading order. When the western knight took up the cultivation of gallantry, the Church urged as a substitute for his earthly lady the Virgin Mother of God, and impressed upon him the Christian virtue of chastity, to combat the troubadour's advocacy of adultery. The Church did indeed attempt to transform the knight into a monk, riding abroad seeking holy adventures, culminating in the vision of the Holy Grail. Knighthood, too, ended in mysticism. The ritual that marked the transformation of the knight into a servant of the Church was that of the Knight of the Bath, substituted for the older Knight of the Sword.

THE "NIBELUNGENLIED"

Anglo-Saxon was the first of the German dialects to be set down in writing.[27] In the twelfth and thirteenth centuries a large store of Icelandic tales, the stories of pagan gods and heroes, and of the expansion and settlement of a people, were written down in the sagas, reflecting a prefeudal world. This literature contained the *Prose Edda* of Snorri Sturluson (1179-1241), a collection of material from ancient legend and history, of rules for poetic composition, and illustrations from earlier verse, all for the use of Icelandic poets. In it is to be found the tale of the *Niblung Hoard*, an early version of the tale of the *Ring of the Nibelungs*. It is this tale that was made over into the epic *Nibelungenlied* by a south German poet writing in the Austrian dialect somewhere between 1190 and 1205. In the *Nibelungenlied* the older pagan and heroic material from the period of the barbarian invasions has been somewhat transformed by the spirit of Christianity and of chivalry.

The setting of the poem is "Worms by the Rhine," in the kingdom of Burgundy, where the noble maiden Kriemhild is guarded by her three

[27]See pp. 424 f.

brothers, Kings Gunther, Gernot, and Giselher, courteous lords of "high lineage, bold, and very strong, each of them the pick of knights." As her husband, Kriemhild acquired Siegfried, the king of Netherland, the great hero who had captured from the family of the Nibelungs their hoard of gold. He had secured her from King Gunther only after having helped the king win the athletic Queen Brunhilde of Issland as his wife. For Brunhilde would have no one as husband who could not beat her at hurling a stone, leaping after it, and heaving a spear. And the spear she threw could scarcely be carried by three of her lords, and the stone by twelve strong knights. Siegfried, wearing a coat that made him invisible, beat the queen at her games, and, after Gunther had brought her to Burgundy, he had been rewarded with Kriemhild, the loveliest of maidens. Siegfried had also been obliged to subdue Brunhilde and, for Gunther, force her to play her dutiful role as married wife. When Brunhilde had repulsed Gunther on their wedding night, he "began to be angry with her, and fought with her and tore her raiment. And the royal maiden seized a girdle, a strong embroidered silk cord that she wore round her waist, and did hurt enow to the knight [Gunther]. She bound his hands and his feet, and carried him to a nail and hung him on the wall. She forbade him to touch her because he disturbed her sleep. He almost perished from her strength," and was left hanging until morning. The following night the loyal Siegfried, in his magic coat, took the king's place. When he "put his arm round the valiant maiden, she threw him onto a bench, that his head rang loud against a foot stool." The conqueror of the Nibelungs then thought to himself, "If I lose my life by the hand of a woman, all wives evermore will make light of their husbands, that, without this, would not dare. . . . Then Siegfried got hold of Brunhilde. Albeit she fought valiantly, her defense was grown weak. . . . She squeezed his hands till, by her strength, the blood spurted out from his nails. Then he broke the strong will that she had shown at the first. . . . Siegfried pressed her down till she cried aloud, for his might hurt her greatly. She clutched at her side, where she found her girdle and sought to tie his hands. But he gripped her till the joints of her body cracked. So the strife was ended. Siegfried rose up then and left her, as though he would throw off his clothes. He drew from her hand a gold ring, without that she was aware of it. He took her girdle also, a good silken band." Gunther then took Siegfried's place and with his mighty queen "abode there till the bright day."[28]

This indelicate matter of Siegfried's substitution for Gunther came to light in a bitter dispute between the two ladies over the relative merits of their husbands. Brunhilde claimed that however reputable Siegfried was as a knight, he was still the vassal of her husband, and thus inferior. Kriemhild retorted that she would like to see anyone keep her from entering the

[28]From *The Fall of the Nibelungs*, translated by Margaret Armour. Everyman's Library, published by E. P. Dutton and Company, Inc. Quoted in Jones, *Medieval Literature*, pp. 437 ff.

cathedral before the queen, whose vassal her husband was supposed to be. "So they met before the minster, and Brunhilde, with deadly spite, cried out to Kriemhild to stand still. Before the queen shall no vassal go." It was at this moment that Kriemhild accused the muscular Brunhilde of having been the mistress of her vassal husband, and then stalked into the cathedral. "There was deadly hate, and bright eyes grew wet and dim." When, after the service, Brunhilde sought proof of the charge against her, Kriemhild produced the ring and girdle that Siegfried had taken from Brunhilde on the night he substituted for Gunther. In spite of his denial that he had boasted of his prowess, Siegfried was not able to placate his enemies at Gunther's court. Hagen of Trony, after hearing Brunhilde's story, "swore straightway that Kriemhild's husband should pay for it, or never would Hagen be glad again." He is represented in the poem as the loyal vassal, loyal to his lord's wife as well as his lord, and unable to support the wealth of the Nibelung hoard, which came to Kriemhild as her dowry and which she used to build up a party in the Burgundian court. Under the pretext that he wished to protect Siegfried under all circumstances, he learned from Kriemhild that Siegfried was vulnerable in a small spot on his back where, while he was bathing in the dragon's blood that had made him invulnerable, a "broad leaf of a lime tree" fell between his shoulders. In the course of a hunting trip in the Odinwald Hagen murdered Siegfried with a stab between the shoulders, and "his heart's blood spurted out on the traitor's clothes."

At this point the *Nibelungenlied* becomes a feud between Hagen and Kriemhild, Hagen seeming to dread what this woman portended for the Burgundian feudal world, both because of her fabulous wealth, and because of her marriage with Attila the Hun, and Kriemhild's seeking a fierce and primitive revenge for the murder of her beloved Siegfried. After the death of Siegfried Hagen seized her wondrous treasure and "sunk it in the Rhine near Locheim." When envoys came from Etzel (Attila), the pagan king of the Huns, seeking Kriemhild as his wife, Hagen was the only Burgundian to oppose the suit. For Kriemhild, the marriage with Etzel was an opportunity to take revenge on Hagen. "Haply I may yet avenge my dear husband's death. Etzel hath so many knights, that, were they mine to command, I could do what I would. Thereto, he is so wealthy that I shall have wherewith to bestow gifts. Cruel Hagen hath taken my treasure from me."

After seven years as the queen of the Huns Kriemhild sought to achieve her maniacal aim, the death of Hagen, by inviting the Burgundians, her kinsmen, to visit the Hunnish capital. When this invitation was brought to Worms, it was opposed by Hagen. He said to King Gunther, "If thou goest to see Kriemhild, thou mayest lose thine honour and thy life. The wife of King Etzel hath a long memory." Hagen went along only when taunted by Gernot: "Because thou fearest death with reason among the Huns, it were ill done on our part to keep away from our sister." Led by

Hagen, the Burgundian court passed through Germany and Austria, stopping to visit Margrave Rudeger in Hun territory. Here Rudeger gave his daughter to Giselher, Kriemhild's brother, and having pledged his friendship to the Burgundians led them on to Attila's capital.

Here the fierce Hagen-Kriemhild rivalry was renewed by the mutual slaughter of the Burgundian and Hunnish knights. Kriemhild sent loyal retainers to attack the sleeping Burgundians in their hall the first night of their stay. The attack was thwarted. "The queen was heavy of her cheer when they told her that her messengers had failed. She began to contrive it otherwise, for grim was her mood."

At a feast tendered the guests on the following day Ortlieb, the young son of Attila and Kriemhild, was brought in to the table at which Hagen sat. When Hagen heard that hostilities had broken out between the two courts, he "slew the child Ortlieb, that the blood gushed down on his hand from his sword, and the head flew up into the queen's lap." In the deadly fracas that followed, "of the Huns that had been in the hall, not one was left alive," and Hagen ordered their bodies carried out. "They did as he commanded, and bore the seven thousand dead bodies to the door, and threw them out." Then "a thousand and four" Thuringians and Danes attacked the Burgundians in the hall and were killed. "When the tumult fell, there was silence. Over all the blood of the dead men trickled through the crannies into the gutters below. They of the Rhine had done this by their prowess." Thereupon Etzel and Kriemhild engaged "twenty thousand or more" men of Hungary to attack the strangers. When the Burgundians sought a truce and were told they could have one only by surrendering Hagen, they refused, and Kriemhild urged the Hunnish knights forward again. "I will requite Hagen's insolence to the full. Let not one of them forth at any point, and I will let kindle the hall at its four sides. So will my heart's dole be avenged." To assuage the thirst caused by the burning hall, Hagen advised the Burgundians to drink the blood of the dead. "Then went one where he found a dead body. He knelt by the wounds, and did off his helmet, and began to drink the streaming blood . . . many more of them drank the blood and their bodies were strengthened." After this holocaust six hundred of the Burgundians were left alive.

Finally, Rudeger, the margrave who had pledged his friendship to the Burgundians, was called upon to fulfill his loyalty to the Huns. He shouted into the hall, "Stand on your defence . . . I would have helped you, but must slay you. Once we were friends, but I cannot keep my faith . . . King Etzel's wife will have it so." He is slain in combat with Gernot— "slain by each other's hand." Then Dietrich of Bern (historically Theodoric the Ostrogoth) and his knights took up the battle. "They smote till the links of their foemen's mail whistled asunder, and their broken sword-points flew on high. They struck hot-flaming streams from the helmets." Finally, of all the knights none were left alive save two, Gunther and Hagen. After giving him "a wound that was deep and wide," Dietrich of

Bern took Hagen captive and brought him to Kriemhild, who put him in a dungeon. He took Gunther captive also, and the queen imprisoned him. When Hagen refused to return the hoard he had sunk in the Rhine, at the promise of life for both him and Gunther, Kriemhild "bade them slay her brother, and they smote off his head. She carried it by the hair to the knight of Trony." She then drew Siegfried's sword "from the sheath. He could not hinder it. She purposed to slay the knight. She lifted it high with both hands, and smote off his head." Then Hildebrand, one of Dietrich's men, to avenge "the death of the bold knight of Trony . . . sprang fiercely at Kriemhild, and slew her with his sword. . . . Her loud cry helped her not.

"Dead bodies lay stretched over all. The Queen was hewn in pieces. Etzel and Dietrich began to weep. They wailed piteously for kinsmen and vassals. . . . The end of the king's hightide was woe, even as, at the last, all joy turneth to sorrow." The rulers were left with nothing to rule. It is hard to refrain from seeing in this mutual slaughter of West and East in the *Nibelungenlied* an early picture of the murderous desolation that, on a much vaster scale, would probably be the outcome of a modern East-West conflict.

THE "SONG OF ROLAND"

An English chronicler reports that at the Battle of Hastings the Normans and their allies went into battle with a minstrel named Taillefer who,

> Mounted on a charger strong,
> Rode on before the Duke, and sang
> Of Roland and of Charlemagne,
> Oliver and the vassals all
> Who fell in fight at Roncesvals.[29]

By the end of the eleventh century the story of Roland, whose death Einhard reports in his *Life of Charlemagne*,[30] had been made the vehicle for the first notable work in the dialect of northern France, the epic *Chanson de Roland (Song of Roland)*. The author who wrote this epic was not a historian, or, if he was, he did not bother to cloak his tale with accurate details of a Carolingian environment. He wrote at a time when feudalism had reorganized the French half of the former empire of Charlemagne, and when the Capetian kings of France, as the overlords of French vassals, were beginning to stabilize the chaos of private feudal war. He wrote, moreover, at a time when the knights of western Europe, under the leadership of the French, were going off to the East on the First Crusade. In terms of the late eleventh century, therefore, the poem carries on the tradition promoted by Charlemagne, with his crusades against

[29]See p. 379. This translation is by Henry Adams, quoted in Jones, *Medieval Literature*, p. 520.
[30]See pp. 378 ff.

Mohammedan Spain. Its spirit, however, is monarchical rather than imperial. Charlemagne, in the poem, is the patriarchial king of "sweet France," some two hundred years old and with a white, flowing beard. He is surrounded by his loyal vassals, the "peers of France," who lead the rest of the French feudality. Charles and his vassals are also eleventh-century crusaders in Spain; the poem expresses the same naïve Christianity as the chroniclers of the First Crusade. The feudal virtues that the poem extolls are the manly virtues of the loyal vassal and the devoted comrade at arms. The *Nibelungenlied*, written a century later, praises these virtues also. Siegfried and Hagen are types of heroes exemplifying the noble vassal. The *Nibelungenlied* also retains some of the atmosphere and legend of a still-earlier heroic period, when the Germans were migrating through the Roman Empire: the amazonian strength and fierce passion of a Brunhilde, the cunning and all-consuming revengeful rage of a Kriemhild, the savage spirit of a Hagen, when not restrained by a vassal's loyalty, and the bloody ferocity of the Hunnish court. Into this primitive and feudal atmosphere, none too well compounded, is introduced something of the cult of the Lady that the French had developed. Before the death of Siegfried, Kriemhild is portrayed as the gentle noblewoman, and Rudeger's daughter Gotelind is beautiful and gentle enough to melt all male hearts. Into the *Chanson de Roland* not much of the cult of romantic love has crept. Roland's fair Aude appears at the very end of the tale to inquire of Charlemagne what has befallen her hero, and dies when she learns of his death. Women do not occupy very many lines of the poem. It is the man's feudal world that is characterized in the strong, valiant knight, astride a noble horse, swinging a powerful sword, as only a French knight can swing it, on behalf of a king of sweet France with whom no other can compare; a world that is sanctioned also by an intolerant, martial religion.

The traitor of this piece is Roland's stepfather Ganelon, who, while on a mission of peace to the Spanish Moslems of Saragossa, betrayed his lord Charlemagne by arranging to have the French rear guard, which Roland was to captain, attacked in the pass of Roncesvalles, while the main French army went on ahead. A rear guard of some twenty thousand French knights thus found itself attacked by 400,000 Saracen cavalry. When faced with such a preponderance, Oliver, Roland's companion, wants him to blow his horn and summon Charlemagne to return, but Roland refuses. "That were the act of a fool . . . God forbid that it be said by any living man that for fear of Pagans I blew my horn! My skin shall not be thus dishonored. When I am in the thick of the fight, I shall strike blows even unto a thousand and seven hundred, and you shall see the steel of Durendal dripping with blood."[1] As Roland crossed the pass of Spain on his swift horse, Veillantif, "He bore his arms, which became him well; and rode brandishing his spear, twirling it, the point toward heaven, the white pennon floating at the tip, with its fringes of gold beating against his hands. Noble was his figure, his face bright and laughing." The nephew of the Spanish Emir Marsile advanced toward Roland, shouting insults. "When Roland heard him, O Lord, how great his grief! He spurred his horse and gave it rein, and rode to smite the Pagan as hard as he could. He pierced his shield and rent his hauberk, cut open his breast, and broke his bones, and severed his spine from his back. With his spear he cast forth the Pagan's soul. He struck him squarely, striking his body, and with the full force of his spear, flinging him dead from his horse. His neck was broken in twain." In a subsequent encounter with Chernuble of Munigre, whose hair swept the ground, and who could, "when he wished, carry, in jest, a greater weight than four laden mules," Roland "pierced his helmet, where the carbuncles shone. He cut through the coif and through his hair, through his eyes and his face, through his white hauberk, fine-linked, through his whole body even to the groin, through the saddle of beaten gold. The sword did not stop until it plunged into the horse, cleaving its spine without seeking the joint, and laying horse and rider dead upon the grass. . . . What a sight to see him cast one dead upon the other, while the bright blood flooded the place."[31]

Meanwhile the martial Archbishop Turpin had taken on one "skilled in evil arts." "There was no man under heaven whom he felt more like hating. He spurred his horse with his spurs of fine gold, and rode in his might to strike him. He pierced his shield, rent his coat-of-mail, and thrust his great lance through the middle of his body. Fairly he struck him, striking him so that with the full force of his spear he flung him dead upon the road. He looked down and beheld the wretch lying there; nor did he refrain from speaking to him." The archbishop then slew Siglorel the Enchanter, who had once descended into hell, whither "Jupiter had led him by magic," and then took on Abisme, than whom "there was none more wicked in the Pagan host. Evil were his vices and heinous his crimes. He believed not in God the Son of Saint Mary. Black was he as melted pitch. Better did he love treachery and murder than all the gold of Galicia. No one had ever seen him play or laugh. . . . The archbishop could have no love for him. As soon as he saw him, he longed to smite him. He spoke softly to himself: 'That Saracen seems to me to be a heretic. The best thing I can do is to go and slay him. Never have I liked a coward or cowardice.' " The archbishop was mounted on "a swift and nimble charger, with hollow hoofs and flat legs, short thighs and broad croupe, long flanks and a straight back, a white tail and a yellow mane, small ears and tawny head. No beast could compare with him for speed. How valiantly the archbishop spurred! He would not fail to attack Abisme. He rode to strike him in his wondrous shield. On it there were precious stones: amethysts and topazes, esterminals and blazing carbuncles. In Val Metas a devil had given it to him as a present . . . Turpin struck his shield, not sparing it at all. I ween after his blow it was not worth a penny. Turpin pressed the Pagan's body from one side to the other, striking him

[31]*Chanson de Roland*, trans. Merriam Sherwood, p. 47.

down dead in an empty spot. Said the French: 'What mighty prowess! The Crosier is indeed safe with the archbishop.' "

Despite such heroism, the French were overcome by Saracen numbers. When about sixty remained, Roland was willing to blow his horn. To Oliver this was now impossible. "To blow it now were cowardice." He then turned on Roland. "This is all your fault; for valor with sense is not madness. Measure is worth more than foolhardiness. The French are dead through your thoughtlessness . . . If you had taken my advice, my Lord would have returned. We should have won this battle . . . Your prowess, Roland, woe the day we saw it." Roland blew his horn, nevertheless. "Count Roland blew his horn, with great effort and in pain, so hard that the bright blood gushed from his mouth and his brain burst from his temples. The sound of his horn carried far. Charles heard it as he crossed the pass." One by one, the peers of France fell: Oliver, Turpin, and finally Roland. When he felt that death was taking hold of him, he confessed his sins and prayed God for mercy. "He offered his right glove to God. Saint Gabriel took it from his hand. On his arms his head was resting. With clasped hands he went to his death. God sent to him His angel Cherubim and Saint Michael of the Peril of the Sea. Saint Gabriel came with them. Together they bore the soul of the Count to Paradise." (p. 70)

The French, to be sure, were avenged when Charlemagne returned with the main French army and "tore his beard as a man grief-stricken" when he saw his slain knights. God made the sun to stand still so that the French did not have to wait for their revenge. They forced the Saracens to withdraw to Saragossa, where "they ran into a crypt, to an idol of Apollo. They upbraided and vilely insulted him: 'Ah, wicked God, why has thou shamed us so? Why hast thou permitted our King to be confounded? To him who serves thee well thou givest evil pay.' Then they took from the god his scepter and his crown, and hung him by his hands to a pillar. They trampled him on the ground beneath their feet, beat and smashed him with great sticks. Then, from Termagant [another Saracen god] they took his carbuncles, and Mahound [Mohammed] they threw into a ditch, where swine and dogs gnawed and trampled him." (p. 106)

Finally, the two-hundred-year-old Charlemagne is made to take on the emir of Babylon-in-Egypt, Baligant, who "had lived longer than Vergil and Homer. . . . Ah, God, what a baron, had he been a Christian." When in the midst of combat the emir offered terms, Charles said, "A vile act that, methinks! To a Pagan I must not grant peace or love. Accept Christianity, the faith that God hath given us, and I shall love thee straightway." The fight went on until finally Charles "pierced his helmet, on which the gems sparkled; clove his face, even to his white beard, striking him dead without hope of recovery." When Saragossa was taken, "the synagogues and the mosques" were "well searched by a thousand Frenchmen. Wielding iron hammers and axes, they smashed the images and all the idols. There should remain neither sorcery nor falsehood. The King [Charlemagne] believed in God. He wished to serve Him. His bishop blessed the water, and the Pagans were led to the baptistry. If there was any who refused baptism, Charles had him made captive or burned or put to the sword. Well over a hundred thousand were baptized as true Christians. But not the Queen. She was to be taken, a captive, to sweet France. The King wished to accomplish her conversion by affection, not by force." (pp. 147–151)

After the victory the French returned home, where Ganelon, having been entrusted to the cooks of the army, was put to death for treason after his champion had lost a trial by combat. It was agreed that he should "die in fearful anguish. Four chargers were led forward. To these they bound the traitor's feet and hands. The horses were proud-spirited and swift. Four of the guards urged them forward toward a stream which was in the middle of a field. Ganelon was utterly destroyed, as his muscles were stretched; all the limbs of his body broken. The bright blood flowed over the green grass. Ganelon died the death of a craven traitor."

That night the white-bearded emperor, having now at great cost completed the conquest and Christianization of another land, wearily went to bed in his vaulted chamber. Then "Saint Gabriel came to him with a message from God: 'Charles, muster the armies of thine empire! Thou shalt enter by force the land of Bire, to succor King Vivien in Imphe, a city besieged by the Pagans. The Christians are calling upon thee and crying out.' The Emperor had no wish to go. 'Oh, God!' said the King. 'How troublous is my life!' He wept with his eyes and tore his white beard." (p. 165)

THE POETRY OF THE TROUBADOURS

At the time when the *Chanson de Roland* was being written there emerged from southern France, in the dialect called Provençal, a body of lyric poetry written by troubadours in which men played the role of the lover-thrall of the high-born and enchanting mistress of the castle. This attitude reversed the normal position of women in feudal society. A man's world, it subordinated woman to the position of the holder of a noble name who could bring property to her husband and give birth to children who could carry on the family name and tradition. In feudal marriage the question of love did not properly enter.

The attitude of the Church did nothing to improve this position. After all, woman had brought about the fall of man, and her physical charms were a constant snare for him. The Church had no place in its system of values for sexual love. Marriage was but a means of reproducing one's kind. For a man to love his wife with passion was adultery.[32] Chastity was the Christian virtue. The clergy were celibate. Saint Jerome had said that the only purpose of marriage was to produce virgins.

[32]See Lewis, *Allegory of Love*, p. 15.

Medieval poets often reflected this clerical attitude toward women:

> Frail woman, never constant save in crime,
> Is fain in mischief to spend all her time.

> A woman has a thousand ways to work her will upon us.
> She prides herself the more, the more of evil she has done us.
> Most mischievous of all created things, the devil in her
> Beholds his perfect instrument, the true predestined sinner.

A monk of Cluny is more outspoken:

> A creature of crime, a thing for all time fleshly evil, just flesh without mind.
> Ever busy to harm, taught to use nature's charm, for mischief in women we
> find;
> The foulest of jakes, the most deadly of snakes, fair outside and corruption
> within.

> A path where you trip, she strips those who strip her, a public incentive to
> sin.[33]

This was not the attitude of the wandering student, nor indeed of the troubadours. It is a far cry from "the great beauty, the good manners, the shining worth, the high reputation, the courteous speech, and the fresh complexion which you possess, good lady of worth, inspire me with the desire and the ability to envy." The effect upon the troubadour of such a perfect creature was extraordinary. "My heart is so full of joy that everything in nature seems changed. I see in the winter only white, red, and yellow flowers; the wind and rain do nothing but add to my happiness; my skill waxes, and my song grows better. I have in my heart so much love, joy, and pleasure that ice seems to me flowers, and snow green grass. I can go out without clothes, naked in my shirt; my passion protects me from the iciest wind." "When I see her, when I consider her eyes, her face, her complexion, I tremble with fear like a leaf in the wind; a child has more sense than I retain in the violence of my transports." Love made a man a better man. "It makes a vile creature into a distinguished man, a fool into a man of agreeable conversation, a miser into a spendthrift, and it transforms a rascal into a man of honor. By it insane men become sages, the gauche become polished, but the haughty are changed into gentle and humble men." "For the ladies always make valiant the most cowardly and the wickedest felons; for however free and gracious a man is, if he did not love a lady, he would be disagreeable to everyone."[34] The troubadour often expressed this love in feudal terms: the lover was the vassal of the lady, rendering her service in accordance with

[33]F. A. Wright, "Medieval Poetry," *Edinburgh Review*, CCXLVIII (October, 1928), 339–340.
[34]Painter, *French Chivalry*, pp. 112–113.

a contract she was also expected to fulfill. While he might think of moments when "free and bold"

> Or even in secret—I could fold
> Within my arms your fair, sweet form,
> And gaze and lavish kisses warm
> On lips, on eyes, until in one
> We melt a hundred—still not done.[35]

he was normally content with less than this. Nor did either feudal nobles or their wives surrender to the poet who was content to make love a matter of verse. Yet what he did propose was a liberation of women from the yoke of feudal marriage, and accordingly a complete reversal in the position she conventionally held. What he did inaugurate was the cult of courtly or romantic love that has dominated western literature ever since, and has contributed to the ascendancy of women in some societies. In any case, it appears to be a first step in the actual emancipation of women from the limitations set up by the male world.

The appearance in Provence of the theme of courtly love as the dominant theme of troubadour poetry is not an easy thing to explain. It is sometimes attributed to similar treatments of the love theme in Arabic poetry, or to the popularity of the cult of the Virgin, or to the revival of Ovid's *Ars Amatoria*. It seems more reasonable to explain it as a result of the transformation of the castle from a fortress, stable, and arsenal into a court where capable ladies with strong personalities displayed their graces and, anxious to be appreciated, eager to tame the rough and boorish vassals who attended them, allied with the poets (and there are always poets) who, as always, were looking for a means of livelihood and found it in the patronage of the ladies whom they praised. Romantic love was a conspiracy between the lady and poet against feudal marriage.

ELEANOR OF AQUITAINE

Such a lady was Eleanor of Aquitaine.[36] Her experience with royal husbands had not led her to be enthusiastic about men or marriage. King Louis VII, her first, turned out to be a monk, she said, and this marriage ended in divorce. Henry of Anjou, her second, was tempestuous and unfaithful, and unappreciative of her desire to be an independent lady in her own right. After all, she came from a family of troubadours, and had had the devotion of a very distinguished one—Bernard de Ventadour. Dissatisfied with Henry's mistress and his policy, she withdrew (*ca.* 1170) to her own land (Poitou) and her own capital (Poitiers) to organize a court in which men would be trained to recognize the superiority of women and do them homage. To help her, she had such influential daughters as Marie, countess of Champagne,

[35]J. H. Smith, *The Troubadours at Home*, I, 174.   [36]See p. 551.

Marie had in her patronage a chaplain named Andreas, who wrote for her a codification of the rules and regulations of the new cult of love called *The Art of Courtly Love*. For this cleric it was clear that love was no Platonic matter. He defines it as "a certain inborn suffering derived from the sight of and excessive meditation upon the beauty of the opposite sex, which causes each one to wish above all things the embraces of the other and by common desire to carry out all of Love's precepts in the other's embraces." "Everyone of sound mind who is capable of doing the work of Venus may be wounded by one of Love's arrows unless prevented by age, or blindness, or excess of passion." This love is a great civilizer. It "causes a rough and uncouth man to be distinguished for his handsomeness; it can endow a man even of the humblest birth with nobility of character; it blesses the proud with humility; and the man in love becomes accustomed to performing many services gracefully for everyone. O what a wonderful thing is love, which makes a man shine with so many virtues and teaches everyone, no matter who he is, so many good traits of character."[37]

But the love that ennobles was for the upper and middle classes. It was not for the peasants. With them "it rarely happens that we find farmers serving in Love's court, but naturally, like a horse or a mule, they give themselves up to the work of Venus, as nature's urging teaches them to do. . . . And even if it should happen at times, though rarely, that contrary to their nature, they are stirred up by Cupid's arrows, it is not expedient that they should be instructed in the theory of love, lest while they are devoting themselves to conduct which is not natural to them, the kindly farms which are usually made fruitful by their efforts may through lack of cultivation prove useless to us. But if you should, by some chance, fall in love with some of their women, be careful to puff them up with lots of praise and then, when you find a convenient place, do not hesitate to take what you seek and to embrace them by force. For you can hardly soften their outward inflexibility so far that they will grant you their embraces quietly or permit you to have the solaces you desire unless first you use a little compulsion as a convenient cure for their shyness. We do not say these things, however, because we want to persuade you to love such women, but only so that, if through lack of caution you should be driven to love them, you may know, in brief compass, what to do."

Andreas fills his treatise with conversations between men and women of the upper and middle classes on the subject of love, and he includes also a number of cases in dispute brought to Eleanor's court of love for settlement. In the course of the conversations twelve chief rules of love are proposed. Among them are

[37]Andreas Capellanus, *The Art of Courtly Love*, trans. John J. Parry, passim.

II. Thou shalt keep thyself chaste for the sake of her whom thou lovest.
IV. Thou shalt not choose for thy love anyone whom a natural sense of shame forbids thee to marry.
VI. Thou shalt not have many who know of thy love affair.
VIII. In giving and receiving love's solaces let modesty be ever present.
XI. Thou shalt be in all things polite and courteous.
XII. In practicing the solaces of love thou shalt not exceed the desires of thy lover.

Subsequently Andreas gives thirty-one more rules for lovers. Among them are

I. Marriage is no real excuse for not loving.
II. He who is not jealous cannot love.
V. That which a lover takes against the will of his beloved has no relish.
VIII. No one should be deprived of love without the very best of reasons.
XIII. When made public, love rarely endures.
XIV. The easy attainment of love makes it of little value; difficulty of attainment makes it prized.
XV. Every lover regularly turns pale in the presence of his beloved.
XVI. When a lover suddenly catches sight of his beloved his heart palpitates.
XVIII. Good character alone makes any man worthy of love.
XXIII. He whom the thought of love vexes eats and sleeps very little.
XXV. A true lover considers nothing good except what he thinks will please his beloved.
XXVI. Love can deny nothing to love.
XXX. A true lover is constantly and without intermission possessed by the thought of his beloved.
XXXI. Nothing forbids one woman being loved by two men or one man by two women.

Andreas was a chaplain writing for a very distinguished noble lady on a subject not usually covered by chaplains. She may well have dictated to him his table of contents and supplied him with material. When he finished two books on the matter, he seems to have become aware that he, a clergyman, had written a description of the ennobling effects of adulterous love. He hastened to add a third book on the *Rejection of Love*, which we must suppose he did not send Marie, or if he did it was well understood that the last book was for the sake of his clerical superiors or general propriety and was not to be taken seriously, and certainly not to be read. He did not, he says, write the early books "because we consider it advisable for you or any other man to fall in love, but for fear lest you might think us stupid." Since "God is more pleased with a man who is able to sin and does not than with a man who has no opportunity to sin," the early books contain very useful information. But it should be understood that "God hates, and in both testaments commands the punishment of, those whom he sees engaged in the works of Venus outside the bonds of wedlock or caught in the toils of any sort of passion. . . . O wretched and insane, to be looked upon as lower than a beast is that man who for the sake of a momentary delight of the flesh will reject eternal joys and strive to bind himself over to the flames of ever-burning Gehenna!" "Woman, it is to be understood, is a thoroughly vile creature, the compound of all the mortal sins. . . . There is nothing in the world more loathsome or more wearisome than to meditate too intently on the nature or the characteristics of a woman. . . . A woman's desire is to get rich through love, but not to give her lover the solaces that please him. . . . You cannot find a woman of such lofty station or blessed with such honor or wealth that an offer of money will not break down her virtue. . . . Every woman by nature" is "a miser. . . . She is also envious and a slanderer of other women, greedy, a slave to her belly, inconstant, fickle in her speech, disobedient and impatient of restraint, spotted with the sin of pride and desirous of vain glory, a liar, a drunkard, a babbler, no keeper of secrets, too much given to wantonness, prone to every evil, and never loving any man in her heart. . . . No woman is ever so violently in love with a man that she will not devote all her efforts to using up his property. You will find that this rule never fails and admits of no exceptions. . . . They will greedily waste their substance to gobble up food, and no one ever saw a woman who would not, if tempted, succumb to the vice of gluttony." "There is no woman who would blush to drink excellent Falernian [wine] with a hundred gossips in one day. . . . Every woman in the world is likewise wanton, because no woman, no matter how famous and honored she is, will refuse her embraces to any man, even the most vile and abject, if she knows that he is good at the work of Venus."

KING ARTHUR AND HIS KNIGHTS

The rules of courtly love, as codified by Andreas, were elaborated in the poetic romances of chivalry by Chrétien de Troyes, another member of the countess of Champagne's circle. They were taken over by the body of Celtic legend that developed about King Arthur, the great defender of Celtic independence from the invading Germans in the early sixth century. It was Arthur and his Knights of the Round Table who became the great exemplars of the virtues of chivalry. Ultimately, under the stress of the crusading orders, the quite unchristian themes of human slaughter and illicit love were transformed in an ascetic manner by making knights such as Parzival and Galahad into holy recluses who pursued, not other men's wives or maidens in distress, but the vision of the Holy Grail, the chalice that, in some interpretations, caught the blood of the Lord as it flowed from his side on the cross.

THE SPREAD OF CHIVALRIC LITERATURE

It was in France, in the twelfth and thirteenth centuries, that the literature celebrating the ideal of chivalry was worked out; and from France it spread, both subject matter and form, in all directions. German poets such as Walter von der Vogelweide took up the theme of romantic love (*Minne*) with great ability, and in the hands of such a poet as Wolfram von Eschenbach, and others, Celtic tales (Tristram and Iseult) were carried eastward, and the ascetic themes (Parzival) embraced with great seriousness. In Italy, where the art of the troubadour spread rapidly and was received with great enthusiasm, such poets as Guido Guinicelli and many others developed the theme of romantic love (*fin amor*) with great delicacy, and made possible the treatment given to it by Dante. As Charlemagne and his peers, Arthur and his knights, and the many incomparable and worshipful ladies of high degree spread out from France into Europe, they became an international company.

THE "ROMANCE OF THE ROSE"

The development of the theme of courtly or romantic love in the vernacular literatures reached a peak in the *Romance of the Rose* and in the *New Life* and *Divine Comedy* of Dante Alighieri (1265-1321). The former, the most popular literary work of the thirteenth century, was written by two Frenchmen: the earlier part by Guillaume de Lorris and the concluding part by Jean de Meun, in what we may call a humanistic treatment of the theme. Guillaume de Lorris, by using allegory, is able to surround the theme with much classical decoration and allusion without depriving it of the emphasis given it by either the troubadours or Andreas the Chaplain. Jean de Meun, adding or emphasizing such allegorical personnages as Reason and Nature, is able, because of his mastery of the new learning of the twelfth and thirteenth centuries, including a wide acquaintance with the classics and a thorough knowledge of the new science, to put a somewhat cynical damper upon the romantic extravagances of Guillaume de Lorris. The whole is a storehouse of lovely poetry and an insight not only into the treatment of the love theme but into the whole medieval literary outlook.

Guillaume de Lorris says that those who "only yearn for love may all its mystery learn from out its [the *Romance's*] page." The poem is cast in the form of a dream vision describing the quest of the Lover for his Love, symbolized by the Rose. The Garden of the Rose is surrounded by a high wall on which are painted representations of those sins and qualities that find no place in the realm of Love, among them Old Age, Hypocrisy, and Poverty. Poverty is not the Lady whom Saint Francis adored and exalted, but a naked wretch who "Down in a corner, on the ground/ Couched, liken a beaten, shamefaced hound." The Lover (it is the "amorous Month of May") is admitted to the Garden by Iolenus, who tells the Lover the Garden is the property of Sir Mirth, who is at the moment present. Every tree of the Garden has been brought from "out the land of Saracens" to make a "place that would suffice for loss of Paradise." Following

> A shaded pathway, where my feet
> Bruised mint and fennel savouring sweet,

the Lover comes to the place

> Where Mirth held joyously high court
> In care-spurned ease for full enjoyment
> Of life's glad gifts, undashed by cloyment
> Or surfeit or revolt.

Here Gladness sang and danced with her companions.

> Her note was clear as silver bell,
> And, gently swaying, rose and fell
> Her supple form, the while her feet
> Kept measured time with perfect beat
>
> . . . . .
>
> Then through my frame I felt a throe
> Of joy to see them dancing go,
> A man and maid in measure trod
> With twinkling feet the springing sod.
>   While minstrels sang, the troubadours
> Kept with the flute due time I ween,
> And rondelettes burst forth amain
> To merry tunes of old Lorraine
> So sweetly, that I doubt if e'er
> Was heard such music otherwhere,
> For that fair province doth excel
> In heaven-born music's tuneful spell.

"A winsome dame, bright Courtesy, / Bewitching, bright and debonair," invites the Lover to "stir his foot in jocund dance." Thereupon the God of Love approaches the Lover. He wears "a robe of flowers":

> To lend its beauty, blue periwinkle
> 'Twixt rose and yellow broom did twinkle,
> With violets, pansies, birdseye blue,
> And flowers untold of varied hue.
> Sweet scented roses, red and pale,
> (Round which flew many a nightingale)
> Festooned Love's head, and every sort
> Of bird seemed there to hold high court,
> The skylark, blue-tit, mock and dove,
> Sang in his ear sweet songs of love,
> Fluttering around his head, and he
> One of God's angels looked to be.

LITERATURE, ART, AND MUSIC 725

Love is accompanied by Sweet-Looks and Dame Beauty, endowed

> With gentle grace, which freely showed
> In all her movements. As the moon
> Makes candles of the stars, her moon
> Paled all her fellows: as the dew
> Her flesh was tender, and ne'er new
> And blushing bride more simple seemed;
> Where'er her skin peeped forth it gleamed
> As white as fleur-de-lis; her brow
> Was clear and fair as virgin snow,
> The while her form was tall and slight.
> No need had she her face to dight
> With paint or other vain disguise,
> As women somewhiles use; despise
> And scorn might she such false allure,
> In nature's decking bright and pure.
> So plenteous grew her golden hair,
> That near her heels it reached, I swear.
> Her nose, her mouth, her beaming eyes,
> Were such that when their beauties rise
> (God help me) in my thought they seem
> To wake once more that glorious dream.
> Forsooth, so sweet she was and fair,
> With perfect rounded limbs that ne'er
> Throughout the world's broad space I ween,
> Aught could surpass her matchless sheen.

The dance finished, the Lover approaches a fountain (the Fountain of Love), in which the whole garden is reflected, and is taken especially with the reflection of a rose bush full of red buds.

> What ardent longing in my breast
> These buds inspired! . . .
>   Amongst them all,
> My rapturous eyes on one did fall,
> Whose perfect loveliness outvied
> All those beside it. I espied
> With joy its lovely petals, which
> Kind Nature's hand had dyed with rich
> Deep crimson hue. Its perfect leaves
> Were formed of two quadruple sheaves,
> Which side by side stood firm and fair,
> With stalk strong grown enough to bear
> The full-grown bloom which did not bend
> Or languish, but most sweetly spend
> Its fragrance on the air around,
> And wrapt my senses in profound
> Yet soft delight. Whene'er I smelt
> Its odour, strong desire I felt
> Possess me wholly that I might
> Snatch for mine own that dear delight.

As the Lover approaches the Rose, Cupid shoots him with the arrows of Beauty, Simpleness, Courtesy, Generosity, Company, and Fair-Seeming, and then approaches to claim the Lover for his vassal. The Lover drops upon his knee with will to kiss his foot, but the God of Love says: "Homage unto me / 'Tis thine to do, and grant I thee / This boon—my very mouth to kiss." The ceremonies of vassalage performed, Love then gives the Lover his instructions:

> 'Fore all beware of Villany,
>
> . . . . .
>
> Both base
> And mean are slanderous tongues.
>
> . . . . .
>
> Be thou careful to possess
> Thy soul in gentleness and grace.
> Kindly of heart and bright of face
> Towards all men, be they great or small.
>
> . . . . .
>
> Watch well thy lips, that they may be
> Ne'er stained with ill-timed ribaldry.
>
> . . . . .
>
>   . . . Have special care
> To honour dames as thou dost fare
> Thy worldly ways, and shouldst thou hear
> Calumnious speech of them, no fear
> Have thou to bid men hold their peace.
> Most richly shalt thou gain increase
> Of glory, if to maid and dame
> Thou givest ready aid;
>
> . . . . .
>
> Above all else, beware of pride,
>
> . . . . .
>
> Let him who would in love succeed
> To courteous word wed noble deed;
>
> . . . . .
>
>   Thou shouldst wear
> Rich habit as thy purse can bear,
> Well formed and fashioned; fair attire
> Is oft good fuel for love's fire.
>
> . . . . .
>
>   Do not leave
> Thy shoes half laced, but have them new
> And sprucely made, . . .
>
> . . . . .
>
> Wear gloves well made; thy purse should be
> Of satin, and, tied daintily
> About thy waist, wear sash.
>
> . . . . .

Use thou as part of gentleness.
Wash oft thine hands, and ne'er forget
Thy teeth to whiten, nor e'er let
Thy finger nails untended be,
But pare and keep them carefully.
Lace well thy sleeves, and comb thine hair,
But painted face and leering stare
Disdain, it suits but women or
Vile men, who get due scorn therefor.

And next remember that, above
All else, gay heart inspireth love.
A laughing mouth and merry smile
May oft a lady's heart beguile:

     . . . . .

If thou shouldst know some cheerful play
Or game to wile dull hours away,
My counsel is, neglect it not,

     . . . . .

If lithe and strong of limb thou art,
Fear not, but boldly act thy part,
And canst thou well a-horseback sit,
Prick high and low in pride of it;
And much with ladies 'twill advance
Thy suit, if well thou break'st a lance.

     . . . . .

And if a voice strong, sweet and clear
Thou hast, and dames desire to hear
Thee sing, seek not to make excuse
But straightway from thy memory loose
Some ditty soft; and shouldst thou know
To wake the viol's voice with bow,
Or tune the flute, or deftly dance,
Such things thy suit will much advance.

     . . . . .

With diligence avoid the name
Of miser;

     . . . . .

         . . . Thou all alone,
Content must be to make thy moan.
Then sighs, and woeful plaints, and tears,
And trembling hopes, and shivering fears,
Within thy breast will thou enfold;
Now parched with heat, now pinched with cold,
And now vermilion red, and now
Wan as a spectre shalt thou grow:
No fevers ever troubled man,
Nor tertian, nor quotidian,
Worse than the throes that lovers feel.

After many vain attempts to reach and pluck the Rose the Lover is again
approached by Reason, who tries to dissuade him from the folly of serving
the God of Love for a single rose. He should turn his attention to the
love of mankind.

> Every living man should be
> Joined in one vast fraternity,
> Loving the human race as one,
> Yet giving special love to none.
> Mete out such measure as ye fain
> From others would receive again:
> Pursue thy fellow in such guise
> Alone, as thou in equal wise
> Wouldst be pursued, and freely give
> Quittance of debt, if thou wouldst live
> By all beloved—such love should sway
> The lives of men from day to day.

In the course of many obstacles put in the way of the Lover's reaching
his Beloved, Jean de Meun gives disillusioning advice on how the women
should keep up their part:

> She's but a fool, who fixes on
> One man, and clings to him alone.
>
> . . . . .
>
> If she be plain, by dainty dress,
> Should she repair ill-favouredness;

If in some way she's lost her hair,

> Then, with a view to clothe her pate,
> Hair must she get of one who late
> Hath died, or yellow silk must tie
> Beneath neat fillets skilfully.
>
> . . . . .
>
> Or if she have the need to dye
> Her hair, she should most carefully
> Choose the right plants; leaves, bark, and root,
> Will each the varied purpose suit.
>
> And lest her bloom of cheek grow pale,
> Whereat her spirit well might fail,
> She should within her chamber keep
> Sweet unguents, that she thence may reap
> A secret freshness;
>
> . . . . .
>
> If she hath neck and bosom white,
> Then let her cut her bodice low,
> Her fair and dazzling skin to show,
> Two palms behind and eke before,
> There's no device attracts men more.
>
> . . . . .

If hands she hath nor fine nor fair,
But corned and blistered here and there,
'Twere well, that with a bodkin she
Should dress and tend them carefully,
Or better still, with gloves should hide
Defects—no man need pry inside.
And if her breasts too ample grow,
A swathe-clothe should she bind below
To bear them up, and hold them tight
Against her chest.

     . . . . .

Is her leg ugly? ne'er 'tis bare.
Too large her foot? 'tis shod with care.

     . . . . .

If she be cursed with noisome breath,
It doth not worry her to death,
But heed she taketh not to speak
To any till her fast she break,
And careful is her mouth ne'er goes
Too closely towards her lover's nose.
When laughter doth provoke her, so
She laughs that two sweet dimples show
About her mouth, on either side,
The which she never opes right wide
In laughing, but conceals beneath
A well-set smile, her doubtful teeth.

     . . . . .

And if her teeth are nothing grand,
But crossed and out of order stand,
'Tis just as well that they remain
Fast hid, would she not win disdain.

     . . . . .

When women cry at will, 'tis not
That they some cruel grief have got,
But mere vexation and chagrin
That some vile trick they're baffled in.

     . . . . .

She should behave her when at table
In manner fit and convenable;

     . . . . .

'Tis well she take especial care
That in the sauce her fingers ne'er
She dip beyond the joint, nor soil
Her lips with garlick, sops, or oil,
Nor heap up gobbets and then charge
Her mouth with pieces overlarge.

     . . . . .

               Then her cup
She should so gracefully lift up
Towards her mouth that not a gout
By any chance doth fall about
Her vesture,

     . . . . .

Nor should she set
Lips to the cup while food is yet
Within her mouth.

. . . . .

And first should she
Her upper lip wipe delicately,
Lest, having drunk, a grease-formed groat
Were seen upon the wine to float.

. . . . .

To pluck the fruits of love in youth
Is each wise woman's rule forsooth,
For when age creepeth o'er us, hence
Go also the sweet joys of sense,
And ill doth she her days employ
Who lets life pass without love's joy.

. . . . .

She shows her figure amorous
To all the gallants that she meets
As sails she through the crowded streets.

. . . . .

Women as free as men are born,
It is the law alone hath torn
Their charter, and that freedom riven
From out their hands by Nature given.

. . . . .

For Nature . . .
Made each for all and all for each
And every one for all alike,
E'en as the taste and fancy strike.[38]

It is only when the God of Love summons his mother, Venus, and when Nature, God's regent, intervenes on behalf of the Lover that he is able, after much allegorical adventure, to reach, and pluck, and possess the Rose.

DANTE'S "DIVINE COMEDY"

If the *Romance of the Rose* is a humanistic treatment of the theme of romantic love, the *Vita Nuova* (*New Life*) and *Divina Commedia* (*Divine Comedy*) of Dante are an ascetic treatment, corresponding to the literary transformation of Roland into Parzival. In their treatment of the theme, the Italian poets before Dante were inclined to emphasize less the formal feudal adoration of the troubadour and the adultery of Andreas the Chaplain than the ennobling spiritual influence of the good and beautiful Lady. It is this characteristic that Dante takes up and brings to completion in a nonreligious sense in the *New Life*. In the *Divine Comedy* the Lady, Dante's Beatrice, is made a source of religious influence that is actually mystical. For she not only inspires Dante's trip through hell, purgatory,

[38]Trans. F. S. Ellis, Guillaume de Lorris and Jean de Meun, *Romance of the Rose*.

and paradise, but when Vergil has led Dante as far as a pagan may, it is Beatrice, as the symbol of Divine Revelation, that guides him to the supreme mystic experience of absorption into the Godhead. At the last moment she surrenders her rôle to Saint Bernard, and, joining Dante, both Lover and Beloved behold in mystic contemplation the Triune God.

DANTE'S "NEW LIFE"

The *New Life* is an account of Dante's love for his Lady Beatrice, and of the Italian poetry it inspired. When he first saw her as a youngster of nine, she was eight. "Her dress, on that day, was of a most noble colour, a subdued and goodly crimson, girdled and adorned in such sort as best suited with her very tender age. At that moment, I say most truly that the spirit of life, which hath its dwelling in the secretest chamber of the heart, began to tremble so violently that the least pulses of my body shook therewith." The trembling and shaking continued for as long as Beatrice lived and as long thereafter as Dante thought on her. "I say that, from that time forward, Love quite governed my soul; which was immediately espoused to him, and with so safe and undisputed a lordship (by virtue of strong imagination), that I had nothing left for it but to do all his bidding continually." As a youth of eighteen, "it happened that the same wonderful lady appeared to me dressed all in pure white, between two gentle ladies elder than she. And passing through a street, she turned her eyes thither where I stood sorely abashed: and by her unspeakable courtesy . . . she saluted me with so virtuous a bearing that I seemed then and there to behold the very limits of blessedness . . . because it was the first time that any words from her reached mine ears, I came into such sweetness that I parted thence as one intoxicated." At a later time, when some lady companions of Beatrice asked Dante, "To what end lovest thou this lady?" he replied, "Ladies, the end and aim of my love was but the salutation of that lady . . . wherein alone I found that beatitude which is the goal of desire." (pp. 710–711, 719)[39]

When Dante thought of writing poetry in her praise he wrote sonnets such as the following:

> My lady is desired in the high Heaven:
>   Wherefore, it now behoveth me to tell,
>   Saying: Let any maid that would be well
>   Esteemed keep with her: for as she goes by,
> Into foul hearts a deathly chill is driven
>   By Love, that makes ill thought to perish there;
>   While any who endures to gaze on her
>   Must either be made noble, or else die.
>   When one deserving to be raised so high
> Is found, 'tis then her power attains its proof,

[39]Trans. Dante Gabriel Rossetti, quoted in Jones, *Medieval Literature.*

Making his heart strong for his soul's behoof
  With the full strength of meek humility.
Also this virtue owns she, by God's will:
Who speaks with her can never come to ill.

Love saith concerning her: "How chanceth it
  That flesh, which is of dust, should be thus pure?"
  Then, gazing always, he makes oath: "For sure,
    This is a creature of God till now unknown."
She hath that paleness of the pearl that's fit
In a fair woman, so much and not more;
She is as high as Nature's skill can soar;
    Beauty is tried by her comparison.
  Whatever her sweet eyes are turned upon,
Spirits of love do issue thence in flame,
Which through their eyes who then may look on them
    Pierce to the heart's deep chamber every one.
And in her smile Love's image you may see;
Whence none can gaze upon her steadfastly.

My lady carries love within her eyes;
  All that she looks on is made pleasanter;
  Upon her path men turn to gaze at her;
He whom she greeteth feels his heart to rise,
And droops his troubled visage, full of sighs,
    And of his evil heart is then aware:
    Hate loves, and pride becomes a worshipper.
O women, help to praise her in somewise.
Humbleness, and the hope that hopeth well,
  By speech of hers into the mind are brought,
  And who beholds is blessèd often whiles.
  The look she hath when she a little smiles
  Cannot be said, nor holden in the thought;
'Tis such a new and gracious miracle. (pp. 720–722)

In 1290 "the Lord God of justice called my most gracious lady unto Himself, that she might be glorious under the banner of that blessed Queen Mary, whose name had always a deep reverence in the words of holy Beatrice." "When mine eyes had wept for some while, until they were so weary with weeping that I could not longer through them give ease to my sorrow, I bethought me that a few mournful words might stand me instead of tears. And therefore I proposed to make a poem, that weeping I might speak therein of her for whom much sorrow had destroyed my spirit":

Beatrice is gone up into high Heaven,
  The kingdom where the angels are at peace;
    And lives with them: and to her friends is dead.
Not by the frost of winter was she driven
  Away, like others; not by summer-heats;
    But through a perfect gentleness, instead.
    For from the lamp of her meek lowlihead

Such an exceeding glory went up hence
    That it woke wonder in the Eternal Sire,
      Until a sweet desire
Enter'd Him for that lovely excellence,
      So that He bade her to Himself aspire:
Counting this weary and most evil place
Unworthy of a thing so full of grace.

       .   .   .   .

With sighs my bosom always laboureth
    In thinking, as I do continually,
      Of her for whom my heart now breaks apace;
And very often when I think of death,
    Such a great inward longing comes to me
      That it will change the color of my face;
      And, if the idea settles in its place,
All my limbs shake as with an ague-fit:
    Till, starting up in wild bewilderment,
    I do become so shent
That I go forth, lest folk misdoubt of it.
    Afterward, calling with a sort lament
On Beatrice, I ask, "Canst thou be dead?"
And calling on her I am comforted. (pp. 731, 733–734)

Dante concludes his *New Life*: "Wherefore if it be His pleasure through whom is the life of all things, that my life continue with me a few years, it is my hope that I shall yet write concerning Her what hath not before been written of any woman. After the which, may it seem good unto Him who is the Master of Grace, that my spirit should go hence to behold the glory of its lady: to wit, of that blessed Beatrice who now gazeth continually on His countenance." (p. 740) What Dante wrote still further concerning her was the *Divine Comedy*, "unapproached by any other work of art dedicated to woman." When Beatrice appears, in the *Comedy*, to become Dante's guide through paradise, she has "a wreath of olive over a white veil" and is "robed with the color of living flame under a green mantle," colors symbolic of faith, hope, and charity. She makes him feel "the great potency of ancient love." When she leaves him, he is in the care of Saint Bernard, who explains to Dante that "To terminate thy desire, Beatrice urged me from my place, and if thou lookest up to the third circle from the highest rank, thou wilt again see her upon the throne which her merits have allotted to her." Dante beholds her and prays: " 'O Lady, in whom my hope is stronge, and who, for my salvation, didst endure to leave thy footprints in Hell, of all those things which I have seen through thy power and through thy goodness, I recognize the grace and the virtue. Thou hast drawn me from servitude to liberty by all those ways, by all the modes whereby thou hadst the power to do it. Guard thou in me thine own magnificence so that my soul, which thou hast made whole, may, pleasing to thee, be unloosed from the body.'

Thus I prayed; and she, so distant, as it seemed, smiled and looked at me."[40]

Dante's *Divine Comedy* is indeed a consecration of the love between man and woman which leads to mystic blessedness. When Saint Bernard, at the end of the *Comedy*, prays to the Virgin Mary on behalf of Dante "for power such that he may be able with his eyes to uplift himself higher toward the Ultimate Salvation," and asks that the Virgin "wouldst dispel for him every cloud of his mortality, so that the Supreme pleasure may be displayed to him, . . . behold Beatrice with all the Blessed for my [Bernard's] prayers clasp their hands to thee." Dante thus joins Beatrice in the mystic contemplation of the Eternal Light. "My mind was smitten by a flash. . . . My desire and my will were revoked, like a wheel which is moved evenly, by the Love which moves the sun and the others stars." (pp. 866–868)

GEOFFREY CHAUCER'S EARLY LIFE

At Eastertide, 1357, it is recorded in the household accounts of the countess of Ulster that Geoffrey Chaucer received a short cloak, a pair of bright breeches in red and black, and some shoes.[41] He who has been called "English poetry incarnate"[42] was then sixteen or seventeen years old. Save for official records of the time, he would not be known as a man of considerable affairs in the world, for he makes scarcely a reference to his busy and crowded life in all his work. To be sure, he did not live in an age when any subject was thought a fit one for verse, and there were always the patrons and the persons who could read to be interested. In *The House of Fame* the talkative Eagle scolds him for his ignorance of far countries and, worse still, of his very neighbors that dwell almost at his door:

> For when thy labour doon al ys,
> And hast mad alle thy rekenynges,
> Instede of reste and newe thynges,
> Thou goost hom to thy hous anoon,
> And, also domb as any stoon,
> Thou sittest at another book
> Tyl fully daswed [dazed] ys thy look,
> And lyvest thus as an heremyte.

Ten years later, in 1367, Chaucer was a yeoman in Edward III's court, and by 1372 a squire in the royal household. During the summer of 1370 he was "abroad in the king's service." He apparently took to diplomacy, for in November of 1372 he was sent to Genoa to treat with the duke of

[40]*The Divine Comedy*, trans. Charles Eliot Norton, quoted in Jones, *Medieval Literature*, pp. 831, 862–863.
[41]Emily L. Johnson is the author of the material on Chaucer.
[42]J. L. Lowes, *Chaucer*.

Genoa and certain merchants with regard to the setting up of a Genoese commercial establishment in an English port. The desire of these Genoese merchants for an English port was to alter the current of English poetry. Chaucer's business took him to Florence, and there an entire world of living art and literature, the most wonderful in the fourteenth century, lay before him. "The pale ghosts of frescoes which we study so regretfully were then in their first freshness, with thousands which have long since disappeared. Wherever he went, the cities were already building, or had newly built, the finest of the Gothic structures which adorn them still, and Chaucer must have passed through Pisa and Florence like a new Aeneas among the rising glories of Carthage."[43]

CHAUCER'S LATER LIFE

Upon his return to England after an unsuccessful mission, but with precious manuscripts of Dante, Petrarch, and Boccaccio, Chaucer was appointed in 1374 Controller of the Customs and Subsidies on wool, hides, and woolfells in the port of London. For twelve years thereafter he lived in lodgings over the tower of Aldgate, and there the magic wrought upon his genius by his Italian visit began to set its spell. He translated Boethius,[44] whose work men had never ceased to read. He wrote, with material from Boccaccio's *Filostrato*, the first great poem in the English language, and one of the most beautiful in any language, *Troilus and Criseyde*. In 1386 he was elected to Parliament as a knight from the shire of Kent, and in 1389 was appointed by the king "Clerk of our works at our Westminster Palace, our Tower of London, the Castle of Buckhampton, etc." This responsible position he kept until 1391, and during these years he probably wrote most of *The Canterbury Tales*. In 1391 he was appointed subforester of the royal forest-park of North Petherton in Somerset, a position he held until 1398. He was back in his own London in 1399, where he died the following year.

CHAUCER'S TRAINING AS A POET OF LIFE ABOUT HIM

The training of an artist is always an interesting and thought-provoking problem, but it is difficult to see how a poet with mankind for his subject could have better developed his perceptions than in these positions of public and court service. Chaucer does not refer to the actual turbulence of his time, the Hundred Years' War, the Peasants' Revolt, John Wycliffe and the Lollards (save perhaps in *The Canterbury Tales*, when Harry Bailly, the host, says, "I smelle a Lollere in the wynd," after the parson had protested about swearing), social practices such as wife and child beating and child marriages, and the filth of the towns, but all these things and much more went to make him the humane and sane English poet he

[43]G. G. Coulton, *Chaucer and His England*, pp. 42–43.
[44]See pp. 414 ff.

was. His presence at Edward III's court at a time when the court was alive with noble French hostages and captives, including even King John himself, and his position as Clerk of the King's Works, where he had to oversee the gathering of all sorts of workmen and materials, gave him ample opportunity to observe human individuality and the interplay of personality upon personality. Only Shakespeare surpassed him in his perception and expression of the life about him.

CHAUCER'S READING

Chaucer added to his knowledge of the world by reading everything he could get his hands on. In addition to English, he read French poetry, the *fabliaux*, the works of Froissart, and, most important of all for his early years, he read and made a part of his thinking the *Romance of the Rose*, written more than a century before.[45] Ignorant of Greek, he did read the *Aeneid* and also Ovid in Latin and in French adaptations. He read Latin tales of the Trojan War, the Vulgate, contemporary works on astronomy, astrology, magic, and alchemy—the list is endless. His reading and his tolerant observation of, and absorption in, contemporary life combined with the white light of imagination to make up his art.

CHAUCER'S LANGUAGE

Chaucer wrote the mixed Anglo-Saxon and Norman French spoken in London by the middle and upper classes, the future language of all English-speaking peoples. He was aware of the constantly changing language of his time, for he pleads toward the end of *Troilus and Criseyde*:

> Go, litel bok, go, litel myn tragedye,
> . . . . .
>
> And for ther is so gret diversite
> In Englissh and in writyng of oure tonge,
> So pre I god that non myswrite the,
> Ne the mysmetre [scan wrong] for defaute of tonge.
> And red whereso thow be, or elles songe,
> *That thow be understonde*, God I beseche!

THE "CANTERBURY TALES"

His masterpiece was *The Canterbury Tales*. What genius could have informed him! There is more zest for life in this marvellously conceived dramatic poem than in anything in English literature—always excepting Shakespeare. The idea of a pilgrimage to Canterbury by twenty-nine travelers with the immortal Harry Bailly, the owner of the Tabard Inn in Southwerk, as host and master of ceremonies and commentator on the proceedings, wears the mantle of genius. Chaucer begins quickly to de-

[45]See pp. 724 ff.

scribe the persons on the trip, and they breathe the air of England. The Knight is a well-traveled crusader, lately returned from some mission:

> . . . he loved chivalrie,
> Trouthe and honour, fredom and curteisie.
> He was a verray, parfit gentil knight.

THE SQUIRE AND THE YEOMAN

When the company drew straws to find who should begin his story first, the Knight drew the short one and began the series of tales with a story of chivalry and romance, originally told by Boccaccio but now with the altering touch of Chaucer's humor and characterization. Along with the Knight was his son, a young Squire, a curly-haired lover and a lusty bachelor (a probationer for the honor of knighthood) of twenty, who wore an embroidered cloak and who sang or played the flute all the day: "He was as fressh as is the month of May." He had been on cavalry expeditions to Flanders and elsewhere. The Squire had with him a Yeoman whose description may have been grounded in Chaucer's own experience as a forester.

> And he was clad in cote and hood of grene.
> A sheef of pecok arwes, bright and kene,
> Under his belt he bar ful thriftily,
> (Wel koude he dresse his takel yemanly:
> His arwes drouped noght with fetheres lowe)
> And in his hand he baar a myghty bowe.
> A not heed hadde he, with a brown visage.
> Of wodecraft wel koude he al the usage.

THE PRIORESS

Madame Eglentyne, the Prioress, is described in a charming, gently satirical manner. She cannot quite forget that she is a woman as well as a religious. She perhaps should not have so displayed her fair forehead. Her small hounds were altogether forbidden, and strictly speaking, she should not have been going on any pilgrimage at all.

THE MONK

Chaucer's critical picture of the hunting Monk is one of his best. This Monk gave not "of that text a pulled hen, / That seith that hunters ben not hooly men." Nor did he hold worth an oyster the idea that a monk out of cloister was like a fish out of water! Why should he study and drive himself mad, pore over a book, or work with his hands and labor as Augustine bids? "Lat Austyn have his swynk [work] to him reserved." The Host feels free to tease the Monk, saying that very often he has heard said that the monk is the ideal type for procreation.

I pray to God, yeve [give] hym confusioun
That first thee broghte unto religioun!
Thou woldest han been a tredefowel [procreator] aright.
Haddestow as greet a leeve, as thou hast myght,
To parfourne al thy lust in engendrure,
Thou haddest bigeten ful many a creature.

. . . . .

God yeve me sorwe, but, and I were a pope,
Nat oonly thou, but every myghty man,
Though he were shorn ful hye upon his pan,
Sholde have a wyf.

THE FRIAR

The Friar, like the friar in the *Romance of the Rose*, but still an English friar, is so closely described, even to the unusual name of Huberd, that Chaucer may have taken him from life. He is a rascal from first to last, finding husbands for the young women he has seduced and giving an easy penance. He knew all the taverns and hostelries in every town better than the lepers and the beggars with whom he disdained to have acquaintance, for it may not advance one to deal with such poor people. He was the best beggar in his order, and from even the poorest widow he would glean a farthing before he left her. He lisped a bit, "to make his Englissh sweete upon his tonge."

THE SUMMONER

This worthy Friar hated summoners,[46] and after his story about an evil summoner, Chaucer introduces his summoner. This man is afflicted with a kind of leprous skin disease, and his pimply visage makes the children afraid of him. No ointment will help him, but even so he is as lecherous as a sparrow; he loves garlic, onions and leeks, and above all he loves wine, "Reed as blood." He would suffre for a quart of wyn,/A good felawe [rascal] to have his concubyn/A twelf month, and excuse him atte ful."

And when that he wel dronken hadde the wyn,
Thanne wolde he speke no word but Latyn.
A fewe termes hadde he, two or three.

These telling descriptions of persons who have life and breath go on in this wonderful way in the general "Prologue," and are often added to in the prologues of the individual tales. There is the hungry Scholar and his equally spare horse. He had as yet no benefice, and the gold he could beg from his friends he spent on books and learning. "And gladly would he learn and gladly teche." There is the Sergeant of Law, who seemed busier than he was, and the Franklin[47] who was in his company—white was

[46]Officials citing violators of canon law before the bishop's court.
[47]A landowning country squire.

the beard of the Franklin, as is the daisy, and of a sanguine complexion, good-humored, generous, and expansive. "Wo was his cook but if his sauce were poynaunt and sharp." There is the Shipman, with a line about his clumsy way of riding a horse, who drank a good deal of the wine he was carrying from Bordeaux, stolen while the captain was asleep—"Of nyce conscience took he no keep." There is the Doctor of Physic, through whom Chaucer gives a good description of the practice of medicine in the Middle Ages. The first professional quality of the Doctor is his grounding in astronomy.

THE DOCTOR

> He knew the cause of everich maladye,
> Were it of hoot, or coold, or moyste, or drye,
> And where they engendred, and of what humour,
> He was a verray, parfit praktisour.

And in quite modern accents with a good deal of irony,

> Ful redy hadde he his apothecaries
> To sende hym drogges and letuaries,
> For ech of hem made oother for to wynne—
>
> . . . . .
>
> His studie was but litel on the Bible.
>
> . . . . .
>
> He kepte that he wan in pestilence.
> For gold in phisik is a cordial,
> Therefore he loved gold in special.

THE WIFE OF BATH

The uninhibited Wife of Bath is surely one of the great characters in English literature. Chaucer distills the extensive body of antifeminist literature in drawing her, but it is still hard to believe that he did not have a particular person in mind. She has had five husbands at the church door, and that is not to mention other "compaignye in youthe." She has a deaf ear, caused by a beating one of her husbands gave her when she tore three pages from one of the antifeminist books he delighted in reading to her. She has been to Jerusalem three times, to Rome, Bologna, and other places on the Continent and likes to tell of these wanderings. She excels even the Flemish in her skill at clothmaking. Hers is a domineering personality. She is a great believer in woman's ruling the household and all those about her.

> And eek I praye Jhesu shorte hir [their] lyves
> That wol not be governed by hir wyves;

Chaucer's ability to communicate his zest for life could not be better shown than by the Wife's exclamation:

> But, Lord Crist! whan that it remembreth me
> Upon my yowthe, and on my jolitee,
> It tikleth me aboute myn herte roote.
> Unto this day it dooth myn herte boote
> That I have had my world as in my tyme.
> But age, allas! that al wole envenyme,
> Hath me biraft my beautee and my pith.
> Lat go, farewel! the devel go therwith!
> The flour is goon, ther is namoore to telle;
> The bren, as I best kan, now moste I selle;

The portraits of the good and Christian Parson, who taught Christ's lore, and followed it himself, and of the hard-working Plowman who paid his tithes regularly and honestly are followed by the descriptions of the Reve, the Miller, and the Pardoner. In creating the Miller, Chaucer is at his best; the man stands before us.

THE MILLER

> The Millere was a stout carl for the nones;
> Ful byg he was of brawn, and eek of bones.
> That proved wel, for over al ther he cam,
> At wrastlynge he wolde have alwey the ram.
> He was short-sholdred, brood a thikke knarre;
> Ther was no dore that he nolde heve of harre,
> Or breke it at a rennyng with his heed.
> His berd as any sowe or fox was reed,
> And therto brood, as though it were a spade.
> Upon the cop right of his nose he hade
> A werte, and theron stood a toft of herys,
> Red as the brustles of a sowes erys;
> His nosethirles [nostrils] blake were and wyde.
> A swerd and bokeler bar he by his syde.
> His mouth as greet was as a greet forneys.

After the Knight has finished his tale, this Miller, "that for dronken was al pale," insists upon telling his tale of a carpenter and his wife and of how a clerk had set the cuckold's cap on this carpenter. This sets off the ire of the Reve, who is also a carpenter. Chaucer prepares us for the tale that is to follow by saying that the Miller must tell his tale in his own manner and that he (Chaucer) must rehearse all the tales as told, "Or elles falsen som of my mattere." Those who do not want to listen to this kind of tale must turn over the leaf and choose another tale. "Blameth not me if that you chese amys."

THE REVE

The Reve from Norfolk rode last in the line of pilgrims, perhaps to get as far away from the Miller as possible. He is represented as a crafty, choleric man, of whom the bailiff, the herdsmen, and other farm laborers were adread "as of the deeth." He seems not to occupy the usual subordinate place of a reve, that is, below the bailiff, in the management of an estate. When the Host cuts off the Reve's speech about the infirmities of old age, the Reve proceeds to tell an equally rough tale of a miller, and so he gets back at the Miller, as he says at the end of his story.

THE PARDONER

With the Summoner rode his friend, a Pardoner of Rouncivale, "That streight was comen fro the court of Rome," or so he would say, with his papal indulgences and his relics. He was beardless—"I trowe he were a geldyng or a mare"—his hair was long and yellow, his eyes glaring like those of a hare, and he had a voice "as small as hath a goat." With his relics he was able to make the country parson and the people his "apes." In the remarkable prologue to his tale he confesses that he preaches of avarice and other wickedness not for the correction of sin but to win gold, and that he has been very successful at this game. If the ignorant will pay for his sermons on avarice and cupidity, should he willfully choose to live in poverty?

> Nay, nay, I thoghte it nevere, trewely!
> For I wol preche and begge in sondry landes;
> I wol nat do no labour with myne handes,
> Ne make baskettes, and lyve therby,
>
> . . . . .
>
> I wol have moneie, wolle [wool], chese, and whete,
> Al were it yeven [given] of the povereste page,
> Or of the povereste wydwe in a village,
> Al sholde hir children sterve for famyne.
> Nay, I wol drynke licour of the vyne,
> And have a joly wenche in every toun.

At the conclusion of his tale, in a revolting interchange of words, he tries to sell his indulgences to the company, and offers the host first chance at kissing the relics! He is perhaps the only really vicious person in the whole company.

HARRY BAILLY, THE HOST

Harry Bailly, the Host, is one of the best of the characters, and we know a great deal about him before the tales are finished. He is a hen-pecked husband—how he wishes his wife would take to heart the tale of the patient Griselda! But on the pilgrimage he is the lord of the gathering and he glories in his estate. He commends and scolds as the individual tales are ended. He tells the Clerk of Oxford not to tell his tale in high scholarly language, but "Speketh so pleyn at this tyme, we you preye,/That we may understonde what ye seye." When Chaucer begins his tale of Sir Topas, a satire on the endless metrical romance, the Host cuts him short with

> "Namoore of this, for Goddes dignitee,"
> Quod oure Hooste, "for thou makest me
> So wery of thy verray lewednesse [ignorance]
> That, also wisly God my soule blesse,
> Myne eres aken of thy drasty [worthless] speche."

He tells the Monk that "Youre tale anoyeth al this compaignye./Swich talkyng is nat worth a boterflye." He had been all prepared for a tale of hunting, and he complains that only the jingling of the bells on the bridle of the monk's horse kept him awake during the story the monk did tell. All in all he is one of the most delightful persons in the merry group.[48]

THE ASCETIC SPIRIT IN MEDIEVAL LITERATURE

The Latin and vernacular poetry of the Middle Ages thus reveals that the ascetic spirit of Christianity was unable completely to suppress, transform, or absorb those passions and outlooks called secular and humanistic. All poets did not subscribe so wholly to Christian views as to exclude all others as worthy of poetic statement. This is not to deny that Christianity succeeded in inspiring a beautiful and powerful poetry, in both Latin and the vernacular dialects, and in absorbing, by the use of allegory and from the reading of Latin literature itself, something of the latter's substance and spirit. It is not to deny that Christianity was influential enough to transform some poetry celebrating secular prowess and earthly love into poetry exalting prowess on behalf of the Church and a religious love. It is simply to deny the ubiquity and the monopoly of the ascetic view. As it did not suppress the lust for political power and wealth, no more did it suppress sexual lust or its refinement in physical love, or its expression in literature. Its ideal of the saint could be held up to the knight and to the lover, but this did not mean that they always accepted the substitute. Indeed, it has been said that "there is hardly an epoch of western history whose literature so revels in descriptions of the beauty of the naked body, of dressing and undressing, bathing and washing of the heroes by girls and women, of wedding nights and copulation, of visits to and invitations into bed, as does the chivalric poetry of the rigidly moral Middle Ages."[49] If migrant clerical poets occasionally made sport of Christian pretensions and values, a gay lover might in a tale reject heaven itself. For Aucassin, in *Aucassin and Nicolette*, paradise was not especially attractive: "For into Paradise go none but such people as I will tell you of. There go those aged priests, and those old cripples, and the maimed,

---

[48]This is to say nothing of the consummate art of the *Canterbury Tales* as poetry, flexible and musical, nor of the sparkling variety in meter and rhyme. For those who examine the work more carefully, a very great treat is in store here, too.

[49]Arnold Hauser, *The Social History of Art*, I, 220

who all day long and all night couch before the altars, and in the crypts beneath the churches; those who go in worn-out mantles and old tattered habits; who are naked, and barefoot, and full of sores; who are dying of hunger and of thirst, of cold and of wretchedness. Such as these enter in Paradise, and with them I have nought to do. But in Hell will I go. For to Hell go the fair clerks and the fair knights who are slain in the tourney and the great wars, and the stout archer and the loyal man. With them will I go. And there go the fair and courteous ladies, who have friends, two or three, together with their wedded lords. And there pass the gold and the silver, the ermine and all rich furs, harpers and minstrels, and the happy of the world. With these will I go, so only that I have Nicolette, my very sweet friend, by my side."[50]

Medieval Architecture

ROMANESQUE AND GOTHIC STYLES

In the field of art the same tension between asceticism and humanism, or secularism, may be observed. Among the arts in the Middle Ages, architecture was supreme. Public and secular architecture found expression in the feudal castle, the royal palace, the guild and town hall; ecclesiastical architecture, in the monastery, parish and cathedral church. In a very general way, the two styles characterizing medieval architecture, the Romanesque and the Gothic, correspond to the chief types of church buildings, Romanesque to the monastery and Gothic to the cathedral. It it, however, primarily the earlier Benedictine and Cluniac churches that embody the best Romanesque. The later orders, the Cistercians and Mendicants, built in the newly created Gothic style and spread it throughout Europe.

THE ROMAN BASILICA

The Romanesque style is so named because it preserved certain features of Roman architecture. For example, it preserved the form of the Roman public assembly hall or basilica. The basilica, rectangular in shape, was divided into a main, central aisle (the nave) and narrower aisles on either side. The nave terminated in a semicircular apse. Separating the nave from the side aisles were arcades of columns, usually topped by Corinthian capitals, and connected by the round or semicircular arch. Into the nave walls supported by these arcades small windows were sometimes introduced to make what was subsequently called a clearstory (clerestory). The roofing of the nave and side aisles of the basilica was in either wood or stone. The stone roofing of the basilica is known as the vault, and this vault the

---

[50]From *Aucassin and Nicolette*, p. 6, translated by Eugene Mason. Everyman's Library, published by E. P. Dutton and Company, Inc.

Romans built in two forms, barrel and groined. The barrel vault is a semicircular, round-arched vault. The groined vault consists of a series of bays whose roofing is made by the intersection of two barrel vaults. The lines of intersection are the groins.

EARLY MEDIEVAL CONSTRUCTION

The early Middle Ages are not conspicuous for their buildings. The skill of the Roman mason was lost, and most of the building was in wood. The early Benedictine monastery may be thought of as a group of primitive wooden farm buildings. For as long as materials could be pilfered from Roman buildings, this was done. The wooden buildings or wooden roofs were of course quite inflammable, and frequently burned. When fireproof stone vaulting was attempted for churches, it was usually the barrel or semicircular vault. Such a vault was heavy, and this, together with its thrust—the force causing it to bulge if not properly supported—required very heavy walls which could not be pierced with windows, or if so, only with small ones. Accordingly, the early Romanesque interiors were low and dark.[51]

THE ABBEY OF ST. GALL

This was all quite proper, for a rigid asceticism had no room for the beauty of man's handiwork or art. The monastery was no place for the artistic titillation of the senses. It was meant to discipline the body and save the soul. But as the landed endowment of the monasteries increased beyond the point necessary to support a community of monks, and as some order was gradually established in the post-Carolingian world, the surplus wealth of the monasteries began to be invested in an ecclesiastical art calculated to make the service of God elegant and lovely, and the abode of the monks impressive and beautiful. The monks of St. Gall in Switzerland, in the ninth century, drew up such elaborate plans for their monastery that they were never able to complete them. They numbered among their congregation Notker, who "was most assiduous in illuminating, reading, and composing," and Tutilo, who was "a delicate carver and painter; musical, with especial skill on the harp and flute." The abbot gave him "a cell wherein he taught the harp to the sons of noble families around." He was "skilled in building and all the kindred arts . . . a most excellent composer of poetry and melodies." Tutilo, indeed, was so well known as a sculptor that he was called to work as far away as Metz, on a statue of the Virgin Mary, and, in a continuation of the tradition of divine aid to artists, did it so well that it was believed that the Virgin herself helped him to complete the work.[52]

[51]Cf. Joan Evans, *Art in Medieval France*, p. 496.
[52]G. G. Coulton, *Life in the Middle Ages*, IV, 51.

By the time of Saint Bernard, many of the older Benedictine and newer Cluniac monasteries had become stunning collections of Romanesque art. The church at Cluny was "the largest and most sumptuous Church in Christendom."[53] Bernard, whom we have met as a severe critic of the Cluniacs, an ascetic "who despised beauty," could not stomach the extravagance of their art. To a Cluniac abbot he complains in a letter (1125) about "the vast height of your churches, their immoderate length, their superfluous breadth, the costly polishings, the curious carvings and paintings which attract the worshipper's gaze and hinder his attention." For monks, he writes, "who have left all the precious and beautiful things of the world for Christ's sake; who have counted but dung, that we may win Christ, all things fair to see or soothing to hear, sweet to smell, delightful to taste, or pleasant to touch,—in a word, all bodily delights,—whose devotion, pray, do we monks intend to excite by these things?" The eyes of the faithful "are feasted with relics cased in gold. . . . They are shown a most comely image of some saint, whom they think all the more saintly that he is the more gaudily painted. Men run to kiss him, and are invited to give; there is more admiration for his comeliness than veneration for his sanctity. Hence the church is adorned with gemmed crowns of light—nay, with lustres like cart-wheels, girt all round with lamps, but no less brilliant with the precious stones that stud them. Moreover we see candelabra standing like trees of massive bronze, fashioned with marvelous subtlety of art, and glistening no less brightly with gems than with the light they carry. . . . The church is resplendent in her walls, beggarly in her poor; she clothes her stones in gold and leaves her sons naked; the rich man's eye is fed at the expense of the indigent."[54]

Even though these things be admitted into the Church to embellish the habitation of God, what are they doing in the cloister itself, the monk's living quarters? Here Saint Bernard breaks out against Romanesque sculpture. "In the cloister, under the eyes of the Brethren who read there, what profit is there in those ridiculous monsters, in that marvelous and deformed comeliness, that comely deformity? To what purpose are those unclean apes, those fierce lions, those monstrous centaurs, those half-men, those striped tigers, those fighting knights, those hunters winding their horns? Many bodies are there seen under one head, or again, many heads to a single body. Here is a four-footed beast with a serpent's tail; there, a fish with a beast's head. Here again the forepart of a horse trails half a goat behind it, or a horned beast bears the hinder quarter of a horse. . . . We are more tempted to read in the marble than in our books, and to spend the whole day in wondering at these things rather than in meditating the law of God. For God's sake if men are not ashamed of these follies,

[53]Evans, p. 25.
[54]Coulton, *Life in the Middle Ages*, IV, 172–173.

why at least do they not shrink from the expense?"[55] Suger, the abbot of the royal Benedictine monastery of St. Denis, whom Bernard urged to reform his house, was of a different opinion. He believed in "super-resplendent architecture," and thought that "men's eyes are set under a spell by reliquaries. . . . They see the shining image of a saint and in the imagination of the people his saintliness is proportioned to its brilliance."[56]

THE GOTHIC CHURCH

At the moment Saint Bernard wrote the above Suger was rebuilding St. Denis in the new Gothic style. For, already, those experiments in Romanesque building had been made and adopted that transformed it into Gothic. Gothic was the creation primarily of French architects of the Île de France. While the original experimentation was done in monastic churches, the mature style was worked out in cathedral churches of the new towns. It was accomplished under the guidance of the secular clergy, the bishops and archbishops, who had no compunctions about the relationship between art and Christianity. In 1401 the cathedral chapter of Seville resolved to "build so great a church to the glory of God that those who come after us will think us mad even to have attempted it."[57] Gothic churches were built by lay workmen organized in masons' lodges and in guilds; they were paid for by the faithful, among whom the new bourgeoisie contributed a large part. Nineteen guilds at Chartres contributed windows to the cathedral. Gothic architecture spread from the cathedrals to the new orders: the friars, for example, who needed churches in which to preach the gospel to large urban audiences. It was also taken up by the older orders, the Cistercians, Cluniacs, and Benedictines. When

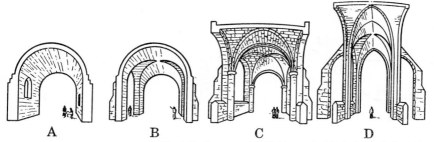

A   B   C   D

After J. W. Thompson and E. N. Johnson, *An Introduction to Medieval Europe*

The evolution of vaulting in medieval architecture. A. A very early Romanesque barrel vault. B. Section through piers of an early Romanesque round-arched groin vault. C. Section through window showing later round-arched and ribbed groin vault. D. Section through window bay showing typical Gothic pointed-arch vault with ribs, piers, and flying buttresses.

[55]Coulton, IV, 174.
[56]Evans, p. 21.
[57]John H. Harvey, *The Gothic World*, p. 8.

the ascetic ardor of the Cistercians waned the Gothic of their churches became less austere than the rule provided. Ultimately they were not averse to using statues of Saint Bernard himself to decorate their churches. "The final stage is represented in the retable made for Clairvaux in the fifteenth century. In the middle, God the Father upholds his Son upon the cross. On either side are panels of the Baptism of Christ and of Christ appearing to the Apostles: a scene of which the supernatural quality is shown by his gilded face, feet, and hands. The end panels show Saint Bernard holding a model of his abbey, and a mitred abbot. When the queen of Sicily visited the abbey in 1517, there were enough reliquaries for each monk to hold one during Mass, and yet to leave sixteen or seventeen for her to see in the sacristy. The high altar was adorned by a frontal of copper gilt, and behind it were three altars of alabaster, one of which was crowned by an image of Saint Bernard under a canopy. There was a bronze candelabrum and a bronze statue of the Virgin nine feet high. A sculptured group of the Resurrection adorned the cloister, and there was a fine library with traceried windows and an elaborately sculptured façade. Men had entered into their inheritance of visible beauty; it had come to form part not only of their daily life but also of their imaginative dreams. The blind austerity of Saint Bernard could no longer prevent it from forming a part of their religion."[58]

GOTHIC STRUCTURE

The successful experiments with Romanesque that transformed it into Gothic developed out of concern for building a fireproof structure, the

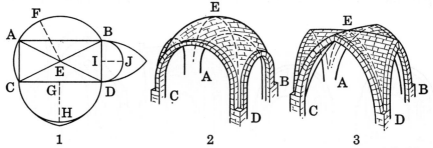

After J. W. Thompson and E. N. Johnson, *An Introduction to Medieval Europe*

The advantages in vaulting with a pointed arch. (1) ABCD is an oblong bay to be vaulted. BC is the diagonal rib; DC, the transverse; and BD, the longitudinal. If circular ribs are erected, their heights will be EF, GH, and IJ. The result will be a domical vaulting (2) irregular in shape because of the unequal heights of the ribs, and with the longitudinal arch too low to admit of a clearstory. A building so vaulted is low and dark. The problem, then, is to bring the crowns of all the ribs to the same height as that of the diagonal rib E. This can be done by pointing the lower ribs. The result is a lighter, more flexible system, affording ample space for a clearstory (3).

[58]Evans, pp. 72–73.

748 CHAPTER FIFTEEN

introduction of more light into the interior, and the building of a church of sufficient height to give artistic expression to the divine aspiration of Christianity. The change from wood to stone took care of the fires. To an eleventh-century French chronicler the new stone churches made it appear as if France were being covered with a clean, white robe. To build stone vaults and at the same time to increase the window space in the walls meant that the stone vaults had to have other than wall support. This was provided in the form of a skeletal structure of ribs for each bay upon which the stones of the vault were set. This framework of ribs carried the weight of the vault to the ground. The early vaults had a framework of six ribs for each bay, four covering the length and width of the bay (two transverse and two longitudinal) and two diagonal. The thrust of the vault was thus carried by these ribs to those points on the nave wall where the transverse, longitudinal, and diagonal ribs met. To these points there were built up from the outside stone supports called buttresses. The stone vault thus rested upon (1) a skeletal framework composed of ribs carried to the ground floor, and (2) buttresses.

After J. W. Thompson and E. N. Johnson, *An Introduction to Medieval Europe*

Showing the skeleton framework of ribs and flying buttresses in Gothic construction. A. Transverse rib. B. Diagonal rib. C. Cross ridge. D. Longitudinal ridge. E. Wall or longitudinal rib. F. Flying buttresses. This also shows the stonework filling between ribs in a finished vault.

Thus walls were no longer necessary; their place could be taken by windows. This left only the problem of height to be solved. Vaulting a square or rectangular bay with round-arched ribbing meant building the vault upon ribs of unequal height and giving it therefore a domical shape. If the pointed instead of the round arch were used, the ribs could all be made of the same height and the domical effect avoided. The pointed arch itself was not a western invention but a borrowing from Islamic architecture. But its use in the very structure of the church, rather than as a mere form of decoration, was a western innovation coming to symbolize Gothic. Once having introduced the pointed arch into the vaulting, there was no keeping it out of other parts of the church. Nor was there any limit, except safety, to the amount of pointing or stilting that could be given to an arch. When highly stilted arches were introduced into the nave arcade, the triforium (the gallery above the side aisles), and the clerestory, as well as into the vaulting, the Gothic church shot upward toward the heavens, changing the line bruptly from the horizontal of the Romanesque to vertical.

COLORED GLASS

When glass was substituted for the wall surfaces, glass held together by ribbing and buttressing, the effect would have been something like a soaring greenhouse, blinding the worshipers, had not colored glass been used. With the use of colored glass to mediate the introduction of the outside to the inside, a Gothic interior became a mystical handling of space. The ever-changing daubs of colored light filtering in from vast stained-glass windows bedeck the floors, and piers, and what is left of walls, and disappear into the dim recesses of the vaults. "The Gothic effect" is "of soaring space—space no longer rational, commensurable, and geometric as in antique and Byzantine interiors, but irregular in volume and expansion, linked with the infinitude of out-of-doors in a union made mystic by the jeweled light of the clerestory, losing the eye of the observer in the shadowy severies of the vaulting—in short, a space in movement. . . . The movement and subtle communication with outer space that links the observer with infinity are potent factors in the spiritual levitation a Gothic interior can give: but give in full measure only when reinforced with its panoply of painted glass. The Gothic window turned the light of day to Christian use and significance, stirring the devout soul with jeweled color, and the devout mind with a panorama of the Christian epos, recorded in the illumined figures and symbols which took the place in Gothic churches of Byzantine mosaics."[59]

GOTHIC SCULPTURE

The Gothic architect did not leave the exterior of the church bare. Its façade and its portals he covered lavishly with a sculpture illustrating

[59]Charles R. Morey, *Medieval Art*, pp. 268, 265–266.

The spacious transitional nave of the monastery church at Vézelay, France. La Made-
leine at Vézelay was an old Benedictine house reformed by Cluny in the eleventh century. The present church was built in the twelfth century after a fire in 1120. It is an
example of the splendor of late Cluniac construction (see p. 746 for Saint Bernard's
protests against Cluniac architecture). The Romanesque nave converges on an early
Gothic choir (1198–1201). Heavy transverse ribs, carried to the floor, help to support
the nave vaulting, which, it can just be observed, is groin vaulting. The dramatic use of
black and white stone may be Moorish in origin. (Text after Arthur K. Porter, *Medieval
Architecture*)

Plate 43

Caisse Nationale des Monuments Historiques

The façade of the cathedral of Notre Dame of Paris at night.

Plate 44
André de Diènes

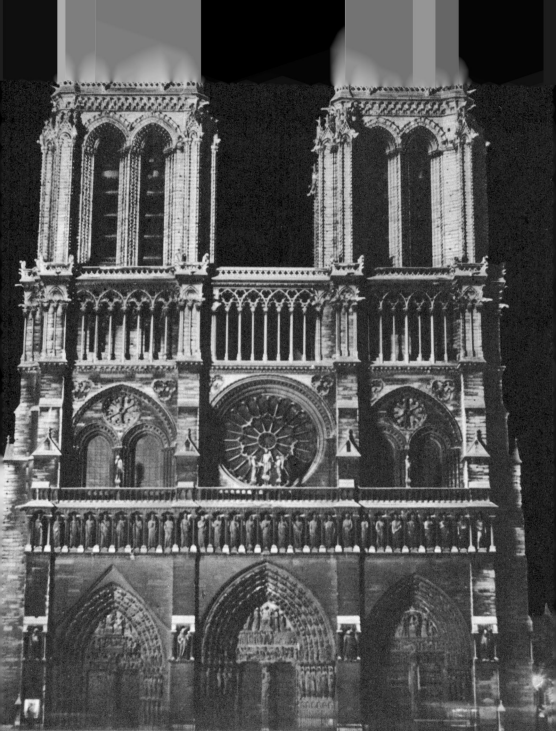

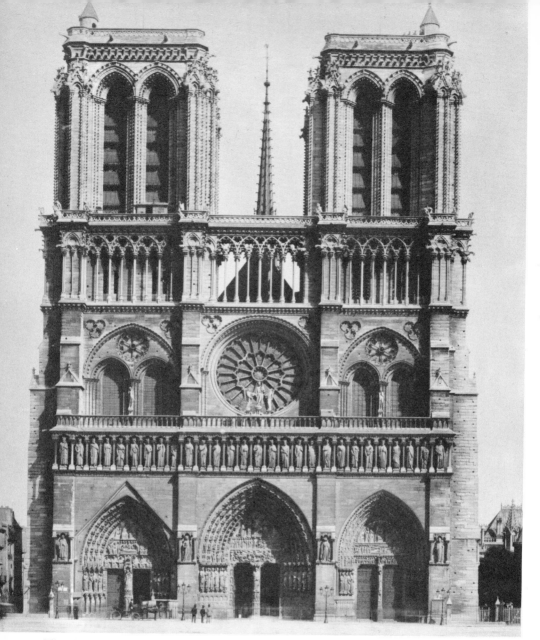

The Gothic façade of the cathedral of Notre Dame (Our Lady) at Paris was begun in 1210 and finished in 1235. The three vertical divisions made by the four wall buttresses are made into three horizontal divisions by the two connecting galleries. The sculptors left some surfaces uncarved. It is a design "of which no words can express the exalted beauty . . . the façade, as a whole, is perhaps the most impressive produced by Gothic art." (Porter, II, 281, 307)

Plate 45

Caisse Nationale des Monuments Historiques

The Gothic façade of the cathedral of Our Lady at Reims was, except for the towers, built in the last half of the thirteenth century. The cathedral was the most lavish in its use of statuary, some two thousand separate figures covering it and leaving little of the surface uncarved. The portals have been made to protrude from the façade to form a porch. "One of the supreme achievements of Gothic art; the façade is rivaled only by that of Paris." (Porter, II, 309)

Plate 46

André de Diènes

A close-up of the central portal of the cathedral at Reims, illustrating the profusion of sculptural detail. A cathedral of Our Lady must devote its main entrance to her. At her left the Annunciation and the Visitation are represented. These saints have lost the rigid, archaic grace of Romanesque sculpture, but seem a very human, friendly, and animated group as they join the Virgin in mingling with contemporary worshipers. "The figures of the façade of Reims are as nearly perfect technically as any which the Middle Ages produced." (Porter, II, 303)

Plate 47

André de Diènes

The rose window of the façade of the cathedral of Notre Dame of Reims.

Plate 48
André de Diènes

The nave of the cathedral at Reims, looking toward the main altar. This nave must be compared with Vézelay to see what the pointed arch, when boldly introduced into the construction of the arcade, triforium, clerestory, and ribbed vault, does to shift the emphasis from the horizontal line of the Romanesque to the aspiring, mystical verticality of the Gothic.

Plate 49

Caisse Nationale des Monuments Historiques

The nave of the cathedral at Amiens, another of France's great Gothic churches. This nave has been called "the most beautiful, as it is certainly the most typical example of French Gothic architecture, and it is hardly too much to say that for inspiration of conception, for perfection of proportion, and for purity of detail, it is equaled by no other edifice ever erected by the hand of man." The architects of Reims raised the height of the nave, bettering the 115 feet of the Paris cathedral, to 125 feet. Those of Amiens went still higher to 140, second to Beauvais' 157. (Porter, II, 305)

Plate 50

Caisse Nationale des Monuments Historiques

The north porch of the cathedral at Chartres (thirteenth century) opens into the north end of the transept (the choir is at the east end of the church). There is also a similar south porch. These side entrances are more elaborately treated with superb sculpture than the main portals of the western façade (twelfth century).

Plate 51

Caisse Nationale des Monuments Historiques

The central portal of the north porch at Chartres is dedicated to the Virgin. To her right stand these imposing figures of Melchizedek, Abraham (with Isaac), Moses, Samuel, and David.

Plate 52

Caisse Nationale des Monuments Historiques

The sculpture on the left portal of the north porch at Chartres contains this beautifully realistic rendering of the Visitation (the Virgin and Saint Elizabeth).

Plate 53

Caisse Nationale des Monuments Historiques

The sculpture of Chartres has to do
with human as well as superhuman
beings: A devil carries off a usurer
and his moneybag to hell, and a
peasant trims his vines.

Plate 54

Georges Viollon (above)
**Caisse Nationale des Monuments
Historiques**

The Tree of Jesse window on the western façade of the cathedral of Chartres (twelfth century). The genealogical tree of Jesus rises from Jesse at the bottom through David and three other kings to the Virgin and Christ himself. The tree is surrounded by fourteen prophets. The blue, red, and green of the central section are repeated again in the intricate border. "The Tree of Jesse stands at the head of all glasswork whatever . . . the most splendid colour decoration the world ever saw. . . ." (Henry Adams, *Mont-Saint-Michel and Chartres*)

Plate 55

Three Lions

A medallion of the Transfiguration of Christ from the Passion window on the western façade of Chartres (twelfth century).

Plate 56

Jim Johnson, from Rapho-Guillumette

Saint Theodore on the south porch of the cathedral of Chartres, one of the masterpieces of late thirteenth-century sculpture.

The tympanum of the central portal of the western façade at Bourges is devoted to a serious reminder of what the Last Judgment will be like. On the awful day Christ presides on his throne (see the *Dies Irae*, pp. 707 ff.); the dead rise from their coffins, awaiting the verdict on their souls. The central panel is dominated by the Archangel Raphael, holding in his hand the scales of justice.

Plate 58

Rapho-Guillumette

15—22.

The sculpture of the Last Judgment above the main portal of the cathedral of Bourges. In the upper section, Christ, approached by intercessors, blesses the awful proceedings. Below, the dead are raised from their graves. In the central panel souls are being weighed in the balance and found wanting or saved. The saved march to Eternity; the damned are hurled into hell.

Plate 59

Georges Viollon, from Black Star

Plate 60

This detail of the Last Judgment from the cathedral at Bourges shows the right halves of the lower and central panels. Below, the resurrected bodies, freed from their tombs, plead with Christ to be merciful. In the upper panel Raphael has his left hand on the head of a soul whom the scales show to be saved. The attending devil appears grim over this disappointment. His fellows are having great sport forcing the damned toward the entrance of hell, whose flames are kept lively by the bellows of two grinning demons.

An example of realistic medieval sculpture at its best is this statue of the German princess Uta, who, together with her husband, Ekkehardt, stands in the apse of the cathedral of Naumburg, Germany.

Plate 61

the doctrines of the faith or the lives of Christ and the saints. An early church council had prescribed that "the composition is not the invention of the artist, but a product of the legislation and tradition of the Catholic Church. The art alone is the artist's: the choice and arrangement are of the fathers who built the churches." If the matter was then prescribed in accordance with an old iconographical tradition, the manner, or art, of presentation was not. The experimentation in structure was supplemented by experimentation in sculptural form and ornament. Gradually the sculpture lost some of its allegory and symbolism, as well as its archaic stiffness, and took on the features and meaning of the real outside world. The classical Corinthian capital was supplanted by a Gothic one, reproducing in stone the foliage, flowers, beasts, and birds of the outside world. Kings and queens, lords and ladies join the saints on the portals. At Bamberg Adam and Eve in all their nudity adorn the left entrance. The saints become real persons modeled from life, serious and noble, coy and smiling. "When Hugh, Abbot of Meaux between 1339 and 1349, ordered a new crucifix for the choir of the lay brethren, he . . . provided the sculptor with a naked man as a model."[60] The medieval sculptor at his best came to equal the Roman and the Greek in his representation of man. The knight came riding into the church on his horse. The peasant and his labors were carried through the seasons. The expanded world of learning of the twelfth and thirteenth centuries was introduced, sometimes, it seems, from the very text of the new encyclopedias. The seven liberal arts were there, and Aristotle and Donatus. When inspiration from the ideal and real world failed, fantasy and humor took their place. The whole creation joined together in the worship of God.

THE HUMANISM OF GOTHIC

It may thus be said that the Gothic cathedral represents better than the *Divine Comedy* or the scholasticism of Saint Thomas Aquinas the spirit of early Christian humanism. Like them, its ultimate justification was mystic—to provide the setting for an emotional absorption into the Godhead. Like them, its spirit was authoritarian. The structural basis for Aquinas's theological edifice was Aristotelian logic. For Gothic, it was the tension of stone vaults resting upon a stone frame supported by flying buttresses. In the Gothic church, however, all is subordinated to the architectural necessity. The painting of the windows or of the frescoes, the sculpture of the portals and the piers were not permitted to have an independent position of their own. Or, if so, it was not to interfere with the total architectural effect. The figures in a stained-glass window must not be permitted to call so much attention to themselves that they interfere with the mystical effect of the colored light that they admit. The sculptured figure on the portal or pier must not stand out so freely that

[60]Evans, pp. 31, 58.

it interferes with, rather than enhances, the vertical line. But given Gothic mysticism and verticality, given the priest at the high altar resacrificing Christ to God on behalf of mankind's sins, given, that is, the basic asceticism of the structure, then there is little that cannot be introduced in a subordinate place to support, enhance, embellish, and enrich. The humanism of antiquity knew how to employ beauty in the form of art to give meaning and delight to existence. The Christian humanism of the Gothic knew how to utilize beauty in all forms of art to make Christianity a wonder and an exquisite, sensuous delight, as well as a faith, a comfort, and a mystical experience.

Medieval Music

THE CHURCH AND MUSIC

Those who have felt the powerful emotional impact of a beautiful liturgy carefully and seriously performed in an environment of great art know how much is contributed to the mystical effect of such a combination by the addition of music. While rejecting the dance as a form of worship, the Church did not hesitate to use the music bequeathed to it from classical antiquity. Except for the organ, the music it had use for was primarily vocal. Drums and horns and flutes were not calculated to enhance the ascetic spirit of the faith.

THE QUESTION OF UNIFORMITY

The Church retained from antiquity the practice of singing or chanting the Latin text of the liturgy in simple melodies. As it spread throughout the West, its services were performed in varying liturgies, and these were sung with differing melodies. Introduced into these services were hymns written by Christian poets and sung by the congregations. The Roman church was not content with the variety of liturgies and music used throughout the West and sought to substitute instead a uniform Latin liturgy sung with the same melodies. By and large, it was successful in spreading its liturgy and music. While it never succeeded in supplanting the Ambrosian liturgy and music at Milan, in the course of centuries it won out elsewhere. Pope Gregory VII, for example, was concerned with getting Spanish Christians to give up their special Mozarabic liturgy.

GREGORIAN, OR PLAIN, CHANT

The music that the Roman church used, and continues to use, to sing the Latin liturgy is called Gregorian, or plain, chant. It is called Gregorian because of the tradition, seriously disputed, that it was Pope Gregory I who finally established the musical foundation for the liturgy. The term plain chant merely refers to the use of simple, unadorned melody to sing the Latin text. The ideal performance of such music requires the subordination of the music to the words and meaning of the liturgy. When sung carefully and patiently by priest and choir in cathedral or monastery, it can be a thing of great beauty, but careless or indifferent chanting at top speed, in order to rush through the service, makes a mockery of the sacred text and mood. Gregorian chant may also be called Romanesque music because it was the only music sung during the period when the architecture of monastery and church was Romanesque.

THE DEVELOPMENT OF HARMONY

Melody is the foundation and permeating substance of the music of all peoples. What is characteristic and unique about the development of western music, however, is not its melodic but its harmonic enrichment. We are so accustomed to singing or playing in a complicated harmony that we do not realize that for other civilizations this is quite unnatural. The development of a harmonic system in the West came as the result of centuries of experimentation. It accompanied those experiments that transformed Romanesque into Gothic architecture, and the results of these early experiments may accordingly be called Gothic music, the music of the Gothic cathedral. Like the experiments in architecture, these in music were made by French composers, and spread out from France as a center. In the later twelfth and thirteenth centuries it was the musical school of Notre Dame in Paris, under the leadership of Léonin and Pérotin, that was the most influential in western Europe.

Given a priest, a choir with voices of many pitches, and an organ with many tones, it might seem inevitable that discontent would arise with the continued limitation of sacred music to the simple melody accompanying the text of the liturgy. So it was. Why, in places at least, if not for the whole text, could not music composed of more than one melody, sung simultaneously, be introduced? Why might not these places be exactly those expansions of the liturgy that were being made at the moment with new poetry and drama in the form of sequences and tropes? In the course of time, special dramatic portions in the liturgy of the Mass (the Kyrie Eleison, Gloria, Credo, Sanctus, and Agnus Dei) were elaborated to constitute a special musical form used by composers ever since.

POLYPHONIC MUSIC

The development of many-melodied, many-voiced, or polyphonic, music from Gregorian, or plain, chant first took the form of writing and singing the same liturgical melody an octave higher or lower. Parallel melodies were then written in what were regarded as especially beautiful or perfect consonances, four and five tones below or above the fundamental liturgical melody. But if four or five, why not three or six or any other possible number? If a second melody could be written to parallel the basic liturgical melody, why could not the parallel begin after the first melody had started (a round, fugue, canon)? Or why need the second melody parallel the first? Could it not be written exactly contrary to the first melody? Need it be written parallel or contrary? Could it not be given an independent value of its own? Why limit polyphonic music to two voices? Could not a second or third voice be added to the basic liturgical melody? And why need the basic melody be liturgical and sung in Latin? Could it not be taken from a song of a troubadour or a Minnesinger and be sung in French or German? That is, why could there not be a secular, as well as a sacred, polyphonic song? And why, indeed, if the sacred or secular basic melodies had a text of their own (Latin or otherwise) could not the additional voices have an independent text as well as an independent melody of their own? Combinations of several voices with independent melodies and texts, whether sacred or secular in character, came to be called motets. It came to the point in one motet where, while the tenor sang a broad smooth melody to a text from the New Testament, a second part was praising in a different rhythm "the pious priests' works," which "shine like stars of the firmament," and a third part, in a far more vigorous rhythm, was cursing the "hypocritical, malicious, drunken, and lecherous priests, tormentors of the Church."[61]

Many different voices singing together introduced problems with which Gregorian chant did not need to be concerned. If it were to be done in the same manner at all times, it had to be written down in permanent fashion. It was, accordingly, during the latter Middle Ages that our modern system of musical notation (lines, spaces, clefs, notes, sharps, flats, rests) was invented. Many different voices singing together brought up the problem of the temporal relation of melody to melody, measure to measure, note to note. Thus, instead of relying upon the imprecise rhythm of the Latin text for the lilt of the melody, precise indication of meters or time-values was indicated for the individual melodies (3/4, 4/4, whole, half, quarter notes). The introduction of many voices also brought up the problem of the harmonic relationship of melody to melody, measure to measure, note to note. If, at one note, the second melody were a fourth above the basic melody, would it be proper, at the next note, to shift the second melody to a third below the basic melody? These problems led to rules and regulations for writing in counterpoint (note against note, *punctum contra punctum*). Composers of Gregorian melodies had used the Greek mode for scales. How adequate were these in polyphonic composition? How far was it desirable to emphasize chordal rather than melodic progression in the course of a composition? The medieval answers to these problems constitute the first chapter in the history of our extraordinary western music, so unlike all other. The basic change from plain chant (monophonic) to polyphonic music was not easily made. The human ear is as averse to change as is the mind. John of Salisbury, other-

[61]P. H. Lang, *Music in Western Civilization*, p. 135.

wise a distinguished humanist, could say that "Music defiles the service of religion. For the admiring simple souls of the congregation are of necessity depraved—in the very presence of the Lord, in the sacred recesses of the sanctuary itself—by the riot of the wantoning voice, by its eager ostentation, and by its womanish affectations in the mincing of notes and sentences."[62]

Neither the development of Gothic architecture nor that of polyphonic music was an exclusively ecclesiastical affair. The glories of Gothic architecture are to be found chiefly in the Gothic church, but that does not mean that they were not extended to the castle or town hall. The beauties of polyphonic music are to be found chiefly in liturgical or sacred settings, but that does not mean that they were not extended to secular song. No more in architecture and music than in Latin and vernacular literature could the ascetic Christian spirit, however vital, exercise a monopoly over the human spirit.

[62]Lang, p. 140.

chapter sixteen

HUMANISM AND ASCETICISM AT THE CLOSE OF THE MIDDLE AGES

CHALLENGES TO ASCETICISM. At the close of the Middle Ages, in the fourteenth and fifteenth centuries, the body of learning in western Europe was so increased as to disturb the prevailing relationship between the humanistic and ascetic points of view. The ascetic spirit of medieval Christianity had been challenged earlier by a political, economic, and social revival. The political revival established a new order in the towns, territorial states, and national kingdoms, after the theocratic experiments of the Holy Roman Empire and the Holy Roman Church had failed. It created new desires for political power which recognized no external restraints. With the economic revival came a western exporting industry and a revival of trade and commerce with eastern Europe, western Asia, and northern Africa. This beginning of western capitalism created new ambitions for wealth and the kinds of power that go with it ill befitting Christian teachings on greed, avarice, interest, and prices. The old monastic orders, when corrupted by corporate wealth, were joined, finally, by the friars. The secular Church, when tainted by these desires and ambitions, suffered criticism and rebellion at the hands of heretics and reformers. The social revival broke up a rigid class structure and helped to stimulate an ambition for prosperity and security in this world, regarded no longer as a mere remedy for sin and a vale of tears. The last two chapters have demonstrated that the Christian outlook was by no means able to inspire all creative activity in the realm of literature, thought, and the arts. Frankly secular or humanistic values entered into the products of creative imagination.

A certain enthusiasm for Latin literature existed in some cathedral schools in the twelfth century. This same century witnessed the enormous expansion of the West's knowledge brought about by the translations from Arabic into Latin of Greek and Arabic philosophical, scientific, and mathematical works. In the fourteenth and fifteenth centuries the labor of translation was increased when the works of Plato, Plotinus, and his Neoplatonic successors, together with the body of extant Greek literature—the epic and lyric poets, dramatists, and historians—were added to the West's store of learning. A large part of what Boethius had once wanted to do,[1] and much more, was now, after one thousand years, accomplished. At the same time the medieval interest in Roman literature was continued by unearthing, from monastic and cathedral libraries, Latin works of which western scholars were generally quite ignorant. The body of extant pagan Latin literature thus became known. Under these circumstances, it could be expected that the West would not remain content with a knowledge of Greek literature in translation. It wanted the full flavor of reading Greek literature in the original. New Greek works were translated not only into Latin but, together with the new Latin works, also into the chief vernacular tongues. This whole new world of Latin and Greek literature and philosophy, whether in Latin, Greek, or translation, found permanence and a wider audience when brought out in the new, printed books and put in new libraries.

UNDERSTANDING CLASSICAL CIVILIZATION

The recovery of ancient Greek and Latin literature stimulated the scholarly construction of a complete picture of the development of classical civilization. Every source of information that would contribute to this end was eagerly and often enthusiastically sought after. Inscriptions on ancient monuments were searched for, copied, and reproduced by artists in their paintings. Classical coins became an object of the collector's passion. Classical buildings ceased being quarries of ready-cut stone. When possible, the fragmentary remains of classical art were stored in museums, and a beginning made of classical archaeology. Scholars began (by comparing one manuscript with another) to consider the problem of establishing sound texts for the study of classical literature and thought. They became expert in detecting whether documents were genuine or not. Every phase of classical civilization, its law (especially Roman law), its art, its religion, its mythology, as well as its literature and thought, became the object of devoted and learned attention. Gradually there emerged, to continue perfecting itself to the present, an understanding and appreciation of the ancient world free from the distortions and misapprehensions that medieval ignorance and Christian prejudice had

[1]See pp. 414 ff.

supplied. The first and pre-Christian chapter in the history of western mankind's experience began to be passionately studied and slowly uncovered.

EDUCATION IN THE CLASSICS

For the education of youth and the training of the gentleman a knowledge of classical civilization, its languages and literature, was now considered indispensable. The children of the nobility and of those who could afford to educate their children were taught their Latin and Greek at an early age, and set to work translating and memorizing the classics, and indeed writing Latin and Greek poetry and prose. They were, as it was put, educated in the humanities or humane letters of Greece and Rome. Until relatively recently, this was the education given to all youth in school. The humanistic tradition of Roman education that prescribed a knowledge of Greek in addition to Latin was now enlarged, for the gentleman was to be educated not merely in his native tongue but in both Latin and Greek. The object of this knowledge was not merely to come to understand theology but to study and delight in literature and philosophy. Thus began anew a task that the later Roman Empire and the Middle Ages had not succeeded in achieving: passing on the best in the cultural tradition of the past to train youth for the future. The Romans had started to pass on Greek, and therewith the Greek inheritance, but in the later Roman Empire the knowledge of Greek was lost. It was not fully recovered in the West until the fifteenth century. The Romans failed to educate, whether in Greek or Latin, all the potential talent of their state. Education in these languages was confined to the nobility and upper classes. The many were illiterate. Medieval education in Latin was also largely confined to the upper classes. The masses were illiterate. The West now began again to train its upper classes in Latin and Greek. Whether it could do any better than the Roman or medieval periods in passing on this brilliant heritage to all who could profit by it, of whatever social class, was a question for the future to decide.

CHRISTIANITY AND THE CLASSICS: CLASSICAL HUMANISM

It must be asked whether this rebirth of interest in, and enthusiasm for, the classics, this increase in the knowledge of the ancient world, modified in any important respect the Christian ascetic view. Like the introduction of Arabic learning, the Renaissance did produce a few individuals who preferred, in some respects, a pagan to a Christian outlook. On the whole, however, the Renaissance did not seek to repudiate Christianity for paganism or asceticism for humanism. It sought merely, in the light of the new knowledge, to liberate Christianity from the limitations of ignorance, the arrogance of dogma, and the narrowness of its circumscribed view of man. It thus took up the tradition of Christian humanism and

CHRONOLOGY — Humanism and Asceticism in the Late Middle Ages

	Political Figures	Italian Humanists	Northern Mystics and Humanists
1200			
			Master John Eckhart (ca. 1260–1328) Duns Scotus (ca. 1265–1308) Henry Suso (ca. 1295–1366)
1300			
		Petrarch (1304–1374) Boccaccio (1313–1375)	William of Ockham (ca. 1300–1349)
	Cosimo de Medici (1389–1464)	Leonardo Bruni (1369–1444) Poggio Bracciolini (1380–1459)	Thomas a Kempis (1380–1471)
1400			
		Lorenzo Valla (1406–1457)	
	Lorenzo de Medici (1449–1492)	Marsilio Ficino (1433–1499) Pico della Mirandola (1463–1494)	John Reuchlin (1455–1522) Desiderius Erasmus (ca. 1469–1536) Crotus Rubeanus (ca. 1480–after 1539) Martin Luther (1483–1546) Ulrich von Hutten (1488–1523)
	Emperor Maximilian I (r. 1493–1519)		
1500			
	Pope Leo X (r. 1513–1521)		

sought to give it a larger content. The classical world, and what it inspired in the contemporary world, was to have a larger place in the Church. Classical art and classically inspired Renaissance art of all genres were to have a larger part in beautifying Christian life. Christian literature was to be adorned as never before by the elegancies derived from an imitation of classical literature. The new classical learning was to be absorbed into the Christian outlook by continuing to emphasize, even if not in the manner of Aquinas, the use of reason. The study of nature was to be justified by a renewed mysticism that made an inquiry into detailed fact lead on to higher realms of truth. Man's moral freedom within the Christian pattern, or even without it, was to be given new emphasis. This did not mean that Christianity was to be abandoned. In claiming the support of classical morality, Christianity did not give up its own outlook.

PETRARCH AND BOCCACCIO

Some detail will illustrate these general statements. Petrarch, Boccaccio, and Lorenzo Valla were the leading Italian humanists in the generations following Dante. Of these, the first two began their literary careers with what they are most read for today. Petrarch is known for his Italian poetry singing of his love for Laura, and Boccaccio for his Italian prose tales, *The Decameron*, which incorporate much lighthearted and even cynical criticism of the Church. Each of these humanists turned from the career of a writer in the Italian vernacular to that of a classical scholar. As a humanist writing in Latin, Petrarch pretended to ignore, if he was not actually jealous of, Dante's popularity as a writer of the Italian tongue. He refers to "the hoarse applause which our poet [Dante] enjoys from the tavern-keepers, fullers, butchers, and others of that class, who dishonour those whom they would praise. But, far from desiring such popular recognition, I congratulate myself, on the contrary, that, along with Virgil and Homer, I was free from it, inasmuch as I fully recognize how little the plaudits of the unschooled multitude weigh with scholars."[2] Petrarch's successors as humanists today may wish that they and their predecessors had not so readily scorned these plaudits of an unschooled multitude that, in its turn, has now chosen to ignore them.

DISCOVERY OF UNKNOWN MANUSCRIPTS

As scholars, both Petrarch and Boccaccio turned to discovering unknown Latin works among the unmolested shelves of monastic libraries. Petrarch tried to uncover lost works of his hero Cicero. He found two speeches at Liège, in 1333, and many of his letters at Verona twelve years later. Boccaccio found works of Ovid, Martial, and Tacitus. We are told that when he visited the library of the mother house of the Benedictine order at Monte Cassino, "being eager to see the library he besought

[2]G. C. Sellery, *The Renaissance*, pp. 65–66.

one of the monks to do him the favour of opening it. Pointing to a lofty staircase, the monk answered stiffly, 'Go up; it's already open.' Boccaccio stepped up the staircase with delight, only to find the famous house of learning destitute of door or any kind of fastening, while the grass was growing on the window sills and the dust reposing on the books and book shelves. Turning over the manuscripts, he found many rare and ancient works with whole sheets torn out, or with the margins ruthlessly clipped. As he left he burst into tears and, on asking a monk . . . to explain the neglect, was told that some of the inmates of the monastery . . . had torn out whole handfuls of pages and made them into psalters, which they sold to boys, and had cut off strips of parchment, which they turned into amulets to sell to women."[3]

POGGIO BRACCIOLINI

Petrarch's and Boccaccio's discoveries of the writings of Latin authors were augmented by the searches of a fifteenth-century papal secretary, Poggio Bracciolini, who attended the Council of Constance. At the monastery of Cluny he found a manuscript of Cicero's speeches; at St. Gall, Quintilian's *Institutio Oratoria*,[4] which he copied in fifty-three days. Elsewhere he found Lucretius, Manilius, Ammianus Marcellinus, Columella, and Petronius. He negotiated with monks of Hersfeld for works of Tacitus, got twelve new plays of Plautus from Germany, and from Monte Cassino Frontinus's work on aqueducts.[5] By the middle of the fifteenth century the present canon of classical Roman authors had been established by efforts such as these. It was then necessary to turn to Greek writers.

GREEK AUTHORS AND MANUSCRIPTS

Although Petrarch never managed to acquire the Greek language, he realized the importance of a knowledge of it for a proper understanding of classical culture. In his library there not only were Latin versions of the *Iliad* and *Odyssey* but also Plato's works in Greek, that Plato whom he though far superior to Aristotle. He urged upon Boccaccio the importance of Greek, and Boccaccio learned it, boasting of being the first of all modern Italians to begin reading Homer again. In the fifteenth century the manuscripts of Greek authors, brought from the East, became available for reading and study. The Sicilian Giovanni Aurispa reached Venice from Constantinople in 1423 with 238 manuscripts, including such authors as Aristophanes, Demosthenes, Plato, and Plutarch. A few years later Filelfo, the secretary of the Venetian legation at Constantinople, brought the manuscripts of some forty Greek authors back home, including Homer, Herodotus, and Thucydides. Lorenzo de' Medici sent an agent to the

[3]G. Highet, The *Classical Tradition*, pp. 91–92.
[4]See pp. 228 f.
[5]J. E. Sandys, *History of Classical Scholarship*, II, 25–34. Also see p. 256.

center of Byzantine monasticism at Mount Athos for manuscripts who returned in 1492 with no less than two hundred.

TRANSLATING AND PRINTING GREEK AUTHORS

This work of re-establishing direct contact with the culture of ancient Greece was aided by Byzantine Greeks who came westward, for the Council of Ferrara-Florence in 1438–1439,[6] and to escape Turkish rule after the capture of Constantinople in 1453. Among the former were men interested in Plato and Neoplatonism, one of whom, Bessarion, actually was made a cardinal of the western Church for his services at the Council on behalf of the papacy. Many of these men, together with westerners who had learned Greek, were employed by the popes to translate Greek authors into Latin. After the Germans Sweynheym and Pannartz had introduced the printing press in Italy (1465) the Latin and Greek classics were quickly printed. Before 1495 only a few Greek books had been brought out, but under the scholarly patronage of the printer Aldus Manutius (1449–1515) of Venice Greek authors also were speedily published. Indeed, by 1501 Aldus thought it possible to issue a pocket edition of the Latin and Greek classics. By 1515, all the major Greek, as well as Latin, authors had been printed.

SPECIALIZED STUDY OF ANTIQUITY

Latin and Greek works in manuscript or printed form were not enough to establish an adequate account of a point of view or of a whole civilization. The authenticity or accuracy of the writers and manuscripts had to be established and what they said related to its historical environment. The ability to do these things had to be learned. Skill had to be acquired in detecting whether a manuscript was a forgery or not, and, if not, in determining the circumstances under which it was written. Scholarly aids to the reconstruction of the past had to be composed. In these things Petrarch and Boccaccio made a start and thus inaugurated the specialized study of classical antiquity. Petrarch was a collector of gems, curios, fragments of sculpture, and inscriptions from the classical past. His *On Illustrious Men* led Boccaccio to write *On Famous Women*, and both may be regarded as early dictionaries of classical biography. Boccaccio wrote the first systematic account of ancient mythology and a work on ancient geography to help in understanding the Roman poets: *Mountains, Woods, and Waters*. It was inevitable that, with the physical remains of the Greek and Roman worlds about them, Italian scholars should become interested in epigraphy and archaeology and put a stop to the plundering of classical monuments for the sake of building materials. A fifteenth-century scholar, Ciriaco of Ancona, traveled extensively in Greek lands in search of Greek inscriptions, after having come to realize the importance of

[6]See p. 633.

Latin ones in Italy. He ultimately published three volumes of them. His contemporary Flavio Biondo of Forli was an early student of archaeology. By the end of the fifteenth century, new libraries and new museums, founded often enough by the despots of Italian cities, were available for the use of the new secular scholars, the humanists. Rome and Greece could now begin to be understood directly from their remains by men willing to try to understand them for what they were.

LORENZO VALLA

A good example of the critical spirit that some humanists brought to bear upon the thought and institutions of their day is contained in the works of the Italian humanist Lorenzo Valla. He went further than most humanists in rejecting an ascetic outlook. In one work, *De Voluptate* (*On Pleasure*), he prefers Epicureanism to Stoicism and extols the frank enjoyment of sensual pleasure, going so far as to compare the prostitute favorably with the nun. In a work on the *Monastic Life* asceticism is still further criticized. He won especial distinction in the scholarly world for his *On the Elegancies of the Latin Language*, a systematic discussion of the virtues of classical Latin and an attack upon medieval and contemporary Latin usage. Such archaistic criticism by humanists of a Latin that was then a living language hastened its death. Yet Valla's knowledge of the history of the style and usage of the Latin tongue made him a sharp critic of important Christian writers and documents. The Latin of Saint Jerome's Vulgate he could not stand. If only for their diction, the Scriptures, he thought, could not be taken as verbally inspired. The Apostles' Creed could not have been written by the Apostles.

THE DONATION OF CONSTANTINE A FORGERY

One of Valla's most successful critical victories was his demonstration that the famous Donation of Constantine[7] was a forgery (1440), the first attack of this kind upon a major historical document.[8] Among the methods he used to demonstrate the improbability of so vast a grant was to demonstrate that Pope Sylvester must have possessed an incredible worldliness to have accepted the ownership and governance of half the civilized world. As the successor of Christ, the pope would certainly have refused the grant, even if a Roman emperor had wished or been permitted to make it. He puts into the mouth of Pope Sylvester, as he refuses the grant, such words as the following: "Do we renounce earthly possessions in order to attain them more richly, and have we given up our own property in order to possess another's and the public's? . . . What are riches and dominions to me who am commanded by the voice of the Lord not to be anxious for the morrow, and to whom he said, 'Lay not up for yourselves treasures

[7] See pp. 389 f.
[8] C. B. Coleman, *The Treatise of Lorenzo Valla on The Donation of Constantine.*

upon earth, possess not gold nor silver nor money in your purses,' and 'It is harder for a rich man to enter into the kingdom of heaven than for a camel to go through the eye of a needle.' Therefore he chose poor men as his ministers and those who left all to follow him, and was himself an example of poverty. Even so is the handling of riches and of money, not merely their possession and ownership, the enemy of uprightness. Judas alone, he that had the purses and carried the alms, was a liar, and for the love of money, to which he had become accustomed, chided and betrayed his Master, his Lord, his God. So I fear, your Majesty, lest you change me from a Peter into a Judas. Hear also what Paul says: . . . the love of money is the root of all evil. . . . And you command me, your Majesty, to accept what I ought to shun as poison. (pp. 51-53)

"Nay more, I should have to use my authority to shed blood in punishing offenders, in waging wars, in sacking cities, in devastating countries with fire and sword. Otherwise I could not possibly keep what you have given me, and if I do this, am I a priest, a pontiff, a vicar of Christ? Rather I should hear him thunder out against me, saying 'My house shall be called of all nations the house of prayer but ye have made it a den of thieves!' 'I am not come into the world,' said the Lord, 'to judge the world but to save it.' And shall I who have succeeded him be the cause of men's death, I to whom in the person of Peter it was said, 'Put up again the sword into his place, for all they that take the sword shall perish with the sword.' It is not permitted us even to defend ourselves with the sword. . . . And do you command us to use the sword for the sake of either getting or keeping riches? . . . I must not accept the things that are Caesar's nor will I ever accept them, though you offer them a thousand times." (pp. 59, 61)

With respect to the phrase of the Donation that "we ordain and decree that he [the pope] shall have the supremacy as well over the four seats, Alexandria, Antioch, Jerusalem, and Constantinople, as also over all the Church of God on the whole earth," Valla remarks, "I will not speak here of the barbarisms in language," but "What Christians could endure this, and not, rather, critically and severely reprove a Pope who endures it and listens to it willingly and retails it; namely, that the Roman See, though it received its primacy from Christ . . . should be represented as having received it from Constantine, hardly yet a Christian, as though from Christ? Would that very modest ruler have chosen to make such a statement and that most devoted pontiff to listen to it? Far be such a grave wrong from both of them! How in the world—this is much more absurd and impossible in the nature of things—could one speak of Constantinople as one of the patriarchal sees, when it was not yet a patriarchate, nor a see, nor a Christian city, nor named Constantinople, nor founded, nor planned!" "Which shall I censure the more, the stupidity of the ideas, or of the words? . . . Does not [a] barbarous way of talking show that the rigmarole was composed not in the age of Constantine but later: 'decernimus quod uti debeant' for the current form 'decernimus ut utantur'? Boors commonly speak and write [this] way now: 'Iussi quod deberes venire' for 'Iussi ut venires.' . . . I contend that not only did Constantine not grant such great possessions, not only could the Roman pontiff not hold them by prescription, but that even if either were a fact, nevertheless either right would have been extinguished by the crimes of the possessors, for we know that the slaughter and devastation of all Italy and many of the provinces has flowed from this single source. . . . Can we justify the principle of papal power when we perceive it to be the cause of such great crimes and of such great and varied evils!" Valla did his job so thoroughly that no one since has ever dared to suggest that the Donation of Constantine was not a forgery. (pp. 93, 95, 115, 121, 179)

THE TURN TO PLATO

The late medieval humanists scorned all Latin that did not approach the style of Cicero. They were inclined to ridicule the scholastic philosophers, who went, they thought, to excessive lengths in utilizing the logic of Aristotle for their theological hairsplitting. Many of them sought relief in the poetry of the newly recovered dialogues of Plato. The relief they sought was not from the principles of a Christian outlook but from the ponderous rigidity of their Aristotelian formulation. In turning to Plato, they sought to substitute him for Aristotle as the classical basis for a Christian view. As the scholastics sought to absorb Aristotle into the substance of Christianity, so now the humanists sought to absorb Plato.

PLATO AND MYSTICISM

To a certain extent this had already been done. The ascetic strain in Plato and the relationship between Platonism and mysticism have been referred to.[9] Neoplatonism, as the last and mystical philosophy of a declining Roman world, has been described.[10] It has been shown how Augustine was able to come to Christianity through the mediation of Plotinus, and how the chief reward of Christianity, the soul's eternity in heaven, is a mystical reward, the perpetual beholding and absorption into the Godhead. The significance of Augustinianism during the Middle Ages has been stated, and such additional aids to the mystic outlook as the works of Dionysius the Areopagite, John the Scot, Saint Bernard, and the school of St. Victor's in Paris have been touched upon.[11]

THE USES OF PLATONISM

Latin translations of the works of Plato and Plotinus and the recovery of the Greek texts of the *Dialogues* and the *Enneads* now poured fresh

[9]See pp. 137 f.
[10]See pp. 298 ff.
[11]See pp. 638 ff.

water into the Christian mystic fount. The late medieval scholastics, such as Duns Scotus and William of Ockham, pointed out that the attempts of such men as Aquinas and Albertus to provide a rational basis for the faith were illusory. God's revelation could be understood only as an act of faith and, accordingly, as a result of a mystical process. Such criticism cleared the way not only for a learned mysticism of Neoplatonic character but for a popular mysticism grounded in simple piety. Some of the artists for whom the streams of allegory and symbolism were running dry, and who, without resorting to realism, were trying to preserve the literary and artistic beauties of the ancient world, to recapture the loveliness of nature, and not altogether to reject a non-Christian sensualism, felt the need of a Platonic approach. If concern with the details of secular or profane love led to an understanding of the mystic transports of divine love, the former could be tolerated. If a description of the naked beauty of one's beloved led to an understanding of her true spiritual worth, its purpose was then clear. A preoccupation with the superficial beauties of the natural world led to a comprehension of the spiritual or ideal forms behind the outward show. In these ways Platonism or Neoplatonism were of use, not only to the tired theologian and Christian eager to widen the foundation and to refresh the inspiration of his religion, but to the plastic and literary artist as well. If piety could become learned, daring deviations from the ascetic outlook could also be made to seem philosophical.

THE NEOPLATONIC ACADEMY AT FLORENCE

The enthusiasm of the humanists for Plato and his Neoplatonic successors led to the foundation of an academy at Florence whose task it was to study their works and translate them into Latin. It was Plethon, one of the Byzantine Greeks to come to the Council of Ferrara-Florence, who urged Cosimo de' Medici to found such an academy. Under his leadership, the battle raged over the relative merits of Plato and Aristotle. Bessarion, in a work of 1469, thought it necessary to free Plato from the charge of being a pagan and "even to make of him an acceptable if involuntary Christian." This Platonic academy at Florence came to be chiefly inspired by two humanists, Marsilio Ficino and the young Pico della Mirandola. Ficino was active as a translator. His translation of the dialogues of Plato into Latin was "the first complete translation of all the dialogues into a western language." He translated Plotinus as well, and then turned to the lesser Neoplatonists and Christian mystics Porphyry, Proclus, and Dionysius the Areopagite. But his larger task was to reconcile anew Platonism with Christianity and Christianity with Platonism, to bring to bear the whole of ancient philosophy upon its Christian successor, and thus to preserve religion from "detestable ignorance." To this end he wrote two works, one called *Platonic Theology* (*Theologia Platonica*) and the other *Concerning the Christian Religion*. In his preface to the former he says, "I believe and this belief is not fallacious, that divine

Providence has decided that the perverse minds of many persons who do not easily yield to the authority of the divine law should be satisfied at least by Platonic arguments that are brought to the aid of religion." He later observes that "Platonic doctrine is related to the divine law . . . as the moon to the sun."[12] Plato thus is put to use in reviving the faith of the weak-minded or sceptical. He, together with Pythagoras and Socrates, should not, Ficino thought, be denied the Christian reward of eternal salvation.

PICO DELLA MIRANDOLA

Ficino's student and disciple, the young and handsome Pico, Count of Mirandola, was completely enthralled by the whole new world of learning. His enthusiasm led him to learn Hebrew and Arabic, as well as Greek and Latin and other languages, and to be unwilling to sacrifice any of the new learning because of its pretended incompatibility with Christianity. As a young man of twenty-three, he appeared in Rome ready and eager to argue with all comers theses he had formulated as a result of his extensive reading. To the papacy some of them were a little too daring. It was no part of wisdom to argue that "no science gives surer conviction of the divinity of Christ than the knowledge of the secrets of heavenly bodies and the Kabbalah [cabala, a medieval collection of Hebrew theosophy]." Pico had to give up his proposed disputation and defend his theses in an apology. Subsequently he engaged upon the Boethian task of bringing together the Aristotelian and Platonic philosophies into one grand synthesis (*Symphonia Platonis et Aristotelis*), but made only a beginning. As an introduction to his planned Roman disputation, however, he wrote a lecture *On the Dignity of Man* that illustrates his hope of denying Christianity the aid of no other learning, and expresses the humanist's trust in man as a creature of reason and free will.

PICO'S "ON THE DIGNITY OF MAN"

When, according to Pico, "God the Father, the Supreme Architect . . . and Craftsman," had finished with his work of creation, he "kept wishing that there were someone to ponder the plan of so great a work, to love its beauty, and to wonder at its vastness. . . . He therefore took man as a creature of indeterminate nature and, assigning him a place in the middle of the world, addressed him thus: 'Neither a fixed abode nor a form that is thine alone nor any function peculiar to thyself have we given thee, Adam, to the end that according to thy longing and according to thy judgment thou mayest have and possess what abode, what form, and what functions thou thyself shalt desire. The nature of all other beings is limited and constrained within the bounds of laws prescribed by Us. Thou,

[12]Paul O. Kristeller, *The Philosophy of Marsilio Ficino.* These sentences are translated by Kristeller, pp. 24–25.

constrained by no limits, in accordance with thine own free will, in whose hand we have placed thee, shall ordain for thyself the limits of thy nature. We have set thee at the world's center that thou mayest from thence more easily observe whatever is in the world. We have made thee neither of heaven nor of earth, neither mortal nor immortal, so that with freedom of choice and with honor, as though the maker and molder of thyself, thou mayest fashion thyself in whatever shape thou shalt prefer. Thou shalt have the power to degenerate into the lower forms of life, which are brutish. Thou shalt have the power, out of thy soul's judgment, to be reborn with the higher forms, which are divine.'

"O supreme generosity of God the Father, O highest and most marvelous felicity of man! To him it is granted to have whatever he chooses, to be whatever he wills. . . . On man when he came into life the Father conferred the seeds of all kinds and the germs of every way of life. Whatever seeds each man cultivates will grow to maturity and bear in him their own fruit. If they be vegetative, he will be like a plant. If sensitive, he will become brutish. If rational, he will grow into a heavenly being. If intellectual, he will be an angel and the son of God. And if, happy in the lot of no created thing, he withdraws into the center of his own unity, his spirit, made one with God, in the solitary darkness of God, who is set above all things, shall surpass them all." Man's nobility therefore consists first of all in his freedom of will. But Pico certainly goes on to suggest that when that freedom is used to acquire the mystic's joy of union with the solitary darkness of God, then man is most noble. This is an undogmatic statement of the orthodox view of the Church. For, Pico says, "it should never be said against us that, although born to a privileged position, we failed to recognize it and became like unto wild animals and senseless beasts of burden" rather than "angels and sons of the Most High. . . . We may not, by abusing the most indulgent generosity of the Father, make for ourselves that freedom of choice He has given into something harmful instead of salutary. Let a certain holy ambition invade our souls so that not content with the mediocre, we shall pant after the highest and (since we may if we wish) toil with all our strength to obtain it."[13]

Many are the past and present aids to attain the mystic's joy: "the light of natural philosophy," the winter of "moral philosophy," and the "felicity of theology," which will make us perfect. "Let us be driven by the frenzies of Socrates, that they may so throw us into ecstasy as to put our mind and ourselves in God. . . . Let us consult the wise Pythagoras. . . . Let us renew . . . the records of the Chaldeans," including Zoroaster. Pico's study of Plato and Aristotle led him to formulate seventy-two new

[13]"On the Dignity of Man," trans. Elizabeth L. Forbes. Reprinted from *The Renaissance Philosophy of Man* edited by Cassirer, Kristeller, and Randall, pp. 224–227, by permission of The University of Chicago Press. Copyright 1948 by The University of Chicago Press.

physical and metaphysical theses, "by means of which whoever holds them will be able . . . to answer any questions whatever proposed in natural philosophy or in divinity by a system far other than we are taught in that philosophy which is studied in the schools and practised by the doctors of this age." With the further aid of a philosophy of numbers, natural magic, and the ancient mysteries of the Hebrews (the cabala) man should be able, if he so chooses, to realize his highest mystical potentiality. It is difficult not to smile at the incoherent cocksureness of Pico's essay on human dignity. But perhaps such extravagances may be allowed the zeal of a young man who is interested in human excellence and in all knowledge leading thereto.

PETRARCH'S CHRISTIAN HUMANISM

Petrarch's view was no less Christian but much less mystical. He could see no reason why he and all others should not gain sustenance for their Christianity from the moral views of Cicero, the great popularizer of Greek philosophy for the Romans. When Cicero, in *De Natura Deorum* (*Concerning the Nature of the Gods*), speaks of a "Divine Being of most outstanding mind, by whom all . . . is ruled," Petrarch is enchanted. For, he says, Cicero describes "one single God as the governor and maker of all things, not in a merely philosophical but almost in a Catholic manner of phrasing it." Indeed, Cicero speaks "like an Apostle. . . . I can hardly tear myself away from Cicero, so much am I fascinated by his genius."[14]

But Petrarch is disturbed when, instead of talking about God and Divine Providence, Cicero talks about the gods "to the point of nausea. . . . He gives an account of the names and qualities of each of these gods, no longer intent on dealing with the providence of 'God' but with that of 'the gods.' Listen please to what he puts in: 'We must venerate and worship these gods,' he says, 'and the best and at the same time the most chaste form of worshipping the gods, that which is overflowing with piety, is adoring them with unabatedly pure, unpolluted, and uncorrupted mind and voice.' Alas, my dear Cicero, what did you say? So quickly have you forgotten the one God and yourself. . . . Who are these new, these recent and infamous gods whom you try to smuggle into the house of the Lord? Are they not those of whom another prophet says: 'All gods of the nations are demons; it is the Lord who makes the heavens.' Just now you spoke of that Maker and Creator of the heavens and all things, pleasing with good reason the ears and heart of a pious hearer. Thus quickly you group Him with rebellious creatures and impure spirits.

"If," Petrarch goes on in his work *On His Own Ignorance*, "to admire Cicero means to be a Ciceronian, I am a Ciceronian. I admire him so much

---

[14]"On His Own Ignorance," trans. Hans Nachod. Reprinted from *The Renaissance Philosophy of Man* edited by Cassirer, Kristeller, and Randall, pp. 83 ff., by permission of The University of Chicago Press. Copyright 1948 by The University of Chicago Press.

that I wonder at people who do not admire him. . . . However, when we come to think or speak of religion, that is, of supreme truth and true happiness, and of eternal salvation, then I am certainly not a Ciceronian, or a Platonist, but a Christian. I even feel sure that Cicero himself would have been a Christian if he had been able to see Christ and to comprehend his doctrine. Of Plato, Augustine does not in the least doubt that he would have become a Christian if he had come to life again in Augustine's time or had forseen the future while he lived. Augustine also relates that in his time most of the Platonists had become Christians and he himself can be supposed to belong to their number. If this fundament stands, in what way is Ciceronian eloquence opposed to the Christian dogma? Or how is it harmful to consult Cicero's writings, if reading the books of heretics does no harm, nay, is profitable, according to the words of the Apostle: 'There must be heresies that they which are approved may be made manifest to you.' "

PETRARCH'S "MY SECRET" AND "ON THE LIFE OF SOLITUDE"

Petrarch's attitude toward the ascetic view may be gathered from his essays called *My Secret* and *On the Life of Solitude*. The first is a dialogue between Petrarch and Saint Augustine, held in the presence of Truth, to determine the value of Petrarch's attachment to Laura. At first Petrarch regards it as one "of the finest passions of my nature. In her face," he says, "unless truth is an empty word, a certain divine loveliness shines out; whose character is the image and picture of perfect honour; whose voice and the living expression of whose eyes has nothing mortal in it; whose very form and motion is not as that of others." Petrarch insists later, "I am not, as you suppose, infatuated with any creature that is mortal. You might have known that I loved her physical charms less than her soul, that what has captivated me has been a life above that of ordinary lives, the witnessing of which has shown me how the blessed live above." But Augustine insists, "She has detached your mind from the love of the heavenly things and has inclined your heart to love the creature more than the Creator; and that one path alone leads, sooner than any other, to death." For a soul crushed by the "miseries of love" cannot "arise to that one and only most pure fountain of true Good."[15] Petrarch admits finally that the saint is correct.

He is then accused by Augustine of pursuing a "false immortality of fame" that may shut for him "the way that leads to the true immortality of life." This false immortality of fame is all the more strong in that "no man more than you abhors the manners and behaviour of the common herd. . . . You write books on others, but yourself you quite forget. And who knows but what, before . . . your works are finished, Death may

[15]*Petrarch's Secret or the Soul's Conflict with Passion*, trans. W. H. Draper, quoted in H. H. Blanchard, *Prose and Poetry of the Continental Renaissance*, pp. 31 ff.

snatch the pen from your tired hand." Petrarch argues that he wants only mortal glory. "Such glory as belongs to man is enough for me. That is all I sigh after. Mortal myself, it is but mortal blessings I desire . . . to follow after human fame as knowing that both myself and it will perish." In the end Petrarch grants that it "would be much safer for me to attend only to the care of my soul, to relinquish altogether every bypath and follow the straight path of the way of salvation. But I have not strength to resist that old bent for study altogether." "Want of will," Augustine replies "you call want of power." And Petrarch prays, "May God lead me safe and whole out of so many crooked ways; that I may follow the Voice that calls me; that I may raise up no cloud of dust before my eyes, and, with my mind calmed down and at peace, I may hear the world grow still and silent, and the winds of adversity die away."[16]

In praise of the life of solitude, "as far as may be from the haunts of men and crowded cities," Petrarch states that it is hardly to be thought of without literature. "Isolation without literature is exile, prison, and torture; supply literature, and it becomes your country, freedom, and delight." Then it is "something holy, innocent, incorruptible, and the purest of all human possessions." Solitude and leisure bring the presence of Christ, for "though he is present everywhere, he never deigns to grace us more fully with his presence, to listen and converse with us more intimately than in solitude . . . the human spirit accustoms itself to celestial contemplation, by continuous intercourse acquires confidence in its salvation, and from a guest and stranger becomes a member of God's household. . . . For from great love and unremitting faithful service there grows up an intimacy between God and man such as is not known between man and man." Withdrawal means that you do not have "to unlearn humanity among men, and through satiety of feeling to hate things, hate people, hate business, hate whom you love, [and] hate yourself." But Petrarch's solitude is not the contemplative solitude of the monk; it is the literary solitude of the gentleman of leisure. "To devote oneself to reading and writing, alternately finding employment and relief in each, to read what our forerunners have written and to write what later generations may wish to read, to pay to posterity the debt which we cannot pay to the dead for the gift of their writings, . . . and with respect to the dead, by cherishing, remembering, and celebrating their fame in every way, to pay them the homage that is due to their genius even though it is not commensurate with their greatness, this is the ideal life." (pp. 48, 49, 79)

SALUTATI AND BRUNI

The view of Petrarch, Ficino, and Pico that the study of ancient authors should serve to enrich, soften, and liberalize the ascetic view has been called Christian humanism. It was supported by other western hu-

[16]Blanchard, pp. 50, 51, 57.

manists of these centuries.[17] Coluccio Salutati remarked that "Human studies are bound up together, and the study of divinity is bound up with them, so that a true and complete knowledge of the one cannot be had without the other."[18] Leonardo Bruni, an early fifteenth-century Italian humanist, begins his treatise *Concerning the Study of Literature* with the remark, addressed to a lady of high lineage, "The foundations of all true learning must be laid in the sound and thorough knowledge of Latin." He goes on to say that "You may naturally turn first to Christian writers. . . . Such a writer, for instance, as St. Augustine affords . . . the fullest scope for reverend yet learned inquiry." If the young lady should turn to "the help and consolation of holy men now living . . . let her not for an instant yield to the impulse to look into their writings, which, compared with those of Augustine, are utterly destitute of sound and melodious style, and seem to me to have no attraction whatever.

"Moreover, the cultivated Christian lady has no need in the study of this weighty subject to confine herself to ecclesiastical writers. Morals, indeed, have been treated of by the noblest intellects of Greece and Rome. What they have left to us upon Continence, Temperance, Modesty, Justice, Courage, Greatness of Soul, demands your sincere respect." "In practical wisdom or moral earnestness" Plato and Aristotle do not "yield to our modern critics. They were not Christians, indeed, but consistency of life and abhorrence of evil existed before Christianity and are independent of it."[19]

THE CLASSICS AND EDUCATION

In being persuaded by humanist educators that the study of Latin and Greek, their literature and thought, should become a part of the training of youth, the western ruling classes were not simply concerned with promoting cultivation or refinement or broadening the religious outlook of the aristocratic classes. Ancient civic life in the city-state demanded contributions and sacrifices from useful citizens. What made Cicero so attractive to the humanist of the Renaissance was his active citizenship, as well as his style and learning. An English humanist-educator could say to his noble pupil that nobility is something that is conferred upon men when "either out of knowledge, culture of the mind, or by some glorious action performed they have been useful and beneficial to the commonwealths and places where they live. For since all virtue consisteth in action, and no man is born for himself, we add, beneficial and useful to his country; for hardly they are to be admitted for noble, who (though of never so excellent parts) consume their light, as in a dark lantern, in contemplation and a stoical retiredness." A literature that contributed to this

[17]See Douglas Bush, *The Renaissance and English Humanism.*
[18]*Life of Solitude*, trans. Jacob Zeitlin, quoted in Blanchard, pp. 63, 67, 73.
[19]Reprinted from *Main Currents of Western Thought*, pp. 136–138, by F. Le Van Baumer, by permission of Alfred A. Knopf, Inc., copyright 1952.

activity contributed to true nobility. "Rome saw her best days under her most learned kings and emperors . . . Plutarch giveth the reason: learning (saith he) reformeth the life and manners, and affordedth the wholesomest advice for the government of a commonwealth."[20]

THE RESTORATION OF CHRISTIAN ANTIQUITY

A more precise conception of the Christian humanism of these centuries may be secured by going back to trace the changes north of the Alps leading to such men as the German Johann Reuchlin and the Dutch Erasmus of Rotterdam. If the intellectual development of these and other northern humanists were to be considered in detail, it would be found that they were all influenced directly by study and travel in Italy, or indirectly by reading the works of the serious Italian humanists. Reuchlin and Erasmus and men like them are often referred to as Christian humanists to differentiate them from pagan Italian humanists. There is not much point to this differentiation, for, as we have seen, there were few if any actual neo-pagan Italian humanists. That is not to say that Christian humanist is not an adequate term for the northern scholar. If the Italian humanists were especially interested in reviving classical antiquity, then the northern Christian humanists, while no less interested for the same reasons in promoting the study of Latin and Greek letters, were especially interested in reviving Christian antiquity. They were interested, that is, in the promotion of Latin and Greek letters for the definite purpose of studying the works of the Latin and Greek Fathers of the Church, and indeed all literature associated with the origin, spread, and victory of Christianity. Since the most important part of this literature was the Scriptures, Hebrew had to be added to Latin and Greek so that the Old Testament might be studied in the original tongue.

Scholarship was thus faced with another huge task. It was not simply that men had to learn to read the Old Testament in Hebrew and the New Testament in Greek in order to understand properly what these sacred texts meant. They also could not be understood properly outside their historical context. What was the relationship of the Old Testament to the history of the Jewish people? What was the relationship of the New Testament to the development of Christianity? What was the relationship of Greek and Latin Christian literature to the whole history of Christian expansion and victory in the Roman world? As Erasmus put it, "If, thanks to works of history, we know not only the situation of the peoples among whom the recorded events happened, to whom the Apostles wrote, and also their origin, their manners, their institutions, their genius, what light—let us say better—what life it puts into the study of the sacred texts!" These are problems with which, of course, Christian scholarship is still concerned. But to study the Scriptures or Christian literature as,

[20]Van Baumer, pp. 131, 133.

among other things, historical documents meant that their allegorical interpretation had to be abandoned for a strictly literal intepretation of the text. Before they could be understood as revelations of God, they had to be understood as the products of man.

THE EARLIER CHRISTIAN RENAISSANCE

The classical revival of the fourteenth and fifteenth centuries was preceded by the lesser revival of the twelfth and thirteenth centuries, making it proper to speak of the gradual recovery of an understanding of the ancient world. The emphasis of the fourteenth and fifteenth centuries upon a restoration of early Christian antiquity was likewise preceded by a similar and lesser demand in the earlier period. Men like Robert Grosseteste and Roger Bacon[21] were aware of the importance of knowing Greek not only to get back of the Latin translations of the twelfth and thirteenth centuries but to read the new Testament in the original language. They were quite convinced of the importance of reading the original Scriptures to penetrate through the elaborate theological façade erected by the scholastic philosophers. Indeed this distinction between the pagan and Christian Roman pasts is artificial and academic. Rome did not develop as two separate societies, one pagan and one Christian. Its imperial history is a story of continuous, interconnected development.

CHRISTIAN HUMANISM AS A REFORM PROGRAM

Scholars were stimulated to read the Scriptures and early Christian literature by the difficulties of the Church in the later Middle Ages: the renewed quarrels with the state, the Avignon papacy, the Great Schism, the heresies of John Wycliffe and John Huss, and the whole conciliar movement.[22] Since these followed earlier criticism of the Church by heretics and the friars, the question was raised: how are Christianity and the Church to be saved, to be reformed, to be protected from the attacks of its enemies? The Christian humanist replied to this question by advocating the salvation of the Church through a return to its premedieval, Roman scriptural form. To know what this early form was required a reading and comprehension of early Christian literature. For the northern humanist, the restoration of a knowledge and understanding of early Christianity was actually a method of reform. In this early Christianity he did not find those medieval accretions of a thousand years that often enough, even without a knowledge of history, he felt to be pagan rather than Christian.

EARLY CHRISTIANITY AND CHRISTIAN HUMANISM

The restoration of a knowledge of early Christian history and institutions revealed the simple organization of Christian communities before

[21]See pp. 660 f.
[22]See pp. 626 ff.

the patterning and building of the theocratic Church. The early Church was without hierarchy and pope, pomp and ceremony, elaborate sacramental rites and hosts of saints. Primitive Christianity was a religion not yet adapted to the gorgeous public character of classical paganism and without a hard and fast or complicated dogmatic system. If, these humanists felt, the clergy knew these things they would have in their hands the instruments of reform. A Christian humanism, leavened by the humanism of antiquity and the simplicity of early Christianity, by what Erasmus called the philosophy of Christ, would save the Church without the necessity of revolution.

THE POPULAR MYSTICISM OF THE RHINELANDS

Accompanying the revival of a learned Neoplatonic mysticism in Italy in the fourteenth and fifteenth centuries was a growth of popular mysticism in the Rhinelands, which influenced many Christian humanists and Protestant reformers. Its background was the same decline of the Church and the mechanization of Christianity that contributed to the reforming spirit of the Christian humanists. Its leaders came from the Dominican friars, whose German leader, Albert the Great,[23] had made Cologne a mystic center. Its devotees came from busy Rhine towns, from Cologne to Strassburg, and from communities in southern Germany and Switzerland. They formed organizations called the Friends of God. They regarded themselves as divinely chosen to lead the Church out of its confusion. They, to whom the privilege of a mystic experience had been granted and who thus shared God's divinity, were obviously a special group of hallowed laymen whose leadership, many thought, should be preferred to that of the clergy. It is hard not to suppose that the simple lay piety of these mystic circles may be traced back to the earlier Waldensians and Albigensians.[24] They aimed to renounce the excessive pleasures of urban life and to discipline their spirits in accordance with definite exercises drawn up by their leaders. Their circles possessed a live literature, often predicting disaster for the Church. Their leaders, moving from center to center as itinerant preachers, were Master John Eckhard, Ruman Merswin of Strassburg, John Tauler, Henry Suso, and in Holland Jan Rysbroeck. In some instances it was a very tender, in others a very realistic, mysticism that these men preached.

THE LANGUAGE OF THE MYSTICS

"When," said Eckhard, "I attain this blessedness of union, then all things are in me and in God, and where I am, there God is, and Where God is, there am I." For Tauler, a layman who has attained the summit of mystical experience, "speaks in the place of God," and has thus an

[23]See p. 659.
[24]See pp. 608 ff.

apostolic authority that puts him above any priest or doctor, who has only the authority of ordination or scholarship. "Those whom God has drawn into the unity of the Godhead are the persons on whom the Church rests. They are divine supernatural men, and they hold up the world and the pillars of it. If they were not in Christendom, it would not last an hour." Henry Suso used extraordinary language to describe the presence of God in his soul. Looking into himself, "he saw as through a crystal in the midst of his heart the Eternal Wisdom in lovely form, and besides Him his own soul leaning lovingly to God's side, and embraced in His arms and pressed to His Divine heart, and lying entranced and drowned in the arms of the God he loved." When the Virgin granted him the privilege of holding her Baby, Suso writes that "he contemplated its beautiful little eyes, . . . kissed its tender little mouth, and gazed again and again at the infant members of the heavenly treasure. Then, lifting up his eyes, he uttered a cry of amazement that He who bears up the heavens is so small, so beautiful in heaven, and so childlike on earth." As a mystic, Suso says, he searches "in silent darkness, in absolute repose, the marvels of Divinity." When one has achieved union with Divinity, he is "like a being which loses itself, in an indescribable intoxication. The human spirit ceases to be itself, divests itself of itself, passes into God, and becomes wholly one with Him, as a drop of water mingles with a cask of wine. As the drop of water loses its identity and takes on the taste and colour of the wine, so it is with those who are in full possession of bliss: human decrees influence them no longer; divested of self they are absorbed in the Divine Will, mingle with the Divine Nature, and become one with it." The product of this mystic school of writing that most influenced Luther was the *German Theology* (*Theologia Germanica*), of unknown authorship. "Next to the Bible and St. Augustine," he said, "no book has ever come into my hands from which I have learned more of what God and Christ and man and all things are." Like the others, it is written in praise of the "partaker of the Divine Nature," for "to be a God-like man, means to be illuminated by the Divine Light, and to be influenced and consumed with Divine Love."[25]

BRETHREN OF THE COMMON LIFE

Dutch mysticism did not content itself with writing devotional literature. Gerhard Groot of Deventer founded a new kind of monastic order called the Brethren of the Common Life, a group of men who set out to remedy what they considered the defects in contemporary religion by reforming the methods of teaching. The best teachers in western Europe in the fifteenth century, they taught such men as Erasmus and Luther. They joined together a scholastic and a religious training grounded in

[25]The selection from R. M. Jones, *Studies in Mystical Religion*, pp. 233, 273, 287, 290, 296, copyright 1909 by The Macmillan Co., and used with The Macmillan Co.'s permission.

mysticism. If not actually from the pen of another of their pupils, Thomas a Kempis, the fifteenth-century *Imitation of Christ* has long been, next to the Bible itself, the most popular of all religious tracts.

THE "IMITATION OF CHRIST"

It appealed especially to those humble people who were the mainstay of the German mystical movement. "Surely an humble husbandman that serveth God is better than a proud philosopher who, neglecting himself, is occupied in studying the course of the heavens. . . . Cease from an inordinate desire of knowledge, for therein is much distraction and deceit. . . . If thou wilt know or learn anything profitably, desire to be unknown, and to be little esteemed. . . . Truly at the day of judgment we shall not be examined as to what we have read, but as to what we have done; not as to how well we have spoken but as to how religiously we have lived. . . . He is truly great who hath great love. . . . He is truly wise that accounteth all earthly things as dung, that he may win Christ. . . . And he is truly learned that doeth the will of God, and forsaketh his own will.

"He is vain that putteth his trust in man, or in creatures. . . . Desire to be familiar alone with God and his angels, and avoid the acquaintance of men. . . . It is a great matter to live in obedience, to be under a superior and not to be at our own disposing. It is much safer to obey than to govern. . . . Go whither thou wilt, thou shall find no rest but in humble subjection under the government of a superior. . . . Fly the tumult of the world as much as thou canst; for the treating of worldly affairs is a great hindrance, although it be done with sincere intention. . . . Perfect security and full peace cannot be had in this world. . . . God will have us perfectly subject to him, that, being inflamed with his love, we may transcend the narrow limits of human reason.

"If thou wilt stand firm and grow as thou oughtest, esteem thyself as a pilgrim and a stranger upon earth. . . . Never be entirely idle; but either be reading, or writing, or praying, or meditating, or endeavoring something for the public good. . . . Who therefore withdraweth himself from his acquaintances and friends, God will draw near unto him with his holy angels. . . . Oh, how great is human frailty which is always prone to evil! . . . Thou oughtest so to order thyself and all thy thoughts and actions as if to-day thou wert to die. . . . Happy is he that always hath the hour of his death before his eyes. . . . Do not think that thou hast made any progress unless thou esteem thyself inferior to all. . . . Thou art deceived, thou art deceived if thou seek any other thing than to suffer tribulations; for this whole life is full of miseries, and marked on every side with crosses. . . . Indeed if there had been any better thing and more profitable to win salvation than suffering, surely Christ would have showed it by word and example.

"If I abase myself, and reduce myself to nothing, and shrink from all self-esteem, and grind myself to the dust I am, thy grace will be favourable to me, and thy light near unto my heart, and all self-esteem, how little soever, shall be swallowed up in the valley of my nothingness, and perish forever. Truly unspeakable is the sweetness of contemplating thee, which thou bestowest on them that love thee. . . . A man ought therefore to mount above all creatures, and perfectly to renounce himself, and to be in a sort of ecstasy of mind, and to see that thou, the Creator of all things, hast nothing amongst creatures like unto thyself. . . . Blessed is the man who for thy sake, O Lord, is willing to part with all creatures, who does violence to his nature, and through fervour of the spirit crucifieth the lusts of the flesh; that so with a serene conscience he may offer pure prayers unto thee, and, all earthly things both outwardly and inwardly being excluded, he may be meet to be admitted into the angelic choirs. . . . O that with thy presence thou wouldst wholly inflame, burn, and conform me unto thyself; that I might be made one spirit with thee, by the grace of inward union, and by the meltings of violent love."[26] These mystical groups sought the comfort of the gospel teachings of Christian love that they could not find in the ministrations or theology of a hierarchic church or in the learned writings of classical humanists.

JOHN REUCHLIN

Their leaders were Dominicans. These friars had become closely associated with the papal inquisition soon after its foundation, and in that capacity were especially sensitive to heresy and near-heresy, and to all writings that deviated from the regular dogmatic positions given by the Church. It can be imagined, therefore, that they were suspicious of the works of humanists, and that, when the humanists undertook to defend the language and literature of the Jewish betrayers of Christ, their suspicion was intensified. Such turned out to be the situation in the case of John Reuchlin (1455–1522). Reuchlin was a German humanist who had first turned to the study of Greek and Roman law. On a journey to Italy he met Pico della Mirandola, and was influenced by his notion that in the Jewish cabala ideas could be found that would show that Platonism and Christianity were but different approaches to the same divine truth. This turned Reuchlin to the study of Hebrew, the importance of which for a proper study of the Old Testament and Judaism he did not have to have pointed out to him. In 1506 he published a Hebrew grammar, and this was followed by other works on the Psalms and the cabala. He was the first learned pioneer of Hebrew and oriental studies in the West, one who through the study of Hebrew and Hebrew literature opened up the world of the Ancient Near East to western scholars and together with it critical study of the Old Testament.

[26]*Imitation of Christ.*

As a Hebrew scholar, Reuchlin was attacked by ignorant, anti-Semitic obscurantists and heretic baiters. One of these was Johann Pfefferkorn, a renegade Christian Jew who sought to lead a campaign against the Jewish faith and literature in Germany. He had secured, in the summer of 1509, from the German emperor Maximilian, a mandate giving him power to require every Jew in the empire to surrender to him all Hebrew books that called in question Christian beliefs or upheld Judaism. "An ancient literature, in short, was to be swept away at the will of the ignorant agent of pedantic bigots who could not read a line of it." Reuchlin refused to support Pfefferkorn in his campaign against Hebrew literature. Later in 1509 Maximilian set up a special commission, including Reuchlin, to examine all Hebrew books dealing with religious subjects, and in July, 1510, the archbishop of Mainz was ordered to collect the opinions of the members of this commission. Reuchlin's opinion differentiated between Jewish writings that openly attacked Christianity and those that did nothing of the sort. The former might be suppressed, the remainder should not be disturbed. Reuchlin argued for more attention to Hebrew and for the establishment of chairs of the Hebrew language and literature at the German universities. For this, Pfefferkorn attacked him in a pamphlet called the *Handt-Spiegel* (*Hand Mirror*). Reuchlin was called "a charlatan in learning," "an apostate in religion," "the Jews' advocate," and "a disseminator of their blasphemies." Reuchlin answered with a pamphlet of his own, the *Augenspiegel* (*Eyeglasses*), "a defense of my character and my writings."[27]

In the course of the pamphlet controversy that followed, Pfefferkorn was supported by the Dominicans and theologians of Cologne, and it became clear that the issues involved were no less than the future of the whole new humanist movement in Germany and elsewhere. Was it to be permitted to follow its reforming and liberalizing bent, or was it to be intimidated by the ecclesiastical authorities supported by the Inquisition? Reuchlin's *Augenspiegel* was in fact sent to the Dominican Jacob von Hochstraten, the "Inquisitor of Heretical Pravity for the dioceses of Cologne, Mainz, and Trier." The inquisitor, after taking steps to humiliate Reuchlin that caused even the emperor to intervene, finally cited him before a court of the Inquisition at Mainz (9 September, 1513). Reuchlin did not appear, and instead appealed to Rome. The case was then sent to the archbishop of Spires, a humanist sympathizer. His opinion was that the *Augenspiegel* was not heretical (March, 1514); Hochstraten had slandered Reuchlin, and had to pay the costs. The Dominican now took the case to Rome (1514), where he tried for a year to get the *Augenspiegel* condemned. The pope now had to decide whether to condemn or support a scholar determined to cultivate a new field of study vital to Christianity.

[27]*Epistolae Obscurorum Virorum*, ed. and trans. Francis G. Stokes, pp. xxiv ff.

Meanwhile, at the end of 1515, and again in 1516 and 1517, there appeared in Germany various editions of a collection of letters called *Letters of Obscure Men*. They were the answer of German humanists to the attack of the Dominicans and their supporters upon Reuchlin. In the spring of 1514 Reuchlin had published a collection of letters written on his behalf which he called *Letters of Famous Men*. Two of the leading German humanists, Crotus Rubeanus and Ulrich von Hutten,[28] conceived the notion of pretending to counteract these with the *Letters of Obscure Men*, which were actually, of course, an unrestrained, crushing, witty, and ridiculing attack upon the ignorance, pettiness, dishonesty, and lechery of the "obscurantist" Dominicans. The letters were written mostly by Rubeanus and von Hutten, with some help from fellow humanists. The laughter they provoked made it impossible any longer to take the anti-humanist charges of Reuchlin's enemies seriously. Pope Leo X, in 1517, ordered that copies of the *Letters* should be turned over to the ecclesiastical authorities for burning, their authors excommunicated, and the heretical book itself denounced from all pulpits. Meanwhile a commission of cardinals, with one dissenting vote, decided in Reuchlin's favor in the matter of the *Augenspiegel*. For the time being, Pope Leo, unwilling to antagonize the Dominicans, did not announce this decision, but rather suspended the whole controversy in the courts. But after Luther had emerged as a European hero in 1517, the pope went over to the Dominicans. He sided with the minority of one, of his commission of cardinals, proclaimed the *Augenspiegel* a dangerous book, and imposed the legal costs of the whole business upon Reuchlin.

Many of the *Letters* were addressed to Ortwin Gratius, the leader of the Cologne theologians supporting von Hochstraten. In one of them Master Hochstraten is described as "a mumping cheese-begging friar." Another refers to the report that "the Pope is minded to confirm the sentence pronounced a year ago at Spires in favour of Doctor Reuchlin. . . . I verily fear me that the Pope is no good Christian—for if he were a good Christian it would be impossible for him not to uphold the Theologers. . . . I have heard that many burgs, and princes, and persons of quality have written letters on his [Reuchlin's] behalf. Now the reason of this is that they are not grounded in Theology, . . . otherwise they would bid the devil take that heretic—for a heretic he is though the whole world should hold to the contrary."[29]

Another letter to Ortwin introduces Erasmus, the distinguished Dutch humanist and one of the most learned men of his day. The writer is a medical student who has come to Strassburg in Alsace, where he hears that "Erasmus of Rotterdam, of whom I had never heard, but who is profoundly skilled in all knowledge and in every branch of learning," was in

[28]See Hajo Holborn, *Ulrich von Hutten and the German Reformation*.
[29]*Epistolae Obscurorum Virorum*, passim.

town. The medical student arranged to be present at a dinner for Erasmus. The host, "a humanist of parts, fell to some discourse on Poetry, and greatly belauded Julius Caesar, as touching both his writings and his valorous deeds. So soon as I heard this, I perceived my opportunity, for I had studied much, and learned much under you in the matter of Poetry, when I was at Cologne, and I said, 'Forasmuch as you have begun to speak concerning Poetry, I can therefore no longer hide my light under a bushel and I roundly aver that I believe not that Caesar wrote those Commentaries. . . . Whosoever hath business with arms and is occupied in labour unceasing cannot learn Latin; but Caesar was ever at war and in labours manifold; therefore he could not become lettered and get Latin. In truth, therefore, I believe that it was none other than that Suetonius who wrote those *Commentaries*, for I have met with none who hath a style more like Caesar's than Suetonius.' . . . Erasmus laughed, but said nothing, for I had overthrown him by the subtlety of my argument."

One letter is from von Hochstraten (Hoogstraeten) at Rome. He regrets that he started his campaign against Reuchlin. "All men deride me and plague me, and Reuchlin hath more friends here than in Germany, and many Cardinals, and bishops, and prelates, and Curialists love him. Had I not entered upon this business I should now be at Cologne enjoying my victuals and drink, whereas here I have scarce a crust." Hochstraten had heard that Erasmus is writing on Theology. "I cannot believe he hath avoided error. . . . If I come back to Germany and read his scribblements, and find in them the very smallest jot on which he hath gone astray—or which I do not understand—let him take heed to his skin! He hath also written in Greek; this is not well, for we are Latins and not Greeks." Hochstraten speaks of walks in Rome during which the "Curialists come and point at us with their fingers, and laugh, and say: 'There go the two who want to eat up Reuchlin. They eat him and then void him again!'" People drop little papers in front of him which seem to be his epitaphs. One of them reads:

> Here Virtue's bane, Hochstratus, carrion lies,
> In life the cynosure of scoundrels' eyes,
> Indignant fled his soul that she had run
> Her earthly course—with evil left undone!

Hochstraten spends a long time trying to figure out if the epitaph was meant for him. "If it mean me—which I cannot believe, for I am not yet dead—I will hold an inquiry, and when I have caught the fellow I will make ready a bath for him that will be no laughing matter; that is easy."

Another letter complains of the new poets at the universities. It was better in "the days when there was not a Poet within twenty miles." Universities have come to a bad end when "now-a-days all the students must needs attend lectures on Virgil and Pliny and the rest of the new fangled authors—what is more, they may listen to them for five years and yet get no degree; and so, when they return home their parents ask them, saying, 'What art thou?' and they reply that they are naught, but that they have been reading Poetry!" In the old days it was a "grave offence to study poetry. If a penitent admitted in the confessional that he had privily listened to a Bachelor lecturing upon Virgil, the priest would impose upon him a thumping penance." All the students want "to study the Humanities. When a Magister [a theologian] lectureth he findeth no audience; but, as for the Poets, when they discourse it is a marvel to behold the crowd of listeners. And thus the Universities throughout all Germany are minished and brought low. Let us pray God, then, that all the Poets may perish, for 'it is expedient that one man should die', that is that the Poets, of whom there are but a handful in any one University, should perish, rather than so many Universities should come to naught."

Another letter returns to Erasmus. Its author speaks of him as "an enemy of the monks: he speaketh much ill of them; he saith they are clumsy jackasses, who hate polite letters, and they can do naught save guzzle, and swill and mumble psalms. . . . He lieth in his throat when he saith these things. He himself is the jackass. He is a sound Latinist and writeth fair Latin—but he knoweth naught else. . . . He hath written many books—notably . . . a commentary on Jerome—and in these he doeth naught but belabour the Regulars. I warn him, pardy, that if he refrain not his hands from them we will do to him as to Reuchlin, though he were in a hundred ways favoured by the Pope and King Charles. We have seen many men as arrogant as he, and yet we have suppressed them."

ERASMUS

Many elements in the Church would have been delighted to have the renowned Erasmus silenced. He can be taken as an excellent example of the outlook and activities of a Christian humanist at the close of the Middle Ages. No one was a more devoted student of the serious literature and thought of pagan antiquity. That there could be any great conflict between this pagan world and Christianity he did not believe. Christianity was but the fulfillment of the law of the Old Testament, the philosophical genius of the Greek, and the political genius of the Roman. The Christianity that Erasmus was devoted to, however, was not the Christianity of his day. It was not the religion of secular-minded popes trying to preserve a papal state in Italy nor of like-minded prelates preoccupied with the accumulation of property and wealth. It was not the religion of sacraments and incense, pilgrimages or relics, the Virgin or indulgences. It was not the so-called asceticism of his monastic contemporaries. Erasmus wanted to reform the Church in the light of the religion of Jesus and of the early Greek and Latin Fathers. It was this end that learning should serve. Learning had no justification in the conceit of the scholar over his fine Ciceronian style. It had no special sanctity because far removed from the interests and needs of the vulgar crowd. Learning had to serve the purpose of reviving a simple, undogmatic Christian piety—the philosophy of Christ. It had to confound a decadent and secularized Church that presided over a religion lost in ignorance, superstition, and mechanical contrivance. The humanist, a believer in the rationality and free will of man, must labor in this world for power to enable learning, avoiding the extreme of revolution, gradually to reform the Church and religion so as to enhance, and not cheapen, the dignity and nobility of human life.

ERASMUS AND THE CLASSICS

A distinguished American scholar has referred to the Erasmian ideal of an undogmatic religion and an ethical piety founded alike on the Sermon on the Mount and the teachings of Greek philosophy. "Plato he soon discovered was a theologian, Socrates a saint, Cicero inspired, and Seneca not far from Paul." "When," Erasmus says, "I read certain passages of these great men, I can hardly refrain from saying, Saint Socrates, pray for me."[30] "I cannot read his [Cicero's] books on *Old Age, Friendship*, and *Duties* without stopping and kissing the manuscript." "To the ancients reverence is due and in particular to those who are commended by holiness of life as well as by learning and eloquence; yet they are to be read with discretion." "A man's studies should strengthen his faith, not undermine it."[31]

ERASMUS AND THE SCHOLAR'S TASK

Erasmus had ideas of being influential among more than a learned coterie. He writes to a French scholar, "You have preferred to be understood by the learned: I, if I can, by the many; your aim is to conquer, mine to teach or persuade." In his desire to see Christianity restored to its original simplicity and made universal, he wished to have the Scriptures translated into all languages and to have "scriptural passages . . . in the mind of the farmer following his plough and the weaver at his loom." But he did not regard it as his task to do this translation. His task was to relate pagan antiquity to contemporary Christianity, to make available sound original texts of the Christian classics, and, finally, by way of criticism to suggest a reform of the religion and Church of his day. "All studies, philosophy, rhetoric, are followed for this one object, that we may know Christ and honour Him. This is the end of all learning and eloquence. . . . It has long been my cherished wish to cleanse the Lord's temple of barbarous ignorance, and to adorn it with treasures from afar, such as may kindle in generous hearts a warm love for the Scriptures."[32]

[30]Preserved Smith, *Erasmus*, p. 20.
[31]*Cambridge Modern History*, I, 608. See also H. Baker, "Christian Humanism," *The Dignity of Man*, p. 260.
[32]Douglas Bush, *The Renaissance and English Humanism*, p. 64.

ERASMUS AND THE CHRISTIAN CLASSICS

Erasmus was the first scholar to give the West a printed text of the Greek New Testament. He accompanied it with a fresh Latin translation and courageous, unconventional notes of his own. He then turned to the preparation of sound texts for the Latin and Greek Fathers. He worked on Jerome for an edition of the Fathers published by the Amorbachs of Basel. He worked on an edition of Cyprian, and, among many others, of Irenaeus. He published four folio volumes of Ambrose and ten of Augustine. It was at this point that he reports, "They tell me that if I am to live, I must give up all writing, indeed study of any sort. But life at such a price is no life, especially as my pains will not give me up."[33] In bed he began work on a Latin edition of the Greek Father Origen.

ERASMUS ON REASON AND FREE WILL

Meanwhile he had been engaged on books and pamphlets containing his ideas on reform. In a work *On the Education of Children* he wrote, "it is the possession of Reason which constitutes a man . . . a man not instructed through reason in philosophy and sound learning is a creature lower than a brute, seeing that there is no beast more wild or harmful than a man who is driven hither and thither by ambition, or desire, anger or envy, or lawless temper. . . . He that provides not that his own son may presently be instructed in the best learning is neither a man nor the son of a man."[34] In his controversy with Martin Luther, Erasmus defended that humanistic principle of freedom of the will that the early medieval Church had adopted in reaction to Saint Augustine's doctrine of predestination.[35] He contended in his work *On Free Will* (1524) that if the will were not free, sin could not be imputed to man. The Scriptures exhort man to do good and promise him rewards or threaten punishments accordingly. These admonitions are addressed to beings capable of moral action, not mere mechanical instruments of the divine will. It is absurd to make God, who is just and good, the author of human wickedness. God co-operates with human action. The evil in the action does not proceed from God but from human choice. If God determines human action, there is no possibility of human merit, and no distinction between good and evil. "For my part," Erasmus says, "I prefer the opinion of those who attribute something to free will, but a great deal to grace."[36]

"THE PRAISE OF FOLLY"

Erasmus' reforming zeal can be best seen in his *Praise of Folly* and his colloquy on the *Excluded Julius*. In the former he takes to task, as the

[33]P. S. Allen, *Erasmus, Lectures and Wayfaring Sketches*, p. 54.
[34]W. H. Woodward, *Desiderius Erasmus*, pp. 186–187.
[35]See p. 589.
[36]Ephraim Emerton, *Desiderius Erasmus*, p. 396. See J. Mackinnon, "Luther and the Humanists" and "The Conflict with Erasmus," *Luther*, Vols. I and III.

disciples of Folly, all those he detests or dislikes. Of war, Folly asks, "What is more foolish than to enter upon a conflict for I know not what causes, wherein each side reaps more of loss than of gain? . . . When armored ranks engage each other and bugles bray with harsh accord, of what use are those wise men, who, exhausted by studies, scarce maintain any life in their thin, cold blood? The day belongs to stout, gross fellows: the littler wit they have, the bolder they are. . . . This famous game of war is played by parasites, panders, bandits, assassins, peasants, sots, bankrupts, and such other dregs of mankind; never by philosophers with their candles of wisdom." On the scholastic philosophers Erasmus exercises his wit. The apostles, he says, undobtedly "consecrated the Eucharist devoutly enough; but suppose you had questioned them about the *terminus a quo* and the *terminus ad quem*, or about transubstantiation—how the body is in many places at once, the difference between the body of Christ when in heaven, when on the Cross, when in the sacrament of the Eucharist, about the point when transubstantiation occurs (seeing that the prayer effecting it is a discrete quantity having extension in time)—they would not have answered with the same acuteness, I suggest, with which the sons of Scotus [Duns Scotus] distinguish and define these matters."[37]

Erasmus pours scorn on the professional ascetics, the monks. "They reckon it the highest degree of piety to have no contact with literature, and hence they see to it that they do not know how to read. . . . Some of them make a good profit from their dirtiness and mendicancy, collecting their food from door to door with importunate bellowing. . . . According to their account, by their very dirtiness, ignorance, want of manners and insolence, these delightful fellows are representing to us the lives of the apostles. . . . Members of certain orders start back from the mere touch of a piece of money as if it were aconite. They do not, however, withdraw from the touch of a glass of wine or of a woman. In short, all orders take remarkable care that nothing in their way of life shall be consistent; nor is it so much their concern to be like Christ as to be unlike others. . . . The greater number of them work so hard at their ceremonies and at maintaining the minutiae of tradition that they deem one heaven hardly a suitable reward for their labors." When Christ comes to demand a reckoning of them, they will provide their "hundred bushels of hymns, . . . myriads of fasts . . . a pile of ceremonies . . . so big that seven ships could scarcely carry" it, and Christ will say, " 'I promised the inheritance of my Father, not to cowls, orisons, or fasts, but to works of charity.' . . . Tell me, what comic actor or mountebank would you rather watch than the monks rhetoricizing in their sermons . . . how they intone, throw themselves about, suddenly put on a new face, and confuse all things by their bawling! They bandy about before an uneducated crowd their syllogisms, majors, minors, conclusions, corollaries, conversions, and such

[37]*The Praise of Folly*, trans. H. H. Hudson, pp. 30, 80.

bloodless and more than scholastic pedantry." Monks are in a "class of men, who with their ceremonials and silly pedantries and bawling exercise a kind of despotism over mortal men, and believe themselves to be Pauls and Anthonies." (pp. 88-89, 91, 93)

The secular clergy no less than the monks are the objects of Erasmus' criticism. The bishops "do well enough by way of feeding themselves; as for the others, the care of the sheep, they delegate that to Christ himself, or else refer it to their suffragans. . . . In raking in moneys they truly play the bishop, overseeing everything and overlooking nothing. . . . As to these Supreme Pontiffs who take the place of Christ, if they tried to emulate His life, I mean His poverty, labors, teaching, cross and contempt for safety . . . who on earth would be more afflicted? Who would purchase that seat at the price of every resource and effort? Or who would defend it, when purchased, by the sword, by poison, or by anything else? Were wisdom to descend upon them, how it would inconvenience them! Wisdom, did I say? Nay, even a grain of salt would do it—a grain of that salt which is spoken of by Christ. It would lose them all that wealth and honor, all those possessions, triumphal progresses, offices, dispensations, tributes, and indulgences; it would lose them so many horses, mules, and retainers; so many pleasures . . . all those copyists and notaries would be in want, as would all those advocates, promoters, secretaries, muleteers, grooms, bankers, and pimps. . . . As it is now, what labor turns up to be done they hand over to Peter and Paul, who have leisure for it. . . . Scarcely any kind of men live more softly or less oppressed with care, believing that they are amply acceptable to Christ if with a majestical and almost theatrical finery, with ceremonies, and with those titles of Beatitude and Reverence and Holiness, along with blessing and cursing, they perform the office of Bishop. To work miracles is primitive and old fashioned, hardly suited to our times; to instruct the people is irksome; to interpret the Holy Scriptures is pedantry; to pray is otiose; to shed tears is distressing and womanish; to live in poverty is sordid; to be beaten in war dishonorable and less than worthy of one who will hardly admit kings, however great, to kiss his sacred foot. . . . And although war is so cruel a business that it befits beasts and not men, so frantic that poets feign it is sent with evil purpose by the Furies, so pestilential that it brings with it a general blight upon morals, so iniquitous that it is usually conducted by the worst bandits, so impious that it has no accord with Christ, yet our popes, neglecting all their other concerns, make it their only task . . . priests, by reason of modesty, leave all pursuit of piety to common folk." (pp. 97-99, 100, 102)

"ON THE RELIGIOUS PILGRIMAGE"

In his *Colloquy on the Religious Pilgrimage* Erasmus makes sport of many features of popular religion. The pilgrimage is terminated by the beholding of many sacred relics, including "the heavenly milk of the blessed Virgin." "O Mother like her Son! for as He has left us so much of His blood upon earth, so she has left us so much of her milk that it is scarce credible that a woman who never had but one child should have so much, although her child had never sucked a drop. . . . Our Lord's cross . . . is shewn up and down both publicly and privately in so many places, that if all the fragments were gathered together, they would seem to be sufficient loading for a good large ship; and yet our Lord himself carried the whole cross upon his shoulders." At Canterbury the relics of Becket were seen. "Upon the altar is the point of the sword with which the top of the head of that good prelate was wounded, and some of his brains that were beaten out, to make sure work of it. We most religiously kissed the sacred rust of this weapon out of love to the martyr." The shoes of Saint Thomas were shown as relics. "I think it a piece of impudence to thrust slipper, and shoes, and stockings upon any one to be kissed."[38]

"JULIUS EXCLUSUS"

The best of Erasmus' *Colloquies*, and one published anonymously, is the *Julius Exclusus* (*Julius Excluded*, 1514). The Julius of this piece is Pope Julius II (1503-1513), one of the most secular-minded and hard-boiled of the Renaissance popes. Saint Peter will not let him into heaven because he does not think he is a Christian. Throughout the dialogue Erasmus is bent upon drawing the contrast between the early Church and primitive Christianity and the Church and Christianity of his day. When Julius approaches the door, Peter refers to him as "some giant, or conqueror. Heaven what a stench!" When the pope refers to himself as Julius, P. M., Peter asks, "P. M.! What is that? *Pestis Maxima?*" and the pope replies, "*Pontifex Maximus*, you rascal." When Peter looks at him closely, he describes him as "not precisely like an apostle. Priest's cassock and bloody armour below it, eyes savage, mouth insolent, forehead brazen, body scarred with sins all over, breath loaded with wine, health broken with debauchery. . . . You are Julius the Emperor come back from hell." The pope threatens to "fling a thunderbolt" at Peter. "I will excommunicate you. I have done as much to kings before this. Here are the Bulls ready." Peter answers, "Thunderbolts! Bulls! I beseech you, we had no thunderbolts or Bulls from Christ." When asked what he had done for the Church, Julius replies, "I raised the revenue. I invented new offices and sold them. I invented a way to sell bishoprics without simony. . . . Nothing can be done without money. Then I annexed Bologna to the Holy See . . . I defeated a schismatical council by a sham council of my own. . . . I have torn up treaties, kept great armies in the field. . . . I owe nothing to my birth, for I don't know who my father was; nothing

---

[38] *The Colloquies of Erasmus*, trans. N. Bailey, quoted in H. H. Blanchard, *Prose and Poetry of the Continental Renaissance*, pp. 520, 529, 533.

to learning, for I have none . . . nothing to popularity, for I was hated all around." When Julius confesses that he wanted the duchy of Ferrara "for a son of my own, who could be depended on to be true to the Church, and who has just poniarded the cardinal of Pavia," Peter asks, "What! What! Popes with wives and children?" "Wives!" answers the pope, "No not wives; but why not children?" Julius insists that under no circumstances may a pope be removed. "A pope can only be corrected by a general council, but no general council can be held without the Pope's consent; otherwise it is a synod, and not a council. Let the council sit, it can determine nothing unless a pope agrees; and, again, a single pope having absolute power is superior to the council. . . . Thus he cannot be deposed for any crime whatsoever." Popes hate councils because they are "apt to throw the majesty of popes into the shade. There will be able men upon them, men with a conscience who will speak their minds, men who envy us and would like my power to be cut down. Scarce a council ever met which did not leave the pope weaker than it found him."[39]

Peter tells Julius, "A vicar of Christ should be like Christ. . . . He has sovereign goodness, sovereign wisdom, sovereign simplicity. Power with you is joined with madness and vanity. If Satan needed a vicar, he could find none fitter than you." Julius says to Peter, "You starved as Pope, with a handful of poor hunted bishops about you. Time has changed all that, and much for the better. You had only the name of Pope. Look now at our gorgeous churches, our priests by thousands; bishops like kings, with retinues and palaces; cardinals in their purple gloriously attended, horses and mules decked with gold and jewels, and shod with gold and silver. Beyond all, myself, Supreme Pontiff, borne on soldiers' shoulders in a golden chair, and waving my hand majestically to adoring crowds. Hearken to the roar of the cannon, the bugle notes, the boom of the drums. Observe the military engines, the shouting populace, torches blazing in street and square, and the kings of the earth scarce admitted to kiss my Holiness's foot. Behold the Roman Bishop placing the crown on the head of the Emperor, who seems to be made king of kings, yet is but the shadow of a name. Look at all this, and tell me it is not magnificent." "To be a Christian," Peter says, "is to be careless of pleasure, to tread riches under foot as dirt, and count life as nothing. And because the rule is hard, men turn to empty forms and ceremonies. . . . If the world saw the gifts of Christ in you, saw you holy, learned, charitable, virtuous, it would think more, not less, of you for being poor. If Christians had no care for riches, or pleasure, or empire, if they were not afraid of death, then the Church would flourish again. It withers now because Christians have ceased to exist except in name. Did you never reflect, you who were supreme shepherd, how the Church began in this world, how it grew, how it strengthened itself?—not by war, not by horses, not by gold ingots; but by

[39] Reprinted from *The Life and Letters of Erasmus*, pp. 249 ff, by S. A. Froude; used by permission of the publishers, Charles Scribner's Sons.

suffering, by the blood of martyrs, my own among the rest, by imprisonments and stripes. You think you have added to the Church's greatness by troops of officials, or raised its character when you have polluted it with sumptuous expenditure, or defended its interests when you have set all nations fighting that priests may divide the spoil. You call the Church flourishing when it is drunk with luxury, and tranquil when it can enjoy its wealth and its pleasant vices with none to reprove, and when you have taught the princes to call killing and plundering by the fine name of defense of the Church." Peter concludes, "We are not of your communion in this place. You have an army of sturdy rogues behind you, you have money, and you are a famous architect. Go build a paradise of your own, and fortify it, lest the devils break in on you." (p. 168)

THE PROGRAM OF CHRISTIAN HUMANISM

Late medieval Christian humanism was thus both a point of view and a program. It held that the Christian scholar should be acquainted with classical literature in the original tongues, Latin and Greek, and especially with those authors who were concerned with moral problems. This was necessary so that Christian literature might not, with respect to linguistic adornment, be put at a disadvantage when compared with pagan literature. This was necessary also in order that, by acquaintance with the moral teachings of antiquity, these might be properly related to Christianity, which correctly interpreted was not antithetical to these teachings and could indeed profit from them. The Christian scholar must also be acquainted with early Christian literature in the original tongues, and this meant, ideally, an acquaintance with Hebrew, as well as Greek and Latin. This was necessary in order that he might get behind those rather devastating scholastic theologians to the original documents of Christianity, especially the Bible. It was necessary, also, so that it might be appreciated how far contemporary Christianity had strayed from its primitive form.

Christianity and its institutional expression, the Church, ought to be reformed from top to bottom in accordance with the guiding principles set forth in early Christian literature. By and large, it needed to be less ascetic in character, concentrating more on spreading love and charity in this world than in rejecting this world for the one to come. A scriptural Christianity literally interpreted would restore the real Jesus to his followers and, together with his noble example, his teachings on the love of God and man. Ideally, Christianity should be an undogmatic religion. It should emphasize individual piety, righteous conduct, and a personal relationship between the individual and his God; not a mechanical piety that brought salvation as a result of the performance of ceremonies in the prescribed way. The mechanics and superstitions of the faith that needed most seriously to be restrained were those connected with the adoration of the saints and the Virgin Mother, relics, pilgrimages, and, of course, indulgences. The whole notion of a specialized Christianity for monks and an unspecialized one for laymen should be revised. Monasticism in its ordinary form had pretty well discredited itself. The whole secular Church, it seemed, had to be done over, from pope to parish priest. It had to turn from its theocratic programs, its wealth and luxury, and confine itself to the spiritual task of saving souls. Had this program, or a large part of it, been taken over by the Church in time, the West might have preserved its religious unity.

SUMMARY

Approximately 1500 years after Christ a creative synthesis of ascetic and humanistic influences, originally stemming from the Ancient Near Eastern and Graeco-Roman worlds, seemed possible. In its characteristic Hebrew expression "What is man that Thou art mindful of him?" the ascetic preoccupation with the City of God seemed far from the confident citizenship in the City of Man implied in the humanistic Greek assertion "Man is the measure of all things." Yet human aspiration has embraced both heaven and earth. The humanistic Greek and Roman societies, under the impact of political and moral failure, turned toward an otherworldly Christianity. Ascetic medieval Christendom found it impossible to forgo entirely the humanistic love of life and the works of man. In the Christian humanism of the late medieval period, with its renewed emphasis on the doctrine of love, and its spirit of good-humored tolerance combined with humility and moral zeal, western society might have found a common program to promote gradually and productively a further reconciliation of God and man. But in human affairs great changes—whether progress or not—rarely occur peacefully and gradually. More often great disruptive surges push society from extreme to extreme. Already, at the time of Erasmus, Christian humanism was being counteracted by the kind of extreme secular humanism dominant at the courts of the popes and princes of the Italian Renaissance. In the north, pietistic and moral zeal was acquiring an impetus that would lead to the extreme asceticism of the Protestant Reformation. The strength of these opposed forces, along with other new developments in political and social life, transformed old institutions and points of view. The Christian humanism of Erasmus was a last medieval synthesis. The new and often inimical movements of the literary and artistic Renaissance and the religious Reformation served, together with expansion overseas, to introduce a new period of rapid growth and adjustment in western life still identified for the contemporary world as the "modern" age.

A Note on Bibliography

Since the books mentioned in the footnotes to the text are to be taken as suggestions for further reading, they will not necessarily be included in what follows. Since, too, the bibliographies of the students' manual accompanying the text will emphasize contemporary works in paper-back editions, they will not necessarily be included in what follows. The student is urged to plunge as soon and as deeply as possible into contemporary materials. It is still possible for him during college days to familiarize himself with a great part of the literature, history, philosophy, and science that constitute our heritage. The sooner he gets into it, the quicker the fun and stimulation begin. Preparation can thus be made for the future pleasure of a second, third, or even annual review of the books he has come to love.

ANCIENT NEAR EAST: A new historical atlas with beautiful maps has been edited by Edward Fox (*Atlas of European History*. New York, 1957). The student who is restless over the limited amount of information in the text on the Ancient Near East or the classical period should go to M. Rostovtzeff, *History of the Ancient World* (Vol. I, *The Orient and Greece*; Vol. II, *Rome*. Oxford, 1928–1930). If he is still hungry he should go to the *Cambridge Ancient History* (New York, 1923–1939), where he will find the material on the ancient world summarized by specialists in twelve large, learned volumes, supplied with elaborate bibliographies. This is not meant to discourage him. W. G. de Burgh's *The Legacy of the Ancient World* (Penguin Books, 1953) is excellent, in much briefer compass, and includes the Ancient Near East. J. A. Wilson's *The Burden of Egypt* (Chicago, 1951), a product of recent scholarship, has been reissued as *The Culture of Ancient Egypt* (Phoenix Books, 1951). In the same series is Edward Chiera's *They Wrote on Clay* (G. G. Cameron, ed., 1938), valuable for material on daily life in ancient Mesopotamia. A. T. Olmstead's volume on Syria and Palestine should be supplemented by his *History of Assyria* (New York, 1923) and his *History of the Persian Empire* (Chicago, 1948). For ancient Israel there can be recommended R. H. Pfeiffer's *Introduction to Judaism and the Old Testament* (New York, 1948), W. O. Oesterley and T. H. Robinson's *Hebrew Religion, Its Origin and Development* (London, 1937), and two books by A. Lods, *Israel from Its Beginnings to the Middle of the Eighth Century* (London, 1932) and *The Prophets and the Rise of Judaism* (London, 1937). While covering more than the ancient period, the summary essays in the *Legacy of Israel* (E. R. Bevan and C. Singer, eds., Oxford, 1928) should be examined. A scholarly discussion of the important ideas to come out of the Ancient Near East will be found in H. Frankfort and others, *The Intellectual Adventure of Ancient Man* (Chicago, 1946).

GREECE: For textbook accounts of the ancient Greek world, together with bibliographies, there is either the first volume of A. A. Trever's *History of Ancient Civilization* (*The Ancient Near East and Greece*. New York, 1935), M. L. W. Laistner's *Greek History* (New York, 1932), or Professor C. A.

Robinson Jr.'s revision of Botsford's *Hellenic History* (New York, 1956). For sympathetic and well-written appreciations of the Greek world the student should first go to accounts like Edith Hamilton's *The Greek Way* (New York, 1930), G. L. Dickinson's *The Greek View of Life* (New York, 1949), or A. E. Zimmern's *The Greek Commonwealth: Politics and Economics in Fifth-Century Athens* (Oxford, 1931). The Minoan age can be studied in H. R. Hall's *The Civilization of Greece in the Bronze Age* (London, 1928), and Greek civilization before the fifth century in G. Glotz's *The Greek City and Its Institutions* (N. Mallinson, trans., New York, 1930). For the Athenian empire W. S. Ferguson's *Greek Imperialism* (New York, 1913) is important. For Greek civilization at its height in the fifth century the following are profitable: F. M. Cornford, *Greek Religious Thought from Homer to the Age of Alexander* (New York, 1923); Gilbert Murray, *Five Stages of Greek Religion* (Oxford, 1925); A. N. Smith, *The Sculptures of the Parthenon* (London, 1910); M. Bieber, *The History of the Greek and Roman Theater* (Princeton, 1939); C. M. Bowra, *Greek Literature* (New York, 1933); and J. B. Bury, *The Ancient Greek Historians* (New York, 1919). Other books to be recommended are Edith Hamilton's *The Great Age of Greek Literature* (New York, 1942) and Gilbert Murray's *Aeschylus, the Creator of Tragedy* (New York, 1940), *Aristophanes* (Oxford, 1933), and *Euripides and His Age* (New York, 1913). Gilbert Norwood has written a *Greek Comedy* (London, 1931) in addition to his *Greek Tragedy*. There is a biography of Socrates by A. E. Taylor (New York, 1933). He has also written on Plato (*Plato: The Man and His Work*. New York, 1927). W. D. Ross has written a good biography of Aristotle (New York, 1924) and there is a short account of Aristotle's subsequent influence in J. L. Stocks, *Aristotelianism* (New York, 1925). For Alexander and the political history of the Hellenistic period see P. Jouget's *Macedonian Imperialism and the Hellenization of the East* (M. R. Dobie, trans., New York, 1928) and C. A. Robinson Jr.'s biography *Alexander the Great* (New York, 1947). W. W. Tarn's article "Alexander the Great and the Unity of Mankind" (*Proceedings of the British Academy*, Vol. XIX) is exciting. For the post-Alexandrian period there is M. Cary's *The Legacy of Alexander* (A History of the Greek World from 323 to 146 B.C. London, 1932). The economic history of the Hellenistic period is covered in vivid detail by M. Rostovtzeff's *The Social and Economic History of the Hellenistic World* (3 vols., Oxford, 1941), and the cultural history in W. W. Tarn's *Hellenistic Civilization* (London, 1930). Hellenistic science is covered by B. Farrington, *Greek Science: Its Meaning for Us* (Penguin Books, 1944) and O. Neugebauer, *The Exact Sciences in Antiquity* (Princeton, 1952). There are also the very solid biographies of T. L. Heath, *Aristarchus of Samos* (Oxford, 1920) and *Archimedes* (London, 1920). For Greek medicine there is the book of A. J. Brock (*Greek Medicine*. New York, 1929) and another by Charles Singer on *Greek Biology and Greek Medicine* (Oxford, 1922).

ROME: For good textbook accounts of the Roman world, together with bibliographies, see A. E. R. Boak, *History of Rome to 565 A.D.* (New York, 1946) and R. Geer, *Classical Civilization* (Vol. I, *Greece*; Vol. II, *Rome*. New York, 1950). Ralph Turner's *The Great Cultural Traditions* (2 vols., New York, 1941) covers the classical period, and while sometimes involved in terminology is learned and stimulating. A very useful collection of source materials on the Republic and Empire is N. Lewis and M. Reinhold, *Roman Civilization, Selected Readings* (New York, 1955). For a favorable account of Roman expansion consult Tenney Frank, *Roman Imperialism* (New York, 1914), and for economic history there is again the beautifully illustrated M. Rostovtzeff, *Social and Economic History of the Roman Empire* (Oxford, 1926). Cyril Bailey has edited a volume in the Legacy Series (*The Legacy of Rome.* Oxford, 1923) and written a fine volume on Roman religion (*Phases in the Religion of Ancient Rome.* Berkeley, 1932). J. W. Duff has done two important volumes on Roman literature: I, *Literary History of Rome from the Origins to the Close of the Golden Age* (New York, 1953), and II, *Literary History of Rome in the Silver Age* (London, 1953). Samuel Dill has two good volumes on Roman social history, *Roman Society from Nero to Marcus Aurelius* (London, 1905) and *Roman Society in the Last Century of the Western Empire* (London, 1921). Other commendable books on the Empire are J. Buchan, *Augustus* (Boston, 1937); A. S. L. Farquharson, *Marcus Aurelius* (Oxford, 1951); M. Cary and T. J. Haarhoff, *Life and Thought in the Greek and Roman World* (New York, 1940); Edith Hamilton, *The Roman Way* (New York, 1932); G. H. Stevenson, *Roman Provincial Administration till the Age of the Antonines* (Oxford, 1949); R. F. Arragon, *The Transition from the Ancient to the Medieval World* (New York, 1936); Ferdinand Lot, *The End of the Ancient World and the Beginnings of the Middle Ages* (New York, 1931); F. W. Walbank, *The Decline of the Roman Empire in the West* (London, 1946); Jacob Burckhardt, *Constantine the Great* (New York, 1949); A. H. M. Jones, *Constantine and the Conversion of Europe* (London, 1948); A. Alföldi, *The Conversion of Constantine and Pagan Rome* (Oxford, 1949); S. Angus, *The Religious Quests of the Graeco-Roman World* (London, 1929); W. R. Halliday, *The Pagan Background of Early Christianity* (Liverpool, 1925); W. W. Hyde, *Paganism to Christianity in the Roman Empire* (Philadelphia, 1946); A. D. Nock, *Conversion: The Old and New in Religion from Alexander the Great to Augustus of Hippo* (Oxford, 1933); J. Weiss, *The History of Primitive Christianity* (2 vols., New York, 1937); and A. E. R. Boak's *Manpower Shortage and the Fall of the Roman Empire in the West* (Ann Arbor, 1955).

CHRISTIANITY AND EARLY MIDDLE AGES: Books such as S. Angus's *The Mystery Religions and Christianity* (London, 1925); W. W. Hyde's *Greek Religion and Its Survivals* (New York, 1923); and Gordon Laing's *Survivals of Roman Religion* (New York, 1931) show in detail the influences of pagan religion upon Christianity. E. R. Goodenough's *The Church in the Roman Empire* (New York, 1931) is an excellent brief discussion of the conversion of the Roman Empire. Good one-volume accounts of early Christian history are F. J. Foakes-Jackson, *History of the Christian Church from Earliest Times to A.D. 461* (New York, 1924) and the first volume of K. S. Latourette's *A History of the Expansion of Christianity* (*The First Five Centuries.* New York, 1937). E. K. Rand's *Founders of the Middle Ages* (Cambridge, Mass., 1928) contains well-written and sympathetic chapters on the Latin Fathers of the Church, among others. There is also Miss E. S. Duckett's *Latin Writers of the Fifth Century* (New York, 1930).

As a bibliography of the European Middle Ages, covering materials written before 1931, L. J. Paetow's *Guide to the Study of Medieval History* (New York, 1931) is indispensable. Within the compass of the bibliography of his *World of the Middle Ages* (New York, 1949) John La Monte brought Paetow up to date. Carl Stephenson (*Mediaeval History*, 3d ed. New York) went to 1951, Sidney Painter (*A History of the Middle Ages, 284–1500.* New York) to 1953, and R. S. Hoyt (*Europe in the Middle Ages.* New York) to 1957.

A large co-operative history of the medieval period in eight volumes, comparable to the *Cambridge Ancient History*, is the *Cambridge Medieval History* (Cambridge, 1911–1936). It has been reduced to two volumes and revised by C. W. Previté-Orton (*The Shorter Cambridge Medieval History.* Cambridge,

1952). There is also a *Cambridge Economic History* (2 vols., Cambridge, 1941–1952) and a *Cambridge History of English Literature* (Vol. I, Cambridge, 1907). All these Cambridge histories have extensive bibliographies. For translations into English of medieval sources there is C. D. Farrar and A. P. Evans, *Bibliography of English Translations from Medieval Sources* (New York, 1946). Other general works to be consulted on the economic history of medieval Europe are Herbert Heaton, *Economic History of Europe* (New York, 1948) and H. Pirenne, *Economic and Social History of Medieval Europe* (New York, 1937). A helpful work on cultural history, with many quotations, is H. O. Taylor's *The Mediaeval Mind* (2 vols., New York, 1925). F. B. Artz's *The Mind of the Middle Ages* (New York, 1954) contains an extensive bibliography. Other phases of medieval cultural history are covered by C. H. McIlwain's *The Growth of Political Thought in the West* (New York, 1932), going back to Greece and Rome, and E. R. Curtius, *European Literature and the Latin Middle Ages* (New York, 1953). For medieval art and architecture consult C. R. Morey, *Mediaeval Art* (New York, 1942) and A. K. Porter, *Medieval Architecture* (2 vols., New Haven, 1912); for medieval science, A. C. Crombie, *Augustine to Galileo, A·D. 400 to 1650* (London, 1952). For the Church there is Miss M. Deanesly's *A History of the Medieval Church, 590–1500* (London, 1954). *The Legacy of the Middle Ages* (Oxford, 1932) has been edited by G. C. Crump and E. F. Jacob. No student should miss Henry Adams's sensitive and warm *Mont St. Michel and Chartres* (Boston, 1922), a masterpiece of American historiography.

For the early medieval period Miss Deanesly has written *A History of Early Medieval Europe, 476–911* (London, 1956), a sharp summary of a vast amount of reading. J. B. Bury's *The Invasion of Europe by the Barbarians* (London, 1928) has separate chapters on the individual German tribes. The best introduction to Merovingian Gaul is O. M. Dalton's translation of Gregory of Tours' often amazing *History of the Franks* (Oxford, 1927). Samuel Dill has also a volume on the Merovingian period (*Roman Society in Gaul in the Merovingian Age*. London, 1926). For Saint Benedict there is E. C. Butler's *Benedictine Monachism* (London, 1924) and J. Chapman's *Saint Benedict and the Sixth Century* (New York, 1929). For the general cultural history of the period M. L. W. Laistner's *Thought and Letters in Western Europe, A.D. 500–900* (New York, 1957) is to be preferred. For early English culture consult in addition to Miss Duckett's book on *Anglo-Saxon Saints and Scholars* (New York, 1947) A. H. Hodgkin's *History of the Anglo-Saxons* (2 vols., Oxford, 1935); C. W. Kennedy, *The Earliest English Poetry* (New York, 1943); and A. H. Thompson, ed., *Bede: His Life, Times and Writings* (Oxford, 1935). For Boniface there are the *Letters* in the translation of E. Emerton (New York, 1940) and W. Levison, *England and the Continent in the Eighth Century* (Oxford, 1946). Miss Duckett has written both a biography of Alcuin (*Alcuin, Friend of Charlemagne*. New York, 1951) and Alfred (*Alfred the Great*. Chicago, 1956).

On the early Irish see L. Gougaud, *Christianity in Celtic Lands* (M. Joynt, trans., London, 1932); R. Flower, *The Irish Tradition* (Oxford, 1947); H. Herbert, *The Greatness and Decline of the Celts* (London, 1934); P. S. Allen and H. M. Jones, *The Romanesque Lyric*, especially for translations of early Latin and Irish poetry; and H. Zimmer, *The Irish Element in Medieval Culture* (J. L. Edmonds, trans., 1891).

For the Vikings the best one-volume work is T. D. Kendrick, *A History of the Vikings* (London, 1930). To be recommended also is G. Turville-Petre, *The Heroic Age of Scandinavia* (London, 1951). Consult also B. S. Phillpotts, *Edda and Saga* (London, 1931) and H. Hermannsson, *Old Icelandic Literature* (Ithaca, N. Y., 1933).

For the Slavs, early Byzantium, and Islam the student should begin with S. H. Cross, *Slavic Civilization through the Ages* (Cambridge, Mass., 1948) and continue with O. Halecki, *Borderlands of Western Civilization* (New York, 1952) and Francis Dvornik's two books, *The Making of Central and Eastern Europe* (London, 1949) and *The Slavs, Their Early History and Civilization* (Boston, 1956). For the conversion of the Balkan Slavs there is M. Spinka, *A History of Christianity in the Balkans* (Chicago, 1933). For early Russia see N. K. Chadwick, *The Beginnings of Russian History* (Cambridge, 1946); G. Vernadsky, *Ancient Russia* (New Haven, 1943); *Kievan Russia* (New Haven, 1948); and the *Mongols and Russia* (New Haven, 1953). The best guide to Byzantine history is A. A. Vasiliev, *History of the Byzantine Empire* (2 vols., Madison, 1952). The distinguished French Byzantinist Charles Diehl has written *Byzantium: Greatness and Decline* (N. Walford, trans., New Brunswick, N. J., 1957), with a detailed bibliography by P. Charanis, and the charming *Byzantine Portraits* (New York, 1927). R. Byron, *The Byzantine Achievement* (New York, 1929) is a brief and enthusiastic account. R. H. Baynes and H. L. B. Moss, eds., *Byzantium, An Introduction to East Roman Civilization* (Oxford, 1948) is in the Legacy Series and to be compared with S. Runciman, *Byzantine Civilization*. The best general work in English on the Arabs is P. K. Hitti, *History of the Arabs* (London, 1953), of which there is a shorter version (*Short History of the Arabs*. Princeton, 1947). B. Lewis's *The Arabs in History* (London, 1950) is an interesting brief account. A *Legacy of Islam* has been edited by Sir T. Arnold and A. Guillaume with stimulating chapters on the influence of the Islamic upon the western European world. There is good material also in *The Arab Heritage* (N. A. Faris, ed., Princeton, 1944). H. Pirenne's views on the importance of the expansion of Islam for the economic history of the early Middle Ages (*Mohammed and Charlemagne*. New York, 1939) should be compared with those of A. Dopsch, *The Economic and Social Foundations of European Civilization* (New York, 1937). In his *Civilization on Trial* (Chapter 9) Arnold Toynbee discusses the Byzantine heritage of Russia, and in his *History in a Changing World* (Chapter 13) G. Barraclough tries to account for the lag in Russian behind western European development.

LATER MIDDLE AGES: For more detailed accounts of the history of the later Middle Ages consult Z. N. Brooke, *A History of Europe from 911 to 1198* (London, 1951); C. W. Previté-Orton, *A History of Europe from 1198 to 1378* (London, 1948); and W. T. Waugh, *A History of Europe from 1378 to 1494* (London, 1932). To these should be added two volumes in the Langer Series, each with voluminous bibliography: E. P. Cheyney's *The Dawn of a New Era, 1250–1453* (New York, 1936) and Myron Gilmore's *The World of Humanism, 1453–1517* (New York, 1952). In the Oxford History of England there are now A. L. Poole, *From Domesday Book to Magna Carta* (Oxford, 1955) and Sir Maurice Powicke, *The Thirteenth Century* (Oxford, 1953). On the growth of Parliament see G. L. Haskins, *The Growth of English Representative Government* (Philadelphia, 1948) and F. Thompson, *A Short History of Parliament, 1295–1642* (Minneapolis, 1953). There should be added to these, G. M. Trevelyan, *England in the Age of Wycliff* (London, 1909) and K. H. Vickers, *England in the Later Middle Ages* (London, 1919). For France and England together Charles Petit-Dutaillis, *The Feudal Monarchy in France and England* (London, 1931) must be used. For France in the later Middle Ages, see E. Perroy, *The Hundred Years' War* (London, 1951) and A. Buchan, *Joan of Arc and the Recovery of France* (London, 1948). For Germany the best recent account is G. Barraclough, *The Origins of Modern Germany* (Oxford, 1947). For feudalism there are two good short accounts: F. S. Ganshof,

Feudalism (London, 1952) and C. Stephenson, *Mediaeval Feudalism* (Ithaca, N. Y., 1942). W. R. Southern's *The Making of the Middle Ages* (London, 1953) should also be consulted in this connection. For Spain there is R. Altamira, *A History of Spain* (M. Lee, trans., New York, 1949) and R. B. Merriman, *The Rise of the Spanish Empire* (Vol. I, New York, 1918). On medieval expansion C. H. Haskins, *The Normans in European History* is almost mandatory; and for crusading expansion R. A. Newhall, *The Crusades* (New York, 1927) is a concise summary. S. Runciman has now finished his *History of the Crusades* (3 vols., Cambridge, 1951–1954), even though he may have thought it "unwise for one British pen to compete with the massed type-writers of the United States." These are the typewriters massed for a five-volume *History of the Crusades* (K. M. Setton, ed.), of which the first, *The First Hundred Years* (M. W. Baldwin, ed., Philadelphia, 1955), is now available. The student will be almost sure to like D. C. Munro's *The Kingdom of the Crusaders* (New York, 1935).

For the economic and social history of the later Middle Ages the student should use G. G. Coulton's *The Medieval Village* (Cambridge, 1931) for its fascinating detail and N. Neilson's *Medieval Agrarian Economy* (New York, 1936) for a succinct scholarly description. He should miss neither A. Luchaire's *Social France in the Age of Philip Augustus* (New York, 1912), Eileen Power's wonderfully human *Medieval People* (New York, 1924), nor, if not all, then the introductory chapter of H. S. Bennett's *Life on the English Manor* (Cambridge, 1937). He will find the merchant and student as well as the noble and peasant in U. T. Holmes Jr.'s *Daily Living in the Twelfth Century* (Madison, 1952). If he is interested in the urban revival he will need to read H. Pirenne's *Medieval Cities* (Princeton, N. J., 1925) and look into the documents of *Medieval Trade in the Mediterranean World* (R. S. Lopez and I. W. Raymond, trans., New York, 1955). There is a brief analysis of medieval society by Sidney Painter (*Mediaeval Society*. Ithaca, N. Y., 1951) in the series of essays in the *History of Our Tradition* edited by Edward W. Fox.

For the history of the medieval Church there is an essay by Marshall W. Baldwin (*The Mediaeval Church*. Ithaca, N. Y., 1953) in the above-mentioned series. The second volume of K. S. Latourette's *History of the Expansion of Christianity* (*The Thousand Years of Uncertainty*. New York, 1938) covers the medieval period. The *Letters* of Gregory VII have been translated by E. Emerton (New York, 1932). The Church at its height under Innocent III can be studied in the brief account of S. R. Packard (*Europe and the Church under Innocent III*. New York, 1927). There is an excellent (non-Catholic) account of the Inquisition by H. C. Lea (*A History of the Inquisition in the Middle Ages*. 3 vols., New York, 1888) and a smaller, excellent (Catholic) one (E. Vacandard, *The Inquisition*. New York, 1924). Post-Benedictine monasticism can be studied in E. S. Davison, *The Forerunners of St. Francis* (New York, 1926) and in two works of D. Knowles (*The Monastic Order in England* and *The Religious Orders in England*. Cambridge, 1940 and 1948). The declining Church of the fourteenth and fifteenth centuries can be reviewed in A. C. Flick, *The Decline of the Medieval Church* (2 vols., New York, 1930); L. E. Binns, *The Decline and Fall of the Medieval Papacy* (London, 1934); and L. B. McFarlane, *John Wycliffe and the Beginnings of English Nonconformity* (New York, 1953).

The student should begin a study of later medieval culture with C. H. Haskins, *The Renaissance of the Twelfth Century*. He could then go on with a second book of Haskins, *The Rise of the Universities* (New York, 1923), and from there to the standard history of the medieval universities, H. Rashdall, *The Universities of Europe in the Middle Ages* (F. M. Powicke and A. B.

Emden, eds., 3 vols., Oxford, 1936). For an introduction to medieval philosophy he should find E. Gilson, *The Spirit of Mediaeval Philosophy* helpful, and he might continue with the same author's *Reason and Revelation in the Middle Ages* (New York, 1938). Medieval science can be pursued in L. Thorndike, *A History of Magic and Experimental Science* (6 vols., New York, 1923–1941), and medieval political theory, in most of its ramifications, in R. W. and A. J. Carlyle, *A History of Mediaeval Political Theory in the West* (6 vols., London, 1903–1936). The history of Latin poetry is contained in the two learned works of F. J. E. Raby, *A History of Christian Latin Poetry from the Beginnings to the Close of the Middle Ages* (Oxford, 1953) and *A History of Secular Latin Poetry in the Middle Ages* (2 vols., Oxford, 1934). The history of the vernacular literatures can be read in such works as U. T. Holmes, *A History of Old French Literature* (New York, 1948) and E. H. Wilkins, *A History of Italian Literature* (Cambridge, Mass., 1954). Translations of Latin (including student) poetry are to be found in J. A. Symonds, *Wine, Women and Song* (London, 1884); Helen Waddell, *Medieval Latin Lyrics* (London, 1929); and George F. Whicher, *The Goliard Poets* (1949). On architecture there is K. J. Conant's *Early Medieval Church Architecture* (Baltimore, 1942) and Otto von Simson's *The Gothic Cathedral* (New York, 1956). There should be mentioned also Sidney Painter's engaging *French Chivalry* (Baltimore, 1940); E. K. Chamber's *The Medieval Stage* (2 vols., Oxford, 1903); Karl Young's *The Drama of the Medieval Church* (2 vols., Oxford, 1933); and P. H. Lang's *Music in Western Civilization* (New York, 1941).

The history of the fourteenth and fifteenth centuries marks the decline of a medieval culture in J. Huizinga, *The Waning of the Middle Ages* (London, 1929) or in R. L. Kilgour, *The Decline of Chivalry* (Cambridge, Mass., 1937). It may also be interpreted as the beginning of a new modern era, as in J. Burckhardt, *The Civilization of the Renaissance in Italy* (New York, 1943). Some aspects of the economic background of these centuries (the advance of capitalism) can be traced in A. B. Kerr, *Jacques Coeur* (New York, 1928) or R. de Roover, *The Medici Bank* (New York, 1948). A good general treatment is G. C. Sellery, *The Renaissance* (Madison, 1950). These centuries mark the beginning of the Reformation in James Mackinnon, *The Origins of the Reformation* (London, 1939). A recent statement on the revival of classical learning emphasizing the continuity of the medieval tradition is P. O. Kristeller, *The Classics and Renaissance Thought* (Cambridge, Mass., 1955). The revival of Christian learning of the classical period, the so-called Christian Renaissance, can be studied in A. Hyma, *The Christian Renaissance: A History of the "Devotio Moderna"* (New York, 1924). As a revival of mysticism this Christian Renaissance is discussed in J. M. Clark, *The Great German Mystics: Eckhart, Tauler, and Suso* (Oxford, 1949). Neoplatonic mysticism is discussed in N. A. Robb, *Neoplatonism of the Italian Renaissance* (London, 1935). E. Gilson, *Dante the Philosopher* (New York, 1949) is a good introduction to this poet as is H. S. Bennett to Chaucer (*Chaucer and the Fifteenth Century*, Oxford, 1947). Italian literature after Dante is covered in J. B. Fletcher, *The Literature of the Italian Renaissance* (New York, 1934). See also E. F. Chaney, *François Villon in His Environment* (Oxford, 1946). L. Thorndike has continued his work on medieval science into the fifteenth century, *Science and Thought in the Fifteenth Century* (New York, 1929). See also George Sarton, *The Appreciation of Ancient and Medieval Science during the Renaissance* (Philadelphia, 1955). For the great fructifying influence of the literary Renaissance one must read Gilbert Highet, *The Classical Tradition* (New York, 1949).

Acknowledgment

I wish to express my gratitude to these publishers and holders of copyright for permission to quote from the following works.

Emily Davenport and Houghton Mifflin Company: *Forerunners of St. Francis* by Ellen Davison.

Jack Lindsay and Curtis Brown, Ltd.: his translation of "Good Friday" by *Abélard*.

Lord Rennell of Rodd and Edward Arnold, Ltd.: Sir Rennell Rodd's translation of Sappho's "Evening" in *Love, Worship and Death: Some Renderings from the Greek Anthology*.

Abelard-Schuman, Inc.: *Man the Maker* by R. J. Forbes.

George Allen and Unwin, Ltd.: E. M. Hulme's translation of *Mystics and Heretics in Italy at the End of the Middle Ages* by Émile Gebhart.

The American Book Company: S. E. Turner's translation of Einhard's *Life of Charlemagne*.

Appleton-Century-Crofts, Inc.: *Essays in Honor of George Lincoln Burr*.

The Baker and Taylor Company: *Medieval Architecture* by A. K. Porter.

G. Bell and Sons, Ltd.: *The Roman History of Ammianus Marcellinus* (Bohn's Classical Library) translated by C. D. Yonge and *Select Historical Documents of the Middle Ages* by E. F. Henderson.

Benziger Brothers, Inc., New York: *The New Roman Missal* (1937), in Latin and English.

William Blackwood and Sons, Ltd.: *Western Christian Thought in the Middle Ages* by S. H. Mellone.

The Thomas A. Boyd Company: Peter Abélard's *Story of My Misfortunes* translated by H. A. Bellows.

Burns, Oates and Washbourne, Ltd.: T. Stapleton's translation of the Venerable Bede's *History of the Church of England*.

The Catholic Education Press: "Pope Gelasius I and His Teaching on the Relation of Church and State" by A. K. Ziegler in the *Catholic Historical Review*.

Chatto and Windus, Ltd.: Notker of St. Gall's *The Early Lives of Charlemagne* translated by A. J. Grant and *Of the Tumbler of Our Lady and Other Miracles* by Alice Kemp-Welch.

Chatto and Windus, Ltd. and S. N. Draper: *Petrarch's Secret, or The Soul's Conflict with Passion* translated by W. H. Draper.

William Collins, Ltd.: *Christianity in European History* by H. Butterfield.

Constable and Company, Ltd.: *Mediaeval Latin Lyrics* by Helen Waddell and *Boniface VIII* by T. S. R. Boase.

Constable and Company, Ltd. and Barnes and Noble, Inc.: *The Wandering Scholars* by Helen Waddell.

J. M. Dent and Sons, Ltd.: Frederick S. Ellis's translation of the *Romance of the Rose* and Philip Wicksteed's translation of *The Latin Works of Dante*.

Walter De Gruyter and Company: *The Acropolis of Athens* by Martin Schede.

The Devin-Adair Company: passages translated by Kuno Meyer in *1000 Years of Irish Poetry* by Kathleen Hoagland.

Gerald Duckworth and Company, Ltd.: *A Survey of Russian History* by B. H. Summer.

E. P. Dutton and Company: *History of the Sciences in Greco-Roman Antiquity* by Arnold Reymond; *Chaucer and His England* by G. G. Coulton; and Margaret Armour's translation of *The Fall of the Nibelungs*.

E. P. Dutton and Company and J. M. Dent and Sons, Ltd.: Sir Frank Marzial's translation of *Memoirs of the Crusades* by Villehardouin and De Joinville; *The Little Flowers of St. Francis*; and Eugene Mason's translation of *Aucassin and Nicolette*.

Harcourt, Brace and Company, Inc.: *History of Ancient Civilization* by Albert A. Trever.

Harper and Brothers: *Sources of English Constitutional History* by Carl Stephenson and F. G. Marcham and *Greek Literature in Translation* and *Roman Literature in Translation* by G. Howe and G. A. Harrer.

Houghton Mifflin Company: Henry Adams's *Mont St. Michel and Chartres* and *The Divine Comedy of Dante Alighieri* translated by C. E. Norton.

Hutchinson and Company, Ltd.: *The Arabs in History* by Bernard Lewis.

Alfred A. Knopf, Inc.: *Main Currents of Western Thought* by F. Le Van Baumer; M. R. Dobie's translation of *The Roman Spirit in Religion, Thought, and Art* by Albert Grenier, and of *Roman Political Institutions from City to State* by Léon Pol Homo; and *A History of the Jews* by A. L. Sachar.

Longmans, Green and Company, Inc.: B. F. Conway's translation of *The Inquisition* by Elphège Vacandard; *The Creative Centuries* by H. J. Randall; *Gregory the Great* by F. Homes Dudden; a fragment of Sappho from *Greek and Roman Classics in Translation* by C. T. Murphy, K. Guinagh, and W. J. Oates; *Luther and the Reformation* by James Mackinnon; F. A. Wright's "Medieval Poetry" in the *Edinburgh Review*; and *Chanson de Roland* translated by Merriam Sherwood (copyright 1932 by Longmans, Green and Company, Inc.).

John W. Luce and Company: *Greek Tragedy* by Gilbert Norwood.

McGraw-Hill Book Co., Inc.: *The Great Cultural Tradition* by Ralph E. Turner.

The Macmillan Company: *Hellenic History* and *The Roman Assemblies* by George W. Botsford; *Adventures of Ideas* by A. N. Whitehead; *The Golden Bough* by Sir James George Frazer; *Christianity, Past and Present* by Charles A. H. Guignebert; *Anglo-Saxon Saints and Scholars* and *Gateway to the Middle Ages* by Eleanor S. Duckett; *Athens and Its Monuments* by C. H. Weller; *Studies in Mystical Religion* by Rufus M. Jones; *Fourscore Years* by G. G. Coulton; *Roman Imperialism* by Tenney Frank; *The Growth of Political Thought* by C. H. McIlwain.

The Macmillan Company and J. M. Dent and Sons, Ltd.: *Greek Poetry for Everyman* by F. L. Lucas.

Macmillan and Company, Ltd. and St. Martin's Press, Inc.: *The Works of Matthew Arnold*.

The Macmillan Company of Canada, Ltd. and St. Martin's Press, Inc.: John Burnet's *Early Greek Philosophy*.

The Mediaeval Academy of America: E. N. Johnson's "Adalbert of Hamburg-Bremen" in *Speculum*; and T. F. T. Plucknett's *The English Government at Work, 1327–1336*, edited by J. F. Willard and W. A. Morris.

The Medici Society, Ltd.: *The Dialogues of Gregory* translated by P. W. Gardner and revised by E. G. Gardner.

Methuen and Company, Ltd.: *Medieval Papalism* by Walter Ullman; *Select*

Documents of European History by R. G. D. Laffan; *The History of the Decline and Fall of the Roman Empire*, by Edward Gibbon, ed. J. B. Bury; and *An Introduction to the Early History of Christian Doctrine* by J. F. Bethune-Baker.

New Directions: *The Goliard Poets* translated by George F. Whicher, copyright 1949, by George F. Whicher. Reprinted by permission of the publisher.

W. W. Norton and Company, Inc.: *Mediaeval Art* by C. F. Morey; *Music in Western Civilization* by P. H. Lang; and *An Introduction to Medieval Europe* by J. W. Thompson and E. N. Johnson.

G. P. Putnam's Sons: Boethius's *Consolation of Philosophy* translated by "I. T."; *The Troubadours at Home* by J. H. Smith; and *Desiderius Erasmus* by Ephraim Emerton.

Random House, Inc.: *Basic Writings of Saint Thomas Aquinas* edited by A. C. Pegis.

Rinehart and Company, Inc.: *England before Elizabeth* (Hutchinson's University Library) by H. M. Cam.

The Round Table Press, Inc.: *Living Religions and Modern Thought* by Alban G. Widgery.

Routledge and Kegan Paul, Ltd.: *The Trial of Jeanne D'Arc* translated by W. P. Barrett; *The Social History of Art* by Arnold Hauser; and *The Autobiography of Guibert* translated by C. C. Swinton Bland.

Charles Scribner's Sons: *A History of the Ancient Egyptians* and *The Dawn of Conscience* by James H. Breasted; *Pioneer to the Past* by Charles Breasted; *History of Palestine and Syria* by A. T. Olmstead; *Reason and Revelation in the Middle Ages* by E. H. Gilson; *History of Christian Thought* by A. C. McGiffert; *The Life and Letters of Erasmus* by S. A. Froude.

Sheed and Ward, Inc.: *The Confessions of St. Augustine*, in the translation of F. J. Sheed, copyright 1943 by Sheed and Ward, Inc., N. Y., and *Christianity in Celtic Lands* by Louis Gougaud.

Society of Authors and the Public Trustee: *Saint Joan* by G. B. Shaw.

The Viking Press, Inc.: *The Dead Sea Scrolls* by Millar Burrows.

The Viking Press, Inc. and Jonathan Cape, Ltd.: Sean O'Faolain's translation of "The Heavenly Banquet" in *The Silver Branch*.

The Cambridge University Press: *Life on the English Manor* by H. S. Bennett; *Desiderius Erasmus* by W. H. Woodward; *Roman Stoicism* by E. Vernon Arnold; *The Medieval Village*, *Ten Medieval Studies*, *Life in the Middle Ages*, and *Four Score Years* by G. G. Coulton; *The Cambridge Economic History of Europe*; *The Cambridge Ancient History*; *The Cambridge Medieval History*; *Studies in Early Celtic Nature Poetry* by Kenneth Jackson; and *The English Church and the Papacy* by Z. N. Brooke.

The Clarendon Press: *The Roman Legions* by H. M. D. Parker; *The Mission of Greece* by R. W. Livingstone; *The Social and Economic History of the Roman Empire* by M. I. Rostovtzeff; *The Oxford Book of Greek Verse in Translation* edited and translated by T. F. Higham and C. M. Bowra; *The Universities of Europe in the Middle Ages* by Hastings Rashdall; Gregory of Tours' *History of the Franks* translated by O. M. Dalton; *A History of Secular Latin Poetry in the Middle Ages* by F. J. E. Raby; *A History of the Anglo-Saxons* by R. H. Hodgkin; *From Domesday Book to Magna Carta* by A. L. Poole; *The Classical Tradition* by Gilbert Highet; J. B. Moyle's translation of *The Institutes of Justinian*; and *The Allegory of Love* by C. S. Lewis.

The Columbia University Press: *Marsilius of Padua, the Defender of Peace* by Alan Gewirth; *The Philosophy of Marsilio Ficino* by P. O. Kristeller; *An Introduction to Contemporary Civilization in the West* prepared by the Contemporary Civilization Staff of Columbia College; Andreas Capellanus's *The*

Art of Courtly Love translated by J. J. Parry; Helmold's *The Chronicle of the Slavs* translated by F. J. Tschan; *A History of Magic and Experimental Science* by Lynn Thorndike; *The Literature of the Old Testament in Its Historical Development* by J. A. Bewer; *Hellenic Civilization* by G. W. Botsford and E. G. Sihler; and *The Letters of Saint Boniface* translated by Ephraim Emerton.

The Cornell University Press: *Constitutionalism, Ancient and Modern* by C. H. McIlwain, and *Freedom and the University* by E. N. Johnson.

The Harvard University Press: *Eleanor of Aquitaine and the Four Kings* by Amy Kelly; *The Mediaeval Mind* by Henry O. Taylor; *Slavic Civilization through the Ages* by S. H. Cross; *The Dignity of Man* by Herschel Baker; and the translations from the Latin and Greek authors of the Loeb Classical Library.

The Johns Hopkins Press: *French Chivalry: Chivalric Ideas and Practices in Medieval France* and *The Reign of King John* by Sidney Painter.

The Manchester University Press: *Bernard of Clairvaux* by Watkin Williams.

The Princeton University Press: Erasmus' *The Praise of Folly* translated by H. H. Hudson; *The First Crusade* by August Krey; and *Roman Rule in Asia Minor* by David Magie.

The Oxford University Press: *Art in Medieval France* by Joan Evans; *Documents of the Christian Church* by H. Bettenson.

The Oxford University Press and Basil Blackwell and Mott, Ltd.: Gilbert Highet's translation of *Paideia: The Ideals of Greek Culture* by Werner Jaeger.

The Oxford University Press and the British Academy: R. W. Chambers's "Bede" in the *Proceedings of the British Academy*.

The Oxford University Press and the Columbia University Press: Ephraim Emerton's translation of *The Correspondence of Pope Gregory VII*.

The Oxford University Press, Inc.: *Aristotle's Metaphysics* by W. D. Ross; *The Mind of Latin Christendom* by E. M. Pickman; *Christianity and Classical Culture* by C. N. Cochrane; *Phases of Thought in England* by M. H. Carré; *Our Perfecting World* by M. N. Dhalla; *The Essence of Plotinus* by Grace Turnbull; *The Legacy of Greece* by Gilbert Murray; and *The History and Religion of Israel* by W. L. Wardle.

The University of Chicago Press: "To Héloïse," translated by H. M. Jones in *Medieval Latin Lyrics* edited by P. S. Allen; *The Goodspeed Parallel New Testament* by E. J. Goodspeed; *Jesus Through the Centuries* by Shirley J. Case; Pico's "On the Dignity of Man" (trans. by Elizabeth J. Forbes) in *The Renaissance Philosophy of Man* edited by Cassirer, Kristeller and Randall; *Pagan Regeneration* by H. R. Willoughby; *The Nature of the World and of Man* by H. H. Newman.

The University of Illinois Press: *Petrarch's Life of Solitude* translated by Jacob Zeitlin.

The University of North Carolina Press: *The Romanesque Lyric* by P. S. Allen and H. M. Jones.

The University of Pennsylvania Press: *Medieval Foundations of England* by G. O. Sayles.

The University of Toronto Press: *The Renaissance and English Humanism* by Douglas Bush.

The University of Wisconsin Press: *History of the Byzantine Empire* by A. A. Vasiliev and *The Renaissance* by G. C. Sellery.

The Yale University Press: *Epistolae Obscurorum Virorum* edited and translated by F. G. Stokes; *The Treatise of Lorenzo Valla on The Donation of Constantine* by C. B. Coleman; and *The Medieval Attitude toward Astrology* by T. O. Wedel.

Index

Index

Knights, of Aristophanes, 71, 72
Knights of the shire, 563
Knights Templars, 599
Koran, 482
Kossovo, battle of, 516
Kurs, 498

Lancastrian dynasty, 568
Langton, Stephen, 578
Laon, 453 f.
Lares and *penates*, 238, 239
Latin, medieval, 685 f.
Latin Kingdom of Jerusalem, 491, 494
Latin League, 169, 171
Latin peoples, 169
Law, Roman, 252 ff.; *ius gentium*, 254;
    natural law, 254 f.; state of nature,
    255 f.
Laws, of Plato, 133, 139, 140
Lay investiture, 528, 531
League, Achaean, 86; Aetolian, 86;
    Delian, 60–61; Hellenic, 81; Latin, 169,
    171; of Verona, 544; Lombard, 544;
    Hanseatic, 567 f.
Legate, papal, 582
Legnano, battle of, 544
Lenten Synod, of 1075, 535; of 1076,
    537
Leo IX, Pope, 470
Lepidus, 214
Letters of Obscure Men, 781 ff.
Letts, 498
Leucippus, 119, 120
Leuctra, battle of, 79
Libation-Bearers, of Aeschylus, 109–110
Life of Solitude, of Petrarch, 771 f.
Lindisfarne, 398
Lithuanians, 498
Liutprand, bishop of Cremona, 472 ff.
Livonia, conquest of, 508 f.
Livonian Brothers of the Sword, 509
Livs, 498
Logos, 324; Jesus as the logos, 330 f.
Lollards, 628
Lombard League, 453
Lombards, 283, 373, 380
Lorenzo de' Medici, 762
Louis IV, of Germany, 621
Louis VI (the Fat), of France, 551 f.
Louis VII, of France, 491, 551
Louis IX (Saint), of France, 494, 555
Louis XI, of France, 570
Louis the Pious, 382 f.
Lucilius, 236

Lucretius, *The Nature of Things*,
    241 ff.; atomic theory of, 242
Lullus, 407
Lupus of Ferrières, 420
Luxemburgers, 566
Luxeuil, 398
Lyceum, of Aristotle, 140
Lysistrata, of Aristophanes, 67, 78–79

Maccabees, 183
Macedonia, and Greek liberty, 80
Macedonian War, Third, 174
Magna Carta, 434 f., 436 f.
Magnesia, battle of, 177
Magyars, 384, 498
Mamelukes, 494
Manfred, 545
Mani, cult of, 40, 286, 297–298
Manilian Law, 210 f.
Manilius, 297
Manutius, Aldus, 763
Manzikert, battle of, 488
Marathon, battle of, 60
March, 380
Marcus Aurelius, 221; and Germans,
    189; as a Stoic, 244–245, 249–250
Mariolatry, 681
Marius, 180 f., 204 f.
Mark Antony, 214; and Cleopatra, 215
Marsh, Adam, 660
Marsiglio of Padua, 621, 624
Martial, 236
Martin V, Pope, 633
Mass, 325
Matilda of Tuscany, 538
Matilda, daughter of Henry I, 551, 557
Maximian, 269
Maximinus, 271
Mayor of the Palace, 378
Medes, 23, 46
Melos, destruction of, 62–63; and *The
    Daughters of Troy*, 77–78
Menaechmus, 150
Menander, 231
Mendicants, 601
Menelaus, 151
Merchet, 442
Merovingians, 378 f.
Mesopotamia, 22; early history of, 23;
    influence upon Hebrews, 23, 24, 25, 26
Metaphysics, of Aristotle, 142
Methodius, 499
Metics (Athenian), 51
Micah, 32

Middle class, rise in Greece, 50; Roman, 198, 199–200; medieval, 449 ff.
Minoans, 47
Mithra, cult of, 40, 41, 286, 294–296; Mithraic ceremonies, 295; and Christianity, 295–296
Mithridates, 181–182; and Sulla, 181–182; and Pompey, 183
Model Parliament, 564
Mohammed, 480 f.
Monasticism, Benedictine, 392 f.; Irish, 396
Mongols, 494; and Russia, 502 f.
Monophysites, 335
Monotheism, ethical, 32; and the Hebrew prophets, 32
Monte Cassino, 391; and Boccaccio, 761
Moravians, 498
Morosini, Thomas, 479
Mort d'ancestor, writ of, 560
Moslem, 379, 384, 450, 481 f.
Mozarabs, 484
Munda, battle of, 212
Museum, of Alexandria, 148
Music, medieval, 752 ff.; polyphonic, 754 f.
Mycale, battle of, 60
My Secret, of Petrarch, 771 f.
Mystery cults, 40, 41; Isis and Osiris, 40, 42; Ishtar and Tammuz, 40, 42; Great Mother, 40, 42; Venus and Adonis, 40, 42; Greek, 111 ff.; Eleusinian Mysteries, 111; Dionysus cult, 111; Orpheus cult, 111; theory of, 112; in Roman Empire, 286 f.; westward spread of, 296; and Christianity, 325–326
Mysticism, Neoplatonic, 302; Christian, 639 f.; Rhineland, 776

Natural History, of Pliny the Elder, 257–258
Natural law, 254 f.; and God's law, 355
Natural theology, 653
Nature of Things, of Lucretius, 238 ff.
Naxos, revolt of, 62
Nebuchadnezzar II, 30
Neckam, Alexander, 664
Nemesis, 104
Neoplatonic academy of Florence, 767
Neoplatonism, 298; and Christian mysticism, 301; Trinity of, 301–302; mysticism of, 302, 303; and Christianity, 303

Nero, 221
Nestorius, 334
Nevski, Alexander, 510
New Life (Vita Nuova), 724, 732 f.
Nibelungenlied, 710 ff.
Nicephorus Phocas, 471 ff.
Nicetas, 479
Nicias, 68
Nicomachus of Gerasa, 149, 415
Nicomedes III, of Bithynia, 183
Nominalism, 644; and relativism, 644
Nominalists, 643
Norbert of Xanten, 598
Notker of St. Gall, 423 f.
Novels, of Justinian, 466
Nureddin, 491

Octavian (Augustus), 214, 215, 216; as *princeps*, 216–217; reforms of, 217; *see also* Augustus
Odo, bishop of Bayeux, 586
Odovacar, 285, 373
Odyssey, 49, 100
Oedipus the King, of Sophocles, 110–111
Old Testament, 17, 19–20, 23, 25
Omar Khayyám, 496
On Interpretation, of Aristotle, 642
On Monarchy, of Dante, 521 f.
On the Dignity of Man, of Pico della Mirandola, 768 f.
On the Religious Pilgrimage, of Erasmus, 787
On the Revolutions of the Celestial Bodies, of Copernicus, 7
Orations against Verres, of Cicero, 173
Ordeal, by cold water, 559
Order of Goliards, 692 f.
Orestes, 285
Organon, of Aristotle, 142–143
Origen, 325, 330
Origin of Species, of Darwin, 8
Original sin, 345
Orpheus, mystery cult of, 111
Osiris, and Isis, 40, 42
Osred of Northumbria, 411
Ostmark, 380, 384
Ostracism, 55
Ostrogoths, 283, 370–373
Otto I, of Germany, 471, 505, 528 f.
Otto IV, of Brunswick, 579
Ottoman Turks, 265, 515 f.
Ottonian dynasty, 527
Our Lady of the Stiletto, 327–328

Socrates, 95; on science (*Phaedo*), 118, 126–132, 135; Xenophon's *Memoirs of Socrates*, 127; in Plato's *Apology*, 127; and Alcibiades, 127; in Plato's *Phaedo*, 129–130; point of view of, 130 f.; and Greek humanism, 131–132
Solomon, 27 f.
Solon, reforms of, 51–52; constitution of, 52
Song of Roland, 714 ff.
Sophists, 121 ff.; and Plato, 122 ff., 135
Sophocles, 107 ff., 110–111
Sophrosyne, 104
Sorbs, 505
Spanish March, 379
Sparta, 64; political institutions, 64; other institutions, 66–67, 79
Spartacus, 210
Stabat mater, 707
States-General, 555 f.
Statutes of Provisors and Praemunire, 627
Stephen of Blois, 557
Stephen II, Pope, 389
Stilicho, 285
Stoic theory, and Christianity, 355
Stoicism, Roman, 244 ff.; man and natural law, 246; and human brotherhood, 247; an ascetic discipline, 247; the Stoic day, 248; views on immortality, 251
Strategoi, 54
Sturluson, Snorri, 710
Subinfeudation, 431
Subsidies, 584
Suburb, 452
Suetonius, 238
Suevi (Swabians), 283
Sulla, 181–182; in Asia Minor, 182, 207–208, 209
Sultanate of Rum, 488
Sumerians, 23
Summa contra Gentiles, of Saint Thomas Aquinas, 653 ff.
Suso, Henry, 776 f.
Suzerain, 429
Sweynheym and Pannartz, 763
Swiss Confederation, 568
Sworn inquest, 557
Sylvester I, Pope, 389
Symposium, of Plato, 137–138
Syracuse, punishment of, 173

Tacitus, 218, 219, 220, 237

Tagliacozzo, 545
Taille, 570
Tammuz, and Ishtar, 40, 42
Tannenberg (Grünwald), battle of, 513
Tartars, 503
Taurobolium, 290
Terence, 231
Tertiaries, Franciscan, 604
Tertullian, 269; on Mithraism, 296, 336
Tetrabiblos, of Ptolemy, 153, 662
Teutoburg Forest, battle of, 188
Teutonic Knights, 510 f.; conquest of Prussia, 511 ff.; end of, 514, 599
Thales, 119
Thapsus, battle of, 212
Theaetetus, of Plato, 123, 132–133
Thebes, 79; destruction of, 82
Themistocles, 60
Theocracy, in the Ancient Near East, 26 ff.; definition of, 26–27; ecclesiastical, 26, 337, 519 f., 571 ff., 619; secular, 26, 337, 519; Hebrew under Solomon, 27 f.; Hebrew after exile, 37; and Alexander, 86; Roman, 270, 367; Islamic, 482; papal, 580 ff.
Theodore of Tarsus, 403
Theodoric, 373; and Boethius, 409
Theodosius, 265; and Christianity, 307; and Saint Ambrose, 341
Theodulph, 413, 415 f.
Theognis, 106–107
Theogony, of Hesiod, 104
Theophrastus, 152
Thermopylae, 60
Third estate, 449
Thomas Becket, 577 f.
Thorn, First Treaty of, 513; Second Treaty of, 514
Three estates, 439
Three-field system, 664
Thucydides, Pericles' funeral speech in, 56–57; on Melos, 62–63; on cause of Peloponnesian War, 63; on the Sicilian expedition, 69; on Pericles, 70; on Cleon, 72; on divine causation, 92
Thuringians, 283
Tiberius Gracchus, 206–208
Tibullus, 231
Timaeus, of Plato, 138–139
Tithed Lands, 189
Titus Flamininus, 176
Totalitarianism, and western tradition, 11; and democracy, 12; and fascism, 12

PRINTED IN THE UNITED STATES OF AMERICA